A013599666

GW00792944

History of European Literature

Appearing here in English for the first time, this unique collaboration between European universities traces the development of literature in Europe. Organised in chronological order, this wide-ranging introductory survey is designed to reveal interconnections and cross-fertilisation amongst writers in Europe from Antiquity to the present day. It is a stimulating compendium of research, bringing together new visions of mankind and international identity, pointing towards a Europe of the future.

Period by period, *History of European Literature*:

- offers a summary of the main events of the era, which impacted upon literature across Europe
- describes events which affected specific countries and their literature
- presents a genre which was particularly important at the time, and discusses its development up until the present day
- discusses a few key authors of the time
- identifies a non-literary figure who had a considerable influence on the literary production of the time
- brings to the fore less widely-known works and writers, as well as discussing more famous classics.

History of European Literature is an inspiring resource for students of comparative literature, and for those seeking to widen their understanding of the cultural context in which major works were written and received.

History of European Literature

ANNICK BENOIT-DUSAUSOY

AND

GUY FONTAINE

Translated by Michael Wooff

ROUTLEDGE
Taylor & Francis Group

London and New York

First published 2000 by Routledge
11 New Fetter Lane, London EC4P 4EE

Simultaneously published in the USA and Canada
by Routledge
29 West 35th Street, New York, NY 10001

Typeset in Plantin by
Keystroke, Jacaranda Lodge, Wolverhampton
Printed and bound in Great Britain by
TJ International Ltd, Padstow, Cornwall

British Library Cataloguing in Publication Data
A catalogue record for this book is available from the British Library

Library of Congress Cataloging in Publication Data
Lettres européenes. English
History of European literature / [edited by] Annick Benoit-Dusausoy
and Guy Fontaine.
p. cm.
ISBN 0–415–17334–5
1. European literature—History and criticism. I. Benoit-Dusausoy, Annick.
II. Fontaine, Guy. III. Title.
PN513.L83 1999
809'.894—dc21

ISBN 0–415–17334–5

Contents

CONTENTS

CONTENTS

CONTENTS

CONTENTS

CONTENTS

CONTENTS

CONTENTS

CONTENTS

Preface

From his ancestral seat in Hainault, Prince Charles-Joseph de Ligne, lover of Marie-Antoinette, friend of Goethe and of Casanova, proclaims his cosmopolitanism: 'I have six or seven homelands: the Empire, Flanders, France, Spain, Austria, Poland, Russia and, at a pinch, Hungary.'

What are we to make of European identity today? Fragmented by the nineteenth-century nationalist movements born of the French Revolution, and more and more influenced by the world as a whole from the beginning of the twentieth century onwards, the cultural coherence of Europe is, nevertheless, to be heard, to be seen, to be touched in the fields of music, painting and the plastic arts. In the Prado Museum in Madrid there is no boundary of nationality or language stopping us from walking out of the Velázquez room into the Rubens room. What does it matter that, in the sixteenth century, there was a war between Spain and Holland? Every art gallery's catalogue is international. But those literary catalogues that are histories of literature, what are *they* like? National – above all, national, sad to say!

We know, of course, that humanists everywhere are indebted to Erasmus, a native of Rotterdam, and remember that a Rumanian, Tristan Tzara, launched Dada, but wouldn't we like to know just a little bit more about Dutch and Romanian literature in general?

More than a hundred and fifty academics from all over Europe have, for three reasons, collaborated in the writing of this book.

First, they wanted to shed light on some hitherto dark corners: the Renaissance in Poland, for example; the work of Fricius Modrevius; and the part played by Rhigas Pheraios in Greece during the Enlightenment.

Second, they wanted to give credit where credit is due, in a pan-European context, to authors who are not recognised as widely as they should be because they are writing in the language of a minority, as is currently the case with the Norwegian Dag Solstad and the Latvian Vizma Belševica.

Third, they wanted to decompartmentalise the study of literature: Molière and Calderón and Milton and Van den Vondel rather than Molière, La Bruyère, Boileau and Malherbe.

How should this history of European literature be read?

A persistent obsession with nationhood, limiting an author to one particular area, linguistically and geographically, is a mindset, passed on to us by the nineteenth century, that dies hard; it prevents us from seeing that a work belongs to a cultural context that is not just European but global. In *History of European Literature* the literary histories of the various countries are lumped together instead of being treated separately. Points of convergence between literatures are spread over 14 chapters providing a synthesis of the literary output of several centuries for the whole of Europe. So does this mean that national differences are sacrificed on the altar of Eurocentricity? No. A strong preoccupation with European identity must not be allowed to detract from the originality of the Russian balagan or the Italian commedia dell'arte. The diversity of literature is forever asserting itself throughout.

After the unfolding of literary events in Europe over a given period have been dealt with, a chronological overview plots the development of a genre (the letter, the traveller's tale) or a theme (marriage, eroticism) which has blossomed at the intersection of all the influences on it and has then evolved as fashions and social structures dictated.

Europe, however, is not to be confused with the world! The part of our heritage that comes from beyond Europe – our Bible, and Greco-Roman and Byzantine roots – are discussed in four introductory chapters which acknowledge the debt and the contribution of European literature to the global exchange of ideas.

And where does all this leave the individual writer? The pleasure we derive from reading comes from what we know about writers themselves as well as what they write. In browsing through these pages we encounter the myths that the satanic Byron, Victor Hugo, writing his thundering diatribes from exile, and D'Annunzio, the tireless iconoclast, created for themselves. A more thorough examination of the work of those who were, or still are, 'beacons' – not only for their own country's literature, but for literature in general – is also included.

This book, consisting of contributions in numerous languages, has been the literary equivalent of the Tower of Babel. The challenge had to be met, however, in order to experience the pleasure of genuinely getting to grips with European diversity and all its various nuances, of which the bilingual quotations are echoes.

So where, all things considered, would the Prince de Ligne fit into this picture? Bear in mind that he was a friend of Voltaire and Rousseau, though a counter-revolutionary himself, and a French-speaking Austrian by adoption. Let us turn for the answer to Italo Calvino's *If on a winter's night a traveller* . . .:

> Lettore . . . , fatti tuoi, veditela un po' tu. Quello che conta è lo stato d'animo con cui ora, nell'intimità della tua casa, cerchi di ristabilire la calma perfetta per immergerti nel libro, allunghi le gambe, le ritrai, le riallunghi.
>
> (Reader . . . , that's your business, for you to know. What counts is your state of mind now as, in intimate surroundings, at home, you try to regain your composure so as to immerse yourself once more in the book, stretching your legs, bending them, stretching them again.)

Annick Benoit-Dusausoy
and Guy Fontaine

1 *Europe and Beyond*

J. WEISGERBER

Now, to return to my purpose, I find, as far
as I have been informed, that there is nothing
in that nation that is either barbarous or
savage, unless men call that barbarism which
is not common to themselves.

Montaigne, Essays

The problem of the heritage that Europe
has been given from beyond its frontiers is
so complex that it defies every attempt at
synthesis. Here we shall merely indicate some
of its more salient features, considerably
simplifying the multifaceted and diverse
contribution made by other continents to
European literature. This proposal already
subsumes *ipso facto* our Judeo-Christian
heritage, as the Bible and the Apostles may be
said to have come to us from the Near East.
This begs a first question: a vital one, for it has
to do with the limits of our subject. There is
nothing harder to define than our linguistic
frontiers. Arabic, for example, which we
normally limit to the Near East and North
Africa, was geographically speaking part of
Europe for centuries; in Spain it put down
strong roots and only at Poitiers in 732 AD
did Charles Martel stem the Muslim tide.
The Ottoman Turks, coming from Asia,
already masters of Constantinople, laid siege
to Vienna in 1529 and again in 1683,
dominating almost the whole of the Balkans
until the twentieth century. The withdrawal of
both Muslims and Turks did not in itself put
an end to the resulting confusion of tongues.
Since the end of the Second World War,
decolonisation, a shortage of manpower in
Western Europe and emigration for political

reasons have led to a veritable melting-pot of
nationalities and languages. Arabic is spoken
in Paris as well as in Algiers. Pakistanis and
Jamaicans have settled in England, and today
there are many Turkish enclaves in Europe
– in Germany and in Belgium – as well as in
Istanbul. More than ever we can say that
languages have no precise boundaries. The
time when homogeneity was the norm has
gone forever. We could even ask whether it
ever existed: we need only consider the Jewish
Diaspora and its Armenian counterpart.

We are also faced with another difficulty:
studies in comparative literature are handi-
capped by the major obstacle posed by the
unsuitability of European literary criteria
– already quite tenuous and uncertain of
application in themselves – to literary
phenomena in Asia, America or Africa. If
it is difficult, even sometimes impossible, to
make distinctions between periods and genres
common to every literature from the Atlantic
to the Urals, how can we compare them to
those of Japan or Mexico? The chronology
or periodicity that more or less lends itself to
a European framework is invalid for these
countries.

The same is true when it comes to European
genres. It is hard to find an exact equivalent,
in any of our literatures, for a particular literary
form, subject to strict rules, which can be
found, for example, in ancient Chinese poetry.
It has been said that the development of
Western-style tragedy was held back by Islam,
since the latter places the whole of man's fate
in God's hands. The modern novel, as we
know it in Europe, did not appear in Arabic

until virtually the beginning of the twentieth century. We need to be careful: the journey from one culture to another is full of pitfalls. We must put aside our Eurocentricity: it is derived from ignorance or, worse still, from a superiority complex, without any foundation in reality other than in an out-of-date colonialism which threatens to cloud our judgement. For almost three millennia, Europe has undoubtedly been a significant source of literary work, but it is not the only source. China, India, Israel and Egypt can lay claim to letters of patent a great deal older than those of France or Russia.

OTHER CONTINENTS AND EUROPE

'Other continents' do not present a united front. Their relationship with Europe as far as literature goes varies according to whether we are dealing with old civilisations and written traditions as worthy of respect as Eastern ones, or with peoples with whom Europe came into contact later and whom she often dismissed as 'savages' or 'barbarians'. The difference here is that between Zadig and Winnetou. The outcome of any dialogue necessarily depends on the status of the participants. Colonial conquests gave rise to societies which were very different, both for the occupiers and for those being occupied. The Portuguese, the British and the French did not implement identical policies over their possessions in Africa. Portugal was very tolerant about racial intermarriage; Britain voluntarily chose to govern through the intermediary of local institutions (Indirect Rule) and safeguard native culture; the French tended to assimilate the ruling classes, bringing about their increasing alienation and, indirectly, paving the way for the concept of Negritude (the quality of being a Negro).

Constant 'comings and goings'

We do not need to dwell here on the ways in which contacts came to be established between cultures. The contacts set up were not so different from those within Europe itself. There were always travellers – from Herodotus to Marco Polo, from Las Casas to Pierre Loti – ambassadors – those sent by Siam to France, for example – missionaries – Saint Paul in Corinth, Francis Xavier in Japan – merchants – the East India Company – invasions and military campaigns – from the Indo-Europeans to Alexander the Great, from the Crusaders to Cortez and Kitchener. Last but not least, books and their translations (sometimes excellent but often unfaithful) have even infiltrated our twentieth century media. Meetings between cultures, cultural interchange or, to be more precise, exchange took place, for these contacts were reciprocal. European visitors neither gave nor took without taking or giving in return, even if the only things exchanged were blows. It is easy to be ironical: to maintain, with justification, that Europe exported alcohol and the Inquisition's *autos-da-fé* while seizing Peruvian gold, that it took advantage of slavery wherever it existed and reaped its benefits. On balance, however, there were more significant happenings than terrible atrocities, however painful their memory. Europe brought with it its knowledge of medicine and technology, its culture, its literacy and its fight against the slave trade. It also acted as host to more civilised emissaries from Asia than Genghis Khan. We need to remember the two-way, positive and negative aspects of the exchange: it is often impossible to separate the degree of indebtedness from the amount given, so closely are they intertwined.

It is hardly surprising, then, that literary relations between continents should tend to boomerang. Those in exile from their native lands, emigrants or dissidents, are not the only ones to hanker after their homeland. The large-scale migration of people from Africa and Asia to Western Europe after 1945 was only a distant echo of its opposite, from Vasco da Gama to Francis Garnier. As far as literature is concerned, this process goes back centuries. This is how Aristotle found himself translated by the Arab philosophers of the Middle Ages, by Averroes among others.

Then, having been translated into Latin, Aristotle was used in this subsequent form, not without reservations, by medieval scholastics, Thomas Aquinas in particular. There are many twists and turns to this long journey, and many linguistic reincarnations to be taken into account. The languages that accompanied their White Caucasian conquerors – English, Spanish, French, Dutch and Portuguese – were, in the long run, adopted and adapted by Indians, Mexicans and Africans who were thus able to add to the literary heritage bound up with European languages: the novel in French in North Africa, for instance, the novel in Latin America, French poetry of the Caribbean, Canadian Indian theatre in English. The Pilgrim Fathers of the *Mayflower* come back to us with the faces of Henry James and T.S. Eliot, all examples of a strange to-ing and fro-ing during the course of which Europe's intellectual capital, at least artistically speaking, increases a hundredfold, and whose evolution needs to be traced. It looks as if these intervening changes have been a series of often contradictory chain reactions.

From the desire for cultural absorption to the attractions of exoticism

On the one hand, European influence led to the imitation of the models it established: for the colonisers this was the phase of carrying on from where they had left off. For the colonised it was the phase of cultural absorption. During this phase literature brought into being 'over there' sought to be included with that of the mother country. Naturally, however, there was resistance to this idea, a tendency to differentiate the homespun product with a view to maintaining a feeling for a national, ethnic, religious or cultural identity. This becomes all the sharper with the passage of time, after a loosening of links with the old country and a growing awareness of other environments, traditions and lifestyles. This can often lead to introspection, to a rediscovery of one's roots and even to 'provincialism' as it has done particularly in

Québec. But there is no reason why regionalism – that awareness of autonomy at the local level – should not open up broader horizons. No one is more of a 'Southerner' than Faulkner nor more universal at the same time. Negritude has also been responsible for the creation of works which are equally universal in their appeal.

On the other hand, knowledge (or lack of knowledge) of faraway places from Lisbon to Moscow helps to determine the nature of exoticism: an assimilation of foreign elements which together make for a species of originality that, aesthetically, as Europeans, we have cultivated since the eighteenth century. In Europe, however, there can be a feeling of satiety or opposition, identical to that to be found under Cancer and Capricorn with respect to 'Western values', which can, unfortunately, take the form of xenophobia or racism more political than literary. But there are also, quite unlike Uncle Tom, caricatures of Negroes, Asians or 'savages' made to look ridiculous – the Turks' heads of Molière or Mozart, for example – or even repulsive, such as Shakespeare's Caliban. 'There's always something about a Chinaman,' says Fontane's Effi Briest, 'that gives you goose pimples.' The sinister Dr Fu Manchu of Sax Rohmer is a case in point.

These antitheses are worth thinking about. Europeanisation and the Americanisation that has taken over from it have spread everywhere, still admittedly leaving intact various backwaters – thinner and thinner on the ground these days – but transforming (and sometimes disfiguring) the entire planet. They have lent to Japanese, Indian or African towns their now familiar appearance by introducing science and technology, the mass media, even Western clothes and customs. This process of cloning which goes hand-in-hand, as in Europe, with the developing Industrial Revolution and empires in search of raw materials and markets, reached its apogee in the nineteenth and twentieth centuries. Turkish, Indian, Chinese and Japanese literature became Westernised and underwent modernisation around 1850, in one place reinvigorating the literary idiom, in another introducing newspapers or hitherto unknown literary themes and genres. Cultural absorption can end in such a seamless acquisition of European languages that these, supplanting local languages (still without a written form), become the favoured, even unique, means of expression of those who have been colonised and their descendants. They can also come to express a sensibility which they have never been responsible for mediating. Naipaul and Rushdie use English with the same verve as Greene. The teaching of French in Africa and the West Indies has brought about an equally impressive harvest: Senghor, Césaire, Depestre . . . These are some of the most striking concrete examples of the return to one's cultural roots which has particularly distinguished the post-colonial era.

A great deal of cultural absorption was made compulsory. We need only think of Black slaves in America and of tribes of American Indians, of which a certain number were exterminated, or as good as. Relatively few cultural contacts between donor and recipient are made in an atmosphere of perfect freedom and on a strictly equal footing, and that includes technological development and the maintenance of a politico-economic *status quo*. A tendency towards assimilation brings out rivalries, even a refusal to co-operate. Levelling and uniformity produce the anguish of losing one's own individuality in the anonymity of a crowd and becoming rootless, unattached, deprived of a personality. All these things encourage a nostalgia for the past. Minority groups in Europe, such as Basques, Catalans and Scots, experience similar problems with regard to the globalisation of lifestyles and cultures; the traditional nation-state is too broad a framework for them to function in, even given that this entity is no longer big enough to deal with the imperatives of the global economy. Faced by the threat of losing their individual identities, Brazil and the United States are reacting on a continental scale, so to speak. The doubts that torture Joe Christmas, Faulkner's tragic hero in *Light in August*, are valuable as a paradigm. Is he

White? Is he Black? He doesn't know. In places like the one in which he lives, questioning one's own identity has to do not only with Europe, but also, taking into account racially mixed marriages, with Africa or with the pre-Columbian past. It is not by accident that 'magical realism' and Carpentier's 'marvellously real', centred on the quest for roots, on what makes things either 'the right way up' or 'upside down', on 'recovering ancient substrata', have flourished in Latin American and Canadian literature. Writers stateside formerly exhibited signs of an inferiority complex with regard to European culture, which was the culture of their ancestors and therefore sacrosanct. What this eventually gave way to, as the political prestige of London and Paris went into decline, and both history and the past, after 1945 especially, became discredited, was a feeling of smugness, an Americanism soon to be confirmed by a universal enthusiasm for Coca-Cola, jeans, Neil Armstrong, Orson Welles, J. D. Salinger and even certain idiomatic expressions. Negritude, the paradoxical consequence of an educational system introduced by France in its colonies, may be attributed to comparable attitudes. In the twentieth century it has penetrated a number of works written in Africa and the West Indies, in English and in Portuguese as well as in French, without, however, obtaining the approval of all Negroes everywhere wanting to shake off the colonial yoke and its aftermath. In the United States, the Harlem Renaissance of the 1920s and a movement like the Black Muslims owe their existence to a twofold experience of alienation: racial with regard to the society of the White man, whose language these writers nevertheless share, and cultural with regard to Africa, their ancestral home.

ASPECTS OF EUROPE'S LITERARY DEBT

Exoticism is at the very heart of our subject. Far from seeing in it something cheap and tawdry – palm trees, geisha girls and glass baubles – we will take it to mean the entire debt contracted by Europe to the outside world: the importing of ideas, themes, forms, genres and, most important of all, myths. For 'myths' read 'illusions'. Exoticism is capable of fulfilling various functions: it is an escape, even a mirage – a mainstay, a safe haven, a libertine's paradise – for all those who are weary of the pleasures of Western civilisation, and a source of nostalgia once the native has been repatriated. Dutch literature abounded in sentiments of this kind after Indonesia became independent. But it is not necessary to board a ship in order to dream of being at sea: stories of a return to our natural state have mostly been invented in bedrooms. We can escape from reality equally well on paper without needing, like Gauguin, to live in a mud hut, the kind of primitivism in action we could call 'going native'. There are some for whom the dream takes on human features in the shape of the noble savage. One step further and we might think we'd caught a glimpse of a golden age. A European's horizon is constantly expanding, so that he goes to the Far East and America to look for what the Elizabethans thought they had found in Italy and writers of science fiction in interstellar space – a disorientating paradise, a Utopia finally able to neutralise all the prohibitions by which he is trapped in his own society. Hence, in one sense, the fantasy of rococo chinoiserie, and Eastern decadence, full of unashamed luxury:

I want to see the madness of a Malabarese and his dances that end in death; wines kill like poisons, poisons are sweet as wines; the sea, a blue sea filled with coral and pearls, echoes to the noise of sacred orgies . .
Flaubert, *November*

The narrator in *The Immoralist* by André Gide recovers his health in Biskra. This is a characteristic touch, for, at bottom, exoticism acts as a corrective to too much civilisation and is merely one of the many guises our stubborn search for happiness assumes. Myths appear under its strange trappings: a Judeo-Christian one – that of the garden of Eden – and a pagan one – that of the 'aurea ætas' or golden age.

Happiness is elsewhere

The need for escape, caused by disgust with the civilised world, can lead well beyond dreams, disguises or the desire to adopt the apparently lax ways of the tropics. Some writers have preferred to hear the sirens singing, succumbing to the irresistible attraction of the desert, of the ocean, of the unexplored wilderness, substitutes for the old solitary retreats in which man was wont to lose himself, to get away, to abandon the painful sense of his own individuality. The last two centuries have offered illustrious specimens of this hands-on, existential exoticism: Rimbaud, of course, then T.E. Lawrence, minus his 'English self', but as incapable as Chateaubriand's René of truly turning over a new leaf; and even that hero of the Dutchman Slauerhoff who sought oblivion among the multitudes of the Great Empire of China: 'to be one of those millions who have never achieved self-awareness – what joy.'

Is happiness always to be found elsewhere? It depends on your viewpoint. Whatever that is, for those who want to put old Europe on trial, for writers during the Enlightenment especially, exoticism yields particularly efficacious lines of enquiry. With Montesquieu, with Voltaire, it served as an observation post, as an instrument of criticism. This philosophical variant consists of placing things in a new perspective: the observer's comments are lucid because he is a foreigner and his way of seeing is revealing because it questions convention and opens the eyes of convention's victims. The American Revolution of 1775, by giving a tangible form to the ideas of Locke and Montesquieu, will render these digressions through a fictitious Persia superfluous. For all that, it is obvious that the Enlightenment did not have a monopoly on the process. In the early years of the sixteenth century, Thomas More's *Utopia* already combines the description of an ideal republic, along the lines of Plato, with the reactions of an imaginary traveller confronted by English society at the time. In similar vein, we cannot lose sight of the fascination exerted later by the philosophies of India, China and Mexico and by 'primitive' religions on Keyserling, Döblin and D. H. Lawrence.

The most interesting form of exoticism from a literary point of view is the first, generative of myths, fascinating images and heroes/heroines. Among the latter we could cite at random the dusky Tahitian maiden, the geisha girl and the Japanese doll (*Madam Chrysanthemum* or *Madam Butterfly*), Uncle Tom and the rich uncle in America, Winnetou and Tarzan, the gaucho and the cowboy (more alive than ever thanks to advertisements and westerns), the guru whose place was formerly taken by the odd abstruse philosopher, good-natured eighteenth-century Chinamen and occasional baddies . . . There is no shortage of landscapes either to grab Europe's attention, whether it be the desert, virgin forests, the rose gardens of Shiraz, warm seas and their islands or cotton and tobacco plantations. As for myths, there are two in particular which deserve further examination, one by virtue of its historical importance, the other by virtue of the pull it still exerts today: the noble savage and the American dream. The use of the word myth almost seems to exclude a correspondence of the real and the imaginary; whether they are positive or negative, these mind's eye views are normally fantasies, tall stories based on misunderstandings. This is all the more true in light of the fact that those who told the stories did not always have first-hand knowledge of far-off lands. Rousseau had not travelled further than Europe; Diderot had never seen Tahiti. Nor had Jules Verne been round the world or, for that matter, had he walked on the moon.

The myth of the noble savage

The concept of the noble savage derives from the shock which accompanied specific contacts between 'civilised' peoples and others. Greco-Roman antiquity was already conscious of it. The Scythian and the German, in comparison, despite being 'barbarians', did not carry less force as examples – they stood, in fact, for courage and, fidelity. The picture

slips into sharper focus during the age of the great discoveries, from the fifteenth century onwards, when Christianity and European thought, frames of reference hitherto considered to be absolute and universal, came to see themselves as relative and contingent. If Eurocentrism continued to assert itself, with bloody programmes of mass evangelisation, for example, it seemed henceforth to be on the defensive.

How could we not admit, after Columbus, that there are people who think and feel differently from us? People who may be – who knows? – less unhappy? This raises an important question. Is our civilisation good? Could it be that it is, in fact, wicked? In one way, it is by contact with it that the 'savage' succeeds in using his natural gifts. But, in many cases, prehistoric times – humanity's infancy – appear to be linked to an innocence and a happiness which have since fallen away, whence a feeling of nostalgia for that pristine state and an embarrassing awareness of decadence in modern societies. The *Colloquies* of Erasmus act as a curtain-raiser to these ideas, which Montaigne expounded at length in two of his *Essays*, 'Of the Cannibals' and 'Of Coaches':

> They are even savage, as we call those fruits wild which nature of herself and of her ordinary progress has produced: whereas indeed, they are those which we ourselves have altered by our artificial devices, and diverted from their common order, that we ought rather to term savage.
>
> Montaigne, *Essays*, 'Of the Cannibals'

From this moment, thanks to travellers' tales, the foundations of the noble savage myth are laid. Although Shakespeare's *Othello* and *Oroonoko, the African Prince* by Aphra Behn are already indebted to them, it is during the following century that the cult of the primitive reached its peak with *Inkle and Yarico* (published by Addison in *The Spectator*) and, strangely enough, Rousseau and Diderot who used it as a weapon against classicism, reason incarnate. As the concept becomes extended, the image of the noble savage came to include all those living on the margins of intellectual, urban and industrial preoccupations. Thanks to Vico, Herder and the Romantics, in the nineteenth century it also blended in with images of childhood, the people and the peasantry of rustic idylls.

This image continues on occasion to persist, in spite of radical modifications, even in the scholarly studies of today's ethnologists. However, this hackneyed association of ideas has not been spared from satire and no chance has been missed to link a state of innocence to silliness – and even to wrong-doing.

The American dream seems to have been rooted in this myth of the noble savage, though it was soon to emerge from it. The two myths share a common ground: an old Europe in decline, a New World rapidly developing. But the latter proved to be a battlefield for civilisation to gain one of its most Pyrrhic victories over nature. The memory of the Pilgrim Fathers imbues personal convictions with a genuinely Biblical, even puritanical quality. The mother country's decadence becomes confused with the idea of original sin, with the fall of Adam to whom God nevertheless wanted to give a 'second chance', an opportunity to redeem himself after the failure of the European experience. In the eighteenth century, with Defoe and Prévost, arrival in America was to become synonymous with personal redemption. White men, once there, would, it was hoped, become 'new men', set free from the weight of the past, from duress and from social condemnation, happy, liberated, equal and rich. Yet, from the start, this idea of moral purging was overlaid by the mentality of the pioneer who clears the ground and makes reluctant nature bear fruit, but, in doing so, succeeds in domesticating it, making use of it, taking it over while forcing the natives who already live there into bondage, thus falling back into the same errors he thought he had escaped. The Bible's message is clear: man's fall is irreversible, his innocence beyond recovery. The American dream, in which negative elements are combined with positive

ones, the material with the spiritual, is flawed: it is undermined by its own success. The love of nature ends in rape; the earth that God made available to all, the free, fair earth 'on which the cursed shadow of Europe has never fallen', bears silent witness to the disappearance of the 'frontier', the limit to the territories settled or, more precisely, pillaged by colonists, from one end of the continent to the other. The White man, not to put too fine a point on it, has made a mess of things: he has divided the land, introduced slavery, indulged in genocide. On the credit side, however, there are still the aspirations to a better life and protest at the worship of Mammon and of the machine which came to replace it, which held out such fascinating promise to so many of the dispossessed in Europe. Conversely, the old continent appears to the average American – another delusion – as a special reserve of the intellect, as the hallowed dwelling of Art and Thought.

Leaving behind the realm of the imagination, and to round off this brief overview of exoticism, let us take account of more substantial borrowings, such as those images and forms in which European literature has sought the cultural displacement of the picturesque since *Les Orientales* of Victor Hugo and the Parnassians: the Japanese haiku and Noh drama, the ghazals of Hafiz, the *Rubáiyát of Omar Khayyám* . . .

The scattering of European languages also raises many problems. Cut off for a long time from their origins, evolving independently, they have departed from the linguistic norms that applied in the areas from which they came: French in Québec and Afrikaans in South Africa are two cases in point. Under the influence of indigenous or imported languages, Creolised languages have grown up in addition to secondary languages like Levantine sabir and pidgin English, a mixture of English, Chinese and Malay. Some of these reincarnated languages have become literary languages by virtue of the new wave of ethnic and national awareness that signalled the end of colonialism. This is exactly what happened at the end of the nineteenth century to Afrikaans, a language which shared its existence for a long time with Dutch, the language of official documents.

The question of bilingualism, even of multilingualism, now emerged. In some African states, such as Nigeria, not only is literature produced in several languages, but there are authors who can move with ease and fluency from one language to another (a phenomenon which also exists in Europe). André Brink has written in English as much as he has written in Afrikaans and he is, like Tagore, his own translator. There are Tunisian writers who publish in French as well as Arabic. These alternations are common practice and formally give the lie to a dated romanticism which argues that we only ever truly possess our mother tongue, that of our childhood, our ancestors, our 'Heimat'. Conrad, who replaced his native Polish with English, is a famous illustration of this contradiction. Those who have emigrated from Turkey, anxious to reach the audiences of their adopted countries, address them in German and in French. Even though this literature belongs to the world outside Europe, culturally speaking, it has its place, linguistically speaking, within Europe. All this reveals that the mobility of the majority of people today has led to a geometric progression of hybrids, thus bringing into permanent disrepute the fiction of 'racial' or national purity.

The importers of exoticism

The importers of exoticism come from all walks of life. They may be Europeans of sedentary habits – Jules Verne, among others – thrown back on the resources of their own imagination and what they have read; travellers returning to the country of their birth; temporary or permanent exiles; the descendants of former colonists (in the USA, in Canada, in South Africa) who, while claiming to be European in terms of their culture, increasingly feel themselves to be different; last, but not least, many Asians, Africans and Indians have been attracted to the learning of European languages. Extreme forms of assimilation can cancel out all possibility of exotic content. Nabokov's *Lolita* does not remind us of the Russian-speaking circles of its author who had become an American citizen; nor, at first sight, can a surrealist poem by Clément Magloire-Saint-Aude appear to have its roots in Haitian landscapes. Then again, even as they swell the literary heritage of their mother countries' languages, many (former) subjects of colonial rule paradoxically make use of the latter to contest Europe's political supervision and to emphasise their independence. We need to sieve through translations carefully, as they often contain errors, distortions, far-fetched images: in a word, inventions. Our translations from the Arabic have tended to be based on rigid stereotypes, from Galland's translation of *The Arabian Nights* onwards. A well-known writer and so-called translator will sign his name without scruple to a literal version of an original work, provided by an impecunious hack, not knowing even the basic rudiments of the foreign language concerned (none of which will prevent him, should the need arise, from doing justice to the original by accident or a stroke of genius).

Europe and beyond: a final assessment

Geographically speaking, the greatest influences on Europe have come from Asia and from Mediterranean Africa, in some ways the cradle of European culture. But there have also been Israel and ancient Egypt, the China and Japan of Hans Bethge, Malraux and Ezra Pound, and the India of Pilpay's fables and of Kipling, not to mention *Floire et Blanchefleur* or the Arab scribes (in Spain!) who might well have exerted an influence on the troubadours of Provence. It is, first and foremost, through the medium of lyricism, theatre and the story that Asian influence is made manifest. As for sub-Saharan Africa, Europeans knew very little about it before settling there in the nineteenth century, although philosophers were interested in its system of slavery. Later, 'Negro art' helped literary and artistic avant-garde movements in Europe to dispense with 'mimesis' and to form a new vision of reality. Still more recently it was the fashion on our continent to read African novels, as it still is to sample Latin American 'magical realism' or the poetry of Pablo Neruda and Octavio Paz. The reception of literature from the USA alone would merit a chapter in itself, for its impact as a literary nation has been felt for a century and a half: from Poe and Melville to Baldwin and Roth. Malaysia and Oceania are to be found in the works of Diderot, Conrad and many authors writing in English.

A chronological presentation does not make the position any clearer. Everything depends on the length of time the contacts have lasted and the situation on the ground. If it is a thankless task to establish any kind of common timescale, we can at least divide these historical processes, which sometimes lasted for centuries, into three phases which do not necessarily overlap in time. They are a function of the two-way movement – expansion, then contraction – made by Europe in its overseas territories, a process of development which was far from being carried out everywhere at the same time and in the same way. Decolonisation, which started in 1775 in the United States and gathered momentum after 1945, has still not been fully achieved even now, especially from an economic viewpoint.

The first phase could be described as colonial. The early days hardly encourage literary endeavours. Before we can write, we must live, make adjustments, survive. Once they have properly settled, White emigrants who decide to become writers adopt the literary code in force in the country of their birth, a code which is already familiar to them. The literary production of North America before the Revolution remained provincial, more or less in conformity with contemporary British models, and a similar dependence on Dutch may be noted in Indonesia and South Africa. The colonist thinks along lines he has brought with him and he pays more attention

to his own class than to the world inhabited by the native. There are exceptions: some settlers, more clear-sighted than the others, denounce the inherent exploitation of the colonial system (*Max Havelaar* by Multatuli). Historically, this phase coincides with the setting-up of empires. It ends – but only in Africa – with the Berlin Conference of 1885, which saw European Imperialism triumph. This era is contemporaneous with military expeditions to China, to Tonkin, to Cuba.

Then there is a transitional stage, whose limits are not well-defined, during the course of which belief in Europe's innate superiority is attacked on two fronts, from within as well as from without. Relativism and doubts entertained from Montaigne onwards finally lead to the apotheosis of the native and the lauding of lands now judged to be better than an Old World that is worn out. While this is happening, colonised élites realise their essential dignity and proclaim their rights in the conqueror's own language. Above all, it is in the third phase, the postcolonial phase, that we observe the harking back to our roots. In literary terms, political independence ends up by putting a stop to the imitation of European models imposed at school. Key concepts like the American dream, Negritude or 'magical realism' can now surface. Whether this literature emanates from the descendants of White emigrants or from the descendants of their former subjects, it exists in abundance. It serves to diversify and revitalise our European languages and to assign to them dimensions that are truly international. The North American novel has been a living testimony to this for many years. Closer to us, there are Senghor, Naipaul, Brink, Nadine Gordimer, Patrick White, Carpentier and García Márquez, authors that no well-read reader can afford to ignore. Europe has not been dealt with ungratefully. On the contrary. The caravels of its navigators and soldiers have come back to it, freed of their canons, floating on the wings of the human spirit.

2 *The Greco-Roman Heritage*

J. RICHMOND

Greek literature is the product of a 'world' that was culturally homogeneous, made up of independent city states who valued their autonomy and who spoke a variety of mutually intelligible dialects. This initial situation developed into one of even greater unification (though not all those affected were in fact Greek) which gradually allowed the adoption of Greek as a lingua franca for both literary and administrative purposes. Ultimately, Rome imposed a political unity which both culturally and linguistically helped to unify the Greek-speaking world. Countries situated in the north-west reaches of the Roman Empire used Latin as a cultural vehicle and created a Latin literature based on Greek models. Most modern literary genres were invented by the Greeks. Up until the nineteenth century, literary higher education was dominated by the study of Latin and ancient Greek. In the world of classical antiquity, Greek, as the language used for study and research, was always more prestigious than Latin, which only took precedence in the field of Roman law.

PRE-CLASSICAL GREECE

In the eighth century BC, the introduction of alphabetical writing in Greece ensured that literature could be disseminated more easily and more reliably. This was when lyrical and epic poetry came into existence in an important way.

Homer and Hesiod

The two great epics, *The Iliad* and *The Odyssey*, which tell of legendary deeds dating back to the Mycenaean period (*c.* thirteenth to twelfth century BC) were probably cast in the form we know them today by *c.*750 BC. Tradition has it that **Homer (*c.* eighth century BC)** was responsible for writing them. The content of the poems accurately describes conditions during the Mycenaean age, but their style is the result of a long process of linguistic development, because of their peripatetic verbal transmission at the courts of petty kings or nobles. The archaic nature of the language and of the conditions described shows that the texts in question are very old. The influence of the aristocracy and of the values of the godlike rulers of Mycenaean states lends to the epic its nobility, its elegant language and its heroic views in which honour is held to be the quality most worthy of admiration. Heroes are subordinated to the gods and to destiny and, in *The Iliad*, an epic on war, a tragic dimension prevails.

Other epics composed during this period, according to the same tradition, have been lost; Homer is therefore regarded as the archetypal epic poet. Remarkable texts were subsequently compiled in imitation of Homer by Apollonius of Rhodes and by Virgil.

Works and Days by **Hesiod (eighth century BC)**, a partly autobiographical poem, contains practical information for peasants who lived, as he did, in the rural community of Ascra, near Mount Helicon. This didactic tradition subsequently had a long history, but only Lucretius and Virgil knew how to make it famous.

Lyrical poetry

The only odes of **Pindar (522–443 BC)** to survive, *The Epinicean Odes*, celebrate the victories won by his patrons at the pan-Hellenic Games in rich language and a very elaborate style. These poems were accompanied by music and dancing which are now inaccessible. Their exposition of deep-rooted myths and their use of a sacred, gnomic language appropriate to the religious function of the Games indicate the high social level of these aristocratic festivities. The odes were usually commissioned by rich aristocrats or ambitions tyrants who sought an introduction to high society. As urbanisation and democracy became more prominent, in the middle of the fifth century BC, choral lyricism lost its pre-eminence. Pindar, or 'the eagle of Thebes' as he was called, had no serious rival in classical antiquity.

Personal lyricism (monody) was illustrated by **Alceus (c.620–570 BC)** who wrote of his life as a soldier and his experience of chequered political events and by **Sappho (c.610–580 BC)**, from the isle of Lesbos, whose few poems were all written for women and much appreciated for their refinement.

Archilocus (c.712–c. 664 BC) was not a lyrical poet in the Greek sense of the term. An innovator and an individualist, he made use of elegiac verses and is supposed to have invented the iamb for his satires. A rebel against traditional values, he led the life of a mercenary, expressing his opinions on war, wine and women with great candour.

These lyrical poets were a source of inspiration for Horace in his *Odes* and *Epodes* which, in their turn, influenced modern literature.

From Homer to James Joyce

> So in the future, the sister of the past, I may
> see myself as I sit here now . . .
>
> James Joyce, *Ulysses*

For a long time Homer's influence was chiefly conveyed to posterity by Virgil, for the simple world that Homer described hardly matched the sophisticated taste of the literary patrons of the Renaissance or the centuries that followed. Pope's elaborate translation into English in the eighteenth century met with well-deserved success, but won for him the following celebrated criticism: 'An extremely fine poem, but one cannot say that it is Homer's.' With the arrival of the Romantic movement, a taste for the natural and the primitive rekindled an interest in Homer. Yet the accent on the naïve and the unsophisticated led to the formulation of works that were basically uninspiring, such as Goethe's *Hermann and Dorothea*. This poem, like others written in English during the next century, followed the pattern laid down by Voss (who translated Homer into German) in the eighteenth century, and consisted of acclimatising Homer's hexameters to modern languages. In the twentieth century, Joyce used *The Odyssey* as a canvas for his *Ulysses*, in which the hero, Leopold Bloom, like a modern Ulysses (or Odysseus), lives through a series of experiences parallel to those of Homer's hero. The meeting of Odysseus with the awful giant, the Cyclops, for example, and his tame ram, during the course of which the monster is blinded by Ulysses by means of a spear thrust into a fire, has as its parallel in *Ulysses* Bloom's meeting with a rabid nationalist and his dog as Bloom brandishes a lit cigar. Just as the Cyclops violently throws a rock at Ulysses, a tin of biscuits gets thrown at Bloom. Kazantzakis's *Odysseus* is presented as a sequel to Homer's in which Odysseus boards ship for one last voyage which takes him in a southerly direction where he re-encounters old companions, founds a new city, has fresh religious experiences and finally dies in Antarctica.

The fact that other lyrical Greek poets only exist in scattered fragments meant that Pindar was the only real model for posterity. In the sixteenth century, Ronsard, in the first four books of his *Odes*, states that: '[. . .] from wearing short pants/The first poet in France/I imitated Pindar.' The absence of dance and music, however, which together served to enhance Pindar's work, coupled with the affectation and lack of good breeding in Ronsard's imitations of his poems, have done him a disservice. Two odes in English in the seventeenth century, however, give some idea of Pindar's artistry: *Ode on the Morning of Christ's Nativity* by Milton and *Alexander's Feast* by Dryden.

CLASSICAL ATHENS

In the second half of the sixth century BC, Athens was ruled by the tyrant Pisistratos who inaugurated lavish new festivities, among them the feast of Dionysus, god of wine, a great favourite with the common people. Events taken from legendary happenings associated with Dionysus were related in 'dithyrambs', a kind of chanting which made use of a poetic language verging on madness. This chanting was accompanied by dances and interpreted by a chorus of fifty people. Around 520 BC an actor wearing a mask was added to play the parts of legendary characters. Out of this innovation sprang Athenian tragedy which Athens then transmitted to the rest of Europe. In Greek antiquity the subject was almost always taken from mythology. Comedy is another form of dramatic art which acts out on a stage everyday life, in absurd and fantastic situations.

The age of Pericles

While Athens was in the ascendant, the first great name to appear was that of **Aeschylus (*c.*525–456 BC)**, the oldest of the great tragic poets. The introduction of a second actor into tragedy is attributed to him. He tried to express his views on theology and morality in language that was measured and slightly stilted, sometimes to the point of grandiloquence. He depicts in theatrical terms divine power and divine justice, the pre-eminence of Zeus, hereditary guilt, the punishment of sin and the possibility of redemption through suffering. His tragedies are grouped into trilogies which take us through the different stages of a legend. The only complete surviving trilogy is *The Oresteia* (the story of Orestes), which consists of *Agamemnon*, *The Libation Bearers* and *The Furies*. His authorship of *Prometheus Bound* is disputed.

His young contemporary, **Herodotus (*c.*484–424 BC)**, who came from Halicarnassus, in Asia Minor, lived in Athens and became a citizen of the Athenian colony of Thurii in southern Italy. He wrote the history of the wars between Greece and Persia, but also tried to go back even further in time to explain how the Persian Empire originally came into existence. He also added long geographical and ethnological digressions to his work. Until then, writers who spoke of past events were known under the generative name of logographers (collectors of reports). Herodotus was the first to describe his work as an 'enquiry' or 'historie', showing that a historian's task inevitably carries with it the critical appraisal of his sources.

The Peloponnesian War

Sparta, formerly the greatest power on the Greek mainland, finally went to war with Athens in 431BC, and their long struggle ended with defeat for Athens and the material and moral destruction of Greece.

Thucydides (*c.*455–400 BC) dedicated his life to writing the history of the Peloponnesian War. Exiled from Athens in 424 BC for having failed as a General, he spent his time travelling among those who were opposed to Athens and in leaving no stone unturned in his enquiries. He cherished the ambition that his history (which he never managed to complete) would be 'a lesson for every age' from which in times of political crisis statesmen could draw inspiration.

Sophocles (*c.*496–406 BC) is credited with the introduction of a third actor in Greek tragedy. As the actors wore masks and each could play several parts, tragedy never used more than three actors in speaking roles. Sophocles concentrated on the human characters in legends; the gods were in the background as mysterious, incalculable but nevertheless omnipotent presences who decided human destinies. His most important play was probably *Oedipus Rex*, a masterpiece of plotting, which shows the terrifying power of the gods over the fate of its principal protagonist, Oedipus. His *Antigone* depicts the conflicts between human and divine law. These plays, which dwell so deeply on eternal problems, are still relevant to modern man. Sophocles' style is subtle and spare, and its underlying strength is always rigorously controlled. Dramatic irony is used with great skill.

Euripides (c.485–406 BC) was the last of the great Greek tragedians. A group of teachers (the Sophists), who taught the art of defeating one's adversary in reasoned argument, emerged in Athens during the fifth century BC. They were very successful and, thanks to the new theories they brought with them from schools of philosophy in Ionia (Asia Minor) and southern Italy, they provided the original yeast for a fermentation of new ideas. Surrounded by this climate of intellectual upheaval, **Socrates (469–399 BC)** imagined conversations questioning traditional Athenian values. The tragedies of Euripides, though set in a mythological past, were anachronistically influenced by the art of rhetoric and current dialectics – and by growing incredulity. His interest in female psychology is particularly apparent in *Medea*. The disasters of the Peloponnesian War had made his public well able to identify with his descriptions of human suffering, and his compassionate humanity ensured the survival of his reputation.

The writer of comedies **Aristophanes (c.445–385 BC)** exhibited great vitality in the realm of the comic, but also a delicacy and an artistic instinct which clash rather oddly with the bawdy elements that are usually found in comedy. He criticised Athenian warmongering vigorously and inimically. This naturally conservative man, though fascinated by Socrates and Euripides, made fun of them in his plays *The Clouds* and *The Wasps*.

The later classical age

Plato (c.429–347 BC), a devoted disciple of Socrates, wrote a series of lucid dialogues portraying the philosopher's discussions with his contemporaries, friends and enemies alike. The real Socrates, it seems, tried to discredit erroneous beliefs, but Plato increasingly made use of him to advance the doctrines which were finally epitomised in *The Republic*. This describes in minute detail an ideal constitution which would ensure justice for all in an ideal State. It is, in effect, an authoritarian oligarchy based on a system of censorship and a rigid class system. Citizens hold their wives and their personal possessions in common so that the interests of the private individual cannot outweigh those of the state. In one of his ultimate dialogues, *The Laws*, Plato modified these doctrines so that there was greater scope for human weakness to be taken into account. In his writings we can see his disillusionment with the democracy which, taken to extremes, brought Athens to its knees in 404 BC. Many other works are about abstract philosophical doctrines (the world of Platonic ideas, in particular). A fascinating person and, at the same time, a brilliant philosopher, Plato bequeathed his land to the Academy near Athens so that a school of philosophy could be established. This college was dissolved by the Emperor Justinian in 529 AD.

Xenophon (c.428–354 BC) is an important Athenian historian, but also a writer who tackled various themes and who spent most of his life with the Spartans and their allies. His masterpiece, *Anabasis*, is an authentic description of the march of 10,000 Greek mercenaries led by the brother of Ataxerxes, Cyrus, against Ataxerxes, King of Persia, and their flight from the area around Babylon towards the Black Sea in the north, then towards the Aegean. Another Athenian, **Isocrates (436–338 BC)**, was an orator who was highly thought of in his time. The impact of his finely crafted prose and his pamphleteering speeches was considerable and lasted all his life. He persuaded the Greeks to accept Philip II of Macedon as their leader in a war of conquest against Persia. His rather longwinded style has had a steady influence on Greek literary prose.

Demosthenes (384–322 BC), a peerless orator, inflamed by patriotic feeling for the past glories of Athens, exhorted the Athenians, in a long series of vehement harangues, the *Philippics*, to oppose the advance of Philip.

From Sophocles to Sartre

For I am a man, Jupiter, and each man has to invent his own way.

Jean-Paul Sartre, *The Flies*

Because of the ever greater dissemination of Greek learning and, especially, the detailed study of Aristotle's *Poetics*, Greek tragedy began to have a profound influence on the seventeenth century. Racine defends them in the introductions to his plays by referring to the theory and practice of Greek drama. His work is marked by strict observation of the rule of the Three Unities (of time, place and action) mapped out by Italian literary theorists on Greek models, by the deliberate use of alexandrines more monotonous and finely wrought than their Greek counterparts and by a style very close to the purism that had been preached by Malherbe. He also pays close attention to his plots in which complications and amorous involvements are more significant than in Greek tragedies. In *Phaedra* Racine has lent more dignity to the heroine (it is her confidante who slanders the young Hippolytus in front of his father and not herself, as in the *Hippolytus* of Euripides) and added to the original plot an amorous involvement between Hippolytus and Aricia to complicate the action of the play still further. The subtle but lasting adaptations that Racine made of his pagan and democratic Athenian originals were designed for the aristocratic, luxurious and Catholic court of Louis XIV. They were to influence French theatre for a long time: Racine was revered, then denounced, but never ignored.

In England, at the end of the seventeenth century, Milton wrote *Samson Agonistes* as a 'dramatic poem' rather than a play. It remained faithful to its Greek precedents – which Milton knew by heart – but its main interest lies in the parallel between Samson, the blind prisoner of the Philistines betrayed by his wife, and the blind author living under an unpopular government and a victim, or so he thought, of his own wife's unfaithfulness. English pragmatism was never favourable to the imitation of Greek tragedy, but we can detect the influence of Aeschylus' *Prometheus Bound* on Milton's *Paradise Lost* in which the character of the rebel angel, Satan, recalls that of Prometheus defying Zeus. In the nineteenth century, Shelley also drew his inspiration from *Prometheus Bound* to write a sequel, *Prometheus Unbound*. This ends not with Prometheus being reconciled to Zeus, as it does in the Greek trilogy, but with Prometheus victorious over his divine captor and with his liberation: an allegory of mankind's future liberation from God secured by the atheism preached by Shelley and his friends. There are also fragments of a tragedy on Prometheus written by Goethe. The twentieth century has seen a reawakening of interest in Greek tragedy based on mythology in the wake of Gide's *Prometheus Improperly Bound*.

This reawakening was signalled by the works of Cocteau, Giraudoux, Anouilh and Sartre whose plays usually remain faithful to the original myths, but treat them in a modern way, the problems at issue being those of today's society. In November 1990 an Irish play, *The Cure at Troy*, by Seamus Heaney, was performed. It is based on the *Philoctetes* of Sophocles and is an allegory of the civil war in Northern Ireland.

Plato's philosophy was destined to undergo substantial changes in late Antiquity brought about by the Neo-Platonists whose works influenced the intellectual development of Saint Augustine, the most famous of the Latin Church Fathers. In the Middle Ages the study of Plato disappeared in the West and, in the twelfth and thirteenth centuries, the Scholastics adopted Aristotelianism. Petrarch, in *On my own Ignorance and that of many Others*, took Plato's side against Aristotle, but it was not until the arrival of Pletho of Constantinople at the Council of Florence in 1439 that the Plato's words became accessible. In 1459 Cosmo dei Medici created the Accademia Platonica and Marsilio Ficino began to translate Plato and to develop a version of Platonism which for him was almost a religion. Pico della Mirandola, in *Of Being and Unity* and in other works, attempted to harmonise and synthesise Hebrew, Platonic and Christian wisdom. Platonism became popular in Italy (despite the fears of the clergy) and deeply influenced the literature of that period. Bembo's *The Asolani* is a case in point: it is a work dedicated to Lucrezia Borgia and written in the form of a popular dialogue on Platonic love which defends marriage and praises women. Then there is *Of the Madness of Heroes* by Giordano Bruno (who hated Aristotle), a text in which belief in the folly of poets, lovers and lunatics is extended to include the seeker after truth.

Greek oratory prospered in free and democratically elected assemblies which debated the burning issues of the day. More or less similar conditions held true for the House of Commons during the French Revolution and the Napoleonic Wars. The *Inaugural Speech* of Lord Brougham at Glasgow in 1825 is evidence of how the concise and effective style of Greek oratory was closer to the actual style of his own generation than the long-winded and somewhat calculated style of Cicero. In his *Speech on the Arming of Russia*, it is interesting to see how Charles J. Fox had to refute an argument of Demosthenes: '[Mr Grant] has told us that, when Demosthenes, who was urging the Athenians to make war on Philip, reproached them with their lack of interest in certain towns that the latter had taken, whose names they scarcely knew, by saying to them that these towns were in fact the key that would allow him one day to invade and conquer Greece itself, he was giving them a salutary warning of the danger looming over them.' In like manner, it had been argued, the Russian occupation of Oksakov would be fatal to the balance of power in Europe! (In 1938, Neville Chamberlain could argue in favour of the abandonment of Czechoslovakia to its fate 'because of a quarrel in a far-away country between people of whom we know nothing'.) Oratory, under more authoritarian regimes in Europe, was not encouraged, but the obituary sermon came of age with Bossuet's *Funeral Orations*. Though Bossuet modelled his speeches on Latin authors, he acknowledged his debt to Plato, Isocrates and Demosthenes.

THE HELLENISTIC WORLD

With Philip of Macedon and Alexander the Great (356-323 BC), the Macedonian Empire extended from the deserts of Libya to the banks of the Indus. The Macedonian culture and the language they spoke acquired an official status and a boundless prestige which continued after Alexander's death. Alexandria, especially, the Ptolemaic kingdom's capital in Egypt and, to a lesser degree, Pergamon, the capital of the kingdom of the Attalids in Asia Minor, became cultural centres to rival Athens thanks to their royal patronage. The Greek language took on a new form known as 'koine' (common language), because of the association of people from different areas who needed a lingua franca for diplomatic, business and administrative purposes. A simplified version of the Greek spoken in Athens – Attic Greek – it lost its more subtle distinctions and was influenced by other dialects: as a result its vocabulary increased considerably.

Hellenistic literature . . .

The Egyptian pharaohs founded and maintained not only the richest library in the world, but also its adjacent Museum – a college for scientific research and a great study centre for Mathematics, Astronomy, Mechanical Engineering, Geography, Medicine and other disciplines. The scientific study of language and literature (Philology) also developed here and one of the librarians, **Callimachus (c.299–210 BC)**, was the source of a veritable revolution in poetry. Writing for the Alexandrian court and a highly educated élite, he concentrated on works which were more limited in scope than traditional epics. He insisted on a linguistic perfection of style and metre, avoided anything he considered banal or hackneyed, and enriched his work with learned but frequently obscure and pedantic allusions. His influence extended to Latin as well as to Greek literature, although many Romans went back to older models for their inspiration. His rival, **Apollonius of Rhodes (c.295–215 BC)**, drew deeply on Homeric sources for *The Argonauts*, the story of Jason's quest for the Golden Fleece, and influenced Virgil's *Aeneid*. **Theocritus of Syracuse (c.300–260 BC)** was content to follow in the footsteps of Callimachus and wrote short stylised poetry on everyday life (*The Idylls*). Most of these graceful and humorous texts describe daily life for the shepherds of his native Sicily and the songs they sang. Pastoral literature was inspired by them.

The comic dramatist **Menander (c.343–292 BC)**, by means of the 'new comedy', depicted daily life while avoiding any reference to politics – a dangerous topic under Macedonian hegemony. He made use of the 'plots based on discoveries' so dear to Euripides. His works soon became classics, appreciated for the subtlety and intelligence of their character analysis. Their variety, so reminiscent of everyday life, prompted the famous question: 'Which came first, life or Menander?' His plays usually have a happy ending: the estranged lovers marry, and the modern reader will be struck by the predictability of the plot. At that time, love had become the overriding theme in Greek literature: the conduct of political matters was no longer a subject for public debate and interest focused the individual.

. . . and its influence

Of all the poetry written during the Alexandrian age, that of Theocritus has probably had the greatest influence on modern life, mainly because of Virgil and his *Eclogues*. The *Idylls* of André Chénier, who wrote at the end of the eighteenth century, owe much to those of his Greek predecessor.

A YOUNG GIRL Another shepherd carried off the prudent Helen.
DAPHNIS Helen, however, of her own free will, preferred to capture the shepherd with a kiss.
A YOUNG GIRL Do not be so confident, young satyr; they say that kisses mean nothing.
DAPHNIS And yet, even in a meaningless kiss, there is a pleasure that is sweet.
(He kisses her.)
A YOUNG GIRL I'm wiping my mouth and spitting your kiss away.
DAPHNIS You're wiping your mouth? Let me kiss you again.
A YOUNG GIRL Your kisses should be for your calves, not for a young maiden.
DAPHNIS Do not be so confident; your youth will fly away like a dream.

Theocritus, *Idylls*

DAPHNIS Helen condescended to follow a shepherd who bore her off;
A shepherd like Paris, I mean to kiss my Helen.
NAÏS It hardly becomes you to take pride in so empty a gesture.
DAPHNIS Ah! These empty kisses are not without their sweetness.
NAÏS Now I've wiped my mouth they're invisible.
DAPHNIS Well then! Other kisses will take their place.
NAÏS Take these wishes of yours elsewhere; their ardour bothers me.
You should have respect for a maiden.
DAPHNIS Imprudent shepherdess, your youth flatters you. Ah! Don't be so proud:
Like an unfeeling dream, it will one day disappear . . .

André Chénier, *Idylls*

Three fine English poems imitate bucolic elegies: Milton's *Lycidas*, Shelley's *Adonais* and Matthew Arnold's *Thyrsis* all commemorate brother poets. In Poland, at the beginning of the nineteenth century, Brodzinski's *Idylls* paint a portrait of rural life in Cracow.

The Poetics, the short, fragmentary text by **Aristotle (384–322 BC)**, though still typical of him, had an almost tyrannical influence on tragedy during the Renaissance and the Baroque period in Italy, France and Germany. Literary critics still analyse it. Its doctrine is transmitted to posterity in some subsequent literary masterpieces: Horace's *Ars Poetica*, Boileau's *Art poétique*, and Pope's *Essay on Criticism*. The fables of **Aesop (sixth century BC)** were imitated and put into Greek verse by Babrius (second century BC) and rendered into Latin by the fabulist Phaedrus (first century AD). The art of writing fables reached its peak with La Fontaine and the twelve books of his *Fables*.

A fox one day spied a tragic actor's mask:
'Oh, what dignity!' he said. 'The brain is
   absent
though.' This could be said of those to whom
   Good Fortune
gave consideration and success, but took
   away their sense.
                    Phaedrus, *The Fox and the Masks*

THE LATIN HEIRS

After the defeat of Macedonia by Rome at the battle of Cynoscephales (197 BC), while the Romans were getting more and more of their own way politically, Greek culture walked at the head of its own victory procession into Rome itself, or, as Horace put it: 'captive Greece has made a captive of her jailer'. The only literary genre that Rome can claim as its own is satire; all the other flowers on its tree of literature have been adopted.

'The age of iron'

Plautus (T. Maccius Plautus, c.254–184 BC) adapted the 'new comedies' of the Athenian Menander as well as other comedies for the Latin theatre. Writing for an unsophisticated and somewhat rough-and-ready audience, he was very free in his use of the original texts. Although the places and the characters' names are Greek, allusions and local colour, present in both the plot and the characters, give his comedies a Roman flavour for a Latin-speaking audience. A writer of comedies, Plautus excels in portraying extraordinary situations and extravagant language. Slaves and the lower orders who plot surreptitiously are depicted with benevolence and understanding. Despite the somewhat stereotyped nature of the characters (impulsive young people, boastful soldiers, grasping go-betweens) they are always presented in a recognisable and lively way.

Plautus' successor as a comedy writer, **Terence (P. Terentius Afer, c.184–159 BC)**, was the protégé of a group of noble Romans that included Scipio Emilianus. The delicacy of his six comedies recalls the elegance of their Greek originals. Because of their charm, their purity of language and the skilfulness of their plot construction, they were always popular with the Roman aristocracy. The absence, in Terence, of the farcical element so dear to Plautus, and a dearth of typically Roman garishness and comic brio (which made people say of him that he was 'half a Menander') confer the status of classics on his plays for readers of taste. The Roman public, however, stayed away from them in droves: they preferred to watch boxers or tightrope walkers.

Two poets mark the end of this first period of Latin literature. The first is **Lucretius (T. Lucretius Carus, 99–55 BC)** who died before he could finish his great commentary on Epicurean philosophy, *De Natura Rerum*, steeped in missionary zeal. Epicurus had decided to alleviate mankind's anxiety by using the atomic theory of Democritus (c.460–370 BC) in order to prove the material, and hence mortal, nature of the human soul, thus removing the fear of punishment after death.

The second part is **Catullus (c.84–54 BC)**, a young provincial with connections to the smart Roman set, but with few prospects. He is considered to be a lyrical poet in the modern sense of the word: his short poems celebrate first his love and then his hate for a woman he calls 'Lesbia'. Some of them also refer to his friends and enemies, whether they were literary, personal or political. His hypersensitivity, his poetic gift, nurtured by many readings of Greek poems, helped him to create his epigrams, along with lyrical or occasional poems and scholarly works, similar to those of Callimachus. Catullus was a member of a group of young avant-garde poets. His premature death was a great loss.

'The age of gold'

The works of **Cicero (106–43 BC)** include speeches, both public and private, treatises on philosophy and rhetoric, essays and a vast correspondence on public and private matters. We are more intimately acquainted with his qualities and defects than with those of any other writer of Antiquity! Most ancient Roman prose writers found in Cicero an ideal model: a style that was balanced and restrained, clear and expressive, harmonious in its cadences, multilayered and moving and never at a loss for words. In the hands of its most slavish imitators, Cicero's style degenerated, becoming artificial, pompous and verbose. His character is attractive when we consider his love of literature and philosophy, along with his attachment to liberal and humanitarian values, but there is a downside to it too: as a politician he was an opportunist and liked to prevaricate and, as he was wont to point out when in melancholy mood, 'We live in the sewers of Romulus, not in the Republic of Plato.' Vanity was another of his personal weaknesses and he was blinded by his hankering after the past glories of the Roman Senate. During the period of crisis triggered off by civil wars, Cicero, like Demosthenes, chose to be on the losing side and, in a series of terrible denunciations of Mark Anthony, called *The Philippics* as a nod to his Greek predecessor, he virtually signed his death warrant, a death that he freely accepted with the courage befitting a Roman.

The reign of Augustus (31 BC–14 AD), the great-nephew of Julius Caesar, who had overturned Rome's republican constitution, encouraged the writing of good poetry. The victorious emergence of Augustus brought to an end a century of atrocities and violent clashes dating back to the challenge that Tiberius Gracchus had thrown down to the Senate in 133 BC. **Virgil (70–19 BC)** and **Horace (65–8 BC)** were victims of the civil wars, but they had Maecenas, one of Augustus' most influential ministers, as their patron, thus enabling them to take advantage of his favours. Both were firm admirers of the new regime, celebrating the return of peace and the greatness of Rome. Virgil, having written his first poems, *The Eclogues*, as an imitation of the bucolic idylls of Theocritus, then wrote a didactic work on agriculture, *The Georgics*, in the manner of Hesiod. These are finely wrought poetic descriptions of work in the fields, written in melodious verse. Above all, it is a work of art and poetry, rather than an agricultural guide. Virgil's masterpiece is his epic poem *The Aeneid*, which connects Rome to the world of Greek mythology. He avails himself of the heritage of his predecessors, from Homer to Lucretius, to make his work pregnant with literary allusiveness. With its symbols, its examples, its prophecies and portents, the poem relates to Augustus and his achievements, considered by Virgil to be the ultimate aim of Aeneas' quest. Despite its hero, who is not particularly likeable, future generations found this vaunting of Rome fascinating and, in Western Europe, until relatively recently, it has held a place in the collective consciousness on a par with the one Homer commanded in the Greek-speaking East.

Horace, on the other hand, was a practical man of his time. His *Odes*, which imitate Greek lyrical poems, were written with great skill. His *Satires* and *Epistles* were inspired by his Latin predecessor, Lucilius (*c.*180–102 BC). They affect offhandedness and a friendly casualness, outlining with restrained humour and relaxed wisdom their author's opinions on life, society and literature.

Rare victims of shipwreck float upon the deep's immensity.

Virgil, *The Aeneid*

The same contrast is to be found in the personalities of three poets whose works, written in elegiac verse, we have also inherited. **Tibullus** (*c.*60–19 BC), melancholic and reserved, writes about two love affairs that each ended badly. **Propertius** (*c.*47–15 BC) had a more complex personality, dark and neurotic, obsessed with death. His poetry reflects his violent mood swings. His relationship with the fascinating but fickle Cynthia takes him from ecstasy to despair. Sometimes he watches himself with cynical detachment; at other times he bemoans his cruel fate.

Ovid (43 BC–17 AD), the youngest of the three, discloses in both form and content some of the fragile elegance of a man of the world in his elegies on his youthful loves. He understands human nature and his linguistic virtuosity allows him to analyse, with detachment and from every angle, the ever popular theme of love, while he adds spice to his poems with malicious footnotes and also, occasionally harsh comments. His masterpiece, *The Metamorphoses*, a collection of stories taken from mythology, has a complex underlying structure and mingles an overlying unity and narrative momentum with a wide variety of tones and registers. During the Renaissance, the vividness of Ovid's descriptions inspired both poets and painters.

The main works in prose of the Augustan age are the thirty-five books (out of a total of a hundred and forty-two) which have come down to us of *The History of Rome* by **Titus Livius (Livy)** (59 BC–17 AD). This enormous work traces the history of the city from its foundation to the time at which its author was actually writing. Livy cannot be considered a critical historian, even by ancient standards, but his compilation of historical themes and legends, sometimes distorted, is a model of storytelling, always readable and often fascinating. It was chiefly intended as a panegyric of Rome.

Plautus, Terence, Calderón, Molière

The works of Terence which survived the Middle Ages were often staged during the Renaissance. Plautus became more accessible in the fifteenth century with the growth of education and the discovery of new plays. Around 1500, a lively but limited comic art form developed in Italy with Ariosto, Machiavelli, Aretino and Cecchi, an art form based on Plautus' most famous comedies. Later, after comedy had developed in London, Shakespeare began to write comedies in the manner of Plautus, but his treatment of the original plot gradually transcended his classical model. *The Comedy of Errors*, for example, derives partly from Plautus' *The Twin Menaechmi* and partly from his *Amphitryon*. The Spanish dramatists Lope de Vega and Calderón relied less on classical influences. In France the tradition of the fabliau and the satirical farce and of inferior versions of Italian comedies slowed down the evolution of a truly national theatre, until Corneille wrote *Mélite*, followed by Molière's *Amphitryon* and *The Miser*, based on plays by Plautus. *The Miser* is vastly superior to its Plautian original, *The Pot of Gold (Aulularia)*, because of its in-depth portrayal of character – especially that of Harpagon, the miser himself – and its underlying seriousness.

Catullus often inspired imitations of individual poems (like that of Cristóbal de Castillejo, for example, *Give me, Love, innumerable kisses*), but never great works.

The philosophical poem of Lucretius was not easy to imitate when philosophy began to be written in prose, but there are bits of Chénier, designed to transmit in poetic form the philosophy behind Diderot's *Encyclopaedia*, which are still extant. Tennyson writes about a legend in his poem *Lucretius* which brilliantly captures the intensity of the Latin poet.

The vernacular writers of the Middle Ages, when they broach abstract subjects, are ineluctably attracted by Cicero's style, whether directly or indirectly, through intermediaries such as Saint Jerome or Saint Augustine, when no precedent exists in their country. During the Renaissance the growing prestige of classical pagan culture led to an excessive admiration for Cicero, as Erasmus' satire *Ciceronianus* reveals. Cicero's style was quickly absorbed into vernacular languages during the Baroque period. Among its greatest exponents were Guez de Balzac, Bossuet, Bourdaloue and Fénelon in France and Jonathan Swift and Edmund Burke in England. Johnson and Gibbon perfected this style at the end of the eighteenth century in a manner that was somewhat monotonous and a trifle pretentious. In the nineteenth century, the taste for a less esoteric style resulted in prose that was simpler and more natural to read. Cicero's art of rhetoric, however, though used less often, was never entirely lost.

Virgil and Horace have had imitators throughout Western culture. Among the disciples of Virgil, certain poets may be mentioned who have written pastoral poems in his style: Spenser (*The Shepherd's Calendar*, much influenced by the Italian school), Clément Marot, Ronsard, Belleau (*The Pastoral*), Garcilaso de la Vega and even the satirical John Gay (*The Shepherd's Week*). The *Aeneid* inspired many epics in the sixteenth and seventeenth centuries: Camoens' *Lusiads* in Portugal; Ariosto's *Orlando Furioso* and Tasso's *Jerusalem Delivered* in Italy; Spenser's *The Faerie Queene* and Milton's *Paradise Lost* in England. These poets generally kept the genre as it was while adapting it to non-classical situations. The echoes of countless passages in Virgil may be found in them. Horace's *Odes* have been cleverly imitated in Spain by Garcilaso de la Vega and in Italy by Bernardo Tasso. France and England followed suit. In the eighteenth century, Klopstock's attempt to put Horace's metre into German is worthy of attention. The *Satires* and the *Epistles* inspired Régnier, Boileau and the free and energetic adaptations of Pope.

The echoes of elegiac poems often occur in love poetry, and authors contemporaneous with Watteau often turned for their inspiration to Tibullus, but the work that was most influenced by the three Latin creators of elegies was Goethe's *Roman Elegies*, which uses the ancient metre and its themes to express his experience of love. Both poets and painters of the Renaissance turned to Ovid for their inspiration time and time again.

For *The Rape of Lucrece*, Shakespeare took his inspiration from Livy, as indeed did Corneille for his tragedy *Horace*. This legendary history is also the source for Machiavelli's *Discourse on the First Ten Books of Titus Livius*. These vivid legends, studied at school and considered, until quite recently, to be historically accurate, together constituted common property for poets, orators and moralists.

THE RULERS OF THE GRECO-ROMAN WORLD

During the age of Augustus, as Latin authors had already managed to assimilate the principal literary genres of ancient Greece, late Latin literature has a tendency to leave Hellenic influences on one side. It was also very critical of the current political situation.

Latin literature

Seneca the Philosopher (c.4 BC–65 AD) wrote in a longwinded, shrill, mannered and uneven style, on a moral philosophy of life which aimed to inculcate stoicism. His imitations of Greek tragedies (probably not written to be staged) were far-fetched and even grotesque, as much in the feelings they portray as in the style used to portray them, which is artificial, declamatory and rhetorical. A brilliant young man who showed great promise, **Lucan (39–65 AD)**, who was also a nephew of Seneca, wrote an arresting epic *On the Civil War (Pharsalia)*, on a historical subject: the war between Caesar and Pompey which took place in 49–48 BC. The poem is unfinished, full of rhetorical flourishes and sometimes grotesque or bizarre. It lacks a logical structure and the prosody is harsh and mechanical. Nevertheless the poet's idealism, combined with his energy, his vigour and his youthful imagination make it an impressive piece of writing. The writer of satires, **Juvenal (*c*.60–140 AD)**, and the writer of epigrams, **Martial (*c*.40–104 AD)**, describe daily life in Rome in striking images. Juvenal, with a wry, sardonic humour, condemns the vices of his era. Martial, less morally committed, describes both saints and sinners, demonstrating great indulgence for the latter. History is represented by **Tacitus (*c*.55–120 AD)**, who lived, with impotent hatred, during the reign of the Emperor Domitian, whose despotism lasted from 81 to 96 AD. In his two principal works, the *Histories* and the *Annals*, Tacitus follows the course of events under the Flavian Emperors (69–96 AD) and subsequently during the Julian and Claudian dynasties (14–69 AD). He recounts their crimes with melancholy pessimism and tells of their repressive measures. When he runs short of facts, he takes recourse in sly innuendoes. His style owes much to **Sallust (86–*c*.34 BC)** and to Thucydides.

The prose *Lives of the Caesars* by **Suetonius (*c*.70–170 AD)**, though lacking objectivity, is nevertheless fascinating, for the author had access to the imperial archives, and his conception of the dignity of history did not prevent him from passing on details which may have been devoid of historical interest, but were titillating none the less.

> I have had no constant dealings with any one book in particular, unless you count those of Plutarch and Seneca, from which I drink as from the barrel of the Danaids.
>
> Montaigne, *Essays*

During this period Latin literature went into decline. The attacks by Barbarian hordes from 170 AD onwards shook Rome's confidence and unravelled the fabric of society. After a period of anarchy in the second century AD, in spite of new institutions founded by Diocletian, who reigned from 285 to 305 AD, the development of Christianity and its official designation as a State religion changed society's centre of gravity. Among the noteworthy figures, it is worth remembering the names of **Ausonius of Burdigala (*c*.310–395 AD)**, who had much to say about the day-to-day life of his time, and **Claudian (*c*.370–404 AD)**, a Greek from Alexandria, who wrote panegyrics and a mythological epic in polished Latin rhetoric and elegant metres.

Greek literature

Greek literature deteriorated during the two centuries before the birth of Christ, though many important non-literary books were written. In the first century AD we have **Plutarch (*c*.46–120 AD)**, an affluent Boeotian who spent several years in Rome. Among his best-known works are the fifty *Parallel Lives* which deal with famous Greeks and Romans (forty-six of them place the life of a Greek and the life of a Roman alongside each other). They were written from a viewpoint that was less historical than moral and biographical. Plutarch had access to well-stocked libraries and with great circumspection made use of many sources. He excelled in choosing details that bring a character to life. Generally less well-known, his *Moralia* were essays on ethics and Antiquity, many of which were written in dialogue form, so dear to Socrates and Plato.

The satirical writer **Lucian (*c*.125–190 AD)** produced a powerful and interesting work which denounced phoney philosophers, religious charlatans and literary hacks in faultless Attic Greek (all the more surprising since he was Syrian). In his *Dialogues of the Dead*, he attacked the pomposity and futility of the living with nihilistic cynicism.

The Emperor **Marcus Aurelius (121–180 AD)** wrote the *Meditations*, philosophical jottings in which he considers the maxims of stoicism. These brief, disorganised reflections, with their many quotations and allusions, give us a sympathetic portrait of him: he was dedicated to the noble idea of doing his duty, conscious of the vain, ephemeral nature of human life, but resolute in his attachment to the counsels of the great minds he had studied.

We also need to mention the Greek novel, the origin of which is partly to be found in

Middle Eastern influences. The most interesting is perhaps the pastoral novel *Daphnis and Chloë* by **Longus (second or third century AD)** which is set on the island of Lesbos. Longer and more unusual is the novel by **Achilleus Tatius of Alexandria (third century AD)**, *The Loves of Leucippe and Clitophon*, and *Aethiopica*, the novel by **Heliodorus of Syria (c.200–250 AD)**. These works, which contain some eroticism, deal above all with thwarted loves and marriages.

The fall of the Western Empire in 476 and the closing of the schools of philosophy in Athens by Justinian in 529 signal the end of classical literature. From this period comes *The Greek Anthology*, a remarkable monument to the persistence of the Hellenistic tradition. Originally, epigrams were verses written to be inscribed on a tombstone or composed as dedications; the genre was adopted into literature because it allowed the writer to say and suggest a great deal in only a few words. The first anthology that brought works together spanning a period of 400 years was edited by **Meleager of Gadara (fl.c.80 BC)**, who compared his collection to a wreath of flowers and each of the poets in it to an individual flower ('anthos'). Later writers edited new collections and, around 900 AD, Cephalas tried to bring together the best poems in the first collections in a new anthology used by scholars to establish the compilations that we recognise today because of their inclusion in medieval manuscripts. There are approximately 4000 short poems in this collection; the most outstanding of them skilfully combine poignant declarations of love with a reticence which is typically Greek.

In the footsteps of the ancients

Seneca's tragedies were the models used by Renaissance dramatists. At a time dominated by tyrannical and unscrupulous leaders, his terrifying tyrants struck a chord in the hearts of their audiences. His plays, full of cruelty, reflect the reality of contemporary life at court, and the compressed force of his pointed powers of expression pleased a society in which a witty remark could determine a courtier's future career. *Orbecche* by Giraldi and *Cleopatra Captive* by Jodelle took their inspiration from plays by Seneca. Later, Shakespeare, in his first tragedies (*Titus Andronicus*, for example), and John Webster, in *The White Devil* and *The Duchess of Malfi*, recreated their terrible atmosphere. The theatre of Racine, who turned directly for his inspiration to the Greek originals, eventually eclipsed Seneca's influence.

Tacitus is a difficult writer who has had a limited influence. He described a period of moral decline and, consequently, appeals to us less than Livy. Nevertheless his work has sometimes been used, notably by Racine for *Britannicus*. Juvenal's *Satires* made a contribution to the work of authors such as Swift and Pope, but we should also mention the adaptation of *Satire 3* by Boileau (in his sixth satire) and by Johnson. Another very good adaptation by Johnson is his *Vanity of Human Desires*.

The influence of Martial ensured the preponderance, in modern times, of the Latin epigram which carries 'in cauda venenum' ('a sting in the tail'). The work which is most characterised by its influence is possibly *Xenien* by Goethe and Schiller, which consists of two-line epigrams in the style of Martial's dedications. The *Parallel Lives* of Plutarch, which have frequently been read, offer a vivid glimpse of a democratic society destined to influence future political life. Shakespeare found inspiration in an English version of Amyot's French translation of it for *Timon of Athens*, *Coriolanus*, *Julius Caesar* and *Anthony and Cleopatra*. The *Parallel Lives* and the *Moralia* greatly influenced Rousseau in his *Discourse on the Sciences and Arts* and *The Social Contract*, as they were to influence the political theorists of the French Revolution.

Marcus Aurelius definitely inspired the publication of Pascal's *Thoughts*, in addition to that of the *Maxims* of La Rochefoucauld and the *Reflections and Maxims* of Vauvenargues.

3 *The Judeo-Christian Heritage*

M. SZABOLSCI

In the beginning, God created the heavens and the earth.

The Bible, Genesis

Although the notion of a 'Judeo-Christian heritage' is often used and quoted, it is difficult to grasp. It has never been defined and there is not even an accurate description of it. The problem becomes that much more intense given the ingenuity employed in previous centuries to show the historical and theological differences between Judaism and Christianity. The question of the Judeo-Christian heritage is not bound up with the problem of Jews who have converted to Christianity (from the first century AD till now) nor with that of Christians who have turned to Judaism. The modern concept of this heritage began to come about with those in the 1920s, like Franz Rosenzweig and Martin Buber, who believed in a personal God; and the conditions favourable to its acceptance date back, in the main, to the time of Vatican II.

A COMMON PROPERTY: THE BIBLE

The foundations of the Judeo-Christian heritage are to be found in one specific geographical and cultural focal point: a small, Middle Eastern country. (In this sense the Judeo-Christian heritage could come under the heading of 'Europe and beyond'.) The land of Israel, the Holy Land and its history with patriarchs, kings, prophets, high priests and the Redeemer became and remains, through the mediation of the Bible, our culture's common property. The Bible, with its collection of stories and narrative materials, is central to our thought.

Starting with the initial themes of this common property, a whole series of variations has developed. Carried at the outset by tribes migrating through the deserts of Arabia, these variants, over the course of the centuries, have led to empires covering almost the entire surface of our planet, establishing as they did so the various schools and sects of Christianity and Judaism: the rabbinic variant, the Kabbala and Hassidism on the one hand; Catholicism, Arianism, Monophysitism, Catharism, Protestantism and Mormonism on the other. The fact that this is not an exhaustive list gives us some idea of the diversity of doctrines and beliefs. Throughout their history, Judaism and perhaps even more Christian thought have tended to absorb influences and thoughts from outside their cultures in order to create new syntheses. Thus 'the Greco-Roman heritage' has sometimes been combined with 'Judeo-Christian' beliefs.

Universalist ideals

We can indicate the general features of this heritage by reducing differing views and currents of thought to certain formulas:

- God exists. He is a God who is unique, transcendent and has created man in His own image and likeness.
- Thus there is a dichotomy between God and man. Man takes part in history, which is teleological in the sense that it has a

well-defined purpose: the coming on earth of God's kingdom. History therefore makes sense, as does each individual life.

- History's purpose is attained by a Messiah or a Redeemer. History ends with the coming of the Messiah, simultaneously bringing about a radical change, for this ending is accompanied by phenomena of an apocalyptic nature.

Arising from this we have a universalist view of history and a conception of history's organic evolution, as well as a conception of man's evolution and of history existing together in an organic unity.

Man, who belongs in this higher unity, participates in his development through his actions, his convictions and his faith. He is also an object of the divine will. He carries the burden of the entire human race on his shoulders and struggles with a sense of personal responsibility and feelings of unworthiness.

God has His elect, a people, a community (as far as the Jews are concerned) or those who believe in His son (as far as Christians are concerned). A strict covenant exists between God and His elect.

Man must always strive towards an ideal. He must surpass himself, be forged in the image of the new man. The ideal of his living in community is to create a state of everlasting peace. Some precepts are derived from these universalist ideals: they concern morality, the behaviour of individuals and the rules of the community. Because moral uniformity is one of its fundamental principles, the Judeo-Christian vision is characterised by moral and existential universalism. This universalist morality was set out in the Ten Commandments which together encompass a community made up of individuals who respect the rights of others and obey rules that have a general application. The foundation of this morality is Faith, and the sundry forms and variants attaching to the practice of this Faith are maintained by the sacraments and prayer. Faith is the prerequisite for individual salvation.

Another fundamental principle is respect for the family, the nation and the community of believers. The group, the community are perceived as higher authorities.

Morality also contains the idea of social justice, which places an obligation on the members of a community to help one another. Fighting injustice or helping the poor, the sick and the old is an important element of this vision. In theory, the absoluteness of the right to life remains the essential basis of all ethical teaching. Mutual respect among a community's members and tolerance of the behaviour and the idiosyncrasies of others is also an important element of this vision of the world.

These principles and elements of the Judeo-Christian tradition vary in accordance with geographical and historical differences. This is why only one of the elements sometimes dominates, forcing the others into the background. M. Löwy considers the Messianic component to be central in Judaism – unlike B.H. Lévy who gives precedence to the component to be central in Judaism – unlike component of prophecy, law and distinctness as a people.

From the viewpoint of European literature, we must therefore separately consider the Rabbinical variant, the Kabbala, Hassidism, Neo-Personalism, the Catholic variant, after the Great Schism in the eleventh century, the Greco-Slavic Orthodox variant, the Hussites, then Luther's Protestantism, Unitarianism and Calvinism, as well as all the other Christian religions from the Armenians to the Copts. All these currents of religious thought add to the common property.

The Bible, a source of European literature

The vehicle of this heritage is a collection of texts which are very different from one another: the Bible – the books of the Old Testament in their entirety – to which Christians have added the New Testament. Here we find the most disparate texts assembled: annals, historical chronicles, psalms and love poetry, stories and anecdotes from all over the Eastern world, hallucinatory visions, prophetic prayers, admissions and confessions, epistles and documents – and even inventories and magic formulas. Certain research has shown that these texts originated from between 1000 BC and the third century AD. For the most part they were devised in Palestine or in neighbouring countries, others in more remote locations – Asia Minor, Greece, Northern Arabia, Iraq – but always in areas in or around the Mediterranean.

As a text the Bible is the basis of the whole of Western Culture. Over the centuries it has not only been integrated into religious ritual, but has also become a part of everyday life. The text itself, written in Hebrew and Aramaic for the Jews, in Latin (the Vulgate) and in Greek (the Septuagint) for Christians, remains the foundation of their entire culture. From the fifth century AD we find evidence of attempts to translate the Bible into 'the languages of the Barbarians' (that of Wulfila the Goth, a monk, dates from approximately 380 AD). These attempts at translation continued throughout the Middle Ages. Around thirty-three partial translations of the text have been discovered. To this may be added paraphrases, as well as other writings of various types.

And God saw all that He had made, and it was good. Not that the works of God possess a certain charm in His eyes . . . but beauty lies in what has been accomplished, and in what is in perfect harmony with the attainment of its ideal form.

Basil of Caesarea, *Homilies on the
Six Days of Creation*

The first historiographical sketches, the 'Chronicles of the World' begin with the narration of Biblical history. In this way the Bible is the starting-point for a country's literature and history.

After the Reformation, new translations of the entire text appeared, as well as the first works of philology which aimed to establish the authentic text. There was an edition of the New Testament by Erasmus (1516 and 1519); a German translation by Luther (1522–31); the Zürich Bible (1529) translated by Zwingli; a French translation by G. de Rely (1487); or, in Calvinist vein, the translation of P. Robert (Oliventanus, 1535). There were also the King James version of the Bible in English, 1525–6, and translations into Czech, Polish and Hungarian among other languages.

Today the Bible is the most widely read book in the world. The whole of it has been translated into 600 languages and, if partial translations are included, into 1100 languages.

Until 'secularisation' took place, almost all European literature can be considered as religious. Of course, there were also non-religious, even anti-religious genres, trends and authors – the beginnings of love poetry bear witness to this. But even in its anti-religious forms, this literature remains impregnated with a Judeo-Christian vision of the world. The independence of secular literature in France goes back to the early Middle Ages, to the eighteenth century in Eastern Europe, and to the end of the nineteenth century, occasionally to the beginning of the twentieth, in national literatures connected with Greek Orthodoxy.

Whether it be in sermons, mysteries, hymns, proverbs and parables, philosophical treatises or popular songs, the Judeo-Christian heritage is present, directly, in all its variants and all its forms, first in Latin, then in the vernacular. The history of each national literature begins with the appropriation and transfer of themes and forms taken from the Bible.

Countless works turn to the Bible for their themes, their motifs and their storylines, creating what may be called 'Biblical literature'. In the strict sense of the term, 'Biblical literature' describes highly literary works which present a Bible story with a religious and didactic purpose: tales in prose or verse, legends, poetry in honour of the Virgin Mary, Biblical dramas, mysteries, miracles, passions, plays representing different schools of thought. A part of these works, while preserving a religious turn of mind, diverges from the text as found in scripture, with permitting itself a certain amount of religious liberty: this is the case, for example, with Milton's *Paradise Lost*,

Racine's *Esther* and *Athalie*, Klopstock's *Messiad*. In a broader sense, the term describes literary works which take as their inspiration Bible stories, but which strip them of their religious meaning to leave them with an artistic dimension only; thus we have *Booz Asleep* by Victor Hugo, Hebbel's *Judith*, Oscar Wilde's *Salomé*, and *The Tidings brought to Mary* by Claudel. Other literary works leave the Bible even further behind. Sometimes there is only a theme, a motif, a turn of phrase, reinterpreted symbolically, or literary transpositions of works of art from other media, to remind the reader of the original passage of scripture (Rilke's *Pietà*, for example, or the influence of canticles on the poems of Saint-John Perse).

Finally, historical or ironical interpretations of Biblical themes, such as the short stories of Anatole France, should be mentioned. Thomas Mann's tetralogy, *Joseph*, in which the Bible becomes the generalisation of a myth, can be taken as the sum total of these efforts.

The durability of Biblical themes and characters

Each protagonist of the Old Testament texts and each motif has inspired a series of works. They begin with Adam and Eve, then go on to include Cain and Abel (remember Byron's poem), Abraham, Joseph (Goethe, Thomas Mann), Moses, King David (the great baroque novel of the German, Lehms, the trilogy of plays by Des Masures, the play *The Young David* by the Austrian, Beer-Hoffmann, and the opera of Morax-Honegger, more recently the novels of Heller and Heym), Jeremiah (Zweig), until we reach the Book of Daniel (*Belshazzar's Feast* by Calderón, the works of the Dane, Stolberg, and the poems of Byron and Heine).

The great figures of the New Testament also appear in literary works. Jesus Christ himself is at the heart of many works from the early Middle Ages to the religious mystics of the seventeenth century, from Saint Ambrose to Silesius. He is re-established in the nineteenth century in the work of Strauss and Renan, in *The History of Christ* by Papini, in the poems of the Expressionists (Holz) until we reach the popular novels of Graves. Character generalisation and transposition, a 'second resurrection', begins with Dostoyevsky (the Grand Inquisitor in *The Brothers Karamazov*), but the antecedents can be found in Balzac (*Jesus Christ in Flanders*). The idea is developed again by Gerhard Hauptmann (*The Assumption of Hannele*), the Spaniard, Perez Galdós (*Nazarina*), Léon Bloy (*The Desperate Man*) and Alexander Blok (*The Twelve*). Mary, the Apostles, and the tragic, contradictory character of Judas, are to be found in hundreds of works. The decapitation of John the Baptist on the orders of Herod Antipas – who, according to the legend, granted in this way the wish of his daughter, Salomé – is repeated with sundry variations throughout European literature: in the nineteenth century, following on from *The Wandering Jew* by Eugène Sue, we have Heine in *Atta Troll*, then Karl Gutzkow. Mallarmé started to write his tragic poem *The Herodiad*: Flaubert in his long short story *Herodias* and Wilde in his drama *Salomé* embroidered on the theme and the Slovak writer Pavel Osiragh-Mirvadoslav wrote a great novel about it, *The Herods and Herodias*. And so it continues to Richard Strauss' opera and the poem by Apollinaire. The conversion of Saint Paul on the road to Damascus became a key motif to indicate the changes in public opinion which intervened in the and nineteenth and twentieth centuries (Strindberg: *After Damascus*; Werfel: *Paul Among the Jews*; the Hungarian Mészöly: *Saul*).

The great religious feastdays, such as Easter, Whitsuntide, Christmas and Yom Kippur, with their rituals, their customs and their atmosphere, also inspired an entire body of literature – songs, plays and works – which have these feasts as their subject Remember too the great symbols: bread, wine, the lamb of God, the menorah, the star of David and the cross, themselves the basis of literary works. A whole series of metaphors that translate the Judeo-Christian vision of the world, of mankind and of history have entered into everyday vocabulary and from there into literature. These are only a few examples of the enormous wealth of literary works inspired by the Bible.

The stylistic influence of the Bible

The Bible has also exerted a linguistic and stylistic influence on European literature. The Hebrew 'machal', the proverb, the brief tale which serves to show a state of mind, a doctrine: all these function as the 'building blocks' of European thought. Biblical figures of speech, metaphors and, above all, comparisons that draw for their content on the agriculture practised in Middle Eastern countries (the innumerable allusions to viticulture, for instance) abound in all our literature. The supremacy of the Biblical metaphor lasts until we reach surrealism.

Similarly the rhythmical forms, the parallelisms of thought in the Biblical text, fashion and transform literary texts. The cadence of the psalms is detectable in the writing of Nietzsche and, subsequently, in that of Gide. Biblical turns of phrase give style to Ramuz or the stanzas used by the Hungarian poet, Ady, in his later poems. Youry Lotman, an Estonian scholar, has written that every age has two ways of expressing itself: that of the sacred Scriptures and that of ancient myth and Greco-Roman Antiquity.

THE SAME VIEW OF THE WORLD

The Judeo-Christian heritage has had an influence on European literature in other ways. In addition to Biblical narrative and style, many literary works have grown out of the deep-seated problems and philosophical insights which underpin this heritage.

Some outstanding features

The Judeo-Christian vision of the world and of history, and universalism, are manifested in great inclusive works: 'poems of humanity'.

After Dante and Milton, Goethe's *Faust*, and later the works of Lamartine (*Jocelyn, The*

Fall of an Angel), the record of a pilgrimage by Mickiewicz, a Polish poet of the Romantic era, the *Fragments of an Epic* by the Czech poet, Jaroslav Vrchlický, *Man's Tragedy* by the Hungarian, Imre Madách, and, as the final link in this chain, T.S. Eliot's *The Waste Land*, all testify to the effort to include everything. These works have as their common starting-point an all-inclusive, universalist concept of history. They admit that history is finite, confront the problem of harmonising reason with faith, dwell on the conflict between the individual and the community and wonder about the role in creation of a God who is one and indivisible. The problem of the individual and history, that of redemption and personal salvation, constitute another leading theme in this kind of literature. Sometimes the problem appears in a sacred light (for example, the legend of Parsifal in Wagner's opera), sometimes in a profane one, as a quest for personal salvation in the case of the German poet and sculptor Barlach, and as a theme that underlies the whole of an author's work, as in Faulkner who constantly searches for the possibility of redemption in the lives of simple people. The deeply religious and Biblical structure of Faulkner's works is not just obvious in his works directly inspired by the Bible (*Absalom! Oh Absalom!* and *Requiem for a Nun*), but also in the great portraits of towns in the Deep South. His worldview is close to that of Dostoyevsky and, to some extent, it is influenced by him.

In Dostoyevsky we have a writer whose work was positively steeped in part of the Judeo-Christian view of the world: the concept of original sin, taken together with that of crime, is reinterpreted in a modern context. The problem of crime and punishment is debated not only in his great novel *Crime and Punishment*, but throughout his work. The question of crime also has a dominant part to play in Kafka whose protagonists are always weighed down by unknown, hidden crimes. Perhaps the roots of this deep feeling of guilt exist in the Jewish notion of life itself. In any case, the problem of crime, which has become more appreciable since Freudian analysis, is central to almost all twentieth-century literature: for example, in Camus' work or in the poetry of the Hungarian Jósef.

Redemption is brought by the Messiah, who relieves men of the burden of their crime. A just reign begins with his appearance. The Messiah puts an end to man's sufferings and brings equality to perfection. This messianic idea is deeply rooted in the European consciousness. For Christians the Messiah came down to earth in the person of Jesus Christ. Mickiewicz formulates a Polish variant of the coming of the Messiah. For him, too, in his great work, *Ancestors*, the Polish people become Christ crucified. This Polish expectation of the Messiah continues in several nineteenth- and twentieth-century authors. Later this messianic attitude, in a secularised, even anti-clerical form, occurs in many of the twentieth-century's thinkers, especially Jewish ones, certain of whom become the theorists behind or the founders of socialist parties: Ernst Bloch, Gustav Landauer, Walter Benjamin, Bernard Lazare. This messianic attitude is one of the chief characteristics of social movements by anarchists and, above all, socialists. The works of literature which developed from these movements – from the so-called revolutionary poetry of Jean Richepin to Richard Dehmel or Mayakovsky and J.R. Becher – bear its stamp.

The prophet is one of the most typical phenomena in the Judeo-Christian world. Although he appears in pre-Biblical civilisations, he becomes the vehicle of a dialogue between God and man, the representative of the covenant between God and His people, the guardian of the law, the defender of the poor as far as the Jews are concerned. Such is his function for the entire Judeo-Christian period. The man who, against his own best interests and risking his life, berates the State's leaders, has become a literary archetype and is turned into a poet-cum-prophet. The prophet appears as a theme in Zweig's *Jeremiah*. On the other hand, heroes are created with a prophetic attitude. In French literature there is a prophetic line from Agrippa d'Aubigné's *Tragic Men and Women*

to Hugo's *Punishments*. In these works a prophetic tone is allied to a manner akin to Juvenal. During the First World War, Ady, and then at the end of the Second World War, his Hungarian compatriot, Radnóti, assumed prophetic attitudes and uses prophetic expressions to describe the apocalyptic nature of their times. From 1940 to 1945, *The Book of Jonah* allowed the Hungarian poet Babits to speak of a clerk's responsibility when faced with oppression.

The role of the individual, the autonomy of the human person within the framework of a world governed by the divine will, and the conflicts arising out of this made possible spoken and written confessions and, later, autobiographies. Saint Augustine's *Confessions* are the first and perhaps the greatest example. It is a Christian story of personal salvation and the subjectively viewed drama of an individual witnessing the development of a Christian personality. We also discover the role that memory has to play in our lives. The *Confessions* reveals an individual's struggle with evil, with his instincts, his remorse and his crisis of conscience. Saint Augustine's work is the first in a long line: those of Petrarch and Dante, for example, certainly the latter's *Vita Nova* and even his *Divine Comedy*. The concept of modern individuality is inconceivable without this Judeo-Christian worldview. The autobiography of Saint Theresa of Avila (*The Book of her Life*) and a whole series of intimate diaries written by Protestants extend that line. Rousseau's *Confessions*, the confession of Stavrogin in *The Possessed* by Dostoyevsky, Gide's *Unless the Seed Dies* are all examples of the strength of confessional literature.

Indirect correspondences

Only a few themes and genres are directly attributable to the Judeo Christian heritage, but there are many indirect correspondences. For example, the concept of an overall unity in Baudelaire (the poem *Correspondences*) is also attributable to a universalist worldview, and in the work of Coleridge or T.S. Eliot there also traces of this concept.

A theme like the clown before God (*Our Lady's Minstrel* by Anatole France or the fundamental attitude in every work by Böll), or the theme of Christ or Barabbas as a parable of the conflict between the individual and the crowd in the Hungarian writer, Karinthy, also belong to this heritage.

The history of religions as a literary theme

The themes inherent in religious history constitute their own chapter in the history of European literature. The history of a religion becomes in itself, from the outset, a literary object; later it gets transformed into a theme, as in, for example, *Jerusalem Delivered* by Tasso. This theme often recurs in the nineteenth century in literature, opera and painting, from *The Temptation of Saint Anthony* by Flaubert to *Quo Vadis?*, the great historical portrait by Sienkiewicz, which was revived towards the end of the twentieth century by Umberto Eco (*The Name of the Rose*) and Marguerite Yourcenar (*The Abyss*).

Variations among different religions

The Judeo-Christian heritage reveals different aspects of itself according to the relevant religion, school of thought and period of time.

Religious literature in its earliest form evolved from Catholicism. This is revealed by the works of the Church Fathers, as well as by medieval literature in general. At the end of the Middle Ages, Thomas à Kempis' celebrated *The Imitation of Christ* encapsulated this evolutionary process and for centuries continued to be required reading for Catholics. After the Renaissance, the Council of Trent brought about ecclesiastical re-structuring. Thanks to the Jesuits, a great Catholic baroque literature was born, whose full potential was shown by Saint Theresa of Avila and Bossuet. The early days of Jansenism heavily influenced the work of Racine and Pascal. At the end of the eighteenth century and the beginning of the nineteenth, a Catholic revival displayed itself in the work of Chateaubriand and later in that of J. de Maistre and Lamennais. During the same period, a new notion of religion became one of the foundations of German Romanticism, conceived as a means of defence against a life experienced as mediocre. A revival of literature inspired by Catholicism signals the start (Henri Bordeaux, Péguy, Léon Bloy, Claudel) and the middle of the twentieth century (Jacques Maritain and Mauriac). During this same period, a strong neo-Catholic tendency emerged in Polish, Slovak and Hungarian literature. Protestantism, in all its forms – Lutheranism, Zwinglism, Calvinism, Puritanism – produced a characteristic religious literature. Milton's *Paradise Lost* and Bunyan's *Pilgrim's Progress* both attest to this, as does all eighteenth-century German pietist literature: the problem of free will and determinism, as well as individual participation in our own salvation, are mirrored in a series of works. The sources of modern existentialism are close to the Protestant variant of a Judeo-Christian outlook on the world. The works of Kierkegaard and the philosophical works of Heidegger are steeped in it. Alternatively, the plays of Ibsen and especially of Strindberg are distinguished by a very Lutheran feeling of guilt and sexual Puritanism. This Protestant view of man has survived and is still current, for example in the work of the film-maker Ingmar Bergman.

The cultural realm of Greek Orthodoxy is a world apart. In Byzantium and, later, in the Slav lands, this church's theology evolved towards eschatology in general. It included the belief in the presence of Christ as an indwelling spirit, a leaning to evangelical expansiveness, a universalism based on absolutes, a mixture of the inspired poverty of the gospels and Biblical prophecy, the coming and going of sectarian movements and the omnipotence of the fusion of Church and State under these auspices. Leaving to one side the religious period of Greek Orthodox literature, we need only to trace a predominant thread in Russian literature, from Gogol and Dostoyevsky to Bulgakov and Solzhenitsyn. This same source of inspiration occurs again in the poetry of Anna Akhmatova, in Pasternak's poetry and novels, and in Rumanian literature, most notably in poetry by Blaga. In the twentieth century, Bulgakov's great novel, *The Master and Margarita*, is constructed around Christology and orthodox theology, and its protagonists convey a message of Biblical significance.

In Judaism. there were mystic undercurrents, above all the Kabbala, which, from the sixteenth century to the twentieth, nurtured literary works from Agrippa of Nettesheim and Böhme to the tales of Poe and the novels of Marguerite Yourcenar. The Hassidic undercurrent, first appearing in the eighteenth century, preached direct contact with God and the abandonment of liturgy. This undercurrent quickly became a religion of the poor and the oppressed and gave rise to hundreds of stories and parables. Hassidic stories, in their literary form, appear in twentieth century – above all with Buber – and their influence can be seen in the tales, stories and novels of Kafka, as well as in a whole literary sub-genre dealing with the life of Eastern European Jews, from Shalom Alechem to the stories of Singer or Chagall's autobiography. To a certain extent this is a triangular theory of the world – I/you/God – which has had an effect, both directly and indirectly, on existentialism in France, certain types of contemporary poetry and even literary theories. The Judeo-Christian view of things is not always accepted automatically. One of the vectors of literary creativity springs from the conflict between Judeo-Christian and other values: those recognised by ancient Greece and Rome, for example, or by science. This conflict, already manifest during the Renaissance, becomes indissoluble from the philosophy of Spinoza, and is also to be found in Pascal and Molière. The Don Juan myth and all the works that take it up afresh by Molière, Mozart, Kierkegaard and Max Frisch, reveal this conflict. In the nineteenth century, almost all of Heine's work bears the imprint of the struggle between Jewish, Christian and 'peasant' values. This struggle becomes wild and gigantic with Nietzsche and is resolved into a smiling scepticism with Renan.

Many thoughts, movements and works which set out to discuss the Judeo-Christian worldview, from Voltaire to Sartre and from Hobbes to Marx, derive their inspiration from this heritage while they also engage in denying or attacking it. In the final analysis, a whole literature exists that deals with persecution, 'concentration camp' literature, 'gulag' literature, literature about the Holocaust – and the tragic nature of this heritage's history is thereby emphasised.

4 *The Byzantine Heritage*

A. VASSILIKOPOULOU

The resiting of the political and administrative capital of the Roman Empire in Constantinople (324–330), and the decline in the economic and cultural importance of the West which followed, pushed Europe's centre of gravity eastward. The Empire christened Byzantine prolonged the myth of world domination and thought of itself as 'Roman' to the bitter end.

From Constantine onwards, Christianity, by now a legally recognised religion with a privileged status, and soon to be a State religion (381), became the central and dominant element in the understanding of life and the world. Dedicated by the Emperor to the service of Christ, the Byzantine people saw themselves as the new 'chosen people'.

Christianity developed in the first centuries after Christ in a Hellenistic setting. The sacred scriptures, canonical or not, were written down directly in vernacular Greek, with the one exception of the Gospel according to Matthew, which was written in Aramaic. Words such as Christus, evangelium, ecclesia, liturgia, eucharistia, angelus, diabolus and ascesis, which described the liturgy, theology and asceticism, derived from the Greek (as, in former times, philosophical and cultural vocabulary had been) entered into Western Church Latin.

THE EARLY BYZANTINE ERA (*c*.330–*c*.640)

The Emperor proclaimed himself heir to a tradition founded by Augustus and Diocletian, thus perpetuating the Roman system of values.

Latin, however, the official language of the imperial administration, was gradually replaced in Byzantium by Greek and was eventually abandoned, as Greek had been in the Western Empire.

Literary continuity in late Antiquity and the beginnings of medieval literature

Christianity was soon in the ascendant, the guiding principle behind the cultural ambience, but the educational system left in place by the Ancients was felt to have a richness of humanity about it which Christians could only aim to perfect (an idea adopted during the Carolingian Renaissance). Rhetoric, inculcated by education, was present in almost every work of literature, whether prose or poetry.

Admiration for the perfection of style led to the veneration of traditional literary forms. Almost all the literary genres of the Alexandrine period of late Antiquity (History, Rhetoric, Epistles, Quantitative Poetry) were represented in Byzantium, a court literature for the highly literate.

Simultaneoulsy, an original literature in demotic Greek was created – the language of the New Testament and the Septuagint – based on spoken language but open to scholarly influence. With the help of the Church Fathers, new links between the religious and the profane were established at this turning-point in Byzantine history. The movement came from Cappadocia and contributed to the definition of the fundamental

31

dogmas of religion and at the same time to the flourishing of new literary genres.

The splendours of the liturgy satisfied the same taste for religious spectacle which had formerly led to the birth of tragedy. Liturgical developments went hand-in-hand with a rapid production of homilies and hymns, several centuries before similar activity in the West.

Inside as outside the Church, distinctive literary genres appeared, a fusion of Eastern and Greek traditions. These genres exercised great influence, first within the frontiers of a unified empire and then, by various external contacts, on other peoples, both in the West and in the East.

> The Word alone is all I am attached to, and I do not complain of the sufferings that I have undergone on land and on sea in order to possess it.
>
> Gregory of Nazianza,
> *Discourse against Julian*

Theology

This genre begins where philosophy ended, making use of all its weapons. The Church Fathers of the fourth century and the beginning of the fifth laid down codes of thought; only what could be assimilated by the spirit of Christianity was retained of the spirit of Antiquity. **Basil of Caesarea (329–379)** and **Gregory of Nazianza (c.330–c.390)** are proof of the high level reached by religious meditation during the Protobyzantine era; **Gregory of Nyssa (c.331–c.394)** was, by temperament and education, a genuine philosopher.

The mysterious author who dared to assume the prestigious name of **Dionysus the Areopagite (c.500)** exerted tremendous influence in the East and above all in the West, where his work read and admired during Carolingian times. His writings left their mark on all the teachings of mysticism. In the West, **Ambrose of Milan (c.340–397)**, having had a traditionally Greek and Latin education, was able to assimilate the thought of his Eastern contemporaries.

Homiletics

In Greek, 'omilia' means reunion, talk, sermon. Preaching takes the place of public debate; the sermon inherits from rhetoric; polemics from dialectics. Preaching is rich not only in quotations from the Bible, but also in quotations from ancient writers (Homer, writers of tragedies, Plutarch) probably taken from school anthologies.

Gregory of Nazianza sought after profane eloquence 'to make it auxiliary to truth'. **John Chrysostom (c.344–407)** criticises the ruling passions of his time.

The homily extended to the West by means of translations by Jerome and by Rufinus Aquileus. With the *Homilies* of Gregory the Great (c.540–604) – he lived as papal nuncio in Constantinople from 579 to 585 – 'omilia' and 'sermo' became virtually synonymous.

Hagiography

The lives of the saints constitute a distinct literary genre which is very common in Byzantium. The perfect life is to be encountered in the desert. The monastic ideal – a life of renunciation and mortification similar to that lived by the angels – added new forms to existing literature. The first expression of Latin monasticism is directly attributable to Eastern sources. Jerome, educated in the East, translated the rule of **Pacomius (287–347)**, Rufinus Aquileus that of Basil of Caesarea. Veneration for martyrs, ascetics and monks is revealed in literature in the proliferation of hagiography: acts, passions, collections, miracles. This literary genre, more or less historical in character, borrows from various sources. A feeling for romantic storytelling found a substitute in the legendary flowering of saints' lives, as in apocryphal writings. The language was popular, the tone familiar. The influential *The Life of Saint Anthony*, written by **Athanasius of Alexandria (c.298–373)** about 360, was soon translated twice into Latin and played the role of model for the future lives of saints. *The Story of the Monks*, written at the end of the fourth century AD by an anonymous writer whose journey took place in 394–395, was circulated in Latin in an amplified translation by Rufinus Aquileus. Mention may also be made of the *Story for Lausos* (419–420) by **Bishop Galates Palladios (c.363–c.431)**, a collection of the edifying lives of Egyptian monks, dedicated to Lausos; the *Story of Philotheus* (437–449), compiled by **Theodoret of Cyr (c.393–c.466)**; the biographies of **Cyril of Scythopolis (mid sixth century)**; and the 'spiritual meadow' (615–619) of John Moschos, a monk in Jerusalem, then in the desert, who was particularly interested in the ascetics who had settled between Jerusalem and the Dead Sea. The 'spiritual meadow' has often been compared to the *Fioretti* or *Little Flowers* of Saint Francis of Assisi.

The universal chronicle

Whereas Byzantine historians recounted the political and ecclesiastical history of their times, choosing for their models the historians of ancient Greece, medieval historiography adopted a new literary genre. Begun in the third and fourth centuries AD, this followed in the footsteps of the Alexandrine novels of late Antiquity and was influenced by Eastern traditions. The chronicler was careful to link history with the Biblical story of creation. The Church of Christ, associated with the Roman empire and Hellenic culture, was established in the empire of the New Rome, which was also the New Jerusalem. The chronicler attempted a global history of humanity, from the creation of the world (about 5500 BC) to the time in which he wrote, without attempting to distinguish between fantasy and truth.

John Malalas (c.491–578), a Syrian from Antioch ('malel' means orator in Syrian), was the most picturesque of the Byzantine chroniclers. His chronicle stretched from legendary times in Egypt to the end of the reign of the Emperor Justinian (563). It served as a model for the chronicles of Latin, Germanic and Slav lands.

Liturgical religious poetry

This differs from traditional poetry both in content and rhythm. Its metre is based on musical accentuation, not on vowel length. Rhythmically adventurous and set free from the straitjacket of prosody, vernacular Greek adopted the harmonies of Hebrew poetry. **Romanos the Singer (sixth century AD)**, poet and composer, a native of Emesus in Syria, lived in Constantinople in the first half of the sixth century. He perfected the form of hymns (Kontakia). The stanzas of his canticles are written in the same flowery style we find in Byzantine homiletics. The continual interplay of antitheses, his taste for pathetic inscriptions, the richness of his imagery, the epic movement of some of his pieces, the dramatic dimension to the interchanges between

Προοίμιον
Ὅταν ἔλθῃς, ὁ Θεός, ἐπὶ γῆς μετὰ δόξης,
καὶ τρέμουσι τὰ σύμπαντα,
ποταμὸς δὲ τοῦ πυρὸς πρὸ τοῦ βήματος ἕλκει,
καὶ βίλοι διανοίγονται καὶ τὰ κρυπτὰ δημοσιεύονται,
τότε ῥῦσαί με ἐκ τοῦ πυρὸς τοῦ ἀσβέστου
καὶ ἀξίωσον ἐκ δεξιῶν σου με στῆναι,
κριτὰ δικαιότατε.

Prooimion
God, when you walk upon the earth in glory, and when the universe trembles, the river of fire flows before the judgement seat, the books are opened and all secrets are revealed, save me then from the fire that burns forever and account me worthy to stand at your right hand, o most equitable judge.

Christian sources

characters (Christ and the Virgin Mary climbing up to Golgotha), the inner struggles that disturb them (Peter's denial of Christ), the sweetness of his pity for the sinner and the joy of salvation elevate this ecclesiastical poetry to a level above the average.

THE 'GREAT BREACH'
(*c*.640–843)

Great events have shaken the Mediterranean world and none more so than the expansion of Arab civilisation. The flourishing Greek communities of Syria, Armenia, Palestine and Egypt were ravaged and, for the most part, destroyed. Later, from 700 AD onwards, the Roman provinces of Africa and the whole of the Iberian peninsula fell into the hands of the 'infidels'. The area marked out by Christianity which, during the Protobyzantine era, grew up around the Mediterranean fringe, was now displaced in a northerly direction.

The Byzantine Empire enters into its medieval period, referred to as the 'great breach'. Avaroslavic invasions, epidemics and religious crises completely changed the face of the Protobyzantine State. Literary genres inspired by religion – homiletics, hagiography and chronicles – were still ardently pursued, but in a language which further distanced itself from the spoken word.

In theology, **Maximus the Confessor (580–662)** was very influential in the East, and subsequently in the West, thanks to the translations of Johannes Scotus Erigenes. **John Damascene (*c*.650–*c*.750)**, in his *Source of Knowledge*, merely set out to complete the work of his predecessors, without even trying to innovate. His mind, devoted to synthesis, and his Aristotelianism, made him the great theologian that the West, and Thomas Aquinas in particular, later remembered. **Theodorus of Stoudites (752–826) and Nicephorus the Patriarch (758–829)** defended true faith in their sermons against the iconoclasts.

The chronicles of Nicephorus the Patriarch, of **George Syncellus (second half of the eighth century)** and of **Theophanes the Confessor (*c*.758–*c*.818)** were later translated into Latin by Anastasius the Librarian (*c*.817–897), who carried out the duties of a papal secretary.

Liturgical poetry added to itself a new literary genre, the canon, whose music is more varied than hymns and whose language is much more erudite. John Damascene, **Andrew the Cretan (*c*.660–740)** and **Cosmas the Singer (born *c*.675)** often composed both the words and the music, still used today in the orthodox liturgy.

With the coronation of Charlemagne in 800, the Empire of Western Christendom was born, asserting the same political pretensions as the Eastern Empire. A parallel development took place of two worlds which both claimed to have assumed the mantle of the Roman Empire, entailing a new geographical division of spheres of cultural influence. The West evolved according to Germanic and Celtic influences, but also Eastern ones, out of which emerged the medieval and the modern Western world.

The Eastern Empire survived for a further seven centuries. Bulgarians, Russians and Serbians owe the fact that they are Christian and a great part of their culture – their alphabet, literary language and genres – to Byzantium. The Christianisation of other nations under Byzantine rule was carried out in their own tongue. The taste for learning grew from the end of the period of iconoclasm in 843. Grammarians, commentators, compilers of encyclopaedias continued the work begun by philologists in the Alexandrine era. Greek Antiquity is revered and, because of this, we can speak of a Renaissance. This philological activity knew no rest. From Byzantium it radiated outwards to Benedictine abbeys, to Florence, to Paris, to Europe in general, both medieval and modern, which, from different historical and geographical perspectives, will speak of a different Renaissance.

5 *The Beginnings of Literature in Europe*

F. SUARD

How is it you are not ashamed of thinking that there are only three languages – Hebrew, Greek and Latin – and of believing that all other nations and peoples must be blind and deaf?

The Life of Constantine

The long period of time that stretches from the eighth to the thirteenth century, from the Venerable Bede, the father of literature in Anglo-Saxon, to Llull, one of the greatest Catalan writers, is rich in European literary treasures. Because of the upheavals during this period, cultural exchanges on various levels allowed a literary style in vernacular languages to emerge and the diffusion of common narrative themes: the result of a fertile interplay between Latin and Greek, the languages of worship and culture.

To describe, however briefly, the luxurious blossoming of this fertile combination would be tantamount to not describing, even succinctly, each individual literature's flowering, irrespective of size. At the risk of neglecting essential authors and texts, we will therefore only consider those elements in this overall flowering which help us to understand how this European literary heritage was formed: a heritage whose lustre and harmony reverberated down the centuries – and ignorance of which would certainly detract from our understanding of any European country's contemporary literary scene.

THE DIFFUSION OF MANUSCRIPTS

In medieval Europe manuscripts were always changing hands. They were translated from one language and literary form to another, serving different purposes, and they highlight the importance of taste and of medieval literary expectations. Three manuscripts in particular exemplify these attributes.

Boethius: a guide to Christian thought

Before the period that now concerns us, the work of **Boethius (c.480–524)**, *De Consolatione Philosophiæ* (*The Consolation of Philosophy*, 524), is inextricably linked to two areas of intellectual endeavour: philosophy and literature. With its roots in Alexandrine neo-Platonist thought, *The Consolation of Philosophy* transmitted to the Middle Ages a philosophical tradition acquired at first hand (Boethius understood Greek) and allowed a Christian spiritual exercise to be defined in relation to the culture of Antiquity. In this work began the theme of meditating on the relationship between Providence and Destiny, on divine predestination and human free will and on worldly infinity, as well as on the question of sovereign goodness:

O qui perpetua mundum ratione gubernas,
terrarum cælique sator, qui tempus ab ævo

O Thou who governest the Universe according to an everlasting order, Father of earth and of heaven, from whose hand, from all eternity, time

ire jubes stabilisque manens
das cuncta moveri,
quem non externæ pepulerunt
fingere causæ
materiæ fluitantis opus (. . .).
Boethius, *De Consolatione Philosophiæ*

trickles like sand, Thou who art immovable,
making all things move,
no external cause
constrained Thee to fashion
Thy handiwork from lifeless matter (. . .).

This book is not a philosophical textbook, even though it marks a return to the dialogue technique so dear to Socrates. It is a moving testament, for Boethius was under sentence of death at the time. A minister for Theodoric the Great, King of the Ostrogoths, Boethius had been accused of plotting against him and after a long time in prison he was tortured to death. The *Consolation* was written while he was a prisoner.

The *Consolation* is a beautiful book in which the allegorical personification not only of Philosophy, but also of various other concepts, fills its argument with vitality. Heir to a literary tradition, Boethius defines the medieval aesthetic once and for all, especially in his depiction of the Wheel of Fortune:

Haec nostra vis est, hunc
continuum ludum ludimus:
rotam volubili orbe versamus,
infima summis, summa infimis
mutare gaudemus.
Boethius, *De Consolatione Philosophiæ*

Here is our nature, here is
the interminable game at which
we play: tirelessly turning
the wheel, taking pleasure in
making what is up descend
and making what is down rise.

The juxtaposition of prose and passages in verse makes it possible to alternate measured reflection and lyricism, and many of the set expressions in the metrical parts reappeared in the works of medieval authors, for example, in prayers.

In the second half of the ninth century the Latin text was translated for the first time into a vernacular language: King Alfred adapted it into Old English, an adaptation in which there is an interesting reminiscence of a golden age.

Later, from 1377 to 1381, Chaucer translates the *Consolation* into Middle English adding a passage in verse: a translation which was printed by Caxton in 1475. A second adaptation was done in German in the second half of the tenth century, the work of a monk, Notker III the German (*Teutonicus*) or the Thick-lipped (*Labeo*) in the monastery of St Gallen. His method was interesting: Notker reproduced the Latin text, translated it into High German, then gave a Christian commentary alongside his translation:

Cum formares mores
nostros, et rationem
totius vitæ
ad exemplar celestis
et angelici ordinis.

Tō dū mīne síte
únd álla dīa uvīsūn
mīnes lībes scáffōtōst
nāh témo bílde dero
éngelo.
Uuánda dāt-umbe
chám christus
dei sapientia hára in
uuerlt táz er
ménnisken
lérti, in terris
angelicam uitam
ducere.

As Thou hast created me,
in my deportment
and in all
the organisation of my life,
modelled on the angels.
For if the Christ, God's
Wisdom, came into
this world, it was
in order to teach
men to lead on
earth the life of angels.

Translations into Romance languages came later. *Boeci* (*Boethius*), in the language of Limoges *c.*1000, is an indication of the interest in Boethius rather than a true translation. We have to wait until 1150 for an anonymous translation into French prose, but there were many translations into French in the thirteenth and fourteenth centuries, especially that by Jean de Meung (at the end of the thirteenth century) and by Renaud de Louhans (fourteenth century) which were very popular. The *Consolation* also inspired many philosophical commentaries, several of which appeared during Carolingian times – notably those of Alcuin and Rémi of Auxerre, who made the work a guide to Christian thought. Also noteworthy in the twelfth century was the commentary by Guillaume de Conches. The *Consolation* also played a decisive role in the thought of laymen: Jean de Meung's meditation, in the final part of the *Roman de la Rose*, on the relationship between God and the world owes much to it, as does the *Tesoretto* (*Little Treasure*, *c.*1260) by Brunetto Latini (*c.*1220–1295). Its influence was felt in Spain in the fourteenth and fifteenth centuries.

The *Navigatio Sancti Brendani* or the importance of the imagination

The fate of *The Consolation of Philosophy* shows how the diffusion and disclosure of the Greco-Roman heritage operated in the Middle Ages and reveals a connection between non-utilitarian literature and a certain kind of speculative reflection. The *Navigatio Sancti Brendani*, or *Voyage of Saint Brendan*, for its part, shows the osmosis between very different contemporary cultures and emphasises the importance to the medieval mind of imagination. The text of this 'voyage', set out in Latin, dates back to the ninth century. Taking as its starting-point the story of a man who lived in sixth-century Ireland – the abbot of a monastery in County Kerry and the founder of many religious houses – the *Voyage of Saint Brendan* is the story of a mystical quest. It borrows from Irish traditional tales of imaginary journeys, the 'immrama' of Irish folklore, which themselves drew on the real-life experiences of seafaring voyages.

Having learned from his nephew, Barinthus, of the existence of a marvellous island promised to God's saints, Brendan decides to go looking for it. He boards a ship with fourteen brothers. After seven years their mystical quest ends with the discovery of the island which symbolises both the promise of eternal happiness and the impossibility of reaching it without dying. Although the quest is punctuated by edifying passages of scripture, it is also a fantastic journey in which amusing encounters alternate with disturbing discoveries. One day, for instance, the travellers start a fire on the back of a whale – an incident which soon involves them in beating a hasty retreat:

Cum autem ministrarent lignei ignem et fervere cepisset cacabus, cepit insula se movere sicut unda. Fratres vero currere ad navim, deprecantes patrocinium sancti patris. *Navigatio Sancti Brendani*	*They had just lit a fire with some wood and the cooking pot had started to boil, when the island began to move as if it were water. Then the brothers ran towards the ship and cried out for divine protection.*

These anecdotes tally with the marvellous episodes described in Irish tales, such as the *Voyage of Bran* or the *Voyage of Maël-Duine*: encounters with islands where people are held against their will, where they are always laughing, where they always have enough to eat and drink. But there are also echoes of ancient mythologies in all this: of Homer's *Odyssey* and Virgil's *Aeneid*.

This mixture of different traditions is the work of Irish monks. They wanted to place an ascetic interpretation on their spirituality by understanding the Christian life as a pilgrimage and, in so doing, to Christianise traditions with which they were already familiar. These 'Scoti' (Irish) had probably fled their country, which had been ravaged by the invasions of Vikings from Denmark, to settle in Lotharingia. The oldest manuscripts were found in Lorraine – and we can also see here in the tenth century AD a tendency to use the various forms of pagan culture in a way which Christianises them. The epic poem of *Waltharius*, is a good example.

The Middle Ages were fascinated by this mixture of edifying characteristics and images propitious to inducing a dream-like state. An impressive number of Latin manuscripts have been preserved: there are almost 120, of which fourteen were copied in the fourteenth century and twenty-eight in the fifteenth. Transpositions of the originals into vernacular languages started early and included a variety of texts.

These transpositions were the most numerous and the longest lasting in German-speaking areas. Around 1150 a text was compiled in Middle High German which embodies an independent version of the Brendan story with many offshoots. It contains deviations from its Latin source material (the voyage lasts for nine years rather than seven) and its fantastic aspect is emphasised in the manner of texts in the 'Spielmannspoesie' (epic minstrelsy) tradition. Several texts in German are derived from this version, including one written in the Lübeck dialect. This same adaptation is also the source of a metrical version in Middle Dutch (*De Reis van Sente Brandane*) which contains original touches. Departure on the quest is motivated by Brendan's incredulity about a book detailing the marvels of creation: an angel prompts the abbot to see them for himself and this is how the voyage is initiated.

Trade with Northern Europe translated by the towns of the Hanseatic League brought the Germanic version of the story to Scandinavia. Later, a fifteenth-century Dutch text served as a model for a version in Middle High German composed at the court of Albert III of Bavaria

and printed in 1468. Many other editions in High and Low German followed in the sixteenth century and the work became a 'Volksbuch' (chapbook).

In countries where Romance languages were spoken, the *Navigatio* seems to have been known first in Brittany, if the similarity of the place names and the plagiarisms in the *Vita Sancti Machuti* (*Life of Saint Malo*, ninth to tenth century) are anything to go by. The sacking and pillaging of the Normans in Brittany forced the monks who had inherited the story to flee eastwards, and the first version in French is in Anglo-Norman, written by one Benedeit at the request of the Countess of Louvain, Adeliza or Matilda, the wife of Henry I. This translation was so popular that it was twice 'translated back' into Latin, its original language. Other versions in Old French – prose time – were also produced.

We know of translations of the *Navigatio* into Old Italian: probably resulting from the position of Venice or Genoa at the intersection of sea-lanes, they were confined to Northern Italy. In the Iberian peninsula we find a Catalan translation and a Portuguese version, the *Navigação de S. Brandano*, the source of a faithful adaptation called the *Conto de Amaro*.

In England, the physical proximity of the Celtic lands explains how the legend found its way there, but as far as we know, there are no translations (which were produced one after the other, in verse then in prose) before the fourteenth century.

Even though Ireland is the country mentioned in the story, texts in Irish are curiously lacking: the tradition was transmitted orally and written versions have disappeared because of civil unrest and invasions. What remains, the *Betha Brennain* (*Life of Brendan*), bears no direct resemblance to the Latin version.

The success of this composite work was such that, till the end of the Middle Ages at least, the genuineness of Brendan's voyages was never called into question, and old maps – the one in Hereford which dates back to 1275, for example – mention the *Insula Brendani* (Brendan's isle).

Alexander, from history to legend

When we come to tales about Alexander, King of Macedonia, we touch on a subject where historical accuracy and the narration of legend can be compared and contrasted. What is worth noting, above all, is the extraordinary spread of the traditions about Alexander in all cultures and in all areas of intellectual activity. We also find ourselves at the meeting of three great vehicles of culture – Hebrew, Greek and Latin – together with vernacular languages.

History or legend? There are plenty of historical biographies of Alexander, whether that by Arion in Greek, or those in Latin by Quintus Curtius, Trogus, Pompeius, Orosius and Justinus. These biographies, however, attest to a legend – that of the conqueror of the world – as much as to an episode in history. The legendary aspect increased in importance in literary works, even when their authors attempted to correct their sources.

The medieval tales about Alexander are a forest dense with trees – or, to use a fifteenth-century expression, 'a sea of stories'. Two main categories can be identified. First, there is the one that originated with historians. This is not the largest category, but it did produce works of value: the *Alexandreis, sive Gesta Alexandri Magni* (*The Alexandreid*, c.1180), for example, by **Gautier de Châtillon (twelfth century)**, one of the best French poets writing in Latin who, reared on Virgil, Lucan and Ovid, produced a kind of model for the medieval Latin epic. Many works in vernacular languages may be bracketed with his text: in Spain we have the *Libro de Alexandre* (*Book of Alexander*, c.1240); in Holland there is the *Alexanders Geesten* (*Alexander's Deeds of Derring-Do*, second half of the thirteenth century) by Jacob Van Maerlant, who set an example for supplements and sequels to Biblical accounts. In Bohemia there is an adaptation in German written in 1287 for the Přemyslid king Otakar II (thirteenth century) by Ulrich von Etzenbach, and another in Old Czech (c.1300) which partially does away with the ancient frame of reference and is striking because of its allusions to the current state of the nation.

The second category is made up of a collection of legends, the most important of which was the *Pseudo-Callisthenes*, the Greek novel written shortly after 200 AD by a native of Alexandria. This was soon amplified and gave rise to adaptations in various languages. Among those relevent to Europe (translations also exist into Hebrew, Syrian, Ethiopian and Armenian) was a life of Alexander in Bulgarian (twelfth century), in Serbian and in Croatian (fourteenth century) and three Greek versions. But in European terms the most important adaptations were two translations into Latin which provided a starting-point for most medieval versions: these were the *Res gestæ Alexandri Macedonis* (*Alexander's Deeds*, c.320 AD) by Julius Valerius and his abridgement of this, the *Epitome*, together with a later, but much imitated version, which demonstrates the literary contacts between the Latin West and Byzantium, the *Nativitas et Victoria Alexandri Magni* (*The Birth and Victory of Alexander the Great*, c.950), better known under the title of *Historia de Preliis* (*The History of Wars*), by the priest Leo of Naples.

A mirror for princes

In addition to the *Pseudo-Callisthenes*, and sometimes included with it, are certain texts which have played an important part in the medieval tradition. First, there are exchanges of letters between Alexander and a Brahmin, *Collatio Alexandri cum Dindimo per Literas Facta* (*An Epistolary Conversation with Dindimus*), in which the Brahmin's asceticism is contrasted with the conqueror's sensuality and desire for glory – though it is the conqueror who has the last word. Second, there is Alexander's letter to Aristotle, *Epistola Alexandri ad Aristotelem Magistrum suum de Itinere suo et de Situ Indiæ* (*A Letter from Alexander to his Master Aristotle on his Itinerary and on India*) and a text on the marvels of India which was probably attached to the former, *Epistola de Mirabilibus Indiæ* (*Letter on the Marvels of India*). Next we find a group of

Jewish texts, the most important of which is Alexander's journey to paradise. The most ancient version of this text is found in the Talmud of Babylon (before 500) and was translated into Latin after 1100 under the title of *Iter ad Paradisum*. Finally, there are a group of Arab texts, separate from the works about Alexander, the *Secret of Secrets*, which supposedly relates Aristotle's advice to Alexander. This was possibly compiled in Syrian during the eighth century and was immediately translated into Arabic; it was considerably augmented and appeared in two versions. The long version, which was to be very successful in Europe, was translated into Latin in the thirteenth century, first and foremost by the Englishman, Roger Bacon (*Secretum Secretorum*, 1257).

The tradition of the *Pseudo-Callisthenes* is the source for most medieval vernacular versions. In the same vein as Julius Valerius, there is the oldest fragment of a novel in French, the fragment of Alberic in the dialect of the Dauphiné (early twelfth century), the oldest poem in German, the *Alexanderlied* by Pfaffe Lamprecht, of which the original version (*Vorau Alexander*) dates from 1155, as do the revisions of the former texts. There is the French *Alexandre* in decasyllables (*c.*1170) and, above all, there is the great novel in alexandrines (*c.*1180).

Linked to *The History of Wars*, we find the *Seelentrost* (*Consolation of Souls*, before 1358) in Middle Low German, and the late text in Middle High German, edited in 1473 in Augsburg, by Johann Hartlieb, the *Histori von dem grossen Alexander* (*The History of Alexander the Great*), a work translated into Danish prose in 1584. The most important derivative text is the French prose novel written in the thirteenth century which went through eleven editions between 1506 and 1630. But *The History of Wars* was also translated into English, German and Middle Swedish and inspired the *Historia Alexandri* (*History of Alexander the Great*, fourteenth century) by Quilichinus of Spoleto, a judge at the court of the Hohenstaufen, which was adapted in Germany and Italy.

Why was Alexander such a fascinating subject? Though he was attacked by the moralists who followed Seneca, and though theological thought, based on *Daniel* and 1 and 2 *Maccabees*, sees in him the forerunner of the Antichrist, he quickly acquired a mythical dimension. From the viewpoint of the ideals of courtly love and of the thirst for knowledge that developed in the twelfth century particularly, he combined conflicting qualities. He was the conqueror of the known world, but also someone whose thirst for knowledge encouraged him to discover the secrets of nature according to the education he had received. The conquest of the world and of knowledge are indistinguishable – and generosity became the primary virtue of this conqueror who only amassed a fortune to dispose of it and only discovered things himself in order to make them known to others.

THE FORMING OF LITERATURE IN EUROPE

The five centuries (Early Middle Ages) which led to the development of the great European States were eventful in terms of political upheavals, which affected not only the international balance of power, but also the concomitant fostering of national and community awareness. Cultural belonging, a country's literature and the language in which it is written, was the result not only of national identity, but of the circumstances attendant on campaigns of mass evangelisation and the propagation of the Christian message. Three distinct cases can be discerned: Byzantium proper, the Slav lands and the Latin West.

The Christian message, a cultural bond

In Byzantium, Greek, which gradually became the official language of the Empire, was a vehicle for a unifying concept of the world: the universal message of Christianity was guaranteed by the Emperor who had a duty to spread the faith.

THE BEGINNINGS OF LITERATURE IN EUROPE

In the Slav lands, the major event was the work carried out, from 863 onwards, by two Greek brothers from Thessalonika, **Constantine-Cyril (826–869)** and **Methodius (815–885)**, who were summoned to Greater Moravia by Ratislav to put the finishing touches to the process of Christianisation already begun by 'Latin' missionaries before 800 AD. In order to make the Christian faith intelligible to all speakers of closely related Slavic dialects, Cyril and Methodius extracted from their own Macedonian dialect of Greek the literary and liturgical language of 'Old Church Slavonic'. On the basis of Greek lower-case letters and other elements, they devised an alphabet of thirty-eight letters – subsequently known as the 'Glagolitic' alphabet – and translated into 'Old Slavonic' such essential texts as missals and prayer-books. Constantine then tackled the translation of the New Testament wholee prologue (*Proglas'*) consisted of 110 duodecasyllabic verses with caesuras: the first great poem in a Slavic language. He then translated both a psalter and a missal. His brother, Methodius, soon helped by translating first a selection, then most of the Old Testament. His distinctive contribution, however, was in the area of civil law, when he collaborated with his brother in drawing up the oldest Slavic civil code, *Zakon sudnyj ljudem* (*Code of Justice for the People*).

Appointed as an archbishop, Methodius and his followers formed a 'Greater Moravian school of literature' (873–885). Because of this, the future leading lights of Bulgarian religious and literary activity – Clement, Constantine and Naum – produced their first writings. The major literary works of this period remain the *Žit'je Konstantina* (*Life of Constantine*), in which Methodius took up the cudgels on behalf of the Slavonic language with the *Žit'je Methodija* (*Life of Methodius*).

Cyril and Methodius' work was not continued in Moravia as shortly after 885, the Latin clergy, ever present and active, banned the Slavonic liturgy and excommunicated its followers. The latter took refuge in Bohemia,

Croatia and above all in Bulgaria, where their literary activity paved the way for the emergence in the cultural hinterland of Byzantium of a national literature in Bulgarian Slavonic. This contributed to the definitive rapprochement of Kiev, the capital of Little Russia, to the Greek Orthodox tradition.

Introduced to Russia at the end of the tenth century, Christianity was rapidly Slavicised in terms of language and culture, but remained indebted to Byzantium for its liturgy. From the beginning of the eleventh century, the Russian Orthodox Church adopted the Bulgarian liturgy, as well as the Cyrillic system of writing created within Bulgarian Slavonic *c*.900 AD. Close to the language spoken by the Eastern Slavs and capable of being influenced by it, Russian Slavonic was not recognised as a foreign language, unlike Latin in Hungary, Poland or Scandinavia. Thus the intermingling of liturgical and spoken language led to the creation of a unique literary one.

Serbia, Christianised at the end of the ninth century by disciples of Cyril and Methodius, remained under the influence of Byzantium. Croatia exemplified a twofold influence, Frankish and Methodian: a symbiosis of Latin, Greek and Slav traditions was its literary hallmark in the Middle Ages.

Bohemia was Christianised during the ninth century by Latin missionaries from Bavaria. It was part of the Great Moravian Empire for a time, influenced by Methodian missionary work and its aftermath. During the tenth and eleventh centuries, it experienced the phenomenon of liturgical and literary Czech Slavonic which was used in hagiographies of Wenceslas and Ludmila, and in homiletic writings, and which existed alongside a preponderance of Latin. After the end of the thirteenth century, however, this period, was followed by an equal insistence on Latin and Old Czech.

In the rest of Europe, the Christianisation of new countries, just like the Christian reconquest of countries devastated by migrating barbarians, was carried out by Latin-speaking missionaries, as had been the case, for Italy, Gaul and Spain from the first century AD.

In the same way that the culture of 'Late Antiquity' had been maintained because of its close ties with Christian thought, especially in the works of Augustine (354–430), so the work of evangelisation effected during this period was accompanied by a cultural content derived from Latin precedents.

A new Christian outreach

From 750 to 850 a renewal of Christian outreach took place in Northern Europe from England to East Frisia and Germany. From Irish monasteries, which had sprung up from the middle of the fifth century at the instigation of Saint Patrick, the 'Scoti' began to evangelise the continent and England from the end of the sixth century. Missionaries travellers, ascetics, reformers, grammarians, poets and Celtic monks in their wanderings *pro Christo* (for the love of Christ) covered the Rhineland and Switzerland, founding important monasteries such as St Gallen, Lorsch and Reichenau. To their pupils they imparted a knowledge of Latin and the basic rudiments of Greek. They copied and preserved Latin authors such as Terence, Horace and Virgil, or those of 'Late Antiquity' such as Boethius, Donatus and Priscian, and later Isidorus of Seville. The monks' cultural outreach continued long after their evangelical campaign. The philosopher **Johannes Scotus Erigenes** (*c.*800–*c.*877), for example, arrived at the court of Charles the Bald in the first half of the ninth century to translate the works of Dionysus the Areopagite which in 827 the Byzantine Emperor, Michael the Stammerer, had offered to Louis the Pious. At the beginning of the tenth century, Marianus Scotus, a hermit in Fulda for most of his life, wrote a chronicle in which he proposed a chronological revision of the Anno Domini system.

Galvanised into action by the Irish and Roman monks sent to England in 597 by Gregory the Great, the English Church, in its turn, became a hub for mass evangelisation. The most significant task was accomplished by Winfrith: coming from monasteries in Wessex, at the beginning of 716, he embarked on intense missionary activity which took him to Frisia, then to Thuringia and Bavaria.

Once again, the English made the first attempts to evangelise Scandinavia. For a long time, the Church in Denmark and Norway retained traces of ancient links with the English Church in their liturgy and religious literature. Christianity, however, also developed to the east of the German Empire: in Greater Moravia and Bohemia in the ninth century, and in Poland and Hungary from the second half of the tenth century. Similarly, the bishopric of Aarhus was founded in Denmark in 947. In all these territories, as in those which had a history of Christianity, Latin was a language of both liturgy and culture. The vernacular was not necessarily despised, at least as a language informed by reflection, in which faith could and should express itself. At the end of the ninth century, King Alfred had already translated into Old English four works that became essential for medieval culture: the *Historia Ecclesiastica* (*The History of the Church in Britain*) by the Venerable Bede; the *Cura Pastoralis* (*The Duties of a Pastor*) by Gregory the Great; Boethius' *Consolation*; and the *Historia Mundi* (*The History of the World*) by Orosius; but here, as elsewhere, the cultural reference was to Latin. Throughout this part of Europe, we are confronted by a bilingual situation which opposed an academic language – Latin – to vernacular languages. In the Eastern empire, however, the Greek of erudition jostled with vernacular Greek, and different forms of Slavonic played the same part in certain Slavic countries such as Bulgaria, Serbia, Russia and, for a time, Bohemia and Croatia.

Hubs of culture and distribution networks for texts

In the footsteps of the indefatigable 'Scoti', the continental movement of knowledge and manuscripts was the key to the formation of a European world of literati from the eighth to the thirteenth century. The aim of this movement was to simultaneously transmit a knowledge inherited from the Ancients and ways of writing and thinking which this apprenticeship to Antiquity had developed in terms of the religious as well as the profane.

> (. . .) an Grece ot de chevalerie
> Le premier los et de clergie.
> Puis vint chevalerie a Rome
> Et de la clergie la some,
> Qui or est en France venue.

Chrétien de Troyes, *Cligés*

On the other hand, thanks to the *translatio*, there was a flowering of national literatures. We should not be taken in by Chrétien de Troyes' enthusiasm for things French: the phenomenon is universal and not even Byzantium was immune. If there is no, or relatively little, geographical movement here, the double standard persists: on the one hand, there is the transmission of the culture of ancient Greece; on the other, the emergence of Byzantine literature. The *translatio* is not just about history: it also encourages a taste for novelty.

The study of how texts were generated is inseparable from close consideration of the places where they were produced. These were centres in which the intellectual wealth inherited from previous generations was preserved and passed on: a school in the widest sense of the word. Though a scholarly tradition was maintained in Byzantium despite the trembles inflicted on it by attacks from outside and the onslaught of iconoclasm during the years of the 'great breach', this same tradition was suspended in the West during the centuries that followed the collapse of the Roman Empire. In the West this gap was filled by monasteries which initiated a system of education where none had existed before: until the eleventh century, centres of culture are synonymous with the great abbeys. **The Venerable Bede (c.673–735)** was a monk from Jarrow, near Newcastle, while the beginnings of Germanic culture were synonymous with the history of St Gallen, the spiritual homeland of the Notkers and the Ekkehards,

On the one hand we have the *translatio studii* (transmission of knowledge), the route of which is plotted in the characteristic manner of that son of Champagne, **Chrétien de Troyes (c.1138–c.1183)**:

> (. . .) the lustre of knowledge and of
> chivalrous valour shone forth first
> in Greece, afterwards they came to
> Rome and now they are found here
> in France.

and that of Tegernsee and Fulda, illustrated by **Raban Maur (c.780–856)**.

In Serbia, the many monasteries, such as Studenica, Zica and Peć, were centres for a variety of literary activities, including the translation and transcription of Biblical and liturgical texts. At the beginning of the twelfth century, the shaping of Serbian Slavonic began in the monasteries of Paska, which gave its name to a school of spelling, and Chilindari in particular where there was a Serbian enclave.

Then came schools connected to a bishop's palace (cathedral schools) or to a college of canons (collegiate schools), such as those at Rheims and Laon (eleventh century), Chartres, Saint-Victor and Sainte-Geneviève in Paris and Bologna. Some of these schools developed their own universities, involving themselves in a process of association which made them independent of episcopal patronage (as in Paris) or of the commune (as in Bologna).

Another essential element of cultural exchange was the court of a prince or a king. Breton storytellers came to the English court of Henry Plantagenet via Ireland or Wales to make their traditions known. The authors of the *Tristan* cycle of novels and Marie de France, a writer of lays, drew from these tales the subject matter of their work. Henry's court in Poitiers heard the troubadours' first songs and Eleanor, the grand-daughter of William IX of Aquitaine, took them into Northern France with her. The court of Frederick II in Sicily became the cradle of Italian lyricism.

Germany also laid claim to brilliant princely courts, like that of the landgraves of Thuringia, as did Bohemia, the Brabant, Aragon and Castille, in which some kings were themselves poets. In all these courts an ideal life of chivalry was expounded, in which the art of loving held a crucial place; hence the characteristic terms of 'cortezia', 'courtoisie' and 'hövescheit'.

Some towns were able to act as catalysts in the development of cultural activities. In France, such was the case with Arras in the thirteenth century, or, in Italy, with large fiefdoms like Florence. The transmission of learning or forms of culture presupposes that a different cultural tradition is made available to a new public in its own language of habitual use, whence stems the importance, for the evolution of literature in Europe in the Middle Ages, of translations and of the border areas in which they originated.

These translations were sometimes the work of actual schools of translators (the school of Alfred in tenth-century England, for example), particularly in regions where many civilisations came into contact with each another. This was the case, in the twelfth century, for Northern Italy which, via Venice, was in contact with Byzantine culture; for Sicily, whose civilisation was founded on a veritable trilingualism (Latin, Greek and Arabic); for Southern Italy with, in the eleventh century, the medical studies of Constantinus Africanus, translated from Arabic and Greek; and for Spain in particular, after 1130 and continuing into the second half of the twelfth century, with its school of translators in Toledo, brought into existence by Archbishop Raymond. This included, in addition to Castilians, Christians, Jews and Arabs alike, and a number of foreigners: Germans (Herman of Carinthia), Englishmen (Adelard of Bath) and Italians (Gerard of Cremona). Because of this school, Aristotelian thought became familiar in the Latin-speaking West.

Translations from one vernacular language to another involve certain paradoxes. This process would seem to be indispensable to the circulation of literary works. The Limburger **Henric van Veldeke (*c*.1175–*c*.1200)** wrote a first copy of his adaptation of *Aeneas* in early Frankish, but when he settled in Thuringia, he had his work transcribed into Old High German, the only language in which his epic manuscripts have survived. Provençal, on the other hand, the language of the troubadours, did not need to be translated either in Italy or in the Iberian peninsula: the Italian **Sordello (*c*.1200–after 1269)**, for example, a native of Goito, near Mantua, wrote in Provençal, as did the Catalan Guillem de Berguedi (1138–1192) and Alfonso II of Aragon (1152–1196). Provençal, in its turn, became a language of culture as far as poetry was concerned for one and a half centuries.

The circulation of certain works can bring with it the formation of a literary language adapted to it; French epics, which crossed into Northern Italy at the end of the twelfth century, were reworked in a language midway between French and Venetian, called Franco-Venetian. Thus *The Song of Roland* and *The Song of Aspremont* were converted into a hybrid language, cobbled together *ad hoc*. sort of way. In this way too new works such as *Huon of Auvergne*, *The Entrance to Spain* or *The Capture of Pamplona* were also composed in the thirteenth and fourteenth centuries.

Obstacles and tribulations

All kinds of obstacles loomed on the road that led to the formation of a European literary heritage. The most obvious concerned the history of migrations or conquests that took place much later than the great barbarian invasions. Literature in Old English flourishing during the tenth century and the first half of the eleventh, but the Norman Conquest considerably reduced the amount of literature produced in the vernacular: the conquerors spoke French – or rather Norman French – which for more than two centuries imposed itself as the language of communication and even as a literary language in the shape of Anglo-Norman. It was not until the beginning of the Hundred Years' War that a new stage in the development of English, Middle English, began to emerge.

In Languedoc, the fight against the Cathar heretics led by Simon de Montfort, various feudal rivalries and, not least, the power of the Inquisition and the atrocities it committed (the wholesale burnings at the stake in Montségur in 1244) effectively dismantled the baronial courts and dispersed the troubadours. No doubt their art was to bear fruit elsewhere for a time, for the greater good of Italy and Castille, but the 'glowing ember' from which the movement had grown was now extinguished, and other forms of culture clamoured to be born.

Other phenomena, in a clearly defined context, succeeded in slowing down the development of certain literatures. Politically speaking, for example, the formation of the German Empire under Otto made for greater cohesion, but only Latin, a language with pretensions to universalism because it was the language of the Church as well as the Empire, took advantage of this fact: works composed in the vernacular were rare in Germany in the tenth century. It had not been thus under Charlemagne, when evangelisation had seemed an urgent task and translations had consequently flourished.

Languages and cultures

Looking at the development of national literatures in Europe, we have to recognise two distinct worlds: the Byzantine sphere of influence (which includes not only an empire with its capital at Constantinople, but also that portion of the Slav lands which received Greek religious and literary traditions and adapted them into its own languages) and the Western sphere of influence. Contacts existed between them, but until the thirteenth century they ran from east to west, even though diplomacy and trade had made Byzantium a familiar concept to the Latin mind before 1204, when Constantinople was conquered by a crusading army.

In the West, Latin remained for the whole of this period, and particularly during the Carolingian Renaissance of the ninth century and the heyday of the monastic schools in the twelfth, a language of literary creativity according to each country's own parameters. It is therefore impossible to study a Western European country's literature and not take into account what was written in Latin, even if there were many works written in the vernacular, as is the case in twelfth-century Germany and France. Latin is, at one and the same time, a common heritage and the property of a specific region or nation.

In the West at that time, there was anything but linguistic unity, even within already existing political entities. France was not only divided into two distinct language zones (the language of *oïl* and the language of *oc*), but there were many languages inside these separate areas, particularly in the north of France where the language of Picardy, a language of both creation and diffusion, spilt over France's geographical borders. In the German-speaking lands, too, we find many different language groups, among them Middle Dutch which detached itself as a separate language supported by the dynamic activity of Flemish towns. The case of the Iberian peninsula is even more interesting. If Mozarabic – 'romancium juxta latinum' (a novel revolving round Latin) spoken in areas of Spain under Arab domination – vanished quite quickly, Leonese and Valencian continued for a long time in certain legal documents (the 'fueros'). In Spain, we can distinguish two totally distinct languages (apart from Basque) both used for producing literary works: Catalan and Castilian. In Portugal, several distinguishing features mark the difference between dialects spoken in Northern Galicia and those spoken in the heart of Portugal. Until the end of the thirteenth century, the vernacular language of literature, and especially of Gallego-Portuguese poetry, was common to both Portugal and Galicia.

Literary originality in the Middle Ages

The intensive circulation of texts, whether diachronic, in the transmission of ancient culture, or synchronic, in the transmission of culture from one region to another, lends to the idea of originality a very peculiar stamp which is liable to disconcert the modern reader: on the face of it, nothing very new can ever appear and everything has been more or less faithfully copied from somewhere else. The constant aim of literature, however, is to say something different on the basis of assimilated elements. The medieval world, marked by the study of the Bible, knows it can say nothing except on the basis of a divine word carefully meditated; thanks to this word of scripture, in the image of Bernard de Chartres, he can see further and better than his predecessors, as dwarves would who were perched on the shoulders of giants. In among so many re-readings, some direct transfers may be found, devoid of inspiration, but what happens most often is that we find adaptations in which we can detect, through significant changes, the hand of a different author and the characteristics of the cultural background in which he lived.

RELIGIOUS LITERATURE: A CHOICE AREA

The most sought-after area in which literary creativity is deployed is that of religious literature. Strictly speaking, it cannot be considered in isolation. It is connected with forms of writing in the field of profane literature (lyrical poetry, for example), it maintains close links with the epic or the history, and it possesses aims which are not exclusively those of faith (the manifestation of national identity, for example). However, because it comes first – it is usually the first kind of thing to be written in a vernacular language – and because of the way in which it evolved, it deserves to have a place to itself.

Biblical texts

Before the beginning of the medieval period, Greek played a vital part in transmitting the text of the Old Testament, while the canonical and apocryphal texts of the New Testament were also being elaborated in it.

Among the non-canonical works, we find principally the work known as *The Acts of Pilate* or *The Gospel of Nicodemus*, which is the origin of the story of Joseph of Arimathea to be found in the Grail legends. There are also traditions that relate to Christ's harrowing of Hell, such as the *Vision* or *Apocalypse of Paul*, which played a large part in medieval literature about visions and speculations on angels, hell and purgatory. These writings were subsequently translated into Latin.

Translations into the Romance languages came later, appearing especially during the second half of the eleventh century. There are interesting works in Anglo-Norman like the adaptation of *The Book of Proverbs* by Sanson de Nanteuil (12,000 octosyllables written *c.*1150) and the anonymous version of *The Four Books of Kings*, written in rhythmical prose, as well as the translations of the psalms from the *Oxford Psalter* and the *Cambridge Psalter*. In 1190, Herman of Valenciennes adapted some of the historical and apocryphal books of his Bible; one of the latter adaptations, the *Evangelium Nicodemi* (*The Gospel of Nicodemus*), was translated into French before 1204. The 'scientific' translation of the Bible was the preserve of orthodoxy as well as scholarship; it was not until 1230 that a complete translation of it appeared under the auspices of the University of Paris.

The source text – the actual Bible – can face serious competition from scholarly paraphrases. Such is the case for the compilation of **Petrus the Eater (Petrus Comestor, *c.*1100–*c.*1179)**, the *Historia Scholastica* (*History of Scholasticism, c.*1170), a veritable manual of Biblical history for 'everyday use', which won for its author the name of 'Magister Historiarum' (Master of Histories) and a place well to the fore in the circle of the sun in Dante's *Paradiso*. This scholastic history, known throughout Europe, was translated into French at the end of the thirteenth century by Guiart des Moulins with the title *Bible Historial*. It remained highly popular until the end of the Middle Ages:

Jacob Van Maerlant adapted the Latin version into Dutch (*Rijmbijbel*) *c*.1271 and, in the following century, it was translated into Czech.

In Slavic hands, the Bible was also the subject matter of translations, as in the Serbian missal *Marijansko Evandjelje* (tenth to eleventh century) and the *Miroslavljevo Evandjelje* (1185), based on a Glagolitic original from Macedonia which already demonstrated characteristics typical of the Raška school of Cyrillic spelling. The first translations into Croat of Bible texts, of which only fragments have been preserved, date from the eleventh century. In Serbia, the flowering of hagiography (*The Life of Saint Simeon*, 1208, and the many lives of Saint Sava, narrator of this story) explains the fact that Serbian kings were canonised after their death and became objects of worship.

The translation of apocrypha is, in many languages, practised early and often. Mention may be made, from this viewpoint, of the Bulgarian texts, *Detsvo Isusovo* (*The Childhood of Jesus*), *Videnie Isaevo* (*The Vision of Isaiah*) and *Kniga Enohova* (*The Book of Enoch*), as well as *The Gospel of Nicodemus* in Old English,

associating with *The Acts of Pilate* the *Protoevangelium* of James (tenth century). Russian and Croatian adaptations of *The Gospel of Nicodemus* came somewhat later, in the twelfth century. Among the most common apocryphal works are *Uspenje Bogorodice* (*The Final Sleep of Mary*) and *Legenda o Svetom Makariju* (*The Legend of Saint Makar*).

Side by side with those two vehicles of culture, Greek and Latin, Gothic, a Germanic language, became the first European language in which a written translation of the Bible developed. The work is attributable to **Wulfila** (*c*.**311–383**), an Arian bishop living between the Danube and the Dnieper who was engaged in important missionary activity. He replaced German runes with a more exact alphabet inspired by the Greek one and used this to transcribe his translation (before 383), of which substantial elements are still extant. It is a remarkable monument to a Germanic tongue. In Germany, a translation of the Gospel concordance of Tatianus (*Evangelienharmonie*) was undertaken in 830, while a Saxon poet, at roughly the same time, made an adaptation of the Gospel message in *Heliand*:

(. . .) Than seggeo ie ii te
uuāron nu,
fullīcur for thesumu folke, that
gi iuuua fīund sculun
minneon an iuuuomu mōde, sō
samo sō gi iuuuva māgos dōt,
an godes namon.
Heliand

(. . .) Now I say to you
verily,
I insist upon it in the presence
of this crowd:
you shall love in your heart
your enemies
as much as you love those
who are close to you.

The main claim to fame of Otfrid of Wissemburg, writer of the *Evangelienharmonie* (*Gospel Concordance*, second half of the ninth century) is to be the author of the first piece of poetry in the German language that we know of. Anxious to make it possible for the Franks to praise God in their own language, he pioneers the use of rhyme in German poetry:

Uuánana sculun Fráncon éinon
thaz biuuánkon,
ni sie in frénkisgon biginnen,
sie gótes lób singen?
Otfrid von Wissemburg
Evangelien harmonie

Why should the Franks alone
abstain from singing in
their own language the praises
of God?

In Anglo-Saxon areas, translation also comes into its own in the ninth century, initially because of the extensive borrowings from the Bible made in the legal corpus set up by Alfred the Great, then because of the Anglo-Saxon versions of fifty psalms, in rhythmical prose, contained in the *Paris Psalter*. In the tenth century, a translation of the four gospels in their entirety is to be found, written in West Saxon, as well as two glosses preserved in the magnificent *Lindisfarne Gospels*.

Poems and Biblical epics

Epic poetry of a Biblical and Christian persuasion soon radiated from Great Britain. **Caedmon (died c.680)**, a shepherd at the Whitby monastery during the third quarter of the seventh century, and his associated school together produced two poems on the *Book of Genesis*, a tale of epic proportions based on the *Book of Exodus*, a story about Daniel and a meditation on the theme of *Christ and Satan*. Later, the poem of *Judith* (tenth century), which was not a product of Caedmon's school, resounded with powerful, epic resonance: 'She struck with all her strength, this courageous heroine, a second time that pagan dog, making his head roll over the ground . . . His ignoble, lifeless body lay where it had fallen. The spirit had departed, caught at the bottom of the pit into which it would ceaselessly fall, tortured by unending tortures.'

Cynewulf (mid-eighth century), a monk in Dunwich, composed, in East Anglian Mercia during the second half of the eighth century, four poems of Christian inspiration celebrating, respectively, the martyrdom of Saint Juliana (*Juliana*), the Acts of the Apostles (*Fata Apostolorum*), the discovery of the Cross by Helena (*Elene*) and the story of the Redemption (*Crist*). The latter contained a compelling evocation of cosmic pain at the death of the Saviour: 'Under their bark, many trees were then rutted by thick and red tears bleeding, their sap changing to blood.'

There were many Biblical poems in Germany, between 1050 and 1160. The oldest is the *Wiener Genesis* (*The Vienna Genesis*),

which relates, in 6000 epic verses, the creation of the world and the history of the Patriarchs. Two tales composed to honour Judith (*Judithlied, The Song of Judith* and *Judithepos, The Judith Epic*) and then the Macchabees adopted the same epic tone, while *c.*1120, Dame Ava wrote a *Life of Jesus*.

In France, the epic muse hovered over the different versions of *La Venjance Nostre Seigneur* (*The Vengeance of Our Lord*) and *Judas Macchabée* (*Judas Macchabeus*) (end of twelfth to beginning of thirteenth century). This adopted the language of the epic saga to celebrate a militant hero of the faith.

Hagiography

With its four formulaic types – lives, passions, stories of miracles and the translation of saintly relics – hagiography, which sets out to celebrate a saint's individual merits, is the most prolific area of medieval religious literature and enjoyed a rich and complex relationship with its profane counterpart.

The arrival of hagiography as a literary genre may be traced back to the *Life of Saint Anthony*, written in the fourth century by Athanasius, bishop of Alexandria. Equally crucial was the influence of *Lavsiaki Istoria* (*The Story of Lausias*) by Palladias, especially on **Gregory of Tours (538–594)** who at the end of the sixth century wrote a *Tractatus in Vita Patrum* (*Treatise on the Lives of the Church Fathers*), which enjoyed great popularity until the fourteenth century. He also wrote *Passio Septem Dormientium* (*Passion of the Seven Sleepers*), the tradition behind which is particularly interesting. It is the story of seven young people of Ephesus, hunted down at a time when Christians were being persecuted by Diocletian. They were walled up alive in a cave where they remained for 200 years before they were able to bear witness to the hope they had in the Resurrection. Several Syrian versions are known to exist, including two homilies by Yacub of Saroug (521) which emphasise the importance of the Resurrection: 'Because of you [. . .] Christ our Lord has woken us / So that you may truly see and recognise the Resurrection.' This is the version of Gregory of Tours and the Muslim version contained in Sura 18 of the Koran called the Sura of the Cave. A Greek original served as a source for both Latin and Syrian versions.

It was also from the Greek that the Neapolitan, Paul the Deacon (ninth century), translated into Latin both the story of Theophilus, famously rendered into French by Gautier de Coinci and Rutebeuf, and the story of *Saint Mary of Egypt*, of which, there are French, Spanish and Italian versions, among others:

A iceu tens n'ert si bele feme kar ele estoit sur tutes gemme, onke cuntesse ne reïne n'ot mes el chief si bele crine.	*De aquell tiempo que ffue ella, depues no nascio ton bella. Nin reyna nin condessa non viestes tal como esta.*	*Or intendi qued voglio dir se vu voli ancor oldir del stao e de convenente si como el era bel e gente.*

Saint Mary of Egypt

In the tenth century, the collection of hagiographies assembled by Simeon Metaphrastes, chancellor at the court of Byzantium, contained 120 lives of the saints. It included a traditional tale of Buddhist origin, *Barlaam and Josaphat*, the Greek version of which is attributed to John Damascenes.

In the West, the largest collection appeared in the second half of the thirteenth century, the *Legenda Aurea* (*Gilded Legend*) by the Dominican friar **Iacopo da Varazze (Jacob of Voragine, 1230–1298)**. Using an enormous amount of hagiographic material, he vividly described the Christian conquest of the pagan world. Translated into several European languages – French, English, Italian, Dutch, Czech – this collection was published several times.

Characterised by the proliferation of the miraculous element in them, hagiographies were among the first to be translated or to be written directly into vernacular languages. Thus, in France, after the *Cantilène de Sainte Eulalie* (*Cantilena of Saint Eulalia*), came the *Vie de Saint Alexis* (*Life of Saint Alexis*), the origin of which is found in fifth-century Edessa. First written in Syrian before being translated into Greek in the eighth century, this text was brought to Rome by Serge of Damascus in 977 and translated into Latin. The story of Alexis is known in Provençal, Spanish, Portuguese, German, Czech, Russian and Old Norse. The French version can be dated back to the end of the eleventh century.

The same phenomenon of hagiographies of Byzantine origin was found in Russia, Bulgaria and Serbia. In Russia there was the life of Theodosus, the founder of a monastic community who lived in grottoes at Pečery near Kiev, by Nestor the Hagiographer (*c*.1080). In Serbia there were the lives of Saint George, Saint Dimitri, Saint Alexis and Mary of Egypt, inherited from Byzantium, and, in Bulgaria, the life of the Bulgarian saint Ivan Rilski (John of Rila), written before 1183.

These texts, devoted to the celebration of God and his saints, bring together various perspectives. They come close to being epics, given we accept the definition of heroic saga by Jean de Grouchy, a thirteenth-century musicologist: 'a song in which the actions of heroes and the works of our ancestors are recorded as well as *the life and the martyrdom of saints.*' These same texts also share in the marvels of the romance, as in the *Life of Saint Gregory* (a twelfth-century Norman text), in which Pope Gregory is the hero of a complicated spiritual journey marked by two stories about incest. This legend, famous throughout the Middle Ages, notably gave rise to the *Gregorius* of Hartmann von Aue, *Daz maere von den guoten sündaere* (*The Tale of the Good Sinner*), before it was taken up again in modern times by Thomas Mann in his novel *The Chosen One*.

The hagiography is, finally, a defender of various interest groups. It can be the apology for a monastery, as in the *Vita Sancti Dionysii* (*The Life of Saint Dennis*) which identifies the abbey's founder with Dionysius the Areopagite. It can also be a defence of the division between Church and State, as in the *Life of Saint Thomas Beckett*, of which there are five versions from the martyrdom of this Archbishop of Canterbury in 1170 to the end of the twelfth century. Last but not least, it can be a defence of national identity, as in the lives of Saint Ludmila and Saint Wenceslas (roughly ten such appear in Czech Slavonic as early as pre-950, then in Latin until the fourteenth century). In these the male martyr reappears as 'rex perpetuus' (everlasting king), 'patron saint and celestial protector of Bohemia'.

Homiletic literature

Aimed as much at the daily teaching of the faithful, in conjunction with the seasons of the liturgy, as at the presentation of important doctrinal problems, sermons form a traditional genre of Christian literature whose most distinguished practitioners in the East were John Chrysostom, Athanasius and Augustine (fourth century) and in the West Leo the Great (fifth century). In the Latin West, sermons, directly linked to pastoral care, were soon translated into vernacular languages.

> It is in every tongue that God is worshipped, and man's prayer granted if what he asks for is righteous.
>
> *The Synod of Frankfurt*, 794

A thriving homiletic literature exists in Old English in which we can hear the echo of the problems caused by the Viking invasions of the tenth and eleventh centuries. Wulfstan, in his *Sermo ad Anglos* (*Sermon to the Angles*), uses the disaster caused by the Danish invasions of the tenth and eleventh centuries as a call to repentance: 'With God's permission, the pirates were so strong that one alone was able to put ten of us to flight (sometimes more, sometimes less) and all that was due to our

sins.' It was not until the end of the twelfth century that France saw collections of homilies appear in the vernacular. In Italy, the *Sermoni Subalpini* (*Sermons from beyond the Alps*) or *Prediche Gallo-Italiche* (*Franco-Italian Sermons*), perhaps from Piedmont, date from the beginning of the twelfth century.

Apart from their stylistic interest – in registers which are both elevated and colloquial – sermons have preserved many *exempla* – anecdotes with a didactic purpose – borrowed from the most diverse traditions: Celtic folklore, for example, as well as Buddhist, Arab and Jewish pearls of wisdom. A famous sermon by Maurice de Sully tells how God, to make a monk understand the sweetness of the joys awaiting him in paradise, sent an angel to him in the shape of a bird, whose song was so charming to him that he forgot all his worries. When he came back to reality a few hours later, or so it seemed to him, no one in his monastery recognised him any more, and he himself was flabbergasted to see only unknown faces. The monk was finally given to understand that he had spent more than 300 years away from his monastery and that God 'by the beauty of the angel and the sweetness of his song, had revealed to him as much as He had seen fit to, the joy experienced in heaven by the friends of Our Lord'.

Accounts of miracles

Among the accounts of miracles, texts connected with the veneration of Mary are popular in the thirteenth century, in the shape of collections of miracles which are attributed to her.

In France, the *Miracula Virginis* (*Miracles of the Virgin Mary*), composed in Laon, Soissons or Chartres, began to be translated in the twelfth century into medieval French. The most interesting work is by Gautier de Coincy (1223) who adapted a collection of the *Miracula* emanating from Hugues Farsit of Soissons. Among the miracles in this collection, the *Miracle de Théophile* (*The Miracle of Theophilus*) stands out, a tale which later inspired Rutebeuf.

In Spain, *Los Milagros de Nuestra Señora* (*The Miracles of Our Lady*, first half of the twelfth century) by Gonzaleo de Berceo celebrate the omnipotence of Marian intercession. Her only aim is to ensure the soul's salvation, as in the fourth miracle in which the Virgin promises a clerk, who has always revered her, the perfect recovery of his health: not bodily health, as the clerk thinks, but a healthy soul.

One of the most celebrated miracles performed by the Virgin is found in the *Dialogus Miraculorum* (*Dialogue on Miracles*, 1218–1223) by the Cistercian Caesar of Heisterbach, a town near Cologne. This is the legend of the female sacristan, the Brabantine version of which, *Beatrijs* (*Beatrice*), is particularly interesting. A nun, who shows great reverence towards the Virgin, leaves her convent out of love for a young man, but just as she is on the point of leaving,

Die couel toech si vte al daer	*Then she took off her veil*
Ende leidse op onser vrouwen outaer.	*And put it on Our Lady's altar.*
Doen dede si vte hare scoen.	*After that she took off her shoes.*
Nv hoert, watsi sal doen!	*Now what do you think she did next?*
Die slotele vander sacristien	*She hung up her sacristan's keys*
Hinc si voer dat beelde marien.	*In front of the image of Mary.*

Beatrijs

Having been made a mother and abandoned by her lover, she becomes a prostitute in order to survive. Fourteen years later she returns to her convent and asks what has happened to the Beatrice who was formerly their sacristan. She is told that the nun is still active in that capacity: during the time of the young woman's waywardness, the Virgin took over her duties because of the reverence that Beatrice had once shown her.

Singing the wonders of God

In Byzantium, as everywhere else in Christian Europe, poetry is the jewel of medieval religious literature and its masterpieces help to sustain liturgical prayer. Developed in the sixth century by Romanos the Singer, who perfected the outward form of hymns (the 'Kontakia'), Byzantine religious poetry, already rhythmical, takes on lyrical, narrative and dramatic traits; meditating on the texts of the Old and New Testaments, it expresses the grandeur of creation and redeeming grace. In the eighth century, John Damascene, in addition to his hymns, distinguished himself in a new form of poetry: the canon. Like the canon of the Resurrection (*Kanón Anastásimos*), it consisted of nine odes, based on scriptural themes.

Κέκριται τοῦ θανάτου, ἡ	*The tyranny of death*
τυραννίς διά ξύλου, ἀδίκῳ	*was condemned by the cross,*
θανάτῳ σου, κατακριθέντος	*Lord, when you were condemned*
Κύριε· ὅθεν ὁ ἄρχων τοῦ σκότους,	*to an unjust death.*
σοῦ μή κατισχύσας, δικαίως	*Also, the Prince of Darkness,*
ἐκβέβληται	*unable to defeat you,*
	was justly cast out.

John Damascene,
Kanón Anastásimos

Religious poetry in Latin was originally inspired by its Greek precedents. The first form to be introduced in Latin, the hymn, was created at the beginning of the fourth century by Hilarius of Poitiers who became aware of its existence in Greek during his four-year exile in Asia Minor. Ambrose of Milan (second half of the fourth century), sensitive to Greek influences, brought perfected the hymn by making the accentuation of certain words – and not the length of syllables – the most important element in its composition. The other major form is that of the sequence, originally a text relating to the particular feast being celebrated on a particular day, adapted to liturgical harmony, then generating its own melodic line and included as a separate element by the celebrant. Among many examples of writers of hymns was **Wipo of Reichenau (c.990–1050)**, personal chaplain to the Emperors Conrad II and Henry III, with his paschal sequence:

Victimæ paschali laudes	To the Easter victim may Christians
immolent christiani.	Offer up their praises.
Agnus redemit oves,	The Lamb has ransomed back the sheep,
Christus innocens patri	Christ in his innocence
reconciliavit	Has reconciled sinners
peccatores.	To his Father.

Wipo of Reichenau, *Paschal Sequence*

Another work, attributed to Iacopone da Todi (1230–1306), the *Stabat Mater*, is an evocation of the sufferings of the Virgin Mary, with a wealth of prestigious musical settings ahead of it:

Stabat mater dolorosa	The suffering mother was standing
Juxta crucem lacrimosa	In tears next to the cross
Dum pendebat Filius;	Where her son was hanging.
Cujus animam gementem,	Her soul there moaning,
Contristantem et dolentem	Sad and aching,
Pertransivit gladius.	Was pierced by a sword.

Iacopone da Todi, *Stabat Mater*

In view of the liturgical use of some of these poems, most of the texts were written in Latin. Certain forms, however, like the 'planctus' (dirge) were sometimes used in non-religious poetry written in the vernacular (the 'planh' in Provençal, for instance). The first poem in Hungarian was an adaptation of a lay yet mystically inspired dirge called *Ómagyar Mária-Siralom* (*Mary's Plaint*, thirteenth century). Great lyric poets cross easily from the profane to the sacred. Peire Cardenal and Folquet de Lunel, Jacques de Cambrai and Thibaut IV of Champagne have left us some very fine religious poems, and the adaptation of troubadour lyricism to Marian poetry is brilliantly illustrated in the thirteenth century in Gallego-Portuguese poetry by the *Cántigas de Santa Maria* (*Canticles of the Virgin Mary*) composed by **Alfonso X o Sabio (Alfonso X the Wise, 1221–1284)**:

Esta dona que tenno por Sennor	This lady that I have as Lord
e de que quero seer trobador,	and whose troubadour I want to be,
se eu per ren poss'aver seu amor,	if I can obtain her love
dou ao demo os outros amores.	I renounce all other loves.
Rosa das rosas e Fror das frores,	Rose among roses, Flower among flowers,
Dona das donas, Sennor das sennores.	Lady among ladies, Lord of Lords.

Alfonso X the Wise,
Canticles of theVirgin Mary

A mystical tradition existed in Germany well before the great fourteenth-century figures of Master Eckhart, Johann Tauler and Henry Suso, with Hildegard of Bingen (twelfth century) and Mechtilde of Magdeburg (1210–1285), a Cistercian Beguine from Helfta. The same tradition also existed in the north of France with Marie d'Oignies (1213) and Marguerite Porete (burned at the stake in 1310) and especially in the Brabant with Beatrice of Nazareth (died 1268), the author of *Van seven manieren van heiliger minne* (*The Seven Stages of Divine Love*) and Hadewijch of Antwerp (mid-thirteenth century) whose work includes visions, letters and, in the main, poems in stanza form whose manner is close to that of poems of courtly love:

> *Dat ic van minnen vele songhe,*
> *Dat hulpe mi niet vele,*
> *maer lettel goet.*
> *Maer dien ouden ende dien jonghen*
> *Coelt sanc van minnen haren moet.*
> *Maer van minnen mijn heel*
> *Hevet so clenen deel:*
> *Mijn sanc, mijn wenen scijnt sonder spoet.*

Hadewijch of Antwerp,
Strophic poems

> Love, having sung of you much,
> has been of no use to me;
> he whose heart is soothed
> by a song of love is neither old nor young.
> But from you I get so little relief
> that songs and tears alike
> seem poured out in vain.

In the Brabant and in Northern France, this mystic undercurrent is connected to movements of mass piety and associations like those of the Beguine nuns. In Italy, mysticism is strongly influenced by the personality of the founder of the Franciscan order, **Francesco d'Assisi (Francis of Assisi, c.1182–1226)** who in a language coloured by Umbrian dialect sings the praises of God's creatures, as in the *Canticle of Brother Sun*:

> *Laudato sie, mi'Signore, cum*
> *tucte le tue creature,*
> *specialmente messor lo frate sole,*
> *lo qual'è iorno, et allumini noi*
> *per lui.*
> *Et ellu è bellu e radiante cum*
> *grande splendore:*
> *de te, Altissimo, porta*
> *significatione.*

Francis of Assisi,
Cantico di frate Sole

> Praise to you, my Lord, with
> all your creatures,
> especially Brother Sun,
> who gives the daylight and,
> with him, you illuminate the world.
> He is handsome and he shines forth with
> great splendour;
> to you, O Most High, he bears
> witness

This mysticism is epitomised by the 'lauda' made famous by Iacopone da Todi, whose tone can be satirical as well as lyric.

Finally, as one of the great mystic poems to be written during this period, we must mention the *Libre del Amich et Amat* (*The Book of the Lover and the Beloved*) which appeared in the fifth section of the *Libre d'Evast et Blanquerna* (*Blanquerna*, c.1286) by the Catalan **Ramón Llull (1235–1315)**:

> *Amat qui.m fas amar: si no.m*
> *ajydes, per què.m volguist*
> *crear? ¿Ni per què per mi*
> *portest tantes langors, no*

> Beloved who makes me love, if you
> will not come to my aid, why did
> you want to create me?
> And why did you desire to suffer

sostenguist tan greu passio?	*for me so much wilting and*
Pus tan m'as aiudat a exalçar,	*such a painful passion?*
ajuda'm, amat, a devallar a	*Since you helped me to become*
membrar, aïrar, mes colpes e mos	*exalted, help me to be humble*
defallimens, per ço que mills mos	*so that I can recollect my*
pensaments, pusquen pujar a	*faults and my defects and so that I*
desirar, honrar, loar tes valors.	*can hate them so as to be able after-*
	wards to raise my mind to wish,
Ramón Llull,	*to honour and to praise your worth.*
Libre del Amich et Amat	

In Byzantium the poetry of **Symeon the New Theologian (949–1022)** aspired towards mystic illumination. In the *Loves of Hymns Divine*, the clarity of God and the darkness of human reason are opposed to each other.

In some religious poetry a feeling of national identity may be embodied. In Czech, for instance, the hymn *Hospodine, pomiluj ny* (*Lord, have mercy on us*), from the third quarter of the tenth century, and especially the invocation of the 'patron and celestial protector' of Bohemia (twelfth century, three stanzas, with six additional stanzas down to the fifteenth century), was sung for centuries as a national anthem:

Svatý Václave,	*Saint Wenceslas, duke*
vévodo české země,	*of the country of*
kněže nás,	*Bohemia, our prince,*
pros za ny Boha,	*pray for us to God*
svatého Ducha!	*and the Holy Spirit!*
Kyrieleison!	*Kyrie eleison!*
(. . .)	*(. . .)*
Pomoci tvé žádámy,	*We ask you for your*
smiluj sě nad námi,	*help, have mercy on us,*
utěš smutné,	*console the sad,*
otžeň vše zlé,	*drive away all evil,*
svatý Václave!	*saint Wenceslas!*
Kyrieleison!	*Kyrie eleison!*

In Poland this role devolves on the hymn *Bogurodzica* (twelfth century):

Bogurodzica, Dziewica,	*Virgin and Mother of God,*
Bogiem slawiena Maryja,	*Blessed Mary,*
Twego syna, gospodzina,	*Of your son, Lord,*
Matko zwolena Maryja,	*Chosen to be mother, Mary,*
Zyszczy nam, spuści nam!	*Give us grace and grant our*
Kyrie eleison!	*prayer. Kyrie eleison!*
Bogurodzica	

DIDACTIC LITERATURE

Didactic literature covers a great deal of ground, in the sense that almost everything that was written at this time had a mission to inform and educate. The 'branches of the tree of knowledge', moreover, were difficult to tell apart, since each one could be an allegory or a metaphor for another: 'science' and 'morality' or reading grounded in religion frequently overlapped as may be seen from the encyclopedias and bestiaries of the time.

The encyclopedic tradition

Nurtured in the Latin-speaking West by the *Etymologiæ* (*Book of Etymologies*, early seventh century) by Isidorus of Seville, the encyclopedic traditi, written for the most part in Latin, embraces work which seek to encompass the whole of knowledge. From *De Naturis Rerum* (*On the Nature of Things*, 856) by the German Raban Maur, to the *Speculum* (*Mirror*) by the Dominican Vincent de Beauvais (thirteenth century), encyclopedias came thick and fast: *Imago mundi* (twelfth century) by Honorius of Autun, for instance (who is more likely to have been from a country traversed by the Danube) was twice adapted into French in the thirteenth century (notably by Gossuin de Metz, in 1246, under the title of *Image of the World*). Then came *De Naturis Rerum* (end of the twelfth century) by the Englishman Alexander Neckham (*c.*1157–1217), *De Natura Rerum* (*c.*1240) by the Brabançon Dominican Thomas of Cantimpré and *Proprietates rerum* (*The Properties of Things*, *c.*1250) by Bartholomew the Englishman. These encycloedias were subsequently translated into vernacular languages, apart from the one by Brunetto Latini, the *Livre du Trésor* (*Book of Treasure*)(*c.*1265), which was compiled directly into French.

Some of these works are characterised by a particular objective, such as the *Fecunda Navis* (*The Ship of Fertility*) by Egbert of Liège (end of tenth to beginning of eleventh century), which describes an allegorical vessel laden with the subjects of an encyclopedic curriculum, or the *Otia Imperialia* (*Imperial Pastimes*) of Gervais of Tilbury (end of twelfth to beginning of thirteenth century) which takes an inventory of the 'wonders of each province'. In Byzantium, the encyclopedic tradition is rich and varied. When it tries to explain in Christian terms the coming into being and development of the universe, it can assume the shape of homilies on the six days of Creation, as in the *Hexaemeron* begun by Basil of Caesarea, completed by Gregory of Nyssa and later continued by George of Pisidia (seventh century). It can also bring together observation and allegorical commentary: *Hexaemeron*, imitated by Ambrose of Milan, then by the Bulgarian John the Exarch (ninth century), whose *Sestodnev* enjoyed great popularity in the Slav lands, was complemented in its viewpoint but based on different models, by the *Hexaemeron* (*c.*1220) of the Dane Anders Svenson, a Biblical and scientific epic poem.

An encyclopedia can also specialise in literary matters, as with the *Miriovivlion* (*Myriad of Books*) by Photius (ninth century). In his grouping together and commenting on all the works, profane and sacred, that he had read and discussed during the course of meetings held in his home, Photius was a precursor of literary criticism ranging from Herodotus to the patriarch Nicephorus.

> Everything that has been written down has been written to instruct us.
>
> Paul

But encyclopedic knowledge can also be about many aspects of public life, as may be seen with the work of Constantine VII Porphyrogenetes (first half of the tenth century). In his *Pros ton idhion ión Romanón* (*The Administration of the Empire*), he gives us information about Byzantium's diplomatic relations with neighbouring countries. He also takes an interest in the bureaucratic and military organisation of the Empire in his *Peri thematon* (*On themas*) – the thema being a unit of administration – and he described Byzantine society from a historical perspective in *Peri vasilíou táxeos* (*Book of Ceremonies at the Byzantine Court*).

Summarising man and changing him

Characterised by its tropological aim – the transformation of the reader's behaviour

– morally edifying literature is everywhere. There is gnomic poetry and the literature of pious maxims. Having recourse to an example which illustrates a moral reflection is a particularly widespread practice in Germany, in 'Spruchdichtung' (epigrammatic poetry). Some great poets, like **Walther von der Vogelweide (c.1170–c.1230)** or **Reinmar von Zweter (c.1200–c.1260)**, have developed it.

Collections of maxims and proverbs were popular throughout the Middle Ages. The Bible served as a model for them, with the *Book of Proverbs* and *Ecclesiastes*, but there was also the culture of the post-classical period to draw on in the *Disticha Catonis* (*Distichs of Cato*, first half of the thirteenth century), an anthology of stoic maxims. These texts were translated and gave rise to many imitations. One of the most curious adaptations is the contrastive dialogue form of *Salomonis et Marcolphi Dialogus* (*Dialogue of Solomon and Marcolf*), possibly of Talmudic origin, a collection of proverbs and enigmas where the wisdom of Solomon is contrasted with the facetious, even outrageous replies of the lunatic Marcolf. This text was known in Germany from the eleventh century and was the basis of a minstrel's epic in the thirteenth (*Salman und Morolf*) and of a gnomic poem in the fourteenth (*Salomon und Markolf*); it was translated several times in France in the twelfth and thirteenth centuries.

Next came collections of moral anecdotes and stories. Three important collections are worth mentioning. First there is the work that Rabbi Moses Sephardi, born in Huesca in 1062 and a Christian convert, wrote under the pseudonym of Pedro Alfonso, the *Disciplina Clericalis* (*Education of the Clerk*), in which an elderly man tells his son about thirty tales, some serious and some facetious, taken from Arab and often Indian sources of wisdom. This 'teaching for the use of clerks' was raided by preachers and compilers of digests and very often translated.

A second remarkable collection was that of the Indian *Sindbad* (eighth century BC). This recounts the dangers incurred by a young prince condemned to be mute for a week because he had been slandered by one of the wives of the king, his father. The young woman in question, having had her advances rejected, accused the prince of having tried to rape her; the defence of the prince, who can now no longer speak, is undertaken by seven wise men who give examples of feminine deceitfulness. On the final day of the trial, it is the prince's turn to speak and he convicts his female accuser of lying. The way in which the Sanskrit original arrived in Western Europe is unclear, but the book's circulation was extraordinary. A tenth-century Syrian version is known of, *Sindban*, which was translated into Greek in the eleventh century (*Syntipas*), several Persian versions, a Spanish version *Libro de los engannos y los asayamentos de las mugeres* (*Book of the Ruses and the Wiles of Women*, 1253), the *Mishle Sendebar* in Hebrew in the fourteenth century and the same century Arabic version of the *Seven Vizirs*. Western versions, which wove new anecdotes into an already existing pattern, were commonly designated under the generic title of *Romance of the Seven Sages* and belong to various traditions. One, represented by a French text in verse, was translated into several European languages and inspired Boccaccio as well as John Gower.

Aesop's Fables

Aesop played a major part in the literary development of fables. A master in the Greek tradition from Alexandrian times to the end of the twelfth century, he became known in the West through the anthology of distichs compiled by Avianus (fourth century) and by the collection *Romulus Imperator* (ninth century). This in turn gave rise to other anthologies, like the *Novus Æsopus* (*New Aesop*) by Alexander Neckham.

These fables were used by preachers, just as the *exempla* had been. They are found in particular in the *Liber Parabolarum* (*Book of Anecdotes*, beginning of the thirteenth century) by the English Cistercian Eudes of Cheriton;

in the *Treatise of Divers Matters on Which to Preach* (*c.*1250) by Étienne de Bourbon and in the *Sermons* (thirteenth century) of Jacques de Vitry. They were also translated into vernacular languages. A tenth-century version of them in Old English is known about, as is a French translation by Marie de France called *Isopet* (*c.*1180). Other translations were made during the thirteenth century and at the end of the Middle Ages.

Moral treatises

Too numerous to count, moral treatises are a combination of ideology, knowledge and practical advice. They can teach us how to make the most of life, as well as about the art of love or the tasks of the prince.

Following an ancient tradition, Bonvesino de la Riva, a Milanese author of the second half of the thirteenth century, sets out in his *De quinquaginta curialitatibus ad mensam* (*Fifty Ways to Behave Well at Table*) a witty manual of 'good table manners':

La terza cortesia si é: no sii trop presto	*The third way of showing good manners is the following: do not be in too much*
De corr senza parolla per assetar al desco;	*of a hurry to sit down at table without permission;*
s'alcun t'invidha a noze, anz che tu sii assetao,	*If someone invites you to a wedding, before sitting at table, try not to make*
per ti no prend quel asio dond tu fiz descazao.	*yourself too much at home, if you do not want to be shown out.*

Bonvesino de la Riva,
De quinquaginta curialitatibus ad mensam

The meditation on love by Andreas Capellanus attempts to codify the ways of love in the form of a scholastic treatise, the *De Arte Honeste Amandi* (*The Art of Perfect Love*, *c.*1185), by using the most varied of sources: the tradition of Ovid, songs, Arthurian romances. The vision conveyed is surprisingly contradictory: love is pure because it is required by nature and calls for the exercise of reason in a courtly context, but it is also at the root of all evils since 'no woman is good'. This work of dark and light was extremely well received. Condemned by the Archbishop of Paris in 1277, it was translated into French in 1290 and was a source of inspiration for many authors: for Albertano da Brescia in his *De dilectione Dei et Proximi* (*On the Love of God and of One's Neighbour*, 1238) and for Juan Ruiz, Archpriest of Hita, in his *Libro de Buen Amor* (*Book of Perfect Love*, fourteenth century).

Finally, there are two attempts to define what constitutes kingship in the Russia where Kiev was the capital. The first is an epistle written in Greek and translated into Slavonic, in which the metropolitan Nicephorus I (beginning of the twelfth century) affirms, with Vladimir Monomaches in mind, the like nature of the power of a Russian prince and imperial power, adding a religious dimension to the first. The second document is a *Poučenie* (*Instruction*) drawn up by the prince himself. Without seeking to give his power an ideological basis and therefore deviating from Byzantine tradition, he recalls the real conditions involved in the exercise of princely power and manifests a desire to apply to them the norms of Christian morality.

Good speech and good writing

Byzantium preserved the rhetorical tradition inherited from Antiquity. The tenth and eleventh centuries were particularly rich in practitioners of the cult of rhetoric, with Photius, Michael Psellos (eleventh century), a statesman, monk and teacher, John Italos (eleventh century), the author of treatises on rhetoric influenced by the writings of Aristotle,

Michael Atalikos (twelfth century, the 'second Plato'), and Theodorus Prodromus (twelfth century), a particularly prolific writer.

This love of public speaking and literature also revealed itself in the preservation of past literary glories, like the precious *Palatine Anthology* of Constantine Cephalas (beginning of the tenth century). Availing itself of the oldest collections at its disposal (the *Crown of Meleager* in particular), this traced the evolution of a well-defined genre – the epigram – from the sixth century BC to the tenth century AD.

In countries of Latin culture, rhetoric first took the form of collections of letters and legal protocols, destined to inspire the drawing up of diplomatic documents, such as the *Codex Udalrici* in the eleventh century. In the twelfth and thirteenth centuries, theoretical research on the art of writing appeared, based on the treatises of Cicero, Horace and Quintilian, although, particularly in Italy, a preoccupation with legal texts kept the aims practical: this was 'the art of composition' by which many authors were tempted.

> Le fiz sainte Marie.
> Nus si oiselet sumes
> E en faiture d'humes,
> Si sumes relevé,
> De mort resuscité
> Par le sanc precïus
> Que Deus laissat pur nus,
> Cum li oiselet sunt
> Ki par treis jurs mort sunt.

Philippe de Thaon,
Bestiaire

THE MEMORY OF BYGONE ERAS

This is one of the most important areas in medieval literature. On the one hand, it often offers the oldest testimonies to a national literature and to the consciousness of a group identity. On the other, in a Christian universe, it sets out to reflect on the work of God through time and seeks to give it literary shape.

Science and allegory

The observation of nature can serve as an excuse for showing off a symbolic technique of interpretation characteristic of the medieval spirit. This is embodied in lapidaries (books on the properties of stones) and volucraries (descriptions of birds). Most important of all, bestiaries were inspired by *Phusiologos* (*The Naturalist*), an Alexandrian compilation of the second century AD, of which we have a version in fifteenth-century Demotic Greek.

Translated into Latin as early as the fourth century, the *Physiologus* was largely transmitted to Great Britain, Ireland, Germany and France. In the chapter on the pelican, we read that the pelican's young rebel against their father who ends up by killing them; at this point the pelican strikes itself with its bill, and its blood, falling on its young, restores them to life. The pelican, according to **Philippe de Thaon (twelfth century)**, the author of the first bestiary in a Romance vernacular (*c*.1130), refers to:

> The son of Saint Mary.
> We are his chicks,
> And, in human form,
> We are lifted up
> And brought back to life from death
> By virtue of the precious blood
> That God poured out for us.
> Just as the chicks are
> Which remain dead for three days.

Medieval history wants to retain, from all that has happened, the memory of bygone eras, hence the importance that it gives to real or imagined chronology. Its purpose, more than that of other literary genres, is educational, often edifying (ecclesiastical histories in the manner of Bede), though sometimes political (Otto von Freising). In collecting the treasure of bygone eras, it does not try to distinguish reality from fantasy: this explains the importance of the mythical material and folklore that can be found in it. It is also pre-occupied with saying things well: 'narratores rerum' (speakers of facts), historians also had to be 'exornatores rerum' (those who adorn facts). Thus the ties of kinship between history and literature are strengthened.

Universal chronicles

The work of the German **Otto von Freising (c.1115–1158)**, *Chronica sive Historia de Duabus Civitatibus* (*Chronicle or History of Two Cities*), offered to Frederick Barbarossa in 1157 is, without doubt, the most represen-tative and accomplished of the global histories of a humanity awaiting salvation. The author's stated aim was to describe the history of his time in the light of humanity's past: 'to build a history in which, by the grace of God, the misfortunes of the citizens of Babylon may be made manifest, but also the glory of the reign of Christ to be hoped for in the next world, and of which the citizens of Jerusalem can expect to enjoy the first fruits in this world'. Otto's originality is to have given new meaning to Augustine's vision of the Celestial City. The Church of Christ, in association with the 'imperium romanum' and all the culture bound up with it, had now come home to roost in Germany, in the empire governed by Barbarossa, where it was possible to have a foretaste of the heavenly Jerusalem.

National histories

This genre was particularly widespread, for it was closely linked to the formation of national consciousness.

In Byzantium, at the beginning of the twelfth century, the work of **Anna Comnenia (1083–after 1148)** called *Alexiás* (*The Alexiad*), is that of a great writer, even if this account of the reign of Alexis Comnenius (1081–1118) lacks historical substance. Later, Nicetas Chroniates, secretary to the Emperor, judge and great wordsmith, described the capture of Constantinople by the Crusaders. His style is erudite and somewhat obscure – and his hate of all things Latin quite pronounced.

The oldest work to come out of England, which was highly thought of in the West in medieval times (164 manuscript copies of it are known to exist), was the *Historia Ecclesiastica Gentis Anglorum* (*The History of the Church in England*, 731) by the Venerable Bede. Written in five sections, it starts with the conquest of 'Britannia' by Caesar and the island's conversion to Christianity. It ends with Bede's own time, placing in close proximity the history of the English people and that of the Church. It is a mine of information on the civilisation and literature of that period and in terms of folklore, it is a significant document. In particular, it contains the vision of Drythelm, a starting-point for many repre-sentations of Hell and Purgatory in the Middle Ages. This work was translated into Old English before 900.

Other important works are similarly the fruit of Anglo-Saxon historiography. There are *The Anglo-Saxon Chronicle*, begun in Old English at the instigation of King Alfred *c.*892 and continued till 1154, and the literary corpus which has won respectability in scien-tific circles for Arthurian legends, including the *Historia Brittonum* (*History of the Britons*, *c.*826) by Nennius, and especially the *Historia Regum Britaniæ* (*History of the Kings of Britain*, 1136) by **Geoffrey of Monmouth (c.1100–1155)**.

In Bohemia, *c.*1115, **Kosmas (1045–1125)**, equipped with a sound classical education, described Bohemia before its historical exis-tence in a lively style, recording popular myths on the arrival of the Czechs there, the founding of the Přemyslid dynasty and the war of the Czech Amazons. He describes the country's development, using all available documen-tation and his own personal experience. This *Chronica Boëmorum* (*Chronicle of Bohemia*), which led to several continuations, played an important part in shaping the Czech national consciousness. The same was true of the *Gesta Hungarorum* (*Chronicle of the Hungarians*) written in the twelfth century by Master P. (surname unknown). From the end of the twelfth century came *Ljetopis Popa Dukljanina* (*The Chronicle of the Monk of Duklja*), written in Latin and containing a Gotho-Slavic genealogical tree down to the tenth century. We also have the legend of Prince Jovan Vladimir (997–1016) and the chronicle of the State of Duklja (eleventh to twelfth century).

In Spain, in 1270, Alfonso X the Wise orderd an extensive search to be carried out in the libraries of his kingdom which allowed compilers acting on his instructions to produce the *Primera Cronica General de España* (*First General Chronicle of Spain*), a thoroughly documented work which made use of recent sources as well as epic poems (at least forty epic 'cantares'). In Alfonso's eyes, royal authority resided not only in the power of the sword, but in a country's collective memory.

In France two works, simultaneously opposed to and associated with each other, deserve to be cited. One is the *Liber Sancti Jacobi* (*Book of Saint James*), written in honour of Saint James of Galicia and finished *c*.1150. This includes, in Part IV, a *Historia Karoli Magni et Rotholandi* (*History of Charlemagne and Roland*), a legendary account of Charlemagne's expeditions to Spain and the death of Roland at Roncevaux, attributed to Archbishop Turpin. This work was soon taken out of context and held to be an independent narrative worthy of belief. One hundred and seventy-five manuscripts have preserved it and it was very early on translated and retranslated into vernacular languages very early on. The second work was quite different. Primatus, a monk at the Abbey of Saint-Denis, translated or adapted at the Saint Louis'

request a weighty collection of chronicles in Latin which had been gradually accumulated over time, from the *Vita Caroli* or *Life of Charlemagne* by Eginhard to the *Gesta Philippi Augusti* or *Deeds of Philip Augustus* by Rigord. This was the official historiography of the French royal house, hence the title of *Roman des Rois* (*Romance of Kings*) given by the author to his work, which he finished in 1274.

In Poland, two chronicles of the twelfth and thirteenth centuries were important literary monuments. The chronicle of the *Gallus Anonymus* (*Anonymous Frenchman*) encompassed the period from the legendary prince Popiel to the 1113. Among other things, it recounts the coronation of King Boleslas the Valiant by Emperor Otho I who, aware of the prince's power, declares that 'it is fitting to gloriously raise him to the royal throne and to place a king's crown on his head'. The *Chronica Polonorum* (*Chronicle of Poland*), by Vincent Kadlubek (beginning of the thirteenth century), also written in Latin, takes the history of the country up to 1206. This work, which devotes a great deal of space to legends, was used in schools as a manual of history and ethics and as a model of eloquence and rhetoric.

Starting from Byzantine sources or from texts which glorify the apostolic work of Cyril and Methodius, Russian historians made of the conversion of pagan Russia a major event in the history of man's salvation. The *Povest' vremenych let* (*Chronicle of Former Times*), in particular, bears this out:

Посем же володимеръ посла
по всему граду, глаголя:
«Аще не обрящеться кто
заутра на рецѣ, богатъ ли,
ли убогъ, или нищъ, ли
работникъ, противенъ мне
да будетъ.» Се слышавше
люцье с радостью идяху
радующеся и глаголюще:
«Аще бы се не добро было,
не бы сего князь и бояре
прияли.»

After that Vladimir had broadcast
the following announcement throughout the
town: 'Whoever
tomorrow is not at the riverside,
be he rich or poor,
wretched or slave, he will be
my enemy.' Hearing these words,
the people came joyfully, making
glad and saying: 'If it
were not something good,
our prince and the boyars
would not have embraced it.'

Povest' vremenych let

In order to strengthen the Danish perception of nationhood, **Saxo Grammaticus (1140–1206)** compiled a history of Denmark from its mythical origins to the reign of Valdemar I the Great.

The sagas

Certain Icelandic sagas, though situated in a no-man's-land between true history and the historical novel, even fantasy, may be categorised as national history. These prose tales, written between the second half of the twelfth century and the middle of the fourteenth, but frequently containing quotations from earlier poems, as well as vestiges of previous oral traditions, claim to give a history of Icelandic settlement into which they offer significant insights.

The 'royal sagas' recount the lives of the Kings of Norway and, collaterally, those of Denmark. Based on more or less legendary oral accounts and on the poems of 'Skalds', court poets who celebrated the great deeds of princes, these sagas are grouped together in collections. The most famous is the *Heimskringla* (the 'orb of the world', the words with which the first saga begins) by the Icelandic writer and statesman **Snorri Sturluson (1179–1241)**, who offers us a picture of Norwegian history from prehistoric times to the end of the twelfth century.

The 'contemporary sagas', written from the first years of the thirteenth century, recount the dramatic events and civil wars in Iceland which ended in 1262 with the country's submission to the King of Norway. The most important of these sagas, sometimes based on stories by eye-witnesses, are contained in the vast compilation of the *Sturlunga Saga*, a meditation on Icelandic history and its lost harmony.

> *Clocán binn*
> *benar i n-aidchi gaíthe:*
> *ba ferr lim dul ina dáil*
> *indás i ndáil mná baíthe.*

The woman's complaint, often on the theme of the unhappy wife, the *aubade*, which evokes

The *Islendingasögur* (*Sagas of the Icelanders*), written at the same time as the contemporary sagas, tell of earlier events using hallowed traditions, but also creating characters. We find in them the lives of remarkable individuals, heroes, 'Skalds' or outlaws, as in the *Saga of Egill* or the *Saga of Grettir*, or the story of a region over several generations like the *Saga of the Leaders in the Valley of the Lake*. Still others – the *Saga of Njall the Burnt* in particular – trace a feud between several people which gets out of hand and ends in a paroxysm of violence.

POETRY: LYRIC, SATIRICAL, MORAL

Poetry is one of the major areas of medieval literature. It simultaneously underlines the wealth of cultural exchange as regards sources, the original and prolific nature of a particular tradition – poetry in Languedoc – and the work of appropriation by various cultures.

Popular poetry and the birth of medieval lyricism

Ancient poetic traditions can be detected in Old English (elegiacal poetry) and in German (Carolingian 'Winieod').

In Ireland, from the eighth century, metrical forms found in Latin are used in the vernacular to express the delicacy and freshness of a feeling for nature and personal emotions. In the margins of manuscripts copied in monasteries, we find these brief poems which can also serve as interludes in prose narratives. Formal sobriety combined with a liveliness of feeling, as in this short anonymous fragment dating from the ninth century:

> *Bell that rings so charmingly,*
> *ringing on a windy night,*
> *I would rather have a rendezvous*
> *with her than with a loose woman.*

the separation of two lovers, and the *pastourelle*, common forms all over Europe, are also of popular origin, but have only been preserved in versions where the influence of erudite poetry is discernible. The greatest of poets have tried their hand at these different genres as in this *Tagelied* (*Dawn Song*) from **Wolfram von Eschenbach (c.1170–c.1220)**:

Den morgenblic bi wahtaeres	*A lady saw the first*
sange erkos	*ray of sunshine,*
ein vrouwe, da sie tougen	*heard the watchman's song, while*
an ir werden vriundes arm lac.	*she was lying*
da von si der vreuden vil verlos.	*in the arms of her noble friend.*
des muosen liehtiu ougen	*Then all her happiness fled.*
aver nazzen, si sprach:	*Her shining eyes filled up*
'ove tac!	*afresh with tears, and she said:*
Wilde und zam daz vrewet	*'Alas, the day!*
sich din	*All that lives feels*
und siht dich gern, wan ich	*joy because of you*
eine, wie sol iz mir ergen!	*and is happy to see you, apart from me.*
nu enmac niht langer hie bi	*What is to become of me?*
mir besten	*Henceforth my beloved can*
nin vriunt, den jaget	*no longer dally*
von mir din schin'.	*long near to me: your shining*
	pushes him far away from me.'

Wolfram von Eschenbach,
Tagelied

The crucial event at the end of the eleventh century was the burgeoning of poetry in Provençal, original in its literary forms and ideology, which borrowed from various sources, but established itself as a model in Northern France and Germany, while being cultivated in its native tongue in Spain (especially in Catalonia) and in Northern Italy. Working in conjunction with it, a vigorous and varied production of poetry in Latin, with signs of cross-fertilisation, was still in evidence, at least during the twelfth century. The sources of it were extremely diverse. Along with the tradition of rhythmical metrical poetry in Latin, a lyrical tradition in Arabic must be taken into account with the great names of Ibn Hazan (994–1063) and Almutamid (1068–1091), and the lyrical forms of the 'zejel' (a poem derived from Mozarabic poetry) and the 'moaxaja'. This ideology celebrates an art of living ('cortezia') based on a system of values ('mesura', restraint; 'jovens', youth) and on the trans-formation of a human creature by perfect love ('fin'amors').

Following from the Mozarabic 'hardjas', the first signs of poetry in a vernacular language derived from Latin, new forms were created, the most important of which was the 'canso' (song). These forms lend themselves to lyric poetry as well as to satire ('sirventés') and present possibilities of dialogue ('tenso', debate; 'partimen', division). Various poetic registers are envisaged: hermetic poetry ('trobar clus'), poetry open to all ('trobar leu'), poetry that values the sensuality of words and versification ('trobar ric'). The writers of this poetry, in which 'vers' and 'so' (text and music) are bound up with each other, were often great feudal lords such as Guilhem IX of Poitou, Duke of Aquitaine, Raimbaut d'Orange or Jaufré Rudel. There were also women among them, the 'trobairiz' Azalais de Porcairagues, Na Castelosa and, above all, the Countess of Die, whose laments of disappointment in love are justly famous:

A chantar m'èr de ço qu'eu no	*I must sing of that which I do not*
volria,	*want to sing of,*

Tant me rancur de lui cui sui
amia;
Car eu l'am mais que nulla ren
que sia:
Vas lui no'm val Mercés ni
Cortezia
Ni ma beltatz ni mos prèts ni
mos sens;
Qu'atressi'm sui enganad'e
trahia
Com degr'èsser, s'eu fos desavinens.

Countess of Die,
Canso

for I have much cause to reproach
him whose friend I am.
I love him more than anything in
the world,
and nothing finds favour with him:
neither Mercy nor Courtesy,
nor my beauty, nor my merit, nor
my wit;
I am deceived and betrayed
as I would be if I
were totally lacking in charm.

The miracle of Occitania

The fact that lyrical poetry in the language of *oc* spread to Spain and Northern Italy may be attributed to the welcome extended to the troubadours at the courts of Barcelona, Aragon and Castille, as well as that of Mantua and of the marquises of Montferrat. An interesting testimony to these 'travels' is contained in the song of **Raimbaut de Vaqueyras (*c.*1155–*c.*1210)**, 'Eras quan vey verdeyar' ('When I am to grow green again'). The first stanza of this is in Provençal, the second in Italian, the third in French, the fourth in Gascon and the fifth in Galician Portuguese.

Lady, I have often begged you . . .

Raimbaut de Vaqueyras

Many Catalan troubadours as well as a few Italians write in Provençal. Elsewhere the lyricism of Provence was transposed into other languages and played a vital part in the over-all development of lyrical poetry. This was certainly the case in France where the determining factor was the acquisition for the lands of the Plantagenets of the traditions of Aquitaine by virtue of the marriage of Eleanor, grand-daughter of Guilhem IX, to Henry II of England. The first *trouvères* appeared in the second half of the twelfth century – Conon de Béthune, Gace Brulé, the Châtelain de Coucy and Blondel de Nesle. The Provençal and French lament of the English king, Richard the Lionheart, on his captivity, is a good indication of the leading role played by the Empire of Anjou:

Ja nuls òm pres non dira sa razon
Adrechament, si com òm dolens non;
Mas per conòrt deu òm faire canson.
Pro n'ai d'amis, mas paure son li don;
Anta lur es si, per ma recenzon,
Soi çai dos ivèrs pres.

Richard the Lionheart,
Rotruenger

A captive will never speak sincerely,
unless as an afflicted man;
but in order to console himself he
must compose a song
I have many friends, but
few gifts of ransom money.
Shame on them if, in order to be
ransomed,
I have to be a prisoner here two
winters.

In Italy Provençal poetry is 'acclimatised' to Sicily thanks to Emperor Frederick II of Hohenstaufen who surrounded himself at Palermo with a glittering court where troubadours recruited new disciples. Among the poets of the Magna Curia writing in Sicilian, we should mention **Giacomo da Lentini (first half of the thirteenth century)**, the inventor of the sonnet, and the Sardinian king Enzo (*c.*1220–1272). From Sicily this poetic current migrates to Tuscany with great poets like **Guittone d'Arezzo (c.1226–1294)**; here, thanks to the meeting of the Provençal tradition transmitted by the Sicilians with the theological works of **Thomas Aquinas (c.1226–1274)** and Franciscan mysticism, an authentically Italian tradition in poetry was born, the 'dolce stil nuovo' (sweet new style), with Guido Cavalcanti (c.1255–1300) and Guido Guinizelli (c.1230–1276). Earthly love is sublimated and the courtly lady becomes an angelic being.

In the Iberian peninsula, Gallego-Portuguese poetry includes more than 1700 profane songs written from the end of the thirteenth century to the sixteenth by more than 150 *trovodoris* and *jograis*, among whom were two kings: Alfonso the Wise of Castille and Dennis of Portugal.

In Germany, where the Provençal tradition was known above all through the songs of the *trouvères*, ideological adaptations were also produced: *Minne* (love in German, hence the term *Minnesänger*) was a sublimated concept in comparison to troubadour love – the lover's reward is, more than physical union, the heady virtue of love itself, *hohe Minne* (sublime love). Henric Van Veldeke, Heinrich von Morungen (died in 1222), Reinmar von Haguenau (c.1160–1210) and Walther von der Vogelweide all sang of this higher love.

In Ireland, the Anglo-Norman invasion of the country in 1169 led to profound social, linguistic and psychological changes. The former world of heroes was swept away by feudal society, and the popularity of Ulster's heroic epic gave way to even more popular Ossianic tales of love and adventure. After Middle Irish became Modern Irish, professional poets worked to establish a standard literary language which also caught on in the Highlands of Scotland. It was used for short elegies, for occasional verse and similarly for the love poems introduced into Ireland by the Anglo-Normans.

Satirical or realist poetry

Among the poetic genres of Provence, the *sirventés* lent itself to moral and political debate or to personal invective. Among its Provençal practitioners, Bertran de Born (c.1137–c.1208) was one of the most adept in cultivating this genre.

The *trouvères* were more cautious in their use of satire. German poetry, on the other hand, set great store by it and the work of Walther von der Vogelweide included a number of political or satirical poems.

The development of courtly tradition evolved in the direction of satire and realism. In Germany, Neidhart von Reuental (c.1180–c.1250), in his 'Dorfpoesie' (rustic poetry), made use of the most sophisticated poetic techniques to recount village loves and discussions: this type of formal literary plagiarism will occured later in France with the *sote chanson* (silly song), a parody of the great courtly lyrics. Such realism is present in thirteenth century Italy in the works of Rustico Filippi (1230–before 1300), Cecco Angolieri (1260–c.1311) and Folgore di San Gimignano (end of thirteenth–beginning of fourteenth century). In France, it corresponds to the personal and often polemical poetry of **Rutebeuf (c.1285)**.

Poetry in Latin

Liberated, like religious poetry, from metrical constraints and striving for novelty in both rhythm and rhyme, poetry in Latin dealt with the same subjects as vernacular poetry. It discoursed on love in a learned and discreet way or, alternatively, in an energetic and sometimes crude way. It sang of bodily joys and pains and engaged in polemics with the secular powers and the Church. It is the work of recognised literati like Baudri de Bourgueil, Hildebert de Lavardin and Gautier de Châtillon or of itinerant and annoying clerics like Primatus or the Archipoet. Their texts are sometimes of great literary value and bear witness to writing that is fully alive and capable of self-renewal.

Here we have the world unworlded: it is indeed quite empty of all the good things that the world consists of.

Gautier de Châtillon

Poetry in Latin and vernacular poetry have several forms in common, like the crusading song. Marcabru, for instance, in his song of the *lavador* (purifying bath of the feat of arms),

Pax in nomine Domini!	*Pax in nomine Domini!*
Fetz Marcabrus lo vers e.l so.	*Marcabru has written both the words*
Aujatz que di:	*and the music,*
cum nos a fait, per sa doussor,	*Listen to what he has to say:*
lo seingnorius celestiaus	*that the Lord of Heaven*
probet de nos un lavador,	*in His kindness*
c'anc, fors outramar, no.n fo	*has built in our proximity a bath*
taus,	*such as there never was*
en de lai enves Josaphas;	*across the sea*
e d'aqest de sai vos conort.	*from here to Josaphat,*
Crucifigat omnes	*and from this bath I am exhorting you.*
Domini crux altera,	*May we all be crucified*
nova Christi vulnera!	*By Our Lord's second cross,*
Arbor salutifera	*The new wounds of Christ!*
perditur; sepulchrum	*The tree of salvation*
gens evertit extera	*Is lost; a foreign race*
violente; plena gente	*Is destroying the Holy Sepulchre*
sola sedet civitas;	*With their violent acts; the city full*
agni fedus rapit hedus.	*of people now stands desolate;*
	The kid has broken its pact with
	the lamb.

Anonymous

Byzantine poetry

The learned poetry inherited from Antiquity was maintained, particularly in the shape of the epigram, with the poetess Cassiané or Cassia (ninth century) and in the eleventh and twelfth centuries with Christophorus Mitylenaios, John Geometres and John Callicles. In the twelfth century satirical, personal and persuasive poetry started to appear, attributed to Theodorus Prodromos (1115–1166) and therefore referred to as Prodromic poetry. The four manuscripts which have been preserved, pitying the poverty or the bad temper of a wife, the cares of a father of many children and the uncomfortable situation of a teacher (such themes continue to be typical), satirise monks. As far as realist poetry derived from personal inspiration goes, there is the *Poem on his Imprisonment* by Michael Glykas (died *c.*1204), written in prison in 1159 and dedicated to Manuel

invites us to abandon tranquillity in life for God, as does the author of this anonymous Latin poem:

Comnenius. The poem is a defence on the grounds of his domestic problems: its author complains of having been locked up because of the slanderous gossip of a neighbour.

THE NOVEL

In the tradition of the novel in Alexandria, Byzantium saw the publication of *Rodanthe and Dosicles*, attributed to Theodorus Prodromos in the twelfth century. Like all Greek novels of its period, this text is faithful to the sophisticated model of Heliodorus' *Aethiopica* and takes place in a pagan world reconstructed for the purpose. The memory of the genre (allegory), like that of the style, has been carefully preserved and the work was written in ancient Greek.

Although it is impossible to prove the prior existence of a Greek version, in the Latin-speaking West the *Story of King Apollonius of Tyre* (second century) demonstrates the importance of the Alexandrian novel tradition and plays an essential part in the evolution of the novel about adventure and love. Having revealed the act of incest committed by the King of Tyre with his own daughter, Apollonius becomes the husband of the King of Cyrene's daughter, from whom he is promptly separated and whom he believes to be dead: she has, in fact, just given birth to a baby girl. Dragged into a series of many dangerous journeys, Apollonius finally becomes King of Tyre. At the same time, he is separated from his daughter who, destined to be a prostitute, succeeds in evading dishonour. After many years, Apollonius finds his daughter and his wife again and reigns over Antioch, Tyre and Cyrene.

Borrowing from various sources – the story of Oedipus, the tale of a persecuted woman – this work holds our attention by the charm with which it tells the story of a voyage and the variety of the often scabrous troubles that journey incurred. At the end of it virtue and true love are rewarded. Known in Gaul in the sixth century, the *Historia Apollonii Regis Tyri*, passed on in more than 60 manuscripts, was regarded in the Middle Ages as being solidly based on historical fact. It was quoted by all the best authors, and translated into Old English in the tenth century (*Apolon of Tyre*). We still possess some fragments in Old French dating back to the twelfth century – the story of *Apoloines* is cited by Chrétien de Troyes – that the epic romance of *Jourdain de Blaives* (thirteenth century) supplemented. In Germany the story is known to Lamprecht, the first man to adapt the story of Alexander (twelfth century). The same story inspired Heinrich von Neustadt at the end of the thirteenth century. One of the most original versions was the *Libro de Apolonio* in Spanish (1235–1240), with all the hallmarks of the 'mester de clerecia' (art of the scholar), a novel which attached some importance to psychological analysis. The work continued to be read and transmitted after the thirteenth century and was particularly famous in England where there was a fourteenth-century version in Middle English, an adaptation by the poet

John Gower in Book VIII of his *Lover's Confession* (a text later translated into Portuguese and then Spanish), a poem in the fifteenth century and two texts in the sixteenth, not to mention Shakespeare's *Pericles*. Following its adaptation into Old Czech in the fourteenth century, the story of Apollonius was included for several centuries among the most popular in Bohemia.

The attraction of a succession of adventures also distinguishes a text in Latin, the *Ruodlieb*, doubtless compiled by a clerk at the monastery of Tegernsee in Bavaria (first half of the eleventh century). This seems to have been the first original medieval novel.

The epic becomes the novel

The writing of novels, by and large, often refers, at its outset, to an ancient tradition which gives it the necessary authority and sometimes makes use of national or royal genealogical claims. Apart from the story of Alexander, two ancient epics in particular attracted vernacular adaptations. First, there were the tales associated with the Trojan War, unknown to the West during the Middle Ages from perusal of the *Iliad* itself, but based on abridgements of this in the fourth and fifth centuries AD, the *Ephemeris Belli Trojani* (*Journal of the War with Troy*) by Dictys of Crete and the *De Excidio Trojæ* (*The Ruins of Troy*) by Dares the Phrygian. Each author was supposed to have actually witnessed what happened: Dictys on the Greek side and Dares on the Trojan.

The second epic to influence the Middle Ages was Virgil's *Aeneid*, which it read directly from the Latin text itself. The history of the destruction of Troy, like that of the arrival of Aeneas in Italy, offered writers an opportunity to interweave amorous adventures and tales of combat. It also lent itself to the illustration of the literary motif of the 'translatio studii': the glory of Greek poets had shone on the Roman Virgil and could in turn be reflected on to the clerks who were preparing to write these tales in their own language. But it could also justify the claim for a 'translatio imperii' (transfer of power) based on Trojan origins, asserted in France by Gregory of Tours and postulated by those close to the Dukes of Brabant in the thirteenth century.

The major work to popularise the legend of Troy in a vernacular language was the novel by Benoît de Sainte-Maure, the *Roman de Troie* (c.1165). Written in French by a clerk employed by Henry II of England, this text mastered the art of description. It included the love story between Paris and Helen together with other love stories destined to become famous, such as Troilus and Cressida, which inspired Boccaccio, Chaucer and Shakespeare. These stories, in which a tragic rather than a pessimistic concept of love appears, allowed their author to construct rounded characters.

Benoît's novel, rewritten in prose in the thirteenth century, gave rise to many adaptations, among which are Segher Diengorgaf's *Trojeroman*, (*Novel of Troy*), preserved in the *Historie van Troyen* (*History of Troy*) by Jacob Van Maerlant, praising love; the *Historia Destructionis Troje* (*History of the Destruction of Troy*), written in Latin by Guido delle Colonne. This inspired two Czech versions of the *Trojanská kronika* (*Chronicle of Troy*, end of fourteenth century and 1410), a work which was the first book printed in Bohemia about 1470, the *Rumanac Trojski* (*Novel of Troy*), translated into Croatian towards the end of the thirteenth century; finally the many German versions, the first of which was the *Liet von Troye* (*Song of Troy*, beginning of the thirteenth century) by Herbort von Fritzlar.

So that those who do not understand Latin can enjoy reading a novel.

Roman de Troie

Though it was adapted less often, the *Aeneid* gave rise to works which were important in the evolution of the novel in the Middle Ages, such as the French *Eneas* of 1160 in which, for the first time, systematic use was made of the analysis of the characters given by the narrator, and the *Eneit* of Henric Van Veldeke, of which only the German version is still extant. The legend of Troy and the story of Aeneas were considered to be closely linked, so Jacob Van Maerlant, in his *History of Troy*, took his story, including the *Aeneid*, up to the foundation of Rome by Aeneas.

Absolute love

The medieval novel found its most inspirational sources in Britain, made up of different Celtic traditions, and two myths whose fascination still holds power over us.

With *Tristan et Iseut* (*Tristan and Isolde*) there was, as Julien Gracq once wrote, 'the temptation of an absolute love'. This was derived from the power of magic (the love-potion) and was insubordinate to the most hallowed institutions and laws: family relationships, relationships within a clan. It found in itself the guiding light of its own destruction – Iseut of the white hands, a seductive and ominous reflection of Iseut the fair-haired – but also found in death itself the perennial flower of triumph in adversity which, for later centuries, governed the Western definition of passionate love.

The most important sources of this myth are in Scotland (Tristan is a hero of Pictish origin), in Wales and in Ireland, with the motif of the 'geis', the challenge-cum-spell which links Diarmaid and Grainne, as the philtre deprives Tristan and Iseut of their liberty. But we can also detect the echoes of other traditions: those of ancient mythology, for example, with the combat against an adversary who ravishes young people and young women (Theseus and the Minotaur), or those of Eastern origin (the Persian tale of *Wis and Ramin*).

The written documents which convey the oldest versions of the legend are themselves diverse. Perhaps has there never been ampler evidence of the 'European' nature of a work, to the extent that our knowledge of the existing texts necessitates the juxtaposition of versions in different languages. We only have fragments, in French and Anglo-Norman, of the first texts which, from 1170 to 1180, give two accounts of the legend: an 'ordinary' version by Béroul, with the accent on dramatic construction, still close to a performing minstrel's work, and a 'courtly' version by Thomas, which concentrates on character analysis and on the celebration of a love 'delicate and true'. It is in German texts – the *Tristrant* (before 1190) of Eilhart von Oberg and the *Tristan* (before 1210) of **Gottfried von Strassburg** **(early thirteenth century)** – and in texts in Norse (the *Saga* of Brother Robert, 1226) that we recognise the novel in its entirety, given over to the celebration of love. For those inspired by it, as Gottfried points out, it was perfect nourishment:

Daz was diu reine triuwe,	It was a perfect fidelity,
diu gebalsamete minne,	a love perfumed with balm,
diu libe unde sinne	which, to body and soul,
als innerliche sanfte tuot,	brings intimate felicity,
diu herze fiuret und muot:	which inflames both heart
diu was ir bestiu lipnar.	and spirit:
	such was their perfect food.

Gottfried von Strassburg,
Tristan

This dispersal of the legend throughout Europe continued during the thirteenth century, notably in Italy *Tristano Veneto* (*Tristan in Venice*). Later it reached as far as Serbia and Croatia (*Tryscan y Izolta*), and Bohemia, where *Tristram a Izalda* (last third of the fourteenth century) is the longest poem to have been preserved in Old Czech. New versions appeared in the countries where the traditional story was formed, such as versions by Ulrich von Türheim, *c.*1230 and by Heinrich von Freiberg, *c.*1300, the prose *Tristan* in French, *c.*1230–1240 and a version in Middle English, *Sir Tristrem*, *c.*1300.

The search for the Grail

The theme of the Grail served as a matrix for works produced independently of one another (the *Conte del Graal* of Chrétien de Troyes, *c.*1180; the *Parzival* of Wolfram von Eschenbach, before 1210) before turning into a cycle (the Christianised trilogy of Robert de Boron, beginning of the thirteenth century) and becoming a recurrent element in the great prose cycle centred on the character of Lancelot (*Lancelot* in French prose, *c.*1220). Because of this, we have the inauguration of a whole configuration of myths, designed to discover an alternative to the ideal of chivalry and at the same time to formulate relationships between individuals and the world in a new way.

The quest for the Grail is suggested to a character who is different to all other heroes of novels. Brought up far away from the practices and conventions of courtly love and chivalry, he becomes, when necessary, a better knight than others because of his natural virtue. But the trial he must endure is not one he can negotiate with valour, strength or even courtly expertise. He must know how to interrupt the vision of a procession in motion – not by fighting, but by asking questions. Why does the white lance carried by a young man let a drop of blood run down it on to his hand? Who will eat from the Grail (a sort of hollowed-out bowl) carried by a young girl? If this moving procession, placed within the hero's reach, is interrupted by these questions, the current misfortune with which the Fisher King and all his lands are being afflicted disappears, while Percival is admitted to unheard-of glory and may well be the next king. If he remains silent, his worth as a knight is of no practical use to him.

From the outset, the Grail theme is a point of convergence for various imaginary and self-contained worlds. These make it surprisingly powerful and interesting. Magical adventures meet initiation rites, for the castle of the Grail is both a place of other-worldly sovereignty to which the hero can gain admittance, and a potential discovery of family ties which the hero did not even know existed. The Fisher King is, in fact, Percival's cousin, so the discovery of an identity is also involved. The objects carried in the procession are marvellous talismans – the Grail, for instance, is a horn of plenty that satisfies and cures – and Christian symbols. The medieval reader, meditating on the bleeding lance, would probably remember Longinus, the centurion at the Crucifixion. Life and death meet at this point, for the lance is the weapon of the Celtic god Lug, and corresponds to the wound sustained by the Fisher King, as to that of Percival's father, but it is also the means of salvation in Christ. Fault and redemption are inextricably linked in every exegesis imaginable: the fault of the hero, who lets his mother die of grief, or of the Fisher King (and Sinner) who, from Wolfram's version onwards, succumbs to the temptations of the flesh. But there is also salvation in magical adventures or in conversion to Christianity.

The literary history of Europe is marked by a succession of texts that put their own slant on this tale. There is the Cistercian and mystical vision of the *Queste du Graal*, the bellicose vision of the Welsh *Peredur*, in which the idea of a vendetta dominates, the truly novelistic vision of the Portuguese *Demanda do Santo Graal* (*Search for the Holy Grail*) and, closer to us in time, the exaltation of compassion to a redeeming virtue in Wagner's *Parsifal*, or a refusal to do away with desire by possessing the absolute in *The Fisher King* by Julien Gracq.

However, beyond *Tristan* and the *Graal*, the whole of Arthurian literature, in verse and then in prose, was widely transmitted and interestingly adapted. The prose *Lancelot* was translated at least three times into Middle Dutch, notably in the rhyming version of *Lantsloot van der Haghedochte* (*Lancelot of the Lake*, mid-thirteenth century), but many original versions were known in Flanders, whose hero was often Sir Gawain (*Roman van Walewein*, *The Romance of Gawain*, by Penninc and Pieter Vostaert). Similarly, the prose *Lancelot* was known in Germany from the middle of the thirteenth century, but only became popular there at the end of the Middle Ages.

The Romance of the Rose

Begun by **Guillaume de Lorris (c.1200– after 1240)** around 1230, and continued by **Jean de Meung (1250–1305)**, who wrote the major part of the work, *The Romance of the Rose* is not easy to classify. It is a didactic treatise as much as a pure narrative, but it had considerable influence on European thought until the sixteenth century. Inspired by an allegorical tradition (the *Psychomachia* of Prudentius at the beginning of the fifth century; the *Marriage of Philology and Mercury* by Martianus Capella, first half of the fifth century; works by Bernard Sylvester and Alain de Lille in the twelfth century), the novel also had recourse to scholastic debate ('altercatio') which allowed for the portrayal of characters in a dialectical framework.

To the lyrical and courtly inspiration of Guillaume de Lorris, underpinning the initial allegory ('wherein the Art of Love is wholly hid') is added, with the contribution of Jean de Meung, a sort of compendium of medieval anthropology in which we can detect the philosophical background of the author (Aristotle, Plato and the problem of universals) and his ideological predilections (the struggle against the mendiant orders of friars). The second part of the work, however, which literary posterity found more to its liking, does not move away from the problem of love. It leaves behind the story form to concentrate on debate. In the choice of his protagonists, the author opposes the different driving forces that regulate love, whether they are internal and psychological, external and social, honourable or reprehensible – and they are all praised for their fecundity and their closeness to the life preached by Nature and Genius. This mirror for lovers is sometimes cynical and crude, but only because its author did not want to ignore a single aspect of love.

At the end of the thirteenth century, the romance, above all the part written by Jean de Meung, was paraphrased in the 232 sonnets of *Il Fiore* (*The Flower*) which may be attributed to Dante. We can find in them the devilish advice of La Vecchia (the Old Woman):

*In nulla guisa, figlia, vo' sia
larga,
né che 'l tu' cuor tu metti in
un sol loco;
ma, se mi credi, in più luoghi
lo larga.*

Il Fiore

*In no way, my daughter,
must you be generous
nor put your heart in one
place only;
if you take my advice, you'll
dole it out liberally.*

And here we have the Romance of the Rose
Wherein the Art of Love is wholly hid.
The matter of it's good and newly-baked.

Guillaume de Lorris,
The Romance of the Rose

From 1290 to 1325, *The Romance of the Rose* was also subjected to two adaptations into Middle Dutch. The first, originating in Flanders, introduced new sections of narrative in the style of the Arthurian romance; the second, more faithful to its original, comes to us from the Brabant and has been edited by Hein Van Aken.

Satirical and slapstick literature

Alhough it is not always easy to tell apart from didactic literature, satirical and slapstick literature is characterised by the importance attached to comic elements, by its polemicising bent and its often colloquial tone.

Diverting tales and fabliaux are short narratives which, calling on themes that are sometimes commonplace, such as the snow-child, are mostly of interest because of their subtle narrative construction, which brings to life quite banal subject matter. Satirising certain social categories, such as peasants and priests, these texts can be anti-feminist, but often make the central character a woman. The tone, normally comic, is only rarely tragic or courtly. This type of story developed in France in the thirteenth century and was still flourishing in the fourteenth. In Germany, a cycle of tales was constructed in the thirteenth century around *Pfaffe Amis* (*Father Amis*); this popular work had some of its motifs repeated in the cycle of *Till Eulenspiegel* (*A Mirror for Owls*), written during the second half of the fifteenth century in Low German and

preserved from the beginning of the sixteenth in a High German version.

Renart's pranks

Founded on the premise of man disguising himself as an animal (and related, from that point of view, to the fable tradition of which it is largely an offshoot), literature about Renart brings together animal perceptions, farce and education in varying quantities. Originally it consisted of works in Latin, the *Ecbasis Cujusdam Captivi* (*Escape of a Prisoner*, c.940), an allegorical tale of a badly behaved calf, captured by a wolf and then saved by a fox. *Ysengrimus* by Nivard was written c.1150 and was personifications of animals to attack the monastic orders. The evolution of the genre in vernacular languages began during the third quarter of the twelfth century with Pierre de Saint-Cloud, whose work describes Renart's rape of a female wolf: his character has become both burlesque and satirical and accessible to a variety of audiences. Many branches (groups of tales) were added to the first at the end of the twelfth century and during the thirteenth which developed on a more and more clearly satirical significance with Rutebeuf, *Renart le Bestourné*, in the middle of the thirteenth century and *Le Couronnement de Renart* (*the Coronation of Renart*) c.1295.

In Germany in 1180, Heinrich der Gelichesaere (Henry the Sly) also developed the satirical potential of the text from a French source, attacking love's vassalage, court circles and the clergy. The central theme here is *untriuwe* (disloyalty).

In Flanders c.1260, Willem created a particularly interesting work rich in consequences, *Van den vos Reynaerde*, from the first branch of the novel. This hero develops the theme of the misuse of language, the 'scalcheit' which now becomes typical, replacing the traditional 'renardie' (ruse). This text was later recast in *Reynaerts Historie* (*Story of Renart, c.*1375), after having been translated into Latin. It was translated into English and printed by Caxton, adapted into Low German as *Reinke de Vos* (*Renard the Fox*) and published in Lübeck in 1498: this is the version that Goethe adapted in his own *Renart the Fox*. The tradition of Reynard entered Italy before the end of the thirteenth century, but accounts of *Rainaldo e Lesengrino* (*Reynard and Ysengrin*) date from the fourteenth.

Later times

At the end of the thirteenth century, in every European country, at different stages of development, there was a literature in the national language. Now, as those who spread the gospel wanted, everyone can pray to God in their own language. They can also describe the world they saw and imbue it with the magic of their imagination without needing Greek, Latin or Hebrew.

Three courses of development was still left to be realised. The first was that of a system of thought which, inevitably nurtured by Christianity, effected an original synthesis between the dominant culture and the main currents of philosophy. This task, began with *The Romance of the Rose* by Jean de Meung, was developed Dante's genius.

The second is that of the perfecting and renewal of literary forms. Some, like the theatre, had hardly been thought of; others, like the 'canso' of the troubadours, had been fully developed. Now miracles and mysteries appeared, together with the sonnet, while the ballad and the rondeau became increasingly popular until the end of the fifteenth century.

The third course is that of new sources of inspiration in the fields of ancient literature and thought. Plato and then Aristotle had already contributed to philosophical and theological pondering. Many authors remained to be discovered and read, independently of the accumulated glosses which they had amassed – above all Greek authors, known up to this point in history through translations into Latin and Arabic. New cultural spheres of influence were to flourish. To the influence of the 'Scoti' during the Carolingian period, to the role played by Byzantium in the birth of Slavic literature, to the brilliance of the twelfth-century Renaissance in Northern France and lyrical poetry in Languedoc succeeds, and for a long time to come, the light now shed by Italy.

The Epic

F. Suard

The epic is not the only literary form practised during the beginnings of medieval literacy but it does indisputably have a connection with those beginnings, as has been demonstrated by Dumézil. A community uses the epic to describe its origins, what surrounds it, what are its expectations. Such a community cannot fail to create the world of the gods in its own image and likeness, but communal myths are not limited to the history that has preceded them. A community rediscovers in the language of the poem, and subsequently in that of prose, a type of 'forgotten language' so that, according to D. Madelénat, it is able to condense 'mythical essence into historical event'. As well as having a story to tell, a community has a way of expressing it which, before it can put it into writing, goes through a long process of being handed down orally, like those 'very ancient poems by Barbarians in which were written down the story and the wars of old kings' which Charlemagne, Eginhard tells us, had transcribed in order to preserve their memory. The epic owes to such a process its stylised quality, its spell-like repetitiveness and its hyperbole.

Among the first literary forms to emerge, the epic tends to make way for types of narrative which are deliberately fictitious, such as the romance, or which prefer to stick to the truth as they see it, such as official histories. However, it was never totally eclipsed.

71

A learned tradition

Greek and Latin epics were studied throughout the Middle Ages and led to imitations which were occasionally destined for great things. The first generation of novels, the novels of Antiquity, drew their inspiration from these. Among them were the *Romance of Troy*, which took up the tradition of the *Iliad* as related by Latin abridgements and which was popular in Europe. Then there was the story of Alexander, which was instrumental in the composition of a very great work, the *Alexandreis* of Gautier de Châtillon, often imitated.

The interest of clerks in the epic was not merely shown by the resumption in hexameters of ancient themes; throughout the Middle Ages current affairs also acted as a spur to the creativity of scholars. Heroic deeds call forth panegyrics or biographies in dithyrambs, such as *Karolus Magnus et Leo Papa* (*Charlemagne and Pope Leo*, ninth or tenth century), the *Carmen in Honorem Ludowici Pii* (*Poem in Honour of Louis the Pious*, ninth century) by Ermold the Black, or the texts written in praise of Frederick Barabarossa, such as the *Gesta Friderici I Metrice* (*Exploits of Frederick I in Verse*) from the twelfth century.

Important battles and large military expeditions naturally furnished ready-made themes. Next to the celebration of the Battle of Hastings (1066) by Gui d'Amiens (*Carmen de Hastingæ Prælio*) or of a victory won by the Pisans in an alliance with the Genoese over Saracen pirates (*Carmen in Victoriam Pisanorum*, 1088), it was, above all, the Crusades which furnished epic subject matter: *Solimarius* for the first Crusade, *De Recuperatione Ptolemaïdiæ* (*The Reconquest of Acre*, 1190–1191) for the third.

Finally, some works demonstrated that access to popular legend from a learned tradition could be possible. The *Waltharius*, the legendary history of Walter, King of Aquitaine, attributed to Ekkehard I of St Gallen, had as its protagonists the heroes of the Anglo-Saxon *Waldere* and the Germanic *Song of the Nibelungs*. The fragment known as The Hague fragment (beginning of the tenth century) describes battles in which the heroes of the epic cycle of Guillaume d'Orange participate. The *Carmen de Proditione Guenonis* (*Poem on the Treachery of Ganelon*, beginning of the thirteenth century) was an offshoot of *The Song of Roland* tradition.

The epic in the community

A second group of works aimed to build the mythical history of the community by drawing on the resources of collective memory. This group can be included under the heading of popular epic, provided that we abandon as untenable the Romantic hypothesis of collective composition: professional poets, sometimes highly literate, wrote these works, but in doing so they drew on the traditions of the group they celebrated.

Mythological and religious epics are found in Germanic and Scandinavian literatures. The *Ancient Edda*, preserved in a thirteenth-century manuscript, certain texts of which were written as early as the eighth century, celebrated in alliterative verses both the exploits of the heroes of the great migrations and barbarian invasions and those of Odin (*Hávámal, Tale of the Most High*) or Thor (*Hárbarosljo, Lay of Hárbaror*). Part of the Irish epic, the cycle of the Dedanann, also fits into a mythological perspective: it describes how the tribes of the Dedanann brought four magical objects to Ireland: the stone of Fal, the unbreakable lance of the god Lug, the sword of Nuada and the bottomless cauldron of Nagde.

In certain works we can see a contact between different religious traditions. For example, in the Scandinavian *Völuspá* (*Visions of the Clairvoyant*, c.1000), in which there is a feeling for humanity's tragic destiny and a denunciation of hubris, there is some Christian influence. This is particularly sharply defined in the Anglo-Saxon epic: out of eight poems of heroic proportions, two are Biblical epics in the strict sense of the word (*Exodus*, *Judith*), two more are hagiographical

(*Andreas*, *Fates of Apostles*) and the most famous work, *Beowulf*, which tells the story of a hero who slays monsters, contains a story of creation taken from the Bible. Heroic epics contain a historical perspective. In Ireland the cycle of the *Ulates*, completed before the early eighth century, offered an interesting picture of pre-Christian Irish civilisation with its tales of raids, feasts and amorous conquests. The cycle of the *Fenians*, on the other hand, is half-way between mythology and history.

The historical nature of the Byzantine epic *Digenis Akritis* (twelfth century) derived not only from direct or indirect allusions to events and people from the seventh to the twelfth century, but also from what it meant to be an 'acrite', whence the name of the eponymous hero. Acrites were soldiers who had received grants of land near the frontier of the Byzantine Empire in exchange for an undertaking on their part not to move from there, to provide themselves with weapons and horses and to be ready to fight for the Emperor whenever the occasion arose. The imperial laws of the tenth century strove to protect the lands of the 'acrites' against the acquisitiveness of large landowners. So it was that the carrying off by Digenis of General Lykandos' daughter, and his marriage to her despite the initial opposition of her parents, symbolised the efforts of these soldier-farmers to redistribute the wealth of the military and landowning aristocracy of the time in Asia Minor.

The *Poema* or *Cantar del Mio Cid* (*Poem of the Cid*, c.1140), the first major work of Spanish literature, relayed interesting information about the relationship between Christians and Muslims at the end of the eleventh century (the Cid takes refuge, after 1081, with the Moorish king of Zaragoza) and on the quarrels between the 'Campeador' and King Alfonso VI of Castille.

In the Slav lands, the *Slovo o polku Igoreve* (*Tale of the Campaign of Igor*) (1185–1187) has as its source a historical fact: the unsuccessful campaign of Igor, Prince of Novgorod, against the Coumans. In it the author develops the political theme of the misfortunes that can befall a country when princes fail to agree.

The French epic developed from a virtual disregard of history to the desire to portray in the song of exploits a genuine experience of life. In comparison with many texts in which there are only 'bits of historical truth transfigured into myth', the *Song of Antioch* (twelfth century) was the versified chronicle of one of the high points of the first Crusade. Two centuries later, the *Life of Bertrand du Guesclin* by Cuvelier appeared in epic form because it was thought to be the only form worthy of the exploits of a hero of the Hundred Years' War.

Although the Germanic epic sometimes had historical figures as heroes – Dietrich von Bern and Etzel, for example, whom we meet in the cycle of Dietrich, are, in fact, the king of the Goths, Theodoric of Verona, and Attila – it cast them in a role which had little to do with their actual role in history and often resorted to motifs in tales and legends: Brunhilde's quest or Siegfried's fight against the dragon in the *Nibelungenlied* (*Song of the Nibelungs*) are elements taken from folklore. With the exception of the *Hildebrandslied*, these texts have come down to us in thirteenth-century revisions and they contain interesting information for that period on the relationship between a sovereign and his vassals, and on chivalry.

Themes

The importance of social links was an essential constant, whether was a predetermined structure (an organisation along feudal lines), the relationship between a prince and the soldiers who depended on him, or the role played by kinship. The struggles that emerged at the heart of these types of organisation and put loyalty to the test created epic action. Without the injustice of the king of Castille towards his vassal, for example there would have been no *Poem of the Cid*; without Ganelon's jealousy of Roland, no ambush at Roncevaux; without Hagen's desire to extend the power of the Burgundian dynasty and to fight Siegfried, no *Song of the Nibelungen*.

Born of struggle, the epic poem developed

a warrior code of honour. The primary social imperative was the armed defence of the community and of the ideological or religious links which bound it together. Tales of mortal combat played a crucial part: they invited the hearer-reader to bear witness with their imagination to the exaggerated feats accomplished.

But matrimonial alliances assured the stability or the expansion of the clan. The epic was also interested in the search for love, and in female characters, particularly to the extent that they were opposed to the good running of the institution and the logic of the clan. Siegfried's love for Kriemhilde led him to indulge Gunther's love for Brunhilde, to take the king's place during the wedding night, and later to expose himself to the bridge's undying hatred. In other contexts, love appears as the hero's prerogative, capable of inspiring a lifelong attachment in a noble heart. How can we imagine the Cid without Ximena? Separation from her was the equivalent of self-mutilation.

> Llorando de los ojos, que non vidiestes atal.
> Assi parten unos d'otros commo la uña de la carne.

> Their eyes shed tears, you never saw such woe.
> They separated from each other like a nail torn from the flesh.

The epic heroine can become a symbol of the value system itself which she reminds the warrior about when he has temporarily forgotten. In the Chanson de Guillaume (Song of William), Guibour is unable to recognise her husband in the deserter who begs to be let into Orange: If you were Guillaume with the bumps on his nose/You would have helped us Christians, God knows. The epic excluded the narration of wonderful adventures, sometimes taken from history, which put the heroic stature of the hero to the test. The German 'Spielmannsepen' (minstrels' epics), König Rother (King Rother) or Herzog Ernst (Duke Ernst) in particular, as well as Huon de Bordeaux in France, describe a fantastical Orient and revert to plots taken straight from folklore.

The epic hero

The epic hero was the community's representative. He was therefore not merely an individual, but a character who stood for the virtues of the group pitted against destiny. However, in spite of the deep ties that unite them, the characters of an epic were not interchangeable.

With the exception of those who were exalted by adventure, they had a special relationship with the tragic. In certain Icelandic sagas, the hero was conscious of the holy nature of his destiny, which he must recognise and take upon himself once he has been permitted to reveal it. Elsewhere, destiny assumed the role played by 'fate' in Antiquity, a power using the efforts of heroes to crush them. So Kriemhilde, in the Nibelungen, tells Hagen, Siegfried's future murderer, just where her husband is vulnerable, thinking to protect him in this way.

In the texts in which Christian influence was felt, the work of destiny put the finishing touches to the sacrificial nature of a freely accepted death. So it was with Roland, whose soul was carried into the divine presence by angels. So it was with Vivian, in the Song of William, who swore before God never to flee in battle.

Displacements, resurgences

Like other medieval literary forms, epics were not limited to a particular cultural area, nor did they disappear when the mental or social structures present at their birth no longer existed. The displacements of epics were doubly interesting: thanks to the comparative approach, they allow us to reassemble legends of which only a part has been preserved in a particular cultural area, while they confirm the popularity of such and such a tale. Thus the Thidrekssaga bears witness to a lost early version of the *Nibelungen*, while the Latin *Waltharius*, linked to the *Nibelungen*, to the Anglo-Saxon *Waldere* and to the cycle of Dietrich von Bern, simultaneously allows us to see the interest in the story of Walter of Aquitaine and to consider the possibility of there having been a lost Germanic epic source.

These displacements can lead to reappropriation or reaction. In Spain, the success of the French *Chanson de Roland* inspired both the revision of *Roncesvalles* and the anti-Frank version of the epic, *Bernardo del Carpio*, preserved in the *Primera Cronica General*: the Spanish hero fights at Roncevaux next to Marsilius against Charlemagne before helping the latter to take Zaragoza.

In the Low Countries the *Exploits of the Lotharingians*, as far as part of the Dutch adaptation is concerned, gave rise to a veritable rewriting of the story in the *Epos der Lorreinen*; while in Italy the transmission of French songs of exploits led to the creation of a hybrid language, Franco-Venetian.

These modified versions are an indication of the ease with which the epic, just as it is giving way to new forms of writing, such as the romance, reappears in different guises, as chronicle, as lyrical poem in the Spanish 'romances' and, above all, as prose translation.

Among the adaptations which, from the Middle Ages to the nineteenth century, assured the revival of the epic form, the work of Italian poets of the Quattrocento and the Cinquecento deserves to be singled out. Thanks to the importance given to love, to the space set aside for marvels and enchantment, to the choice of new verse forms, Pulci, Boiardo, Ariosto and Tasso recreated a heroic poetry of chivalry. They established, particularly with the *Orlando Furioso* and *Jerusalem Delivered*, a constellation of new characters – Ruggero and Angelica, Bradamante, Tancredi and Clorinda – who, along with the heroes of tradition – Orlando, Rinaldo – inspired dramatists and poets.

The unique contribution of chivalrous Italian poetry was to maintain the epic tradition as a cultural value for three centuries both for the public and the literary theorists.

Pedlars' editions and 'Volksbücher' (chapbooks) continued to keep the epic popular. So today medievalists, the general public and the cultivated public can all appreciate the charm of a heroic tale.

The Misfortunes of Abelard

J.-L. Solère

There was nothing second-rate about Pierre Abélard (Peter Abelard, 1079–1142). He was exceptional, a man of peerless intellectual prowess whose life was nevertheless romantic. His fortunes were as resounding as his misfortunes. He experienced fame as well as infamy in his eccentric career: as a student giving lessons to his masters, as the castrated husband of a nun, as a monk whose excommunication ban could never be lifted, as a dialectician to be feared and a theologian persecuted by the Church, you either loved him or loathed him. Can we be impartial about him, even today? His autobiography, *The Story of My Misfortunes* (*c.*1136), reveals an uncompromising character endowed with many talents – including the ability to get himself into trouble.

Abelard the philosopher

Pierre Abélard was born in the village of Le Pallet, not far from Nantes. The eldest in a family of minor nobles, he gave up bearing arms to devote himself to his studies, especially to that philosophy. He went to Paris to follow a course of lectures. Exceptionally gifted, he forced his master to abandon first his teachings, then his chair, having emptied his lecture hall by opening a school to rival it! 'This,' Abelard wrote, 'was the start of my misfortunes.' He brought enmity and envy on himself, all the more so as he repeated his strategy. Not content with his success as a philosopher, he wanted to study the queen of sciences, theology. He went to Laon to follow the courses of a famous old teacher of the subject. Still as insolent, he declared himself disappointed and took the teacher's place: his Bible commentaries surpassed those of the latter on the strength of his talent and dialectical ability alone. On his return to Paris, he became rich and famous.

Abelard's innovations gave rise to mis-interpretations. In the nineteenth century he was portrayed as a champion of free thought, a forerunner of Descartes. In fact, his audacity did not break with scholasticism, but opened up new possibilities for it. If Abelard's influence on methodology was enormous, his doctrine did not pass directly to posterity.

Abelard and Heloise

Another misunderstanding has to do with what contributed to his celebrity in spite of himself: his relationship with Heloise. From Villon to the Romantics, by way of Rousseau, this couple became the symbol of a starcrossed love stronger than anything that stood in its way. The story began with a seduction, pure and simple. In 1118, at the height of his fame, Abelard noticed Heloise, a young woman already recognised for her fine mind and her love of study. He took up lodgings in her uncle's house where she lived, offered to give her private lessons and won her love. The escapade came to light. Abelard married Heloise in secret, but did not live with her in order not to lose his clerical status. Her uncle felt that the fault had not been atoned for and caused Abelard to be castrated. Hiding his face in shame, Abelard decided that he and Heloise would take religious vows.

From that moment on, another story begins, which we know about through the moving letters they wrote to each other. Abelard's passion had been carnal and unworthy of the pure love Heloise had had for him. This passion now became transformed into an affection that was wholly Christian, a brotherly solicitude for a young tormented nun. Abelard fully accepted what he thought was a just punishment visited on him by God and his conversion was total. Heloise, on the other hand, merely obeyed her husband and remained in a state of inward rebellion against God. She led a hard, irreproachable monastic life, not because she loved God, but because she continued to love Peter as passionately as before. The letters the two sent each other are tragic and sublime: on the one hand, there are the efforts of Abelard to bring Heloise round to an acceptance of faith and hope; on the other, there is Heloise's desperate love as she goes on repeating to Abelard that she belongs to him more than she does to God.

> I do not complain that my merits have diminished, knowing that yours are increasing. And now you have me as your servant, who formerly you held to be your master. You are greater than the sky, greater than the world, you whom the Creator of the world has ransomed.
>
> From Abelard to Heloise

Abelard and the Church

During this time, Abelard's public life continued to be tumultuous. He had entered the Abbey of Saint Denis to find peace and forgetfulness. But his uncompromising nature and his critical acumen involve him in quarrels with the other monks. On two occasions he had to leave the abbey. As he had not given up his vocation as a thinker and teacher, he continued to write and to teach. He was first condemned at the Council of Sens (1121). Aware of renewed threats of persecution, in 1125 he accepted the post of abbot in a remote monastery in Britanny. There he encountered debauched monks who tried to kill him and he had to run away again. He returned to Paris and experienced new triumphs.

But, with this upward turn in his fortunes, as his peculiar fate would have it, storm clouds appeared. His students maintained that with him they perfectly understood the mystery of the Trinity. Theologians got upset and alerted a fearsome opponent, St Bernard of Clairvaux. The Cistercian reformer had the dialectician condemned – without Abelard really being able to defend himself – by the Council of Sens and then by the Pope (1140). From then on, Abelard was mortally wounded: his doctrines were censored, his books condemned to be burnt, he himself reduced to silence. He gave up the struggle and asked for asylum with the Venerable Peter, abbot at the famous Benedictine monastery of Cluny. This important figure in Western Christendom brought about a reconciliation with St Bernard and the Pope and eased Abelard's final years. He finally found peace. The former proud, fiery teacher spent what little time remained to him in a state of perfect humility. He died on 21 April 1142. Heloise, who had never stopped loving him, laid his body to rest and had herself buried next to him.

Chrétien de Troyes (c.1138–c.1183)

T. Hunt

Arthur, the good king of Britain,
Whose royal prowess fits us
To be gallant, perfect knights.
The Knight with the Lion

After François Villon, Chrétien de Troyes was the most famous French poet of the Middle Ages. His personal details, however, are a good deal less clear than those of the *enfant terrible* of fifteenth-century poetry. Instances of his name being mentioned are disconcertingly few and far between and his relationship with his two patrons, Marie de Champagne (one of the daughters of the celebrated Eleanor of Aquitaine) and Philippe de Flandre, was vague and shrouded in mystery. Nevertheless, we know that Chrétien de Troyes moved in aristocratic circles and that his way of handling tales of chivalry helped to strengthen the aspirations of the minor nobility during the second half of the twelfth century. The marriage of the ideals of chivalry and those of courtly love had a civilising influence on the turbulent social grouping of young, unmarried nobles, both attracting and placating them. Second-born sons deprived of an inheritance by the right of the eldest son to inherit sought fame and fortune through violent action and

dreamt of marrying rich heiresses. Chrétien de Troyes, who used his moral sensitivity to depict the ethics of chivalry, put a new gloss on this idea.

At the same time, he manifested an insatiable curiosity about the highs and lows of human love, and took great delight in creating the comical bathos that resulted from superimposing on them the poses and lamentations he found in the love poems of the troubadours. We find in his works the note of seriousness and the moral preoccupations that characterise works of his time on the art of ruling, what have been called 'mirrors for princes', and, coexisting with this, the humorous note, verging on parody, of Ovid and Provençal poetry, applied to the psychology of love. In his five novels of chivalry, written in verse in the 1170s and 1180s, Chrétien juxtaposed humour and seriousness, love and chivalry, with such mastery of both writing and intellectual thought ('clergie') that he deserves to be recognised as the first true man of letters to express himself in a European vernacular.

Chrétien's 'clergie'

Chrétien used irony and had recourse to many different viewpoints: intervention on the part of the narrator – sometimes highly complex intervention – and the use, within the story itself, of repetition and counterpoint. His audience needed to concentrate. Three brief examples show the importance of these innovations.

In his first work, *Erec and Enid* (c.1160), Chrétien hid from readers precisely those things that they want to know. As if in playful imitation of his literary creator, Erec recounts his adventures to King Arthur in chronological order, accompanied by the narrator's running commentary:

Erec started to tell him of his adventures, without leaving out a single one of them. But do you honestly think that I plan to remind you of the reason for his departure on a quest? No, for you know the truth about this as about so many other things, since I have already explained it to you. To go through it again with you would bore me, for the tale would certainly not be short were I to go back to the beginning to set out everything he said to them.

Why has Erec taken his wife with him on this quest? The reader wants to know, but despite what his narrator tells us, Chrétien never gives us the reason: a fact which still fuels critical debate about the work.

The later novel, *Yvain or the Knight with the Lion* (*c*.1170), full of irony, has a conclusion which is even more challenging to a reader willing to suspend disbelief. Having provided us with copious evidence to the contrary, the narrator then assures us that the hero and his wife are wholly reconciled to and full of affection for each other.

The author has so little confidence in the plausibility of this statement that he foresees that those who recite or copy his story will be tempted to alter the ending of it, so he adds some verses designed to affix tangible limits to his text, to guarantee its authenticity:

And so Chrétien draws to a close his novel of The Knight with the Lion; this is all he has heard said about this story, and you will not learn anything more unless some lie is added.

It was when trees burst into flower,
And greenery bedecks each bower,
When the birds in plainsong Latin
Sweetly sing their gracious matins,
When joy inflames the universe.
                    Percival or the Story of the Grail

In this same work, Chrétien makes use of the dialectical patterns which make his audience reflect on the direction of the story. At the beginning of the novel, the narrator declares in his preamble that a 'chivalrous man, even when dead, is worth more than a living boor'. The first adventure the hero experiences leads him to fall in love with the widow of a paragon of chivalry whom he has killed. Later, the hero marries this widow and, just as the marriage feast is at its height, the narrator observes:

Sir Yvain is now the master here, and the dead man has been completely forgotten. His murderer is married: he has tied the knot with the wife of the deceased and is sleeping with her, and the man who is still alive is universally loved and respected much more than the dead man was.

In this delicate situation, what has become of the narrator's assertion in the preamble? This problem, as well as certain other details, oblige a hearer to envisage the possibility that, despite appearances, the hero has in fact been implicitly portrayed as a boor; indeed his conduct was far from exemplary during the fight that led to the death of the knight he killed. At a key moment in his tale, Chrétien awakes certain memories that make us doubt the veracity of the story. This moment of intense reflection, brought about by the opposition chivalrous-dead/boorish-living, is an example of another aspect of his literary virtuosity: the art of veiled allusion to other works. For someone with a knowledge of tales in Old French, the narrator's comments hint at an episode in the marriage of Œdipus and Jocasta in the *Roman de Thèbes* (*Novel of Thebes*). Just as Chrétien seems to be emphasising his hero's good fortune, he puts a doubt in our minds. This is where his greatness as a writer lies: his technique constitutes a permanent challenge and an invitation to interpret what actually happens.

The subject of Britain

Chrétien's originality of form should not blind us to the particular interest of the themes he introduced. Although his education made him familiar with the works of Ovid and Virgil, and he himself tried to adapt certain works of Ovid, in his maturity (the 1170s and 1180s) he turns away from Antiquity, the happy hunting-ground of previous verse tales in Old French, to glean inspiration from Celtic tales, the subject of Britain, characterised by the presence of the marvellous and the supernatural, and by frequent allusions to the Celtic afterlife.

Together with his contemporary, Marie de France, Chrétian did most to introduce Celtic mythology into French literature. Many images and motifs which occur time and again in his novels to illustrate the knight's quest are of Celtic origin: malevolent dwarves, dangerous fords, enchanted castles, welcoming hosts, to name but a few. From each of the novels we take away the memory of an image which plays an essential part in the hero's enterprise: the joy at court (*Erec*), the flaming lance and the Bridge of the Sword (*Lancelot or the Knight with the Cart*, *c.*1170), the Fisher King and the procession of the Grail (*Perceval or the Tale of the Grail*, *c.*1175), the magic fountain (*Yvain or the Knight with the Lion*). The exception to this rule is found in *Cligés* (*c.*1170), Chrétien's second novel. This work, of a dazzling preciosity whose action takes place in Byzantium, was probably his response to the popularity of the story of Tristan and Isolde.

It is perhaps paradoxical that a typically French author should find the essence of what he writes about in the Celtic tradition. Three of Chrétien's stories – *Erec*, *Yvain* and *Perceval* – exist in a version in medieval Welsh, in the famous work called *Mabinogion*. These adaptations seem to have been based on Chrétien's novels from which they doubtless derive their inspiration. However, they do contain some curious anachronisms which seem to point to an earlier origin. Whatever the truth of the matter, these Welsh works are of great interest. Although they have the same narrative thread as the novels, they employ a completely different storytelling technique: that of the popular legend.

In Chrétien's novels the knight's first adventure takes place far away from court and results in a crisis. This is followed by a period during which the knight serves a new apprenticeship and is anxious to make up for his past mistakes. Then he recovers both his personal identity and his social status. The hero is simultaneously alone in his personal quest and integrated into a group which is trying to find its own place in society. The fusion of these two quests and of their aims marks the end of the knight's adventure.

The considerable influence Chrétien had on the way in which the medieval novel in Europe was later to be structured is entirely due to Erec and *Yvain*. *Lancelot* and *Perceval* are unfinished works (*Lancelot* was finished by a different hand). In *Perceval*, Chrétien experiments with two plots – the story of Percival on the one hand, that of Gawain on the other – thus laying the foundation of the technique of intermingling multiple adventures which will be adopted in the great prose novels of the thirteenth century. In this way he establishes the typical structure of the medieval novel. His critical study of the links that can exist between love and chivalry gave his successors ample food for thought. He was not a moralist pursuing a single objective throughout his work; each of his novels poses a new and interesting problem for which he endeavours to find a new solution. With the exception of *Erec*, all his works bear witness to his keen sense of humour and it is clear that, intellectually speaking, he transcended the limits and conventions of the courtly society that he was partially responsible for creating. His portrait of King Arthur, for example, is far from flattering.

Chrétien and Europe

Chrétien de Troyes was known all over Europe. The Swabian poet, Hartmann von Aue, whose other works were based on religious legends, wrote faithful adaptations of *Erec* and *Yvain* barely twenty years after their original composition. Wolfenbüttel's *Erek* is another version in Middle High German of Chrétien's first novel. *Cligés*, not as well appreciated, was translated into German in verse form around 1230 by Ulrich von Türheim; Rudolf von Ems also notes another version of the same work by Konrad Fleck. In Schmalkalden and Rodeneck there are murals showing scenes from Hartmann's *Yvain*. Shortly after Hartmann, Wolfram von Eschenbach responds to the invitation extended by *Perceval*, Chrétien's unfinished work on the quest for the Holy Grail, by writing his monumental *Parzival* which mixes a good deal of humour with the deeply pious outlook of a layman. The fact that copies of Chrétien's novels fell into such expert hands is a phenomenon worthy of emphasis.

Towards the middle of the thirteenth century, *Erec* and *Yvain* travelled north: they were two of the five works in Old French (which also included *Perceval*) translated by the Norwegian king Hákon Hákonarson. *Yvain* later appeared in a detailed Swedish translation, *Herr Ivan Lejonriddaren* (*Sir Ivan, Lion Knight*), written in 1303 for the wife of Haakon V of Norway by a Swedish clergyman who had studied in Paris and put to good use his knowledge of French and his perusal of an *Ivenssaga* already in existence. Conversely, there was only one adaptation into Middle English of a novel by Chrétien: it was *Yvain*, the popularity of which had never waned. *Ywain and Gawain*, written *c*.1350, and of which one copy only is still extant, gives a fairly humdrum version of Chrétien's story, devoid of what made it so original: the accent is on the theme of chivalry, while the love element almost completely disappears. Finally, Chrétien made his mark on Arthurian romances in Middle Dutch. The *Roman van Perchevael* is a fairly faithful translation of the original *Perceval*, but only fragments of it remain. The determining influence of certain episodes in Chrétien's novels can be found in the *Roman van Walewein* (*Novel of Gawain*), as it is in other novels originating from Flanders. The most striking episodes were abundantly illustrated in medieval art: illuminated manuscripts, sculptures, misericords and frescoes. So the tradition of the medieval European novel only developed its full meaning because of Chrétien. If the great prose romance frescoes of the thirteenth century, *Lancelot* and *Tristan*, were destined to nourish European culture down to and including the eighteenth century, while the works of Chrétien were eclipsed by classicism, it is to him that these texts owe their imaginary world and their fictional structure. The clerk from Champagne well deserved the title of 'meister' (master) bestowed on him by Wolfram von Eschenbach.

Saxo Grammaticus (1140–1206)

K. Friis-Jensen

I prefer to go to Denmark which has given us Saxo Grammaticus, the man who was able to bring to life the history of his people in all its splendour and magnificence.

Erasmus, *Colloquies*

An idealised and dramatised version of Danish history, the *Gesta Danorum* (*Chronicle of the Danish People*, *c*.1200) by Saxo Grammaticus is one of the founding texts of Danish literature. Saxo restored the tales, myths and legends handed down from pagan times in Scandinavian countries with the consummate art of a storyteller, and its fame spread beyond Denmark's frontiers. Since the Renaissance, his tales have been a source of inspiration for poets from all over Europe: Shakespeare's tragedy *Hamlet, Prince of Denmark* is the most celebrated example.

Saxo sided with the international literary culture of his time and wrote in Latin a history of Denmark which made of the Danish and the Danish royal line a people as old as the Romans and their first kings. By imitating the style of classical Roman writers, he introduced a temporal dimension. He peopled the beginnings of Danish history with conqueror kings and legislators, with great bards (extracts from whose works he gave in Latin), great explorers and beautiful women beseiged by suitors. In his description of the history of later centuries, from the introduction of Christianity to Denmark *c*.960 to 1185, Saxo emphasised the role of Danish kings as defenders of the realm, as well as the importance of the collaboration between Church and Royalty. According to Saxo, the high point of this collaboration was reached with King Valdemar I the Great (died 1182) and Archbishop Absalon, who after long struggles against the Venetes together contributed to a national revival.

Latinate, Christian, Danish

We have little information about Saxo's life and what we do have is often unreliable. Saxo came of a great military family with a tradition of service to the king. He became a parish priest and the secretary of Archbishop Absalon (died 1201) in Lund, probably securing the post of canon of Lund's cathedral chapter. The library there was filled with manuscripts on historical subjects. By virtue of its archdiocese and because it was part of the royal domains, Lund was a frequent destination for clerical and secular delegations as well as for occasional sojourns by the Danish court. Anyone with a mind as alert and inquisitive as Saxo's could collect oral testimonies to contemporary events from various locations. It was Absalon who asked Saxo to write a history of Denmark which would make it possible for it to be ranked among civilised European countries and, in this way, to counterbalance the one-sided picture of barbaric pagan pirates that medieval chroniclers had given of the Vikings; Saxo was already working on this before 1190. But Absalon died before the *Chronicle* was finished. Shortly after 1208, Saxo dedicated his work to Anders Suneson, Absalon's successor as Archbishop of Lund, and to King Valdemar II the Victorious.

Saxo's mastery of Latin points to the fact that, like so many other rich young Danes at the time, he had received a solid grounding in book learning at a centre of higher education, no doubt in the north of France. He was familiar with the Latin epic of Alexander, written in Rheims *c*.1180 by Gautier de Châtillon, and his own versification bears a close similarity to it. His admiration for and imitation of classical Latin models is indicative of the direct influence of a cultural trend often referred to as 'the twelfth century Renaissance' whose epicentre was in France.

The triumph of Latin culture

In the preface to his work, Saxo sets out certain guidelines to its interpretation. Latin literature came quite late to Denmark, during the period of its introduction to Christianity. But already, during the pagan period of their history, just like the ancient Romans, the Danes composed poems boasting of their prowess and that of

their ancestors and etched stones with runic inscriptions. These were the raw materials that on his own admission Saxo used as the foundation for his *Chronicle*, together with the stories of Icelandic scholars and those of Archbishop Absalon. For Saxo, the Roman Empire had not entirely passed away. He considered the Holy Roman Empire of his time as the Roman Empire's heir apparent by way of the Empire of Charlemagne: a way of thinking wholly in accordance with the imperial ideology of the time. But in his preface and in the body of the work itself Saxo often insisted on the fact that Denmark had always been independent of the temporal power of the Roman Empire. He praised King Valdemar II, for instance, for 'not having, in his campaigns, spared the lands of the Holy Roman Empire from armed attack'.

This attitude only applied to civil authority. For spiritual authority, the Pope in Rome represented the old Christian Empire and in Denmark the leader of the Danish Church, the Archbishop of Lund, was its current representative. Saxo was no agnostic: he believed that Christianity provided man's one and only salvation.

The story of a people

The sixteen books of the *Chronicle* are structured symmetrically, in harmony with the basic idea of the work. The first eight evoke the era of paganism in Denmark and here, in the first half of the work, poems are interspersed with text. The last eight books describe the introduction of Christianity and the period of Christianisation which ensued. Inspired by the universal chronicles of late Antiquity and medieval times, Saxo went further in his own conscious structuring of the course of history.

The Danish royal line of the *Chronicle* began with King Dan and his brother Angul. One of Saxo's predecessors had made Dan contemporaneous with the Emperor Augustus, but, thanks to bold surmises, Saxo put him more than twenty generations before the birth of Christ – about the time of Romulus and

Remus. The first quarter of the book (Books 1–4) describes a period of Roman history which extended from Romulus to the reign of the first Emperor, Augustus. In the manner of Virgil, Saxo describes the fall and destruction of the royal house of Lejre through betrayal, as well as the death of King Rolf Krake, and includes a translation of the poem *Bjarkamál*. There is also the story of Prince Amlet, or Hamlet, who takes vengeance on his father's murderer by pretending to be mad. A narrative equivalent is to be found in the story of the first consul, Brutus, who also exacted revenge by pretending to be mad, and Saxo may have borrowed some of these elements for his story of Hamlet.

Book 5 is exclusively about the long reign of King Frode, presented as the Danish equivalent of the reign of the Emperor Augustus. Frode is a great conqueror and a great legislator, just like Augustus. The last thirty years of his life were a long period of peace, comparable to the *pax romana* of Augustus ('pax Augusta'). Saxo spoke of the birth of Christ coming at the end of this period and insisted on there being peace over the rest of the world to celebrate the arrival of the Saviour. At this point Saxo chose to insert great poems which are spoken by Scarcatherus, warrior and bard. He makes them into approximations of poems by Horace and Juvenal. At the end of Book 8, he mentions the victory of Charlemagne over the Saxons as well as the conversion of the latter to Christianity – the border between Christianity and paganism, from now on, is the south of Denmark. Summoned southward by the Pope to defend Rome, Charlemagne avoided the threat of a pitched battle with the Danes. This expedition ended in 800 with Charlemagne being crowned as head of the Roman Empire.

Books 9–12 contain the introduction of Christianity to Denmark. From a Christian point of view, the country depended on the Archbishop of Hamburg and Bremen in Northern Germany, but retained its autonomy with regard to the Roman Empire where Charlemagne's successor was now enthroned. The great Anglo-Scandinavian Empire of King Canute (Knud the Great) was regarded as a high point. At the end of Book 12, Denmark obtained its ecclesiastical autonomy. The Pope authorised the creation of an archdiocese and the papal legate chose the town of Lund (1104).

The last part of the work (Books 13–16) deals with the period from 1104 to the submission of Duke Bugislavus of Pomerania to the Danish king (1185). Freedom of religion is thereby acquired, but later in the century Emperor Frederick Barabarossa became a real menace to Danish independence. King Valdemar I was forced to swear an oath of allegiance to the Emperor in 1162, an event whose importance Saxo attempted to play down. The narration of the many seagoing campaigns of Valdemar I and Archbishop Absalon against Wendic pirates is superb. Its high point is the conquest of the town of Arkona on the Rügen, including the destruction of its most important pagan temples such as that of the god Svantovit. The campaign conducted by the Danes was justified here as a crusade. In 1177, the schism between Pope and Emperor came to an end and King Valdemar elected his ally Bishop Absalon, as Archbishop of Lund. Saxo related these two events which together constitute a kind of universal harmonisation of relations between paganism and the Church, and celebrated this fact by bringing down the curtain on it in Book 14. Diametrically opposed to Saxo's usual practice, the end of this book did not correspond to the death of a king.

The *Chronicle* described Denmark as a remarkable Nordic counterpart, both political and cultural, to the Holy Roman Empire of the time.

Saxo's influence on Europe

In the centuries that preceded the first printed edition of the *Chronicle* (Paris, 1514), its influence was limited to Scandinavia and Northern Germany, even if some researchers thought that the medieval legend of William Tell, for example, was derived from a tale about the master bowman Toko. In the fourteenth century, a Latin abridgement was written. This quickly soon became popular and was soon translated into Low German. The humanist Albert Krantz, a native of Hamburg, had access, c.1500, to Saxo's work in its entirety while he was working on his own *Chronica Regnorum Aquilonarium* (*Chronicle of the Nordic Kingdoms*, printed in Latin and a High German translation in the 1540s). Krantz took all the most interesting tales, often literally, and put them into his work, becoming another sixteenth-century source of knowledge about Saxo. Hans Sachs, for instance, one of the meistersingers of Nuremberg, found in Krantz themes for a tragedy and several poems, all material to be found in Saxo's original. The Parisian edition of Saxo won him an international reputation and his expertise as a writer was celebrated by Erasmus. The two Swedish humanist brothers Johannes and Olaus Magnus, compiled historical and cultural works, on Sweden and Scandinavia basd on Saxo. These which were printed in Rome in the 1550s and were much sought after. François de Belleforest put some of Saxo's tales into his collection of *Histoires Tragiques* (*Tragic Stories*, 1559), and it was probably though him that the subject of Hamlet reached Shakespeare. In the seventeenth and eighteenth centuries, German and Italian dramatists took their inspiration from Saxo, but it was above all with the advent of Nationalism and Romanticism in Danish theatre that his work reached the pinnacle of its importance, with *Rolf Krage* (1770) and *The Death of Balder* (1773) by Johannes Ewald and *Hagbard and Signe* (1815) by Adam Oehlenschäger.

Walther von der Vogelweide
(c.1170–c.1230)

U. Wyss

Alas! My life's years, whither have they fled?
Walther von der Vogelweide

Walther von der Vogelweide was undoubtedly the most complex lyric poet of the Middle Ages, not only in Germany, but anywhere in Europe. Other poets today may hold a greater fascination for us – the boldness of Guilhem IX, Count of Poitou, the lyricism of Jaufré Rudel or the melancholic narcissism of Heinrich von Morungen may appeal to us more directly – but Dante himself did not investigate the possibilities of lyrical discourse more thoroughly than Walther.

A little-known poet

We only know of Walther's life what his poems tell us about it. Only one official document testified to his existence: in a list of expenses for journeys undertaken by the Bishop of Passau's household there is a note to the effect that, on 12 November 1203, at Zeiselmauer on the Danube, a minstrel by the name of von der Vogelweide received five crowns for the purchase of a mantle. He must have been an itinerant musician, a scion of the most lowly of minor aristocratic families, poorly provided for, trying his luck at one court after another. There is some dispute about where he was born. Perhaps he was born in the Tyrol, south of the Brenner Pass, in Lower Austria, in Franconia or somewhere between Nuremberg and Würzburg: none of these opinions has been satisfactorily proved. About 1190 he was at the court of the Duke of Austria in Vienna. In an elegy he wrote that he had 'worked as a poet for some forty years or more', which means that he would have reached the end of his career c.1230. According to a written testimony from the 1350s, whose truth we cannot verify, he was buried in Würzburg.

Walther began his career as a medieval court poet in Vienna, where his rival was the celebrated Reinmar von Haguenau. 'Will someone tell me what is courtly love?' Walter asked – and devoted himself to taking part in this endless troubadour debate. Even to this day, medievalists continue to study and argue about his work. By introducing nuances of meaning, Walther went beyond the fixed framework which kept courtly love firmly in the realm of unsatisfied desire, as Reinmar had done. According to Walther, a love worthy of the name should bring happiness and pleasure, not suffering. In taking this stance, he infringed a basic rule of the exposition of the 'Minnesang'. Because it never reached its avowed aim, the troubadour's love was a metaphor for many social, political, religious and aesthetic aspirations. One hundred years after Walther's death, in the 'dolce stil nuovo' as well as in Dante, it became a point of departure for philosophical and theological knowledge. Walther himself also established a link between the self's reward for taking up love as a theme and the wages of the poet for performing at court. He also sang of how chimerical an erotic happiness can be which rests on a desire divided between man and woman, notably in songs inspired by dreams of shepherd girls in which the knight asks for the favours of a young woman from a less privileged social background. For Guilhem IX of Poitou there was a chasm between affected virility and the agony of castration. Walther invents a whole gamut of erotic alternatives. In thinking these up, he makes a distinction between a woman ('wîp') and a lady ('frowe') with a role to play in society. While accepting the joy of real experience, he did not take this to its logical conclusion of sexual love, making metaphor superfluous. 'Alas, what can I say, I who am deaf and without eyes? How can one whom love makes blind see clearly?' he wrote at the end of a poem in which he wonders about the nature of love.

An almost mythical figure

It is, however, Walther's political and didactic poems above all which made him an almost mythical figure in Germany during the Middle Ages. These poems were something totally new, even in comparison to French poetry of the period. Walther addressed the princes who must have been his patrons. Among them were not only the Austrian Duke Leopold VI of Babenberg, Landgrave Hermann of Thuringia, and Dietrich von Meißen, but also two emperors, elected by opposing factions among the imperial elector and crowned in

1198. The first was Philip of Swabia, the brother of the recently deceased Henry VI, a member of the house of Hohenstaufen; the second was Othon IV, a Guelph on whom the French king Philippe Auguste inflicted a crushing defeat on 27 July 1214, at Bouvines.

Walther's last imperial patron was Frederick II of Hohenstaufen, crowned in 1215. Walther thanked him for having given him a small fief to overcome his material poverty. In his political poems – to distinguish them from his poems of courtly love they are called, paradoxically, 'sung words' – Walther described the Emperor's relationship with the Church, promoted the Crusades and exhorted princes to be generous to their retinues. In the nineteenth century, the medieval poet was considered to be a counsellor of princes and a spokesman for the myth of imperial greatness. This, of course, remains surmise. Certainly Walther wrote for his patrons and defended their interests, but he also attached importance to his own role.

The picture of the poet sitting by himself on a stone, his head resting on his hand, and reflecting on the instability of the world order is a famous one:

Deheinen rât kond ich gegeben,
wie man driu dinc erwurbe,
der keines niht verdurbe;
diu zwei sint êre und varnde guot,
daz dicke ein ander schaden tuot;
daz dritte ist gotes hulde.

I could not manage to find out
how to acquire three things
that would never pass away;
two of them are honour and good fortune,
which often clash with each other;
the third is God's favour.

Sometimes Walther defended himself against all kinds of opponents at court or complained that great nobles lacked hospitality. With the lay, Walther attempted to acquit himself – only once – in the richest and most complex of lyric forms. This was a poem composed of several different stanzas, probably modelled on liturgical sequences in honour of Mary and the Trinity. In this respect he was to be much imitated in the thirteenth century. A great poem written at the end of his life, however, remains unique and incomparable; using once again the rhyme scheme used in the *Song of the Nibelungen*, he regrets that earthly beauty and desire are ephemeral:

> *Oswê war sint verswunden alliu mîniu jâr?*
> *Ist mir mîn leben getroumet, oder ist ez*
> *wâr?*

> *Alas! My life's years, whither have they*
> *fled?*
> *Is my life just a dream, or real instead?*

It was a call to go crusading, for there, over the sea, a knight, as a soldier of God, could dislodge with his lance the heavenly crown of beatitude . . .

Saint Thomas Aquinas (*c.*1226–1274)

J.-L. Solère

O Godhead hid, devoutly I adore thee,
Who truly art within the forms before me.
Thomas Aquinas

If it is not *a priori* ridiculous for a philosopher or a theologian to appear in a history of literature, for a 'Scholastic' to do so is perhaps likely to raise more than a few eyebrows. Plato or Saint Augustine have a right to be included, but the presence of Thomas Aquinas in such august company needs to be justified.

Thirteenth-century Latin scholarship

Born near the town of Aquino in Italy, Thomas, a Dominican and teacher of theology, belongs to a time and place in which the cultivation of eloquence for its own sake is no longer a priority. In as much as the twelfth century was distinguished by a Renaissance in the love of fine literature, the thirteenth

century, a period which saw the rebirth of a different sort of learning, devoted itself to making another part of the heritage of classical Antiquity bear fruit: that of the science of the ancient Greeks which the Arabs were helping it to rediscover. From this moment on, all effort to assimilate and develop this knowledge would be based on a made-to-measure technical language that sacrificed ornateness for precision, and beauty and emotion for clarity and intellectual rigour.

We must not let the enormous philosophical and theological output of Thomas, from which all pretension to literary style has been banished, make us forget that he was also a poet, one of the greatest of the Middle Ages writing in Latin according to Rémy de Gourmont. He to perfected both the rhyme and rhythm characteristic of Christian poetry 'as if with the hammer blow resounding from the clapper of a bell':

> *Lauda Sion salvatorem*
> *Lauda ducem et pastorem*
> *In hymnis et canticis.*
> *Quantum potes, tantum aude*
> *Quia major omni laude*
> *Nec laudare sufficis.*

> *Praise, Zion, your Saviour,*
> *Your ruler and your pastor,*
> *In your hymns and your songs.*
> *Do as much as you are able,*
> *For He is greater than all your praise*
> *And you will never praise Him enough.*

The profound intuition of the divine presence in the Eucharist also comes through this prosody, expressed not in passionate exultation, but in rounded, considered, measured, crystal-clear formulas, like all that this saint ever thought, and 'with such a sonority in the words,' according to Gourmont, 'that doubt is panicked into flight.'

It would seem that this medieval Scholastic lacked neither a poetic technique nor a discriminating ear for words that sound mellifluous. It is not because he is incompetent that the prose which made up most of his work was so austerely wrought. Scholastic philo-sophy was sparing, even finicky with its language, but it was precisely calculated to serve its purpose, and was never used to such telling effect as by this friar Thomas whose 'beautiful Latin' was praised by Dante.

Writing at university level

The expression 'school Latin' is sometimes used, but the connotations of the word 'school' are new ones in thirteenth-century Europe, at least where universities, those schools for which there is no antecedent, are concerned. The university was a professional community of masters and students, an urban legal entity, very different from the traditional monastic educational system. Thomas Aquinas cannot be understood outside a university setting, for his public life, coordinated and dedicated to the pursuit of knowledge, is almost indis-tinguishable from his personal ministry as educator and academic researcher, which he practised at those new institutions of still unified Latin-speaking Christendom, the universities of Paris and Naples.

The first task of the master is to 'read' texts: to make sense of them in a cursory, then in a more reasoned way. Thomas, accordingly, has given us a series of commentaries, both on the Bible and on theological and philosophical works. Above all he has written on Aristotle, whose philosophy, like his teacher, Albertus, he tried to render accessible to Christians and comprehensible to those who understood Latin. The commentary is a major genre for, by tracing its evolution in the Middle Ages, we can discern the appearance of a theory on text interpretion. Respect for an already estab-lished way of proceeding can be found in that other great genre which nurtured scholastic literature in general and the work of Thomas in particular: the 'quæstio' (question). Derived from Aristotelian dialectics, it begins by setting out opinions backed by written authority, but mutually exclusive, not to encourage scepticism, but rather to set in train a process of analysis based on the methodical doubt arising from a confrontation. According to St

Anselm's formulation, medieval belief in search of reason had decided to do without it, despite the received wisdom, where the demands of a rational conviction could be met. Initially it posed the problem by recognising the existence of contrary opinions and pro-ceeding to overcome these difficulties in order to solve the initial problem. Before it was written down, the 'quæstio' was a 'disputatio', bringing supporters of opposite views to grips with each other under the guidance of a master. This form of oral jousting which was the principal method of teaching and contributed to the intellectual ferment of university life. A scholarly as well as a military phenomenon, the art of the joust found its echo in literature, so that it can be considered as an ingredient of civilised life. Certain literary forms and certain situations to be encountered in medieval novels and romances 'also reflect, in their way, how far-reaching in society then was this model of intellectual argument: such was the case with the "jeux-partis" in the North of France and the "partimens" in the South, types of debate or poetic tournaments [. . .], it was also the case for the "ambivalent" oaths sworn in French novels of the 1180s [. . .]' (A. de Libera). So it is not surprising if most of Thomas Aquinas' works are structured around this device. Some of them, in fact, are nothing more than retranscriptions of disputes he originally organised, grouped thematically, such as *Questions on Truth*.

But his most famous book, the *Summa Theologiæ* (*Theological Summary*, c.1266–1273), employed the same method, even though – a rarity where Aquinas was con-cerned – it did not spring directly from his university lectures. The various points of doctrine were divided into questions about the existence of God, God as a perfect being, and themselves divided into sub-headings. Each one was introduced by a dialectical inter-rogation ('utrum . . .'), whose two sides are each backed by 'authorities' (quotations from the Bible, the Church Fathers, philosophers, human reason). Those authorities which tended to rebut the thesis that Thomas had chosen to defend are listed first ('videtur . . .'), then contradicted by a 'sed contra' which acts as both a counterbalance to them and a spur to discussion. The latter began with a re-examination of the problem ('respondeo . . .') that led to Thomas' own conclusion. The discussion was then brought to a close by answering each of the initial objections in turn ('ad primum dicendum . . .') which either refuted them, or suggested a way of reconciling them to the conclusion.

The imperatives of clear and reasoned argument, of systematic and integral analysis which guided this unchanging procedure were not the spontaneous product of timeless 'common sense'. If the medieval way of going about things seems natural to us, it is because we are 'the unwitting heirs of Scholasticism', as Panofsky has it. He attributed this search for the organic whole and for making things explicit to a habit of thought of medieval civilisation, a leading principle which he called the principle of 'manifestatio', of clarification or elucidation. Order must be visible in every-thing. The pure forms that populate Thomas' work are rooted in his civilisation. They are related to those forms embodied in Gothic cathedrals, whose strongly delineated archi-tectural lines are self-explanatory as far as their structure goes. But they are also related to the literature of his time, since the same requirements of enumeration, making distinctions and satisfactory coordination are included.

From aesthetics to metaphysics

The three requirements which have just been mentioned and the principle of 'manifestatio' itself can be compared to the three criteria that Thomas uses to define beauty: 'integritas, consonantia, claritas'. The *Theological Sum-mary*, though it is not a work of art, has often surprised people with its beauty. This is because, by a sort of habitual process of reflection, Thomas applied to his own writing the rules of his aesthetic theories, in which it is possible to find the whole of his metaphysics, founded on the primacy of form and action.

For Thomas the notions of unity, order, harmony, proportion and form are the foundations of a theory (in the Greek sense of 'contemplation') in which artistic and perceptible beauty is merely a particular instance of the intelligible beauty which illumines the whole of Creation and secretly animates it. Beauty, in effect, is omnipresent in its radiance: it is what the Scholastics call a 'transcendental', a property of being. Every-thing is beautiful because it is perfect. None of those properties are lacking which give it its essence (organised in terms of its form, its intelligible structure), when this essence has effectively been realised, when it has fulfilled all its inner potential. Aristotle, who gave Thomas these ideas, then calls it 'in action'. An essential prerequisite for this state is for an element of creation to be brought into existence, for it cannot cause itself to exist as it owes its existence to its causes and, in the final resort, to its primary cause. This is its 'integritas' its: first constitutive element.

Each being is endowed with an intelligible harmony of proportions or 'consonantia': its second constitutive element. By the word 'proportion' we must understand a connection between parts which correspond to one other and which form an organic unity, born from inside itself as if from a seed of reason planted there. Beauty, according to Plotinus, is the agreement of parts between themselves as well as with everything surrounding them. Each being so constituted is endowed with 'claritas' – the third constitutive element. This is the ontological property of the form, and of the order it belongs to, to manifest itself in accordance with that in the object which seizes and holds our gaze, and which is the foun-dation of our perception of the beautiful. Joyce, who took up Thomas' three criteria to found his own poetics, maintained that the moment when this radiance is perceived by the mind is 'the luminous and silent stasis of aesthetic pleasure'.

Beauty is then a light emanating from the form or, more usually, from the plenitude of the object 'in action', that gives to each thing its measure, its number and its weight, to make use of the Biblical phrase. But each particular form and its existence are themselves included in among all others. In other words, the three criteria which together define individual beauty can also be applied to the whole of Creation. This is at least how Thomas views Creation: as an overall unity finished in accordance with the principle towards which it tends. Whereas in every creature there is always a residue which eludes actuation, in God everything has realised its full potential. He is the Being whose essence is to exist, whose essence is never just potential, but existence actuated for all eternity. God is the pure state of being. The things on which He confers the gift of life are analogous to Him: they are partially imitative of Him, each in its own way. So God's creatures are arrayed, rank on rank, in a vast and continuous hierarchy according to the degree of actuation each one carries with it. Beings are coordinated with one another in an intelligent arrangement of species and types, for all are subordinated to the same purpose. Thus the world constitutes a vast synergy, an intrinsic disposition that makes all the activities of created things tend towards their good, and the whole ultimately towards absolute perfection as 'all things tend to be assimilated into God'. All levels of this God-given order radiate a 'claritas' which approximates to the reflection of the divine glory. With this vision Dante's *Paradiso* begins: 'The glory of Him who moves all things penetrates the universe and shines forth in one place more than in another.'

Poetics and culture

Beginning with Thomas Aquinas' way of writing, we have laid bare the outline of his metaphysics: such is the cohesion between what he says and the way in which he says it that the two are inseparable. The order of the *Theological Summary* recreates in its way the order present in the real world (God, Creation, the return to God), and the orthodox canon which regulates the finest detail of its architecture is the same one that serves to reveal the beauty of beings and of the world. When

Cajetano, a Thomist commentator of the Renaissance, said of him that 'Saint Thomas always speaks in a formal way', it was not a reproach, but an indication of the latter's eminent aptitude for defining 'formalities': the properties of created things. Dry and abstract, his style nevertheless conforms to a way of thinking which places beauty in the realm of forms, for does not 'formosa in Latin mean the same as 'beautiful'? It is this aesthetic viewpoint that Thomas brings into play when he has to pray or praise. Can it be argued that his poetics or his thinking in general had an influence on other writers? Certainly, here and there, there are doctrinal elements, as we saw with Dante and Joyce. But, by the same token, Claudel would not have been Claudel if he had been content to versify the *Theological Summary*, which he nevertheless used to read assiduously. It is, no doubt, preferable to seek in Thomas the foundations of a philosophy of art rather than a literary vade-mecum as, for instance, Jacques Maritain and Étienne Gilson have tried to do. His metaphysics, the leading principle of which is action, being both existing and acting, certainly provided an adequate framework for seeing art as 'poïetic': as production, as 'making', and not as knowledge or imitation.

But rather than look for hypothetical direct influences, we can also try to disengage affinities from cultural tendencies. So it is with Jean de Meung, who was Thomas' contemporary and neighbour in Paris. It is not possible to equate the philosophical substratum of the second part of the *Romance of the Rose* with Thomism, since there are significant points on which the two part company. What is clear, however, is that the *Romance* conveys ideas belonging to the same current of thought. It was the thirteenth-century equivalent of 'modernism' that tried to acclimatise to Western Christendom all the Greco-Arab knowledge which had just sprung up to threaten old certainties.

To end this portrait of Thomas Aquinas, (who always seems younger when we view him in the context of his time) let it be clear that to claim Aristotle as an 'authority' then was to claim for human reason the right to be exercised freely in those areas where it could be exercised, in spite of theologians mixing everything up. Unlike previous theology which based itself on external appearances and treated things as symbols devoid of reality, trying to attain directly to the supernatural, Jean de Meung and Thomas Aquinas were interested in a nature that had its own consistency, fertility, laws and comprehensibility. This was no longer the age of lapidaries and bestiaries, nor of the miraculous world of the novels of courtly love. Thomas Aquinas meditated on a cosmos which was well defined in terms of its structure and its movements, the causes of which could be apprehended by a reason that dominated his thought and life. He would have appreciated the following verses by Jean de Meung:

> *Nature is more fair than I know how to*
> *   say,*
> *For God whose beauty is beyond all*
> *   measure*
> *When He put the beauty into Nature,*
> *Made of her a fountain head*
> *always spurting water, never dry,*
> *from which all beauty flows:*
> *no one can reach*
> *bottom or the edge.*

6 *From the Middle Ages to the Renaissance in Italy (1300–1450)*

F. ORSINI

Now every enlightened individual can thank God for having permitted him to be born in this new age, so full of hope and promise . . .

Matteo Palmieri, *On the Life of the Citizen*

The year 1300 was the Roman Catholic Church's first jubilee, officially declared by Pope Boniface VIII. The year 1453 marked the Turks' capture of Constantinople. Between these two dates, we can only stand and watch as two great institutions, the Empire and the Papacy, gradually declined. Christian belief remained deep-rooted, despite the crisis of authority within the Catholic Church and the first inklings of the Reformation. The major event during this period, so favourable to new endeavours in the arts, was the noticeable increase in towns with an independent status and a growth in the accumulated wealth of the business community.

Almost everywhere in Europe, three cradles of culture emerged. First, there were the universities which began to multiply in the fourteenth century. Universities were founded in Prague and Perugia (1347), Cracow (1362), Heidelberg and Perpignan (1386), Cologne (1388), Ferrara (1391), Poitiers (1421) and Louvain (1425).

Second, there were the courts of kings and nobles – those of France, England, Castille and Aragon, Portugal, Bohemia and Poland – together with the duchies of Berry, Burgundy and the Brabant. There were the earldoms of Holland and Flanders and the Italian seignories of Milan, Ferrara and Mantua, to which we can add the 'court' of the Pope at Avignon.

Last, there were the towns with cultural structures peculiar to themselves: France had its 'literary societies' and 'brotherhoods'; England its 'guilds'; the Northern Netherlands their 'chambers of rhetoric'. Towns saw the development of the plastic arts, particularly architecture, and had a monopoly on theatrical performances during the main annual religious festivals. One of the crucial distinguishing marks of culture during this period lay in its secular nature. The new educated élite came less and less from the ranks of the clergy; it was made up of 'lay priests' belonging to the urban middle classes and the university educated. In many countries, the cultured man became a 'professional' employed by a lord or a sovereign. He was a notary, a secretary, a chancellor, an official historian or a court poet.

Literature because more personal: if, before this period, there were works, from now on there were authors who preferred to write in the vernacular and who had a greater sense of realism.

Lyrical poetry: the music of words

The courtly lyricism of the troubadours and their Northern French counterparts took love as their theme, not only in words but also in accompanying music. Although this form of lyricism was practised until the end of the fourteenth century, it gradually gave way to a different sort of music – more personal, more intimate – in which the artificial music of the instrument was replaced by the natural music of words, rhythms and rhymes: what Eustache

Deschamps called 'mouth music', produced 'en *prouférant* paroles métrifiées' ('by *uttering* metrified words'). This new art led naturally to a science of language, a type of rhetoric described as 'secondary' to distinguish it from the 'primary' rhetoric of Latin poetry.

Called on to play a part in the corridors of power, the poet, increasingly conscious of his potential, became a straightforward word craftsman. This approach to the art of using words turned 'authors' into 'writers'. In parallel with court poetry, a lyrical poetry developed whose readers lived in towns.

During the last two centuries of the Middle Ages the poetic influence of France was still being exerted over other European countries, but it lacked the vigour that had characterised it in the twelfth and thirteenth centuries. The torch of lyricism, in the new sense of the word, passed to Italy where the poetry of **Dante Alighieri (1265–1321)** and **Francesco Petrarca (Petrarch, 1304–1374)** reigned supreme. In the *Vita Nova* (1291–1293) and the *Rime* (*Rhymes*), Dante forced courtly love to undergo a gradual transformation, until it became what it achieved in *La Divina Commedia* (*The Divine Comedy*, 1304–1321): a totally spiritual love.

An unearther of ancient classics and a precursor of humanism, Petrarch was, first and foremost, a sublime lyrical poet who wrote the *Canzoniere* (1342–1374). His influence on Western poetry was immense. Petrarch's love for Laura, coloured here and there by troubadour-like touches and snatches of the 'stil nuovo', displayed a new, essentially subjective quality. The fruit of introspection, it expressed its author's underlying 'ego' in verses whose subtle musicality and refinement of imagery, sometimes to the point of preciosity, of imagery were virtually unknown until then.

Lyrical poetry in France: ballads, lais and virelais

French lyrical poetry in the years 1300 to 1450 was markedly different from that of the troubadours and *trouvères*. It made increasing use of the scholarly ornamentation – allegory, erudition – inherited from the *Romance of the Rose*. It continued to sing of courtly love, but, in terms of form, it obeyed strict rules of composition as each genre carried with it its own fixed form.

The undisputed master of this new poetic technique was **Guillaume de Machaut (*c*.1300–1377)**, the 'noble rhetorician'. A native of Rheims, he belonged to the retinues of John of Luxembourg, King of Bohemia, of Charles the Bad, King of Navarre, of Charles V, the French king, and of the Duc de Berry. A poet-musician – the last one of the Middle Ages – he was looked up to in his time as a leading light and was presumed to have founded a sort of literary school.

> Love then, willynilly . . .
>
> Guillaume de Machaut, *True Tale*

As a musician (*Mass for Our Lady*, *Two-part Motet of David*) Machaut revolutionised the art of polyphony. As a poet he perfected the ballad, the rondeau, rhymes royal, lais and virelais and defined their forms. His poetry included lyrical pieces for which he composed musical accompaniments, roughly 250 poems on courtly themes collected under the overall title of *In Praise of Ladies*. His work also contained lyrical/narrative works such as the *Tale of the Orchard* (*c*.1342–1343), the *Tale of the Lovelorn Fountain* (*c*.1360) and, above all, the *True Tale* (1364), an autobiographical idyll in which the sixty-year-old author tells of an amorous adventure with one of his female admirers, the young Péronne d'Armentières. The book is made up of letters in prose and exquisitely charming verse, as in this scene from *The Kiss in the Orchard*:

> *However on her sweet young mouth*
> *I planted then my loving lips*
> *And kissed her just a little bit,*
> *But afterwards I felt remorse.*
> *Because, once she had taken in*
> *My boldness and presumptuousness,*
> *She spoke to me in lowered voice:*
> *'My friend, I think you want too much.*
> *Have you no other way to touch?'*

But, saying this, she gave a smile
That played upon her mouth the while
And my imagination's scope
Increased to feel the certain hope
We might be more than just good friends,
By silence she would gain her ends.
Guillaume de Machaut, True Tale

Eustache Deschamps (c.1346–1406), who followed in Machaut's footsteps and may have been related to him, spent most of his life in the service of Charles V and the house of Orléans. He left behind a considerable literary legacy – 1500 poems in all, including lais, virelais and nearly 1000 ballads. In 1392 he wrote an *Art of Writing*, the oldest 'ars poetica' in French. While his highly personal and melancholic lyricism paved the way for Charles d'Orléans, his experiments with form, sometimes highly sophisticated, remind us of the many users of rhetoric who were to come. Christine de Pisan, who called him her 'dear master and friend', admired him, and Chaucer also held him in high regard.

Christine de Pisan (1364–1430) was the daughter of a Venetian doctor and astrologer, Thomas de Pisan, who had entered the service of Charles V, the King of France. A widow with three children at the age of twenty-five, Christine de Pisan earned her living by writing. She wrote for a number of noble patrons: for Jean, duc de Berry, Philip the Bold, Duke of Burgundy and Charles VI and his wife, Isabel of Bavaria. Her varied work included philosophical and moral treatises, historical works, verse tales, letters and hundreds of poems. Her facility and virtuosity, the importance she attached to autobiography and to the fact of her being both a writer and a woman, made Christine de Pisan a unique in lyrical poetry in France at the end of the Middle Ages. She can be illustrated by the first stanza of the following ballad, in which, after 1389, she expressed her loneliness and the pain of widowhood:

I am alone, alone I want to be,
alone, of my companion bereft,
I am alone with none to comfort me,

alone and aching, angry left,
alone in boredom hard to bear,
alone and hardly knowing where,
alone, no single friend is there.
Christine de Pisan, Ballad

Alain Chartier (c.1385–1433), royal notary, is the author of the *Book of the Four Ladies* (1415), written in verse, of the *Quadrilogue Invectif* (1422) in prose, and, most memorably, of a long poem called *La Belle Dame Sans Mercy* (1424). Original and subversive, this caused a scandal at the time. Contrary to the Lady in courtly literature before this, Chartier's 'Dame sans mercy' does not allow herself to love. She proclaims her freedom not to love. She refuses to let herself be swayed by the arguments, which she regards as sham and conventional, put by her lover who, rejected, dies of his grief.

Charles d'Orléans (1394–1465), the son of the Duke of Orléans and an Italian bluestocking, Valentina Visconti, was the leader of the Armagnacs faction after his father was assassinated by John the Fearless. He fought at Agincourt and was taken prisoner by English until 1440. Once free, he retired to his castle at Blois and devoted himself to literary pursuits. The finest poets of the time, including François Villon, were his guests. Charles d'Orléans wrote most of his courtly poems, some of which are in English, during his captivity. With a cultivated mind, he was the most delicate and attractive of all the writers who wrote using fixed forms. Few poets of his time knew how to speak as he did of nature, weather and the seasons. There are no great passions in his work, but feelings expressed in half-tones – languor, sadness, 'nonchaloir' (heedlessness) – which cause him to sink into the deep well of his melancholy:

From the deep well of my melancholy
The water of Hope I constantly draw,
My Comfort's thirst is what I want it for,
Though often I find dryness in my folly.
Charles d'Orléans, Rondeau XXX

Othon de Grandson (1330–1397), born a gentleman in Vaud, was a man for war and tournaments, and for a time a crusader in the East. He was also the author of lais, ballads, songs and laments, in the style of courtly poetry and amorous wordplay. His is the first lyrical voice to be heard on the frontiers of Savoy and Burgundy, regimented and impersonal, for whom love and death are interchangeable:

My highest good, my sovereign dear,
My only wish, my joyous thought,
My one true love, the fountain of all good,
Beauty from whom joy is given to me,
Which will be increased a hundred
*   thousandfold,*
When it pleases you to crown me with the
*   victor's wreath*
That I have often sought of you.
But you have always answered no.
                        Othon de Grandson,
                        The Book of Sir Ode

French lyrical poetry continued for a time to have a decisive influence. Chaucer, for example, took his inspiration from Machaut to write his ballads and rondeaux. **John Gower (1325–1408)**, towards the end of his life, wrote an anthology called *Cinkante Ballades (Fifty Ballads)* in which he sang of courtly love in Anglo-Norman. King James I of Scotland (1394–1437), a soulmate of Chaucer, wrote with great poetic aplomb of his captivity under the English and of his love for the beautiful Anne de Beaufort in his *Kingis Quair (The Book of the King, c.1423)*.

Courtly lyricism was highly prized in the Northern Netherlands. The court accounts of Albert of Bavaria (1358–1404), in The Hague, mention frequent visits from minstrels and musicians from the Rhineland, Southern Germany, Burgundy and France. The *Haags*

Liederenhandschrift (The Hague Songbook), written just before 1400, has courtly love as its principal theme. French influence is particularly noticeable in the *Gruuthuse Manuscript*, dating from the same period. This second songbook marks an appreciable step forward: even though it was not composed at a court, it developed courtly themes but in circles close to the ruling élite in Bruges.

The cancioneiros

French influence, that of Northern France and that of Languedoc, was also present in the Portuguese and Galician 'cancioneiros' (songbooks) which brought together lyrical poems written between the beginning of the thirteenth century and the middle of the fourteenth: the *Cancioneiro Português da Vaticana (Portuguese Songbook of the Vatican,* end of the fifteenth century), the *Canzoniere Portoghese Colocci-Brancuti,* before 1549, today called the *Cancioneiro da Biblioteca Nacional (Songbook of the National Library)* and the *Cancioneiro da Ajuda (The Songbook of Ajuda,* end of the thirteenth century). The pieces contained in these songbooks are divided into 'cantigas de amor', songs sung by men in which a knight complains of the hardship he is made to endure by his lady, and 'cantigas de amigo', songs sung by young women, full of the melancholy of *saudade.* In these final pieces, the best ones, a young woman in love weeps for her absent lover. Her solitude leads her to apostrophise nature: trees, flowers, beasts and birds. King **Dinis I (1279–1325)** enjoyed dabbling in such songs. The following verses, with their stark subjectivity, their simplicity and their obsessive rhythm of repetition and symmetry, have the indisputable force of incantation:

Ai flores, ai flores do verde pino,	*Ah! Flowers! Flowers of the green pine,*
Se sabedes novas do meu amigo?	*Do you have any news of my friend?*
Ai, Deus, e u é?	*Ah! God! Where is he?*
Ai flores, ai flores do verde ramo	*Ah! Flowers! Flowers of the green branch,*
Se sabedes novas do meu amado?	*Do you have any news of my beloved?*
Ai, Deus, e u é?	*Ah! God! Where is he?*

Dinis, *Cantiga de amor*

Another type of poem contained in these songbooks are the 'songs of mockery and cursing', satirical, burlesque pieces directed against aristocrats, the newly rich, tax collectors and doctors.

In the Iberian peninsula, French influence began to be replaced by Italian influence, which became dominant from the second half of the fifteenth century. At the beginning of the period 1300–1450, Spanish lyricism was still under the twofold influence of Franco-Provençal and Portuguese lyrics. After about 1350, Gallego-Portuguese lyricism made way for Gallego-Castilian lyricism. The courts of the Spanish kings were ones in which poetry was well established and courtly love particularly favoured. The *Cancioneiro de Baena* (*The Songbook of Baena*, 1445), a vast compilation containing 576 compositions under the editorship of Juan Alfonso de Baena, brought together songs in Castilian composed by poets during the reigns of Peter I, Henry II, John I, Henry III and John II. The display two tendencies. The first is illustrated by Alfonso Alvarez de Villasandino, whose verses oscillate between satire and flattery, while the second is conveyed by Francisco Imperial (born *c*.1360), who introduced the allegorical poetry of Dante into Spain. The 'cantigas', fixed-form pieces designed to be sung, have either love or devotion to the Virgin Mary as their main theme. The 'decires' are lyrical-cum-narrative compositions made to be recited, redolent of everyday life, with a somewhat didactic aim. In the *Cancioneiro de Stúñiga* (*The Songbook of Stúñiga*, *c*.1458), which takes its name from the author of the first piece in the collection, Lope de Estúñiga, the poetry takes on a tone at once more plaintive and more precious. It becomes more erudite. The old 'cantiga' becomes the 'canción', a more learned piece, or the 'villancico', a more colloquial composition. In this collection, there are many 'serranillas' (mountain songs), quite close to the French pastourelle.

Working independently of the poets represented in the songbooks, two major figures of fifteenth-century Spanish lyricism need to be mentioned: **Iñigo López de Mendoza, Marquis of Santillana (1398–1458)**, and **Juan de Mena (1411–1456)**. Juan de Mena borrowed from Dante's *Paradiso* the layout of his principal work, which was allegorical and didactic: *El Laberinto de Fortuna* (*The Labyrinth of Fortune*, 1444). Though he admired Guillaume de Lorris and Provençal writers, the Marquis of Santillana nevertheless preferred to go to Italy for his inspiration. *El Infierno de los Enamorados* (*The Lovers' Hell*) returns to the allegory of Dante's *Inferno*, and his *Comedieta de Ponza* (*The Little Comedy of Ponza*, *c*.1436) is directly inspired by Dante's masterpiece. Santillana also remembered Petrarch when he wrote his forty-two sonnets. His songs, his tales, and above all his 'serranillas' are tiny poetic gems:

La Vaquera de Bores

Moçuela de Bores,
allà do la Lama,
púsome en amores.

Cuydé que olvidado
amor me tenía,
como quien s'avía
grand tiempo dexado
de tales dolores,
que más que la llama
queman amadores.

Mas vi la fermosa
de buen continente,

The Cowgirl of Bores

A young maiden from Bores,
the other side of Lama,
made me fall in love.

I thought that love
had forgotten me,
not having felt
for quite a long time
those sufferings
that more than flame
burn lovers.

But I saw my beautiful one,
with an engaging air about her,

la cara placiente,	*a pleasant face,*
fresca como rosa,	*refreshing as a rose,*
de tales colores	*with a complexion*
qual nunca vi dama	*never before beheld in a lady*
nin otra, señores.	*or another woman.*
Por lo qual: ‹Señora,	*'Beautiful one,' I said to her, 'truly*
(le dixe), en verdat	*such grace*
la vuestra beldat	*cannot be hidden*
saldrá desd'agora	*among these hills;*
dentre estos alcores,	*it will leave them behind,*
pues meresce fama	*deserving of renown*
de grandes loores.›	*and great praise.'*
(. . .)	*(. . .)*

The Marquis of Santillana,
Serranilla

'Minnesang' and 'Meistersang'

In Germany the 'Minnesang' (song of courtly love) remained popular with poets. It was particularly so with a great lord, Hugo von Montfort (1357–1423) and Oswald von Wolkenstein (1377–1445). The latter's poems heralded a new phase in German lyricism. Returning to the themes of courtly love poetry, he boasted of the gentle condition of his lady to whom he promised total fidelity. He also dwelt on her physical charms with a great deal of sensuality, deviating, in this respect, from strict courtly orthodoxy. Real-life amorous experience impinged on the stylised performance of the minstrel. Wolkenstein was also a pioneer of linguistic experimentation. His use of colloquial or dialect expressions, the attention he attached to plays on words, to bold neologisms, to meaty metaphor, lent his many songs an undeniable character of their own.

Gradually in the fourteenth century the 'Minnesang' underwent a transformation. It became the 'Meistersang' (song of master singers). If the former was aristocratic in tone, the latter was middle class. Although they had scrupulous respect for the forms and themes of the 'Minnesang', the poems of the 'Meistersänger' are of limited interest. Often moralistic, they are too much the same. Closely scrutinised by *Merker* (markers), even

the most gifted of the 'Meistersänger' – Behaim, Heinrich von Müglen, Muscatblüt – were unable to express themselves freely.

Towards the middle of the fourteenth century, secular and courtly lyrical poetry, normally sung, took off in Bohemia, practised by members of the nobility and, often, itinerant students. Apart from a certain number of poems of native extraction, the vast majority of songs were of foreign inspiration and provenance. Their mediators were the German 'Minnesänger'. The most frequently chosen theme of these poems, written towards the middle of the fourteenth century, was love: *Dřevo se listem odievá* (*The tree is covering itself with leaves*), Račtei Foslúchati (*Deign to listen . . .*), *Milostný list* (*Love letter*). The finest example came from a former student of the University of Padua, *Záviš ze Zap: Jižt'mne vše radost ostává* (*Already all my joy is leaving me*).

Popular lyricism: songs, ballads and snatches

Alongside this learned lyricism, a lyricism developed which originated from popular sources. In Germany it was called the 'Volkslied' (folk song) and performed by itinerant singers who gave renderings of straightforward, light, tripping texts. One of their favourite themes was that of love, conceived of in the manner of the 'Minnesänger'. But folk poets had simpler and more sentimental ways of expressing themselves. In their poems the knight was replaced by the youth; the beloved was no longer a noble lady, but a young woman of humble origins. Words are used expressively and the images are arresting: the lover appears as 'a poor fledgling' who has fallen out of his tree, while the unfaithful beloved is depicted as 'an apple', red and inviting on the outside, but gnawed by a worm from within. In the fourteenth and fifteenth centuries, the 'Volkslied' encompassed the most varied subjects: epics, politics, religion. Surprisingly uninhibited, it did however hesitate to make the Angel Gabriel into a hunter sounding his horn, or the Virgin Mary into a hostelry hostess! As the following anonymous song reveals, this popular poetry was lively and charming:

Got gebe im ein vurdreben jar	*I hope that God will punish the one*
der mich machte zu einer nunnen	*who has made of me a nun,*
und mir den swarzen mantel gap,	*who has given me a black habit to wear*
den wissen rock darunden.	*and a white undergarment*
Sal ich ein nunn gewerden	*under it!*
sunder minen willen,	*If I have to be a nun against my will,*
so wel ich eime knaben jung	*I will comfort a young man*
sinen komer stillen.	*in his distress.*

Volkslied

In England and Scotland the popular lyricism of ballads developed. These are narrative poems designed to be sung, in which rhyme, refrain and melody all play an important part. Many themes are raised: epics, legends, stories, border struggles, amorous adventures. Among these ballads, two are particularly famous: *A Gest of Robyn Hoode* (end of the fourteenth century) and *Chevy Chase* (beginning of the fifteenth).

The most original contribution from Denmark, Norway and Sweden during the Middle Ages was their sung legends. Much was produced in this genre from 1400 to 1500. The folk song in Scandinavia consisted of stanzas two to four verses in length. This form was primarily a song-cum-narrative; it was danced to, recited and sung. It told a story of epic or dramatic character, praising the exploits of a whole pantheon of historical and legendary heroes with various Christian, pagan and courtly elements thrown in for good measure. The lyrical element was normally limited to snatches. In Denmark, the 'Folkeviser' (folk songs) tell of the dangers encountered by young people when they leave their first home at the age of fourteen or fifteen in order to marry and set up home. In *Elver*

Høj, a young man, on the eve of his wedding, crosses a heath haunted by female vampires, identifiable as such because they have no back. Having managed to give them the slip and to find his bride-to-be, he just has time enough to kiss her before he dies. The Scandinavian folk tale was admired by the Brothers Grimm. Still popular even now in the Faeroe Islands, interest in it is being rekindled in the rest of Scandinavia.

THE LITERATURE OF CHIVALRY

During the last two centuries of medieval times, there was a decline in the popularity of the epic of chivalry and the novel of courtly love in most European countries, because of the loss of prestige associated with being a knight and the increasingly important role being played by the urban middle class in literary production. On the whole, there were relatively few innovations. Writers were content to adapt and rework existing texts or to compile collections of them. The most noteworthy phenomenon is the putting into prose of the songs of exploits and the novels in verse of preceding centuries. Printing began to make these prose versions popular in the second half of the fifteenth century.

Epic poetry

In France, at the end of the Middle Ages, many songs of exploits were still being written, but their quality degenerated. Some of these songs, still being written in verse, belong to the tradition of songs about crusades; others emphasised love and adventure; others, yet again, were strongly linked to contemporary history, such as the *Song of Bertrand du Guesclin* and the *Exploits of Philippe and Jean, Dukes of Burgundy*. The writing of songs of exploits was not limited to verse. To keep abreast of contemporary tastes and trends, songs of exploits in prose were also written, such as *Renaud de Montauban* (1462) and *Florent et Octavien*.

French songs of exploits retained a certain amount of prestige in other European countries: in Germany, towards 1320, the *Karlmeinet* (*Charlemagne*), written in the area around Cologne, brought together five poems in the Charlemagne cycle. The work of Countess Elisabeth von Nassau-Saarbrücken was also significant: four prose novels recalled the time of Charlemagne and took their inspiration from the French epic tradition.

In Italy, epic poetry found an outlet in 'cantari' (sung poems of chivalry), popular narratives often full of pungent realism, sung at crossroads. Usually anonymous, they derived their inspiration from Carolingian and Breton cycles of romances, holy legends, the history of Troy or Rome. The oldest of these poems, *Fiorio e Biancifiore* (*Floire and Blanchefleur*) dates back to 1330. It went through various editions and alludes to a celebrated medieval legend, possibly of Eastern origin. Piero di Viviano (1343–1410), from Siena, called after his occupation the 'canterino' (singer of poems of chivalry), wrote *La Bella Camilla* (*The Beautiful Camille*, 1370–1390). From 1362 to 1364, Antonio Pucci (*c*.1310–*c*.1390) recast and adapted legends to which he added an unashamedly popular twist: the *Apollonio di Tiro* (*Apollonius of Tyre*), the *Brito*

di Brettagna (*Brutus of Britanny*), the latter based on an episode from *De Arte Honeste Amandi* (*On the Art of Loving Honestly*) by André le Chapelain, and, last but not least, the *Reina d'Oriente* (*The Queen of the East*).

In Spain, especially in Castille, the 'mester de juglaría' (the career of minstrelsy) produced the last songs of exploits in the fourteenth century. Written in the vernacular, designed to be recited and sung in the streets and squares, the epic poems of the 'juglares' (minstrels) glorify the warring deeds of national heroes.

The novel of courtly love

Enthusiasm for this genre knew no bounds. New titles, however, were rare in comparison to retellings, adaptations and prose versions of the tales: according to a medieval saying, 'great princes and their peers were fain good prose than rhyme to savour'. The Arthurian cycle remained a source of inspiration for many authors. *Lancelot* was translated into Catalan; the *Romance of Pierceforest* (1314–1323) was copied by a friend of William I of Hainaut; *Lancelot-Queste-Mort* was twice adapted into Middle Dutch: in the *Lancelot-compilatie* (*Lancelot Compilation*, before 1326) and in the *Rotterdamse Fragmenten* (*Rotterdam Fragments*, before 1320). The *Saga of Eric* (*c*.1320) and the *Saga of Percival* (after 1320) appeared in Norway. The *Eufemiavisorna* (*Euphemia Poems*, *c*.1300) were love stories and adventures written in Swedish. *Tristram a Izalda* (*Tristan and Isolde*, *c*.1400) was a Czech version of the French original, written by an anonymous poet on the basis of German adaptations. *Sir Gawayne and the Green Knight* (*c*.1370), appearing in Great Britain, dealt in a somewhat subversive fashion with the values and premises inherent in the classical novel of chivalry relating to the invincibility of the hero.

Material from ancient times is also at the root of many texts: the influence of *Apollonius of Tyre* was considerable and the *Novel of Alexander* went through various adaptations. Many novels were devoted to the history of

Troy; many novels of chivalry, tinged with eroticism, were written in Demotic Greek, such as *Kallimakhos ke Khrisorroï* (*Callimachus and Chrysorrhea*, twelfth century).

Other subjects were also extremely popular: a number of travelogues (or exotic 'romances') were written in praise of the mysterious East and the spells it cast over travellers. The celebrated *Travels of Sir John Mandeville* (1356), which was translated into several languages, was often held to be a kind of pilgrim's guide to the Holy Land.

The finest novel of chivalry in Castilian was an anonymous and composite text called *La Historia del Caballero de Dios que había por nombre Cifar* (*The Story of the Knight of God who was called Cifar*, c.1300). Its central idea was already present in 'The King who lost Everything' in the *Arabian Nights*. The author recounted the legend of Saint Eustace, of Greek origin, as well as Breton legends. True to the edifying vein of the period, the second part of the novel was more didactic. The character of Squire Ribaud appeared, in whom some have seen the original of Sancho Panza and others a precursor of the 'picaro' of Spanish sixteenth and seventeenth century literature.

The prose story and the verse tale

Arising out of middle-class preferences, the short narrative form began to prosper in Europe in the fourteenth century. It assumed either the name of short story* or tale. Its structure, usually simple, traced the development of a single, unique action, often happening in the present. A critical attitude towards the customs of the day, polemical comments and realism are its other distinguishing marks.

Short narratives are enshrined in two medieval masterpieces. First, there is *The Decameron* (1350–1355), a collection of short prose novellas by the Italian **Giovanni Boccaccio (1313–1375).*** Then there are the tales, in verse, of the English writer **Geoffrey Chaucer (c.1340–1400),*** *The Canterbury Tales* (1387). In the fourteenth and fifteenth

centuries, this type of narrative commanded the undivided attention of several writers.

In Italy, in a roughly direct line of descent from Boccaccio, three Tuscans – Sachetti, Sercambi and Ser Giovanni – described in their novellas the minute details of everyday life in Italian towns. The Florentine, Franco Sachetti (1332–c.1400), the author of a collection called *Trecento Novelle* (*Three Hundred Stories*, 1392–1396), often described the familiar middle-class world into which he was born. His stories, though rambling, are full of charming anecdotes and juicy gossip about ordinary people's lives.

> The twelfth joy of marriage occurs when the young man has gone backwards and forwards so much that he has found the entrance to the trawl and has entered thereby and has found a woman to his liking.
>
> *The Fifteen Joys of Marriage*

In each of the short prose narrations of the *Libro de los enxiemplos del Conde Lucanor o Libro de Patronio* (*Book of the Examples of Count Lucanor or Book of Patronio*), finished in 1335 – thirteen years before the *Decameron* – Count Lucanor, who is young and inexperienced, goes to his adviser and mentor Patronio with a difficult moral and social problem. Patronio solves it and the Spanish author of this work, **Don Juan Manuel (1282–1348)**, concludes each tale with a moral in verse.

In the second half of the fifteenth century the short narrative form, as a definite genre, made its appearance in France in no uncertain terms, for example in 1462 with the *Cent Nouvelles Nouvelles*. Until this date there was a paucity of texts. There were works like *Floridan and Elvida*, told before 1437 by Nicolas de Clamanges and *The Story of Griselidis*, translated by Philippe de Mézières, between 1384 and 1389, from the Latin version of the tale of Griselda, the last novella in the *Decameron*, by Petrarch in 1374. To this may be added the fifteen short stories called *Les Quinze Joyes de Mariage* (*The Fifteen Joys of Marriage*, end of fourteenth century), in which the narrative formula adopted, while perpetuating with its brevity the tradition of the lai and the fabliau, had something in common with that of the short story. Despite the hardly original subject matter – marital tiffs and infidelities, frequent occurrences in works at that time – the tales related in the *Quinze Joyes de Mariage* are miniature masterpieces of late medieval French prose, thanks to their verbal dexterity, the relevance of their metaphors and the perceptiveness of their psychological insights:

> The twelfth joy of marriage occurs when the young man has gone backwards and forwards so much that he has found the entrance to the trawl and has entered thereby and has found a woman to his liking. And it may be that he ought to have found another, yet he would not want her for the world, for it seems to him that his lot could not be better and that fate smiled on him when God willed him to meet the woman he met, for in his opinion she hath not her equal, and he listens to her talk, takes pride in her, in her prudence such that she knows when she is daydreaming [. . .] Henceforth he will do great things, since he controls his wife, for the wisest woman in the world, as far as common sense goes, has as much of it as I have gold in my eye or an ape has a tail, for she needs sense before she can be up to half of what she wants to say or do [. . .]
>
> *The Fifteen Joys of Marriage*

John Gower owed his reputation to a series of tales called *Confessio Amantis* (*A Lover's Confession*, c.1390). Like Chaucer, who used the idea of a pilgrimage to lend continuity to the stories told by his characters, Gower made use of the literary device of the lover's confession to Genius, the priest of Venus, to knit together the 141 exemplary tales designed to facilitate his examination of conscience. In the Middle Ages, all writing, in the final analysis, had an educational purpose. Short stories and historical chronicles were no exception.

HISTORIOGRAPHY

Historiography was perhaps the area in which changes were most noticeable and a reforming spirit most in evidence. The sheer volume of the writing became important. Latin was replaced by the vernacular for the most part and the rhyming chronicle was often abandoned in favour of the chronicle in prose. World history tracing the origins of human life on earth continued to flourish, but was no longer the most important literary work. From now on there was more interest in national history and current affairs. Local chronicles about towns and local rulers were popular, while other chronicles lingered over the exploits of heroic figures who worked to defend and liberate their homelands. If legends and divine providence still played a major part in explaining the course of events, some progress had been made: the historian now checked his sources and made sure his documents were genuine. Nonetheless, the fact that a chronicler had personally witnessed the events he related introduced a subjective element into his writings which, impaired their impartiality. Their literary quality, on the other hand, was enhanced.

Official histories, new histories

French historiography of the period 1300–1450 was driven by a deep desire for innovation. The *Great Chronicles of France* added to official history. Alongside this official historiography, 'new' ways of recording history developed. Jean, Sire de Joinville (1225–1317) completed his *Livre des saintes paroles et des bons faits de notre saint roi Louis* (*Book of Holy Words and Good Deeds of our Holy King Louis*) in 1309, an eyewitness account of the Seventh Crusade as much as a book of memoirs on the reign of Saint Louis. Crammed with fascinating detail about the Crusaders themselves, Joinville's chronicle is especially worth reading for its fine portraits of the king and of Joinville himself. Canon of the cathedral church of Saint-Lambert in Liège, Jean le Bel (c.1290–1370) wrote a *Chronicle* (1352–1361) about the beginning of the Hundred Years' War, written for Count Jean de Beaumont whom he accompanied on his military expeditions. Despite its revelation of pro-English sympathies, the work of Jean le Bel is distinguished by the quality of its observations and its sober analysis. Jean d'Outremeuse (1338–1400) wrote *Geste de Liège* (*Epic of Liège*) which contains no less than fifty thousand alexandrines and of a prose chronicle, the *Myreur des Histors* (*The Mirror of Histories*, end of the fourteenth century), strongly biased towards the Walloons. In these two works the author's objective was to tell the history of the principality of Liège from the most remote times to the present. For the far past he drew on various sources, particularly *chansons de geste* (songs of exploits). For the more immediate past he mainly used chronicles of the locality in Latin which he 'embellished' to tell a good story, filling in the gaps with a logic of his own. A repository for countless old legends, the work of Outremeuse also created new ones. Down to the nineteenth century it was used, by other historians of the principality of Liège, sometimes with excessive credulity.

The most 'European' of French historians of his time was undoubtedly **Jean Froissart (1337–1410)**. From 1361 to 1369 he was in the service of Queen Philippa of Hainaut in England. After Philippa's death, he established close links with Wenceslas of Bohemia, then became chaplain to Guy de Blois and gravitated in the orbit of the French court. Froissart was a great traveller, visiting Scotland, Savoy, Béarn, Avignon and Italy. He met Petrarch and doubtless knew Chaucer. His work as a historian consists of a monumental *Chronicle* in four books covering the years 1325 to 1396. Froissart was principally interested in relating the events of the Hundred Years' War, but with very little objectivity. The causes which produced the events almost always eluded him. He was fascinated by 'wars, captures, stormings, incursions, battles, rescues and all fine feats of arms' performed by knights whose taste for adventure and physical prowess he shared. He even sympathised with their

prejudices, so much so that he presents as exploits the pillaging carried out by noble men-at-arms during their military forays!

German historians were no longer interested in world history, but rather in the political realities of their time, in the territorial powers born out of the decay of empire. In 1310 Ottokar von Steiermark (*c.*1260–*c.*1320) illustrated this evolution towards the particular with his *Österreichische Reimchronik* (*Austrian Chronicle*). Written in verse, this dealt with the quarrels between the Dukes of Austria and their vassals. Towards 1340, Nikolaus von Jeroschim (first half of the fourteenth century) wrote a *Chronik von Preußen* (*Chronicle of Prussia*) in twenty-seven thousand verses on the rise and fall of the Teutonic order of knights. The development of history in prose was linked to the huge increase in urban chronicles at the end of the fourteenth century. The oldest of these, the *Straßburger Chronik* (*Chronicle of Strassburg*) by Fritsche Closener (fourteenth century) dates from 1362. Its author vividly described the political struggles and the customs that took place in the town and that were prevalent in different social classes.

> Wars, captures, stormings, incursions, battles, rescues and all fine feats of arms.
> Prologue to the *Chronicle* of Froissart.

Historiography in Middle Dutch was dominated by chronicles originating from the courts of Holland and the Dukedom of Brabant or from great aristocratic families. The most important of these was the one by **Jacob Van Maerlant (1225–1291)**, the *Spieghel Historiael* (*The Mirror of History*, 1283–1288). This was completed by the Brabançon priest, Lodewijk Van Velthem (died 1326). **Jan Van Boendale (1279– c.1350)**, a senior public official in Antwerp and a disciple of Van Maerlant, wrote the *Brabantsche Yeesten* (*Deeds of the Brabant*, from 1316 to 1347), a history of the Dukedom of Brabant from the year 600 to 1347. A tribute to the dukes, the work also presents the viewpoint of townsfolk about the policies being implemented in the dukedom.

The first chronicle in Czech, *Kronika Dalimilova* (*Chronicle of Dalimil*), dates from 1310. In 106 chapters, the author, an unknown noble, painted a picture of all that had happened to the accession of the Luxembourg family to the Czech throne since the Flood. Passionately patriotic and traditional, the author reacted badly to the arrival of German colonists, to their presence at the royal court, and was critical of the imported customs of chivalry. Other chronicles were in Latin, beginning with the massive and exceptional *Chronicon Aulæ Regiæ* (*Chronicle of Zbraslav*, 1305–1338). We owe this to two abbots of the royal Cistercian abbey south of Prague. It related Czech national history from the Přemysl king Otakar II (died 1278) to 1338. Charles IV wanted to have a chronicle sympathetic to his views. Přibík Pulkava z Radenína compiled his *Chronica Boemorum* (*Chronicle of the Kings of Bohemia*) which, for Charles, was worth waiting for. The historicity of this chronicle, immediately translated into Czech and German, was guaranteed by documents taken from the royal archives.

Before Jan Długosz (Longinus, 1415–1480), the author of the *Historia Polonica* (*History of Poland*, 1455–1480), compiled in the second half of the fifteenth century, Poland had only had one worthwhile historian in John of Czarnków, Archdeacon of Gniezno and Vice-Chancellor of King Casimir the Great, the author of two chronicles. His *Kronika Wielkopolska* (*Chronicle of Greater Poland*, 1377–1384) traced the history of Poland from its origins to 1271. For the first time Polish ethnic identity was mentioned, together with that of other Slav peoples: the Czechs and the Russians, for example. This chronicle also contained the story of 'Bold Walter of Tyniec and the Fair Heligunda', of Western origin, which Sienkiewicz, Lange and Zeromski developed in the nineteenth century.

The English exhibited a conspicuous taste for the historical genre. This gained a new lease of life with the compilation of many chronicles in the vernacular. **Robert Mannyng of Brunne (1288–1338)** finished his *Rhyming Chronicle of England* in 1338.

Written in simple English, it was dotted with personal observations. John of Trevisa (1362–1402), a Cornishman, the parish priest of Berkeley and the canon of Westbury in Gloucestershire, completed his translation in 1387 of Ranulph Hidgen's *Polychronicon*, a history of the world in Latin which began with the origin of the world and finished in 1352. John of Trevisa added a history of events from 1352 to 1360 and, in 1385, a famous passage in which he defined the new Oxford teaching method, which aimed to use Middle English rather than French for educational purposes. In Scotland, **John Barbour (c.1316–1395)**, Archdeacon of Aberdeen, wrote his great historical poem *The Bruce* in 1376. The *Paston Letters* deserve a place apart. This correspondence in Middle English between three generations of the Paston family covered the years 1422 to 1509. Part literature, part history, it was an exceptional document on the English middle classes in the fifteenth century. The *Letters* tell us about the importance of business and money, of leases and rents on farms, about the running of an estate and the respective roles of a wife and husband in the home. Information may be gleaned from it about a household's favourite books and rules for the education of children.

Two Swedish chronicles have retained their right to fame. One of them, *Erikskrönikan* (*The Chronicle of Eric*, c.1440), compiled towards 1330 by an unknown author, traced a century of national history under the Folkungar dynasty. The other, *Frihetsvisan* (*Poem of Freedom*) – or *Engelbrektskrönikan* (*The Chronicle of Engelbrekt*) – written by Bishop Thomas Simonsson (died 1443), makes much of the popular insurrection against the Danes which was led by the miner, Engelbrekt. This chronicle is a classic of Swedish literature: it exalted, the ideal of freedom for Scandinavian peoples in majestic verse and rich, pure language.

The *General Estoria* (*The General History*, after 1272) and, above all, the *Primera Crónica General de España* (*First General Chronicle of Spain*), begun by the King of Castille Alfonso X towards 1270 and continued under the reign of Sancho IV, are two of the original works of Spanish prose historiography. They included the four chronicles written by Pero López de Ayala, and the *Poema de Alfonso Onceno* (*Poem of Alfonso XI*), written *c.*1348 by the Leonese Rodrigo Yáñez, who inaugurated the metrical form of historical 'romances'. In the fourteenth century, Spanish kings and dignitaries had their own chroniclers. People were interested, first and foremost, in contemporary history, but also in individuals who moved in princely circles and who inspired genuine biographies: *El Halconero de Juan II* (*Juan II's Falconer*, 1435–1455) by P. Carrillo de Huete, and the *Crónica de Don Álvaro de Luna* (*The Chronicle of Don Alvaro de Luna*, 1453–1460) by Gonzalo Chacón. The most important of the Catalan chronicles, relating to the reigns of James I, Peter III, Alfonso III and James II, was the only one by Ramón Muntaner (1265–1336) who took part in the expedition of Roger de Flor and the Almogavares in Anatolia, Thrace and Macedonia. The author flaunts his patriotism and enthusiastically sings the praises of his fellow countrymen's courage and devotion.

Portuguese historiography began in earnest with the works of Fernão Lopes (*c.*1380–*c.*1459). He compiled the *Crónica de D. Pedro I* (*The Chronicle of D. Pedro I*), the *Crónica de D. Fernando I* (*The Chronicle of D. Fernando I*) and the *Crónica de D. João I* (*The Chronicle of D. João I*), all of a high literary and historical standard and all written between 1434 and 1443.

In Italy, in the fourteenth century, historiography was mainly confined to Florence and reflected, above all, the current political struggles of the City States. The *Cronica delle cose occorenti ne' tempi suoi* (*Chronicle of Things that Happened in his own Lifetime*, 1310–1312) by **Dino Compagni (*c.*1225–1324)**, a witness to and actor in the events he related, traced the course of the famous intestinal struggles between the White Guelphs and the Black Guelphs at the end of the thirteenth century and during the opening years of the fourteenth. Less personal and of more mediocre literary quality was the *Nuova Cronica* (*New

Chronicle, 1308–1348) by the Florentine merchant **Giovanni Villani (1276–1348)**.

Many chronicles also appeared in Byzantium. At the beginning of the fourteenth century a chronicle was written in Demotic Greek, in non-rhyming verse, no doubt by a Greek-speaking Frank, called *Khronikón tou Moréos* (*Chronicle of Morea*). Half-way between history and a song of exploits, this chronicle told the story of the conquest of the Peloponnesus by the Franks and of the reign of Guillaume II Villehardouin (1246–1278). Another anonymous chronicle, *Khronikón tou Tokkon* (*Chronicle of Toccos*) also in verse, covered the period 1375–1422: it was a kind of epic about the royal family of Leukas Tocco who extended their dominion as far as Epirus. Its author, probably a native of Joannina, seems to have been in the service of Charles Tocco, who died in 1422. During the first half of the fifteenth century, Leontios Macheras, who held an important position at the court of the Lusignans in Cyprus, wrote a prose chronicle in Cypriot dialect with the title *Exighisis tis ghlikías khóras kíprou* (*An Exegesis of the Pleasant Land of Cyprus*). Macheras discussed the events that occurred in the years 1359 to 1432.

In Russia, more than any other genre, historiography is firmly in the tradition of the *Rus'* of Kiev. Each compilation ('svod') undertaken at this period takes up the themes of universal history (based on the Bible) and the origins of the state of Kiev. Though they were compiled in different political centres around Kiev, they all harked back to the *Povest' vremenych let* (*Chronicle of Former Times*), the masterpiece of medieval Russian historiography, the oldest versions of which are given by the *Lavrent' evskaya letopis'* (*Chronicle of the Monk Lawrence*, 1377) and *Ipat' evskaya letopis'* (*Chronicle of the Saint Hypatius Monastery*, fifteenth century). They were all conceived to an identical pattern, to provide a written record of local, dynastic, political, military and ecclesiastical events. Occasionally, there were even digressions on meteorological phenomena and their economic consequences. They included a few events that happened in other Russian-speaking areas but, for a long time, a pan-Russian approach to historiography was difficult to achieve. It was only after the restoration of religious unity that, at the instigation of the head of the Orthodox Church, the Metropolitan Cyprian, a huge compilation was embarked on encompassing the history of the Eastern Slavs in its entirety, whether under Mongol or Lithuanian influence. This 1408 compilation, partially attested to by the *Troitskaya letopis'* (*Chronicle of the Trinity*), introduced no new way of treating the narration of past events, but was more objective in its treatment of the more recent events which happened in rival Russian-speaking spheres of influence. A new pan-Russian compilation was conceived in the same spirit of objectivity in 1448, when the Church in Russia attained genuine self-government. This was borne out in copies of the work made in Novgorod (*Novgorodskaya*

četvertaya letopis', The Fourth Chronicle of Novgorod; *Pervaya Sofiskaya letopis'*, First Chronicle of Saint Sofia). This new compilation, constructed around the Metropolitan Bishop's throne, served as a primary source for later, essentially Muscovite, historiography.

The victory gained in 1380 by the Muscovite army of Dmitri Donskoi over the Tartars of the rebel Khan, Mamai, was reported in a restrained way in works close to the event, such as the 1408 compilation, *The Chronicle of the Trinity*. However, roughly at the same time, an otherwise unknown author, Sophonius of Ryazan, wrote a prose poem on the 'battle beyond the Don' (*Zadonščina*). According to the most commonly held theory, this text was inspired by a twelfth-century work, *Slovo o polku Igoreve* (*The Song of the Campaign of Igor*), to which it probably owed its epic quality, as in the following passage on the gathering of the Russian forces before the battle:

тогды аки орли слетоша ся со всея полунощныя страны. То ти не орли слетошася, съехали ся все князи русскыя к великому князю Дмитрию Ивановичю Ча пособъ, а ркучи такъ: «Господине князъ великыи, уже погании Татарове на поля на наши наступають, а вотчину нашю у нас отнимають. Стоять межю Дономъ и Днепромъ [. . .]. И мы, господине, поидемъ за быструю реку Донъ, укупимъ землямъ диво, старымъ повесть, а младымъ память.»

Sophonius of Ryazan,
Zadonščina

Then it was as if eagles had come together in flight from all over the North. But they were not eagles that had gathered, rather were they all the Russian princes who had gone together to assist the Grand-Duke Dmitri Ivanovitch, saying: 'Lord Grand-Duke, already the pagan Tartars are marching through our lands and they are taking from us what is ours. They are in the area between the Don and the Dniepr [. . .]. And as for ourselves, sir, let us go beyond the Don, the fast-flowing, to obtain for our lands things to marvel at, for the old things to talk about, and for the young things to remember.'

Later, as Moscow's supremacy became more established in the areas of religion and politics, the narrative of the chronicles boasted about the Battle of Kulikovo as a victory of the whole of 'Russian Christendom' over the Infidels – a

prelude to the shaking off of the Mongol yoke, which only happened in 1480. The chronicled, partly mythic, version of the event was presented in the fifteenth century in the *Skazanie o Mamaevom poboišče* (*The Chronicle of Mamai's Defeat*), a veritable 'piece of propaganda' which anticipated the politico-ecclesiastical literature of the following period in Russian history.

DIDACTIC LITERATURE

Whether it was in prose or in verse, religious or secular in inspiration, edifying, moral, satirical or encyclopedic in nature, didactic literature, in the broad sense of the term, continued to flower in the fourteenth century and during the first half of the fifteenth to such an extent that this period was often referred to in histories of literature as the 'didactic period'. Heir to a Christian system of herme-neutics – this was particularly true for Dante – and to the *Romance of the Rose*, didactic literature from 1300 to 1450 found its most appropriate expression in allegory, either from the viewpoint of Biblical exegesis or rhetoric.

Edifying works of religious inspiration

Written by both lay people and clerics, these works, in which the moral element was closely linked to a spiritual dimension, continued to cater for a wide audience. With Dante's *The Divine Comedy*, Italy produced a masterpiece of religiously inspired didactic and allegorical poetry at the beginning of the fourteenth century.

Many writers borrowed from Christian dogma, as did the Frenchman Guillaume de Digulleville (died 1380). In his three *Pilgrim-ages*, written between 1330 and 1358, he based his work on the evolutionary unfolding of 'journeys'. Highly attentive to the precedent of the *Romance of the Rose*, Digulleville's *Pilgrimage of Human Life* (*c*.1330) made use of the convenient fiction of a dream and personified Nature, Reason and God's Grace.

Across the English Channel, the Gilbertine monk, Robert Mannyng of Brunne, translated into English a twelfth-century Anglo-Norman treatise on the seven deadly sins and seven cardinal virtues called *Handlyng Sinne* (*c*.1303). In this work women are held responsible for leading men astray, while the clergy are sternly

taken to task for their love of luxury and frivolity. Writers of this period used the Bible as the basis of their teaching. Two alliterative poems, attributed to the author of *Sir Gawain and the Green Knight*, were inspired by Scripture. *Patience* (*c*.1360–1370) was a paraphrase of the story of Jonah and the whale. There are questions here about the value of life and death, the importance of faith and the relationship between God and man. *Purity* (*c*.1360–1370) was symbolically arranged around the opposition between purity and impurity: the impurity of the fallen angels and the inhabitants of Sodom and Gomorrah, the purity of Christ and the Virgin.

In Germany, at the beginning of the four-teenth century, a poem known as *Des Teufels Netz* (*The Devil's Net*) taught men good conduct. All those who wandered down the path of sin ended up as lost and were ensnared by the Devil.

Commissioned by Albert of Bavaria, Count of Holland, (1358–1404), and appearing *c*.1404, was the work of the learned Domini-can and master of theology, Dirc Van Delft (*c*.1365–*c*.1404), called *Tafel van den Kersten Ghelove* (*Picture of the Christian Faith*). This impressive work, a veritable theological summary in the vernacular, explained to lay people, in rich, clear prose, the entire universe in the light of the church's spiritual and moral doctrine. Its repercussions were considerable, even outside the Low Countries, although perhaps less with the aristocratic audience for whom it was intended than with simple, devout believers: nuns, Beguines, lay brothers who assiduously studied and emulated it.

In Bohemia, many moral writings meant for personal edification were compiled, for the most part as 'exempla'. Bound together in anthologies, used primarily by preachers, the 'exempla' gradually escaped from a religious setting and become more entertaining. So, towards 1400, there was a compilation of a cycle containing thirty-five 'exempla' of this kind called *Olomoucké povídky* (*The Tales of Olomouc*). The same genre in Hungary was epitomised by the anthology *Példák könyve* (*Book of Examples*).

Practical morality, general morality, learned literature

During the last two centuries of the Middle Ages, moral education ceased to be the prerogative of clerics and began to include lay people. In Europe, many works were still being written on practical and general morality, and there were also books of aphorisms. The most important author in the Brabant at this time was Van Boendale. *Der leken Spieghel* (*A Mirror for the Secular*), written between 1325 and 1333, way not just only a four-book history of the world, but also devoted plenty of attention to the way society worked, to court etiquette, to love and, of course, to morality. The work also contained Europe's first art of writing poetry in the vernacular.

In Flanders, literature and morality rubbed shoulders. This is especially true of the *Spieghel der Wijsheit* (*The Mirror of Wisdom*, c.1350) by Jan Praet (active before the middle of the fourteenth century), an allegorical poem that betrayed the influences of the *Roman de Fauvel* (*Romance of Fauvel*) by Gervais du Bus and of the *Pilgrimage of Human Life* by Digulleville. We must also mention the 'Sproken', short moral tales in verse, that itinerant performers – the 'storytellers' – recited or read at the court of the Counts of Holland, reminding courtiers of their duties towards God and criticising, in more or less veiled terms, what was wrong the world.

Treatises on morality also flourished in England. Gower, christened by his friend Chaucer 'moral Gower', was the author in French of the *Mirour de l'Omme* (*Mirror of Man*, 1376–1379), a close examination of

virtues and vices in thirty thousand verses. Gower also wrote a collection of edifying pieces of advice called *Traité pour essampler les amantz mariez* (*Treatise exemplifying Married Couples*, 1397). One of the finest didactic/allegorical works in Middle English was the poem *Pearl* (written between 1350 and 1380), attributed to the anonymous author of *Sir Gawain and the Green Knight*. A tearful father falls asleep on the grave of his daughter, his well-loved 'pearl'. In a dream he sees her on the bank of a river, dressed in white, radiant with joy and dazzlingly beautiful. She tells him she is now one of the brides of the Lamb in the City of God. The man, in transports of ecstasy, tries in vain to join the lovely apparition. Suddenly he wakes up. Placated, he takes heart, for his child has led him to understand that death could not be regarded as 'theft' since life was not a 'gift', but rather a 'loan' agreed to by God.

In fourteenth-century Spain, the main representatives of the 'Mester de Clerecía' (the clergy) also practise didacticism with a moral point. To make their 'chastisements' or teachings more efficacious, and so that they could be accessible to the people, these well-educated poets use the vernacular. In stanzas of four verses ending with a single rhyme (the 'cuaderna vía') and containing fourteen syllables, clerical poetry provides, in its regularity, a contrast with the popular art of the minstrel, the 'Mester de Juglaría' which is far less refined. The most representative poet of the clerical tendency was **Juan Ruiz** (*c.*1293–*c.*1350), Archpriest of Hita. The first version of his greatest work, the *Libro de Buen Amor* (*Book of True Love*), one of the most original works of the Middle Ages in Spain, dates back to 1330:

Ensiemplo del alano que llevaba la pieza de carne en la boca

Alano carnicero en un río andaba,
una pieza de carne en la boca passaba,
con la sombra del agua dos tanto.
I semejaba
cobdicióla abarcar, cayósele la
que levaba.

The example of the mastiff that carried a piece of meat in its mouth

A hunting mastiff was heading
towards a river,
and had sunk his teeth
into a piece of meat.
Its reflection in the river made it
appear to be double,

105

> *Por la sombra mintrosa e por su*
> *coydar vano,*
> *la carne que tenía perdióla el alano,*
> *non ovo lo que quiso, no. I fué*
> *cobdiciar sano,*
> *coydó ganar; perdió lo que tenía*
> *en su mano.*
> *Cada día contesce al cobdiciosso atal,*
> *coyda ganar contigo, e pierde su* cabdal;
> *de aquesta raíz mala nasce todo*
> *el mal;*
> *es la mala cobdicia un pecado mortal.*
>
> Juan Ruiz, *Libro de Buen Amor*

> *he coveted it, tried to grab it, letting*
> *fall the piece he was already carrying.*
> *Because of the fallacious shadow*
> *and its false reflection, the mastiff*
> *dropped the meat that he was holding;*
> *he did not get what he wanted, his*
> *covetousness was of no avail.*
> *He thought he would gain something,*
> *but lost what he already had.*
> *Every day the same thing*
> *happens to the greedy man,*
> *he thinks he'll get one up and loses what he*
> *has; all evil springs from this bad origin:*
> *cupidity is a mortal sin.*

Ruiz was by no means a boring moralist. Humour constantly invigorated his work which was a veritable hymn to Nature and the zest for life. The *Book of True Love* was an indication of important texts to come in Spanish literature. The character of Trota-conventos, for example, prefigures that of La Celestina, the heroine of the tragi-comedy *Calixto and Melibea* by Fernando de Rojas.

The Chancellor **Pero López de Ayala (1332–1407)** was the last in the line of Spanish poets to use the 'cuaderna vía'. A servant to several Kings of Castille, his principal legacy is a long poem in 8200 verses, traditionally known as the *Rimado de Palacio (The Book of Palace Verse,* after 1385). The first part was a biting satire on life at court, the second a long lamentation on human destiny, and the third was a series of reflections on vice and virtue.

The Byzantines also attached some importance to moral and didactic literature. The fourteenth century marked the appearance of two texts, both interesting and both anonymous. The first was a short poem called *Loghos parighoritikós perí dhistikhías ke eftikhías (A Comforting Story about Happiness and Unhappiness);* the second the *Istoría tou Ptokholéontos (The Story of Leo the Poor).* This tells of the misfortunes of wealthy Leo who then goes on to lose his wealth after his country is invaded by Arabs. Eventually he asks to be sold as a slave, where, in a palace, he demonstrates his wisdom. He is rewarded by the Arab Emperor who sets him free and showers him with presents.

Also included in this genre were stories about animals that occurred all over Europe. A highly original text in Czech, *Nová rada (The New Council,* 1395), by **Smil Flaška of Pardubice (died 1402),** is an allegory in 2126 verses in which animals give good advice to their king (the lion), Wenceslas IV, at the time of an uprising of the nobility.

The education of women and princes, treatises on etiquette

As far as treatises designed for the education of women are concerned, France laid claim to the *Livre du chevalier de La tour Landry (Book of the Knight La Tour Landry),* written between 1371 and 1373 by the country gentleman Geoffroi de La Tour Landry to be used in educating his daughters from a first marriage. The *Ménagier de Paris* (1394), a work by an 'honest' burgher, was intended for his wife in the event that, left a widow, she should start a new home. In a treatise in verse mixed with prose, *Reggimento e costumi di donna (The Conduct and Customs of Women,* 1318–1320), the Italian Francesco dei Neri, called 'da Barberino' (1264–1348), enumerated a whole series of rules for the use of young women from various backgrounds on how they should behave, on the duties they needed to perform and on how they should dress and be educated.

Writings about the education of princes proliferated. The Spaniard, Don Juan Manuel, for example, wrote *El Libro del Caballero y del Escudero* (*The Book of the Knight and his Squire*, 1326). The Portuguese king, Duarte I (1391–1438) gave us the *Leal Conselheiro* (*The Loyal Counsellor*, *c*.1437), a hotchpotch in which pages on moral and political virtues alternate with memories of the monarch's family.

Among the many works which perpetuated the writings of previous centuries on the art of good conduct in company, the didactic poem *O zachowaniu się przy stole* (*On Good Table Manners*) by Słota appeared in Poland at the beginning of the fifteenth century. A treatise on social etiquette, a compendium of advice on how to behave at table, this is a useful document on the study of manners. It is also considered to be the first courtly love poem in Polish literature because of its fine eulogy on woman.

Social satire and satire against women

In the Middle Ages satire often went hand-in-hand with didacticism. In France in the fourteenth century, the combination sizzles in an imitation of the *Romance of Reynard*, *Reynard the Misshapen* (1319–1322; 1328–1342) by the Grocer of Troyes. More than sixty thousand verses make up this acerbic denunciation of the century's peccadilloes, but this time Reynard has become the defender of Good against Hypocrisy. In the north of the Low Countries, *Reynaerts Historie* (*The Story of Reynard*, *c*.1375) was a well-known text which took its inspiration from the first branch of the French *Roman de Renart*. It closely followed Willem's *Van den vos Reynaerde* (*Reynard the Fox*, *c*.1260). *The Story of Reynard* was very successful: it was translated into German and English and then, on the basis of the German edition, versions were produced in Icelandic, Danish, Norwegian and Swedish. Satirical verve is even stronger in the French morality story *Fauvel* (1310–1314) by Gervais du Bus (the end of the thirteenth century–*c*.1338). The author, a royal notary, constructed a

moral tale around the allegory of Fauvel, a fawn-coloured horse that epitomised cunning and dishonesty.

A desire to instruct coupled with satire and parody was at the heart of the poem *Der Ring* (*The Ring*), written *c*.1400 by the German Heinrich Wittenwiller (end of the fourteenth–mid-fifteenth century), a knight from the St Gallen area. According to the author's stated intentions, the first part of *The Ring* 'gives instruction on how to pay court to ladies', the second 'is full of good advice on how to take care of one's soul and one's body' and the third 'sets out the best ways of conducting oneself in battles'. To avoid becoming tedious, however, Wittenwiller piles up bizarre propositions and obscenities in the purest traditions of the farce and the fabliau. Thematically, *The Ring* presents us with an almost encyclopedic cross-section of the various types of knowledge then current: religious, ethical, philosophical and practical. In terms of literary form, particularly in its use of comedy and wordplay, *The Ring* heralded in a new aesthetic which Fischart and Rabelais later made famous.

The most important text in English of this popular satirical literature so typical of the waning of the Middle Ages was *The Vision of Piers Plowman* (1377) by **William Langland (*c*.1331–*c*.1400)**. The poet has a dream during which the Holy Church appears to him, teaching him that it is everyone's duty to seek out Truth and that only Charity leads to Heaven. Lady Meed, the symbol of corruption, promised in marriage to Falsehood, is fiercely taken to task by Theology and Conscience. In the following scene, Peace arrives in Parliament to level accusations against Wrong and Reason. Another scene revolves around the Seven Deadly Sins. Later we are introduced to the mythical figure of Piers Plowman. Piers is a ploughman, but he is also the model of the true Christian: one of those ordinary people in whom God has become incarnate. Representing Christ, his mission is to lead his brothers to a golden age. Finally, three passages depict the three stages of the spiritual life: Do-well, Do-better, Do-best. The work is an unflinching condemnation of social injustice and vigorously defends constitutional liberties. It also makes a heartfelt plea for an in-depth reform of society and the Church. By its use of a vision and allegorical characters, it belongs to the same tradition as the *Romance of the Rose*.

Satires in Old Czech were popular in Bohemia, especially during the second half of the fourteenth century. Some of the best-known texts were a cycle of seven satires, which include *O řemeslnících a konšelích* (*Of Craftsmen and Aldermen*), *O ženě zlobivé* (*On a Bilious Woman*) and *Podkoní a žák* (*The Student and the Groom*).

The Spaniard **Alfonso Martínez de Toledo (1398–1470)**, the Archpriest of Talavera, was the author of a famous work written in 1438, the *Reprobación del Amor mundano* (*The Reproval of Worldly Love*), also known as *El Corbacho* (*The Riding Crop*). The originality of the 'examples', the quaintness and the realism of many of its scenes, the use of vivid colloquial language and the high quality of its reasoning added interest to this acerbic critique of love. Another important satirical text in Spain was written at the end of the fourteenth century: the *Danza de la Muerte* (*The Dance of Death*). It includes a moving dialogue between Death and the representatives of various classes of society terrified by what they hear. This is the first work in Spain on a theme common to many European literatures: the 'danse macabre' in France, for example, and the German 'Totentanz'. We find this theme of collective satire again in the *Diálogo de Mercurio y Carón* (*Dialogue of Mercury and Charon*, 1528) by Alfonso de Valdés (1500–c.1532), as in the *Cortes de la Muerte* (*The Courts of Death*), a drama to which Cervantes alluded in *Don Quixote*.

Satirical intent is at the heart of the poems by two Cretan writers who, at the end of the fifteenth century, were the first to introduce rhyme into neo-Hellenic poetry. *Graphi ke stikhi* (*Verse and Writing*) by Stephanos Sachlikis made a corrosive allegation against 'political' women, calling them 'prostitutes'; *Istoria ke oniro* (*The Story and the Dream*) by Marinos Phalieros, is an erotic satire, in rhymed verses of fifteen syllables like the former work.

Encyclopedic writings: science and philosophy

Under the influence of *The Divine Comedy*, often considered in the fourteenth and fifteenth centuries as a veritable encyclopedia of human knowledge and not as a monument to individual poetic achievement, Italy produced a number of didactic/allegorical works which aim to teach science or philosophy. Among these poems, *Intelligenza* (*Intelligence*), written c.1300, is attributed to Dino Compagni. Falling in love with a beautiful noble lady – Intelligence – Compagni describes in detail the luxurious palace in which she lives and the precious stones that adorn her diadem. He counts the blessings she showers on mankind.

Everywhere short scientific treatises in verse and prose appeared: texts on astrology, physiology and medicine. Written in the vicinity of Ghent, *Natuur-Kunde van het gheheelal* (*The Science of the Nature of the Universe*, end of the thirteenth century) was the oldest cosmological treaty in Dutch. *Cyrurgia* (beginning of the fourteenth century) by the Fleming Jan Yperman (c.1300) was remarkable and ahead of its time because it valued observation and experiment over and above the authority of the Ancients.

Codes of courtly love, 'arts of loving'

The *Romance of the Rose*, which was hugely popular in fourteenth- and fifteenth-century Europe, remained the obligatory point of reference. Chaucer began a partial translation of it: *The Romaunt of the Rose*. In the north of the Low Countries, where the didactic side of courtly love was extremely important, there were two translations: *The Flemish Rose* (c.1290), a free adaptation of the French original, and *Die Rose* by Hein Van Aken, written between 1278 and 1325, which is faithful to its source. Although we are not sure just how influential *The Romance of the Rose* was in Germany, as there was no translation of it, many lays, debates and judgements of love began to appear in the fourteenth and fifteenth centuries. These describe allegorically the various stages the lover has to pursue to attain his goal. Among the most significant embodiments of the 'Minneallegorie' (the Allegory of Love) in the fourteenth century were *Die Jagd* (*The Hunt*) by Hadamar von Laber (*c*.1300–*c*.1355), written *c*.1315, in which the 'hunter', helped by his 'bloodhounds', tracks the 'doe', the object of his lover's quest; and *Minneburg* (*Love's Castle*, *c*.1356), whose author, after several fruitless attempts and thanks to the aid of Wisdom and some of the Virtues, manages to enter the castle of Freudenberg (Monjoie), where to reward his efforts Love is born.

Towards the middle of the fifteenth century, the 'Minneallegorie' occupied a prominent position in a poem by Hermann von Sachsenheim (1365–1458), *Die Mörin (The Negress*, 1453). As well as the usual events – lovers walking together, receipts of aid, obstacles encountered, the court of Love, Love's judgement and the conquest of the Beloved – *The Negress* gives us with a picturesque portrait of current German customs.

A STILL-FLOURISHING RELIGIOUS LITERATURE

Religious literature continued to be a genre much in demand at the end of the Middle Ages. Mystical literature developed and took on a particular form: the 'devotio moderna'. Sermons and homilies remained fashionable and those who wrote them strove to outdo one another in their eloquence.

Mystical literature: contempt for worldly things

Mystical literature was in its heyday in the fourteenth century, often because of remarkably able women. In Sweden its most worthy representative was **Birgitta Birgesdotter (or St Bridget of Sweden, 1302–1373)**. A strong, self-willed, even aggressive individual, obsessed with the problem of Charity, this saint was Swedish literature's first great visionary. Her mystical experience was distilled in *Uppenbarelser* or *Revelationes Celestes* (*Celestial Revelations*, after 1340–1373). Written first in Latin under her dictation, the 'visions' of St Bridget always had a moral purpose. Believing herself to be Christ's instrument, she was never frightened of judging those accounted great among her contemporaries: kings, princes, cardinals, the Pope himself. Her style is cutting, personal, full of explosive energy, expressive of her unceasing moral indignation when faced by the corruption of her time.

Italian mysticism was represented by **Caterina Benincasa (St Catherine of Sienna, 1347–1380)**. A woman of the people and a member of the Third Order of St Dominic, Catherine of Sienna left behind 333 letters in which she expressed forcefully, even with 'virility', her flawless piety and her wish to see Peace triumph on earth in the name of Truth. She wrote hundreds of letters to the princes and Popes of her time, never hesitating to take them to task. Her mystical experience was expressed in *Dialogo della Divina Provvidenza* (*Dialogue of Divine Providence*, 1378) and in a collection of prayers.

England also had its visionaries and its holy men. **Richard Rolle of Hampole (*c*.1300–1349)**, a Yorkshire, hermit, was the most influential writer in this area of mystical revelation. He wrote many devotional works, both in Latin and in English. *The Form of Perfect Living* (1348) is a prose epistle and *Ego Dormio et Cor Meum Vigilat* (*I Sleep while my Heart Keeps Watch*, 1343) a treatise on the perpetual vigilance required of the Christian in relation to his faith. With Richard Rolle, mystical experience pervades English letters. His purpose was to sustain and encourage devotional practices, in the most rigidly orthodox way, just when **John Wycliffe (*c*.1320–1384)** was violently attacking the authority of Rome and opening up the way for a confrontation which, by way of Jan Hus, led to Luther's Reformation. After Rolle, Walter

Hilton (died 1395) was the most famous of the English mystical writers. The best of his writings was *The Scale of Perfection* (c.1390) which spoke of the elevation of the soul and its union with God. Two English women also wrote about their mystical experiences in the form of revelations and visions. Margery Kempe's (1373–c.1440) *The Book of Margery Kempe* is a kind of journal in which she relates her life of piety as a married woman. Mother Julian of Norwich (1342–c.1412) wrote *XVI Revelations of Divine Love*.

Mysticism flourished in the northern Netherlands with the great **Jan Van Ruysbroec (called the 'Admirable', 1293–1381)**. The author of eleven treatises and many letters, Ruysbroec wanted to map out a spiritual path for those who felt called to the contemplative life, whether they were lay people, nuns, Beguines or hermits, as the Church all too often paid little heed to them. Because of its clear and harmonious structure, *Die Chierheit der gheesteliker brulocht* (*The Adornment of the Spiritual Wedding*, c.1335), is generally held to be his masterpiece. The little treatise called *Van den Blinckenden steen* (*The Sparkling Stone*, c.1336) was a synthesis of Ruysbroec's doctrine. His best-known text in the Middle Ages, *Van den Gheesteliken Tabernakel* (*The Spiritual Tabernacle*, 1336–1345) was an allegorical explanation of the ark of the covenant. Thanks to many translations, Ruysbroec's work was rapidly disseminated all over Europe.

> Flee the tumult of men as much as you can; for the talk of worldly affairs is a great hindrance, even when they are talked of with a sincere intention . . .
>
> Thomas à Kempis, *The Imitation of Christ*

It had a marked influence on the founder of the 'devotio moderna' ('modern devotion'), **Geert Groote (called Gerard the Great, 1340–1384)**. The 'devotio moderna', however, preached a less speculative concept of faith than Ruysbroec's: more practical, founded on prayer and, principally, on the imitation of Christ's life. Indeed, it is in the work of **Thomas à Kempis (1380–1471)**, the *Imitatio*

Christi (*The Imitation of Christ*, 1410–1420), that the spirit of this movement was best captured. The 'devotio moderna' spread quickly throughout the Netherlands and a good part of Germany.

The Czech 'devotio moderna' developed in parallel to that in The Netherlands and was constantly in touch with it. Its prime movers were the bishops and archbishops of Prague, as well as the devout Charles IV himself. Among its many writings, the Latin dialogue, *Malogranatum* (*The Pomegranate*, c.1350) was written by a Cistercian from the Abbey of Zbraslav. This text pointed the reader towards an essentially internal perception of faith, independent of the established Church. As such it appeared in Czechoslovakia as a forerunner of the Reformation.

During this period in Portugal, three mystical works of high literary quality were written anonymously: the *Bosco Deleitoso* (*The Delightful Grove*, beginning of the fifteenth century), in which monastic spirituality was shaped by a partial translation of Petrarch's *De vita solitaria* (*On the Solitary Life*, 1346–1371); the *Horto do Esposo* (*The Bridegroom's Garden*, end of the fourteenth century), slightly pessimistic in tone, devoted considerable space to the *exemplum*; and the *Livro da Corte Imperial* (*The Book of the Imperial Court*, end of the fourteenth century) which was a huge allegory acting as an apologia for the Catholic Church.

> Raise your heart above this mire [. . .]. You are stuck in that miserable vale of tears where pleasure is mixed with sufferings, [. . .] where no heart has ever found total joy, for joy deceives and lies . . .
>
> Henry Suso

The contribution of German mysticism was equally remarkable. Its most distinguished representatives were **Meister Eckhart (Master Eckhart, 1260–1327)**, **Johannes Tauler (John Tauler, 1300–1361)** and **Heinrich Seuse (Henry Suso, 1295–1366)**. Mysticism prospered as a counter-attraction to the materialism cultivated by the well-off bourgeois.

Meister Eckhart, a Dominican, carried out important duties for his order in many German towns. He taught in Paris before settling in Cologne where he directed the Dominican 'Studium generale'. The mystical component in Meister Eckhart's work consisted of many sermons, written for those who attended his lectures and, above all, *Mystische Schriften (Mystical Writings)*. This includes three treatises: *Reden der Unterscheidung (A Discourse on Spiritual Discernment)*, *Buch der göttlichen Tröstung (The Book of Divine Consolation)* and *Von der Abgeschiedenheit (On Detachment from the World)*. Here Eckhart gave an account of his own visionary experience, explaining the mystery of the oneness of the human soul with the Godhead. He taught that man must be detached from everything, give everything up, both the world of appearances and himself as a part of that world, in order that the union can take place.

Sermons

Religious eloquence was distinguished in the fourteenth and fifteenth centuries by high calibre writers who abandoned Latin in favour of the vernacular. If Germany had in Meister Eckhart, Tauler and Suso three great givers of sermons, France had in **Jean Charlier** (also known as **Jean Gerson, 1363–1429**), a theologian and chancellor of the Sorbonne, a first-rate preacher. Sixty of his sermons have come down to us.

> Man is nothing in himself, if not a corrupter of all that is good.
>
> John Tauler, *Sermons*

Two Italians, one in the fourteenth century, the other in the fifteenth, distinguished themselves with the quality of their collected sermons: **Iacopo Passavanti (1302–1357)** and **San Bernardino da Siena (1380–1444)**. Passavanti, a Dominican friar, produced a treatise called *Specchio di vera penitenza (Mirror of True Penitence*, first edition 1495) mostly containing the sermons he had delivered during Lent in 1354. The *Mirror* has remained justly celebrated for its incisive, vigorous prose, rich in humanity and poetry, and also for its narratives enlivened by *exempla*, which the author introduced by way of commentaries. Saint Bernardino of Sienna's sermons were often long-winded, but their colloquial tone was brisk and lively. He knew how to be subtle and pertinent when he decried the vices and errors of man. He avoided the monotony of the seriousness of his subject by including in his sermons popular, naïve and amusing anecdotes.

Homiletic literature was a genre well-loved in Poland. *Kazania Gnieźnieńskie (Gniezno Sermons)*, a collection from the end of the fourteenth century, consisted of 102 sermons in Latin and ten in Polish. In its crossings-out and amendments, which go to show how much the preacher wanted to be accessible to his hearers, this work was an important document, both linguistically and psychologically. The Hungarian Franciscan Pelbárt Temesvári (1440–1504) provided a source of several adaptations into Hungarian in his *Pomerium sermonum*.

In the Bohemia of the second half of the fourteenth century, we find many great preachers supported by Charles IV. **Jan Milíč of Kroměříž (c.1305–1374)** stood out because of his ardour and audacity. He preached mainly in Czech, but wrote his treatises and books of sermons in Latin. One of the many people who came to hear the fiery words of this precursor of Jan Hus was **Tomáš ze Štítného (or Tomáš Štítný, c.1333–c.1405)**. After writing treatises on religion and a book of discourses, his *Řeči nedělni a sváteční (Sermons for Sundays and Feastdays, c.1392)* connects to Milíč's tradition. Tomáš Štítný was one of the first European laymen who dared to broach religious questions by using the vernacular.

Lives of saints, pious legends

Hagiographies were always fashionable and, in their ever increasing numbers, were very like an art form.

The Kiev period bequeathed to the various 'Russias' two types of saint: the prince and the monk. In the first of these cases especially, the notion of sainthood was vague: canonisation, pan-Russian or local, often only occurs to give official sanction to a pre-existing cult. So it is hard to make distinguish between lives and panegyrics, especially when the latter are dedicated to living princes. These texts were often included in chronicles. Such was the case with the life of the Lithuanian prince, Dovmont, baptised Timothy, who fought for the town of Pskov. For services rendered, after his death in 1299 he was venerated there as a saint. The story of his life was linked to that of Alexandr Nevskii and belongs to the genre of military history. The story of Mikhail Yaroslavič, Prince of Tver' and Grand-Duke of Vladimir, killed at the Battle of the Golden Horde in 1318, returns to the theme of the prince-martyr, created in the eleventh century by the two brothers, Boris and Gleb. If, in this case, a prince is called 'Tsar' in memory of the crucified 'Tsar' – Christ – elsewhere the name has a political connotation: in the panegyric of the Grand-Duke Vitovt (died 1430), whose reign marks the high point of the Lithuanian-Slav state or in that of the Grand-Duke of Tver', Boris Aleksandrovič (died 1462). The composition was realised in his lifetime by Pseudo-Thomas and was more inspired by the glorious past of the dukedom than by its true political standing in the mid-fifteenth century. The same period also marked the composition of the *Slovo o žitii i o prestavlenii velikogo knyazya Dmitriya Ivanoviča, tsarya Russkago* (*Discourse on the Life and Death of the Grand-Duke Dmitri Ivanovič, Tsar of Russia*). The hero of this text, better known by the name of Dmitri Donskoi (died 1389) was simultaneously portrayed as the conqueror of the Tartars at Kulikovo (1380) and an ascetic, a prince-monk.

The last two texts were written in the complex style, characterised by the 'plaiting of words', imported from the Balkans and originally disseminated, in monastic circles. It was introduced at the beginning of the fifteenth century by the Metropolitan Cyprian, particularly in the life of one of his prede-cessors, Peter (died 1326), and the technique was developed by a Russian monk, Epiphanias the Most Wise ('Premudryi'). The latter made use of all the procedures involved in the 'plait-ing of words' in order to give his hagiographic works an added dimension which made them different from others. He wrote in a Slavonic already marked by colloquial speech. His masterpiece was the life of Stephen of Perm (died 1396), a missionary bishop who invented an alphabet enabling him to note down their language in order to evangelise the Finno-Ugric tribe of the Zyrians.

At the beginning of the fourteenth century, *The Life of Saint Brendan*, translated from the French, introduced to England the realm of the marvellous and the philosophical opti-mism of that magnificent Celtic legend. *The Life of Saint Dunstan*, attributed to Robert of Gloucester, charmed the reader by its treat-ment of the saint as a familiar friend as well as by the joy and cordiality that emanated from the text. John Lydgate wrote *The Life of Saint Edmund* and *The Life of Saint Margaret*. The Italian Domenico Cavalca (1270–1342), in his *Vite dei santi Padri* (*Lives of the Holy Fathers*), took up from where his 'model', *The Lives of the Fathers*, left off, giving it a new dimension. In Italy, in the fourteenth century, the anony-mous author of the *Fioretti di San Francesco* (*The Little Flowers of Saint Francis*, 1370–1390) was an artless and tactful poet. The *Fioretti* were a collection of legends in Italian, trans-lated from a Latin text of the end of the thirteenth century: *Actus beati Francisci et sociorum ejus* (*The Acts of Blessed Francis and his Companions*).

Strictly speaking, these legends are not tales but *exempla*. If they teach us nothing new about the saint's life, at least they give us useful information about what the 'Poverello' (the 'little poor man') stood for in the eyes of medieval men. The reader is transported to an atmosphere of sainthood and perfection where everything has taken on the colour of a fable full of light, grace and gentleness. Among the tales of the *Fioretti* was the one in which St Francis performed a miracle by taming the fierce wolf of Gubbio:

Ed ecco che vedendo molti cittadini, li quali erano venuti a vedere cotesto miracolo, il detto lupo si fa incontro a Santo Francesco con la bocca aperta: e appresandosi a lui, Santo Francesco, gli fa il segno della santissima Croce, e chiarmollo a sè, e disselli così: Vieni qui, frate lupo; io ti comando dalla parte di Cristo, che tu non facci male nè a me, nè a persona. Mirabile cosa! immantinente che Santo Francesco ebbe fatta la Croce, il lupo terribile chiuse la bocca, e ristette di correre; e fatto il comandamento, venne mansuetamente, come uno agnello, e gittossi alli piedi di S. Francesco a giacere.	*And there, in the presence of many inhabitants of the town assembled to see the miracle, the wolf approached Saint Francis with open mouth. Saint Francis went towards him, making a sign of the most Holy Cross as he did so, asked him to come nearer and said to him: 'Come here, brother wolf; in the name of Christ, I order you to do no harm, either to myself or anybody else.' Hardly had Saint Francis made the sign of the Cross when, wonder of wonders! the terrible wolf closed his jaws and stopped running. And then, having heard the order, as gentle as a lamb, came to throw himself at the feet of Saint Francis and lay down.*

I Fioretti

Towards 1360, two pious legends were born in Bohemia. The *Pasionál* (*The Book of the Passion*) was a remarkable adaptation into Czech prose of the *Gilded Legend* to which had been added the legends of five Czech saints. The work of a Dominican in Prague, it became extremely popular and went through two editions before 1500. The second of these legends, the *Legenda o svaté Kateřině* (*The Legend of Saint Catherine*), is a magnificent verse adaptation by an unknown poet of two Latin 'lives' which together give us the plot. A veritable *compendium* of medieval Czech poetry, this legend holds us spellbound with the quality of its dramatic dialogues, the beauty of its ecstatic visions and the finesse of the interweaving of courtly themes (*Tristan and Isolde*) with mystical ones (*The Song of Songs*). *Tkadleček* (*The Weaver*, c.1400) derived from the *Ploughman of Bohemia* by the German Johannes von Saaz. This allegorical dialogue in prose between the Weaver and the person-ification of Misfortune on what has caused the object of his affections to be unfaithful to him quickly becomes transformed into a philosophical argument on the subject of man's free will and its limitation by the will of

God. The text in Czech is four times as long as the text in German and its structure is more complex. Given the high quality of both its thought and its style, *The Weaver*, along with the writings of Tomáš Štítný, represented the summit of fourteenth-century Czech prose.

An important cultural phenomenon during this period is that translations of the Bible into vernacular languages began to multiply all over Europe. In Germany, they were extant from the mid-fourteenth century onwards. Thanks to one of these translations, made in Nuremberg in 1350, the Bible of Jean Mentel was printed in Strasbourg in 1466. Around 1388, at Wycliffe's instigation, the translation of the entire Bible was undertaken in England. In Bohemia in the 1370s the same task was accomplished by a group of ten scholars. Linguistically and stylistically excellent, the Czech translation played a major part in future literary endeavours. Either directly or indirectly, it later had an influence on translations into other Slavic languages.

The ups and downs of Saint Alexis' life, already described so often in Europe, were repeated in Poland, in 1454, in the *Legenda o Świętym Aleksym* (*The Legend of Saint Alexis*).

We find in this a very fine psalter, the *Psalterz Floriański (Psalter of Saint Florian)* or *Psalterz Królowej Jadwigi (Psalter of Queen Hedwiga*, end of the fourteenth century) which contained 150 psalms of David, in Latin, Polish and German, on richly illuminated parchment.

RELIGIOUS AND SECULAR DRAMA

Religious drama developed rapidly in the fourteenth and fifteenth centuries in an increasingly secular and popular way. There were many reasons for this transformation, one of them secular culture's reinforcement with the rise of the bourgeoisie. They were effectively responsible for the organisation of public entertainment under the auspices of the powerful city 'guilds', who represented various key professions, and for the increased emancipation of the vernacular in relation to Latin.

Religious drama, morality plays and mysteries

In France, the growth of religious drama was little short of remarkable. The 'Puys' – brotherhoods who were both religious and literary, run by respectable burghers – were heavily involved. Theatre companies were formed: the 'Brotherhoods of the Passion'. In 1402 the most company in Paris were given a monopoly for to stage religious mysteries there.

In the fourteenth century both the morality play and the mystery became increasingly popular. Serious, comic or satirical, the morality play gave its audiences allegorical characters, usually in order to convey a moral or religious message. The spectator was invited to discover the hidden meaning, the forces that governed his existence, behind the literal meaning, the 'senefiance'. The oldest and best-known English morality play was *The Castle of Perseverance* (1425), whose whole plot recurs in all the plays in this genre. The accent was on the quest for personal salvation and the hurdles to be overcome to achieve it.

Personified abstractions always dominated: Humanus Genus, under the thumb of Pleasure and Folly, takes refuge with the Virtues in the Castle of Perseverance. Greed, slipping into the castle by the back door, drags him outside. Just as he is about to die, Humanus is saved from Hell fires by the timely intervention of Peace and Mercy.

In the episcopal principality of Liège, theatrical performances clustered around the Feast of the Nativity. The valley of the Meuse, Huy above all, was the most active. Here, continuing their tradition of liturgical and semi-liturgical drama, two fascinating morality plays were written in the fourteenth century. The first, *The Coming Together of Faith and Loyalty*, discussed the political struggles in the Liège diocese and preached reconciliation. The second, *The Seven Sins and the Seven Virtues*, adapted from the *Mirror of Life and Death* by Robert de l'Omme, was about the two paths that are offered to man in this life: the narrow one and the wide.

The stories of Christ's passion told by minstrels and the semi-liturgical dramas of the previous period inspired the first Passion plays. By the fourteenth century, the genre of the mystery – which in this context means 'dramatic performance' – included long sacred dramas based on saints' legends, on the Old and, above all, the New Testament. The Nativity and the Resurrection were at first the most popular subjects, but gradually the emphasis shifted to Jesus' sufferings and the Redemption. Soon the whole of Christ's life and death were being acted out. With their educational purpose and their three mansions – Hell below, Heaven above and Earth in the middle – the mystery plays eventually incorporated as many as 400 parts. Their scenes took place simultaneously, they employed some impressive stage machinery and they lasted for several days. The fifteenth century saw the golden age of mysteries, with the *Passion of Semur* (1430), the *Passion of Arras* (1440) by Eustache Marcadé (beginning of the fifteenth century) and, above all, the *Passion* (1450) by Arnoul Gréban (*c*.1420–1471). As the secular element in these dramas eventually concealed the sacred, their performances began to attract the condemnation of the Church. On 17 November 1548, the Paris town council banned them altogether.

The liturgical element in the *Innsbrucker Osterspiel* (*Easter Play of Innsbruck*, c.1350) is littered with light relief. Pilate claims to have but one purpose: 'to make the Jews sweat'. Christ hands over to the Devil a cobbler and a butcher, pathetic figures who lamentingly confess their sins. One of the most famous mysteries in German was the *Spiel von den klugen und törichten Jungfrauen* (*The Play of the Wise and Foolish Virgins*), performed in Eisenach in 1322. Mysteries in German were often crude and basic, a reflection of the new realism among the citizens of chartered towns who made religion subservient to force. Nevertheless, at the beginning of the twentieth century, the technique of the medieval mystery will emerge, that of the expressionist 'Stationendrama' (drama with stops).

Throughout the fourteenth century and up until the 'Hussite Revolution', many mysteries were performed in Bohemia. Among them were *Hry tři Marii* (*The Plays of the Three Marys*), *O Kristově zmrtvýchstání a jeho oslavení* (*the Play of the Resurrection of Christ and His Glorification*) and *Hra o Maři Magdalěně* (*the Play of Mary Magdalen*). Dating from the second half of the fourteenth century the latter dealt with of the New Testament sinner's conversion, a theme rarely tackled in European drama of that time.

In Italy, the equivalent of the mystery was the 'Sacra rappresentazione': sacred performance. It had originated partly from liturgical drama, partly from the laud which had succeeded the lyrical laud born in Umbria with the rise of the Franciscans. It had fairly loose ties with clericalism and a pronounced secular character, like that of the brotherhoods responsible for its staging. Sometimes accompanied by music, edifying and moralising, the fast-moving action of the 'Sacra rappresentazione' contained little by way of psychological development. Based on the Old and New Testaments, the scenes, often farcical, were unashamedly low-brow.

The English public's love of scripture, especially among ordinary working people, led to the formation of 'cycles' of mystery plays. These were performed in large towns on the main religious feastdays, thanks to the work of the 'guilds'. Among these cycles, the *Chester Plays* and the *Towneley Plays* stand out: both were compiled between the end of the fifteenth century and the beginning of the sixteenth. The former contained twenty-five scenes about the fall of Lucifer, the death of Abel, the adoration of the Shepherds and the triumphal entry into Jerusalem. The latter were the 'plays' of Woodkirk near Wakefield. They consisted of thirty-two scenes including the Flood, the greeting of Elisabeth and the purification of the Virgin Mary. The staging of English mystery plays was characterised by the use of 'pageants': stationary or sometimes mobile platforms over which the actors moved. When the platforms were mobile, they were mounted on wheels and paraded about in front of the spectators who saw the plot of different plays unfold before thier eyes. English mystery plays were aesthetically superior to those in France. Their restrained emotion and their vivacity guaranteed their popularity and ensured their survival into Elizabethan times. The comically incongruous, particularly to be savoured in the *Towneley Plays*, made them unique. In the *Play of Noah*, 'Goodman Noah' is obliged to give his wife a good hiding to make her decide to enter the ark. From this moment on, the querulous and recalcitrant Mrs Noah turns into the most docile wife imaginable, actively cooperating with the smooth running of the operation . . .

When Castilian Spanish replaced Latin in Spanish liturgical drama, mysteries called 'Autos' were written, inspired by the Gospels and showing the Biblical episodes of the Annunciation, the Nativity and the Resurrection. Only a fragment of 157 verses remains of the earliest Auto, from the end of the twelfth century, called the *Autos de los Reyes Magos* (*The Auto of the Three Wise Men*). With the exception of the work by Gomez Manrique (*c.*1412– *c.*1490), the *Representación del Nacimiento de Nuestro Señor* (*The Performance of the Birth of*

Our Lord, *c.*1458–1481) was undoubtedly the most representative example of the genre before the fine productions of Juan del Encina.

Secular drama: the comic and the serious

Not everyone recognised the secular drama as a distinct and independent genre between the years 1300 and 1450. It existed in embryo in some 'discussion' dialogues, in parodies of sermons on popular feastdays and, above all, in the realistic scenes, bordering on farce, which were included in mystery and miracle plays. At the end of the Middle Ages, comedy was fashionable in Germany, thanks to the farces performed during carnivals called 'Fastnachtspiele' (carnival plays). Originally a simple diversion, farce developed dramatic traits which revealed comic trials, domestic scenes and popular stories to its shopkeeper-craftsman audience. Cuckolded husbands, shameless wives and lecherous monks were these carnival plays favourite protagonists.

Their language was often vulgar to the point of obscenity.

Serious secular drama was also being hatched during this period. The Brabant, however, was one bit of Europe which became a major exception to the norm and produced high-quality work. Four plays dating from *c.*1350 contained in the 'Van Hulthem manuscript' (*c.*1410), made up the oldest example of serious secular drama to have been preserved in Europe. Described as 'abele spelen' (excellent or well-made plays), they are called *Esmoreit, Gloriant, Lanseloet van Denemerken* (*Lancelot of Denmark*), *Van den Winter ende den Somer* (*Play of Winter and Summer*). The first three plays are set in the world of chivalry in which courtly love plays an important part. The last play, in the tradition of the 'Discussion', was an adaptation of Alcuin's *Conflictus veris et hiemis* (*Debate of Spring and Winter*). The simple plot, the spontaneity of feeling and its lyrical language made *Lancelot of Denmark* a fine piece of writing:

Sanderijn	*Sandrine*
Ic salt al laten ende gaen mijnder straet	*I shall leave all behind and go my way*
Dolen in vremden lande.	*wandering through foreign lands*
Ic bidde Gode, dat Hi mine scande	*and asking God if He will please*
Wille decken, die ic nu hebbe ontfaen,	*hide the shame that has been inflicted on me,*
Want ic hebt sonder danc ghedaen;	*for the act was barren*
Dies es mi te moede wee.	*and the pain too hard to bear.*
Lanseloet, ghi en siet mi nemmermee:	*Lancelot, you will see me no more:*
Ic wille gaen dolen in dit foreest.	*I shall lose myself in the forest.*
Lanseloet van Denemerken	

NEW WAYS FORWARD AND NATIONAL DIFFERENCES

During the period 1300 to 1450, Italy, Bohemia, Byzantium and Bulgaria experienced a situation cultural like that of other European countries, but developed it in specific ways. Italy rediscovered Classical Antiquity, advocated the abandonment of the vernacular in favour of a return to Latin, drifted away from Scholasticism and Aristotle and paved the way for the acceptance of

a different philosophy: Neo-Platonism. Bohemia, aggrieved by the death sentence passed on Jan Hus at Constance, engaged in a struggle to 'reform' the Christian life and even the Church itself. This led to a literary output that was atypical in European terms. In parallel with a vernacular literature strongly influenced by the West Byzantium continued its ancient traditions and wrote erudite works. The Byzantine culture of this period, apart from its closeness to ancient roots, reflected an important phenomenon whose influence transcended the Empire's frontiers: the emergence of an essentially contemplative view of religion, the hesychasm of Mount Athos. In Bulgaria, monasteries became the busiest cultural centres, heavily influenced by Byzantium with hesychasm a leading component.

The first Italian humanists

The terms 'Renaissance' and 'humanism' are ambiguous. 'Renaissance' means, in effect, that the period which extended from the last third of the fourteenth century to the middle of the sixteenth century was placed under the sign of a renewal, a 'ri-nascita' (re-birth): a positive value judgement. It relegates the preceding period, that of the early Middle Ages, to outer darkness where everything must have been immutable, stiff and dead.

Thanks to the rediscovery of Classical Antiquity, the Renaissance was distinguished culturally speaking by a massive leap forward in the arts, letters and sciences. But things were otherwise in the areas of politics and economics, especially in Italy. Even if they did not put their knowledge to the same use as the humanists, medieval clerks were not ignorant of either Latin or classical authors. The Renaissance was not created *ex nihilo*. France experienced two 'renaissances', albeit limited and imperfect: the Carolingian renaissance and that of the twelfth century. The Italian Renaissance was the end of a long period of gestation, of a gradual process of trans-formation that had begun within the society of the early Middle Ages, with one important difference: the Middle Ages had made use of Antiquity, the Renaissance was its servant; the Middle Ages sought support for its religious faith in Antiquity, the Renaissance explored it for its own sake.

The word 'humanism' is hard to define. In its broadest sense, it takes into account all the reflections that make man a privileged subject of study. But if that were the case, all philosophy could be defined as 'humanist'. From a strictly literary point of view, the term means the study of Greek and Latin language and literature: the 'Studia humanitatis' (humanities). In a historical sense, it does not refer to a specific time period. If humanism first appeared in Italy *c.*1375 – some might even say in the middle of the Trecento with Petrarch – in a number of European countries it only saw the light of day much later, above all in the sixteenth century, when Italian humanism had already yielded its best results.

We see two main trends in the Italian Renaissance. There was a literary, philological and 'committed' humanism connected to 'civic' duties, and a more abstract variety practised by courtiers. The first developed under a republic, the second at a time of seignories and princedoms.

Civic humanism ('l'umanesimo civile') and philological humanism are typical of the years 1375–1450: they were also called 'the first humanism' and had their birth in Florence. They were mainly expressed in critical com-mentary on ancient texts, epistolography, historiography, the pedagogical treatise and the ethical and political discourse. One of the basic contributions of the first humanists lay in the discovery – or rediscovery – of Greco-Roman Antiquity in arts, languages and civilisations. Petrarch was the great precursor in this area: he pioneered research into ancient manuscripts. Motivated by a genuine passion for Antiquity and in the course of his journeys and sojourns in France – at the papal court of Avignon – in The Netherlands, in the Rhineland and in Italy, he exhumed many works which enabled him to found uniquely important library. Helped by friends and correspondents who were driven by the same curiosity, Petrarch rescued from oblivion rare texts, among them Cicero's discourse *Pro Archia* (*For Archias*). Petrarch's passion opened the way for Italian humanists at the end of the *trecento*, who continued his work and began the search for manuscripts which had lain covered with dust in convents and monasteries since the early Middle Ages. A veritable hunt for the unpublished took place in Italy: teams of zealous researchers criss-crossed Europe, admirable masterpieces made their reappear-ance. Ambrogio Traversari (1386–1439) and

stimulate the ideal of the active life. While the Middle Ages subordinated all realms of thought to theology, which was slanted towards the revelation of Divine Truth, humanists themselves were resolutely matter of fact about the acquisition of knowledge. In their eyes, knowledge was useful for the individual's education for his personal enrichment and spiritual development. So 'litteræ humanæ' (humanities) were of prime importance. They shaped the individual by developing all his faculties and the citizen by preparing him for an active life.

Humanists praised wealth and economic activity, indispensable to a nation's general wellbeing reputation. Their attachment to 'socialitas' (society) led them to glorify marriage and the family as the basic social unit: a radical change in thinking from previous centuries. The ascetic ideal of the Middle Ages excluded the prospect of marriage for a hero who was often a saint. Courtly love, 'fin' amor', could only be fully realised outside marriage.

Leon Battista Alberti (1404–1472), the son of one of the richest Florentine families of merchants and bankers, was also one of the first universal minds of the Italian Renaissance. He was an architect, a theoretician of the figurative arts, a mathematician, a physician, an archaeologist, a musician and the author of many works in Latin: *De commodis atque incommodis litterarum* (*Advantages and Disadvantages of Literary Activities*, c.1430), *Intercœnales* (before 1438), *Momus* (1443–1450). He also wrote texts in the vernacular, whose value relative to Latin he defended by organising in Florence, in 1441, a literary contest in which he participated. The bourgeois and lay ideology of the time and the vision of humanism were brilliantly illustrated in *I libri della famiglia* (*The Books of the Family*) that he wrote between 1437 and 1441. This was a resolutely 'modern' economic and moral treatise in which our twentieth-century values were spelled out. Alberti maintained that money was the very foundation of life in society. He gave advice on how to acquire wealth and how to make it work, recommending, in particular, the pursuit of commerce and industry and insisting on the preciousness of time:

Giannozzo	Giannozzo
Adopero tempo quanto più posso in essercizii lodati; non l'adopero in cose vili, non spendo più tempo alle cose che ivi si richiegga a farle bene. E per non perdere di cosa si preziosa punto, io pongo in me questa regola: mai mi lascio stare in ozio, fuggo il sonno, né giacio se non vinto dalla stracchezza . . .	*I use my time, as much as possible, in noble activities and not in unworthy ones. I never devote to tasks more time than is necessary to carry them out. And, so as not to lose the smallest atom of that precious commodity, I impose on myself the following rule: I avoid letting myself slide into idleness, I elude sleep and only go to bed when I am worn out with exhaustion.*

Leon Battista Alberti,
I libri della famiglia

Alberti described parental duties in detail. He established rules for children's education, declared himself strongly opposed to celibacy and outlined the ways in which a household should be run. He approved specifically human qualities: reason, wisdom, intelligence, prudence. Thanks to them, man is master of 'Fortuna' (fortune, coincidence) and becomes a kind of demigod. Alberti examined human activities for their exclusively social implications, for what they meant in terms of civic pride. Financial profit, he asserted, must work for everyones benefit. Language itself was above all a communication between individuals, a vehicle of conviviality. Like other humanists, Alberti set great store by dialogue because it encouraged an exchange of views. For him, friendship was a social 'virtue' beyond price.

The humanists based a new conception of man on their rediscovery of Antiquity. During the early Middle Ages man was seen as a weak creature, tainted by original sin. His life on earth was an ephemeral progress amid the vanity and falsehood of appearances. His real home was in heaven. Humanists, brought up with the realism and dynamism of economically thriving city states, had an optimistic vision of man, which the *Decameron* had already described. In their eyes, man was free, enterprising, capable of asserting himself thanks to his intelligence, his reason and his will. Though he is not indifferent to his future salvation, he fulfils his destiny during his life on earth.

Towards the middle of the Quattrocento, Giannozzo Manetti (1396–1459) wrote a treatise with the important title *De dignitate et excellentia hominis* (*On the Dignity and Excellence of Man*, 1451–1452), in which he listed all the typically human qualities of both the mind and body. He insisted on the importance of free will, which puts man in charge of his own destiny and renders him immune to all determinism and to Providence. Contrary to those who had nothing but contempt for worldly things, he praised the beauties and joys of earthly existence. Manetti did not believe in the nobility bestowed by wealth; for him true nobility derives from the exercise of admirable activities.

Although the first humanism was mainly Florentine, between the end of the Trecento and the end of the first half of the Quattrocento it spread to other Italian cities. As most of these were ruled by authoritarian monarchs, humanists were less committed than in Florence to becoming involved in State affairs, and were more interested in teaching and research.

The humanist revival in the field of education was remarkable and not just because of the spread of universities. It was very involved with schools attached to chanceries and royal courts. Teaching methods changed. Reflective reading, designed to form the pupil's judgement, took place of the learning by heart and the 'cramming' advocated by practitioners of the scholastic tradition. Humanist teachers, faithful to the maxim of Juvenal – 'a healthy mind in a healthy body' – combined physical and intellectual activity. Educational support systems changed. The old books that had been used to educate previous generations, for example the *Disticha Catonis* (*The Distichs of Cato*) and the *Liber Æsopi* (*The Book of Æsop*) were abandoned. The witty Merlin Cocai (Teofilo Folengo, 1496–1544), a defrocked Benedictine, later said of them that they were only good for 'for cooking sausages'. The new 'auctores' were the Greek and Latin classics, principally Plutarch and Quintilian. To ensure the education of both men and of citizens, humanist schools favoured the teaching of Grammar, Rhetoric, Dialectics, Philosophy and Moral Education.

In Milan, humanist pedagogy was made famous by Antonio Loschi (1368–1441), the chancellor of Gian Galeazzo Visconti, by Francesco Filelfo (1398–1481), an outstanding example of the courtier who was also a man of letters, and by Pier Candido Decembrio (1392–1477). Padua, Ferrara and Mantua established schools in which people from all the large European cities came to study. The great Neapolitan humanists were at the service of the court of Aragon: Antonio Beccadelli (1394–1471), Giovanni Pontano (1426–1503) and Masuccio Salernitano (1410–*c*.1475). Roman humanism was represented by Bracciolini and Valla, but also by the historian Flavio Biondo (1388–1469) and by Popes Nicholas V (1397–1455) and Pius II (Enea Silvio Piccolomini).

Pre-humanism in other European countries

From 1350 to 1450 Italy had an undeniable influence over several European countries. Already on the road to humanism, it communicated to them something of its passion for Classical Antiquity. This was a passion which was marked not by the emergence of a new conception of mankind and earthly life as inherited from the Ancients, but by translations of Greek and Latin texts or of those of the great forerunners of the Renaissance proper, Petrarch and Boccaccio.

A pre-humanism evolved in France at the end of the fourteenth century and during the first quarter of the fifteenth century. At the papal court of Avignon, Petrarch played a decisive role in the French discovery of Latin culture, mostly the work of Cicero. He was seen as the scholar who was passionately interested in the literature of the Ancients, the stylist who handled classical Latin to perfection, the moral orator. In Avignon, thanks to Italian scholars and translators, the French discovered the importance of philology. They learned to associate the critical commentary with the translation of ancient texts, to examine the work of pagan authors in their own right and not with the sole purpose of finding useful principles of government in them.

At the French court, many translations were reproduced. Jean II the Good asked Pierre Bersuire to translate Livy's *History of Rome*. Around 1370, Charles V set up to an entire team of translators. Renewed hostilities against England in 1420 and the troubles brought about by civil strife in France prevented this French version of pre-humanism from evolving further. It will, however, have developed just enough to prepare the ground for the 'rhétoriqueurs' of the second half of the fifteenth century.

Petrarch's embassy for the Viscontis of Milan to the King of Bohemia and Holy Roman Emperor, Charles IV, in 1356, and the letters written in Latin that Petrarch exchanged with the Royal and Imperial Chancellery of Prague, had important implications for the culture of the German-speaking lands in Europe. Taking his inspiration from Petrarch's correspondence, whose consummate elegance he so admired, Chancellor Johannes Novofirensis (John of Neumarkt, died 1380) drew up a collection of model letters in Latin to be copied by his scribes. But it fell to one of his emulators, another Bohemian German, **Johannes von Saaz** (or **von Tepl, 1350–1414**), to create an original work in which pre-humanism's unmistakable features can be seen. A German prose masterpiece, his work *Der Ackermann aus Böhmen* (*The Bohemian Ploughman*), also known as *Der Ackermann und der Tod* (*Death and the Ploughman*), written in 1401, preached the hope of happiness in this world and provided an apologia for man's existence:

> Tell me where is there a craftsman who has wrought so fine and rich a work, a little ball as knowledgeable as the head of man?
>
> Johannes von Saaz, *Death and the Ploughman*

Der Ackermann	*The Ploughman*
Herr Tod, lasset Euer nutzloses Kläffen! Ihr schändet Gottes allerfeinstes Geschöpf. Engel, Teufel, Schrätlein, Totenvögel, das sind Geister in Gottes Banngewalt; der Mensch ist das allervornehmste, das allergeschickteste und das allerfreieste Werkstück Gottes. Ihm selber gleichend, hat es Gott gebildet, wie er es selber auch bei der Schöpfung der Welt ausgesprochen hat.	*Lord Death, cease your useless barking! You are insulting God's noblest creature. Angels, demons, gnomes, birds that scavenge, are all spirits under God's orders. Man is the noblest, most skilful and freest work of God, who made him in His own image, as He said Himself when He created the world. Tell me where is there a craftsman who has*

> *Wo hat je ein Werkmann ein so*
> *geschicktes und reiches Werkstück*
> *gewirkt, eine so kunstvolle kleine*
> *Kugel wie das Menschenhaupt?*
> *In ihm sind kunstreiche, allen*
> *Geistern unbegreifliche Wunderbräfte.*
>
> Johannes von Saaz,
> *Der Ackermann und der Tod*

> *wrought so fine and rich a work,*
> *a little ball as knowledgeable*
> *as the head of man? It is*
> *inhabited by wonderful*
> *forces, beyond the understanding*
> *of every spirit.*

Interrupted in Bohemia by the Hussite Wars, Czech humanism resurfaced at the end of the fifteenth century, while German humanism developed in other parts of the Holy Roman Empire, above all in its south-west corner, where the Councils of Constance and Basel enabled German men of letters to meet the Italian humanists who made up the papal retinue. **Nikolaus Krebs (1401–1464)**, a theologian, went in search of ancient manuscripts. Translations of works by Petrarch and Boccaccio began to appear. Enea Silvio Piccolomini had a marked influence on the Imperial Chancery of Vienna where he was secretary from 1443 to 1455.

From the second half of the fourteenth century, the penetration of French and Italian culture into Spain created a predisposition to translate the texts of Antiquity. This was especially true of the vassal states of Aragon, at the instigation of its sovereigns Peter IV and John I 'the Humanist'. In Castille humanism arrived later. Apart from translations, Spanish pre-humanism was graced by the writings of the Marquis of Santillana and of the Catalan **Bernat Metge (between 1340 and 1346–1413)**. As John I's secretary and treasurer, the latter left behind a highly original work, *Lo Somni* (*The Dream*, 1398), in which we can see the influences of Cicero, Petrarch and Boccaccio.

Bohemia: a literature of struggle, Hussite literature

In Bohemia, the Hussite eruption – the culmination of a crisis at the heart of the Church – was caused by abuses of the system among the clergy and the growing moral laxity of their Christian life. It led rapidly to general discontent and hostility. Literary production took a radical change of direction and a function specific to the service of the 'Czech Reformation'. Thus, after more than a century of Czech literary output coexisting with writing in Latin and embracing nearly all the genres and themes of other Western literatures, the realm of Czech literature was limited to the religious sphere, perceived however from a different viewpoint than that of the established Church. The Hussites' objections to certain ways of interpreting dogma, even to the very foundations and practices of the Roman Catholic Church, were scripturally based, aiming to apply God's word to realistic daily situations.

A 'committed' literature of struggle and criticism, of defence and propaganda, was organised, which targeted the working classes and the bourgeoisie. Latin, almost eliminated as a language of worship, remained indispensable for certain academic writings. It was retained by Catholics: now in a minority they were every bit as vehement in their beliefs as the Calixtine Hussites – whose symbol was the chalice – and the Utraquists – who believed in 'communion under both kinds'. The debit side of this 'ideological' orientation and democratisation was, on the one hand isolation from the rest of Europe and, on the other, an aesthetic impoverishment, a formal simplification, the final disappearance of several literary genres. The rejection of the two dominant medieval figures – the saint and the courtly warrior – led to the disappearance of legend, poetry and lyrical prose, as well as liturgical and semi-liturgical 'plays'. The new orientation of Czech literature favoured oratory, declamation and song – and the treatise, the moral polemic and the satire.

The substance of the Hussite problem – the need to reform Christianity – was expounded in many theoretical texts. The ones that make essential reading are those of **Jan Hus (c.1369–1415),**★ who wrote either in Latin, *Questio de indulgentiis* (*The Problem of Indulgences*, 1412), *De ecclesia* (*On the Church*, 1413), or in Czech, *Výklad Viery, Desatera a Páteře* (*The Great Explanation of the Confession of Apostolic Faith, The Ten Commandments and the Our Father*, 1412), or in both languages, *De sex erroribus, O šesti bludiech* (*On the Six Errors*, 1413). It is worth adding the writings of Jerome of Prague (died 1416), of Jakoubek ze Stříbra (died 1429) and of Jan Rokycana (died 1471).

As at the time of Hus' precursors, preaching was the main way of reaching a wide audience. The texts of sermons were bound together in books called 'Postillas'. The one that Hus compiled during his stay in Southern Bohemia in 1413 is invaluable.

Jan Hus also made his mark as a great stylist in the art of letter writing. In Constance, before he was burned alive as a heretic there in 1415, he wrote a series of letters in which he launched poignant appeals to his friends, to the University of Prague and to the Czech nation, dealing as he did so with various religious and moral questions. Undeniable literary qualities were also contained in the letters of the Hussite military leaders, Jan Žižka (died 1424) and Prokop the Great (died1434).

Another genre, the polemic in dialogue

form, though old, tried and tested, was completely revitalised, with an ideological bonus, at the hands of Utraquists and Catholics. One of the most accomplished examples was *Hádáni Prahy s Kutnou Horou* (*The Dispute of Prague and Kutná Hora*, 1420). This was an allegorical polemic of almost 3000 verses between the Hussites – personified by the capital – and the Catholics – represented by the rich mining town of Kutná Hora – in the presence of the Supreme Judge, Christ, who gave his approval to the former, enjoining them to be more perfect. On the Catholic side, there was a work called *Václav, Havel a Tábor čili Rozmlouvaní Čechách roku 1424* (*Wenceslas, Gall and Tabor or the Conversation about Bohemia in 1424*). The Catholic arguments were also taken from the Bible, nor was their patriotism any less heartfelt than the Utraquists.

But the main Hussite genre was the popular song. There is nothing more natural than to praise, condemn or parody an event, person or action in a song. The Hussites marked the beginning of the tradition of the spiritual canticle, so beloved of the Czechs, with Hus himself. The oldest collection of Hussite songs dates to *c.*1420: the *Jistebnický Kancionál* (*The Jistebnice Songbook*). It contained many liturgical texts, most of which were anonymous, apart from the ones we know were by Hus and Jan Čapek). Among the marching songs was the famous canticle *Ktož jsú boží bojovníci* (*You who are the soldiers of God*). This frightened invading Crusaders with its simplicity, solemnity and calm confidence:

Ktož jsú boží bojovníci *a zákona jeho,* *prostež od boha pomoci* *a ufajte v něho,* *že konečně vždycky s ním* *svitězite.*	*You who are the soldiers of* *God* *and of His law,* *ask God for His help* *and hope in Him:* *in the end, you will conquer with Him.*

Ktož jsú boží bojovníci

The compromise solution set up by the 'Compactata' of Basel (1433), the tragic end of the Hussite Wars (1434) and the uncertain political situation until thee arrival of George of Poděbrady – Lieutenant General of the

Kingdom, then king from 1458 to 1471 – did not manage to end the arguments between Utraquists, Catholics and the new arrivals, the Bohemian Brothers.

In the general climate of disenchantment, a

singular religious and social thinker emerged with firm opinions: **Petr Chelčický (c.1390–c.1460)**. At the sack of Prague, 1419–1420, Chelčický immediately reacted by writing his treatise *O boji duchovním* (*On Spiritual Struggle*, 1421), in which he affirms that the only acceptable form of struggle is the spiritual kind. In another of his writings, *O trojím lidu řeč* (*Discourse on the Three Estates*, 1425), he attacked social injustice and rejected the traditional division of society into clergy, aristocracy and peasantry. His two master-pieces were *Postilla* (c.1435) which described his reflections as a layman on the Gospel texts, and a long treatise, *Siet'viery pravé* (*The Net of True Faith*, c.1440). Here he gave a relentless analysis of the malevolent forces at work in the Catholic Church, and expressed his own vision of the Church of Christ and of society. Chelčický condemned the State, rejected its justice and its army and disapproved of commerce, private property and higher education. This uncompromising reader of the Bible believed that the Christian must rigorously adhere to the precepts of the Gospels.

Even before his death, groups of peasants organised themselves to put into practice Chelčický's ideal life based on evangelism and pacifism. In 1467 they formed the Union of Bohemian Brothers (or 'Moravians'). Half a century later, having abandoned the Utopian part of their spiritual journey, the Brothers remained enthusiastic defenders of the culture of humanism. Bohemia rejoined the West. Thanks to its radically Christian ideas, soon supported by the idea of tolerance – enshrined in law by the Diet of 1485 – the 'Reformation' became a powerful spiritual leaven and a major factor in cultural and human progress. Through its influence, awareness of a Czech national identity took hold – an identity of which Jan Hus, who often maintained that 'truth will win', remained the perfect representative.

Scholarly Byzantine literature

During this period, Byzantium continued to produce its own literature in scholarly Greek, distinguished by a taste for erudition, a nostalgia for ancient Greece and a strong religious bias.

In the fields of philosophy and theology there were two marked tendencies. The first sought common ground with Rome and practised a kind of 'theological humanism' by treasuring the legacy of the ancient world, even in its 'scientific' aspects. The second is 'contemplative', irreducible to rationalism and introverted. It is represented by hesychastic spirituality, born in the monasteries of Mount Athos.

Two important personalities illustrated this culture of Byzantium: Gregory Palamas (c.1296–1359), a monk who became Archbishop of Thessalonika, and Nicholas Cabasilas (c.1320–c.1391), the two most fervent defenders of hesychastic mysticism. **Gemisto Plethon (c.1360–c.1452)**, a philosopher and humanist, strove to rekindle an awareness of Hellenism in his contemporaries. His *Nomoi* (*Treatise on Laws*) expressed complete confidence in philosophical thought which, over and above religious differences, must contribute to the revelation of a truth valid in everyone's eyes. He also wrote a work which compared Plato's philosophy with Aristotle's. An opponent of Latin influences, Plethon contributed to the development of Platonism in Florence. Demetrius Cydones (c.1323–c.1397), from Thessalonika, passionately Latinate, translated Thomas Aquinas' *The Theological Summary*. He was the author of a work which tried to synthesise Aristotelian metaphysics and Plato's ethics. His correspondence with the literati of his time is a key document for the understanding of intellectual life in fourteenth-century Byzantium. John Bessarion (1403–1472), from Trebizond, the Metropolitan bishop of Nicaea, was a proponent of union with Rome and became a cardinal of the Roman Catholic Church. A theologian with a background in scholasticism, he was drawn towards Platonism in which he perceived 'some of the principles of true theology'. He was the author of several historical works.

Bulgaria: literature and hesychasm

The creation of the second Bulgarian kingdom, in 1185, was favourable to the development of literature which reached its peak in the fourteenth century. The reign of Ivan Alexander (1331–1371) contributed to the building-up of the cultural potential of monasteries in which many schools were formed near the capital, Tărnovo in particular. Bulgarian culture began to assert itself in the Balkans and the Slavic lands. In the total absence of a secular intellectual élite or an urban intelligentsia, monasteries were the only centres of literary and artistic life. This monastic culture is closely linked to Byzantine hesychasm, a movement whose eminent practitioner was Theodosius of Tărnovo. A disciple and translator of Gregory of Sinaï, he founded a school of hesychasm in the monastery of Kelifarevo where he taught Bulgarian, Serbian, Wallachian and Hungarian seminarists.

Under the reign of Ivan Alexander, hesychastic mysticism became an official doctrine and expanded with **Euthymius (c.1320–c.1402)**, the Patriarch of Tărnovo from 1375 to 1393. Euthymius was a brilliant theologian, an excellent Hellenist, a translator and an educator who vigorously and single-mindedly defended the traditional forms of the cultural and spiritual life of his country and disliked anything to do with Western Europe. After a long stay in Constantinople and on Mount Athos, he went back to Bulgaria where in 1371, he founded a study centre, later called the school of Tărnovo, in the monastery of the Holy Trinity. He pioneered a reform which altered not just religious perceptions but also linguistic and literary ones. At his behest, sacred books of the Church which had variant readings were revised, not only in the translations made by Cyril and Methodius and their followers, but also in the Greek originals. A modification of the spelling was undertaken and new translations of Greek religious texts were made. Aspiration to an elevated style, by making use of the resources of Byzantine eloquence, was one of Euthymius' constant preoccupations. Euthymius's reform coincided with the activity of Western European humanists in the areas of philology and translation.

As for the genres practised, the school of Tărnovo preferred the lives of saints and panegyrics. The most celebrated were those by Euthymius, particularly *Žitie za Sveti Ivan Rilski* (*The Life of St John of Rila*), *Žitie za Sveta Petka* (*The Life of Saint Parasceva*) and *Pohvalno slovo za Sveti Konstantin i Elena* (*Panegyric for St Constantine and St Helena*).

Grigorii Camblak (c.1364–c.1419), Euthymius' most famous disciple, spread the Tărnovo school principles to Serbia, where he wrote two important works: *Žitie za Stefan Dečanski* (*The Life of Stephen Decanski*) and *Razkaz za prenasjane moštite na Sveta Petka* (*The Story of the Transfer of the Relics of St Parasceva*). In 1409 Camblak went to Russia and became Metropolitan Bishop of Kiev in 1414. At the Council of Constance he tried in vain to reconcile the Eastern and Western Churches. His lives of saints and his many sermons and panegyrics assured him of an important niche in Bulgarian, Serbian and Russian literary history. His best-known composition, *Pohvalno slovo za Evtimii* (*Panegyric for our Father Euthymius*), presents his master not only as a theologian, moralist and writer of the highest calibre, but also as a man of action, a courageous defender of the Bulgarian capital and its inhabitants against the Turkish invader. The description of the patriarch's attitude, full of dignity and nobility at the fall of Tărnovo, is a moving and beautiful scene.

At the beginning of the fifteenth century, the Bulgarian cultural élite suffered a tragic fate in the aftermath of its conquest by the Ottoman Empire: most intellectuals were killed and only a few writers were able to flee abroad. Few educated people remained and scholarly culture lost all its prestige in favour of a strengthening of popular culture. The school of Tărnovo, however, left a lasting influence on the development of language and literature in Russia and particularly in Serbia. In Rumania Bulgarian Slavonic was used for a long time as a liturgical language. The works of Euthymius and his disciples spread from Mount Athos to Jerusalem.

The dawn of better things

It was from Venice that Marco Polo set out and to Venice that he returned in order to promote his incredible *Book of Wonders* (1298–1299), written in French. Turning towards the commercial and intellectual riches of the East and driven by the dynamism of the West, Italian towns were the first to favour the rebirth of literature. Dante, Petrarch and Boccaccio were all born in Tuscany, all wrote in the language of its opulent capital, Florence, and were known all over Europe. The gaiety of *The Decameron* found an echo in its joyous English counterpart, *The Canterbury Tales*. The growth of this Renaissance, 'the dawn of better things' hailed by Palmieri, can be illuminated in an anecdote about Petrarch. Despite a warning that he himself had only brought back knocks and bruises from such an adventure, Petrarch climbed Mount Ventoux, and discovered, with rapture, the Alps, the Rhone and Marseilles.

The downward slope of this new impetus given to thought that the Roman Catholic Church could not wholly regulate could be seen in Jan Hus who found it out at the cost of losing his life. Christendom was not ready to be reformed. The end of the fifteenth and the beginning of the sixteenth century continued to follow this double path. On the one hand, there was humanism, evolving in Italy and expanding in Europe. On the other there was a desire, which became increasingly marked, to reform the Church, to make it accept the position that man wants to occupy on earth.

The Short Story

M. Guglielminetti

The short story, of all short forms of literature, is the most difficult genre to define: its border with the tale is not always clearly delineated and the function assigned to it has changed considerably over the centuries. However, as we move through its various incarnations from the Middle Ages to the present day, from Boccaccio to Torgny Lindgren, Sean O'Faolain or Costas Takstis, we can focus on some of its defining features. One thing is sure: the land of the short story written in a language other than Latin is Tuscany.

Tuscany: the cradle of the 'novellino'

The 'novellino', an anonymously compiled collection, dates back to the closing decades of the thirteenth century. Why should the first collections of short stories have chosen Tuscany to make their appearance? At that time, thanks to its high level of literacy, this region had been responsible for translating quickly and on a large scale many religious, didactic and historical texts from Latin into the vernacular. There was obviously a deep-seated need to make available to the enthusiastic new reading public in the towns a body of knowledge which until then had been the exclusive prerogative of those who understood Latin. General culture stopped being clerical and became middle class. The transformation extended to those genres which were intended to entertain as well as those whose aim was to educated. A prime example of the former was the *exemplum*, the Latin ancestor of the short story.

Multiple origins

Other, more attractive materials were available to those who took part in this transformation of the narrative. So, in Tuscany, two texts of Eastern origin had been translated into the vernacular. The first one by Pedro de Alfonso (1062–1100), a Jewish doctor who had converted to Christianity, was the *Disciplina clericalis* a rewritten version of the *Panchatantra*, an Indian book of the second century AD, in which tales had already been set in a frame. The second was the *Libro dei Sette Savi di Roma* (*The Book of the Seven Sages*), an anonymous work translated into

Persian, Arabic, Greek, Hebrew and Latin. If we add to this list the simultaneous translation of the *Conti di antichi cavalieri* (*Tales of the Knights of Old*), drawn from other translations of historical compilations of material in Latin and French, we can see that the short story known as 'Tuscan', inaugurated by the 'novellino' and soon to achieve its masterpiece with Boccaccio's *Decameron*, did not originate from just one source.

In the introduction to the 'novellino', the author addressed the élite of his bourgeois public: those who were 'noble and worthy in their words and in their actions' and who could therefore hold up 'a mirror to the destitute'. So that they may learn the art of pleasing with words, he gave examples 'of certain flowers of fair language, politeness and appropriate replies, and of fair exploits, fair generosity and fair tales of love'. In such a way the culture gap which existed at the heart of the middle classes would be filled, thus providing 'profit and pleasure (to) those who are ignorant and who wish to know things'.

The themes of the 'novellino'

The subject matter of the 'novellino' is extremely varied: from classical authors such as Cicero, Ovid, Valerius Maximus and Diogenes Laertes to the *Disciplina clericalis* and the *Book of the Seven Sages*, from the legend of Barlaam and Jehosaphat (a Western rendering of the life of Buddha) to the apocryphal epistle of Prester John (the mythical Christian monarch of India) and to fabliaux and the *Novel of Renart*. It could be an unpalatable mixture, but its charm lay in its style founded on 'brevitas'. Some critics have equated this pursuit of brevity with the short story's main distinguishing mark, at least to begin with.

In each story an emphasis is given to the kind of speech that makes the knight, the gentleman and the man of culture stand out from the crowd. Everyone is called on in various ways to defend the values the author himself holds dearest: courtesy, generosity and conspicuous consumption. Characters from Antiquity and the contemporary world, kings and courtiers, lords and knights give way to one another in a hundred tales and anecdotes, without showing any sign of their actual literary origin, perfectly integrated into a narrative in absolute harmony with current values.

Boccaccio and the *Decameron*

Fifty years later, the reasons which prompted Boccaccio to write the *Decameron* were more pressing than those that contributed to the writing of the 'novellino'. Boccaccio imagined that a group of young people had taken refuge from the plague in a villa in the Tuscan hills. There, every day for ten days and under the guidance of one of the company – members of which take it in turn to be king or queen – everyone told a story on a different theme. Each day ended with a song and included dancing, meals and all kinds of agreeable worldly distractions.

Boccaccio promoted all the values that are continued in the 'novellino' – courtesy, liberality, munificence and, above all, eloquence – but with more heartfelt feelings of regret for their passing, for these values were threatened by a new, profit-orientated mentality.

The *Decameron* set the pattern for a new literary genre: the collection of stories united inside a framework, or 'Rahmen', that soon found its counterpart in England with Chaucer's *Canterbury Tales*. This collection of tales organised its framework differently, entrusting each of the tales to individual members of a band of pilgrims making their way from Southwark to Canterbury. Each pilgrim was the subject for a thumbnail sketch – that of the good Wife of Bath is justly famous – and the tales remind us of medieval romances, fabliaux and fables.

In Boccaccio's footsteps

In Italy several writers followed in Boccaccio's footsteps. Among them were Giovan Francesco Straparola (died after 1547) from Caravaggio near Bergamo, the author of the

Piacevoli notti (*Agreeable Nights*, 1550–1553); Giovan Battista Giraldi, also known as Cinzio, from Ferrare, the author of the *Ecatommiti* or 100 tales (there are actually 113); and Giovan Battista Basile, a Neapolitan, the author of *Lo cunto de li cunti* (*The Tale of Tales*), also known as the *Pentamerone* (1634–1636).

During the three centuries over the course of which the formative influence of the *Decameron* lasted, there was only one occasion (in Giraldi's book) when a serious historical event justified the retreat of the narrators to a safe place: the sack of Rome by German mercenaries in 1527. As far as everyone else was concerned, withdrawal from the daily grind and the choice of an idyllic retreat so as to be able to narrate to their heart's content are tributes paid to Boccaccio's inventiveness.

He has also been imitated in tragic or comic stories, but less slavishly than has far too often been asserted.

Others did not follow the model of the *Decameron*, preferring to insert after each tale a letter of dedication which was also a key to how to read it. Salernitano wrote a second 'novellino' (1476), a work in which the anticlericalism of the *Decameron* was particularly apparent. Matteo Maria Bandello, from Castelnuovo Scrivia, wrote a collection of *Novelle* (*Short Stories*, 1555–1572) which, together with those by Giraldi, soon became the best-known Italian short stories in France and England and were often translated and adapted. Shakespeare took from Bandello the material for *Romeo and Juliet* and *Much Ado About Nothing* and from Giraldi *Othello* and *Measure for Measure*, while *The Merchant of Venice* came from the *Pecorone* by Ser Giovanni Fiorentino. Of those responsible for stage adaptations we can add the names of Lope de Vega, who found in the *Decameron* the subject matter for eight not very good comedies, and Molière who went to him for the third act of *Georges Dandin* (1668).

The future of the genre

Marguerite de Navarre, the author of the *Heptameron*, deviating from the Boccaccio's path, proclaimed that she had set herself the task 'of writing no story which is not a true story', making good her promise in a framework where characters who speak their mind come and go, but where, ultimately, Parlamente, the authorial mouthpiece, who constantly urges honesty and truthfulness on others, prevails. The moral and the real are confused and take the shape of stories which are, above all, tragic. In a sense, Marguerite's tales complement Boccaccio's: the *Heptameron* belongs to the same lineage as the *Decameron*. As La Fontaine later said to justify his *Stories in Verse taken from Boccaccio and Ariosto* (1665), and particularly the second part of his *Tales and Stories* (1666), we can mine the 'divine spirit' of the Tuscan as much as the skilful presentations of the 'Queen of Navarre'. The same could be said of other tales adapted from Boccaccio, not quoted here, which owe their popularity to La Fontaine. By the middle of the seventeenth century, irrespective of translations (in England, for example, the *Decameron* was only translated in its entirety in 1620), the short story created by Boccaccio and copied by the whole of Europe is no more than a narrative diversion for worldlings. The prevalence of titillating lecherous tales in La Fontaine's collections was hardly coincidental.

In the seventeenth century, in order to find works outside the magic circle of the *Decameron*, we need to turn to Spain. There was already *Count Lucanor* by Juan Manuel, a moralistic collection of tales taken from Eastern tradition and Castilian legend, designed to educate its eponymous protagonist. This revealed a unique capacity for expanding on narrative material in Spain, later confirmed by *The Book of True Love* by Juan Ruiz, Archpriest of Hita. This autobiographical poem was devoted to love in its various manifestations. It abounded with 'examples' inserted into the text to illustrate and drive home its author's opinions. The first series of *Exemplary Novels* by Cervantes dated from 1613. The frame and all other supports for a story were lacking. Although it took a leaf out of the Italian tradition, this book reflected the reality of certain towns in Spain (Seville, for instance) and revealed, above all, a knowledge of two literary structures quite foreign to Boccaccio: the picaresque novel and Erasmian dialogue. The central characters – a student who thinks that he is made of glass (*The Glass Graduate*) and dogs engaged in thinking about the world they inhabit (*The Canine Colloquy*) – were indicative of the anxieties and upsets with which Cervantes began his post-Boccaccio narratives.

The short story from Romanticism to naturalism

The short story developed from the eighteenth century. Only in the nineteenth century did it possess characteristics that marked it off from the novel, in the shadow of which, until then, it had lived. The new fate awaiting the short story came into being during the Romantic era with the vogue for tales which were historical and fantastic. In the 1820s France unearthed a fundamental contrast between the picturesque and medieval manner of Walter Scott in his historical novels and the ironic and whimsical manner of the tales of Hoffmann: *Fantasies in the Style of Callot* (1814–1815), *Nocturnes* (1817), *Tales of the Brothers Serapion* (1819–1821). The originality and liveliness of these works, which emphasised the greyness of area between the short story and the tale, are recognised throughout literary Europe by the mid-nineteenth century. Nodier's tales of the fantastic and the narratives of Théophile Gautier were inspired by Hoffmann. *The Queen of Spades* (1836) by Pushkin and the St Petersburg tales of Gogol, as well as those of Italian writers called 'scapiglati' (writers who could be described as 'Bohemians') were equally indebted to Hoffmann.

Made famous by Baudelaire's translations, Poe's tales exerted an influence comparable to that of Hoffmann. The French version of Poe's *Tales of Mystery and Imagination* (1845) Europeanises the first great narrative work to come out of America with its fantastic tales of *The Masque of the Red Death*, *The Gold Bug* and *The Black Cat*. The 'incunabula' of the detective story were particularly appreciated.

The 'detective' Dupin was the central character in two cases called *The Murders in the Rue Morgue* and *The Purloined Letter*. Over time, the detective story lost the disturbing fascination of these works, becoming at once more technical and more mechanical. This is what endeared it to a wider public who were less discriminating and more easily pleased.

But towards the middle of the century, the most popular tale was the one born of the 'experimental' novel, particularly by Zola, the foremost exponent of naturalism. For a time, Maupassant was drawn towards naturalism, but he remained, above all, a disciple of Flaubert, who wrote three exceptional, long short stories in *Trois Contes* (*Three Tales*, 1877). After *Boule de Suif* (1880), Maupassant created a total picture of French society, almost on a par with that offered to us by Balzac in *The Human Comedy*. There were the tales of *La Maison Tellier* (1881), then *Mademoiselle Fifi* (1882). Maupassant also published tales of the fantastic: tales about madness, *Fear*, *A Madman*, *The Horla* (Flaubert had himself written *The Memoirs of a Madman*) which corresponded to Balzac's *Droll Tales*. During this same period, the master of the Italian realist short story or 'bozzetto', the Sicilian Giovanni Verga, published *Life in the Fields* (1881) and *Peasant Tales* (1883). To this may be added *Tales of Pescara* (1904) by D'Annunzio, but he tended to dilute the story with poetry, which detracted from the short story's independence as a distinct genre in twentieth-century literature.

The short story in the twentieth century

Rather than draw premature conclusions about the pre-eminence of the novel over the short story at the start of the twentieth century, we need to be reminded of two great short story writers from the end of the nineteenth and the beginning of the 20th centuries, both of whom published short story collections. First, there was Chekhov, who gradually moved away from the comic elements in Gogol to prefer a style that was elegiac (*The Steppe*,

1888) or symbolist (*The Black Monk*, 1896). Then came Pirandello whose *Tales for a Year* range from the grotesque (*When I was Crazy*, 1902) to the description of an existential crisis which entails the breakdown of a personality, destroyed by the alienating aspects of life in society (*A Day in the Life*, posthumous).

Today, mirroring the changes in the pace of life and reading habits, the short story's share of the Western literary market is growing. Interest in the short story form in the English-speaking world in general, in Scandinavia and in North America make it a genre with a mission. Short stories are appearing on all the shelves of the library of Babel. *The Dream of a Staircase* (1971) by the Italian Dino Buzzati, *The Nice Little Crime of a Customs Officer* by the Spaniard Camilo José Cela, show the importance, for Mediterranean Europe, of a genre practised by Takstis in Greece and Sophia de Mello Breyner in Portugal.

In Northern Europe the phenomenon is even more explosive as the stories of Siegfried Lenz in Germany and Sean O'Faolain, Dermot Bolger and Edna O'Brien in Ireland indicate. Is the 'short story' the way of writing which best harmonises with the world in which we live? This is what Scandinavian writing would seem to suggest. In the wake of Danish writers such as Andreas William Heinesen or Karen Blixen, a whole generation now looks on the short story as a unique way in which to express events and feelings with few words. Tarjei Vesaas in Norway, Eeva Kilpi and Rosa Liksom in Finland, Eyvind Johnson, Stig Dagerman, Lars Ahlin, Torgny Lindgren in Sweden . . . out of their pared-down style comes the impact of the short story. The contemporary short story has retained some of its original traits, including brevity, but the tone has changed. A long way removed from the pleasant, flowery, sometimes bawdy anecdotes in the manner of Boccaccio, today it is often a narrative which is concise and, excluding the point at the end, devoid of any striving for effect. Its main theme is the solitude of the individual and a denunciation of society's violence.

Jan Hus (*c.* 1369–1415)

V. Peska

In the Middle Ages, among so many men who were tortured as heretics, Jan Hus (*c.*1369–1415) paid with his life for his total commitment to the internal reform of his Church and, because of that commitment, his opposition to its chief representatives, including the Pope.

The authority *per se* of scripture

Hus acted in the name of truth, the truth of Scripture, 'authority *per se*' in his opinion for any and every Christian. He invoked the right to delve into Holy Writ and to interpret it freely. He consequently also claimed the right to dissent from an authoritative interpretation of it and the right of an individual conscience to disobedience.

At the Council of Constance, the former Rector of the University of Prague gave precise answers to each accusation – frequently unfounded – that was levelled against Hus and asked his judges, above all Jean Gerson and Pierre d'Ailly, to enlighten him with 'the word of God'. They invariably responded by repeating their invitation to him to retract, but his conscience, in his own words, would not allow him to deny himself.

Four years after his death on 6 July 1415, when the secular arm of the Church in the shape of the Holy Roman Emperor, the King of Bohemia's own brother, had the 'heretic' burned alive at the stake and his ashes thrown in the Rhine, the city of Prague, soon to be followed by the whole Czech nation, rose up in the name of 'Master Jan' against the oppression of Church and Emperor. For the first time in European history, a whole nation took up the cudgels on behalf of its national martyr.

In 1485, after years of struggle, the Imperial Diet negotiated a religious non-aggression pact between Utraquists and Catholics, Hus introducing and legalising the idea of religious tolerance. It was to be jealously guarded until Czech Protestants were crushed by Hapsburg

Catholics at the Battle of the White Mountain (1620): a signal for the enforced reoccupation by Catholics of the Czech lands.

A pre-Reformation

Western historians are only willing to see in the Hussite Rebellion a prelude to the Reformation proper. Its role in a larger, international context was expressed, somewhat crudely, by a famous saying: 'Wycliffe begat Hus – Hus begat Luther.' Luther wrote that 'we are all Hussites without knowing it' and he propagated the German edition of Hus' *De Ecclesia*. He also ensured that the reformer's letters were translated into Latin.

In France it was only with Bossuet and Lenfant that the 'Czech heretic' began to be better known and appreciated. Rehabilitation came with the first historians of the French Revolution, the novels and studies of George Sand and the poems of Victor Hugo, who placed him alongside humanity's most noble figures: 'Christ, Socrates, Jan Hus, Columbus'. For the Czechs themselves, Hus remained a symbol, a herald of truth and freedom of conscience, an ethical and universal figure. In the nineteenth century the historian Palacký considered the Hussite period to be the high point of Czech history and the philosopher Masaryk took the essence of the Czech Reformation as the humanist axis of his philosophy of nationhood.

As for Catholics, setting aside what separated them from Hus, they have begun to insist that 'The heart of Hus never stopped being Catholic.' They are now asking Rome to rehabilitate this son of the Church who always heeded the promptings of his reason and his conscience and who was subservient only to human dignity.

Dante (1265–1321)

C. Ossola

The sacred poem in which heaven and earth have both had a hand.

Dante, *Il Paradiso*

To make a person knowable, assuming that a person can be known, a modern novel needs five or six hundred pages. To Dante one single moment is enough. And, in the time it takes for one single moment to elapse, a character is indelibly defined. Unconsciously Dante looks for the fulcrum. I have tried to do the same thing in a number of my stories and this discovery, which consists in summarising in an instant a person's whole life, and which was what Dante discovered in the Middle Ages, has always fascinated me.

Jorge Luis Borges, *Seven Nights*

La Commedia: the ink of eternity

La Divina Commedia (*The Divine Comedy*, 1307–1321) was an allegorical poem in three parts with 100 cantos that took the poet, and through him all humanity, from *Hell* to *Purgatory* and finally to *Paradise*.

Words of destiny, written with the ink of eternity, 'the sacred poem in which heaven and earth have both had a hand', condensed the history of men and books in a gesture, a feature, an epigram, as if *The Divine Comedy* were eternity's register of births. Everything, places and books, the Bible and the classics, the history of Florence and the life of Dante Alighieri, was fixed, judged and placed within the architecture of infinity which, from the depths of the earth (the deep conical cavity of Hell), rose to the summit of Eden (where the ascent of the mountain of Purgatory finished) and extended 'with open wings' to the glory of the heavens (in Paradise).

But more important to Dante than the allegorical approach to God was his intention to root his writing in the fixity of the celestial bodies, in the 'firmamentum æternitatis'. This is why Dante ended each of the three sections into which his work was divided by a reference to the stars.

A humble ode

This text was a *Comedy* for all that, a poem inscribed as a 'sermo humilis' (a humble ode) in everyday language. Although Dante rejected the language of Virgil, he was nevertheless, the model to follow. 'A comedy, almost a popular song', Dante himself said, referring to his poem's subject and to his choice of the language of Tuscany. The choice of the medium was equally valid given the nature of the route to be followed: 'Comedy takes as its starting point the difficulties of a situation, but ends with a joyful epilogue, as Terence shows us in his own comedies.' In order to describe the 'harshness' of Hell, Dante wanted us to make use of 'harsh and raucous rhymes/as would befit this lugubrious hole'. He sought a perfect match of language and subject: 'This is why we have called our poem *Comedy*. If we consider its subject matter, it is, to begin with, horrible and disgusting, for it concerns Hell, but it becomes, in the end, happy, desirable and welcome, for it is then about Paradise, and if we look at the writing, it is straightforward and familiar since it is couched in the popular parlance of housewives when they talk to one another.' This 'horrible and fetid' matter, described with sustained realism, is characteristic of all *L'Inferno*. There are 'the horrible threshold', the 'horrible sands', the 'horrible noise' announced in a mounting cacophony at the entrance to *Hell* in the third canto:

Diverse lingue, orribili favelle,
parole di dolore, accenti d'ira,
voci alte e fioche, e suon di man con elle
facevano un tumulto, il qual s'aggira
sempre in quell'aura senza tempo tinta,
come la rena quando turbo spira.

Various languages and horrid tongues,
words of souls in torment, shrieks of rage,
loud, rasping voices, sounds of hands
  righting wrongs
were making a din that naught could
  assuage,
turning around in that ever sombre air
like a whirlwind-driven sandstorm lasting
  an age.

But this matter is also 'in the end happy, desirable and welcome', guiding our desire beyond that which is expressible, beyond memory, 'for as it gets closer to what it desires/our intellect goes down so deep/that memory is unable to follow it.'

Interpretations

This twofold register of the *Comedy*, where 'the awful mixture/of rain and shadows' was allied to 'the angelic singing' of a mystical vision, the trivial to that which transcended the trivial, the 'cesspool' to the place 'in which joy lasts forever', did not merely conform to the model suggested by Terence. It did not just revolve around the classical dictum that 'nothing of what is human is alien to me'. It also aimed to transcend the limits laid down by the theory of literary genres. This fact was first remarked on by Boccaccio in his *Life of Dante*, in giving an explanation of the premonition experienced by the poet's mother to whom 'a splendid peacock' had appeared. This peacock, Boccaccio tells us in his allegorical interpretation, was endowed with four remarkable 'properties': 'The first appertains to the fact that its feathers are those of an angel and each feather has a hundred eyes; the second relates to the fact that it has muddy feet and a silent gait; the third appertains to the fact that its voice is horrendous to the ear; its fourth and final property consists in its flesh being perfumed and incorruptible. These four attributes are the very ones that our poet's *Comedy* possesses fully.' The colourful plumage, the feathers of the angel were the elevated style of Dante's 'vision' of Paradise; the muddy feet represented 'the vulgar speech in which and above which the whole architectural structure of the *Comedy* is centred': a humble system of roots which nevertheless sustained 'the tree that draws life from its topmost branches'. The poet's gaze from on high, from the edge of the mystic Rose, constantly returned to the paths and strands of life on earth, 'to the tiny threshing floor that makes us all so fierce'. His judgement on history was delivered from the pit of eternity in a magnificently loud voice. Dante's voice reverberated like an apocalyptic trumpet. Boccaccio presented the *Comedy* as the book of the 'Dies irae' – of the Last

Judgement – written unchangeably by the great scribe, 'the book to be presented/in which all things are judged'. By applying the image of the peacock to Dante, Boccaccio was using a simile applied to Holy Writ in the ninth century: 'Scotus Erigenes said that the Holy Scriptures contain an infinite number of meanings and compared them to the changing plumage of the peacock.'

Above all, the image of the peacock confirmed the fact that the readers of the *Comedy* were conscious of being in the presence of an author destined to become the 'Christian Homer'. This was not only because of what Dante tells us about 'Homer the sovereign poet'; it also harked back to a tradition associated with Homer and the peacock to the effect that 'Homer was transformed at his death into a peacock which meant, for followers of Plato, that he had been able to adorn with the colours of poetry a wide variety of subjects.' Having expressed the inexhaustible variety of the cosmos, Homer earned the right to be turned into a peacock. Dante, on the other hand, according to the wonderful dream reported by Boccaccio, was born one.

The 'Christian Homer' was only the 'scribe' of his immortal book so that, assured of the book's everlastingness, as its author he could afford to be self-effacing: his work was merely to transcribe 'this sacred poem/in which heaven and earth have both had a hand'. The life of Dante was like his writing: not a single line of hand-written text, not a single genuine signature remain. There is no trace of his passage through time, as if he had decided to abolish his biography, to be totally contained within the pages of his book; as if he had chosen to make of his life an expiation for the sin of pride – 'for the sin of pride is the root of all evil' – which he believed he would have to atone for a while longer in Purgatory, once again faithful to the symbolic premonition: 'A peacock sitting on green grass betokens a man filled with pride.'

The *Vita Nova*

Dante retained in his *Comedy* something of the poetry he had written earlier: above all the verses of the *Vita Nova* (1291–1293). The *Vita Nova* alluded to Dante's meeting, at the age of nine, with Beatrice Portinari ('already comes the dawn of your beatitude') which was to remain, after Beatrice's premature death, engraved in his memory.

Beatrice is manifested in Dante's life as 'beatitude'. She reappears in *The Divine Comedy*, at the beginning of time and the human race, in the Garden of Eden, from whence she will lead the poet to joy eternal. After she appears ('Here is a god stronger than myself who has come to be my lord'), everything is reduced to a memory, the book of memory, of a memory which, from *La Vita Nova* to *Il Paradiso*, changed the past to a permanent present.

We rediscover *Vita Nova* in *The Divine Comedy* through an awareness of the novelty of new verse forms. The first verse of the first 'canzone' of the *Vita Nova* is repeated in *Il Purgatorio* when Dante meets those who have gone before him as poets in Tuscany, much as other formulas were repeated virtually unchanged from one work to the next. In this respect, the *Vita Nova* already more inaugurated than prepared that realm of 'last things' that we find in *The Divine Comedy*.

The continuous weave of Dante's work, which takes us from his *Rime* (*Rhymes*) to his *Divine Comedy*, also included the *Convivio* (*The Banquet*, 1304–1307), a doctrinal work which was never finished. The 'canzone' announcing Tract III of *The Banquet* was quoted and recited by the poet's friend, Casella, in *Purgatory*: 'Love which reasons in my heart/began then so gently/its gentleness still echoes in me.'

Theoretical works

'And if, in the present work, which I have just called *The Banquet*, and earnestly desire it should be so named, the subject should appear to have been treated in a more manly fashion than in my *Vita Nova* . . .' The plan Dante mapped out at the beginning of *The Banquet* reminds us of a 'fervent and passionate' work of his youth (the *Vita Nova*) and a 'manly and restrained exposition' (*The Banquet*), a mature work open to inspection by everyone, but destined to remain unfinished because from then on everything converged on that universal slice of life embodied in the *Comedy*. The altarpiece of a cathedral has been substituted for the atmosphere of a scholarly gathering that reigns in the *Banquet*, a fresco of the Last Judgement, a register of all time and all names. The language of this register is furnished by *De vulgari eloquentia* (*On Eloquence in the Vernacular*, 1303–1305), dealt with in two books which reveal the dignity of 'the illustrious common herd' that underscored the *Comedy*, while its royal seal comes from the treatise *De Monarchia* (*On Monarchy*, 1310–1317), written to defend the primacy of the emperor 'in temporal matters' and of the Pope 'in spiritual matters': 'Indeed it is clear that the whole human race inclines towards unity [. . .] and therefore it is needful that there be one to rule and govern, and he shall be called Monarch or Emperor. And it is clear that worldly wellbeing makes the existence of Monarchy or Empire necessary.' As the *Epistolae* (*Epistles*) of Dante showed this dream would not be realised. At the poet's instigation, Emperor Henry VII came to Italy, but he did not attack Florence. So Dante remained, banished in exile for the rest of his life.

Mysticism and memory

In accomplishing his ascent to the radiance of the divine glory, after beholding the dazzling mystery of the Holy Trinity and having attained to perfect contemplation of the Heavenly Kingdom, Dante seems in the final verses of his *Paradiso* to share his mystical stupefaction with us. But the only way in which he can do it is to quote what is inscribed in his memory, his first poem: 'Such I was at that new sight:/I wanted to see the join/of the image to the circle, how it was knotted there.' The 'new life' reappears to become 'new sight'. It is a 'sight' that turns 'life' into 'vision'. Struck down by the dazzling vision of the ultimate mystery, the 'scribe' is blinded to

such an extent that he forgets everything: 'Here the strength to sustain my sublime vision was lacking.'

So the mystical vision, anticipated and desired all the way through this cosmic poem of 100 cantos ('So my soul suspended/stared unmoving and attentive,/and continued to burn as it went on to gaze'), does not appear in the 'unifying oneness' dear to mystical tradition, but rather as the shadow of a memory that cannot be erased.

The last classical myth evoked in *The Divine Comedy* is that of Neptune who, in the ocean's depths, was stupefied, as Dante was now, at the end of his 'voyage', to see the shadow of the ship, the Argo, pass over him: 'And an instant brought me more forgetfulness/than the twenty-five centuries it took to forget the enterprise/which made Neptune marvel when he saw the Argo's shadow'.

The dream of the peacock, which, according to Boccaccio, prefigured the life of Dante, provides us with the last symbolic vestige of the *Comedy*, the deep intuition of a night into which melt the darkness of Hell, exposed to a hope, the twilight of Purgatory, exposed to the appearance of a divine being, and the clarity and lustre of Paradise, exposed to the prospect of a return, with, along the way, a sigh and the tenderness of the stars looking down: '[. . .] for the peacock signifies the Argo and the Argo is, in its turn, the sky which, during the night, seems only to be lit by the eyes of the stars.'

Petrarch (1304–1374)

C. Ossola

Eyes, nothing other than the eyes of memory, filled with memory.

Giuseppe Ungaretti

In a celebrated passage of the *Confessions* of Saint Augustine, 'it is, my heart, by you I measure time', we find a model and a spur for Petrarch's whole poetic vision of life. A generation after Dante, Petrarch (Francesco Petrarca) no longer believed in an eternal afterlife, in a journey whose end was signalled by a beatific vision. To conquer the boredom and the disrespect of a period of spiritual decadence, he found himself obliged to rediscover the classics, lost manuscripts and their voices; he conquered death by rediscovering the memory of a past love. Like Saint Augustine who declared: 'My thought entertains not things which are no longer there, but traces of them, permanently left behind,' Petrarch took refuge in the fixity of a memory which was still alive as he demonstrated in the opening sonnet of his *Canzoniere*:

> *Alma felice, che soventi torni*
> *a consolar le mie notti dolenti*
> *con gli occhi tuoi, che Morte non ha spenti.*

> *Oh happy soul, returning frequently*
> *To comfort me in nights of suffering*
> *With eyes that Death has not known how*
> *to make not see.*

As Ungaretti, Petrarch's literary heir, said, he was able to express everything in terms of memory: 'Eyes, nothing other than the eyes of memory, filled with memory.'

An absolute gaze

Time which carries us away with it ('we are dying as we live and, though we remain, we are still carried off') is transposed into an inner space, into a profound silence. Only the movement of the pen across the page, gliding over it like a stirring of leaves, inhabits and causes this silence to vibrate, as the following extract from one of Petrarch's *Verse Epistles* has it:

> *Dum levis aura papirum verberat*
> *et faciles dant carmina pulsa*
> *susurres.*

> *When a breath, a breath of air*
> *raises with a rustling noise a leaf, and*
> *verses imitating this tremble slightly.*

In this retreat of pure writing, time and death are finally abolished. The silence that buries monuments and fame is vanquished, according to the epic Latin poem *Africa* (1338–1342), by the silence of an absolute gaze that dissolves time, 'a silence white as snow papers over time'.

Time fed by memory

The age of humanism began and the Middle Ages ended with Petrarch. This is not just because of the intellectual repercussions of the Papacy's move from Rome to Avignon (the end of God's city on earth, formerly eternal and untouchable, was 'central' to things), repercussions more or less foreseen by Dante and often mentioned by Petrarch. But Petrarch put a distance between himself and some of the great medieval metaphors: life conceived of as a way forward, both as a 'peregrinatio' to Jerusalem and a journey into God. Petrarch did not abandon the journey. But he did not accept the aims that the medieval mind assigned to it of walking through the streets of Jerusalem and raising up one's writing to be pleasing to God. He refused to accompany his friend, Giovanni Mandelli, on his tour of the Holy Places, but instead, provided him with a guidebook, the wonderful *Itinerarium ad sepulchrum Domini* (*The Route to the Holy Sepulchre*).

Like Dante's Ulysses, Petrarch called himself a 'restless spirit, driven by an insatiable desire to see new things', but his borders were modern – those of Europe – and no longer the routes used by pilgrims and the crusading knights of medieval romances: 'It will be enough for me to travel over Europe and in Italy,' he wrote. His writing was remarkable for its reticence in the face of the mystery of the Trinity, seeking rather to dwell in 'un dolce fuoco', a gentle and intimate fire, fed by memory rather than by vision.

Fragments of a Discourse on Love: the desire for Laura

Writing shrank henceforth to the dimensions of the days of the year: Petrarch's *Canzoniere* was made up of 365 poems, one for each day of the year: a tireless prayer of love with an opening sonnet dedicated to readers whose ears are attuned to 'scattered rhymes', to verses as copious as tears, to 'fragments of a discourse on love' as the original title of *Rerum vulgarium fragmenta* seems to indicate. This rootedness in time came mainly from the reading and teaching of Saint Augustine, particularly from Petrarch's favourite work, Augustine's *Confessions*. Petrarch heralded humanism, not just because he placed the seal of time on writing – hence the themes of Death and Glory – but also because he travelled the length and breadth of Europe as if the latter were merely a vestige of time to be rediscovered. He was only twenty-nine in 1333 when he visited Flanders and the Brabant to rescue Cicero's *Pro Archia* from oblivion. Petrarch's journeys and retreats were interspersed with his love of letters and his desire for Laura, the young lady whom he saw and admired on 6 April 1327 in the Church of St Claire in Avignon, the town to which he had followed his patrons, the Colonna family.

The journeys and 'retirement'

Petrarch's journeys to Naples and Rome (in 1341), where he was crowned and anointed as a poet in accordance with an ancient and solemn rite, to Parma and Padua (1349–1351) and back to Rome in 1350, were always followed by a return to his beloved retreat in Vaucluse.

Even when he left Vaucluse to enter the service of Giovanni Visconti (1353–1361) in Milan, he always had a haven of tranquillity outside the town itself, near the charterhouse of Garegnano. There he spent his twilight years in the silence of another country retreat, that of Arquà. So Petrarch's itinerary was identical to Lucan's: 'the itinerary of a soul thrust into love'. His writing unfolded as a journey through the history of fame, whether this took the form of the procession of Roman heroes in his poem *Africa* (published posthumously in 1396) or the portrait gallery contained in *De viris illustribus* (*Of Famous Men*, written after 1338). The same thing

occurred in the *Bucolicum carmen* (*Rustic Song*) and in the letter *Posteritati* (*Posterity*), his biographic and literary last will and testament, where he was torn between the desire for glory and the call to a religious life. At the same time his writing carved out for itself a way down to the soul's inmost silences. His triptych of serious treatises bears this out: *Secretum* (*The Secret*, 1342–1358) and *De vita solitaria* (*On the Solitary Life*, 1346–1356), *De otio religioso* (*On the Happiness of the Religious Life*) are equally revealing of the fusion he managed between Classical morality, the Christian model established by the Church Fathers and his own spiritual meditations, which his brother Gherardo's 1342 entry into a monastery strengthened and brought into closer focus. To reach 'the intimate secret of truth': such was the hope evinced by a spirit of enquiry which could listen as attentively to Classical colloquies as it could to conversations with friends. Ample evidence of this was provided by Petrarch's books of epistles: *Familiares* (*Epistles to Friends*), *Seniles* (*Epistles of Old Age*), *Metricae* (*Verse Epistles*), *Sine nomine* (*Untitled Epistles*). Petrarch retained from this exploration an echo of the depths he has been to: 'I carry in myself my secret, my treasure and my wound.'

This internal retreat was above all a condensation of writing into the minimal space of sounds, into the music of words. The world unfolded by Dante was reduced to the dimensions of a small flask filled with the ink of memory, to an onyx light which radiated from the very depth of being. Petrarch was only too conscious of this contest with Dante. He wanted to gain eternity by writing in the vernacular and in *terza rima* as Dante had done. The *Trionfi* (*Triumphs*, 1352) were characterised by a progression that started and ended with Laura:

Se fu beato chi la vide in terra, or
che fia dunque a rivederla in cielo?

If he who saw her was happy on the earth,
what will it be like for him to see her again
in heaven?

The conceptual ascent happened under the auspices of beauty and concluded with it. Beauty, however, appeared as the contemplation of a gaze which had already achieved its 'intention'. The 'beautiful and charming faces' of *The Triumph of Eternity* possessed 'in addition to immortal beauty, everlasting glory'. This was the final, solemn consecration of Petrarch's ideals, the very ones the voice of Saint Augustine had reproached him with in the dialogue of the *Secretum* between the poet and the Father of the Church: 'love and glory'.

Laura's eyes

To enter the world of the *Canzoniere*, we must close our eyes to everything extraneous, according to the admirable suggestion of Gianfranco Contini, who has evoked 'Petrarch's special greatness, alchemy within four walls, unimaginable without them'. Contini was only translating into an act of writing the intention that Petrarch himself had concentrated on: Laura's eyes. Even if, in the mental space of the sonnet, the hands of the beloved entered the picture, blocking our view, the act of contemplation never stopped.

This is why, at the heart of this light, Petrarch's voice is so subtle: to understand it calls for 'long experience of life, extremely sharp senses and a prolonged process of mental staring' (Ungaretti). Fixity of the gaze and fixation 'of' and 'in' the gaze amount, in the literal sense, to that 'exorbitatio mea' mentioned by the *Secretum*. An 'unexpected flash' blinds the poet, plunging him into a 'splendid abyss'. Perhaps too much emphasis has been placed on the 'vaghezza' (vagueness) of the *Canzoniere* as this is compensated for by a tension which held the text together and the sonnet form which retraced its initial meanderings.

We must recognise two distinct elements in Petrarch's poems: the 'intentio' and the 'exhorbitatio', the 'piango e ragiono' (I weep and I talk) of the first sonnet. The halo of fiction, which Petrarch already knew hot to grasp so well, passed over perfectly controlled, 'fixed' diction: 'You will tell me that I have invented the name of Laura, that everything is artificial, even the sighs. If only in this you were right, would that it were a simulation and not true madness!' Certainly the name 'Laura', his laurel ('lauro'), the gold ('l'auro') of her hair, and the gentle breeze ('l'aura') belonged to an ancient tradition dating back to Ovid and the poets of Provence. What was new, in Petrarch, was that this imagery is formed by the fixation of a gaze and the fixity of memory.

Scattered fragments of the soul

The wish with which the *Secretum* drew to a close, 'let the world be silent', is the prerequisite of reading, and the vibrationless resonance of a word burning itself into other words like vitriol. It is a radiant peace emanating from the eyes of the beloved, from their adorable laughter: 'tranquil peace, devoid of torment,/eternal like the peace that reigns in heaven'.

The world has become noiseless, apart from the echo of private thoughts.

The poem of a single name, the writing of a single thought, Petrarch's poetry was a desire to store everything up, life and soul, memory and consciousness, in our hearts. The procedure decided at the end of the *Secretum* – 'I will gather up the scattered fragments of my soul' – was taken up again in the *Canzoniere*, a poem sealed inside Petrarch's heart, engraved like a medallion, set there like a diamond. Petrarch's poetry shed light on silence and out of these mirrors of silence Western poetry was born. 'Not only Góngora and Racine, Camoens and Shakespeare derive from Petrarch,' Ungaretti insists, 'but also Goethe, Leopardi, Mallarmé.'

In his *Sonnets*, Shakespeare knew better than anyone how to make this silence last into infinity, a wing and a wave bringing back all we thought lost:

When to the sessions of sweet silent thought
[. . .]
All losses are restor'd and sorrows end.

A veil spread with thoughts, an 'eternal wind of sighs', the voice of Petrarch.

Boccaccio (1313–1375)

M. Guglielminetti

I invoke here the testimony of all victims, present and past, of Love.

Boccaccio, Prologue to the *Decameron*

Giovanni Boccaccio (or Boccaccio) was universally known as the author of the *Decameron* (1349–1351) which has remained in the collective memory as an erotic and an anti-clerical work. Although this cannot be denied, it does not tell the whole story. After the *Decameron*, Boccaccio wanted to paint a portrait of himself very different to the one which has been handed down to us over the centuries – that of a natural poet whose literary vocation was undermined by his father, Boccaccio di Chellino. The latter, an agent of the Bardi trading company, wanted his son to be a merchant or, at the very least, in order to respect his love of humanistic studies, a lawyer.

A poet rather than a merchant

But Boccaccio thought of himself as a poet first and foremost, quite remote from the world of merchants and lawyers. Dante had already railed against lawyers in his *Banquet*; Petrarch, in turn, had declared himself the enemy of doctors in an *Invective* directed against them. They claimed for poetry the merit of not being a source of profit – poetry could not be bought. This was true to such an extent, Boccaccio added in his *Genealogia deorum gentilium* (*Genealogy of Pagan Gods*, 1350–1367), that all great poets, both ancient and modern, from Homer to Virgil, from Dante to Petrarch, were poor. If we take into account the fact that in the thirteenth and fourteenth centuries Florentine merchants were, to all intents and purposes, their city's paymasters and sometimes those of a number of European courts, we can understand the potency of Boccaccio's faith in poetry. To live for poetry meant to be opposed to the economic tendencies of his own society.

The struggle between Boccaccio and his father had nothing Oedipal about it. We know nothing about his mother other than the fact that she was not married to his father. He had a stepmother who supported his father by putting a spoke in the young poet's idealistic plans, but eventually she too had to acknowledge defeat.

The Lover of Love

It was between 1330 and 1340, in Naples and then in Florence, that Boccaccio deferred to his father's wishes the most. But of everything he could then have known of the business and commercial world, nothing appeared in the works of this period. Nothing of it appeared in the *Filocolo* (*The Lover of Love*, 1336), which told of the amorous problems and vicissitudes of Floire and Blanchefleur, two pagans who had converted to Christianity; nor in *Fiammetta* (1343–1344), an evocation full of the pathos of a desperate love: the heroine, a Neapolitan widow, weeps because she has been abandoned by her lover who has been recalled to Florence by his father (note the autobiographical elements). None of this knowledge of the world of high finance appears either in *L'Ameto* (or 'comedy of nymphs in Florence', 1341–1342), a novel and a poem at the same time. This sometimes harked back to autobiographical elements, but was mostly allegorical. It told the story of a long, complex rite of purification which transformed a shepherd, an 'animal', into a 'man' with the help of a nymph and her companions, servants of Love. As was evident from these three novels, and was also demonstrated by *Il Ninfale fiesolano* (*The Nymph of Fiesole*, 1344–1346) and other short poems (*Il Filostrato, Philostratus*, 1337–1339; *Teseida, The Theseid*, 1339–1340), Boccaccio adapted to his work a literary mishmash of language and situations derived from many different sources, but all indebted to Latin or post-Latin originals. The courtly novels of France, the reworkings of classical poems to suit courtly taste and the Italian epic poems of chivalry (the 'cantari') were the models he followed.

But he already knew Petrarch and of his plan to revitalise classical poetry. In 1339 he wrote Petrarch a letter in Latin, full of affectation, in which he declared himself 'surrounded by the darkness of ignorance, clumsy, like an inert mass barely licked into shape'. He expected to obtain from Petrarch, a master whose doctrine shone like the sun, the means to rid himself of his social clumsiness, his lack of harmony, his ignorance, so that in his turn he could be supple and admirable. This was a clear admission of his cultural inferiority to someone acquainted with and well versed in the Latin classics of Cicero, Livy and Virgil.

The *Decameron*

However, Boccaccio did not immediately abandon the culture of his youth. Apart from the *Genealogy*, he wrote, as a disciple of Petrarch, the lives of Dante and Petrarch, the biographies of particularly unfortunate famous men, *De casibus virorum illustrium* (*On the Misfortunes of Famous Men*, 1355–1360) and famous women, *De mulieribus claris* (*On Ladies of High Renown*, 1360–1362) and a catalogue of geographical place names taken from classical authors: *De montibus, silvis, fontibus . . .* (*On Mountains, Woods and Fountains . . .*, finally published in 1481).

Before he became Petrarch's disciple Boccaccio launched himself into a genre – the short story – to which neither Dante nor Petrarch had ever paid attention.

Boccaccio's *Decameron* (the ten days) was published soon after 1348 when the plague had sown death and destruction in Florence and was a response to the civil and social chaos caused by the epidemic. To tell the stories in his book (ten a day, therefore a hundred altogether) Boccaccio imagined that seven young women and three young men had left the town to seek refuge in a villa in the Tuscan hills where they discovered a life of leisure and elegance. They interspersed their stories with songs and dancing, recreating the time and space of a comfortable social life made pleasant by good meals and tasty morsels. Our first impression of the *Decameron*, particularly for anyone who has been through the manu-

scripts which were quickly circulated all over Europe, is that a small core of people have been exalted. Without being noble by birth, they practise the virtues of the upper aristocracy, rolled, at that time, into the one magic word of 'courtesy' and undermined, more than anything, by the vice of 'avarice'. This key to reading the work is suggested by the first series of ten stories: i.e. the first day. Rather than celebrate commercial virtues, or retrace their epic value, Boccaccio took pains to denounce the desire shown by this section of society to assert itself. So the story of Ser Ciappelletto recounted the skilful transformation of a usurer into a saint, without making fun of those who, like the friar confessor and the man in the street, fell into the trap of misjudging him.

The second and third days have as their protagonists people who have managed to achieve difficult aims and objectives, sovereigns and merchants, sailors and monks, nuns and widows. The most famous is Andreuccio of Perugia, a rich, clumsy horse-trader, received in Naples by a prostitute he has stupidly taken to be a great lady; he falls into a barrel of night soil after having been stripped of everything, including his clothes.

Is this book of stories really a mercantile epic? Is not the merchant, on the contrary, subjected to physical degradation and his way of earning a living held up to contempt? On the third day, we are ushered into the presence of Masetto di Lamporecchio, a gardener in a convent who 'sows' his own seed in the sisters as well as the seed of plants, and the monastic recluse Rustico, who teaches the naïve Alibech the best way to have his 'devil' enter her 'hell' with a success that goes beyond his wildest dreams. The *Decameron* has always been thought of as a satire on the clergy and Boccaccio himself was terrorised by a Carthusian monk who threatened him with divine punishment unless he stopped writing profanities: he did, in fact, take minor orders and found himself entrusted with the care of souls. To make of him a medieval Voltaire is absurd, even if the idea was endorsed by Voltaire himself on the basis of the story of Ser Ciappelletto. The main intention of the work was to satirise behaviour and value systems normally taken for granted, such as the prudence of merchants, the virginity of nuns, the continence of hermits. The fourth day is devoted to telling about tragic loves – stories that included the possibility of women as heroines in a world turned upside down. Indeed, the *Decameron* was dedicated to women in order to provide them with a diversion as they were not allowed to practise male activities like catching birds, fishing, riding or setting up in business.

The day begins with the story of Gismonda, a widowed princess in love with a servant. After her father, obsessively jealous (he has been described as a 'voyeur'), has barbarically killed her young lover, cutting out his heart to send it to his daughter in a goblet, Gismonda, before poisoning herself, delivers a magnificent speech on the rights of the 'flesh', equally divided between men and women, and on 'virtue', the sole criterion in the choice of a partner companion:

Sono adunque, sì come da te generata, di carne, e sì poco vivuta, che ancor son giovane, e per l'una cosa e per l'altra piena di concupiscibile desiderio, al quale maravigliosissime forze hanno date l'aver già, per essere stata maritata, conosciuto qual piacer sia a così fatto disidero dar compimento [. . .] Di che egli pare, oltre all'amorosamente aver peccato, che tu, più la volgare opinione che la verità seguitando, con più amaritudine mi riprenda, dicendo, quasi turbato esser non ti dovessi, se io nobile uomo avessi a questo eletto, che io con uomo di bassa condizione mi son posta; in che non t'accorgi che non il mio peccato ma quello della Fortuna riprendi, la quale assai sovente li non degni a alto leva, abbasso lasciando i degnissimi.

Part of you, I am a thing of flesh. And I have lived so little that I am still young: all the more reason to feel deep within myself that appetite for love that an early marriage, revealing to me the joy of a desire fully satisfied, only served to whet. [. . .] I have committed a sin of love admittedly. But are you not closer to

public opinion than to the truth by blaming me so harshly for having stooped to love beneath me? You seem to be saying you would not have been so put out had I chosen a lover of noble descent! Can you not see that I am not on trial here but Fortune? All too often it is Fortune that elevates the least worthy and leaves the most worthy to eke out a lowly existence.

A woman is the mouthpiece of a polemic against the 'Fortune' of a social hierarchy. Once again, Boccaccio takes it on himself to modify the social pyramid. To disturb an already established vertical perspective is only hypothetically possible for a princess, and even then it is no easy task. In the case of women from more modest backgrounds, like Elisabeth of Messina whose lover was murdered by her three brothers (all merchants), again because of class differences, Boccaccio reasserted his protest against the unnatural values of a male-dominated society differently, and with greater delicacy. Elisabeth learns in a dream where the body of her lover is buried. She goes there, cuts his head off and buries it in a terracotta vase. Then she plants basil in the vase and waters it with her tears until she dies of grief. Their suspicions aroused by her sorrow and by the fuss she makes of the basil plant, her brothers steal the vase and discover the macabre truth. The description of the silent suffering of Elisabeth means as much if not more than the protest voiced by Gismonda.

Boccaccio had based this fine story on a popular song, in which a woman laments the theft of her basil plant. However, he has made it a metaphor for a now impossible sexual relationship, so that Elisabeth's brothers also attack the symbolic plant and, by killing it, destroy both the woman and her love.

The fifth day, still given over to loves that proved difficult but this time had happy endings, narrates complicated land and sea adventures experienced by old-world characters from days gone by with the personal charm befitting knights and courtiers.

Similar, but confined to the nearby town of Florence itself, is the sixth day on which names like Giotto and Guido Cavalcanti, the poet of the 'dolce stil nuovo' and Dante's friend appear, two intellectuals well able to defend the dignity of their profession against the attacks of benighted bourgeois philistines. We also find, in their vicinity, the cook Chichibeo, the baker Cisti and the irresistible Brother Cipolla. These heroes of a moment are past masters when it comes to talking and calculated gestures. The same is true of the perpetrators of hoaxes who inhabit the seventh, eighth and ninth days, mostly men, but occasionally women who excel in the art of preventing their husbands from finding out about their illicit, but scarcely secret, love affairs. The *Decameron* thus runs the risk of dissolving into laughter. Even if, among the objects of ridicule, there are priests, judges and abbesses, Boccaccio wanted to take his leave of the reader in a way that underlines the seriousness of his aspirations to a new and better world.

The tenth and final day celebrates love's great deeds and other events in which the people involved were, for the most part, doubly aristocratic in both soul and birth – sovereigns and nobles past and present, from both East and West. But a bandit and a peasant woman, Griselda, were also included. The story of the peasant woman who becomes the wife of a marchese, but who is forced to undergo the most terrifying tests before she can be truly married to him, shows that 'heaven can cause to be born in thatched cottages spirits endowed with divine grace'. Yet again, a polemical stance refused to accept passivity and took on a powerful hierarchy in the name of open-mindedness. It is not surprising that the story of Griselda was a runaway success throughout Western Europe.

The *Corbaccio*

In the *Corbaccio* (*The Ugly Crow*, 1354–1355 or 1364–1365), the author imagined that he had met the soul of a widow's dead husband in a fictitious location with the symbolic name of Love's Pigsty. The deceased denigrates his wife, both physically and morally, which

perhaps suggested the work's title (in medieval bestiaries the crow symbolises love because it pulls out the eyes and the brains of its victims). In passing, the husband also finds a way to praise the life Boccaccio had chosen, wholly devoted to the love of letters. Such a life did not brook female company. Hence, the road to misogyny becomes possible with the corollary, in Boccaccio's case, of giving the impression that *The Ugly Crow* is a kind of recantation for *The Decameron*, at least as far as any fundamentally positive view of women and their rights are concerned. However, one of the stories contained in the *Decameron* discusses the vengeance of a 'clerk' on a widow indifferent to his love and who cruelly punishes him for his misplaced passion. This notion of 'recantation' can, in this light, be seen as excessive.

Posterity has long preferred the Boccaccio of the *Decameron* to the Boccaccio of the *Genealogy* and the other Latin writings, where he draws the ideal portrait of a man of letters exclusively devoted to study. Even the language of the *Decameron* ended up by seeming overly literary, for example, to Stendhal, who came to prefer Bandello as a source for his *Chroniques italiennes* (*Italian Chronicles*). He referred to Boccaccio, in *Promenades dans Rome* (*Walks in Rome*), as 'a professional man of letters'. In such a way literary reputations are sometimes eclipsed. Indeed it is through the cinema that our contemporaries have rediscovered certain stories of Boccaccio in Pasolini's film version of the *Decameron*

Chaucer (c.1340–c.1400)

J. Smith

Unknowe, unkist and lost that is unsought.
Geoffrey Chaucer, *Troilus and Criseyde*

On the list of obligatory places the modern tourist should visit in London is Westminster Abbey, where many of the men and women to whom Great Britain owes her national heritage are buried. At the heart of this pantheon of great people of the past is Geoffrey Chaucer, laid to rest in 'Poets' Corner'. The place seems ideal for the man John Dryden called 'the father of English poetry'. However, it is not only because of his literary talents that Chaucer lies buried here: it was for a servant of the Crown that the solemn funeral service was held, in 1400, in Westminster Abbey. Chaucer carried out the orders of his royal paymasters not only within the kingdom itself, but also abroad, where he served as both soldier and diplomat.

This combination of individual ability and a flair for public service is a characteristic of the great humanists: Petrarch, Erasmus, Budé, More and Casaubon to name but a few. This is why Chaucer also occupies a place in this select company of 'Renaissance men'. It is thus inevitable that his works should be steeped in early European Renaissance culture. Nevertheless, recent criticism has tended to focus on the medieval, 'Gothic' aspect of his work, both thematically and stylistically. Chaucer was, as it were, half-way between two worlds – the Middle Ages and the Renaissance – and two philosophies of life: his own peculiar genius allowed him to express the tension between these two ways of seeing.

An exemplary destiny

We do not know exactly when Chaucer was born. In 1386 he was called as a witness to give evidence at a trial and stated he was 'forty years of age and upwards', partly satisfying our curiosity about him and displaying a typically medieval vagueness about dates. He was probably born some time between 1340 and 1345. His father, John, was a London wine merchant whose business prospered. In his youth Chaucer enjoyed the benefits conferred on him by London's cosmopolitan culture in the Middle Ages: he had as neighbours Gascons, Italians and Flemings. He may have been a pupil at St Paul's Almonry. While still in his teens he worked as a page in the household of Elizabeth de Burgh, Countess of Ulster, wife of Lionel, one of the sons of Edward III. An incomplete book of accounts

mentions clothes and gratuities bestowed on the young Chaucer. He followed Prince Lionel to France, along with the invading army of Edward III. Around 1359 to 1360 he was taken prisoner at Rethel, near Rheims, but the king set such great store by his services that £16.00 were withdrawn from the royal coffers to defray the cost of the enemy's ransom and he was released. From 1360 to 1380, or thereabouts, he acted as the king's messenger: there are still traces of certain diplomatic missions that he undertook to France, Navarre and Italy.

In 1365 Chaucer married Philippa de Roet, one of the queen's ladies-in-waiting, subsequently enjoying a position of some privilege at court. The king appointed him Comptroller of Customs and Subsidies on Wools, Skins and Hides. This was an important administrative post in London, connected to the payment of duty on wool, England's main import. Up until the late 1370s Chaucer apparently carried out his duties with great efficiency, but, during the following decade, he started to delegate his authority to subordinates. In this way he found time to forge political links with the county of Kent, and was eventually elected its Knight of the Shire. He may then have left London to settle in Kent. In 1389 Richard II gave Chaucer the post that was destined to become the most important post of his career, that of Clerk of the King's Works, responsible for the building and upkeep of all properties belonging to the Crown. After Richard II was deposed in 1399, Chaucer's services were retained by Henry IV. In the same year he moved house to be near the court, taking a fifty-three-year lease on a house near the Chapel of St Mary, Westminster. He died not long afterwards, in 1400.

The father of English poetry

Chaucer led a very active life. Nevertheless he found time to write for the court circles in which he moved the poems that made him famous, from his translation of *The Romaunt of the Rose* to *The Parlement of Foules*.

Chaucer was the first great poet to write in English since the Norman Conquest (which raised French to the status of most prestigious tongue for almost the whole of the medieval period) just at a time when English was becoming the native language of the descendants of the Norman conquerors. The literary use to which Chaucer put English was therefore almost without precedent. The choice of English for a work not lacking in philosophical depth drew attention to itself from the first 'literary critic' to cast an eye over Chaucer's writings: the French poet, Eustache Deschamps. Around 1386 he sent Chaucer a ballad written in his honour. Addressing himself to Chaucer directly, Deschamps exclaimed: 'Thou Socrates, full of philosophy . . .' and even: 'Great as Ovid in thy versifying . . .' Chaucer is 'eagle of the heights', contemplating sublime truths, and a prolific love poet. According to Deschamps, Chaucer had 'planted the rosebush and scattered the flowers/For those who but know the tongue of Pandras'. The 'tongue of Pandras' probably means French. Pandras, in medieval legend, was a Greek king vanquished by Brutus, the Trojan founder of Great Britain, to whom it owes its name. Deschamps thought that, Chaucer had endowed with nobility a language which, until then, had only been used by yokels and the ignorant.

The Book of the Duchesse

In some ways, Chaucer was a 'translator' of European literature. Though it is no longer fashionable to speak of a 'French' or an 'Italian' period in his work, he was obviously familiar with literary works written in both these languages. His career as a poet began with *The Romaunt of the Rose*, a straightforward translation of *Le Roman de la Rose* by Guillaume de Lorris and Jean de Meung. We have yet another partial translation into Middle English of this work, but we are not sure if it was Chaucer's. *The Book of the Duchesse* (1368–1369), undoubtedly by Chaucer, was written to commemorate the death of Blanche, Duchess of Lancaster and

wife of the all-powerful John of Gaunt. The narration of this incident has been worked into the courtly style of poetry in France at this time, that of Guillaume de Machaut in particular. However, it is more a case of allusion than plagiarism. As a counterpoint to the narrative, Chaucer adds the story of Ceyx and Alcyon, taken from Ovid's *Metamorphoses*. He also deliberately draws our attention to other passages in other works which dealt with similar misfortunes, so as to partly alleviate his noble patron's grief. *The Book of the Duchesse* can be thought of as the 'translation' of a situation in 'French' into an 'English' idiom. In the first lines of the poem, stock phrases and padding refer back to the ancient oral traditions of the romance in Middle English. Chaucer was trying to use the literary English at his disposal to convey concepts hitherto unexpressed in it.

The House of Fame

In *The Book of the Duchesse*, Chaucer revealed very little of his knowledge of European literature. Quite the opposite is true when we come to *The House of Fame*, probably his next work. Here he showed signs of a personal culture exceptional in a medieval Englishman. Apart from Ovid and Machaut, he alluded to Virgil, Boethius, the Bible, Jean de Meung and Froissart as well as to Dante and Boccaccio, indicative of a strong Italian influence. The subject of *The House of Fame* was one of the topics most frequently broached during the Middle Ages: the problem of authority. Chaucer, however, reached a far from medieval conclusion. The eagle, one of his most successful comic inventions, shows itself only too willing to enlighten the apprehensive narrator about the perfectly orderly structure of the universe, but the categorical assertions of the bird are somewhat undermined by what happens in the House of Fame. Surrounded by statues representing the poets of the past with their unimpeachable reputations, Dame Fortune condemns both the good and the bad in this world to a reputation not necessarily related to anything in real life. We can see just what uncertainty that implies about the notion of authority. In his perplexity, the narrator finds himself face-to-face with a man of great authority about to express an opinion – but this is where Chaucer's poem breaks off.

The Parlement of Foules

The House of Fame treated the theme of love with great dexterity. The theme, which had also been touched on in *The Book of the Duchesse*, appeared again in Chaucer's third 'dream vision', *The Parlement of Foules* (*c*.1382), a poem written in celebration of St Valentine's Day. In this sense it is merely an 'occasional work' which nevertheless contained the same level of philosophical complexity as a work of art such as Botticelli's *Spring*. Just like Dante, guided through hell by Virgil, the narrator of *The Parlement of Foules* is given a conducted tour by another guide from Antiquity, Scipio Africanus, the principal protagonist of Cicero's *Somnium Scipionis*. Scipio leads the narrator to a wonderful garden where everything seems to function in perfect harmony with its own essential nature. Discordant elements, however, soon rear their ugly heads: the Temple of Venus with its embodiments of lust and its decorations call to mind tragic love affairs. Also in the garden is the central thrust of the poem: the birds' debate before the noble goddess Nature. According to a legend current in medieval times, all the birds chose partners on St Valentine's Day. In the poem this is indeed what happens in most cases, but three male 'tercel' eagles fight for the female 'formel' eagle perched on Nature's wrist. The three males make use of the exaggerated language of 'courtly love'. Since this 'fair love' is characterized by an object that remains out of reach, it is hardly surprising that none of the male birds manage to win the hand of the female: she asks for a year's grace to ponder her decision. The other birds, delighted to see the debate drawing to a close, make such a din with their singing that the narrator wakes up.

Shortly after he had finished writing *The Parlement of Foules*, Chaucer set himself the task of translating Boethius' *Consolation of Philosophy*.

It was in *Troilus and Criseyde* (*c*.1385), Chaucer's most important work of the 1380s, that poetically speaking he harvested the fruits of his translation of Boethius. The main source for *Troilus and Criseyde* was Boccaccio's *Philostratus*, written at the end of the 1330s. This time, however, Chaucer had no compunction about totally transforming his Italian original. Using as his starting point Boccaccio's sad, cynical narrative, Chaucer constructed a tragedy worthy of Boethius, centred on the motif of the Wheel of Fortune. The subject of the story is well-known: Troilus, a Trojan prince at a time when Troy was at war with Greece, falls in love with Cressida, the daughter of Calchas the traitor, a Trojan high priest who has defected to the enemy leaving Cressida in Troy. Pandarus, the friend of Troilus and Cressida's uncle, encourages the two young people to become lovers. Calchas, however, arranges an exchange of prisoners and Cressida is handed over to the Greeks in exchange for Anthenor, a Trojan prince whom the Greeks have captured – and who will, finally betray his country. Cressida promises to remain faithful to Troilus, but she is rapidly seduced by Diomedes, a leader of the Greeks. Chaucer, who looked on man with deep compassion, punctuated his narrative with reflections on the ephemeral nature of the things of this world and on the importance of everlasting spiritual truths.

The Canterbury Tales

The Canterbury Tales is Chaucer's final work and also his longest, even though it remained unfinished. These tales are an almost perfect synthesis of the conventions asociated with the period and a realistic portrayal of itinerant humanity. The work is so rich and varied that it is impossible to summarise it in detail. Chaucer passes seamlessly from the novel of courtly love to the fabliau, from homily to parody and penitential tract, thanks to the unifying frame of the pilgrimage to Canterbury, and the tomb of Thomas à Becket. In

The Legend of Good Women Chaucer had already attempted to find a narrative thread to connect the different stories, but the unifying principle was too narrow: there were not enough stories about truly 'good' women – like Dido – and few occasions to display even the gentlest of ironies – with the exception of the story of Cleopatra. *The Legend of Good Women* was never finished. Perhaps Chaucer was taking up Gower's idea which consisted in providing an overall framework based on an activity linked to religious observance. He was probably also inspired in his research by the group dynamic as well as the relationships between individual characters in Boccaccio's *Decameron* – which he only knew indirectly.

Chaucer was a complex individual, difficult to identify with any one culture: he embodied the transition between two ways of looking at the world. After his death, the critical debate about him moved on. Each historical period is sensitive to a particular aspect of his work. So, for example, in the fifteenth century, John Lydgate, who considered himself a disciple and imitator of Chaucer, admired his master for his lexical ability. William Caxton, England's first printer, took a similar view. Although he paid discreet homage to the 'philosophical' value of Chaucer as a poet, Caxton was interested, above all, in Chaucer's language as well as his refinement of the 'crudity' of English. In the editions of Speght (1598) and Urry (1721), Chaucer enjoyed the well-established renown of a man who, part of a now venerable past, gave the English language dignity. Dryden, one of Chaucer's most perceptive critics, compared him to Ennius, the poet of ancient Rome, but he also saw the full extent of Chaucer's poetic powers: 'Here is God's plenty.' Romantic critics such as Leigh Hunt, a friend of Keats, emphasised Chaucer's passionate nature or his imagination. It may be because of this somewhat limited vision of poetry that in his famous criticism of Chaucer Matthew Arnold reproached him with his lack of 'seriousness'. The vision of Chaucer which has best stood the test of time is that of Eustache Deschamps. The latter pointed out not only Chaucer's rhetorical qualities, but also his talent for philosophising, his undeniable common sense and the interest he took in the power of love. In the final analysis, it was only natural that the most cosmopolitan of English poets should have found his most far-sighted critic on the Continent.

7 *Renaissance Humanism (1450–1550)*

H. BOTS AND C. HEESAKKERS

I have placed you in the middle of the world
to make it easier for you to examine the things
that are around you in the world.

Pico della Mirandola,
The Dignity of Man

The dream of a great Christian Europe foun-
dered in 1453 with the fall of Constantinople.
The world of Islam gained a permanent
foothold in the south-eastern Mediterranean
and the Balkans. Western Europe started
to turn in on itself. Until then, Eastern Slavs
had had the feeling of belonging to a united
Christendom, even if their liturgical dependence on Constantinople drove them further
and further away from their 'Latin' co-
religionists, considered to be heretics by the
Greek Orthodox hierarchy, and the use of
Slavonic as a liturgical language confined
them, culturally speaking, to the Orthodox
fold. Some of these Slavic practitioners of the
Greek rite found themselves in the fourteenth
century under the tutelage of Lithuanian
princes, pagans to begin with, then converts
(in 1386) to the Latin strand of Christianity.
This religious pluralism helped to turn this
part of Europe into a bastion of tolerance.

The abdication of Emperor Charles V in
1555 brought this period to an end. It provoked a new geographical division of Europe
with Emperor Ferdinand I and the King of
Spain, Philip II, sharing Charles' erstwhile
empire. This division coincided with the split
in Western Christendom: after the Peace of
Augsburg, the Reformed Church was openly
recognised politically and enjoyed the same
rights as the Roman Catholic Church in

certain states. At the Council of Trent, Rome
started to reform its Church's inner workings
and reformulated its articles of faith.

But for European literature and thought, the
breaking in two of the West and its turning
in on itself was a process of fermentation
generated by a return to original sources. It
contained the triumph of humanism and the
proliferation of new universities. It heralded
the birth of a veritable community of literature
and culture which went beyond all frontiers:
the Republic of Letters. A new interpretation
of the Bible and the rise of printing favoured
the furthering of the Reformation.

EUROPEAN HUMANISM OR THE RETURN TO ORIGINAL SOURCES

The literary world of the second half of the
fifteenth century was largely influenced in
Europe by Renaissance humanism as it had
developed in Italy during the preceding
period. There were the 'studia humanitatis',
the return to original sources – 'ad fontes' –
and the new method applied to Biblical texts,
involving the dedicated study of Hebrew.
These were practised by many literati while
humanists in Italy continued the work of their
predecessors.

Humanism in Italy

Humanists not only edited and pruned the
texts of classical authors, but themselves wrote
works in which they applied the methods of
creative imitation. Poggio Bracciolini was a

good example. His *Liber facetiarum* (*Humorous Anecdotes*, 1438–1452), a collection of spicy, amusing tales that papal secretaries would tell to one another by way of diversion, gave rise to many imitations in the vernacular in various countries all over Europe.

Equally characteristic of the spirit of humanism was an encyclopedic thirst for knowledge of the world. **Enea Silvio Piccolomini (1405–1464)**, elected Pope in 1458 with the name of Pius II, visited many European countries as a diplomat and devoted certain treatises to the history and geography of some of them. Among his works the short story *De duobus amantibus* (*The Two Lovers*, published in 1531), has often been translated and imitated in national literatures. In Florence, the town of the Medicis, some humanists founded a Platonic Academy in 1457. Marsilio Ficino, Leon Battista Alberti and Pico della Mirandola were its most prominent members. **Marsilio Ficino (1433–1499)** made the complete works of Plato more accessible with a translation into Latin. **Giovanni Pico della Mirandola (1463–1494)** wrote what was later considered to be a humanist manifesto, *De hominis dignitate* (*The Dignity of Man*, published in 1486): man is the only being who can decide his own fate. God the Father speaks in the following terms to Adam:

> *Medium te mundi posui, ut circumspiceres inde commodius quidquid est in mundo.*
> *Nec te cælestum neque terrenum neque mortalem neque immortalem fecimus, ut tui ipsius quasi arbitrarius honorariusque plastes et fictor, in quam malueris, tu te formam effingas.*
> *Poteris in inferiora quæ sunt bruta degenerare; poteris in superiora quæ sunt divina, ex tui animi sententia, regenerari.*

Pico della Mirandola,
De hominis dignitate

> *I put you in the middle of the world to make it easier for you to examine all that is around you in the world. You have been created neither a celestial nor a terrestrial being, neither mortal nor immortal, so that, master of yourself and having as it were the honour and the duty to fashion and to model your own being, you may make unto yourself the form you yourself would have chosen. You are able to degenerate into lower, animal forms, you are also able, by virtue of your own will, to regenerate yourself in higher forms which are divine.*

In Italy, a section of artistic and literary life was determined by the courts. The papal court included several humanist writers, such as Bembo or Iacopo Sadoleto (1477–1547). The court of Naples, with its humanist kings of the houses of Aragon and Anjou, attracted poets such as Giovanni Pontano (*c.*1426– 1503) and Sannazaro. In Ferrare the court of the d'Este family made it possible for Ariosto to complete his masterpiece, and the court of the Montefeltros in Urbino inspired **Baldassare Castiglione (1478–1529)** to write his famous *Cortegiano* (*The Courtier*, finished in 1518, published in 1528), a work devoted to the education and behaviour of the typical courtier. Here four serene discussions held in 1507 are described for four successive nights at the court of Urbino, about the physical and moral qualities that the good courtier should possess, and the way in which he should behave towards other courtiers, his superiors and women. Great value was attached in particular to the literary education of the courtier. The work ends with a eulogy of Platonic love for women delivered by Bembo, himself a courtier at the court of Urbino from 1506.

In Florence, the cultural radiance emanating from the Medicis took on the attributes of a court under Lorenzo the Magnificent. Here **Niccolo Machiavelli (1469–1527)**⋆ conceived and wrote *Il Principe* (*The Prince*, finished in 1513, published in 1532). Here too Guicciardini worked on his histories.

Other European courts fostering literary activity evolved along the same lines. The court of Burgundy, for example, played a considerable part in developing Romance language literature in areas which make up present-day Belgium. In the official court circles surrounding Philip the Good, *c.*1460, the still anonymous collection of the *Cent Nouvelles Nouvelles* was written, deriving from Boccaccio's *Decameron*, without its structure, together with the *Humorous Anecdotes* of Il Poggio. The narrators were the Duke of Burgundy himself and some of his advisers and servants, who took their inspiration from everyday life. This work gives us 100 bawdy stories satirising women and religious. In the final phase of Philip the Good's reign, literary exchanges with other courts, with those of Charles d'Orléans and René d'Anjou, for example, became more intense. Margaret of Austria kept a brilliant literary circle going at the court of Malines. She was, in particular, a patron of Jean Lemaire, one of the precursors of Renaissance French literature.

During this period literature was not just the prerogative of those who lived at court. A new social class, beside the nobility, the clergy and the bourgeoisie, grew up at this time, that of intellectuals and learned people, among whom were lawyers, doctors and teachers. The literature we owe to them is as often about erudite themes as about daily life, far from court, dominated by ordinary people.

This humanistic, sometimes intellectually complex literature was usually produced in large centres of urban population in which universities and academies had pride of place. Italy also had the Platonic Academy of Marsilio Ficino in Florence, the Accademia Pontaniana of Pontano in Naples and the Accademia Romana of Giulio Pomponio Leto (1428–1498). These institutions were meeting places where humanists discussed philological and stylistic problems. The Accademia della Crusca, founded in 1583 with a view to purifying and enriching the Italian language, belonged to the same tradition.

The republic of letters

In all the centres of intellectual excellence of the period, secular and religious literature was elevated to cult status. As Italy attracted a great number of travellers, and because of the political and ecclesiastical influence of the Papal States, Italian humanists became the tutors of Europe. The lessons of their humanism were universally accepted, and men of letters soon came to constitute a veritable literary and cultural community, a transnational superstate called the 'Respublica literaria et christiana': literary and Christian republic. The members of this republic of letters felt duty bound to transcend regional, political and religious differences. Sharers of a common language – Latin – writers and scientists of all shades of opinion formed friendships and devoted themselves to the pursuit of literature and science. They were proud of their free State which was considered to be the true home of all 'viri boni' (good men): all those who cultivated the 'studia humanitatis' (humanities) and belles-lettres.

For those who lived in the republic of letters, a literary exchange of views 'communicatio' (communication) was an indispensable priority. Meetings between humanists, however, were only possible for a privileged group. Among them were students on their 'peregrinatio academica' conducting them to various universities and centres of intellectual excellence, members of diplomatic missions, a number of priests, both secular and regular, or other members of the clergy travelling through Europe to take part in ecclesiastical conferences. Most humanists often had to be content with writing letters as a way of participating in a Europe-wide exchange of views. In this way the letter, considered from the outset as an authentic literary art form, became the preferred means of communication between the denizens of the republic of letters. Many treatises were written on the subject of letter-writing, including Erasmus' *De conscribendis epistolis* (*The Art of Writing Letters*, published in 1521). Those who cultivated this art did not hesitate to polish their letters, even after they were sent. Erasmus and many of his contemporaries, from youth onwards, considered editing their own correspondence.

Humanism also developed outside the most famous centres of intellectual excellence: in Poland, in Bohemia, in Hungary, as well as in towns on the Dalmatian coast of Croatia, where the use of Latin did away with all linguistic obstacles.

> Ipse ego te, rediens etiam paulo ante,
> saluto A Batavis [. . .].

Johannes Dantiscus,
Ad Herbenstenium Solera

> I myself, who have just come back from a journey to Holland, greet you [. . .].

This was written by **Johannes Dantiscus (Jan Dantyszek, 1485–1548)** after his first trip to The Netherlands. This Polish poet, who wrote in Latin and left behind didactic and morally edifying works, contributed to the acceptance in Louvain of the discoveries of Copernicus, who, in 1543, had published his major work containing the theory of heliocentrism, *De revolutionibus orbium cœlestium* (*The Revolutions of the Heavenly Bodies*).

The greatest neo-Latin poet of Central Europe was undoubtedly, the Hungarian **Janus Pannonius (Csezmiczei, 1434–1472)**. A faithful servant of King Matthias Corvinus – humanist and patron of the arts – had been educated in Ferrara at Guarino's Guarini well-known school of humanism. He was famous for his eulogies of his tutor, Guarini, and of the painter Mantegna.

Universities and humanities

From the second half of the fifteenth century in Europe, new, modern monarchies came into existence which needed sizeable bureaucracies. This soon led to groups of qualified civil servants, which in turn gave considerable impetus to secondary and higher education.

Alongside certain big towns with well-established university traditions, like Paris or Prague, new universities were founded in Europe. The German-speaking countries had Freiburg-im-Breisgau (1455), Mainz (1476), Tübingen (1477), Basel (1459), Wittenberg (1502), Frankfurt-am-Main (1506), Marburg

(1527) and Königsberg (1544). Scandinavia had Uppsala (1477) and Copenhagen (1479). In Scotland there were Glasgow (1453) and Aberdeen (1493); in France, Nantes (1463) and Bourges (1465); in Spain, Barcelona (1450), Valencia (1501), Seville (1505) and Granada (1531). In Hungary there were Buda (1465) and Debrecen (1531) and in Portugal in 1537 the University of Coimbra was reorganised.

Many universities remained bastions of old-style scholasticism, inimical to the methods of humanism, especially in countries dominated by Catholic theology. Such was the case, for example, in Paris and Louvain: both universities were unceasingly criticised by Erasmus. In countries where old universities remained very conservative, the cause of literature and science was advanced by the new academies of humanist persuasion. Renaissance humanism did not exert its influence everywhere simultaneously.

In France humanistic studies gathered momentum with the creation of a chair of Greek at the University of Paris in 1456, when Gregorio Tifernas arrived to teach rhetoric and Greek language. But humanism only really devevloped several decades later, thanks to direct contact with Italians, among whom were Fausto Andrelini, the great friend of Erasmus, and Girolamo Aleandro (1480–1542), made responsible in 1521 for obtaining from the Emperor the banishment of Luther at the Diet of Worms. **Jacques Lefèvre d'Étaples (c.1450–1536)**, a former pupil of

Pico della Mirandola, laid claim to fame with his annotated edition of Aristotle and his studies of scripture, including an edition of the Epistles of Saint Paul. He also translated into Latin a work by Ruysbroec, *De ornatu spiritualium nuptiarum libri tres* (*Three Books on the Adornment of Spiritual Weddings*, 1512). The influence of the hellenist **Guillaume Budé (1467–1540)**, educated, like Lefèvre d'Étaples, by Hermonymus of Sparta, the exiled teacher from Greece, was such that in 1530 he persuaded the King of France, François I, to found the College of Royal Readers, the present-day Collège de France. Lefèvre thought the study of Greek was essential in order to confirm the orthodoxy of the Roman Catholic Church. Stating the opposite view, Budé, in his *De transitu hellenismi ad christianismum libri III* (*Three Books on the Transition from Hellenism to Christianity*, 1529), affirmed that too much enthusiasm for secular classical literature harmed both the study of scripture and the Christian tradition.

In Spain, **Antonio de Lebrixa**, better known under the name of **Nebrissensis (1444–1522)**, after twenty years in Italy, returned to his country to teach Salamanca and Alcalá de Henares, in Seville, and to publish Latin, Greek and Hebrew grammar books. The Colegio de San Ildefonso at the University of Alcalá was an important centre for humanism. Here the *Biblia complutensis* was compiled, a multilingual Bible in which the Greek version of the New Testament was composed and printed in 1514, two years before that of Erasmus, but only published in 1520 because of censorship.

The Dominican **Lucius Andreas Resendius (de Resende, *c*.1500–1573)** was a friend of Erasmus whom he met while studying in Louvain. On returning to Portugal he taught in Lisbon and Evora. He defended a humanist education in his poem *Adversus stolidos politioris literaturæ obtrectatores* (*Against Elegant Literature's Stupid Detractors*, 1531), and published a Latin grammar in 1540.

In The Netherlands, humanism was partly promoted by the brothers of the 'devotio moderna' who welcomed poor pupils into their schools. On graduating from one of them, **Rodolphus Agricola (1444–1485)** undertook a long and peripatetic university education, visiting in close succession the universities of Erfurt, Cologne, Paris and Louvain. He then went to Italy to complete his humanistic education in Pavia and Ferrara. The most important contribution by this influential humanist was *De inventione dialectica* (*On Dialectical Invention*, 1479), a systematic guide to humanist rhetoric.

Erasmus (*c*.1466–1536)★ is himself supposed to have benefited from the good offices of a brothers' monastery in Bois-le-Duc ('s-Hertogenbosch). In 1517, he attended the founding by Hieronymus Busleyden of the Collegium Trilingue (Trilingual College) in Louvain, where the accent was placed on Greek, Latin and Hebrew and on the reading of authentic source materials. Erasmus no doubt contributed to the nurturing of humanities at this university founded at the beginning of the fifteenth century, in which medieval and scholastic methodology had previously dominated as it had in other universities of the time. The Spaniard **Juan Luis Vives (1493–1540)** left Spain in 1509 to pursue his studies in Paris. Several years later he began to study philology at Louvain, met Erasmus there *c*.1516 and settled down permanently in the Netherlands. In his major work *De disciplinis* (*On Disciplines*, 1531), Vives emphasised the importance of a humanist education by describing the decline of scholastic erudition and by indicating the ways in which courses of study could be improved. Although Latin remained for him a universal language of first use, the vernacular also had a place in his eeducational system. Moreover, the practice of the humanities must go hand-in-hand with an individual's moral and religious education. In his treatises *De institutione Feminæ christianæ* (*On the Education of the Christian Woman*, 1524) and *De subventione pauperum* (*On the Upkeep of the Poor*, 1526), Vives pleaded for better education for women and a better system of relief for the poor.

Italian humanism was also recognised in

Vienna. Piccolomini spent more than ten years there, from 1442 to 1452, compiling an important treatise on education. Four years later, a Chair of Humanities was established at the university in Vienna. The impetus to humanism in German-speaking countries was given by Reuchlin, Celtes and Melanchthon. **Johannes Reuchlin (1455–1522)**, a celebrated scholar of Hebrew and author of a handbook and dictionary of Hebrew, fostered study of the Cabbala. He also composed two humanist comedies (*Sergius*, 1496; *Henno*, 1497) from which Hans Sachs later borrowed material. Conrad Celtes (1459–1508) unearthed old Latin documents and composed the lyrical verses of the *Amores* (*The Loves*, 1502), inspired by Ovid, as well as Horatian odes, works published posthumously in 1513. The reforming plans proposed by the humanist and theologian **Philipp Melanchthon (1497–1560)** for a humanist education in Protestant schools and universities won him the name of Præceptor Germaniæ (Tutor of the German-speaking Lands). Thanks to his *Elementorum rhetorices libri II* (*Two Books on the Elements of Rhetoric*, 1531), he strongly influenced the teaching of the Latin rhetoric used by succeeding generations.

The paradoxical title of *Enconium Moriæ* (*In Praise of Folly*, 1511) by Erasmus is also a eulogy of Thomas More, homophonic similarity making possible this play on words. More, Grocyn, Latimer and Colet, all Erasmus' friends and contemporaries, cultivated the study of humanities in England. The theologian John Colet (1467–1519) persuaded Erasmus to devote himself to 'sacræ litteræ' ('sacred literature'), to the study of Greek and that of the Bible.

Thomas More (1478–1535), the most original humanist in England, achieved immortality with his masterpiece *Utopia* (1516), a work which criticised contemporary English society by contrasting it with an idealised and fictitious one. Inspired by Vespucci's *New World*, Saint Augustine's *City of God* and Plato's *Republic*, More delved into sources both ancient and modern, religious and secular, although it is not always easy to discern his true intentions. *Utopia* has been hijacked by various ideological movements, all of which found in it a statement of belief in keeping with their own ideas. More's social critique is indirect but effective. Many virtues preached by Christian Europe were in reality hardly respected. A good part of the Christian way was travelled in *Utopia*, in a land where Christ was unknown. Utopians had no fear of death, enjoyed their work, honoured their friends and disliked outward show, conspicuous consumption and wealth. They eliminated dirt and poverty and avoided war. They adopted a rational approach to marriage but, once entered into, it was held to be sacrosanct. Divorce, however, was accepted: religious tolerance was a basic principle for them, which is quite surprising on the eve of the Reformation.

Vtopus enim iam inde ab initio, quum accepisset incolas ante suum adventum de religionibus inter se assidue dimicasse, atque animaduertisset eam rem, quod in commune dissidentes singulæ pro patria sectæ pugnabant, occasionem præstitisse sibi uincendarum omnium, adeptus uictoriam in primis sanxit uti quam cuique religionem libeat sequi, liceat; ut uero alios quoque in suam traducat,	*Utopus at the beginning of his reign learnt that before his coming the inhabitants had had bitter debates on the subject of their beliefs. They were divided into sects that, hostile to each other, fought separately for their country. Thus they presented him with an opportunity to conquer them all at once. Once victorious, he decided that each should be able to profess freely the religion of their choice, but could not proselytise other than by expounding, with calm*

hactenus niti possit, uti placide ac modeste suam rationibus astruat; non ut acerbe ceteras destruat, si suadendo non persuadeat; neque uim ullam adhibeat, et conuiciis temperet; petulantius hac de re contendentem exilio aut seruitute mulctant.

Thomas More, *Utopia*

and moderation, their reasons for believing, without acrimoniously attacking those of others, and, if gentle persuasion was of no avail, without resorting to force and to insults. Whoever engages with excessive fanaticism in quarrels of this nature is punished by exile or slavery.

The influence of humanism: writing in one's first language

In contrast to the first wave of Italian humanism, Renaissance humanism had an influence on the vernacular languages and literatures of various European countries. During the second half of the fifteenth century, Italian was cultivated afresh, subject to the direct influence of Latin as written by classical authors. The new Italian literature of this period evolved because of the artistry of authors whose knowledge of classical Latin literature was equal to their familiarity with great Italian writers such as Petrarch or Boccaccio.

Angelo Poliziano (1454–1494), an influential neo-Latin poet and philologist, contributed to the flowering of Italian literature with his *Favola di Orfeo* (*The Fable of Orpheus*, 1480), a play staged in Mantua, in which he elaborated a classical theme in a literary form borrowed from Christian tradition. This was considered to be the first secular Italian play. Its inspiration, however, was more lyrical than dramatic, reminiscent of Virgil's rustic idylls. In the *Stanze per la giostra* (*Stanzas for a Tournament*, 1475–1478), Poliziano took his inspiration from classical Antiquity, adding fourteenth-century lyrical elements.

Pietro Bembo (1470–1547), a neo-Latin writer who cultivated Cicero's classical rhetoric in its most unadulterated form, pleaded for the use of his mother tongue in *Prose della volgar lingua* (*Prose in the Vernacular*, 1525). Bembo – who was almost too servile in his imitation of Petrarch – recommended the use of the Tuscan dialect employed by fourteenth-

century writers, a special pleading which had a marked effect on the development of the Italian language. Bembo's 'Petrarchism', known also as 'Bembismo', also revealed itself in *Gli Asolani* (1505), dialogues about the influence of love on morality. Bembo made a significant contribution to the dissemination of Petrarch's work and to the consolidation of its influence, not only in the *Asolani*, but also in his *Rime* (1530). Spaniards, Englishmen, Portuguese, Greeks, Croats and Frenchmen, poets from all over Europe saluted a master in Petrarch.

In France the movement to promote French language was spread over two distinct phases. First there were attempts by the humanist Christophe de Longueil, whose prose style had been strongly influenced by Cicero and according to whom, in his eulogy of Saint Louis (c.1508–1509), France and French could hold their own in every respect with Italy and Italian. This was a thesis taken up in 1513 by Jean Lemaire de Belges in his *Concord of Two Languages*.

The second phase of this promotion of the use of French took place in the reign of François I. It culminated in the work of **Joachim du Bellay (1522–1560)**, *Deffence et Illustration de la langue françoise* (1549), largely inspired by the *Dialogo delle Lingue* (*Dialogue between Languages*, 1542) by the Italian Sperone Speroni. French was only just beginning to flourish and still required nurturing with the imitation of ancient authors and the use of all available sources of vocabulary: provincial, archaic and technical. Du Bellay encourages young poets not only to seek out the company of learned people, but also 'sundry mechanicals, like sailors, foundry workers, painters, engravers and others; to know their inventions, the names of their tools and materials, and the terms used in their crafts and professions so as to make fine comparisons and lively descriptions of all that is therein'. He proclaimed that French was a language of philosophy. Evidently encouraged writers to write in their first language, particularly poets, advice which was taken by the poets of the Pleiad. Thus **Jacques Peletier du Mans (1517–1582)** dedicated the following verses to 'a poet who wrote only in Latin':

J'écris en langue maternelle	*I write in my native tongue*
Et tâche à la mettre en valeur,	*And try to do it justice*
Afin de la rendre éternelle,	*So as to make it immortal*
Comme les vieux ont fait la leur,	*As the Ancients did theirs,*
Et soutiens que c'est grand malheur	*And I maintain it to be a great misfortune*
Que son propre bien mépriser	*To despise one's own property*
Pour l'autrui tant favoriser.	*To prefer someone else's.*

Jacques Peletier du Mans,
Oeuvres poétiques

The promotion of literary language in the vernacular was quite different in the southern Netherlands. Here it was rather chambers of rhetoric which, in the context of their 'literary competitions', contributed to the formation and purification of a single ubiquitous literary language.

In Spain the influence of humanism enriched Catalonian culture with knowledge of classical authors and those of the Italian Renaissance – Dante, Petrarch and Boccaccio. At the same time, this humanism tended to further the cause of Latin as a vehicle of culture at the expense of Catalan. **Garcilaso de la Vega (c.1501–1536)**, influenced by both Italian and classical models, initiated a new lyricism in poetry with his sonnets and elegies. His *Egloga* (*Eclogue*, published in 1543) was inspired by Sannazaro's *Arcadia* (1502) and the bucolic poetry of Virgil.

Is there a more vibrant profession of faith in Portuguese than the *Diálogo em Louvor da Nossa Linguagem* (*Dialogue in Praise of Our Language*, 1540) by **João de Barros (c.1496–1570)**? The author of *Ropica Pnefma* (*Spiritual Merchandise*, 1532) placed his humanist education at the service of social, moral and religious criticism along the lines of Erasmus' *In Praise of Folly*. His historical work was inspired by the Decades of Titus Livius. In 1540 his *Dialogue* contributed to the defence and illustration of the Portuguese language, as did his *Gramatica da Lingua Portuguesa* (*Grammar of the Portuguese Language*), published at the same time. In the sixteenth and seventeenth centuries, this work became the indispensable model for all those who tried to defend the national language. **Francisco de Sá de Miranda (1481–1558)**, a poet and letter-writer, spent some time in Italy, where he discovered the new poetic forms of the Renaissance such as the sonnet, the elegy, the eclogue and the epistle. Back in his own country, he introduced these new forms while continuing to cultivate the old traditional ones.

Some great works had a lasting effect on their country's language. Such was the case for *Orlando furioso* (1516) by **Ludovico Ariosto (1474–1533)**[*] in Italy, for the translation of the *Psalms* by Clément Marot and for *Gargantua* by Rabelais in France, and for *The Ship of Fools* by Sebastian Brant in German-speaking lands. From now on, native languages, elevated to the level of literary languages, were no longer considered unworthy of being used to treat religious subjects.

Literature and the Reformation

A return to original sources was an invitation to Christians of the fifteenth and the sixteenth centuries to rediscover the unblemished quality of original texts and that of the original Church in the first centuries of the Christian era. This new humanist mentality, born of a different way of reading Biblical and patristic texts, and the errors and abuses characteristic of the Church at that time, led to the twofold Reformation, both Protestant and Catholic, of the first half of the sixteenth century. The philologists of this time reread the Bible critically and in the original languages: the Old Testament in Hebrew, the New Testament in Greek. This return to reading the Bible increasingly took place at the expense of the authority of received tradition and liturgy.

> *Optarim, ut omnes mulierculæ*
> *legant Evangelium, legant*
> *Paulinas epistolas . . .Utinam*
> *hinc ad stivam aliquid decantet*
> *agricola, hinc nonnihil ad radios*
> *suos moduletur textor, hujusmodi*
> *fabulis itineris tædium lenet viator.*

Erasmus, *Paraclesis*

Martin Luther (1483–1546),* who also promoted the reading of the Bible, was responsible in 1522 for a German translation of the New Testament, and then in 1534 of the entire Bible. This translation served as a model for many other non-German-speaking areas of Europe. First it was imitated in The Netherlands by Jacob Van Liesvelt (*c.*1489–1545), who published his edition of the New Testament in 1526, partly availing himself of a previous translation published in Cologne in 1480. In Sweden, Olaus Petri (1493–1552) collaborated on the first Swedish translation of the New Testament published in 1526, as well as on the first official Lutheran translation of the Bible (*Gustav Vasas Bibel*, 1541), thus making an important contribution to the creation of modern Swedish. In Denmark, Christiern Pedersen (1475–1554) translated the Bible in 1550. Other translations followed in Icelandic (1584), Slovene (1584) and Hungarian (1590).

It is from the sources themselves that doctrine must be drawn.

Erasmus

The Reformation needs to be considered as another given characteristic of the literature and culture of this period. For a humanist like Erasmus or a reformer like Luther, the motto 'ad fontes' or 'It is from the sources themselves that doctrine must be drawn' implied that every believer should read and inwardly digest the sacred message of the Bible so that the Word of God could speak directly to them. Those who had a good knowledge of Biblical languages could respond to this invitation, but for most Christians such a reading of the Bible was out of the question. Erasmus wrote in *Paraclesis*:

> *Moreover I should like*
> *women to read the Gospel and*
> *the Epistles of Saint Paul, for the*
> *farm labourer and the weaver to*
> *sing them as they work,*
> *and for the traveller to recite them to himself*
> *to alleviate his travelweariness.*

Certain translations were not exclusively traceable to that of Luther. William Tyndale (*c.*1494–1536) drew up an English translation of the New Testament, which appeared in printed form in Worms in 1525. Although Miles Coverdale (1488–1568) could not read Greek or Hebrew, he translated the Bible on the basis of the Vulgate and versions established by Zwingli and Luther; his edition was published in Zurich in 1535. The second 1537 edition appeared in England with the king's approval. This translation formed the basis for the Anglican authorised version of the Bible in 1611. These two translations by Tyndale and Coverdale had a marked effect on the language of the Anglican liturgy, and were often quoted in literary English. In France, Lefèvre d'Étaples undertook the translation of the New Testament in 1524 and that of the Old Testament in 1530, followed by the whole Bible in 1534. The Calvinist Pierre-Robert Olivetan (1506–1538) translated the whole

Bible into French in an edition which appeared in Neuchâtel in 1535. The translation of the *Psalms* by Clément Marot in 1543 was a major literary event because of the quality of its language. It was immediately accepted by Calvin for the purposes of worship, which carried with it a considerable audience.

Jean Calvin (1509–1564), like all humanists, had read the Bible in its original languages. In 1541 he published a French version of his 1536, *Institutio*, under the title *Institution chrétienne (Christian Institution)* In it he outlined the fundamentals of his theology 'to be of service to we French'. His personal translation made a major contribution to the advancement of French prose. Alongside this summary of dogma – a veritable body of doctrine based on scrupulous exegesis – he promoted the reading of the Bible with many commentaries on the Old and New Testaments. In conjunction with this, Calvin organised the life of the emerging Church in Geneva (1536–1537), in Strasbourg (1537–1541) and again in Geneva (1541–1564). He promulgated *Ordinances* (1541), drew up a profession of faith and set out his *Catechism* (1537, revised in 1542) in the form of questions and answers, a kind of charter for the young community. Preoccupied with education and training, he founded the College of Geneva in 1541 and then, in 1559, the Academy of Geneva for the training of pastors, of which Théodore de Bèze was the first rector. Calvin thus because one of the greatest architects of the Christian Reformed Church.

Translations of the Bible by Eastern Slavs were of quite a different order. In the eleventh century they were already familiar with certain books of the Bible – the New Testament, the Pentateuch, the Psalms – in Old Church Slavonic. The attempt at translation discernible at the end of the fifteenth century was linked to the appearance, first in Novgorod, of the heresy of the so-called 'would-be Jews'. In order to fight it more effectively, Gennadius, the Archbishop of Novgorod, decided to commission a rendering of the whole Bible into Russian Slavonic for which it was necessary to translate all the missing books on the basis of the Vulgate version of the Bible. Gennadius' initiative had nothing to do with the aspirations of Reformers or Pre-Reformers: rather it was indicative of the efforts of the Counter-Reformation. This Slavonic Bible, finished in 1499, was the foundation for a printed edition which appeared in 1581 in Ostrog, in the kingdom of Poland, and was then reprinted in 1633 in Moscow. An edition which is still used by the Russian Orthodox Church.

The work of the Byelorussian **Francis Skorina (c.1490–1541)** hardly stands up to comparison either with movements aimed at religious reform. From 1517 to 1519 in Prague he published a large part of the Old Testament in a Slavic translation. Even though this was designed for 'the moral instruction of the common people', its language was still Slavonic, despite the odd word here and there borrowed from Old Byelorussian. Slavonic, wrongly thought of as a vernacular language, was still revered as a liturgical language. Maximus the Greek (1480–1556) learned this to his cost: a former pupil of Italian humanists, he became a monk on Mount Athos and was called to Moscow in 1525 to amend Slavic Biblical manuscripts. Having tried to correct them by referring to versions in Greek, in 1531 he was accused of 'failing to respect all sacred Scriptures in our land of Russia, of having been critical of them and of having asserted that there are no books in Russia, neither Gospel nor Psalter'. He was condemned to life imprisonment.

Cyril and Methodius' audacity with regard to the Slavs had led to a linguistic and cultural petrified forest which left the Russian Orthodox Church almost totally severed from humanism and the Reformation. Even today, Russian is the only literary language in Europe not used as a liturgical language.

New ideas and the acquisitions of humanism were disseminated thanks to secondary education, then given through the medium of Latin schools and colleges. This dissemination was accelerated by the invention of typesetting which humanists and reformers made able use of to communicate their new ideas. This new art, which permeated the whole of Europe, changed beyond recall the way in which information was disseminated and ideas exchanged.

The art of typesetting

From the last quarter of the fifteenth century, the art of typography developed all over Europe. The process had begun with Gutenberg's invention in Mainz. The printing c.1453 of forty-two lines of the Bible, the first great achievement of the new art, demonstrated the possibility of producing texts cheaply in a series. Immediately after the invention was patented, Gutenberg's associates, Fust and Schoeffer, started to conquer a European market. The town of Mainz itself soon lost its monopoly and typographers were to be found throughout Europe. Around 1460, Fust and Schoeffer settled in Paris where they opened a shop. They also sold their books in Frankfurt, Lübeck and Angers. Others opened small offices with printing presses: from 1464 to 1466 in Cologne, then in Basle, Constance and Augsburg in 1468 as far as German-speaking countries went. In Italy in 1465 the printers Conrad Sweynheym and Arnold Pannartz set up in Subiaco, near Rome. In 1469, John of Spiers was to be found in Venice, where he printed Cicero's *Letters*. The first book to be printed in France came off a printing press in Paris in 1470: the *Letters* by the Italian humanist Gasparino Barzizza. Lyon followed suit in 1473, Angers and Toulouse in 1476, Poitiers in 1479. In Bohemia printing began c.1470 with the *Trojanská kronika* (*Chronicle of Troy*). In The Netherlands the first books were printed in 1473 in Utrecht, at the premises of Nicolaus Ketelaer and Gerard Van der Leempt, and in Aalst, near Antwerp, at the premises of Dirk Martens – who later published More's *Utopia* – and Johann Van Westfalen. In Poland the first printing press was set up in Cracow in 1474. England had its first printing press in 1476, when William Caxton, who had learned the new art in Cologne and worked in Bruges, came home to set up shop in Westminster.

So printing developed apace in Europe and, towards 1500, books like other merchandise became subject to the laws of the market. Many centres of printing sprang up. There was one in Venice where Aldo Manucci set up shop in 1494. Paris and Lyon had theirs in the print shops of Josse Bade, Jean Petit, and a little later those of Robert Estienne, Sébastien Gryphe and Étienne Dolet. There was one in Basle, where Jean Froben managed a print shop from 1513. There was also one in Antwerp, where almost half of the printers who settled in The Netherlands between 1500 and 1540 (sixty-six out of 123) were found. From the first half of the sixteenth century, these workshops produced a mass of printed literature for a growing group of customers. If printing immediately lent itself to the dissemination of ideas, it also made it possible for the Renaissance to have access to the great literary works of Antiquity. Many ancient texts were printed together with imitations of them in Latin and vernacular languages.

EPIC LITERATURE

The great literary genres of the period continued to be epic and didactic literature. Poetry and theatre continued to develop while one-off phenomena appeared from time to time: Dutch chambers of rhetoric, for example, and the 'romancero' in Spain.

Neo-Latin epic literature

During this period when Renaissance humanism penetrated all corners of culture, 'imitatio' and 'æmulatio' were the basic building-blocks for all literary activity. Many humanist writers aimed to write a Latin which could rival, in terms of both form and content, the great models of Antiquity: Cicero, Virgil and Livy. Epic literature was no exception.

In 1513 the Neapolitan humanist **Iacopo Sannazaro (1456–1530)** wrote *De partu virginis* (*The Motherhood of the Virgin*), an epic poem in three books along Virgilian lines. Although Christ's birth was the principal theme, the poem contained allusions to classical and pagan mythology. It was one of the first epic poems to be written in neo-Latin. It was generally well received, despite critical carpings about its mixture of sacred and secular elements and some overdramatisation of what was merely hinted at in the Gospel account. Sannazaro used a phrase from the

Gospel according to St Luke as his starting point: 'The Holy Spirit will come upon you, and the power of the Most High will over-shadow you.' He then dramatised this text by making the Annunciation concrete in a way which was almost impertinent:

Tantum effata, repente nova	*Hardly had she spoken than*
micuisse Penates	*suddenly, she saw the dwelling*
Luce videt [. . .], nitor ecce	*shine with a supernatural*
domum complerat: ibi illa,	*radiance, the whole house*
Ardentum haud patiens	*being filled with it. Unable*
radiorum ignisque	*to bear the hot flame of the*
corusci,	*rays and the flashing glints*
Extimuit magis. At	*of this fire, she became afraid. But*
venter [. . .] sine vi, sine labe	*her womb [. . .], without being in the least*
pudoris,	*subject to violent attack or the slightest*
Arcano intumuit Verbo: Vigor	*affront to her modesty, was*
actus ab alto	*impregnated by the mysterious Word.*
Irradians, Vigor	*A force from above,*
omnipotens, Vigor omnia	*radiant, an omnipotent*
complens	*force, an all-pervasive*
Descendit, Deus ille, Deus,	*force comes down on her:*
totosque per artus	*it is God, God Himself*
Dat sese miscetque utero:	*who is united with her whole being and*
quo tacta, repente	*who mingles with her womb; her entrails*
Viscera contremuere . . .	*tremble at His coming . . .*

Iacopo Sannazaro,
De partu virginis

Christiados libri VI (*The Six Books of the Christiad*, 1535) by the Italian Marco Girolamo Vida (1485–1566) was an epic poem characterised by this same mixture of Christian and pagan elements. Vida's style is so like Virgil's that it sometimes seems as though we are reading him instead. Despite an overly intrusive rhetoric and servile imitation of its model, this Christian epic influenced the work of other Christian epic writers such as Tasso, Milton and Klopstock. The reprints and translations of this work into several languages proved to its popularity. The Croatian humanist Jakov Bunić (1469–1534) also wrote an epic devoted to the life of Christ.

The Latin epic poem which was the most accomplished of its age was *Syphilis sive de morbo gallico* (*Syphilis or On the French Disease*,

1530) by the doctor Girolamo Fracastoro (1478–1553). This work, dealing with such a curious theme for a poem, was dedicated to Bembo and was reprinted many times. Sixteenth-century critics thought that only Sannazaro's epic could be compared to Fracastoro's. Its author had wanted to show that even such an unprepossessing subject could lend itself to poetry.

Epic literature in the vernacular

Apart from authors who wrote in Latin, the number of those who wrote in the vernacular also increased. The themes that had inspired epic writers in the Middle Ages also continued to play a part in literature during this period. Thus we find in Polish literature (1510) as in

Hungarian (edited *c*.1572), Greek and Czech literature a pseudo-historical romance: *The Story of Alexander*.

We also find ancient themes in Russian epic literature which, at the end of the fifteenth century and the beginning of the sixteenth, had a short-lived revival. Collections of Old Testament apocrypha, known as *Paleja*, and their novelistic elements were also a source of the production of epics.

The first epic to be written in Croat, called *Judita* (*Judith*, 1501), published in 1521, was by **Marko Marulić (Marulus, 1450–1524)**. Biblical legend was reinforced by real life: the siege of Jerusalem served as a dramatic metaphor for the threat of a Turkish invasion.

The inspiration of the Middle Ages played a major part in the Italian poetry of chivalry. The character of Roland had been celebrated before Ariosto by Luigi Pulci (1432–1484) in *Morgante Maggiore* (*Morgante the Giant*, 1460–1470). Matteo Maria Boiardo (1441–1494) returned to the theme of Roland in his *Orlando innamorato* (*Roland in Love*, 1486). This poem of chivalry took its inspiration from the epic poem of Carolingian times and from the novel of courtly love of the Arthurian cycle: the theme of physical prowess went hand-in-hand with that of love.

Italian epic poetry from previous centuries continued to influence Europe: the *Teseida delle nozze di Emilia* (*The Theseid of the Wedding of Emilia*) by Boccaccio was faithfully translated into Greek *c*.1500.

From the epic to the novel

Derived from the romance in verse, prose fiction began to develop in France from the middle of the fifteenth century. Only the form was new; novels of adventure and chivalry were much appreciated by the reading public and were disseminated in large quantities through the channel of printing in its infancy. Such was the case for *Fierabras*, a novel which recounted Charlemagne's adventures, mixing sources from history, legend and poetry and taking up from where former accounts had ended. The first prose novel to be printed

(1478), it went through twenty-six editions from 1478 to 1588. This text was a good example of the songs of heroic deeds revamped for contemporary tastes, revised and adapted, which Cervantes ridiculed in *Don Quixote*.

The success of these novels encouraged some writers to publish a sequel to satisfy public demand. *Renaud de Montauban*, having gone through twenty-seven editions, contained additional episodes in some editions.

The vogue for novels of chivalry was only rivalled by that for adventure stories, for *Robert the Devil* or *Huon of Bordeaux*. These texts were translated and adapted to satisfy the demands of an increasingly voracious public: *Amadis of Gaul*, compiled by Montalvo in Spain in 1518, was adapted by Nicolas Herberay des Essarts from 1524. It took several years to publish its twelve folios. The translator tried to prove the existence of a French original and took every opportunity to glorify Gaul.

there is no doubt that he was first manifested in French, being Amadis the Gaul and not the Spaniard. And that such is the case I have found as evidence a remnant of an old hand-written manuscript in the dialect of Picardy, on which I surmise that a Spanish translation was based.

Amadis of Gaul, translated by
Herberey des Essarts

In Dutch literature, the same phenomenon could again be seen. Medieval texts such as *Floire and Blanchefleur*, *Renaud of Montauban* or *The Chatelaine of Vergi* were adapted, modernised and put into prose in printed books. The adventures and their meanings were looked at 'from the outside', which led to a much more explicit narrative mode. The gradual transition from reading aloud to silent, personal reading perhaps also elucidated the use of narrative techniques designed to play on the reader's emotions.

An English variant was found in *Morte d'Arthur* (*The Death of Arthur*) by Sir Thomas Malory (*c*.1410–1471). This prose novel, completed *c*.1470, was about the fictitious reign of King Arthur and about his knights in search of the Holy Grail, a symbol of the aspiration to Christian perfection. Apart from this, prose novels in English were clearly subject to French influence. Some of them, such as the *Prose Merlin* or *Valentine and Orson* were, as in Dutch literature, translations or adaptations of French originals. As well as quite free Russian translations of medieval epics, there was also an original work dating back to the first half of the sixteenth century, *Povest' o Petre i Fevronii* (*The Tale of Peter and Febronia*), by the monk Ermolai-Erasmus. Originally conceived as a hagiography, it belonged to the novel genre, as it included a belated echo of the theme of Tristan and Isolde.

DIDACTIC AND SATIRICAL LITERATURE

Literature of this period in Europe was strongly redolent of humanism, whose great representatives were frequently tutors and teachers. Traces of it were everywhere discernible. Literature aimed to improve both the individual and society, either with morally edifying and educational works, or with critical, even satirical works, which condemned human vices and the abuses inherent in ecclesiastical and social institutions.

> One can, in general, say of men that they are ungrateful, changeable, hypocritical, ready to run away from danger and always wanting to be on the winning side.
>
> Machiavelli, *The Prince*

Satire and social criticism

In the neo-Latin literature of this period, the satires of Horace and Juvenal were the great models to follow. Taking his lead from their example, the Italian humanist Filelfo was the first to publish a collection of satires in verse in his *Satyrarum opus* (*Book of Satires*, 1476), in which he was severely critical of his enemies and the abuses current in his time. In Northern Europe, the genre was represented by the neo-Latin historian **Gerardus**

Geldenhauer (called **Noviomagus, 1482–1542**), who published the *Satyræ octo* (*Eight Satires*) in 1515. Less subtle and more biting is satire by the German humanist Ulrich von Hutten (1488–1523) and by certain other German scholars, expressed in the *Epistolæ obscurorum virorum* (*Letters from Lowly Men*, 1515–1517). Here the sterile pedantry of scholastic theologians at Cologne University is held up to ridicule, after the latter had cast aspersions on the work of Reuchlin with the princes of the Church.

Erasmus' *In Praise of Folly* was the most important satire of this period. It unmasked the wisdom of this world as the lunacy it really is, singling out as the highest wisdom the ultimate lunacy in men's eyes: that of the Crucifixion.

Didactic treatises

Renowned for their teaching, humanists were more than once entrusted with the education of young princes. Many treatises on children's education, were attributable to Piccolomini, Erasmus and Vives. Humanists believed that a good education for a prince was a way of building a better society, governed by a wise, just king. The *Institutio principis christiani* (*Education of a Christian Prince*), drawn up by Erasmus when he was official adviser to Charles V in 1516, is the most influential example. It is quite astonishing that this calm, balanced discourse, which focused on a prince's Christian piety, should have been written at almost the same time as another mirror for princes of a totally different kind: Machiavelli's *The Prince*. Ethical considerations did not count for this political theorist: for him politics was an end in itself.

In contrast to these realistic works, Greek didactic literature of this period was imbued with a religious character. At the end of the fifteenth century, the Cretan Georgios Chumnos wrote a long poem, *Cosmogenesis*, dealing with the first two books of the Old Testament. The dream poem of Joannis Pikatoros (fifteenth century), another Cretan poet, called *Rima thrinitiki is ton pikron ke akoreston Adhin* (*Rhyming Lament on Bitter and Insatiable Hades*) revolved around the hauting theme of death, like many other works of the period. Another well-known poem by Giustos Glykys in Greek, on the same theme, was called *Penthos thanatou . . .* (*The Mourning of Death . . .* , 1524). The later work of Markos Depharanas, a sixteenth-century poet, was more concerned with everyday life, *Loghi dhidhaktiki* (*Words of Edification from a Father to His Son*), while his *Istoria tis Sosanis* (*The Story of Susannah*), dealt with a well-known passage from the Bible.

Travellers' tales

Europe's cultural and intellectual élite was shaken during this period by the discovery of a New World, the Americas. From the voyages of Christopher Columbus to those of Magellan, our perception of geography was completely changed, even if most Europeans only became aware of the existence of this New World much later, in some cases only at the end of the seventeenth century. The discovery of the Americas signalled the beginning of a new era for the traveller's tale.*

Emblematic literature

A new form of didactic discourse, emblematic literature was an acquisition peculiar to this period. The emblem is an intimate marriage of symbolic image and motto. In the *Emblematum Liber* (*Book of Emblems*, 1531) by the Italian humanist and jurist **Andrea Alciato (1492–1550)**, a new teaching aid was introduced thanks to a series of models, ordered semantically, symbolically representative of moral realities and abstract concepts.

Alciato's book of emblems was so popular that almost 170 new editions of it were published in various languages. His example was followed, particularly in the seventeenth century, by a number of writers in the German-speaking countries and The Netherlands. Among his imitators were Pieter Corneliszoon Hooft with *Emblemata Amatoria* (*Emblematic*

Loves, 1611) and Visscher with *Sinnepoppen* (*Allegorical Images*, 1614). But the genre had already appeared much earlier in The Netherlands in a translation by the printer and rhetorician Frans Fraet of Antwerp of Guillaume La Perrière's *Good Brainteasers containing 100 Moral Emblems* under the title of *Tpalays der gheleerder ingienen oft der constiger gheesten* (*The Palace of Learned Geniuses or Ingenious Minds*, 1554). The new genre, however, was only recognised and promoted in its own right in 1566 in the dedication to the reader that preceded the Dutch translation of the *Emblemata* (1564) by the Hungarian neo-Latin philologist Johannes Sambucus.

Tales and short stories

In France, **François Rabelais (c.1483–1553)**,* the author of *Pantagruel* (1532) and *Gargantua* (1535), was a master of the narrative genre and an eminent satirist.

Alongside the great laughter of Rabelais, there was a whole literature of merriment taken from Boccaccio, breathing new life into the short story. His influence made itself felt in the *Cent Nouvelles Nouvelles* (*100 New Stories*), an anonymous work that was the first collection of short stories in French literature.

The tales by **Marguerite de Navarre (1492–1549)**, brought together after her death under the title *Heptameron*, were published for the first time in 1559. She was indebted for her structure to the *Decameron*; she not only described her epoch's social life, but at the same time sketched a critical picture of society with all its different social classes. Gathering round her a literary circle with liberal and religiously unorthodox ideas, she influenced her own generation, notably her protégé and manservant Bonaventure des Périers (1510–1544), the author of *Cymbalum Mundi* (1537) and *New Games and Happy Pastimes* (1558). In the first of these, in the form of dialogues imitated from Lucian, Des Périers was sharply critical, of Christianity and abuses of it then current, albeit in veiled terms. The book was condemned by the Sorbonne in 1537, shortly after it was published.

Also influenced by Boccaccio, Jakovos Trivolis, a native of Corfu, wrote in the first half of the sixteenth century his *Istoria tou re tis Skotsias me ti righisa tis Ingliteras* (*Story of the King of Scotland and the Queen of England*), an adaptation of the seventh story of the *Decameron*. The *Novelle* (*Short Stories*, 1554–1573) by **Matteo Bandello (1485–1561)** were reminiscent of Boccaccio and Bandello was also a wonderful storyteller. These stories were very popular and served as models for Shakespeare and Lope de Vega, and even for Byron and Musset.

The Portuguese writer **Bernadim Ribeiro (1482?–1552?)** seems to have been influenced by Boccaccio's *Fiammetta* in his famous tearjerker *Menina e Moça*, written *c.*1525 and almost lyrical in character. The book contained two chivalrous love stories which were independent of each other; both ended tragically.

In Bohemia the poet and diplomat **Hynek z Poděbrad (1452–1492)**, the son of King George of Poděbrady, was the first to translate, towards 1490, a dozen stories by Boccaccio which subsequently proved a source of inspiration to him.

The amusing situations in which the characters in the *Decameron* were embroiled, often in spite of themselves, captivated a large and literate public. The pranks of Till Eulenspiegel making fun of affluent burghers also met with great popular success in the German-speaking lands. Inspired by Poggio Bracciolini's collection of amusing anecdotes, *Till Eulenspiegel*, a collection of farces published in Strasbourg in 1515, was almost immediately adapted for a Dutch audience around 1519 in Antwerp and expanded to include new adventures for its leading character. Till Eulenspiegel was portrayed as a vagrant who sometimes appeared as a craftsman, a showman, a peripatetic student or a debauched clerk. He appeared in a Czech version *c.*1550.

Belonging, like *Till Eulenspiegel*, to the realm of popular literature, *Das Narrenschiff* (*The Ship of Fools*) by **Sebastian Brant (1458–1521)**, published in 1494, had a considerable influence on European literature. The vessel in question carried a cargo of personified stupidities and vices to the accompaniment of the applause and derision of fools on shore, among whom was the author himself:

Hier is an narren kein gebrust,	*Stupid folk are not in short supply here,*
ein yeder findt das in gelust	*all of them find what they want*
und ouch warzuo er sy geboren	*and what they were destined for. That*
und war umb so vil sindt der doren,	*is why there are so many stupid people.*
was ere und freyd die wiszheit hat,	*The high esteem and joy with which*
wie sörglich sy der narren stat;	*wisdom is adorned and the comfortable*
hie findt man der welt gantzen louff,	*situation stupidity finds itself in will all*
disz büechlin wurt guot zuo dem kouff.	*be found in this book, the whole of*
Sebastian Brant,	*human life. This little book*
Das Narrenschiff	*will be a good seller.*

By the use of maxims, proverbs and quotations borrowed from the Bible and classical authors, the author imparted a moral message in accessible language. As Brant thought that the recognition of folly was a principle of wisdom, he hoped that *The Ship of Fools* would contribute to the betterment in his own lifetime of morals and manners. Thanks to the

Latin translation by Jacob Locher, *Stultifera Navis* (1497), Brant's work was widely disseminated all over Europe. Several translations into vernacular languages soon followed: *La Nef des fols du monde* in French in 1497; *Der zotten ende der narren scip* in Dutch in 1500; and *The Shyp of Folys of the Worlde* in English in 1509. This work was undoubtedly an important source text for Erasmus when he wrote *Praise of Folly*.

In Scotland the poet **Robert Henryson (c.1425–1508)**, who belonged to the circle of 'Scottish Chaucerians' and was the author of the *Testament of Cresseid* (printed in 1593) – a continuation of the poem *Troilus and Criseyde* by Chaucer – wrote thirteen fables with a moral, *Morall Fables of Esope the Phrygian* (printed in 1621); they occupy an important place in the history of European fabulism and the best of them was taken on board by La Fontaine. In Hungary, Ferenc Apáti depicted his country in his satirical writing (*Feddöének, c.1523*). A satirical vein was also in the many poems written to advance the cause of the Reformation, such as those of András Szkhárosi Horvát, *Az fejedelemségröl* (*On Principalities*, 1541).

In Bohemia, Czech satirical literature gained an addition with an anonymous work, *Frantova práva* (*The Rule of Franta*), a social and popular satire derived from a parody of the statutes of the guild of drunkards, printed in 1518. The book was also very popular in Poland. The father of Polish letters, **Mikolai Rej (1505–1569)**, one of the first writers in Poland to use the vernacular, started his career in 1543 with a satirical dialogue in verse, *Krótka rozprawa* (*A Short Argument between Three People*), in which he condemned the corrupt customs of his society.

LYRICAL POETRY

In the realm of lyric poetry, the neo-Latin literature of this period also emulated the great classical models of Catullus, Tibullus, Propertius and Ovid. The humanist poets had ambitions to become an 'alter Catullus' or a 'nostri sæculi Tibullus'. The anthology collected by the Dutch poet **Janus Secundus (1511–1536)**, consisting of nineteen poems, the *Basia* (*The Kisses*, 1539), was directly inspired by two poems of Catullus and had much influence not only on other neo-Latin poets, but also on lyric poets who chose to write in their mother tongue, such as the poets of the Pleiad.

Non dat basia, dat Neæra nectar, [. . .]	*Neæra does not give kisses, she gives nectar, [. . .]*
Sed tu munere parce, parce tali,	*Go easy with this magnificent present,*
Aut mecum dea fac, Neæra, fias:	*go easy with it or else*
Non mensas sine te volo deorum,	*become a goddess too, Neæra! Without*
Non, si me rutilis præesse regnis,	*you there, I want nothing from the table of*
Excluso Jove, dii deæque cogant.	*the gods, no, even if, to*
	offer me the golden sceptre of their
Janus Secundus,	*sway, the gods and goddesses*
Basium IV	*dethroned Jupiter and made me accept it.*

The editor and translator Thierry Sandre has counted three imitations by Pleiad poets from the closing stanzas below:

Hold back a little, prithee,	*I leave upon my plate the choicest fare*
The good things with which I am sated,	*The gods themselves do eat. I leave what's rare,*
Temper my joy as you ought:	*Nectar, Ambrosia, Honey and Manna.*
I would be like a god,	*To refrain from all food I'd be able*
And 'twould seem something odd	*If the gods made me eat at their table,*
If you were not my consort.	*For heaven without you would be a gehenna.*
Pierre de Ronsard,	Rémi Belleau,
'Kisses for Cassandra', Odes	*'Second Day of the Pastoral', Kisses*

This divine ambrosia
Deifies
Whosoever may taste it,
And it may be such a meal
So tasty
Makes us more than men.

Give me no more of it, mistress
If goddess
You'll not consent to be with me;
For with the gods I want no reign
As God or master,
Lest it be with you beside me.
Jean Antoine de Baïf,
Divers Loves

Without you there, I want nothing from the table of the gods . . .

Janus Secundus, *Basia*

The *Elegiæ* (*Elegies*, 1541) by Janus Secundus, a more important work, are characterised, as are his *Odes* and *Epistles*, by the exceptional candour of the feelings expressed and by a distinctive mellowness and grace. Janus Secundus did not just go for inspiration to the models of Antiquity, but continued in the tradition of his great lyric predecessors, the Renaissance Italians such as Pontano, Michele

Marullo (1453–1500), a native of Byzantium, and Sannazaro. In the sometimes erotic lyricism of Pontano we find the piquant grace of Catullus, but this Neapolitan poet also defended and sang the praises of conjugal and family virtues in *De Amore conjugali* (*Of Conjugal Love*). The personal lyricism of Marullo was sometimes melancholic and patriotic. The autobiographical element that we find in him was even more striking in Sannazaro's Latin elegies.

Lyricism was also expressed in vernacular languages. Three tendencies were clear among the poets who chose to write in their first language: some kept to medieval fixed forms; others were interested in the verbal acrobatics of the rhetoricians; the rest were influenced by Italian literature, especially by Sannazaro and Petrarch.

Spain: from tradition to modernity

In Spain **Jorge Manrique (*c.*1440–1479)** was a good example of the transition from the Middle Ages to the modern era. He became famous with *Coplas por la muerte de su padre* (*On the Death of His Father*, 1476), part two of his *Cancionero*, in which he expressed deeply felt emotions on the reality of death and the vanity and brevity of human life:

Nuestras vidas son los ríos	*Our lives are the rivers*
que van a dar en la mar,	*which flow into the sea,*
qu'es el morir;	*which is death;*
allí van los señoríos	*great lords go there*
derechos a se acabar	*straight*
e consumir;	*and are consumed; big*
allí los ríos caudales,	*rivers,*
allí los otros medianos	*rivers of average size and the*
e más chicos,	*smallest,*
allegados son yguales	*on arrival all are equal,*
los que viven por sus manos	*those who work with their hands*
e los ricos.	*as well as the rich.*

Jorge Manrique,
Coplas

France: Villon to Clément Marot

Also midway between the medieval period and modern times, the Frenchman **François Villon (1431–after 1463)**, author of the *Legacies* (1456) and the *Testament* (1461), created a poetic corpus of great power and sincerity. As far as form and inspiration were concerned, the work remained medieval, but at the same time it was modern because of its personal lyricism and its direct confrontation of the solitary individual with other people, time and death. Villon made his own existence the sole source of a poetry in which the tragic alternated with the grotesque. In pictorial fashion, sardonically and ironically, he parades the themes of fortune, stupidity, vanity, evil and above all death, which echoes throughout his poetry:

> *I know that paupers and the wealthy,*
> *Wise and foolish, priests and lay,*
> *Noble, wicked, open, selfish,*
> *Small and great, and fair and fey,*
> *Dames with turned-up collars, say,*
> *From whatever walk of life,*
> *Wearing finery and jewels today.*
> *Death shall seize on with its knife.*
>
> François Villon,
> *The Testament*

For many years the idea was current that, between Villon's *Testament* and Marot's poetry, French literature lived in a poetic vacuum. The formal aspects of language were completely ignored. The so-called 'grands rhétoriqueurs' ('great rhetoricians') were too easily dismissed. Their art, however, which evolved between 1470 and 1520, played a large part in the literary life of the time. The rhetoricians created poetic forms in abundance without abandoning the use of certain medieval forms such as the rondeau or the ballad. Treatises on rhetoric, which flourished at the end of the fifteenth century and the beginning of the sixteenth, provided poets with formal precepts. The most important of these treatises was by Pierre Fabri (1450–1535), *The Great and True Art of Total*

Rhetoric. Published for the first time in 1521, by 1544 it had been reprinted seven times. The treatise insisted on the use of rhyme, listed the possibilities of verbal acrobatics, defined the main literary genres and, for the first time, gave indications about the number of syllables in a verse and the placing of the caesura. Court poets, in an aristocratic world that was virtually immutable and in which everything became a spectacle, made language into a spectacle by cunningly manipulating its sonorous, lexical and rhythmic properties. Among its most distinguished authors were Georges Chastelain (*c*.1415–1475), Jean Molinet (1435–1507), Jean Marot (*c*.1450–1526), Jean Lemaire de Belges and Pierre Gringoire (*c*.1475–1538).

Chastelain added dignity to poetry and was the great model for **Clément Marot (1496–1544)**. Heir – literally and figuratively – to the rhetoricians, Marot guaranteed the change to new poetic forms and concepts. Son of the French rhetorician Jean Marot, Clément assimilated the precepts of the poetry generated by his father and recognised the court as his 'schoolmistress'. His verbal virtuosity was arresting, as in the following famous *Short Epistle to the King* (1517–1518):

> *As I frolic I make rondeaux and make*
> *rhymes,*
> *And quite often in my rhyming I make*
> *rhymes;*
> *In short, it's a shame between we*
> *poetasters,*
> *That you yourself of poets are a*
> *taster,*
> *And, when you want to, rhyme better*
> *than I do,*
> *With fine observations and well thought-*
> *out haiku . . .*
>
> Clément Marot,
> *Short Epistle to the King*

If Marot made use of traditional forms like the rondeau, the ballad and the epistle, at the same time he introduced new poetic genres, the sonnet and the blazon, as well as the eclogue and the epigram, forms borrowed from classical literature. Much of his poetry, such as the *Epistle to the King during his Exile in Ferrara* (1536), in which he tried to defend himself against the charge of heresy, has a significant religious and political dimension. In *Hell* (1526), a long poem of 500 verses, he allegorically condemned the legal system of his time. Repeatedly condemned for his evangelical stance, not dissimilar to that of Luther, he ended his life in exile in Geneva where, in 1540, he wrote his famous translation of the Psalms of David.

The Netherlands: committed lyricism

Dutch lyricism was partly characterised by social or religious connotations. The rhetorician from Bruges **Anthonis de Roovere (c.1430–1482)**, the town's poet laureate, did not hesitate to oppose social injustice in his sometimes bitter poetry.

His ballad *Vander Mollen feeste* (*The Banquet of the Moles*) presented death as an invitation to a subterranean banquet given by moles; like some dance of death all social classes are invited to this feast. Dying young was most movingly evoked. By means of this tableau of society, de Roovere depicted the dark side of life in the States of Burgundy.

The Antwerp schoolmistress **Anna Bijns (1493–1575)** also wrote as a rhetorician. She owed her fame to three collections of poems published in 1528, 1548 and 567. Ardently Catholic, she revealed the full extent of her religious commitment, making use of all the resources of language and poetry then available to her to proclaim her pain and anger at the progress of Lutheran heresy:

Cloosters en abdijen	*Those wicked Lutherans*
Bederven dese boose	*corrupt convents and corrupt*
lutherianen;	*abbeys;*
Als Heidenen, Turcken ende	*like pagans, Turks or*
Soudanen	*Sultans*
Brecken sij beelden in kercken,	*they break statues in*
in capellen.	*churches and chapels.*
Hoe sal icse best noemen na mijn	*How shall I say*
wanen?	*what I really think of them?*
Tsijn eertsche duvels, die den	*They are devils put on earth*
menscen quellen.	*to torture men.*

Anna Bijns,
Refereinen

The third collection by this poet was less polemical: it consisted of religious poems in which she tirelessly sang the praises of Jesus and the Virgin Mary and meditated on death and the Last Judgement. Today she has become the symbol of the Dutch Women's Liberation Movement thanks to a poem in which she celebrated the life of a single woman.

The Italian influence

Works by two Italian authors, Sannazaro and Petrarch, were sources of inspiration for many European lyricists. Sannazaro wrote in the neo-Latin tradition of the rustic idyll, adding to it his *Eclogæ piscatoriæ* (*Fishers' Eclogues*, 1526). His *Arcadia* (1485), one of the most important works in Italian literature of that period, was not only a collection of lyrics written independently of one another, but a well-structured pastoral novel which had a Europe-wide influence:

Sovra una verde riva
di chiare e lucide onde
in un bel bosco di fioretti adorno,
vidi di bianca oliva
ornato e d'altre fronde
un pastor, che 'n su l'alba appiè
d'un orno
cantava il terzo giorno
del mese innanzi aprile;
a cui li vaghi ucelli
di sopra gli arboscelli
con voce rispondean dolce e gentile.

Iacopo Sannazaro,
Arcadia

On the edge of a green riverbank, where
the water was clear and limpid, in a
pretty wood patterned with flowers, I saw
a shepherd, girt with the white
branches of an olive-tree and other
foliage as well, who, at dawn, on the
third day of March, was singing
at the foot of an elm;
charming birds perched on
bushes answered him
with sweet and melodious
birdsongs.

The novelty and originality of this pastoral novel come from its mixture of prose and verse; the landscapes of Arcadia resemble those of Eden, in as much as they exist in isolation from the real world.

Pastoral poetry in Italy was also written by Boiardo in his eclogues, though he was better known for his love poems, published under the title of *Sonetti e Canzoni* (*Sonnets and Songs*, 1499), in which he imitated Petrarch.

The poetry of Juan Boscan (*c.*1490–1542) was published by his widow in 1543, along with that by Garcilaso de la Vega, under the title *Poesias de Juan Boscan y su amigo Garcilaso de la Vega* (*The Poetry of Juan Boscan and his friend Garcilaso de la Vega*). Boscan, whose lyricism was less pronounced than Garcilaso's completed an excellent translation into Spanish of Castiglione's *The Courtier* (1534). English poetry of this period was more indebted to Petrarch. **Sir Thomas Wyatt (1503–1542)** introduced the sonnet into English literature by translating some of Petrarch's and writing twenty-one himself. **Henry Howard (1517–1547)**, like Wyatt, gave much thought to the achievements of the Renaissance in Italy, which he tried to emulate. His poetic technique was more sophisticated than Wyatt's, especially that of his octosyllabic couplets. The rhyme scheme of his sonnets even set an example that Shakespeare followed.

Published in 1516 by Garcia de Resende (1470–1536), the *Cancioneiro Geral* (*General Songbook*) gave access to a range of current Portuguese lyrical offerings. Poetry had freed itself from music, courtly love had been replaced by passing fancies. Spanish and Italian influences were very noticeable. This poetry looked for new ways forward without entirely giving up traditional themes and forms. The poet Ribeiro, who contributed eleven unremarkable poems to the *Cancioneiro*, made a name for himself in the rustic idyll genre, particularly in the eclogue which, subject to close analysis, was sometimes transformed into a soliloquy of unremitting introspection.

Literature in Greek at this time was doubtless influenced by works in Italian, given the diplomatic relations between Greece and Venice. It was distinguished by the *Rimadha koris ke niou* (*Ballad of the Young Woman and the Young Man*, fifteenth century), a rhyming love poem by an anonymous Cretan poet in the form of a dialogue which included elements of Greek folklore.

The imitation of Petrarch continued to attract a dedicated following in Croatia, above all in Dubrovnik (Ragusa) and most notably in works by **Šiško Menčetić (1457–1526)** and **Džore Držić (1461–1501)**, which embellish the theme of a young man in love with an ideal lady. Despite the conventional framework of this Petrarchan poetry, these texts replicate the versification and figures of speech used in popular literature.

In the sixteenth century, when France was

still decentralised, the town of Lyon stood out because of its admirable vitality: it was a cosmopolitan crossroads, a commercial metropolis, a hotbed of humanist and intellectual activity and an important centre for printing. Many French writers – Marot, Rabelais, Des Périers and Marguerite de Navarre – came into brief contact with this urban milieu, open to suggestions from Italy, where Petrarchism and Platonism had a field day. Among the poets who prospered in Lyon were **Louise Labé (1524–1566)**, whose house was a meeting-place for artists and poets, and **Maurice Scève (c.1501–1564)**. Louise Labé's work includes a collection of poems and a prose text: the *Débat de Folie et d'Amour* (*Debate of Love and Madness*, 1555) speaks the passionate language of love to perfection and its verses often deal with unhappiness in love. Maurice Scève thought he had rediscovered the tomb of Petrarch's Laura in Avignon. In 1544 he published *Délie, objet de la plus haute vertu* (*Delia, Object of the Highest Virtue*). This work, which is not easy to read, was influenced by the occult and by the theories of neo-Platonism (certain critics have put forward the view that the first word of the title could be an anagram of the word 'l'idée' [the idea]). Poles apart from this erudite poetry, Czech literature witnessed Hynek z Poděbrad's highly original lyricism, characterised by great candour and a free, sensual, personal, unaffected understanding of love (*Májovy sen, May Dream*), and by a sceptical, ironic and irreverent attitude to religion.

DRAMA

Like other literary genres, drama manifested itself in two ways: in neo-Latin drama, which became popular in the sixteenth century, and a vernacular drama frequently inherited from the Middle Ages in mystery plays, farces and slapstick comedy.

Neo-Latin drama

In neo-Latin literature, drama was given a facelift influenced by Greek tragedy. Erasmus, with his translation from Greek to Latin of two plays by Euripides, introduced to the world of sixteenth-century literature *Iphigenia in Aulis* and *Hecuba*. Thanks to this new model, humanists found inspiration in a less sentimental and more structured theatre than that of Seneca. In 1544, the Scot **George Buchanan (1506–1582)** translated into Latin a third tragedy by Euripides, *Medea*, and also composed a tragedy in neo-Latin on a Biblical theme, *Jephtes sive Votum* (*Jephtha or the Vow*).

There were many theatrical productions in this period in the Latin schools and colleges set up by humanists, especially in The Netherlands and in German-speaking countries, where the top classes regularly performed plays which were often written by their own teachers or by those of a neighbouring establishment. So it was that the headmaster of the Latin school in The Hague, **Gulielmus Gnapheus (1493–1568)** distinguished himself with his *Acolastus* (1529), a Biblical drama on the Prodigal Son, which owed a good deal to Plautus and Terence. This play was very popular and was even translated into English in 1540. According to the Dutch teacher and humanist **Georgius Macropedius (1487–1558)**, himself the author of twelve plays, school plays were the best mirror on life, an excellent grammatical exercise and a good illustration of good and evil. This is why he took his themes from the Bible and from everyday (college) life. In the German-speaking countries, this genre was practised by **Jacob Wimpfeling (1450–1528)**, the author of a comedy called *Stylpho* (1480), and by Reuchlin, the author of *Henno* (1497), a comedy of manners.

Drama in the vernacular

Before 1550, French theatre was, above all, a popular theatre inherited from the Middle Ages, with mystery plays, slapstick, moralities and farces, the latter being the only medieval form of drama to survive after 1550.

The popularity of the mystery play began to decline in the sixteenth century. The stereotyped imitation of models, the greater intrusion of the secular on the sacred and the appearance of a theatre aimed at a more literate public went some way towards explaining its demise. Socially disruptive, mystery plays were officially condemned around the middle of the sixteenth century, and only survived in the provinces. The morality play, always diverse in its forms, appeared in the fourteenth century and had a certain popularity up until the end of the sixteenth century; it pursued an end that was edifying, often religious. The historical morality play borrowed from legend or from history gleaned from Ovid, Pliny the Elder or Valerius Maximus. The morality play could have a comic twist to it, as in the *Happy Moral with Five Characters*, or found its inspiration in current events, as was the case for *The New World* (1508) by André de la Vigne (died 1515). The sotie, a short, abstract play, which nevertheless had recourse to a comedy in which carnival elements prevailed, showed us clowns on stage. The *Sottie du Prince des Sots* (*Clowning of the Prince of Clowns*, 1512) by Pierre Gringoire condemned Pope Julius II and paved the way for the acceptance of Louis XII's foreign policy. The farce, a short diversion of 500 verses, was always very popular and survived after 1550. Deeply rooted in the real world that it caricatured, it flayed humankind with the scourge of laughter. The masterpiece of the period was *La Cornette* (*The Cornet*) by Jean d'Abondance (first half of the sixteenth century).

More or less the same genres existed in Dutch theatre, with mystery plays, miracles and 'spelen van sinne' (morality plays). Among the mystery plays there were *De seven bliscappen van Maria* (*The Seven Joys of Mary*): a cycle of seven plays, one of which, from 1448, was staged every year in Brussels. Only two plays have survived from this unique cycle: the first, devoted to the Fall and the Annunciation, and the last, devoted to the death and the Assumption of Our Lady. *Mariken Van Nieumeghen* (*Mariette of Nijmegen*), from the end of the fifteenth century, was the most famous miracle play. It tells the story of a young woman who, after having lived for seven years with the Devil, is redeemed by the intervention of the Virgin Mary. The psychology of the situation is handled with subtlety and the language of the piece is remarkably spontaneous. The story of Mariette was adapted into English in 1518. Since the nineteenth century, the text has been translated into German, French, English and Norwegian, and has been made into an opera and a film.

The 'spel van sinne' was a genre peculiar to Dutch rhetoricians without its like elsewhere in Europe. These were more serious plays often woven around a particular theme. If there was a competition, the themes of the 'sinnen' would be given. Theatre-goers would then go to a performance of different plays linked by the same theme. There was a certain similarity between the 'spelen van sinne' and French morality plays, but the former were much shorter (often 500 to 700 verses, never more than 1200) and included features which set them apart. One of these was the appearance on stage of 'sinnekins': a theatrical role born from a fusion of the devils of medieval theatre and personifications of human vices, who often intervened to comment on the action. Another distinguishing mark of these plays was in their use of *tableaux vivants* during the play – the staging of a situation or an action at a different level from that of the main storyline. *Elckerlijc* (*Everyman*) was the rhetoricians' play which had the best reception. The play shows that when they die all men must justify to God the way in which they have managed their earthly goods. When Death, sent by God, introduces himself to Elckerlijc, he addresses him thus:

Rekening wilt Hij van U ontvaan,	*God wants you to give an account*
zonder enig verdrag. [. . .]	*of yourself without delay. [. . .]*
Brengt U geschriften ende pampieren	*Bring your documents and*
met u ende overziet ze	*papers and study them closely,*
bedachtig.	*for of this you can be sure, you will have to*

Want gij moet voor God Almachtig
rekeninge doen, des zeker zijt,
van hoe gij bestaad hebt uwen tijd,
van uwen werken, goed ende kwaad.
Elckerlijc

give an account before God
Almighty of how
you have spent your time and of
your works, both good and bad.

Written *c.*1470 and printed in 1495, the play was enormously popular and an English version, *Everyman*, followed before 1500. During the fifteenth century there were several Latin translations. The one by Macropedius called *Hecastus* (1539) was the best known, an adaptation which was, in its turn, translated into German by Hans Sachs towards 1550. In 1911, Hugo von Hofmannsthal puts on a *Jedermann* in Salzburg, inspired by the medieval text.

One of the most remarkable secular plays, *Spiegel der Minne* (*The Mirror of Love*, *c.*1480), by the Brussels rhetorician Colijn Van Rijssele (second half of the fifteenth century–beginning of the sixteenth), had as its subject a passion which led to the destruction of the lovers. In such a case, only self-restraint – reason – could save a person. In European literature *The Mirror of Love* is the first psychological drama in which middle-class characters take centre stage.

In England, religious theatre retained its importance until virtually the middle of the sixteenth century. Mystery plays continued to be staged during this period. It was only after King Henry VIII severed all ties with Rome that these plays, considered to be a part of the Church that had been superseded, became increasingly morally suspect. A decree published in 1540 forbade them from being printed or staged. Like continental literature, English literature of this period had morality plays, such as those by John Skelton (*c.*1460–1529). In *Magnyfycence*, a social satire that mocked the king's counsellors, the sin of ambition and the virtue of self-restraint were portrayed as the main characters. *Everyman*, an adaptation of the Dutch *Elckerlijc*, *Mankind* and *Nature* by Henry Medwall (second half of the fifteenth century) belonged to this same literary category. The plays by John Heywood (1497–*c.*1578), such as *The Play of the Weather*

(*c.*1525–1533), were a preparatory phase for the development of secular Elizabethan theatre.

Despite the catalyst of the Renaissance, Italian theatre had not yet begun to prosper. Politian's *Fable of Orpheus* was certainly a play, but the work was more lyrical than dramatic: the characters had little personality and there was no genuine action. Only Machiavelli wrote a play worthy of the name. In *La Mandragola* (*The Mandrake*, 1520), he exhibited his great knowledge of human nature and a remarkable imagination as he scrutinised in detail the behaviour of men dominated by different passions. The play was an immediate success and, according to Voltaire, was worth more than all the plays of Aristophanes put together. Lorenzo the Magnificent (1449–1492) wrote *Sacre Rappresentazioni*, the Italian equivalent of mystery plays.

The theatre in Spanish only came into existence *c.*1500. Its main work was *La Celestina* (*Celestina*, 1499) by **Fernando de Rojas (*c.*1465–1541)**,* a student at Salamanca. The dramatic works of **Juan del Encina (*c.*1468–after 1529)** gathered together simple popular pieces, still medieval in inspiration, and several more modern dramas which revealed the influence of the Renaissance, such as *Egloga de Fileno* (*Eclogue of Fileno*). Towards the middle of the sixteenth century, Lope de Rueda (*c.*1505–1565) wrote four comedies, remarkable for their spontaneous style and thought, and ten 'pasos' – one-act plays – with quick-fire dialogue that appealed to popular taste.

Of the forty-six plays by the Portuguese **Gil Vicente (*c.*1465–*c.*1537), eleven were in Spanish, nineteen in Portuguese and sixteen in both languages. Difficult to classify, the plays can be separated into four distinct categories: mystery plays, morality plays, farces and comedies. Vicente's theatre is to some extent a magnificent altarpiece on which man's chief concerns are painted and analysed realistically and imaginatively not only in Portugal, but also in Spain, where Spanish became, the second literary language of many Portuguese writers right up to the end of the seventeenth century. In the *Trilogia de las Barcas* (*Trilogy of the Boats*, 1516–1519), Vicente criticised society, the Church and representatives of all social classes, not without humour. In these three plays he wrote about themes of diverse provenance: folklore, the Dance of Death, the classical theme of Charon – the ferryman in Hades – St Ursula's boat and the eleven thousand virgins, as well as Brant's *Ship of Fools*. In the *Auto da Barca do Inferno* (*The Play of the Boat from Hell*, 1517), a large number of characters are sent to Hell, among them a usurer, a pimp, a Jew, a priest and his mistress and a corrupt policeman. Only a simple, honest man and four knights who died serving God in Africa are saved: they are the rare chosen ones who have gained the reward of Paradise.

At the other end of Europe, two Croatian writers won a more singular title to fame. Hanibal Lucic (1485–1553) wrote the first secular play, *Robinja* (*The Captive*, 1556), which took a political event of the period for its theme. **Marin Držić (1520–1567)** was an important Renaissance writer of some pastorals published in Venice in 1551 (*Venera i Adon*, *Venus and Adonis*), in which he mixed sentimental elements with rustic comedy. In a cycle inspired by Plautus (*Skup*, 1554, and *Dundo Maroje*, *Uncle Maroje*, 1556), he went beyond erudite comedy to give a wide overview of Dubrovnik society.

HISTORICAL LITERATURE

There was no lack of literary output in the shape of historical writings. Many humanists contributed to the historical documentation of their country or their place of origin. Most Italian States had their own historiographer: Poggio in Florence, Bembo in Venice and Pontano in Naples. This was also a time when,

in many European countries, the 'national' origins of countries were being sought after, a search which sometimes resulted in the formation of myths.

Neo-Latin chronicles

The humanist Wimpfeling gave German history a boost with *Germania* (1501) and *Epithome rerum germanicarum* (*Digest of Things German*, 1505); **Robert Gaguin (1423–1501)** did the same for France with *Compendium de origine et gestis Francorum* (*Abridgement of the Origin and History of the Franks*, 1497). In Poland, Matthew of Miechow (died 1523) introduced historical myth into neo-Latin Polish literature with *Tractatus de duabus Sarmatiis* (*Treatise on the Two Sarmatias*, 1517). The Croatian humanist Ludovik Crijevic Tuberon (1459–1527) wrote a chronicle on the modern history of Christian countries under Ottoman rule, *Commentaria de rebus quæ temporibus eius . . . gesta sunt* (*Commentary on What Happened During the Time of . . .*, 1490–1522). In Hungary, the Archbishop of Esztergom, Miklós Oláh (1493–1568), tried to console his country by recalling in his works (*Hungaria* and *Attila*, 1536–1537) the great deeds of Attila, tacitly accepting the medieval myth that made the Huns and the Hungarians brothers-in-arms. On the origins of the northern Netherlands and the myth of Batavia, there was a debate between Cornelius Aurelius, the author of the *Defensio gloriæ batavinæ* (*Defence of the Glory of the Batavians*, *c*.1520), and Noviomagus, the author of *Historia batavica* (*The History of Batavia*, 1533). Writing about Scandinavia, the Swedish humanist Olaus Magnus (1490–1557) brought out in 1554 *De gentibus septentrionalibus libri XXII* (*On the Northern Peoples in XXII Books*).

A more explanatory and critical historiography

Historiography in the vernacular during this period took to heart the precepts on which humanism insisted: to compile information harmoniously and to observe the rules of rhetoric. The official historian also became increasingly critical: he took more interest in political and diplomatic events and the analysis of their causes and interconnections. Official histories provided explanations, though they did not as yet take account of sociological and economic factors.

In Italy, Machiavelli and Guicciardini were representative of this trend. In *Storie Fiorentine* (*A History of Florence*, c.1525), Machiavelli, with great perspicacity, explained the political reality of Florence, even if he was biased against the papacy which he thought was an obstacle to Italian unity. He wanted to find a way to set up a republic strong enough to defend the State against its enemies and restore its independence. **Francesco Guicciardini (1483–1540),** for his part, wrote another history of Florence in 1508–1509 called *Storie Fiorentine* (*A History of Florence*). Guicciardini ignored current literary conventions. His primary concern was contemporary Florentine politics, in the description of which he exhibited surprising lucidity of critical judgement and a relatively impartial approach to his subject matter. In his other major work, *Storia d'Italia* (*A History of Italy*, 1532), for the first time as far as historical studies were concerned, Italy was considered as a national and geographic entity. There were some concessions to literary conventions, but the scope of Guicciardini's subject allowed him to describe the interaction between different Italian city states and the character of international relations.

In France, memoirs were the order of the day. The memorialist **Philippe de Commynes (1445–1511),** who owed much to his Burgundian precedents – he served Charles the Bold – thought form was unimportant. His documentation and critical acumen both left a lot to be desired, but he recorded facts accurately. His realistic turn of mind resembled Machiavelli and Guicciardini; sometimes he reveals the same cynicism, when he expressed admiration for the cunning of certain princes. His *Memoirs* (1489–1498) and the *Chronicle of the Dukes of Burgundy* by

Chastelain were of great historical interest. In his work, half history, half novel, *The Illustrations of Gaul and Singularities of Troy* (1511), Jean Lemaire de Belges tried to prove the fundamental unity of all the great European dynasties by tracing them back to a common ancestor.

The fall of Constantinople inspired many Greek historians to write an account of it. John Doukas (1400–1470) described the history of Byzantium from 1341 to 1462, up to and including the fall of Lesbos. In his opinion, the fall of the Byzantine Empire brought in its wake the collapse of the religious ideology which had guaranteed and ensured its greatness. The glory and the fall of the Empire formed the subject of the 'chronicles' of George Sphranzes (1401–1477). In Greece, the fall of Constantinople encouraged the composition of 'historical laments', often anonymous poems in fifteen-syllable metre without rhyme. Emmanuel Georgilas of Rhodes described in a verse chronicle c.1500 the plague which had devastated his country in 1498. In Cyprus, George Boustronios wrote a chronicle in dialect in which he related the political and social events of the years 1456–1489, continuing after a fashion the work of Leontios Macheras.

The discovery of a New World had an important influence on Spanish historiography. Among the authors who wrote about South America, the Dominican bishop Bartolomeo de las Casas (1474–1566) distinguished himself with *Historia de las Indias* (*History of the Indies*, only published in 1875) and *Brevísima Relación de la Destruición de las Indias* (*Very Short Account of the Destruction of the Indies*, 1542). He defended the indigenous population and criticised the European conquerors for their cruelty to primitive people. Portuguese expansionism was the main preoccupation for the historian João de Barros. Despite his ambitious plan to compile a systematic description of all Portuguese discoveries and conquests in Europe, Asia, Africa and America, accompanied by geographical and economic information on these four continents, he only completed the three first sections of his *Decadas da Asia* (1552–1563).

Russian historiography carried on where the Middle Ages left off, but it also reflected something of the political development leading to the unification of all the Russian territories by the kings of Moscow. From *c.*1472, there is evidence of Muscovite compilations, characterised by biased accounts of recent and historical events.

About the same time, the series of chronicles in Czech was increased by a translation of the chronicle of Piccolomini (1510), by two chronicles with a Utraquist viewpoint and by *Kronika česká* (*Czech Chronicle*) by the Catholic priest **Václav Hájek z Libočan (died 1553)**, published several times after 1541 and three times in German. The main value of this popular chronicle was in its artistic, colourful and interesting narration and its truly patriotic tone. Certain chapters of *Magyar krónika* (*The Hungarian Chronicle*, 1575) by Gáspár Heltai (1510–1574), an adaptation of a Latin work by Antonio Bonfini, an Italian who settled in Hungary in the fifteenth century, can be considered to be the first short stories in Hungarian literature.

In Bulgaria, in the second half of the fifteenth century, Vladislav the Grammarian wrote compilations of sermons and lives of saints by Bulgarian and Byzantine authors, accompanied by some interesting historical comments. He was noted for his *Story of Rila* (1479) which described the transfer of the relics of John of Rila, the most popular Bulgarian saint.

However strongly united the Republic of Letters may have been, the emancipation of vernacular languages at the expense of Latin favoured the development of distinctive national traits.

TWO UNIQUE PHENOMENA

In addition to the literary trends then widespread throughout Europe, The Netherlands and Spain developed two original approaches to literature. In the first were the Dutch chambers of rhetoric; in the second, the Spanish romancero: both unique literary phenomena.

The chambers of rhetoric

The Dutch term 'rederijker' was popularly derived from the word 'rhetorycker' (rhetorician). From about 1400, chambers of rhetoric developed: associations of rhetoricians which, from 1430 until the second half of the sixteenth century, when the influence of the Renaissance in The Netherlands was at its height, determined the course of literary development. These chambers gained ground in the south-west of this cultural area, spreading first to Flanders and the Brabant, then to Zealand and Holland. The chambers probably originated in the fraternities who assisted the clergy in mounting religious plays or processions. Members of theatre committees and corporations of harquebusiers (civil guards) mingled with these 'Church servants'. Carnival associations may also have played a part, together with the potential influence of the 'puys' of Northern France. The chambers were gradually recognised by the civil authorities. A dean and an advisory council together constituted their ruling body. The 'factor' set subjects for the composition of verse; the 'prince' acted as patron and subsidised the activities; the 'fool' or 'jester' provided light entertainment on feastdays. Servants wore a 'blazon' with a 'motto' on their livery during walks and processions. The members were selected according to their literary talents, personal merits or because they belonged to a particular social class.

The rhetoricians appreciated complicated poetic techniques: of melodious recitation vied with musical performance. They were drawn to 'oratorie', a dialectic connected with matters of precedence and religious or social viewpoints. Language was not just a means of communication, but also a way of creating aesthetically valid works of art. Rhetoric, the Holy Spirit's daughter, was kept from the defilement of the rabble and inferior poets. Out of the chambers of rhetoric developed many poetic forms such as the refrain, the ballad, the acrostic, the chronogram, the retrograde and the impromptu. Matthijs de Castelein (c.1485–1550) published a handbook in 1548 for those who were addicted to this recondite art: *De Const van rhetoriken* (*The Art of Rhetoric*).

The rhetoricians had a lasting influence on Dutch theatre and produced a great deal of theatrical work. Their greatest masterpieces were *Everyman* and *Mariette of Nijmegen*. Their theatre consisted of several genres such as 'frolics', parlour games, plays about saints, historical plays, moralities and mysteries, miracles, comedies of manners.

Brabançon rhetoricians organised drama and poetry competitions in Brabant in which the various guilds and corporations took part. Similar events were also organised outside Brabant, but the ideas of the Reformation were soon being voiced in them, as in Ghent in 1539, for instance. The chambers became more strictly controlled, and certain works were put on the Index. Many rhetoricians became martyrs during the revolt against Spain. Many 'geuzenliederen' ('beggars' songs') were written to commemorate them. During these years of revolt, many rhetoricians from the south took refuge in the north, notably in Amsterdam and Leyden, where they established their own chambers. Amsterdam, consequently, had two chambers: Hooft and Bredero frequented the old De Eglantier chamber, and Vondel that of the immigrants

Het Wit Lavendel. In 1617, Samuel Coster left the De Eglantier chamber, troubled by internal rifts since 1615, and founded with Hooft and Bredero the first Dutch Academy, heralding the start of a new era.

Chambers of rhetoric lost their dominant position in the north, though they maintained their activities until the eighteenth century. In the southern Netherlands, the chambers took on a new lease of life in the second half of the seventeenth century.

The Spanish romances

At the beginning of the fifteenth century, new poetic compositions, or romances, developed in Spain and became one of its most fertile genres. It was first thought that the romances were the most ancient manifestation of Castilian poetry; the fifteenth-century romances, described as 'ancient', could have been a source for songs of deeds which, in their turn, would only have been a polarisation of romances around a single character or theme. Today we think that, on the contrary, the first poetic creations were the long songs of deeds transmitted orally. With the decline of the epic genre and the appearance of shorter lyrical texts, popular memory only preserved fragments in the form of epic and traditional romances. On the basis of one of them popular tradition wove the image of the Cid as a young hero ready to revolt against his king:

[. . .] los trescientos hijosdalgos;	*[. . .] three hundred gentlemen.*
entre ellos iba Rodrigo,	*Among them was Rodrigo,*
el soberbio castellano.	*the proud Castilian.*
Todos cabalgan a mula,	*They were all mounted on mules;*
sólo Rodrigo a caballo;	*only Rodrigo was on horseback:*
todos visten oro y seda,	*all wore cloth of gold and silk;*
Rodrigo va bien armado.	*Rodrigo went well-armed.*

Romance del Cid

Rodrigo and his men go like this to Burgos to see the king. The latter's men-at-arms complain that Rodrigo has killed Count Lozano in a duel. Rodrigo challenges them to avenge the dead man. They disappear. The

romance ends when Rodrigo's father obtains his permission to kiss the king's hand.

The success of these poems encouraged minstrels to compose others along the same lines: minstrel romances. In these two types of romances, quite different from the solemn atmosphere in songs of deeds, there was a predominant taste for the concrete, the subjective and the sentimental. Recited or sung, these poems with their simple metrical structure have expressed many themes and incorporated many aesthetic variants.

The Gutenberg galaxy

During the fifteenth and sixteenth centuries, knowledge left the scriptorium, the monastery and the clerk's library. Masterpieces which were now accessible to a larger public rolled off the presses of Gutenberg, the Estienne, the Plantin. Books now allowed their readers to experience the pleasures of the company of colourful characters such as Ariosto's Roland, or to meet new, racy ones such as Rabelais' Gargantua and Rojas' Celestina. An editor and at the same time, a book stockist, the printer also played a part in the theological debates that questioned the authority of the Church. Without printing, what effect would the theses of Luther or Erasmus have had? What effect would the tales of the great travellers have had during the era of Christopher Columbus' sailing vessels?

The Traveller's Tale

M.-C. Gomez-Géraud

Where am I going? Where does anyone want to go in winter? I'm going in search of the spring, I'm going in search of the sun, [. . .] it burns like a torch before my eyes in the colourful mists of the East.

Gérard de Nerval, *Voyage to the East*

The traveller's tale is a difficult literary genre to define. Everything was grist to its mill: verse or prose, the scientific approach of the geographer, the botanist, the archaeologist, the ethnologist, the intentions of the explorer or the missionary, the intimist or mystical quest. The traveller's tale made no distinction between types of discourse. Sometimes it was graced by the attentions of famous writers

such as Montaigne or Goethe; sometimes it was handled clumsily by Grub Street's most obscure inhabitants. A mercenary sub-genre, vilified since time immemorial and considered to be little more than a tissue of lies, it has nevertheless always been popular – under the protection no doubt of Hermes, god of travellers . . . and bandits.

Precursors

If we want to trace the traveller's tale to its origins we must look to Antiquity. We are not even sure that the title of father of the genre can be attributed to Herodotus who, in the fifth century BC, pushed the limits of his *Inquiry* as far as the Araxes and the Indus, though he did leave behind descriptions which were useful to Renaissance geographers among others.

In the thirteenth century, Europe was already looking eastwards; travellers were returning from the East with tales full of marvels and surprise. The Italian Franciscan, Giovanni del Plano Carpino, sent by Innocent IV as an emissary to the Great Khan from 1243 to 1246, gave his impressions and descriptions of Batu and Karakorum. Shortly afterwards (1252–1254), the Fleming, William of Rubrouck, sent by Saint Louis, confirmed what his predecessor had written about Mongolia; Montecorvino, then Marco Polo, had reached China. On returning from his travels, the Venetian merchant dictated *The Book of Wonders* (1298) which startled its readers with its strangeness. Marco Polo, however, admitted he had not revealed half of what he had seen in the lands of the Great Khan! The information that he did provide was supplemented by the *Itinerary* of Brother Odoric of Pordenone, compiled on his return from a long journey to parts of the Far East: Tartary, India, Sumatra, Borneo, China and Tibet (1314–1330). The influence of these works was relatively modest in comparison to the unprecedented success of the *Voyages* by the English doctor, John of Mandeville – though it is now thought he was only an armchair geographer – compiled in 1356 or

1357, where manuscripts, translated into various languages, circulated throughout Europe. This geographical *compendium*, which conjured up a picture of both the Holy Land and China, attracted readers with its fabulous elements and the prodigious characteristics with which it endowed far-off countries. The viewpoint of Afanasy Nikitin, a merchant of Tver, is quite different: he set out for the Caucasus in the reign of Prince Mikhail Borisovitch (1462–1485) and made his fortune in Persia and India. In his *Itinerary* he lists a series of observations on the religious practices of the people he met, revealing a sympathetic curiosity.

The fate of these explorers before the word had been formulated, impelled to go beyond the trade-routes of the Levant in search of new wealth or for the greater glory of God, was the exception rather than the rule. On the other hand, from early Christian times and throughout the Middle Ages, a throng of pilgrims, merchants and religious men composed, against a never-changing backdrop, tales of their halts and tribulations on the way to Compostella or Jerusalem.

New worlds, new tales

The Renaissance heralded a new era for the travellers tale. The world of the mid-fifteenth century, when the Portuguese, pushed ever further south beyond Cape Bojador (1434) – beyond which stretched the uninhabitable torrid zone described in Ptolemy's geography – then the southernmost tip of Africa (1497). The frontiers of the known world were pushed back westward when the Genoan Christopher Columbus, commissioned by the King of Spain to find a sea passage to the Indies, stumbled across some of America (1492) and pioneered the way to the 'fourth part of the world'.

From then on, overseas travel took on new dimensions: knowledge, conquest, conversion. Such was the dream come true of a Europe which, sure of itself and its own values, set out to conquer a world and established an empire for centuries to come. The traveller's tale

recorded and paid lip service to its ambitions. The tribute paid to navigation by humanists summed up these hopes in the name of a Christian vision of history. The French geographer and traveller Nicolay (1517–1583) wrote:

> God the Creator made and established Man in His likeness as lord and master over all lands and seas and everything contained therein, giving him an instinct to find out the extent of his temporal possessions in their totality [. . .], so that by means of peregrinations and communications, all the various countries of the world might learn to live in peace and grow familiar one with another, mutually amending any barbaric vices and teaching one another true religion, [. .], communicating with each other and distributing wealth by reciprocal trading and equal and gracious exchange of their common goods [. . .], so fertile seem all fields [. . .]. And that, due to such symbolic peregrination, a city common to all men may be made of this one earth, yea, even a family, the father of whom will be God and the eldest son Jesus Christ.

Travellers' tales were written as and when discoveries were made. In thrall to its first readers – the rulers who commissioned long voyages – their primary vocation was to impart geographical and strategic information. It gauged the possibilities of conquest or of commerce in view of the new countries' resources or indigenous customs; it smoothed over the difficulties of getting to places by providing cartographic landmarks to steer by. Such was the appeal given to the celebrated *Carta de Pêro Vaz de Caminho* relating to the voyage of Pedro Alvarez Cabral (1500–1502), which stood out from the rest of Portuguese geographical literature in which we can distinguish between chronicles, 'roteiros' and ships' logs, nautical guides and descriptions of new lands. These traits persisted in Christopher Columbus' *Cartas*, or the narration of Amerigo Vespucci, known as *Carta sobre las islas recién halladas en cuatro viajes suyos* (*Letter on the Islands recently discovered on Four of his Voyages*), published in 1505 and embellished with woodcuts; or, a little later, in the accounts that the Frenchman Jacques Cartier addressed to François I, in particular his *Bref Récit* (*Short Account*, 1545), in which this native of Saint-Malo painted Canada as a land every bit as promising as Peru.

Conscious of what was at stake in the New World, the kings of Spain decreed that the advance of the Conquistadors through the new continent should be recorded in detail. Eyewitnesses were told to put each episode of the Conquest in writing. Every expedition had its official recorder: Coronado for the territories in North America, Bernal Díaz del Castillo and Hernán Cortés in Mexico, Alvarado in Central America, Jiménez de Quesada in Colombia, Cieza de León in Peru, Valdivia in Chile, Federman in Venezuela. The chronicles of such men had their own axe to grind, particularly noticeable, for instance, in the *Historia verdadera de la conquista de la nueva España* (*The True Story of the Conquest of New Spain*) by Bernal Díaz del Castillo (*c.*1500–1581), written many years after his return to Europe. Here scant regard was given to chronology or geographical detail; instead we find a patriotic fervour and a strong religious bent that constantly attributed military victories to God, and a mixture of factual description with chivalrous motif. Steeped in a history dominated by the spirit of the Reconquista, Spain repeated in its American epic the ideals it espoused throughout the Middle Ages, pushing back the infidel from the shores of the New World. According to Francisco Lopez de Gomara:

En acabándose la conquista de los moros, que había durado más de ochocientos años, se comenzó la de los indios para que siempre peleasen los españoles con infieles.

When the conquest of the Moors, which had lasted more than eight hundred years, was over, that of the Indians started so that Spaniards could continue to fight against Infidels.

In the second half of the sixteenth century, the traveller's tale became an accessory to the picturesque and the romantic. The *Singularitez de la France Antarctique* (*The Curiosities of the French Antarctic*, 1557) by André Thevet or the *Histoire d'un voyage fait en la Terre du Brésil* (*Story of a Brazilian Journey*, 1578) by Jean de Léry (recognised by Claude Lévi-Strauss as the 'ethnologist's breviary'), gave the curious reader a precise picture of the cannibalistic customs of the Tupinamba tribe, while the engravings they contained show 'for free' a portrait of primitive peoples who have not yet acquired the name of noble savages. On the other hand, *The Peregrinations* (1614) by Fernando Mendes Pinto, a masterpiece of Portuguese literature, which transported the reader to China and the East Indies in journeys full of storms and attacks by pirates, turn the traveller's tale into an adventure story. This particular vein was mined for years, especially in tales of shipwreck which became popular in Portugal in the second half of the sixteenth century, reaching a pinnacle with the collection of Bernardo Gomes de Brito, known as *Historia Tragico-Maritima* and published in 1735–1736.

A reasoned inventory of the earth

The Renaissance saw the development of overseas travel as a phenomenon that would change the course of European history, opening up new perspectives for every nation.

The travel books that people were then reading are proof: by trying to gather together the whole of geographical knowledge and display, by means of travellers' tales from all over Europe, a reasoned inventory of all the territories scattered over the face of the earth, these weighty tomes attempted if only symbolically, to possess the world. The Venetian Ramusio (1485–1557), whose *Navigations and Voyages* was published between 1550 and 1559, was at great pains to describe the part Italians had had in the adventure of the long voyage. He hoped he could convince them to set out in search of the wealth that the New World also held for them. Richard Hackluyt (*c.*1551–1616), whose

Principal Navigations, Voyages and Discoveries of the English Nation, published in 1589–1590, was famous for its breadth of information, set out to show how, thanks to trade with the New World, England could eventually attain true economic independence.

A hymn to the power of nations that discover new potential for development as the limits of the known world recede, collections of travels are also a mirror of reflected European awareness of what discovery can entail. The *Grands Voyages (Great Journeys)* edited in Frankfurt by the de Bry family between 1590 and 1634 chronicled in a series of several hundred engravings the destruction of the Americas by the Conquistadors and depicted the natives of countries across the seas. We can understand why 'from these plates [. . .] a feeling of melancholy rises: death is there already and we cannot help but notice. De Bry too seems to have sensed it: his engravings are a sort of funeral dirge in honour of the Indian's passing and fix in the mind of posterity images that hint at atrocity and cruelty' (M. Duchet).

From the banal journey to the tall tale

As long as the discoveries are made, the traveller's tale preserves its function of privileged informer about strange lands. Until the eighteenth century, it remained the prime tool of geographic research and the servant of nations who went to find new sources of wealth across the seas. We must wait for Wilhelm von Humboldt and the thirty volumes of his *Voyage to the Equinoctial Regions* (1807–1834) to see a definitive end perhaps to that era of accounts designed to extend our knowledge. The traveller's tale, however, went on to conquer an audience enthralled by exoticism, an important factor when it came to selling books, whether it was the *New Voyages* of the Baron de Lahontan in North America (1703), the *Journey via Muscovy to Persia and the West of India* by Cornelis de Bruin (1718), or the travel narratives of James Cook, published after 1772. Anthologies like the *General History of Travel* by Prévost (1746–1759) were a good example of the

success of this genre. In *Circumnavigation* by Bougainville (1771) we are as interested in finding out about distant lands as we are in dreaming of the coasts of islands where 'the air that one breathes, the songs, the dances almost always accompanied by lascivious postures, everything recalls at all times the tender caresses of love, everything cries out to us to abandon ourselves to it'.

The literary vogue for long journeys was associated with another phenomenon which developed during the Romantic period, when the English launched the 'Grand Tour' in continental Europe: travel became an escape from boredom. For twenty or thirty months people travelled through France, Germany, Switzerland, Italy, Spain and sometimes Greece. No writer came back without having replenished his store of impressions: Thackeray, Shelley, Goethe, Hugo, Théophile Gautier or even Stendhal. But because the world was getting smaller, Walpole could declare:

> The farther I travel, the less I wonder at anything: a few days reconciles one to a new spot, or an unseen custom; and men are so much the same everywhere that one scarcely perceives any change of situation.

The East, however, never stopped yielding up its charms to natures uncompromising in their search for the absolute. The *Voyage to the East* (1848–1850) by Gérard de Nerval was the perfect symbol of an initiatory quest which led the individual to the revelation of the mystery of his origins. The world's passing show was merely a pretext for an interior journey. The huge world of the self consoles us for the claustrophobic frontiers of the outside world. It was not gratuitously that the ethnologist Claude Lévi-Strauss placed the following words at the beginning of *Sad Tropics* (1955):

> I hate travel and explorers, yet here I am getting ready to relate my expeditions. How long it was though before I made my mind up! Fifteen years have gone by since I left Brazil for the last time, and for all these years

I have often planned to write this book and, each time I did, something akin to shame and disgust prevented me. What? Am I to describe in detail so many things that are anodyne, so many trivial events?

The loss of interest in the genre was connected with the narrowing of horizons. Instead of the traveller's tale we now have tales of achievements or of journeys accomplished in record time as if today we have to reinvent space.

Machiavelli (1469–1527)

P.-M. Sipala

In a celebrated letter written in 1513 to his friend Francesco Vettori, Niccolo Machiavelli, angry and mortified, described the life he had to endure in the countryside near Florence. He spent his days in humiliating occupations and in games with ordinary folk. Only during the evening, wearing formal dress, could he establish an ideal dialogue with the writers and leading lights of the classical age. He was the Secretary of the Republic of Florence for fifteen years and, entrusted with successive diplomatic missions to Duke Cesare Borgia, the King of France, Louis XII, and the Emperor Maximilian, he sharpened his powers of observation to the point of writing accounts of 'things' in Germany and France and on the Duke's methods of eliminating enemies.

The Prince: a theory of the State

During these years Machiavelli wrote *Il Principe* (*The Prince*, 1513), in which he recalls his 'long experience of things modern' and the 'continual lessons of Antiquity'. We owe to this piece of writing the extraordinary influence of Machiavelli in the European ideological debate and the survival of its key ideas: first and foremost the analysis of Italian political reality, characterised by the weakness of individual fiefdoms in relation to great international States, such as France and Spain,

who, between them, competed for domination of the Italian peninsula. This premise led Machiavelli to imagine a prince and a non-mercenary militia capable of liberating Italy from 'barbarians' by creating a central northern State. There follows a definition of methods to set up and maintain a state.

Political science

How can a prince build and preserve a State? Should he make himself loved or feared? Should he keep faith and 'live with integrity' or is he allowed to violate moral principles? Machiavelli's answer to these questions was that the prince should do good but also evil 'if necessary', that he should be as cunning as a fox and as strong as a lion, that he should make people love him (if possible) or fear him (if unavoidable). Machiavelli considered these criteria as norms, but without going as far as to say that 'the end justifies the means', a saying with which he was later incorrectly credited. This phrase is, in fact, a travesty of his thinking, in as much as the justification of means (political) by an end (moral) re-establishes between politics and morality that link which Machiavelli had broken to lay bare the autonomy of political action.

Machiavellianism

Machiavelli's thinking was misinterpreted and his works were put on the Index in 1559. The Catholic polemic against him began in 1535 with a pamphlet by the English cardinal, Reginald Pole, and an accusation of impiety. In France, in 1573, the 'Machiavellianism' of the Italian advisors of Charles IX was condemned. Political, Catholic and Protestant polemics all vented themselves on Machiavelli and the adjective 'Machiavellian' became a synonym for atheistic and free thinking. At the same time another interpretation of Machiavelli, equally misguided, came to light: that of him as a democrat who, ostensibly reinforcing the prince's power, actually showed people how violent and cruel he was.

Erasmus (c.1466–1536)

J. Ijzewijn

Let us try not to act violently or turbulently!

Erasmus

In his letters Erasmus used two images to designate the twin poles of his literary pursuits: on the one hand the 'Musarum Vireta', the green mansions of the Muses; on the other the 'Theologorum spineta', the thorny bushes of the theologians. These names corresponded to the titles he conferred on himself: 'poeta', i.e. humanist, in his youth; 'theologus', theologian, following on from his first stay in England at the end of 1499. These titles, in turn, corresponded to the two ideals of his life and of all his intellectual striving: 'bonæ litteræ' or classical literature and its humanist continuation, and 'pietas', genuine, true faith through the mediation of a theology free from scholastic accretions and based on first-hand knowledge of the Scriptures.

Humanist and theologian

A great love of the beautiful, the pure and the genuine underpinned the life of this scholar and writer. It was the immediate legacy of the Italian humanists of the Trecento and the Quattrocento that Erasmus of Rotterdam, as a student, was able to read in Deventer, thanks to printing, the great invention of his childhood. Petrarch, Leonardo Bruni, Valla, Francesco Filelfo and others had rescued the literature of Antiquity from obscurity, reintroduced its study and propagated its message. They wanted to restore the timeless beauty of the classical Latin language and literature, return to the unsullied sources of Greek culture and root out everything that was barbarous in their age. All this can be read in Erasmus' early works, for example in the remarkable dialogue *Antibarbari* (*Against the Barbarians*, 1494). But these ideas were the leading principles of classical rhetoric restored to pristine purity: a good writer writes correctly; he expresses himself clearly, adapts his style to the needs of his subject and knows how to adorn a text discreetly.

For the whole of his life, from his first eclogue in the style of Virgil to the last great work of his career, his treatise on Christian rhetoric – the art of the preacher – Erasmus described his principles and, an admirable stylist, revealed the lasting value of having a good style. His work inevitably attracted not only the praise and enthusiasm of his humanist brethren, but also often the hostile criticism of those – mostly theologians – who did not share his humanist ideas and who therefore saw no reason for changing their style or for adopting more scientific methods in the study of Greek and Hebrew.

Poetry, prose, translations

As a humanist, Erasmus was above all an 'orator': a prose writer. But he started out as a humanist poet and also made a contribution to the drama of his time, another prime area of humanist literary endeavour. Although he published many original works, he was also an eminent translator. Like all the great humanists from Leonardo Bruni, he translated into Latin an impressive array of Greek texts: Euripides, Lucian, Plutarch, Galenus, Libanius, as well as innumerable fragments of poems and proverbs that we find scattered through *Adages*. He followed in the footsteps of the Italians whose efforts were made known to him in his youth from his reading and from precursors like the Frisian Rodolphus Agricola and, later, in Venice, Bologna and Rome. He maintained a certain distance from his models, especially in the second half of his life. A famous dispute made him oppose a certain school of humanistic style originating in Italy, that of the Ciceronianists: prose writers who regarded Cicero as the only admissible model for good humanist prose style. In his dialogue *Ciceronianus* (1528) Erasmus mocked in a witty way the extremist and absurd insistence on purity of style by this school. Unfortunately too many readers came to the wrong conclusion that Humanism and Ciceronianism were one and the same thing. They did not notice that this dialogue, in certain passages, was a settling of grievances for Erasmus with certain academic circles in Rome who in his opinion did not give humanism its due. Subsequently, Erasmus was taken literally, even though historical facts indicate that he was sometimes a master of misinformation.

As a true humanist, Erasmus had a deep affection for classical poetry: Virgil, Horace, Ovid, Juvenal. He knew them by heart and even remembered them when working on his works of piety like the *Commentaries* on the Psalms. At the cost of long hours of reading and practice, Erasmus learned to manipulate with ease the most varied and sophisticated metres of classical poetry. All his life he had a penchant for Latin prosody: the last piece we know of his was written in verse, in Basle, barely weeks before his death.

Erasmus did not, however, become a great humanist poet. Perhaps he did not have the rich poetic vein of his contemporary Johannes Secundus. The Northern European monastic and ecclesiastical milieu in which he lived and on which he was dependent was often hostile to the culture of humanism. While he was still a student, Erasmus dreamed of being a poet, but one of his fellow students pointed out that, for a Christian, poetry was a total waste of time unless he chose to write religious verse. Not a very encouraging comment for a young man with artistic aspirations! To some extent, Erasmus accepted this state of affairs by composing, for example, a long religious poem on Christ's resurrection and his descent into Hell (1499?). The most interesting thing about this is that it imitates an Italian model, the *De Triumpho Christi* by Macarius Mutius (1499). This characteristic of Northern European humanist literature should be emphasised: many works had at their source not only a classical model but, even closer to home, some Italian ancestor, the name of whom, more often than not, was kept secret.

The translation of two tragedies by Euripides, *Hecuba* and *Iphigenia in Aulis* (1506), made it possible for Erasmus to become one of the original pioneers of the rediscovery of Greek

tragedy in the West. These translations were a turning point for the return of Euripides (and later Sophocles and Aeschylus) to the European stage. Also in 1506, an Italian, Giorgio Anselmi, published *Hecuba* in Latin in Parma. It was the first time since Antiquity that a Greek dramatist had been accessible to a larger audience, ancient Greek being the privileged possession of a few rare scholars. After Erasmus and Anselmi, other humanists carried on the work of translation, among them the German reformer Melanchthon and the Scottish poet Buchanan.

The *Colloquies*: humour and irony

Theatrical performances in schools aimed to teach pupils how to express themselves fluently in Latin. Another work by Erasmus had the same aim and its author's genius was able to make of it, not just some college handbook, but one of his masterpieces and a book that the modern reader can still read passionately and profitably: the *Colloquia* (*Colloquies*, 1518) – dialogues. At the beginning of the collection, which included new pieces over the years, were simple elementary formulas for beginners such as greetings and thanks. But the dialogue quickly became more dense, as the interlocutors discuss all kinds of contemporary problems, some of which remain live issues today: religion and the Church, politics, war and peace, literature, social life, women – in a word, all the important and interesting aspects of human life. These texts were written in a lively way, in a rich and unstuffy style, so we can surmise that the pupils who learned their Latin with the help of these *Colloquies* were indeed privileged. Unfortunately the powers-that-be could not see the humour in the critical and independent cast of Erasmus' thought, and before long the book was bowdlerised, censored and banned. Here, for example, are a few lines of a colloquy between a priest and a young woman called Magdalia; it is an exchange of ideas wholly typical of Erasmus as much for the content as for the humorous, ironical style:

P. *What is this furniture I can see here?*

M. *Don't you find it to be in good taste?*

P. *I don't know. In any case it is hardly suitable for a girl or a lady.*

M. *Why not?*

P. *Because everything is filled with books.*

M. *Well, as you are of noble birth and a priest and a courtier to boot, surely you must have seen books in the homes of great ladies?*

P. *Of course, but they were in French. Here I can only see Greek and Latin books.*

M. *Is it only books in French that teach us wisdom?*

P. *What noble ladies need is to have something to pass their time on pleasantly.*

M. *But can only noble ladies be wise and live agreeably?*

P. *You are mistakenly connecting being wise with living agreeably. Wisdom is not something women should have and living agreeably is only right for noble women. [. . .]*

M. *Does not everyone have the right to live well?*

P. *Of course.*

M. *So how can you live agreeably if you don't live well?*

P. *Ask rather how he who lives well can live agreeably.*

M. *So you approve of those who live badly as soon as they live agreeably?*

P. *As far as I'm concerned, whoever lives agreeably lives well.*

M. *But where does that agreeableness come from; from externals or from the mind?*

P. *From externals.*

M. *You're a delicate priest, but a crude philosopher!*

In Praise of Folly

Because of their humour and irony, the *Colloquies* are similar to another famous work by Erasmus, the *Moriæ Encomium* (*In Praise of Folly*, 1511). This eulogy belongs to a distinct literary genre, the declamation or fictitious discourse. These discourses have been extremely popular since the Greek sophists of the sixth and fifth centuries BC made use of them. In *In Praise of Folly*, Dame Folly speaks out to sing her own praises before her followers – men. In a style which is sometimes light and sometimes pedantic, she rattles off a whole string of sarcastic remarks on human stupidity in general and on that of various social classes and professions in particular. Here Erasmus is visibly inspired by classical texts, for example by a well-known satire by Horace. But Folly does not limit herself to these kinds of stupidity and dwells on the folly of Christianity, the folly of the Cross, the folly of those who in the eyes of the world seek God, that fundamental paradox of Christian faith. This part of the discourse, based on the Bible this time, became longer and more important with each new edition. It would be an exaggeration to say that Erasmus succeeded in amalgamating these two disparate themes into a harmonious unity. The marked dichotomy of the work sums up the two essential preoccupations of Erasmus's life and work: humanism or the cult of classical literature on the one hand, genuine, unspoilt religion on the other.

If this lack of unity was an obvious defect of *In Praise of Folly* the work was also much too long. It contained too many proverbial expressions and adages. This is hardly surprising as all his life Erasmus collected thousands of Latin and Greek proverbs. This is so blatantly true that even quite recently it was possible to say that 'the *Adages* (1500–1536) will prove to be his greatest work, the one that he was constantly revising all his life'. Each expression in this tome is furnished with a philological, historical, philosophical or other kind of explanation; occasionally their development stretched to the dimensions of an essay and become a foretaste of Montaigne. These essays, like many colloquies and treatises, are devoted to important problems in society, in culture, in education.

Erasmus's final work was *Correspondence*, perhaps the one which is closest to our modern tastes. In his letters, Erasmus spoke to the world in general from Pope and Emperor to the most unassuming literature teacher, to his admirers as well as his detractors. He was one of the great letter-writers of Western literature, a peer of Cicero, Voltaire and Madame de Sévigné. He knew how to write a fine letter; he composed a treatise on epistolary art. But he was not only a theorist. He had something to say about the great upheavals that shook and transformed the Europe of his time and he often used letters to make his opinions known. He was a key figure in the clash of ideas that opposed humanism to scholastic traditionalism and theologians to one another. People came to ask his advice, to support and give him encouragement in his cause or to attack and condemn him. His *Correspondence* was a stage over which the whole of Europe passed and on which were played out the great struggles of humanist culture with the Church, events that alternated with the story of his own life: his journeys, his friendships, his illnesses, his financial problems. Here too we find the human being and his weaknesses. In the *Colloquies* he makes us laugh at superstition and the naïveté of worshipping saints. One fine day, however, on the way to Ghent, he fell off his horse and hurt his back really badly. Immediately he called on St Paul to help set him free from his paralysing pain. He was on the point of promising to go on a pilgrimage. In this way his letters indicated the limits of a critical mind to be found in physical pain. Stoicism had no attraction whatsoever for Erasmus! Anyway, he was not the only one not to be always logically consistent: the German humanist Hutten used to pray to the Virgin Mary when he suffered with his feet!

Erasmus tuned into the message and the great intellectual conquests of Italian humanism and transmitted them to the rest of Europe, from Spain to Poland. He also played a major role in ecclesiastical controversies. This last point is fundamental: not only did he transpose his humanist love of genuine and uncorrupted sources on to the religious level, but the struggles that followed gave an enormous resonance to his writings. This is what made him different from his friend Vives, who was a thinker no less energetic and original than Erasmus, but who had a way of

writing that was more impenetrable. Because he was a lay person and of Jewish extraction, Erasmus was careful not to get mixed up in theological arguments: 'Speak to me of anything you like, apart from theology,' he wrote in 1521. Consequently his works were not banned and he did not benefit from the publicity that such a condemnation would inevitably have brought about. Traces of Erasmus can be found almost everywhere in Europe, whether you follow him as a master or reject him as a heretic. But many writers could have repeated what Rabelais wrote to him in a letter in Latin: 'I have called you my father, I should also like to call you my mother . . .'

Ariosto (1474–1533)

P.-M. Sipala

He walked along the streets of Ferrara
And, at the same time, was walking on the moon.

J.L. Borges, *Ariosto and the Arabs*

In Chapter VI of *Don Quixote*, Cervantes imagines that a priest is examining the books of chivalry and poetry of the protagonist, 'from whence came all the harm'. He throws most of them in the fire, apart from a select few, among which – but with the stipulation that it be in the original language – is the *Orlando furioso* (1516, published 1532) of the 'Christian poet' Ludovico Ariosto. We could wonder why this book was withheld from the flames, for the work, of which Don Quixote knew certain stanzas by heart, introduced into the weft of poems of chivalry the red thread of folly, Erasmus' great theme. But folly in the work of the Italian poet was not considered, as in the *Praise* of the Dutch philosopher, 'iucundus quidam mentis error' ('a pleasant aberration of the mind'); it took on dramatic aspects which altered the face of the valiant paladin to the point of making it inhuman.

Perhaps the indulgence of Cervantes' priest was justified because, in the *Orlando furioso*, madness is considered by the 'Christian poet' as a punishment from God for the hero's having forgotten, by reason of his love for Angelica, his God-given mission to fight against the Moors.

Love is madness

Madness was the new ingredient that Ariosto brought to literary tradition by openly associating himself with *Roland in Love*, another epic poem of chivalry in octosyllables by Boiardo and published in 1495. It allowed him to proclaim in the 1516 introduction to his work:

> *Dirò d'Orlando in un medesmo tratto*
> *cosa non detta in prosa mai né in*
> *rima*
> *che per amor venne in furore e matto*
> *d'uomo che sì saggio era stimato*
> *prima.*

> *At the same time I will say of*
> *Roland*
> *something that was never said before*
> *in prose or in verse*
> *that love drove him to distraction and*
> *madness*
> *though he was held to be wise till then.*

Doubtless love was always madness as Ariosto himself wrote with elegant autobiographical references (he was for a long time in love with Alessandra Benucci, a noble lady whom he married in secret so as not to lose the small ecclesiastical income he enjoyed). But Roland's love led to a paroxysm of jealousy when he discovered that the daughter of the Emperor of Cathay (the beautiful Angelica), whom he has pursued all over the world to no avail, had, in her turn, developed a crush on an ordinary wounded soldier, Medoro the Saracen, and married him. A mixture of sadness and envy, of disappointed passion and wounded pride, painstakingly described in all its stages and successive psychological developments, ranging from attempts to deny the reality of the situation to the irremediable acceptance of the truth, it eventually exploded with dramatic effects, as self-destructive as

they are devastating with regard to nature, people and animals. However, the theme of the love of the Christian Roland for the pagan Angelica, with its disastrous outcome, voluntarily placed at the centre of the poem, has another symmetrical and complementary counterpart which is parallel to it: the amorous quest of the Christian lady Bradamante for the pagan Roger. This quest ended in a happy union out of which emerged the d'Este family, that of the lords of Ferrara, at whose court lived Ariosto, who had inherited his father's obligations and administrative functions.

While tragic events were causing upheavals in the Italian political system, Ariosto's life in comparison appears modest and provincial, in particular in a spiritual autobiography, in his *Letters* and above all in his *Satires* written between 1517 and 1524 (while he was working on his great fantasy), the everyday reality of which formed a counterpoint to his *Mad Roland*. He declined to continue in the service of the Cardinal Ippolito d'Este to avoid having to follow him to his new post in Hungary. He gave spurious practical reasons for his decision, but sketched as he did so an ironical portrait of the situation of the courtier who 'wants to contradict his lord [. . .] but who, because of his humble station, does not have the courage to open his mouth'. With equal equanimity, he refused the post of ambassador to Pope Clement VII: he declared his attachment to provincial habits, the physiological necessity for him to immerse himself for at least two months a year in the crowd milling about in front of Ferrara's cathedral, the sheer impossibility of being sent away from the narrow horizons of his home town (*Satire*, VII).

Ariosto did not stop at expressing his view of the world from this private angle. His smile, now tinged with irony, now with compassion or nostalgia for bygone values, prevailed over moments of emotional crisis in his characters and in the events he portrayed. All belonged to a chivalrous and epic world, endowed by definition with a higher, superhuman dimension. But in the same way that Ariosto understood the humanity and the inhumanity of madness, brought back to a human level the behaviour of his heroes and magicians. Even the epic theme – the war of the Christians against the Arabs that formed the backbone of the poem – bore the imprint of the recent history which had witnessed the end of Moorish domination in Spain with the fall of Granada (1492) and the realisation of the Reconquista begun seven centuries before.

The irony of *Mad Roland*

For Hegel, the irony of *Mad Roland* marked an essential point in the process of attrition of the ideals of chivalry. Voltaire, who saw in Ariosto 'his god', wrote in 1742: 'Ariosto is a charming poet, but not an epic one.' Yet the exaltation of physical strength, warrior virtues, loyalty and the 'sterling qualities of knights of old' were not lacking in the poem. A modern reading of it highlights other aspects. During a meeting between Voltaire and Casanova, mentioned by the latter in *The Story of My Life*, the two men vied with each other in reciting from memory cantos from the *Orlando furioso*: Voltaire chose to recite 'the two great set-pieces of the thirty-fourth and thirty-fifth cantos of this divine poet'; Casanova chose the last stanzas of Canto XXIII.

What can we deduce from this choice? The Italian libertine, for sentimental reasons, preferred those stanzas which depicted with psychological verisimilitude Roland's disappointment in love and, in gradual stages, his descent into the long tunnel of madness. The French philosopher, for intellectual reasons, chose the episodes which narrate Astolfo's journeys out of this world, his descent into Hell, his ascent to the Garden of Eden and, from there, with St John the Evangelist as his guide, to the Moon in order to recover Roland's reason, lost among all the things that were mislaid on earth, but can then be rediscovered up there: the sighs of lovers, the praises of the powerful and, above all, men's reason.

The memory of the journey Dante made to the Beyond has an almost familiar ring to it in Ariosto's work and this, in itself, is the source of its irony. Critical reflection attacks the whole apparatus of social relations and especially once again the power structure and the situation of the courtier. The religious foundations of the Heaven–Hell dichotomy were violently shaken. Even the image of St John the Evangelist was unhallowed: he called himself a writer no different from any other and, while he celebrated, not without objectivity, the humanist myth of the poet who conferred immortality on only a privileged few in the ranks of those who were adulated, he portrayed the construction of human history as a 'literary fiction'.

Astolfo's travels, quite apart from his vertical displacement from the subterrestrial world (hell) to the extraterrestrial world (the Moon), have covered, horizontally, a large part of the globe. His winged horse, the hippogryph, 'the offspring of a mare and a griffin', has transported him from one end of the Earth to another.

The adventures of Ariosto's heroes did not recognise frontiers. To compensate for this, they displaced them, with great freedom of movement and invention, from one part of the world to another. This fantastic dimension was also nurtured by the geographical discoveries of Columbus, Vasco da Gama, Cabral and Magellan, who themselves pushed back the limits of the known world.

All these events encouraged an atmosphere in which the marvellous, already present in medieval literature, found new possibilities for realisation. Ariosto never tried to hide the many sources of his work, which included Homer's epic poems and medieval French romances.

A novel in verse

The composition of the poem lasted more than thirty years, interspersed with three versions of it in 1516, 1521 and 1532. Ariosto also carried out its linguistic and stylistic revision. This aimed to eliminate all traces of dialect from its literary language and to elaborate a work in verse capable of rediscovering in the long sweep of its stanzas the rhythm, harmony and fluidity of prose and of a smooth, interesting narrative, easy to read and to listen to.

In order to avoid the monotony which could arise from the 38,000 verses moulded into a closed octosyllabic structure, the poet adopted a narrative syntax, thus combining cadences gradually breathed out, constructed by means of subordinate clauses, and making evocative use of reported speech. It is, in fact, almost a novel in verse, which, as far as prose goes, is based on Boccaccio's *Decameron* and, poetically speaking, on Petrarch's *Poesie*. Like the 'good musician' who often changes the key signature and varies the sounds, sometimes using a low note and sometimes a high-pitched one, Ariosto alternated the tone of the narrative, passing in turn from the heroic to the prosaic, from the comic to the elegiac, from the marvellous to the everyday. In order to obtain these effects, he did not hesitate to interrupt an episode to continue with an earlier one or to introduce a new one. The nonchalant alternation of interruptions and reminders keeps the reader alert. Ariosto achieved a subtle balance between narrative thread and rhythmical harmony.

The poem of anxious wandering

The many characters in *Mad Roland* were not all clearly psychologically delineated. Each character was important, for each followed the pattern of their own adventure which somehow brought them into contact with the main characters. The symbolic meeting point for some of them is the palace of Atlanto the magician where 'Each one seems to find the thing/That they desired or looked for most'. The palace represents the anxious wandering of the man who runs after his delusions. This is one of the main themes of the work, but there are many others: the cult of friendship elevated to heroism, fidelity in love elevated to sacrifice, passion to madness, the marvellous to the fantastic. We also find the representation of negative, though no less real themes: betrayal, female infidelity, blood lust and, through it all, a theme that embraces and

encapsulates all the others, that of their overall harmony. This consisted not just in the winning of the higher values common to all poetry, but also, historically, in the Renaissance concept of harmony between man and nature and between feeling and reason.

It was not by accident that this noble and serene concept of existence grew weaker and darker during the last years of the poet's life. In an appendix to the 1521 edition, Ariosto wrote five pessimistic cantos which he did not include in the third and final edition of *Orlando furioso* in order to preserve the ideal harmony of an age that had disappeared forever.

Ariosto's influence

Mad Roland has often been reworked, integrated with other works, continued, and not just in Italy where, in the sixteenth century, Roland was depicted as having finally become wise and Astolfo as being mad and in love instead. Ariosto even found admirers and disciples in Central and Eastern Europe, albeit somewhat later. In eighteenth-century Germany, Wieland was considered to be the 'German Ariosto'; in the Hungarian epic *The Peril of Sziget* (1651) by Miklos Zrinyi, and in Poland in the work of the Romantic poet Słowacki, affinities can be traced to a common Italian predecessor. There are traces of Ariosto's influence in Shakespeare, and Byron declared his personal admiration for him.

But for obvious reasons of physical proximity and cultural continuity with the 'song of exploits' and the 'romancero', it was in France and Spain that *Mad Roland* had the widest repercussions in the areas of imitations, translations and literary judgement. One volume gathered together in 1572 all the imitations that various French poets had made of certain cantos of Ariosto. Montaigne admired in him his fervent imagination which allowed him 'to flutter and hop from one story to another'; the characters of Alcina and Olympia were taken up by the poets of the Pleiad; La Fontaine made use of certain moral themes in his *Fables*.

Madame de Staël observed that 'Ariosto is the first modern painter and consequently the greatest modern poet perhaps' and, judged by the principles that inspired her own conception of literature in its relations to social institutions, at the beginning of the Romantic movement (1800), she considered him to be the expression of the Italian character which unites 'in the very objects that are of greater importance, the gravity of form to the lightness of feelings'.

In Spain, in 1549, *Mad Roland* appeared in Castilian in a translation by Captain Jeronimo de Urtea that annoyed Cervantes. The latter felt the attraction of many themes in Ariosto. The character of Angelica, the symbol of sought after, elusive femininity, was taken up by various authors, including Lope de Vega in an epic poem, *The Beauty of Angelica* (1602), and in his first plays. The influence of Ariosto on Spanish lyricism was present in the language and the imagery of Garcilaso de la Vega and in a 'romancero' by Góngora that treated afresh the theme of the amorous encounter between Angelica and Medoro. The most successful imitation of *Orlando furioso* was in the Baroque epic of 40,000 verses by Bernardo de Balbuena, the Bishop of Porto Rico, *Bernardo or the Victory of Roncevaux* (1624). From the world of Latin America, still open to the attraction of chivalrous subjects, came the most recent sign of interest in Ariosto. Borges, in a poem of twenty-four quatrains, *Ariosto y los árabes* (*Ariosto and the Arabs*, published in a 1969 volume), touched on the universal themes of literature that Ariosto resuscitated :

As for every poet, fortune
Or destiny gave him a rare experience;
He walked along the streets of Ferrara
And, at the same time, was walking on the moon.

Fernando de Rojas (1465–1541)

A. Diaz-Muñoz

Oh love, love, I did not think you endowed with the strength and the power to kill your own subjects!

Fernando de Rojas, *La Celestina*

The *Tragicomedia de Calisto y Melibea* (*Tragicomedy of Calisto and Melibea*, 1499), by Fernando de Rojas, is better known by the name of its main character: *La Celestina*. In terms of its ideology, aesthetics and style, it is a pivotal work between the Middle Ages and the Renaissance. It does not belong completely either to the novel genre or that of the drama: it is armchair theatre, following in the wake of a mode launched by Petrarch, very common in the Italy of the fifteenth and sixteenth centuries, and which already had its antecedents in the Middle Ages in the leisured classes.

Fernando de Rojas, born in Puebla de Montalbán, in the province of Toledo, probably in 1475, lived mostly in Talavera de la Reina. A lawyer, he was also the mayor of this town where he died in 1541. He was a converted Jew, which explains his opinions and those of his characters with regard to certain precepts of Christianity.

La Celestina

The author of *La Celestina* tells how, as a student in Salamanca, he found a manuscript. In it we discover a rich young man, Calisto, who is running through the town in pursuit of his hunting falcon and who strays into the garden of Melibea, with whom he falls in love. This was Act One of his work. Taking advantage of a fortnight's holiday, Fernando de Rojas decided to add to this little tale, which had so captivated him, at the rate of a chapter a day; the first edition of the book therefore contains sixteen chapters. Having returned home, Calisto realises that he cannot live without his lady, and one of his servants,

Sempronio, suggests he use the services of the old go-between, Celestina. She becomes the central character in the work as she sustains the plot: to make Melibea fall into the arms of Calisto. We are present at the unfolding of a female passion, of the initial refusal of Melibea to abandon herself to Calisto one night in her room. Calisto pays Celestina with a gold chain, but the young man's servants begrudge this reward to the old woman whom they murder; they will be brought to justice for this crime.

The following night obliged to flee through the window of Melibea's room, Calisto falls and kills himself. Melibea commits suicide out of desperation. The work ends with the lament of Pleberio, the young girl's father, which supplies a moral. The enthusiastic public reproached the author with the rapidity of the punishment that befalls the lovers. Fernando de Rojas added five more acts.

Its popular success earned the work the severest strictures. According to the moralist Luis Vives, it was a book to avoid like the plague. Cervantes commented: 'A book which would be, in my opinion, divine/If only it were less human.'

The human tragedy

In his prologue Rojas affirmed that the work was 'composed to criticise the folly of lovers who, prompted to disorderly conduct by their desire, make a goddess of its object. It also puts one on one's guard against the deceitfulness of go-betweens and the treacherous flattery of servants.' Rojas' intention, however, was not to write a work of Christian didacticism, but to express the tragedy of what it is to be human.

The work offers a new concept of man and of the world which surrounds him: Renaissance society in which everyone asserts themselves and everyone is intent on personal pleasure and material gratification. In the suicide scene, Melibea seems to be unrepentant ('I lost my virginity and we enjoyed our delightful sin of love for nearly a month'), nor does she seem to suffer from the loss of her lover. Disappointed, what she reproaches

herself with more than anything is not having taken more and better advantage of the pleasure love afforded her.

The dialogue form gives life to the action, revealing the existence of amorous passions and involving the reader in the lovers' pleasure or in the grief of Melibea's parents. The language varies with the social class: that of Calisto, Melibea and her parents is a living example of the speech of the moneyed classes during the time of the Catholic kings. In the language of Celestina, the servants and the prostitutes, there are the vivacity and colour of the lower classes, often enriched by proverbs and the humour of popular wisdom. That is why it was said at the time that there was no language more natural, more fitting or more elegant than that of *La Celestina*.

La Celestina belonged in Europe with the books that contributed with their realism to the birth of the modern novel, by unifying medieval and classical characteristics, Italian and Spanish traditions of popular literature, the influences of Petrarch, Boccaccio, Boethius, Andreas Capellanus and those of the Greco-Roman classics. The work was so popular that it was immediately translated into almost all European languages – there were more than 187 editions before 1600 – and imitated by other Spanish writers, Torres Naharro, Francisco Delicado, and Portuguese writers, Feliciano da Silva, Jorge Ferreira de Vasconcelos. Adapted for the stage by Camilo José Cela, the work still appeals to us today because of its vitality and the inexhaustible capacity for enjoyment of La Celestina.

Rabelais (*c*.1483–1553)

M.-C. Gomez-Géraud

Find me a book in any language, conveying any faculty or knowledge that you want, possessing comparable virtues, properties and characteristics, and I'll stand you a round of tripe.

Rabelais, prologue to *Pantagruel*

Rabelais was hailed by Flaubert in the nineteenth century as 'sacrosanct, immense and finer than fine', but for most people since then his work has been overshadowed by Gustave Doré's engraved illustrations to the major texts. The readers of Rabelais fully understood the gastronomical excesses of the heroes of 'that Aeschylus of overindulgence' (Hugo) and their almost mystical taste for wine which brings men together, unchains minds and presides over the act of writing. His readers created Rabelais in the image and likeness of his heroes, celebrated his irreverence towards institutions, saluted his Gallic genius and satirical verve and would willingly have raised their glasses in the company of that altarboy of the 'wine service'. It is true that Master Alcofribas Nasier (an anagram of François Rabelais) resembled the characters in his work. He was insatiable in his appetite for knowledge, just like his giants, free as Panurge and, weather permitting, ready to cast off, tossed, like Pantagruel's companions by the waves of a Renaissance at its height, where man is learning to put his trust in man and in his ability to manage his own destiny.

The seven lives of Rabelais

Destined for the monastic life, François Rabelais left the Cordeliers of Fontenay-le-Comte to live with the Benedictines of Maillezais in 1524, where he had more freedom to devote himself to the pleasures of study. But the young monk soon hankered after 'the perfect knowledge of that other world, which is man'. He began to study medicine in Montpellier, then practised in Lyon, a centre in France for humanist printing and the gateway to Italy. Here he published certain scholarly works: the *Letters on Medicine* by Manardi (1532) and a *Topography of Ancient Rome* (1534), translated by the Italian Marliani. He also edited *The Testament of Cuspidius* (1532), a comprehensive forgery which, in his fervent love of Antiquity, Rabelais had taken for an archive piece dating back to the days of the Roman Empire that had suddenly come to light. From Lyon he set out

on his first two journeys to Rome with the diplomat, Jean du Bellay (1534, 1535–1536). It was, above all, in Lyon that *Pantagruel* (1532) and *Gargantua* (1535) were born: the adventures of these two giants and their all too human companions began with these two stories. The *Tiers Livre* (*Third Book*, 1546), banned as soon as it was published, forced Rabelais into exile in Metz in imperial territory.

But the journeys and tribulations soon came to an end with the final stay in Rome (1549) and the final ecclesiastical appointments. Rabelais was happy to take the income from the parishes of Meudon and Saint-Christophe-de-Jambet. He finished the *Quart Livre* (*Fourth Book*, 1552) before dying in March 1553 with the words: 'Bring down the curtain, the farce is over' – if legend is to be believed.

Rabelais' death, however, did not stop Panurge and his companions from continuing their journey of discovery in search of the oracle of the Divine Bottle. In 1562 there was a new book in the bookshops, *L'Isle sonante* (*The Ringing Isle*). The book had got longer by 1564 and appeared under the title of the *Cinquième Livre* (*Fifth Book*), signed François Rabelais. This 'resurrection' was the cause of much discussion. Should we believe the work to be apocryphal? Today critics believe that its editors called 'fifth Book nothing more than rough drafts of previous books or notes made while reading' (M. Huchon). But what proof, if any were needed, of the extraordinary vitality of an author whose popularity, more than ten years after his death, did not waver.

Deeds of giants

Was the monk-cum-doctor-cum-humanist who carried on a correspondence with Budé and Erasmus seeking diversion when he came to compose the gluttonous and larger-than-life doings of giants in which the body and its needs took centre stage? Was it simply the obscenity of the work that justified its first ban by a Parliament in 1543? We would do better to believe with Daniel Ménager that 'the religious ideas of the author were targeted, whether seriously or facetiously expressed.' If Rabelais' work was indeed a river that fed on the mud of popular tradition, this river simultaneously carried with it the aspirations and reflections of humanist circles and was regenerated at the fountainhead of personal experience. We can listen to the advice of Rabelais when, in the prologue to *Gargantua*, he refers to the work as a Silenus and a juicy bone, inviting the reader to 'open the book and carefully weigh what matters are touched on therein. Then you will know that the drug it contains is more valuable than what the box seemed to promise, that the matters here under discussion are not as silly as the title makes out.'

The giants did not spring directly out of Rabelais' creative genius, but came from the *Chroniques gargantuines*, one of those novels of adventure and chivalry among so many at the end of the Middle Ages in which the wizard Merlin recruited the giant Gargantua into King Arthur's service. From this popular material, simply drawn and designed to satisfy the expectations of a readership hungry for marvels and adventures, Rabelais took 'the support of a scenario' (M. de Dieguez). He departed from his model, however, in that his giants are an incarnation of mankind as visualised by humanist thinkers and also because as the books continue, that they serve an apprenticeship to being human.

The structure of *Pantagruel* and *Gargantua* follows the pattern of the novel of chivalry which describes the hero's youth before narrating his deeds of physical prowess as a warrior. The marvellous accounts of the 'nativity' of the giants (Gargantua comes out of his mother's womb by way of the 'left ear') are followed by the exploits of their childhood – the raised rock, the invention of toilet paper, the theft of the bells of Notre-Dame – that time of life during which the inner man is still under the domination of the body. The enthusiasm of the Renaissance then made its appearance in the encyclopedic programme of studies for the use of two adolescents. Rabelais had read Erasmus: he knew both the treatise on *Youthful*

Civility and *The Education of the Christian Prince*. He wanted to build a fully rounded individual: a 'well of learning', a good servant of God, for 'knowledge devoid of conscience is merely ruin for the soul', and a doughty knight capable of defending his home and his friends 'against the assaults of malefactors'.

Having received his education, the giant is called on to prove himself, for war tests not only the knight's aptitude for combat, but a king's ability to govern his subjects. Having beaten Picrochole, Gargantua must decide the fate of the vanquished and punish those who have disturbed the peace. Humanist optimism radiated even through the punishment Gargantua metes out to them, for 'Gargantua did them no harm, other than to order them to run the presses in his printing establishment, which he had recently founded.' Can we read into this the hope that Gutenberg's invention, thought up 'by divine inspiration', will one day get the better of artillery given to men 'by diabolic suggestion'?

Belief in a human race on the road to perfection is made flesh, it has been said, in the Utopian fiction of Thelema at the end of *Gargantua*, where 'freeborn men and women, of high birth, well educated, conversing in honest company' apply the motto 'fais ce que voudras' ('do as you will'). But Utopia is not the favourite resort of the Rabelaisian hero: neither Brother Jean, who has received Thelema as a reward for his exploits, or any of his companions go into this new-style abbey, where man, deprived of his body, has become a shadow, and where individuals fade away into an ethereal humanity, sheltered from the conflicts, the questions and the tribulations of history.

During the twelve years that elapsed between the publication of *Gargantua* and that of the *Tiers Livre*, the humanist horizon darkened. The great inspirers of the movement had disappeared, Thomas More had been beheaded by Henry VIII's executioner's axe in 1535; then, in 1536, Erasmus had died. In France, Rabelais lived through religious fanaticism's burnings at the stake and the hardening of repression against evangelical Christians. His own books were also banned. Perhaps these circumstances went some way towards explaining the new orientation of his work. Behind the question of Panurge who, thinking about getting married, wants to make sure that he will not be cuckolded, other problems were hidden. All the learned men of the period were assembled in vain, for Panurge does not just consult dreams, 'Virgilian castings', the sibyl of Panzoust and lunatics, but also a theologian, a doctor, a jurist and a philosopher. None of them can answer Panurge's questions with absolute certainty and the latter saw himself irremediably thrown back on his own resources and anxieties.

He reads into the gesture of the jester Triboulet, who 'put the bottle in his hand', the need for him to set out on a journey, to open himself up to the world to get closer to the oracle of the Divine Bottle. This quest was the theme of the *Fourth Book*, then of the *Fifth*. The voyage from island to island gives the reader a mirror reflecting a world in which the unknown offers countless opportunities for wonder: fabulous animals, strange monsters, unicorns and physeteries. But these islands were also the reflection of a universe which has lost its harmony, the 'abode of a mania, the refuge of characters who have made themselves ridiculous by entertaining an idea that determines their bodily features, their way of dressing and what they talk about' (A. Glauser): Ennasins of curious ancestry, Chitterlings sworn enemies of the sinister Shrovetide, Gastrolaters and Papimanes. The satirical account of the voyage reminds us that areas of scandal are ever near.

'Trinch' is the word that the bottle proffers to Panurge's ear; not a tribute to wine, but an invitation: 'taste and see for yourselves your enterprise'. This not a call to drunkenness, but to poetic fervour, for Pantagruel, Panurge and Brother Jean, under the influence of enthusiasm, start to 'rhythmise', possessed no doubt by the intuition that 'only Poetry [. . .] can account for a world that eludes the categories of reason by its dark splendour' (D. Ménager).

A writing laboratory

An obscure splendour lived in Rabelais' language. Far from elucidating the world's mystery, it suggested new mysteries. Aiming to express the world in its infinite richness and its infinite density, it experimented with the possibilities of language without ever excluding any form or style.

So the text was a constant medley of colours, a mixture of verse and prose, a marriage between laughter and seriousness, between scatology and humanist philosophy. The text was that barrel (prologue to the *Third Book*) that Rabelais invites us to empty by the jar, but which turns out to be inexhaustible, for 'it has a living and perpetual source'.

The presence of lists in Rabelaisian texts, like the clever entanglement of anecdotes that slow down the main action, revealed his extraordinary fertile imagination. There are lists of the books in the library of Saint-Victor, of Gargantua's games, of the dozens of different uses to which toilet paper can be put. Abandoned to the writer's whims and fancies, the reader walks into a labyrinth symbolic of the infinitely open nature of narrative creativity. All that is needed for this to happen is, for example, for the narrator who is writing these 'true stories' to enter into Pantaguel's mouth. He finds another world there and sees 'big rocks like cliffs in Denmark [. . .] those were his teeth, and big meadows, big forests, large and fortified towns, no less large than Lyon or Poitiers' (*Pantagruel*, Chapter 23). The narrator does not cease to wonder at the universe that he is simultaneously creating and discovering. Rabelais, just like modern writers, gives us to understand in this way that writing opens on to perspectives of immensity, surprise and questions.

The never-ending banquet

Rabelais enjoyed the posthumous fate of writers of genius. Slated by St Francis de Sales who spoke of 'the infamous Rabelais', he was appreciated no better by La Bruyère who declared his work 'incomprehensible', adding 'It is a monstrous assembly of a delicate and ingenious morality and a sullied corruption.' Rabelais was rehabilitated during the French Revolution by Guinguené who, in his *Rabelais' Authority in the Present Revolution*, chose to see in Master Alcofribas a critic of the Ancien Régime. Rabelais was only truly appreciated in the nineteenth century. Flaubert saluted 'a work as fine as wine whose mystery it possesses'. Chateaubriand praises 'one of the founding spirits of humanity'. Michelet and Hugo saw in Rabelais a 'laugher of fearsome proportions'. Hugo asserted that 'his laughter is one of the abysses of the human mind', while Michelet declared: 'A bold explorer over the deep sea engulfing old gods, he journeys in search of the great *Perhaps*.'

Despite these latter judgements which gave Rabelais' work a veritable philosophical status, his first imitators retained his more spectacular aspects. In the sixteenth century, the German Johann Fischart adopted *Gargantua* in 1575. This disciple of Luther, no doubt frightened by his turbulent model, watered down the religious message of the work, laying particular emphasis on the funny episodes, especially the scatological ones (he invents graffiti on the wall of the latrines in a Thelema rechristened *Willigmut*!), and derived enjoyment from increasing the already copious lists of words.

Henceforth would-be satirists were decorated by some kind of reference to Rabelais. So, in The Netherlands, Marnix de Sainte-Aldegonde, a great destroyer of the scandals associated with the Catholic Church, 'turned religion into A Rabelaisian mockery' according to De Thou. In England, Thomas Nashe proposed an adaptation of the *Pantagruelian Almanach* (1591). In 1589 Gabriel Harvey celebrated his satirical genius humorously: 'Pity me for having entered into the lists with a Gargantuist who will swallow me up raw in a salad.' In recognition of possessing similar qualities, Swift obtained from the Abbé Lejeune the title of 'the English Rabelais': his critique of the establishment and the monarchy encountered motifs of travel and the gigantic that were omnipresent Rabelais.

We can understand the annoyance of Alfred Jarry, a faithful disciple of Alcofribas, when his Père Ubu, the definitive satirist, was reduced to a scatological mask: 'the reading public, illiterate by definition [. . .] has levelled against *Ubu Rex* the charge of being a vulgar imitation [. . .] of Rabelais, because [. . .] a certain word is repeated in it. [. . .] Moreover, people have seen in *Ubu* a work "written in Old French", because we had fun printing it in old-fashioned characters, and thought that "phynance" was a sixteenth-century spelling.'

Rabelais constantly reminds the general public of his presence – even a public not acquainted with his work. He lives in everyday language. We find traces of his giants not only in French dictionaries, but also in English ones (*gargantuan*: huge, enormous), Flemish ones (*Pantagruëlist*: joyful drinker), Italian, Spanish and Portuguese ones. Portuguese speakers have even retained a proverbial expression, 'a quarter of an hour of Rabelais', to mean a difficult situation that has to be faced up to which it is not easy to get out of. We have here an allusion to the adventurous life of a creative writer whose heroic banquets continue to be a feast for the mind.

Luther (1483–1546)

H. Ch. Graf von Nayhauss

> We are beggars, that is true!
>
> Martin Luther

'He it was who, with his translation of the Bible, woke and set free the German language, a sleeping giant; with his Reformation, he raised the consciousness of a whole nation to the point where it began to think and feel.' This is how Herder, the father of German romanticism, hailed Luther's legacy.

A prophet in his own language

Goethe wrote with similar respect to Blumenthal: '[. . .] for what God says in the Koran is true: we have sent no prophet to any people unless he spoke their language. And so it was that, thanks to Luther, the Germans became a people.'

'Whoever would speak of new German literature must begin with Luther,' according to Heine. In *Religion and Philosophy in Germany*, he declared that with the translation of the Bible, 'thousands of copies of which printing in its infancy, that magic art, disseminated among the people, the language of Luther spread, in a matter of a few years, throughout Germany and was elevated to the rank of a universally accepted formal written language. This written language still reigns supreme in Germany and gives this country, as divided politically as it is religiously, its literary unity. This one old book is a fountain of eternal youth for our German language.'

Luther did indeed spark off the Reformation, a process which, in the realm of theology, had already begun 300 years before. The Reformation proper began with the overwhelming question which never left Luther alone: 'How do I find a God who is merciful?' The 'monastic little friar', as Charles V scornfully referred to him, wanted to go to Heaven and not to Hell.

Nevertheless the Reformation would not have had the repercussions that it did without the new German language raised by Luther to the level of literature and the literature that ensued in all German-speaking countries as a result of his translation of the Bible. All Luther's literary and journalistic work, always to be read in the light of his activity as a reformer, covered a veritable gamut of genres: lectures, discussions, defending theses, programmes for reform, tracts, homilies, letters, hymns, a religious literature aimed in its entirety at initiating and edifying. The many fables translated into German also form part of this œuvre, not to mention the *Tischreden* (*Table Talks*, 1566).

Luther's life

Martin Luther was born on 10 November 1483 in Eisleben and studied his 'septem artes' (seven arts) at the University of Erfurt. After his master's degree in 1505, he should have devoted himself to the study of law but, for personal reasons, he gave up the chance of a worldly career in 1505 to become a monk in the monastery of the Augustinian hermits of Erfurt where he became a prior in 1507. In 1508 he took a chair at the University of Wittenberg where he lectured in moral philosophy and the study of Scripture. In 1510 and 1511, because of the lawsuits in which his order was involved, Luther left for Rome. On his return to Wittenberg he obtained the title of Doctor of Divinity and in 1512, he succeeded his patron, Johann von Stampitz, as Professor of Holy Scripture, a post he held until his death.

Luther was also a preacher, considering this occupation to be 'the most elevated function of Christendom'. He constantly strove, in consequence, to be easily intelligible, for 'we must tell the poor that what is white is white and that black is black in the most straightforward way possible, just as it is, with clear and simple words, and, even then, they barely understand.'

In 1515 Luther took charge of a district that administered eleven monasteries in Saxony and Thuringia. Despite his outward show of success, man's relationship with God remained for Luther an open-ended, unresolved and painful question. He became a monk to serve God and to obtain the salvation of his soul. During his monastic period, the question of predestination plunged him into the depths of anguish, bringing him to a state of inner collapse. One part of humanity was destined for eternal happiness, the other for eternal damnation, according to God's own inscrutable edict. Luther feared he would be among the rejected; because of little things like praying distractedly or sins of thought and omission, he believed that he was no longer capable of total love towards God, of complete abandonment. His pitiless sounding of himself may be explained by the idea, shared by Ockham, of a God of majesty who demands perfect justice. In his lectures he rediscovered the mysticism of Bernard de Clairvaux, Bonaventure, Gerson, Anselm of Canterbury, Tauler and *German Theology*. His deep imagination and sensitivity increased his fear of eternal damnation.

Luther first tried to resolve his conflicts by accusing himself, declaring God's judgement right in the hope that He would no longer judge someone who has judged himself. Such an attitude was in opposition to the scholastic doctrine of nominalism, to the idea that God does not refuse His grace to whoever shows Him love through good works. Luther would not allow the individual to share in the divine grace. He was sure that everything on earth depended on God's mercy: 'I am Yours, make of me one of the blessed.' In his lecture on *The Epistle to the Romans* a moral certainty suddenly appeared: 'God's justice is shown in the Gospels.' Man only needs to believe in the Good News to know what divine justice is. This absolute pre-eminence of faith abandoned to God's will over all pious works, this direct communication of the soul with God remained the central core of Luther's personal faith throughout his life. Everything henceforth depended on salvation in Christ alone. This was 'the one article of faith on which the Church stands or falls.'

The practice of selling indulgences therefore appeared to Luther as a cut-price redemption from sin. He denounced this trade in forgiveness of sins in his ninety-five theses, which, following a tradition inherited from Melanchthon, he nailed to the door of the chapel of Wittenberg Castle on 31 October 1517 as an invitation to theological debate.

Written in Latin and soon translated into German, these theses sparked a huge popular movement. The anti-Vatican lobby of the imperial States, whose demands had already been expressed in Erasmus' *Complaints of the German Nation*, also backed Luther. Called on to retract by the Diet of Worms and faced by the Emperor Charles V himself, Luther refused to abjure his theses and concluded his refusal with the words: 'So help me God! Amen!'

Luther was excommunicated and banished. In order to protect him, his overlord, Frederick, Elector of Saxony, had him brought in secret to the castle of Wartburg. There Luther translated the New Testament from Hebrew and Greek into German. In 1522, he returned to Wittenberg, devoting the rest of his life to strengthening his theological arguments and locally forming evangelical communities and churches.

Luther died on 18 February 1546 during a journey to Eisleben, his family's original home. Two days before his death, as a sort of summary of his life, he wrote: 'We are beggars, that is true!'

From theses to Reformation

Luther was reluctantly drawn more and more into the struggle against the Church of Rome. The more he had to defend himself, the more visible the nefarious evolution and weaknesses of the Papacy appeared. In 1519, in a debate with the theologian Johann Eck, Luther disputed the divine origin of the Papacy. He said about Jan Hus, burnt as a heretic in 1415, that 'among the articles of faith [proposed by the Czech contingent] condemned by the Council of Constance, some were truly Christian and in keeping with the spirit of the Gospel.' He even proclaimed that Church Councils may also be fallible. This was enough for Eck to denounce Luther as a heretic: a denunciation which increased Luther's popularity not only in humanist circles, but also among ordinary people.

In the years 1520–1521, in three great works in prose, Luther elaborated reforms on a massive scale. From being a reformer he became a driving force behind the Reformation. He began the first of these writings, *An den christlichen Adel deutscher Nation. Von des christlichen Standes Besserung (To the Christian Nobility of the German Nation on Improving the Condition of Being a Christian*, 1520), with an appeal to Emperor, princes and the minor nobility, asking them for their help. The Papacy made all reform impossible, hemmed in as it was by three high walls. The first wall was the power of the Church, superior to temporal power. The second was the doctrine that only the Pope could be infallible in his interpretation of Holy Scripture. The third was the monarchical power of the Pope, who alone had the power to convene a Church council.

> A Christian is free, master of all things and subject to no-one. A Christian is a servant in subjection to everything and everyone's subject.
>
> Martin Luther, *On a Christian's Freedom*

For Luther all believers, and all baptised Christians, were ecclesiastics: each and everyone was himself priest, bishop and Pope. The priest was not an intermediary between God and men. It is for the Christian to decide what is good or bad in his faith, as he is his own priest. Luther called on the temporal powers to convene a council open to everyone, for nobody is better able to do this than 'the secular arm of the Church'. He concluded with the wish: 'May God grant to all of us a Christian discernment and to the Christian nobility of Germany in particular true spiritual courage so it can do what is best for the ailing Church!'

In his second great writing, originally in Latin, *De captivitate Babylonica ecclesiœ prœludium* (*The Babylonian Captivity*, 1520), Luther, kept only the Word of God and three sacraments in a pared-down form – Baptism, Penance and the Holy Eucharist – instead of the old seven sacraments. He thought that by refusing to give communion to lay people under both kinds, and by defending the dogma of transubstantiation and the sacrificial nature of the mass, the Church was placing itself in chains. In expressing such an opinion, Luther struck a heavy blow at the exclusive nature of the priesthood.

His third great work, *Von der Freiheit eines Christenmenschen* (*On a Christian's Freedom*, published in November 1520), was a response to an attempt at mediation on the part of Karl von Miltitz, the papal secretary. In this new attack on the foundations of the Roman Catholic Church, Luther again asserted that, as far as the Christian is concerned, only God's own Word is authoritative in matters of faith.

From 1521 to 1525 the Reformation in Germany gathered momentum. Luther found a huge audience in the German-speaking countries: peasants, burghers and the nobility immediately applied the teaching of Luther's polemical writings to their own social and political situation. But Luther preached against such 'dissolute spirits' and in 1523 he wrote the tract *Von weltlicher Oberkeit, wie weit man ihr Gehorsam schuldig sei* (*On Temporal Authority, to What Extent We Owe Obedience to It*). Here he demanded that Christians recognise authority as part of the divine order.

Yet he had written that Christians should depose regents who 'have acted in a non-Christian manner towards us and are therefore tyrants'. This is why Thomas Müntzer (1489–1525) and the peasants accused him of only being radical in his words. In 1524 Müntzer circulated a *Hochverursachte Schutzrede und Antwort wider das Gaistloße, Saufft-lebende Fleysch zu Wittenberg* (*A Strongly Justified Defence and Answer to the Witless Lump of Meat Living an Easy Life in Wittenberg*). With the revolt of the German peasants, Luther answered these charges and took up a position in *Wider die mordischen und reubischen Rotten der Bauren* (*Against Bands of Peasants Who Murder and Pillage*).

Luther's Bible

With each new work by Luther, one thing became increasingly clear: the need to make the Word of God accessible to everyone. Since 1517, Luther had translated nineteen of the psalms into German, but it was only in the seclusion of his retreat in Wartburg that in ten weeks he wrote the New Testament in German. Beginning in the summer of 1522, he undertook his main work, the translation of the whole Bible into German, eventually achieving the 'crowning glory of German prose' (Nietzsche). In the autumn of 1534, Hans Lufft published the first whole Bible in High German in Wittenberg. From 1534 to 1574, Lufft sold 100,000 copies (without taking into account facsimiles). The translation was accomplished with the help of the new scientific approach of humanism, by referring to texts in Hebrew and Greek. A truly hermeneutic translation, it sought to restore the most accurate overall meaning without becoming the slave of the word in isolation. In the interests of this appropriateness for the text, Luther was sometimes obliged to 'sacrifice the literal meaning'. His principle was that 'the sense should not be subservient to the words, but the other way round'.

In contrast to the mystics who preceded him in forging the German language, Luther was devoted to the concrete meaning of words. His language, with its harmonious rhythms, did not shade into the abstract, but remained visual, potent and fresh. According to Luther, in order to know how we should speak German, we need to 'ask the mother in the home, the children in the streets, the ordinary man in the marketplace, and see on their face how they speak, and translate accordingly, and, in this way, they will understand and notice that we are speaking German with them.' Luther's human side is nowhere more apparent than in his letters to his wife and children, as well as in his *Table Talk*. This consisted of conversations with friends and contemporaries, written in an agreeable mixture of Latin and German.

Luther's influence

Lessing, Klopstock, Herder, Hamann, Goethe and even Brecht lifted things straight from the Bible, straight from Luther's language. The *Book of Evangelical Songs*, the *Collected Sermons* and the catechism exerted the strongest influence on Protestants. In Luther's thirty-eight canticles, which are still sung today, the great reformer revealed himself to be as linguistically creative as he was in translating the Bible. In his thousands of sermons which still used fourfold meanings and allegory, Luther remained in close contact with the tradition current at the end of the Middle Ages. But at the same time he succeeded in raising to a level of rationality didactic literature and the literature of personal improvement. He dared to think, as Kant, later, and on a different plane, would dare to know.

8 *The Second Half of the Sixteenth Century*

A. BENOIT AND G. FONTAINE

I can tell you, reader, that, in all good faith, the poet I am currently looking for in our language will be the poet who can make me feel indignant, calm or joyful, make me feel his pain, his love, his hate.

Joachim du Bellay, *Defence and Illustration of the French Language*

'Cujus regio, ejus religio' ('Religion depends on who rules'). After the compromise arrived at by the Peace of Augsburg (1555), what was left of European cultural unity in a grievously divided Christendom? Initially it seemed as if the message of artists and men of letters had transcended the great ideological rift in Western culture. The Protestant Rembrandt completed an engraving showing *The Death of the Virgin* for the Catholics among his admirers. The books of Erasmus and even of Melanchthon, one of Luther's disciples, were used in Jesuit colleges. But in the second half of the sixteenth century, what was there to turn to when the Earth was no longer the centre of the cosmos and the Church no longer indivisible and universal? In science, as in religion, the most contradictory ideas coexisted, so that neither could reign supreme. In this atmosphere of confusion, of intellectual and spiritual anarchy, the anger of heated debate gave way to the violence of armed intervention. The whole of Europe was thrown into turmoil with wars of religion, the rise of nationalism and with Turkish domination in the Balkans. Everyone everywhere was haunted by a horror of the plague. Death, omnipresent, became an obsession, arousing in people feelings of fragility and melancholy.

The Reformation and the Counter-Reformation engaged the attention of the whole of Europe, apart from countries under the sway of Greek Orthodoxy who were not directly affected by the Protestant schism. Literature, naturally enough, weighed in on the side of ideologies. The act of writing added fuel to the fire begun by the wars of religion; opinion, according to Ronsard's formula, became 'the wet-nurse of conflict' (*Discourse to the Queen*). In a Europe convulsed by war, which literary forms could exorcise the violence of the times? There was the theatre, a genre in which the world was portrayed as an illusion and a 'shifting sand' (Shakespeare, *Macbeth*). There was the pastoral, a type of writing harking back to a 'lost age fair' (Tasso, *Aminta*). There was poetry to the accompaniment of a lute, the strings of which 'are passing sweet' (Kochanowski, *Hymns to God*).

OPINION, WET-NURSE OF CONFLICT

On both sides, all means of imposing beliefs were legitimate. Literature was muzzled because the Church suspected it of failing to act in accordance with dogma; a religious literature evolved in tandem with the many translations of Biblical texts. Texts stating a particular position cut across one another wherever there was confrontation between Catholics and Protestants, armed with sword or pen. The mocking laughter of satire mingled with the clash of steel on steel. So the number of books multiplied and, what is more, the number of books in the vernacular. At least religious tensions had encouraged implications for the arts because they encouraged the development of national literatures. In the midst of all this sound and fury, few rejected fanaticism, preached tolerance or extended an olive-branch.

Literature muzzled

With the exception of Venice, Italy never really questioned the authority of the Pope, despite protests organised by Juan de Valdés and the appearance of centres of Calvinism, such as the one at the court of Ferrara. On the other hand, the Italian peninsula was the birthplace of that important movement of spiritual renewal that we know as the Counter-Reformation, brought about by the Council of Trent (1545–1563). The Church formulated several measures to combat the reformed religion. New religious orders were created: the Oratorians, the Ursulines, the Lazarists and, above all, the Jesuits, intended by preaching and teaching to labour for the restoration of the Catholic Church's good reputation. Apart from the Company of Jesus, the Congregation of the Supreme and Universal Inquisition and the setting-up of the Index of Forbidden Books both served Rome's purpose: the purification of consciences.

This disciplinarian mentality, enforced by measures which aimed to check the emancipation of thought, put obstacles in the way of the free circulation of ideas and hampered literary production. Authors who refused to toe the line were in dire danger. The Renaissance in Italy, reaching its zenith before 1550, went into terminal decline after this date. Italian individualism was stifled by the rules of the now fashionable Aristotelian poetics. Tasso studied both the precepts of Horace and Aristotle's *Poetics*, following them with enthusiasm in *Arte Poetica* (*The Art of Poetry*, 1565). The same was true of Giulio Cesare Scaligero (Scaliger, 1484–1558) in *Poetices Libri Septem* (*The Seven Books of the Poetics*, 1556). What should have been the logical outcome of Quattrocento humanism degenerated, more often than not, into a sterile,

slavish imitation of Greek and Roman authors. Only Gian Maria Cecchi (1518–1587), Anton Francesco Grazzini (also known as 'il Lasca', 1503–1584), Giovan Battista Gelli (1498–1563), Giovambattista Della Porta (1535–1615) and Giordano Bruno (*Il Candelario*, *The Chandelier*, 1587) tried to break free of classical influences. On the other hand, in the field of lyric poetry, the most frequently imitated model was not an ancient author, but Petrarch: the poet who celebrated Laura remained the undisputed yardstick. The epic enjoyed great success for, as a genre, it could only be encouraged both by the Church and by monarchies: it denounced the enemies of Catholicism – and not only the Islamic infidels – and flattered rulers who were celebrated as mythical heroes. Narrating a Christian epic, however, while at the same time being faithful to Aristotelian rules, proved difficult. Works lacked spontaneity and freshness; characters were two-dimensional; heroic deeds were unconvincing.

However, there was one important exception: Tasso. **Torquato Tasso (1544–1595)** dreamed while still very young of writing an epic on the conquest of Jerusalem, but the subject seemed too arduous. At this stage he gave up the idea. In 1562 he published a poem of chivalry, *Rinaldo*, which made him famous overnight. At the court of Duke Alfonso II, sensual, sophisticated and affected by the Reformation, Tasso lived the happiest years of his life, despite the pain of his tempestuous love affairs with Ferraran princesses. *Aminta*, a pastoral performed on 31 July 1573, dates from this period. This hymn to love, which expressed the feeling of time passing, is founded on a bold moral, far removed from the rigorous precepts of the Counter-Reformation.

In spite of the popularity of *Aminta*, Tasso had not entirely forsaken the project he had had in his head for many years. In 1575 he finished *Gerusalemme liberata* (*Jerusalem Delivered*). A Christian epic of chivalry, this long poem in twenty cantos, which tried to reconcile the sacred with the profane, related the capture of Jerusalem in the hands of the

Saracens by an army of Crusaders under the command of Godefroi de Bouillon. If there were many echoes in the poem of Homer, Virgil and Ariosto, the expressive sweetness and delicacy of feeling undoubtedly belong to the tender, melancholy temperament of Tasso himself. Witness, for example, the following moving scene in which Tancred, a Christian knight, just has time to baptise the woman he loves, Clorinda, a Saracen princess whom he has mortally wounded in single combat, her armour having rendered her unrecognisable:

Non morì già, ché sue virtuti accolse	*[Tancred] does not die just then,*
tutte in quel punto e in guardia al cor le mise	*but gathers all his strength around his heart,*
e premendo il suo affanno a dar si volse	*and, fighting back his despair,*
vita con l'acqua a chi con 'l ferro uccise.	*he rushes to restore, with the waters of baptism,*
Mentre egli il suon de' sacri detti sciolse,	*life to the woman that his sword has killed.*
colei di gioia trasmutossi, e rise;	*While he pronounces the words of consecration,*
e in atto di morir liéto e vivace,	*Clorinda smiles, and, as if happy to be dying,*
dir parea: 'S'apre il cielo; io vado in pace.'	*she seems to say: 'Heaven is opening up to me, I go there in peace.'*

Torquato Tasso,
Gerusalemme liberata

Often attacked, notably by Galileo, *Jerusalem Delivered* was one of the most popular works of Italian literature. Tasso was conscious of having produced a poem vastly superior to the feeble attempts of Il Trissino and Alamani. Nevertheless he was soon racked by doubts. A former pupil of the Jesuits, he questioned the quality of his faith. Had he written an impious work? Had he made it overly sensual? Torn and anxious, he wrote a new version of *Jerusalem*. Robbed of its romantic episodes, *Jerusalem Delivered*, which he was now unwilling to acknowledge, became a didactic and wholly edifying work: *La Gerusalemme conquistata* (*Jerusalem Conquered*, 1592–1593). Pope Clement VIII promised to have him crowned at the Capitol, a reward reserved for truly great Italian poets. But the ceremony did not take place as Tasso's health had deteriorated, and he died on 25 April 1595.

Discordant voices were raised within the Italian Church itself. A dialectician with a lively mind and a feared polemicist, **Giordano Bruno (1548–1600)**, in his philosophical writings (*Della causa, principio ed uno, On the Cause of Principles and Unity*, 1584), criticised Aristotelianism, advocating a knowledge of the world based on experience and reason. He was sent to the stake for his pamphlets, in particular, *Spaccio della bestia trionfante* (*Expulsion of the Beast in Triumph*, 1584), in which he described a firmament purged of its constellations of evil omen in the forms of a Bear, a Dragon and a Lion and subsequently inhabited by Wisdom, Truth and all the other benevolent entities. The Jesuits saw in this an allegory for the purging of Rome and the Church.

> The sentence that you have just read out is more of a problem for you to say perhaps than it is for me to hear.
> Giordano Bruno at the Inquisition's stake

This visible face of the Counter-Reformation, in which the only culture to be disseminated was one which was officially approved, should not hide another major aspect of the Catholic Reformation – the fact that it also led to a spiritual renewal. In Italy, Palestrina created a new musical genre, the oratorio, for the gatherings of the Congregation of the Oratory founded by Philip Neri. Throughout Europe both Catholics and Protestants published many translations of the Bible which, from a literary viewpoint, were masterpieces.

Translations of the Bible

Translations of the Bible, which had been under way at the time for several decades and in some cases for several centuries, all rested on the same desire: to make the Holy Scriptures accessible to the masses and, in each case, vernacular languages were considerably richer for them. Marnix de Sainte-Aldegonde, for example, with his translation of the Psalms (1580), made an important contribution to Dutch prose.

> *Jsemt' roztržen na vše strany,*
> *Nevím, co činiti . . .*

Ján Silván, *Písně nové na sedm žalmů Kajících i jiné žalmy*

Torn between the search for absolute certainties and human happiness, between pessimism and repentance, in 1571 the Slovak poet Ján Silván (1493–1573) published *Písně nové na sedm žalmů Kajících i jiné žalmy* (*New Songs – Paraphrases of the Penitential Psalms and Other Lamentations*). Apart from the paraphrases of the seven psalms of David, the essence of the collection was in the twenty-three spiritual and meditational poems that reflected Silvan's own anxiety. These moving texts were written in Czech with a Slovakian accent, one of two literary languages in Slovakia, but Martin Rakovský (1535–1579) preferred to write in Latin. His humanist synthesis of the ancient roots and the Christian understanding of the world, from the reforming perspective of Melanchthon, reflected on the organisation of the State and of society.

Catholics also played a part in the development of hymns in Czech, a new phenomenon in Europe: we owe a hymnal to Jan Rozenplut

In the same year, in which he published a collection of hymns, 1564, *Kancionál* (also known as the *Hymnal of Ivančice*), Jan Blahoslav (1523–1571), one of the Bohemian Brethren, undertook, on the basis of linguistic comparison, a translation of the New Testament, with specific reference to the Vulgate, the translation by Théodore de Bèze and previous Czech translations. His work prompted the Protestant Unity of Brethren to bring to perfection a translation of the Scriptures different from all previous ones. Making use of Hebrew, Greek and Latin texts, and taking on board the latest findings of homegrown and European Biblical exegetists, a group of scholars produced a work of reference, *Biblí česká* (*The Czech Bible*, 1579–1594), known as *the Bible of Kralice*. For two centuries it remained a standard version for Czechs and Slovaks, even Catholics.

> *I am torn apart on all sides,*
> *I know not what to do . . .*

of Švarcenbach (died 1602), for example, compiled after that of Šimon Lomnický z Budče.

The Reformation touched Northern Croatia, Hungary and Transylvania. For many Hungarians, the fact that they were Protestants was an expression of their national identity and independence: Christians against the Turks, Protestants against the Catholic Hapsburgs. In Croatia the Reformation was quickly stifled by the Hapsburgs, but a few names have survived: Matija Vlacic (Flacius Illyricus, 1520–1575), one of the founders of hermeneutics, Stjepan Konzul Istranin (1521–after 1579) and Antun Dalmatin (beginning of the sixteenth century–1579) who translated the New Testament into Croatian. Primož Trubar (1508–1586) was the central character in Slovenia during this period. Strongly influenced by the works of Erasmus and prompted by Lutheran and Zwinglian ideas, he argued for Slovene to be the language of the liturgy in *Slovenska cerkovna ordninga* (*Church Order in Slovenia*, 1564). In 1557 Trubar published a translation of the New Testament. In order to carry out his translations, he built a literary language on the Slovene spoken in Ljubljana and founded the first Slovene grammar school. But the 'Protestant Renaissance' only lasted a short time: as the sixteenth century drew to a close, the Counter-Reformation destroyed most Protestant books.

In Poland the Reformation progressed in leaps and bounds. Protestants – Calvinists for the most part – even managed to be the majority in the Polish parliament. Bishop Ján Laski, effectively the head of the Reformed Church in Poland, tried to bring together all the Protestant denominations in Little Poland and Lithuania. But the alliance between Calvinists, Czech Brethren and Lutherans only really came about after 1560, the year in which Ján Laski died. The publication of the first complete Bible in Polish by Jan Leopolita, a Roman Catholic priest, was the fruit of this religious fervour. Other translations were subsequently compiled, first by Calvinists in 1563, then by Arians in 1572. In any event, it was the Bible of the Jesuit, Jakub Wujek, that provided a version for Roman Catholics. The appearance of this last Bible in 1599 was an indication of the desire on the part of Poles won over by the spirit of the Counter-Reformation to equip themselves with a national literature appropriate to their religious denomination.

A preacher at the court of King Sigismund III and King Stephen Bathory, founder of several Jesuit colleges and rector of the Jesuit Academy of Wilno, **Piotr Powęski** (known as **Piotr Skarga, 1536–1612**) used sermons in their most exquisite literary form to exhort the Polish nation to abandon heresy. His *Kazania Sejmowe* (*Sermons to the Polish Parliament*, 1597), a moral and political treatise, warned the faithful about the evils of the country's internal dissension. In *O jeności Kościoła Bożego* (*On the Unity of God's Church*, 1577), the basis of the Uniate Church brought about by the Union of Brześć in 1596, which ensured the expansion of Catholicism eastward at the expense of the Orthodox religion, Skarga invented a Biblical style which influenced Polish literature for many centuries. His *Żywoty Świętych* (*Lives of the Saints*, 1579) was also extremely popular, bearing the stamp of the Messianic concept which the great Polish Romantics remembered.

Messianic religion, made possible by the prevailing religious atmosphere of the century, had the same effect on Hungarian minds and was later the source of a whole literary tradition which blossomed with Romanticism.

In the Iberian peninsula, where the writ of the Holy Inquisition was vigilantly observed, religious literature, no less fine or rich, chose a less direct relationship to Scripture. The mystical tradition that evolved in Spain was more of a gloss on the Bible than a translation.

Mystical literature

In Portugal the Counter-Reformation created conditions which encouraged the development of inspirational prose. Frei Heitor Pinto (1528?–1584?) wrote *Imagem da vida cristã* (*Image of the Christian Life*, 1563–1572) which testified to the influence of Renaissance humanism.

Aspiring to be contemplative, but rooted in action, simultaneously idealist and realist, spiritual and human, mystical Spanish literature retraced the steps of the inner quest of a soul filled with the desire to know God. A soul on fire spiritually, **Teresa de Cepeda y Ahumada (Theresa of Avila, 1515–1582)**, wrote simply, sincerely, sometimes humorously works that were mystical and didactic, accomplishing her plan to reform a religious order. Her autobiography, *El Libro de la vida* (*The Book of her Life*, 1588), like her other prose writings, *Camino de perfección* (*The Road to Perfection*, 1583), and *El Castillo interior o Las Moradas* (*The Interior Castle or the Mansions of the Soul*, 1577), described her visions as a heavenly lover. 'I pine away because I do not die,' she wrote in *Aspirations to Eternal Life* (1571).

Following in the footsteps of Santa Teresa, whose disciple and co-worker he was, the 'little saint', as she called him, **Juan de Yepes y Alvarez (John of the Cross, 1542–1591)** did for monks what she had done for Carmelite nuns. His poetry, wholly given over to mysticism, was that of a soul in ecstasy, who felt his pen to be guided by a higher power. According to the poet Valéry, 'These poems give the impression of a very tender love song, initially evocative of an ordinary love and I know not what sweet pastoral escapade lightly sketched in by the poet almost furtively and sometimes mysteriously. But one must not be taken in by this initial clarity: the gloss enables us to return to the original text and to find in its charm hidden depths of supernatural passion and a mystery infinitely more precious than any amorous secret locked inside the human heart.' The amorous lyricism of Saint John of the Cross' poems was literally a pre-text for theological exposition: if each work was relatively short, it was surrounded by a long commentary and detailed glosses. The dark night of the soul was an attempt to explain 'the way of climbing to the top of the mountain which is union with God', but it was also one of the most delicate evocations possible of a night of physical love. *Flame of Living Love* was the most intensely mystical poem by St John of the Cross, its erotic tone unmistakable. In the *Song of the Soul and Jesus Christ its Bridegroom* there was a mixture, as in *The Song of Songs*, of spirituality and libido: the soul – the spouse – goes off into Nature in search of the loved one, God, and questions His creatures until she finds Him and becomes united with Him.

Noche oscura | Dark Night

(Canciones del alma que se goza de haber llegado al alto estado de la perfección, que es la unión con Dios, por el camino de la negación espiritual.)

(Songs of the soul that rejoices in having attained the high state of perfection, which is union with God, by the way of spiritual negation.)

¡En una noche oscura,
con ansias en amores inflamada,
oh dichosa ventura!
salí sin ser notada
estando ya mi casa sosegada.

In the shadow of a dark night,
Anguish all in flames of love consumed,
Oh happy fate not slight!
I went out, I presumed,
Unseen, my home in peaceful calm subsumed.

¡Oh noche, que guiaste,
oh noche amable más que la alborada:
oh noche que juntaste
Amado con Amada,
Amada en el Amado transformada!

Oh night that to me served as guide,
Oh night more loveable than dawn,
Oh night which side by side
Beloved with a love new-born
Placed next to Lover,
Both into each other
Quite transformed!

Juan de Yepes y Alvarez,
Noche oscura

If religion was a source of literary creativity in Spain, elsewhere it was a military and literary battlefield. France was the scene of the most violent confrontations: Ronsard's *Discours* (*Discourses*) were a reflection of the deeply polemical nature of the literature of the time. How could it be otherwise when Blaise de Monluc and Agrippa d'Aubigné, literary champions of Catholicism and Protestantism respectively, openly proclaimed themselves to be heads of factions?

Militant literature

A self-professed enemy of pleasure and the would-be destroyer of the Roman Catholic Church temporal because it made religion into something material and brought God down to a human level, John Calvin, the Savonarola of the North, added to Luther's doctrine and made of the Reformed Church a highly structured organisation. He translated his principal work into French under the title of *The Institution of the Christian Religion* (1560). Against this cogently argued text, in which the theology of predestination was elevated to the status of a doctrine, Ronsard, a fervent Catholic, entered the lists.

Ronsard's first *Discourses* were written in 1560, before the first wars of religion, when there was still hope of an accord – at least political, if not religious – between the two opposing camps. In France, Ronsard was already unanimously recognised by his contemporaries as the 'prince of poets', showered with favours by King Henri II and his successor Charles IX. His polemical writings were a response to the poetic and dramatic works of **Théodore de Bèze (1519–1605)**, who fought in Geneva for Calvin's ideas. With the sincere aim of rescuing the kingdom of France, Ronsard established himself as the leader of the Counter-Reformation. For him Protestants were mutinous dissidents disrupting the peace and the God-given order of things. He accused them of preaching 'an armed Gospel' which, far from spreading the faith, merely sowed the seeds of terror and sedition, portraying the Son of God as 'A pistol-toting Christ blackened all over with smoke.'

The *Discourses*, whose images, myths and allegories contained great powers of evocation, had a certain influence, even with Protestants themselves. They recognised that by putting himself on the side of the Roman Catholic Church, Ronsard had achieved more than the whole of the Sorbonne. **Théodore Agrippa d'Aubigné (1552–1630)**, educated in Geneva by Théodore de Bèze, was the first to acknowledge his debt to Ronsard. *The Scapegoat in the Desert*, the title under which he published *Les Tragiques* (*The Tragic Ones*, 1616), was a soldier-poet who placed both his sword and his pen at the service of the Reformation ('We abort our songs in the midst of armies') without ever denying Ronsard's influence. His allegorical description of France during the wars of religion recalls the *Continuation of the Discourse on the Miseries of this Time* in which Ronsard addressed the members of the Reformed Church:

*I want to paint France as a mother full
  of sorrow,*
*Who has, between her arms, the burden
  of two babes.*
*The strongest, who is proud, takes hold of
  the two nipples*
*Of the nurturing breasts; then, by dint of
  scratches,*
*Blows from fists and feet, he stems the
  flow of milk*
*Which Nature also gave to his twin
  brother.*

Agrippa d'Aubigné,
Les Tragiques, 'Miseries'

You are also like those baby vipers,
*That open up in being born the stomachs
  of their mothers:*
*Thus, by your miscarriage, you have
  killed*
*Your mother, France, instead of feeding
  her.*

Ronsard, *Continuation of the
Discourse on the Miseries of
this Time*

Still very young at the beginning of the wars of religion, this nobleman's son, destined for a brilliant future by virtue of his extraordinary intellect, grew up surrounded by violence. He was eight years old when his father took him to Amboise where the leaders of the Huguenots were executed and made him swear before their corpses not to spare himself 'in avenging these honourable leaders'. He began to write *The Tragic Ones* in 1577, only to complete it forty years later, when the Edict of Nantes, which had stipulated religious freedom, was once again called into question. For d'Aubigné there was just time to ask the Protestants to prepare themselves once again for battle.

Catholics who persecuted Protestants were, for d'Aubigné, a lot of 'false and foolish tongues' whom he accused of levelling abuse at heaven. In the Protestant camp, there was unanimous blame for the Roman Catholic Church, for its lying, hypocrisy and debauchery. In The Netherlands, Germany and Hungary, pamphlets and satirical writings flourished like those by Théodore de Bèze, that derided the Catholic clergy. They were written in the vernacular to have sharper and swifter effect: the abandonment of Latin was a religioius and political act of protest.

Satirical literature

'The school of Geneva offered well-educated teachers and strict codes of behaviour; it was the temple of the new faith; there the Renaissance combined with the Reformation; advanced literary studies went hand in hand with the teaching of theology; Marnix drew from both these sources; his mind was fortified by contact with teachers called Calvin, Théodore de Bèze, etc.' In his edition of the *Works of Marnix de Sainte-Aldegonde* (1857), Edgar Quinet insisted on the influence that Geneva had at this time on noble families in the Low Countries. So it was natural that, after his years at university in Louvain, Paris, Dole and Padua, during which **Filips Van Marnix Van Sint Aldegonde (Philippe de Marnix de Sainte-Aldegonde, 1540–1598)** became familiar, as did many humanists, with six foreign languages – Latin, Greek, Hebrew, Spanish, French and Italian – this young cosmopolitan went on to study theology in Geneva. Once back in his native country, this dyed-in-the-wool Calvinist with the razor-sharp pen, just as sharp in Flemish as it was in French, first published a pamphlet against a Lutheran who dared to cast doubt on the legitimacy of Calvinist iconoclasm: *Van de Beelden afgheworpen in de Nederlanden (On the Destruction of Holy Images in The Netherlands,* 1566). Later he published *Den Byencorf der H. Roomsche Kercke (The Beehive of the Holy Roman Church,* 1569). This biting satire depicted Catholic monks and nuns as 'honey bees':

Van den Byencorf, waer van hy ghemaecht wordt	*Of the Beehive and what it consists of*
De Byencorf dan, dar onse Byen in woonen, swermen ende hare Honich maken, wordt met taye ende stercke Lovensche of Parisische Horden ende Teenen onder een ghevlochten: sy noemense ghemeynlijck te Loven Sophismata oft Quotlibeta, ende men vindtse by de Corfmakers der Roomscher Kercken veyl: als by Joannem Scotum, Thomam de Aquino, Albertum Magnum ende andere dierghelijcke, die seer subtijl in deser Conste gheweest	*The beehive in which our bees are housed, come together and do their work, is made of strong and supple wickerwork from Louvain, Paris or Cologne, subtly interwoven: such stuff is commonly referred in Louvain as sophisms or gibes and is found for sale on the stalls of the basketmakers of the Roman Church, such as John Scotus, Thomas Aquinas, Albertus Magnus and other masters of this ilk who were*

*zijn. Dese Horden alsoo
ghevlochten, moet men noch tot
meerder dichticheyt te samen
binden, met grove Joodtsche oft
Thalmudische kabelen, ende dan
daer over een clevende
Mortelplaester trecken, ghemaeckt
van oude Puyne oft
Kalckscherven (daer de oude
vervallen Concilien voortijdts
mede ghemetselt waren) wel cleyn
tot pulver ghestooten ende dunne
gewrocht, met ghecapt story, dat
de Aptekers noemen:* Palea
Decretorum, *begietende het
t'elcken met schuym der oude
Leeraers: ende daer onde oock
wat nieuwe Calcks van Trenten
vermengt.*

*fine and subtle in these matters. For
greater safety, one should bind
this wickerwork together and join
it up with thick
ropes or Jewish cabbalas, or something
Talmudic, and throw
on top some good cement
made up of old ruins, from which
old and decrepit Councils were
fashioned, broken up and ground down
fine, and mixed with
cut straw that the apothecaries
call* palea decretorum,
*watering it time after time with
the saliva or sputum of ancient
Doctors of the Church, and mixing in too
a bit of fresh quicklime from
Trent.*

Filips Van Marnix, *Den Byencorf
der H. Roomsche Kercke*

Just as vigorously, but with more bias to his virulence, **Johann Fischart (1547–1590)**, a native of Strasbourg, supported the Huguenots in France and attacked the Counter-Reformation. His pamphlets, such as *Das Jesuiterhüttlein* (*The Jesuits' Little Hat*, 1580) were aimed, first and foremost, at monks and Jesuits. In his satires he also attacked the tyrant, Philip II, claimed political freedom for all and marked astrology. Fischart made use of Rabelaisian energy in a free adaptation of *Gargantua* and *Pantagruel* (*Affentheuerliche und ungeheuerliche Geschichtklitterung vom Leben, Rhaten und Thaten der Helden Gargantua und Pantagruel*, 1575). He set part of the action in Germany, denouncing moral decadence and the decline in the current state of the Church and society. But whereas Rabelais, convinced that Nature is good, left plenty of room for individual freedom, Fischart saw man chiefly as a sinner. His satire often had fantastic, grotesque dimensions; this feverish imagination was combined with great erudition. His racy, inventive language seems had a life of its own, chaotic and bursting at the seams, a reflection, as Fischart himself liked to say, of the complex reality that surrounded him. Where Rabelais wrote 'to dance', Fischart went one better with an enumeration of verb forms, a veritable variation on the theme of dancing: 'Da danzten, schupften, hupften, lupften, sprungen, sungen, hunken, reieten, schreieten, schwangen, rangen, plöchelten, fusslöpfelten, gumpelten, plumpeten, rammelten, hammelten, gaukelten, rädleten, burzleten, balleten, jauchseten, gigagelten, armglocketen, handruderten, armlaufeten, warmschnaufelten . . .' Fischart's work represented an important stage in the development of German prose and heralded the exuberance of the Baroque.

National literatures

Germany and Denmark searched for their identity through popular and nationalist literature: generally because of the breakdown of the Holy Roman Empire, Denmark because of constant war with its powerful neighbour, Sweden. The 'Volksbuch' enjoyed extraordinary popularity in the sixteenth century. Considered by the Romantics to be a creation of the collective imagination, it appears today rather as a literary creation that became increasingly popular with most people. There were often collections of little humorous anecdotes designed to poke fun at the failings of small German towns: *Die Schildbürger* (*The Burghers of Schilda*, 1598) tells how the inhabitants of the imaginary town of Schilda, famous for their skilfulness and wisdom, decided to pretend to be stupid so they would no longer be pestered by the mighty of this world and sent away from their town where they could no longer carry out their functions. But they actually become stupid by dint of pretending too well.

We have also inherited *Die Historia von D. Johann Faustus* (*The Story of Faust*), published in Frankfurt in 1587. This 'Volksbuch' took up the legend of Georg or Johannes Faustus (1480–1540), a native of Wurtemberg. After studying theology in Wittenberg, he gained a reputation for being a magician, an astrologer and a charlatan; he was also supposed to have led a life of debauchery and died an unpleasant death. The meaning read into Faust's fate proved that the anonymous author was a convinced Lutheran: he derived a moral lesson from this legend, warning his readers against magical practices and idolatry. Faust gave in to a twofold temptation: he was led astray by both his senses and unedifying books. He abandoned theology for medicine and magic. To enhance his powers, he conjured up demons and signed a pact with Mephistopheles. Remorse, worry and despair finally took their tole, but he died unshriven. His lack of moderation and his insatiable curiosity were his downfall: knowledge could not override faith. Faust's story was marked by current religious preoccupations: satire on the Papacy and the Roman court. Already set apart by the taste for knowledge for its own sake characteristic of the Renaissance, Faust was nevertheless poles apart from Goethe's Faust, the symbol of a human race in search of truth and longing to be saved.

Hans Sachs (1494–1576), a master shoemaker in Nuremberg, tackled the most varied genres of poetry (gnomic poems, fables, 'Meisterlieder'), prose dialogue, humorous anecdote and drama in some five hundred thousand verses. Having attended the 'Singschule', where he learned how the songs of masters ('Meistergesänge') were made, he drew inspiration from current events and his own personal experience, enriched by peregrinations through Bavaria, Austria and Western and Northern Germany, in order to compose his own work. Attracted by the Reformation, Sachs came out in 1523 for Luther, to whom he dedicated a 'bar' – a poem overladen with allegorical meanings: *Die Wittenbergisch Nachtigall* (*The Wittenberg Nightingale*). His religious pieces, designed to edify above all else, sometimes contained sermons about marriage, for example. Their characters, borrowed from Greek epic, Roman history, Teutonic legend or Italian short stories, spoke in the language of the Nuremberg shopkeeper: they were not as yet subject to propser psychological analysis. On the other hand, Sach's humorous anecdotes ('Schwänke') and his farces and carnival plays ('Fastnachtspiele') hold the reader. These short plays in rhyming couplets, with four stressed syllables to the line, limited to a few characters, present everyday pictures, dealing in an unusually lively fashion with the setbacks and quarrels of conjugal life. Sachs preached a rather utilitarian morality. In his eyes, sin was folly and the sinner was a fool.

Anders Sørensen Vedel (1542–1616) affirmed the existence of Denmark as a nation and laid the foundations for a national literature. In 1575, he was responsible for translating the *Gesta Danorum* of Saxo Grammaticus. This Danish version fuelled Danish nationalism and gave birth to a Danish literary language. The artificial character of the language perfected by Vedel and his original style made the language powerful enough to be a viable substitute for Latin. Vedel aimed to compile a new chronicle of Denmark, but in 1593 he had to abandon this plan: he lost his position as historiographer royal after his principal benefactor's death. Vedel made another important contribution to the development of a national literature in Denmark by collecting and editing an anthology of popular songs, *Et hundrede Danske Viser* (*A Hundred Danish Songs*, 1591).

A literature of appeasement

Most countries were involved in the violence aroused by religious questions. The principle of religious tolerance, established for the first time in Europe by the Diet of Bohemia in 1485, and excluding the application of the maxim 'cujus regio, ejus religio' (religion depends on who rules), was ratified by Bohemia. Poland also agreed to freedom of worship. In this 'Paradisus hereticorum', a paradise for heretics, King Sigismund I and his son, Sigismund-Augustus maintained the privilege of contact with their Protestant councillors while adopting positions formulated by the Catholic clergy. The life and the work of **Andrzej Frycz-Modrzewski (Andreas Fricius Modrevius, 1503–1572)** illustrated the royal policy of tolerance. A disciple of Erasmus, the latter embodied the spirit of the Renaissance in Poland. Having finished his studies in Cracow, Modrzewski travelled to Wittenberg, where he encountered Martin Luther and Melanchthon. Back in Poland where he brought Erasmus' library, he became the secretary of King Sigismund-Augustus and went on diplomatic missions to the Netherlands and Bohemia. Persecuted by the Church, which placed his work on the Index, he benefited from the protection of the king, thus eluding ecclesiastical jurisdiction. However, he did not break with Roman Catholicism, even though he freely interpreted its dogma and went further in his criticism of the Church than some Calvinists. All his writings attacked the defects of Polish society: *Lascius, sive de pœna homicidi* (*The Punishment of Homicide*, 1543) denounced the inequality of punishment according to States, as well as the abuses certain nobles made of power. In his masterpiece, *De republica emendata* (*On the Cleaning-Up of the Republic*, 1554), he sketched out his great plan to reform institutions, pleading the cause of the peasantry against oppression from their feudal lords and preaching that every citizen was equal before the law. As a guardian of Christian ethics, Modrevins vigorously opposed religious struggles and advocated tolerance, democratisation of the clergy and secular education.

Respecting freedom of thought, some thinkers denounced the fanaticism and intolerance shown in both camps and the part that both the Reformation and the Counter-Reformation played in extinguishing original thinking. Coornhert, for example, by political action and writing, bitterly opposed the execution of heretics in The Netherlands.

A poet, prose writer, engraver, theologian, moralist, notary public, musician and fencer, **Dirk Volkertszoon Coornhert (1522–1590)** began to study Latin after the age of thirty so that he could read the works of the Fathers of the Church in the original. A man of the Renaissance, well-read in the books of Classical Antiquity and of the Great Reformers, he admired Erasmus, 'the unique Phoenix of all Europe', but objected to his scrupulous submission to the Church's authority. He kept his distance from the Catholic Church, whose Roman idolatry he deplored, but he also had reservations about Protestantism. His humanist belief in the perfectibility of the individual made him reject notions such as the unmitigated corruption of the poor sinner.

A notary public in Haarlem in 1561 and, three years later, its town clerk, he became familiar with politics and cultivated the Prince of Orange who subsequently appointed him as parliamentary secretary to Holland. However, after many struggles and a period in exile, disturbed first by one party, then by another, he abandoned politics to devote himself to his work. This impressively contained 145 different titles. His ideal was a combination of tolerance and freedom of conscience, which, in *Van de toelatinge ende Decreten Gods* (*On God's Permission and Decrees*) led him to reproach Luther with having made of the Bible 'a paper Pope':

Elck wil des anders gheloof regeren	*Each one wants to have a say over someone else's faith.*

Dit doen, diemen voormaels	Those who do this taught
fachleeren	in former times
Dat sulcx den Christen niet	That such behaviour was not fitting
betaemt;	for Christians.
Maer soo ootmoedich was haer	Their spirit then was humble,
gedacht	When, weak, they lay
Alst noch ondert Cruys Lach	beneath the Cross.
sonder macht	But now they make
Nv thoonet syn macht	an impudent display of their power.
onbeschaemt.	

Dirk Coornhert,
Van de toelatinge ende Decreten Gods

Coornhert attempted to write comedies, hymns and theological treatises among other things. His most important work was *Zede-kunst dat is wellevenskunste* (*Morality or the Art of Living Well*, 1585), considered to be the first moral guide in Europe composed in a vernacular language, and deeply indebted to both Stoicism and Christianity. Here we learn how a human being can live virtuously. Coornhert developed the theme of man's perfectibility, man who has free will, moral judgement, knowledge and a conscience to master the four cardinal virtues of wisdom, justice, strength and temperance. 'Weet of rust' – know those things that it is important to know and leave the rest alone – is an adage dear to Coornhert, emblematic of the intel-lectual struggle he had chosen. It found an echo in Montaigne's sceptical approach.

In a part of France where Catholics and Protestants clashed with particular vio-lence ('I was bombarded on all sides: to the Ghibelline I was a Guelph, to the Guelph a Ghibelline'), **Michel de Montaigne (1533–1592)** * kept his head when confronted by fanaticism: 'What truth is it that ends with those mountains, which is a lie to the world beyond them?' This philosophical prudence revealed how troubled late sixteenth-century man really was. The escalation of religious and political struggles, a downturn in the economic situation and the deterioration in standards of living fractured the contented image of man spread by humanism. There was greater sensitivity to the succession of deceptive appearances that constitute the world, to the disappointment of delusions and make-believe.

ON THE EARTH'S SHIFTING SAND: THE THEATRE

At the end of the sixteenth century, the Renaissance had done its work in depth as far as the masses were concerned. Many plays were brought into being by the expectations of a public starved of public spectacles. Italian, Spanish and English playwrights and actors satisfied the taste of their contemporaries for the larger-than-life. To the starkness of reality they opposed a theatrically stylised, codified and acceptable type of violence. Spectators felt an affinity with the characters of Shakespeare, for whom man was merely a strolling player and the world here below 'the earth's shifting sand'.

Didactic theatre

If the medieval heritage was maintained in Germany with edifying plays, Latin drama was also in its element: humanists made use of it to disseminate their ideas. The Jesuits made their theatre into their main pedagogical tool. In the twenty-one Jesuit colleges of the region of the Lower Rhine, 502 plays were performed between 1597 and 1761.

In Scandinavia, after a period of cultural lethargy induced by the Reformation, interest in the theatre was rekindled with Biblical dramas and student comedies, an extension of the college drama taught in schools. There were, for instance, the *Tobiæ comedia* (*Comedy of Tobias*, 1550), attributed to Olaus Petri (1493–1552) and *Samson Saengsel* (*Samson's Prison*) by Hieronymus Justesen Rauch (1539–1607).

The influence of the classics

The Protestant preacher **Péter Bornemissza (1535–1584)** transposed the quarrels between different religious denominations on to the Hungarian stage. In *Tragédia* (*Tragedy*, 1558), freely adapted from Sophocles' *Electra*, he put forward a synthesis of reformed religion and humanism. A theorist of the classical theatre, but also a dramatist, **Antonio Ferreira (1528–1569)** created his own niche with his tragedy *Castro*, an example of the adaptation in Portugal of tragic models from ancient Greece. Its plot was revived in the twentieth century in Montherlant's *The Dead Queen*. Composed in 1558, *Castro* was dedicated to Inez de Castro, the secret wife of the Infante Peter of Portugal, who was killed on the orders of King Alfonso IV.

Dramatic art

This period of European theatre witnessed an explosion of liberating theories of the drama that crystallised the tastes and wishes of a huge audience. In France, the cultivated public enjoyed plays of Robert Garnier (1534–1590) and the aristocratic public those of Étienne Jodelle (1532–1573), which are more like court poetry than drama. But the idol of most theatregoers was Alexandre Hardy (*c*.1570–1632) who satisfied contemporary taste for violence and action.

This enthusiasm for dramatic art was manifested in Italy, England, Spain and France by the construction of many playhouses: architecturally and aesthetically different, the Corral de la Cruz (Spain) and the Olympian Theatre of Vicenza (Italy) were built at the same time, 1584–1585. The invention of the Italian-style stage was symbolic current taste. Architecturally the actors were separated from the public. This made for a twofold spectacle,

one happening on stage, the other in the auditorium: people went to the theatre to see and be seen. The one place that combined make-believe, optical illusions and scenery, the theatre became the fashionable place to be for a society which believed in deceptive appearances and ephemeral dreams. The 'Theatrum mundi' makes us think of transcendental truth: life is merely an illusion, genuine reality lies in the beyond. For the duration of the performance, the burden of social and religious constraints can seem lighter. Perhaps this was why a protest movement that refused to submit to the principles of Aristotle as applied to drama shook Italian theatre to its foundations: a new genre appeared, which turned both Italian and European dramatic techniques upside down: la commedia dell'arte. England meanwhile chose to ignore Aristotelian theories and instead promoted the beginnings of a theatre which released hidden imaginary power.

The commedia dell'arte

The first troupe of professional actors appeared in Mantua in 1545. It was not until 1567, however, that the 'comedians of the art', abandoning the formal script, estures and mimicry as a stage language. Originally, commedia dell'arte contrasted with 'commedia sostenuta' (elevated comedy), written down, learned, declaimed and constructed on ancient models. In addition to improvisation, the commedia dell'arte required of an actor a highly physical, agile and expressive style. The player had to be 'in the profession', and this, in fact, is the meaning of 'of the art'.

The characters of this art embodied universal, immutable types whom the spectator can identify thanks to their mask and costume. In order to fill the gaps in the action, the actor also has a repertoire of proverbs, tall stories, buffoonery and monologues carefully prepared which he can supply at an appropriate moment.

The main characters, or 'masks', had a marked regional origin: there were many 'zanni' or servants, inherited from Latin comedy and catalysts of the action, that come to us from Bergamo, Arlequino, Pedrolino (the French Pierrot), Brighella, Beltrame, Mezzetin, known in France under the names of Scapin, Pasquin and Turlupin. Pulcinella (Punch), heir to the Maccus of the Romans, comes from Naples; his two mirror images, Meo Patacca and Marco Pepe, come from Rome. Il Dottore, the doctor, an ignorant pedant, comes from Bologna. Pantalone embodies the grumpy old Venetian bourgeois: he became Gorgibus and Géronte in French comic theatre. The Southern European braggarts Capitano, Spavento, Scaramuccia, Fracassa, Giangurgolo and Coviello are all blood brothers to the Spanish captain Matamoros. The female roles, that were actually played by women, which was quite exceptional, wore fanciful costumes, and the actresses played unmasked the parts of the maids, Colombina and Silvia, and the female lovers, Isabella and Flaminia.

The commedia dell'arte swiftly replaced regular comedy. Its popularity can be explained by the importance it gave to inventiveness, to direct observation of life and, above all, by the quality of the acting. Its universality of gesture ensured that it made a name for itself far beyond the frontiers of Italy. Actors of the commedia dell'arte who went to perform in Spain contributed to the rise of Spanish popular drama.

The theatre in Spain

The Spanish nobility's ideal was to impose Christianity by fire and sword, to serve and revere the king and to cleanse insults to honour in blood. This ideal was faithfully reflected in theatrical productions, as was the taste of an entire people for marvellous, funny, sentimental and spectacular situations. Whether the drama was popular, literary or religious, the religious undertone was obvious and the great Spanish dramatists were, sometimes fleetingly, priests. Such was the case for Lope de Vega, Tirso de Molina, and then for Calderón and Moreto.

The religious theatre kept up the medieval tradition of the 'Autos sacramentales': plays with an allegorical content which ended with a glorification of the Eucharist and were performed in the porticoes of cathedrals or on carts transformed into stages. In places and the houses of nobles, literary or courtly theatre was more appreciated: in 1588, Juan de la Cueva (1543?–1610) successfully put on, *Libertad de España por Bernardo del Carpio* (*The Liberation of Spain by Bernardo del Carpio*). But it was the Sevillian **Lope de Rueda (1505–1565)** 'who took away the mantilla from comedy, gave it luxurious garments and maintained it sumptuously'. The first Spanish actor-cum-professional playwright, Lope de Rueda founded the first Spanish theatre company to stage theatrical classics. To widen the company's repertoire, he wrote sketches called 'pasos': very short pieces, studies of manners, entertainments or satires which delighted their spectators. *Las Aceitunas* (*The Olives*, 1567) showed a family of stereotypical peasants. The father, the mother, the daughter, who are all a trifle silly, build castles in the air. They fall out over the administration of an imaginary fortune: how best to make use of all the money they are going to accumulate . . . thanks to the olive-tree cutting they have just planted.

The 'Corral de Comedias'

Circumscribed by a popular reality, theatres in England and Spain invented stages in accordance with local conditions. In Spain theatrical works were put on in 'corrales de comedias': courtyards surrounded by houses. The stage was erected for the performance at one end of the courtyard. The bareness of the stage was a clear indication of the evocatory power of the script and the acting. Nobles and people of leisure hired balconies to see the performance, while ordinary folk stood in the courtyard itself. Each courtyard had its audience, whose partiality sometimes interrupted the performances. In Madrid, at the beginning of the seventeenth century, the general public gave its approval to the Corral de la Cruz upheld by the 'Poles', to the Corral del Príncipe applauded by the 'Sausages' and to the Corral de los Canos del Peral defended by the 'Stale Breads'. Some of these buildings, like the Corral del Carbón in Granada, and especially the Corral de Almagro in Ciudad Real, are still used for theatrical performances, particularly during the annual Week of Spanish Theatre. The taste for perspective, however, soon ensured that the Italian-style stage was preferred, in Spain as in the rest of Europe.

> All the world's a stage and all the men and women merely players.
>
> William Shakespeare, *As You Like It*

Elizabethan and Jacobean drama

At the end of Queen Elizabeth's reign a type of drama came into being which gave free rein to the power of the imagination ('we'll put our dreams to work', proclaims the prologue to Shakespeare's *Henry V*), and which was, at the same time completely artificial. The great period of Elizabethan and Jacobean theatre began after 1580. But the sixteenth century experienced all kinds of theatrical creations: didactic sketches, slapstick in which actors told jokes and acted the fool, edifying tragedies in which the great lost their dignity. The writers of Elizabethan dramas drew from the well of popular tradition or found inspiration in their professional colleagues.

The theatrical space

Before the Elizabethan era, the theatre was held to be a commercial enterprise run by charlatans to entertain the really ignorant. Performances of plays involved public gatherings which were considered to be potentially disruptive. According to 1570s laws, actors were thought of as vagabonds. In 1616, when Ben Jonson published his plays in a folio volume, calling them his collected 'works' (a term associated with serious artistic activities), he was ridiculed. But, before long, English audiences saw in the actor a representative of the human condition and the stigma with

which he had been burdened gradually disappeared. A theatre was ordered to be built, and in 1567 the Red Lion, the first playhouse of its type, was erected in the north London suburbs. In 1576, James Burbage, a carpenter and part-time actor, built The Theatre outside the London city walls. Its commercial success encouraged many other theatres all over London. Dramatic art prospered during the 1590s despite the disapproval of the faithful, the open distrust of the authorities, omnipresent censorship and, in the summer, the fearful threat of plague which led to the banning of all public meetings. By the end of the sixteenth century, the theatres on the South Bank of the Thames, at some distance from the city centre, were regularly visited by one in eight Londoners. The most famous theatre was The Globe where most of Shakespeare's and Ben Jonson's plays were performed.

The only document of the period showing an Elizabethan theatre has come down to us from a Dutchman, Johannes de Witt, who drew it in 1596 on a visit to London during which he went to the Swan Theatre. The inside of the auditorium is circular. There is a raised stage, protected from rain by a kind of canopy supported by columns. The spectators are standing on all three sides of the stage, or seated in the two or three balconies which encircle the room. Behind the space where the actors perform looms a 'tower' with covered rooms sheltering the foyer and all the troupe's stage properties. Theatres without a roof were sometimes very big, with room for more than two thousand spectators; the price of admission varied according to whether the spectator remained standing around the stage or sat down in one of the circular galleries above the stage.

Theatre troupes in the Elizabethan era were made up exclusively of men and young boys, all under the patronage of a great lord. William Shakespeare and Richard Burbage, at The Globe, belonged to the Chamberlain's Men, the Chamberlain being their protector. When James I came to the throne in 1603, this troupe became the King's Men. The theatre and all its accessories were the property of the actors: they were shareholders theatre's business, and received a fixed proportion of the theatre's profits. This principle of property held in common was related to the principles that governed Italian commedia dell'arte troupes.

Thanks to Kyd and Marlowe, both of whom were influenced by Seneca, drama occupied a place in literature as important as lyrical or narrative poetry. A single play by **Thomas Kyd (1558–1594)**, *The Spanish Tragedy* (1594?), has come down to us. There is a tragic irony in the fate of this man who had such brutal treatment meted out to him by the courts six years after having written *The Spanish Tragedy*. At the beginning of the 1590s, Kyd had a brush with the law; his house was searched by the watch who found irreligious and seditious pamphlets. In 1593, Kyd was imprisoned and tortured. He tried to put the blame on Christopher Marlowe, making out that the pamphlets in support of the 'monstrous ideas' which were responsible for his incarceration had been left at his house by Marlowe in 1591 while the two of them were lodging together. Kyd managed to have Marlowe arraigned, but he never recovered from the affair and died the following year.

Christopher Marlowe (1564–1593), the son of a shoemaker, studied at school in Canterbury, then at the University of Cambridge. From 1587 to 1593 he wrote seven plays, including *The Tragedy of Dr Faustus* (1588–1593). Only *Tamburlaine* was published in his lifetime. During his studies he worked as a spy for Sir Francis Walsingham, the head of the Queen's secret service. Then he went to London to become a dramatist. With his free-thinking atheistic ideas and riotous behaviour he acquired a reputation for scandal. He was killed by a dagger through the eye during a quarrel in a tavern where he had refused to pay the bill.

The thrust of Marlowe's plays is simple: his protagonists stride towards worldly success which is as grandiose as it is immoral until the final act which records their tragic fall. *Tamburlaine* shows us a shepherd at the beginning, driven by an insatiable thirst for conquest. Thanks to his strong personality and his talent as an orator, Tamburlaine finds allies, makes war, triumphs over his enemies, then undertakes new conquests. This basic pattern is constantly repeated. Those who would resist Tamburlaine and those he puts to flight swear vengeance on him, but he remains miraculously untouched. At the end of the play he has conquered the heart of Princess Zenocrate, who becomes his wife and ally, and he seems called to be the master of all the known world.

For a sixteenth-century public, the play owed much of its appeal to the fact that the story of Tamburlaine flew in the face of current conventions. It was commonly held, in the tragedies of the Middle Ages and of the beginning of the Tudor period, that odious tyrants ended up as the victims of a well-deserved fall from grace. Marlowe anticipated this in his prologue, but failed to deliver it in his first play. In the sequel, which he wrote in 1588 to capitalise on the success of the original, Tamburlaine experiences several reversals of fortune: his wife dies, one of his sons shows signs of cowardice, and Tamburlaine himself has to accept that he is only mortal. But Marlowe did not give his play a truly tragic twist; indeed, Tamburlaine transforms these painful events into manifestations of personal triumph. This arrogance has something irresistible and fascinating about it, and Tamburlaine's success seems assured right until the end of this second play: he dies, apparently the victim of his own orders: 'Tamburlaine, the scourge of God, must die.'

Vengeance furnished the main theme for the tragedies of this period and provided a stimulating moral debate. A greater variation in theme can be seen in comedy. Shakespeare's own taste for romantic comedy came from John Lyly's example. At the beginning of the 1590s, Lyly wrote a series of light comedies for young actors with a talent for both acting and music. But *c.*1600, biting satire was the dominant note in dramatic writing, a note struck most forcibly by Ben Jonson.

While Lyly and most of his contemporaries located the action of their plays in distinct times and places, **Ben Jonson (1572–1637)** looked at London and its inhabitants. He felt bitter at not having been to university. To make up for it, he strove to become one of the writers who paid most attention to the three classical unities and, in conformity with a literary theory inherited from classical tradition, he unmasked men's follies and vices in order to correct them. This is why he sometimes used characters with the role of an ancient chorus, who comment on the action so that the play's moral lesson was universally understood. Jonson's theatre depicts a hard world where there is no place for finer feelings. In *Volpone* (1605), the story of a rich scoundrel who pretends to be terminally ill to force all those who hope to inherit something from him to redouble the care with which they treat him, the most powerful scene is that of the trial, during which the guilty are summarily led off to be put in prison or thrown to an angry crowd.

Actor and dramatist, **William Shakespeare (1564–1616)*** was a member of the troupe that staged Jonson's *Every Man in His Humour* (1598) and *Sejanus* (1603), which was virtually his last role. By 1590 some of his own works had been staged. He used every genre, aiming above all for popular success. The sombre, tragic tones of his historical plays mingle with the light, pleasing effects of his comedies, appealing to a public made up of nobles as much as groundlings.

The Jacobean style

Jacobean tragedy was tinged with bitterness. It attempted to show the complex ramifications of corruption stemming from the perversion of central power. Comedy concentrated on the fascination riches, honours and sexual favours held for their devotees. Few plays directly alluded to the court of King James. Those which did were immediately banned and their authors promptly placed under lock and key. Tragedy was often critical of Italy, while comedy writes generally took as their target the world of London merchants and decadent aristocrats. In both cases, the

choice was a judicious one. On the one hand, Italy had for a long time stood for vice, sin and religious deviance in the popular imagination. Daily life in London, on the other hand, offered everyone the spectacle of debauchery. In keeping with this, dramatic language became denser, full of ambiguous and difficult turns of phrase. Tragedy had an obsession with death and disease.

There is one play which forms a sort of catalogue for almost all the practice in force in the dramatic writing of this period: *The Revenger's Tragedy* (1606) now thought to be by Thomas Middleton (died in 1627). To the court of an Italian duchy comes Vindice, seeking revenge on the Duke who has poisoned Vindice's betrothed Gloriana. Vindice dons the guise of a pander (Piato) to Cussurioso, the Duke's son, who comically pursues Castiza, Vindice's sister. Vindice murders the Duke by having him kiss the posioned skull of the long-dead Gloriana, and so begins an ever-increasing spiral of violence which eventually wipes out the entire court. At the end the stage is strewn with bodies as even Vindice and his brother are themselves put to death for their part in the slaughter. Despite the play's moral ambiguity, there is an acknowledgement that revenge and blood lust lead inevitably to chaos.

More or less the same thing can be said of the tragedies by **John Webster (1580–c.1634)**, who shows us life as an anxious and febrile search for security in a constantly menacing world. Men delude themselves and their happiness is ill-founded. *The Duchess of Malfi* (1614) described the persecution then the murder of a noble widow who tried to find happiness by marrying her steward. Pitted against her are two of her brothers, a mad duke and a bloodthirsty cardinal, who have hired the malcontent Bosola to torment and murder the unfortunate woman. Later, prey to remorse, Bosola undertakes to avenge the woman whose murder he arranged.

Diametrically opposed to this drama of violence and cynicism, a new genre appeared in royal and aristocratic entertainments in England, France, Spain and Italy: the pastoral

213

drama, natural heir to the eclogue. This is a theatrical version of the pastoral, sometimes with simple dialogue.

THE FAIR GOLDEN AGE: THE PASTORAL

Heir to the ancient eclogue, the pastoral, whose protagonists – shepherds and shepherdesses – live in a stylised Nature, was a genre that rapidly evolved and that was particularly appreciated by the nobility. Far removed from the artificiality of court life, it symbolised a model of Utopia for a different lifestyle in a natural setting redolent of a golden age, both a paradise lost and a joyful future for a society reconstructed on new relationships between individuals.

Couples come together and drift apart throughout the story in a pastoral poem. Each partner feels pain at not understanding the other's soul, only to be united at the end in real, lasting harmony. The plot elements favour the interplay of appearances, disguises and fickleness, all characteristics of the Baroque aesthetic of the Counter-Reformation. To contemporaries, the eulogy of Nature seemed to be a deliberate negation of all forms of pessimism, whether inherited from medieval thought or inspired by Calvinism. Contrary to a sombre vision of the world that immediately decided if somebody was chosen or damned, the pastoral unswervingly affirmed that to follow Nature is to follow the natural order of things, the joyful order of the universe.

Pastorals written at the end of the sixteenth century and during the seventeenth century were influenced by Sannazaro's Italian *Arcadia* which relates the poet's tragic love affairs; and by *Los siete libros de la Diana* (*The Seven Books of Diana*, 1559) by the Portuguese writer, Jorge de Montemor (or Montemayor, 1520–1561), which retraced the adventures of various shepherd couples, in particular the adventures of Sireno who loves and is loved by the shepherdess Diana, but who, after a year's absence, finds her married to the shepherd Delio. Petar Zoranić (1508–1569) wrote the first pastoral novel in Croat, *Planine* (*The*

Mountains, 1569), which takes place on the Dalmatian coast and whose characters are the heroes of Slavic folk legends. Tasso published *Aminta*, a charming tale of the unrequited love of the shepherd Aminta for Sylvia, a cold, distant nymph; the latter, assaulted by a satyr, escapes thanks to the shepherd's intervention, but she shows him no gratitude and runs off into the woods. The shepherd, in despair at her coldness, tries to kill himself. He is prevented from doing so, but learns shortly afterwards that Sylvia has been devoured by wolves. He throws himself off the top of a cliff. Sylvia, in fact, is not dead and, moved by these tangible proofs of the shepherd's love, she wants to join him in death, when a passer-by reveals that Aminta has miraculously survived.

Enthusiasm for these pastorals encouraged translations and imitations. In Spain there was *La Galatea* (1588) by **Miguel de Cervantes Saavedra** (known as **Cervantes, 1547–1616**);* in Italy, *Il Pastor Fido* (*The Faithful Shepherd*, 1590) by Giovan Battista Guarini (1538–1612); in Poland *Idylls* (1614) by Szymon Szymonovicz (Simon Simonides, 1558–1629); in France *L'Astrée* (*Astrea*, 1607) by Honoré d'Urfé; in England *The Two Gentlemen of Verona* (*c.*1594) by Shakespeare; and, above all, *Arcadia* (1580) by Sidney, which, in England, was one of the most widely read works.

Sir Philip Sidney (1554–1586) represented the ideal man of his time. He thought it was an aristocrat's duty to be above reproach and to serve as an example to the rest of society. In 1572 he went to Europe on a 'Grand Tour' which became obligatory for well-born young Englishmen. Back in England, he took an active part in national politics and soon became the centre of a literary circle whose mission was to enrich the English language. In 1585 he took part in a military expedition to The Netherlands, but the following year he was mortally wounded in a skirmish with Spanish soldiers. He declared on his death bed: 'Everything in my life has been vain, vain, vain.' But we can recognise in him the archetypal Renaissance man: scholar and politician, poet and courtier, critic and soldier. These qualities, combined with the success of *Arcadia*, held a genuine fascination for his contemporaries and future generations; in the eighteenth century, Fielding and Richardson derived much of their inspiration from him.

For Elizabethan readers, *Arcadia* was both a source of entertainment and a model to be imitated. The two successive versions of the novel can be considered as an increasingly penetrating investigation into the conditions necessary for an ideal community, peopled by poets-cum-shepherds. The first *Arcadia*, begun in 1577 and finished in 1580, tells a simple story in five books. Despite the warnings of his councillors, Basil, King of Arcadia, consults an oracle. When he learns of the appalling fate his family can expect, the king abandons his duties and retires to the Arcadian countryside; by doing so he fulfils his destiny rather than escapes it. Because of the king's madness, the whole of Arcadia falls prey to sedition. Two wandering princes, Pyrocles and Musidorus, fall in love with Basil's daughters and are forced to disguise themselves in order to reach them. Eventually they are dragged before a court, accused of Basil's murder and the rape of his daughters. Ultimate tragedy is only avoided by a totally improbable dramatic turn of events.

The pastoral sounded the death-knell of the novel of chivalry which at the beginning of the century still had the power to enchant a huge readership. More than a genre, the pastoral had a tone and a content that were always associated with another form – be it literary, dramatic, lyrical or romantic – which combined verse and prose. In the realm of poetry and the novel, it was very fashionable, as prolific a source of inspiration as Petrarch.

YOUR STRINGS, MY LUTE, ARE PASSING SWEET: POETRY

The influence of Petrarch – even his linguistic idiosyncracies – continued to be felt in Portugal. The melancholic, disenchanted, pessimistic tone of Portuguese poetry is utterly unlike any other. How many bitter reflections on the traps and evils in the world come in the wake of the rout at Alcacer Quibir in 1578, the ensuing nationwide crisis and the loss of independence in 1581! Many poets turned towards religious texts. Frei Agostinho da Cruz (1540–1619) evoked with nostalgia Paradise, the Cross, the presence of the Creator. His sad poems were lit by descriptions of the lush Serra da Arrabida he adored. But the poet who set Portugal on fire and gave it back a feeling of national pride was **Luis de Camões (1524–1580)★** with his epic *Os Lusiadas* (*The Lusiads*, 1572). Petrarch's influence is still found in his lyrical poems.

To disclaim the formal experiments of poets following in Petrarch's footsteps, as Du Bellay does, is still to recognise how strong Petrarch's influence was on the aesthetics of love poetry. In search of an original poetic language, the poets of the Pleiad cannot deny their Italian ancestry: in France as elsewhere, it was under Petrarch's influence that a national poetry was formed.

The Pleiad

They were aged between twenty and thirty. They came mostly from the banks of the Loire or from Lyon to stoke the boiling cauldron of humanist ideas that were splashing over Paris and Europe. At first they came together as the 'Brigade' to put an end to 'old-fashioned nonsense such as rondeaux, virelais, chants royaux, chansons and other such merchandise'. They were called Ronsard, Du Bellay, Étienne Jodelle (1532–1573), Jean Antoine de Baïf (1532–1589), Peletier du Mans, Rémi Belleau (1538–1577) and Ponthus de Tyard (1521–1605): seven of them, like the constellation of the Pleiades or the members of the group of poets who had taken that name in ancient Greece. Creation, not versification, was the watchword of these poets who christened themselves the Pleiad in 1556. Poetry, the essence of language, was no longer versified prose or simple translation, but a recreation which tended towards beauty. If they returned to the Italian sonnet form, they enriched its possibilities and, with an ear for the musicality of the verse, they allocated the lion's share of space to rhyme.

When he was twenty, **Joachim Du Bellay (1522–1560)** met Peletier du Mans and Ronsard, his future classmates at the Collège de Coqueret in Paris. Directed by the humanist Dorat, they enthusiastically discovered the finest Greek and Latin texts. Du Bellay obtained the post of secretary to an uncle who lived as a diplomat in Rome and set out joyfully for that city so full of the past and of meaning for a humanist. The reality was deeply disappointing. His work was boring and Rome, a hotbed of ecclesiastical intrigue, was far from being the model of grandeur and virtue he had dreamed about. After his return to France, Du Bellay published in 1558 *The Various Rustic Games, The Regrets, The Antiquities of Rome* and *The Dream*. Elegiac, like Ovid's *Tristia*, Du Bellay's *Regrets* sang of his nostalgic obsession with going home. 'Blessed be the day, and the month, and the year when I met my beloved,' Petrarch had written. Du Bellay's feeling of regret inverted and transposed the acclamation of Laura's lover into a different context:

Malheureux l'an, le mois, le jour, l'heure et le point
Et malheureuse soit la flatteuse espérance,
Quand pour venir ici j'abandonnai la France:
La France, et mon Anjou, dont le désir me point.

Joachim Du Bellay, *Regrets*

Unhappy the year, the month, the day, the hour, the point in time,
Misfortune to my hope obsequious,
When to come here I left behind my France:
My France and my Anjou, desire for which hurts me.

From one sonnet to the next, the poet did not stop singing of the emptiness of Rome, his life, even his poetry: 'And the Muses like strangers fly from me.' He proclaimed his lack of inspiration, but carried on writing just the same. His poems were not just his 'surest secretaries' or the verse diary of his sadness, but a celebration of the magic of poetry.

Just when he seemed sure of a brilliant career at court, **Pierre de Ronsard (1524–1585)** had his future wrecked by premature deafness. He devoted himself from then on to poetry which, in his eyes, was the noblest activity man could pursue, placing the poet on an equal footing with the king whom he advised. His first publications, the *Odes* (1550), inspired by Pindar, and *The Love of Cassandra* (1552), influenced by Petrarch, offended courtly taste with their pomposity. But Ronsard swiftly emerges with simpler anthologies: *Bocage, Mixtures* (1554) and *The Second Book of the Loves* (1556). In 1558 he became poet laureate to the French king, Henri II, and then to Charles IX. On Charles' death, Ronsard, rich and famous, but disappointed by the recent failure of his epic

The Franciad (1572), left the French royal court, replaced as court poet to Henri III by a young poet, Desportes. Living in retirement in his priory in the Vendômois, Ronsard published *Sonnets on the Death of Marie* and the *Sonnets to Helen* (1578). Before his death in 1585, he tirelessly revised his work.

Four registers dominated this work: occasional verse in honour of kings and courtly events (*Bocage royal*); poetry committed to the ideal of defending royalty against the Protestants (*Discourses*, 1562–1563); philosophical poetry that dealt with primordial myths and strove 'to cover the truth of things / With a fabulous coat.' Last but not least, Ronsard wrote poems about love.

I have forgotten how to imitate Petrarch,
I want to speak of love quite openly.
Joachim Du Bellay, *Various Rustic Games*

The collections by Ronsard which sing of loves, more literary than real, revolved around the Christian names of three women: Cassandra, Marie and Helen. Cassandra Salviati and Hélène de Surgères were real women, but we know nothing. It is unlikely that Ronsard really loves any of them. Their names had a is symbolic and creative value rather than a referential one. It was only belatedly that the names Cassandra and Marie appeared in the titles of the relevant collections, and many poems were shuffled about from one collection to another. What makes the works different has less to do with the woman who inspired them than their tone: Cassandra was celebrated in odes with an elevated style; with Marie, Ronsard coined

what he called his fine low style, Marie being less inaccessible than Cassandra. Lively and dynamic – she was symbolic of the Anjou countryside – Hélène was always accompanied by the serious framework of the court of the Louvre, scholarly, solemn and proud. From one poem to the next, the lover, getting older, never stopped singing of love and the fleetingness of beauty: 'Cueillez dès aujourd'hui les roses de la vie' ('Gather ye life's roses now today').

Le temps s'en va, le temps s'en va, ma Dame
Las! Le temps non, mais nous nous en allons
Et tôt serons étendus sous la lame
Et des amours desquelles nous parlons
Quand serons morts n'en sera plus nouvelle.
Pour ce, aimez-moi cependant qu'êtes belle!
Pierre de Ronsard,
Second Livre des Amours

Time passes, time goes by, my love.
Alas! Not time but we ourselves go by
And soon we will be stretched out underground
And of the loves we talk about today
When we are dead there will be no more news.
Love me then while you are beautiful!

The influence of Petrarch and the Pleiad

The search for the perfect love, for which the Hungarian poet Albert Gergei had also found the theme in Italian literature, dominated the

work of his contemporary, **Bálint Balassi (1554–1594)**. Influenced by Petrarch, he wrote the thirty-three poems of the cycle Julia (1588) for a married woman he was in loved. This new type of stanza was called the Balassi stanza.

Vagy àll, ül, nevet, sir,
Örül, levelet, ir,
Szerelem is ast teszi;
Vagy mùlat, énekel . . .
Bálint Balassi,
Julia

She stands up or sits down, she laughs,
Cries, makes merry, writes,
Always limited by Love,
Comes and goes, sings some refrain . . .

The *Poems for Julia* were the second cycle of a work in three cycles. The first included poems on various subjects, written before she was married: love poems, martial poems and poems dedicated to the 'sacred season', Pentecost or springtime. The inspiration for the third cycle was religious. Balassi sometimes alluded to his eventful life: the eldest son of a family of Hungarian aristocrats, he studied at Nuremberg, then went to Italy. Mastering, Latin, Italian, German, Turkish, Slovak, Polish and Rumanian, apart from Hungarian, he was inspired by the cadences of love songs

composed in these various languages to write his own poems. Politically his fate led him to Poland in the wake of Stephen Bathory, the Prince of Transylvania, who had just become. Back home, on the death of his father, he was disinherited by his family. Poor, always at loggerheads with his relations, the founder of modern Hungarian poetry lived and died a soldier, and was killed at the siege of Esztergom. There, in the last verses he wrote, paraphrasing Théodore de Bèze, he spoke to God, the fount of 'infinite mercy':

Ime kioldoztam	*In order to present her to you,*
S teelöbden hoztam	*You see, I have laid bare*
Fene ötte sebemet.	*The rankness of my festering wound.*

Bálint Balassi

The influence of Ronsard

To establish a pedigree for the Polish language by virtue of poetic speech: this wish, so typical of Renaissance writers generally, belonged to **Jan Kochanowski (1530–1584)**, who met Ronsard while he was in Paris. Kochanowski was a humanist whose personal culture was universal. He studied at Cracow, Königsberg and Padua where he composed, in Latin, his

first poems inspired by Horace. Subsequently he used both Latin and Polish. Back in Poland, he spent time at the courts of powerful lay and ecclesiastical rulers and was appointed secretary to King Sigismund Augustus. In 1570, he retired to his estate of Czarnolas, near Lublin. Its name, which means 'Dark Forest', became the name of a symbolic site in Polish letters. For Kochanowski, to be a poet was to share the fate of Proteus:

Dziú żak spokojny, jutro	*Today a fine upstanding scholar and*
przypasany	*tomorrow, sword strapped to thigh,*
Do miecza rycerz; dziś między	*A knight; today to be found*
dworzany	*among courtiers*
W pańskim pałacu, jutro zasię	*In a marble palace: and*
cichy	*tomorrow, for a change,*
Ksiądz w kapitule, tylko że nie	*A priest, but in a chapter, and not*
z mnichy	*a monk greyly*
W szarej kapicy a z dwojakim	*In a cage. A priest, yes, but with*
płatem;	*a padded coat.*
I to czemu nic, jesliże opatem?	*A horse for the soldier, for the priest*
Taki byl Proteus, mieniąc się	*gladrags..*
to w smoka.	*Proteus was what he felt like*
To w deszcz, to w ogień, to	*being too,*
w barwę obłoka.	*A dragon, or rain, or a fire, or*
Dalej so będzie? Śrebrne	*a cloud with a rainbow.*
w głowie nici,	*When I am older, my forehead will be covered*
A ja z tym trzymam, kto co	*with wise snow,*
w czas uchwyci.	*Since every season needs its personage.*

Jan Kochanowski,
Do gór i Lasów

Kochanowski's stay at court in Cracow was marked by occasional works: *Satyr albo Dziki Mąż* (*The Satyr or the Wild Man*, 1564) denounced the shortcomings of the nobility; *Proporzec albo hold Pruski* (*The Standard or a Homage to Prussia*, 1569) recalled the ceremony of Prussia's act of submission to the King of Poland; the epic poem, *Gallo Crocitanti* (*To a Frenchman Crowing like a Cock*), whose hero was the French Valois, King Henri III, fleeing Poland, was a response to *The Farewell*

to Poland by Philippe Desportes. Through his life Kochanowski composed witty 'fraszki' (from the Italian 'frasca'): short epigrams which combined lyricism, humour, morality, politics and even eroticism. The first collection of poems in Polish was a skilful adaptation of the Psalms *Psalterz Dawidów* (*The Psalter of David*, 1579). After this there were many *Pieúni* (*Songs*), bucolic in tone, in which Kochanowski imitated the Ancients while working on the sensuous style of his native language. He tested his talent as a dramatist with *Odprawa posłów greckich* (*The Dismissal of the Greek Ambassadors*, 1578), the first tragedy in Polish, which portrayed current events on an ancient backdrop. In *Treny* (1580) he poured out his despair after the untimely demise of his only daughter, Ursula. The logic of emotion conquered prosody: a new, purer, codified language had been born in Poland.

From 1546 to 1570, Italy continued to reach out to Cyprus, which was governed by the Doge of Venice. One hundred and fifty-six fine lyrical poems, influenced by Petrarch, were composed by one or more anonymous poets, the *Kipriaka erotica piimata* (*Cypriot Love Poems*). They were either original pieces, paraphrases, or translations into Greek of Italian poems from a particular anthology, typical of those in circulation in sixteenth-century Italy. Apart from their purely aesthetic value, these poems were of philological interest: they were written in Cypriot Greek, a dialect consciously developed to become a worthy literary tool. A fourteen-syllable line, typically Italian, appeared instead of the usual Greek fifteen-syllable verse, as well as fixed forms of Italian origin such as the sonnet, the canzone and the madrigal. This promising work was rudely interrupted in 1570 by the Turkish invasion. Throughout the sixteenth century, Dubrovnik allowed the Renaissance to seep in: poems by Mavro Vetranović (1482–1576), Dinko Ranina (1536–1607) and Dominiko Zlatarevic (1558–1613), translator of Tasso's *Aminta* in 1597, were all written with Petrarch in mind.

In England, in Germany and in the southern Netherlands, the Renaissance made its appearance thanks to the work of **Jan Van der Noot (*c*.1539–*c*.1595)**. Van der Noot's Calvinism forced him to leave Antwerp for England. In London and later in Cologne, he published radically innovative books. Inspired by the poems of Petrarch and Du Bellay, those in *Het Theatre oft Toon-neel* (*The Theatre*, 1568) described the miseries that await the worldly. Each was accompanied by an illustration by Coornhert and by a prose commentary. Around 1570, *Het Bosken* (*The Grove*) appeared in print in London: a collection of sonnets, elegies and epigrams, followed by a Dutch transposition of the psalms that Marot had translated into French a few years earlier.

Even more important was *Das Buch Extasis* (1576), an epic poem more than two thousand verses long, the first great work in German in the Renaissance style. The Franco-Dutch edition only contained 1044 verses; the French version predates the Dutch which is held to be Van der Noot's masterpiece. The epic celebrated the poet's victory over the power of Hell, his coronation and his marriage to Olympia, the embodiment of beauty and goodness. The poem unfolds with clarity and sublimity, lively and assured, majestic yet pleasing. The boldness and the proud grace of the iambic foot, vigorous and firm in its progress, resounds through a rich vegetation of novel images, surrounded by pretty allegorical edifices in the manner of Colonna. Van der Noot embraced the ideas and the style of the Pleiad, adapting them to circumstances prevalent in Holland. Having met the members of this group in Paris, he described, like Ronsard's *Hymns*, the 'fury' and the frenzy of inspiration:

Io, je sens une fureur lancée	*Io, I feel a fury launched*
En mon esprit, au fond de ma pensée,	*Inside my mind, at the bottom of my thought,*
Qui nuit et jour m'enflamme tellement	*Which, night and day, inflames me*
D'un gracieux et doux forcènement	*With a sweet and gracious mania*
Que tout mon sens et mon esprit se trouble	*That my senses and my mind are troubled*
Du zèle ardent qui dans moi se redouble.	*By the ardent zeal which is redoubled in me.*
Ô quel plaisir! Ô quel bien souverain	*Oh what pleasure! Oh what sovereign good*
Quand Dieu descend au coeur d'un pauvre humain.	*When God comes down to dwell in a human heart.*

Jan Van der Noot, *Olympiade*

that poesy, thus embraced in all other places, should only find in our time a hard welcome in England, I think the very earth lamenteth it, and therefore decketh our soil with fewer laurels than it was accustomed.

With these words, Sidney cuts his readers to the quick in his *Apology for Poetry or Defence of Poesy* (1579, published in 1586). Here he reviewed Greek and Latin theories on poetry with erudition and humour, recalled the quasi-divine function that the Ancients conferred on their poets and described some of continental Europe's poetry. Despite what Sidney says, the England of previous generations was not indifferent to works from abroad: the influence of the Ancients and Petrarch had already had an effect on Henry Howard, Earl of Surrey, who introduced blank verse into English, and on Sir Thomas Wyatt who made his fellow countrymen familiar with the sonnet form. We owe to Thomas Watson, who began his career as a poet by translating Petrarch into Latin, the first sequence of 'quartorzains' or 'fourteen-liners', as Elizabethan sonnets were called, with the publication, in 1580, of a collection of 100 love poems, *The Hecatempathia or Passionate Centurie of Love*. However, these were the exception rather than the rule, and had little immediate impact. English poetry only really blossomed at the end of the century.

Towards 1582, Sidney, an admirer of Henry Howard, composed *Astrophel and Stella* (published in 1591), a sequence of 107 sonnets written by a lover to the traditionally distant object of his love. The feelings of the lover invite us to reflect on death and the passage of time. The collection is also an anthology implementing the various ways of writing a courtly sonnet. The poem which opens the collection, 'Loving in truth, and fain in verse my love to show', describes the art of composing courtly poetry, eliminating all overly erudite methods. With a humorous affirmation of his poetic independence, Sidney draws our attention to the originality of his prosody by sometimes setting aside the traditional iambic pentameter form to write sonnets in hexameters or alexandrines.

Other poets also differentiated themselves from the English poetic tradition and turned to Italian poetry for their inspiration: the *Amoretti* (1595) and the *Epithalamium* (1595) by **Edmund Spenser (c.1552–1599)**, written for his wife, Elizabeth Boyle, celebrated a love that found fulfilment in marriage. The verse form Spenser adopted in his sonnets is particularly complex: he built his sonnet round just five rhymes – difficult to achieve in English. Spenser was a friend to Sidney, and dedicated his first major work to him: *The Shepherd's Calendar* (1579). This was composed of twelve eclogues written in an archaic language as a tribute to Chaucer, whom he admired, and in order to create a rustic language appropriate to his subject matter. This technique did not find favour either with Sidney, who criticised it in his *Apology*, or with Ben Jonson, for whom Spenser wrote in no known language! Braving this hostility, Spenser continued to develop his own style. He wrote a poem which attempted to synthesise the whole Elizabethan era, *The Fairy Queen*: of the total twelve volumes, only the first six were published in 1590 and 1596. In the dedication of his poem to Sir Walter Raleigh, Spenser explained that 'The general end therefore of all the book is to fashion a gentleman or noble person in virtuous and gentle discipline.' Each volume was the allegory of a virtue: Holiness, Temperance, Chastity, Friendship, Justice and Courtesy. An epic novel in verse, *The Fairy Queen* celebrated Queen Gloriana – Elizabeth I – monarch by Divine Right over a people chosen by God, sought by Arthur, the Prince of the Virtues, who had seen her in a dream. *The Fairy Queen* invites us to read fascinating tales, to see fantastic landscapes in dark forests and vast wastelands as so many metaphors with more than one meaning. With this work, a veritable laboratory of poetic experiment, Spenser used for the first time the stanza of eight decasyllables prolonged by an alexandrine that Keats, Shelley and Byron later used:

A gentle Knight was pricking on the plaine,
Y cladd in mightie armes and silver shielde,
Wherein old dints of deepe woundes did
*   remaine,*
The cruell markes of many a bloody fielde;
Yet armes till that time did he never wield.
His angry steede did chide his foming bitt,
As much disdayning to the curbe to yield,
Full jolly knight he seemed, and faire did
*   sitt,*
As one for knightly giousts and fierce
*   encounters fitt.*

Edmund Spenser,
The Fairy Queen

During the following decade, **John Donne (1572–1631)** pushed back the frontiers of sonnet conventions when he composed nineteen *Holy Sonnets*, written mostly between 1609 and 1616 and published in 1633. Donne replaced the traditional relationship of lover to beloved with the love of the true believer for God. The anguish of a passionate doubt was expressed through the rigorous constraints imposed by the sonnet form.

At the end of the sixteenth century, traditional Irish poetry was still very much alive, created by professional poets supported by the king. But in 1603 the king was deposed by the English and courtly poetry died. All that survives is a highly literary poetry, circulating privately in manuscript form. Culturally crushed, Ireland failed to be influenced by Petrarch as continental Europe had been so profoundly.

Euphuism

The major works of English literature in the second half of the sixteenth century, with the exception of plays, were aimed at an aristocratic, sophisticated public. Like Spenser's *Fairy Queen*, Sidney's *Arcadia* also benefited from *Euphues or The Anatomy of Wit* (1578) by **John Lyly (c.1553–1606)**. Lyly's style was so popular in the 1580s that the bookseller, Edward Blount, wrote of him a few years later: 'All our ladies were then his scholars, and that beauty in court who could not parley *Euphuism*

was as little regarded as she who now there speaks not French.' Euphuism testified to an Elizabethan need to create novel, curious forms of expression, innovations capable of satisfying both the mind and good taste. This style consisted essentially in using sentences which contained two propositions of equal length: a balance highlighted by alliteration, assonance and other rhetorical devices:

Though the style nothing delight
the dainty ear of the curious
*   sifter,*
yet will the matter recreate the
mind of the courteous reader.

John Lyly, *Euphues or*
The Anatomy of Wit

This elaborate style was used to demonstrate paradoxes. It can lend a veneer of coherence to the most absurd statements: in the above quotation, Lyly used a bombastic construction to demonstrate that his style suffers from too much simplicity! Another characteristic of euphuism is its piling up of examples, often taken from Pliny's *Natural History*, aimed at illustrating fallacious arguments.

The resounding success of *Euphues or The Anatomy of Wit* meant that Lyly abandoned all hope of obtaining the post that he wanted at Oxford University. He devoted himself entirely to literature, joining the group of the 'University Wits': Oxbridge writers whose playful use of knowledge dominated prose and dramatic writing at the end of the 1580s. Thomas Lodge (1557–1625), Robert Greene (c.1560–1592) and Thomas Nashe (1567–1601) were also admired. For about a decade, Lyly wrote brilliant comedies. Once again, however, he was frustrated in his ambitions and apparently abandoned literature to take up a seat in Parliament at the beginning of the 1590s. He died in 1606, completely forgotten and, it seems, destitute. Euphuism continued to fascinate English writers for many years, even if its popularity was eclipsed by that of Sidney's *Arcadia* at the end of the 1580s.

There are areas in which, for aesthetic or political reasons, literature lags behind and is virtually untouched by ideological conflict. Russia, Greece and Bulgaria, politically closed to the rest of Europe, developed intense feelings of national and religious pride which their literature echoed, while Rumania was reduced to silence.

THE ORTHODOX PART OF EUROPE

Far from the literary currents that captured the imagination of Western Europe and the struggles between Catholics and Protestants, the Orthodox part of Europe also experienced a renewal of religious fervour, linked to the political situations of Russia, Greece and the Balkans. In Russia and Greece, which were almost totally deprived of political, economic and artistic relationships with the rest of Europe, nationalism became exacerbated, whipped up by rulers in Moscow who wanted to unify the whole of Russia around their capital and aroused in Greece by Turkish occupation. The power of the Orthodox Church was thereby reinforced – calculatingly in Russia and out of historical necessity in Greece and Bulgaria, where the clergy maintained the only national tradition tolerated by their Turkish occupiers.

In the grip of Ivan IV

For Muscovy the second half of the sixteenth century felt like a continuation of what had gone before, of the whole medieval tradition, and like the modest beginning of a new era in literature. Historiography still occupied a prominent place, but literature was more marked by contemporary events. Foremost among these was the solemn crowning of the young Ivan IV (1547), the first Czar of Russia. The ceremony was organised by the Metropolitan Macarius in the spirit of the political doctrines expounded from the start of the century. This new empire had to be given a historical foundation, a religious content, a political – and moral – organisation. The very nature of absolute power was to raise

discussions all the more passionate because the Czar himself took an active part in them, making his mark, in the eyes of posterity, as the most original of current writers.

Historical compilations which bracketed together the Muscovite Empire to the Rus' of Kiev reached their zenith with *Stepennaja kniga* (*The Book of Degrees*, 1563), written under the supervision of Father Andrei, the Czar's confessor and future metropolitan (Athanasius). In a process of development which was meant to be continuous, the work encompassed the history of the Eastern Slavs from the 10th to the sixteenth century, associating princes and prelates in a common task, of which the reign of the first Czar was the final stage. To glorify the ruling dynasty and monarchical power, the writers did not hesitate to promote certain legends at the expense of historical truth. A little later, Ivan IV commissioned an illustrated historical encyclopedia, *The Illuminated Compilation*, 1568–1573, and the *Licevoj svod* (*The Great Menologist*, 1547–1552) on the basis of the *Chronicle of Nikon*, a legacy of the previous epoch. At the same time, 'Holy Russia' (the expression would soon be used, discreetly at first) had to honour its saints. The canonisations of 1547 and 1549 inspired the Metropolitan Macarius to compile the *Ceti Minei* a volume for the twelve months of the year, a veritable encyclopedia of hagiography.

At the same time the Czar wanted to regulate the liturgical side of life in the Church, which had always dominated religious life in Russia, and its place in society. A synod approved the *Stoglav* (*One Hundred Chapters*, 1551) for this express purpose. Perhaps Ivan also wanted to regulate the lives of his subjects: Father Sylvester, one of his boon companions, compiled *Domostroj* (*Home Companion*, 1556) in a language close to spoken Russian. This handbook for the perfect paterfamilias went into detail about how a pious man should manage his household. It set down common norms for family and social life for all sections of the population: how a man should carry out his religious duties, be thrifty, hospitable and how he should conduct himself with his wife, children and servants, knowing how to handle a whip to punish them if necessary. An ideal of orderliness, restraint, cleanliness, saving, mutual respect, family peace and quiet, hospitality and work was conjured up in a detailed description of daily life.

With its often legendary compilations, to which may be added contemporary historical works such as *Kazanskij letopisec* (*The Chronicle of Kazan*, 1528–1583), and its utilitarian texts, Russian literature of the second half of the sixteenth century would have cut a poor figure in the literature of Europe overall had it not been for the Czar and his political opponent, Prince Andrei Mikhailovitch Kurbski. The latter, a descendant, of the former rulers of Russia, like Ivan, had been one of the best leaders in the kingdom before he fled to Lithuania (1564) ahead of the reign of terror that overtook Moscow. From exile he sent Ivan a letter full of reproach. The Czar – who corresponded with Stephen Bathory, King of Poland, and Elizabeth I of England – replied. This began their celebrated *Correspondence*: three letters by Kurbski and two by the Czar. The most spontaneous writer was **Ivan IV the Terrible (1530–1584)**. In a style both expressive and powerful, his two letters state caustically, ironically and passionately his right to do as he sees fit as a sovereign. To prove this right, the Czar did not hesitate in his choice of arguments. So, for example, to refute Kurbski who claimed a local power for nobles, he wrote:

и что от сего случишася в Руси, егда быша в коемждо граде градоначальниць и местоблю стители, и какова разорения быша от сего, сам своима беззаконьма очима видал еси. От сего можеши разумети, что сие есть. К сеиу пропок рече. «Горе мужу, им же жена обладает, горе граду, им же многи обладают». Видиши ли, яко подобно женскому безумию владения многих? Аще не под единою властию будут, аще крепки, аще и крабри, аще и хразумни, но обаче женскому безумию подобни будет, аще не под единою властию будут.

Ivan IV, *Perepiska Ivana Groznogo s Andreem Kurbskim*

And what happened then in Russia when in each town there was a governor and a lieutenant? You saw for yourself with your impious eyes the ruin that ensued: after that you could understand for yourself that parlous situation. On this subject a prophet had this to say: 'Cursed be the husband dominated by his wife, and misfortune to the town where several reign.' Can you see that the reign of several is similar to female folly? If warriors are not under the command of a single leader, their strength, their bravery, their common sense will be in vain, they will be no less like a madwoman if they do not have a single leader.

Prince Kurbski's style was more sober. It owed more to literary Slavonic and, after his exile, to Polish. This characteristic appears strikingly in *Istorija o velikom knjaze moskovskom eže slyšachom u dostovernych i eže videchom očima našima* (*The story of the Great Prince of Moscow as we have heard it from people worthy of trust* *and seen it with our own eyes*, 1573). This pamphlet against Ivan the Terrible in favour of more freedom for the nobility marked a turning point for Russian historiography and became a major literary work of the period.

The last part of the sixteenth century included no significant work. The ruin of the country, as a result of the reign of terror to which it had been submitted, seems to have extended to literature. We witness the breakdown of a system of cultural values borrowed exclusively from the Middle Ages, just when Europe is entering modern times.

Under the yoke of the Ottomans

From the fall of Constantinople, Greece, Serbia, Bulgaria and the principality of Rumania along the Danube, without a governor or hand to guide it, endured the yoke of the Ottoman Turks. This not only hindered political and social development in these countries, but also their intellectual and literary life. Literature was written in small pockets where there remained some freedom of expression: in the monasteries of Peč, Miloöevo and especially Chilandari; in Greece, in the Greek diaspora, revolving around the Orthodox Patriarchs; and in Cyprus until 1570 when the island was conquered by the Turks. Among the many ethnic groups who lived in Sofia – the town with a hundred mosques and a thousand Orthodox churches that became an Ottoman centre of administration and the main town in Bulgaria in 1587 – Bulgarians also managed to maintain national cultural activity. Bulgarian literature, like Rumanian literature, then consisted mostly of hagiographies, such as *The Legend of Sunday*; *The Journey of the Virgin into Hell*. In Rumania sacred scriptures, in particular those of the Deacon Coressi, were translated into Rumanian. The new lease of life accorded to the diocese of Pecˇ in 1557 coincided with a brief flowering of Serbian literature. At the end of the sixteenth century, the Patriarch Pasije wrote the last hagiography of the Serbian kings, *Život cara Uroša* (*The Life of Czar Uros*).

The scholars of the Greek diaspora

Fleeing from Turkish domination, many Greek scholars found asylum and protection in the Christian countries of Western Europe, above all in Italy. They brought with them ancient Greek manuscripts that had been copied and recopied in Orthodox monasteries for centuries. With the start of the Renaissance, many of them were employed as teachers and tutors in noble Italian families. They wrote works in ancient Greek, composing hymns and letters according to rules laid down by the Ancients, such as the *Epistle on the Death of Valvinus* (1564) by Francisco Portos.

Religious prose literature

In continental Greece, people clustered round the Patriarch of Constantinople, national character and religious feeling mingling together. This is why Greek literature of this period had such a strong religious tone. Prose texts, works mostly by great bishops, patriarchs or priests, served a dual purpose: to reform the Orthodox Church and to strengthen the people's faith. The Church had to be renewed so that it would be ready to perform its role as guardian of the faith and of Greek national language and tradition. Theological texts began to appear. Their enlightened authors, who intended to change the inflexibly conservative character of the Church, did not hesitate to contact European reformers, especially those in The Netherlands and England. Among them was Cyril Loukaris (1572–1638). On the other hand, there was an obligation to strengthen the people in their Orthodox faith so that they could resist Turkish pressure to secure conversions to Islam and also the efforts of the Jesuits who wanted to bring Greece back to the heart of the Catholic Church. In ordinary straightforward language, the clergy addressed the crowds in great urban centres of population such as Alexandria and Constantinople, as it did people in the provinces. In these moral and didactic sermons, which emphasised the value of Christian living and righteousness as preserved by Orthodox Christianity, we can find the origins of neo-Greek prose. The most famous orator of this period, Meletios Pigas (1550–1601), preached the truths of a reformed Christianity in no uncertain terms.

This active Greek religious preaching also supported the faith and historical consciousness of Bulgaria. The *Kontakion*, a hymn by Theodorus the Studite, was anonymously translated into Bulgarian. So was the *Treasure* (1568) by the Greek preacher Damascene the Studite at the end of the century: a collection of thirty-six sermons for priests. A literary text, *The Life of the New Saint Nicholas of Sofia* (*c.*1560) bore witness to the culture shock of the clash of Christian and Ottoman cultures. Its author, Matthew the Grammarian, was an eye-witness to the martyrdom of Nicholas Marinov, stoned to death by the Turks in 1555.

Similarly, if half of the population of Albania were forced to convert to Islam, the other half remained faithful to the Orthodox religion. The priest, Gjon Buzuku, published a book of hours (1555) in Albanian to help his community survive.

A twin birth

For most of Europe, the sixteenth century ended in conflict: internally or externally, individually or collectively, oppression either derailed or stifled humanism. Nevertheless, a twin birth showed just how much this century belonged to the modern era in literature: that of vernacular languages which, at the expense of Latin, acquired the status of literary languages, and that of the picaresque novel,* a narrative genre born of a brutal reality experienced by more than one contemporary of Fernaõ Mendes Pinto (1510?–1583). His autobiographical tale, *Peregrinaçaõ* (*Peregrinations*, 1614) included reminiscences of the trials and tribulations of Spanish picaros.

Four figures in particular stand out on the cusp of the sixteenth and seventeenth centuries. First, there was Camões, who sang in his *Lusiads* of Portuguese national pride and the feeling of having contributed to the progress of European civilisation by discovering new lands. Second, there was Montaigne who, in his *Essays*, also celebrated man's greatness – the greatness of the average man rather than the mighty. Third, there was Cervantes,

who holds up to his reader the distorting mirror of *Don Quixote* to allow him to see the illusory truth that much more clearly. Like Montaigne, Shakespeare placed man at the centre of his concerns, in the infinite variety of his dramatis personae. All four had heard Erasmus' message. The concerns of humanism were their concerns, even if they could no longer share its optimism. All four looked for wisdom, through the imprecations that the old man of Rostelo hurls at the sailors whose arrogance has driven them mad in *The Lusiads*, the 'Que sais-je?' ('What do I know?') of Montaigne, the heroic and pitiful struggle of Don Quixote and Shakespeare's 'the sound and the fury'.

The Picaresque Novel

A. Benoit and G. Fontaine

Travel is really quite useful, it broadens the mind. Everything else is just disappointment and weariness. Our own journey only exists in our imagination. That's what makes it so potent!

Louis-Ferdinand Céline, *Journey to the End of Night*

This was the picaresque credo of Louis-Ferdinand Céline who launched Bardamu, his ragged hero, on to the broken down roads of the twentieth century. Lazarillo de Tormes, Guzmán de Alfarache, Simplicius Simplicissimus, Gil Blas, Moll Flanders, Thyl Eulenspiegel and Schweik had all ventured down those potholed roads before him.

My name is Lazarillo de Tormes

For a cultivated sixteenth-century reader, who knows about the importance of a name, this novel's first words were provocative! Like the heroes of chivalrous romances, the narrator's name is foreordained but, in this case, it is Lazarus, the patron saint of lepers and rogues, who watches over him. In a Spain mindful of the purity of its bloodlines, Lazarillo impudently asserts the hybrid nature of his own: his father is sentenced for having 'slashed a few holes in the sacks of those who came to grind their wheat'. His mother is maltreated for having had sexual relations with a shady Moor, whose visits became so frequent that she 'ended up giving him a little black baby loveable to look on'.

Without the benefit of title, wealth or noble birth, who is this upstart who boasts of his dubious lineage as if it were a gift to be savoured? A beggar! A vagabond! In 1554 a short anonymous biography, *La Vida de Lazarillo de Tormes* (*The Life of Lazarillo de Tormes*), was published simultaneously in Burgos, Alcalá and Antwerp – a work to be wondered at since it related not the customary loves of a shepherd or the exploits of a knight, but the life of a tramp. The career of the book was as chequered as that of its hero. After its initial triumph, it was soon on a list of banned books. In 1573 a censored version appeared in which all irreverent references to the behaviour of the clergy had been suppressed. This anti-obscurantism, which verged on the anti-clericalism of many medieval fabliaux, took on other connotations after the fifteenth century in a Europe riven by religious issues.

While still a child, Lazarillo is entrusted to a blindman as his guide. This avaricious, bad-tempered, cunning master gives him his education and, paradoxically, from their first meeting, opens his eyes to life.

Salimos de Salamanca, y llegando a la puente, está a la entrada della un animal de piedra, que casi tiene forma de toro, y el ciego mandóme que llegase cerca del animal, y, allí puesto, me dijo: 'Lázaro, llega el oído a este toro, y oirás gran ruido dentro dél.' Yo, simplemente, llegué, creyendo ser ansí, y, como sintió que tenía la cabeza par de la piedra, afirmó recio la mano, y diome una gran calabazada en el diablo del toro, que más de tres días me duró el dolor de la cornada, y díjome: 'Necio, aprende: que el mozo del ciego un punto ha de saber más que el Diablo.' Y rió mucho la burla.

We went out of Salamanca and when we arrived at the bridge, at the entrance to which is a stone animal something like a bull, the blindman told me to go up to the animal, and when I was next to it, said to me: 'Lazarillo, put your ear against this bull and you'll hear a big noise inside it.' And I, like a simpleton, advanced, thinking he was telling the truth, and when he felt that my head was almost touching the stone, he pushed me roughly with his outstretched arm and made me hit the head of that damned bull so hard that the pain from its stone horn lasted for more than three days. And he said to me: 'Learn, silly lad, that the blindman's helper must be one step ahead of the Devil.' And he had a good laugh at the prank he had played on me.

Once bitten twice shy: after his first lesson, Lazarillo knows that he is on his own. He learns to get by without the help of others. Before leaving his first master, however, he is determined to show him how much he has learned by making him collide with a pillar: 'What! You were able to smell the sausage and couldn't smell the post! Use your nose! Use your nose!' After his second outing, Lazarillo enters the service of several masters. He finally makes his fortune thanks to the patronage of the Archpriest of San Salvador who appoints him to the royal office of town crier in Toledo. From then on, he is a paragon of respectability who turns a blind eye to his wife's relations with the Archpriest and every day eats as much as he likes.

The life of a beggar

Lazarillo de Tormes introduces us to a new literary character, the picaro, led by his wretchedness to make the most of the little he has and to make a laughing stock of the values of faith and honour on which Spanish society was founded. There were antecedents in Spanish literature: Lazarillo is in a direct line of descent from the characters in *La Celestina* or the treatise called *Centurio* – and even more so from *The Happy Andalusian Woman* by Delicado. Going back even further, Lazarillo

226

recalls the tradition that stretched from *The Satiricon* by Petronius and *The Golden Ass* by Apuleius across the Middle Ages in Europe with the *Romance of Reynard*, *The Decameron*, *The Canterbury Tales* and the French fabliaux. But Lazarillo is a poor Spaniard in a country made poor by all the gold of the Americas. The economic and ideological background – the disappearance of the skilled middle-class worker, the aristocrat's contempt for work – explains the creation of this new literary type. The ironical glance that Lazarillo casts at society unmasks the hardness, the hypocrisy and the cynicism of the world in which this child grows up, qualities he makes his to find his own place in the sun. A sausage-stealer and a safe-cracker, the picaro knows that words cannot be trusted: the truth is far from what people say it is. In order to survive the picaro must see what the other side of life has to offer, according to Céline's hero, Bardamu. And so the picaresque came into being.

Lazarillo de Tormes spawned many imitations, in Spain as in the rest of Europe: Spanish picaros of the seventeenth century, the German soldier of the Thirty Years' War, a young seventeenth-century English woman of easy virtue, a Flemish beggar-cum-revolutionary, a French 'misfit' and a 'good soldier' in 1920s Bohemia. Guzmán, Simplicius, Moll Flanders, Thyl Eulenspiegel, Bardamu and Schweik are all Lazarillo's next of kin.

The picaresque in Spain

Fifty years after the publication of *Lazarillo*, a novel appeared by Mateo Alemán (1547–c.1614), *Guzmán de Alfarache* (1599). In it the term picaro is used for the first time to designate the beggar Guzmán, a man without honour, ready to do anything to become rich. It laid down the ground rules for the picaresque genre: it was both a story – of a journey to the end of hunger, with its proper conventions – and a narrative rhetoric. The story of the picaro, with all kinds of variations, included a number of themes that recur in one novel after another: the tale of where the rogue came from, his childhood and what reduced

him to a life of ceaseless wandering, his obsession with hunger and money, his development in a caricature of a society which, in gradual stages, makes him less naïve and more cynical. This story also implied recourse to expected procedures: we have an autobiography recounted by an experienced narrator whose pessimistic commentary pitilessly picks up on the hypocrisy and nastiness of society and on the hero's credulity.

Guzmán de Alfarache consists of three books. The first tells of 'Guzmán's departure from his mother's house', the second of the beggarly life he led and the third of the poverty to which he was reduced. Much more elaborate than *Lazarillo*, this work is characterised by long didactic digressions; the ascetic rubs shoulders with the aesthetic. These moral reflections are not in the *Story of Don Pablo de Segovia*, written by Francisco de Quevedo between 1603 and 1608. Irony sets in with the notice to the reader: 'God keep you safe from bad books, sergeants and tricky, flattering blondes!'

Many novels or tales of picaresque inspiration were published in Spain in the first half of the seventeenth century: *Justina la Picara* (1606) by Francisco Lopez de Ubeda; *Celestina's Daughter or the Ingenious Elena* (1612) by Salas Bardadillo; *The Colloquy of the Dogs, Rinconete y Cortadillo* and *The Lame Devil of Velez de Guevara* by Cervantes. The circumstances that favoured the birth of the picaresque then changed and it would be more correct to speak of picaresque traits. The publication of the *Life and Deeds of Estebanillo Gonzalez* (end of the seventeenth century), for example, is not so far away in time from that of the first picaresque novel *The Adventures of Simplicius Simplicissimus* (1669) by Grimmelshausen, which takes place within the same setting of the Thirty Years' War.

The picaresque genre

Simplicissimus, the superlative of simplicity, lives in a frightening world where his simplicity of spirit conveys innocence and absence of sin. After contact with the world, he goes to the dogs and becomes a sinner. When he withdraws from the world, he turns to God. The dualism between the world and the soul, close to medieval concepts of them, cannot be circumvented. In this portrait of a good-for-nothing who is used as an example for the whole of humanity, the most famous German novel of the seventeenth century reveals a harsh version of reality.

Alain-René Lesage's hero Gil Blas de Santillane, is a more openly comic creation, owing something to the Pulcinea of the commedia dell'arte, Rabelais' Panurge and Guzmán de Alfarache; but the irony dear to the seventeenth century gives unity and specificity to the *Story of Gil Blas of Santillana*. With this protagonist, the naiveté of the first picaro gives way to sarcasm. His wanderings in Spain are described in twelve books.

An opportunist like Gil Blas, born in the gutter, eager to succeed: now we have Moll Flanders, a picaresque heroine from Daniel Defoe: a picaro in skirts who was twelve years a whore and five times a wife. But how can she escape from the alleyways of London without hitching up her skirts?

'Long live the Beggar!' shouts Eulenspiegel, revolting against the tyranny of Philip II. Was not this nickname that Flemish followers of the Prince of Orange proudly gave to themselves the translation of the word picaro? Thyl Eulenspiegel was its Romantic and Northern incarnation. In 1867 the Belgian writer, Charles de Coster, who based his character on its sixteenth-century German forebear, published *The Legend and the Heroic, Joyful and Glorious Adventures of Eulenspiegel and of Lamme Goedzak in Flanders and Elsewhere*. The mischievous Thyl denounced 'the stupidity, ridiculousness and crimes of an era'. The storms that broke over Europe at the beginning of the twentieth century gave rise to a new generation of brothers to the picaros: in the Austro-Hungarian Empire, as in France, modern anti-heroes stand up to their waists in mud and bullets. *The Good Soldier Schweik* (1922), by Hašek, rediscovers the picaresque vein to relate the hero's misadventures. Schweik possesses the innocence of the picaresque hero, which he never lost, unlike Bardamu

who, when the first shots are fired in the First World War, stops being a 'virgin to Horror'. Bardamu's chaotic wanderings leave him no richer either in terms of money or ideals. So, from the sixteenth to the twentieth century, the picaro is left without a handle on fate. All things considered, at the end of a picaresque narrative, the only conclusion to draw is the totally disenchanted one with which *Journey to the End of Night* closes:

> How many lives would I need to find an idea stronger than anything else in the world? There was no way of saying! It was too late! My ideas [. . .] were like little cheap flickering candles trembling all life long in the middle of an utter cesspit of a universe . . .

Camões (*c.*1524–1580)

L. Sà Fardilha

Fate has caused my genius, from which I no longer derive either joy or pride, to freeze up.

Luis de Camões

In 1569 the historian Diogo do Couto, heading out to Mozambique, met one of the many Portuguese emigrants who took ship every year to seek fame and fortune in the East Indies. This man spent his time polishing the verses of an epic poem, *Os Lusíadas* (*The Lusiads*, 1572), while at the same time putting in order a collection of lyric poems called *The Parnassus of Luis de Camões* with a view to publication. Unfortunately for the poet and for us, this manuscript was stolen and irretrievably lost. Fate, once again, had struck at him. The following year, Luis de Camões went back to Lisbon, which he had left in 1553, with only his manuscript of *The Lusiads*. He returned to his homeland without having made his fortune, disappointed and undermined.

The Lusiads: A lifetime's work

His loves and youthful hopes in Lisbon and Coimbra, his seventeen years of fighting battles, sailing and having adventures on Eastern oceans, frivolity and poetic entertainments: all these henceforth were things of the past. It was during these very years, however, that the Camões wrote the poetry that he tried to have published on his return to Portugal. *The Lusiads* were a lifetime's work, in which wide humanist education mingled with real poetic talent and a rich experience of what it is to be human. During his life Camões experienced war and oriental luxury, prison and hunger:

A fortuna me traz peregrinando,
Novos trabalhos e novos danos:
Agora o mar, agora experimentando
Os perigos mavóreios inumanos,
Qual Canace que à morte se condena,
Numa mão sempre a espada e noutra
a pena;
Agora em pobreza avorrecida,
Por hospícios alheios degradado;
Agora da esperança já adquirida,
De novo mais que nunca derribado.

I go where destiny leads me,
Enduring new trials and new injuries;
Sometimes experiencing heavy seas,
sometimes
The inhuman perils of the god Mars,
Like Canaceus condemned to die,
I always have my sword in one hand and
my pen in the other;
Sometimes I am exiled in foreign places,
With importunate penury for companion;
Sometimes deprived yet again,
And more than ever, of experiences already
acquired.

In the East, Camões experienced the dangers and agonies that Vasco da Gama's sailors had endured and surmounted, men who, having departed from 'the western strand of Lusitania [. . .] went, through seas hitherto never navigated, beyond Taprobane'. Mixing his own personal experience with memories of the exploits of Portuguese navigators, Camões became the faithful interpreter of collective feelings and concluded the epic that the Renaissance in Portugal had so eagerly

awaited. Traveller, scholar, humanist, a troubadour in the time-honoured tradition, an aristocrat who went hungry, Camões reflected on the experience of a whole civilisation with whose contradictions he was familiar, seeking to transcend them in artistic creativity. Camões and *The Lusiads* were a poet and a poem that belong to the Renaissance.

The Camoensian epic speaks to us of man's greatness and the nobility of his triumph over worldly things. This work was not merely a historical narrative. The text certainly has its basis in reality, but it transcends that reality. It is a drama about transcendence: men fight with gods to attain immortality; men measure up to the gods and eventually conquer them. The arrival of Vasco da Gama in the Indies marked the victory of the Portuguese over their opposing gods. This is why the captain and his companions claim the right to be immortal. Men become gods: are not the latter men in a previous life whose reputation has made known 'their works of valour'?

But the spirit of the Renaissance which animated *The Lusiads* did not limit itself to the exaltation of Man as the central person in History and the driving force behind its development. Camões also wanted his epic to be an encyclopedia of natural history, a didactic and pseudo-scientific work. To achieve this, he describes geographical areas, strange situations and little-known natural phenomena. In Canto X, he described the accumulated wisdom of Ptolemaic geography, still flourishing in the sixteenth century.

In the field of geography, the nautical experience of the Portuguese often questioned the authority of the authors of classical Antiquity and opened up new maritime trading routes. *The Lusiads* expressed a new conception of the world and the marvels of nature. The exaltation of pagan eroticism, characteristic of the Renaissance, is latent throughout the poem and surfaces in the episode of the Utopian 'Island of Love' where Portuguese mariners copulate with nymphs so that, obedient to the desire of Venus, 'from the womb of Neptune's realm a generation strong and fair of aspect may emerge':

Ali, com mil refrescos e manjares,
Com vinhos oderíferos e rosas,
Em cristalinos paços singulares,
Fermosos leitos, e elas mais fermosas,
Enfim com mil deleites não vulgares,
Os esperam as Ninfas amorosas,
D'amor feridas, para lhe entregarem
Quanto delas os olhos cobiçarem.

That the amorous and lovelorn nymphs
shall make them welcome with a
thousand sweetmeats and
refreshments, with perfumed wines and
roses in precious palaces of crystal, in
gorgeous beds (and they themselves
even more gorgeous!) and, all in all,
serve them with a thousand
extraordinary delights and let them
have whatever their eyes covet.

With *The Lusiads*, Camões revived the classical Homerian epic, thus realising one of the aesthetic aspirations closest to the heart of humanism. The work's main theme, the sea-going voyage, brings it close to *The Odyssey* and to the first part of *The Aeneid*. Its existential optimism prolonged the groundswell of a humanism that vigorously asserted man's value as an individual and his ability to build a new stage in his history.

The disorderliness of the world

Contrasting with the optimism of his epic, Camões' lyric poetry was distinguished by confessions of the misfortunes, the uncertainties and the despair that dogged his personal life, above all the cruelty of fate:

O dia em que eu nasci, moura e pereça,
não o queira jamais o tempo dar,
não torne mais no mundo, e, se tornar,
eclipse nesse passo o sol padeça. [. . .]
O gente temerosa, não te espantes,
que este dia deitou ao mundo a vida
mais desgraçada que jamais se viu!

May the day I was born pass away and
  perish,

may it never be renewed by time,
may it never return to the world and,
if it does return,
may the sun be eclipsed when it does.
[. . .] Do not be surprised, ye fearful,
for that day gave unto the world
the most unhappy life that has ever
been seen!

The multiplicity and diversity of his work allow us to follow a journey through life made up of disappointments in love and disillusion with powerful men. The 'disorderliness of the world' is a central theme for Camões, summed up in various sonnets, in the eight-line stanzas to Dom Antonio de Noronha or in the 'esparsas' – ancient poems usually composed in hexasyllabic verse, as brief as they are bitter.

The causes of this chaos are identified by the poet in the last eight-line stanza of the poem dedicated to Dom Antonio de Noronha:

Fortuna, enfim, com Amor se conjurou
contra mim, porque mais me
magoasse:
Amor um vão desejo me obrigou
só para que a Fortuna mo negasse.

Finally Fortune and Love conspired
against me
in order to bruise me even more:
Love submitted me to vain desires
so that Fortune could refuse them to me.

Unlike *The Lusiads*, in Camões' lyric poems the theme of love is tackled from the viewpoint of suffering. According to the tradition established by Petrarch, woman is unattainable. The beloved appears irradiated by a supernatural light which transfigures her appearance in the flesh. Her luminous golden hair and shining gaze have the power to calm the wind; her presence makes flowers grow, melting the heart of even inanimate objects. Her whole being is the physical incarnation of an ideal: she breathes serenity, gravity, elevation. Camões merely follows the example of Laura, developing the Platonic theme of the 'dolce stil nuovo'. Even if the model is foreign, however, the poet quickly frees himself from the poetry which has inspired him to fly using his own wings, thus realising an original synthesis from disparate elements. Not content with a purely spiritual love similar to that sung by Petrarch, Camões' poetry takes up the struggle between carnal desire and an ideal, disinterested love which is purely contemplative, developing it still further. The poet wants to make a synthesis, continually sought after, sometimes glimpsed but never reached, between what is finite in love and what is infinite. His lyricism is the expression of a tension between spirituality and carnal desire:

Manda-me Amor que cante
  docemente
o que ele já em minha alma tem
  impresso
com pressuposto de desabafar-me,
e porque com meu mal seja contente,
diz que ser de tão lindos olhos preso,
contá-lo bastaria a contentar-me.
Este excelente modo de enganar-me
tomara eu só de Amor por interesse,
se não se arrependesse
co a pena o engenho escurecendo.
Porém a mais me atrevo,
em virtude do gesto de que escrevo;
e se é mais o que canto que o que
  entendo,
invoco o lindo aspeito,
que pode mais que Amor em meu
  defeito.

Love orders me to sing
  sweetly
what he has already printed on my
  soul
with the intention of setting me free;
and so that I can be satisfied to be
  so sick,
he says: to be able to relate
how you are a prisoner of such pretty
eyes must suffice to please me.
I would have accepted from Love
this excellent manner of deceiving
myself through self-interest

if he had not repented
with pain obscuring genius.
However, I dare more,
by virtue of the face of which I write;
and if what I sing is above
what I understand,
I invoke her beautiful aspect
which can do more than Love for my
  defectiveness.

One of the most interesting aspects of Camões' poetry lies in the alternation of these two poles, in the tension thus created, in the never-ending and ever-renewed attempt to forge them and to give them global meaning. With Camões love and the world appear to be fragmented, contradictory, problematic. His poetry expressed an anxiety far removed from the assurance and the optimism that normally characterise the height of the Renaissance. Camões is disturbed. He is full of foreboding when he sees the breakdown of the Ptolemaic system, a cosmos made up of concentric spheres, limited in time and space, constituting a unique system in which man and the earth occupied the middle ground. After this elegant construct had broken down, the known continents and the planet itself were lost in an expanding universe possibly infinite and without a centre, where space, time and causality could no longer be expressed by simple visual images.

Camões' lyric poetry becomes the echo of a sharp intuition in which the world consists of opposing forces out of man's control, whose sense he does not grasp:

Mudam-se os tempos, mudam-se as
  vontades,
muda-se o ser, muda-se a confiança,
todo o mundo é composto de
  mudança,
tomando sempre novas qualidades.

Times change and desires change,
And people change and so does
  confidence;
The whole world is made up of change,
Always taking on new qualities.

The prince of poets

When Camões died on 10 June 1580 (a date commonly acknowledged), his greatness as a poet was still barely recognised. But his fame spread and, in both Spain and Portugal, he was christened the 'prince of poets'. *The Lusiads* were immensely successful; many editions were published and with them scholarly commentaries. The first edition of *Rimas* (*Rhymes*) was published in 1595. Their success was such that subsequent editors sought to include in the body of work attributed to Camões everything he appeared to have written. Manuel de Faria e Sousa, a Camões 'fanatic', did most to swell this body of work with extraneous additions, giving the criterion he had followed: 'I have attributed to my poet all I have found containing even as much as a shadow of his genius.' In the absence of rigorous selection criteria, the *Rhymes* became longer with each succeeding edition: victims of their own success. The poets of the seventeenth century paid homage to Camões by calling him the 'Lusitanian swan', the 'Iberian phoenix' or the 'Lusitanian Homer' and copiously annotated him. In the seventeenth century, Bocage proclaimed that Camões was his model and his master, while in the nineteenth century, Almeida Garrett inaugurated Portuguese Romanticism with a poem called 'Camões'.

In Europe Camões was known above all as the author of *The Lusiads*, a work which, according to the words of its first French translator, 'can be considered as one of the finest poems ever to be read since Homer and Virgil'. The Spanish were the first to read Camões's epic in their own language: two editions were published in 1580, followed by a third in 1591. In the seventeenth century the first translations into English (1655) and Italian (1658) appeared but it was not until the eighteenth century that *The Lusiads* would be known in nearly all the civilised languages of Europe: French (1735, 1768, 1776), Dutch (1777), Russian (1788), Polish (1790). With these translations, to which others were added in the nineteenth century – German, Swedish, Hungarian, Danish – Camões' poetry ceased to be merely a part of Portugal's literary heritage and became incorporated into European culture.

Montaigne (1533–1592)

A. Benoit
and G. Fontaine

So, dear reader, I am myself the subject of my book.

Montaigne, *Essays*

From his library, Michel Eyquem, Lord of Montaigne, travelled the world through books and his own personal experience. Sometimes surprised, sometimes amused by the diversity of the universe, his curiosity examined everything, for everything that can shed even unaccustomed light on human behaviour interested him. Caring not a fig for distances in time or space, he collected anecdotes, reflections and thoughts all the better to focus on his one true theme: man, whose reasons for behaving as he does he never tired of analysing. Over the years and by dint of continual reading, Montaigne modified his original opinions. His *Essays*, re-read, revised, added to, were the fruit of a critical intelligence which aimed at a way of thinking that had nothing to do with dogmatism and was based on freedom of thought. A veritable compendium of current knowledge and tending to promote a new humanistic attitude, the *Essays* had notable repercussions in France as they did abroad, with varying fortune however: their translation, in certain countries, far from facilitating their dissemination, led to their being put on the Index! All of which would have made their author smile.

A mind curious about everything

'We were born to seek the truth,' said Montaigne. And he listens to and scrutinises the world. *On Cannibals*, *On Glory*, *On Thumbs*, *On an Expression of Cato's*, *On*

Friendship, *On the Education of Children*, *On Liars* – Montaigne, always wide-awake, 'sieves everything through the muslin' of his judgement. He took note of the arrival of three savages in Rouen or of the road from Quito to Cuzco, of the change to the Gregorian calendar or of the cleverness of animals. He noted and found something in them to reflect on. He liked to discuss everything that preoccupied a gentleman of the late Renaissance, going for his subjects to the Ancients or the chronicles of his contemporaries.

Montaigne's ability to encompass the world in all its variety was not only acquired from his trips outside the Gironde or from his own human experience, varied as this was, but from the breadth of his reading. Seneca or Copernicus, Homer or Ariosto: everything was a source of personal enrichment. He was well-read in the classics and, to the end of his life, kept up with new publications. As one of his time's leading intellectuals, and because of his father's influence, he was familiar with Latin and Latin literature. His thought developed with his reading. First he was haunted by the Stoic Seneca, the first writer who taught him how to think, and by Cato whom he wished to imitate. Then knowledge of Plutarch, in Amyot's translation, and of Sextus Empiricus had a marked effect on him. For a time he was tempted by scepticism. Montaigne carved on a beam in his library the famous motto 'Que sais-je?' ('What do I know?'). He always valued Latin poetry. The works of Lucretius, Ovid, Martial, Virgil and Horace went with him everywhere; he likes their 'poetic gait, all hops and gambols'.

He also liked to read the testimonies of his contemporaries: *The History of the Great Kingdom of China* (1588) by Gonçales de Mendoza, *The History of the West Indies* (1584) by Lopez de Gomara, *A Short History of Persia* (1583) by George Lebelski. Pasquier, Tasso, Thomas More and Erasmus were his contemporaries. Montaigne wrote about all the works he read. He discussed them, illustrated them, went from one to the other to see them in a fresh light. He humorously admitted to what he called his 'thefts'.

At the heart of this swarm of thoughts, anecdotes and quotations reflecting on the variety of the world, one question obsessed him: what is man? The question was asked in various ways because 'Man is a wondrously vain, diverse and changing subject. It is hard to have constant and uniform ideas about him.'

The depiction of man

From this accumulation of examples and opinions Montaigne puts together a vision of man diametrically opposed to the humanists before him. In *The Dignity of Man*, Pico della Mirandola emphasised man's intrinsic worth. In God's terms, man must be the architect of his own fate; Montaigne makes him 'the joker in a farce'. This fall from grace in less than a century is a hard one for humanity! Man cannot be certain of anything since the senses are scarcely to be believed and our reason is 'a free-ranging and ill-defined instrument'. Montaigne's conclusion was irrefutable: 'Most of our occupations are laughable.' Once we have admitted that knowledge and customs are relative, Montaigne suggested that we see man in all individuals: 'I think of all men as my compatriots and embrace a Pole as I would a Frenchman.'

The knowledge that we have of the world can come to us from no *a priori* teaching but depends on personal experience: the only definitive certainty.

So, in 'this only book in the world of its type', Montaigne tells his own story: 'If I set before you the example of a lowly and lacklustre life, it's all one: the whole of moral philosophy can be just as easily attached to an ordinary private life as to a rich fabric; each man carries in himself the human condition in its entirety.' We must not take this overly modest declaration too literally: this 'lowly and lacklustre life' was that of a noble from the area around Bordeaux who could live well and was called on to play a part in politics in the entourage of the French King Henri IV.

After completing his studies, Montaigne entered parliament in Bordeaux. Here he met

Étienne de la Boétie, a local magistrate, whose influence on Montaigne was decisive. La Boétie was the author 'of a discourse to which he gave the name of *Voluntary Slavery* . . . He wrote it as a sort of essay, in the first flush of youth, in honour of freedom from tyrants,' said Montaigne, adding 'If I were pressed to say why I liked him, I think that I could only answer: Because he was himself and I was myself.'

Montaigne's functions led him to undertake journeys to Paris where he took part in court life. In 1570 he sold his post as councillor and retired to his estate in south-west France. He had carved on the joists of his library Greek and Latin maxims that he liked to ponder – and he set to work on the first volume of the *Essays*.

In 1578 Montaigne contracted gravel, the stony malady as renal colic was then called. The resulting pain was the beginning of a personal reflection on the body. Montaigne called on philosophy so that 'in the face of colic, it might keep the soul able to know itself, to follow its accustomed train of thought'. At the end of this period, towards 1579, the essays were more personal than those of 1572. This is when he compiled the 'Notice to the Reader' in the first edition: 'I want to be seen in my unaffected, natural and usual way, without contentiousness or artifice, for it is myself that I am depicting, My faults will be easy to spot [. . .]. So, dear reader, I am myself the subject of my book.'

The image that Montaigne gave of himself is that of a man who knew how to get the best out of life: 'Speaking for myself, I like life and cultivate it as it has pleased God to bestow it.' The last book of the *Essays* was a hymn to life. Montaigne replaced a morality of perfection with the morality of the average man, close to the ideal of the 'honnête homme' in the century that followed, whose experience and wisdom were well worth that of Cato or Plato. He restored to his reader the totality of free will, possibly without the latter's being aware of it. Could he have gone any further in respecting the ideas of others, he who never stopped trumpeting the claims of his own

personal freedom? Without fanaticism, in the name of ordinary common sense, Montaigne often opposed opinions that were generally accepted by his contemporaries: for example, in a century of forced conversions and religious intolerance, he condemned the use of torture.

The freedom of Montaigne the gentleman was echoed by that of Montaigne the writer; the originality of his project was linked to his freedom as a writer. His book evolved from a compilation to a conversation with the reader. In the essay *On Drunkenness*, Montaigne digressed to present a picture of his father, then, abruptly, and not without humour, says: 'Let us get back to our bottles!' Digressions, far from being an involuntary weakness, were a conscious decision: 'This embroidering takes me a little bit away from my subject. I am wandering, but more by design than by mistake.'

With the additions, so plentiful and characteristic of the *Essays*, aesthetics and ethics were united: truth, one of Montaigne's major and constant preoccupations cannot be reached until it is written down. There is no everlasting truth, there are only things that are true in the here and now. Hence the commentaries that were constantly added to different editions. Hence the outgrowths whose hidden roots have so disconcerted readers of the *Essays*.

The fate of a book, the fate of a genre

Marie de Gournay hoped that the 1595 edition of the *Essays*, which contained her preface, would find 'good stomachs' 'to digest it' and 'not to partake [of it] superficially'. In the sixteenth century and at the very beginning of the seventeenth, Europe's appetite for Montaigne increased. A wider public soon existed for it, and remained over the centuries: the *Essays* disturbed Catholic thinkers, the Enlightenment assimilated the ideas contained in them for its own theses. The Romantics were divided: suspicion on the part of Rousseau, boundless admiration from Byron. 'With Montaigne,' wrote Stefan Zweig in 1942, 'I do not feel myself in the company of a book, but of a man who is my brother, who counsels me and consoles me, of a man I understand and who understands me.' Editions one after the other in the sixteenth and seventeenth centuries, translations of the *Essays* into English and Italian, by John Florio as early as 1603 and by Marco Ginammi some years later, give some idea of the work's popularity. Shakespeare was so impressed by the *Essays* that a scene in *The Tempest* repeats a passage in *On Cannibals* almost verbatim. According to Ben Jonson, London theatres echoed to the sound of frequent 'flights' of Montaigne.

In 1597, Francis Bacon was the first to use the title of *Essays*, already chosen by Montaigne, to designate short prose writings. Joseph Addison defined the readers to whom his essays were dedicated in the following terms: 'I want it said of me that I brought philosophy out of studies, schools and colleges to make it dwell in clubs, around tables where tea is taken and in cafés.' This recalls what Montaigne had to say about his audience: the *Essays* would not please 'either common and vulgar minds or singular and fastidious ones[. . .]. They would muddle through between these two extremes.' An agreeable genre, for any reputable reader, humorous and yet profound, from Addison to Hazlitt, from Thackeray to Chesterton, the essay has prospered in England.

Montaigne recycled?

'The most useful books are those whose readers supply half of their contents,' wrote Voltaire in the preface to the *Philosophical Dictionary*. How useful that would make the *Essays*, with each succeeding generation, were they to be measured by that yardstick! In 1601, the theologian Pierre Charon decided to 'put them in order': he made them a work called *Wisdom*, designed to control 'the vicious nature of man, the wildest and most difficult to tame of all animals'. Attempts to appropriate the work then began to gather momentum. In the worldly moral teaching of Montaigne, Epicureans and libertines in the

seventeenth century found a justification for their thoughts and lifestyle. During the same period, Montaigne's Spanish translator, Diego de Cisneros, purged his book 'of the vices of pagan licentiousness', yet kept 'what is exquisite and perfect' as he called it in his translation. In spite of the precautions taken beforehand, the Inquisition condemned the *Essays*. But the placing on the Index of 1676 was prepared above all by the repeated attacks of Bossuet, Malebranche, Nicole and Pascal. Pascal, who found fault with Montaigne because of 'his silly plan to paint his own portrait', often took from the *Essays* examples in support of his own arguments.

The Encyclopedists of the eighteenth century saluted in Montaigne the precursor of the Enlightenment, as did Melchior Grimm in his *Literary Correspondence* (1753–1773): 'The divine Montaigne was a man who was unique, who spread the purest and most vivid light through the darkness of the sixteenth century, though his merit and his genius have only been recognised in our own century, when truth and philosophical inquiry have taken the place of superstition and prejudice.' Certain themes in the *Essays* particularly interested the Romantics: in *On the Education of Children*, for example, which Rousseau severely criticised Montaigne came close to appearing in *Émile*, next to La Fontaine, as one of the worst teachers. Emilia Pardo Bazán, however, in late nineteenth-century Spain, excused Montaigne's 'anti-sentimentalism' about children in her treatise called *Teachers of the Renaissance* (1889): 'I can forgive Montaigne for thinking that all a woman had to know how to do was to tell the difference between a jerkin and knee breeches because of the pleasant discourses he wrote on childhood and youth, on the authority of fathers and on those hateful pedants he himself forgave nothing.'

If virtually every current of thought has tried to recycle for its own use the author of the *Essays* – free-thinkers, rationalists, even followers of Nietzsche, including Gide who found in Montaigne a brother in immoralism – the twentieth-century image of the un-hampered Montaigne, always at pains to reject dogmatism, has survived. The self-confessed heir to the founding culture of Europe, Montaigne is also one of its disseminators as Élie Faure pointed out in *Montaigne and his three first-born: Shakespeare, Cervantes and Pascal* (1926):

> I could easily show, in Montaigne himself, the traces and the fruits of a thousand years of unconscious assimilation of Christian doctrine. But here, once again, he scotched dogma which indicates that the task of the religion of his fathers, at least in noble souls, had been accomplished, which his sons, it seems to me, understood perfectly. If Montaigne appears to be completely outside the Christian and other faiths, Shakespeare is so much above them that he seems not to suspect so much as their existence. Cervantes, of course, is inside religion, but he seems to ignore the presence of the bars through which he discerns even the most distant perspectives of space and daylight. [. . .] *Hamlet* and *Don Quixote* belong more or less to the same year, the second or third of the new century. Two madmen bring into the world acerbic moral truth, the knowledge of which leads to lyrical wisdom, the only wisdom that can replace hiding behind a received truth, at least for highly individual minds. Montaigne, in the *Apology of Raymond Sebonde*, playing with his own arguments like an ironical juggler with sharp swords, had already established the effectiveness of this strategy.

Cervantes (1547–1616)

Don Andrés Soria-Ortega

> What could a mind as barren and uncultivated as mine give birth to, if not the story of a dry, weak, stunted and capricious son?
>
> Cervantes

In contrast to other authors, both ancient and modern, who carefully ordered or forged their lives before submitting it to the scrutiny of others, Miguel Cervantes – as the poet Antonio Machado said later – merely accepted what life gave him: extraordinary things on occasion, 'with that humility that yields / only to the law of life / which is to live as best you can.'

The one-handed man of Lepanto

In the sixteenth-century, Alcalá de Henares, where Cervantes was born, was a famous university town. But, from his earliest years, the young Miguel knew other towns in Castille and Andalusia – Madrid, Toledo, Valladolid, Cordoba, Seville – where his father, the surgeon, Rodrigo de Cervantes, lived. At school he met López de Hoyos, a master steeped in the teachings of Erasmus own early work.

Later Cervantes discovered the world beyond Spain: the *dolce vita* in Italy as he called it, in Rome, la Via Julia, then Sicily and Naples. He had adventures and even encountered war. The battle of Lepanto, in which both Cervantes and his brother Rodrigo fought as soldiers in Diego de Urbina's company aboard the galley *Marquesa*, was a memorable episode. Miguel was left an invalid by an injury to his left hand, but he considered it an honour to have been involved in one of Christendom's greatest military actions. He remained with the army in Naples for four years, took part in the expedition to Tunis (1573) and one year later, became, like his brother, 'a well-paid soldier' in Palermo.

But, on the other side of the Mediterranean, misfortune awaited him. In 1575, returning to Spain on the galley *El Sol* with Rodrigo – both of them furnished with glowing testimonials – they were attacked and taken prisoner by Barbary Coast pirates and taken to Algiers. For five years Cervantes was plunged into another world, humiliated and degraded, held captive in unspeakable, hellish conditions from which only a ransom would free him. This period of captivity was a watershed: he had left the heroic empower-ruled Spain with its high ideals and firm beliefs, only to return to a much altered country where there was no room for the mutilated veteran who had been away for five years.

Cervantes could not accept the fact that fate had made him a prisoner. He hatched plans to escape, trying but failing several times. He had shown his mettle as a professional soldier and, once in captivity, his self-denial made him still greater: he assumed responsibility for all escape plans and, in spite of the scourging and impalement to which he was subjected, he gave no one away and never weakened. In 1612, he was cited for this valorous action in the report published after the official enquiry made in Algiers by Diego de Haedo. By the time his family scraped the ransom money together, Cervantes was thirty-two years old.

Paradoxically, the tale of his captivity – the 'live' broadcast by someone who has lived through the events – did not come immediately after the euphoria of his homecoming. It was only thirty years later that Cervantes condensed it into the short story inserted into the first part of his masterpiece: the eventful story of the Captive, Chapters 39, 40 and 41 of *Don Quixote*.

On his return to his Spain, taking advantage of friendships fostered during his captivity, Cervantes asked for a position as a civilian. In 1582, he wrote to Antonio de Eraso, the king's secretary, to ask him for a post in the West Indies and, at the same time, to commend to him the work that he was writing: *La Galatea* (1585). From now on his two main occupations were the administrative service of the Crown – and writing.

We know little about his family or his love life: there are no letters, no diary or any other records of an intimate nature. There are only a few official documents, all relating to economic questions, all hinting at a difficult daily life in a shabby-environment. Cervantes' mature years, which normally mean a settled existence, planned output and reasonable stability, may be summed up in one word: failure, in social if not literary terms.

Cervantes became a professional writer and moved in Madrid literary circles. The theatrical world offered him more flexible contacts. In his exemplary novels *El Coloquio*

de los perros (*The Colloquy of the Dogs*) and *El licenciado vidriero* (*The Glass Graduate*), he gave us caricatures of the poets, actors and authors he knew at this time. A writer in the full sense of the word, he spoke to the public in traditional ways, devoting himself to writing in conventional registers. He tried the pastoral novel as it suited him, occasional verse and plays, practising these genres in all their variety. But he was always a modest craftsman, clearly acknowledging his limitations. He maintained he needed exceptional gifts – which he did not have – to compose 'great poetry, on a par with celestial grace'. In the area of stagecraft, he recognised the exceptional superiority of Lope de Vega, crowning him 'king' of the stage. In the field of letters, Spanish literary life in all its fullness offered him a niche he thought he could occupy. In his administrative activities, however, he was a pawn in a game of chess that did not remain a game.

Poetry and theatre, comic and creative

Cervantes' literary career oscillated between verse and prose in accordance with the norms of his time – those of the classical Renaissance. Throughout his career he composed poems that were an integral part of his prose; nevertheless, thinking perhaps of Garcilaso whom he admired, he knew he did not have a true poet's gifts. In spite of everything, his occasional works were admirable. The *Canto de Caliope* (*Calliope's Song*), in *La Galatea*, the pastoral novel he wrote at the beginning of his career, unfinished like the *Viaje al Parnasso* (*The Journey to Parnassus*, 1614), written at the end of his life, were admired by the poets of his time.

Cervantes fervently explored his other great interest: the theatre. In his childhood he had known Lope de Rueda, the actor-playwright, one of the most active promoters of primitive street theatre. Cervantes remembered him for a long time, and was always enthusiastic about the art of his 'comedias' and 'pasos'. After 1580 his own first plays for the stage were produced, but their overall quality was uneven.

Cervantes followed classical models and was influenced by Torres Naharro, a precursor of Lope de Rueda. We find the theme of captivity in *Los Tratos de Argel* (*Life in Algiers*). But, in tragedy, a genre where imitation is obligatory, classicism received from Cervantes' genius an extraordinary addition with *El Cerco de Numancia* (*The Siege of Numancia*, 1581–1583), also known as *La Numancia* (*Numancia*), which depicted the courage of a people. Cervantes' feeling for a whole nation was transmuted into concentrated, tragic and stoical art, especially at the moment of the Numancians' collective suicide when men and women, the allegories of Hunger, War, the river Duero and Spain itself mingled in a sombre, beautiful scene.

In the dramatic works of the second period, Cerevantes revealed his consummate ease in various registers: the dramatist embroidered on the theme of captivity (*La gran sultana, The Great Sultana*, 1615; *El gallardo español, The Valiant Spaniard*), and dealt with intrigues in the Italian manner (*La casa de los celos, The House of Jealous People*). At the same time he wrote for the usual repertoire: the 'comedia de santos' or the 'comedia de picaros'. However, these works may have belonged to the first period of his dramatic production, and were possibly brought up to date to resemble Lope de Vega, the model then dominant in Spain.

Alongside comedy and tragedy, casual theatre existed in which Cervantes distinguished himself: the comic, astute, lively, deep, sentimental art of the *Entremeses* (*Interludes*, 1615). Unlike most of the anonymous writers of these little plays, Cervantes drew attention to his signature. He declared that he had written six of these pieces, but published *Ocho entremeses nuevos nunca representados* (*Eight New Interludes Never Before Performed*). Many others have also been attributed to him, including *El hospital de los podridos, La cárcel de Sevilla* and the best-known *Los Habladores*. Cervantes preserved the traditions of the genre and had recourse to the different mainsprings of comedy; he also knew how to present real-life situations in miniature, introducing elements of the fantastic into his work in a pleasingly harmonious way.

In Lope de Rueda's 'pasos' Cervantes had admired the comic characters of classical extraction (the ruffian and the fool) and those taken from actual life (the negress and the Basque), but he added types of his own to this mix and reworked it, gives a carnival feel – as later defined by Bakhtin – to the malice of farce.

Domestic intrigue, a true reflection of his own family problems, was resolved in laughter (*El juez de los divorcios, The Divorce Judge*) and raciness (*El viejo celoso, The Jealous Old Man*). Like Erasmus he mocked the solemn professions of being a soldier and being a writer as practised by young Cristina's two suitors (*La guarda cuidadosa*). Cervantes adopted special effects like the ones in the fabliaux (*La cueva de Salamanca*), or verbal magic (*El vizcaino fingido*), or the magic of total caricature (*El rufián viudo*). Imagination scales the heights and a play overflows with inventiveness, even if the theme is conventional, when the writer characters, Chivinos and Chanfalla, whose comic wit constantly provokes laughter, conjure up for a village an invisible world, that of the *Retablo de las maravillas* (*The Wonderful Altarpiece*). In this work and also in *La elección de los alcaldes de Daganzo* (*The Election of the Mayors of Daganzo*), Cervantes' laughter is directed at hot gossip, scabrous events in small villages, mocking with a positively Cartesian malice problems both real and imaginary arising from the notion of the 'purity of bloodline'.

Cervantes exercised his ability to revamp a traditional genre in the novel too, whether it was his youthful pastoral novel, *La Galatea*, or, at the end of his life, the Byzantine novel, consisting of journeys, reunions and conversions (*Los trabajos de Persiles y Sigismunda, The Labours of Persiles and Sigismunda*, published posthumously in 1617). In the twelve *Novelas Ejemplares* (*Exemplary Novels*, 1613), Cervantes boasted of having introduced the Italian-style 'novella' to Spain.

Don Quixote

Spain appreciated Cervantes' work in its entirety, but for the rest of the world he was the author of one book only, *El Quijote* (*Don Quixote*). This was immediately popular, both its first part (1605) and its second (1615). Editions and translations rapidly followed during Cervantes' own lifetime. There was even an apocryphal *Don Quixote*, by Avellaneda, circulating in 1614.

Cervantes' aim was to parody the novel of chivalry. He ridiculed this genre, still very popular in the sixteenth century, the main form of escapism condemned by learned writers and sometimes by churchmen ('devilish sermons' as Alejo Venegas called them). The comic impact on his readers was tremendous: they loved the works themselves as as much as the parody. Around 1605 the production of 'new books' (which, some years before, had worried the future Saint Theresa of Avila herself) had substantially decreased. Intimately linked to the genre being parodied, the parody, which should have disappeared when novels of chivalry died out, nevertheless survived them. Two contrasting worlds encountered each other: the imaginary world of the literature of chivalry and the real familiar world of daily life. The mechanism that dissociated and superimposed them was Don Quixote's folly. Ariosto and his *Orlando Furioso* was the most important literary antecedent for it, but there was also a strong influence from medieval literature – Roland, the heroic archetype and the courtly novel of Chrétien de Troyes, the driving force behind which was adventure.

Like all knight errants, the hidalgo sets out three times. His first outing includes the episode at the inn in which he is made a knight. He is then beaten with sticks; despondently he laments his lot, becoming a character in chivalrous literature and a character from the 'romancero' folk tradition.

His second outing leads to the meeting with Sancho, the character who allows us to learn more about Don Quixote. A series of adventures begins interpreted differently by the two different protagonists: where the knight sees giants, his squire can only see windmills. But the dialogue between madness and common sense gradually becomes more important and is one of the book's most original features.

With the last outing of the hero and his squire, novelistic development, ludicity, the settings and the vitality of the work are even greater than in the 1605 edition. The moral is clearer too: know that life is merely dreams and shadows, but live it as if it were real.

Cervantes in Europe

'Prince of wits', Cervantes was perhaps the most European of the great writers. Risking his life, not only did he discover Rome in his youth, but his last novel, *Persiles and Sigismunda*, after its hero has been to Scandinavia, ends in the Eternal City which he celebrates in medieval verse. The anxieties of his youth and his last artful gaze come together in Rome, the microcosm of an ideal Europe.

All over Europe in the sixteenth century people had read books of chivalry in prose and the verses of courtly poems. Cervantes parodied what was at the heart of European literature, in Britain as well as in Germany, Italy, France and the Iberian peninsula. Cervantes not only transformed this novel tradition, but he opened the way to another: his masterpiece, born out of literature, gave birth to new kinds of literature. This can be measured in the imitations engendered by the fashion he launched, as in the various copycat novels and the spate of new heroes in other modern languages. Here we have a book dealing with the influence of literature and the dangers of abusing it (the Man of La Mancha grows mad as a result) which itself enjoys a massive and decisive influence. This affirmation takes us back to the heart of the work itself where Cervantes has concentrated all his literary games. The invention of 'the book within a book' – Cid Hamet Benengelin, an imaginary chronicler who becomes the believable narrator of the story of the Captive, or the readers of the adventures of Don Quixote who in their turn become characters in the book – is a game worthy of Pirandello. *Don Quixote* received the support of French and English literary critics in the seventeenth century and had an influence on the English novel of the eighteenth century, on Fielding, Smollett and Sterne.

But the crowning achievement of Cervantes' novel in Europe, that of becoming a myth, only gradually happened with Romanticism. Schelling saw in it the real battle with the ideal; Jean-Paul the game that transcended madness. Byron asserted that, of all our stories, *Don Quixote* was the saddest because it makes us laugh.

At the other end of Europe, Turgeniev portrayed Hamlet and Don Quixote as the two opposing poles of the literary hero: the first embodied doubt, the second hyperactivity. Dostoyevsky discovered in *Don Quixote* 'the bitterest irony that man is capable of expressing'. Stendhal, Dickens, Flaubert, Thomas Mann and many other famous writers join in the procession that accompanied the parading of Cervantes' great work. Cervantes himself died on 23 April 1616, the very day on which Shakespeare also died.

Shakespeare (1564–1616)

K. Brown

The works of William Shakespeare (thirty-seven surviving plays are normally credited to him today: at least another two, or perhaps three, are partly his) are England's greatest contribution to European literature. Not only is Shakespeare the master of four genres – Tragedy, History-play, Comedy and Romance – but even within these forms he exhibits great variety. As a result, no matter how the cultural climate of our civilization changes, there always seems to be a Shakespearean drama that speaks directly to it. Thus nineteenth-century romanticism saw the glamorous, self-doubting figure of Prince Hamlet as Shakespeare's supreme tragic hero; while since 1945 the bleaker Absurdist world of King Lear is most often felt to be Shakespeare's supreme creation. Yet the neo-classical eighteenth century felt a need to rewrite the ending of *King Lear* for performance, and eminent nineteenth-century critics also thought the play poorly suited to the stage.

Shakespeare was born in 1564, the son of a Stratford-on-Avon merchant. His father, at first prosperous, suffered humiliating financial troubles during Shakespeare's teenage years and early twenties. Even so, the scanty evidence suggests that the home was harmonious, and the playwright's loyalty to his family and to his home town seems a feature of his life. Echoes of the standard Elizabethan grammar-school syllabus in his writings suggest that he must have left school at about sixteen: he did not go on to university. However, the grammar-school syllabus was remarkably ambitious, reflecting all the earnest aspirations of High Renaissance scholarship, and offered an education quite comparable to that received by other young men at English universities in later, less strenuous times. There is therefore no real mystery about the quiet awareness of the classical roots of our culture, or of the contemporary world of letters, discernible under the surface of Shakespeare's works, despite his lack of university training.

Before he was twenty-one, Shakespeare was the father of three children by his wife Anne Hathaway, about eight years his senior, who had already been pregnant when they married. Some time afterwards, he seems to have left Stratford, and for much of the following seven years his whereabouts cannot now be documented. In 1592 he re-emerges, already well-enough established as a London actor and playwright to be attacked in print by an older rival. Play-writing in English, however, was at this time an activity that did not really count as 'literature', and Shakespeare soon made a clear bid for higher literary, and social, status by publishing two long non-dramatic poems (*Venus and Adonis* and *The Rape of Lucrece*), dedicated to the youthful Earl of Southampton. Both won rapid admiration. He also began to privately circulate the first of his sonnets: very much a gentleman's form of 'publication'. These seem to afford fascinating glimpses of Shakespeare's own private life in the 1590s – the famous Dark Lady, a stolen mistress, a rival poet – as it is impossible not to feel that the sometimes moving and powerful feelings expressed are genuinely the poet's own. Then in 1596 the Shakespeares, doubtless financed by William, successfully revived a long-abandoned application for the grant of a coat-of-arms: a further step towards social status.

But a man so clearly determined to rebuild his family's lost position in his native town (Shakespeare early bought for himself Stratford's finest house, and spent his years of retirement as a Stratford rentier) could hardly turn his back on the unique financial opportunities offered by the Elizabethan theatre. In 1594 Shakespeare became a partner in one of London's two leading companies of actors. (The company is most often referred to as The Lord Chamberlain's Men, but it became The King's Men in the next reign.) It staged its plays at court when required, but mostly put them on in ordinary public theatres. From 1599, Shakespeare and other members of this company were also joint owners of the famous Globe Theatre (recently recreated near the original site on London's South Bank). The first Globe could hold more than 3,000 people; and in 1609 the company also took over a smaller indoor theatre, The Blackfriars, where higher prices could be charged. Thus for more than half his career Shakespeare would be paid for writing a play, and paid whenever he acted, while also drawing his share of his annual profits made by both the Chamberlain's company and by the Globe's proprietors. Most of this substantial income was channelled back home to Stratford.

Such practical details perhaps throw some light on the near-universal success of Shakespeare's work. To fill the Globe, the company needed to attract spectators from most levels of London's highly stratified society: yet many of the same plays also had to satisfy a court that was still in many respects the country's cultural focus. That Shakespeare could meet such diverse requirements, year after year, in work that also has the aesthetic and intellectual coherence of great art, is a striking example of the capacity of great intelligence to be lifted by unusual challenges to unusual heights. Had he been solely a court playwright, or purely a popular entertainer, the results could hardly have been the same.

As You Like It – generally considered, along with *Twelfth Night*, to be one of the greatest of Shakespearean comedies – illustrates the point. Its title, quite unrelated to the plot, is a shameless advertising gimmick. And the play's contents are as advertised. The more literary-minded among the audience would be amused by the fun had with the conventions of the pastoral. The many law-students and apprentices likely to be present (often the younger sons of country gentlemen) were bound to be hooked by the story of Orlando, a knight's younger son cheated of his rights by his elder brother. Noticeable too is the play's consciousness of the popular culture of the English countryside, where most Londoners of all classes had either been born or had close family contacts, renewed each summer. The tales of Robin Hood are explicitly evoked, along with other motifs redolent of the world of ballad and folk-tale, and we are treated to a wrestling-match – the favourite village sport. It is a genial work from a man who knows what his public will like; but it is not merely whipped together into the usual kind of semi-farcical situation comedy. Shakespeare had early proved his mastery of that form, in *The Comedy of Errors* (a reworking of Plautus), and thereafter took little interest in it except in *The Taming of The Shrew* and the slightly laboured *The Merry Wives of Windsor*, supposedly a royal commission. (In *A Midsummer Night's Dream*, though, the form is daringly interwoven with the haunting creation of a magical, fairy world.) By contrast, *As You Like It* seeks less to raise laughs than smiles of reflective sympathy, or of sheer delight at the seemingly casual effortlessness of the play's transitions from mood to mood. There is in fact a quasi-musical quality about this, as in so many other of Shakespeare's works: a quality almost impossible to analyse, since it is a matter of pace and timing as well as of interweaving of theme and motif. It stirs curiosity about the knowledge of music apparently implied by occasional phrases in Shakespeare's plays.

Women formed a substantial and economically important part (perhaps 40 per cent) of the Globe and Blackfriars audiences, where Shakespeare's liking for putting his comedies' heroines into male disguise must have offered pleasant escapist fantasies to many an over-confined gentlewoman. The playwright himself seems to have regarded the women of his day with clear eyes: respectful of their intelligence and capable of quiet anger at their oppression. Thus Ophelia is a perfectly trained and schooled young lady whose mental conditioning leaves her defenceless against the psychological brutality with which she is treated by her father and Hamlet. In *Othello*, Desdemona dies because she has been conditioned to value self-preservation less than wifely submission. In *King Lear*, Cordelia triggers disaster by taking with full seriousness the ideals of honesty and good taste urged on every well-bred young woman. Even in Lady Macbeth, wicked though she is, can be felt the maddened frustration of a powerful yet helpless woman, denied – like so many in real life – all outlet for her ambitions save through an inadequate husband's career.

None of Shakespeare's great comic heroines, however, could ever have suffered the fate of Ophelia or Desdemona. Beatrice of *Much Ado About Nothing*, the ladies of *Love's Labours Lost*, Viola of *Twelfth Night*, Rosalind of *As You Like It*, are all witty, well-balanced, enterprising young women, capable of self-irony and mentally a match for any man around them. The role-model they present is far superior to that offered by the conventional wisdom of Shakespeare's day – and further improved by his unfussed recognition, without Petrarchan sentimentalising, puritanical prudery or vulgar snigger, that women are creatures of flesh and blood no less than men. Thus Rosalind's warm reaction to the spectacle of the wrestling-match in *As You Like It*, for instance, serves to legitimate – to 'make

respectable', as it were – any similarly erotic response privately felt by the female part of the audience: the episode is not there just for men to 'like'. The same friendly Shakespearean unsentimentality shows again in the fact that it is the well-bred Ophelia's repressed *sexuality*, not just a conventional romantic broken heart, to which her subconscious gives bawdy expression in the first Mad Scene.

Reference was made above to the traditional division of Shakespeare's dramatic work into four genres: Tragedy, Comedy, History, and Romance. But sometimes, in various ways, he seems deliberately to place a work between two genres. Thus the powerful tragic figure of Shylock the Jew in *The Merchant of Venice* is incapsulated in what is otherwise a comedy sharing several elements with *Twelfth Night*. And *Measure for Measure*, with a seemingly typical Shakespearean comic plot, has nevertheless a wry and bitter mood that is far from comedy and tragedy alike. More normally, though, Shakespeare's dramas belong clearly enough to one of the four genres, while showing with equal clarity the continuity between them in his own mind.

That a history play, concerned with the rise and fall of princes, can take on a tragic dimension, is of course self-evident. And obviously the romances, with their tales of lost princesses found again and so forth, essentially expand the idea of *reconciliation*, a necessary element in any comedy, into one overriding theme. Less obvious, though, is the highly diversified debt of both Shakespearean tragedy and the maturer history plays to the comic drama. This is not simply a matter of what critics used to call 'comic relief'. Far subtler in its effect is Shakespeare's knack of filtering the concept of the tragic, as it were, through the forms of comedy. (Late Roman analyses of the structure of Terentian comedy were in fact presented to Elizabethan schoolboys as the model for all types of drama.) Thus the underlying design of *King Lear*, despite its echoes of Oedipus, suggests a classical comedy turned black: instead of the happy love-poems of two young gentlemen, the appalling outcome of the family problems of two elderly gentlemen. *Romeo and Juliet* and *Othello* can be seen as tragedies generated by letting loose in the familiar world of classical comedy (a young man, say, in love with a girl with a ferociously hostile father . . .) persistent bad luck and obsessive malignity. Even in *Hamlet*, Polonius – the mildly ridiculous old father – echoes the ancient comedies.

Shakespeare has in the past often been called a philosopher. Much depends on what is meant by this. He is not a preacher, and has few outright 'messages', though of course his psychological insights have ethical implications. But his plays do often serve to raise the general level of our moral awareness, not least because of the open-ended reflectiveness with which part of his mind seems to explore the concepts his plays are built around. Thus *Hamlet* quietly notes the paradoxes and complications of the revenge-ethic. Comedy is generally concerned with Love, and hence Fidelity: so *As You Like It* ends like a demonstration, with four couples on stage, all in love in different senses; while *Twelfth Night* amounts to a light-hearted parade of varieties of fidelity. The later Histories quietly chart the pros and cons of heroic chivalry.

Apart from occasional passages of prose, Shakespeare's plays are almost entirely written in 'blank verse': unrhymed iambic pentameter. As time went on, he tended progressively to loosen the form, increasing the number of broken or imperfect lines. Scholars have found this useful when seeking to determine the chronology of his plays.

9 *Baroque Triumphant and French Classicism (1618–1715)*

R. HORVILLE

Since we live in a world so strange and life is nothing more than a dream.

Calderón

The seventeenth century in Europe was dominated by the aesthetics of the Baroque. These apply for the whole of this period, leaving Classicism within narrow geographical confines and with limited timespan for its development. Located where many influences intersect, the Baroque was made up of several components.

The birth of the Baroque was closely linked to the Catholic reaction to the Protestant Reformation. Set in motion by the Council of Trent (1545–1563), the Counter-Reformation strongly raffirmed the great principles of Catholicism and advocated a movement of ideological reconquest. The Jesuits played a decisive role in this enterprise, especially in their substitution of a vision of salvation in which a human being could exercise their own personal freedom for the Protestant concept of predestination. Aesthetically and architecturally, the Jesuits evolved a style based on sumptuousness and ornateness.

At the same time, libertines celebrated a world marked by diversity, subject to every kind of change, open to curiosity and sensuality. A paradoxical consensus existed between the libertines and the Jesuits, who exalted communion with the beauty of an inexhaustibly rich universe, a living testimony to the perfection of its Creator.

It was to these two currents of thought that the name of Baroque was given, but it was a belated christening. The word certainly existed in the seventeenth century, but at that time it referred to an irregularly shaped pearl. In the eighteenth century, it was used to denote the style of architecture born in Italy at the end of the sixteenth century, marked by formal and decorative exuberance. The extension of the word's meaning to literature is quite recent.

BAROQUE IN THE ASCENDANT

In the seventeenth century, Europe was beset by ideological power struggles and armed conflicts. This permanent state of flux explains one of the underlying principles of the Baroque: the world is constructed through the eyes of man. Nothing is fixed. Movement reigns supreme: in the architectural achievements of the Italian Gian Lorenzo Bernini (1598–1680), in the music of Claudio Monteverdi (1567–1643) and in the warriors' tales of *Astrea* (1607–1627) by the Frenchman Honoré d'Urfé.

An aesthetic of movement and appearances

Attracted to movement, Baroque man was naturally drawn to water, the very image of flow, or to fire with its fleeting forms. These two elements inspired the poets. They were used in a concrete way during court entertainments, in fountains and fireworks. If, on the other hand, Baroque man was sensitive to Nature, it was because the changes that occured in it were tangible signs of the permanent process of change that characterised the world. Like the Frenchman Théophile de Viau, Baroque man praised the charms of the countryside. These constant changes gave him a heightened sense of life's complexity. In order to define what was real, one had to take account of everything that makes up the diversity of reality. In his historical work, the Italian Sarpi tried to take account of both Catholic and Protestant viewpoints. This is how intolerance is avoided: everyone has their own version of the truth, without condemning anybody else's.

In this open-ended world, God does not map out for man the ways he must follow or impose imponderable laws. A human being can fight the external forces he has to confront and have some chance of success. He has the ability to change the world. He comes to believe in Utopia, like the Italian Campanella who imagined the City of the Sun a society based on 'communist' principles.

Nothing is irreversible and the element of chance governing the world offers man continued new opportunities. So the heroes of tragi-comedies are not prey to a fate they cannot control; on the contrary, they can choose their own destiny. In *The Cid* (1636) by Corneille, Rodrigo chooses knowingly between the honour of his family and his love for Ximena. Similarly, in *La Vida es sueño* (*Life is a Dream*, 1634), the Spaniard Calderón makes the point that, after an inexorable struggle, man's will triumphs:

Segismundo	*Sigismund*
[. . .] pues reprimamos esta fiera condición, esta furia, esta ambición, por si alguna vez soñamos; y sí haremos, pues estamos en mundo tan singular, que el vivir sólo es soñar.	*[. . .] Well then, let us repress these fierce instincts, this anger, this ambition, in case we have another dream. That's agreed then, that's what we'll do since we live in a world so strange and life is nothing more than a dream.*

Calderón,
La Vida es sueño

Open to the outside world, Baroque man exercises his curiosity about everything around him. The heroes in the novels of the period resemble him: faced with a multiplicity of happenings, they are interested and active. In the same way, the emotion of love is never powerful enough to limit Baroque man to one exclusive passion: he is often desperately smitten but he rarely dies of love.

Baroque man does not believe in the existence of the absolute here on earth, but thinks that everything is appearance. Even death is merely a moment of transition in the unceasing transformation of matter. This rejection of the absolute explains the development of the decorative. In architecture, the main lines of a building were hidden under the decor, appearances veiled the 'truth' of the edifice. Baroque decorative artists were past masters in the art of deceiving the eye. In literature, the decorative was just as prominent, in particular in English poets who, like Milton, continued the Elizabethan tradition.

In love with life, Baroque man was drawn by the thousand details which lent savour to things. He had a taste for the lyrical and the pathetic which allowed him to express his emotions and his individuality. However, he did not abandon realism, which he often used to describe the ravages of death. He was also drawn to the fantastic, by all that occult knowledge that satisfied his curiosity. In *Il Conto dei conti* (*The Tale of Tales*, 1634–1636), the Italian **Giambattista Basile (1575–1632)** took up the folk tradition of the marvellous, introducing, for example, the character of the 'cat Cinderella'.

Modernity, irregularity, freedom and eclecticism

The Baroque bore the stamp of modernity. Baroque creative artists knew how to adapt their writing to their times and cast off the shackles of tradition. This struggle between two aesthetic tendencies – that of the imitation of the Ancients and a search for new solutions – manifests itself in several countries: in France, the quarrel of the Ancients and Moderns broke out in the 1680s; in England it was known as 'the battle of the books' and in The Netherlands as 'de poëtenstrijd' ('the quarrel of the poets').

Irregularity is another factor in the Baroque sphere of influence. Baroque writers refused to make their writing comply with functional rules. In the first half of the seventeenth century, dramatists in France and Spain wrote plays characterised by extravagance, action that burst the bounds of the unities of time and place. Burlesque writers refused to be confined within a hierarchy of genres, claiming freedom of creation. In their search for artistic renewal and imaginative values, Baroque writers rejected hard and fast academic rules. There were no limits to their freedom. But their refusal to follow the rules did not mean they practised irregularity for irregularity's sake: the French dramatist Mairet had no compunction in writing plays which were both regular and irregular.

Eclecticism was one of the guiding principles of Baroque thought. Baroque writers prefered pluralism to dualism. They did not think that, in a world consisting of a multiplicity of elements, good and evil were radically opposed to one other. This rejection of Manicheism was at the heart of Jesuit philosophy.

Baroque diversity

European Baroque was not homogeneous either geographically or chronologically. Linked to the Counter-Reformation, it began in Italy and developed in countries where the reaction against Protestantism was particularly strong. Its great flowering was in Spain and Central Europe. The Hapsburgs, who jealously guarded Catholic orthodoxy, promoted the dissemination of the Baroque, the speed of which varied according to the area. In Croatia, the seeds of the Counter-Reformation fell on fertile ground thanks to the relaxation of Turkish domination and to the existence of the free city of Dubrovnik in Ottoman territory.

In France, the opposition between Catholics and Protestants always lurking just beneath the surface, the rise of libertinism and the ideological dominance of the Jesuits nurtured Baroque's coming into flower during the first part of the seventeenth century. In England, the Anglican compromise – a stand-off between Catholicism and Protestantism – led to the flowering of a watered-down Baroque.

Protestant Baroque, which was more evident in the United Provinces than anywhere else, was inextricably linked to the still-surviving literary current of the Renaissance. It was characterised by elements of heroism, mystical love and pathos, by ecstasy and exaltation, by an attitude which had its roots in the reformed religion. Among its most famous representatives were Jacobus Revius, who composed the *Over-Ysselsche Sangen en Dichten* (*Songs and Poems of Overijssel*, 1630), and Pastor **Joannes Vollenhove (1631–1708)**, the author of *Kruistriomf* (*The Triumph of the Cross*, 1656). The religious poetry and love poetry of Huygens or Jan Luyken (1649–1712), distinguished by hyperbole and antithesis, developing the themes of vanity, instability and metamorphosis, also belongs to the Baroque.

> There are as many tastes as faces, and as much difference between some as between others.
>
> Baltazar Gracián, *The Courtier*

In Poland this trend had aspects which set it apart. In contrast to courtly baroque, refined and cosmopolitan, local baroque appeared conservative and xenophobic. It was called 'barok sarmacki' (Sarmatian Baroque) because of a medieval tradition according to which the Poles had sprung from the glorious tribe of the ancient Sarmatians, whose customs, lifestyle and political institutions they had retained. Rowdy and quarrelsome Polish nobles, given to heavy drinking, by virtue of this juxtaposition, liked to consider themselves independent of Polish royalty. They were fond of pomp and circumstance, eloquence and keeping up appearances. Through their regular contact with oriental splendour they had inherited a love of luxury and a fascination for shiny fabrics, weapons and jewellery. This was the era of constant warfare against the Muscovites, the Turks and the Swedes. Writing was considered as a particularly indispensable asset in social relationships. Many writers, members of the middle aristocracy, paraded their narrow, provincial views in a language adorned with Latin quotations, the fruit of a picturesque combination of disparate elements.

In Russia a conservative Baroque movement developed: the 'Starovery' (Old Believers) fiercely defended their national traditions. A similar movement, but of a lay nature, sprang up in Scandinavian countries. There was a will to renew ties with the nation's past and with the Middle Ages. This movement, a distant precursor of Romanticism, was particularly important to Rudbeck, the great figurehead of Swedish Gothicism, who claimed a connection with the culture of the ancient kingdom of the Goths.

A MINORITY CLASSICISM

In the seventeenth century the expansion of classicism was limited. This aesthetic movement only affected France in the years 1660–1680 and, marginally, Protestant countries. It was only in the eighteenth century that its influence was acknowledged and impinged on Europe in general.

Like the Baroque, classicism began in Italy. It held sway during the first half of the sixteenth century only to be replaced by the Baroque. In France the opposite occurred: classicism followed the Baroque and became the benchmark of seventeenth-century letters. Indeed, some critics have called the preceding period pre-classical.

The word classical is even more ambiguous than the term Baroque. In the seventeenth century it was not used in its current sense, referred to two different states of affairs. There were two types of classicism: the first was linked to Protestantism and Jansenism, religious concepts marked by austerity; the second was worldly, revealed in the ideal courtier embodied in the 'honnête homme'. Despite this diversity, it remains possible to isolate certain characteristics of classical writing.

An aesthetic of stability and the absolute

Classical writers believed that human beings find themselves thrown into a completed universe, subject to strict laws which cannot be circumvented. Man must accept the permanent, inviolable, fixed world just as it is. He cannot change it and must therefore turn progress into something relative. This thinking was at the heart of Jansenism. It suited the social organisation peculiar to the reign of Louis XIV subject to strict rules making it work. The predictability of human behaviour as classical writers conceived of it was a step in the same direction: character development could only happen within the logical framework governing a character's actions. French dramatists therefore rejected endings to plays that hinged on a change of heart – that introduced radical modification into behaviour.

In this inflexible world, classical man appeared to be tragically divided by his internal contradictions. He is torn between conflicting impulses he cannot reconcile. His chances of transcending these contradictions are limited. The 'honnête homme' boasts of his concern for openness and compromise in vain, since he is powerless to alter his destiny. Fate makes his decisions for him. Despite his attempts to resist, it sets him on an inflexible path to a predetermined destination. Racine's *dramatis personae* cannot choose exultantly because they cannot choose at all.

For classical writers, if appearances are strong, if they have an unavoidable effect on the imperfection of human life, truth will always out. Classical writers hankered after permanence. In taking account of their contemporaries who were their audience, they want to compose works which would valid. To reconcile these two imperatives, classicists submitted their art to precise rules which observed three major principles: the writer had to show respect for a rationality synonymous with common sense, imitate nature and take as his inspiration a truth acceptable to most of his contemporaries. In order to succeed, he needed to adopt a moderate form of expression and to pay attention to the lessons taught by the Ancients.

Imitation, regularity, determinism and unity

Four key ideas serve as guides to the way classical writers go about things. First, they prefer the permanence of ancient models to Baroque modernity. These models must be taken as points of reference at the expense of modern Italian and Spanish authors who, during the first half of the seventeenth century, had themselves constituted the principal sources of inspiration. La Bruyère states it clearly in his *Characters*:

Tout est dit, et l'on vient trop tard depuis plus de sept mille ans qu'il y a des hommes, et qui pensent. Sur ce qui concerne les moeurs, le plus beau et le meilleur est enlevé; l'on ne fait que glaner après les Anciens et les habiles d'entre les Modernes.	*Everything has been said, and we have arrived on the scene seven thousand years after men who thought. As far as standards are concerned, the fairest and the best have been gathered in; all we are doing is picking up after the Ancients and those among the Moderns with skill.*

Jean de La Bruyère,
Les Caractères

Regularity was one of the effects of imitation. Since the Ancients were our examples, we must extract from them the necessary rules to reach the perfection they exemplify. With this in mind, academies developed in France whose role was to make scrupulously sure that different types of creativity adhered to those rules. For literature the Académie Française, founded in 1635, exercised that function. In England, the Royal Society, formed in 1660, also tried to purify language and literature, but without much success. In The Netherlands, in 1669, Spinoza's follower, Lodewijk Meyer (1629–1681), entrusted the task of giving new momentum to Dutch literature to the nine members of the Nihil Volentibus Arduum Society ('Nothing is difficult to those who want to do it').

Restrictions on freedom emanated from this theory of imitation and regularity. The creative artist had no right to follow his own imagination. Carefully curtailed, he was forced to adapt himself to the imperatives of literary creativity in the same way that man had to be subservient to a transcendent fate.

This determinism, finally, was included in a perspective that claims to unify. Art, like the world, appeared as composite, as a whole, made up of elements brought together in a coherent and harmonious way.

The limits and contradictions of French classicism

Classicism was at its most representative in France. But even at its height, its triumph was mitigated. Great writers, fortunately, knew how to bend the rules and thus managed not to descend into the stereotyping and academicism which 'experts' demanded. The 'quarrel' of the Ancients and Moderns, which broke out at the end of the seventeenth century, confirmed classicism's fragile nature. Opposing those who cast their vote for the Ancients to those who affirmed the superiority of the Moderns, the quarrel emphasised the contradictions of a period which harked back to a monolithic past and exalted present greatness. Life at court, organised around Louis XIV, illuminated another type of contradiction. The court's taste for keeping up appearances and for outward show, its often self-conscious sophistication, the composite and complex entertainments which were performed there were all diametrically opposed to the classical ideal.

The emergence of Protestant classicism

Can we talk of Protestant classicism? The attempts of the English Royal Society or the Dutch literary circle Nihil Volentibus Arduum were not closely linked to the movement of the Reformation. It seems, however, that Protestant countries were the first to benefit from the dissemination of French classicism. In The Netherlands, in particular, Protestant writers who based their work on a mentality nurtured by Calvinists, Non-Jurors and Anabaptists, used the classical rules formulated by Boileau, but this tendency was most marked in the eighteenth century. Certain works by **Joost Van den Vondel (1587–1679)**,★ like the Biblical epic *Joannes de Boetgezant* (*John the Prophet*, 1662), cannot be considered as Protestant classicism because their author had converted to Catholicism.

THE CONDITIONS SURROUNDING CREATIVITY

The dominant expression of the Baroque was dependent on the social class of both artists and their public. On the one hand works were influenced by the court and literary salons; on the other a scholarly approach to literature was influenced by the Church and the educated middle classes. A third trend sprang from popular tradition, while the opposition between ruler and ruled gave literature a productive theme.

Worldly literature

The brilliant flowering of court and salon life encouraged the blossoming of worldly literature. This led to many works characterised by stylistic experimentation, particularly in the literary movement called Mannerism. During the second half of the seventeenth century, it favoured psychological analysis and the discussion of love so prized in circles full of gentlemen and ladies of leisure. It gave rise to forms designed to please, influenced by a sense of social nicety. There was even an epistolary literature designed to be read in public: in France, work by Madame de Sévigné offered a typical example. The fashion for personal memoirs may be included in the same perspective.

The public to which this literature was addressed consisted mostly of refined aristocrats, together with a few worldly clerics and bourgeois culture vultures. A moral code gradually gained credence in these well-off circles: the code of the *honnête homme*. Mapped out in Italy by Castiglione in *The Courtier*, this lifestyle found a sequel in Portugal in *Corte na aldeia e noites de inverno* (*The Court in a Village and Winter Nights*). Published in 1619, Francisco Rodriguez Lobo (*c.*1580–*c.*1622) expounded in dialogue all that was potentially interesting to the *honnête homme*: pedagogy, poetry, love and the rules governing correct behaviour in society. In France, these preoccupations were taken up and concluded by Nicolas Faret (*c.*1596– *c.*1646) in *The Honnête Homme or How To Please At Court* (1630); then by the Chevalier de Méré (1607–1684) in *Conversations* (1668) and *Discourses* (1671– 1677); and in Spain by **Baltazar Gracián y Morales (1601–1658)** in *El Oráculo manual* (*The Courtier*, 1647).

Conscious that everything is relative, the *honnête homme* is endowed with an infinite capacity for blending in:

He needs to be able to cut a fine figure in every social circle and all circumstances. To achieve this aim, he must avoid too much specialisation, too detailed a display of knowledge. Avoiding pedantry like the plague, he knows something about a certain amount of everything, which allows him to shine unostentatiously. A past master in the art of conversation, he knows how to proscribe excess and adopt a neutral position. This ideal, first confined to the countries of Southern Europe, only belatedly reached Northern Europe, in particular England and The Netherlands.

Erudite literature

Erudite literature slowly became lay literature rather than religious. In many countries in Europe, it continued to be the Church's monopoly. But the place of the bourgeoisie became increasingly important and, especially in France and Italy, preponderant. Often still written in Latin, erudite works gradually come to be written in vernacular languages, and authors revealed an ever-increasing concern for popularisation. In the prolongation of Renaissance humanism, whose influence remained strong in The Netherlands, there was the will to unite knowledge and diversion, theory and practice. In France, dramatists began to preface their plays with preambles in which they justified their dramatic choices. As in the previous century, philology played an important part. The Dutch school of Leyden carried on where the Pleiad in France left off, influencing, in its turn, the German Opitz. In a famous treatise on German poetics, he laid down the rules for writing poetry – rules that he observed himself in his abundant and varied work.

Popular literature

A third influence made itself felt in European literature: popular tradition. It was in the folk song, frequently practised by poets of the time. The Frenchman Malherbe liked this genre, and in The Netherlands, the song collections,

Friesche Lust-Hof (*The Friesian Pleasure Garden*, 1621) by **Jan Jansz. Starter** (**c.1593–1626**), and *Zeeusche Nachtegaal* (*The Zeeland Nightingale*, 1623) by Cats enjoyed great success. In this branch of literature, anonymous popular authorship had an important place. The Czechs developed a twofold tradition. On the one hand, a folk-song tradition of rural inspiration evolved, rich in lyrical and epic themes, buzzing with dramatic happenings at the level of the individual and the family or complaints about fatigue duties and military service. On the other hand, there was a whole urban tradition with an emphasis on satire and gallantry.

The blossoming of the emblem – an important symbolic link between image and motto – was also included in this popular tradition. The combination of painting, engraving and literature was particularly striking in Dutch writing. In the Southern Netherlands, the Jesuit Adriaen Poirters (1605–1674) was its past master. He left behind popular books of religious emblems which were infused with the spirit of the Counter-Reformation. The ingenious intellectual technique involved in unveiling and decoding the emblematic image was used to unmask sin, vice and human frailty. The texts that accompany the pictures were presented in a variety of ways: in verse, in prose, their tone alternated from comic to austere, tearful, triumphal, spicy, meretricious. Adriaen Poirters' first collection, *Ydelheyt des werelts* (*This World's Vanity*), was published in Antwerp in 1645. For the 1646 third edition, he radically reworked the text, publishing it under the new title *Het masker van de wereldt afgetrocken* (*The World Unmasked*). The work took on its definitive form with the 1650 seventh edition and, going through two dozen reprints to the end of the nineteenth century, it remained Adriaen Poirters' most popular work.

The survival of farce and the rise in popularity of the realist novel were other manifestations of the importance of popular tradition. The development in tales which contained elements of the marvellous was equally noticeable: in Italy, Basile published

The Tale of Tales; in France **Charles Perrault (1628–1703)** published *The Tales of Mother Goose* (1697); while Czech literature increased its output of fairy tales. At their heart was the typical Czech peasant Honza (Johnny), a simple, honest village lad, concealing beneath his apparent simplicity much cunning and subtlety.

The growth of commerce and towns promoted a cultural life on the margins of intellectualism all over Europe. In Scandinavia, many flourishing activities were linked to the guilds. Initiation rites included a spectacular public ceremony, distinguished by parades of mythological characters. The customs of the ruling class were parodied and an inverted world came into being inspired by the carnival traditions of the Middle Ages. Meanwhile, a suggestive comic style, full of sexual innuendo, peppered the travelling shows, while in the broadsheets handed out to passers-by, ballads were printed on subjects inspired by love, monsters, bloody murders or other exciting themes. Lars Wivallins (1605–1669), a wandering student, composed most of his songs and poems in prison. The joys of drunkenness and the pathos of death were constant themes in the drinking songs and love poems by Lasse Lucidor (1638–1674), nicknamed the 'Swedish Diogenes'. The tradition of the marvellous, which was later developed by the Romantics, also played an important role. But in the seventeenth century, this popular culture aroused the growing opposition of the ruling powers who thought the use of a non-literary vernacular retrograde.

However, despite this attempt at regimentation, common everywhere in Europe, the existence of a popular reading public was pouched by the development of books for peddling. These were sold in country towns and villages, as was the case for 'blue' books in France, printed in Troyes.

Rulers versus ruled

European literature was crisscrossed by a whole series of interplays between rulers and ruled, majority and minority ideologies. This interplay revealed itself in religious matters, sometimes connected to Protestants, sometimes to Catholics, sometimes to libertines, depending on the country and the event. In Germany, it led to the development of the familiar theme of the confrontation between absolute power and its individual victim.

The political and religious aspects of a situation often combined as they did in Bohemia. After the defeat of the Protestant States at the White Mountain (1620), the victorious Hapsburgs set repressive measures in train. The Jesuits were given the task of spreading the Counter-Reformation and stamping out all traces of Protestantism. This process of normalisation split literature in two. While an officially sanctioned Catholic literature prospered in Bohemia, Protestant writers retreated into exile. Refugees in Poland, Germany, Hungary and Slovakia, they produced an émigré literature consisting essentially of religious and polemical works, consolatory writings, prophecies, laments and history. Among them **Jan Amos Komenský (Comenius, 1592–1670)*** embodied and symbolised the tragic fate of Czech exiles. After the Peace of Westphalia (1648), he lost all hope of returning home and was inexorably absorbed into his countries of refuge. He was also the only one to surmount and transcend his émigré status by virtue of his work. To whip up national feeling in his fellow countrymen, the Albanian Frang Bardhi (1606–1643) composed an apology for Albania's national hero, Skanderberg (1636).

MANNERISM AND BURLESQUE; REALISM AND IDEALISM

The political and ideological complexity that characterised seventeenth-century Europe led to the development of ambivalent aesthetic functions, sometimes opposed to one another, sometimes connected within a particular work. In this way there was friction and cohabitation between Mannerism and burlesque, realism and idealism. This diversity, at first perceived as an indication of the world's richness and variety, progressively gave way to value judgements based on a hierarchical classification of genres ranging from the sublime to the prosaic, from the noble to the bourgeois.

Part of the sphere of Baroque influenc, both Mannerism and the burlesque gave pride of place to form, virtuosity and ludicity. But whereas Mannerism wanted continued mental activity, the burlesque allowed for man's diversity by revealing the contradictions that make us distinct from one another and by showing the influence of man's body over his behaviour.

The scintillations of Mannerism

Mannerism appears as a sophisticated ideal, closely connected to the development of life at court and in literary salons. Developing from an imitation of Petrarch, it gave special place to the theme of ethereal, spiritual love. As in medieval novels of chivalry, woman was idealised. She became the perfect, ideal being, whose beauty testified to her moral perfection. But because she represented an absolute, she was also cruel and inaccessible. Mannerism developed these twin themes of perfection and inaccessibility *ad nauseam*. This alienating situation might seem tragic, but this was not the case. Banter and lightness demystified the pain of unrequited love. Love itself was no more than a game game played by those at court and in salons to relieve their boredom. Amorous conquest involved an entire strategy which, like war, had its own rules. The lover, in his long journey to the beloved, had to follow that symbolic itinerary of the 'Carte du Tendre' ('Chart of Tenderness') contained in *Clélie* (*Clelia*, 1654–1660) by the French writer, **Madeleine de Scudéry (1607–1701)**: to reach the village of New Friendship, he needed to avoid Lake Indifference and the villages of Lukewarmness and Inequality and instead to make his way via the villages of Diligence and Little Attentions. To express all the nuances of feeling, Mannerism made good use of the resources of rhetoric. It adored hyperbole, which included multiplying the instances of fulsome praise lavished on the loved one's perfections. It played on contrasts, notably on antitheses that unexpectedly brought together opposing expressions and idea. It preferred meandering circumlocutions to simple, straightforward meaning. It made ready use of personification that gave life to objects or to ideas. It sought the surprise effect, paradox, amazing endeavours, in particular ending a poem on a high note.

> Yield to that neck, that brow, those lips, that hair.
>
> Luis de Góngora, *Sonnets*

Mannerism flourished particularly in those European countries where court and salon life flourished. Poetry was its mainstay, but it also occasionally emerged in the novel. It had various names. In Spain, there was *gongorismo* or *cultismo*. **Luis de Góngora y Argote (1561–1627)**, a cleric with a maverick, worldly life, was its initiator. In the *Soledades* (*Solitudes*) – the first volume appeared in 1613, the second remained unfinished – a luxuriant, finely wrought poetry appeared, full of sumptuous imagery, unexpected juxtapositions, striking contrasts and often enigmatic ellipses. His *Sonetos* (*Sonnets*) of love, which he composed throughout his life, glittered with a thousand sequins of sophistication and stylistic experimentation:

Mientras por competir con tu cabello,	*While, in order to tarnish the sheen of your hair,*
oro bruñido el Sol relumbra en vano,	*The sun, polished gold, sparkles in vain;*
mientras con menosprecio en medio el llano	*While, slightingly, in the middle of a plain,*
mira tu blanca frente al lilio bello;	*Your white brow stands comparison with the beauty of a lily;*

mientras a cada labio, por
cogello,
siguen más ojos que al clavel
temprano,
y mientras triunfa con desdén
lozano
de el luciente cristal tu gentil
cuello;
goza cuello, cabello, labio y
frente,
antes que lo que fué en tu edad
dorada
oro, lilio, clavel, cristal luciente
no sólo en plata o viola troncada
se vuelva, mas tú y ello
juntamente
en tierra, en humo, en polvo, en
sombra, en nada.

Luis de Góngora,
Sonetos.

While, in order to pick
each of your lips
More eyes go after you
than after the early carnation,
And while your delightful neck
triumphs
with cool disdain
over gleaming crystal,
Yield to that neck, that brow, those
lips, that hair,
Before what was in your age
of radiance
Pure gold, and a lily, a carnation, gleaming
crystal,
Not only become
silver or withered
Violet, but you yourself become part of
Earth, smoke, dust, shadow,
nothingness.

In Italy **Giambattista Marino (1569–1625)** practised a style characterised by complexity, outrageousness and fantasy. An exile in France, where he was known under the *nom de plume* of Cavalier Marin, he had a great deal of influence on poets before returning to Naples in 1623 where he became the Duke of Alba's favourite. He wrote a long mythological poem, *Adone* (*Adonis*), in which he mixed many invented episodes with the tale of the love of Venus for Adonis. In *Lira* (*The Lyre*, 1602–1614), he excelled in embellishing the trivial, as in the following eulogy on a beauty spot:

Quel neo, quel vago neo,
Che fa d'amate fila ombra
vezzosa
A la guancia amorosa,
Un boschetto è d'Amore.
Ah! Fuggi, incauto core,
Se pure cogliervi brami o giglio
o rosa!
Ivi il crudel si cela, ivi sol tende
Le reti e l'arco, e l'alme impiaga
e prende.

Giambattista Marino,
Lira

This spot, this charming beauty
spot
Which, with its well-loved hairs, throws
a pretty shadow
Onto an amorous cheek,
Is a little wood of Love.
Flee, imprudent heart,
If you are burning to gather there
lilies or roses!
For it is there that the cruel one is hiding,
It is there he spreads his nets and draws back
His bow, wounding and capturing souls.

With Spain and Italy as its power bases, Mannerism launched itself during the first half of the seventeenth century, to conquer a Europe where it met a mixed reception. In France, *précieux* or 'precious' poetry and novels were influenced by it. This writing survived during the classical period, despite being a target for vociferous attacks, notably those of Molière and Boileau who advocated naturalness and restraint. Radiating from the salon of Madeleine de Scudéry, French preciosity had as its undisputed leader **Vincent**

253

Voiture (1597–1648). This bourgeois, the 'âme du rond' (soul in the round) of Mme de Rambouillet (1588–1665), the driving force behind her aristocratic circle, left to posterity a poetic legacy full of banter and brilliance, bearing the stamp of a real talent for writing.

In Germany, **Martin Opitz (1597–1639)** expressed ideas about writing which were close to those of Mannerism. In the *Buch von der deutschen Poeterei* (*Treatise on German Poetry*, 1624), he portrayed poetry as a social diversion. A frequenter of court life, he wanted to find a brilliant way to express himself which was both finely wrought and flexible, in which the form of the work was its essential ingredient. This aesthetic bias shines out in his many lively sonnets.

Mannerism had a strong influence on Portuguese poetry. Góngora's influence permeated two anthologies of poems published belatedly: *Fenix Renascida* (*Phoenix Reborn*) and *Postilhão de Apolo* (*Apollo's Messenger*). Both contain mythological allusions, exquisite metaphors, violent contrasts, scholarly diction: all reminiscent of Góngora's style.

Mannerism appeared in England in the 'metaphysical' poets and in Holland in Dutch love poetry and the work of Pieter Cornelisz Hooft (1581–1647). In Poland it had an admirable pupil in **Jan Andrzej Morsztyn (c.1613–1693)**. This courtier and diplomat, keen on everything Western, the favourite of Queen Maria Luisa de Gonzaga and the translator of Corneille's *Le Cid*, was the author of two collections of poems: *Kanikuła albo psia gwiazda* (*Dogdays*, 1647) and *Lutnia* (*The Lute*, 1661). Full of current literary fashions, he orchestrated a whole interplay of linguistic transformations:

Niestałość

Oczy są ogień, czoło jest
zwierciadłem,
Włos zlotem, perla ząb, płeć
mlekiem zsiadłem,
Usta koralem, purpurą jagody,
Póki mi, panno, dotrzymujesz
zgody.
Jak się zwadzimy, jagody są
trądem,
Usta czeluścią, płeć blejwasem
bladym,
Ząb szkapią kością, włosy
pajęczyną,
Czoło maglownią, a oczy
perzyną.

Jan Andrzej Morsztyn,
Kanikula albo psia gwiazda

Inconstancy

Your eyes are a blazing fire,
your brow is a noble mirror,
Your hair is golden, your teeth
pearls, your complexion milk of ivory.
Your mouth is of coral and your
cheeks are of the deepest vermilion
As long as you are getting on with me,
beautiful lady, like a house on fire.
But, when we quarrel with
each other, your cheeks become leprous,
Your mouth cavernous, your complexion
deathly pale,
Your teeth mare's bones,
your hair a spider's web,
Your brow a washing board and
your eyes burning embers.

In the free enclave of Dubrovnik, on Ottoman territory, a Mannerist circle developed. Its chief members were Ivan Gundulič (1589–1638), the author of *Suze sina pazmetnoga* (*The Tears of the Prodigal Son*, 1622) in which vanity was contrasted with piety, and **Ivan Bunic Vucic (1592–1658)**, who published the religious epic *Mandaliena Pokornica* (*Mary Magdalen Repentant*).

Burlesque games of contrasts

Burlesque writers were sensitive to the contradictions of their varied, troubled world. To express these contrasts, they established a series of procedures to make use of antonymous juxtapositions. For example, they used a humorous style to go with a supposedly sublime topic. This subversive desire to call styles into question was clearly seen in the many parodies of ancient epics. **Paul Scarron (1610–1660)** excelled in them. In *Virgil Travestied* (1648–1652), he parodied the *Aeneid* by transforming the heroes of this masterpiece into middle-class grotesques whose only concern is material things. This work was widely imitated, among others by the Dutchman **Willem Godschalk Van Focquenbroch (1640–1675)**, the author of *De Aenas in syn Sondaeghs-pack* (*Aeneas in his Sunday best*, 1678).

Demystification can also develop from mock heroic writing, which treats prosaic subjects with an elevated style. Influenced by Cervantes' *Don Quixote*, the Italian **Alessandro Tassoni (1565–1635)** published *La Secchia rapita* (*The Stolen Bucket*, 1622). On the basis of the rivalry between Bologna and Modena, he embroidered a whole poem about robbers from Modena who stole a Bolognese bucket. This is a pretext for recounting fantastic exploits, some taken from epic tradition, others borrowed from historical facts, brought together as it pleases their narrator with no respect for chronology while chivalrous characters rub shoulders with realistic picturesque ones.

Burlesque was not merely about the opposition of form and content. At a deeper level, it revealed the frequent gulf between what a character would like to appear to be and what they really are. This contrast lies at the heart of the depiction of lightweight, colourful characters in European comedy. These were built on Italian models of the scholarly commedia erudita and the popular commedia dell'arte. Thus we have the Matamoros, courageous when he speaks, cowardly when he puts words into deeds; the Pedant, whose erudition cannot hide his stupidity; and the Poet, who sponges off people for all his spiritual pretensions. The revelation of these contradictions was a redoubtable tool in the hands of the satirists. While La Bruyère revealed the dangers of appearances and bogus values in *Les Caractères* (1688), Dutch political weekly periodicals of the eighteenth century often need this style to denounce abuses and injustices. Utopian writings, such as *La Città del Sole* (*The City of the Sun*, 1623) by the Italian **Tommaso Campanella (1568–1639)**, *The Man in the Moon* (1638) by the Englishman **Francis Godwin (1562–1633)**, or *Les États et Empires de la Lune* (*The States and Empires of the Moon*, 1657) and *Les États et Empires du Soleil* (*The States and Empires of the Sun*, 1662) by the Frenchman **Savinien de Cyrano de Bergerac (1619–1655)**, made subtle use of discrepancies: they confronted the reality of European life with the manners and customs of imaginary countries.

In order to reveal man's divisive oppositions, burlesque writers vigorously emphasise real life. The Mannerists were idealists, the Burlesques were realists. They attached great importance to the material and the human body. They were incapable of self-censorship. Their descriptions included the most prosaic details, real life at its most crude. In The Netherlands many poets practised this kind of writing. Van Focquenbroch left several collections of poems distinguished by realism, cynicism and black humour: *Thalia of de geurige zanggodin* (*Thalia or the Comic Muse*, 1665, 1669) and *Afrikaense Thalia* (*African Thalia*, 1678). **Gerbrand Adriaensz Bredero (1585–1618)** wrote *Boertigh, amoureus en groot lied-boeck* (*Collection of Humorous, Amorous and Devotional Ditties*, 1622) a whole series of compositions remarkable for their direct and verbal inventiveness:

Aanspraak van een getrouwde vrouw, an een gevrijde Vrijster	*Address to a married woman and to a young woman whom one is courting*
Neen Trijntje, doet't niet,	*No Catherine, don't do it,*
Wilt op het goed niet kijken,	*Beware of all its benefits.*
Ik ra je dat je ziet	*I would advise you to wait for*
Na een uw tijds gelijken,	*someone of your own age,*

Wagt neem je een oude rijke
en afgeleefde man,
Diens krachten vast bezwijken,
Gij bent er kwalijk an.

Gerbrand Adriaensz Bredero,
Boertigh, amoureus en aendachtigh groot
lied-boeck

for if you take a rich
old lover, a decrepit old man
whose strength will soon
give out,
then you'll be sorry.

In this same realistic vein, but much more spontaneously, much closer to ordinary speech, the Pole **Jan Chryzostom Pasek (1636–1701)** composed *Pamiętniki (Memoirs)*. Racy and peppered with colourful anecdotes, this described how the burlesque had travelled widely in Europe. Published in 1836, it told the story of Polish history from 1656 to 1688. Pasek was the initiator of a particular literary genre: the 'gawęda' (historical conversation) is the basis of the nineteenth-century Polish historical novel. A series of mock heroic adventures gives us an admirable portrait of Pasek and his life and time. Minor details, insignificant to the historian, suddenly come to life and speak to us amusingly, as in the following tale of the how the Kolding fortress was taken:

Skorośmy tedy do fosy przyszli,
okrutnie poczęły parzyć owe snopy
słomy. Już się czeladzi trzymać
uprzykrzyło I poczęli je ciskać w
fosę; jaki taki, obaczywszy u
pierwszych, także czynił i
wyrównali ową fosę tak, że już
daleko lepiej było przeprawiać się
tym, co naostatku szli, niżeli
nam, coúmy szli w przodzie z
pułku królewskiego; bo źle było z
owemi snopami drapać się do
góry po śniegu na wał; kto
jednak swój wyniósł, pomagał, i
znajdowano w nich kulę, co i do
połowy nie przewierciała.
Wychodząc tedy z fosy, kasałem
ja swoim wołać: 'Jezus
Marya!', lubo insi wołali:
'hu, hu, hu!', bom się
spodziewał, że mi więcej pomoże
Jezus, niżeli ten jakiś pan Hu.

Jan Chryzostom Pasek,
Pamiętniki

When we got to the ditches, the bales
of straw that our men were carrying
grew to be such a burden to them
because of the heat they were
causing, that they threw them away,
each of them following the example
of someone else. And they ended up
by filling in the ditch, so well that those who
followed our royal regiment crossed it with
a lot less trouble than
we had. It wasn't easy
to climb up the slope with that
straw, walking through the snow; but
it was a good thing for those who
kept their bale, for they found in it
bullets which had not even
penetrated to the middle. On
emerging from the ditch, I ordered
my men to shout: 'Jesus
and Mary!' This while the besieged
were shouting on their side: 'Hu!
Hu! Hu!' For I counted on
Jesus helping us more
than their Hu.

During the Middle Ages two types of narrative writing had developed. The realistic tale described licentious amorous intrigues, often in crude terms. Novels of chivalry idealistically narrated the adventure of a hero who accomplished the greatest exploits to win a fair maid. These two genres persisted, but were gradually replaced by others whose exposure to Baroque influence underlined their realism or idealism.

The way of the picaresque and the burlesque

The European realist novel of the seventeenth century absorbed the influence of both the picaresque and the burlesque. It often involved the tale of a long journey in time and social class by someone on the margins of society: a picaro. But this picaro was no longer merely an adventurer of doubtful integrity. He could also be a student, an actor, even a pilgrim. Wanderings allowed the main character to look askance at the social functioning of his time and to show, with a burlesque approach, its contradictions and absurdity.

In Spain, after the great works of the preceding century, the picaresque novel had some interesting sequels. *La Vida del Buscón* (*The Rogue's Life*, 1626) by **Francisco Gomez de Quevedo y Villegas (1580–1645)** tells in a vigorous, lively style the story of Don Pablo, a student, then a bandit, then an actor, fleeing from justice and experiencing the baseness of the human soul. In *El Diablo cojuelo* (*The Devil with a Limp*, 1641) by **Luis Vélez de Guevara (1579–1644)**, a demon gives student the ability to raise the roofs of houses and observe the moral baseness and madness of his contemporaries.

In France the combined influence of the Spanish picaresque novel and the work of Cervantes produced the comic novel which survived throughout the seventeenth century. By means of quaint, amusing adventures society was described, in particular its under-privileged and marginal. This technique emphasised the importance of everyday life, throwing harsh light on mundane existence. In the *Histoire comique de Francion* (1623), **Charles Sorel (1602–1674)** describes young Francion's in the squalid waters of both town and countryside. *The Comic Novel* (1651–1657) by Scarron recounts the adventures of the persecuted lovers Destiny and the Star, who under borrowed names join a theatre troupe as actors and share in the troupe's peripatetic life.

The picaresque and the burlesque are also in the German novel: for example, in *Der Abenteuerliche Simplicissimus* (*The Adventures of Simplicius Simplicissimus*, 1669) by **Hans Jakob Christoffel von Grimmelshausen (c.1621–1676)**. In a series of episodes during the Thirty Years' War, the author tells the story of the eventful life of this precursor of Voltaire's Candide. A foundling, he grows up in a peasant's home. After soldiers murder his adoptive father, he takes refuge with a hermit. Page and jester to a Swedish governor, he goes on to discover the world, leads a wild life and grows rich. Tempted to become a brigand, he finally comes to his senses, realises the fickleness of earthly things, walks the path of virtue and non-violence and retires to a desert island. Through its description of the world's imperfections, the work invites the reader to climb the ladder of redemption. This allows the innocent who has been led astray by sin through his contact with society, to rediscover purity thanks to punishment and penitence. Thus we find a radical separation between the spiritual – a source of truth and clarity – and the material – the realm of appearance and the indecipherable.

Da sagte ich zu mir selber: Dein Leben ist kein Leben gewesen, sondern ein Tod, deine Tage ein schwerer Schatten, deine Jahre ein schwerer Traum, deine Wollüste schwere Sünden, deine Jugend eine Phantasei und deine Wohlfahrt ein Alchimistenschatz, der zum Schornstein hinausfähret und dich verläßt, ehe du dich dessen versiehest. Du bist durch

Then I said to myself: 'Your life hasn't been a life, but a kind of death; your days have been spent in a thick shadow, your years have been nothing but a bad dream, your pleasures grave sins, your youth a chimera, and your prosperity the treasure of an alchemist which goes up in smoke when you least

viel Gefährlichkeiten dem Krieg nachgezogen und hast in demselbigen viel Glück und Unglück eingenommen, bist bald hoch, bald nieder, bald groß, bald klein, bald reich, bald arm, bald fröhlich, bald betrübt, bald beliebt, bald verhaßt, bald geehrt und bald verachtet gewesen. Aber nun, du o meine arme Seele, was hast du von diesen ganzen Reise zuwegen gebracht? [. . .]

Hans Jakob Christoffel
von Grimmelshausen,
Der Abenteuerliche Simplicissimus

expect it. You have survived the dangers of war in which you were both very fortunate and unfortunate, now exalted, now abased, rich and poor, happy and sad, loved and hated, respected and despised. But now, my poor soul, what have you gathered from your journeying?
[. . .]

In The Netherlands the picaresque genre appeared only belatedly. It produced, notably, *Den vermakelyken avanturier* (*The Dutch Adventurer*, 1695), written by **Nicolaas Heinsius (1656?–1718)** in a satirical style with burlesque elements. The story, set in Russia, denounces Muscovite society and institutions – even the Orthodox Church – in a series of satirical anecdotes. In England, the picaresque and realist veins were closely intermingled with spiritual preoccupations in *The Pilgrim's Progress* (1666–1678) by **John Bunyan (1628–1688)**. He describes the parallel journeys of Christian and his wife Christiana who during their pilgrimage from the Town of Perdition to the Heavenly City encounter all humanity, whose behaviour and vices are described in a lively, precise way. Based on realist writing, this novel unfolds as an allegory: the topography of the journey takes on a symbolic aspect as the pilgrims travel through the Valley of the Shadow of Death and Vanity Fair.

In the Italian novel, a realistic study of manners and character supplants a picaresque taste for adventure and the burlesque search for contrasts. **Girolamo Brusoni (1614?–1687?)** brilliantly described the life of people in high places and their peccadilloes, notably in *La Gondola a tre remi* (*The Three-Oared Gondola*, 1657) and *Il Carrozzino alla moda* (*The Fashionable Carriage*, 1658).

The novel of ideals: flowering and withering

In the seventeenth century the novel found it hard to assert and define itself. It did not exist at all in Scandinavia, nor in Eastern or South-East Europe. Where it did develop, it was subject to disease. As a reaction to it, the realist novel developed. Opponents complained that the novel of ideals was artificial: it relied on literary conventions, turned its back on reality and was flawed by improbabilities. As a defence against this criticism it used parody as a weapon, but its status remained high in certain countries.

Five broad characteristics, either separately or together, characterised the novel of ideals: a pastoral setting, ethereal love, a symbolic aspect to meanings, adventures and a historical dimension.

The pastoral novel was important during the first half of the seventeenth century. Set in the country, it never tried to describe it realistically. Shepherds and shepherdesses talk like courtiers, developing an idealised concept of love. This romantic genre was based on a system of unequal and frustrated love: a productive one for all seventeenth-century literature. A character loves another, but is not loved in return; the latter loves a third who does not return the love either but who is in love with the first character –

unrequitedly. These incompatibilities, at first sight tragic, are eventually resolved and end in happy loving relationships.

Practised by the Italians and the Spanish during the second half of the sixteenth century, the pastoral novel in France produced a masterpiece: *Astrea* (1607–1627) by **Honoré d'Urfé (1568–1625)** which influenced several European countries. This huge five-volume novel describes the mutual love of the shepherdess Astrea and the shepherd Céladon. Their families hate each other and oppose the union. To confuse the issue, Céladon pretends to love Aminthe. Sémire, in love with Astrea, exploits the situation by making the young shepherdess believe that Céladon really is being unfaithful to her. Confronted by Astrea's indignation, Céladon throws himself into the river Lignon. Rescued by three nymphs and after many exploits, he finds happiness with the woman he loves. The main plot is enhanced by several sub-plots that often introduce an atmosphere of adventure. One book is devoted to Chryséide's love for Arimant. Chryséide tells the shepherd Hylas how King Gondebaut seized the town where she had taken refuge with Arimant, all of which allows Honoré d'Urfé to evoke the typical misfortunes of war.

This pastoral pattern encouraged a prolific output in Europe. Authors often gave pride of place to sentimental plotlines and adventures in which romantic episodes interweaved with warlike exploits. The English **John Barclay (1582–1621)** wrote *Argenis* (1621), a gallant, heroic *roman à clef*. Opitz, having translated it, published *Schäferei von der Nimfen Hercynia* (*Pastoral of the Nymph Hercynia*, 1630). Here in writing very familiar to short-storytelling, he exploits all the formal potential of the genre.

Sometimes the pastoral supported morality and didacticism. In Germany, where the genre was most successful, many anonymous pastoral novels were published, using love interest for educational purposes. Love is always eventually tamed by reason after a journey at the end of which man relinquishes his freedom and assumes responsibility for his

actions. In The Netherlands, *Arcadias* develop. One of them, *Inleijdinghe tot het ontwerp van een Batavische Arcadia* (*Preface to a Blueprint for a Batavian Arcadia*, 1637), by Johan Van Heemskerck (1597–1656), was particularly remarkable: erudite historical and geographical descriptions succeed one another at every turn, slotted into the tale of a long journey.

The novel of ideals was clearly steeped in symbolic significance. Astrea and Céladon appear as symbols of the faithfulness and self-sacrifice of love. With *Labyrint světa a ráj srdce* (*The Labyrinth of the World and the Paradise of the Heart*, 1631), which described the wanderings of a pilgrim in search of his vocation, Comenius expressed a vision of a torn, confused humanity looking for elusive certainties.

The importance that the novel of ideals gave to adventure owed a great deal to medieval novels of chivalry and to Spanish literature of the preceding period. This romantic atmosphere, full of menace and danger, influenced the heroic genre which gradually took over from the pastoral, borrowing its interest in love and war and introducing an historical dimension. But whereas the French pastoral was set in Celtic times, the heroic novel's preferred backdrop was Antiquity. Against this it paraded its fictitious or real characters who were totally transformed by the creative imagination. The heroic novel dominated France throughout the seventeenth century: *Le Grand Cyrus* (*The Great Cyrus*, 1649–1653), by Madeleine de Scudéry, was set in fifth century BC Persia, while the action of *Clelia* happens during the revolt in 509 BC which ousted Tarquin, King of Rome. The French heroic novel spread across the Channel. Inspired by the works of Madeleine de Scudéry, which were frequently translated, many writers tried their hand at this genre. The Irishman **Roger Boyle (1621–1679)** published *Parthenissa* (1654–1655), distinguished, like its French models, by the stilted nature of its sentiments. In England **Aphra Behn (1640–1689)**, with *Oroonoko* (1688), elaborated a more original work from the premise of unrequited love. The African prince Oroonoko loves Imoinda, with whom the king, the young man's grandfather, is also in love. In order to rid himself of a rival (his grandson), he sells him to English slave-traders. Deported to Surinam, the captive leads a rebellion and, in spite of Governor Byam's promises of pardon, is cruelly punished after the revolt fails. With her consent, he then decides to kill Imoinda and the governor – and then to commit suicide. He kills the woman he loves, but he is captured and executed before he can carry out the rest of his plan. In Italy **Ambrosio Marini (c.1594–c.1650)** used the heroic layout to build a work of complex structures, *Colloandro fedele* (*Loyal Colloandro*, 1640), an interplay of writing cleverly put together and constantly interrupted by exciting events. In its 1635 version, he gave this work a didactic flavour. In Germany, the heroic novel also met with considerable success: Grimmelshausen tried his hand at it with *Keuscher Joseph* (*Joseph the Chaste*, 1666) and *Proximus und Lympida* (*Proximus and Lympida*, 1672).

For **Madame de La Fayette (1634–1693)**, the action takes place in Renaissance France. *La Princesse de Clèves* (1678), set during the end of Henry II's reign, describes the Princess of Cleves' repressed passion for the Duke of Nemours. It placed special emphasis on the historical dimension – only to evoke, in fact, the actual period of the work's publication – and on psychological analysis, but the work was only accepted belatedly in the rest of Europe. Little by little, the novel began to bridge the temporal gap that separated it from its author's actual life.

The introduction of history revealed a desire by writers to retain the support of actual facts. To some extent this compromises the independence of the novel and indicated a crisis. The fictitious letters of the exile **Giovanni Paolo Marana (1642–1692)**, living in Paris from 1683, which he published both in Italian (*L'Esploratore turco*) and in French (*L'Espion du Grand Seigneur, The Great Lord's Spy*, 684, 1686), simultaneously drew attention to this phenomenon. It was also revealed in *Letters of a Portuguese Nun* (1669) by Gabriel Joseph de Lavergne, comte de Guilleragues (1628–1685): published at the time as letters actually translated from the Portuguese, until comparatively recently they were taken at face value as a genuine testimony, a heartfelt cry of suffering from a nun seduced and abandoned by a French officer.

THE BLOSSOMING OF IDEOLOGICAL LITERATURE

During the prolongation of Renaissance humanism throughout the seventeenth century, the literature of ideas experienced considerable expansion. The most popular and important literary genre, it constituted a complex, diverse mix that could be divided into three major categories: the literature of psychological analysis, historiography, and scientific and religious literature. These various perspectives were often combined within a single work.

The literature of psychological analysis

Understanding man – making sense of what motivates him – was one of the main concerns of seventeenth-century thinkers. In some countries this type of psychological analysis, which often has to do with moral aims, becomes 'worldly', gradually abandoning scholarly forms to encompass more attractive moulds.

Moral treatises continued to flourish throughout the seventeenth century. Human passion was a constant subject of reflection among contemporary thinkers who described it in detail, gleaming various lessons from its analysis. In France, Descartes, in *The Passions of the Soul* (1649), described the interdependence of body and mind. Father Senault (1601–1672), in *On the Use of Passions* (1641), wrote an educational work by contrasting the positive and negative ways in which man can respond to his impulses. The Dutchman

Jacob Cats (1577–1660) devoted two of his works, *Houwelick, dat is het gantsche Beleyt des echten staets* (*Marriage consists of the Precepts of the State of Marriage*, 1625) and *'s Werelts Begin, midden, eynde, besloten in den Trou-ringh* (*The Beginning, the Middle and End of the World in a Wedding Ring*, 1637), to giving matrimonial advice. Moved by a spirit of moderate Calvinism, he discussed the choice of the ideal partner and the behaviour to be adopted before and after marriage. From a Catholic viewpoint, the Portuguese writer **Francisco Manuel de Melo (1608–1666)** published *Carta de guia de casados* (*Guide for Married People*) in 1651, a practical manual in which he expounded most diverse considerations. In Italy, **Paolo Sarpi (1552–1623)**, in *I pensieri medico-morali* (*Medical and Moral Thoughts*, compiled between 1578 and 1597), revealed the psychosomatic character of human passions. In a wholly modern way he concluded that mental illnesses did not differ in nature from bodily afflictions. In England, **Thomas Hobbes (1588–1679)**, in *Leviathan* (1651), showed how man's behaviour derived from the fact that he is matter, that he possesses a body: 'Homo homini lupus' ('man is a wolf to man'), because the demands of his body, in the grip of desire and fear, lead him to defend his integrity against his fellow men. Hobbes concluded that, for society to run smoothly, man must give up his freedom and submit himself to a State with absolute power:

> To this war of every man against every man, this also is consequent: that nothing can be unjust. The notions of right and wrong, justice and injustice, have there no place. Where there is no common power, there is no law; where no law, no injustice. Force and fraud are in war the two cardinal virtues. Justice and injustice are none of the faculties neither of the body nor mind. (. . .) They are qualities that relate to men in society, not in solitude. It is consequent also to the same condition, that there be no propriety, no dominion, no mine and thine distinct; but

> only that to be every man's, that he can get; and for so long as he can keep it.
>
> Thomas Hobbes, *Leviathan*

'Worldly' writers became involved with the psychological and moral analysis which developed to an exceptional extent: an experimentation in form and an inventiveness which was already present in sixteenth-century Italian literature and which only seeped slowly into Europe.

Taking as his inspiration *The Courtier* by Gracián, **François de la Rochefoucauld (1613–1680)**, in his *Maxims* (1664), perfected this concise form on which he placed the seal of paradox. He shows how human behaviour is subordinate to self-esteem. This is a kind of vital instinct which helps the individual ensure his survival and maintain his identity in the face of his environment and, in particular, in society, by reducing everything to himself, by always making his self-interest uppermost. This eminently social behaviour ends up by distorting virtue. Every virtue is self-interested and aims to make whoever practises it stand out in some way or hide his true feelings. Given this premise, virtue and vice are no longer radically opposed to each other: virtue is often vice in disguise. Thus transfers are made in a system in which dissimulation plays a major part. Man is imposed on by appearances, reality's masks and chance, the great orderer of circumstances.

Madame de Sévigné (1626–1696), in her *Letters* (1640–1696), showed the complexity of human existence. She mixed concrete and abstract, comic and tragic, objective statement and lyricism. Portraits, descriptions of landscapes, anecdotes and dialogues all have their place in a veritable panorama of literary forms, the variety of which echoes the diversity of human kind. She adds to all this the spontaneity of an often impressionistic writing which, in standing back and laughing at itself, is often borderline parody: as in this announcement of an astounding event in French high society, the marriage of the Duke of Lauzun to the Grande Mademoiselle:

Je m'en vais vous mander la chose la plus étonnante, la plus surprenante, la plus merveilleuse, la plus miraculeuse, la plus triomphante, la plus étourdissante, la plus inouïe, la plus singulière, la plus extraordinaire, la plus incroyable, la plus imprévue, la plus grande, la plus petite, la plus rare, la plus commune, la plus éclatante, la plus secrète jusqu'aujourd'hui, la plus brillante, la plus digne d'envie.

Madame de Sévigné,
Lettres

I am going to tell you the most astonishing piece of news, the most surprising, the most marvellous, the most miraculous, the most triumphant, the most bewildering, the most unheard of, the most singular, the most extraordinary, the most incredible, the most unexpected, the greatest, the smallest, the rarest, the most common, the most shocking, the most secret until today, the most brilliant, the most likely to occasion envy.

Jean de La Bruyère (1645–1696) perfected the intimate portrait genre. In *Characters* (1688), inspired by the work of the ancient Greek author, Theophrastus, this seventeenth-century French writer devoted himself to violent social satire. He showed how individuals are trapped in manias which alienate them from society, whether they be victims of absent-mindedness like Ménalque, of gluttony like Cliton, or of hypochondria like Irène. He denounced the abuse of power, the power of money, the wretchedness of the peasant and the horrors of war, thus opening the way for Enlightenment philosophers.

From anecdotal to reasoned history

Throughout the seventeenth century various concepts of history existed simultaneously. A divide appeared between a subjective, event-orientated approach and one that allowed more space for analysis.

The chronicle tradition continued: it consisted rattling off facts and neglecting their explanations. While in France Madame de La Fayette recounted the *History of Henriette d'Angleterre* (only published in 1720), in which she introduced an element of fantasy, works in England sometimes covered the whole of the country's history, like Milton's *History of Britain* (1670) or sometimes dealt with the reign of a certain king, like *The Life and Raigne of King Edward the Sixth* (1620) by **John Hayward (1564?–1627)**. In Moldavia, **Miron Costin (1633–1691)** gave pride of place to event-orientated history in a Polish work,

Kronika Moldawii (*The Chronicle of Moldavia*, 1677), which described civil strife and warring episodes. In Crete, which still had Venice as its overlord, a singular style was evident in *Thrínos is tin eaftoú Kritomítora pátrin tis apasis nisou katastrophis éneken* (*A Lamentation for his Motherland, Crete, on the Catastrophe that has befallen the Whole Island*, 1645–1660) by **Athanassios Skliros (1580?–1664)**. This included much information on the first stage of the conflict between Venice and the Ottoman Empire.

In the oppressed countries of Central and Eastern Europe, historiography became a claim and a defence of national identity. In this light **Bohuslav Balbín (1621–1688)** published, in Latin, an abridged history of Bohemia, *Epitome historica rerum bohemicarum* (*A Digest of the History of Bohemia*, 1677). He then began work on a twenty-volume project about to the Kingdom of Bohemia, *Miscellanea historica regni Bohemiæ* (*A Historical Medley of the Kingdom of Bohemia*), but he only completed half of it (1679–1693). Comenius contributed to the collective work of the Bohemian Brethren: his denunciation of Hapsburg intolerance, first published in Latin, *Historia persecutionum ecclesiæ bohemicæ* (1647–1648), was translated into Czech (*Historia o těžkých protivenstvích církve české, A History of the Persecutions suffered by the Church in Bohemia*, 1655) and its many new editions and translations proved its importance and popularity. The historical and geographical works of the Bulgarian **Petăr Bogdan Bakšič (1601–1674)** shared a comparable perspective;

Archbishop of Sofia he was a convinced freedom fighter for Bulgaria's political liberation, with the support of the Catholic countries of Europe. The Dominican Juraj Križanić (1618–1683) posed the problem of the recognition of the Croats: in *Politika ili razgovor o vladatlystum* (*Politics or a Conversation on Government*), written between 1661 and 1676 during his exile in Siberia, he advocated the solution of pan-Slavism; while Pavav Ritter Vitezović (1652–1713) declared himself in favour of pan-Croatianism. This use of history took on an original aspect with the Swede **Olof Rudbeck (1630–1702)**. In *Atlnd eller Manheim* (*Atlantis*, 1679), a major work which enjoyed considerable success, this professor of medicine created a curious hotchpotch of history and mythology; in vigorous prose he described the ancient kingdom of the Goths which he takes to be Atlantis, from which Sweden inherited its civilisation and spread throughout Europe.

Works in the form of travellers' tales or memoirs were often very subjective. The Slovak **Ján Simonides (1648–1708)** described the persecutions he had suffered for staying faithful to Lutheranism in *Incarceratio,*

liberatio et peregrinatio (*Incarceration, Liberation, Peregrination*, 1676): condemned to exile and the galleys, placed in solitary confinement after an attempted escape, he was ransomed by a German merchant, travelling through Europe before returning to his own country. An excellent observer and narrator, he described his travels, commenting on the social situations in which people find themselves, mentioning particular buildings and lingering over real-life happenings.

In Russia, this autobiographical approach was demonstrated by **Avvakum Petrovič (c.1620–1682)**. A sincere believer in the reform of liturgical customs and usages, he rejected foreign models. His unwillingness to compromise and especially his celebrated autobiography *Žitie* (*Life*, 1672) resulted in his excile. He was then imprisoned and condemned to be burnt at the stake (1682). Using colloquial Russian, Avvakum engaged in violent polemics, in which there is sometimes a brutal, sarcastic note. But he was not a militant fanatic. Conscious of his own weaknesses, he focused much attention on 'the humiliated and the offended', as in this following scene which is touchingly simple:

Протопопница бедная бредет-бредет, да и повалится, вольско гораздо! Выную пору, бредучи, повалиась, а иной томной же человек на нея набрел, тут же и повалился; оба кричат, а встать не могут. Мужик кричит: «матушка-государыня, прости!» А протопопница кричит: «что ты батько, меня задавил?» Я пришол, на меня, бедная пеняет, говоря: «долго ли муки сея, протопоп, будет?» И я говорю: «Марковна, до самыя до смерти!» Она же вздохня, отвечала: «Добро, Петрович, ино еще побредем».	*The poor archpriestess hobbles forward, and then falls down: it was terribly slippy! Once, out walking, she fell over and someone else just as tired out stumbled and fell down on top of her: both of them cried out and were unable to get up again. The man cried: 'Sorry, mother!' And the archpriestess cried: 'Hey, good father, you're crushing me.' I came up and it was me that the poor woman turned on: 'Do we have to go on suffering for a long time, archpriest?' And I said: 'Daughter of Mark, until we die!' And she, with a sigh, replied: 'Well, son of Peter, let's carry on walking then.'*

Avvakum Petrovič, *Žitie*

In Denmark, **Leonora Christina (1621–1698)** wrote *Jammers Minde* (*Memories of Misery*, 1673–1674), memoirs interspersed with historical references and personal reminiscences. She was the daughter of King Christian IV and his court favourite, compromised by and imprisoned in the wake of a conspiracy of which her husband, the Chancellor Ulfeldt, was the ringleader. She describes her life in prison, expresses her thoughts on the world and notably pleading for equality between men and women. Her way of expressing herself mingles realism and subjectiveness, as in the following evocation of her retinue during her years of captivity:

thi grove Ord og fuul Tale	*for it is with rough*
var deres Venligheds og Mildheds	*language and drunken*
Tegn, og blodige Eder deres	*arguments that these people*
Usandfaerdigheders Smykke og	*show their friendliness and*
Beprydelse, saa at deres	*their good nature, while*
Omgaengelse var mig meget	*monstrous oaths*
uangenem. Jeg var inte gladere,	*make up the jewel and ornament*
end naar Dørene imellem mig og	*of their falsehood. You*
dennem vare lukte.	*will therefore understand how*
	disagreeable their company could
Leonora Christina,	*be to me, and I never felt happier*
Jammers Minde	*than when the doors between myself*
	and them were closed again.

In England, **Samuel Pepys (1633–1703)** adopted a resolutely autobiographical approach in his *Diary* which he kept methodically from 1 January 1660 to 31 March 1669. He expressed his thoughts, his states of mind, his experiences, giving us a unique interpretation of the great historical events of his time.

Along with this subjective vision of history, another objective and more 'reasoned' approach gradually developed. Sarpi's *Istoria del concilio di Trento* (*History of the Council of Trent*, 1619) did not stop at describing historical events, but tried to disentangle their causes and explain their consequences. This approach was also popular in England. Bacon's *History of the Reign of Henry VII* (1622) developed a way of understanding power. Many other works, like *The History of the Rebellion* (1702) by **Edward Hyde, Earl of Clarendon (1609–1674)**, tried to find the causes of revolution and the factors distinguishing a republic from a monarchy. In *Nederlandsche Historien* (*Histories of the Netherlands*, 1642– 1654), the Dutchman Hooft set out an array of sources. Describing events both for and against the Spanish, he obtained information from eye witnesses or their direct descendants.

In France, this evolution of history is equally noticeable. In *Memoirs* (only published in 1717), Cardinal de Retz (1613–1679) mingled a novelist's manner with deep, relevant analyses of the Fronde (1648–1652), in which he himself had participated. Charles de Saint-Denis de Saint-Évremond (1613–1703) took this tendency still further: *Reflections on the Variety of Genius among the Citizens of Rome* (compiled *c.*1664, published in 1668 and 1684) were one of the first attempts to elaborate a philosophy of history which took into account both moral and sociological data.

The riches of philosophical, scientific and religious literature

Philosophical and scientific literature flourished throughout the seventeenth century. Connected to religion, it only gradually moved away from it. Sometimes learned, sometimes more accessible, it was a European constant, reflecting the ideological diversity current on the continent.

René Descartes (1596–1650) had a decisive influence on the entire Western world. He lived as a citizen of Europe. Born in Touraine, he travelled Europe from 1618 to 1628 to complete his apprenticeship. He saw the sights of the countries he visited, frequenting court circles and meeting scholars and artists. In 1628 he settled in The Netherlands where he felt he would be allowed more freedom of expression than in France. There he wrote most of his work. But religious authorities considered his ideas were dangerous, so he accepted the Queen Christina of Sweden's invitation to live there. She was passionately interested in science and extremely learned. Descartes died of pneumonia in Sweden on 11 February 1650.

Cartesianism was a rigorous philosophy. The image that Descartes used in the *Principles of Philosophy* (1644) emphasised its coherence: science 'is like a tree'. Its roots lay in metaphysics for, as he points out in *Metaphysical Meditations* (1641), all human knowledge is subordinated to the existence of God, who created truths and revealed them to man. Physics, which formulates the principles the universe obeys, forms the trunk of the tree. The branches are the other sciences which follow on from the rules of physics. Morality, provisionally expounded in the *Discourse on Method* (1637) and investigated in more depth in *The Passions of the Soul* (1649), was the system's crowning glory.

Descartes perfected a strict method, outlined in *Discourse on Method*. Making use of methodical doubt which consists in making a *tabula rasa* of all certainties, he posits the existence of a thought: in denying something, we think. And if we think, it is because we exist. Descartes concluded this reflection with his famous 'I think, therefore I am' which amounts to admitting the reality of reason:

> But, immediately afterwards, I took note that, while I thus strove to think that everything was false, it was necessary that I myself, who thought it, was something. And I noticed that this truth: I think, therefore I am, was so solid and so assured that all the wildest suppositions of the sceptics could not avail to shake it, so I judged that I could definitely accept it as the first principle of the philosophy that I was seeking.
>
> René Descartes, *Discourse on Method*

Reason also needs to function correctly. Descartes outlined the method to follow in the apprehension of facts. First, truth is guaranteed by the clarity with which God illumines it, whether it be attained by intuition or deduction. Reason must put into practice analysis, which consists in breaking down complex facts into a series of simple data. Then comes synthesis, whose function is to reconstruct a complex coherence on the basis of isolated elements. Then comes verification, designed to put errors right and make up for possible omissions.

Many seventeenth-century European philosophers were influenced by Descartes. Sometimes they restricted themselves to spreading Cartesianism in their own countries, like the Hungarian **János Apáczai Csere (1625–1659)**, the author of *Magyar Enciklopédia* (*Hungarian Encyclopaedia*, 1655). Sometimes they retained their own spirit, while making an original contribution. Author of *Principia philosophiæ cartesianæ* (*Principles of Cartesian Philosophy*, 1663), of *Tractatus theologico-politicus*, 1670), of *Ethica* (*Ethics*, 1677) and of *Tractatus de intellectus emendatione* (*Treatise on the Reformation of the Understanding*, 1677), the Dutch philosopher, **Baruch de Spinoza (1632–1677)** considered that God, endowed with an infinite number of attributes, thus contained in himself the totality of creation. In these conditions, we must be careful not to ascribe human behaviour to the Creator and, particularly, not to think that he organised the world with precise aims in mind. By explaining everything by the divine will, man takes refuge, in fact, in ignorance: the easy way out. Spinoza therefore thinks that he should avoid continually looking for the causes of causes of physically observed phenomena, but find truth directly in God.

The German Leibniz made his own contribution to the renovation of Cartesian thought. In *New Essays on Human Under-standing* (1704), *Attempts at a Theodicy* (1710) and *Monadology* (1714), written in French, he conceived of the world as a reflection of God's existence. God was the great organiser, under whose protection the unity of the universe was effected.

Alongside Cartesianism, Europe witnessed the seventeenth-century development of thought focused on the analysis of sense data, refusing to apprehend the nature of things. Science emerged slowly from its metaphysical and religious chrysalis. It did not so much break its ties with philosophy, but entered into a new relationship with it. Scientific reflection on the laws governing the universe brings it to express a philosophical vision, but the founding of scientific laws is done, to some extent, independently, marginally to a philosophical worldview. This increasingly lay treatment of science went hand-in-hand with a tendency towards popularisation. Scientists wanted their works to be known in cultured, non-specialist circles. They preferred ver-nacular languages to Latin, the use of concrete terms, a recourse to less daunting forms, a multiplication of examples, comparisons and images: these were all the distinguishing marks of seventeenth-century scientific works and testify to a desire on the part of their authors not to remain confined to narrow educational boundaries.

This approach favoured the development of experimental science, whose prime aim was the objective observation of the world. Bacon in England, Galileo and Torricelli in Italy, Kepler in Germany, Descartes and Pascal in France, Huygens in The Netherlands all laid down methodological rules of analysis, synthesis and verification. Experimental sci-ences gave birth to a scientific literature which flowered in Italy. **Galileo Galilei (aka Galileo, 1564–1642)** opened the way with *Sidereus nuntius* (1610), in which he published his observations of the Moon and his discovery of Jupiter's four satellites. Later, he proposed an explanation of sunspots in *Istoria e dimos-trazioni intorno alle machie solari e loro accidenti* (*A History and Demonstrations concerning Sunspots and their Changes*, 1613). His con-demnation by the Church in 1616 led him to change course. He abandoned the image of the Renaissance magician and scholar to take on the aspect of the modern man of science, who informed the scientific community as well as the ordinary reader not only about the results he obtained but also how he had arrived at them.

Galileo's disciplined approach was some-times also humorous. *Il Saggiatore* (*The Assayer*, 1623) and *Dialogo sopra i due massimi sistemi del mondo* (*Dialogue on the Two Main World Systems*, 1632) displayed a polemical and ironic force against Aristotelian tradition, and became a veritable model for modern European prose.

After the condemnation of the *Dialogue*, philosophical reflection and critical polemics lost something of their force, but seventeenth-century Italian scientific literature remained productive. Between Galileo's last work, *Discorsi sopra due nuove scienze* (*Discourses on Two New Sciences*, 1638), and the end of the century, there was a veritable flowering of research and works of fundamental significance.

In England, **Francis Bacon (1561–1626)**, in *Novum organum* (*The New Logic*, 1620) and *Instauratio magna* (*The Great Restoration of the Sciences*, 1623), put forward an empirical theory of knowledge. Only experience can reveal the world's reality. The use of the senses plays a decisive role in grasping the complexity of the universe. On the basis of this initial perception, thought functions to put order back into that diversity by proceeding to a structural synthesis of the data provided by perception and analysis:

> Man, being the servant and interpreter of Nature, can do and understand so much only as he has observed in fact or in thought of the course of nature; beyond this he neither knows anything nor can do anything.
>
> Francis Bacon, *Novum organum*

Hobbes took observation as his starting point to reduce everything to material terms and in

France materialist thought gave rise to a marked tendency: libertinism. Extremely complex, it informed the whole of the period and exercised a decisive influence on eighteenth-century philosophers. If, however, all libertines claimed to have their roots in materialism, they were far from forming a homogeneous whole. Atheism or anti-clericalism, the questioning of political and social organisations, the quest for pleasure: such were the consequences of this form of dissident thought which, in literary writing, did not hesitate to use burlesque weapons. The broad school of the French libertine movement includes 'scholars', such as the priest Pierre Gassend, known as Gassendi (1592–1655) as their leader, 'creative writers' like the poet Théophile de Viau or Cyrano de Bergerac, 'socialites', moral Libertines, like the gambler Damien Miton (1618–1690) to whom Pascal adressed himself in *Thoughts* (1670).

This libertine expression of materialism was essentially French, although we can find some traces of it in Italy, especially in Venice. In The Netherlands, the Dutch Academy functioned in part as a centre for opposition to the Protestant *status quo*. Among its members, Hooft appeared as a libertine believer who, influenced by both Stoicism and Epicurean-ism, pursued sophisticated social pleasures.

In the seventeenth century, the Jesuit doctrine represented the dominant ideology at the heart of Catholicism, but it soon came into conflict with Jansenism. Elaborated by the Dutch theologian, **Jansenius (1585–1638)**, who expounded its principles in *Augustinus* (published posthumously in 1640), this religious concept had some influence in The Netherlands and Italy, but developed above all in France.

The bone of contention between Jesuits and Jansenists was initially the problem of grace. While Jesuits believed that salvation and dam-nation depended on an individual's actions, Jansenists tried to elaborate a concept half-way between that of the Jesuits and the Calvinists: God will only grant his grace to those he knows deserve it. Human freedom could still be exercised, for theoretically man can oppose the divine will. But, in fact, man's free will is limited. He who is the object of grace feels such a deep joy that he cannot resist it. He, on the contrary, who is inhabited by the forces of evil cannot be saved because he does not have that impulse towards good that is given by divine grace.

French literature of the second half of the seventeenth century was full of this conflict. **Blaise Pascal (1623–1662)**, a universal genius in both the literary and the scientific sense, was close to the Abbey of Port-Royal, the hub of Jansenism. He vigorously defended Jansenist positions in a polemical work, *Letters to a Provincial Father* (1656–1657). In these eighteen fictitious letters, which discuss grace and criticise the easygoing nature of Jesuit religious practices, Pascal did not want to denounce them in an erudite, heavy-handed way. He knew how to use the power of per-suasion. He style was lively and ironic. He could expose the incoherence of his oppo-nents' ideas by pushing their logic to extremes and showing them its ultimate consequences, as in the following evocation of the lax nature of casuistry:

if someone comes to them absolutely determined to give back ill-gotten gains, do not think that they will deflect him from this aim: on the contrary, they will praise and confirm such a saintly resolution; but if someone else comes to them who wants to have absolution without restitution, that will be difficult, unless they put up capital for which the Jesuits can stand guarantors.

Blaise Pascal, *Letters to a Provincial Father*

In *Thoughts*, Pascal expressed a Christian faith inspired by original Jansenism, in piece-meal form, marked by lyricism, which the incomplete character of the work helps to make truly striking.

Another French writer, Racine, was deeply influenced by Jansenism. A pupil of the Little Schools of Port-Royal, he constructed a theatre in which the machinery of fate owed a great deal to the Jansenist concept of grace.

The idea according to which the unity of the world is the reflection and consequence of the unity of God, had a profound effect on European thought in the seventeenth century, particularly on German philosophy. In this perspective, philosophers worked to grasp universal harmony by establishing constant parallels between nature and religious dogma. As **Johannes Kepler (1571–1630)** pointed out in *Harmonices mundi libri* (*World Harmony*, 1619), the human microcosm is an image of the macrocosm that makes up Creation. In order to be virtuous, we must therefore be integrated into the divine harmony. Only in this way can man fight against chaos, the symbol of evil, and recreate celestial order on earth. Johann Andreae (1587–1654) and Jakob Böhme (1575–1624) took up this concept, while poets began with the evocation of visible nature which bore witness to the divine, invisible world.

In tandem with this Protestant mysticism, **Philipp Spener (1635–1705)** elaborated the doctrine of pietism, which advocated the fusion of the individual in God. This concept of faith had a major influence on German writers and also on those in The Netherlands, such as Luyken, the author of *Jezus en de ziel* (*Jesus and the Soul*, 1678). Within Catholicism, the Spaniard **Miguel de Molinos (1628–1696)**, particularly in *Guia espiritual* (*The Spiritual Guide*, 1676), expressed the great principles of quietism which considered as the highest virtues were the peace of the soul and its fusion in God. One of his most famous disciples was the Frenchman Fénelon who, in 1697, defended this doctrine in *Explanation of the Maxims of the Saints on the Inner Life* (1697), subsequently condemned by royalty.

This reflection of the unity of the world appeared in the work of many other European philosophers. The Rumanian Dmitrie Cantemir (1673–1723) published *Gâlceava înteleptului culunea, Jiutedetrul susletului, cutrupul* (*The Talk of the Wise Man with the*

World, or the Dispute of the Soul with the Body) in 1698, a work whose title clearly revealed its preoccupations.

Religious literature sometimes adopted 'socialite' aspects and encouraged a flourishing art of sacred rhetoric. In France, **Jacques-Bénigne Bossuet (1627–1704)**, close to royal circles, gave many sermons (*On the Eminent Dignity of the Poor*, 1659; *On Death*, 1662) and funeral orations (for Henriette d'Angleterre, 1670; for Michel Le Tellier, 1686; for Condé, 1687), in which he revealed the vanity of material things when man is confronted by death and by God.

> A disastrous night! A frightful night, in which reverberated all of a sudden, like a clap of thunder, that astounding piece of news: The Mistress is dying, the Mistress is dead!
>
> Bossuet, *Funeral Orations*

In Portugal, **António Vieira (1608–1697)** made this art of sacred rhetoric famous. A Jesuit priest, missionary, diplomat and statesman, Vieira the writer and the man of action appeared to be inseparable. He placed his eloquence at the service of his campaigns against the brutalities of the Inquisition or against the slavery Portuguese colonists imposed on Brazilian natives. According to tradition, Vieira organised his sermons around a Biblical quotation which he commented on to illustrate his themes and ideas. For him, scripture was endowed with a mystery that the preacher had to try to elucidate. Superficially evolving according to strict inferences, Vieira's poetic language actually followed the many arbitrary paths of fantasy. In order to convince his hearers, he had recourse to every means of pressure and persuasion, while appearing to follow the straight-forward paths of self-evident truth. So, in this extract from *Sermão das lágrimas de S. Pedro* (*Sermon on the Tears of Saint Peter*, 1679–1699), he subtly combines analysis and subjective considerations:

Vede quão misteriosamente puseram as lágrimas nos olhos a Natureza, a Justiça, a Razão, e

See how mysteriously Nature, Justice, Reason and Grace bring tears

a Graça. A Natureza para remédio; a Justiça para castigo; a Razão para arrependimento; a Graça para triunfo. Com pelos olhos se contrai a mácula do pecado, pôs a Natureza nos olhos as lágrimas, para que com aquela água se lavassem as manchas; como pelos olhos se admite a culpa, pôs a Justiça nos olhos as lágrimas para que estivesse o suplício no mesmo lugar do delito; como pelos olhos se concebe a ofensa, pôs a Razão nos olhos as lágrimas para que onde se fundiu a ingratidão, e desfizesse o arrependimento; e como pelos olhos entram os inimigos à alma, pôs a Graça nos olhos as lágrimas para que pela mesma brecha por onde entraram vencedores os fizesse sair correndo.

António Vieira,
Sermões

to our eyes. Nature to heal us, Justice to make us mend our ways, Reason to make us repent and Grace so that we can be triumphant. The stain of sin may be seen in our eyes, so Nature brings tears to our eyes so that, like water, they wash away the stains. Our eyes betray our sin, so Justice brings tears to our eyes so that our penance can be carried out where the crime has been committed. A sin may be born from a look, so Reason brings tears to our eyes so that remorse can drain away and repentance run out. Through our eyes, our enemies get into our soul, so Grace brings tears to our eyes so that the breach whereby the conquerors have entered be that by which they will take to their heels.

In Hungary, another Jesuit, Cardinal **Péter Pázmány (1570–1637)**, encouraged sacred rhetoric. Deeply marked by a stay in Rome, an eminent propagator of the Counter-Reformation, he left behind a large collection of sermons (1636). Above all, in his polemical texts directed against Protestant preachers that he expressed the full oratorical force of a language animated by the breath of persuasion (*Felelet, Response*, 1603; *Öt levél* [. . .], *Five Letters* [. . .], 1609).

The art of sacred rhetoric developed strongly in Greece. **Elias Migniatis (1669–1714)**, influenced by Bossuet, wrote *Dhidhakhé* (*Sermons*, published in 1716). This taught traditional moral values and expressed his patriotic wish to see his country liberated. In Crete, religious literature revealed the complex relationships between Orthodox Christianity, Catholicism and Protestantism. **Kyrillos Loukaris (1572–1638)**, a native of Candia, gave a characteristic testimony to this effect. Named Patriarch of Alexandria in 1602, he vigorously opposed the Catholics and aligned himself with the Protestants. In his principal work, *Omologhia tis khristianikis pisteos* (*Confessions of the Christian Faith*, 1633), he raised many theological, historical and political problems. Although he expressed a doctrine which adopted certain points in Calvinism, he remained loyal to his Orthodox faith – the only faith he thought could save the identity of Hellenism.

In Europe overall, dogmatic religious literature was still very much impregnated with the spirit of the Middle Ages, but a desire to popularise also made itself felt, as we can see in the Bulgarian 'damaskini'. These anonymous collections, handed down in manuscript form from generation to generation, were veritable encyclopedias. They contained sermons, the lives of the saints, interpretations of the Gospels, educational stories, legends, long historical narrations and apocryphal works which attempted a kind of psychological analysis. In these 'damaskini' we find the famous *Fiziolog*, an allegorical and symbolic theological work offering an interpretation of Christianity based on ancient and oriental sources. The Albanian Pjetër Budi (born 1556) published in 1621 the poetically excellent *Speculum Confessionis* (*Mirror of Confession*) Despite its religious and moralising content, this work proved the new trends, contributing to the awakening of national awareness as well as to the evolution of a linguistic and literary taste.

THREE CONTRASTING STYLES OF WRITING

While regular and irregular theatre were starkly opposed to one other, poetry experienced mixed fortunes. Going through a serious crisis in France, poetry developed successfully in most countries, where it appeared in many different guises. Fragmentary literature was undoubtedly a speciality of France and was only marginally practised elsewhere.

Theatre: from irregularity to regularity

Seventeenth-century theatre did not constitute anything like a homogeneous whole. A dominant form of expression countries such as Spain, France, even England and The Netherlands, it went through a period of stagnation in Italy, which paved the way to it in the sixteenth century and still exerted a great influence in Europe. In Central and Eastern Europe, the theatre began to regenerate itself and cast off the traditional forms of the Middle Ages. Theatre as an art form was split by aspirations to irregularity and a quest for what was regular.

Seventeenth-century European theatre bore the seal of irregularity. Many dramatists boasted of their freedom to create as they saw fit. They refused to be hemmed in by strict rules of composition and tried to adapt their art to current realities. In Spain, this concept of theatre inspired the brilliant succeeding generations of dramatists throughout the century. **Lope de Vega (1562–1635)**, in *Arte nuevo de hacer comedias* (*The New Art of Making Plays*), formulated the flexible, open-ended creativity of the new Spanish drama in 1609. Made up of three acts, metrically varied, marrying tragedy with comedy, the latter cultivated in particular by the *gracioso*, the play was built up around a complex plot. The themes it treated were diverse, making reference to religious, epic and folk traditions. But the dominant note was, nevertheless, a popular sense of honour. The author of some 1500 plays, Lope de Vega put his own principles into practice in *Peribañez y el comendador de Ocaña* (*Peribañez and the Commander of Ocaña*, 1614), in which a peasant is determined to kill the Commander of Ocaña to stop him maltreating his wife. In *Fuenteovejuna* (1618) a village revolts against the tyranny of a feudal lord; at the end of it Mayor Esteban formulates the following significant moral:

Fuente Ovejuna, señora,	*Fuente Ovejuna, madam, humbly*
que humildes llegan agora	*comes to assure you of its*
para serviros dispuestos.	*love and loyalty.*
La sobrada tirania	*The insufferable tyranny*
y el insufrible rigor	*and the excessive cruelty of the*
del muerto Comendador,	*Commander, who committed against us*
que mil insultos hacía,	*every day a thousand injustices, were*
fue el autor de tanto daño.	*the cause of much harm.*
Las haciendas nos robaba	*Incapable of feeling*
y las doncellas forzaba,	*any pity, he used to take our property*
siendo de piedad extraño.	*and force himself on our wives and daughters.*

Lope de Vega, *Fuenteovejuna*

Don Pedro Calderón de la Barca (1600–1681) continued to use the contributions of his predecessor. He transformed Spanish drama, simplifying the plot and placing the accent on the play's philosophical dimension. These two dramatists had many imitators. In the line of succession to Lope de Vega, there was Guillén de Castro (1569–1631), the author of *Las Mocedades del Cid* (*The Youth of the Cid*, 1618), which served as a model for Corneille; Antonio Mira de Mescua (1574?–1644), a forerunner of Goethe whose *Faust* took up the theme of *El Esclavo del demonio* (*The Devil's Slave*, 1612); Ruiz de Alarcón (1581–1639), the creator of a theatre of manners later adapted by Corneille and Molière and by the Italian Carlo Goldoni; Tirso de Molina (1581–1648), who, with *El Burlador de Sevilla* (*The Joker of Seville*, 1624), created the character of Don Juan, who has become a part of literary mythology. In Calderón's sphere of influence, two playwrights were very much imitated by succeeding European dramatists: Rojas Zorrilla (1607–1648), a master of comic realism, and Agustín Moreta (1618–1669), a witty stylist, all nuances of meaning and psychological analysis.

In France theatre, until *c.*1640, was distinguished by a lack of concern for rules which continued throughout the century in court entertainments. Alexandre Hardy (1570–1632) was a good example.

This irregularity asserted itself in many other European countries. While in England, during the first half of the seventeenth century, the Elizabethan manner continued, notably with Thomas Middleton (*c.*1570–1627) and Ben Jonson, Baroque theatre was the order of the day in Germany. **Andreas Greif (Gryphius, 1616–1664)** was one of its best practitioners. In sombre dramas he depicted the martyrdom of a queen (*Katharina von Georgien*, *Catherine of Georgia*, 1647), the torture of a king (*Carolus Stuardus*, *Charles Stuart*, 1649) and the life of a stoic hero (*Papinianus*, 1659). In comedies full of fantasy, he also gave us characters with something of the marvellous about them (*Peter Squentz*,

1663) or a boastful soldier (*Horribilicribrifax*, 1663). While Vondel found his inspiration in the Bible – a source of emotionally intense dramas – Spanish influence was felt in The Netherlands. In his tragi-comedy *Griano* (1612), Bredero was inspired by a Spanish novel, enhanced by realistic interludes rooted in his country's social context. In *Spaanschen Brabander Jerolimo* (*The Spaniard from Brabant*, *Jerolimo*, 1618), he adapted *Lazarillo de Tormes* bringing into it a whole new Dutch dimension. This play, which depicts an impoverished Antwerp noble with affectations and an ordinary young lad from Amsterdam, obtained comic effects from the contrasts between characters, the palpable difference between the realistic preoccupations of the northern working-class people and the vanity of emigrants from the southern Netherlands. This Spanish inspiration was also found in Poland in *Komedia Lopesa starego* (*The Comedy of Old Lopez*, *c.*1674) by Stanisław Lubomirski (1642–1702), full of colourful characters.

Alongside this irregular theatre, under the influence of sixteenth-century Italian theatre, the regular theatre gradually gained ground in France. Its supporters held that, in order to create valid theatrical works, some rules should be applied. The play had to be unified around a main plot which should remain dominant: this was the unity of action. It had to last a length of time approximately comparable to that of the performance: this was the unity of time. This limited the events that took place in the play to twenty-four hours. It had to take place in a single space synonymous with what was on stage: this was the unity of place. To emphasise the underlying tone, the regular theatre rejected the mixing of genres. Tragedy portrayed eminent people whose fate could influence the destiny of nations. It unfolded in a tightly controlled way and its heroes came to an unhappy end. Comedy portrayed characters of middling or low birth, describing their everyday life. It had a happy ending with sympathetic characters.

After a generation of transition in which Jean Mairet (1604–1686) and Jean Rotrou

(1609–1650) distinguished themselves, three great names dominated the regular theatre in France. Corneille, who gradually emerged from irregularity, **Jean-Baptiste Poquelin**, also known as **Molière (1622–1673)**,* whose theatre was at a crossroads of influences and was not always regular and Racine, the undisputed master of regular theatre. The theatrical career of **Pierre Corneille (1606–1684)** dominated the century. It began in 1629 with the comedy *Mélite* and ended in 1674 with the tragedy *Suréna*. His diverse and contrasting dramatic productions were nevertheless marked by a few constants. Although he supported rules, he was not their slave; he gave himself an opportunity to 'cunningly domesticate them with our theatre' (epistle to *La Suivante*, 1634). He wanted to please his audience. He also wanted to instruct, depicting his characters so that spectators were attracted by their virtues and repelled by their faults.

Heroism set its seal on Corneille's theatre. The greatness of man consisted in keeping a watchful eye on his 'gloire' – his honour – so that it always corresponded to his own self-image. This individual behaviour brought about the intervention of collective values sanctioned by history and society. In *Le Cid* (1636), Rodrigo's honour, which consists in avenging his father, is both his personal honour and the honour of his caste.

The choice was not always easy and often made after much soul-searching: Cornelian dilemmas. In *Horace* (1640), for example, the fight to the death organised between the three Horaces, champions of Rome, and the three Curiaces, representing the rival city of Alba, to determine the supremacy of one city or the other, divides the protagonists between their patriotism and the family ties that unite them. But heroism presupposes mastery over one's personal impulses. Because characters choose the path of honour, they assume their condition, reject alienation, pose as free men in a world where fate does not exist. So, in *Cinna* (1641), the Emperor Augustus cuts short his hesitations between pardoning and punishing the plotters, crying:

I am master of myself as of the world;
I am so, and I want to be so.

Corneille, *Cinna*

If Corneille was influenced by Jesuit ideas, **Jean Racine (1639–1699)** was exposed to the influence of Jansenism. His theatre was marked by both passion and restraint. The driving force behind his plays was the confrontation between different feelings. This introduced a moral dimension, alerting the spectator to the negative consequences of these impulses. The strict application of the rules conforms with the manifestation of fate. The unity of tone emits tragedy. The unity of time makes for concentration. The unity of action places events in a moment of crisis. The unity of place traps characters in an insufferable cohabitation with others and an alienating self-absorption.

Fate is at the centre of Racinian tragedy. Man is not master of his own existence. He must be resigned to the fate he has been assigned. This alienation is all the stronger and more unbearable for the characters because it is a mass of unresolved contradictions. They are divided between individual impulses, stemming from personal desires, and social taboos, based on reason. In the play named after her (1677), Phaedra is impelled by her desire for Hippolytus, but her reason prompts her to renounce her passion. She lucidly expresses this inner division when she declares to the forbidden subject of her love:

I love you! Do not think that now I love
* you,*
Innocent in my own eyes, I approve of
* myself;*
Nor that this foolish love which troubles my
* reason*
Was fed by the poison of my cowardly
* complacency;*
Unhappy object of celestial vengeance,
I execrate myself more than you detest me.

Racine, *Phaedra*

This game of contradictions takes on a particularly tragic dimension when it opposes love to power. Power then enlists in the service of passion. In *Britannicus* (1669), Agrippina has designated her son, Nero, to succeed her rather than Britannicus, the legitimate heir. But she takes Britannicus' part in his love for Junia, with whom Nero is also in love. Nero wants to use his power to break down her resistance: he abducts Junia, has his rival poisoned and his mother arrested. Junia denies the tyrant victory by taking refuge as a vestal virgin.

After the Civil War and the return from exile of the court of Charles II, England experienced the growing influence of regular French theatre. In *Essay of Dramatic Poesy* (1668), **John Dryden (1631–1700)** adopted some practices of regular drama, rejecting others. The use of rhyme and the application of the unities tended to become the rule in tragedies, like *Cato* (1713) by Joseph Addison (1672–1719). Comedy set more store by the study of manners rather than characters and love occupied an essential place. Sometimes it described naïve behaviour, as in *The Country Wife* (1675) by William Wycherley (1640–1715). But most of the time the manners of fashionable people were ridiculed by playwrights. Wycherley in this vein wrote *The Plain Dealer* (1676); George Etheredge *The Man of Mode* (1676); while **William Congreve (1670–1729)**, in *The Way of the World* (1700), depicted a society wedding.

In The Netherlands a whole dramatic tendency took its cue from Antiquity. A theatrical concept which embraced the Aristotelian theory of catharsis developed under the influence of the treatise of Daniel Heinsius (1580–1655), *De tragoediæ constitutione* (*On the Constitution of Tragedy*, 1611). In the preface to *Jephthah* (1659), Vondel pronounced himself in favour of a dramaturgy based on the application of Aristotelian theories and supported by Seneca's good practice. At the same time, Latin authors provided Dutch dramatists with the models that they imitated, while adapting them to conditions in their country. On the basis of Plautus' *Aulularia*, **Pieter Cornelisz Hooft (1581–1647)** wrote the comedy *Ware-Nar, dat is Aulularia van Plautus* (*The Real Fool is the Aulularia of Plautus*, 1617), in which avarice was invested with the characteristics typical of The Netherlands at the beginning of the seventeenth century. Conversely, in the southern Netherlands, **Michiel de Swaen (1654–1707)** wrote the classical comedy *De gecroonde leerse* (*The Boot Crowned*, 1688) based on a popular episode in the life of Emperor Charles V.

In Crete, a regular theatre developed under Italian influence. Comedies took over the plots and subject matter of works of the Italian Renaissance, adapting them to the reality of Crete during the years 1600–1669, like *Katsurbos* (between 1595 and 1600) by George Chortatzis (*c*.1545–1610) or *Fortunatos* by Marcos Antonios Foskolos (died 1662). Tragedy in Crete was also close to Italian models: *O Basileús Rodolinos* (*King Rodolinos*, 1647) by Joannis Andreas Troilos (1590–*c*.1648), for example, inspired by Tasso's *King Torrismond*, shows us the King of Egypt torn between love, friendship, fidelity and treachery. At the same time as the regular theatre aimed at the ordinary public, college theatre, developed by the Jesuits, becomes the order of the day in many European countries. Relying on Greek and Latin models, it was often as in Eastern European countries, the only theatre there was before the birth of national inspiration.

The poetic explosion

Like the theatre, European poetry was distinguished by diversity. Despite certain writing constants supported by the major trends of the age – the Baroque, Mannerism and the burlesque – it was heterogeneous in nature. Although it was in crisis in countries such as France and Crete, it flourished in England, in Germany and in The Netherlands, where it split into many sub-genres – metaphysical, lyrical, epic, satirical or didactic.

In a lyrical way, metaphysical poetry asked after the place of man and his role in the universe. For German poets, the beauty of creation was the reflection of the beauty of its Creator. This concept gave rise to a blossoming of spiritual poetry inspired by Catholicism or Protestantism; **Angelus Silesius (1624–1677)** and **Paul Gerhardt (1607–1676)** were its main representatives. One of their favourite themes was of man's journey through the deceitful, unpredictable sea of life. This is illuminated by the Divinity, who alone can guide man through it. In this conflict between the gratuitousness of the world and God's permanence, death, the domain of the intangible and the essential is contrasted by a set of contradictions: the realm of the fluctuating and the relative. These antagonisms of self-abnegation and voluptuousness sometimes lead to deep movements of the soul. These in turn result in the fear of a vacuum ('horror vacui'), sometimes in a lust for life – an expression of the desire to make the most of each moment of existence ('carpe diem') – sometimes to the stoic attitude which aims to reach happiness by mastering the passions. At the same time, the need for security produced by the instability of the world explained the pre-eminence of the closed structure of the sonnet. All these phenomena, already apparent, but under control in Mannerist writing, were evident in Gryphius. The Thirty Years' War made a deep impression on him and he left behind a work in which we are struck by the desperate quality of life. In a style both poetic and realistic, he depicted a sombre world tortured by a suffering that the light of salvation does not alleviate.

> Magnificence in flower is quickly trampled down!
> But none want to open their eyes to the Eternal God.
>
> Andreas Gryphius,
> *Vanity, Vanity*

The term 'metaphysical' used to characterise English poets' work during the first part of the seventeenth century had another meaning, originally pejorative. Dryden first applied it to John Donne, who 'prides himself on his metaphysics', or expounds complex thoughts in a pretentious way, instead of arousing emotion and passion. In fact, Donne closely intermingled the intellectual and the emotional dimensions of poetry. In both his love poetry (*Songs and Sonnets*, 1611) and in his religious poetry (*Holy Sonnets*, composed between 1607 and 1614), Donne's manner is forceful: he uses elaborate arguments and juxtaposes striking ideas, which act as a counterpoint to his emotional strength. So, in 'A valediction: forbidding mourning', the strength of the emotions of two parting lovers gives rise to sharp observation which, mediated by reflection, accentuates the poem's emotional intensity.

This spectacular poetry adapted Elizabethan verbal outlines and conceits, to hold our attention by the powerful depiction of the whole range of human emotions. While many poets such as Henry King (1592–1669), Thomas Carew (1595–1640) and Richard Crashaw (1612–1649) travel this road, Ben Jonson chose a simpler style, believing that the poet should respect decorum, balance and measure. He gathered round himself 'the tribe of Ben', including, notably, Robert Herrick (1591–1674).

Some poets wavered between these two influences, revealing themselves to be either affected or simple, sometimes varying their effects in the space of a single poem. This was, in particular, the case with **John Milton (1608–1674).** In *Poems* (1645) he revealed two faces: he followed Donne in his extravagant aspect (*The Passion*), but he also knew how to attain a lyrical simplicity (*Song on May Morning*). This mixture of styles was also found in his major works, *Paradise Lost* (1667) and *Paradise Regained* (1671).

In some European countries, poetry often had a specifically religious aspect. In the southern Netherlands, **Justus de Harduijn (1582–1636)** published *Goddelicke Lof-sanghen* (*Divine Hymns*), in which a Baroque sensitivity to movement and colour blended with the fervour of medieval poetry. Similarly, in the United Provinces the Catholic priest Joannes Stalpart Van der Wiele (1579–1630) composed melodious hymns close to medieval popular song (*Gulde-laers Feest-dagen*, *Feast-*

days of the gilded year, 1634–1635). These collections of religious songs, produced throughout Europe, took a special direction in Bohemia and Slovakia. Among these hymnbooks various ones shine out, including *Cithara sanctorum. Písně duchovní staré i nové* (*The Harp of the Saints. Old and New Spiritual Canticles*, 1636) by the Lutheran Jiří Třanovský (1592–1637); *Cantus catholici. Písně katholické latinské i slovenské* (*Catholic Hymns in Latin and Slovak*, 1655) by the Jesuit Benedikt Szölössi (1609–1656); or even the one published by Comenius in 1659 in Amsterdam. Also a hymnbook writer, the Czech **Bedřich Bridel (1619–1680)** left a long metaphysical poem, *Co Bůh? Člověk?* (*What is God? What is Man?*, 1658), in which he expressed all the anguish of the human soul, guilty, frivolous and vile, in the presence of God's majesty:

> Já jsem zarytou skrejší
> badův, jenž se ve mně plazí,
> já, v' němž jako v peleši
> rádi zlí duchové vězí:
> já jsem pekla pochodně,
> věčné vždy hořící svíce,
> neskonČeného ohně
> pokrm, potrava a píce.

Bedřich Bridel,
Co Bůh? Člověk?

> I am merely a mean bed
> crawling with vermin.
> Snakes slither over my breast,
> A den where evil spirits
> Enjoy taking up residence.
> I am a torch in hell,
> A candle burning for ever and ever,
> Food, grub and nourishment
> For a fire incessantly renewed.

In another register, **Albert Szenci Molnár (1574–1634)**, a Hungarian living in Germany, adapted the psalms, published in 1607 under the title *Psalterium Ungaricum* (*The Hungarian Psalter*). Inspired by the French models of Clément Marot and Théodore de Bèze, his rich poetical texts are still sung today in Hungarian Protestant churches and have greatly influenced modern poetry.

In The Netherlands, **Jacobus Revius (1586–1658)** wrote *Over-Ysselsche Sangen en Dichten* (*Songs and Poems of Overijssel*, 1630), deeply religious in their lyricism, while **Dirck Raphaëlsz. Camphuysen (1586–1627)** conceived *Stichtelycke Rymen* (*Religious Rhymes*, 1624), whose asceticism is much appreciated in Anabaptist and Remonstrant circles. Vondel composed *Bespielingen van Godt en Godtsdienst* (*Meditations on God and Religion*, 1662), a long text of 7352 verses, in which he fights several forms of paganism and opposes Spinoza's ideas.

In Denmark, **Thomas Kingo (1634–1703)**, in his pompous *Aandelige Sjungekor* (*Psalter*, 1674–1681), marked a deep sense of God's majesty and the sacred. He reconciled this with a concern for popular psychology and a desire to adapt to the daily life of his time.

Jesuit religious lyricism occupied an important place in seventeenth-century European poetry. In Poland, **Maciej Kazimierz Sarbiewski (1595–1640)** was its distinguished representative. A poetics teacher at the Academy of Pololsk, he wrote *Lyricorum libri* (*Books of Lyric Poetry*, 1625), which in Europe earned him the name 'Christian Horace'. Written in Latin, it combined pagan lyricism and Biblical influence, mixing a spirit of neo-Platonism with a sense of solitude and a nostalgia for paradise lost and interpreting nature as a divine hieroglyph. It went through sixty editions in various European countries. Sarbiewski had considerable prestige in England where his writings, translated in 1646 as *The Odes of Casimire*, became an inexhaustible source of inspiration for the Metaphysical poets.

Lyrical poetry was profoundly marked by Mannerism and some contrast continued to lay claim to the lessons of the French Pleiad which had a considerable influence over European poetry in the seventeenth century.

This applied to the southern Netherlands poet De Harduijn: *De Weerliicke liefden tot Roosemond* (*Profane Love, Poems for Rosemonde*, 1613) is a cycle of elegiac poems dedicated to the woman he loved. In the northern Netherlands, love poetry developed in an important way. Apart from Hooft, influenced by Mannerism, Bredero wrote lyrical poems (1622), in which he describes the joys and pains of love in a Christian perspective.

In Poland a pastoral trend was represented in particular by **Szymon Zimorowicz (1608–1629)**. *Roksolanki* (*Young Ruthenian Girls*), only published in 1654, was a collection of madrigals around the conventional themes of fire, ashes, flowers and doves. The local colour of Ruthenia, present-day Ukraine, was somewhat eclipsed by mythological allusions. Unusual metaphors led to images which are sometimes jolly, sometimes sad, even macabre. Pastoral writing was also produced in Bohemia. Václav Jan Rosa (1620?–1689) wrote *Pastýřké rozmlouvání o Narození Páně* (*Pastoral Dialogue on the Birth of the Lord*, 1672), a long idyll. He also left an allegorical poem, *Discursus Lipirona, to jest smutného kavalíra, de amore aneb o lásce* (*The Discourse of Lipiron, the Sad Cavalier, de amore or on Love*, 1651).

In France, lyricism came to life itself during the first third of the seventeenth century. On the margin of Mannerism, two poets in particular illustrate this style: **François de Malherbe (1555–1628)** developed the themes of death, love, time passing and nature, noting melancholically, on the occasion of the death of one of his friend's daughters:

And, a rose, she lived what roses live,
  The space of a morning.
        François de Malherbe, *Consolation for*
                  M. du Périer

His predominantly Baroque writing made him a transitional writer who paved the way for classical regularity and modernity. The libertine **Théophile de Viau (1590–1626)** placed a feeling for nature at the centre of *Poetic Works* (1621–1624). Sensitive to the ephemeral and the fluctuating, he knew how to appreciate the subtle changes in a landscape which make it moving, because each moment is unique and unforgettable. He was open to all impressions, his senses alert, eager to take advantage of the life he was offered.

The medieval tradition of epic poetry persisted in part of Europe. It was still very much alive in the north, the east and the south-east of the continent, where it often contributed to a country's national identity if it was growing or under threat. We can place *Osman* (published in 1826) by the Croat Ivan Gundulić (1589–1638) in this perspective: a Baroque fresco exalting the struggle of Christianity against the evil forces of Sultan Osman II supported by Lucifer. In the same web of ideas, the Hungarian **Miklós Zrinyi (1620–1664)**, in *Szigeti Veszedelem* (*The Zrinyad or Siege of Szizet*, 1645–1646), exalted the sacrifice of his grandfather who, by defending the fortress of Szigetvár besieged by the armies of Suleiman (1566), avoided the fall of Vienna and the domination of the West by the Ottoman Empire. Taking his inspiration from Tasso's *Jerusalem Delivered*, Zrinyi appeared as a convinced patriot and a poet steeped in humanism.

In an analogous perspective, the Croat and Serb epic called 'burgarštica' can be allied to a resistance movement against the Turks and is a glorification of patriotism. Two Polish poems also reflect national preoccupations. *Transakcja wojny chocimskiej* (*The War of Chocim*, 1670) by **Wacław Potocki (1621–1696)** was a glorification of the victory over the Turks that Chodkiewicz the Pole won in 1621. To the detailed description of the battle, the author mixed lyrical digressions and contemporary political considerations. *Psalmodia Polska* (*Polish Psalmody*, 1695), by **Wespazjan Kochowski (1633–1700)**, is a cycle of religious and patriotic meditations celebrating the triumph of Polish arms over the Turks. The conviction that God had entrusted Poland with a special mission made Kochowski adopt a sneering, fanatical tone towards the Turkish enemy. In another register, the exile **Jakub Jakobeus (1591?–1645)** published in Latin *Gentis Slavonicæ lacrimæ, suspiria et vota* (*The Tears, Sighs and Wishes of the Slovak People*, 1642), a long elegiac epic poem exalting the Slovakian past. In Crete, *Erotokritos* (written between 1645 and 1660), by **Vicenzo Cornaros (died 1677)**, ten thousand verses in five sections, related the conflict between love and heroism which raged in Erotokritos who was in love with Arethusa. The action takes place in ancient Athens, but was heavily influenced by the medieval tradition of chivalry. From this work an aspiration for a new Hellenism emerged, conjured up by a curious alliance of ancient mythology and popular hopes of the time.

The epic by the Swede **Georg Stierhielm (1598–1672)**, *Hercules* (1658), was written in quite a different way. Hercules, who cannot make his mind up between sensuality and asceticism, encounters Dame Joy, escorted by her three daughters, Pleasure, Lechery and Vanity. Ready to follow the advice they give him to enjoy life, he is finally saved from perversion by the goddess Virtue, who sets against this Epicurean vision a Stoical conception of life. This long allegorical poem, written in a very archaic language but observing a classical metre, was very original beecause its inspiration was entirely secular.

In Denmark, **Anders Arrebo (1587–1637)** in his poem *Hexaemeron* (*The Six Days*, written between 1630 and 1637) drew on the Bible for inspiration. Inspired by *The Week* (1578) by the Frenchman Du Bartas, he drew up a kind of inventory of the world over the course of Creation, thinking about living conditions in Denmark. Arrebo's great talent lay in his attempt to make Danish poetry stress-timed, which he preferred to the metrical rules of versification. Apart from work by Milton, epic poetry only appeared in Western Europe as an artificial survival, cut off from historical and sociological realities.

Metaphysical, lyrical and epic poetry attempted to move the reader. A much more rational desire to convince, based on didacticism, developed, tinged with moral concerns. This manner quite naturally found its most fruitful soil in France, where the growing importance of Reason gradually rendered individual outpourings morally suspect.

Towards the end of the century, **Nicolas Boileau (1636–1711)**, who appeared on the European stage as a classical theorist, produced work in line with this function. In his satirical poems (*Satires*, 1666–1716; *The Lectern*, 1674–1683; *Epistles*, 1670–1698) or didactic ones (*The Art of Poetry*, 1674), he banished what he considered to be imaginative excesses, and put technique before inspiration.

Jean de La Fontaine (1621–1695) used the didactic genre of the fable in an original way. Published between 1668 and 1696, the *Fables* were 'a wide-ranging comedy with a hundred different acts', as the author himself commented in *The Woodcutter and Mercury* (1668). Whether man was directly portrayed as himself or indirectly through animal, vegetable and mineral, La Fontaine depicted the whole human comedy. Each fable was constructed like a play, taking place against a quickly sketched but precise background and is situated in a well-defined time-period. It represented characters described in their picturesque actions, but also delineated in their most inward thoughts. It ends with the statement of a moral, often condensed into a brief precept.

> *Depending on whether you are powerful or*
>   *wretched,*
> *The judgements of the court will make you white*
>   *or black.*

> La Fontaine,
> *The Animals Sick with the Plague*

Lyricism constantly animated the coldness of the fable, whether La Fontaine was expressing his melancholy at the transience of time or praising friendship. He also asserted a complex philosophy which included both Epicureanism and Stoicism. Enjoy life in moderation, take account of others without becoming too committed to any one person, accept the inevitable without being resigned to it: such were the essential lessons of the *Fables*, often expressed with a nostalgia for a way of life both regretted and longed for:

Solitude, in which I find a secret sweetness,
Places that I always loved, will I never be
   able,
Far from the world and its noise, to enjoy
   there shade and cool?

La Fontaine, *The Dream of an*
Inhabitant of the Mogul Empire

La Fontaine cast a lucid, often cruel gaze at the society of his time. He denounced injustices and abuses. He unmasked incongruities. Above all, he dissected the relationship between oppressors and oppressed. He described how governments abused their powers, bringing a modern point of view to this denunciation. He revealed the perversion inherent in all power, which is misused and exercised in the defence of individual interests. Even those who are oppressed consent, to paying the price for others without too much resistance: the donkey in *The Animals Sick with the Plague*, having owned up to a minor infraction of a rule, serves as an expiatory victim, taking the place of those who were really responsible. Thus La Fontaine revealed the infernal dialectic which unites torturer and tortured, master and slave.

Satirical and didactic poetry was not the sole prerogative of France. Present in Hungarian poetry, it was also much practised in the northern Netherlands, where **Constantijn Huygens (1596–1687)** willingly exploited it. In *Batava-Tempe, dat is't Voor-Hout van's Gravenhage* (*Batava-Tempe, the Voorhout of The Hague*, 1621), he takes to task and mocks the frequenters of the Voor-Hout, a famous alleyway in The Hague; in *Kerkuria Mastix, satyra. Dat is't Costelick Mal* (*Kerkuria Mastix, the Costly Folly*, 1622), he amusingly criticised the excesses of fashion.

In Spain, Quevedo, in *La Hora de Todos* (*Everyone's Hour*, 1636), both epic and satirical, criticised a whole series of picturesque characters: doctors, thieves, receivers of stolen goods, phoney aristocrats and coquettes. He then attacked the great of this world, often expounding bold theories.

A little in the style of the first part of Quevedo's work, Potocki, in Poland, brilliantly described, with alacrity, the manners of the Sarmatian middle aristocracy (*Moralia, Writings on Manners*, 1688–1696).

Didactic poetry, widespread throughout Europe, was practised in Russia by **Simeon de Polock (1629–1680)**. This tutor of Czar Alexis' children introduced 'virši' (syllabic verses), to Moscow. These had been imported from Poland to the Ukraine and Byelorussia. This system of versification, is built on a number of fixed syllables, the presence of a caesura and an obligatory feminine rhyme, went hand-in-hand with the use of Slavonic, a learned language. Polock used this system in his didactic and panegyric poetry, divided up between two collections, *Vertograd mnogo-cvetnyj* (*The Many-Coloured Garden*, 1677) and *Rifmologion* (1679).

In Scandinavian countries, a 'scientific' type of poetry flourished. The Norwegian **Peter Dass (1647–1707)** was a distinguished representative. In his long poem *Nordlands Trompet* (*Trumpet of the Northland*, 1700), he portrayed the geography, climate, flora and fauna and the inhabitants of north Norway in a spiritual fashion.

The high fashion of fragmentary writing in France

During the seventeenth century, fragmentary writing was in great demand in France. This modern technique, which consists of having a series of remarks or reflections succeed one another in no particular order and without any apparent connection between them, was interesting for three reasons. Worldly readers, not very assiduous or not disposed to making an effort, could easily break off in the middle of reading. They could then return to their book without having to remember exactly what had happened before. Conversely, those who sought a more enriching approach could reconstitute the succession of ideas and thus collaborate with the author. Also, by avoiding a rigorous construction, by turning his back on closely reasoned argument, the writer avoided being accused of pedantry, an unforgivable accusation for socialites and for the *honnête homme*.

Epistolary literature was a first form of fragmentary writing. The collections of letters by Madame de Sévigné contain some 1400, written between 1640 and 1696. Many people are written to, but this body of correspondence is held together by the personality and concerns of their author.

'We confess our failings to remedy by our sincerity the disservice that they do us in the minds of others'; 'There are heroes of evil as there are of good'; 'We do not despise all those who have vices, but we do despise all those who have no virtues': so say maxims 184,185 and 186 by La Rochefoucauld. Readers can contemplate the sense of each of these maxims individually. They can also try to recreate the twists and turns of the author's own thought. The 641 maxims and nineteen reflections on various subjects which make up the work, reorganised and augmented from 1664 to 1678, follow on from one another in no particular order. But these comments on human behaviour do in fact convey a coherent system of thought. La Rochefoucauld cruelly deconstructs in them man's true motivation, by showing that every human action may be explained by the promptings of self-esteem.

In *The Characters*, La Bruyère practised this technique of splitting things up in a more moderate way. The 1120 numbered elements, which appear as maxims, reflections or portraits, are regrouped into sixteen themes schematised under headings like *On Intellectual Work*, *On Women*, *On Living in Town*.

Pascal's *Thoughts* are different. The 800–900 sheets of paper that he left behind – that puzzle made up of a series of notes and fair copy – were not meant to stay like that. They were just some of the materials compiled for an *Apology for the Christian Religion*, an unfinished defence and illustration of the faith. They were to fit into an overall plan with four main elements: the picture of the wretchedness and greatness of man and societies; the realisation of the ignorance of true happiness from which man suffers; the need to search for God; and proofs of God's existence. The work's impact and its strange fascination come, paradoxically, from its unfinished state, perhaps more penetrating and more polished than a definitive version would have been:

> Man's greatness lies in the fact that he knows himself to be wretched. A tree does not know itself to be wretched. Knowing oneself to be wretched amounts to being wretched, but it is a mark of greatness to know oneself to be wretched.
>
> Blaise Pascal,
> *Thoughts*

In the rest of Europe, apart from a flourishing epistolary literature, fragmentary writing was rather despised. It was seen as a sign of weakness in writers incapable of substantial work. The exception, however, was the Spaniard Gracián. The maxims of included in *The Courtie*, which inspired La Rochefoucauld, were not rationally catalogued, as shown, for example, in the titles of texts 98 to 101:

Cifrar la voluntad; Realidad y apariencia;
Varón desengañado: cristiano sabio, cortesano filósofo; La metad del mundo se está riendo de la otra metad, con necedad de todos.

Baltazar Gracián,
El Oráculo manual

Dissimulation; Reality and appearance;
Man undeceived: the wise Christian, the philosophical Courtier;
One half of the world is laughing at the other, and both are laughing at the folly that they have in common.

A flowering heralds a new age

The seventeenth century in Europe simul-taneously marked an ending and a period of transition in the evolution of literary writing. It was primarily the age in which the Baroque came to fruition. But it was also the age during of the elaboration of theories of French classicism that would spread over the entire continent. This coexistence of two great opposing trends was particularly revealing of the diversity of a period which rejected the monolithic. Ideological oppositions – notably between Catholics and Protestants, Jansenists and Jesuits, supporters of an absolute power and upholders of liberty – gave rise to divergent types of aesthetics. Irregularity and regularity confronted each other, a confrontation which produced the quarrel between the Ancients and Moderns towards the end of the century. Mannerism and burlesque each made their suggestions. The realist novel resolutely took the opposite view to the novel of ideals.

This flourishing and its exceptional variety and a literature of ideas are partly explained by the hectic activity of this period. Prolonging the effervescence of the Renaissance, this type of writing continued to flower throughout the eighteenth century. This phenomenon is all the more important in the seventeenth century for its being paired with a twofold liberation. The literature of ideas became secular, gradually freeing itself from the heavy hand of the Churches. It also began to reject pedantry, to eschew specialisation in a desire to appeal to ordinary people. This made it more attractive and more accessible to enlightened amateurs.

The seventeenth century marked an aesthetic reflection of life leading to a definition and a practice of literary genres that heralded their modern function. Different poetic forms were brought into sharper focus. The novel began to escape from the destabilising temptations of history. The theatre severed the ties binding it to religion.

The eighteenth century magnified these tendencies, limited in the seventeenth to certain authors and certain countries, but already clearly defined.

Theatre, Marriage and the Bourgeoisie

A. Piazecki

Let us be as strange as if we had been married a great while.
William Congreve, *The Way of the World*

From the seventeenth century, marriage, as portrayed in European theatre, reflected the way in which the institution had evolved and the rise of the bourgeoisie. In both comedies and tragedies, the theatre signalled the resist-ance of the end of feudalism to an economy based on money rather than land. In front of an increasingly bourgeois audience, the theatrical portrayal of marriage was also a way of celebrating the manners and values of a rising middle class. It became the ideal vehicle for criticism of their attitudes.

The theatricality of marriage

The act of marriage is in itself a theatrical one. It is therefore normal for some forms of theatre to be intimately linked to the celebration of marriage, whether it be the spectacular masquerades put on for aristocrats in the six-teenth and seventeenth centuries, or the rituals characteristically associated with peasant weddings during the same period. In *Fuenteo-vejuna* (1618), for example, the play by Lope de Vega, traditional songs and dances are exploited for their innate theatricality, without compromising the author's freedom to communicate his ideas about honour, an omnipresent theme in Spanish literature. The peasant hero and heroine's wedding feast is at its height when it is brutally gatecrashed by the tyrannical lord of the manor who tries to rape the bride. In order to overcome such provocative behaviour and to safeguard their honour, the peasants have to bring down the tyrant and reunite the couple. Marriage and honour are here inextricably linked to a 'natural' fear of God, which somehow makes it possible to reaffirm the existence of an ideal feudal society. Indeed, although it is in opposition to the hierarchy of the landed aristocracy, the revolt of the peasants was finally pardoned by the king, the highest authority in the land.

Like Lope de Vega, Shakespeare dramatised the lives of characters from every social class, from kings to vagabonds, while retaining a fundamentally aristocratic vision of life. This is particularly noticeable in his last plays, the tragi-comedies *Pericles* (1608), *Cymbeline* (1609–1610) and *The Winter's Tale* (1623), whose plots revolve around aristocratic characters.

All these plays end in royal marriages, themselves potent symbols of unions announcing order and harmony within families and States, after a period of tyranny, separation and suffering. So, in *The Tempest*, the marriage between Miranda and Ferdinand is the ultimate dramatic happening to reinforce Prospero's power and benevolence. Shakespeare lived during a period of increasing social instability: less than thirty years after his death, England was plunged into the horrors of the English Civil War. It is almost as if, in response to the challenges increasingly directed at the social order, Shakespeare wanted to take refuge in a reaffirmation of orthodoxy, an essential element of which was the institution of marriage.

Theatre, marriage, class struggle

Molière's *Le Bourgeois gentilhomme* (*The Bourgeois Gentleman*, 1670) shows just how much the struggles between the classes had increased over the century in the most economically advanced European countries, even while the king's power remained strong. Monsieur Jourdain, the target of Molière's satirical comedy, is absurd in his attempt to use marriage to climb the social ladder. The assumption is that his daughter Lucile, constantly encouraged by Madame Jourdain, is right to want to marry someone from her own class: 'Marriages to those greater than ourselves always have tiresome disadvantages.' Monsieur Jourdain will be punished for his

delusions of grandeur, and everything will turn out for the best in the best of all possible worlds, since, thanks to a trick, Lucile and Cléonte are finally able to marry. All this confirmed what common sense seemed to dictate from the beginning: in terms of behaviour, etiquette and culture, the aristocracy and the bourgeoisie are as different as chalk and cheese. Does Molière's play make us aware of a certain underlying anguish undermining the seventeenth century? Social mobility began to threaten traditional structures. Are the differences between classes more a question of social conditioning than inherited qualities? At the end of the day, what matters most of all is money.

These tensions were vividly demonstrated in English Restoration comedies in which marriage, placed in the context of money and sex, explored both the battles which oppose the classes and those which divide the sexes. The audiences – above all, aristocratic audiences – for these plays were entertained by this vision of a new world order (after the 1660 restoration of Charles II) which appeared cynical and, some people thought, decadent. In these plays marriage could not embody an ideal relationship. More often than not, it was considered as a contract, bound up with problems of freedom and power. The most striking example of this is the scene from Act IV of *The Way of the World* (1700), by William Congreve, in the course of which Miss Millamant and Mirabell set out the clauses for a premarital contract, similar to one we could imagine between two Hollywood movie stars:

> Let us never visit together nor go to a play together, but let us be very strange and well-bred as if we were not married at all.

With Beaumarchais, in *The Marriage of Figaro* (1778), the rivalry between the great aristocrat, Count Almaviva, and his servant, Figaro, is played out and resolved to the latter's advantage in a 'crazy day' which ends with the wedding of Figaro and Suzanne – only a few years before the French Revolution.

The beginnings of bourgeois tragedy

In the eighteenth century the theatre became one of the favourite forms of bourgeois diversion. The values of this social class were demonstrated in the plays of the period. In Germany as in France, with Lessing as with Diderot, the beginnings of bourgeois tragedy were in the air, a form that Ibsen developed so powerfully in the nineteenth century.

When it first began, as in *The London Merchant* (1731) by George Lillo, the tragic thrust of this type of theatre tended to be frustrated by sentimentality. George Barnwell's incorrigible desire to seduce women leads him into crime, preventing him from marrying the daughter of his boss. In the eyes of the upwardly mobile bourgeoisie, such a marriage represented the perfect union of love and wealth. Social life and morality were idealised and only human life itself was imperfect. For the moment, the moral virtues affirmed by this new class remained too sacred to be themselves the source of a drama.

Yet these same values were the subject of criticism in comedies. The most classic illustration of this is John Gay's satirical musical *The Beggar's Opera* (1728). The heroine, Polly Peachum, daughter of a receiver of stolen goods, falls in love with a highwayman, Macheath. Though the play ends with their wedding, it is only a case of producing a comic effect by giving a twist to the plot: Macheath was going to be hanged for his crimes, but he is pardoned at the last minute. His marriage to Polly, one of the many women he has ardently pursued, is merely a parody. Two hundred years later, this vigorous satire of the eighteenth-century bourgeoisie gave Brecht the ideal subject matter for his *The Threepenny Opera* (1928) which he transposed to Victorian London and, indirectly, to Germany's economic chaos in the 1920s. The closer we get to nineteenth-century melodrama, the more various social types are defined, the more stereotyped the notions become of 'good' and 'evil'. Marriage represents the high point of harmonious human relationships, legitimising physical desire and laying the necessary foundations for an honest, hard-working, prosperous life. Other themes are touched on, such as social injustice, but the bottom line remains a study of bourgeois values and principles, allied to a rarely questioned conventional morality.

> You who are girls, know this anyway, that at the end of a fortnight of marriage, your husband will leave your bed for a table, then a table for the tavern, and that you have to resign yourself to it or nurse your tears in a corner.
>
> Federico García Lorca,
> *The House of Bernarda Alba*

During the nineteenth century, Scandinavian society, conservative and ponderous, saw the emergence of two significant dramatists of contemporary theatre: Ibsen and Strindberg.

Ibsen and Strindberg

In *The Pillars of Society* (1877), *A Doll's House* (1879), *Ghosts* (1881) and *An Enemy of the People* (1882), Ibsen assailed bourgeois complacency. He revealed its principles as so many deceptions; the struggles between the individual and their social context reveal the weakness and inflexibility of society's moral rules. In *A Doll's House*, which takes place in the Norwegian countryside, the plot owes much to the traditional mechanisms of melodrama, but, towards the end of the piece, there a new dimension of social tragedy is linked to bourgeois life. Nora Helmer shows an individual sense of responsibility which is directly opposed to the more conventional vision of her role as wife and mother. In order to assert her own identity, she finds herself obliged to break up her family and leave a husband who is incapable of treating her as a mature woman. There is no place for her in a society in which the institution of marriage is a repressive iron collar.

Strindberg's vision of marriage is even more pessimistic and in total opposition to bourgeois conventions. In describing human relationships as an incessant battle of the sexes for power, he shows that marriage is anything but a state of happy harmony. In *Miss Julie* (1888), for example, social classes and the sexes are involved in a fight described from a deeply misogynistic viewpoint. As Strindberg emphasised in his preface: 'Miss Julie is a modern character – not that the woman who is only half a woman, who hates men, has not always existed: but she has just been discovered, she has put herself forward and is making a noise. The half-woman is a type who elbows a way for herself, who sells herself for power, decorations, distinctions and diplomas as she did in former days for money: a testimony to her decadence.'

In terms of the evolution of the theatre in Europe, as much in terms of form as content, Strindberg was one of the most influential authors of the twentieth century. The German expressionist movement, which developed between 1912 and the early 1920s, owes a lot to works like *A Dream Play* (1902). As a theatre movement, it was one of the first artistic revolts against bourgeois society.

Expressionism

Expressionism was passionate, tragic, iconoclastic. Often voluntarily irrational, it incited people to rebellion. On a practical level, the areas implicated by this rebellion remained vague; not surprisingly, some aspects of the movement were involved in fascism. As with many subsequent avant-garde movements, the main aim was to attack the *status quo* and to aggressively defy the conventions of a respectable bourgeois existence in which marriage represented a solid tradition of order and stability. In *Murderer, Hope of Women* (1907) by Oscar Kokoschka, relationships between men and women are described as a bestial struggle for power. In *From Dawn to Midnight* (1917) by Georg Kaiser, marriage was considered as the basis for a materialist society stifling all hope of freedom and personal growth. Such ideas became fashionable again in the 1960s. Though it was often openly sexist, not to say fascist, the expressionist movement was, above all, liberating, for it did

not hesitate to oppose the traditions and the naturalism which dominated art at that time. Most of the authors of plays which attacked the bourgeoisie with such vehemence were themselves products of it – just like their audience! But as an experimental movement in opposition to the 'establishment', it prepared the way for a politics of theatre developed in Weimar Germany by Piscator and Brecht. During this same period, Federico García Lorca similarly attacked the particularly repressive orthodoxy of Catholic Spain. He also chose avant-garde forms like surrealism to distance himself from the conventional bourgeois theatre, the predominant form of which was naturalism.

While attacks against conventional bourgeois morality had been repressed in the nineteenth century, they became the rule in what we call 'serious' theatre.

In former times marriage offered a happy end to comedies, providing for a time the very substance of the element of comedy. What today we would consider to be 'serious' theatre was nothing more than the reflection of a profound pessimism about the future of human relationships. How many European dramatists earned their living by defending traditionally bourgeois values and principles like a stable marriage, the family, private property and work? Nevertheless, whether it was the irony of fate or the dialectic of history, dissident authors were encouraged by their public and financial aid committees who themselves emerged from the ranks of the bourgeoisie.

Van den Vondel (1587–1679)

K. Porteman

Without God, nobody feels safe.
Joost Van den Vondel, *Lucifer*

It is no easy task to present Vondel as a 'monumental' figure in Western literature: he just about survives, if that, in the collective European memory. His work originated from a small language area, which, in its time, made no great international stir, except in Germany. It was only translated later into the major European languages in a fragmentary and mediocre way. In its most important parts, this work belongs to a stylistic and ideological trend that exerted very little influence on literary tradition: Catholic baroque, self-confident and exuberant. In the final analysis, set alongside the tragedies of Shakespeare or Racine, which revolve around the effects of human passions, Vondel's tragedies give the impression of being theoretical constructs, rich in poetry, it is true, but, above all, well thought-out intellectually. Because the plays deal with problems of conscience with strong metaphysical and religious repercussions, their staging often encountered deeply rooted prejudices.

However, in the specialist circles of this period there is surprising unanimity: Vondel's varied work is of a high level of quality and is pre-eminently important for Europe from a cultural historical viewpoint.

A Dutch Catholic's destiny

Joost Van den Vondel was born on 17 November 1587 in Cologne. His Anabaptist parents had fled there from Antwerp and, in 1595, they also had to leave the city on the Rhine. After wandering through Germany, the family settled in Amsterdam in 1597 where it started a silk and hosiery business which Vondel later inherited. His first poems, some of which were in French, date from 1605. In the 1620s Vondel distanced himself from his fellow Anabaptist immigrants, at the cost of a long period of discouragement. He then embraced a tolerant form of humanism before converting to Catholicism around 1640. This self-taught man, surrounded by literary friends, gradually became Holland's greatest poet. When Vondel's son, who had taken over the business, was declared insolvent in 1656, Amsterdam granted Vondel a sinecure in a firm of pawnbrokers. He continued to write to a ripe old age and died on 5 February 1679.

Vondel's presence made itself felt for many years in the subsequent development of Dutch intellectual life. During the spiritual adventure of the remarkable seventeenth century, the poet played a significant part in asserting Holland's cultural awareness and in the intellectual and social emancipation of Dutch Catholics. One of the most curious things in the tribute still rendered to Vondel is the annual performance, in Amsterdam, in January, of his play *Gysbrecht van Aemstel* with which he had inaugurated the town's new theatre on 3 January 1638. This is quintessentially a tragedy about Amsterdam life constructed around a surprising mixture of motifs taken from Virgil, Christianity and national history.

The master of Biblical tragedy

Vondel made a unique contribution to European drama in the seventeenth century as the author of twenty-four original tragedies. He was undoubtedly one of the great originators of modern Biblical tragedy (one of his lifelong ambitions) and the first to conceive of it along the lines of Greek tragedy in *Gebroeders* (*The Brothers*, 1640). In this richly dressed, colourful and moving play, the subject of which is the revenge of the Gibeonites (2 Samuel 21: 1–14), David finds himself forced to have seven young men in his family executed. Vondel concentrates on the theme, borrowed from Sophocles, of suffering deferred, on David's inner struggle to carry out this 'unnatural' punishment and on the complex pathos of conflicts within a single family.

David's tormented family also serve Vondel as a counterpart to the Greek Atridae. In the introduction to his play *Jephthah*, he called for the application of Aristotelian theories to theatrical works. Several dramatic masterpieces, the titles of which have become household words in Dutch literature, grew from this desire to create a 'modern' tragedy based on a marriage between Aristotelian rules and a view of life in keeping with the period.

Vondel's dramatic work came to fruition

gradually. He began by writing various devotional plays, in which he drew attention to himself as a talented innovator within a strong national tradition of forceful rhetoric. His vocation as a 'modern' dramatist really began after 1620 with translations of Seneca. From 1640, with his discovery of Greek tragedy, Vondel became obsessed by Seneca's themes. By now he had abandoned his pretensions to write epics and had converted to Catholicism. This slow process bore fruit in an impressive series of original plays in which he continually swam against the prevailing fashionable tide. As a result, after many resounding successes, he distanced himself from the stage.

The different stages of this process are easily traced. Vondel began with plays about martyrs which were Catholic in character, and with tragedies that articulated a universal principle and in which the atmosphere was increasingly of Classical Greece. He went on to dualist dramas about the life-and-death struggle between good and evil. He finally wrote plays that hinged on the representation of a real-life episode the last of which, *Noach* (*Noah*, 1667), was an original synthesis of the old Christian drama of the Redemption and Greek tragedy. Few European dramatists, like Vondel, have justified and explained their own evolution by means of lengthy introductions to their plays. This poetic theorizing formed part of the most interesting metatexts on seventeenth-century theatre, particularly as it served to introduce works which were a major part of the collective imagination of Western Baroque: stories of sons who rebelled, fathers who were humbled and raised, the assertiveness of the individual, the fascination with pride and the fall, reason, passion and faith.

First there was the scintillating *Lucifer* (1654), a dualist drama about Satan's fall and the heavenly angels who were with him. Act V contains what is possibly Baroque literature's most memorable catastrophe. The juxtaposition of the verse's priestly grandiloquence and a daring setting – the scene takes place in heaven! – which, at the time, met with a certain amount of disapproval, give this typically political drama extraordinary depth. The great conflicts of the seventeenth century appear in a cosmic light: revolt against the established order in society, frictions between an absolutist state and feudalism, humility and arrogance, the danger of overly seductive rhetoric. Calvinist ministers, for whom it constituted blasphemy, had the celestial setting of the play banned after only two performances. *Lucifer* was, nevertheless, reprinted seven times in a single year. The play *Adam in ballingschap* (*Adam Exiled*), published in 1664, which Vondel called 'the tragedy to end all tragedies', belongs to the same celestial cycle, not merely because it is about the fall of the first human couple, but also because its author succeeded in presenting in its original form the event he considered after the publication of *Jephthah* as the tragedy at the heart of things. The absolute happiness of paradise is opposed to a state of the most abject grief. Vondel wrote this when he was nearly 75 years old, the most lyrical and poetic of his tragedies, full of exquisitely sensual verses on conjugal love. In a vision of magnificent reach and scope, he placed eros alongside divine love.

A variety of poetic inspirations

Vondel's monumental didactic poems are another often neglected contribution to European Baroque. There are didactic poems on the Eucharist (1645), on the greatness of the Catholic Church (1663) and, above all, there are the *Bespielingen van Godt en Godtsdienst* (*Meditations on God and Religion*, 1662) – a pinnacle of poetic achievement, an accumulation of lyrically phrased reflections on God and religion in 7352 verses. This theodicy was greeted, too hastily perhaps, as the first orthodox Catholic refutation of Spinoza's monism. There is more to this work, however, than theological and philosophical erudition. Fear of the transcendent and religious fervour go hand-in-hand with intelligent, pleading polemics. The third book of the *Meditations* is a masterly exposition of a Catholic and Baroque world view.

The most captivating part of Vondel's poetic output is still, even today, the hundreds of poems in various genres (occasional works) in which he loyally praised or pitilessly castigated Amsterdam and the United Provinces, a republic unique in the way it was governed at that time. In these occasional works Vondel was an uncompromisingly painstaking observer passionately seeking peaceful solutions to problems. He drew attention to the often difficult political situation of the Low Countries both at home and abroad, the atrocities committed during the Thirty Years' War, the execution of the King of England and the Turkish threat. Vondel was a staunch and provocative defender of national liberty, religious tolerance and freedom of conscience. These three considerations formed the basis for an impressive series of satirical poems in various genres which became an integral part of Dutch culture's classical heritage. The most telling poems are the many texts in which, at considerable personal risk, Vondel defended Oldenbarneveldt, the Great Pensionary of Holland who was beheaded in 1619 on the orders of Maurice of Nassau acting under pressure exerted by Calvinist fundamentalists. For Vondel this statesman was a symbol of peace, of resistance to religious sectarianism, of opposition to the rampant opportunism of the Princes of Orange (Maurice of Nassau and later William II). In this respect his *pièce à clé* of 1625, *Palamedes*, is a European curiosity. Taking his inspiration from ancient Troy and writing in a Senecan manner, Vondel secularises the type of tragedy concerned with religious martyrdoms, and creates the kind of hero we shall often meet again: faithful to his principles but destroyed because of them.

Vondel was not just a dissenting voice. His hymns celebrated the great achievements of Holland's golden century, commerce and shipping in Amsterdam, the political peace-making role it played, architecture, music and painting. In 1653, the painters of Amsterdam paid him tribute and crowned him as their new Apollo. No poet has ever described with such lyricism so many works of art and pictures. All Vondel's work was tremendously visual: descriptions of nature and representations of the human face are often formulated in the

phraseology current in an artist's studio. He presents his play *The Brothers* under the guise of a fictitious Rubens accompanied by detailed explanations. His poetry has often been compared to Ruben's paintings: both the poet and the painter can be seen as the pre-eminent representatives of European Baroque.

Comenius (1592–1670)

V. Peska

The time will come, Comenius, when the majority of good men will honour you, and honour your works, your hopes and your wishes.

Gottfried Wilhelm Leibniz in a 1671 poem

Born on 28 March 1592 in Nivnice in Southern Moravia, into a family of Bohemian brethren, orphaned at the age of twelve, sent to finish his studies at the Protestant Academy of Herborn and at the University of Heidelberg, ordained pastor in 1616, the young Jan Amos Komenský – Comenius – had as his one single aim to serve his country and his church which had developed from the Hussite tradition and the teaching of the pacifist Petr Chelčický. His country's fate would decide otherwise.

A work of unusual destiny

Pastor, preacher, theologian – Comenius was the first bishop of the Bohemian brethren – teacher, author of school textbooks, educational theorist and the inventor of a grand idea for the original and global reform of humanity, Comenius produced a huge amount of work in all these areas: more than 200 brochures and pamphlets. Like his eventful and tragic existence, the destiny of his work was exceptional and unusual. He was immediately recognised for his language handbooks, then for his didactic works. After his death, his didactic works were neglected, only to reappear in the second half of the nineteenth century; his ideas on agricultural enrichment were reread after 1930. There were various reasons for this: a dearth of national intellectual support (exiles became assimilated into their host countries); the almost complete eviction of scholars in his homeland where the 'outlaw' only reappeared with the 'national Renaissance' after the end of the eighteenth century; the nobility's distrust of his democratic and egalitarian educational system; the disastrous effect that accusations of 'mysticism' had on him, and his misfounded trust in 'revelation', contrary to the rationalism of the Enlightenment.

Even before finishing his university studies, Comenius undertook two huge works: a dictionary (*Poklad jasyka českého*, *Treasury of the Czech Language*, compiled between 1612 and 1656, lost in the fire in the Polish town of Leszno) and a first encyclopedia in Czech, the *Theatrum universatis rerum* (1624–1627, twenty-eight volumes planned), incomplete and for the most part lost. He also compiled and published several treatises, notably his reflections on the poor in society, *Listové do nebe* (*Letters to Heaven*, 1619), and enriched the theory of oratory and Czech poetry.

After the defeat of the White Mountain, which ended independence for the kingdom of Bohemia in revolt against the Catholic Hapsburgs, Comenius refused to go into exile, hiding on the lands of noblemen who had escaped confiscations. He carefully prepared a new edition of *Kancionál* (*Songbook*, 1659) about the Bohemian brethren with translations and his personal creations. Some of his writings were still published in Prague by the clandestine printing press of the Bohemian brothers, like his *Přemyšlování o dokonalosti křesťanské* (*Reflections on Christian Perfection*, 1622) or the first two volumes of *Truchlivý* (*The Afflicted One*, 1623–1624) written in dialogue. These began a series of 'consolatory' books that he wrote after 1648.

A creator of allegories

In this secrecy, Comenius also wrote his most important work, *Labyrint světa a Ráj srdce* (*The Labyrinth of the World and the Paradise of the Heart*, written in 1623, published abroad in 1631 and 1663). In this allegory, an honest young man in search of his vocation, trying to make sense of his life, travels through a town in which he observes all social categories: corporations, professions and trades. He is accompanied by two strange characters: one, 'I-know-all-pass-through-all', explains wordly matters to him with assurance and optimism. The other, 'Illusion', provides him with deforming lenses which, badly focused, nevertheless allow him to glimpse the reality of men and of their affairs. Later the young pilgrim arrives at the castle of Queen 'Wisdom' to learn, in the presence of Solomon, that truth and wisdom do not belong in this world. Disillusioned and desperate, the young man then hears an inner voice inviting him to return 'to the house of his heart'. There, far from temptations, blindness and the tumult of the world, his soul finally experiences peace with God.

Thanks to its special features and undeniable qualities, this work was published in Bohemia from 1782 and became increasingly popular in Europe generally. Drawn to the English translation, the father of Marguerite Yourcenar translated it and published it in Lille in 1906; his daughter borrowed the first part of the title for her memoirs.

Comenius prolonged his meditation with a philosophical/theological treatise in which he came close to the theories of Jacob Böhme, *Centrum securitatis* (*The Centre of Security*, written c.1625, published abroad in 1633 and 1663). Here he conceived of the world as a disc turning around its God-axis; the more men stray from the centre, the more they expose themselves to troubles, disorders and uncertainties.

As the situation became more dangerous in the Czech homelands, Comenius went into voluntary exile in 1628, never imagining that his exile would last for forty-two years. His three sojourns in the little Polish town of Leszno, between 1628 and 1656, were broken by a visit to London (1641–1642), a stay in The Netherlands (marked by an encounter

with Descartes, an invitation to Paris superseded by the death of Richelieu), educational
missions for Sweden at Elblang (1642–1648)
and for the Prince of Transylvania Rákoczy
in Hungary (1650–1654). After the fire of
Leszno and the resulting destruction of his
library and of most of his manuscripts,
Comenius found a final refuge in Amsterdam
thanks to the generosity of the businessman
Lawrence de Geer.

The author of school textbooks

Comenius' international reputation was solidly
established by manuals which revolutionised
the teaching of Latin and foreign languages,
of grammar and the sciences and also the
publication of pedagogical works.

The masterpiece remains the first illustrated
school textbook *Orbis* (*sensualium*) *pictus* (*The
World in Pictures*, 1658, in Latin–German).
This was, in fact, the 'Janua' restructured and
perfected, all chapters in which were preceded
by an illustration of the particular theme and
in which the figures designating things, people
and activities refer us to the text. The success
of this manual-cum-encyclopedia was immense
– even Goethe praised it! – and persisted
into the nineteenth century with about 300
bilingual, trilingual and quadrilingual editions
and adaptations.

Gradually left unread after his death, the
work was rediscovered during the nineteenth
century. Calling Comenius 'a genius of light,
a powerful inventor, the Galileo of education',
Michelet grasped the fundamental significance
of his work. According to Illich, Comenius
remained 'one of the greatest precursors of the
theories of the modern school'.

Towards 1648, the pedagogical and didactic
axis of Comenius' work was, to all intents
and purposes, complete. Now – between the
conclusion of the Treaty of Westphalia and
its ratification two years later – all hopes of
return for the exiles vanished and the Czech
nation, crushed by the Hapsburgs, was left to
its fate. The last bishop of the Bohemian
brethren wrote new 'consolatory' pamphlets,
particularly the heart-rending *Kšaft umírajíci*

matky Jednoty bratrské (*Last Will and Testament
of the Protestant Unity of Brethren, Dying
Mother*, 1650). Here he took leave of his
country, to which his scattered church left
a spiritual message. Comenius inserted the
following prophetic words, never forgotten
by Czechs: 'once the storm of anger that our
sins have drawn down on our heads has
passed, the government of your affairs will
revert to your hands, Czech people!' In 1668,
in *Unum necessarium* (*The One Thing that is
Necessary*), 'the man of ardent aspirations'
drew up the last balance sheet of his life,
alluding to his bitter memories, his love, his
faith in the human spirit and his continual
hope for the future.

As he had done fifty years earlier, Comenius
found some 'consolation' in the 'revelations'
or 'prophecies' of various seers who predicted
the end of the persecution of the Protestants.
He collected these thoughts in *Lux in tenebris*
(1657) and *Lux e tenebris* (1665). He sent a
copy of the latter to Louis XIV, asking him to
convene a 'council' to solve the problems of
Europe. Such 'revelations' kept alive the hopes
of the oppressed and the outlawed by giving
them the promise of a future Kingdom of God
on earth. Shortly before his death, Comenius
was brutally attacked for these debatable ideas,
but his teaching and philosophical works were
also unjustly criticised.

The reform of human affairs

Apart from these publications, Comenius
carried out other historical, metaphysical and
polemical research, prepared the edition of his
complete didactic works, and increasingly
concentrated on what he thought of as his
essential work. From the beginning of the
1630s, he had reflected on the idea of bringing
together, classifying and synthesising human
knowledge in order to attain truth, wisdom
and the reformation of human affairs, to
rescue men from 'the labyrinth of the world'
and to promote universal peace and harmony.

Before inviting Comenius to discuss his
project, his friends in England published
Pansophiæ prodromus (*Prodromus of Pansophia*,

1637 and 1639), which circulated among European intellectuals. Mersenne told Descartes about it and Descartes himself discussed it with Comenius in 1642. Richelieu wanted him to found a 'pansophical school' in Paris. After several other preparatory works, notably *Via lucis* (*The Way of Light*, written in London, only published in 1668), Comenius formulated his ideas in seven volumes collected as *De rerum humanarum emendatione consultatio catholica* (*The Universal Consultation on the Reform of Human Affairs*). Only two volumes were published in his lifetime. The others were not completely finished and were only rediscovered in manuscript form in 1934 in Germany and published in Prague in 1966.

Comenius situated his project in the light of a neo-Platonic metaphysic. Reason and the light of spirituality went hand-in-hand to achieve, thanks to man's active, creative role, a peaceful, reconciled, tolerant community made up of equal individuals who were brothers in solidarity.

Comenius' project – a Utopian one? – was organically linked to education. This is particularly apparent in Volume IV of the *Consultation, Pampœdia*. Only the consistent education of mankind can lead humanity to a general awakening (Volume I, *Panegersia*, with an introduction addressed 'to Europeans'), enlighten minds with faith and reason (Volume II, *Panaugia*) and be conducive to universal wisdom 'based on human nature itself' (Volume III, *Pansophia*). Such an education can also enable a perfect understanding between men thanks to a universal language (Volume V, *Panglottia*) and result in a general reform of the affairs of the human race, managed by various supreme institutions (Volume VI, *Panorthosia*). The final volume (*Pannuthesia*) was an ultimate 'universal admonishment' to action and to bring about this 'reform'.

Known only in its broad lines and in its first two volumes (1662), the dynamic and open 'pansophical' thought of Comenius attracted Leibniz and many other representatives of the German Enlightenment. It also made its mark on 'Pietism' (Francke). It impressed Herder with its humanism. The work and philosophical and educational thought of 'the teacher of peoples' occupied a special niche between humanism, Baroque and the Enlightenment in the seventeenth century. They were the object of a rebirth of interest and a well-deserved gratitude. Europe. The Czechs themselves saw in Comenius one of their most worthy cultural and ethical figures. Between Hus and Masaryk, this exile who believed in universalism remains to this day one of their fundamental points of reference.

Milton (1608–1674)

A. Yearling

Regarded for generations as a literary figure to be ranked only with Chaucer and Shakespeare, John Milton nevertheless presents problems for the modern reader who lives in a world of weakened religious faith and whose certainties are no longer those of the seventeenth century. Even by the standards of his own time, Milton was a man remarkable for his learning, his ambitions and the force of his personality. In some ways embodying the thought and tendencies of seventeenth-century puritanism, he was a radical in the cause of liberty; yet he also upheld artistic ideals carried on from Antiquity and from the previous Elizabethan era. He showed in both his verse and prose writings the force of genius. And as he writes with such massive conviction, so the twentieth-century reader may find himself resisting and arguing: an appropriate response, since Milton's is a combative art. His styles, too, are elevated, and strange to the modern taste: epic verse and the lengthy prose sentences of Ciceronian rhetoric coexist with an ornate manner harking back to the beauties of Spenser and Shakespeare. His classicism is softened by that lyricism and ingenuity of thought associated with the English Renaissance.

That he should write in these ways is easily accounted for. Naturally gifted in his youth, he received a thorough education in both the classical and recent authors at St Paul's School and Cambridge University. On graduating, he devoted six years to perfecting his studies at his father's house in the country: 'I gave myself up with the most complete leisure to reading,' studying mathematics, music, and theology as well as literature. In effect his ambition was the same as Spenser's in the previous century: to prove that English could be as noble and poetical a language as those – Greek, Latin, and Italian – that had conveyed the greatest flowering of European culture. He toured Europe, spending much time in Italy where he visited the aged Galileo as well as 'contracting intimacy with many noble and learned men, assiduously attending their private academies'. But he cut short his visit in 1639: 'the sad news of the English Civil War recalled me: for I thought it shameful, while my countrymen were fighting for their liberty at home, that I should be peacefully travelling for culture.'

By this time Milton had composed sonnets, elegies, odes, a masque and other verse of various sorts, often in direct emulation of traditional forms in which poetical virtuosity was required; he now turned his attention to writing prose pamphlets, idealistically setting forth a vision of a society reformed in its religious and civil customs.

Bishops should be removed from the church; kings may be overthrown; divorce laws should be liberalised; censorship of the press abolished; education reformed. A commonwealth under a properly understood Law of God would give example in these matters to the rest of Europe. And when the English king had indeed been deposed and beheaded, and a commonwealth established under Cromwell, Milton found himself offered the post of official spokesman for the nation. As Secretary for the Foreign Tongues in the Council of State, he had the duty of justifying the puritan regime and replying to the barrage of hostile propaganda emanating from the European mainland to which the defeated Royalists had largely fled. He did this in Latin, the international language, in a series of massive *Defences*. And despite the fact that he was now blind, his confidence was such that he began

work on his epic poem *Paradise Lost*, dealing with the primal war between God and Satan which led on to the Fall of Man. To write a genuine epic would forever install his name in that select pantheon alongside Homer and Virgil: the summits of his ambition would be largely conquered. Towards the end of his life he consolidated his aspirations with a tragedy after the ancient Greek models, *Samson Agonistes*, as well as with a 'brief epic' on Christ's temptations in the desert, *Paradise Regained*. England's spokesman would also prove to be her loftiest poet.

Yet there is another side to all this. The sheer force of Milton's individuality, his manifest superiority to those around him, his perpetual certainty that he was in the right, made him into someone that no set system could ever accommodate: a natural rebel by energy and temperament. His early pamphlets were illegal (we would call them the 'underground press'): in an age when all publications had to be officially licensed, his radical opinions made him unacceptable even to his fellow puritans and to their regime that was willing to go as far as countenancing regicide. In these pamphlets he boldly reinterpreted history and manipulated the doctrines of the Bible, certain of his justification in his own vision of what God intended for man. Those who argued against him were abused and held up to ridicule. All this led to petitions to have him imprisoned. And when the regime did eventually absorb him and use him, and when that regime collapsed with the restoration of the monarchy in 1660, Milton again became a rebel in another sense, with the death penalty for treason hanging for a while over him. His violent energies, his uncompromising confrontations with orthodox opinion, make all of his major works fascinatingly unstable. A witty and acute remark is that if Milton had been placed in the Garden of Eden, he would at once have eaten the forbidden fruit, then written a pamphlet justifying his action: *Paradise Lost* is perpetually divided between the heroic but evil dynamism of Satan, and the duty of obedience owed to the authority of God. In the same way, his early masque known as *Comus* had rendered its provocatively tempting enchanter more attractive than the essentially passive Lady, the force of goodness he seeks to corrupt; and the great pamphlet on the evils of censorship, *Areopagitica*, collapses into spectacular self-negation when Milton's urge towards universal liberation comes into conflict with his horror of allowing the Roman Church to spread its doctrines.

The coexistence of these tensions in Milton's work takes various forms. In his epic he allows a reference to Galileo's telescopic discoveries to sit alongside the archaic cosmos of Ptolemy, with the Earth at the centre of a universe of crystalline spheres. In his tracts on divorce he sets forth proposals more generously radical than have even to this day been adopted in most lands, but always with the underlying supposition of women's innate inferiority to men. When he writes of Christ in *Paradise Regained* he makes him simultaneously the figure recognizable from the Gospels, and a learned theorist with a cast of mind distinctly similar to that of his author. Milton shows himself devout, yet independent. William Blake was only exaggerating slightly when he wrote, more than a century later, that 'Milton was of the devil's party without realizing it.'

It would be wrong to see in this self-divided Milton a figure given to unconsidered blunders, for he thought deeply about the nature of his literary undertakings. *Paradise Lost* is the outcome of years of preparation in religious and literary studies. Yet the divided impulses remain, and it is fascinating to watch Milton wrestling painfully with them. The subject that he chose for his epic is the sin of disobedience, and in casting it into extended narrative form Milton consciously encountered his divided urges head-on. *Paradise Lost* was originally intended to be a sacred tragedy; the epic poem was to concern King Arthur. In the end, Milton decided on a sacred subject as the only proper one for a latter-day epic, 'to justify the ways of God to men', but the traditional procedures of such poems – the elevated recounting of heroic actions, lengthily described with digressions and flashbacks

against the background of an ordered cosmos – had to be applied almost forcibly to the brief story of Creation and Fall found in the Book of Genesis. To allow any heroic action at all, material from elsewhere in the Bible, and from theological tradition, had to be added. Milton's story thus begins with Satan, cast into Hell with his rebel angels after making war in Heaven, deciding on revenge by corrupting the newly-created Adam and Eve. All this is foreseen in Heaven, and God the Son offers himself as atonement for mankind's fault. Satan's first attempt is repulsed by guardian angels, but he succeeds when he later returns to Eden in the guise of a serpent. Adam and Eve are expelled from their paradise into a fallen world, but not before they have been granted a consolatory vision of God's eventual triumph through Christ. Into this narrative Milton slots accounts of the war in Heaven and the creation of the world, as recounted to Adam by angelic messengers. He thus gives himself opportunities for as various a range of episodes as possible. The restless and tormented Satan has a dramatic function closest to that of the classical hero. But heroic action is not confined to Satan: Christ's offering of himself to save mankind and Adam's decision to join Eve in disobedience rather than lose her are examples of individual heroism, though of very different moral worth. And there are full-scale battles, as in the *Iliad* and *Aeneid*. But whereas in those epics the actions were those of humans on a grand scale, the majority of Milton's personages are divine; he must continually remind us that his descriptions are a sort of code, reducing transcendental events into comprehensible terms. Often this is effective: the reader understands Satan by the humanness of his passions, and is impressed by their superhuman intensity. Such empathy becomes dangerous, though, for the forces of good do not emerge well from this sort of reductive treatment. God the Father argues, jests, defends himself against possible criticism and deceives the rebels about the extent of his power. He thus becomes quite untranscendental, and less the fount of all positive qualities required by the poem's scheme. The Son, for all that he is shown as the architect and saviour of the world, is by his very divinity made to seem like someone going through the motions of significant action only. When all the host of Heaven shrink back from offering themselves up to death for man's sake, the Son's self-sacrifice is undercut by his prompt admission that 'death' for him will be no more than a temporary inconvenience. At such moments, the vast issues at stake dwindle into play-acting, and our natural reaction is to find the poem's chief value in the depiction of Satan and his straightforward fortitude. Even worse than arguing with Milton's religious and moral theme, we are tempted to discount it.

That he should not succeed in attempting 'things unattempted yet in prose or rhyme' is not altogether surprising. What do succeed in his epic are many other things, from the scene-painting of the 'darkness visible' of Hell, to the brilliantly confusing yet persuasive rhetoric of Satan's speeches of temptation to Eve; from the vividly-imagined catalogue of the works of the world's creation, to the psychologically acute portrayal of Adam's and Eve's behaviour after they fall from innocence. And Milton's language, with its strong Latinate bias (which has caused some commentators to query how far Milton is a genuine writer of English at all), achieves in a multitude of passages not only the necessary generalized grandeur, but also an expressive precision remarkable on such a large scale. If he usually lacks Homer's sublime plainness, he emulates Virgil's more subtle and selfconscious artistry. If *Paradise Lost* – perhaps inevitably – fails in its avowed intention to explain God to men, its poetic power remains hugely imposing. Religious thought in England was to move on from the enlightened fundamentalism of Milton as the eighteenth century succeeded the seventeenth; but Milton as a poet of grand designs was to impress and influence whole later generations of writers.

The falling-off in poetic power that many have felt in the final two books of the poem may be accounted for by Milton's shattering disappointment at the restoration of the monarchy. To him it must have seemed that everything he had championed had been lost in what he called 'a game of folly'. The traumatic shocks for many Englishmen of revolution, regicide and commonwealth were absorbed and gradually healed in a new constitutional hierarchy of king, bishops, factional politics and the national habit of compromise. Milton was left stranded: aesthetically and spiritually, his reaction was two-fold. His tragedy *Samson Agonistes* returns to an Old Testament world of simplicities. God tells his elect what to do: they disobey and are wretched, or obey and win through to fame. The situation, with a hero now blind and powerless betrayed by those he trusted most, may have attracted Milton by its relevance to his own position; and anger and bitterness are much on view. In this world God's champion may justifiably be violent in the cause of a black-and-white morality where pity for human frailty finds no place: 'all wickedness is weakness', as the hero tells his treacherous wife Dalila. These primitive certitudes echo the crusading spirit of the civil wars twenty years earlier. Yet at the same time, and published in the same volume, *Paradise Regained* cele-brates a submissive and inward doctrine of 'new heroism', characterised by Milton as an essentially passive attitude of patience and fortitude: 'who best can suffer, best can do'. This is exemplified in Christ, who resists Satan's offered temptations with stern obe-dience to the will of God. The old Miltonic harshness is still present, as when Jesus is made to say that he has not come to save men 'enslaved' by the sins of their own appetites; and this Christ remains aloof and unloveable. For many readers this, along with the failure in *Paradise Lost* to present a deity who is truly a God of Love, makes Milton a champion of a false version of Christianity; but in truth it is a mark of how far English, and European, culture has travelled since that seventeenth-century heyday of Jansenist and Puritan. Milton, archaic in his conception of the poet's role as an inspired seer, celebrator of the rugged religion of the Reformation, impure classicist of the Baroque era, was in many ways a majestic termination, and the mid-seventeenth century was the last point at which his doctrines could have been so whole-heartedly expressed, and in language so elevated from normal usage.

Calderón (1600–1681)

A. Sanchez-Trigueros

One cannot get from paper either the sonority or the visual splendour of the boards.
                    Pedro Calderón de la Barca

Don Pedro Calderón de la Barca, one of the most important figures of the Baroque or classical period in Spain, first followed the ways opened up by Lope de Vega, who originated what is called the 'Spanish national theatre'. To be able to describe Calderón's work we must compare it with the theatrical inheritance that the dramatist, consciously and progressively, reorganised, refined and deepened. Calderón's theatre concentrated the plot-lines of the action. He thus simplified the basic framework and clarified the exposition of the conflict. His plays reduced the number of characters, placing them in a hierarchy and giving them greater contrast, depth and reality. The topics tackled and the underlying ideology were more clearly marked than in the theatre of the preceding age: Calderón put pure philosophy on stage. He often had recourse to symbolism and allegory, thus giving the religious play a new direction. He made use of a literary language new to the stage, far removed from the spontaneity and transparency of his predecessors. Above all, he took limitless advantage of stage architecture and the increasingly elaborate techniques of staging that were at his disposal.

A new art of writing comedy

Calderón has, in a way, been over-confined to the precincts of a literary history which particularly emphasised the stylistic, literary and ideological value of his work. However important these values were, we now recognise that they were less important than his purely theatrical greatness, his complete understanding of the visual impact of how a scene, his ability to experiment with various genres and themes which allow him to use new forms and stage effects. For those of us who have Wagner's 'Gesamtkunstwerk' in mind, we can say that Calderón conceived of his theatre as a total piece of art which is why he was one of the initiators of opera in Spain. We can only appreciate Calderón's theatre when it is performed, in the presence of its stagecraft and its choreography. The dramatist himself told his readers: 'One cannot get from paper either the sonority or the visual splendour of the boards.'

Let us imagine the splendid possibilities for staging offered by the court of the last kings of the House of Austria – Calderón was their private chaplain – by the ecclesiastical and municipal authorities and also by the guilds. Let us also imagine the palace precincts, whose construction was overseen by Italian engineers, or the magnificent setting of the religious and popular celebrations of Corpus Christi. The facilities for stage effects placed at Calderón's disposal were far superior to those afforded by the 'corral' of the popular theatre – which, however, Calderón never despised or abandoned. So when Calderón imagined and composed his plays, he not only included the original stage effects which a popular audience would have expected. He also had new opportunities to change the stage scenery and to make use of acoustics and footlights. The wings and the lighting, choral and instrumental music, the interplay of light and shadow, the right props, life-sized mechanical dolls and other inventions: everything could offer a thousand surprises in a new dramatic style. All this was linked to Calderón's conception of himself as a demiurge who, magically, like God, presided over, dominated and governed the world of theatrical performances.

A dramatic style of writing

Calderón's writing, outside the constraints of the popular theatre, became complex, attempting to find its place beyond spontaneity. He abandoned spontaneity to create a new language on stage, demanding that we pay attention to it, that we take pleasure in the drama itself, a language expressive of a character's inner world. Hence he used a kind of monologue in dialogue form which made it possible to reveal the problems and contradictions with which a character had to wrestle. When there is a surprise in the action of a play, it thus finds an ideal space in which the audience can perceive the violence of the contrast. It is a language in itself totally adapted to the stage by virtue of its visual and pictorial character, by its rhetorical brilliance and by the sonorous and musical intensity of the verse.

The undeniable opacity of a language as elaborate as Calderón's also created a climate of mystery propitious to the interest of the plot. It gave an added dimension to themes and subjects. It strengthened the transcendence of problems which, on the limits of the inaccessible, fascinated even the ordinary spectator. Because of his heightened awareness, such a spectator participated in the performance. Calderón also regaled his audience with alienation effects in his best plays. Even if the natural and mental space occupied by his characters seems very close, the spectator was transported into odd and exotic situations and atmospheres. This encouraged creative dysfunctionalism that defied any kind of routine way of seeing.

In the plays about honour, for example, instead of the conventional, naturalist treatment of the action, Calderón used exaggerated tones, and rhetoric, hyperboles that left the excessive nature of the proposed solution to resolve a dramatic crisis visible in all its nakedness. Cutting the Gordian knot by a character's death appeared as an inevitable consequence of the social pressure which makes characters turn to crime against their will. Directors who try to tone down Calderón's wild excesses do him a disservice; they emasculate the effects he wanted and make credible and human what is purely pathological and monstrous. In *El Médico de su honra* (*The Doctor to his Own Honour*, 1637), for instance, there is a scene worthy of Antonin Artaud's theatre of cruelty: the innocent victim is subjected by her jealous husband to repeated blood-lettings, which make her die slowly – medically if you like. The vengeance for this act is all the more terrible because it is only revealed at the end of the play by the king who confirms that it has taken place.

A wide variety of inspiration

Among Calderón's work, *La Vida es sueño* (*Life is a Dream*, 1635), a masterpiece of dramatic composition, stages the poetical and philosophical story of Sigismund, a warm, human yet symbolic character. The action takes place between Destiny and Liberty and Dream and Reality in an exposition close to modern critical philosophy. The anecdote which inspired this is reminiscent of an oriental fairytale and traditions of asceticism and stoicism. But it is also related to historical facts, which the dramatist handles objectively: the tragic relationship between Philip II of Spain and his son Don Carlos. Reflections on the vanity of life, predestination and free will are interspersed with the question of absolute authority, revolt in the face of injustice and the courage born of a strong will.

El Alcalde de Zalamea (*The Mayor of Zalamea*, 1636) was the work in which the direct connection between Calderón's theatre and the New Art of Lope de Vega was at its most visible: an undiluted concentration of characters and actions, the clear assertion of certain national values and of a just and conciliatory monarchy. Equality between men is also defended against the notion of class when revenge for an act which dishonours the mayor of Zalamea, carried out by a man of low birth, is fully justified. This impressive character has the stature to confront the soldier-aristocrat, Don Lope de Figueroa; their confrontation gives structure to the drama.

One of Calderón's most appealing works, *El Príncipe constante* (*The Constant Prince*, 1636), has always been described as a religious drama. The psychological and physical passion of the hero, played in the 1960s by the Polish actor, Ryszard Cieslak, was a revelation to the whole of Europe. The plot was borrowed from a Portuguese chronicle: the Infante, Don Ferdinand, the king's brother, prefers to give his life rather than surrender the town of Ceuta to the Muslims. The religious theme is transmuted into an apology for the hero's self-sacrifice, determined to the point of death to defend principles that mean more to him than anything else. The prince leaves no scope for negotiation; his sacrifice brings about the victory of the Christian army and the triumph of his own ideas.

La Devoción de la Cruz (*The Devotion to the Cross*, composed *c*.1633) stimulated the interest of the Romantics and, later, of Albert Camus who translated it. Everyone has admired the dynamism of the action, its violence, its passion, its exceptional situations steeped in a tension between temporal and supernatural forces, between a reality rendered substantial by abnormality and transcendental beliefs which harmonise and resolve everything.

A large part of his work reveals Calderón's taste for symbolism, particularly in the 'autos sacramentales' which his creative imagination, his Baroque language and theological background revitalised as a genre. The most representative of these plays is perhaps *El Gran teatro del mundo* (*The Great Theatre of the World*, created *c*. 1640). In this synthetic staging of human life, this example of theatre within theatre – a typically Baroque approach – the world is the stage on which the characters (the Rich Man, the Labourer, the Poor Man) play their parts. The play is their own life (Do good, for God is God) and they are finally judged by a critic and spectator who is out of the ordinary: the Author, no other than an allegory of God.

To develop the religious theme of these plays Calderón used many different arguments. Among the most important and the most frequently performed, *La Cena del Rey Balthazar* (*King Balthazar's Feast*, created in 1634) was inspired by the passage in the Bible about the profanation of the sacred vessels which led to a tragic punishment. *El Divino Orfeo* (*The Divine Orpheus*, 1663) was a religious play which included mythology to attain its edifying aim. *Life is a Dream* illuminated the way in which Calderón created allegories and, conversely, the underlying complexity of the problems in the original play.

A universal classic

Calderón was a highly successful playwright, recognised in his own lifetime. In 1659, the French traveller Bertaud declared: 'He is the greatest poet and the finest mind that they [the Spanish] currently possess.' An emulator of Lope de Vega, Calderón constantly saw his plays being performed and overtook a whole circle of imitators and disciples. After the neglect and relative oblivion of the neo-classical period, Calderón was rediscovered by an enthusiastic Goethe, whose *Faust* has been compared to *El Mágico prodigioso*, a 1637 Calderón play, and by those German masters of Romanticism, the Schlegel brothers, who made him a universal classic. Later Schack and Grillparzer, among others, deepened and enriched his prestige. Through Calderón they discovered the richness of the Spanish national theatre.

After Calderón's Romantic and European rehabilitation, in which Spain somewhat belatedly joined, Calderón became a major focus for Hispanic Studies throughout the world. Today there are countless works which affirm his constant presence on the European stage and his influence in Germany, Italy, England, Poland, France, Russia, Sweden and Belgium.

In the twentieth century, works by Calderón still take their place in the repertoires of European directors and some of his plays have become emblems of the avant-garde. Even now, at the end of the twentieth century, his plays attract and challenge other dramatists. It is still possible to remember Charles Dullin's staging in 1922 of *Life is a Dream*, in which Antonin Artaud played King Basilio and for which he designed the costumes and the scenery. *The Crown of David* had a constructivist slant in a version performed by the Jewish Habima theatre troupe from Moscow in 1929 during a European tour which became permanent exile. Giorgio Strehler's *The Wonderful Magician* (1947) was mentioned by the critics in the same breath as existentialism. *The Great Theatre of the World* by José Tamayo (1952) was a production only exceeded in pure spectacle by *King Balthazar's Feast*, another production mounted by Tamayo, which took Rome by storm in 1953. The slightly expressionist staging of *La Dama Duende* (*The Scatterbrain*, written in 1629) by Ulrich Bettac (1955) was produced by Stephan Hlawa at the Wiener Burgtheater. Jerzy Grotowski's version of *The Constant Prince* (1966) in his theatre–laboratory in Wroclaw, captured the European imagination by proposing, in a revolutionary fashion, to concentrate on the actor's interpretation of the role. *Autosacramentales* by Victor García (1974) is a delirious exploration through human bodies of the allegorical world of Calderón seen from the critical and aphrodisiac angle of May 1968 in France. *Calderón* by Luca Ronconi (1978) is an original Pasolinian re-reading of the drama of Sigismund which underlines the importance of Rosaura's role. The staging of *Life is a Dream* by José Luis Gómez (1981) has been described as a new way of scenically reading the classics, while *The Devotion to the Cross* by Daniel Mesguich (1986) is a perfect example of neo-Baroque treatment.

Molière (1622–1673)

R. Horville

And the school of the world, the air we
  breathe to live
Give us much more of life than any book can
  give.

  Molière, *The School for Husbands*

Under this tombstone lie Terence and
  Plautus,
Though only Molière is really buried here.
One spirit they formed with their three
  talents sheer
And here in France their fine art thrilled
  and taught us.

In this epitaph, La Fontaine alerts us to the contribution made by Latin comedy to the comedy of Molière. But many other influences helped to form it. Molière's culture and experiences, often portrayed as typically French, made him a dramatist for the whole of Europe.

Molière's French roots

Molière was deeply influenced by his country's traditions. His origins and education were similar to those of most French dramatists of his time. Born in Paris into the Poquelin family, well-off tapestry-makers, he was, like virtually all his fellow playwrights, of bourgeois extraction. He was educated by Jesuits and then studied law. Eloquence in pleading a case then constituted in France a good preparation for secular dramatic writing, whose adepts, unlike Spain, had severed all ties with the Church. Influenced by libertine thinking, Molière broke with religion to the point of having nothing further to do with it, a decision which provoked violent attacks from practising Catholics during the arguments sparked off by *The School for Wives* (1662), *Tartuffe* (1664–1669) and *Don Juan* (1665).

In his youth, Molière was already attracted to the theatre. He went to the Parisian theatres of the hôtel de Bourgogne and the hôtel du Marais, where he got to know the French repertoire. He was interested in the performances of tumblers who continued the French medieval tradition of farce. Soon the armchair pleasures of the well-informed amateur were no longer enough. He preferred the nomadic uncertainty of theatrical engagements to the monotonous security of trade. In 1643 he signed a contract with the Béjarts to set up a troupe, the Illustre Théâtre, based in Paris.

Despite crushing financial problems which resulted in his imprisonment for debt, he was undeterred. From the date of his release, in the autumn of 1645, he enrolled in a troupe of strolling players. For more than thirteen years he toured the French provinces, leading an unpredictable existence. He learned his trade as an actor, playing all kinds of roles in comedies, tragi-comedies and tragedies. He observed the people around him and those he met, adding to his experience of being human, noting those tiny details with which he created the colourful characters so typical of seventeenth-century France: the doctor, the miser, the blue-stocking, the hypochondriac.

When Molière began to write, he looked first to French farce for inspiration: *La Jalousie du Barbouillé* and *Le Médecin volant* (from 1645 to 1658) rely on visual comedy and jokes. Molière remained faithful to this register of broad comedy even in his 'serious' comedies (*Don Juan*, for example) and which he hones to perfection in *Les Fourberies de Scapin* (1671), notably in the scene during which Scapin, passing himself off as a swordsman, beats Géronte who is hidden in a sack:

> *(He gives several blows to the sack.)*
> There. This is what I think of him. 'Ah! Ah! Ah! Ah!' Yes. He might well say that. Ah! Go easy! Ah! Ah! Ah! 'Give him that on my behalf, Adieu!' Ah! The devil take this Gascon! Ah!
> *(Moaning and moving his back, as if he had received the blows.)*

The practice of comedy, Italian-style

Another influence, that of the commedia dell'arte, was superimposed on this tradition of the French farce. From the start of his career, Molière had had the opportunity to watch performances by Italian theatre troupes. In *La Jalousie du Barbouillé* and *Le Médecin volant*, he took up the scenarios of the improvised comedies of their repertoire. This influence became still stronger when, in 1658, Molière began to live in Paris. He shared first the playhouse of the Petit-Bourbon, then of the Palais-Royal, with an Italian theatre troupe, whose acting techniques he had the time to observe.

The contribution of the Italian theatre generally was considerable. The auditoria where Molière gave performances were inspired by what was called Italian-style theatre with a proscenium-arch stage.

Like his contemporaries, Molière adopted the arrangement of the Italian-style plot-based comedy, central to which were the couple of sympathetic young lovers. But there were obstacles in the way of their marriage: their parents have partners in mind more suited to their own aspirations for their children. From then on, the action is built around the efforts of the young leading lady and the young leading man to foil these troublesome plans. Still in the first flush of youth and inexperienced, they find precious allies in the shape of a cunning maid or a diligent servant who take their interests in hand and give the play its rhythm. After many twists and turns, the positive characters triumph in an ending where one or more impending marriages will be announced. This was the plot of most of Molière's plays, but he knew how to inject it with fresh life. He also used the plot to air the major problems that existed in society, particularly relationships of power within the family.

Molière was also inspired by Italian comedy in the elaboration of his characters. His servants, whether they were clumsy – like Georgette and Alain in *The School for Wives* – or cunning, like Scapin in the *Fourberies*, owe much to his models. He often gave them Italian names: Scapin, Polichinelle (*The Imaginary Invalid*, 1673), Sganarelle (*The Flying Doctor; The School for Husbands*, 1662; *Don Juan*). Picturesque characters, distinguished by their absurd outlandishness, built around contrasts between appearance and reality, intentions and actions, or avowed aims and actual results, were also anchored in the Italian tradition. In *The Imaginary Invalid*, for instance, Thomas Diafoirus cannot resolve to abandon his half-Latin mode of speech, even when he is courting the lady he loves. Nor can he manage to hide the paucity of his knowledge of medical terminology. But, once again, Molière knows how to elaborate on his sources. He reveals the dangers of the power of science and the alienation that manias and obsessions can lead to. Molière's staging, which gives great scope to often gratuitous gestures, whose function is to spice up more than illustrate the text, was inspired by the practice of the commedia dell'arte. In the end, he uses in his own way the tradition of lazzi, that broad sometimes even slightly risqué humour, the audience loved. So, in *Tartuffe*, Orgon makes the following answer to his mother who reproaches him for not having looked sufficiently into the intentions of the hypocrite in the process of paying court to his wife:

> *Great God! How could I look into them better?*
> *Should I then, mother, have waited till under my very eyes*
> *He . . . You'll make me say something silly.*

The attractions of Spanish fantasy

Molière was also attracted by Spanish tragi-comedy, the genre he would have liked to specialise in. But his aspiration to engage in 'serious' theatre was not to his public's taste. Although they appreciated his comic talent, the heroic comedy *Dom Garcie de Navarre* (1661) was poorly received. In the light of this failure, Molière reverted on high comedy in which, as in tragi-comedy, he skilfully mixed comic register and tragic tone. *The School for Wives*, *Tartuffe*, *Don Juan*, *The Misanthrope* (1666) all aired society's major problems. But the attacks from theoreticians and practising Catholics to which he then fell victim obliged him to return to a more regular, prudent style. He did not abandon his Spanish examples. In many of his plays, he spiced up the stagecraft of the Italian-style plot-based comedy with a fantasy borrowed from Spain. Thus *Les Fourberies de Scapin* ends with an unexpected act of recognition: Hyacinthe, the poor young girl married by Octave, is in fact Géronte's child, whose son Léandre has fallen in love with a gypsy girl, Zerbinette, who turns out to be the daughter of Argante, Octave's father. Under these circumstances, the two fathers, friends into the bargain, can only joyfully approve of their children's choice of partner:

> LÉANDRE Father, do not complain that I love a mystery woman, lacking high birth and lacking wealth. Those from whom I redeemed her have just revealed to me that she is from this town and of good family, that they stole her when she was four years old, and here is a bracelet that they have given me, which will help her to find her parents.
> ARGANTE Well! If this bracelet is anything to go by, it's my daughter, whom I lost when she was the age you say this girl was.

Molière often closely combines French, Spanish and Italian influences. In *Don Juan*, for instance, he takes as his examples the French tragi-comedies of Dorimond (1658) and Villiers (1659), introduces a Spanish picaresque dimension and returns to the comic slapstick of the commedia dell'arte, which Domenico Biancolelli had staged at the Palais-Royal in 1662.

The Western tradition of court entertainments

'Their majesties had for the first time the entertainment of a ballet with six entrances, accompanied by comedy, which began with a wonderful overture, followed by a dialogue set to the most agreeable of music. The decoration of the theatre and everything else evinced the splendour customary in these court entertainments.' With these words the *Gazette* of 14 October 1670 evoked the performance in the presence of the king of *Le Bourgeois gentilhomme*, thus testifying to another facet of Molière's genius. In Western Europe, court life had a dominant cultural role, leading to the production of sumptuous spectacles which mingled text, music, song and dance, complex staging, fireworks and fountains. In the French court, Molière appeared as the authorised jester, good at organising these spectacles that the king so admired. But he knew how to innovate, creating the comedy–ballet, which united comic attractions with the prestigious effects of great spectacle. From the *Fâcheux* (1661) to *The Imaginary Invalid*, Molière's work included many hybrid compositions.

Molière's function at court meant he could take advantage of the good relationship he had with the king. Louis XIV protected him because he was grateful for the entertainments he devised, and because his condemnation of excess and his middle-of-the-road tastes were in keeping with royal policy. But the king failed to recognise Molière's literary worth and considered that his status as a court jester did not warrant him becoming a member of the French Academy.

Molière's prestige in Europe

Molière's European dimension was also revealed in the international prestige he had during his lifetime and which increased over the centuries. He was particularly influential in Restoration England. Dryden wrote a version of *The Scatterbrain* (1667); Otway offered an adaptation of the *Fourberies de Scapin* (1677); Fielding adapted *The Unwilling Doctor* (1732) and *The Miser* (1773).

In Germany, Molière's reputation was assured. Characteristically, when the anti-classical Romantic reaction developed with Lessing and Schlegel, Molière was chosen as a target. He was accused of being a jester without imagination or, in a somewhat contra-dictory way, a didactic pedant. Shakespeare or Calderón were preferred. But Goethe praised him unstintingly.

In England, in Germany: these are just two examples of Molière's international reputation in European countries. For example, *Les Fourberies de Scapin* encouraged twenty adaptations up to the end of the nineteenth century: one in Latin, two in Modern Greek, four in Italian, one in Portuguese, one in Rumanian, two in English, two in Dutch, one in Swedish, two in Danish, one in Hungarian, one in Polish and two in Russian.

10 *The First Half of the Eighteenth Century: the Enlightenment*

P. MALANDAIN

Dare to know!

The first half of the eighteenth century was called the Age of Enlightenment. This word did not have the same meaning throughout Europe: the attitudes, values and work it included did not develop uniformly or synchronically. The Enlightenment, however, remains the most appropriate term to describe the thirst for knowledge, the desire to appropriate the world for humanity and the feeling of self-satisfaction which then took hold of people in Europe. Even though living conditions were often hard, religious struggles and superstitious practices still existed, and certain art forms were still highly controversial, European man was happy – or rather he was someone who thought that happiness was possible, that it was in his nature to be happy, that happiness represented a kind of duty. From its performance would inevitably flow peace of mind, progress and social equilibrium. According to Kant's assessment of the situation (*Was ist Aufklärung? What is the Enlightenment?* 1784), the individual was now coming of age at the end of a minority that he himself had been responsible for by heeding the injunction: *Sapere aude! Dare to know!* This magnificent formula simultaneously expressed a desire for knowledge, the mastery of the means to implement it, the mutual encouragement of those advancing down its path, and even the joyful audacity contained in this attitude. Happiness, freedom, action and secularisation are the key terms for understanding this period.

WHAT IS 'THE ENLIGHTENMENT'?

Three problems manifest themselves if we are to give an account of the century of the Enlightenment from a literary viewpoint on the European level: the unequal spatial distribution of the phenomenon, its temporal limits and the particular place that literature then occupied in human activities.

An unequally distributed phenomenon

The inequality of the phenomenon's distribution is glaringly obvious when we come to consider how advanced certain countries were in north-west Europe (England in economic and political fields, the United Provinces philosophically and scientifically, France as regards arts and letters and, to a lesser extent, Italy) in comparison with northern, central and southern Europe. The German-speaking lands had to wait for Lessing to affirm their cultural autonomy; Sweden took a long time to recover from the foray into war launched by Charles XII; the Austrian regency of Maria Elisabeth shackled all intellectual activity in the Austrian Netherlands; Spain was in total decline under the Bourbon French dynasty and only began to recover with Charles III and Aranda (1759); Portugal, under John V, depressed by a long sleep out of which only Pombal, swept into power by a reform movement, could awaken it after 1755. In the East, Peter the Great's reforms only bore fruit in 1725 in Russia forty years after his death;

Poland, enfeebled and ruined, remained in 'Saxon darkness', or 'Sarmatism', until its great, dramatic awakening, the reign of Stanislas II Augustus Poniatowski (1764) and the three divisions that it then had to undergo; Bohemia, muzzled by the Austrian Hapsburgs, shone in the realm of the 'Baroque', but its letters, thought and language were dangerously close to extinction until the great leap forward of its national Renaissance in the second half of the century; the Hungarians were slowly recuperating from the Ottoman yoke which still weighed down on Serbs, Rumanians and Greeks.

Early signs of emancipation were no less visible for all that, but there is a danger of reading them with hindsight – a bad way to read history. It is nevertheless true that, in various guises in those countries, what we now call the Enlightenment nurtured casts of mind similar to those of the advanced European countries. It created real convergence between rich and poor European countries. This was encouraged by the many exchanges made possible by the dissemination of writings and the practice of tourism – the 'Grand Tour' of Europe undertaken by many young upper-class people.

I like luxury and even ease,
All pleasures, arts of every kind . . .
What a good time to be had in this iron
  century!

Voltaire, *The Socialite*

The birth of the Enlightenment: 1680–1750

An ideological and tactical weapon of the Enlightenment was first introduced in the 1680s. With the founding of Philadelphia by Penn (1682), it was also the moment when new perspectives enlarged in the colonies, where this same Enlightenment soon encountered its blind spot. Our survey ends in 1750. With rare exceptions, such as Russia, this middle of the century in effect constituted a strong punctuation mark. It suggests the

disappearance from the European stage of Bach, Muratori and La Mettrie, Madame de Tencin, whose place was immediately taken by Madame Geoffrin, and Madame de Châtelet. This signalled the beginning of Voltaire's second career. There was also the reconversion of Swedenborg from scientist to mystic. The victory of the Enlightenment was a long way off: in Prussia, deserters' noses and ears were cut off; in France Machaut's attempt at fiscal reform failed and the campaign of 'confessional letters' began. The 'philosophical' adventure took a new turn. Voltaire had celebrated a fine 'international community':

> The English have profited much from works in our language, and we ought, in our turn, to borrow from them after having lent to them. The English and ourselves came after the Italians who were our masters in everything and whom we have since surpassed in something. I do not know which of the three nations to prefer, but happy whoever knows how to appreciate their diverse merits!
>
> Voltaire, *Philosophical Letters*

From now on we have to deal with a Europe mobilised along national lines as regards its past, its specific genius and its sensibility. Man had been relieved of his theological cope and here, scarcely himself again, he saw his identity shaken by the first elements of an evolving system of thought. The years 1749 to 1750 witnessed the beginnings of Condillac, Buffon and Marmontel, of Gray and Sterne, of Lessing, Wieland and Klopstock, and of Gessner. In France libertinism began a downhill path from Crébillon Junior to Sade. A return to classical antiquity emerged with *Collection of Antiques* (1752–1767) by the Count de Caylus (1692–1765); *Æsthetica* (*Aesthetics*, 1750–1758) by Alexander Baumgarten (1714–1762) distanced itself from rationalism. Above all, two Parisian events created conditions favourable for a radical renewal of society: the launching of the *Encyclopédie*, and the illumination of Vincennes, which gave Rousseau the idea for a totally new philosophical viewpoint.

What is 'literature' between 1680 and 1750?

It was symptomatic of the new state of affairs that Charles Batteux (1713–1780) republished his 1748 *Course of Belles-Lettres* in 1753, adding the sub-title 'Principles of Literature'. Something appeared on the European cultural horizon at this turning point that the first part of the century could not describe, even while it was preparing for it. During this period, what today we call 'literature' was still hard to distinguish from the ideological, theoretical, scientific and artistic works which helped to nourish it and which it illustrated in an outstanding way. Before we examine an 'effervescence' of writing in traditional literary genres, we need to see under what circumstances, from the 1680s, there was 'a new era for philosophical and religious thought' and how 'an implementation of the tools of critical thought' was effected up to 1750. This preliminary examination of ideological, scientific and aesthetic surroundings, puts us at the heart of literary activity for this period, for the surroundings are not the framework for our discourse but its subject matter and theme. Everything was muddled under the heading 'belles-lettres'. We are on the threshold of a period which is preparing the achievement of the *Encyclopédie* and in which, in all realms of thought, science and art, information, arguments and propositions were raised and composed like a Bach fugue.

A NEW ERA FOR PHILOSOPHICAL AND RELIGIOUS THOUGHT

During the 1680s, when the new balance of power brought by the Peace of Nijmegen had barely begun to take effect, Europe was shaken by three important events which had a destabilising influence: the invasion of the Turks who besieged Vienna (1683) and were saved at the last moment by Jan Sobiecki; the revocation of the Edict of Nantes (1685) by King Louis XIV, which forced into exile many French Protestants, especially welcomed in the United Provinces, in Switzerland, in England, in the German countries and in Hungary; and the Glorious Revolution (1688–1689), which chased from the English throne the Catholic king, James II, and replaced him with the Stathouder of Holland, William of Orange. This triple fracture in the established order, coupled with the necessities of economic development, gave the idea and the means for the old systems to joyfully reassert themselves. The weakening of the House of Austria, the revival of religious intolerance in France and the transformation of political power in England into a constitutional monarchy were bad enough. To all this, however, may be added the formation, with Frederick William, Great Elector of Brandenburg, who died in 1688, of a new power in Prussia, and the seizing of power in Moscow by Peter Romanov, determined to become Peter the Great and make of Old Russia a modern State. These events not only began to undermine the European political order, but they also created conditions for a radical re-examination of the principles on which that order had been founded.

The United Provinces, an epicentre of movement

It was not by chance that the epicentre of this diplomatic earthquake and change in mentality was found in the United Provinces, where there was the greatest possible freedom of conscience and expression. Since the sixteenth century, it had become the publishing house of the world. The most brilliant intellectual activity had continued there virtually without a pause since the heyday of humanism. At this period, it developed around Huygens, Graevius, Cuper, Gronovius and Burman. To this 'place of sanctuary', driven out by the turmoil in their respective countries, came Furly (1680), Bayle (1681), Jurieu (1682), Lord Shaftesbury (1682), his secretary Locke (1683), Leclerc (1683). Ribeiro Sanches a Portuguese doctor and disciple of Boerhaave, was sent by him to the Russian court, then to furnish documents for Buffon and an article for the *Encyclopédie*. There were also others. Without setting themselves an 'agenda', they effected a division of labour. Despite the genius and ardour of those whom Fontenelle called 'the little band of chosen ones', they were only able to secure the exceptionally large audience they immediately enjoyed because they appeared on the horizon of an epoch eager for change and ready to make it.

Pierre Jurieu (1637–1713), a Calvinist pastor, was responsible for the indignant denunciation of the misdeeds of persecutory dogmatism and an open polemic with Catholic theologians: *Pastoral Letters* (1686), *The Accomplishment of Prophecies or the Impending Deliverance of the Church* (1686) and *The Sighs of the Slave France Pining for Liberty* (1689). **Pierre Bayle (1647–1706)**, the son of a Protestant minister in the county of Foix, after a youth spent between Toulouse, Paris, Geneva and Sedan, became 'the philosopher of Rotterdam' and began by attacking prejudice and superstition. There is irony in *Miscellaneous Reflections on the Comet* (1682), *General Criticism of M. Maimbourg's History of Calvinism* (1682), and *What has become of All Catholic France under the reign of the Great Louis?* (1686). Then, in *Philosophical Commentary on the Following Words of Jesus Christ: Compel them to Enter* (1686), he distanced himself from his Protestant friends, dismissing one by one all doctrines, in the name of freedom of conscience. Finally, he patiently worked out a historical criticism systematically applied to everything, and which crowned all previous efforts at free thinking in Europe in *Historical and Critical Dictionary* (1695–1697; ten editions up to and including 1760). In his research into the human causes of error, based on an examination of religious truths themselves and the texts which have made them venerable, he followed the way opened up by Richard Simon (1638–1712) in *Critical History of the Old Testament* (1678) and *Critical History of the New Testament* (1689). Among the many who were inspired by his thought were the Dane Holberg, the Spaniard Feijóo and the Russian Tatichtchev – who discovered in him a rational justification for Czar Peter

– reforming efforts and even the German Johann Jacob Brucker (1696–1770), whose *Historia critica philosophiæ* (*Critical History of Philosophy*, 1742–1744) Diderot's main source for his articles on philosophy in the *Encyclopédie*. Today Bayle remains for all Europeans the symbol of intellectual and moral maturity, when they exercise it in a tolerant way: with respect for and interest in each other.

> Mohammedans, according to the principles of their faith, are obliged to use violence to ruin other religions; yet they have tolerated them for several centuries. Christians have only been commanded to preach and instruct, and, nevertheless, from time immemorial, they have exterminated by the fire and the sword those who are not of their religion. [. . .] The conclusion I wish to draw from all this, is that men seldom abide by their principles.
>
> Pierre Bayle, *Historical and Critical Dictionary, the article 'Mohammed'*

Philosophy's triple agenda

> 'Try everything, retaining what is good' is a divine commandment.
>
> John Locke

John Locke (1632–1704), who was called the 'Hercules' or 'the Newton of metaphysics', was the first of the 'philosophers': defined at that time as those who wanted to remake all speculation both critical and 'useful' – another key concept of the Enlightenment. Scientifically and medically educated, initiated into political and economic affairs by Lord Shaftesbury, in 1670 he conceived the idea of beginning all quests for knowledge by an examination of its instrument: the human mind. Both tolerant and committed, modest and ambitious, serene and determined, in 1689 he wrote *An Essay concerning Human Understanding* which, translated into French in 1700, became one of the Englightenment's Bibles. In this work he refuted the *a priori* nature of ideas, all separation of concrete ideas, born of sensual experience, and abstract ideas, which were the fruit of reflection, all solution of continuity between simple and complex ideas, the origin of which he saw not in the mystery of the inaccessible, but in the infinite possibilities of combination of which the human mind is capable, once the senses have served their apprenticeship.

Returning to London with William of Orange, he took part in political reform, in particular with his *Two Treatises of Government* (1689). Here he expounded the theory of the contract, which until then had been buried in the scholarly works of theorists of natural right. He rejected Hobbes' famous idea according to which the natural state corresponds to a state of anarchic savagery and needs a State to be brutally repressive. He also rejected still current theory of the divine right of kings. He steered a middle way between the state of nature and the social State. Both were ruled by the same principles of liberty and reason, but the latter was merely the former's well-defined and freely accepted organisation, involving the delegation and separation of powers. To open the floodgate of the century's liberal political and social thinking, Locke added two more works, aiming to negotiate the obstacle of religion by adopting a position soon to be qualified as 'Deist': *Letters concerning Toleration* (1689) and *The Reasonableness of Christianity* (1695).

A whole system of thought way rocked to its foundations, the system that was solidly founded on the literal interpretation – often little known – of Scripture, on the principle of divine authority, on the divine guarantee for the power of princes and for the distribution of wealth in society, on a morality of obedience and submission. The popularisation of these ideas was soon assured by journalists such as Bayle, Basnage and Leclerc, with an intellectual readership, and, above all, with men of the world such as **Anthony Ashley Cooper, Earl of Shaftesbury (1671–1713)**, son of the politician and Locke's pupil, in *An Inquiry concerning Virtue and Merit* (1699) – translated and adapted by Diderot in 1745 – and *A Letter*

concerning Enthusiasm (1708). **Bernard de Fontenelle (1657–1757)** also contributed to the debate with *Conversations on the Plurality of Worlds* (1686), *History of Oracles* (1687) and *The Origin of Fables* (1687). All these writers described the essential ingredients of a new vision of the world in an accessible way.

Voltaire (François Marie Arouet, 1694–1778)* gave a good description of this manner, which was not far from being his own:

> *He opened the gate to a brand-new world;*
> *Of infinite worlds being born all around*
> *   him,*
> *Measured by his hand, growing at his*
> *   order,*
> *He traced the path before our startled eyes;*
> *The ignorant understood him, the scholar*
> *   admired him:*
> *What more do you want? He wrote an*
> *   opera.*
>
> Voltaire, *Complete Works*

The following fifty years accomplished the triple agenda 'philosophy' had set itself: the fight to extirpate all aberrations, historically locatable and ever present, of the human mind; the launching and acceleration of its progress; the abandonment, energetically, but also with nostalgia, for all belief in general and absolute truth.

The question of religion

> God is the first reason for things being there.
>
> Leibniz, *Theodicy*

As far as religion was concerned, the critical vein continued with the Dutchmen Filip Van Limborch and Balthazar Bekker, the Englishman Toland and Collins, the Danes Holberg and Arpe, and throughout Voltaire's work. The upholders of traditional values, however, were still making themselves heard: Bottens produced *Het goddelyk herte* (*The Divine Heart*, 1710) and Bunyan wrote *The Pilgrim's Progress*. In France many works were nurtured by quarrels between sects: the quarrel with Protestantism, especially with the revocation of the Edict of Nantes and when it involved Bossuet (*History of the Variations between Protestant Churches*, 1688); the quarrel with Jansenism which the papal bull *Unigenitus* (1713), in which Pope Clement XI condemned Father Quesnel's *Moral Reflections* (1693), reopened for half a century; the quarrel with quietism: Madame Guyon, *The Short and Very Easy Way to Pray*, 1688; Fénelon, *Explanation of the Maxims of the Saints*, 1697. Bossuet responded to both these in *A Relation concerning Quietism*, 1697. These were just so many reactions by the established Church to Christians. By preferring personal contact with God and the inner life of the spirit, they weakened the Church's authority and participated in the general movement of liberation brought about by the Enlightenment.

Despite the discredit into which mediocre popes had dragged Roman Catholicism, religious faith and practice were not neglected. None of the leading minds of the time – Newton , Bach, Leibniz, Feijóo, Montesquieu, Vico, neither Dutch scholars nor Rococo architects, nor even the Phanariotes – questioned religious belief. Free thinking tending to atheism was still more or less exclusively an English phenomenon; free thinkers were very much in a minority, in the same way that anti-clericalism was typically French. In Catholic countries, as in Protestant and Orthodox ones, the aim was a reconciliation between Reason and Revelation. With a wholly bourgeois prudence of investment, people hedged their bets, interested both in the chance of substantial benefits d from 'philosophy' and in the security that a level-headed religion brings to morally stabilise society. Locke showed the way. He was followed by Samuel Clarke (1675–1729) in *The Obligations of the Natural Religion* (1706) and André Michel de Ramsay (1686–1743) in *The Philosophical Principles of Natural and Revealed Religion* (1748). The Swiss writers Marie Huber (1695–1753) and J. Vernet, and the German poet Barthold Inrich Brockes (1680–1747) in *Irdisches Vergnügen in Gott* (*Earthly Pleasure in God*, 1721–1748) followed suit. The Croat Rudjer

Bošković (1711–1787), a friend of Ramsay, published *Theoria philosophiœ naturalis* (*Theory of Natural Philosophy*) in 1758. It was not at all in a spirit of 'anti-Enlightenment' – no more than in a 'nationalist' spirit (German, for example), since the phenomenon was a general one – that less formal and more genuinely lived models of the religious life sprang up: the German pietism of Spener and August Francke (1663–1725), the Danish pietism of Hans Adolf Brorson (1694–1764), the 'Moravian Brethren' of Nikolaus Zinzendorf (1700–1760), the Methodism of John Wesley (1703–1791), Italian Jansenism and the fanatical Protestantism of the Hungarian Kata Bethlen (1700–1759). In Portugal we need to compare all this with the role of the Oratorians who fuelled a strong tendency towards the reconciliation of Faith and Enlightenment. The criticism of the Baroque (by Padre Vieira, Frei Lucas de S. Catarina and Bluteau) and that of the Inquisition at the heart of the Spanish Church itself also tended in the same direction. The religious humanism of the Greeks Anthrakitis, Kyminitis and Notaras worked in a similar way. In Russia, the polemic on religious reform raised the same questions: Feofan Prokopovitch (1681–1736), unlike Stephan Iavorski (1658–1722) approved of the Czar's efforts to prune the Church's power in order to modernise the country. In the very countries where the new-found spirit shone most brightly, these attempts at reconciliation were most active. In the United Provinces, reconciliation merely continued the tradition of Erasmus and Coornhert; in Scandinavia, science and mysticism combined with Emanuel Swedenborg (1688–1772): *De cultu et amore Dei* (*Of the Worship and the Love of God*, 1745). Then *Swenska Psalmboken* (*The Swedish Psalter*, 1694) by his father Jesper Swedberg (1653–1735) already mingled boldness with prophecy. From Malebranche to Leibniz and Wolff, then Rousseau, this attempt represented the main thrust of speculative philosophy.

This was the line of Bacon's empirical epistemology: we do not know and do not learn to know except by experience. It was reactivated by Locke and Newton, followed by Francis Hutcheson (1694–1746) and especially by **David Hume (1711–1776)**: in *A Treatise of Human Nature* (1739–1740), prolonged by an *Inquiry concerning Human Understanding* (1748) and *An Inquiry concerning the Principles of Morals* (1751), he refuted the notions of substance and cause, restoring the role of passion in the activity of reason and opening the way as much to the sensualism of (Elenne Bonotde Condillac (1715–80), who saw in our sensations our only source of knowledge *An Essay on the Origin of Human Knowledge*, 1746, *Treatise on Sensations*, 1749) as to Kantian criticism, which fixed the potential and the limits of 'pure reason'. On the other hand, **George Berkeley (1685–1753)**, with *An Essay Towards A New Theory of Vision* (1709), *A Treatise concerning the Principles of Human Knowledge* (1710) and *Three Dialogues between Hylas and Philonous* (1713), made a clean break with the ingenuously optimistic objectivism of the nascent Enlightenment. His idealism rejected the existence of matter and abstract ideas outside the mind that conceives them and God who contains them. His was the last rampart against materialism and atheism, and the foundation of a constructive theism (*Siris*, 1744). Harmonising the truths of faith with the certainties of reason had been attempted by **Nicolas de Malebranche (1638–1715)**, an Oratorian, a disciple of Descartes, who made of man's thought a 'vision of God' and of his will an 'occasional cause' of the movement that only God can achieve (*Treatise on Morality* and *Christian and Metaphysical Meditations*, 1683; *Treatise of the Love of God*, 1697; *Conversations on Metaphysics and Religion*, 1688–1698). Above all it had been attempted by **Gottfried Wilhelm Leibniz (1646–1716)**. Leibniz was a universal genius, mathematician, theologian, jurist, historian, diplomat, librarian, chemist (he took part in the discovery of phosphorus), engineer (he conceived plans for a calculating machine, air compressors and a submarine), a traveller (he was in contact with Malebranche, Huygens, Arnauld, Newton, Boyle and Spinoza), the guiding spirit of a review (*Acta Eruditorum, Acts of Scholars*, in Leipzig, founded by Mencke in 1682) and of the Academy of Berlin. He also worked in vain with Bossuet on the reuniting of Churches, was fascinated by China and composed an ecumenical prayer for Christians, Jews and Muslims. His work was immense and multifarious. Its philosophical part (*Discourse on Metaphysics*, 1686; *New Essays on Human Understanding*, 1704; *Essays on Theodicy*, 1710; *Monadology*, 1714; *Principles of Nature and of Grace*, 1718) reconciled the principle of individuation (monads) with the existence of the universe (pre-established harmony). Their relations were ruled by an interplay of sufficient grounds of which the last is God, who chooses to create at each moment 'the best of all possible worlds'. The hierarchy of monads and their inclusion in a coherent whole allowed for a harmonisation of two images of the world, physical (mechanical) and spiritual. We know the fate that Voltaire gave to these notions in *Candide*: notions which had been clumsily taken up by Christian Wolff (1679–1754). Wolff's *Philosophia prima sive Ontologia* (*First Philosophy or Ontology*, 1729) established *a priori* a perfect affinity between being and its attributes: between the human mind and the objects to which it attaches itself. Almost everywhere the productions of philosophy directed their efforts to harmonise the conquests of reason with the traditions of faith and the maintenance of moral standards: Baumgarten, a disciple of Wolff, Arevedo Fortes, André Panckoucke, Nikolas Mavrokordatos all played their part. The Italian school occupied a prominent position with Michelangelo Fardella, Giovanni De Soria, Antonio Genovesi, Muratori, mindful as it was of critical erudition and animated by a reforming fervour. In France, however, Diderot's early works (*Philosophical Thoughts*, 1746; *The Walk of the Sceptic*, 1749; *Letter on the Blind*, 1751) make us aware of the progress of atheistic materialism.

AN IMPLEMENTATION OF THE TOOLS OF CRITICAL THOUGHT

The application of Cartesian rationalism henceforth extended to all areas – philosophy, science, history, politics and sociology, aesthetics, morality and religion – with all kinds of interrelationships incessantly established. The conquest of Newtonian thought and the development of empiricism concurrently asserted themselves. Outside England, the United Provinces and France, Descartes' influence was felt in Greece (Phanariotes), in Scandinavia (Holberg and Swedenborg) and in Portugal (Fortes). Newton's influence made its way more slowly, but was noticeable in Italy by 1735 (Algarotti).

These tools were used in three complementary directions: the theory of knowledge, its exercise (all sorts of sciences and arts), its popularisation and its applications (techniques). Everywhere there dominates, in a surprising mixture of serious audacity and wilfully licentious frivolity, what J. Starobinski has called 'the invention of freedom' which corresponds to the wishes of all. It was the last chance for an aristocracy worried about the decline of its fundamental values and the progress of the centralisation of power which was gradually eroding its prerogatives. It was the interest of the masses. They were still oppressed, but they saw some improvement in their living conditions and the opening up of all kinds of ways to 'personal merit'. The aspiration of the bourgeoisie who, gaining control of administration, industry and banking, finally completed an ascension begun at the end of the Middle Ages. There was unanimous agreement that man should dwell on the other side of the 'discoveries' made in the sixteenth century: not on terror, destabilisation and anarchy, but on constructiveness, optimism about ends and means and about the ultimate reconciliation of bitter opponents.

Literature, science and art

In France, a country which enjoyed at this moment in time the greatest literary prestige, the last years of Louis XIV's long reign saw the illustrious intertwining of two genres generally considered as secondary, but then given prominence for obvious symbolic reasons. On the one hand, as if to give sumptuous burial to a world coming to an end, there were the *Funeral Orations* by Bossuet, Mascaron and Massillon. On the other, opening up minds to new objects of knowledge, there were popular works by La Fontaine (*Discourse to Madame de la Sablière*, 1683), by Fontenelle and Bayle, as we have seen, as well as by Saint-Évremond (*Conversation of Marshal d'Hocquincourt*, 1687; *Saint-Evremoniana*, 1700). The juxtaposition of these works is an indication of the transition, throughout Europe, though at different rates, from a literature based on faith to one based on reason; from a taste for pageantry to a taste for things of the mind; from a preoccupation with death to an exaltation of life. To Bossuet's 'Christians, pay attention and come to learn to die' the answers came in unison with the impertinent glee of Voltaire, Montesquieu's serenity, Pope's optimism and Linnaeus' curiosity.

Linnaeus invented systems of classification, travelled and wrote; Pope developed from pastoral and satirical poetry to great philosophical poetry. Montesquieu, as well as being a brilliant writer, was an active member of the Academy of Science of Bordeaux. Voltaire spent fifteen years of his life in Cirey conducting experiments in physics and studying, then popularising Newton's system in France. He also supplied an opera's libretto for Rameau and posed for La Tour. It is often quite difficult, during this period, to distinguish a writer from a philosopher, an artist from a scholar. The activity of writing not only makes known ideas, theories and inventions and their applications, but praises and celebrates them, orchestrates and prolongs them. Never perhaps has literature so much coincided with all the 'arts' – applied art, the art of living, decorative arts, liberal arts.

An example of this overlapping can be seen in the three 'quarrels' which aroused all sorts of passions. One was essentially concerned with literature, and was a manifestation of a kind of growing pain. It was called the 'war of the poets' in the United Provinces. Certain works by Swift (*The Battle of the Books*, 1697–1704) and by Pope (*The Dunciad*, 1728, 1743) made it famous in England. In Germany it was the opposition of Bodmer and Breitinger to Gottsched. In Paris it was called the quarrel of the Ancients and the Moderns (1687–1694, then 1713–1716). Another quarrel was about genetics and biological theories, the quarrel about 'spontaneous generation'. This continued for several decades before it was definitively resolved in 1765 by Spallanzi's refutation of Needham. The third quarrel had to do with music and singing, opposing the supporters of French music to those of Italian music. This culminated in 1752 with the quarrel of the Bouffons.

In every case, these fertile crises opened up for knowledge the field of the future. A certain concept of European man and his destiny, of his vocation to conquer the world and be actively happy was then forged in the polyvalence and collaboration of theorists and practitioners, of scholars and poets, of great lords and adventurers. This was the period of Newton and Papin, of Bach and Stradivarius, of Euler and Réaumur, of Feijóo and Linnaeus, of Bering and Vico. It was not just a question of isolated initiatives, as this series of famous names might have us believe, but of a concerted operation, taken in hand by all kinds of institutions.

Universities, clubs and salons

A plague on all literary coffee houses!
They have ruined more young people than
  the royal lottery.

William Congreve,
Love for Love

In France, universities, set in their ways, lagged behind, but they were relieved by the Royal College, the King's Garden, technical schools and learned societies. In parts of Europe, some universities are far from being so traditional: Basel, for instance, where Euler had begun to work; Bologna, which equipped itself with laboratories and observatories and where, for the first time, a woman taught – Laura Bassi; Leipzig, where Thomasius introduced rationalism in 1687; Göttingen, where a completely 'new' university was founded in 1737. Berlin, after 1740, became a meeting-place for every scholar in Europe: Bernoulli, Maupertuis, Euler, d'Alembert and soon Lagrange among them. The entire continent of Europe was marked by this surge of activity and everywhere academies spring up: in Moscow (1685), Lisbon (1717), Saint Petersburg (1724), Stockholm (1739) and Copenhagen (1745). While in London more and more clubs addressed themselves to intellectual problems, in Paris, where intellectuals had traditionally been socialites, a wholly exceptional phenomenon developed in the salons where writers met and welcomed visiting foreign scholars. There was the Club de l'Entresol (1720–1731), based on the English model, that met at the home of Hénault, the salons of Madame de Lambert (1710–1733) and of Mme de Tencin (1726–1749). With Madame du Deffand (1740–1780) and especially Madame Geoffrin (1749–1777), openness to the rest of Europe would become even more apparent. To this may be added the teaching efficiency of the Jesuits who, in their colleges throughout Europe, made a contribution to fostering a uniformity of outlook and to broadening intellectual horizons by making minds all the sharper because the content of their education remaining totally scholastic. The activity of the masonic lodges in Europe (London, 1717; Russia, 1730; Paris, 1733; Hamburg, 1733; The Netherlands, 1734; Lausanne, 1739) and spread in it a rationalist, progressive and cosmopolitan ideal also contributed as did the role played in the dissemination and circulation of ideas by the periodic press.* In large towns, coffee houses had a similar function, making possible joyful, bold confrontations, animated discussion about the latest works and a feverish exchange of news.

Suddenly, what was happening in the universities of Halle, Leyden and Padua, in the opera houses of Vienna, Paris and London, in factories and academies became infinitely more important in the eyes of that new force to be reckoned with – public opinion – than the agitation of 'sackers of provinces' or the wild imaginings of 'metaphysicians'. Voltaire stated in his *Lettres philosophiques* of 1734:

> The portrait of the Prime Minister (of England) is on the mantelpiece in his study; but I have seen that of Mr Pope in twenty houses. Mr Newton was honoured during his lifetime, and has been so after his death as he deserved to be. The chief men of the nation fought over the honour of carrying the pall at his funeral procession. If you go to Westminster, it is not the tombs of kings that are admired, but monuments that a grateful nation has erected to the great men that have contributed to its glory.
>
> Voltaire,
> *Philosophical Letters*

The Newton effect

An apotheosis: this is how the funeral of the great English scientist, Isaac Newton, in 1727 appeared to outsiders. Gradually displacing metaphysics as a model of reasoning, and henceforth considered as a precondition of all progress – not only material, but moral and political too – science, which no longer appeared incompatible with the spirit of religion and was not yet an occasion for charlatanism or a radical cultural mirage, was then the object of unrivalled interest and enthusiasm. In mathematics, there was infinitesimal calculus, gradually discovered at the same time by Newton and Leibniz (1684), the work of Rolle, the Bernoulli brothers, Clairault, Euler, and d'Alembert, the balance sheets drawn up by Heilbronner, Gordatos and Anthrakitis.

In astronomy, the passage of the comet, on 26 December 1680, excited both the curiosity of the philosophers (Fontenelle, Bayle, Bekker, then Whiston and Feijóo) and the emulation of the scientists, to which the work of **Isaac Newton (1642–1727)**, in particular the *Philosophiæ naturalis principia mathematica* (*Mathematical Principles of Natural Philosophy*, 1687), offered a fabulous theoretical illustration. Cassini and La Hire refined the theory of triangulars (1680). Louis XIV visited the new Observatory in Paris (1682), and another was built in Berlin (1700). Picard, by measuring the diameter of the earth exactly, made it possible for Newton to develop his theory of universal gravitation, and invented the micrometer (1682); Cassini measured the meridian in Paris (1702); Haley calculated the first orbit of a comet (1705) and worked out the movement of fixed stars (1718), for which Flamsteed compiled a catalogue (1725); Bradley discovered the periodic rotation of the earth on its axis (1748). And **Georges de Buffon (1707–1788)**, keeper of the King's Garden from 1739, started his work with *Treatise on the Formation of the Planets* (1745) and *History and Theory of the Earth* (1749).

Also stimulated by the laws of gravitation, physics gradually freed itself from Cartesian whirlwinds. It is enough to allude here to the work of Mariotte, Boerhaave, Musschenbroeck, s'Gravesande, Taylor, Maclaurin, Nollet, Maupertuis and Huygens, and to recall the fine example of European collaboration: by fixing the boiling point of water at 100°C, the Swede Celsius paved the way for the graduated centigrade scale of the thermometer (1742) which the Englishman Fahrenheit (1713) and the Frenchman Réaumur (1731) invented between them. In opposition to Newton, the Russian **Mikhail Vassilievitch Lomonossov (1711–1765)** advanced an argument against the theory of colours that Newton had put suggested.

Chemistry did not lag behind: it prepared the decisive advance it would make in the second half of the century. In Paris, lectures by Rouelle (from 1738) directly inspired Diderot, d'Holbach and Lavoisier. A new phenomenon gave rise to experiments destined to have a vital future: electricity. Here again, research was Europe-wide: Gray discovered the existence of conductors and non-conductors (1729); Du Fay observed the electrical charge of lightning (1730), then discovered the existence of two poles – positive and negative; Musschenbroeck and Cuneus built the first accumulator with their famous 'Leyden flask' (1745); Nollet dreamed up some applications, particularly therapeutic (electroshock), of electricity (1739–1746). Was this symbolic? Soon the American, Franklin, studying all the previous research, used it to invent the lightning-rod (1752).

Natural sciences became an object of fascination for scientists and for the public.

Woodward suggested a 'natural history of the Earth' (1702); Haller studied the flora of Switzerland (1742); Réaumur compiled a history of insects (1734–1742) and Swedenborg an 'economy' of the animal kingdom (1741). The greatest of these natural scientists was the Swede **Carl von Linnaeus, 1707–1778** who discovered the reproductive capacities of the vegetable kingdom: *Nuptiæ arborum* (*The Marriage of the Trees*, 1729) and worked tirelessly to lay the foundations of botany and to refine his plant classifications. Here is a fragment of these nomenclatures of European garden plants, drawn up in five languages:

Latina	Gallica	Anglica	Belgica	Germanica
Jasminum	Jasmin	Jasmine	—	Jaßmin
Ligustrum	Troëne	Privet	Keelkruyt	Beinhülzen
Olea	Olivier	Olive	Olyfboom	Oliven
Veronica	Véronique	Speedwell	Eerenprys	Ehrenpreiß

By thus revealing its richness, variety and history, Nature furnished the argument for an apology, sometimes naïve as with the Abbé Pluche (*The Spectacle of Nature*, 1732–1750, which was immensely popular throughout Europe), sometimes very enlightened, as with the English 'Christian virtuosi' (Boyle and Newton) or with the Dutch theologian-physicist Nieuwentyt (*Regt gebruik der werelt-beschouwingen, The Existence of God proved by the Marvels of Nature*, 1715). This tried to prove the existence of the divine architect by the arguments of natural perfection and teleology.

However, the most spectacular leap forward was that realised by the science that was not yet called biology. Leeuwenhoeck refreshed it completely with the discovery of red blood cells and circulation in the capillaries (1688); then, after Hamm, with the discovery of spermatozoa (1699). The works of Malpighi were published in London in 1688, and his *Esercitazioni sulla strutura dei visceri* (*Experiments on the Structure of Viscera*) in Frankfurt in 1691. Réaumur studied the regeneration of a crayfish's claw (1712) and Bonnet the

parthenogenesis of the aphid (1740), while Needham confirmed the microscopic observations from whence 'emerged' his famous 'eels' (protozoan cilia). Much of Diderot's thinking was based on these discoveries.

Papin's emulators

New instruments, new techniques, new lands, new products: the science of the time was particularly interested in its immediate applications, likely to improve man's lifestyle, and was therefore an active participant in the philosophical movements of the century. Before any one in Paris had thought of translating Chambers' *Cyclopaedia* (1728), and calling on Diderot (1746) to accomplish this project (*Prospectus for the Encyclopaedia*, 1750), this period witnessed the refinement of the use of steam for mechanical energy by Denis Papineau (first machine 1690), then further refinements by Newcomen and Cooke. After Réaumur's 1722 perfection the formula for steel, the first steelworks appeared (Huntsman, 1740) and industry developed: Le Creusot (1742). The textile industry used technical inventions by Leblond, Kay and Vaucanson. Glass manufacturing made progress thanks to the Mirror Factory of Saint-Gobain (1692), celebrated by Lomonossov, whose genius as a poet and engineer perfectly illustrates the period (*Pismo o pol'ze stekla, Epistle on the Usefulness of Glass*, 1752). Porcelain, manufacture after its invention by Böttger (1708), was perfected by the Meissen engineers (Saxony, 1710), Sèvres (1748) and Berlin (1750). After Gusmao had built the first hot-air balloon (1709), the Russian Ryasan attempted the first ascent.

In the field of food science, Porter and White perfected a preserving method (1691) and Tull invented a machine for sowing seed (1733). The use of coffee, introduced by the Dutch in Java (1686) and by the Portuguese in South America (1710), spread to Vienna, Amsterdam and Paris. Margraff managed to make sugar from sugar beet (1747). A sophisticated symbol of this sparkling period, champagne made its appearance under the hands of Dom Pérignon (1681), about the same time as sherry, port and gin. Europe witnessed the arrival, one after the other, of the first eraser and the first camellia (1739), snow-shoes (the Alps, 1689) and cuckoo-clocks (the Black Forest, 1726), the typewriter (Mill, 1712) and postmen for delivering the post (Berlin, 1698), eau de Cologne (Feminis, 1692) and the toothbrush (Germany, 1749). Europe also amused itself with Vaucanson's automata (*The Flute Player*, 1737).

Medical applications were in full swing: vaccination against smallpox was introduced in England by Lady Montagu (1721), the measuring of arterial tension by Hales (1726), the first dental care by Fauchard (1728), the treatment of venereal disease by Boerhaave (1735) and Astruc (1736), the first cataract operation by Daviel (1745). Also in advance of the rest of Europe in this respect, England taught it sport and melancholy. The latter, also called spleen, was studied medically by Cheyne (*The English Malady*, 1733). One of the first works of social medicine, Muratori's *Del governo della peste e della maniera di guardarsene* (*The Plague: How to Keep it under*

Control and how to avoid It, 1714) was often republished. With *Natural History of the Soul* (1745) and *The Man-Machine* (1748), La Mettrie opened the way to materialism.

Bach, Handel, Vivaldi, Rameau and others

It was a great period for the development of the applied arts and the art of living – and also for art itself. There were many theoretical works in this field. After the death of Félibien (1695), opinions on what constituted the 'Beautiful' were exchanged throughout Europe by Roger de Piles, Jean-Pierre de Crouzas, the Abbé Dubos, Jonathan Richardson and son, Bodmer, Hutcheson, Father André, the Abbé Batteux, Baumgarten and Hogarth. Optical and acoustic studies gave new life to the theory and practice of the arts of the eye and ear. Father Castel's 'ocular harpsichord' (1740) and Rameau's theory of harmonic generation (1737) opened the way for new aesthetic concepts, while new instruments come to enrich musical creativity: the hammer piano or pianoforte (Christofori, 1709), the tuning fork (Shore, 1711), the violin (Stradivarius, 1714).

Music flowered as never before. First there was instrumental music, with a list of distinguished names: Corelli, Delalande, Marais, Purcell, Couperin, Handel, Telemann, Rameau, Bach, his son Karl Philipp Emanuel, who fixed the form of the classic sonata, Vivaldi, Pepusch, Leclair, Domenico Scarlatti. From Rome, Venice, Naples, Vienna, Paris, London, Weimar and Leipzig, sonatas, concertos, cantatas, pieces for organ, harpsichord or viola inundated Europe. Against the background of this Baroque music, the intellectual life of the emerging Enlightenment was acted out and great literary works were written.

What distinguished the period above all was the extraordinary development of choral music. Opera-ballet, lyrical tragedy, interlude, comedy-ballet, melodrama, oratorio, 'opera buffa' (Naples, 1718), tone poem or musical drama, there are hundreds of works which, with librettists such as Quinault, Campistron,

Fontenelle, Voltaire, La Motte, Jean-Baptiste Rousseau, Addison, Gay, Fielding, Metastasio, even Dryden, Guarini, Cervantes, Molière or Shakespeare, attracted composers of the stature of Lulli, Charpentier, Alessandro Scarlatti, Purcell (*Dido and Aeneas*, 1689), Campra, whose *Europe galante* (1697) laid down the rules of composition for opera-ballet, Handel (*The Messiah*, 1741), Porpora, Vivaldi (*L'Olympiade, The Olympiad*, 1734), Hasse, as well as Pergolese (*La Serva padrona*, Naples, 1733; *The Servant Mistress*, Paris, 1746, 1752), Rameau (*Les Indes galantes, The Gallant Indies*, 1735), Arne, Jommelli, Gluck and Jean-Jacques Rousseau (*Le Devin du village, The Village Seer*, 1752). The extraordinary success of these lyrical productions can be explained less in terms of a frivolous taste for escapism, for flights of fancy of the imagination, for a kind of pastoral fantasia than in terms of the vision they offered of human society where harmony, beauty and happiness could be achieved.

Watteau, Hogarth, Piranese and the architects

Compared with such a musical profusion, the other arts might seem to have trailed behind, was wholly relative. In painting, Ruben's imitators dominated Poussin's classicism. The French school was distinguished by Rigaud, Mignard, the Coypels, Nattier, Lemoyne and Lancret, and especially by Watteau (*Gilles*, 1716, *The Embarkation for Cythera*, 1717, *The Italian Players*, 1720), Chardin (*The Skate Laid Bare*, 1728; *The Grace*, 1740; *The Philosopher in his Laboratory*, 1744), Boucher (*Renaud and Armide*, 1734; *Diana Getting Out of the Bath*, 1742; *The Rape of Europa*, 1747) and La Tour (*Maurice of Saxony*, 1747).

In England, the age was Hogarth's and his satirical and didactic engravings (*The Four Hours of the Day*, 1736, *Marriage à la mode*, 1744). The modernity of his series of observations of contemporary life, such as *The Harlot's Progress* (1732), or *The Rake's Progress* (1735), made into an opera by Stravinsky in 1951, is so relevant that they seem to be the ancestors of our cartoons. Gainsborough also began his career. He led English painting from the 'rococo' to Romanticism. In Italy, there were Canaletto, the engraver Piranese (*Le Carceri, Prisons*, 1740–1760, and *Piccole vedute delle Antichità romane, Small Glimpses of Roman Antiquities*, 1748), and the start of Tiepolo's and Guardi's careers. In Germany, after the creation of the Berlin Academy of Fine Arts (1696), the brothers Asam and Zimmermann executed their frescoes and stucco work (Bavaria, 1732). Mengs distinguished himself in portraiture in Dresden before going to Rome (1747).

French sculpture was also extremely brilliant, with Puget, Coysevox, Girardon, Bouchardon, Coustou and Pigalle. In Berlin, Schlüter made the *Equestrian Statue of the Great Elector* (1699). But it is above all in the fields of architecture, urban planning and decorative art that Europe enjoyed incomparable fecundity. In Paris and Versailles, Le Brun, Hardouin-Mansart, Courtonne and Giraldini designed the last great classical buildings, imitated by Caratti in Prague, and by Vanbrugh and Wren in England. But, after 1715, the classical French model had a rival in a new style, known as 'rococo', characterised by fussiness, ornamentation and dissymetry, and which transposed on to architecture, then on to literary works, the clever fantasies of silversmiths, interior designers and decorators (Oppenordt, Meissonnier, Pineau, Slodtz). Bérain had already demonstrated an idea of this style in 1711 with his yellow 'grotesques' which had great success throughout Europe. Mingling with the Baroque which had persisted in many places, this new style spread through Europe. It was more appropriate than severe, regular classicism for a taste for comfort and pleasure and closer to the current instinct for freedom. With the emerging vogue for English landscaped gardens (William Kent) and Sonfflot's journey to Italy (1749), the century swung towards its second half, prepared by the theoretical works of Guarini (*Architettura civile, Civil Architecture*, 1737), Blondel (*Cours d'architecture, Course on Architecture*, 1741) and Piranese (*Prima parte di architetture e prospettive, Part One of Architecture and Perspective*, 1743). In restoring his mansion on Strawberry Hill in the Gothic style, Horace Walpole announced in his own way a new age for taste.

Man and Vico

Gravity, steel, insects, harmonic generation, prismatic colours: all these were interesting subjects for the deepening of a rational, empirical, critical and practical knowledge of the world. But there was an even more interesting subject: man. Human sciences began with **Giambattista Vico (1688–1744)**, a thinker not well known in his time, but whose works, and especially his *Principi di una scienza nuova* (*Principles of a New Science*, 1725, 1744), set themselves the task of attaining the deep truths of history, art and human destiny against Cartesian geometry and quantification. The work was huge. Sometimes unsystematic in its scholarship, certain principles emerged from it, the very ones to which the whole age was ready to adhere. They only found their true philosophical application at the end of the century with Kant and Hegel: knowledge is action; the development of the human race is analogous to that of the individual; humanity is a work unto itself.

Ma, in tal densa notte di tenebre ond'è coperta la prima da noi lontanissima antichità, apparisce questo lume eterno, che non tramonta, di questa verità, la quale non si può a patto alcuno chiamar in dubbio: che questo mondo civile egli certamente è stato fatto dagli uomini, onde se ne possono, perchè se ne debbono, ritruovare i principii dentro le modificazioni della nostra medesima mente umana. [. . .]	*But in the midst of that darkness which covers up the most remote times of Antiquity, there appeared a light which could not go out, a truth which could not be called into doubt: the civil world is certainly the work of man, and it follows therefore that one can, one must rediscover the principles of it in the modifications of one's own intellect. [. . .]*
Or, poichè questo mondo di nazioni egli è stato fatto dagli uomini, vediamo in quali cose hanno con perpetuità convenuto e tuttavia vi convengono tutti gli uomini, perchè tali cose ne potranno dare i principii universali ed eterni, quali devon essere d'ogni scienza, sopra i quali tutte sursero e tutte vi si conservano in nazioni. [. . .]	*Since the civil world is the work of men, let us see on what they have always and still are agreed; it is from thence that we will take our principles which, like those of every science, must be universal and eternal, principles destined to show the formation and the preservation of societies. [. . .]*
Anzi ci avvanziamo ad affermare ch'in tanto chi medita questa Scienza egli narri a se stesso questa storia ideal eterna, in quanto – essendo questo mondo di nazioni stato certamente fatto dagli uomini [. . .], e perciò dovendosene ritruovare la guisa dentro le modificazioni della	*We will go even further and affirm that, this civil world being the work of man and his nature necessarily reflected in the very constitution of the human spirit, whoever meditates on the subject of this Science merely tells to himself this ideal eternal story of which he is the author; and this is the sense of the formula that*

*nostra medesima mente umana
egli, in quella pruova
«dovette, deve, dovrà», esso
stesso se'l faccia; perché, ove
avvenga che chi fa le cose esso
stesso le narri, ivi non può essere
più certa l'istoria.*

Giambattista Vico,
Principi di una scienza nuova

*sums up the preceding argument
'things had to be as they are, must be as
they are and will be'; for there
cannot be a history more
certain than when the person who creates
things is, at the same time, the person
who tells them.*

These principles are applied to all kinds of areas where European thought and productivity were highly active in the early eighteenth century. Vico, even if he had not directly inspired them, was certainly their guideline.

> For there cannot be a history more certain than when the person who creates things is, at the same time, the person who tells them.
>
> Giambattista Vico, *The Principles of a New Science*

In geography, the great explorations continued. Cavalier de La Salle travelled down the Mississippi and discovered Louisiana (1682), where 'New Orleans' (1718) was soon established. Roggeveen discovered Easter Island and Samoa (1721). Bering went beyond the straits that bear his name (1728) and drew maps of Siberia (1741). Tcheliuskin discovered Asia's most northern promontory (1740). Packe drew the first geological map (1737) and the temperature of the ocean depths was measured (1749). We know about the impact of the many scientific voyages of the period by Linnaeus (1732) and Maupertuis (1736) in Lapland, by Bouguer and La Condamine in Peru (1737–1745). Linnaeus published *Öländska och Gotländska resan* (*The Journey to Öland and Gotland*, 1745) and *Skånerejsen* (*The Journey to Scania*, 1751): the quality of their language, lyricism and the humour made them some of the great examples of Swedish prose.

In exploring already-known countries, other travellers blazed an anthropological trail. Tavernier, Chardin, Challe, Child and Bernier described Persia and the Indies. Galland translated *The Thousand and One Nights*

(1704) into French and Pétis de La Croix *The Thousand and One Days* (1710). Leibniz took an interest in China, as did Herbelot, Silhouette and the Jesuits: Fathers Lecomte, Varo, du Halde describes Chinese customs, history and language, and the *Edifying and Curious Letters* (1702–1743) tried to harmonise them with the truths of the Christian religion. America was the source of many a narrative: the splendour of its virgin territory does not allow us to forget the problem of peopling and cultivating it (La Hontan, Fathers Labat, Lafiteau and Charlevoix). Even if he set out to refute the system of Copernicus, Chrysanthos Notaras was caught up in this forward surge with *Isaghoghi is ta Gheoghraphika ke ta Spherika* (*Introduction to the Study of Geography and the Globe*, 1716) as was Costin (*Opisanie ziemi Moldawskiey i Multanskiey*, *A Description of Moldavia and Wallachia*, 1684), as was André Panckoucke (*Elements of Astronomy and Geography*, 1740).

The alter ego which eighteenth-century man observed could be far removed in space: weighty tomes were there to prove it such as the *Great Geographical, Historical and Critical Dictionary* (1739) by La Martinière, or the *General History of Travel*, compiled, mostly with translations of passages from English, by Prévost (1745–1760). This alter ego could also be very ancient: Warburton, for example, wrote an *Essay on Hieroglyphs* (1737), Herculaneum was discovered (1738) and Pompei excavated (1748). He could also be very close to us, this alter ego, and then Europeans learned how to know one another better. They felt the need and the taste for it as the popularity of the *Narration of the Journey to Spain* (1681) by Madame d'Aulnoy proved.

There were also the *Journey to Spain and Italy* (1730) by Father Labat, the *Letters on the English and the French* (1725) by Muralt, the *Narration* [. . .] of a Journey to Holland (1719) by Marcilly, *A Tour through the whole Island of Great Britain* (1724–1726) by Defoe, the poem *Die Alpen* (*The Alps*, 1728) by Haller, *Memoirs* (1735) by Pöllnitz, *Nordlands trompet* (*The Trumpet of the North*, 1739) by the Norwegian Dass, *Informal Letters from Italy* (1739, published in 1799) by President de Brosses and *Letters* (published in 1764) by Lady Montagu, the first-ever woman journalist. Fictitious letters by the Hungarian Kelemen Mikes (1690–1761) (*Törökországi levelek, Letters from Turkey*, published in 1794) chronicled the melancholy of an exile.

History demands not only man's total presence, but also very great perceptiveness on his part.

Ludovico Muratori,
Writers about Things Italian

For historical science, the break was more or less complete with the theological and providential concept expounded by Bossuet in *Discours sur l'Histoire universelle* in 1681, the same year as the publication of the *Great Historical Dictionary* by Moreri. The history of religion was actively researched (Arnold, Tillemont, the Abbé Fleury) and in orthodox countries, it served for the defence of Christian specificity: *Istoria peri ton en Ierosolimis patriarcheusanton* (*History of the Patriarchs of Jerusalem*, 1715) by Dositheos Notaras, *Istoria Iera* (*Holy History*, 1716) by Alexander Mavrokordatos. But was relieved by the interest shown in non-Christian civilisations – the Chinese, for example – and also the Muslims: the translation of the Koran into French by Du Ryer (1685), into English by Sale (1734), and part in Latin, part in Russian by Dimitri Cantemir; the essays of Reland, *De Religione Mohammedica* (*The Mohammedan Religion*, 1717) and de Boulainviller's *History of the Arabs and Mohammed* (1731). The field of historical research was widened by the interest taken in people worldwide – Lambert,

A General History of all the Peoples of the World (1750) – and by a renewed interest in Antiquity. It was also marked by the emergence of national histories, more sensitive to regional peculiarities than to great general laws, to the adventure of ethnic minorities than to the examination of God's plan for humanity. In Hungary, the Jesuit Samuel Timon (1675–1736) suggested a critique of historical sources in *Synopsis novæ chronologiæ* (*Synopsis of the New Chronology*, 1714–1719). More often than not, although motivated by varying local circumstances, these works had in common that they promoted a secular and relativist notion of history. The Slovaks reacted against Hungarian historiography and exalted their Slav past, notably Matej Bel, a scholar with an international reputation, in a huge, unfinished encyclopaedic work, *Notitia Hungariæ Novæ historico-geographica* (*Historical and Geographical Information on New Hungary*, 1735–1742). The phenomenon touched Italy with *Rerum Italicarum scriptores* (*Writers on Things Italian*, 1723) and *Annali d'Italia* (*Annals of Italy*, 1744) by **Ludovico Antonio Muratori (1672–1750)**. He directed an entire team of researchers and informants and, together with Voltaire, was the man who entered into the largest correspondence with other Europeans (*Lettere inedite, Unpublished Letters*, published in 1883: more than twenty thousand letters sent and as many received). There was also Giannone's *Istoria civile del regno di Napoli* (*Civil History of the Kingdom of Naples*, 1723). The phenomenon touched Scandinavian countries with *Danmarks Riges Historie* (*History of the Kingdom of Denmark*, 1733) by Holberg and *Svea Rikets Historia* (*History of the Kingdom of Sweden*, 1747–1761) by Dalin. France was not far behind with the works of Father Daniel, the President Hénault, Duclos, the Abbé du Bos, Dom Dantine and, above all, Voltaire. The personal development which led him from the individual adventure in *The History of Charles XII* (1731) to that of a whole society in *The Century of Louis XIV* (1751) and finally to that, conjointly, of all nations in *The Essay on Manners* (1756) reveals the progressive opening-up of historical curiosity. The latter gave full meaning to local history which flourished everywhere.

The study of law, particularly the importance attached to natural law, leaned for support on the earliest work of Grotius and Pufendorf, translated into French by Barbeyrac. Gravina, Holberg, Muratori, Wolff and Burlamaqui take critical reflection forward at this point. The masterpiece was *De l'esprit des lois* (*The Spirit of the Laws*, 1748) by **Charles de Secondat, baron de la Brède et de Montesquieu (1689–1755)**. The author undertook the analysis of an enormous mass of facts and ideas about the institutions and social habits of all times and all countries. Instead of compiling, as a moralist, a picture of human stupidity and fickleness to illustrate the reign of the gratuitous or to glorify that of Providence, he postulated their intelligibility as a philosopher. He took from his material some outlines which have remained famous: the three possible forms of government (republican, despotic, monarchical) and their respective principles (virtue, fear, honour); the theory of climate (which makes customs depend on the multiplicity and relativity of the various factors acting on them); the non-preferential situation of religion (as one of the components, among others, of the life of societies in history); and the need for intermediaries and for the division of powers.

Public law is better known in Europe than in Asia; however . . .

Montesquieu, *Persian Letters*

Montesquieu was the inspiration behind political sociology. He can be considered the father of liberalism, although he was conscious of its dangers. The way in which *Persian Letters* was composed – a 'chain' rather than a 'plan' – shows his care not to enclose himself in a system, but to make his reader reconstitute a number of 'intermediary ideas', implying a necessary moral dimension in his intellectual understanding of certain mechanisms.

It is in the government of a Republic that we need all the power of education. The fear engendered by despotisms speaks for itself amid threats and punishments; the honour of monarchies is fostered by passions, and, in its turn, fosters them: but political virtue is self-renunciation, which is always a very painful thing.

Montesquieu, *The Spirit of Laws*

For economic matters, we have to wait for the second half of the century, the ground for which was laid by Du Monceau (*Treatise on the Cultivation of Land*, 1750), the Abbé Galiani (*Della Moneta, On Money*, 1780) and, shortly afterwards, Hume (*Political Discourses*, 1752). But politics called forth a plethora of works, based above all on the idea of the contract launched by Locke and criticism in France of Louis XIV's absolute monarchy. Despite Boussuet's *Politics taken from the Holy Scriptures* (1709), this criticism revealed a chorus of voices, in turn anxious, polemical and pathetic: the voices of Boisguilbert, Vauban, Saint-Simon, Boulainviller, Fénelon and Ramsay. Their opinions were repeated, in various contexts, not only by Englishmen (Bolingbroke, Mandeville, *The Fable of the Bees*, 1705), but by Germans (Wolff, Frederick II, *Anti-Machiavelli*, 1739, composed in French), Danes (Holberg), Poles (Stanislas Leszczyński, *Głos wolny wolnosc ubezpieczajacy, The Free Voice of the Citizen*, 1749), Greeks (Konstantin Mavrokordatos) and Russians (Possochkov, *Kniga o skudosti i o bagatstve, The Book of Poverty and Wealth*, 1724). Wars continued to tear Europe apart (the War of the League of Augsburg, 1688–1697; the War of the Spanish Succession, 1701–1714; the Northern War, 1701–1721; the War of the Polish Succession, 1733–1738; the War of the Austrian Succession, 1740–1748), without taking into account the permanent pressure exerted by the Turks on the Austrian and Russian Empires, the Russo-Persian War (1722–1723), the colonial struggle for supremacy between France and England (1744–1748) and the Jacobite risings in Great Britain. Fewer than twenty-five years of peace separated the treaties of Nijmegen (1678) and of Aix-la-Chapelle (1748). Nevertheless, plans for peace in perpetuity sprang up everywhere (William Penn, 1694, the Abbé de Saint-Pierre, 1713).

Educational problems were at the centre of the theories propounded by the Enlightenment in those countries which were first to be illuminated by it. Before *Telemachus*, (1699) Fénelon composed *Treatise on the Education of Girls*, (1651–1715) (1687), de Crouzas published *Treatise on the Education of Children* (1722), Rollin wrote his famous *Treatise on Study* (1726–1731) and Morelly, before publishing his explosive *Code of Nature* (1755), brought out his *Essay on the Human Heart or Natural Principles of Education* (1745). In the countries where the rays of the Enlightenment were slower to break through, education appeared all the more important: it was wholly in the hands of a Church which often proposed the most solid of obstacles to new ideas. In Poland, educational standards had declined during the 'Saxon night' to reach its low point around 1750 (see the almanac disturbing in its pious, even crude stupidity, *Nowe Ateny albo Akademia Wszelkiej scjencji pełna*, *New Athens or the Academy Full of All Knowledge*, 1745, by Chmielovski).

The beginnings of reform emerged with Stanisław Konarski (1700–1773), whose Collegium Nobilium, founded in 1740, aimed, with new teaching methods, to educate an élite able to pull the country out of the morass of obscurantism into which it had plunged (Konarski was later decorated with a 'Sapere audi' medal by Stanislas-Augustus Poniatowski). Later reforms centred around the progressive Jesuit Bohomolec and the brothers Załuski who opened the first public library in Poland in 1747 and, in their *Programma literarium* (*Programme of Letters*, 1743) planned a vast publishing project involving Polish writers. Russia was so backward that the efforts of Czar Peter to raise the educational level of his ruling élites by founding schools and institutes, learning Western languages and publishing many translations only bore fruit later, under Catherine II. Only questions relating to language usage

and poetry were fit subjects for active personal reflection.

In Spain, there is not much to say about the 'French century' imposed by Philip IV other than that classical principles served to keep a tight rein on the excesses of a frenzied Baroque. But there was one man, **Benito Feijóo y Montenegro (1676–1764)**, who bore witness to the progress of critical rationalism. His major works, *Teatro crítico universal* (*Theatre of Universal Criticism*, 1726–1760, sub-titled 'In order to destroy common errors') and *Cartas eruditas y curiosas* (*Erudite and Curious Letters*, 1742–1760), which tackled everything from astronomy to philology, with a wealth of erudition, a delicacy of judgement and a remarkable freedom of expression was considered to be a veritable encyclopedia, heralding the intellectual awakening of Charles III. This theatre was also progressive enough to provoke a reaction from traditionalists, including Mañer's *Anti-teatro crítico* (*Anti-Theatre of Criticism*, 1729).

In Portugal, under John V, the dominance of the Company of Jesus and of the Baroque tradition, especially in preaching, would have prevented all intellectual development for many years had it not been for the education of the Oratorians, who were very open-minded, and the intervention of exiled intellectuals – the 'extrangeirados' – who astutely asked economic, social and pedagogical questions. Oliveira wrote *Cartas*, *Letters*, 1742, Martinho de Mendonça *Apontamentos para a educacão de um menino nobre*, *Notes for the Education of a Young Nobleman*, 1734 and **Luis Vernei (1713–1792)** wrote *Verdadeiro Metodo de Estudar* (*True Method of Study*, 1746), which aimed to bring about a complete cultural reform, sparking the liveliest argument of the entire century.

Greece was very interesting. There was a twofold struggle: the defence of the Christian community against the Ottoman invader and the defence of the specifically Orthodox against the Catholic or Protestant ideology which accompanied the new knowledge offered by the seventeenth century in the West. This is why the progress and dissemination of ideas were both against and with the Church. They were made by 'religious humanists' such as the two Notaras, Comninos, Kyminitis, Palladas, Anthineos of Iberia, Grigoras, Kalogeras, Gordatos, Mandakasis, the Phanariotes (Greeks from Constantinople had become governors in territories bordering the Danube) like the family of Mavrokordatos. Philosophers, developed education not only in Greece (Damodos founded a school in Cephalonia where he taught the philosophy of Descartes, 1720; Anthrakitis taught modern science in Ioannina until 1725), but in territories bordering the Danube and as far as Moscow. Academies were organised on the twin models of the University of Padua and the patriarchal academy of Constantinople: an enlightened example at fusing the principles of traditional religion – not without a reaction from Orthodox conservatives – with the spirit of openness of 'learned Europe'.

The fields of linguistics and poetics were blossoming, not only because the origin and evolution of language were preferred subjects in social sciences, but also because the emancipation of vernacular languages in relation to Latin – even to French, the language of culture, diplomacy and the courts – was a long way from being a fact of life everywhere. This was the period in which dictionary production multiplied, as did contributions to the history of national languages and to the rules governing their prosody.

To return to Vico: he was one of the first to try a kind of writing – autobiography (1725–1731) – in which the individual became the measure of all things. With the Russian Avvakum (*Žitie protopopa Avvakuma im sammim napisannoe, Life of the Protopope Avvakum written by Himself*, 1682), the Swede Swedberg (*Lefwernes beskrifning, Autobiography*, published in 1941), the Germans Francke (*Anfang und Fortgang der Bekehrung A.H. Franckes, Beginning and Continuation of the Conversion of A.H. Francke*, 1691) and Bernd (*Bernd's eigene Lebensbeschreibung, Bernd's Own Account of His Life*, 1738), the Hungarians Miklós Bethlen (1642–1717), Önéletírása (*Autobiography*, 1708–1710) and

Ferenc Rákóczi (1676–1735) (*Confessio peccatoris, Confessions of a Sinner*, 1716–1719), when memoirs, real or imaginary, were popular, we see the launch of a genre to which Rousseau later gave its most striking form with *Confessions*.

AN EFFERVESCENCE OF TRADITIONAL LITERARY GENRES

After seeing such a wide cross-section of intellectual and innovative activities, we may find it surprising that Enlightenment man was still able to think about and find enough leisure to devote himself to traditional literary genres. Perhaps because the period was dominated by texts containing ideas, the Enlightenment writer prepared us for the emergence of what today we would call literature. Without separating them from this fertility, this simmering critical and practical knowledge, the writer had the talent to continue the dramatic and poetic forms he had inherited, to modify and enrich the great romance tradition, and to create new genres, better adapted to the new expression of his taste. We can understand why the period was characterised by an expansion of literary life at every level: a multiplicity of writers, a widening of the reading public, a renewing of genres. We can also understand why dramatic forms, which appeal to an immediate audience and respond to a need for collective diversion and exaltation, were generally well received. Nor was this reception in any way diminished by the popularity of lyrical drama. In this century won over to rationalism, poetry enjoyed an enigmatic status and a paradoxical attraction. Prose fiction revealed an exceptional vitality and inventiveness. It will be in this order that our 'Grand Tour' of texts of European literature will progress.

Forms of drama: from Racine and Congreve to Lessing and Goldoni

The life of European drama was marked by several events which clearly indicated the direction in which it was going. The foundation of the Comédie-Française (1680), for example, symbolised the general prestige of the great French dramatists who were everywhere translated, adapted and imitated: Corneille by Michiel de Swaen, Richard Steele and Whitehead; Racine by Philip and Cammaert; Molière especially by Girolamo Gigli, Cibber and Holberg, 'the Molière of Denmark'. Theatre in Spain, still dazzled by Calderón, was gradually reduced to this imitative activity and, as in Portugal, it was anxious to prune the excesses of the Baroque frenzy. In Lisbon a polemic at the end of the 1730s opposed the representatives of the Spanish Baroque theatre (Valença) to those working in the classical French tradition (Gusmaõ). French influence also dominated the French-speaking Low Countries (the tragedies of Walef, from 1708 to 1724) and, indeed, the Dutch-speaking Low Countries – most of the hundred plays by the Brussels playwright Cammaert have been lost – but Michiel de Swaen (1654–1707) was much admired for *Andronicus* and *De zedhige doodt van Carel den Vyfden* (*The Moral Death of Charles V, c.*1704). French influence was strong in the United Provinces, where the group Nihil Volentibus Arduum reformed the theatre in Amsterdam, scintillating from the seventeenth century, in the direction of discipline and naturalness. Andries Pels (1631–1681) sketched out its theory in *Gebruik en Misbruik des tooneels* (*The Use and Abuse of the Theatre*, 1681). Tragedy is exemplified by Rotgans, Schermer, Huydecoper. Comedy's great practitioner was Pieter Langendijk (1683–1756), 'the Dutch Molière' (*Het Wederzijds Huwelijksbedrog, The Mutual Deceit of Marriage*, 1714).

There was a second series of symbolic events: while the fervour of the literati and that of the people militated in favour of the movement of travelling players and for the creation of new theatres (Copenhagen, 1722; Edinburgh, 1736; Stockholm and San Carlo in Naples, 1737), intimidatory and repressive measures cracked down on this genre whose subversive power was felt by the ruling powers. In the name of Christian morality, Bossuet condemned the theatre irrevocably in *Maxims and Reflections on the Comedy* (1694); the Italians were expelled from Paris in 1697, only to return, thanks to the Regent, in 1716. Christian VI, rigorously moral, closed down the 'diabolical contraption' in Copenhagen (1730). In London, Robert Walpole, no doubt irritated by Fielding's impertinence (*Historical Register for 1736*), promulgated the 'Stage Licensing Act' (1737), which brought back the severe censorship that had disappeared in 1695.

A third characteristic of the life of the genre was the production of collections of plays for each country. These gathered together the existing wealth of drama and made it accessible to others: the *Anthology of Italian Theatre* (1700) by Gherardi, one of the most celebrated Harlequins; *Il Teatro alla moda* (*The Fashionable Theatre*, 1721) in which Marcello reviews the traditions of the lyrical drama of his country to mock and reform them; *Deutsche Schaubühne* (*German Theatre*, 1740–1745) by Johann Christoph Gottsched (1700–1766) which, though still under the tutelage of classical theory, paved the way for a new chapter in the history of German theatre, helped by Neuber's actors. There was Fontenelle's *Life of Monsieur Corneille with the History of the French Theatre down to Him* (1742) which emphasised the period before Louis XIV. Baretti translated the same into Italian (1748). There was the *English Theatre* (1748) by La Place, and *Verhandeling over de redenvoering* (*Essay on Declaiming*, 1751) in which Francis de La Fontaine, after Luigi Riccoboni, encompassed the history of Western theatre. This even included the theatre in China: Father Prémare produced the first translation from the Chinese in Europe, *The Orphan of Tchao-che-koueul* (1736). Finally, while Shakespeare was unrecognised almost everywhere, the English prepared a spectacular resurrection for him at the end of the century: Nicholas Rowe (1674–1718) published his *Complete Works* (1709), and the actor, Garrick, who arrived in London in 1737, produced the plays of the great Elizabethan after 1747 with fresh vigour.

Although the period had lost the sense of the tragic at the same time as that of the sacred – even if the forms of a 'moral' or 'intimate' religion were preserved – it maintained its nostalgia for the greatness of tragedy and an admiration for its formal perfection. So this genre triumphed once again on every European stage. In France, where Racine ended his career with *Esther* (1689) and *Athalie* (1691), his torch was taken from him by many emulators, including Crébillon, who took fury and violence to extremes (*Atreus and Thyestis*, 1707; *Rhadamistes and Zenobia*, 1711), and Voltaire, who began and ended his career with huge tragic successes (*Œdipus*, 1718; *Irene*, 1778) adding to them other major achievements, known and imitated throughout Europe. Among them were *Zaïre* (1732), *Alzire* (1736), and *Mahomet* (1741) which all in their way took part in the great battle of the Enlightenment. Despite Voltaire's poetic talent, his skill in philosophical propaganda and the innovations he brought to his choice of themes, staging and acting, this was not the part of his work which has passed down to posterity.

In England, the tragic vein was also illustrated by authors memorable for their work in other genres: Joseph Addison (1672–1719) with *Cato* (1713), Young (*The Revenge*, 1721) and Thomson (*Sophonisba*, 1730; *Tancred and Sigismunda*, 1745) which dealt with oriental subjects, or even Smollett (*The Regicide*, 1739) and Samuel Johnson (1709–1784) with *Irene* (1749). From Germany came the famous *Sterbender Cato* (*Cato Dying*, 1732), which illustrated in Alexandrines Gottsched's classical theories. The Austrian Low Countries gave us *Iphigenie ofte Orestes* (1722) by Krafft; Scandinavia *Brynhilda* (1738) by Dalin; Russia *Xorev* (1747) and *Sinav and Truvor* (1750) by Alexander Soumarokov (1717–1777), which took its themes from national history, and *Tamir and Selim* (1750) by Lomonossov. Poland only saw the rebirth of its theatre slightly later, with *Tragedia Epaminondy* (*The Tragedy of Epaminondas*, 1756) by Konarski.

What happened in Italy revealed Europe's relationship with the tragic. It was venerated in its pure form – Gravina published five 'Greek' tragedies in 1712 – and French models were not only followed, but they had Italian rivals. Maffei published *Merope* in 1713, which was the best Italian tragedy before Alfieri and which served as an example for Voltaire. Language was turned in the direction of sentimentality: Metastasio, a protégé of Gravina and Zeno, been with a tragedy, *Giustino* (1712), before inaugurating sentimental melodrama in Italy with *Didonne abbandonata* (*Dido Abandoned*, 1724). His triumphant career lasted more than thirty years. A similar development took place in England where Rowe invented the 'domestic tragedy', 'a sad story of unhappiness in private life', with *The Fair Penitent* (1703), which inspired Richardson, and *Lady Jane Grey* (1716). In his own way, sometimes judged to be 'excessive', George Lillo (1693–1739) took the genre in the direction of 'bourgeois' realism in his popular prose tragedies *The London Merchant* (1731) and *Fatal Curiosity* (1736).

Enlightenment man was indeed more concerned with current moral and social problems than with the grandiose misfortunes of legendary kings. So it was rather in the genre of comedy that he exercised his mind, his satiric verve, his reforming energy and his partiality for pleasure. Molière's French successors preferred the comedy of manners – the cynicism of financial circles, the absurdity of socialites, wordly upward mobility, matrimonial ballets: Dancourt (*The Cavalier à la mode*, 1687; *The Speculators*, 1710), Regnard (*The Gambler*, 1696; *The Sole Beneficiary*, 1708), Dufresny (*Contrariness*, 1700; *The Village Coquette*, 1715), Destouches (*Ingratitude*, 1712; *The Boaster*, 1732), Allainval (*The School for Bourgeois*, 1728), Piron (*The Mania for Measuring*, 1738) and Gresset (*The Bad Man*, 1747). The best example of its kind was *Turcaret* (1709) by Lesage, who also produced several vaudevilles at the popular theatre of La Foire. Manners were also the main field of investigation for the English playwrights John Vanbrugh (1664–1726) in *The Relapse* (1696) and *The Provoked Wife* (1697, translated into

French by Saint-Évremond), and George Farquhar (1678–1707) with the verve of the very devil in *The Recruiting Officer* (1706) and *The Beaux' Stratagem* (1707). Suzanna Centlivre wrote *The Busy Body* (1709) and *A Bold Stroke for a Wife* (1718). Above all, there was **William Congreve (1670–1729),** the author of *The Double Dealer* (1694), *The Way of the World* (1700) and *Love for Love* (1695). In this play, one of the protagonists, Valentine, thinks of becoming a writer, a 'poet', to become rich and seduce the beautiful Angelica:

SCANDAL *Aye? Why then I'm afraid Jeremy has wit; for wherever it is, it's always contriving its own ruin.*

JEREMY *Why, so I have been telling my master, sir. Mr Scandal, for heaven's sake, sir, try if you can dissuade him from turning poet.*

SCANDAL *Poet! Why, what the devil, has not your poverty made you enemies enough? Must you needs show your wit to get more?*

JEREMY *Aye, more indeed; for who cares for anybody that has more wit than himself?*

SCANDAL *Jeremy speaks like an oracle. Don't you see how worthless great men, and dull rich rogues, avoid a witty man of small*

> *fortune? Why, he seems commissioned by heaven to seize the better half.*
>
> VALENTINE *Therefore I would rail in my wrightings and be revenged.*
>
> SCANDAL *At whom? The whole world? Impotent and vain! Who would die a martyr to sense in a country where the religion is folly?*
>
> William Congreve,
> *Love for Love*

Molière's model for the comedy of manners was not the only one to be exploited. Comedy also chose history as its theme (De Swaen, *De gecroonde Leersse, The Crowned Boot,* 1688) or in the great Spanish repertoire (Kerrickx, Langendijk and Fielding adapted *Don Quixote*). When the Danes wanted to establish a genuine national theatre, they addressed themselves to **Ludvig Holberg (1684–1754).** He went for inspiration to the whole of European theatre from Antiquity to Spain, from Molière to the commedia dell'arte, only overlooking Shakespeare. Holberg's *Theatre*, published in 1731, contained thirty-four plays, including *Erasmus Montanus* (1724) and *Jeppe paa Bierget* (*Jeppe of the Mountain,* 1722). This tells the story of a drunken peasant who, believing himself to be a baron, begins to exercise a tyrannical power, revealing the conservativeness of the genre, despite his boldness 'for a laugh':

> *Naar Bønder Handvaerksmaend man Regiment vil give*
> *Da scepteret til Riis kan snart forvandlet blive [. . .]*
> *Vi derfor Øvrighed fra Ploven meer ei tage.*
> *plough.*

Ludvig Holberg, *Comoedier*

> *When to peasants, and to craftsmen we wish to give power, their sceptre quite quickly will turn into a whip [. . .]*
> *Let us no longer look for our masters among those who push the*

It is difficult to place the comedies by **Pierre Carlet de Chamblain de Marivaux (1688–1763)** either in the usual categories of the genre (intrigue, manners, characters), or in any formal tradition. The titles of the thirty-five comedies which he put on in Paris from 1720 to 1746 usually indicates their content: *The Surprise of Love* (1722), *Double Inconstancy*

(1723), *Prince in Disguise, The False Maid-servant, The Unexpected Ending* (1724), *The Game of Love and Chance* (1730), *The Happy Stratagem* (1733), *The Mistake* (1734), *False Confidences* (1737), *The Test* (1740). He was a philosopher, a psychologist, even a sociologist, which he showed in the 'journals' and the novels that he also published. Marivaux particularly had all theatre's resources, all the ambiguities which form its basis: game/seriousness, reality/illusion, being/appearance, convention/surprise, truth/falsehood. What he has sometimes been reproached with – always writing what amounts to the same comedy – appears today as his greatest merit. Making practical use in his dramatic art of the lessons of philosophical empiricism, he proposed a series of variations. These allowed him to transform the situations in each of his plays into as many experiences. Their juxtaposition ends by giving a complete picture of the conflicts between love and self-esteem, individual desire and the law, outward or inward, the security of regulations and the pleasure of leaving them behind, if only fleetingly. The dramatic 'moment' he favours is no longer that in which the lovers have to overcome the obstacles which prevent their love being made official in marriage, but that in which love – a pure and delightful surprise – seeks to set itself up as a reason, as an existential value, as a law of society's functioning. This is why there is no break between the sentimental comedies, in which the lovers resist their own desire to put it to the test, and the plays dealing with political utopias (*The Island of Slaves*, 1725; *The Island of Reason*, 1727) in which the deep solidarity between the sentimental encounter with the other and social cohesion is revealed. Still experimental was the alternation between French theatre, which maintained the rules and traditions of the Great Century, and Italian theatre, which was more flexible in its combination of the realism of gesture and the fantasy of dream. The language of Marivaux, in which the affectation of a 'new preciosity' had for a long time been denounced, was the melting-pot of that experience: it is at the very heart of the surprises that it contrives, the twists and turns it suggests, that the truth of feelings is tested. In *The Game of Love and Chance*, Silvia poses as her maid Lisette, and Dorante as his manservant Bourguignon:

SILVIA *Bourguignon, I can't be angry*
with the way you talk to me; but, I beg

you, let's change the subject of conversation
to your master. You can do without
speaking to me of love, I imagine?
DORANTE *You could do without making me*
feel it.
SILVIA *Oh! I'm going to lose my temper. You*
exasperate me. Once again, leave your love
where it is.
DORANTE *Take off your face then.*
SILVIA (To herself) *In the end I think he*
amuses me . . .
(Aloud) *Well, Bourguignon, don't you*
want to finish? Will I have to leave you?
(To herself) *I should have done already.*
DORANTE. – *Wait, Lisette, I wanted to talk*
to you about something else, but I've
forgotten what it was.
SILVIA *I too had something to tell you, but*
you've driven it right out of my head.
DORANTE *I remember asking you if your*
mistress was as nice as you are.
SILVIA *You've come back to your road at a*
tangent. Goodbye.
DORANTE *What? No, Lisette; I'm only*
interested in my master.
SILVIA *Well, so be it! I wanted to talk to you*
about him too [. . .].

Marivaux,
The Game of Love and Chance

Marivaux was a singular and inimitable dramatist. His degree of success was often disputed at the time, and the true greatness of his genius was only realised in the twentieth century.

It was from England that the germs of comic theatre's transformation came, from three directions. The first, following in the footsteps of the Frenchman Scarron and the Dutchman Focquenbroch, was the burlesque and violently satirical parody by Fielding: *Tom Thumb* (1730), *The Mock Doctor* (1732) and especially *The Grub Street Opera* (1731). This had become the symbol of a literature which had left the salons of polite society to win over and divert the streets. The second of these directions was a mixture of genres and tones, with John Gay (1685–1732), a member of the insolent 'Scriblerus Club' together with

Arbuthnot and Pope. Gay wrote *What d'ye call it?* (1715), a 'tragi-comi-pastoral-farce', and the famous *Beggar's Opera* (1728), a pleasing satire against the aristocracy, in which the author mocked the vogue for the Italian opera of Handel, considered to be a perversion of the taste of the world at large. In the penultimate scene of *The Beggar's Opera*, Captain Du Butin is about to be hanged:

PLAYER [. . .] This is a deep tragedy
[. . .] for an opera must end happily.
BEGGAR Your objection, Sir, is very just;
and is easily removed. For you must allow
that in this kind of drama, 'tis no matter
how absurdly things are brought about. So
– you rabble there – run and cry a reprieve
[. . .] let the prisoner be brought back to his
wives in triumph.
PLAYER All this we must do, to comply with
the taste of the town.
BEGGAR Through the whole piece you may
observe such a similitude of manners in
high and low life, that it is difficult to
determine whether (in the fashionable vices)
the fine gentlemen imitate the gentlemen of
the road, or the gentlemen of the road the
fine gentlemen. Had the play remain'd, as I
at first intended, it would have carried a
most excellent moral. 'Twould have shown
that the lower sort of people have their vices
in a degree as well as the rich: and that
they are punished for them.

John Gay, *The Beggar's Opera*

The third direction was that of 'sentimental comedy'. Its invention is usually attributed to Colley Cibber (1671–1757), *Love's Last Shift* (1696), *The Provoked Husband* (1728), but it was also distinguished by Richard Steele (1672–1729) in *The Tender Husband* (1705) and *The Conscious Lovers* (1722). This kind of comedy, which appealed more to sentimentality than to mockery and was more interested in moralising than in depth of character, was taken up in France under the name of 'comédie larmoyante' ('tearful comedy') by La Chaussée (*Prejudice à la moded, 1735; Pamela,* 1743). This last play was inspired by

Richardson, as was Goldoni's *Pamela nubile* (1750). Goldoni had already shown his willingness to reform the commedia dell'arte (*Momolo cortesan, Momolo, the Accomplished Courtier,* 1739; *Donna di garbo, The Good Woman,* 1743), offering a glimpse of how prolific it was (sixteen plays in Venice in 1750). He only gave a full indication of his worth in the second half of the century. The gradual abandonment of models, even the rules of classical theatre, the mixing of genres and giving works a moral paved the way for the coming of the drama towards which, in their own way, Lessing and Diderot oriented European theatre after 1750.

The paradoxical status of poetry

Throughout Europe at the end of the seventeenth century, poetry was the occasion, the means and the stake of a confrontation between rules inherited from ancient tradition and the new needs for self-expression of sensibilities whose relationship with the world, heaven and the city was undergoing profound change. This was first revealed by many theoretical essays on poetic art. The one by Boileau, taken together with his *Reflections on Longinus* (1694) and the ideal of which is illustrated by his final *Satires* (1705) and *Epistles* (1696–1698) and by the publication of his *Works* (1716), was copiously translated, commented on or adapted, by Gottsched in Germany, Ericeira in Portugal, Labare in The Netherlands, Luzan in Spain and Bisshe in England. But quite soon we pull away from this model in two opposing directions, though they both pretend to fight classical 'artificiality'. Valadares e Souza, in *Silva Poetica* (*The Poetic Wood,* 1739), criticised the very principle of poetic representation in the name of scientific truth. Bodmer, on the contrary, in *Critische Abhandlung von dem Wunderbaren in der Poesie (Critical Treatise on the Marvellous in Poetry,* 1740), restored rights to the imagination, anticipating and preparing for the movement of poetic language towards creative autonomy. This revenge of the madwoman at home, this liberation of the word was also what Breitinger wrote about in *Kritische Abhandlung von der Natur, den Absichten, und dem Gebrauch des Gleichnisses* (*A Critical Essay on the Nature, Aims and Use of Metaphor*, 1740), and was Akentide's theme in *The Pleasures of Imagination* (1744).

However, at the beginning of the century, there were still arguments about the way in which the Ancients should be translated. *The Iliad* by La Motte (1714) took an opposing view to that of Madame Dacier (1699), while Pope published an English translation (1715–1720) as Rowe did for Lucan (1718). Madame Dacier and Pope also published an *Odyssey*, in 1716 and 1726 respectively, Cocquelet brought out an *Aeneid* in Antwerp (1747), and the Abbé Conti translated it into Greek and Latin (1739). Reflections on the importance of the literal meaning of the ancient text depend, according to the places, on two types of motivation: either a 'modern' philosophy of autonomy, in conformity with the all-conquering spirit of the Enlightenment or a promotion of vernacular languages. Into the first category fall the interventions of Saint-Évremond, Fénelon, La Motte; into the second fall all kinds of attempts to adapt the rules for measure, balance, good taste and naturalness promulgated by Horace for various national traditions. In this way Holberg began his career as a poet with *Peder Paars* (1719), a comic parody of the *Aeneid* along the lines of Boileau's *The Lectern*. Similarly **Olof von Dalin (1708–1763)** took his inspiration from Voltaire's *The Henriad* to write in alexandrines *Swenska Friheten* (*Swedish Freedom*, 1742). Antioch Kantemir (1708–1744), with his nine *Satires* (1729–1738) – imitated from Horace, Juvenal and Boileau and translated into Italian, French and German – was one of the pioneers of secular Russian literature, together with Vassili Trediakovski (1703–1769), *Epistola ot rossijskoj poezii k Apollonu*, *Epistle on Russian Poetry to Apollo*, 1735, and Soumarokov who, basing himself on Boileau, fought against what he called Lomonossov's 'delirium'. The latter mixed an elevated style, rigorous composition and mythological allusions to a Baroque taste

for exuberant metaphor and theatricality (*Oda na vzjatie Xotina, Ode on the Capture of Khotin*, 1739; *Razmyšlenija o Božûem veličestve, Meditations on the Divine Majesty*, 1743). Jan Pieter Van Male (1681–1735) enriched his country's poetry with *Gheestigheden der Vlaemsche Rhymkonst* (*The Diversions of Flemish Poetry*, 1708–1718), full of humour and freshness. Friedrich von Canitz (1654–1699), in the manner of Horace and Boileau, wrote verses against the vogue of the pastoral poem (*Nebenstunden unterschiedener Gedichte, Hours of Poetry*, 1700). Johann Günther (1695–1723) protested at Baroque artificiality and restored the tradition of the 'Clerici vagantes' of the poetry of the Goliards (*Gedichte, Poems*, 1723–1735).

Two countries organised this adaptation of classical taste to their own tradition by founding a militant school armed with theories. In England there was the 'Augustan' school which included Arbuthnot, Swift and Gay, in orbit around **Alexander Pope (1688–1744)** and the latter's principles expounded in the *Essay on Criticism* (1711):

> True wit is Nature to advantage dressed;
> What oft was thought but ne'er so well
>   expressed.
>
> Alexander Pope,
Essay on Criticism

Pope's *Pastorals* (1709) and *Windsor Forest* (1713), formally perfect but fairly conventional descriptions of nature, applied this programme, while the unusual *Eloisa to Abelard* (1717), based on Bussy-Rabutin's reworking of the letters of Héloïse, allows a sensuality and a suffering of solitude to show through. These sound like the heart-to-heart confidences of a man ill-favoured by nature and abused by critical opinion. Without giving up his classical aesthetics, Pope became the great poet of the Enlightenment, universally admired as such because of the ease, finesse and serenity of his writing. He did not write old-fashioned verse about new thoughts, but mellifluous and superbly crafted verse on explosive topics.

In Italy, the Academia dell'Arcadia, founded in Rome in 1690, set itself the task of eliminating bad taste and the then dominant pomposity of Marinism. It found its chief theoreticians in Gian Vicenzo Gravina (1664–1718), *Della Ragion poetica* (*On Poetic Reason*, 1708) and Muratori, decidedly polyvalent (*Della perfetta poesia italiana*, *On Perfect Italian Poetry*, 1706; *Riflessioni sopra il buon gusto*, *Reflections on Good Taste*, 1715). Favouring pastoral simplicity, this school poetry was sometimes banal and mawkish, but it favoured and exalted 'naïve' talents. It was popular in the Iberian peninsula: Freire's *Arte Poetica* (*Art of Poetry*, 1748) was a manifesto of Portuguese Arcadianism. The best representative of this school was **Pietro Trapassi**, known as **Metastasio (1698–1782)**, who had published a collection of poems in 1717 in Naples and bequeathed to melodrama texts full of charm and emotion. Despite their lightness and a certain monotony in the arguments, these works won considerable success for him all over Europe, particularly in Vienna where he was for a long time 'poeta cesareo'. They are still enough to make this poet one of Italy's national glories.

Aria	*Air*
L'onda, che mormora *tra sponda e sponda,* *l'aura, che tremola* *tra fronda e fronda,* *è meno instabile* *del vestro cor.* *Pur l'alme semplici* *de' folli amanti* *sol per voi spargono* *sospiri e pianti,* *e da voi sperano* *fede in amor.*	*The stream, which murmurs* *from bank to bank,* *the breeze, which ruffles the surface* *from foliage to foliage,* *are less inconstant than your* *heart.* *And yet the pure hearts* *of insensate lovers* *shed for you alone* *sighs and tears,* *and from you hope for* *fidelity in love.*

Metastasio

The Hungarian László Amadé (1704–1764), the singer of a precious love, was influenced by Italian dance and the German courtly song, but also by Magyar folksongs, as was Ferenc Faludi (1704–1779) who, before Herder, collected the poetry of the people. In this manner known as 'Anacreontic' – straightforward, graceful poetry, singing the pleasures of the table, wine and love as the Greek poet Anacreon did – adapted to rococo taste, German poets also had a part to play. They include Friedrich von Hadegorn (1708–1754) in *Moralische Gedichte* (*Moral Poems*, 1750), Johann Peter Uz (1720–1796) in *Lyrische Gedichte* (*Lyrical Poems*, 1749) and Johann Wilhelm Gleim (1719–1803) in *Versuch in scherzhaften Lieder* (*An Attempt at Joyful Songs*, 1745). The manner was connected to that of the French poets known as 'light': the Fontenelle of *Pastoral Poems* (1688), Chaulieu (*Poems*, 1724) and Voltaire, who excelled as much in minor genres as in major ones.

The major genres continued to produce much interesting work. If Latin verse was on the wane, even in countries where it was still being used for religious or scientific works (Poland, Hungary, Scandinavia), we still see it appearing in France (Santeul, Huet, Ménage). And, in this light and mocking century, great official poetry, solemn and conventional, continued to have if not popular enthusiasm at least the favour of the great and good whose virtues and exploits it praised. In France, Boileau (*Ode on the Capture of Namur*, 1693), Perrault (*Ode for the King of Sweden*, 1702) and even Voltaire (*Poem for Fontenoy*, 1745) or

Marmontel mined this vein. It was copiously exploited elsewhere, for example by Matthew Prior (1664–1721) in *Ode to the Queen* (1706) or Thomson (*Poem on the Death of Sir Isaac Newton*, 1727). Arnold Hoogvliet (*Zydebalen, Sacks of Silk*, 1740) was a distinguished representative of the genre of Georgic poetry also cultivated by De Marre (*Hof en Mengeldichten, Georgics and Various Poems*, 1746).

Religious poetry also saw the continuation of the great tradition of the sixteenth and seventeenth centuries, although it weakened. Perrault and then Racine kept it going in France, without great success. With *The Hind and the Panther* (1687), Dryden pressed for ecumenism. Emblem books, which remained popular, were published in Holland (Luyken, *Jezus en de ziel, Jesus and the Soul*, 1678) and in Antwerp (Franz Nerrincq, 1638–1712, *De Goddelycke Voorsienigheydt, Divine Providence*, 1710). In Germany, for the edification of souls, Tersteegen rhymed pietist formulas and songs. Two of the best Polish poets of the period, both of them women, also wrote religious poetry: Elżbieta Drużbacka (1695–1765), *Zbiór rytmóv duchowych* (*Anthology of Spiritual Rhythms*, 1752) and Konstancja Benisławska (*Pieśni sobie śpiewane, Songs addressed to Himself*, 1776, inspired by Kochanowski's *Psalter*) were rediscovered in the twentieth century. Finally the epic, that we might have expected to be wholly defunct, still provided an appreciable output with Rotgans, De Meyer, Hoogvliet and Walef. With the poem *The League* (1723) which became *The Henriad* (1728), Voltaire gave back to the genre a certain efficaciousness: he hijacked it to make it a double-edged sword of philosophical warfare by publishing initially on English soil this glorification of the legendary king of France, Henri IV, and by enrolling him in the cause of religious tolerance. The Germans had to wait for Klopstock and *Der Messias* (*The Messiad*, 1748–1773), which was the first great epic in German since the Middle Ages. The Southern Slavs saw in *Razgovor ugodni naroda slovinskoga* (*Familiar Conversations with the Slav People*, 1738, 1756) by Andrija Kačić-Miošić (1704–1760), an epic

chronicle signalling the awakening of their national conscience. And in *Sagan om Hästen* (*The Horse Grolle and his Riders*, 1740), Dalin offered the Swedes a political allegory which summed up and exalted their historical destiny. It remains one of their literature's greatest achievement.

Reduced to going over old quarrels, to old-fashioned sources of inspiration, to the belated readjustments of a classical theory that had already produced its best results and could only now repeat itself, European poetry went through some of its leanest years. Poetry was written by exiles. Its symbol could well be that of Jean-Baptiste Rousseau (1671–1741). He was banished from France in 1712 for a satire which he had probably not written, given amnesty in 1716, but preferred to live in the Austrian Low Countries, after sojourns in Switzerland and Vienna, as if it were enough to go to Tomis or Guernsey to be Ovid or Hugo. An author of epigrams, cantatas, sacred odes, then considered as a very great poet, today he would be almost forgotten were it not for his having the same surname as Jean-Jacques. The poetry of the Enlightenment does exist, however. It was found where it was not looked for, primarily in the impertinence of wit, then in a fervent didacticism and finally in an obscure inspiration which, paradoxically in this age which wanted and felt itself to be luminous, paved the way for a time of tempests and torments.

When Shaftesbury wrote *Essay on the Freedom of Wit and Humour* (1709), he set the tone for a half-century in which wit in all its forms, from the subtlest to the most profound, had to season all activities, make shine the happiness of the moment, ensure social complicity, to break down one by one, joyfully, all the bastions of resistance to new ideas. And it was not by chance that the English were the first to set this tone. For example, Dryden's satire, *A & A* (1681), had already demonstrated efficacy in this genre: this poem was instrumental in bringing about the fall of the Whigs and frustrating their project to prevent James II from succeeding Charles II. Going beyond the merely academic to devote himself to the most ironical of fantasies, often biting and always witty, attacked bad poets in *The Dunciad*, Defoe targeted William of Orange's enemies (*The True-Born Englishman*, 1701), John Arbuthnot (1667–1735) satirised European politics (*The History of John Bull*, 1712). Even Young, before the success of *Night Thoughts* (1742), paid tribute to this happier genre (*The Universal Passion*, 1728), whose undisputed master, both in prose and verse, was the Irishman **Jonathan Swift (1667–1745).**★ He was followed by Sterne. His sermon *The Abuses of Conscience* (1750) was a first sketch for what became *Tristram Shandy*. In France, the aggressiveness of Gacon or of Lagrange-Chancel was eclipsed by the omnipresent talent of Voltaire, whose short epigrams killed the person they were aimed at more surely than a list of detailed accusations.

(À Boyer, un évêque qui demandait le chapeau de Cardinal au pape Benoît XIV)

En vain la fortune s'apprête	*Fortune in vain readies itself*
À t'orner d'un lustre nouveau;	*To adorn you with new lustre;*
Plus ton destin deviendra beau	*The fairer your destiny becomes*
Et plus tu nous paraîtras bête.	*The more stupid you appear.*
Benoît donne bien un chapeau,	*Benedict may well give you a hat,*
Mais il ne donne point de tête.	*But he won't give you a head.*

Voltaire, *Œuvres complètes*

The genre also touched the United Provinces (Jacob Zeeus, 1686–1718, *De Wolf in't schaepsvel*, *The Wolf in Sheep's Clothing*, 1711) and Spain (Isla y Rojo, *Triunfo del amore y de la lealtad*, *The Triumph of Love and Loyalty*, 1746). Another use of victorious derision was parody, in the tradition of the burlesque, given added piquancy by what the English called the 'mock heroic' or 'mock epic'. Pope, here again, led the way with his famous *The Rape of the Lock* (1714). This revealed him to be divided between a fascination with materialism and reproof of it. This was followed by Gay's *Trivia or the Art of Walking the Streets of London* (1716) and Lady Mary Wortley Montagu (1689–1762) with *Town Eclogues* (1716). The young Marivaux amused himself with a *Homer Travestied or the Iliad in Burlesque Verse* (1717). In *Il Ricciardetto* (*Little Richard*, 1738), Niccolò Forteguerri (1674–1735) disguised a clever satire of contemporary manners under the adventures of Charlemagne and his paladins.

However, if mockery conquers sympathy, it does not always force adherence. With more seriousness and comparable ardent zeal, poetry found in didacticism a weapon of gentle persuasion, wholly appropriate to the essential message of the Enlightenment: to understand, to love and to improve the inner harmony of man with his being (what is referred to at the time is his 'nature'), his time, his setting, his fellow men. Voltaire celebrated this harmony in *The Socialite* (1736) and, more profoundly, in *Poem on Natural Religion* (1756).

In this didactic vein we have Giambattista Spolverini (1695–1762) with *Coltivazione del riso* (*The Cultivation of Rice*, 1746), but, yet again, the English taught best in verse. John Philips (1676–1709), for instance, explained the manufacture and benefits of strong drink (*Cyder*, 1706), and William King (1663–1712) did the same for food (*The Art of Cooking*, 1708). The greatest writers did not disdain to follow Virgil's footsteps of Virgil in the *Georgics* or *Lucretius* – on loftier themes. With *The Seasons* (1726–1730), the Scot **James Thomson (1700–1748)** coupled a learned language full of classical reminiscences and a versification recalling Milton's sublimity with an enthusiasm for the rural world and natural phenomena. This made him a precursor of Romantic nature poetry. Pope wrote *Essay on Man* (1733), the very stuff of the poetry of optimism. It was immediately translated and imitated throughout in Europe. In this 'philosophical' poetry, the philosophy is often rather summary, but the poetry is of a very high quality and celebrates independently the human condition, mortal happiness and the expressive power of language itself.

> *All Discord, Harmony not understood;*
> *All partial Evil, universal Good;*
> *And, spite of Pride, in erring Reason's*
>   *spite,*
> *One truth is clear, WHATEVER IS, IS*
>   *RIGHT.*
>
> Alexander Pope,
Essay on Man

With *The Vanity of Human Wishes* (1749), Johnson turned this inspiration in the direction of a certain anxiety. This is not at all the case with Gay's *Fables* (1727) which illustrated a genre which had been much in vogue since La Fontaine. All Europe was enchanted by the fables of Fénelon (1690), La Motte (1719), Krafft (1734), Hagedorn (1738), Crudeli (1746), Gellert (1748) and Holberg (1750). Nevertheless, despite its success, the fable in verse soon gave way to a new genre which took over from it the functions of diverting and educating: the philosophical tale as Voltaire created it *c.*1746. Another didactic vein, with a wonderful future, appeared in England, where the transition to an urban and industrial society happened more swiftly. Stephen Duck (1705–1756) with *The Thresher's Labour* (1730), Collier with *The Woman's Labour* (1739) made the description of the working classes a definite subject for poetry.

The scintillation of wit and the will to instruct and edify have never by themselves been enough for the birth of great poetry. What characterised poetry in the Enlightenment was the coexistence of these elements – carried to a kind of perfection in their ordering – and a type of new anxiety, more existential than metaphysical. Its first manifestations announced the following period though still retained solidarity with this one. It was 'nature', so euphorically invoked by the philosophers, that poets began to take for their theme – we have seen this already with Thomson – but a nature given to being

nocturnal, and conducive to reverie rather than epistemological curiosity: Anne Finch (1661–1720) with *A Nocturnal Reverie* (1713), and above all **Edward Young (1683–1765)**. His famous poem *The Complaint or Night Thoughts on Life, Death and Immortality* (1742–1745) travelled all over Europe and was known, translated and imitated in France as *Les Nuits* (*Nights*). Celebrating night, death, ruins and tears, Young offered a radical alternative to Pope's rationalism and opposes to his terrestrial optimism the double mystery, both awful and consoling, of death and immortality.

> *Night, sable Goddess! from her*
>   *ebon throne,*
> *In rayless majesty, now stretches*
>   *forth*
> *Her leaden sceptre o'er a slumb'*
>   *ring world.*
> *Silence how dead! and darkness*
>   *how profound!*
> *Nor eye nor list'ning ear an*
>   *object finds.*
> *Creation sleeps. 'Tis as the*
>   *general pulse*
> *Of life stood still, and*
>   *nature made a pause;*
> *An awful pause!*
>   *prophetic of her end.*
>
> Edward Young, The Complaint or Night
Thoughts on Life, Death and Immortality

A poetry of local cultures lost in the mist of time developed in the same vein, those of Scotland and Wales with Thomson again, announcing Ossian and *Liberty* (1736), *The Castle of Indolence* (1746) or with John Dyer (1699–1758) and *Grongar Hill* (1726); a poetry of the dark places of the soul: Thomas Warton (1728–1790), *The Pleasures of Melancholy* (1747), of the darkness of oriental mysteries (Warton, *The Triumph of Isis*, 1749; William Collins, 1721–1759, *Persian Eclogues*, 1742); a pantheist poetry: Klopstock, *Oden* (*Odes*, after 1747); a poetry of death and tombs: Hubert Kornelisz. Poot (1689–1733), *Op de Doot van myn dochtertje* (*On the Occasion* of my Daughter's Death, 1733), Robert Blais (1699–1746), The Grave (1743), Thomas Gray (1716–1771), Elegy Written in a Country Churchyard (1751). We may perhaps interpret in the same sense another triumph of 'sensibility', the development of writing by women, very marked in England in the novel, and also in poetry.

Like the theatre, poetry, despite being weighed down by a somewhat cumbersome tradition, remained a genre which was relatively lively and varied, in which the man of the Enlightenment managed to combine a memory and a conquest, fidelity and innovation. However, it was in prose fiction that he found the freest, most flexible and appropriate form for the expression of his hopes, his questions and his fantasy.

The inventiveness of prose fiction

With some exceptions, the novel was not yet a European genre, but an English and French one. The exceptions, however, were interesting, for they demonstrated the potential of the genre, even in countries where it was hardly practised. They also explained the huge success of Defoe, Voltaire and Fielding. The Philothéou Parergha (The Pamphlets of Philotheus, published in 1800) by Nikola Mavrokordatos was the first neo-Hellenic novel. In Spain, José Francisco de Isla de la Torre (1703–1781) tried to destroy from the inside the pretensions of preaching, as Cervantes had done for the novels of chivalry. His Historia del famoso predicator Fray Gerundio (History of the Famous Preacher, Brother Gerundio) was popular after 1750. With Den vermakelyken avanturier (The Amusing Adventurer, 1695), Nicolaas Heinsius Jr (1620–1681) prolonged the tradition of the picaresque novel, while the burlesque vein found an outlet in periodicals. The universal genius of Holberg attacked pietism and intolerance in al Latin nove, Nicolai Klimii Iter subterraneum (The Underground Journey of Nils Klim, 1741). Hydra mystica (The Mystical Hydra, 1691) by Giovan Vincenzo Gravina (1664–1718) was only a prose satire against

Roman corruption and Jesuit casuistry. Johann Gottfried Schnabel (1692–1750) wrote a utopian travel book, Wunderliche Fata einiger See-Fahrer (The Curious Destiny of a Few Seafarers, 1743). With his gallant, historical novel Grossmütiger Feldherr Arminius (The Magnanimous Condottiere Arminius, 1689), Daniel Casper von Lohenstein (1635–1683) launched a theme destined for great things: that of the vigour of Germanic heroism as opposed to the feebleness engendered by Roman virtues. But we have to wait for Wieland for the true German novel to be born, according to Lessing, with the Geschichte des Agathon (The Story of Agathon, 1766).

These examples show that novel-writing had distanced itself from all the seventeenth-century 'disorientations' to deal with the problems of contemporary society, still recognisable under the playful disguises of fairy-tales or travel, of the confidences vouchsafed in memoirs or exchanges of letters. Under these four headings we can list literary productions in both English and French, before seeing the pleasing inventions of their fantasy and the pitiless precision of their realism in the most original fictional forms of the period, those by Swift and Voltaire.

Once upon a time there was a Woodcutter and a Woodcutter's wife . . .

Charles Perrault, Tom Thumb

The world of faery, in its pure form of the fairy tale, was very fashionable in France. Perrault gave it its unforgettable form in Tales of Time Past (1697), which doubtless owe their popularity with children worldwide for having fixed classical writing, the scattered elements of a popular and immemorial oral tradition with the distinction of naïve and sophisticated. The genre later evolved towards a somewhat gratuitous marvellousness, the beginnings of the fantastic, an exploitation of the exotic vogue opened up by The Thousand and One Nights, but its most important developments were those imparted by libertinism and philosophy. **Claude Jolyot de Crébillon** (known as **Crébillon Junior, 1707–1777**) began with *L'Écumoire* (*The Skimmer*, 1732) and *Sopha* (1740), a depiction of the licentious customs that he would refine, after *Aberrations of the Heart and Mind* (1736), removing its Eastern garb and magical aspect. Diderot retained them in *The Indiscreet Jewels* (1748), but erotic adventures were henceforth, and up to Laclos' *Dangerous Liaisons*, placed directly in the framework of the society of the time. We are far removed, it seems, from the world of Little Red Riding Hood! The philosophical tale also seems to stray away from it, addressing itself nevertheless to the same need in readers to conjure up deep traumas and to rediscover, through the most unbridled wonders, quite simple and quite useful truths.

> Calypso could not get over Ulysses leaving her . . .
>
> Fénelon, *Telemachus*

Travel was another popular narrative framework during this period in which we have already seen the interest aroused by 'real' accounts of journeys. With *Adventures of Telemachus* (1699), the most widely read book of the entire century, **François de Salignac de La Mothe-Fénelon (1651–1715)**, with his royal pupil the Duke of Burgundy uppermost in his mind, organised in a didactic novel the stages in the odyssey all over the Mediterranean accomplished by the son of Ulysses in search of his father. The sage Mentor (Minerva in disguise) who accompanies him does not miss an opportunity to derive for him all kinds of moral, social and political lessons from the people they meet and the customs they encounter. Apart from its own success, due to its elegant language which smoothly combined nobility with simplicity, persuasiveness with erudition, this novel inspired several imitations, such as *The Travels of Cyrus* (1727) by Ramsay and *Sethos* (1731) by the Abbé Terrasson (1660–1750).

The journey also made it possible to gain access to the world of Utopias, whose tradition was continued into the Enlightenment after Denis Veiras with Foigny, Gilbert, Tyssot de Patot and Legrand. Is this a real journey or a didactic journey, a Utopian journey? The genius of **Daniel Defoe (1660–1731)** was to make this question impossible to answer when it came to *The Life and Strange Surprising Adventures of Robinson Crusoe of York, Mariner* (1719), immediately translated and known throughout Europe as *Robinson Crusoe*. The real-life experiences of a sailor may have provided him with the initial idea, but no more. But many readers believed in the actual existence of this Englishman shipwrecked on an island and reconstructing in its entirety, at first alone, then helped by Man Friday, a young native, a framework and conditions of life worthy of the practical genius of the British in terms of industry, economy and social organisation.

> I consulted several things in my situation which I found would be proper for me: 1st. health and fresh water [. . .]; 2dly. shelter from the heat of the sun; 3dly. security from ravenous creatures, whether men or beasts; 4thly. a view to the sea, that if God sent any ship in sight, I might not lose any advantage for my deliverance, of which I was not willing to banish all my expectation yet. In search of a place proper for this, I found a little plain on the side of a rising hill, whose front towards this little plain was steep as a house-side, so that nothing could come down upon me from the top; [. . .] on the flat of the green [. . .] I resolved to pitch my tent.
>
> Daniel Defoe, *Robinson Crusoe*

We can interpret this novel in various ways. We can highlight the courage of a man thrown back on his own resources, who is able to rediscover in himself the true meaning of his relationship to nature. We can emphasise the arrogance of a bourgeoisie sure of its own merit, all-conquering and colonialist. Despite or because of these multiple meanings, this book remains both one of the most characteristic works of the time and one of the most decisive in world literature. Defoe produced a sequel and other novels, without managing to find the same richness, except in *The Fortunes and Misfortunes of the Famous Moll Flanders*

(1722), the adventures of a five-times married prostitute. She is deported to Virginia and then returns to England where she settles down and begins to write her memoirs.

> In a chest discovered in breaking down a wall, a manuscript was found in several notebooks containing the story you are now about to read, and the handwriting was a woman's throughout.
>
> Marivaux,
> *The Life of Marianne*

A third novelistic mode consisted of describing someone's life story. This is the most usual, going from a real persons biography – Anthony, Count of Hamilton (1646–1720), *The Story of the Life of the Count of Grammont* (1713) – to the 'memoirs' that their authors try to pass off as authentic documents written by their heroes. This peculiarity, which aimed to get rid of the 'literary' artifice behind real-life testimony, was proper to the eighteenth century, which thus invented first-person narration. It is noticeable in the *Memoirs of Monsieur d'Artagnan* (1700) by Gratien de Courtilz de Sandras, to which Alexandre Dumas went for most of his *The Three Musketeers* documentation. In the still-flourishing tradition of seventeenth-century historical novellas (Madame de Tencin, *The Siege of Calais*, 1739; La Vieuville, *Gaston de Foix*, 1741), 'secret histories' also blossomed. Under cover of unveiling hidden aspects of history, these empowered female novelists especially to obtain a *succès de scandale* by exploring the realms of politics and sexuality and making the connections readable. Mary de la Rivière Manley (1663–1724), with *The Secret History of Queen Zarah and the Zarazians* (1705), denounced the influence of Sarah Churchill and the Whigs on Queen Anne; her *Memoirs from the New Atlantis* (1713) resulted in her imprisonment, but her example was followed by Eliza Haywood (1693?–1756) in *Memoir of a Certain Island* (1725). The production of novels by women was very prolific in England, divided between a fiction of transgression and one of conformity, in which virtue triumphs over multifarious attacks.

The tale from life was the fictitious but realistic framework which five novelists of the period all chose, adapting it to individual needs. In *Les Illustres Françaises* (*Famous Frenchwomen*, 1713), **Robert Challe (1659–1721)** interwove seven 'true stories' in which each of the young people he has brought together tells a part of their own life. The framework of the minor aristocracy or the ennobled bourgeoisie is familiar, with its money problems, its affairs of the heart and the family, its quest for happiness. Challe's realism was epoch-making in the history of the European novel, as much in what affected the material provincial scene as in what concerned the psychology of the heroes. The narrative structure only revealed this progressively and in an evolving way, to become finally an inseparable part of the mystery. **Alain René Lesage (1668–1747)** borrowed two characters from Spanish tradition. He gave them the job of crossing all the layers of French society in lively scenes, so that he could depict the most secret and most picturesque behaviour with a pitiless lucidity tinged with good humour. For example, there is the demon Asmodeus in *Le Diable boiteux* (*The Lance Devil*, 1707, 1726), and above all Gil Blas in *L'Histoire de Gil Blas de Santillane* (*The Story of Gil Blas of Santillana*, 1715–1735). Blas totally transformed the picaro model by removing that constant sordidness which, at the time of the Counter-Reformation, had made him instrumental in the opposite of redemptive edifications. As he rises in society he manifest by all the means that this redemptive edification suggests to him, an availability and an irony which make him Voltaire's true contemporary. He acquires a kind of practical wisdom, disillusioned but without cynicism. Lesage makes this the century's first apprenticeship novel, thereby creating a type whose essential characteristics will be found again in Figaro. This is the model that the Scot Smollett imitated in *Adventures of Roderick Random* (1748) – attributed at the time to Fielding – before he found a more personal manner in *The Adventures of Peregrine Pickle* (1751), which became the origin of the 'dark novel'. Lesage's subsequent works, still set in Spain (*The Story of Guzman de Alfarache*, 1732, *The Bachelor of Salamanca*, 1737), did not rediscover the freshness and the verve which, in *Gil Blas*, remind us that he was also a skilful comedy writer. The same association between the two genres applies to Marivaux. After some early works which parody the Baroque novel, Marivaux used genuine realism in *The Life of Marianne* (1731–1741) and *The Upstart Peasant* (1735–1736). The realism of the speech is that of the two heroes describing the stages of their entrance into the world. The realism of the settings is that of the Parisian streets, shops and salons. Moral realism covers all the possible aspects of the judgement prompted by each line of conduct in long analyses. Sentimental realism is there for Marianne and Jacob who have sensitive, delicate hearts, and through masks and time, excel at restoring, the exact emotional quality of the scenes they have experienced. Psychological realism is there in their mixture of cunning and naiveté, of spontaneous generosity and the aptitude for calculation that they demonstrate, which gives them a credibility and a sympathy rarely reached before. We could even go so far as to talk of philosophical realism: it gives a frankly optimistic vision of the world which is entirely in keeping with the Enlightenment. It is described paradoxically but victoriously, by a young woman who achieves things in spite of men, and by a young man who realises through women a destiny in harmony with their nature and their conscience, which is never jeopardised by perils or compromises. The unfinished nature of the two novels places them inside the reality of an ongoing story and outlines the developments which led to Richardson or Restif de la Bretonne. Deplored as histrionic, Marivaux's novels nevertheless had a great resonance, translations, sequels and adaptations throughout Europe.

In comparison with Marivaux's quiet, discreet life, that of **Antoine François Prévost d'Exiles** (known as the **Abbé Prévost, 1697–1763**) was itself a novel. Something of the wild eventfulness of his career, his feelings, his travels, his encounters is in his fiction, without detracting from its vigorous realism, as much about the depiction of social customs as about the human heart. His heroes are in the grip of three forces they ardently try to understand and surmount through their tale which they give, after the event, of their adventurous outbursts. The story of a society which both suggests and represses a morality of happiness; of a destiny which cannot always be thought of as providential as they are so much its playthings, satisfied and disappointed in turn; of an inner anxiety which juxtaposes the natural, innocent character of passion – ambition or love – and the need to give it up to escape its destructive violence. Law, providence and desire organise and vie with each other to thwart this search that the heroes recall. The enquiry which justifies and incessantly relaunches this recollection gives it an intensity and a tension that Sade illuminated in his *Ideas on Novels* (1800). In general, Prévost's works were divided into a multitude of interconnected episodes, as in *The Story of Mr Cleveland* (1731–1739), the 'memoirs' of Cromwell's bastard son and *The Dean of Killerine* (1735–1740). But on two occasions they were concentrated on a short, simple plot, whose purity of design makes it similar to a tragedy and the unity of its harmonies like an opera. *The Story of the Chevalier des Grieux and Manon Lescaut* (1731) has taken its place among the great European myths of absolute love linked with death. *The Story of a Modern Greek Woman* (1740) pushes failure even further, since love itself can find no way through. At a time when scepticism was most often found in fundamental optimism, Prévost lucidly heralded the age of anxiety over the mystery of souls.

We had passed a part of the night peacefully. I believed my dear mistress to be asleep and dared not breathe out even slightly as I was afraid of troubling her sleep. I noticed at dawn, when I touched her hands, that they were cold and trembling. I bore them to my breast to warm them up. She felt this movement, and, making an effort to seize my hands, she told me, in a feeble voice, that she thought herself to be in the hour of her death. First of all I took this speech as the ordinary language of misfortune, and answered it with the tender consolations of love. But her frequent sighs, her silence in response to my questions, the squeezing of her hands, in which she continued to hold mine made me aware that the end of her misfortunes was approaching. Do not ask of me that I describe my feelings to you, nor for me to report her dying words. I lost her; I received from her tokens of affection at the very moment of her death. This is all I am able to tell you about this fatal and deplorable event.

Abbé Prévost, *Manon Lescaut*

Byron said that **Henry Fielding (1707–1754)** was the 'prose Homer' of England; Walter Scott described him as the 'father of the English novel'. Fielding, who was also a dramatist and journalist, promoted his talent for satire – which he shared with many of his contemporaries – making it both the food and the driving force of his long novels. Apparently for a joke, he transformed Richardson's virtuous Pamela into a hussy who got round her master (*An Apology for the Life of Mrs Shamela Andrews*, 1741) and then contemplated a riposte, *The History of the Adventures of Joseph Andrews* (1742), in which masculine virtue is misused by women's wiles. *The History of the Life of the late Mr Jonathan Wild the Great* (1743) deforms to the point of monstrosity the cynical banditry of a hero who resembles Robert Walpole. Less bitter, *The History of Tom Jones, a Foundling* (1749) accumulated with energetic verve the rise and fall of a life complicated by family and romantic intrigues, and by wanderings and tribulations. It displays fashionable sentimentality, but frames this with a lively and mischievously humorous narrative style

As we determined when we first sat down to write this History, to flatter no Man; but to guide our Pen throughout by the Directions of Truth, we are obliged to bring our Heroe on the Stage in a much more disadvantageous Manner than we could wish; and to declare

honestly, even at his first Appearance, that it was the universal Opinion of all Mr. Allworthy's Family, that he was certainly born to be hanged.

Indeed, I am sorry to say, there was too much Reason for this Conjecture. The Lad having, from his earliest Years, discovered a Propensity to many Vices, and especially to one, which hath as direct a Tendency as any other to that Fate, which we have just now observed to have been prophetically denounced against him. He had been already convicted of three Robberies, viz. of robbing an Orchard, of stealing a Duck out of a Farmer's Yard, and of picking Master Blifil's Pocket of a Ball.

Henry Fielding, *Tom Jones*

A magistrate, Fielding attacked the social abuses that he knew well, with the sharpness of Hogarth, whom he admired. His rivalry with Richardson, very noticeable in *Amelia* (1751), is seen today to his advantage: he opened the way for the modern novel's audacity. But Richardson exercised the greatest influence in the short term. He closed this chapter in order to open it for Diderot, Rousseau and Goethe, his admirers.

In the form of letters [. . .] the author has given himself the advantage of being able to join together philosophy, politics and morality in one novel, and to bind the whole thing together by a chain which is secret and, to some extent, unknown.

Montesquieu, *Persian Letters*

One of the most eloquent manifestations of the function played by the novel genre in the conquest of the Enlightenment was the use of the letter to which it had recourse. A writing of exchange, of spontaneous verve and the relativisation of points of view, of the reciprocal influence of the public and the private, the letter is a natural way of expression used by 'philosophers' anxious to make readers receptive to their ideas. By bringing to its fulfilment at this point the efforts of many predecessors (Marana, Cotolendi, Dufresny,

Bonnet) Montesquieu gave to *Persian Letters* (1721) the appearance of 'a sort of novel'. He made his Persians' sojourn in Paris something other than one more satirical collection on Western society seen by foreign eyes. Beneath our eyes, Rica and Usbek live out a true adventure of the senses and feelings. Their narrative in letters recounts the transition from old man to new man of which the age was dreaming.

Less 'novelistic', Voltaire's *Philosophical Letters* (1734) are no less an invitation to an exchange of ideas, to the understanding of others, to the rational boldness which, impelling us to sympathise for them, makes it possible to transcend our own prejudices and routine beliefs. When the others are English, when they have the features of Locke or Newton, we can see how overwhelming the project can be for a Frenchman, who can only be freed from Pascal by this method and, without any more religious scruples, launch into the modifying action of the 'world as it is'. In such a context the novel in letters, natural heir to a tradition illustrated by Bussy-Rabutin, Madame de Villedieu and Guilleragues in the previous century, became the preferred form of prose fiction for Anne Bellinzani (*The New Story of the Loves of the Young Bélise and Cléante*, 1689), Fontenelle (*Love Letters of the Chevalier d'Her . . .*, 1699), Madame de Graffigny (*Letters from a Peruvian Lady*, 1747) and above all for **Samuel Richardson (1689–1761)**.

Richardson was a printer who had come to writing by the discovery and systematic exploitation of his letter-writing talents. In 1740 he enjoyed enormous success with *Pamela or Virtue Rewarded*. This type of title in two parts, very common at that time, indicated the twofold dimension of the project: to evoke interest in a particular case and to illustrate a general lesson. Hounded by a libertine, the heroine manages to persuade him to make an honest woman of her. In spite of Fielding, Richardson persevered in this vein and published *Clarissa or the History of a Young Lady* (1747–1749), the longest novel in all of English literature. Clarissa Harlowe, however,

is not a second Pamela Andrews, but rather her opposite. The innumerable misfortunes that her virtuous nature brings down on her occupy the entire novel. Eventually she dies of grief. The wicked – her parents, the libertine Lovelace whom she thought she could trust – are not punished other than by the reader's own rejection of them.

Exactly fifty years passed between republication of *Telemachus* and *Clarissa*. This period saw prose fiction experiment with all the possible configurations of the opposition of good and evil in the real world, and question the problematic compatibility between these three expressions of a 'nature' which reason suggests we should trust: passion (for knowledge, for growth, for love), virtue (as a rule for both the personal and the collective life) and happiness (always postulated, always threatened). Two writers knew how to find a formula entirely appropriate to this questioning. Bringing into simultaneous play the techniques of the fairy-tale, the framework of the journey, the structure of the tale taken from life and, sometimes, the epistolary manner, Swift, with *Gulliver's Travels* (1726) and Voltaire, in his tales, presented the strongest, most memorable images of the Enlightenment hero.

ON THE EDGE OF THE ENLIGHTENMENT

The drastic mobilisation of energies and talents which is characteristic of the period considerably reduce the part played by local diversity. It can be argued that the eighteenth century only became the century of the Enlightenment by hindsight, and insist on a recognition of divergent trends in the period – between 'Lumières', 'Enlightenment', 'Verlichting', 'Aufklärung', 'Illuminismo', 'Ilustración', 'Ilustraçaõ', 'I periodos ton photon', 'Oświecenie', 'Prosveščonie'. This impulse in one case leads us to cosmopolitanism, in another to patriotism, in a third to impiousness, in a fourth to pietism, in a fifth to the defence of absolutism and on, in a sixth to an attack on it. But we may also accentuate what transformed these forces into a dynamic, and recognise that literature everywhere played a decisive role in this transformation. There were only two exceptions: one is of two great French writers curiously isolated in their century; the other, that of the Southern Slavs, relatively isolated within Europe.

In France, Saint-Simon and Vauvenargues

> Reason deceives us more often than nature.
>
> Vauvenargues,
> *Reflections and Maxims*

Several things connect **Louis de Saint-Simon (1675–1755)** and **Luc de Vauvenargues (1715–1747)**: their bad health, their shortened military careers, their pride as gentlemen, their high moral standards, their ambition and their solitude. But their works were completely different. A single small book, the *Introduction to the Knowledge of the Human Spirit*, followed by *Reflections and Maxims* (1746) sufficed for Vauvenargues. Thousands of pages of *Memoirs* (1729–1754, published in 1830) and various essays for Saint-Simon. A fragment for the moralist, a fresco for the memorialist. We could take the former for a replica of La Rochefoucauld, though he was rather a precursor of Diderot, Rousseau and Chamfort in the anticipatory apology he made for emotional denseness, enthusiasm and genius. As for the latter, who did not know the names of Bayle, Locke, Newton and Leibniz and had never heard of Marivaux or Defoe, he was suspended between two worlds: that of the court of Louis XIV which he insisted on portraying as dysfunctional – not because of his liberal tendencies but out of respect for the old feudal model – and that of the great nineteenth-century novelists who, from Stendhal to Proust, saluted in him the creator of a world ferociously observed and vigorously reorganised around an 'essential passion'.

Bulgaria and Serbia

Bulgaria had just emerged from the Middle Ages. The manuscripts of the monk Bradati (1690–1757), preserved in Belgrade, bore witness to a meditation on contemporary Bulgarian reality, but the gulf between these writings and Western literary output remained deep. The content was historical, didactic and religious, without any proper literary concern. This only developed during the nineteenth century. A Renaissance began around two centres in particular: the first was that of the Bulgarian Catholic writers who had emigrated to Vienna, Zagreb or Novi Sad, or stayed inside the country where their activity in the organisation of the Church and of education was very important for renewal. They wrote in Latin or 'Illyrian', a mixture of Serbo-Croat and Bulgarian. J. Pejačević distinguished himself in Baroque Slavic writing and published a thesis, *Veteris et novæ geographicæ compendiosa congeries* (*Compendium of Ancient and Modern Geography*, 1714). K. Pejkič wanted to prove the superiority of Christianity over Islam in *Mohametanus dogmatice et catechice in Lege Christi alcorano suffragante instructus* (*The Muslim Instructed in Conformity to the Koran in the Dogmas and Principles of the Christian Faith*, 1717). This school developed an interesting poetry in the second half of the century, mainly in Thrace, around Plovdiv (Philippopolis). The second centre was the literary circle of the Southern Slavs of Sremski Karlovici, where Bulgarians rejoined the Serbian movement that will be mentioned later on. P. Pavlovič produced a considerable amount of work, including an *Avtobiografica* (*Autobiography*), which derived from the best humanist traditions. A little later, in 1762, the monk of Athos Paisij of Hilandar (1722–1798) wrote *Istorija slavenobulgarskaja* (*History of the Bulgarian Slavs*), a veritable platform for national liberation from the twin yoke of the Turks and the Greek Phanariotes of Constantinople who, motivated by the best of cultural and administrative intentions, threatened to assimilate the Bulgarians.

After Emperor Leopold I's failed attempt to reconquer Christian countries occupied by the Ottomans, there was a new incursion by the Turks which provoked a full-scale migration of the Serbs (in 1690, then in 1739) to Southern Hungary, Voïvodina as it is now. At that time the Serbian Church was the centre for patriotic feelings and national culture. In 1695, it opened the first Serbian schools. The town of Sremski Karlovici, the seat of the patriarchy, established itself as an important cultural centre, through which passed many writers of the first generation of the Serb literary renaissance. The towns of Becej, Novi Sad and Subotica also contributed to the renaissance, not to mention Buda(pest), with its Serb university and printing press. In the first generation of the diaspora were a group of monks called Račani (keepers of the tradition of the monastery of Rača, destroyed by the Turks in 1688), whose most important representatives were K. Račani and G.S. Venclovič. The latter introduced Baroque rhetoric into his religious writings, as well as the colloquial language which existed along-side Serb Slavonic; he was the last figure in the old literary tradition and the herald of the new one. The Church ensured the continuity of genres such as biographies and chronicles inherited from the Middle Ages. The chroniclers gradually abandoned the history of mythical times in favour of contemporary history. Count Gjorgji Brankovič (1645–1711), a politician and scholar, wrote *Slaveno Serbske Hronike* (*Slavo-Serbian Chronicles*, 1705). It was banned but it circulated for a long time under the counter. Beginning with Genesis, it retraced the history of the Serbs, to tackle in the end the events of contemporary history. The author revived the idea of the Ilyrian Empire, this time under the aegis of Austria. In 1741 Hristofor Zefarovič published *Stematografia* (*Stematography*) in Austria, a summary of heraldry accompanied by portraits of Serbian and Bulgarian dignitaries. This was not an original work: it was a translation and a transposition into Church Slavonic of a book written in 1701 by the Croat Pavao Ritter Vitezovič. In the 1730s, the

Serbs were strongly influenced by Russian and Ukrainian literature. In 1727, Russians and students at the Academy of Kiev opened the first religious schools; the first schoolbooks came from 'Muscovy'. The scholastic high school of E. Kozacinski, in Sremski Karlovici, was the centre for 'Russo-Serbian' literature.

These intense contacts altered the linguistic situation. The introduction of Russian Slavonic, mixed with Serb in writings and liturgy, accentuated the decline of Serbian Slavonic, replaced by 'slavenoserbski jezik' (Slav-Serbian), strongly influenced by Russian. It was used until the attempt at linguistic reform by Dosítej Obradovič (1742–1811). In this 'Russo-Slavic' period, poetry went through its 'Baroque Renaissance', evolving under the influence of the Russian and Ukrainian Baroque of the seventeenth century. The most important person of the half-century was **Zaharija Stefanovič Orfelin (1726–1785)**, poet, historian and physician. His collection of poems, *Plač Serbii* (*The Tears of Serbia*, 1761), was steeped in anti-clericalism and is anti-Austrian. It existed in two versions, one in colloquial Serbian, the other in Church Slavonic. In 1768, Orfelin again published in Venice *Slavenoserbski Magazin* (*Slavo-Serbian Magazine*), a journal firmly Enlightenment-orientated. He also wrote *Zitia Petra Velikog* (*Biography of Peter the Great*, 1772), the first Slavic biography of the Russian Czar.

Emergent Enlightenment, militant Enlightenment

Voltaire's influence grew throughout Europe. Towards the middle of the century, in Spain, Portugal, Poland, Bohemia and Italy, political conditions favoured the acceptance of new ideas and the reformation of mentalities they included. With Lessing, Klopstock and Wieland, German culture prepared for the prodigious with leap which it leaped, from Gottsched to Goethe in the space of a few years. From a strictly literary viewpoint, the age of the emergent Enlightenment decanted classical forms and experimented with new models: nature poetry and the poetry of anguish, the serious drama, the epistolary novel, the anthropological summary, the philosophical tale. Towards 1750, everything was ready for Europeans to launch themselves on a conquest other than that of knowledge and happiness. Sensitivity was revealed not as an alternative to the exercise of critical faculties but, according to the language of sensuality, a means of expanding the life of the mind. At the same time, there was organised resistance against this movement. Enlightened despotism tilted into sheer despotism; religion understood that it no longer had to deal with the insubordination of free thinking, but with the lethal alternatives of pantheism or atheism. Institutions, privileges, 'prejudices' saw their ideological foundations eroded. They closed ranks. On all fronts, literature was about to enter an openly militant phase.

Periodicals

H. Bots

Without freedom to censor,
there is no flattery.

Beaumarchais,
The Marriage of Figaro

When, in the course of the last decades of the seventeenth century, the Enlightenment began to shine in most European countries and mass education became increasingly the norm, periodicals became popular as never before. Around 1700, they were already almost a century old. In many countries we can see the emergence of newspapers and gazettes. After the end of the seventeenth century, not only a political and intellectual élite, but also ordinary middle-class people will have the chance of being well informed about current affairs worldwide. Apart from that, the Republic of Letters was enriched, on the eve of the Enlightenment, by a whole series of new literary journals thanks to which the latest discoveries in the arts and sciences could be disseminated and popularised.

A story which begins in the seventeenth century

It is surprising that news reporting remained restricted for so long. Censorship and a low level of literacy no doubt contributed to this delay. It was also necessary to wait for the beginning of the seventeenth century for the emergence in Europe of a new middle class, the bureaucratisation of the administrative apparatus and the development of all kinds of more efficient and cheaper printing techniques so that periodicals could replace a fortuitous and irregular dissemination of news.

For the new extended bourgeoisie, it was no longer the needs of commerce or political interests which came into play, but the search for rapidly delivered and appropriate information which only periodicals could satisfy. In this kind of writing, the author-journalist, thanks to staggered publications, tried to give an account of current events in any field. It is clear that 'corantos', the existing manuscripts, could not hope for large-scale distribution and that loose sheets, slim volumes or printed brochures, composed for an important social or political event, were most of the time aimed at another public, the masses and even the illiterate, thanks to the self-explanatory pictures which accompanied the text of these broadsheets.

The first two printed periodical newspapers appeared in Germany in 1609: *Aviso* and *Relation*. The *Nieuwe Tijdinghe* (*Latest Tidings*) by the 'news journalist' Abraham Verhoeven, in Antwerp, first published in 1605, cannot be considered as an example of a periodical until after 1621. It was only then that Verhoeven began to number his papers, that new editions appeared at regular intervals and that each sheet was dated: three defining characteristics of periodicals.

In the United Provinces, in Amsterdam, a journal had appeared three years earlier with all these characteristics: the *Courante uyt Italien, Duytslandt, etc.* (*The Italian and German Mail, etc.*), a simple printed sheet in small folio format divided into two columns and compiled by Caspar Van Hilten. This journal was such a success that bookshop colleagues soon started to follow his example. After 1620, Van Hilten himself decided to publish translations of his journal in French and English. *The Italian and German Mail* was therefore the first French newspaper to be printed in Amsterdam, a town which, from the 1620s, became an important centre for typography in Europe. Thanks to a fully expanding economy and trade it can claim to be the largest and the best equipped European news agency. It is true that at that time Amsterdam enjoyed particularly favourable conditions: in the Republic of the United Provinces censorship was never applied to manuscripts: it could only be applied to printed books, but in the absence of a centralised government it was not unduly repressive. Moreover, a privileged economic and geographical situation allowed Dutch booksellers and journalists to quickly obtain the monopoly of periodicals in Europe for a long period.

Gazettes

The birth in 1631 of the *Gazette*, published in Paris by Théophraste Renaudot, hardly made a difference to this situation. This new journal, almost immediately the government mouthpiece, did not compete with the gazettes in Holland, which alone were able to ensure independent, candid and relatively impartial information. These gazettes were, on the one hand, broadsheets in Dutch, the knowledge of which, in the seventeenth century, was wide enough for them to be read by a 'European' readership. On the other hand, there were French journals which appeared during the century, not only in Amsterdam, but also in Leyden, The Hague and Rotterdam. Nearly all compiled by French Huguenots living in political exile in the United Provinces, these journals were very popular in France, and in other European countries. We can read the truth in them on political and military events in Europe, distorted or swept under the carpet by the official press, such as the *Gazette de France*. Louis XIV himself could not do

without the 'gazettes of Holland', sometimes the source of information that was painful to read, but which complemented the material that reached him via the usual diplomatic channels.

Many journals which, originally, all limited themselves to providing news of current affairs – a press for information – were founded during the seventeenth century in many European countries: the *Lepziger Zeitung* (*Journal of Leipzig*) in 1631, which became a daily after 1660; the *Ordinar Posttijdender* in 1645, a Swedish journal which has continued under various titles; the *London Gazette* in 1665, originally the mouthpiece for the English government. It was only after the suppression of the 'Licensing Act' (censorship), in 1695, that many other journals began to appear in England, among which the great daily newspaper published from 1702, the *Daily Courant*, deserves particular mention. In Italian towns many weekly gazettes also sprang up: in Florence in 1636, in Rome in 1640, in Bologna, Milan and Venice in 1642. In Turin, from 1645, the *Sincero* appeared, compiled by the Italian journalist Lucas Asarino. *La Gaceta* was born in Madrid in 1661, while the Austrians had to wait for the beginning of the eighteenth century, as did Russia where the gazette made its first appearance in 1703.

The Scholars' Journal

Thanks to the foundation in Paris in 1665 of the *Journal des Savants* (*The Scholars' Journal*), the scholars and literati of Europe had a means of communication which told them about everything that was happening in the Republic of Letters. The latest literary and scientific events and the main books printed in Europe are reviewed in it. The Parisian example set off a chain reaction. It was first followed in England, where Henry Oldenburg, the secretary of the Royal Society, created in 1665 the *Philosophical Transactions*, a periodical which, because of its almost exclusively scientific character, can be considered as the first specialised journal. Three years later, this was followed in Rome by the publication of *Il*

Giornale de' Letterati, modelled on the French version. From 1682 the German Otto Mencke published in Leipzig a Latin journal, the *Acta Eruditorum*. This allowed a scholarly community to learn about many German publications taken up subsequently by other contemporary newspapers.

In 1614, taking advantage of Holland's freedom, the journalist and philosopher Pierre Bayle launched the *News of the Republic of Letters*. In this new periodical, a true herald of the Enlightenment, the journalist presented his European readers with an impressive plea for tolerance. He denounced all kinds of prejudices and all forms of irrational superstition. This journal also allowed a privileged glimpse of the best books appearing in the 'intellectual and cultural warehouse' that the United Provinces constituted during this period. The success of the *News* was so great that dozens of newspapers followed Bayle's example after the end of the seventeenth century, including the *Libraries* (1686–1726) by Jean Leclerc, the *History of the Works of Scholars* (1687–1709) by Henri Basnage de Beauval, the *Literary Journal* (1713–1737) and the *Reasoned Library* (1728–1753).

Besides these journals between 1717 and 1746 Dutch booksellers published specialised periodicals such as the *English Library*, the *Germanic Library*, the *Italian Library* and the *French Library*, which make known the main works of these different countries to readers who generally did not need the other country's language. Most newspapers in Holland were compiled in French, but there were also Dutch periodicals: many gazettes, as well as many learned and literary journals. *De Boekzaal van Europe* (*The European Library*), compiled by Pieter Rabus, inaugurated this scholarly series in 1692.

In the eighteenth century, the phenomenon of 'scholarly' journalism, along Parisian lines and that of Pierre Bayle, was known in most European countries. After 1672, less erudite and more fashionable readers, however, could enjoy themselves with *Le Mercure galant* (*The Gallant Mercury*). Apart from gallantries, they found, news in brief and gossip columns,

political and literary information between a learned periodical and a gazette. This mercurial genre was much followed and imitated in France and abroad in the following decades. Christoph Martin Wieland, when he founded the *Teutsche Merkur* (*The German Mercury*), and Anden Bording, when he created in Denmark *Den Dansken Merkurius* (*The Danish Mercury*), took the *Mercure de France* as their model.

The English renaissance

A veritable renaissance occurred in England thanks to three periodicals: *A Review of the Affairs of France and of all Europe . . .* (1704–1713), edited by Daniel Defoe; *The Tatler* (1709–1711) and *The Spectator* (1711–1712; 1714), edited by Addison and Steele. In the first, Defoe pleasantly instructs his readers in knowledge – political and economic – of the world, while offering them a column with 'readers' letters' which dealt with all sorts of moral and social questions. The two papers by Addison and Steele were enormously successful and were translated into French, Dutch and German. What we have here, in fact, is a new genre in which the journalist, under different forms – letters, dreams, tales – gives his opinions on all sorts of questions, with the intention of combatting and mocking man's defects and vices. In these journals, which reviewed society, the 'spectator' also cast his gaze on women, too often ignored in learned periodicals. There were even 'female spectators', *The Female Tatler* (1709–1710) and *The Female Spectator* (1744–1746), with variant versions in Holland and Germany written by female journalists.

These various 'spectatorial' broadsheets, journals and gazettes not only disseminated the latest news, but during the eighteenth century they did more and more to form public opinion and played an important part in the preparation of the revolutionary spirit, even in France despite all the government measures against those who took too many liberties. This is what the *Journal de Paris*, the first French daily, founded in January 1777, sometimes experienced. Censorship in France was severe until the Revolution, and a periodical like the *Journal encyclopédique* (1756–1793), compiled by Pierre Rousseau, which disseminated the ideas of philosophers and encyclopedists, was published outside France, first in Liège, then, after 1760, in Bouillon.

The French Revolution

The French Revolution momentarily introduced a large measure of press freedom, but journalists soon were obliged to acknowledge that it was a pseudo-freedom and that they could hardly afford to disagree with the new leaders; something which the Figaro of Beaumarchais in *The Marriage of Figaro* emphasised:

> FIGARO I am told that, during my economic retirement, a system of freedom on the sale of productions, which even extends to those of the press, has been established in Madrid; and that, as long as I do not speak in my writings about authority or the church or politics or morals or people in high places or firms in credit or the Opera or other spectacles or of anybody who counts for something, I can print anything I like, subject to the inspection of two or three censors. To avail myself of this sweet liberty, I am announcing publication of a periodical, and, thinking not to trespass on the rights of any other, I am calling it the Useless Journal. Ugh! I can see a thousand poor devils waving their sheets at me, they're suppressing me, and here I am once again without a job!

In Sweden, in 1766, freedom of the press became a fundamental law. It was only towards the middle of the nineteenth century that most of the countries of continental Europe obtained real freedom of the press, in the modern sense of the term: Belgium in 1831, Holland in 1848, France as late as 1881.

The emergence of great international news agencies during the first half of the nineteenth century contributed a great deal to the improvement of newspapers. The press office of Charles Havas in Paris, founded in 1832, was the oldest, followed in 1851 in London by the British press agency of Julius Reuter, who had collaborated with Havas. These agencies made possible a better and a faster distribution of news at affordable prices for a wider public.

The press and the Industrial Revolution

The technical improvements in printing made it possible to considerably lower the production costs of newspapers which, from the middle of the nineteenth century, were more and more dailies. In England the steam engine was introduced in 1814 in the printing of *The Times*, and, after 1847, 'rotary presses' were used which allowed for much longer printing runs. The speed of printing, which increased during the second half of the nineteenth century, was complemented by the invention of the linotype in 1885, which made possible more rapid typesetting. Economic prosperity meant that publicity occupied an increasingly important place in newspaper printing. The income which it brought in would subsequently cover the development costs of a newspaper. All these new technical acquisitions not only contributed to the production of prestigious periodicals of information and opinion, but also to the appearance of a popular press for all those who knew how to read.

By publishing *La Presse* in 1836, the journalist Émile Girardin had already demonstrated that the readership for a cheap newspaper was larger. The periodical press truly became a product for the masses, not only when the price was very low, but also when it was addressed to a different readership which was happy with quite simple information, having to do especially with news in brief. Such is the 'popular' journal, like the *Petit Journal* founded in 1863 and the *Petit Parisien* which first published in 1876, had a circulation of more than a million by 1905. In England, where great political newspapers continued, there was also a comparable 'sensational' press such as *Daily Mail* since 1896 and, some years later, the illustrated *Daily Mirror*.

Other European countries followed this pattern. In The Netherlands, for instance, alongside a serious press dealing with information and opinion, there was a journal for mass consumption, *Het Nieuws van de Dag* (*The News of the Day*). This same type of paper appeared in Germany from the end of the nineteenth century, such as the popular *Lokal Anzeiger* in Berlin from 1883, or the *Berliner Morgenpost*. If European journalism, little by little, managed to liberate itself after the upheavals of the eighteenth century, a tendency in the opposite direction manifested itself in Russia, where Czarism made it virtually impossible for there to be a more liberal press up to the beginning of the twentieth century.

During the first decades of the twentieth century, particularly after 1920, the periodical press' field of activities widened even further. Everywhere in Europe, there were all kinds of specialist reviews, serving literature or different religious confessions. There were also reviews on fashion, finance, sport, theatre and cinema, founded as weekly or monthly publications. This development only ground to a halt during the Second World War, when almost everywhere in Europe papers were again submitted to a severe and repressive censorship regime, which engendered a clandestine press – sometimes a source for important postwar newspapers.

Today, thanks to increasingly sophisticated printing technique the possibilities for the modern press have become almost limitless. Even if it has to suffer competition from other media such as television, the force of the written word will always out.

Swift (1667–1745)

M. Foot

When a true genius appears in the world, you will know him by this sign: that fools are all in league against him.

Jonathan Swift

At first sight, Jonathan Swift can appear to be the most provincial of great English writers. He spent nearly all his life in his native Ireland and never succumbed to the temptation, which he admits to having experienced from time to time, to go a little further than just England to visit contemporary Europe. He takes pleasure in giving advice and admonitions to the leaders as to the peoples of these neighbouring countries. He has no personal knowledge of their way of life, but this ignorance does not make him feel the least bit embarrassed. If the term had existed at that time, he would have deserved the name of 'little Englander', assuming he had not been led, reluctantly, it seems, to become a 'little Irelander', the very first representative perhaps of that singular race.

A Tale of a Tub

Many of the books in which Swift gives us the full measure of his genius seem, at first, to be about subjects which have not the least chance of reaching a universal audience. His *A Tale of a Tub* (1704) claims to defend the Anglican Church to which Swift belonged, or rather, the Irish branch of this very English institution, against all other religious denominations. We can forgive Voltaire, an expert on the subject, for having taken this book for a critique of every form of religion. Such is also the interpretation that Queen Anne put on it, who swears that the author of such a book will never be promoted in the Church that she reveres. And if she judges the offence to be unforgivable, we can easily imagine the feelings of those whose faith Swift has singled out for attack. Nevertheless, we must not deduce from the most virulent pages of this *Tale of a Tub* that the religion to which Swift pays such a discreet tribute that it is almost imperceptible is an object of contempt, or even think that these pages prove the unacceptable character of the author's demands in this area. In reality, we need to recognise that Swift devotes a large part of his time – which a man possessed of his genius could have made better use of – to trying to get, if necessary by scheming, a high post in the Church, which meant then basely flattering politicians. He applies himself to become 'that happy combination of lawn and black satin that we call a bishop'. He steeps himself in all the obligations and all the tricks peculiar to political animals in a sphere in which he notes that 'getting on demands the same bodily posture as grovelling'. Many poems in which he expresses the growing fury that the crimes and follies of the world inspire in him attack targets without true substance: one of the most celebrated examples is the poem called 'Legion Club', which lays into the Irish parliament; the equivalent of setting about a scarecrow for sparrows. We sometimes have the impression that Swift is always tied up with sordid political intrigues, as much on the side of England as that of Ireland. Even the famous epitaph that he chose for himself, and which looks down on us from the height of its black marble plaque, on the wall of St Patrick's Cathedral in Dublin, contains an implicit retort for those who think that his last message to humanity should have been more cosmopolitan. Eminent people, particularly known for their devotion, qualified as 'abominable' the terms that Swift had chosen so carefully. For Yeats, however, it is 'the most remarkable epitaph in the whole of recorded history', a judgement which, fortunately, does not prevent him from giving his own version of this epitaph: the latter denounces 'the traveller besotted with the world' who would dare to reproach Dean Swift with having loved his country, or at least for having stayed in it. We return to this short sermon later. Here, we insist on the fact that Swift himself saw a close link between his fidelity to Ireland and the essence of his personal convictions.

Swift and Ireland

We have been reminded of the exacerbated sensitivity of Swift on this subject even more cogently by Herbert Davis in his opening address to the symposium convened for the tercentenary of Swift's birth, which happened in Dublin in April 1967. 'I have insisted,' he wrote, 'on the Irish works of Swift, not only because it behoves us to evoke them today in this place, but because it appears that the success of his books made him feel joy and pride for the people of Ireland.' In effect, of all his works, he only thought it appropriate to offer a single volume, in a very fine binding, to the Bodleian Library in Oxford: the book was published in Dublin in the autumn of 1725 to celebrate the success of his campaign against Wood who had received the authorisation to mint Irish coins of a real value below their nominal value. Here is the title page, with its triumphal accents, of *The Drapier's Letters* (1724):

THE SWINDLE UNMASKED OR THE
HIBERNIAN PATRIOT
Containing all the letters of the
draper to the people of Ireland
concerning Wood's patent, etc.
Also contains a new poem for the draper, as
   well as songs
sung at the Draper's Club,
situated in Truck Street,
Dublin, unpublished till now.
With a preface
explaining the usefulness of
everything.

According to Davis, Swift, as a good Irishman, was partial to fine fights, and would no doubt have particularly enjoyed a fine victory: slightly more than twenty years after the celebration of his tercentenary, the Irish government decided to adorn its pound notes with a portrait of M.B. Drapier: in other words Swift himself.

Settled in Ireland, Swift was truly a father figure for the Irish nation, and the instigator of the fight for independence. Ordinary people – an expression to which Swift himself gives the value of a compliment – understand him. In Dublin, he becomes an even better-known writer than he was in London. Henry Grattan and Thomas Davis salute in him their guide in matters of patriotism; Wolfe Tone and James Finlan strive to imitate the virulence of his pamphleteering style, and Michael Davitt, the most sincere of patriots, but also the wisest and the most disinterested, sees in him the prophet of the fight for an Irish homeland and the triumph of moral strength. John Redmond declares: 'He did more than anyone else in history to give to Ireland the status of a nation.' In Ireland, for the whole of the nineteenth century and beyond, he was openly a revolutionary figure. James Joyce puts Swift next to Parnell, and sees in these two men the two greatest characters in modern Irish history. And yet it is quite rare for Swift to address himself just to the Irish. As he likes to say in the too obvious manner of a jest, he writes for the universal improvement of humanity.

Gulliver's Travels: a pacifist pamphlet

Political philosophers of all tendencies have shown that the most ardent nationalists can also be considered to be the most convinced of internationalists. Swift, a great Irish patriot, is perhaps the most precocious and convincing example that can be found to illustrate this somewhat optimist theory. He derives great inspiration from the new theories of humanism, a modern form of religion, which were then winning over the whole of Europe. Montaigne, in a France torn apart by civil war, had been the principal representative of this school of thought, and Jonathan Swift was his most sincere disciple. 'Your old loquacious friend', such is the way in which Henry St John, Swift's friend, alludes to Montaigne, thus trying to deny the latter's influence. Indeed, St John merely confirms the existence of the most trustworthy source from which Swift takes his new vision of who man is. It is a vision which embraces the whole world and not just his well-loved country of adoption.

Swift vigorously denounced man's brutality and beastliness towards his fellow men. He had a horror of tyranny exerted by the State. He was revolted by the efforts which a country determined to impose its will on another can make in this direction: by what we would today call a policy of imperialism. He denounced, more vehemently than anyone, the crimes committed in the name of a rampant and boastful patriotism. Gulliver wonders if our

'conquests in the countries that I speak of would be as easy as those of Ferdinando Cortez faced with naked Americans' (where had he picked this up, if not in the works of Montaigne?), then gives free rein to his anger in terms which have lost nothing of their topicality in the final pages of *Gulliver's Travels* (1726):

> But I had another Reason which made me less forward to enlarge his Majesty's dominions by my discoveries. To say the truth, I had conceived a few scruples with relation to the distributive justice of princes upon these occasions. For instance, a crew of pirates are driven by a storm they know not whither; at length a boy discovers land from the topmast; they go on there to rob and plunder; they see an harmless people, are entertained with kindness, they give the country a new name, they take formal possession of it for the King, they set up a rotten plank or a stone for a memorial, they murder two or three dozen of the natives, bring away a couple more by force for a sample, return home, and get their pardon. Here commences a new dominion acquired with a title by divine right.

The most loathsome crime for Swift is war, with its long procession of horrors: it carries within itself all other forms of suffering and vice. *Gulliver's Travels* still constitute today the most powerful of pamphlets on pacifism; and this aspect of Swift's iconoclastic personality has won for him the constant sympathy of left-wingers. It is hardly surprising that Hazlitt, Cobbett, Leigh Hunt and Godwin, at the heart of another great war during which spies and informants were in the service of an authority making exorbitant demands, during a period of enforced military conscription and the Peterloo massacre, should have attached so much weight to *Gulliver's Travels* which they thought of as a subversive work. In fact, it uttered truths which had at the time to be kept silent under pain of being condemned for high treason. It celebrated with clarion calls the anarchist rebellion at a time when support for this same cause meant those who defended it were deported to Botany Bay. It called into question the powers-that-be, whether they were Whigs or Tories (what Cobbett called 'the Thing'), and put all these pretentious people in the modest place they should never have left.

All this fully justifies Swift's reputation as a revolutionary of world stature: had he not attacked the apostles of war and the builders of empires at the height of their glory, in England as in Ireland? Was not his voice the first to be raised with vehemence? And this was not all. He observed the conflict between 'ordinary people' and their leaders, their landlords, their oppressors. He understood that 'freedom implies that a people be governed according to laws promulgated with its consent. Slavery implies the absolute opposite.' He understood that 'poor countries were hungry and rich countries proud', and that hunger and pride would never be in the same camp together. He understood what was really at stake in politics. He had a premonition of what would happen if the new moneyed classes, or 'economic man' came to power. 'Swift showed himself remarkable,' said F.W. Bateson, 'in the sense that he denounced liberal capitalism and all the values that it represented, while it was still no more than a cloud no bigger than a man's hand.' *A Modest Proposal for Preventing the Children of Poor People* . . . (1729) was not just addressed to the Irish themselves. It was 'the language which was really spoken in Cheapside and in Threadneedle Street' (the headquarters respectively of the Stock Exchange and the Bank of England). It was the most terrible of curses pronounced against moneylenders since Jesus of Nazareth chased the merchants from the Temple. Let us go back to the 'most remarkable' of epitaphs to give Yeats' version of it:

Swift has sailed into his rest;
Savage indignation there
Cannot lacerate his breast.
Imitate him if you dare,
World-besotted traveller; he
Served human liberty.

Similar words could have been inscribed on the walls of the tower of Montaigne. The heart of the latter was perhaps less exposed and less easily bruised, but Swift and Montaigne defended the same cause. In his time, Swift nevertheless borrowed – unless he contributed to suggesting it in the first place – the active tone of a writing whose wit and impertinence kill more surely than modesty and reflection.

For two centuries, Swift has been held up to public obloquy without the slightest hesitation, but, today, he is almost a part of the celestial phalanx. The Church lays claim to him, but so too in his time did Voltaire. Swift liked England, but it was Ireland that inspired him. He knew how politicians can be base and ambitious, but he also knew that politics dealt with the major problems of poverty and wealth. He understood that human nature can be fundamentally conservative, seeing also that, sometimes, the most elementary decency led men to throw themselves headlong into a revolutionary struggle. He derived moral lessons from the spectacle he saw around him, while speaking a language accessible to all. He 'worked for the freedom of mankind', and, in his lifetime, took great pride in such a mission. Even posthumously, he continues to fulfil it.

Voltaire (1694–1778)

P. Malandain

After having lived with kings, I became king in my own home.

Voltaire

'An amazing revolution in the way people think has taken place in Europe,' wrote Voltaire to the Prince de Ligne in 1766, pretending to ignore the part that he himself had played in it. Voltaire was everywhere at once and he cannot truly be grasped or shut in at any one point: such was his significance in his age for the world and the human mind. His activity, tireless and impossible to categorise, had as its field of operations the whole of Europe, as much for its inspiration and its aspirations as for its reception and influence. His monument is his character, his career, his immense and varied production, his primordial importance, first disputed then indubitable. His influence was that of his style, both diverse and immediately recognisable among a thousand others, or, as has also been said in the critical approach to him, of his 'taste', of his 'mind', of his 'tempo'.

Bourgeois, libertine, writer

The son of a solicitor in Paris, François Marie Arouet was a typical representative of that middle class which, while maintaining privi-leged contacts with the world of the nobility, wanted to gain its independence and make a name for itself (he created that of 'Voltaire' in 1718). From his Jesuit education he retained a solid classical culture. He found in liber-tinism and the development of scientific thought hope for the development of a new world. In fighting against social injustices he did not neglect to have himself recognised by institutions and to build up his own personal fortune. But Voltaire owed his success to his talent as a writer.

An *enfant terrible* but a spoilt child, incredibly precocious and altogether talented, Voltaire established himself as a skilful poet before the age of twenty. By the age of twenty-four he was Racine's successor in tragedy; the time he was twenty-nine he was a great national poet. He was seen to hold the first rank in tragedy, the epigram, didactic or commemorative, the epic (*The Henriad*, 1723, the only French epic between Ronsard's *Franciad* and Hugo's *The Legend of the Centuries*, went through no fewer than sixty editions in his lifetime, and another sixty-seven between 1789 and 1830), not to mention the historical tale. At the end of the emerging Enlightenment he perfected a short genre that worked extremely well, nicely adapted to the coming age of the militant Enlightenment. This genre, which would ensure his fame, was the philosophical tale. It is an almost impossible genre, in which hardly anybody after him was able to succeed. It was a genre which required that the reader be both naïve

and sly, 'innocent' or 'ingenuous', and 'escarmentado', taught by experience. This took fiction to such a point and dragged it into such a bewildering spiral that it ended up by making the current certainties of reality appear as fictitious. All the objects on which the curiosity of the Enlightenment have been fixed are thus redistributed, as in an adventure playground, placed within everyone's reach, transformed into so many victorious argu-ments for freedom, action, tolerance, zest for life, hope. There was oriental wisdom (*Zadig*, 1747; *Memnon*, 1749; *The Princess of Babylon*, 1768), scientific discoveries (*Micro-mégas*, 1751), philosophical reflection on the problem of evil (*Candide*, 1759), the organisation of society (*Jeannot et Colin*, 1764; *The Ingénu*, 1767), the atheistic hypothesis (*The Story of Jenni*, 1775). Candide's itinerary took him from Westphalia to the Utopian outer limits of America, then to the gates of Asia, after detours via Holland, Portugal, France, England and Venice. Europe found itself invited to take its place in a larger world and to there regenerate its old values, so as to preserve its leading role in the con-struction of a worldwide civilisation. It was not only the fact that the circumstances of Voltaire's adventurous existence, full of flights, imprisonments and exiles, had put him at the centre of a whole network of European exchanges, but that an ardent awareness of a cultural identity had been threatened by its own disorders.

Ferney, a centre for European thought

This awareness manifested itself during Voltaire's stay in England (1726–1728) where the exile paid back his punishment with provocation. With *Philosophical Letters* (1734) he launched an insolent but vibrant appeal for cultures to collaborate, beyond all national or religious sectarianism. This same awareness turns for consolation to Lorraine, to the estate of Stanislas Leszczyński, in Cirey (1734–1749) where Voltaire along with Madame du Châtelet, devoted himself to studying, experi-ments and writing treatises on physics, metaphysics and morality (*Elements of the Philosophy of Newton*, 1738). It was further tested by the stormy relationship that Voltaire had with Frederick II, after 1736, and especially during his stay in Berlin from 1750 to 1753, then, by correspondence, to the end of his life. Voltaire's awareness finally came to rest, from 1759, in Ferney, near the Swiss frontier, where he occupied a position as eloquent in its way as that of Victor Hugo later in Guernesey, but quite different. He was not a sublime exile on the margins of empire, but a rallying point and an obligatory place to cross in the heart of the continent; not in an island off the coast of a forbidden country, but in a garden which he could leave, in case of need, while living there with a liberty renewed each day. In the garden we can come in as we go out: the whole of Europe walks through it meeting one another frequently at this geographical and philosophical cross-roads. For twenty years, Ferney became a centre for European thought. There were discussions with publishers in Geneva and in Amsterdam, intrigues in the political and literary institutions of the 'Welches' (the French), advice for German princes and the Empress of Russia, encouragement for all those who, like the Italian Beccaria, fought for justice and freedom. Still more important, there were interventions in judicial affairs to defend the victims of fanaticism and, above all, from that of the Catholic Church (against which Voltaire launched his famous battle-cry: *Écrasez l'Infâme: Crush the Unspeakable*. He raised his voice in support of Sirven, Lally-Tollendal, the Chevalier de la Barre and gained an outstanding success in 1765 with the rehabilitation of Calas, executed in 1762 after having been wrongly accused of killing his son who wanted to stop being a Huguenot. And there was always his ceaseless literary activity: tragedies, poems, tales, epistles, pamphlets, dialogues, satires and miscellanies were all added, at the end of his life, to 'alphabetical' works, of which the most celebrated was the *Portable Philosophical Dictionary* (1764).

Voltaire achieved all this with a health which he said was always precarious and which only gave out during his last stay in Paris, at the age of eighty-four, in the middle of a sort of apotheosis. This ceaseless activity is still accessible to us through the 20,000 letters which made up his *Correspondence*, one of the most extensive of all time. One example will suffice to illustrate it: the letters he sent and the poem he composed after the Lisbon earthquake (1755) kindled a debate not only with Rousseau, as we know, but in the Iberian peninsula, in Geneva, in Frankfurt where the young Goethe was touched by it, in Königsberg where the young Kant took notice of it.

An inimitable irony

We know the 'words' of Voltaire, and the strange power they had to make an opponent look ridiculous or to discredit a system of thought. We have often seen in them the almost diabolical exercise of a systematic and irresponsible criticism, without mentioning the worry and the permanent search it revealed and nourished in a man less occupied with the dubious pleasure of sneering and destroying than with the joy of understanding, making understood, and constructing. If we had to sum up in a few formulae what was never a system – he hated them – but a lucid and fervent accompaniment to the whole intellectual and sensual adventure of the century, we could do worse than choose the following, which make clear, through an evolution in the diagnosis that he makes of the world, the enduring will to live in it intensely and to constantly improve it: 'Heaven on earth is where I am'; 'But, said Zadig . . .', 'You have to admit it, evil is on the earth'; 'Children of the same God, let us at least live as brothers'; 'I have done a little good, it's the best thing I've done'. And, judging by the faculty of distance that made it possible for such a 'French' genius to widen the horizons of his humanism, we can read again his famous *Discours aux Welches* (*Discourse to the Frenchies*) of 1764:

Frenchies, my fellow countrymen! If you are superior to the ancient Greeks and Romans,

[. . .] admit that you were always a little barbaric. Despite this wretched state of barbarity, those who have compiled your history, whom you take to be historians, often call you the finest people in the world. [. . .] That is hardly just to other nations. You are a brilliant and likeable people, and if you joined modesty to your endowments, the rest of Europe would be very pleased with you. [. . .]

Imagine that, for six hundred years, hardly anyone among you, apart from some of your druids, could read or write. [. . .]

I should like to agree with you, my dear Frenchies, that your country is the finest in the world: you do not however possess the largest land in the smallest of the four continents. Consider that Spain is a little bigger, that Germany is bigger still, that Poland and Sweden are bigger, and that there are provinces in Russia which the country of the Frenchies would fit into more than four times over. [. . .]

First people of the universe, consider that you have in your realm of Frankreich about two million people who walk in clogs for six months of the year and go barefoot for the other six. [. . .]

You give yourselves a round of applause because you see your language almost as universal as Greek and Latin were formerly: to whom are you indebted for this, I ask you? To about twenty good writers you have almost all neglected, or persecuted, or harassed during their lives. You owe especially this triumph of your language in foreign countries to that crowd of emigrants who were obliged to leave their country circa 1685. The Bayles, the Leclercs, the Basnages [. . .] and so many others went abroad to distinguish themselves in Holland and Germany. [. . .] Is not your lack of imagination demonstrated by those dry and barbaric words that you use for everything? [. . .] It has already been objected that you say an arm of a river, an arm of the sea, un cul d'artichaut (an artichoke bottom), a cul-de-lampe, a cul-de-sac. You would hardly allow yourselves to talk about a real ëculí (=arse) in front of respectable women; and yet you have no other expression to mean things to which an arse bears no relationship.

Voltaire and the future of Europe

We would need a whole chapter to give an idea of the influence that the person, work and myth of Voltaire exerted all over Europe, as much before the great upheaval of the French Revolution – to the idea of which, rightly or wrongly, these things remain firmly wedded – as during the nineteenth century – during which 'Voltairianism' exalted and betrayed them in turn – and up to our own time which, without totally extinguishing the passions they arouse, tends to do them justice. The example of two countries can illuminate their nature and scope. In Greece, where Choiseul-Gouffier was welcomed in 1776 by the following anguished question from a monk on Mount Athos: 'Is Voltaire still alive?', his name was first closely associated with the movement of intellectual emancipation which was to bring about political liberation. Translated and commented on by Vulgaris, quoted by Moesiodax, fervently admired by Coray, he served as a symbol for the whole of that forward movement of European thought which ended by making forms of oppression intolerable everywhere. But Turkish oppression was only the most spectacular of these forms: that of religion would soon have to worry about the risks that the stalwart opponent of 'the Unspeakable' was making it run. After the 1790s, the Patriarchate of Constantinople launched a series of attacks on and refutations of Voltaire, which began to construct the myth of a 'ridiculous clown', of a 'mask with a snub nose'. A book by Theotokis was largely responsible for spreading this myth, carried on by Cavvadias and Parios, while, in the years that preceded the War of Independence, Voltaire's tragedies galvanised the will for struggle and rebirth. The whole of Voltaire is in his triple role of rouser of freedom, worrier of the powers-that-be, inciter to action. In the Dutch-speaking Netherlands, we find the same blueprint: the

347

great success of Voltaire's ideas, above all through his plays, known thanks to F. de La Fontaine and Cammaert; a spiteful refutation of these ideas, adjudged 'materialistic', by Hellynckx (1762); finally the use of Voltaire's model for the heady freedom of national and democratic feeling in the 1780s.

One of Hellynckx's arguments, thanks to his ingenuity, would have us definitely plump for the writer rather than the thinker. He reproaches Voltaire with brilliant and dangerous writing became it is seductive. Our age has learned to recognise the dangers and limits of the confidence with which the first part of the eighteenth century thought it could resolve the problems of humanity with just the weapons of reason and irony. But our age too is no less fascinated by the scintillating form that that age was sometimes able to give to dreams that still haunt us.

11 *The Second Half of the Eighteenth Century*

U. JANSSENS-KNORSCH
AND H. CH. GRAF VON NAYHAUSS

Here sensations mingle with ideas, life as a whole is lifted from the same source, and the soul like the air expands to fill the earth and sky. Here genius feels itself at ease.

Madame de Staël,
Corinna or Italy

Three intellectual currents predominated in the Europe of the second half of the eighteenth century: the Enlightenment, sentimental rebellion and classicism. They have all profoundly affected and influenced politics, culture and society and were, in their turn, affected by them. Their development and evolution have varied according to political and social events. So, for example, the Enlightenment affected all of Europe until the 1770s. At the end of the century, revolutionary movements caused an upheaval in the political map, and contributed to a significant change in mentalities and cultures: sentimentality opposed to the omnipotence of reason the primacy of nature and sensibility. Finally, classicism triumphed from 1795 to the Congress of Vienna, which in 1815 determined the new European order.

The Enlightenment as a backdrop

A movement of scepticism and rationalism, the Enlightenment dominated the eighteenth century. The theoretical and philosophical foundation of the age, this movement preached an intellectual attitude of mind which tried to break free of the guardianship over thought exercised by the Church and theology by raising reason (rationalism), the senses (sensualism) and experience (empiricism) to the rank of exclusive sources of knowledge. The Enlightenment leaned above all on the philosophy of 'bon sens' ('gesunder Menschenverstand', 'common sense'). What does not hold water logically was rejected as error, prejudice and superstition.

In their fundamental optimism, the representatives of the Enlightenment believed that reason based on clear ideas, education and the sciences would allow them to steadily improve their knowledge of the world.

There was an important variation on the Enlightenment: the 'reformed' or Christian Enlightenment. Its representatives, faithful to the spirit of the Gospel, tried to take up a position which avoided the pitfalls of unbelief and superstition. This stance in effect made possible the successful fight against prejudice and superstition. During this period, the reformed Enlightenment became closely associated with empiricism and the scientific attitude, taking its lead from Newton's theological physics. This trend became very popular thanks to the work of 's Gravesande and Van Musschenbroek, teachers in Leyden. Strongly rooted in the United Provinces, the movement influenced the whole of Europe and even beyond. The *Kathechismus der Natuur* (*Catechism of Nature*, 4 volumes, 1777–1779) by pastor **Johannes Florentius Martinet (1729–1795)**, translated in an abridged form in German, French, English, Malay and even Japanese, was a good example of this trend.

Rebellion: sentimentality and uniqueness

Revolutionary movements were an uprising against absolute and unconditional faith in the power of reason; they fought against the established order and a society which, because of its prohibition of a rational and lawful order, was opposed to the free development of the personality. Above all they were hostile to a power which was not only limited to Europe, but which spread to all parts of the world under her domination, as is shown, for instance, by the American Revolution. Finally, these movements wanted to rid life of all obstacles, and to leave behind a bookish, sterile and dusty learning to make more room for Nature. Sentimentality, pietism and sensibility ('Empfindsamkeit'), hostile to the predominance of reason, took less note of what men have in common, their universal character, than the uniqueness of individuals and peoples, their originality and nationhood.

Classicism

In terms of the history of culture, Rome was replaced by Athens; the classicism of the period was characterised by Philhellenism or Neo-Classicism, since the important thing from now on was to imitate Greek antiquity. Tribute was paid to a Greece that never existed and which, in the eighteenth century, was merely a myth. A mania for things Greek set in all over Europe, manifesting itself in artistic and cultural fields. From the middle of the century, the three currents revealed themselves with significant and characteristic texts: the *Encyclopedia*, *The Social Contract* and the *History of Ancient Art*.

The *Encyclopedia*: a shining example

The editorial launch of the *Encyclopaedia or Reasoned Dictionary of Sciences, Arts and Occupations* took place, initially, in 1751. It was a monumental work which, in alphabetical order, answered questions about philosophy, religion, literature, aesthetics, politics, eco-nomics, natural sciences and technology. But, in fact, it hid an important arsenal of sub-versive and atheistic ideas, which the authors disguised in articles with an apparently neutral title. The object of the exercise was expressed in the article on the *Encyclopedia* which is full of the Enlightenment spirit:

> The purpose of an Encyclopedia is to gather knowledge scattered over the surface of the earth; to expound the general system under-pinning it to the people with whom we live, and to transmit it to the people who come after us; so that the work of centuries past may not have been useless works for the centuries to come; so that our nephews, in becoming more knowledgeable, may become at the same time more virtuous and happier, and so that we will not die without having deserved well of the human race.

In 1772, the *Encyclopedia* already encompassed twenty-eight volumes. The editor and driving force behind the enterprise was **Denis Diderot (1713–1784)**. The philosopher and mathematician **Jean le Rond d'Alembert (1717–1783)** carried out the function of assistant editor but, hostile to Diderot's overly radical materialism, he withdrew from the project. With Voltaire, Diderot was one of the most influential authors of the second half of this century of the Enlightenment.

The Social Contract: towards the revolution

> Man is born free, and everywhere he is in chains.
>
> Rousseau, *The Social Contract*

In 1762, one year before the end of the Seven Years' War, when Frederick II of Prussia, the first 'enlightened despot' in Europe, waged against Austria, France and Russia the first world war (for the colonies – what was really at stake – were far-flung), *The Social Contract* by **Jean-Jacques Rousseau (1712–1778)*** appeared. Between the criticisms aimed at religion and the Church, and the struggle that would overthrow social structures, this text was an important landmark, perceived as the expression of the revolutionary movements of the age. Rousseau's introduction, 'Man is born free, and everywhere he is in chains', and the doctrine of popular sovereignty which he religiously defends already gave one to understand that the French Revolution would sanction the least deviation from the collective will to defend an ideal of liberty and equality. Some years before, other major works had also presented analyses of how society functioned: the *Discourse on the Origin of Inequality* (1755) by Rousseau, *The Century of Louis XIV* (1751) and the *Essay on the Customs and the Spirit of Nations* (1756) by Voltaire.

The *History of Ancient Art*: the Bible of German 'Klassik'

Geschichte der Kunst des Altertums (*The History of Ancient Art*, 1764) by **Johann Joachim Winckelmann (1717–1768)** can be considered as the Bible of classicism, if German 'Klassik' is included in this European notion. The English Hellenists Stewart and Revett, members of the Society of Dilettanti, had, in 1755, with *The Antiquities of Athens* laid the foundations for an accurate theory of Greek architecture. The same year Winckelmann published *Gedanken über die Nachahmung der griechischen Werke in der Malerei und Bildhauerkunst* (*Thoughts on the Imitation of Greek Works in Painting and Sculpture*), a work in which he celebrated with renewed conviction the spirit of classical Antiquity: 'Good taste was born under Greek auspices.' Winckelmann emphasised that the only way to become inimitable was to imitate the Greeks. His *History of Ancient Art*, a veritable guide to neo-classical aesthetics, depreciated modern art to praise the works of Antiquity, and introduced throughout Europe the process of idealising the Greek 'classical golden century'. This Greek culture of antiquity became alienated from its roots because of Turkish domination. We can only 'look for it with our soul', as Goethe's Iphigeneia says from her rock in Tauris.

Certainly literary Europe formed a cultural unity in the eyes of intellectuals: 'Nowadays we must be Europeans,' Madame de Staël (1766–1817) would say, and Voltaire cried: 'Whoever wants to write the history of one of the great European states will need to write the history of all of Europe.' 'I have six or seven homelands: the Empire, Flanders, France, Spain, Austria, Poland, Russia and, at a pinch, Hungary,' wrote the Prince de Ligne in his *Memoirs*. The Enlightenment had even more. Their distribution invites us to make a tour of Europe.

THE ENLIGHTENMENT: A PANORAMA OF EUROPEAN LITERATURE

France and England are the starting point for this exploration: the first conveys the ideas of the Enlightenment, the second renews the novel genre. But from Scandinavia to the Balkans, from Russia to the Iberian peninsula, it was only slowly that their innovations exerted a decisive influence over the awakening of patriotism or artistic choices.

The initiative: France and England

The Century of Louis XIV and the *Essay on the Customs and Spirit of Nations* by Voltaire bear witness to what point historiography can give men the necessary distance to break free of superstition, fanaticism and despotism. Voltaire's *Treatise on Tolerance* (1763) defended this position afresh; he preached reason and, in the name of humanity, encouraged peace and tolerance, particularly in the area of religion. Apart from this, Voltaire wrote 20,000 letters to friends all over Europe. He produced the best of his work in his philosophical tale *Candide* (1759), in which he links the travel motif to a Utopian one. Candide, the innocent hero, faced with physical and moral sufferings, realises that we need to make the world a better place. Through Pangloss, Voltaire laughs at Leibniz and his philosophy according to which our world is 'the best one of all'. Diderot's *Rameau's Nephew* (1762–1774) also belonged to this philosophical literature. In this novel, written in the form of dialogues, the nephew of the musician Rameau displays a certain cynicism, styling himself the representative of eighteenth-century Parisian society. This satire contains several conversations full of 'wit' on education, virtue, happiness, art and genius, which are the themes of a middle class on the road to freedom. *Jacques the Fatalist and his Master* (1773), a labyrinthine tale, narrates the adventures of Jacques, a credulous servant, and of his noble master; this couple evoke Sancho Panza and Don Quixote. In the ironic commentary of the narrator, a game with fiction becomes the theme of the novel, as in Sterne's *Tristram Shandy*, which served as a model for Diderot.

Enlightenment France produced many Utopian works. If, in the seventeenth century, only some works deserved this description, we can list eighty-three of them in the eighteenth century. Apart from the works of Voltaire, *Usong* (1772) and *Alfred* (1775) by the Swiss Albrecht von Haller (1708–1777), *Der goldene Spiegel* (*The Golden Mirror*, 1773) by the German Christian Marin Wieland (1733–1813), *The History of the Ajaoians* (1768) by Fontenelle, and *Arcadia* (1788) by Bernardin de Saint-Pierre. These tales were called political novel, philosophical novel, system of government, imaginary republic. *The Year 2440, a Dream if ever there was One* (1771), by Louis Sébastien Mercier (1740–1814), was the first Utopian novel to project its ideal into a precise future. The success of Utopian literature, in the second half of the eighteenth century, coincided with the crisis of the Ancien Régime. The desire for Utopia became radical and concrete in the hopes carried by the Revolution of 1789.

The trilogy by **Pierre-Augustin Caron de Beaumarchais (1732–1799)**, *The Barber of Seville* (1775), *The Marriage of Figaro* (1778) and *The Guilty Mother* (1792), gave a good idea of the historical and social turning point then experienced by the drama in France. These three plays indicate the trend towards a middle-class outlook which society and art were experiencing. Beaumarchais depicted in them the three historical phases of society: postfeudal, prerevolutionary and bourgeois.

The bourgeois novel appeared very early in England where the bourgeoisie prospered. This type of novel had its place in the Enlightenment from the beginning of the century, to the extent that it no longer portrayed man as a member of a nation, but as an individual whose personal and cultural importance was duly emphasised. The novel of education or of apprenticeship (*'Bildungsroman'*) is realistic since the author introduces recognisable characters and situations which therefore appear plausible. At the same time, this English novel, unlike classicism and French rationalism, was inspired above all by empiricism. English writers demonstrated pragmatism, preferring to the notion of Cartesian reason the vaguer notion of 'common sense'. In so doing, they showed a strong propensity to balance opposites and to harmonise extremes. From the middle of the eighteenth century, beyond a classical and pragmatic concept of art, it was above all Fielding's chronological narration which had become exemplary, and was distinguished from Richardson's sentimentality. Like Fielding, **Tobias George Smollett (1721–1771)** cultivated in his first novels of manners the tradition of the novel of adventures (*Peregrine Pickle*, 1751). **Laurence Sterne (1713–1768)**,* on the contrary, in *The Life and Opinions of Tristram Shandy, Gentleman* (1759–1767), juxtaposed states of consciousness out of chronological order and so opposed the novel form of Fielding which was determined by chronological order. He multiplied authorial interventions and commentaries, anticipating the style of the 'stream of consciousness'.

'Verlichting': the Enlightenment in The Netherlands

In the Southern Netherlands, under Hapsburg domination, Francophone Belgian literature was marked by the cosmopolitanism of the Enlightenment. The French and Austrian spirit of the Enlightenment spread there quickly and with fewer obstacles once the Jesuits had been banished in 1772. In Brussels the Academy of Sciences and Belles-Lettres sprang up. In 1756, **Pierre Rousseau (1725–1785)** published his famous *Encyclopedic Journal*. In 1771 he completed it, in collaboration with Rey and Pancoucke, with the five-volume *Supplement to the Encyclopedia*. In 1787, Pancoucke and Plomteux added *The Methodical Encyclopedia*, known all over Europe. A dominant figure in literary cosmopolitanism, Charles-Joseph, Prince de Ligne (1735–1814), a French-speaking Austrian, successfully tried all literary genres. His novel *Letters from Fédor to Alphonsine* (1814) owes much to the spirit of the Enlightenment.

In Flanders, to make a stand against Gallicisation, there was an insistence on national character and local culture, which have to be expressed in their own language. Hence the paradox: on the one hand, the ideas and the principles of the Enlightenment had been transmitted in a French medium of instruction (d'Alembert, Montesquieu, Voltaire and Rousseau); on the other, French language and culture were an obstacle to the creation of a national identity. **Jan Baptist Chrysostomus Verlooy (1746–1797)** established the pedigree of his own language, Dutch. In 1788, like the specialist in canon law, Pierre Lamoot, a native of French-speaking Flanders, he published *Verhandeling op d'onacht der moederlyke tael in de Nederlanden* (*Treatise on the Indifference shown to the Mother Tongue in The Netherlands*), which notably had as its consequence the publication, during the French Revolution, of the *Journal of the Constitution* in French and in Dutch.

In The Netherlands, the rationalist and sentimental tendencies of literature were synthesised by **Betje (Elisabeth) Wolff-Bekker (1738–1804)** and **Aagje (Agatha) Deken (1741–1804)**. They lived together from 1777 and composed four epistolary novels. The first, *Historie van Mejuffrouw Sara Burgerhart* (*The Story of Sara Burgerhart*, 1782) was undoubtedly the best Dutch novel of the eighteenth century. Aimed in particular at

young ladies, it advocated the tolerant practice of Christianity and emphasised the importance of trade for the country. It also criticised 'people who mince their words', the 'little masters' who mumble in French, and 'rationalists'.

National feeling in Scandinavia

In Denmark, during the second half of the eighteenth century, the Enlightenment parted company from Holberg's 'French' classicism. Propagated by Sneedorff and Tullin, the Scandinavian Enlightenment carried with it its opposite: Pietism. In 1747, an institute of secular education Det Ridderlige Akaemi i Sorø, was set up, which taught modern philosophy (particularly Wolff), natural sciences (Newton), Deist theology, and the history of the Danish nation. **Jens Schielderup Sneedorf (1724–1764)**, still under the influence of Montesquieu and Voltaire, was the principal representative of rationalism. From 1761 to 1763, he edited *Den patriotiske Tilskuer*, a revue (*The Patriotic Observer*) which contributed in the spirit of Addison and Steele to the moral education of the people. **Christian Braunmann Tullin (1728–1765)** wrote an erudite literature full of restrained feelings, a rococo literature of which the classicist tradition and aesthetics took on rationalist appearances. The writers Ewald and Baggesen were equally indebted to French classicism. We only need to consider *Adam og Eva* (*Adam and Eve*, 1768), a drama by **Johannes Ewald (1743–1781)**, or *Harlekin Patriot* (*Harlequin the Patriot*, 1777) which already heralded the crisis of classical drama, or even *Komiske Fortaellinger* (*Comic Tales*, 1785) by **Jens Baggesen (1764–1826)**. These two authors later wrote sentimental literature. Towards the end of the eighteenth century, a kind of Jacobin literature also developed in Denmark, but its authors fall out of favour during the Terror.

Norway, an integral part of Denmark since 1387, began to break free of the Danish stranglehold towards the end of the eighteenth century. The awakening of Norwegian patriotism was particularly encouraged by the historian **Gerhard Schoning (1722–1780)** and the dramatist, preacher, then bishop of Bergen, **Johan Nordal Brun (1745–1816)**. In his role as secretary of the Learned Society of Norway founded in 1760 in Trondheim, he had advocated the founding of a Norwegian university in 1771 in Copenhagen. In poetry texts, songs and nursery rhymes spread rapidly, inspired by popular language. The *Almuens sanger* (*Peasant Songs*, 1790) and the anthology *Den syngende soemand* (*The Singing Sailor*, 1793) by Claus Frimann (1746–1809) were famous, as was *Doleviser* (*Village Songs of the Valleys*), published by Edvard Storm after 1800. For the first time, this used colloquial language to artistically describe nature and life in the countryside. The members of the Norwegian Society, created in 1772 in Copenhagen, took their lead from Holberg's example, a Norwegian precursor of the Enlightenment. Among members, apart from Brun, were the critic and dramatist Claus Fasting (1746–1791) from Bergen, the writer-cum-satirist Johann Herman Wessel (1742–1785) and the dramatist Niels Krog Bredal (1733–1778).

In Sweden, classicism was the dominant literary trend during the second half of the eighteenth century. As in Denmark, rationalism and the Enlightenment went hand-in-hand with the secularisation of intellectual life. King Gustav III (1746–1792) encouraged the arts, literature and particularly the theatre. He himself wrote dramas and operas and founded the Swedish Academy. In his eighty-four *Fredmans Epistler* (*Poems of Fredman*, 1768–1772), **Carl Michael Bellman (1740–1795)**, the king's protégé, described life in the closed houses and bars in eighteenth-century Stockholm. When, in his poems, he mingled local colour with parodies of mythological figures to show the lack of harmony in the world, Bellman moved away from his classical education to express the essential feelings of a whole socially underprivileged class. **Johan Henric Kellgren (1751–1795)** was a convinced Voltairian who defended French classical style. His satirical poem *Mina löjen* (*My Smile*, 1778) expressed his ideas on reason, his openness to the outside world,

good taste and rationalism. Several years later, a quarrel about the permanence of Swedish national literature put him in opposition to the poet **Thomas Thorild (1759–1808)**, the celebrant of English, German and Danish sentimental poetry. Eventually he distanced himself from French classicism by drawing near to Ossian and Milton. The eighty stanzas of *Den Nya Skapelsen* (*The New Creation*, 1789) by Kellgren foreshadowed Romanticism. **Anna Maria Lenngren (1754–1817)**, the only woman in a circle of Voltairians and satirists, also turned later to the genre of the sentimental idyll. Her poems were collected posthumously (*Skaldeförsök*, *Essay on Poetry*, 1819). In Finland (which belonged until 1809 to Sweden), the enlightened **Henrik Gabriel Porthan (1739–1804)**, surrounded by Finno-Swedish men of letters, inspired with his critical work (*De poesifennica*, *On Finnish Poetry*, 1766–1778) a collection of popular poems. However, this work was not published until 1819, thanks to the famous 'Turku Romantics', under the title of *Runen* (*Runes*).

'Aufklärung': the Enlightenment in Germany

In the German States, during the second half of the eighteenth century, the rationalist Enlightenment thought found its main expression in the novel. Excluded from the spheres of politics and power, limited to the family, the individual and private feelings, the bourgeoisie expressed itself and was accurately reflected in this genre. In the eighteenth century, it was still defined as a simple 'love story'. In contrast to the epic, it was still not considered to belong to the realm of literature. Blanckenburg, in the first theoretical German treatise devoted to this form, *Versuch über den Roman* (*Essay on the Novel*, 1774), as well as Mendelssohn (*Schriften*, *Letters on Literature*, 1761) and Johann Adolf von Schlegel (the father of the two Romantics Friedrich and August Wilhelm von Schlegel) tried to have the novel recognised as an independent literary genre. But it was only with Wieland's novel, *Geschichte des Agathon* (*The Story of Agathon*, 1766), the first significant philosophical novel, considered by Lessing to be the best German novel of the period, that the genre broke free of the epic. Wieland's novels were still influenced by the spirit of rococo art. *The Story of Agathon* and his epic *Musarion* (1769) bear witness above all to the way in which Greek antiquity was then perceived in Germany. Wieland also gave a definition of the short-story genre in his preface to *Novelle ohne Titel* (*Untitled Short Story*, 1772).

In the literature of Central European countries of the German Holy Roman Empire, interest began to be shown in Greek Antiquity at the end of the 1760s. Until then, there had not been either classical literature or classical aesthetics. Although Gottsched preached the imitation of French classicism in new German literature, it was only with Lessing and Winckelmann that German discussion of the value and significance of ancient art became important. The Germans were thus able to enter into a debate without difficulty, in which the French had only managed to enter at the cost of quarrels.

'Oświecenie': the Enlightenment in Poland

In Poland, the age of the Enlightenment coincided with the thirty-year reign of King Stanislas II Augustus Poniatowski (1764–1795). It was marked by crises and reforms, such as the global reform of education in 1773 which imposed Polish as a medium of instruction in schools and colleges and, at court, replaced Latin with Polish. One of the first to fight for correct, clear, logical and lucid Polish was Konarski. In the literary field, the Frenchmen Montesquieu, Voltaire, Diderot, Bouffon and Rousseau were models; they were read in the original as young educated Poles no longer spoke either Latin or Italian, but French. Among the languages he used with ease, Count **Jan Potocki (1761–1815)**★ chose French to write his fantasy, the *Manuscrit trouvé à Saragosse* (1804–1814).

Influenced by the works of the French encyclopedists, Polish literature during the Enlightenment fought against Sarmatism, the élitist national and religious ideology which emerged in the sixteenth century. **Ignacy Krasicki (1735–1801)** was the most brilliant intellectual of this movement of emancipation of the second half of the eighteenth century. He was called both the Polish La Fontaine and the Polish Voltaire. In a poem called *Monachomachia czyli wojna mnichow* (*Monachomachia or the War of the Monks*, 1778), he denounced the drunkenness and stupidity of monks, which earned him indignant protests on the part of the clergy. Krasicki made use of satire and had recourse to the fable to veil his criticisms: *Bajki i Przypowieści* (*Fables and Parables*, 1779) and *Bajki nowe* (*New Fables*, 1802). Kajetan Węgierski (1756–1787), Voltaire's disciple and translator, was another representative of the rationalist confraternity.

The establishment of a public theatre in Warsaw under Stanislas II favoured the revival of many plays, above all French ones, and the mounting of Polish comedies. Franciszek Bohomolec (1720–1790), a rhetoric teacher at the Jesuit College of Warsaw, composed twenty-five plays collected under the title of *Komedie* (*Comedies*, 1755–1760). In Warsaw, during the years 1780–1788, Franciszek Zabłocki (1754–1821) dominated the stage with fifty-four comedies he translated from the French and adapted to Polish taste. *Powrót posła* (*The Return of the Deputy*, 1791) by Julian Ursyn Niemcewicz (1757–1841) was the first Polish political comedy. Wojciech Bogusławski (1757–1829), who was the director of the Polish National Theatre in 1790 and remained so for thirty years, also founded theatres in Lemberg (Lvov) and Wilno, among others. He himself translated and 'Polished' great foreign authors such as Molière, Diderot, Beaumarchais and Lessing. He wrote the first historical prose comedy in Poland, *Henryk VI na łowach* (*Henry VI Hunting*, 1792), as well as the peasant play *Cud mniemany czyli krakowiacy i górale* (*The So-Called Miracle or Men of Cracow and Mountain Dwellers*, 1794), in which he paid tribute to 'the heroes of events to come': the peasant revolt of Koúciuszko in 1794.

During this age of national awakening, the production of drama dominated committed literature. In poetry, classicism and Anacreontic lyricism dominated. In his odes, Adam Naruszewicz (1733–1796), the official royal historian, tried to reconcile Sarmatian and Baroque traditions with the Enlightenment spirit. At the same time he praised the virtues of the State. The epigrams and descriptive poetry by **Stanisław Trembecki (1739–1812)**, frivolous and saucy at times, had a certain rococo style. A disciple of Voltaire, he went to the Thursday dinners at the court of Stanislas II, fighting for the supremacy of reason in his ballads, odes and fables (*Bajki, Fables*, 1776).

> He who can breathe the air of Ferney
> broadens his mind and loses crude
>   prejudices.
>
> Stanisław Trembecki,
> Ballads

'Prosveščenie': the Enlightenment in Russia

Peter the Great brought about a radical transformation of Russian society, where his reforms made possible the dissemination of the Enlightenment. The second half of the eighteenth century coincided with the three phases of the reign of Catherine II (1762–1796): the liberal phase, which lasted until the revolt of Pugačev (1773), the conservative phase up until the beginning of the French Revolution (1773–1789), and the repressive phase after the Revolution. The Czarina's relationship with writers and literature varied according to these phases of political life. At the beginning of her reign an unknown liberal intellectual climate prevailed thanks to which a Translating Society, a Society for Publishing Books and the Russian Academy came into existence. After the French Revolution, writers were threatened with exile to Siberia for insubordination. French influence in Russia was at its strongest from 1765 to 1780. The poet and literary theorist Vassili Kirillovitch Trediakovski

(1703–1769), the poet-grammarian Lomonossov and the dramatists Alexander Petrovitch Soumarokov (1727–1777) and Fonvizin laid claim to the poetic doctrine of French classicism. The Empress Catherine herself edited literary reviews and distinguished herself by writing moral comedies. The liberal **Nicolaï Ivanovitch Novikov (1744–1818)** published satirical reviews in which, for the first time in Russia, an independent critical spirit expressed itself, which criticised, in the name of reason, the corruption of certain aristocratic circles and religious obscurantism. But the materialism of the Encyclopedia who foreign to him; he impugned French models and exalted Russian patriotism. Later, the responsibilities he exercises at the heart of Russian freemasonry earned him a fifteen-year prison sentence (1792). Alexander Nikolaïevitch Radichtchev (1748–1802), the author of the revolutionary ode *Vol'nost'* (*Freedom*, 1783), was condemned to death for having written the famous travelogue *Putešestvie iz Peterburga v Moskvu* (*Journey from Petersburg to Moscow*, 1790), in which he castigated serfdom and the arbitrary rule of feudal overlords; but his sentence was commuted to life imprisonment. **Nicolaï Mikhaïlovitch Karamzin (1766–1826)**, in his travelogues *Pis'ma russkogo putešestvennika* (*Letters of a Russian Traveller*, 1799–1802), propagated the ideas of the Enlightenment while sentimentalising them. Russian poetry was also influenced by Western poets; during the last decades of the eighteenth century, the 'old-fashioned' were nevertheless obliged to increasingly defend the doctrine and the classical norms of literary language against the rising tide of sentimentalism.

The Enlightenment from Bohemia to Bulgaria: the voice of the people

The Czech lands experienced at this time a 'national Renaissance' in several phases. 'Enlightened' historians first tried to rediscover the real, hidden national past. This was notably the work of **František Martin Pelčl (1734–1801)** with his *Nová Kronika česká* (*New Czech Chronicle*, 3 volumes,

1791–1796). His friend **Josef Dobrovský (1753–1829)**, an outstanding critical and scientific mind, remained the essential figure of the first generation of 'awakeners': writing in German or Latin, he established a first literary history (1792), rectified Czech grammar (1809) and founded the scientific study of Slavic languages (1822). At the same time, Czech theatre experienced a resurgence in Prague (1786). Prose slowly regathered momentum and poetry began again with the five 'almanachs' (1785–1815) by a group of Czech and Slovak poets under the leadership of **Antonín Jaroslav Puchmajer (1769–1820)**. They worked in classical genres and themes – patriotic odes, comic and heroic epics, love poetry, fables – then abandoned German models and turned towards Western and Polish examples.

In Slovakia, the Enlightenment hastened the transition from the Baroque to a national Renaissance born of the desire for cultural assertiveness to set it apart from Germany and Hungary, and linguistically apart from the Czechs. The priest **Josef Ignác Bajza (1755–1836)** discovered the ideas of the 'Josephine' Renaissance while studying theology in Vienna. Imitating the *Adventures of Telemachus* by Fénelon, Bajza threw himself into the writing of a 'Bildungsroman' in Slovakian dialect: *René mládenea príhodi a skusenosti (The Adventures and Experiences of Young René*, 1783–1785). This attempt to create a Slovakian literary language was taken up by the Catholic priest **Anton Bernolák (1762–1813)**, but the Lutheran minority opposed it and instead ardently cultivated Czech. Poetry by Augustin Doležal (died 1802) and Bohuslav Tablic (1769–1832), published from 1806 to 1812, reflected the spirit of the Enlightenment. During the second half of the eighteenth century, however, there was only one important poet: **Hugolín Gavlovič (1712–1787)**. The author of many religious and moral works (unpublished), he also wrote a vast cycle of philosophical and didactic poems, *Valaská škola mravriv stodola (The Shepherds' School of Wisdom, a Granary of Customs*, 1755, published in 1830–1831).

Gyorgy Bessenyei (1747–1811), a follower of Voltaire, was the most important precursor of the Enlightenment in Hungary. A translator and poet in the classical style, he called on his contemporaries to rediscover the Hungarian national identity. The first novels written in Hungarian were by Andras Dugonics (1725–1801), *Etelka* (1788), a historical novel about the Middle Ages, and by Josef Gvadanyi (1725–1801), *Egy falusi notariusnak budai utazasa (A Journey to Buda by a Village Notary*, 1790), a satirical novel. During the same period, the inspector of schools, translator and journalist Ferenc Kazinczy (1759–1831) tried to renew the literary language and to have Hungarian officially recognised as the national language. His collection of epigrams *Tövisek és viragok (Thorns and Flowers*, 1811), reflected his classical ideas. When radical political movements overrode literary evolution, Kazinczy joined the Hungarian Jacobins. In 1795 he was condemned to death, then pardoned, and remained in prison until 1801. Then he wrote *Pálayán emlékezete (Memoirs*, 1828) as well as *Fogságom naplóje (The Journal of My Captivity*, 1831).

The most important representative of the Enlightenment in Croatia was Matija Antun Reljković (1732–1798), the author of *Satir Iliti divlji ćovik (The Satyr or the Savage*, 1762). Tito Brezovački (1757–1805), a dramatist, wrote his works in the Kaïkavian dialect before he adopted Slovak: the predominant speech of Croatian literature. His plays offered a kind of caricature of society and his own age. He is considered to be the Croatian Beaumarchais. In the second half of the eighteenth century, writers and historians became aware of the treasure of popular literature. The Serbian writer **Dosítej Obradović** (1742–1811) preached the use of the popular language in literature and gave great impetus to novel writing. Simeon Piščević (1731–1797) wrote above all historical and autobiographical novels. His prose has been emulated among novelists up until the twentieth century. Serbian poetry remained classical; the poet Lukijan Musicki (1777–1837) took his inspiration from Horace, and his influence way felt in the Montenegrin poet Njegoš, the last prince-bishop of Montenegro.

Albanian literature of the second half of the eighteenth century, still separate from the Enlightenment, was completely limited to the Christian genre of moral literature. All Christian authors were clergymen. In 1762, **Jul Variboba (1725–?)**, the first true Albanian poet, published the *Life of the Virgin and the Holy Family*. During this period the first works of Muslim writers, such as Nezim Frakulla started to appear.

Religious literature was equally dominant in Bulgaria, where writers were all churchmen. The awakening of the Bulgarian nation took place in stages. First, it discovered a taste for patriotism, giving greater importance to the Christian traditions of the Middle Ages, as expressed in the *Slavo-Bulgarian History* by the monk of Mount Athos Paisij of Hilandar, written in 1762 and published in the nineteenth century.

'I periodos ton photon': the Enlightenment in Greece

During the eighteenth century, the awakening of patriotism became concrete in Greece with the desire for emancipation and membership of Enlightenment Europe. The Enlightenment in Greece was represented by two symbolic figures: Vulgaris and Theotokis. **Eugene Vulgaris (1716–1806)**, from Corfu, taught astronomy, philosophy and new sciences in Ioannina, in Kozani, on Mount Athos as well as in Constantinople. After a short stay in Berlin, he was appointed head librarian at the Imperial Library of St Petersburg, at the court of Catherine II, and later became Archbishop of Slavoni and Cherson on the Black Sea. There he translated works by Locke and Voltaire, pleaded for the use of the vernacular as opposed to Latin, and carried on a correspondence with Leclerc about rivalry of the Churches of Rome and Constantinople. **Nikiphoros Theotokis (1731–1800)**, also a bishop, spent most of his time in exile in Russia. Rhigas Pheraios (1757–1798) was known for his novel *Skholion ton delikaton*

eraston (The School of Delicate Lovers, 1790), inspired by the libertinism of Restif de La Bretonne. His work's chief aim was to spread enthusiasm for the French Revolution throughout Greece, but this cost him his life. Adamance Corais (1748–1833) took up the torch of liberty. His *Adelphiki dhidhaskalia (Brotherly Teaching,* 1798) inspired Greek youth to fight with the French against the Turks. His letters may be numbered among the distinctive works of neo-Hellenic literature. In the linguistic debate which divided Greece, he was in favour of the homogenisation of the language of scholars and colloquial language. For his part, the Athenian Panagiotis Codrikas (1760–1827) defended ancient Greek against the katharevusa or scholarly language. In 1794 he translated *On the Multiplicity of Worlds* by Fontenelle into Greek.

'Illuminismo': the Enlightenment in the country of light

The 'Illuminismo' in Italy was prepared by the work carried out on Vico's philosophy of history, by the historiographical work and the theological criticism of Pietro Giannone, as well as Muratori's literary and social criticism. 'Illuminismo' brought together on the one hand the cosmopolitan objectives of the European Enlightenment, of which France was the focal point, preaching a political and ethical commitment so as to significantly improve living standards. On the other hand, it reevaluated regional traditions: so a distinction was made between 'Illuminismo' in Lombardy, in Naples, in Piedmont, in Venice and in Florence. In his poem *Il giorno (Day,* 1763), **Giuseppe Parini (1729–1799)** painted a satirical picture of the lying and levity of the Milan aristocracy. In his neo-classical odes, on the other hand, he exalted the poet who is poor, yet honest and faithful to his principles, hostile to a corrupt society. Goldoni's work put him in the Enlightenment tradition, to the extent that he expressed his confidence in reason, his desire to see men equal and his hope for a better world. If Goldoni counted on the intelligence of the public, **Carlo Gozzi (1720–1806)** tried to make himself understood by means of fairy-tale and fantasy, remaining faithful to the tradition of the old Italian theatre.

'Ilustración', 'Ilustraçao': the literary emancipation of the Iberian peninsula

In spite of the many bans placed on them by the Inquisition, cultured minds in Spain read the writings of the French Enlightenment, and the number of translations at this time considerably increased. The Enlightenment in Spain was, simultaneously, an opening up to the Enlightenment in Europe generally and a process of emancipation. The revision of literary beliefs came from French classicism and Italian influences. The Benedictine Feijóo encouraged the reading of Descartes, Bayle and Newton. His prose was a model for the religious satire *Historia del famoso predicator Fray Gerundio de Campazas* (*The Story of the Famous Preacher, Brother Gerundio de Campazas*, 1758–1770) by Juan Francisco de Isla, as well as for Pedro Montegons (1745–c.1825), whose educational novel *Eusebio* (1786–1788) took Rousseau's *Émile* as its inspiration. In the realm of the theatre, the victory of neo-clasicism began in 1764 with the banning of 'Autos sacramentales'. But the plays that respected the classical doctrine of the three unities had no impact and were devoid of poetic inspiration. Among successful writers were **Ramon de la Cruz (1731–1794)** who described life in Madrid in a series of dramatic sketches. The pastoral poetry of Juan Meléndes Valdés was a model to follow until the Romantics. The ironical poems of **José Cadalso (1741–1782)** inspired Goya with their mastery of form.

A political figure dominated literary life: the Marquis of Pombal. In his capacity as Chancellor of José I, he contained the influence that enlightened intellectuals started to exert under John V with his political reforms. With the modernisation of education, taken out of Jesuit hands, whose order was sup-pressed in 1759, Pombal's reforms influenced all walks of public life. The *Verdadeiro méthodo de estudar* (*The Right Way to Study*, 1740), formulated by Vernei, first brought with it a polemical atmosphere (especially connected to the teaching of Latin which the Jesuits continued to dispense with Latin grammar books, while the Oratorians put them forward in Portuguese). With *The Right Way to Study*, the foundations for a global reform of education were laid down from 1759. The academy of Arcadia-Lusitania, founded in 1756, became a rampart against the official Baroque style, and at the same time brought together all neo-classical tendencies. Its texts and theories obeyed the Latin motto 'Inutilia truncat' (it omits what is useless), as illustrated by the poet Pedro Antonio Correia Garção (1724–1772) and the dramatist Manuel de Figueiredo (1725–1801). His tragedies dealt with classical themes, while his comedies criticised aristocratic prejudices and instead put forward bourgeois morality. Towards the end of the century a new academy was founded, Nova Arcadia, and the audience for Arcadians reached as far as Brazil. However, this did not prevent centres of literary life being displaced ever further in the direction of salons and cafés, in which a new style distinguished by poetic sensibility was born.

SENSIBILITY AND GENIUS

After Descartes, the Enlightenment method of investigation, founded on reason and experience, had increasingly repressed heartfelt feelings and natural aspirations. But, in the middle of the century, just when rationalism was at its zenith with the publication of Volume One of the *Encyclopedia* (1751), a return to sensibility was perceptible. This revolution in the feelings, however, cannot be considered as a break with Enlightenment ideas, but rather as a rationalist movement. The rediscovery of feelings was nothing more than the logical outcome of the idea that man henceforth had of himself as a rational and emotional being.

The repressed returns

If during the last third of the century people started to cultivate sensitivity where once they cultivated reason, it was perhaps the sign of a necessary search for a new balance of forces, or even of the 'repressed returns', according to the historian George Gusdorf, but a return accompanied by passionate claims. The Enlightenment tried to illuminate the dark side of human nature and the world. It could not stand for shadow, mystery or anything irrational; it could only admit the existence of a positive world, that only the senses were able to know. In order to triumph, it needed to make this standpoint as radical as possible. Henceforth another source of experience would be opposed to its unilateral epistemology: the 'inner sense', the spontaneity of feelings which, it is commonly believed, do not allow themselves to be regulated by any law. It is significant that d'Alembert spoke in his preface to the *Encyclopedia* of an anthropological dualism:

> It is not that passions and taste have a logic which is peculiar to them; but this logic has principles quite different from those of ordinary logic: it is these principles that we need to unravel inside ourselves, and this is, it must be admitted, something that normal philosophy is virtually incapable of.
>
> D'Alembert,
> Preface to the *Encyclopedia*

If d'Alembert treated feelings and reason with a certain equanimity, his opponent Rousseau went even further. He does not stop with suggesting that inner and outer senses were complementary, but gave priority to feelings: 'For us to exist is to feel,' he wrote in *Émile*, 'our sensitivity undoubtedly precedes our intelligence, and we had feelings before we had ideas.'

Rousseau was able to build his theory on the basis of half a century of British philosophy. This began with Shaftesbury – who established a link between man's moral intuition and the concept of the beautiful – and extended to Adam Smith (1723–1790), whose *Theory of Moral Sentiments* (1759) was based on the idea of innate goodness, the foundation of all moral and social behaviour. There was an attempt to anchor religious belief in feelings, as well as ethics. People would rather listen to the voice of their own heart than follow an official religion fixed in the outward appearance of its rites and dogmas. This 'religion of the heart', called 'pietism' in the Protestant countries of Northern Europe, and going hand-in-hand with a certain amount of exaltation, gained ground. Pietism made an impression on the young Goethe, whose *Wilhelm Meisters Lehrjahre* (*The Apprenticeship of Wilhelm Meister*, 1795–1796) was steeped in it. Rousseau, for his part, encountered it in Switzerland through Madame de Warens. The imprint of pietism on the inner life stimulated in literature the observation of self and the description of the most intimate affective impulses, finally leading to sentimentalism. *La Nouvelle Héloïse* (1761) by Rousseau and Goethe's *Werther* (1774) testify to this, while Sterne's *Sentimental Journey through France and Italy* (1769) led to jokes like the following: 'Sentimental?' wrote John Wesley. 'What is that? The word is not English. The author could just as easily say: continental.'

But was not Richardson's *Clarissa Harlowe* already a striking example of sentimentalism? The popularity this novel enjoyed throughout Europe demonstrated the ravages of love in this 'sentimental century'. A permanent theme of literature, love had to wait for the eighteenth-century novel to become its prime subject.

We may distinguish two principal tendencies about the picture of love given in the eighteenth-century novel: the first, idyllic or elegiac, developed from *Manon Lescaut* to *Paul et Virginie* (*Paul and Virginia*, 1788), via Richardson, *La Nouvelle Héloïse* and *Werther*; the second, a sombre double of the first, went from the myth of Don Juan to the corrupt anti-heroes of the Marquis de Sade, via Lovelace (*Clarissa Harlowe*) and Valmont (*Les Liaisons dangereuses*).

The omnipresence of love with all its nuances, from the heights of passion to the deepest perversion, was symptomatic of a phenomenon which has been called 'the discovery of the ego'. The ego was thought to be the nexus of all experience and a reference point for all values. It is therefore not surprising that narratives at this time favour the auto-biographical form or the epistolary novel.★

New forms of the novel

Richardson and Sterne opened the way for Goldsmith, Fanny Burney and Jane Austen. Smollett owed much to Sterne in his final work, the epistolary novel *Humphrey Clinker* (1771), which has as its setting a pessimistic world completely different from that of his first novels. The protagonist, Matthew Bramble, an extremely sensitive and benevo-lent man, hides his feelings under a mask of scepticism. His niece, Lydia, is all feeling, and his nephew also finds difficulty in concealing his emotions behind the irony and wit typical of an Oxford student. Humphrey, the peasant servant employed during the course of a jour-ney through England, is a fervent Methodist. He will turn out to be Bramble's son and end up by marrying the servant, Winifred Jenkins, who combined religious ardour and sexual desire. Her letters are full of misnomers that today would be called 'Freudian slips'.

The Irishman **Oliver Goldsmith (1728–1774)**, essayist, dramatist, poet and novelist, studied medicine and then turned to literature for financial reasons. His best-known novel, *The Vicar of Wakefield*, written in 1761–1762, was published in 1766. This realist novel retraced the setbacks of an Anglican pastor and his family. The hero is often prone to introspection. The description of family life in the country is full of humanity and tender feeling. Madame d'Arblay, known by the name of **Fanny (Frances) Burney (1752–1840)**, was the daughter of the celebrated musician and musicologist Charles Burney. She grew up in an artistic circle frequented, among others, by Samuel Johnson, Joshua Reynolds (1723–1792) and David Garrick (1717–1779). In 1778, she published her first epistolary novel, whose title, *Evelina or a Young Lady's Entrance into the World*, already

announced her favourite theme that she returned to in all her novels (*Cecilia*, 1782; *Camilla*, 1796). Fanny Burney's novels offered a paradigm for the woman's novel. They des-cribed the life of a young lady inexperienced in the ways of the world, from her first out-ings into polite society to her marriage. The heroine is exposed to all sorts of testing social situations. Marriage is at the centre of the social organisation and the plot; what is at stake is knowing if love is compatible with the outward forms of social life. In her social criticism, Fanny Burney anticipated **Jane Austen (1775–1817)**, who enjoyed a period of great creativity during the last five years of the century. The first version of *Sense and Sensibility* (1811) was written in 1796 under the title *Elinor and Marianne*. The first version of *Pride and Prejudice* (1813) dates from 1797. *Northanger Abbey* was written in 1798 and published in 1818 after much revision. It was an ironic response to Sir Walter Scott and the 'Gothic' horror novel which prospered during this period in England, like *Vathek* (1786) by William Beckford (1759–1844), *The Mysteries of Udolpho* (1794) by Ann Radcliffe (1764–1823) and *The Monk* (1796) by Matthew Lewis (1775–1818).

> Charming as were all Mrs Radcliffe's works, and charming even as were the works of all her imitators, it was not in them perhaps that human nature . . . was to be looked for.
>
> Jane Austen, *Northanger Abbey*

Sense and Sensibility begins like a satire of sensibility: two sisters, Elinor and Marianne, embody the two extremes of reason and feeling. Jane Austen, however, manages to avoid a Manichean development in the plot; Marianne, possessed of great sensibility, finally recovers her reason and serenity by marrying a former suitor, the wise Colonel Brandon. *Pride and Prejudice* is Austen's best-known work. There again the opposition between pride (in the person of Darcy) and prejudice (in the person of Elisabeth) is not as schematic or as simple as the title could lead us to suppose. Jane Austen's art resides, first and foremost, in her subtle, nuanced handling of dialogue. The world of her novels is limited to the upper-middle classes and landed gentry, but this fringe is described in all its nuances and even, on occasion, roundly criticised. Although the position of women is the principal theme of her novels, as with Fanny Burney, Jane Austen never subsided into unadulterated feminist propaganda. Being an object of exchange on the marriage market at the end of the century is in her eyes only a symbol of a problem common to anyone endowed with intelligence and feelings, whatever the society they are surrounded by: this is the conflict between individual desire and the respect of social norms.

The English novel found a major echo on the Continent, particularly in Germany and France. A new world opened up with Richardson which Diderot describes most appositely in his *Eulogy of Richardson* (1761):

Ah Richardson! We take, in spite of ourselves, a part in your works, we get involved in your conversations, we approve, we blame, we grow irritated and become indignant. How many times have I not surprised myself, as happens with children that have been taken to the theatre for the first time, crying out: 'Don't believe him, he's deceiving you [. . .]. If you go there, you're done for.' [. . .] The world in which we live is where the scene is set; the background of the drama is real.

Diderot,
Aesthetic Works

With *Jacques the Fatalist*, Diderot explored a new novelistic technique which interferes with the tale's unfolding in time. For Diderot, grasping reality is, first, in the true sense of the term, 'experiencing sensations'. In *The Nun* (1760, published in 1796), we are essentially dealing with physical pleasure, but in the dialogues of *Rameau's Nephew*, Diderot tried to find a balance between vital forces and spiritual ones. In his work, thought asserts itself and sensitivity is refined in line with actual experience – admirably demonstrated by the shock of conversational exchanges.

If Diderot was the novel's extrovert, Rousseau was the introvert. The latter, who intellectualised the emotions more, created life thanks to the power of his writing. In other words, emotional life with Diderot came before writing, while it is progressively built up with Rousseau.

Between these two poles of French literary life, **Jacques Henri Bernardin de Saint-Pierre (1737–1814)** and Restif de La Bretonne (1734–1806) expressed in various ways the emotions aroused by the spectacle of exotic nature (*Paul and Virginia*, 1788) or dreams of a better life as a reaction against urban perversions (*The Peasant Perverted or the Dangers of the Town*, 1775). The reality of evil is written into the novels of Restif as in the series *Justine* by the **Marquis de Sade (1740–1814)**.* The inner workings of the psychological and perverted refinements of libertinism were taken up a few decades later by **Pierre Choderlos de Laclos (1741–1803)** in *Dangerous Liaisons* (1782).

In Russia, the influence of Richardson and Rousseau was perceptible in the novel *Pis'ma Ernnesta i Doravry* (*The Letters of Ernest and Doraure*, 1766) by Fedor Aleksandrovič Emin (1735–1770), who uses the epistolary genre to introduce subjects of topical interest into his love story. Emin, a traveller and polyglot, is considered to be the creator of the Russian psychological novel. But, artistically speaking, he comes a long way behind Karamzin, whose style, shorn of all the archaic usages which clutter the work of classical writers and enriched by foreign loan-words judiciously integrated into Russian, elegantly captured all the movements of the soul. One of the reasons for the huge success of the author's sentimental short stories was that their affective narration established direct communication with the reader.

The poet Rhijnvis Feith (1753–1824), with his novel *Julia*, published in 1783, introduced sensibility to The Netherlands. *Julia* is the story of a sentimental love, the outcome of which, forbidden by society, is projected into the beyond by its two protagonists. This novel, translated into several languages in the eighteenth century, was compared to Goethe's *Werther*, but its excessive sentimental outbursts also provoked many parodies.

The Hungarian writer Jósef Kármán (1769–1795) took his inspiration from *The Sufferings of Young Werther* in 1794 to write a sentimental pastiche called *Fanny hagyomanyai* (*Fanny's Heritage*).

In Italy, prose was still held captive by academicism, and the long novels of Pietro Chiari (1711–1785) too often sacrificed a sentimental plot to a moral demonstration. There were also rhapsodies that constituted formal hybrids, *Avventure di Saffo* (*The Adventures of Sappho*, 1780) and *Notti romane* (*Roman Nights*, 1792–1804) by Alessandro Verri (1741–1816), an essayist and collaborator on the important Milan review *Il caffè* published by his brother, Pietro Verri.

The Prince de Ligne wrote a sentimental epistolary novel, *The Letters of Gustave de Linar to Ernest de G.* (1807), many letters and autobiographical fragments (*My Lapses*, *Letters to the Marquise de Coigny*, 1787; *Fragments of the Story of My Life*, posthumous papers published in 1928). Influenced by the German poet Klopstock, Ewald wrote some poems of pietist inspiration and dramas in which he took up mythological and ancient themes. His greatest prose work, *Levnet og Meeninger* (*Life and Ideas*, only published in 1914), was a pseudo-autobiographical fragment in which the narrator plays the main role. But as the story is itself fiction, the reader cannot distinguish reality from the world of dreams. The analysis of his love for a woman, Arendse, is at the centre of the plot. However, her existence in reality interests him less than the image he tries to keep of her in the 'dark room of his heart', wherein he has aesthetically sublimated it after their first encounter. Like Don Quixote between his chosen one Aldonza Lorenzo, an uninteresting woman from a modest social background, and Dulcinea de Toboso, the symbol of female perfection, the narrator vacillates between the real Arendse, who lives in Copenhagen, and an aesthetic world of dreams. If Don Quixote's Dulcinea was the product of an Arcadian dream, Arendse comes

directly from the Utopian fantasy of Ewald's youth: an Arcadian landscape in which life is happy, as opposed to the miserable existence he led himself. The author's digressions, his intrusions into the narrative, recall Sterne's *Tristram Shandy*. *Labyrinten* (*The Labyrinth*, 1792) by his compatriot Baggesen seems rather to have been inspired by the *Sentimental Journey*. *The Labyrinth* is a travel journal in rhapsodic fragments which express Baggesen's penchant for the Gothic and his adherence to Rousseauist ideas of nature. An excessively sentimental character, though a passionate defender of Enlightenment ideals, Baggesen celebrated the idea of philanthropy as well as universal cosmopolitanism.

The 'ego' which awakes inside the life within, the 'sensibility' of the writer, occupied an even more important place in prose of the last third of the eighteenth century. With *Confessions* (1766–1782/88), Rousseau adopted a completely new tone:

> I am embarking on an enterprise for which an example has never been set, and which will not be imitated. I want to show my fellow men a man in all the truth of his nature; and that man is myself. Myself alone. I feel my heart, and I know mankind. I am made like no one else I have seen; I dare to believe that I am not made like anyone else alive. If I am no better than anyone else, at least I am different.
>
> Jean-Jacques Rousseau,
> *Confessions*

The *Confessions* are distinct from all previous autobiographical publications, such as memoirs and intimate journals, which are essentially intellectual or historical chronicles, and seek to conjure up the person and the author's life. Rousseau's autobiography, similar to the apprenticeship novel, described a process of happy adaptation to society. The intimate narration of his own psychological and emotional development met with great success towards the end of the century. This vogue, confirmed by Romanticism, was caused by the close link established between poetry and truth. Autobiography and the 'autobiographical novel' offered the reader the possibility of identifying with the main character: Pamela, Clarissa, Julie, des Grieux, Saint-Preux, Lovelace, Valmont or Werther. If Italian 'Illuminismo' did not provide a novel to equal ones in English or French, autobiography was raised to their level with the projection of the individual conscience into history. So, after Vico's *Life*, we see the appearance in Italy of the *Vita scritta da lui medesimo* (*Life Written by Himself*, 1736–1737) by Giannone; then, at the end of the century, *The Story of My Life* (1790–1798) by Giovanni Giacomo Casanova de Seingalt (1725–1798), Goldoni's *Memoirs* (1787) – both written in French – the *Vita de Vittorio Alfieri, scritta da esso* (*Life*, 1790–1803) by Alfieri and the *Memorie inutili* (*Useless Memoirs*, 1781–1797) by Gozzi. *Life* gives us the gripping portrait of a passionate, anxious man, who seeks in his childhood memories for the causes and premonitory signs of what he would be as an adult, expecting from his hasty, adventurous journeys through Europe an impossible easing of his existential anguish. Among important autobiographies in German were *Lebensgeschichte* (*Life Story*, 1777) by Johann Heinrich Jung-Stilling, the autobiographical novel *Anton Reiser* (1785–1790) by Karl Philipp Moritz (1756–1793), which recalls *Werther*, and *Ardinghello* by **Johann Heinse (1746– 1803)**, an imaginary autobiography set in sixteenth-century Italy. Heinse painted a colourful, sensuous, passionate picture of Italy in which he portrays himself as a typical genius of the 'Sturm und Drang'. What brings together these three authors, despite their differences, is their care not to sacrifice observation and vision to the subjectivity of their feelings.

> *Wen beim Ursprung seiner Existenz nicht die Fackel der Gottheit entzündet, der wird weder ein hohes Kunstwerk noch eine erhabene Handlung hervorbringen.*
>
> Wilhelm Heinse, *Ardinghello*

> *Whoever the divine torch has not illuminated from the dawn of his existence will never be capable of either a great work or a sublime action.*

The dramatic portrayal of the bourgeois

> What folly it was to go looking for dramatic models among the French, those banal imitators of the Ancients, when we had Shakespeare.
>
> Lessing,
> *Hamburg Treatise on Dramatic Art*

During the second half of the eighteenth century, drama was the genre in which tradition and renewal clashed most violently. We could personalise this quarrel by saying that it was Racine and Shakespeare who were opposed to each other. It is true that French-style tragedy was maintained until the end of the century, especially in countries where vernacular literature had not yet attained its full maturity, such as Russia, Poland, Hungary, Greece and Sweden. In France, on the other hand, as in England and Germany, Shakespeare, who had been described as a 'barbarian' by classicism, experienced a new lease of life. Many new editions and translations of his complete works prove it. 'What folly it was to go looking for dramatic models among the French, those banal imitators of the Ancients, when we had Shakespeare.' Lessing's cry heralded a new concept of theatre. Strictly speaking, theatrical novelty did not take place in tragedy, but in a new genre: the sentimental drama. The model for it was English: the 'domestic tragedy', an intimate, middle-class version of Elizabethan tragedy. Two playwrights of the first half of the eighteenth century exerted a decisive influence on the continent: the first was George Lillo with *The London Merchant*; the second Edward Moore with *The Foundling* (1748) and *The*

Gamester (1753). These plays served as models for Lessing and Diderot. *The Natural Son* (1757) and *The Father* (1758), as well as their respective prefaces, *Discussions on the Natural Son* and *Discourse on Dramatic Poetry*, made Diderot the principal theorist behind a renewal of French theatre. Renouncing the legendary heroes of classical tragedy, the drama, according to Diderot, depicted more ordinary people, nevertheless faced with grave concerns. From certain viewpoints, the unravelling of the action can be reminiscent of comedy, but it differs from it in the emotion it arouses in the audience. The public recognises itself and vicariously lives through situations consonant with real-life ones.

A great success of bourgeois drama was *The Philosopher without even knowing it* (1765) by Michel Jean Sedaine (1719–1797). His choreography created emotion and plays with emotional responsiveness: that of the characters and that of the audience. After having written a drama of sensibility, *Eugénie* (1767), Beaumarchais turned in 1775, with *The Barber of Seville*, towards a lively version of the drama. The sequel, *The Marriage of Figaro*, contained so much that was politically explosive that it was banned from being performed in public until 1784. And yet it is less the spirit of revolt which gives this work its revolutionary quality than the historical situation. So Mozart respected the reservations of the absolutist court of Vienna when he transformed the comedy into an opera (1786).

In the field of the drama, **Gotthold Ephraïm Lessing (1729–1781)** was the culmination and the transcending of the 'Aufklärung' in Germany. In the seventeenth letter of the epistolary review *Briefe die neueste Literatur betreffend* (*Letters on Modern Literature*, 1759–1765) which he published with Nicolai and Mendelssohn, he settled his account with Gottsched, Voltaire and the French. He reproached Gottsched in particular with having wanted to create a new 'Frenchified' theatre, without asking himself 'if this theatre was in conformity with the German way of thinking'. According to Lessing, Gottsched should have noticed that

German theatre was closer to the English than the French, for the great, the horrible and the melancholic had a greater effect on the Germans than the pious, the gentle and the lover. Shakespeare, not Corneille and Racine, should have been translated into German. In comparison with the Ancients, Shakespeare, the paragon of genius, was 'a tragic poet much greater than Corneille'. According to Lessing, if the Greek spectator emerged from a tragedy purged thanks to the fear and pity it had inspired in him, the modern spectator transformed these affections into 'virtuous faculties'. Because it was necessary, for Lessing as for Diderot, to have 'middling characters': human beings neither too perfect nor too spineless, for only these were capable of being regenerated. It was via this rationalist and moralising concept seeking to render tragedy – in which psychological interest was essential – more human and more touching, that Lessing came to middle-class drama. Until then, only very favoured social classes had been judged capable of acquiring tragic dimensions, while the problems of the middle classes were dealt with in comedies. Henceforth the bourgeois earned his place in drama as a fully-fledged tragic character. With Lessing the adjective 'bourgeois' meant touching, familiar: it had no political significance. Before Lessing, comedies could be in prose, tragedy had to be in alexandrines. With his youthful drama *Miss Sara Sampson* (1755), taken from Richardson, Lessing inaugurated bourgeois drama, demonstrating this new genre's capacity to express tragic effects.

Emilia Galotti, Lessing's masterpiece in the genre, was performed for the first time in 1772. In it, virtue and morality are diametrically opposed to the immoral world of politics and the court. Prince Hettore Gonzaga falls in love with Emilia who is preparing to marry Count Appiani. The world of the count and of the Galotti family is deeply moral. The prince draws Emilia into an ambush, but not everything goes according to plan and Count Appiani is killed. Under the pretext of protecting her, the prince offers Emilia the hospitality of his palace. But

Countess Orsina, used to court intrigues, reveals the prince's crime and informs Emilia's father, Odoardo Galotti. To preserve her

> *Ehedem wohl gab es einen Vater,*
> *der seine Tochter von der Schande*
> *zu retten, ihr den ersten, den*
> *besten Stahl in das Herz senkte*
> *– ihr zum zweiten Male das*
> *Leben gab. Aber alle solche Taten*
> *sind von ehedem! Solcher Väter*
> *gibt es keinen mehr!*

Gotthold Ephraïm Lessing,
Emilia Galotti

Odoardo contradicts her and knifes her. Emilia then evokes the image of virtue: 'A rose is cut down, before the storm unleaves it.' Her father announces his intention to give himself up to the magistrates.

With *Minna von Barnhelm* (1767), Lessing created the first German comedy. The deep merriment, closely related to tragedy, comes neither from conflict nor action, but from a contradiction between the characters conceived along realistic lines. From one play to the next, virtue is put to the test. With *Nathan the Wise* (1779), subtitled 'the school of humanity', Lessing presents the ideals of the 'Aufklärung': human dignity, devotion and tolerance. In this play he calls for reason and for a behaviour dictated by mutual comprehension and the conviction that we cannot find solutions to existential problems in our understanding alone. Finally, he rejects deism and atheism: this is how he transcends the 'Aufklärung'. We note it in his treatise *Die Erziehung des Menschengeschlechts* (*The Education of the Human Race*, 1780).

The Venetian **Carlo Goldoni (1707–1793)** was the European dramatist who came closest to the concepts of Lessing and Diderot. He wrote more than 150 plays with a wide variety of themes and forms. Goldoni strove above all to create a new genre in the theatre, explicitly copying the traditional commedia dell'arte. As a sensible professional, he nevertheless proceeded with a great deal of circumspection, at first taking up tried and tested techniques to

virtue, Emilia recalls to him the story of Virginius, the hero of Livy's tale which is at the source of the drama:

> *Once there was a father*
> *who, to save his daughter from*
> *dishonour, plunged the*
> *first knife he laid hands on straight*
> *into her heart – and gave her life*
> *a second time. But all these*
> *acts are ancient history! There are*
> *no longer such fathers!*

progressively reform them afterwards. He obtained his first European success with *Il Servitore di due padroni* (*The Servant of Two Masters*, 1748), particularly appreciated in Weimar in Goethe's theatre. Although they are called 'comedies', not all Goldoni's plays aimed to be funny in the literal sense of the word; their strength resides rather in the gravity which makes of traditional comedy a 'serious genre' (in the sense that Diderot understood it) with realistic effects in the manner of genre painting.

As in the traditional comedy, Goldoni ridiculed the aristocracy. He did not oppose to their viewpoint the ordinary intellectual horizon of the 'honnête homme', but a representative of the bourgeoisie who had, until then, been the epitome of ridicule. In *La Famiglia dell'antiquario* (*The Family of the Antique Dealer*, 1750), it is Pantalone who, having risen to the status of a rich Venetian merchant, defends with great conviction economic and family order. After 1748, his 'reformed' comedies, now written in their entirety, offered a unique example in the literature of this period of 'realist' art. They left room for situations and characters from contemporary society; at the same time, they were stylistically sophisticated. In the natural, lucid dialogue (in Italian as well as Venetian), he mingled the reality of life and the order of literature. In his great plays, *La Locandiera* (1753), *Il Campiello* (*The Public Square*, 1756), *Gli Innamorati* (*The Lovers*, 1759), *I Rusteghi*

(*The Peasants*, 1760), *La Casa nova* (*The New House*, 1760), *Sior Todero brontolon* (*Master Todero the Grouchy*), the trilogy of *Villegiature* (*A Trip to the Countryside*, 1761) and *Le Baruffe chiozzotte* (*A Squabble in Chioggia*, 1762), we see, as in a veritable human comedy, the decline of the aristocracy with its prejudices and the virtues and concerns of a middle class with which the author sympathises, but which he still considers unable to assume hegemony, and to be the vitality and the people's appetite for happiness. Between 1762 and his death in 1787, Goldoni lived in France. He furnished plays for the Théâtre des Italiens, then became a court tutor in Italian. During his stay in Paris, he wrote in French *L'Avare fastueux* (*The Miser in the Lap of Luxury*, 1773), *Le Bourru bienfaisant* (*The Surly Do-Gooder*, 1771), and his important *Memoirs to Serve for the Story of His Life and for that of His Theatre* (1787).

In Spain, on the two great stages of Madrid, the Corral de la Cruz and the Corral del Principe, in conformity with public taste, plays were put on in which an old-fashioned aristocratic ideology survived in the most complicated and unlikely plots. It is only at the end of the century that a new taste can be imposed: 'emotion', which is supposed to provoke more of a response than beauty. The mixture of feelings and reason was characteristic of the theatre of **Leandro Fernández de Moratín (1760–1828)**. His one-act comedy *La Comedia nueva o el café* (*The New Comedy or the Café*, 1792) criticised Baroque taste which was then dominant. His handful of plays – *El Viejo y la niña* (*The Old Man and the Young Girl*, 1790), *El Barón* (*The Baron*, 1803), *La Mogigata* (*The Female Hypocrite*, 1804) and *El Sí de las Niñas* (*The Young Ladies' Yes*, 1806) – paid particular attention to the theme of the education of young women, particularly the problem of choosing a marriage partner. Like Goldoni, Moratín preached the stabilisation of social relationships, and above all the strengthening of the middle-class family, the crucially important social building-block. The senti- mental, melodramatic colouring of the central scenes in *The Young Ladies' Yes* made of it

one of the greatest theatrical successes of the nineteenth century. Moratín's comedies were essentially solemn in their presentation of characters and their problems. In dealing with them in this way, he broke with the national tradition of Spanish 'comedia' and subscribed to the theory of Diderot's 'serious genre'. Gaspar Melchior de Jovellanos (1744–1811) was a 'committed writer'. He put forward the idea of penal reform in *El Delincuente Honrado* (*The Honest Delinquent*, 1774), the only Spanish melodrama of this period.

In 1748, Danish theatre began in earnest with Frederick V's foundation of the Theatre of Copenhagen. Ludvig Holberg put on there six philosophical and allegorical comedies, inspired from Antiquity. Ten years after Holberg's death, in 1764, Charlotte Biehl (1731–1788) makes her début with *Den Kaerlige Mand* (*The Nice Man*, 1764), a senti- mental family comedy inspired by Marmontel, close to La Chaussée's style of 'commode larmoyante' ('tearful comedy'). In the 1770s Ewald wrote the historical and mythological tragedies *Rolf Krage* (1778) and *Balders Dod* (*The Death of Balder*, 1773), in the vein of Shakespeare and Klopstock, followed by the bourgeois drama *Fiskerne* (*The Fishermen*, 1779) which contained the future Danish national anthem.

The Russian **Dennis Fonvizin (1745– 1792)** began with some translations of Holberg and Voltaire, and may be considered as the founder of the Russian National Theatre. In his first comedy, *Brigadir* (*The Brigadier*, 1769), he tried to adapt classical comedy to the Russian context. In *Nedorosl'* (*The Minor*, 1782), the provincial nobility appeared as a class hostile to all attempts at emancipation, leading a parasitical existence thanks to their serfs. In this comedy, the author's recourse to pathetic or didactic scenes made him a repre- sentative of the new 'serious genre'. **Mikhaïl Kheraskov (1733–1807)** went further in this direction by introducing more intense emo- tional effects into his plays. In his dramas – *Drug nesčastnych* (*A Friend to the Unfortunate*, 1771) and *Gonimye* (*The Hunted*, 1775) – he tried to awaken 'compassion and admiration for the misfortune of virtuous men'. In order to do this, he made use of violent special effects such as night scenes, torchlight or thunder and lightning. His dramas are considered to be the first sentimental dramas in Russia.

While the signal for the renewal of drama on the European continent came from England, dramatic activity there considerably diminished towards the middle of the century. It was only towards the end of the 1760s and in 1770 that new talents and plays appeared in which a critical spirit showed itself hostile to the ambient sentimentality. Goldsmith, the author of *The Good-Natured Man* (1778) and *She Stoops to Conquer* (1773), reproached sentimental comedies for their excess of tears and absence of laughter (*A Comparison between Laughing and Sentimental Comedy*, 1773). His theatre is in the tradition of Shakespeare's amusing comedies and struck a balance between sentimentality and farce. The comedies in which his Irish compatriot **Richard Brinsley Sheridan (1751–1816)** unequivocally parodied sentimental drama were less sophisticated and more effective. Sheridan, the son of an actor and a woman writer, had a chequered career. At the age of twenty-four he eloped with a famous singer, married her and twice fought a duel with her former suitor. In 1776 he was named manager of the Drury Lane Theatre, which he left in 1780. He then launched himself on a parliamentary career and became a famous orator in the House of Commons. His first play *The Rivals* (1775) had the worldly atmosphere of Bath for its setting. The duels, abductions and amorous intrigues were a brilliant transposition of his own past. In 1777 he put on in his own theatre his masterpiece *The School for Scandal*. In this satire of sentimental drama, the hypocrite Joseph Surface makes virtuous speeches, while his brother Charles, the good-for-nothing, reveals an upright, kindly character. The action takes place in London, in the frivolous ranks of the upper-middle classes with its omnipresent slanderers. *The Critic* (1779) was a humorous mockery of the fashionable theatrical style and mocks the critics. The second act presents a play within a play, which in turn parodies contemporary pseudo-Shakespearean tragedy. It was such a success that for several years no tragedy could be performed on the English stage.

The cult of genius: a new poetics

It says something for the complexity of the eighteenth century that the European continent discovered in England alone two distinct 'happy islands'. The first, the England of empiricism and rationality – a source of the Enlightenment – the second, the England of sensitive anti-rationalism – the precursor of European Romanticism. The concept of nature holds them together and differentiates them at the same time: nature has a different meaning for the poet of the second half of the century than for the philosopher of the first half. If the Enlightenment refused to see a divine imprint in nature, the poets of the second half of the century, on the contrary, 'deify' it, and even turn it into a myth.

Like Rousseau's *Émile*, henceforth the natural man, the 'noble savage', will be opposed to the man deformed by culture. Literature no longer needs to be a simple imitation of nature, but its equal: it is credited with a creative and original power. It is clear that the classical model was thus to lose all the authority it had exerted for so long. Henceforth the individual looked for ideals which he drew from himself or his own past: a past which is certainly less old than Antiquity, but much more mysterious, unknown, and therefore more 'original'. The dark Middle Ages become popular, and with them the Gothic era, held for a long time to be barbaric. Then a study of regional literature's past was made and the poetry of the Middle Ages was collected, popular songs and ballads, to reassert their value. The civilisations of Northern Europe, buried for a long time by neglect, was born again: those of the Celts, the Scots, the Welsh, as well as their poets, the bards. In matters of aesthetics, the objective criteria of beauty were abolished to be replaced by the notion of individual taste. Thinkers such as Burke, Hume, Young, Gerard, Kant, Breitinger,

Baumgarten and Diderot occupied themselves with questions of taste. But in England the question of the relativity of criteria had already been pointedly asked: Shakespeare and then Milton had reached a pinnacle with their art. As Shakespeare was for the theatre, Milton became for poetry the exemplar of original genius and divine inspiration. Like Shakespeare, he became the myth, the catalyst and the symbol for liberation from the chains of classicism.

Milton exerted a decisive influence in Germany, particularly on **Friedrich Gottlieb Klopstock (1724–1803)**, who gave a new impulse to poetic language. His imitation of the English poet in *Messias* (*The Messiah*, 1773) conquered all hearts, earning for him the name 'German Milton'. Goethe's poetic universe would have been poorer without Milton's visions, and his *Faust* almost unthinkable without the Satan of *Paradise Lost*. Schiller was perhaps even closer to Milton, in the amalgam of the didactic and the sublime of his early poems and dramas.

The notion of the sublime was already present in Antiquity with Longinus and was taken up by Boileau's *Treatise on the Sublime* (1674). But England elaborated on it considerably: what was merely a stylistic category became subjective feeling and a mode of sensibility. The increasing interest in free, untamed nature, its volcanoes, its tempests, its mountainous landscapes and oceans, became the preferred form of psychological experience. In *The Spectator*, Addison already mentioned the 'agreeable horror' he felt on seeing the Alps and the sea. Gazing at a huge expanse of space or a force of unleashed nature gave the soul a greater idea of its own strength, raising it to infinity by evoking its kinship with the universe. For Burke, the feeling of the sublime did not come directly from suggestion, but was associated with the spectator's anguish. In this, terror and grandeur were sources of the sublime. The aesthetic experience at the basis of the concept of the sublime was close to the Platonic doctrine according to which poetic inspiration was the result of 'enthusiasm' and of a 'divine manifestation'.

The cult of genius which travelled from England (Young) to France (Diderot) culminated in Germany with the 'Sturm und Drang' movement, represented, in essence, by Herder, Lavater, Hamann, Goethe, Schiller and Lenz.

The cult of genius proclaimed the absolute originality of the artist. In *Conjectures on Original Composition* (1759) Young cited Homer, Shakespeare and Milton as examples of supreme poetic originality. **Johann Gottfried Herder (1744–1803)** scrutinised the remotest times of world literature looking for 'original' witnesses and cited the Bible as the 'natural and ancient poetry of the earth', as did *Prealectiones de Sacra poësi Hebraerorum* (*Lessons on the Sacred Poetry of the Hebrews*, 1753) by Robert Lowth. The popular songs and ballads gathered together and published during this period – *Reliques* (1765) by Thomas Percy (1729–1811), and *Fragments* (1760) by Macpherson – became for Herder models of a perfect originality. Herder marked the contours of a necessary regeneration in literature by reasserting the value of ancient literature and 'the voice of the people'.

Under the pseudonym Ossian, the Scot **James Macpherson (1736–1796)** initiated the major literary event of the period. The first *Fragments of Ancient Poetry collected in the Highlands of Scotland and translated from the Gaelic or Erse language* (1760) were barely published when a violent quarrel erupted over the authenticity or forgery of this Gaelic manuscript, the original of which went back to the fourth century, and of which Macpherson only claimed to be the translator. This unexpected success encouraged Macpherson to publish two other epic fragments, *Fingal* (1761) and *Temora* (1763), which he also attributed to Ossian, a Scottish bard-hero, half-historical, half-mythic. Ossian's poetry contained all that is supposed to strike the sensitive soul: wild and anguished landscapes, fog and solitude, storms at sea, death and distress, spirits, heroes and doomed love.

Genuine or not, Ossian was read and revered throughout Europe. The force and authenticity of his poetic language placed him, in contemporary opinion, on the same level as Milton, above Homer and Pindar and even suggested comparisons with Old Testament prophets. Goethe depicted him once and for all in *Werther*'s 'Journal':

Ossian hat in meinem Herzen den Homer verdrängt. Welch eine Welt, in die der Herrliche mich führt! Zu wandern über die Heide, umsaust vom Sturmwinde, der in dampfenden Nebeln die Geister der Väter im dämmernden Lichte des Mondes hinführt. Zu hören vom Gebirge her, im Gebrülle des Waldstroms, halb verwehtes Ächzen der Geister aus ihren Höhlen und die Wehklagen des zu Tode sich jammernden Mädchens um die vier moosbedeckten grasbewachsenen Steine des Edelgefallenen, ihres Geliebten . . .	*Ossian replaced Homer in my heart. What a world, the one to which this superb poet directs me! I walk in the heath, around me blows a storm, which, in the thick fog, in the livid light of the moon, accompanies ancestral spirits. I hear, coming from the mountain, covered by the noise of torrents, the half dispersed gnashing of spirits in their caves and the moans of the young girl, groaning in front of four stones covered up with moss and grass from the tomb of him who died as a hero, her beloved . . .*

Goethe,
Werther

Ossian's reception on the continent followed the vogue for sad poetry with the Miltonic echoes of Thomson, Young and Gray, who found their subjects in nature and in death. In *Odes*, Klopstock let himself be carried away by these echoes and thus conferred on German lyrical discourse new musical and rhythmical possibilities which inspired a whole group of young German poets. Among them were Goethe, Herder and Claudius who made up the 'Hainbund' (circle of the sacred wood) in Göttingen. The 'popular tone' (Herder), the English ballads (Percy), and the myth of the bard (Macpherson) were taken up by the Hainbund poets, who were also attached to conventional lyrical subjects. Another emulator of Klopstock was the Swiss **Salomon Gessner (1730–1788)** who, inspired by Klopstock's *Messiah*, created the 'idyll', an independent poetic genre. His *Idyllen* (*Idylls*) had many admirers (eighty translations between 1762 and 1846).

Bucoliques (1792) by **André Chénier (1762–1794)** was written in the tradition of an idyllic return to the state of nature, but the tragedy of the Revolution inspired his finest pages. His sensibility, exacerbated by injustice, found the right accents in which to express his personal revolt (*Iambs*, 1794). His work was only brought together after his death (he was guillotined) and published in 1819. Fragmentary and difficult to classify, it contained odes, elegies and hymns which testified to a spirit of classicism and, using traditional forms, we nevertheless marked with sensitivity.

The first poet to transgress the poetic conventions of Italian classicism was **Melchiore Cesarotti (1730–1808)**. A teacher of ancient languages and rhetoric in Padua, Cesarotti used his time to rewrite classical authors and translate English ones. His free adaptation, superior to the original, of the fragments of Macpherson's *Ossian* brought him overnight fame. In his letters to Macpherson, he admitted he could not resist the inspiration he derived from Ossian: 'I was totally taken with your *Ossian* – Morven has become my Parnassus!' His *Poesie di Ossiani* (*Poems of Ossian*, 1763–1772) exerted a lasting influence on the evolution of the language of Italian poetry which, until then, had been imprisoned by the preciosity of classicism. Cesarotti's anti-rationalist poetry, proceeding by association, liberated poetic discourse and renewed lyrical expression. Cesarotti's role in Italian literary life can be compared to that of Herder's in German literature. Like Herder, Cesarotti reflected on the genius of the language and the foundations of taste. His *Poems of Ossian*, like the 'Visions' and elegies of Vincente Monti (1754–1828), who in his youth imitated the Bible, Dante and Goethe's *Werther*, offered Italian readers a substitute for the primitive and original poetry that Herder invoked in Germany.

Melancholy and rationalist pessimism combined in *Noches lugubres* (*Lugubrious Nights*, 1789–1790). The Spaniard Cadalso, considered until then as a classical poet, wrote this after the death of his sweetheart, inspired by Young's *Nights*:

Lorenzo	*Lorenzo*
Ya he empezado a alzar la losa de la tumba: pesa infinito. ¡Si verás en ella a tu padre! Mucho cariño le tienes cuando por verle pasas una noche tan dura . . . Pero ¡el amor de hijo! Mucho merece un padre.	*I have already raised a little the stone that closes the tomb: it weighs a ton. Perhaps you will find your father again! Your love for him must have been quite tender, since you are spending such a cruel night so that you can see him again . . . But what can the love of a son not do! A father deserves as much!*

José Cadalso,
Noches lugubres

There was a similar transition from classicism to sensibility with the Dutch theorist and essayist **Rijklof Michael Van Goens (1748–1810)**. After 1786 this author lived in Switzerland under the name 'Cuninghame'. He was the driving force behind the intellectual life of the time, thanks to his friendship with Lavater and Jung-Stilling. **Hieronymus Van Alphen** **(1746–1803)**, who converted to a Christianity tinged with pietism, revealed in *Gedichten en Overdenkingen* (*Poems and Poetic Treatises*, 1777) a sensibility comparable to that of Young, Klopstock and Lavater. It was characterised by its emotional nuances and dealt with death, immortality and the triad formed by religion, virtue and love:

Gij, heerschende Stilte, gebiedt ons te luisteren: Ontzagelijk zwijgen van hemel en aard! 'k Hoor niets, dan de stem van mijn eigen geweten, De stem van mijn God.	*You, sovereign silence, order us to listen to the mighty silence of the sky and of the earth! I only hear the voice of my own conscience, the voice of my God.*

Hieronymus Van Alphen,
Bloemlezing

Rhijnvis Feith, endowed with a melancholy temperament, was also attracted by the sensibility of Young and Klopstock; in his poem *Het Graf* (*The Grave*, 1792), he introduced the poetry of personal confession to Holland. The strong personality and the anti-revolutionary ideas of Willem Bilderdijk (1756–1831) exerted a profound influence on the nineteenth century. Poetry, a divine gift, was essentially for him, as for the poets of the German 'Sturm und Drang', a spontaneous outpouring of the heart demanding a state of ecstasy.

Russian lyrical poetry went through a spectacular renewal with work by Gabriel Derjavin (1743–1816). He began a prestigious career with original poems which combined a rhetorical and colloquial style with a melancholic and elegiac lyricism, redolent of Ossian. His innovative odes *Bog* (*God*, 1784) and *Vodopad* (*The Waterfall*, 1794) described his deep faith and love of nature.

In Poland, after the third partition, there was a blossoming of what has been called 'the

poetry of pain': sentimental and idyllic, it was marked by a deeply sincere patriotism. One of these poems, *Bard Polski* (*The Polish Bard*, 1795), was written by the young prince Adam Jerzy Czartoryski (1770–1861), while he was waiting to be assigned his place of exile in Russia. **Franciszek Karpiński (1741–1825)** together with the prince's governor, Franciszek Dionizy Kniaünin, was one of the principal representatives of Polish sentimentalism. In his idylls, operas and religious poems, he was the first to introduce the people of the Polish countryside, its legends and its beliefs as well as a sort of religious patriotism which prefigured the Messianism of the 1840s:

Przypomnienie dawnej miłości	*Memory of a former love*
Raz się chmura sebrała, *Piorun skruszył dębinę,* *Tyú mię drząca úciskała* *Mówiąc: 'Sama nie zginę!'*	*Ah! The evening when thunder and* *lightning rumbled – Knocking down that* *large oak, a grandfather;* *You trembled, squeezing me in* *your arms,* *Crying: 'I do not want to die alone!'*

Franciszek Karpiński,
Wybór poezji i prozy

'Poet of the heart' is the name he was known by. Between 1782 and 1787 he published seven volumes of *Zabawki wierszem' i prozą* (*Diversions in Verse and in Prose*) which brought him immediate success. The heroes of his finest idylls, *Do Justyny* (*To Justine*) and *Laura i Filon* (*Laura and Philon*) are in the image of those imaginary shepherds and shepherdesses who unite the features of tender sentimentalism with accents of deep sincerity. In his courses at the Collège de France, Mickiewicz would say: 'Everything is national, Polish: the landscape, the barking of the dogs which forms the evening music of each village, the forest on the horizon, everything is taken from the daily life of the country.' In meditating on the ruins of the glorious castle of Casimir the Great, Jan Pawel Woronicz (1757–1829), a young priest and frequent guest at the court of Pulawy, was supposed to have found his vocation as a poet. His first works – lyrical poems and idylls – called *Pieúni wiejskie* (*Rustic Songs*, 1782–1784), are full of anxiety,

patriotism and a Messianic vision of Polish history.

In the Czech-speaking part of Europe, a national renaissance made itself felt towards the end of the century. Dobrovský published a 'defence of the Czech language', and Jacob Felix Dobner (1719–1790) took an interest in the nation's past. Pelčl published texts in Old Czech and compiled his prestigious *New Czech Chronicle*. The popular theatre re-emerged and prose made slow progress with the creation of a first Czech newspaper. Poetry was brought together in the first almanach (1785) by a group of young Czech and Slovak poets, lead by Puchmajer. After having initially published classical genres and themes – odes, heroic and comic epics and love poetry – the imitation of Polish and Western examples was quickly understood.

From the end of the sixteenth century, many collections of patriotic, love and religious poetry, often in manuscript and anonymous, circulated in Hungary. Their series was crowned by Adám Pálócz Horváth's anthology (1760–1820). This half-popular, half-literary poetry retained its inspirational force until the end of the eighteenth century. Learned poets raised on foreign traditions, such as Berzsenyi, Csokonai Vitéz and Fazekas, also echoed it. On his estate in Transdanubia and far from all literary life, Daniel Berzsenyi (1776–1836) – called the 'Hungarian Horace' – wrote philosophical elegies whose classical style managed with difficulty to hide the poet's sensitive soul. The epic poem by **Mihály Fazekas (1766– 1828)**, *Lúdos Matyi (Matthew the Geese*, 1815), belonged to universal folklore: the poor man takes vengeance three times over for the harm done to him by the rich man. **Mihály Csokonai Vitéz (1773–1805)** was above all a lover and a philosopher who dedicated a cycle of poems to his beloved. His songs of *Lilla* (1805) were directly linked to the popular song tradition. They have the grace of rococo and a trace of philosophical sensibility, but remain close to popular song.

'Let he who has not known how to live know how to die,' wrote the Portuguese poet **Manuel Mario Borbosa Bocage (1765– 1805)** in one of his finest poems, a religious sonnet, having cursed eternity all his life as a 'frightening illusion'. Bocage had an eventful life: against his parents' will he took ship to Goa, deserted in 1789 and finally resurfaced in Lisbon. A member of the New Arcadia in which he was called the 'Elmano', he also attended the salon of the Marchioness de Alorna where he formed his last literary contacts in Europe. In 1797 he was arrested for his subversive contacts with Lisbon's literary 'lower depths'. He was banished by the Inquisition to an isolated convent, where he spent his time translating, After his release, he retraced the experience of his long solitude and his penchant for the lugubrious and the 'gothic' in sensitive sonnets, melancholy elegies and songs in the manner of Camões and the Ancients. His work and life make Bocage an almost Byronic character.

In Britain the second half of the eighteenth century only produced, apart from Burns and Blake, second-rate poets. Some of them,

martyrs to acute melancholy, became mad, like William Collins (1721–1759), Christopher Smart (1722–1771) and William Cowper (1731–1800). In his love of alcohol and women, with his provocative attitude to manners and prevailing morality, even by his precocious death, **Robert Burns (1759–1796)** was the son of a Scottish peasant and – given his life story – already a Romantic. He did not belong to the English literary tradition, but to that of the Scottish Highlands, which had come from Dunbar and Henryson. His genius was expressed in his poems and verses written in dialect and rooted in Scottish popular traditions, songs and dances. We have an example in *Coming thro' the Rye* (1792) – a title taken from a famous song – from which Salinger drew inspiration for his cult novel *The Catcher in the Rye* (1951), or yet again in his finest love lyric *A Red, Red Rose* (1787). A stanza taken from this poem reveals how Burns succeeded in transforming the raw material of a simple popular song into a complex metaphor:

As fair art thou, my bonnie
  lass,
So deep in luve am I;
And I will luve thee still, my
  dear,
Till a' the seas gang dry.

Till a' the seas gang dry, my dear,
And the rocks melt wi' the sun:
I will luve thee still, my dear,
While the sands o'life shall run.
              Robert Burns, *A Red, Red Rose*

In his satires, Burns humorously attacked religious and bourgeois hypocrisy, not without a certain acerbity. Such is the case, for instance, in *Holy Willie's Prayer* and *Tam O'Shanter*, written in Lallans dialect; there is as much Scottish derision as satirical English humour in the manner of Pope. In the poem *Love and Liberty*, better known under the title *The Jolly Beggars*, his sympathies for Jacobinism were reflected.

William Blake (1757–1827), poet and painter, also showed Jacobin sympathies. His poetry had little success during his lifetime.

His literary isolation was shown in works which were increasingly mystical and incomprehensible. The famous *Prophetic Books* (published in 1804) containing his 'anti-Swedenborgian' vision, and *The Marriage of Heaven and Hell* (1790) were composed in a pseudo-Biblical and metaphorical language so personal that he was probably the only one able to understand it.

> One thought fills immensity.
>
> > William Blake,
> > *The Marriage of Heaven and Hell*

Blake was known initially for his illustrations of Young's *Nights*, of Blair's *The Grave* and the *Book of Job*. He illustrated his own poems, for he thought that a drawing expressed a thought as well as a poem. This concept makes it possible to see his symbolic short pieces as cameos. *Songs of Innocence* (1789) and *Songs of Experience* (1794) appeared as collections illustrated by etchings in which text and image form a unity. Above all, we should not consider these two collections as the expression of a vision of a world respectively innocent and joyful or heavy with experience and sadness, but, on the contrary, as a unity which illustrates the dualism of nature and the paradoxical nature of every life on earth. Along with 'liberty', 'nature' and 'genius', 'passion' becomes a key term of the period, particularly in the context of 'Sturm und Drang'.

The 'Sturm und Drang'

The German 'Sturm und Drang' appeared in the 1770s. The unexpected meeting of Goethe and Herder in Strasbourg is normally considered as a point of departure for this fleeting but violent movement, whose other vital centres were Frankfurt and Göttingen.

In Frankfurt in 1772, the *Frankfurter Gelehrte Anzeiger* (*Frankfurt Scholarly Gazette*) was launched. Its new editorial staff consisted of Mercks, Schlosser, Herder, Goethe, Leuchsenring and Claudius. Göttingen, a university town, became the meeting place for some poets who formed the Hainbund. The 'Sturm und Drang' had no manifesto, but existed on written and oral exchanges between writers, among whom Herder probably played the most important role. The word 'freedom', the one on which Goethe's play *Götz von Berlichingen* ends, took on special importance in every field. The practitioners of 'Sturm und Drang' were not only trying to escape from French classicism, but also laid claim to political freedom in a Germany broken into 300 seigniories and, moreover, divided into two religions. This national feature of the 'Sturm und Drang' was translated into a revaluing of the German language (Herder). A fresh interest was also taken in folk poetry: such, at least, was the motto of the Hainbund poets of Göttingen. The idea of genius as an 'original force', a 'divine creative spirit', made it possible to break down all social barriers and break free of all restrictions. The new generation aspired to an individuality which the Renaissance had discovered: it saw man as a unity composed of body, soul and spirit. It preached pure nature in Rousseau's understanding of it. It chose its themes among children, simple and good-hearted folk, Biblical characters, Homer's heroes and those of the Germanic past.

The representatives of 'Sturm und Drang' celebrated passion as a force which, in spite of many dangers, liberated and intensified in man all the forces of the soul. They sought the straightforward, spontaneous expression of passion. This desire was best realised in drama. In this way, prose drama became the dominant genre of 'Sturm und Drang'. The conflict between natural man and existing civilisation went through all themes and all motifs. It also revealed against whom and against what the young generation was rebelling. They were fighting for political freedom, for the freedom of love in the face of social barriers and against society and its deceptive morality. They were also laying claim to a natural religion in the face of the Church's despotism.

The dramatic repertory of 'Sturm und Drang' extended from Goethe's *Götz* to Schiller's *Die Räuber* (*The Robbers*, 1781) via dramas by Klinger, Lenz, Wagner and von Leisewitz.

Der Mut wächst mit der Gefahr,	*Courage increases with*
die Kraft erhebt sich im Drang.	*the danger,*
Das Schicksal muß einen großen Mann	*vigour with constraint.*
aus mir heben wollen, weil's mir	*Destiny no doubt wants*
soqueer durch den Weg streicht.	*to make of me a great man*
	since it is barring my route
Friedrich von Schiller,	*in this way.*
Die Räuber	

The Italian genius: Vittorio Alfieri

The personality of **Vittorio Alfieri (1749–1809)**, considered by the writers and patriots of the Risorgimento as the restorer of civic and political consciousness in Italian literature, embodied the veritable genius of the Italian 'Sturm und Drang'. After 1775, and up to the eve of the French Revolution, his tragedies encouraged in audiences in Turin and Rome, Venice and Florence, a hatred of despots and a taste for liberty. Taken from Renaissance chronicles (*Filippo* and *La Congiura de Pazzi, The Conspiracy of Madmen*) as well as from the Bible (*Saul*, 1782), but above all from Greek mythology and Roman history (*Polinice* and *Antigone, Agamemnon and Orestes, Virginia* and the two *Brutuses*), the plot was reduced to essentials, opposing, in grand solitude, the oppressor and his victim, the tyrant and the tyrannicide. The quickfire, spare language of the dialogues is of a rare, inimitable dramatic force. It does not matter if it is a 'tragedy of freedom' as in *Saul*, in which an ageing king is torn between a jealous desire to exercise power and the presence of a terrible God who haunts him, or the conflict of a young girl in love with her father and, at the same time, horrified by her incestuous passion, as in *Mirra* (1786). Alfieri knew how to sound the soul of his characters: by finding in their subconscious the dark impulses the Greeks had attributed to Destiny, he managed to restore the sense of the tragic to the theatre.

THE GERMAN 'KLASSIK': BEYOND CLASSICISM

We refer to as 'classical' a period which included works representative of a society which expressed a people's spirit. Through these works, people 'attain to the maximum of their culture' (Herder). For Kant, the classical German age, the 'Klassik', went beyond classicism. It was no longer a question of imitating foreign models and norms, but of creating poetry 'in the Greek spirit'. The aim of poetry was not imitation ('imitatio'), but admiring emulation ('æmulatio'). The German 'Klassik' wanted to sublimate and perfect French classicism. It saw itself at the same time as a refined result of the cult of genius and a return to rationalism.

The representatives of the 'Klassik', while recognising the natural and social order, aspired to an inner and an outer harmony. They tried to consciously recreate, in a modern and sentimental way, the great original forms of nature and art, as the Greeks would have executed them, in all simplicity: what Winckelmann called 'noble simplicity and silent grandeur'.

The harmony of body and spirit became the ideal aim. Too many feelings (as during 'Sturm und Drang') or too much intellect (as during 'Aufklärung'), too much nature or too much reason harm that harmonious unity of the individual: the ideal of an Apollonian beauty represented in Antiquity. The period of the 'Klassik' raised the contradiction which opposed Christian asceticism and the sensual enjoyment of pagan Antiquity – a synthesis already needed by the Baroque.

Goethe and Schiller; Richter and Hölderlin

Two writers above all represent the German 'Klassik': **Johann Wolfgang von Goethe (1749–1832)** and **Johann Christoph**

Friedrich von Schiller (1759–1805). The beginning of the period was marked by Goethe's journey to Italy (1786–1788). This led him to discover clarity and harmony thanks to the human and artistic models offered by Antiquity. The period of the 'Klassik' ended with Schiller's death in 1805.

While Goethe went from studying Winckelmann to the real-life experience of the great Italian authentic forms of art and nature, Schiller, giving his allegiance in the first place to 'Sturm und Drang', came to the 'Klassik' through the study of Kantian philosophy. He set himself the task of reconciling morality and reason in an aesthetic harmony. According to him, grace and beauty were linked to morality. To rediscover the harmony formerly existing in nature, to rechannel it into the new harmony of a civilisation which has become nature itself, this concept (which Schiller expounded in *Über naïve und sentimentalische Dichtung, Treatise on Naïve and Sentimental Poetry*, 1796) already pointed in the direction of the disharmony which, for the Romantics, was the basic principle of modernity. In his treatise *Über das Marionettentheater (On Marionettes,* 1810) Kleist tried to overcome this disharmony with 'a different naïvety and recklessness'.

The man of the 'Klassik' believed in a nature traversed by God's spirit. The artistic work represented in its structure the works of nature. This is how we come to think of beauty as the expression of the secret laws of nature. The aesthetics of the 'Klassik' are based on a pantheist concept. Art does not reveal life, but rather the laws of life, not reality, but rather truth. The world is the reflection of absolute categories, the concrete expression of the divine. To look, to guess, to believe, to know, according to Goethe, are the 'cornucopias by which man, haltingly, learns to know the universe', by which the division of 'self' and the world can be made. Baroque poetry dressed the idea in metaphors, looking for the particular in general allegorical representations. Classical authors in Germany, on the other hand, sought to make the idea present and

obvious, and to see the general in the particular, by means of symbols, in which the idea and its representation coincide.

As for language, classicism looked for fixed forms and preferred verse. Drama dealt with fundamental problems: Schiller evoked liberty, destiny, man's guilt and purification, great historical figures. The novel of the 'Klassik', as a *'Bildungsroman'*, conceived of as a symbolic expression of the period, depicted the evolution and blossoming of an individual 'according to the law established at his birth'. Overly attached to reality and therefore incapable of making the archetypal classical, the novel was only considered as 'the half-brother of poetry'. Goethe's *Wahlverwandtschaften (Elective Affinities*, 1809) the prime example of a classical work, nevertheless referred back to Romanticism in its recognition of the secret laws of nature. The lyrical poetry of classical authors puts into verse the order of human society, the laws of the world, the responsibility of the 'self', the purity of humanity: witness Schiller's *Lyrik des Gedankens (Philosophical Poetry*, 1795).

Next to Goethe and Schiller, **Johann Paul Friedrich Richter** (known as **Jean-Paul, 1763–1825**) and **Friedrich Hölderlin (1770–1834)** went beyond the classical model and made their own way. Richter's novels, *Das Leben des vergnügten Schulmeisterleins Maria Wuz in Auenthal (The Life of the Joyful Schoolmistress Maria Wuz in Auenthal*, 1793) and *Siebenkäs* (1796–1797), demonstrated a new attitude about to the world: that of Romantic humour. Beauty, liberty, humanity, the basic values of the German 'Klassik', all disappeared and Hölderlin's *Hyperion* (1788) was already deploring their disappearance. Heinrich von Kleist and Johann Peter Hebel (1760–1826) no longer formed part of the 'Klassik' period, but did not yet figure among the Romantics. The ideal of classical humanism burst forth under the impulse of Richter's subjective sensitivity, Hölderlin mythical experience of divine forces and Kleist's demoniac and tragic obsessions.

The Epistolary Novel

C. Brant

I was going to hide the letter in my bosom when, seeing me all of a tremble, he said to me with a smile: who have you just written to, Pamela?

Samuel Richardson,
Pamela or Virtue Rewarded

The letter appears under various forms in eighteenth-century literature and especially in the novel during the second half of this period. But in the area of personal correspondence and of 'intimate letters', many letter-writers expended a considerable amount of creative energy. Voltaire's correspondence or that by Horace Walpole, for example, may be counted in dozens of volumes; thousands of letters to friends, to mistresses, to lovers attest to the genre's popularity. The letter offers, in effect, the double advantage of not imposing any formal restraint and of being a sure way to make known one's opinions. It was also an integral part of European culture: Pliny or St Paul gave their opinions on politics and religious education, Voltaire took an interest in philosophical speculation, John Keats, Virginia Woolf or Vincent Van Gogh spoke of their aesthetic inspiration, Beatrice Webb and Václav Havel the social upheavals around them. In the eighteenth century, the letter was a potent ideological vehicle, perhaps because it was no longer addressed to a single correspondent, but deliberately designed to be printed for a general audience.

After the success of the *Letters of a Portuguese Nun* all through Europe in the seventeenth century, the letter became the preferred genre for presenting arguments and feelings. In this short novel several key aspects of epistolary fiction are found: the events of the plot are less important than the emotions because the emotions are themselves events, the characters are dramatic because they are only voices, and the person is found in the reflection the writing gives them. Personal correspondence imitated the dialogue of polite conversation, while the fictitious letter had only its voice and its writing to give the identity of the character, making truer than ever Buffon's phrase: 'The style is the very man himself.' Was the nun a character or an author? In the novel of letters, the author plays on the link between reality and fiction to sow seeds of doubt. Many novels have subsequently used the convention that makes the author just the finder and publisher of the letters – not in a clumsy desire to believe this trustworthy fiction, but because it made it possible to pose the fascinating problem of knowing how to create a realistic effect with a new technique.

Letters multiplied in France and England because of the ever stronger taste for feelings, compassion and sincerity as philosophical and psychological concepts with social and political implications. During the eighteenth century, different combinations of reason and feeling appeared as the best way to reconcile an individual's aspirations with social restraints. This dynamic crops up again in the double social function of letters, made up of duty and pleasure. A real letter can contain imagined elements and a sober analysis; in the same way a fictitious letter can mix narrative and moralising, in agreement with the aesthetic axiom of the eighteenth century, taken from Horace, according to which literature must instruct and distract. To this dual function may be added, towards the middle of the century, the idea that literature should also move. The letter is the ideal form with which to tell sentimental stories, for it is a place where we react rather than act, and where more ample scope is given to feelings.

Farewell, I cannot leave this missive, which will fall into your hands, and I would like to have the same good fortune: alas! crazy woman that I am, it is clear to me that that will not be possible.

Guilleragues, *Letters of a Portuguese Nun*

Richardson as letter-writer

One of the main writers of epistolary novels was Samuel Richardson. In 1740 he published

Pamela or Virtue Rewarded, an extraordinary story which had extraordinary success. The heroine is a servant who, in her letters to her parents, describes her master's attempts to seduce her. Pamela is attracted to Mr B. despite his violent behaviour – he tries to rape her and is only stopped from doing so by the fact that she opportunely faints. However, she refuses to become his mistress. After having taken and read the letters she was not able to send to her parents, Mr B. is impressed by the young lady's virtue and asks for her hand in marriage. A public reading of these letters persuades the local squires that Pamela's moral delicacy is such that she can be a part of their world. Celebrated as a model, she triumphantly passes the final tests that confront a middle-class woman by becoming an exemplary mother.

Richardson did not just have enthusiastic readers. The parody written by Henry Fielding, *Shamela* (1741), presents us with a manipulative heroine whose only virtue is to be found in her so-called virginity.

Pamela and other epistolary novels of the same type provided evidence of the fact that relationships between a man and a woman were similar at that time to relationships between classes. The letter was a typically feminine form of writing as it only demanded a small amount of culture and a good deal of leisure. In the hands of a woman, Richardson remarked, 'a pen is as pretty as a needle'.

Richardson's next novel, *Clarissa*, depicted the battle of the sexes through the friction of correspondence. The longest novel to be written in the English language (eight volumes, more than 1500 pages) combines multiple strands of correspondence with extraordinary virtuosity. Clarissa is the virtuous daughter of ambitious parents who are constantly pressing her to marry a man she hates. She opposes the marriage and leaves her home in the company of Lovelace, a rake who drugs and rapes her. She escapes and, as her family refuse to forgive her, prepares to die a virtuous death. Lovelace is killed in a duel. This exemplary story, which is also a warning, created huge interest: even before the last volume was

published, readers begged Richardson to give them a happy ending. The text uses letters for moral purposes: it shows, in a very attractive way, that plot has been sacrificed to detailed moral scrutiny. Reading and writing become moral and narrative events in themselves.

The letter is by nature a monologue. This means that the psychological fluctuations of the protagonists are reduced. Characters are formed as a reflection of the writing itself. Whereas *Pamela* showed writing rewarded (as later would Rousseau's *La Nouvelle Héloïse*) *Clarissa* denounces writing betrayed and which itself betrays (as subsequently Laclos' *Dangerous Liaisons*). But the need to believe in the power of words is symbolised by letters, even when they reveal the fragility of this belief. Richardson's novels were translated by the Abbé Prévost, who adapted them somewhat to French taste by increasing the amount of feeling and reducing moral reflection. Diderot's *The Eulogy of Richardson* increased the influence of the English writer's works, 'which raise the spirit, touch the soul and everywhere breathe the love of goodness'.

The internal dynamic of the letter

The welcome reserved for Richardson on the continent came from the fact that the letter was freely used there, not only to recount intrigues and love stories, but for all kinds of other subjects. *The Letters of a Peruvian Lady* (1747) by Madame de Graffigny (1695–1758) turn to good account the apparent sincerity of a letter to give the opinions of an ingenue on a society foreign to her – a plot device also found in Fanny Burney's, *Evelina or the Story of the Entrance made by an Orphan Girl into the World*, in which the heroine talks about her *faux pas* to a gamekeeper. The character of the foreign observer was very often used in epistolary satire after the publication of Montesquieu's celebrated *Persian Letters*. The letters can give an indication of the differences that exist between society and individuals by exposing their respective follies and by striking the right balance between the reader's wisdom and the author's absence.

The eighteenth-century novel speaks in general terms of the choices and constraints placed on young people when they make the transition from childhood to adulthood. Love and friendship, the principal themes of letters to people close to us, make it possible for us, under cover of fiction, to define what types of behaviour, in the bosom of a family, are desirable or undesirable. To exchange letters in epistolary novels allows us to acquire experience, for it develops the personal relationships and favours an analysis of the characters' state of mind. The necessarily static situation that the art of writing letters implies is compensated by the psychological overlapping and exchanges they offer. This dynamic contrasts with the picaresque novel, in which the subjectivity of the characters, by nature restless, is often stereotypical.

A new use of the letter to deal with the domestic, family and female running of a household appeared in print with Rousseau's *Julie ou la Nouvelle Héloïse* cult novel. There were seventy-two editions in French between 1761 and 1800; the English translation was reprinted at least ten times in the same period. This novel traces the progress of the passionate love between Julie and her young tutor, Saint-Preux. Yielding to the pressure of paternal hostility and her own remorse, Julie spurns her tutor and marries the discreet, respectable Mr de Wolmar. When Saint-Preux returns, he is welcomed to their estate where he finds his passion transformed into an elegant virtue he is invited to share. The transformation of the young, rebellious Julie into an exemplary mother recalls the conversion – according to legend – of the medieval Heloïse who experienced passion, then piety.

Rousseau maintained that there was neither a villain nor villainy in his novel, but Laclos' *Dangerous Liaisons* explores the possibilities of evil. As the letter is a place for reflection, it excels in revealing everything which springs from premeditation in a plot: so the intrigues organised by the libertine Valmont and his partner Madame de Merteuil may be seen to be premeditated. If there is any sincerity in this novel, it lies in the exchanges of confidences – thus evil is exposed the better to be destroyed. Without sincerity, there is the reign of hypocrisy, the mainspring of all attempts at seduction. It is not events which are criminal, Laclos suggests, but the complicity of minds: virtue is a state of mind.

Fictional letters gain in credibility when the style in which they are written is nonchalant. Heartfelt writings are convincing when not too much care has been taken over them, and the authors, like the publishers, sometimes draw attention to inconsistencies and grey areas. A certain disorderliness can speak volumes, particularly in the storms of passion, but it can also be expressed in a structured way, by interruptions and interceptions, for example. In *Dangerous Liaisons*, order is suggested by complicated plotlines and a scrupulous formal organisation which makes the presence of disorder even more anarchical.

The letter in the European novel

The effect and influence of Richardson and Rousseau in Europe made itself felt as far as Russia, where Richardson was translated in the 1790s. Before Goethe, epistolary fiction flowered to some extent in Germany thanks to *The Story of Fräulein von Sternheim* by Sophie von La Roche. This was republished eight times in the 1770s and translated over the same period into Dutch, French and English. An orphan heroine sent to court is suspected of being the prince's mistress, and so she is abandoned by the man she loves. Trapped into a false marriage with another gentleman, she takes on a new identity and settles in England, but her false husband carries her off to Scotland where she is eventually found. At this point she agrees to marry her original suitor. Mixing sensitivity and realism, the novel insists on the exemplary and eloquent experience of women, in stark contrast to the 'Sturm und Drang' movement in which femininity was silent.

The Sufferings of Young Werther focus the reader's interest on the tormented soul of a young man. He meets Lotte, a young woman who is like a mother to her brothers and sisters. He becomes obsessed with her, even though she is engaged to be married to Albert, who is still away. When Albert appears, a triangular friendship is formed, but it is not enough for Werther who goes off to work for a legation. His absence fails to cure him; he returns and is unable to bear seeing Albert and Lotte happy together or to improve on his middle-class lifestyle. He blows his brains out with Albert's pistol. While in *La Nouvelle Héloïse* passion, if it is controlled, teaches virtue, for Werther it is not passion if it is controlled. A *ménage à trois* would be possible for Saint-Preux; it is made impossible by Werther's instability. Although readers responded enthusiastically to the melancholy and the alienation of the character, the editor's occasionally caustic comments emphasised certain ironic aspects of the book. Some things which had become clichés in letters are parodied: Lotte, for instance, uses sand to dry the ink on her notes, and when Werther kisses the sheet of paper, he finds himself with a mouth full of sand.

One fiction with two or several voices can constitute the microcosm. Richardson and Rousseau had recourse to the novel because there can be no harmony without distinctions and some of these distinctions can only be harmonised by death. For Goethe, the use of the letter-monologue shows that a single voice can be dissonant, as can its echo after death. Seeking to know what people think and feel, but are not perhaps capable of expressing, epistolary fiction, for the time being, contravenes social conventions, relaxing somewhat the tensions which exist between the individual and society at the end of the eighteenth century. Letters can express transgressive elements which their nature as fiction neutralises by situating them in the realm of the imagination, all of which carries with it an interesting ambivalence between the real and the imaginary.

In this way epistolary fiction played an important part in the history of ideas, particularly in the awakening of sensibility. For writers, to be able to organise a narrative around a complex network of letters was a challenge requiring diversity of tone and skill. For readers, the pleasure of diversity was reinforced by that of evaluating the sincerity of the letters and discovering their irony.

Closely linked to the drama, to conversation, to memoirs and to history, the epistolary novel remained popular until the beginning of the nineteenth century, when the genre died. Ideological changes broke with that vague consensus which had encouraged the readers of letters to distinguish between different voices and to piece together a story divided between several texts.

Sade (1740–1814)

M. Delon

The Marquis de Sade, like Byron half a century later, challenged opinion with his life and his work. His libertine escapades (the sacrilegious thrashing of a young woman on Easter Sunday; homosexual and heterosexual sodomy; the corruption of minors) struck his contemporaries as so many symbols of a detestable Ancien Régime. His family and royal power preferred to leave this man, who was an embarrassment to them with his refusal to submit, in jail.

Confinement . . . and the imagination

Confinement became Sade's destiny. Held prisoner by sealed orders in Vincennes, then in the Bastille, he was liberated by the Revolution in which, for a time, he seemed to believe. His militant commitment to the cause did not prevent him from being arrested again under the Terror. Saved from the guillotine by the fall of Robespierre, he enjoyed a few years of freedom under the Directory before falling victim to the return to a moral order which accompanied Bonaparte's coup d'état. He died thirteen years later in the Charenton hospice without having regained his freedom. Hemmed in and cheated out of his desires, broken in body, Sade took refuge in his imagination. In prison he constructed fantastic fortresses where libertine lords of the manor would be able to satisfy their most unbridled impulses. A compulsive reader, he asked for numerous books. In treatises he looked for arguments on which to base his materialism and atheism. From travellers' tales he solicited proof of the relativity of morality. Stimulated by contemporary fiction, he threw himself into literary creativity, exchanging his high and mighty arrogance for the new rights of a man of letters. He tried writing for the theatre and attempted to have his plays staged during the Revolution, but he found a privileged space of intellectual freedom in philosophical dialogue and the novel. Three examples of the latter genre were coterminous with Sade. *Les Cent Vingt Journées de Sodome* (*The 120 Days of Sodom*, published in 1904) were a collection of tales built into a narrative framework, according to the technique illustrated by the *Decameron* or the *Heptameron*; *Aline et Valcour* (*Aline and Valcour*, 1795) followed the epistolary model of Richardson and Rousseau; *Les Infortunes de la vertu* (*The Misfortunes of Virtue*, 1787) are like a tale by Voltaire.

Sick mind or genius?

Banned, pursued by censorship, all Sade's work was clandestinely disseminated through Europe. In France imitators of Flaubert and Baudelaire, Decadents following the example of Huysmans, and Surrealists in the wake of Apollinaire, took from Sade the example of an uncompromising otherness. The English Swinburne sang in his verses of the inspired débauché, worthy of the Caesars of Suetonius, and made his fellow writers flinch by implying he was having Sadian orgies again in his Étretat villa. *The 120 Days of Sodom* was published for the first time in Berlin under the watchful eye of the psychiatrist Iwan Bloch, under the pen-name of Eugen Dühren. Peter Weiss embodied all the debates of the years which preceded the explosion of 1968 in the figures of Marat, the militant revolutionary,

and Sade, the rebellious individualist: the play *Marat/Sade*, dubbed into all languages, was filmed by Peter Brook.

Madman or poetic genius, apologist for all terrors past and to come or liberator of humanity, feudal lord or revolutionary, Sade, shimmering with contradictions, has become one of the obligatory figures of European modernity.

Potocki (1761–1815)

M. Tomaszewki

He files the silver ball of his teapot lid.
It's still too big.
A strange occupation which punctuates
the last three years of his life.

A curious destiny

A young Polish aristocrat, **Jan Potocki** inherited the wealth of the eighteenth century. A cosmopolitan, he spoke eight languages fluently and quickly threw himself into a whirlwind round of travelling: beyond Poland and Europe, where he felt at home, Turkey and Egypt fascinated him. In 1805, he became a member of a Russian expedition to China, on the recommendation of the Russian Minister for Foreign Affairs, the Polish Prince Adam Czartoryski.

Possessed of an encyclopedic education, he devoted himself to different kind of scientific research, whether it was looking for the roots of the Slavic world in an astonishingly erudite work, *Research into Sarmatia* (1789–1792), or participating, with the aeronaut Blanchard, in a hot-air balloon ascent above Warsaw, accompanied by his Turkish valet Osman and his dog Lulu. A dabbler in political intrigues, a member of the Polish parliament in favour of reforms, he expended an intense amount of political activity during the four-year Diet in Poland. Suspected of sympathy for the Jacobins, he left Poland for Spain and Marocco, where he flattered himself that he was the 'Suetonius of a new reign'.

An initiatory tale

The literary output of Potocki's mind, curious about everything, was placed under a wandering star. Real journeys were followed by an imaginary one. His novel *The Manuscript Found in Zaragoza* (1804–1814) was the final fruit of his many wanderings. It is an initiatory tale relating the Gothic adventures of the young officer Alphonse Van Worden. Written in French, translated into Polish in the nineteenth century, this collection of unusual incidents – picaresque, fantastic and philosophical – recalled Arab tales in its sliding compartment structure. In the haunted mountains of the Sierra Morera, characters telling their life stories are, in spite of themselves, frequently displaced in space and time thanks to the help of mysterious forces embodied by two beautiful Tunisians, female messengers of the night.

The *Manuscript Found in Zaragoza* had an exceptional fate. Published in fragments in Saint-Petersburg in 1804, admired on publication by Alexander Pushkin, this vast novel travelled anonymously days around Europe in sixty-six days in the form of hand-written copies. Plagiarists, and famous ones at that – Charles Nodier, Washington Irving – under their own names, made best-sellers of some of these days. So the bizarre passions, close to mysticism, even Satanism, which haunted Potocki appealed to the general public in the following century, eager for dark novels.

The silver ball had finally attained the requisite dimensions. It slid without difficulty into its holder. On 20 November 1815, Count Jan Potocki put a bullet in his head.

Rousseau (1712–1778)

C. Habib

The will still speaks when nature is silent.
Jean-Jacques Rousseau, *Discourse on the Origin and Basis of Inequality*

Rousseau was born in Geneva, in 1712, into a family of clockmakers. His mother died as a result of the difficult birth, and the little boy, passed like a parcel from one person to another, too often left to his own devices, experienced the unstable and precarious fate of orphans, First fed by an aunt, he was brought up until he was ten with a father who, reading between the lines, often neglected him despite the protestation to the contrary in the *Confessions* (1764–1775). Rousseau was then sent to boarding-school with a cousin, before becoming an apprentice at the age of twelve. Two years later, his father remarried in another town. However, in Geneva, the apprentice went astray: he began pilfering and other criminal activities. At the age of sixteen, decidedly too miserable to stay in the workshop, he left Geneva and took to the open road. The young runaway did not leave much behind. Who was there to stop him? Who would want to care for him?

The young vagabond

Like Rimbaud in the nineteenth century, like the more recent Beat Generation authors, Rousseau 'went on the road'. This experience of youthful vagrancy was decisive, not only for the immediate happiness it gave him – that intoxicating feeling of reverie and independence which is related in the *Confessions* – but also for the people he met and the chance to learn unforgettable lessons which the open roads gave the young adolescent.

The opportunity of his life was to meet Madame de Warens: he was first and for a long time her protégé before being her lover. This encounter made him aware of himself for the first time; practically speaking, it allowed him to acquire a vast, self-taught store of culture between the ages of twenty and twenty-five. To make a career for himself, Rousseau tried careers: tutor to children of the nobility, embassy secretary in Venice in 1744, private secretary to well-off people like Madame Dupin. It was only when he was almost forty that he penetrated the world of letters with the *Discourse on the Sciences and Arts* (1755). It received the prize of the Academy of Dijon and made him famous overnight. Two years later, he experienced a triumph with his opera, *The Village Soothsayer*, which delighted both court and town. But he did not rest on his laurels. A convinced supporter of Italian music against French music, Rousseau soon made an enemy of Rameau and fell out with the opera performers. His reactions to success were disconcerting: after *The Village Soothsayer* has been performed, he refused to be presented to the king. With unrelenting consistency he spurned pensions and remuneration. This attitude annoyed people, making him a thorn in the side of an intellectual group who attacked the ruling powers in writing but had no scruples about living off their generosity. For Rousseau, fidelity to himself was realised through austerity. Doubtless this is also true of his fidelity to his youth. In twenty years he had travelled from the gutter to the salons of the moneyed aristocracy, then the uppermost echelons of the aristocracy; he made it a point of honour to receive no personal advantage out of it. On this subject, the revolutionary legend is accurate: Rousseau, the defender of the poor, remained poor himself all his life, limiting his expenses to the £600 or so which the sales of his books and sheet music produced annually. The result is that Rousseau wrote 'poor' where Voltaire would write 'beggar'.

An independent spirit

There is a school of the road. This separated Rousseau from the men of letters he encountered during his second period in Paris (1745–1756). Rousseau spent his childhood roaming in the open air. When he and Voltaire talked about freedom, did they mean one and the same thing? The word was not supported by the same human experience for them and did not stir the same memories. We could say the same thing about the word 'humanity'.

He who became 'Judas' in Voltaire's eyes never unconditionally espoused the stance taken by the *Encyclopédie*. While the battle raged, opposing progressives, free thinkers, and the Catholic and conservative faction, Rousseau refused to adopt partisan logic. This refusal made him the pet hate of both factions and he found himself deprived of all support when his works were attacked by censorship. Whatever happened as a result, he never agreed to give up his freedom of thought. On many points – notably materialism and determinism – his philosophical sensibility opposed him to those around him. Even if his Christianity had nothing orthodox about it, there is no doubt that he was deeply devout and was utterly revolted by everything that smacked of atheism.

Rousseau belonged to the second generation of 'philosophers': he was almost the same age as his friend Diderot, but eighteen years separated him from Voltaire and twenty-three from Montesquieu. This age difference was relevant: all his life Rousseau preserved a profound respect for Montesquieu and kept something of his youthful admiration for 'the illustrious Arouet', despite all the harm the latter did him.

Rousseauist philosophy

In 1755, the *Discourse on the Origin of Inequality* deepened the intuitions of the first *Discourse*: what presented itself in the first work in the form of antitheses evolved in the following work to an inquiry into origins. The denaturation which the first work was content to note was henceforth explained by a genesis which takes man from the state of nature to the social state – from liberty to oppression and from an original state of innocence to generalised evil. Through *La Nouvelle Héloïse* (1761) Rousseauist themes were propagated to a wider public: the thwarted love of a young lady of noble birth and her plebeian lover form the framework of a work which, together with the love of nature and a taste for domestic happiness, spread the yeast of revolt against an ordered society. This epistolary novel was tremendously successful throughout Europe.

Having become a pariah for the Encyclopédistes, Rousseau was no longer in step with his contemporaries. He no longer wrote with them or for them, but continued to produce masterpieces, like *Émile* (1761), which laid the foundations of a non-authoritarian style of teaching, and *The Social Contract* (1762), a decisive philosophical work. Here Rousseau established the principles of a radically democratic and fundamentally anti-liberal politics by opposing the absolutism defended by Hobbes. Seizing on the tradition of natural law, above all Dutch and German, Rousseau sought to base power on human freedom. He tried to bring a political solution to the evils of the modern world that he had diagnosed in his previous works. Little read when it first appeared, *The Social Contract* became the Gospel for the French Revolutionaries, though at the cost of inevitable distortions of meaning. Rather than in France, it was in Germany, through the intermediary of Kant, that Rousseau's philosophy found its real readers.

These two masterpieces were condemned in 1762 and he had to flee the country. Exiled from France, then hunted from successive retreats in Switzerland, Rousseau became affected by a persecution complex which his only too real misfortunes constantly fuel led. He returned to France, where he was still outlawed, then fled to England at Hume's invitation. He quarrelled with Hume during several dramatic incidents, and in 1767 he returned to France to end his days in semi-obscurity. The forced wanderings of the outlaw made a tragic pendant to his free youthful wanderings. Rousseau took refuge in solitude and became the exclusive theme of his work during the autobiographical enterprise he compiled to rehabilitate himself.

The *Confessions*, whose title he borrowed from Saint Augustine and which he completed in 1770, *Les Dialogues de Rousseau juge de Jean-Jacques* (*The Dialogues of Rousseau, Judge of Jean-Jacques*), compiled between 1770 and 1777, and *Les Rêveries du promeneur solitaire* (*The Reveries of the Solitary Walker*), unfinished at his death in 1778, remained unpublished during his lifetime. These works had a deep influence on autobiography, and even more so on contemporary forms of individualism. If, in the nineteenth century, Rousseau's moral influence acted powerfully on writers ani-mated by philanthropic ideals – George Sand, Hugo, Tolstoy – in the twentieth century that dimension had probably stopped being a living source of inspiration. On the other hand, the relationship with the self which Rousseau determined continued to strike the imagination, to which contemporary works such as those by William Boyd bear witness.

Rousseauist morality

Traditional literary history lists Rousseau as a turning point. Often presented as the person mainly responsible for the century's turning-point, he would have us pass from the values of criticism to those of feeling, from irony to effusiveness, from barbs of wit to the outbursts of noble souls. Not everything is false in this way of looking at things. Breaking with the daring pranks of the libertines, castigating the banality of vice, he paved the way for the explosion of virtue at the end of the century, and there is good reason for revolutionary moralism to be constantly stimulated by reference to this writer. However, to keep ourselves from the mirage of historical continuity, we must bear in mind the two following points. On the one hand, moralism and the exaltation of sensibility had coexisted from the start of the reign of Louis XV. People did not wait for Rousseau to shed torrents of tears; Prévost's novels and Voltaire's theatre both attest to this, each in its own way. On the other hand, of Rousseau's rationalism there is no room for doubt, even if certain commentators have misinterpreted him, backing up their arguments with phrases taken out of context, and particularly the overly famous formula of the *Second Discourse* (1755): 'Contemplative man is a depraved animal.'

It is true that the anti-intellectualism of Rousseau has lent a degree of credibility to these false readings. Did he not make an apology for man in his natural state, whom he never tired of contrasting with his vicious and civilised counterpart? In his capacity as a teacher, he distrusted bookish knowledge and language. He proclaims this in *Émile* with unprecedented vehemence: 'I hate books; they only teach you to talk about what you do not know.'

In *The Reveries of the Solitary Walker*, to return to his opinion on contemplative thought, he recognised his singularity: 'I have seen many who philosophised more learnedly than I do, but their philosophy was, so to speak, alien to them.' Through his work and the tests that he had to face because of it, truth – what is most universal – became his seal, what was most personal to him. This was expressed by the motto that he made his own: 'Vitam impendere vero', to 'consecrate one's life to truth'.

From his first work, and following an intuition which dictated the course of all his work, he linked intellectual development to moral and political decadence. Each of his last books had to reaffirm, but also to deny and to displace the initial and basic paradox which consisted of writing a book that was anti-book learning. This state of being out of alignment was characteristic of Rousseau's writings, and one of the mainsprings of their extraordinary tension. The work, which is peppered with farewells to the world of letters, evolves in fits and starts, almost against its author's will.

Since no activity is less natural than writing, he had to justify doing it, not so much to his reading public, but to himself. This self-justification is a new phenomenon. With Rousseau, writing became *per se* a problematic activity. Rousseau wrote on the razor's edge, at the risk of losing his self-respect. And it is perhaps by virtue of this new tension in his writing, this painful, wounding and wounded acuity, this personal risk that he never stops running, that he is close to us: strangely, but deeply, modern.

Goethe (1749–1832)

H. Blank

'Voilà un homme!' ('There is a man!') Napoleon is said to have exclaimed after the first of two interviews he had with Goethe, on 2 October and the 6 October 1808. One week

later, he decorated the poet with the Legion of Honour.

The life . . .

Goethe was born on 28 August 1749 in Frankfurt-am-Main. His father, Johann Caspar Goethe, was a Doctor of Law and an imperial cousellor (an honorific title); his maternal grandfather was also a jurist and the mayor of Frankfurt. Goethe's education was ensured by his father and by tutors. At the age of seven, the child learned Latin, at nine French, at ten Greek, at eleven Italian, at thirteen English and Hebrew. In 1765, his father decided he should study law in Leipzig. There he wrote his first poems, light compositions in the Anacreontic style. In 1768 tuberculosis obliged him to return to Frankfurt. He resumed his studies in Strasbourg in 1770. But, as in Leipzig, he only studied law through a sense of duty, while his curiosity led him to a cross-section of various branches of knowledge: philosophy, medicine, chemistry, history, theology and geology.

In Strasbourg, Goethe met Herder who introduces him to European folk poetry. In 1771, having obtained his licence to practise law, he returned to Frankfurt, established a law practice, but devoted himself mainly to literary creativity. At his father's request, he went to Werzlar from May to September 1774 to work for the highest court in the land. His friends suggested to him the theme of *Die Leiden des jungen Werthers* (*The Sufferings of Young Werther*, 1774). Back in Frankfurt, in November 1774, Goethe was presented to Crown Prince Charles Augustus of Saxe-Weimar, who invited him to settle in Weimar. Wieland was there already, and Herder, Schiller and others followed shortly afterwards. These writers made this small capital of a duchy (a Grand Duchy in 1815) a first-class intellectual centre. Appointed a member of the Privy Council – the government – in 1775, a councillor in 1779, Goethe looked after various departments: mines, bridges and roads, military, castle reconstruction. Later, he became director of the ducal theatre (from

1791 to 1817) and, until his death, super-intendent of scientific and artistic institutions: in charge of the administration of the University of Jena and all museums, libraries and conservatories in Weimar and in Jena.

As the burden of these functions as a public servant was taking him away from his literary activity, in 1786 without saying a word to anyone Goethe began his great journey in Italy. He only returned to Weimar in 1788. Contact with Italy gave him the decisive inspiration which was to bear fruit in the work of the future classic. But, with the exception of a few brief visits to Venice, Switzerland, Valmy (during the Revolution) and in the direction of the Rhine, and annual summer visits to spa-towns in Bohemia, Goethe remained in Weimar, paying close attention to events in Europe. When he died on 22 March 1832, he had never been to Paris or London.

. . . and the work

Goethe's extra-literary intellectual and artistic pursuits were very varied, but particularly included the fine arts and sciences. It was initially for the fine arts that he developed the analytical criteria that were later useful for literature. His point of departure was observation ('Anschauung'), not a historical approach. He considered Leonardo da Vinci, for instance, whose *Treatise on Painting* he had read, as 'an artist who looks at nature directly, observing and penetrating the phenomena themselves'. In 1817 he devoted a brief treatise to Leonardo's *Last Supper*.

It was not just a natural leaning in that direction that led Goethe to study the sciences, but his duties as administrator of the University of Jena, where he gathered information on the most diverse subjects: astronomy, botany, chemistry, geology, meteorology, mineralogy and zoology. During his research he discovered the intermaxillary bone in man. One idea which greatly preoccupied him was that of the origin of plants (works on plant morphology and metamorphosis in 1790). But the work on which he lavished most attention was the *Zur Farbenlehre*, 1791–1792 and 1810)

in which he conducted a polemic against Newton.

Goethe's literary work reflects the different periods that succeeded one another during his long life at an important turning-point for German literature. His first poems written in Leipzig echo the rococo style (1765–1768). During the interval forced on him by tuberculosis in Frankfurt, he was influenced by pietism (1768–1770). After his stay in Strasbourg (1770) and up to his first stay in Weimar, he was a member of the 'Sturm und Drang' ('storm and stress') movement. In the end, however, direct contact with the works of Antiquity, on the classical soil of Italy (1786–1788), provoked Goethe's conversion to classicism. He laid the theoretical foundations of this style in collaboration (after 1794) with the philosopher and poet, Schiller. By producing exemplary classical works, on the one hand, and vehement criticism of contemporary literature on the other, Goethe and Schiller imposed themselves as leaders of the new school. After Schiller's death in 1805, after the Napoleonic and anti-Napoleonic Wars, Goethe's late work emerged – sometimes on the edge of Romanticism, a movement that Goethe nevertheless hated. More than any other European poet, in his work as in his life, Goethe embraced the most varied tendencies, even poles apart, which came together in a moral and artistic unity of singular calibre.

'Sturm und Drang'

Goethe took part in the 'Sturm und Drang' movement, from 1770 to 1785, by composing hymns to Prometheus (*Prometheus*), Moham-med (*Mahomets Gesang, Song to Mohammed*), Kronos, and by writing lyrical poems. He also composed a discourse on Shakespeare, a treatise on Strasbourg Cathedral and, above all, two works which made him famous. The first was the play *Götz von Berlichingen mit der eisernen Hand* (*Götz von Berlichingen with the Iron Hand*, 1773), a play that laughed at the classical unities. The second was the epistolary semi-autobiographical novel *The Sufferings of Young Werther* the entire younger generation of the time recognised itself in Werther's nostalgia, his passion, his desire to identify with nature and in the demands of a life that was self-determined to the point of suicide.

Italy, where Goethe followed in the footsteps of Winckelmann, became the measuring rod for his later literary output. Ancient architecture and sculpture, as well as the naturalness of Southern European life, suggested the canon of a harmony bringing together all the human faculties: the mind (formerly favoured by the Enlightenment) just as much as sensibility ('Sturm und Drang'), body and intellect, Christian asceticism (above all Protestant) and ancient pagan sensuality.

Works begun before this journey now found their definitive classical form. *Egmont* (1788), *Torquato Tasso* (1789), *Iphigenie auf Tauris* (1779–1789) and *Faust* (1790) took their inspiration from the 'Sturm und Drang', but later acquired a more universal character: this was the case for *Egmont*, the prose of which still preserved the cachet of the 'Sturm und Drang', and for the definitive version of the first part of *Faust*. *Iphigenie* had been played in Weimar, in 1779, in its first prose version; but it was not until the fourth version (1786), respectful of the unities and composed in regular verse, that we have the purest of classical German tragedies, rivalling the best of Racine. *Torquato Tasso* aimed, like *Iphigenie*, at artistic perfection and also at a moral perfection sustained by the ideal of a new humanism.

These classical convictions were enriched by Schiller's philosophical contribution. The collaboration of the two men resulted in a new aesthetics, fuelled by Winckelmann's concept taken from Antiquity: a concept summed up by the word 'kalokagathía' (the quality possessed by a being that is both beautiful and good). Thanks to Schiller, this aesthetic was also influenced by Kant's philosophy. However, Schiller twisted the Kantian categorical imperative in the direction of aesthetic freedom, of a more natural harmony between duty and inclination. He finally elaborated the distinction between naïve and sentimental poetry, the first being supposed to be that of the Greeks, the second that of modern times. The name naïve poet was also attributed to Goethe by Schiller, a compliment which brought the latter closer to the ancient Greeks.

The classic

Goethe and Schiller adopted a classical veneer. They systematically discussed and composed certain literary genres such as the ballad, the tragedy, the novel, the epic, aiming at the general and the universal in the Aristotelean tradition, whose *Poetics* they reread with surprise. This aesthetic, brought about in the first place by their creative work, was, theoretically speaking, flanked by criticism: sometimes pitiless analyses of contemporary literary output, or simple invectives against mediocrity, in the *Xenien* (1797), the epigrams they wrote together.

One of the manifest characteristics of classical style was its form. Goethe replaced the free rhythms of his youth – Germanic verse – by metres inspired by Latin: iambs, trochees, dactyls. The prose of the dramas of the 'Sturm und Drang' gave way to blank verse – the verse of Shakespeare's tragedies which Lessing introduced into German drama. The tragedy conformed to the five acts required by Horace, and sometimes even to the unities of time and place – the validity of which was usually denied in Germany, even by classical writers.

These stylistic demands, however, were not binding for Goethe, who moves easily from the regularity of *Iphigenie* to the free composition of *Faust*, from the iamb to Germanic verse or to a structure suited to breathing, an important element in his poetry. In the exordium to *Iphigenie*, the female protagonist suggests a feeling of nostalgia for her Greek homeland with the beauty, the serenity and the musicality of her words:

Heraus in eure Schatten, rege Wipfel
Des alten, heilgen, dichtbelaubten
  Haines,
Wie in der Göttin stilles Heiligtum

Tret ich noch jetzt mit schauderndem
  Gefühl,
Als wenn ich sie zum erstenmal
  beträte,
Und es gewöhnt sich nicht mein
Geist hierher. {. . .}
Denn ach! Mich trennt das Meer
  von den Geliebten.
Und an dem Ufer steh ich lange
  Tage,
Das Land der Griechen mit der Seele
  suchend.

Going forth under your shade, trembling
  summits of the thick wood, holy, ancient,
  I still feel,
  as when I enter the peaceful
sanctuary of the goddess, a secret shiver: it
  seems to me still that my steps touch these
  places for the first time, and my spirit
  cannot
attune itself to them. [. . .] For, alas!
The sea separates me from those I
  cherish; I spend long days on the
  shore, where my heart seeks in vain
  the land of Greece.

Faust, however, looking for the absolute, and scrutinising many a science to the point of unfathomability, cannot present himself to an audience in this way. Germanic verse, less calm, though still rhyming, is more suitable:

Habe nun, ach! Philosophie,
Juristerei und Medizin
Und leider auch Theologie
Durchaus studiert mit heissem
Bemühn.
Da steh ich nun, ich armer Tor,
Und bin so klug als wie zuvor!

Philosophy, alas! Jurisprudence,
medicine, and you too, sad
theology! . . . I have studied you all
thoroughly with ardour and patience:
and now here I am, poor fool,
no wiser than I was before.

In lyrical poetry, there is little difference between regular metre and personal verse. The same kind of simplicity is expressed in the second *Wanderers Nachtlied* (*Traveller's Song at Night*), whose form was inspired by the Italian madrigal. The verse moves with the natural rhythm of breathing:

Über allen Gipfeln
Ist Ruh,
In allen Wipfeln
Spürest du
Kaum einen Hauch;
Die Vögelein schweigen im Walde.
Warte nur, balde
Ruhest du auch.

Over all mountain tops
Peace reigns.
In the tops of trees
You can hardly feel
A breath of air:
The birds are silent in the wood.
Patience, soon
You too will rest.

The works known as post-classical (written after 1805, the year in which Schiller died) expanded yet again on conventional forms, acquiring a more abstract diction and disengaging their symbolic value from everyday occurrences.

This value emanated from the novel *Die Wahlverwandtschaften* (*Elective Affinities*, 1809) and from *Wilhelm Meisters Wanderjahre* (*Wilhelm Meister's Years of Pilgrimage*, 1821, 1829), the second part of the novel *Wilhelm Meisters Lehrjahre* (*Wilhelm Meister's Years of Apprenticeship*, 1795, 1796).

The notion of symbol still dominates the third tale of Goethe's old age, his autobiography *Dichtung und Wahrheit* (*Poetry and Truth*, 1811–1814).

Distinct from the first part of *Faust*, the second part consists of five acts, but transcends classical structures. It brings together in one work all the varieties of Goethe's versification, descends into the inmost depths of time, and reunites Antiquity, the Middle Ages and the modern period, marrying Northern nature (Faust) to Southern nature (Helen): It reminds us, in the completeness of its panorama, of Dante's *Divine Comedy*. *Faust II* was not published until after Goethe's death in 1832.

Goethe had a prodigious knowledge of European literature – not only of *belles-lettres*, but also of scientific publications generally. He was probably familiar with the works of about 650 French writers and 300 Italian writers, not to mention German, English and Oriental writers. From the lending records of the Weimer library, we know that Goethe read, on average, one *in-octavo* volume a day. He also knew about what was happening abroad with French reviews (*Le Globe*, *The Globe*; *Le Temps*, *The Time*), Italian, English and Scottish ones, and was in contact with their representatives: Victor Cousin, Manzoni, Lord Byron, Thomas Carlyle. He also enriched his knowledge by translating foreign works, something he adopted in his youth, and which he continued (*The Essay on Painting* and *Rameau's Nephew* by Diderot), often to meet the needs of the Weimer theatre (Voltaire's tragedies *Mahomet* and *Tancrède*). A translation of the Persian poet Hafis, which appeared in 1814, encouraged him to imitate oriental poetry. In this way he conceived the *West-östlicher Divan* (*The Western-Eastern Divan*, 1819), a collection of profound poems, marvellously light, yet marked by spirituality.

What we could call Goethe's philosophy – eclectic, pantheist, listening to nature – was not just to be found in his work and theoretical studies, but also in his conversations with several friends and, above all, after 1823, with his secretary Eckermann, who wrote down these discussions with Goethe's consent and published them after his death.

In order to commemorate the centenary of Goethe's death, Valéry made a speech at the Sorbonne in 1932 in front of the then French president. His opening words were:

> Some men give an idea – or an illusion – of what the world, and particularly Europe, might have become, if political and spiritual power had been able to interpenetrate one another, or, at least, to develop less uncertain relations. [. . .] Among these men that I have been talking about, [. . .] the last ones, who were born in the eighteenth century, disappeared with the last hopes of a certain type of civilisation mainly based on the Myth of Beauty, and on that of Knowledge, both creations or inventions of the ancient Greeks. Goethe was one of them. I must say right away that I can see no-one else after him.

Laurence Sterne (1713–1768)

T. Keymer

I wrote not to be *fed*, but to be *famous*.

'Oh rare Tristram. Shandy! – Thou very sensible – humorous – pathetick – humane – unaccountable! – what shall we call thee? – Rabelais, Cervantes, What? – .' Thus the *London Magazine* of February 1760, giving early voice to the bewilderment with which Sterne's wayward masterpiece *The Life and Opinions of Tristram Shandy, Gentleman* was greeted on the appearance of its first instalment. What to call *Tristram Shandy*, how to read, place and explain a text resistant to every expectation and defiant of every convention: these are questions posed by Sterne with such inscrutability that even the shrewdest critics were baffled. 'This is a humorous performance, of which we are unable to convey any distinct ideas to our readers', wrote another perplexed reviewer. Its capricious and fragmented narrative manner left Sterne's fellow novelist Samuel Richardson with a sense only of 'unaccountable wildness; whimsical digressions; comical incoherencies'. Samuel Johnson, by now the nation's leading arbiter of literary taste, pronounced it simply 'odd'. Yet even as the novel bemused its readers it also captivated them, conferring on Sterne such renown that he was soon able to boast that a letter addressed simply to 'Tristram Shandy, Europe' would reach him without delay. Many English editions, which were widely disseminated at home and abroad, were followed before the century's end by German, French, Dutch and

Danish translations, each extending the vogue of 'Shandeism' and sowing new confusion.

And these, it seems, were precisely the goals that Sterne had in view. 'I wrote not to be *fed*, but to be *famous*', he tells one correspondent (*Letters*, p. 90). To another he jests, bumptiously, ''Tis enough if I divide the world' (*Letters*, p. 126).

A conjuror of the self

Much of the puzzle of *Tristram Shandy* lies in its author's very identity – an identity hardly typical of the future novelist, and one moreover that in his writing is questioned, fractured and displaced.

There is a sense in which all the great pioneers of the British novel were unlikely in their origins. Yet Defoe the projector and journalist, Richardson the master printer, Fielding the playwright turned magistrate and Smollett the doctor of medicine were all Londoners by birth or choice, and by virtue of their professional, literary or merely social activities they all moved at the very centre of literary production and debate. Sterne, by contrast, proclaims his isolation in *Tristram Shandy*'s opening pages, stating with jarring melancholy that the novel 'is written in a bye corner of the kingdom, and in a retired thatch'd house, where I live in a constant endeavour to fence against the infirmities of ill health, and other evils of life, by mirth' (*Tristram Shandy* [*TS*] I, Dedication, p. 3).

Though descended from an Archbishop of York, Sterne's immediate background was as humble as these words suggest. He was born in 1713, the son of an impecunious ensign stationed in County Tipperary. By 1759 he had become the comfortable but obscure incumbent of a Yorkshire parish, his only literary work of any note being a short satire on local ecclesiastical politics, entitled *A Political Romance*, printed in York early that year. Prudence had forced the work's hasty withdrawal, however, and a contemporary of Sterne reports that 'it was to this Disappointment that the World is indebted for Tristram Shandy'.

From this point on, Sterne's biography and bibliography combine to suggest a bizarrely multiple existence. The novel he then began and continued to issue in irregular instalments for the rest of his life was 'a picture of myself', as he told the actor David Garrick, and it is certainly the case that he threw himself into his hero's persona with unusual determination. Many novelists can be said to project a part of themselves into the voices of their narrators, but few have taken the exaggerated measures by which Sterne sought to confuse his very existence with Tristram's. When he came to London in 1760 to be fêted by the literary world, he did so not as Laurence Sterne but as Tristram Shandy himself; back in Yorkshire, his new house was renamed 'Shandy Hall'. Such playful gestures ingeniously sustained the basic fiction from which the text had begun: Tristram, his readers were to believe, was a real autobiographer, who had resolved, at the start of his *Life and Opinions* to write 'two volumes every year, provided the vile cough which then tormented me . . . would but give me leave' (*TS*, VII, i, p. 385). Tristram's life, and his chaotic efforts to write it, would go forward in parallel with the reader's own, while *Tristram Shandy* itself would be no fixed, stable or finished text but instead a continuing event, a literary process that might last 'these forty years' (ibid.). Only his own mortality, 'that death-looking, long-striding scoundrel of a scare-sinner, who is posting after me' (*TS*, VII, vi, p. 391), would curtail an otherwise interminable text – and so indeed it proved. For the 'vile cough' with which Sterne afflicts Tristram was also his own disease, and what closes the novel at the end of its ninth volume is not the usual tying up of plot-strings but the death from consumption, simultaneously, of narrator and author alike.

By that time, however, Tristram had long been supplanted as Sterne's favourite alter ego by one of the novel's lesser characters, the concupiscent sentimentalist Parson Yorick. The shift begins in *Tristram Shandy*'s first instalment, which quotes in full a sermon of Sterne's own, attributes it to Yorick, and then, in a typically topsy-turvy move, alleges it to have been stolen and actually preached in York Minster 'by a certain prebendary of that church' (*TS*, II, xvi, p. 113) – that is, Sterne himself, who had indeed preached it there years before. With brilliant opportunism, Sterne then issued more of his sermons as *The Sermons of Mr Yorick*, and although the irreverence of the ploy offended many – 'Would any man believe that a Preacher was in earnest, who should mount the pulpit in a *Harlequin's coat*?' thundered one – he persisted in it. 'The world has imagined, because I wrote Tristram Shandy, that I was myself more Shandean than I really ever was' (*Letters*, p. 402 or 403), he later protests, and in his last years he preferred to recast himself, in Yorick's mould, as an ardent man of feeling. Having travelled abroad he published, weeks before his death in 1768, *A Sentimental Journey through France and Italy by Mr Yorick*, and in the posthumously published *Journal to Eliz* he again uses Yorick's persona in a series of letters written to advance his vain courtship of a married woman in 1767.

Although this last work is sometimes seen as Sterne's most artless and authentic self-portrait, its studious mimicry of Swift's *Journal to Stella* in fact continues the highly literary and deliberate processes of self-fashioning common to all his writing. Each text constructs and anxiously explores a new self, always endeavouring to fix and define, always aware that to do so with anything like completeness or certainty is a task beyond reach. 'There is not a more perplexing affair in life to me, than to set about telling any one who I am', writes Yorick (*Sentimental Journey*, p. 85), and Tristram too finds the self too various, volatile and enigmatic to catch and fix in words. Asked the simple question 'And who are you?' the reply he gives is scattily profound: 'Don't puzzle me; said I' (*TS*, VII, xxxiii, p. 42).

Plagiarist, imitator, original

Given this proliferation of selves in Sterne's writing, it is all the more paradoxical that his most hostile critics should allege his work to have *no* personality of its own. The most damaging such charge begins with the formidable catalogue of his literary indebtedness drawn up by John Ferriar in the 1790s, Ferriar's implication being that his extensive borrowing amounted not simply to legitimate literary influence but to plagiarism or straight theft. More recently it has been estimated that up to a third of *Tristram Shandy* was plundered with little alteration from the shelves of Sterne's study, notable sources being Montaigne's *Essais*, Burton's *Anatomy of Melancholy* and such later repositories of esoteric knowledge as Ephraim Chambers' *Cyclopaedia*. Yet Sterne was no ordinary plagiarist. Indeed, there is a paradoxical sense in which his borrowings and allusions constitute perhaps his most original literary practice, an intricate form of intertextual play addressed to a learned reader. A mischievously deadpan example comes in Book VII of *Tristram Shandy*, which silently plagiarises from *The Anatomy of Melancholy* an attack on plagiarism itself largely plagiarised by Burton from sources of his own.

Where Sterne's forebears exert a heavier pressure on his writing he declares the fact himself, as in Tristram's famous invocation of 'my dear *Rabelais*, and dearer *Cervantes*' (*TS*, III, xix, p. 151). The influence of the former begins to be felt in the bawdy humour of 'A Fragment in the Manner of Rabelais' (an unpublished manuscript dating from 1759 or 1760), but it is most fully and creatively worked out in the gleeful havoc *Tristram Shandy* plays with learning, language and manners. 'This book so mad, so wise, and so gay is the English Rabelais', wrote Diderot; while for Voltaire its author was, after Swift, 'England's second Rabelais'. Yet Sterne himself seems to have seen Cervantes as his prime literary model, above all for the witty mismatch of narrative pedantry and bathetic incident he found in *Don Quixote*'s mock heroic. Commenting on his own minute particularisation of trivial business (the passage in question comes where Dr Slop topples from his horse 'diagonally, something in the stile and manner of a pack of wool' (*TS*, II, ix, p. 86), Sterne succinctly explains the debt to his Spanish master: 'the happiness of the Cervantic humour arises from this very thing – of describing silly and trifling Events, with the Circumstantial Pomp of great Ones' (*Letters*, p. 77).

For all these continuities with Renaissance writing, however, it is hard not to agree with Wieland, one of Sterne's foremost German admirers, who called *Tristram Shandy* 'this original work which cannot be compared with any other' and condemned the analogy with Rabelais in particular as superficial. It is more useful to look instead for discontinuities, and to read Sterne in the more immediate context of the eighteenth-century norms and traditions that his writing works to subvert.

Most obviously, *Tristram Shandy* is a text in which the Augustinian ideology of order, both as an aesthetic principle and as a world view, is challenged and cast aside. Where the harmonious couplets of Pope affirm the concord of a world 'Where order in variety we see, / And where, all things differ, all agree' (Pope, *Windsor Forest*), the sprawling and disjointed text of *Tristram Shandy* attests the very reverse. The world it describes is 'scurvy and disasterous', a 'vile, dirty planet . . . which, o' my conscience, with reverence be it spoken, I take to be made up of the shreds and clippings of the rest (*TS*, I, v, p. 9). It is a world of mishap and misrule, bereft of all coherence save the tenuous and fleeting order imposed on it, arbitrarily, by the consciousness of the beholder. 'Beset all sides with mysteries and riddles' (*TS*, IX, xxii, p. 517), it obstinately refuses to yield up lucid or intelligible meanings. It refuses, indeed, to admit of any adequate description in human language – for words too, as Walter Shandy laments, are 'falling themselves by piece-meals to decay' (*TS*, V, iii, p. 284).

It is here that Sterne most markedly resists the confident assumptions of his fellow novelists, in whose work experience rarely fails to form itself into coherent patterns, and more rarely still exposes the insufficiency of what Tristram calls 'tall, opake words' (*TS*, III, x, p. 158). Well might Locke write a chapter upon the imperfection of words', he exclaims elsewhere (*TS*, V, vii, p. 288), citing the

philosopher's gloomy view of human language as irreparably corrupt and unstable, riven by ambiguity. Where others remained untroubled by the gulf between words themselves and the world they seek to encompass, Sterne's emphasis on the sheer futility of his hero's project continually exposes their deficiency. Tristram's efforts to write his life and shape from it an orderly narrative line suffer perpetual obstruction: words prove too slippery and unsteady for the task, while experience proves too complex, diffusive and unknowable to be adequately recovered in even the most prolix text. 'The more I write, the more I shall have to write' (*TS*, IV, xiii, p. 228), Tristram laments as four volumes of increasingly desperate representation bring him no further than his first day of life. Even without the 'scare-sinner's' approach (*TS*, VII, vii, p. 39) his autobiography can only fail; and the defeat to which he finds himself condemned is nowhere better expressed than in the famous blank page he leaves in despair at the inability of words to catch the beauty of Widow Wadman. With his usual wry combination of seriousness and jest, he asks the reader to fill the gap himself: 'Sit down, Sir, paint her to your own mind – as like your mistress as you can – as unlike your wife as your conscience will let you – 'tis all one to me – please but your own fancy in it' (*TS*, VI, xxxviii, p. 376).

Tristram Shandy and the modern novel

Few readers of the next generation seem to have recognised the explosive narratological implications of Sterne's text. Both Goethe, who repeatedly cites 'Yorick-Sterne' as a formative influence, and Foscolo, the first Italian translator of *A Sentimental Journey*, saw him primarily as a sentimentalist, and neither *Die Leiden des jungen Werthers* nor *Ultime lettere di Jacopo Ortis* shows more than a limited grasp of the unremitting irony in which this sentimentalism is couched. The hectic Shandeism of Diderot's *Jacques le fataliste* is a notable exception, but it was not until the twentieth century that the novel's implications for the practice of fiction were fully perceived and developed. For Virginia Woolf, Sterne's innovative explorations of subjectivity and representation made him 'singularly of our own age', 'the forerunner of the moderns', while the recurrent play on the names 'Sterne' and 'Shandy' in *Finnegans Wake* shows something of his impact on Joyce. For these modernists, as later for the *nouveau romancier* Michel Butor, the unblinkingly sceptical gaze cast by Sterne on the methods and conventions of literary representation made him the novel's exemplary exponent. He was seized on similarly by the pioneering theorists of Russian formalism, who saw in his writing a calculated exposure of the structures and. mechanisms on which the genre was based. By parodying the novel, Sterne had shown it for what it was; as Viktor Shklovsky, wrote with whimsy learned from Sterne himself, '*Tristram Shandy* is the most typical novel of world literature'.

12 *The First Half of the Nineteenth Century*

M. R. FERRÉ AND J. SALVADOR

Man might know with certainty who he is and understand the earth and the sun.

Friedrich von Schlegel,
Debate on poetry

The death of absolute monarchy, the exaltation of fraternity, and the affirmation of the rights of the individual and all peoples to liberty and equality – pillars of the French Revolution in 1789 – were at the heart of all European debates in the nineteenth century. Various ideologies, conservative, liberal or democratic, attacked, upheld or radicalised these principles. In an almost uninterrupted dialectic, revolutions and counter-revolutions succeeded one other.

Liberalism and nationalism were the two key ideological movements of this period. A middle-class phenomenon, liberalism dates back to the Enlightenment – which assumed that man ensured progress by his own efforts – and to the French Revolution. Nationalism, for its part, rested on the exaltation of the historical and cultural entity which makes up a nation, in the face of arbitrary divisions brought about by royal successions. The cultural standard of the ideological and aesthetic crisis of this period was Romanticism. This trend always maintained an individual and national character which brought it closer to liberalism and nationalism: we cannot measure its exact composition, design and evolution in time and space.

Nationalism and regionalism engendered a 'renaissance' of literature, written in languages and dialects hitherto limited to domestic use, such as Catalan, Ukrainian, Finnish, Norwegian, Irish and Dutch. There was no Romantic ideology, despite Romanticism's affinities to metaphysical idealism. But there was an embryonic Romantic spirit, notwithstanding variations in time and contradictions which this cultural movement could not escape as its sphere of influence was so vast: art, philosophy, politics, religion, fashion This spirit was the expression of the Romantic concept of Nature and man, of poetry, imagination and style. Friedrich von Schlegel wrote on the subject of literary creativity: 'Romantic poetry is progressive and universal.' In other words, it took part in the on-going dialectic of history, and its role consisted in unifying and making poetry out of everything.

THE CULTURAL STANDARD: ROMANTICISM

The Romantic spirit is difficult to pinpoint, so we must turn first to the semantic evolution of the term which describes it. The French word 'rommant' (twelfth century), originally used in the expression 'langue romane', afterwards came to mean a genre of heroic and gallant tales, compiled in the vernacular in prose or verse. In the seventeenth century, the adjectives 'romanesque' in French and 'romantic' in English meant 'in the style of the novels of yesteryear'. They conjure up certain landscapes, certain monuments or the burlesque epic of the Italian Renaissance, tinged with fantasy, as in Ariosto's *Orlando Furioso*.

During the Enlightenment, 'romantic' meant unreal, absurd, out of all proportion: anti-classical. As a pre-Romantic sensibility established itself, however, and the imagination rediscovered its birthright, it was increasingly used to refer to the 'moving' aspects of Nature in its grandeur and melancholy – for example in Rousseau's *The Reveries of the Solitary Walker* – as well as medieval fiction and part of the fiction of the Renaissance, both of which were anti-classical. The adjective 'romantic' in English passed into French, then into other languages. At the dawn of the nineteenth century, a few German Romantics used the word 'Romantic' to describe a certain type of literature in the past – Dante, Ariosto, Cervantes, Calderón, and especially Shakespeare. Following on from Schiller, A.W. von Schlegel contrasted the hybrid character, the mystery and the agitation that went with the 'Romantic' art of Christian modernity to the clarity and serenity of the 'Classical' art of Greco-Roman Antiquity (*Vorlesungen über dramatische Kunst und Literatur, Lectures on Dramatic Art and Literature*, 1809), a distinction that Madame de Staël will later make exquisitely plain (*De l'Allemagne, On Germany*, 1810). The adjective 'romantique' took its current meaning in Germany from 1798, and later in Great Britain. In 1818 the Frenchman, Stendhal ,declares himself to be a Romantic.

Enlightenment, sensibility and Romanticism

Romanticism, liberal or conservative, was both the fruit and the mirror of the upheavals that shook Western society at the time of its transition from Ancien Régime to bourgeois liberal State. Though it denied the supremacy of reason and neo-classical poetry, it was nevertheless a manifestation of the Enlightenment, of it's ideal of human autonomy and of the defence of sensibility, the natural and the irrational. Those on the margin of the atheism of the Encyclopédistes, however, the Deists and the Mystics, preached a different way. All this constituted a foundation for Romantic sensibility and individualism.

Sensibility did not lead to the formation of a whole movement. Only certain authors made use of the thematic and stylistic elements of Romanticism – egotism, excessive, melancholic or desperate sentimentality, a taste for the dark and the lugubrious, a penchant for necrophilia in the broadest sense – the result of a spiritual dissatisfaction which it only served to heighten. There were also a pathos of expression and a new vision of Nature with which Romanticism identified and which was now released from its former role as passive scenery.

The 'occult' origins of Romanticism also had a decisive effect: The illuminism of Catholics, Protestants and Pantheists thus made its appearance on the European stage. Its adherents rebelled against the rational, incredulous explanations of the Encyclopédiste tradition, replacing them with faith, magic or other irrational phenomena. There was a new individualistic mysticism, marginal to the official Church, which reconnected to early and medieval Christianity, inward and occult. Among its representatives were Martines de Pasqually (1727–1779), Swedenborg and the Illuminated Ones of Copenhagen. In these trends, we already find traces of individualism and of the intuitive knowledge of innermost truth.

Goethe claimed to expound a humanism placed under the aegis of reason, which carried out a synthesis of demonic, irrational elements on the one hand, and divine elements on the other, since 'we are the product of the one and of the other'. Romantic sensibility, heightened into amorous passion and a painful quest for personal identity, guided their steps.

The romantic *Weltanschauung*: philosophy and history

> Made to love, to suffer.
>
> Friedrich Hölderlin

Born out of Kantian philosophy, German metaphysical idealism asserted the absolute supremacy of mind over matter and supported the aesthetics and psychology of German and, in part, European Romanticism. **Johann Gottlieb Fichte (1762–1814)** replaced God with the ego, creative and absolute, balance and dialectical synthesis between the empirical self and non-self. Knowledge and reality were internal to man, for only the self is real (*Wissenschaftslehre*, *Science of Knowledge* 1794–1795).

> Turn your gaze away from what surrounds you, look into yourself, this is the first demand that a philosopher makes of his disciples.
>
> Johann Gottlieb Fichte

Like the scientific poets and philosophers of the Middle Ages, the idealists looked on the cosmos as a secret, symbolic book founded on the union of opposites. All German Roman-

> *Ich bin der Mittelpunkt, der heilige Quell,*
> *Aus welchem jede Sehnsucht stürmisch fließt.*
> *Wohin sich jede Sehnsucht, mannigfach*
> *Gebrochen, wieder still zusammensieht.*

Heinrich von Ofterdingen, *Novalis*

Friedrich Wilhelm Joseph von Schelling (1775–1854) was on of the adepts of this metaphysics: truth is in man; the absolute can only be apprehended by self-contemplation and only expressed through the medium of art. The founder of the Romantic philosophy of nature, he declared that the world soul was the unifying principle in which all differences are abolished. The brothers **August Wilhelm von Schlegel (1767–1845)** and **Friedrich von Schlegel (1772–1829)**, the leading lights of Jena Romanticism, were the theorists of the new art. They described it in their *Fragmenten (Fragments)* (17898), published in their review *Athenäum* (1798–1800). August Wilhelm inaugurated the theory of the metaphor which proposes an analogical–magical knowledge of the world.

The movement of philosophical and social ideas contained certain constitutive elements of Romanticism. Georg Wilhelm Friedrich Hegel (1770–1831) preached an idealism which identified the real and the rational.

ticism had its source in this innate intuition of a cosmicunity in which opposites complement each other. Thus the German Romantics laid claim to the unity of inside and outside, reason and passion, dream and reality, science and art, which put them out of alignment with the scientific rationalism of the seventeenth and eighteenth centuries.

By appealing to intuition and analogical knowledge, the idealists discovered a hidden similarity between all the beings in the universe. They considered man, a microcosm of the macrocosm, to be the focal point of all these analogies. To know oneself therefore is to know the Whole:

> *I am the centre, the hearth, the sacred source*
> *From whence torrentially springs all desire*
> *And towards which all desire, diverse when it breaks,*
> *Ends up by returning, once appeased, to reconnect with it.*

Phänomenologie des Geistes (Phenomenology of the Mind, 1807) described the development of the 'Weltgeist' ('world spirit') with a view to seeing it attain a state of full awareness. Paradoxically, Hegel's philosophy found its prolongation in a form of materialism. Ludwig Feuerbach (1804–1872) considered that material reality produced ideas, and that God and religion were alienating concepts. Max Sterner (1805–1856) defended absolute individualism, the forerunner of anarchism. Co-authors of *Die deutsche Ideologie (German Ideology*, 1845–1846), Karl Marx (1811–1883) and Friedrich Engels (1820–1895) began from a position of left-wing Hegelianism before breaking away from traditional philosophy. Their materialistic and dialectical concept of history was already apparent in *Manifest der Kommunistischen Partei (The Communist Party Manifesto*, 1848). As a reaction to philosophical idealism, positivism exerted a considerable influence. In *Cours de Philosophie positive (Course on Positive Philo-*

sophy, 1830–1842), the Frenchman Auguste Comte (1798–1857), who had a deterministic and humanitarian concept of the world, declared that knowledge can only be found in science and that man cannot gain access to absolute truth.

The Dane Søren Kierkegaard (1813–1855), almost unknown during his lifetime, went beyond romanticism and announced existentialism. Man is anguished by the absurdity of his existence and by his remoteness from God. Intuitive knowledge is a source of truth, conceived of as an objective truth (*Om Begrepet Angest, The Concept of Anxiety*, 1844). In *Enten–Eeller* (*Either–Or*, 1843), Kierkegaard's two character types confront each other: the aesthete devotes himself to the intense enjoyment of momentary sensual pleasures; the moralist maintains that duty represents the individual's liberation. In *Stadier paa Livets Vei* (*Stages on Life's Way*, 1845), he adds a new character type: the believer. The work of the irrationalist Arthur Schopenhauer (1788–1860) also remained obscure when it was published. His nihilistic determinism conceived of life as an absurd phenomenon, ruled by a blind, cruel fate. The isolated individual can only escape through art and contemplation. God (or reason or history) is dead, and man is helpless and alone.

The study of the evolution of peoples to which history now devoted itself developed as a result of the substitution of a particular, living individual for the rationalist concept of universal, abstract man. Herder's spirit of nationhood, the 'Volksgeist', refers to the immutable essence of the nation. Many historians – Macaulay, Michelet – followed nationalism and Herder. By the same token, many philologists studied and disseminated the popular oral literature of the Middle Ages. For example **Vuk Stefanović Karadžić (1787–1864)** codified the language, introduced Romanticism into Serbia and published the anthology *Srpske narodne pjesme* (*Serb Popular Poetry*, 1841–1862). The Dane Nicolaï Frederik Severin Grundtvig (1783–1872) rediscovered the tradition of the Eddas.

The brothers Schlegel thought the Romantic revolution of the spirit and the French Revolution would bring about a total revolution in man and his relationship with the world. Freedom was the essence of mankind: freedom to politically organise the world, in accordance with reason; freedom to create it according to the dictates of our own imagination. Romantic man had faith in historical progress – and writers have never been so involved in politics. The Romantics deliberately misinterpreted the Fichtean theory of the self. They identified this self, the spirit of humanity, with the individual self that reaches out to inaccessible infinity. From the idea of this infinity emerged man's existential malaise, hemmed in by a finite, transitory world which he rejects and scorns because he thinks he is unique.

Melancholy: *le mal du siècle*

The friction between the outer and the inner world generated anguish as well as an ardent wish to transform reality into desire. The passionate Romantic artist was often a visionary whose own works made him anxious, then put him, with renewed enthusiasm, on the road to creation which will lead him to his ultimate objective: the unity of his life and work, of reality and desire. Anguish will then cease and, according to Friedrich von Schlegel, 'man might know of a certainty who he is and understand the earth and sun'. As this is impossible, Romantic irony and anguish emerge ('a clear awareness of perpetual motion, of the infinite plenitude of chaos'). So do a proper feeling of distance from the artist who feels superior to his work and knows that each victory is only the beginning of a new struggle.

The dominant feeling in Romanticism was 'Sehnsucht': an ardent, insatiable desire to know and to reach absolute plenitude; a longing for a lost paradise where reigned a harmony of contraries (*Heinrich von Ofterdingen* by Novalis, *René* by Chateaubriand, *Don Alvaro* by Rivas). From an unquenchable desire for an absolute came *le mal du siècle*, the existential agony that provokes an absence of willpower and, sometimes, leads to death. As Leopardi said: 'Even the pain which is born of disgust and of the feeling of the vanity of all things is relatively more bearable than the disgust itself.'

Existential torments, excessive idealism, the feeling that we cannot escape our fate, lead to the individual's profound frustration. The characteristic uncertainty of this time of general crisis is the basis of anguish, of the fear of a liberty which both ennobles and condemns a human being. It is possible to calm this unbearable state of soul – worsened by the additional struggle against bourgeois mediocrity – by taking refuge in literature, in dreams or, like young Werther, in suicide. The Romantic's dearest wish is to be exceptional: to live intensely and to die a violent death. Kleist, Nerval and Larra committed suicide; Pushkin and Lermontov were killed in duels; Byron and Petöfi died in battle; Leopardi and Král ended their lives in sickness and disappointment; Hölderlin went mad and Poe became an alcoholic; Novalis, Tieck and López Soler give themselves up to ecstatic states of meditation. Unlike the Goethe of the *Elective Affinities*, all of them despised a certain type of bourgeoisie, its money and its idea of marriage; all of them favoured free love. Anguish is sometimes dissolved by the sad contemplation of ruins and night scenes: the Romantic endeavours by these means to mingle in with nature and to rediscover peace accompanied by death. On other occasions, anguish unleashes impotent cynicism and sarcasm, or inspires macabre pleasures (ghostly apparitions, kisses to rotting corpses, frightening voices), and the search for a way to die which may serve as a protest. Thus we find a whole aesthetic of terror and the demonic – a metaphor for the failure of our deepest aspirations – of which the English Gothic novel had given precursory signs with Horace Walpole and Ann Radcliffe. **Giacomo Leopardi (1798–1837)** spoke bitterly and with a cold scepticism of the disgust and despair caused by 'the infinite vanity of everything'.

Or poserai per sempre,	*Rest forever*
stanco mio cor	*poor weary heart*
Non che la speme, il desiderio	*Not only hope, but desire*
è spento.	*is extinguished.*
Posa per sempre. Assai	*Sleep forever. You have*
Palpitasti. Non val cosa nessuna	*fought long enough. Nothing is*
i moti tuoi, né di sospiri è degna	*worth your excitement, and the*
la terra. Amaro e noia	*earth is unworthy of your sighs.*
la vita, altro mai nulla: e fango	*Bitterness and boredom*
è il mondo.	*are what life is, nothing more: and*
	the world is merely mud.

Giacomo Leopardi,
A se stesso

Escape through literature, allied to love of the natural and the primitive, tempted the Romantics towards exotic countries or areas such as Spain, Italy, America or the East, which many travellers' tales truthfully describe in minute and painstakingly detail. The lost paradise of childhood (Nerval's *Chimeras*), dreams, drugs or the heroes of fiction (Julien Sorel in Stendhal's *Scarlet and Black*) are just so many ways of escaping reality. Similarly, there is a return to the mysterious, idealistic Middle Ages, an enticing period for the first 'reactionary' generation of Romantics, born of the recently dispossessed Catholic nobility. Their names were Novalis, Kleist, Byron, Shelley, Bilderdijk, Chateaubriand, de Vigny, Manzoni, the liberal Pushkin and Thijm, among others. Nevertheless, many of them develop (Lamartine, de Vigny, Shelley, Byron) and drew closer to the ranks of the Romantic liberals, moderate or radical, supporters of Enlightenment reforms or of Utopian and

Saint-Simonian socialism. The genius of each nation saw the light during the European Middle Ages, before being contaminated by classical rationalism. They then returned to original sources, which revived folk traditions and literature. National identities asserted themselves here and there – in Bohemia, Slovakia, Poland, Hungary, Italy, Belgium, Bulgaria, the Rumanian principalities. Thus, next to the Bulgarian intellectuals who defended Hellenism, the nationalists rejected Russia and the West, favouring the exaltation of the national past as in *Mati Bolgaria* (*Mother Bulgaria*, 1846) by Neofir Bozveli (1785–1848).

The Romantic hero acts as a Titan in revolt against society, the world and God himself (Shelley, *Ode to the West Wind*, 1820). Prometheus becomes the symbol of the rebel setting himself against the gods and involved in the work of humanising the world (Shelley, *Prometheus Unbound*, 1820). His constant refusal to accept defeat, commanded by a force of character that fate cannot bend, is the sign of his triumph. The aesthetics of originality and a contempt for conventions correspond to this behaviour. One of the variants of this attitude was Satanism – whose representatives will be Shelley and Byron, as well as various Byronic rebels such as Espronceda, Lermontov, Mácha, Král and Mickiewicz – a negative religiosity which stands up against God and the limits imposed on all created things. This movement brought a distorted art which tried to reflect the moral reality of man by expressionist, blasphemous and sarcastic means.

Literature magnifies defiance and pride in marginal beings: Cain, Don Juan, the pirate, the man seduced by evil, the poet who is cursed and even the beggar: 'Titans' confronted by fate or society, like Nodier's Jean Sloogar.

Traditional Catholicism also has a high profile, with Novalis, Chateaubriand and Zorrilla. Christian religious feeling was sentimental and intuitive, emulating medieval example. Mysticism, occultism and especially pantheism were the most frequent forms of a

phenomenon with multiple aspects, among which the only thing they have in common is the inwardness of religious feeling and the certainty that man discovers God in himself and in the world. For Friedrich Schleiermacher (1768–1834), 'the contemplation of the universe [. . .] is the most common and the most elevated form of religion'.

Sing in your cage, creatures!
Miguel de los Santos Alvarez,
Maria

The Protean unity of Romanticism

In his attitudes, the Romantic can be liberal or absolutist, Satanic or ultramontane, melancholic or sarcastic, socially active or anti-social, a visionary or a realist, irrationalist, ironical and intellectual. Hence his influence over the most diverse forms of literature – realist, symbolist, surrealist or existentialist. These opposites are sometimes present, simultaneously or successively, in a single country, in a single author, even in a single work. As for form, we find the mutually exclusive use of declamatory as well as intimate style, of the historical novel that celebrates the aristocracy as well as brief, sarcastic genre scenes.

Nevertheless we find unifying factors: the concept of the poetic imagination, the symbolic and mythical style, the world seen through the lens of nature and individual freedom, as well as points held in common by a few authors which make it possible to speak of a somewhat traditional and superficial orientation (Lamartine, Scott, Feith, Zorrilla), of an orientation romantic in its own right, constructed on the expression of the self in crisis (Byron, Keats, Shelley, Eichendorff, Brentano, Mácha and, to a certain extent, Hugo), of a third orientation, in the final analysis, more visionary and more avant-garde (Hölderlin, Coleridge, Nerval).

In the second half of the eighteenth century, the concept of literature as a passive mirror had fallen into disuse and was making room for the poem perceived as a heterocosm, or second nature created by an inspired poet–god. Eventually we conceive of poetic creativity as a mysterious, untameable force, born of the imagination and the subconscious mind, of innate, passionate and rebellious genius which aims at the sublime.

Leaving the object behind, attention is now focused on the subject. It abandons the imitation of nature to concentrate on the expression of the poet's inner life. 'Poetry is the spontaneous outpouring of powerful feelings,' as Wordsworth was the first to point out, for it is born from the creative forces of genius and, quite often, from suffering:

> *Know full well it is the heart that speaks*
> *and sighs,*
> *When the hand writes it down, it is the*
> *heart that melts.*
>
> Alfred de Musset,
> *Namouna*

For Romanticism, poetry's most elevated ambition was not to reproduce a world, but to illuminate it and, above all, to create it. So, for example, Novalis declared that 'poetry is genuine and absolute reality'; others, such as Hugo (*The Contemplations*, 1856) and Nerval, considered themselves to be visionaries and prophets who hold the key to the mysteries of the universe and reinvent reality by means of art. Aesthetic creation is ontological. The poet is a demiurge.

The Romantics considered the creative imagination ('queen of all the faculties') as the foundation of art, as a superior form of knowledge which made it possible to gain access to ideal and universal beauty, and to true reality, of which tangible nature was merely a symbol (Shelley, *Defence of Poetry*, 1821). Without refuting the existence of objective reality, as German idealism did, Coleridge, in *Biographia Literaria* (1817), made a distinction between fantasy, or the ability to reorganise in an arbitrary manner the givens of experience, and the imagination, a veritable tool of creativity. The latter can be primary: this is the vital power, equivalent in man to divinity, which gave birth to the universe. Or it can be secondary: limited to the poet, it allows him to

re-elaborate and to express symbolically the elements that primary imagination has placed at his disposal: 'I describe what I imagine,' said Keats.

Sometimes, dreams become assimilated into poetic creation and terrorise or fascinate, according to whether they are related to inner abysses or to the divine. In a wakeful state, the poet–medium transcribes the oniric elements of artificial paradises engendered by music, drugs (Coleridge, *Kubla Khan*, 1797) or dreams: 'the world is transformed into a dream and the dream is transformed into a world', according to Novalis' formula.

The purity and truth of language, by analogy, conceals the essence of things and even the magical power of raising them. From this viewpoint, if the narrator is knowledgeable, there is no longer any distinction between the experience itself and the experience acquired by reading. From this stem two fundamental literary genres; the *'Bildungs-roman'*★ or 'novel of education', the model for which is Goethe's *Wilhelm Meister*, and the folk tale, which harks back to the *'Volksgeist'*.

Conceiving of art as an autonomous form of knowledge, alone able to reveal the infinite and life's mysteries, Romanticism recognises in art a justification which is intrinsic and total. In the eyes of Schelling, Hegel or Keats, art has an absolute value; it is a world apart. Keats wrote of it: 'Truth is beauty, beauty truth.' However, as their morality rested on the intensity and authenticity of the emotions, the Romantics rarely fall fully into the aesthetic engendered by 'l'art pour l'art' ('art for art's sake') – life and art would thereby be estranged from one another.

These ideas had an exceptional resonance in France, where they were introduced during the first decades of the nineteenth century by Victor Cousin (1792–1867), an adept of eclecticism. **Théophile Gautier (1811–1872)** vehemently defended 'art for art's sake' and attacked classical moralists, as well as modern utilitarians and Utopian socialists, who claimed to give art a useful purpose: 'Only what can serve no useful purpose is truly beautiful; all that is useful is ugly, because

[. . .] human needs are ignoble.' Art and beauty are the ivory tower in which the artist takes refuge.

Founded on the absolute freedom of genius and on the organic unity of form and content, 'Sturm und Drang' had rejected the classical theory of genres. The same applied to Romanticism, in the name of spontaneity of expression and homology between all literary forms. The Romantics nevertheless recognised the diversity of works in themselves, wanting to distinguish existing genres by means of philosophical criteria (Friedrich von Schlegel). The theory of Romanticism invites the creation of hybrid genres, for the life which art has to express is a mixture of things: sublime and grotesque, corporal and spiritual. This is why Hugo broke with tragedy and neo-classical comedy, to raise drama to the genre *par excellence*. We can spot this tendency in other areas, such as the novel and poetry epic, lyrical, philosophical and religious. Classical genres (tragedy, eclogue, Pindaric or Sapphic ode), metrical forms and mythological subjects fall into disuse. The novel and poetry admit all types of subjects: we encounter among them the drama, the historical novel, the psychological novel, the novel of manners, intimate and philosophical poetry, the prose poem.

Authors write in the most diverse registers and, in spite of frequent rhetorical excesses, they fight against the noble, pompous style in favour of a freer and more familiar language, closer to reality. Adjective and metaphor are considerably enriched. The aesthetics of inspiration and the heterogeneity of reality engender the imperfect, the fragmentary, the hybrid and the synthesis of opposites.

LYRICISM:
THE ARCHETYPAL FORM
OF ROMANTICISM

A form favoured by the Romantics, poetry derives from no one particular art of prosody. Creative imagination, intimate outpourings direct or reformulated, a fresh perception of nature, religious feeling, melancholy, love, rebellion and irony: such are the values the Romantics hold in common. In general, the aim of writing is to be natural and spontaneous, but the results vary. Neo-classicism and classicism are of more weight in some countries – France, Italy, Greece – than in others. In Great Britain, for instance, where there is no break with tradition, as the previous tradition was not as close to neo-classicism stylistically as it was on the continent, and because the trend towards sensibility had a deep influence. In Germany, where the 'young Romantics', such as Heine, Brentano, Eichendorff, Rückert and Mörike, derive inspiration for their lyrical poetry from popular ballads, or lieder. In Spain popular poetry harked back to the romanceros. Greece, Scandinavia and the Slav countries experienced something comparable. An obsession with the ineffable inner world, which the Russian **Fiodor Tiutchev (1803–1873)** so lucidly expressed, is the hallmark of lyrical poetry.

> Live in yourself, alone and proud.
> Your soul is a vast universe
> Of mysterious and bold thoughts. [. . .]
> Listen to their song and say nothing.
>
> Fiodor Tiutchev,
> *Silentium*

Lyricism crops up in a variety of genres, seeking fusion with the reader, for he is the one who warrants concern: 'Ah! Fool if you think that I am not you!' Hugo exclaims in the preface to *Contemplations*. Never before had subjective poetry shown the deepest and most personal aspects of the soul. This was a tendency began by Rousseau with *Confessions* and taken to extremes by Byron, who makes it popular among the last Romantic generations of many countries. The majority of Romantic poets, however, did not go as far as Byron, Shelley, Hugo, Musset, Mácha or Heine in baring their soul. Lermontov, Pushkin, Zhukovsky, Słowacki, Espronceda and Garrett maintained a certain distance.

Elegiac poetry

The most common feelings are melancholy and sadness engendered by a hankering after the ideal (as in Shelley or Novalis), by acute awareness of the destructive effect the passage of time has on every human being, by frustration in love and by a lack of freedom both at national and individual level. These feelings are found in different types of poems. The Serb **Branko Radičević (1824–1853)** mingled in his poetry melancholy lyricism with patriotic inspiration, along with the rhythms of popular melodies.

> *Courage! Fallen child of a heavenly race,*
> *You carry your proud origin upon your*
> *face!*
>
> Alphonse de Lamartine,
> *Poetic Meditations*

Melancholy, sometimes bordering on hypersensitivity, was gentle and dreamy with Alphonse de Lamartine (1790–1869), who was consoled by Nature's everlastingness. In Vigny, Lenau, Kölcsey and Leopardi, the same melancholy was tinged with profound philosophical pessimism.

In *Les Contemplations* (*The Contemplations*), Hugo described the excruciating pain that overwhelmed him when, submissive but not resigned, he complained to God about his daughter's death:

> *Lord, I acknowledge that man is out of his*
> *mind*
> *If he dares to complain:*
> *I no longer accuse you, I no longer curse*
> *you,*
> *But let me weep!*
> *[. . .]*
> *Let me lean over this cold stone*
> *And say to my child: Can you feel I am*
> *here?*
>
> Victor Hugo,
> 'At Villequier', *The Contemplations*

In this work, as in *Voix intérieures* (*Inner Voices*, 1837) and *Les Rayons et les Ombres* (*Sunbeams and Shadows*, 1840), Hugo gives us the complete record of this period of his life. From *Odes* (1822) to *Contemplations*, he uses every register and tackles a variety of situations, from the burning enthusiasm of youth to the pathetic reflection of maturity. Like Musset, he finds in memory the remedy to the melancholy engendered by the destructive effects of time ('Tristesse d'Olympio', 'Olympio's Sadness', *Les Rayons et les Ombres*).

Leopardi's despair is absolute in the poem *La Ginestra* (*The Broom*, 1836), a plant to be found in historical ruins, a symbol of the decrepitude of human glory, but also of life itself, a commonplace of Baroque poetry. In this poem, the classical tradition meets Romantic sensibility at its most typical, sensitivity combined with disappointment:

E tu, lenta ginestra,	*And you, slow broom-plant*
che di selve odorate	*which, in sweet-smelling forests,*
queste campagne dispogliate	*decorates stark countryside,*
adorni,	*you too will yield, in a*
anche tu presto alla crudel	*time not far off,*
possanza	*to the cruel force of a buried fire.*
socomberai del sotterraneo foco.	

Giacomo Leopardi,
La Ginestra

Some years after the death of his friend Arthur Hallam, Tennyson collected in *In Memoriam* (1850) poems dedicated to the dear departed. Only beauty consoled **John Keats (1795–1821)** for the ephemeral character of this world. A pure poet who sets out in search of the soul of nature, who is nostalgic for Grecian Antiquity, he felt his faith in life was tarnished by the power of death. The Grecian urn of his poem comforts him – 'A thing of beauty is a joy forever' (*Endymion*, 1818) – for its beauty is immortal in the eyes of people who contemplate it:

> *Heard melodies are sweet, but those*
> * unheard*
> *Are sweeter; therefore, ye soft pipes, play*
> * on;*
> *Not to the sensual ear, but, more*
> * endear'd,*
> *Pipe to the spirit ditties of no tone.*
>
> John Keats,
Ode on a Grecian Urn (1819)

Love poetry

Romantic love poetry suggests tenderness allied to affection, rather than sensuality. Many Scandinavian poets, in the wake of the German Romantics, celebrated the idealised, even disembodied beloved, like the Swede Per Daniel Amadeus Atterborn (1790–1855). The poetic transcription given by **Alfred de Musset (1810–1857)** of his brief but painful passion for George Sand is of quite a different nature. In *Nuit de mai* (*Night in May*, 1835), while still suffering from his infatuation, his muse inspires him to put his pain into words and to be reborn to life thanks to the comfort afforded by art. In *Souvenir* (*Memory*, 1841), the love that he remembers acquires genuine value and brings him happiness:

> *I merely said to myself: 'At this hour, in*
> * this place,*
> *One day, I was loved, reciprocated, she*
> * was fair.*
> *I have buried that treasure in my*
> * immortal soul,*
> *And I bring it now to God!'*
>
> Alfred de Musset,
Memory

A tone both passionate and restrained distinguished the verses by Lamartine, Leopardi and Marceline Desbordes-Valmore (1786–1859), and *Sonetni venec* (*Garland of Sonnets*, 1833) by the Slovene **France Prešeren**

(1800–1849). **Elizabeth Barrett Browning (1806–1861)** dedicated *Sonnets from the Portuguese* (1847), tinged with amorous devotion, to her husband. The originality of the love poetry by **Friedrich Rückert (1788–1866)** lies in the simplicity of the object of his affections (*Amaryllis, ein Sommer auf dem Lande, Amaryllis, a Summer in the Country*, 1812). Love poems, in Germanic or Slavic languages, revive the popular traditions of the Middle Ages. The lieder genre in Germany had exceptional success. **Heinrich Heine (1797–1856)** * produced its most famous collection, *Intermezzo* (1823).

> *Why am I now so sick and so sad, my*
> *dearest, tell me? Oh! Tell me, dearest of*
> *my heart, why have you abandoned me?*
>
> Heinrich Heine,
Intermezzo

Heine writes of the pain and bitterness kindled by an unrequited love or the death of the loved one. The acute sensitivity and individualism of the Flemish poet Theodoar Van Rijswijck (1811–1849) were expressed in *Volksliedjes* (*Folk Songs*, 1846). Other examples are Vasili Andreievitch Zhukovsky (1783–1852), Byron, the Slovakian **Ondrej Sládkovič (1820–1883)**, the author of the long poem *Marína* (1846), and the Swede Erik Johann Stagnelius (1793–1823) who take their inspiration from the same sources. Nostalgia is important in *Folhas Cahidas* (*Fallen Leaves*, 1853) by the Portuguese writer, **João Baptista de Almeida Garrett (1799–1854)**, in which we can see the influence of Luso-Galician songbooks and the oral tradition of folk poetry.

The tone is sometimes violent or sarcastic when faced with the frustration brought about by the loved one's infidelity or social constraints, as in Heine's early poems. The long *Canto a Teresa* (*Song for Theresa*, 1840) by **José de Espronceda (1808–1842)** is a strange elegy, rhetorical during its first pages, interrupted by accents of great sincerity initially suggesting happiness and then the pain caused by her disappearance. Misogynist insults and the cruelty of cheating on someone combine in this work with a satanic and exalted Romanticism. It ends with a cynical question: 'What does another dead body matter to the world?'

Philosophical and religious poetry

While philosophical and religious prose in Europe often have a didactic and objective character, the Romantics confer emotion and subjectivity on abstract poetry with an erudite mixture of metaphysics, epic, lyricism, drama and religious feeling. Often visionaries, they write in a descriptive or narrative framework, traditional or innovative, their reflections on destiny, life, society and the life beyond. They have recourse to symbols, an ideal literary procedure to communicate ideas and to transform the austerity of the message into aesthetic pleasure. Their use of symbols corresponds to the symbolic concept of the world proper to Romanticism.

> O stream!
> Whose source is inaccessibly profound
> Whither do thy mysterious waters tend?
> Thou imagest my life.
>
> Percy Bysshe Shelley, *Alastor*

Anxious about the meaning of life, the problem of evil and the destiny of humanity, these poets base their philosophy on their religious feelings. They answer their questions in a variety of ways normally ranging from more or less orthodox spiritualism to pantheism. Mysticism and faith in moral progress is obtained at the cost of great suffering.

> Tam prázdno pouhé
> – nade mnou
> a kolem mne i pode mnou
> pouhé tam prázdno zívá. [. . .]
> Bez konce ticho – žádný hlas –
> bez konce místo – noc i čas [. . .]
> A než příští skončí den,
> v to pusté nic jsem uvedem.

Karel Hynek Mácha, *Máj*

> Down there, there is only nothingness,
> beneath me
> there is nothing but nothingness
> [. . .]
> Infinite silence and night and time
> [. . .]
> And even before tomorrow
> is over
> I will be swallowed by this empty void.

However, there are, some notable exceptions: **Alfred de Vigny (1797–1863)** shows himself to be a pessimist in *Destinées* (*Destinies*, 1838–1863): in *La Mort du Loup* (*The Wolf's Death*, 1838) he expresses compassion for humanity whose fate is to impassively contemplate ungrateful Nature. In *La Bouteille à la mer* (*The Bottle in the Sea*, 1847), fatalism gives way to faith in the redemption of mankind, supported by the impending triumph of science and the human soul. In the Schopenhauer tradition, the Russian **Evgeni Abramovitch Baratynsky (1800–1844)** wonders about the passage of time, the tragic condition of modern man, alone and without traditions, whose only viaticum is solitary meditation. The Austrian **Nikolaus Lenau (1802–1850)** sympathises with the misfortune suffered by the victims of fanaticism in *Savonarola* (1838).

Lord Byron (George Gordon, 1788–1824), the author of *Cain* (1821) and *Heaven and Earth* (1821), rebelled against theological tradition. In *Queen Mab* (1813) and *Alastor, or, The Spirit of Solitude* (1816), **Percy Bysshe Shelley (1792–1822)** affirmed his faith in humanity and his confidence in liberty, love and moral progress. The Czech **Karel Hynek Mácha (1810–1836)**, in his long philosophical poem *Máj* (*May*, 1836), introduced the theme of metaphysical despair by contrasting the sadness of human destiny with the splendour of nature in springtime. His protagonists are anti-social, malevolent and parricidal 'anti-heroes'.

The Pole **Juliusz Słowacki (1809–1849)** allocated a lot of space to spiritualism and symbolism in his unfinished poem *Król-Duch* (*The Spirit-King*, 1847). In this lyrical and fantastic epic steeped in mysticism and ego-centrism, the poet himself is inhabited by the Spirit-King. The Romantic poet attached symbolic values to flowers: *Blommorna* (*The Flowers*, 1812) by Atterbom, *Liljor i Saron* (*The Lilies of Sharon*, 1822) by Stagnelius, the poems in the complete works of the Swedish atheist writer Carl Jonas Almqvist (1793–1866), *Törnrosens bok* (*The Book of the Eglantine*, 1849). *Luča Mikrokozma* (*The Light of the Microcosm*, 1845), by **Petrovic Njegoš (1813–1857)**, the last Prince-Bishop of Montenegro, is a philosophical epic which describes man's cosmic destiny and his union with God.

Many epic and philosophical poems, written in Europe during the 1830s and 1840s were influenced by Goethe's *Faust* (the versions of 1808 and 1832) and by 1830s revolutionary liberalism. The hero usually embodied human-ity or its main characters, playing allegorical, historical or legendary characters in turn: God, Christ or the Devil. The action also takes place in symbolic or Utopian locations. *Skabelsen, Mennesket og Messias* (*Creation, Man and the Messiah*, 1830), by the Norwegian **Henrik Wergeland (1808–1845)**, lyrically evokes in love with freedom, Creation, his love for a woman and redemption through Christ. Browning, an English lyric poet, published *Paracelsus*, in 1835 a dramatic poem which presents the Renaissance scholar as a man eager to discover the Absolute. Espronceda died before being able to finish his long poem in free verse, *El Diablo Mundo* (*The Devil World*, 1840), a lyrical, philosophical and social epic about humanity, symbolised by an Adam confronted with the mystery of his destiny and society. Characters as diverse as Satan, a symbol of evil and rebellion, Faust and the Wandering Jew also appear. *The Demon* (1838), a long poem by **Mikhaïl Yurievitch Lermontov (1814–1841)**, has as its hero an independent spirit who refuses to surrender.

During the same period, social problems invade the philosophical poetry of Hugo who, in *Les Rayons et les Ombres* (*Sunbeams and Shadows*) and subsequent works, sets himself up as a guide and a prophet: 'Peoples! Listen to the poet! / Listen to the sacred dreamer!'

Les Chimères (*The Chimeras*, 1854) by **Gérard de Nerval (1808–1855)**, a hermetic collection of sonnets, alternate between anguish and hope, heaven and hell. The sonnets contain mythological and esoteric elements, and look forward to symbolism and surrealism. The poet places illuminism, onirism and madness at the service of his aspiration to the sacred. In this way, he marks thematically and chronologically, a new stage in Romanticism.

> *I am the dark one – the widower – the*
> *unconsoled,*
> *The Prince of Aquitaine in exile in the*
> *tower.*
>
> Gérard de Nerval,
> *The Chimeras*

The poetry by **Friedrich Hölderlin (1770–1843)**, clearly and classically written, marked by Hellenism, is nevertheless Romantic in its refusal of the real and the pathetic. *Hyperions Schicksalslied* (*Hyperion's Song of Destiny*) reflects the tragic destiny of man:

Doch uns ist gegeben	*It is our lot*
Auf keiner Stätt' zu ruhn.	*Never to be able to rest anywhere.*
Es schwinden, es fallen	*Suffering men*
Die leidenden Menschen	*Stumble and fall*
Blindlings von einer	*Blindly from one*
Stunde zur andern,	*Hour to the next,*
Wie Wasser von Klippe	*As water, thrown*
Zu Klippe geworfen,	*From rock to rock*
Jahrlang ins Ungewisse hinab.	*Over the years into an uncertain chasm.*

Friedrich Hölderlin,
Hyperions Schicksalslied

405

Poetry and nature

*Nature is a delight, a dream of beauty
    and grace.
Springing from a thousand sources,
    calling with a thousand voices,
Even in the soul of man.
He who dies today, dies a thousand
    times.*

Solomos

The reference to nature, introduced by the English, French and German current of sensibility, dominated Romantic literature. Many idealistic and mystical authors see in Nature the embodiment of the hidden language of God and, very often, the symbol of their emotions: this is the case with *Spruch* (*Sentence*) by the German Josef von Eichendorff (1788–1857) and poetry by Alexandre Herculano (1810–1877) in Portugal. In poetry by Keats and Wordsworth, the soul of the landscape penetrates the heart of the poet.

Nature is also at the heart of poetry by **William Wordsworth (1770–1850)**, for whom the mystical apprehension of the universe was impossible unless imagination illuminated the perception of everyday realities. His language is often simple, as in his long autobiographical poem *The Prelude*, published posthumously in 1850 and dedicated to his friend Coleridge:

Summer Vacation

*As one who hangs down bending from
    the side
Of a slow-moving boat, upon the
    breast
Of a still water, solacing himself
With such discoveries as his eye can
    make
Beneath him in the bottom of the
    deep.
Sees many beauteous sights – weeds,
    fishes, flowers,
Grots, pebbles, roots of trees, and fancies
    more,*

*Yet often is perplexed, and cannot
    part
The shadow from the substance.*

William Wordsworth,
The Prelude

We also find this fusion of the natural and the supernatural in Solomos. In *L'Infinito* (*The Infinite*, 1819), Leopardi passes from the contemplation of his native soil to the vertigo of imagined infinity.

Hymnen an die Nacht (*Hymns to the Night*, 1800) by **Friedrich von Hardenberg** (known as **Novalis, 1772–1801**), the most lyrical of all the early Romantics, brings together rhythmic prose and blank verse and mystically reflect the themes of love and death in the ineffable realm of night:

*Noch weckst du, muntres Licht,
den Müden zur Arbeit – flößest
fröhliches Leben mir ein – aber
du lockst mich von der
Erinnerung moosigern Denkmal
nicht. Aber getreu der Nacht
bleibt mein geheimes Herz, und
der schaffenden Liebe, ihrer
Tochter.*

*Happy Light, you wake me
yet again, you summon my weary
body to work – you instil in me
life and joy – but you will not
tear me away from the mossy
stone of memory. But my heart,
inside me, remains
dedicated to the Night
and to her daughter,
creative Love.*

Novalis,
Hymnen an die Nacht

The contemplation of the night, the moon and the stars inspires Musset, Shelley, Mácha, Hölderlin and Ludwig Tieck (1773–1853), and becomes a pretext for sentimental or meditative poetry. Other poetic leitmotifs are sky, woods, mountains, wind and autumn, 'season of mists and mellow fruitfulness', for Keats.

Słowacki associates a description of Alpine beauty with an elegy of love in *K Szwajcarji* (*To Switzerland*). The pantheist Shelley, seduced by exoticism and fascinated by the grandeur of the Alps, sings of his poetic ideal of beauty, freedom and the absolute in the symbolic poem *Mont Blanc*. The mountains also inspired Byron, Hugo and Lermontov: the latter saw a symbol of beauty and freedom in the Caucasus. What matters, however, is not the beauty of the landscape, but the freshness of the gaze directed at it and its hitherto unsuspected horizons. Poems by the Hungarian Petöfi describe landscape in a simple, poignant way. The Rumanian Vasile Alecsandri (1821–1890), who reconciled Western influence with the rural tradition of his country, whose rehabilitation and revival he himself began, described in almost Virgilian fashion a winter landscape in *Paintings in Pastels*, 1868–1870.

Political poetry

Political lyricism, exalting the homeland's past greatness and exhorting it to independence and freedom, was born in Spain under the Napoleonic yoke, before becoming established in France, Germany, Italy, Poland, Hungary and Greece. Most of these poems predate the Romantic period and fall into the neo-classical vein, like *Pavec vo stane russkih voïnov* (*Bard in the Camp of Russian Warriors*, 1812) by Zhukovsky, and Manzoni's patriotic odes to Italy. Others are Romantic to varying degrees, like the sonnets contained in *Slávy dcera* (*Sláva's Daughter*), by the Slovak **Ján Kollár (1793–1852)**, the poems by his compatriot Ján Hólly (1785–1852) or the odes *I lira* (*The Lyre*, 1824) and *Lirica* (*Lyrics*, 1826) by the Greek **Andréas Kalvos (1792–1869)**. These are a patriotic exaltation of freedom and, under their old-fashioned form, spark off Romantic lyricism and fervour. The syntheses of his fellow countryman **Dionysos Solomos (1798–1857)**, *O Kritikos* (*The Cretan*), *I eleftheri Poliorkimeni* (*The Besieged at Liberty*, 1834–1844) and *O Porfiras* (*Porphyras*), published after his death, are Romantic in their

patriotism, their realism, their fragmentary character. Written in Demotic Greek, they constitute a 'mixed but legal genre', in which Romantic inspiration is clothed in a sober, pure form, in which the moral and the sublime coincide with the beautiful. In contrast to this tradition of the Ionian isles, a Romantic school sprang up in Athens which carried on the poetic traditions of the Pharnariotes and used the katharevussa. This same patriotic sentiment dominated poetry by the Serb Radicevič, the Croat Petar Preradovic (1811–1872), the Bulgarian Dobri Čintulo (1823–1836) and the Slovaks Janko Král (1822–1876) and Ján Botto (1829–1881). Poems by Hugo, Pushkin – the author of political epigrams and odes to liberty – and Leopardi, the author of the ode *All'Italia* (*To Italy*, 1818), were more creative and more personal.

Democratic inspiration and belief in human solidarity appear in work by Shelley, Petöfi and Hugo, and in the Swede Erik Gustaf Geijer (1783–1847), the author of *Odalbonden* (*The Peasant of Alen*, 1811). In the vein of liberal and humanitarian Romanticism, the Junge Deutschland (Young Germany) movement, stifled for many years by censorship, appears belatedly because of the dominance of the bourgeois Romanticism expressed by Biedermeier. Opposed to this liberal Romanticism, the Dutchman Bilderdijk warned against the consequences of the French Revolution.

Everyday poetry

Romantic poetry tackled new themes or ones that had been neglected for many years. Wordsworth introduced the description of familiar and rustic realities into poetry, whose poetic value was revealed to him while he was in the country. It is not so much poetry that is realistic, but a poetry that is intimate, in which the poet's sensitivity dominates and seeks to move the reader by revealing the soul of the everyday.

In The Netherlands, poetry by Hendrik Tollens (1780–1856) celebrated the home and childhood. The ballads by this patriotic poet offer an image of the themes that poets preferred to treat between 1800 and 1830: exalted and sentimental love, simple family life. The Flemish-speaking Belgian **Hendrik Conscience (1812–1883)** wrote rustic idylls. We rediscover the famous *When I was a Child*, originally by the Dane Baggesen, in the idealised vision of childhood contained in the beginnings of Swedish poetry (Atterbom). Hölderlin conjured up the happiness of childhood in *Da ich ein Knabe war* (*When I was a Child*). This theme reverberates through work by Hugo and the nostalgic Zhukovsky. In Hungary, the themes of the countryside and the family are broached by a whole poetry of popular inspiration, notably by **Sándor Petöfi (1823–1849)** in his intimate poems. A visionary and a revolutionary, the most Rimbaud-like figure of Romanticism, Petöfi, haunted as he is by the spirit of uncompromising freedom, conjures out of everyday events a world of dreams and nightmares.

Epic–lyric poetry

The success of old literary forms, which owe to their nature as folklore their rootedness in a collective culture, rests on the attraction of an idealised past, elevated to the rank of Eden by Ossianism. This is one of the most virulent reactions to the style imposed by neo-classicism: the folk element versus the aristocratic; spontaneity and the intermingling of genres versus respect for rules; the fantastic and the idyllic versus the likely and the probable.

The principal sources of inspiration for this poetry were the Scandinavian sagas, the Spanish romancero, newly adapted to current taste by **Angel de Saavedra, Duque de Rivas (1791–1843)** in *El moro expósito* (*The Moorish Bastard*, 1834), which relates the history of Lara's children; the English work of Robert Southey (1774–1843), *Roderick, the Last of the Goths* (1814), and the Scottish verse novels of **Walter Scott (1771–1832)**,* tales of love and war set in the world of Scottish chivalry, *Marmion* (1808) and *The Lady of the Lake* (1810):

> *Ellen, I am no courtly lord,*
> *But one who lives by lance and sword,*
> *Whose castle is his helm and shield,*
> *His lordship the embattled ship.*
> *What from a prince can I demand,*
> *Who neither reck of state nor land?*
>
> Walter Scott,
> *The Lady of the Lake*

These works had a considerable influence, notably on Garrett, who wrote *Dona Bronca* (1826), an epic tale unfolding at a period of Arab domination.

We must not overlook the attraction exerted by the world of oriental legends, as in *Thalaba the Destroyer* (1801) by Southey, and in the works of **Alexander Pushkin (1799–1837)**★ and of Lermontov. There is also the attraction of the fantastic or imaginary as in *The Rime of the Ancient Mariner* from *Lyrical Ballads* (1798) by **Samuel Taylor Coleridge (1772–1834)**; of the medieval as in most of Tennyson's poems inspired by the cycle of King Arthur and the Knights of the Round Table. *El Estudiante de Salamanca* (1836) was by Espronceda associates, in a poem of historical and medieval inspiration, the myth of Don Juan with satanism, the perversity of Felix de Montemar with the anguish of the infinite:

Segundo Lucifer que se levanta	*Secondly Lucifer, who gets up,*
del rayo vengador la frente herida,	*His brow wounded with vengeful lightning,*
alma rebelde que el temor no espanta,	*A rebellious spirit who does not fear fear,*
hollada sí, pero jamás vencida:	*Trampled down but never vanquished:*
el hombre en fin que en su ansiedad quebranta	*Man finally who in his anguish breaks*
su límite a la cárcel de la vida,	*The walls of life's prison,*

> *y a Dios llama ante . . . l a darle*
> *cuenta,*
> *y descubrir su inmensidad*
> *intenta.*

José de Espronceda,
El Estudiante de Salamanca

> *who asks accounts of*
> *God,*
> *And tries to discover his*
> *immensity.*

The passions and crimes described by Byron in *The Corsair* (1814) and *The Bride of Abydos* (1813) were equally typical of this period. In Serb and Croatian literature, the theme of the fight against the Turks was reinserted into Romantic epics such as *Gorsk Vijenac* (*The Garland of the Mountains*, 1847) by Njegoš, who paraded therein several centuries of national history, and *Smrt Smail-Aga Cengica* (*The Death of Smail-Aga Cengic*, 1857) by the Croat **Ivan Mažuranič (1814–1890)**. In Hungary and Poland, ballads and epic tales became a national genre based on ancient history: *Zalán futása* (*The Flight of Zalán*, 1825), for example, by the Hungarian **Mihály Vörösmarty (1800–1855)**, was an evocation of Hungary's conquest.

In works from Scandinavian, Slavic and Germanic countries, the heroes of Nordic mythology again become popular and serve as a counterpoint to a society which was considered evil. In Sweden, **Esaias Tegnér (1782–1846)**, in the *Frithiof Saga* (1825), returned to the Icelandic epic: the twenty-four lyrical cantos of his poem present a picture of the Northmen with their pirate lifestyle, popular assemblies and pagan worship. In Finland, **Johan Ludwig Runeberg (1804–1877)** wrote *Fänrik Ståls sägner* (*Tales of Ensign Staal*, 1848–1860), a cycle of romances describing Finnish resistance to invasion in 1808. The legendary themes of the Scandinavian sagas inspired the ballads by the German **Ludwig Uhland (1787–1862)**, by Lermontov, by the Dutchman Tollens and by the Italian Giovanni Prati (1814–1884).

In Poland, **Adam Mickiewicz (1798–1855)*** made his presence felt with *Konrad Wallenrod* (1828), a poem whose action takes place in Lithuania, and *Pan Tadeusz* (*Sir Thaddeus*, 1834), part national epic, part historical novel. In the Czech lands, **František Ladislav Čelakovský (1799–1852)** collected Slav folk poetry, taking his inspiration from it in *Ohlas písní ruských* (*An Echo of Russian Songs*, 1829), which has a predominantly epic and heroic note, and in *Ohlas písní čestých* (*An Echo of Czech Songs*, 1839), with a lyric and satirical note. **Karel Jaromír Erben (1811–1871)** goes deeply into folk poetry in the ballads of his collection *Kytice* (*Garland*, 1853). In Germany, the late Romantic, Friedrich de La Motte-Fouqué (1777–1843) made his contribution to this genre with a chivalrous epic that unfolds in the idyllic and Germanic world of the Middle Ages (*Rittergedichte*, *Poems of Chivalry*).

The Spanish Romancero is also a reflection of a mythical Middle Ages, the time of the Cid, of the Infantes de Lara, of doughty knights and virtuous damsels. The worthy Count Benavente belonged to this golden age of honour and speaks in the following terms to Emperor Charles V:

> *Soy, señor, vuestro vasallo;*
> *vos sois mi Rey en la tierra,*
> *a vos ordenar os cumple*
> *de mi vida y de mi hacienda.*
> *Vuestro soy, vuestra mi casa,*
> *de mi disponed y de ella,*
> *pero no toquéis mi honra*
> *y respetad mi conciencia.*

The Duke of Rivas, *Romances históricos*

> *I am, sir, your vassal;*
> *You are my King on earth,*
> *it is for you to order*
> *my life and my affairs.*
> *I belong to you, my house*
> *is yours.*
> *It and I are yours to dispose of,*
> *but do not offend my honour*
> *and respect my conscience.*

By their popular character, these works favoured literary creation in languages until then reserved for oral communication. In this spirit the emancipated former serf Taras Grigorievitch Chevtchenko (1814–1861) wrote a collection of poems in Ukrainian *Kobzar* (*The Juggler*, 1840), an evocation of the Ukraine's popular past, which was already a place for social criticism. By composing the *Kalevala* (1835), a long poem inspired by myths and legends, the Finnish poet **Elias Lönnrot (1802–1884)** gave to Finnish its letters patent of nobility and its national poem:

Noita saamia sanoja,	*These are the words of our heritage,*
Virsiä virittämiä	*runes turned with the baldric*
Vyöltä vanhan Väinämöinen,	*of old Väinämöinen,*
Alta ahjon Ilmarinen,	*under the forge of Ilmarinen,*
Päästä kalvan Kaukomielen,	*the sword of Lemminkäinen,*
Joukahaisen jousen tiestä,	*the bow of Joukahainen*
Pohjan peltojen periltä,	*right at the bottom of the fields of Pohja,*
Kalevalan kankahilta.	*the moors of Kalevala.*

Elias Lönnrot,
Kalevala

The Renaissance of the Norwegian language, the mortar of nationalism, was helped by popular Norwegian tales written by Peter Christen Asbjørnsen (1812–1885) and Jørgen Ingelbrechtsen (1813–1882), working in collaboration with each other, as well as the work of the grammarian Ivar Aasen (1813–1896). The versification and the demotic Greek used in Greek popular songs, edited by Fauriel in 1824 influenced Solomos' poetry. They were the basic element in neo-Hellenic ideology and literature.

Belgium achieved independence in 1830. Literature became a political instrument no longer destined to defend the struggle against the oppressor, but to encourage nationalism, already well established. Belgian Romanticism placed itself at the service of the nationalist ideology of the ruling class. The Duke of Brabant, the future Leopold II, put it in these terms: 'Literary glory is the crowning glory of any national edifice.' Writers were pleased to describe a rediscovered past and plead in favour of a free Belgium. Popular education and the national emancipation of Flanders were the first objectives of Flemish writers, and foreign literary influences were looked at askance. As a consequence, the great European currents of thought only had a moderate influence, the priority being given to socio-logical criteria. Jan Frans Willems (1793–1846), who wrote and promoted Flemish, was a key figure in the Flemish movement. The first generation of Flemish writers were essentially scholars and philologists, centred on Ghent. Their literary production bore the stamp of pseudo-classicism, as much in its themes and mythological sources as in its form. The most Romantic figure of all was, perhaps, the poet Karel Lodewijk Ledeganck (1805–1847), author of *De drie Zustersteden* (*The Three Sister Towns*, 1846), written to the glory of Ghent, Bruges and Antwerp.

'Primitive times were *lyrical*, ancient times were *epic*, modern times are *dramatic*,' declared Victor Hugo in his provocative preface to *Cromwell* (1827). In fact, the theatre, together with poetry, was the literary genre in which the Romantics introduced the greatest number of innovations.

THE ROMANTIC THEATRE

The Romantic theatre required a radical shift in direction. It needed either to create a form of dramatic art compatible with the new Romantic spirit, or to overhaul completely the rules of the genre.

The dramatic poem

Innovation in the theatre began with works which, for practical reasons, could not be performed: dramatic poems, fantastic dramas or historical tragedies. These ignored the problems of staging and gave free rein to fantasy, following the example of Goethe's *Faust*. The themes vary. In Slav countries, the homeland is the central theme of plays by Mickiewicz, *Dziady* (*Ancestors*, 1832) and by Zygmunt Krasiński (1812–1859), *Nie-Boska Komedia* (*The Non-Divine Comedy*, 1835), prophetic dramas in highly pessimistic poetic prose. In others, the hero's passions stem from the anxious, even tormented soul of the poet. In *Manfred* (1817) and *Cain*, Faustian and symbolic poems, Byron hides his own spirit of revolt, his deep solitude and his massive ego behind the Titanic dimensions of his heroes. Musset's theatre, 'a show in an armchair', written only to be read, seems to contradict the very essence of the dramatic genre. His *Lorenzaccio* (1834), however, portrays a rebel who abases himself to save Florence, his home town. Inspired by the myth of the Titan punished for his rebellion and love of humanity, *Prometheus Unbound* (1820) by Shelley expounds the author's atheism and desire to see justice done in the purest poetic style. Thus, the dramatic poem gave birth to a series of legends like *Faust* (1836) by Lenau and *Don Juan und Faust* (1829) by the German Christian Grabbe (1801–1836).

The fantastic or legendary drama, characteristic of Scandinavian countries, found its inspiration in folklore, local mythology, the Middle Ages and oriental tales. With its sentimentalism, fantasy and sumptuous backdrops, this genre was the perfect antithesis of the neo-classical spirit. *Aladdin eller den forunderlige Lampe* (*Aladdin or the Wonderful Lamp*, 1805), by the Dane **Adam Oehlenschläger (1779–1850)**, brings together exoticism and mystery:

Aladdin embodied the inspired poet, the lamp the genius of intuition which reveals all treasures. Scandinavian mythology inspired *Der Held des Nordens* (*The Hero of the North*, 1808–1810) by La Motte-Fouqué. The dramatic poem and metaphysical tale *Csongor és Tünde* (*Csongor and Tünde*, 1831) by the Hungarian Vörösmarty is the story of two lovers and their quest for love pursued in spite of the harmful influence of Mirigy the witch.

Historical or pseudo-historical tragedies are another stage in the renewal of the drama. These are dramas inspired by Shakespeare plays and by the Spanish golden age, where the combination of passion and exoticism produced plays that were strictly Romantic in character. In 1844, **José Zorrilla (1817–1893)** put on *Don Juan Tenorio*, a marvellous conservative version of the myth of the seducer. In Italy, tragedy was closely linked to the ideas of the Risorgimento – political censorship forbad the performance of certain plays by Giambattista Niccolini (1782–1861) – which all writers respected. Even though he did not succeed in applying all his theories in his works, **Alessandro Manzoni (1785–1873)** explained his ambition to write a historical tragedy in a 1822 letter addressed to the French critic Victor Chauvet, who had objected to the overly great liberty taken in *Il Conte di Carmagnola* (*The Count of Carmagnola*, 1816–1820) from the standpoint of French theatre. In this letter, for Manzoni, the only thing that will pass muster is a historical tragedy in its entirety, which has to reflect man's innermost feelings and passions. In *Adelchi* (1820–1822), which retraced the defeat, destitution and execution of Desiderio, King of the Lombards, Manzoni managed to apply some of his theories: he does not adhere to the historical facts, but offers a lyrical, desperate vision of life. Before he dies, Adelchi says to Desiderio:

Godi che re non sei, godi che chiusa
all'oprar t'é ogni via; loco a gentile,

Be glad you are no longer king, be glad you no longer have to act when there is nothing generous or innocent to be done,

> ad innocente opra non v'é;
> non resta
> che far torto o partirlo.

Alessandro Manzoni, *Adelchi*

> when all one can do is to suffer
> evil or commit it.

We find the same inspiration in the Czech lands with Mácha, in Hungary with József Katona (1791–1830), in his tragedy with overtones of Hamlet *Bánk bán* (1819), in England with *Hellas* (1821) by Shelley, and poems by Byron, in Germany with Eichendorff and von Platen.

Historical drama

European theatre did not really wake up until the years between 1820 and 1850, through the mediation of the historical drama. This was the ideal vehicle for political dissidence and patriotic pride before the invader, and a theatrical form perfectly adapted to the stage. So, at a in time when the theatre of the post-Renaissance and the Baroque theatre of Shakespeare, Lope de Vega and Calderón were fashionable again, we note a clear break with neo-classicism.

In the German-speaking lands, **Heinrich von Kleist (1777–1811)** wrote his last drama, *Der Prinz von Homburg* (*The Prince of Homburg*) in 1811, opposing to the young sleepwalker of a prince in love, disobeying orders, the strict defender of the law. **Franz Grillparzer (1791–1872)**, the Austrian author of *König Ottokars Glück und Ende* (*The Good Fortune and End of King Ottokar*, 1823), introduces an unscrupulous prince who comes up against a just and generous monarch. We find works in the same vein in Denmark with *Palnatoke* (1807) by Oehlenschläger, in Sweden with Carl A. Nicander, 1799–1839, in Russia with *Boris Godunov* (1825) by Pushkin, a Shakespearean tragedy inspired by an aesthetic and philosophical reflection on the nation's past, and in Poland with *Kordian* (1834) by Słowacki, heavily

influenced by Calderón, whose work illustrates the struggle of the people against its oppressors.

If the Romantic movement appeared later in France than in England and Germany, it was because of the political situation: the first edition of *De l'Allemagne*, by Germaine Necker, Baroness de Staël (1766–1817), was destroyed. It only reappeared in France after the fall of Napoleon, who only swore by the literature of the 'Ancien Régime'. The neo-classical tradition was more solidly rooted in France than anywhere else. It was only after the first performance of Hugo's *Hernani* (1830) that the genre of the historical drama took permanent root there. The first performance of the play was a notorious scandal: the audience, accustomed to classical plays, were shocked by the provocative nature of the new play. If it took time to establish itself, French historical drama nevertheless inspired Spanish, Hungarian and Italian dramatists. So works by Vörösmarty imitated those by Hugo in their smallest details. The late appearance of the historical drama in Spain was caused by the censorship imposed by Ferdinand VII, an absolute monarch: we have to wait for the homecoming of liberals exiled in France and England for Romantic literature to gain a right of abode in Spain. In 1830, Martínez de la Rosa (1787–1862) had a success with *Aben Humeya*, but it was in 1835, with the performance of *Don Alvaro o la fuerza del sino* (*Don Alvaro or the Force of Destiny*) by the Duque de Rivas, that the genre became a part of Spanish life. The play's theme is the drama of destiny or 'fatum', a genre created by the German Tieck in 1795, then taken up by the Dutchman Van der Loop. Man is subject to the fate that governs his life.

> ¡Qué eternidad tan horrible
> la breve vida! ¡Este mundo,
> qué calabozo profundo

> How horrid is our
> short life's eternity! And what
> a deep dungeon

para el hombre desdichado *a quien mira el cielo airado* *con su ceño furibundo!*	*is this world* *for the unhappy man* *an angry sky observes* *furrowing its brows!*

The Duke of Rivas,
Don Alvaro o la fuerza del sino

Romantic drama had many successes despite its cohabitation with neo-classical dramatic genres. In the Czech lands, the 'national revival' movement gained ground until 1849 (the year which marked the beginning of an ultra-reactionary regime, which mocked censorship and Metternich's police state). **Josef Kajetán Tyl (1808–1856)** wrote many historical plays, among which were *Jan Hus* (1848) and a play which relates the life of the miners of Kutná Hora, literary expressions of his liberal and democratic ideas. In Portugal the civil wars and the internal politics of Don Miguel forced many men of letters into exile. It was not until they returned that

Romanticism found its literary niche. Though Garrett, in 1820, had tried to adapt the theories of German Romanticism disseminated by Madame de Staël, we must await the founding of the Conservatory, in 1839, to be there when Romantic theatre finally triumphed in Portugal. The Portuguese Romantic drama took its inspiration essentially from national history. There are cases, however, when the plot strayed from historical veracity and let itself be swayed by expressions of emotion. *Frei Luís de Sousa* (*Brother Luis de Sousa*, 1844), for instance, based on the theme of fatality, ends on these words:

¿Que Deus é este que está nesse *altar e quer roubar o pai e a mãe* *a sua filha? (Para os* *circunstantes.) ¿Vós quem sois,* *espectros fatais? ¿Quereis-mos* *tirar dos meus braços? . . . Esta é* *a minha mãe, este é o meu pai . . .* *¿Que me importa a mim com o* *outro, que morresse ou não, que* *esteja com os mortos ou com os* *vivos, que se fique na cova ou* *que ressuscite agora para me* *matar?*	*What is this God on this* *altar who wants to deprive a* *father and a mother of their* *daughter? (To the altar boys) And* *you, who are you, fatal* *spectres?. . .* *You want to tear them from my* *arms? . . . Here is my mother, here* *is my father . . . What do I have to do* *with the Other? Dead or not,* *with the living or the dead, let him* *stay in his grave, or let him come* *back to life now to kill me! . . .*

João Baptista de Almeida Garrett,
Frei Luís de Sousa

The bourgeois drama and the Romantic comedy

Strange as it may seem, contemporary themes held little interest for dramatists, while the historical drama swept on to momentous success. This was perhaps because the themes of daily life were more systematically associated with the novel. Apart from that, the past haloes events with mystery, particularly fitting for dramatic purposes, while reality limits

fantasy, lyricism and dreams. The bourgeois drama almost disappeared during this period, only to reappear under a new light in the middle of the nineteenth century.

Romantic comedy can be historical, folkloric or poetic. It is sometimes the fruit of an unbounded, overflowing imagination, as in *Der gestiefelte Kater* (*Puss-in-Boots*, 1797) by Tieck, the epitome of Romantic irony. It is sometimes satire on contemporary society, as in *Revizor* (*The Government Inspector*, 1836) by

413

Nikolaï Vasilyvitch Gogol (1809–1852),* and *Gorie ot ouma* (*The Misfortune of Having Too Much Wit*, 1822) by **Alexander Sergeivitch Griboyedov (1785–1829)**. Under a classical exterior, this play is resolutely modern in its association of sentimental intrigue with a satire on manners, thus announcing the advent of realism. Written in free verse, it made use of the rhythmical resources and vigour of spoken Russian and acted as a vehicle for the protests of the Decembrists. In his comedies (*Tvrdica ili Janja, Tartuffe*, 1837), **Jovan Sterija Popović (1806–1856)** depicted the manners of the newly arrived middle classes, thus opening the door to Serbian realism. Tyl owes his reputation to his comedies and farces derived from fairy-tales and everyday life: *Fidlovačka* (*The Cobblers' Fair*, 1834), in which, for the first time, we hear the song *Kde domov můj? Where is my Country?* which became Serbia's national anthem.

In Italy, the most fashionable theatrical genres were the melodrama and operas by Bellini, Donizetti, Rossini and Verdi. These account for the Italian Romantic sensibility better than any other art form.

THE NOVEL: THE MODERN BOURGEOIS EPIC

The renewal of dramatic and poetic genres had happened via a total break with the past, but for the art of narration it was quite different, with the possible exception of the historical novel, the archetypal Romantic genre. In Germany, France and England, where the novel occupied the high ground in the literary production of the eighteenth century, it would be more accurate to talk about a process of evolution. But in countries without a true novel tradition, the development of the novel in the framework of Romanticism was like a revolution.

On the other hand, we can speak of a break to the extent that the hierarchy of literary genres found itself turned upside-down. Despised by classical writers for its lack of artistic rigour, the novel henceforth became the centre of attention. In *Vorlesungen über die Aesthetik* (*Lectures on Aesthetics*, 1820–1829), Hegel defined it as the 'modern bourgeois epic': a genre which simultaneously reflected an individual's story and a global, organic world vision. This characteristic may explain the success of the genre and its prodigious development from the beginning of the century. The novel had to adapt to new sensibilities, be conceived of subjectively and give rise to new narrative forms. The ambition expressed by Hugo in the preface to *Cromwell* – to make of drama a total genre – was realised in the novel, which embraced all genres and gave an overall image of the real. So the claim for artistic freedom seems to have found in the novel its favourite means of expressing. On the margin of impersonal stories, the intimate novel and the novel of escapism (exotic or fantastic) particularly lend themselves to the direct, intense expression of the passions which animated the Romantic soul. Because of this, they met with increasing success.

The intimist novel

The intimist novel, heir to the eighteenth-century tradition of sentimentality, brought into the realm of fiction its author's real-world experience. This kind of novel was usually presented in an autobiographical and epistolary form. The way is opened by *Werther*, whose narrative technique – the journal – was an example to be imitated when it came to exploring the human soul: *Lucinda* (1799), for example, a subjective novel by Friedrich von Schlegel, *Godwi* (1801), a novel about barbarians by **Clemens Brentano (1778–1842)**, and *Ultime lettere di Jacopo Ortis* (*The Last Letters of Jacopo Ortis*, 1798), an intimist novel by **Ugo Foscolo (1778–1827)**.

26 ottobre	*26 October*
L'ho veduta o Lorenzo, la divina fanciulla, e te ne ringrazio. La	*I have seen her, Lorenzo, the divine child, and I thank you. I*

trovai seduta, miniando il propio ritratto. Si rizzò salutandomi como s'ella mi conoscesse, e oridinò a un servitore che andasse a cercare di suo padre. [. . .] Io tornavo a casa col cuore in festa. – Che? lo spettacolo della bellezza basta forse ad addormentare in noi tristi mortali tutti i dolori? Vedi per me una sorgente di vita: unica certo, e chi sa! Fatale. Ma se io sono predestinato ad avere l'anima perpetuamente in tempesta, non è tutt'uno?

Ugo Foscolo,
Ultime lettere di Jacopo Ortis

found her sitting down, embellishing her own portrait. She got up, welcomed me as if she had always known me, then sent a servant in search of her father. [. . .] And I went back home, my heart rejoicing. What? Might the spectacle of beauty be enough to placate all our sufferings, poor mortals that we are? That is for me a source of life, the only one, assuredly, and who knows? Fatal perhaps! But if my fate has destined me to perpetual inner storms, is it not all one?

The intimist novel was very successful in France, thanks to Étienne de Senancour (1770–1846), the author of *Oberman* (1804), an introspective novel in the form of a monologue in letters and a symbol of the *'mal du siècle'*, and to Madame de Staël, the author of *Delphine* (1802), a long epistolary novel with feminist overtones; last but not least, to **François René de Chateaubriand (1768–1848)**. *René* (1802) was a pathetic confession in which the author relived his youth and described the ravages 'a wave of passions' can provoke.

> But how can I express that crowd of fleeting sensations that I felt on my walks? [. . .]
>
> Sometimes I should have liked to have been one of those warriors wandering through winds, clouds and ghosts; sometimes I would envy the shepherd I saw warming his hands at the humble brushwood fire he had lit at the edge of a wood. I listened to his melancholy songs, which reminded me that, in every country, the singing of the natural man is sad, even when it expresses happiness.
>
> The sounds that passions make in the void of a solitary heart resemble the murmur that winds and waters generate in the silence of a desert; we enjoy them, but we cannot depict them.
>
> François René de Chateaubriand, *René*

These works, which associate the cult of nature with Romanticism, the pathetic, the revolt against society, psychological introspection, the inner development of characters, even the defence of a thesis, determined the rules of the genre. *Geroi nashego vremyeni* (*A Hero of Our Time*, 1840), by Lermontov, is a collection of five stories. Its main character is Petchorin, cold yet passionate, cruel yet generous, described from a variety of viewpoints. The dramatic intensity of situations, the precision of psychological analysis, the authenticity and the variety of characters make this work a masterpiece of Russian literature. Garrett, in *Viagens na Minha Terra* (*Travels in My Country*, 1846), mingles the description of nature and immediate reality, and the evocation of an intimate drama in a simple and flexible style. At the same time as his poetic work, Mácha published short novels: *Marinka* (1834) and *Cikáni* (*The Gypsies*, 1835). The Hungarian **Jozsef Eötvös (1813–1873)** published the novel which made him famous, *A karthusi* (*The Carthusian*, 1839). Mixing psychological analysis and Romantic themes, Aurore Dupin, better known as **George Sand (1804–1876)**, wrote her first novels in passionate defence of women and love, denouncing social inequalities and the hypocrisy of marriage: *Indiana* and *Valentine* (1832), *Lelia* (1833). This literary feminism aroused the most extreme reactions, ranging from passionate enthusiasm to total condemnation. Their polemical tone went some way to explaining the success of these novels in Europe and their influence on Polish, Russian and Spanish writers.

The exotic novel and the fantastic tale

The ceaseless search for escape routes from everyday life took fiction in the direction of the exotic and the fantastic – even the horrible. The exotic vein had already been tapped by English and German writers, but only as a pretext for tales of intrigue and passionate adventures. *Colomba* (1840) by **Prosper Mérimée (1803–1870)**, took place in Corsica; and *Carmen* (1845) describes an ardent and subjective Spain. Pushkin fits into this category, and Lermontov sets the scene of his tales in the Caucasus.

Other literary genres facilitate such escapism: there were folk legends, mixtures of the supernatural and the marvellous which, before giving birth to the fantastic tale, were the prerogative of poetry. Although the Frenchman **Charles Nodier (1783–1844)** is considered to be the precursor of the genre with *Smarra or the Demons of the Night* (1821) and *Trilby* (1822), this genre was developed, above all, by German and Danish writers, inspired by Nordic legends. The tales of the Dane **Hans Christian Andersen (1805–1875),*** of the **Brothers Grimm (Jacob, 1785–1863**, and **Wilhelm, 1786–1859)** and of Hoffmann are known throughout the world. **Ernst Theodor Amadeus Hoffmann (1776–1822)** had a very personal sense of fantasy. In his tales, the apparently real world, becomes excited under the influence of a never very clearly defined magic and the self is embodied in several characters: *Die Elixiere des Teufels* (*The Devil's Elixir*, 1816), *Der Doppelgänger* (*The Double*), *Lebensansichten des Katers Murr* (*Tomcat Murr*, 1820–1822) and *Der goldene Topf* (*The Golden Pot*, 1814). Here there is a world of dreams, of caricatures, of misshapen beings and of extraordinary facts. However, the progressive adoption of a more intellectual type of humour prepared the ground for realism.

> Yes, run, go on – keep running – fiend – you'll fall – on glass – it's in the order of things!
>
> Hoffmann,
> *The Golden Pot*

Among German writers of fantastic tales, La Motte-Fouqué recreated the myth of the siren who lived and loved like other women in *Undine* (1811). **Adalbert von Chamisso (1781–1838)**, in *Peter Schlemihls wundersame Geschichte* (*The Wonderful Story of Peter Schlemihl*, 1814), presents a hero who sells his soul to the devil to realise his craziest desires. Tieck, a forerunner of the genre, collects folktales with fantastic elements (*Volksmärchen*, *Folk Tales*, 1796–1799). He is close to the marvellous world of dreams of Novalis' lyrical novel *Heinrich von Ofterdingen* (1802), which tells the story of a prince in search of the inaccessible 'blue flower', a symbol of Romantic irony and desire.

In Večeri na čatore bliz Dikan'ki (*Village Evenings near Dikanka*, 1831) by Gogol, the descriptions in lyrical prose in no way detract from the picturesque virtuosity of the narrator's chatter, the bee-keeper Ginger Panko. It is an exotic and stylised Ukraine, where witches and demons rub shoulders with ordinary people, who are shown to us in a fantastic and humorous style full of original touches.

In England, horror stories and Gothic tales multiplied, novels dominated by the theme of the forces of the occult and death. *The Monk* (1796) by Gregory Lewis (1775–1818) and *Frankenstein or the Modern Prometheus* (1818) by Mary Shelley (1797–1851).

> When, by the dim and yellow light of the moon, as it forced its way through the window shutters, I beheld the wretch – the miserable monster whom I had created. He held up the curtain of the bed; and his eyes, if eyes they may be called, were fixed on me. His jaws opened, and he muttered some inarticulate sounds, while a grin wrinkled his cheeks. He might have spoken, but I did not hear; one

hand was stretched out, seemingly to detain me, but I escaped, and rushed downstairs.

Mary Shelley, *Frankenstein*

The historical novel

The birth and circulation of the historical novel in Europe were motivated by the same reasons as the appearance of the historical drama. The historical novel was a narrative genre which found its inspiration in patriotic and medieval themes, without always showing respect for the truth, and integrating these themes with passionate love stories. Walter Scott created this genre in 1814 with *Waverley*, published anonymously, and he made use of it until he died. *Ivanhoe* (1820) was situated in a traditional, remote Middle Ages, while *Old Mortality* (1816) and *The Heart of Midlothian* (1818) described more recent periods in Scottish history. Maria Edgeworth (1767–1849), a friend of the Scottish writer, set out to paint a portrait of life in Ireland in *Castle Rackrent* (1800). Inspired by popular ballads and faithful to historical truth, novels by the Dane Bernhard Severin Ingemann (1789–1862) were devoted to the great period of the Valdemars. France was quick to imitate Walter Scott: *Cinq-Mars* (1826) by Vigny, *Chronicle of the Time of Charles IX* (1829) by Mérimée, *The Chouans* by **Honoré de Balzac (1799–1850)**,* *Notre-Dame de Paris* by Hugo. If they were dubious historically, the novels by **Alexandre Dumas (1802–1870)**, *The Three Musketeers* (1844) and *The Count of Monte-Cristo* (1846), achieved great popular success.

In The Netherlands, the historical novel followed an extraordinary trajectory. *Het leven van Maurits Lijnslager* (*The Life of Maurits Lijnslager* (1808) by **Adriaan Loosjes (1761–1818)**, an unusual novel whole story takes place in the seventeenth century, was the first example of the genre. But it is only after 1830 that we can truly talk about the Romantic historical novel, with works by Geertruida

Bosboom-Toussaint (1812–1886), as well as works by Jacob Van Lennep (1802–1868): *Het huis Lauernesse* (1840), drawn against a background of the Reformation, and *Ferdinand Huyck* (1840), devoted to the life of eighteenth-century patricians.

A particular treatment must be retained for countries in which Romanticism is a synonym for the defence of patriotism. In moments of oppression, the echo of far-distant history returns – notably in Italy, Poland, Hungary, Bohemia and Slovakia – to raise aloft the standard of liberty, for example with the Hungarian **Miklós Josika (1791–1865)**, who wrote more than 125 volumes. He had great success after the appearance of his first historical novel (*Zoliomi*, 1836). The Polish novelist **Josef Ignacy Krasewski (1812–1887)** was considered to be the creator of the historical novel in Poland. **Henryk Rzewuski (1791–1866)**, Madame Hanska's brother describes in an amusing way the court of Stanislas Augustus in *Pamiąpki Soplicy* (*The Memoirs of Severin Soplica*, 1839). Manzoni, in his novel *I promessi sposi* (*The Betrothed*, 1827), re-created the Lombardy of 1630 – then under Spanish domination – starving and ravaged by the plague. The story does not focus on aristocratic characters, portrayed in all their moral decadence, nor great historical events, but rather on humble folk, like the two peasants who eventually marry after a series of setbacks, described against the background of momentous events. Manzoni's aim is clear: he needs to defend the Risorgimento. However, his knowledge of the French Revolution made him distrust rebellion and the use of force. His books are not exempt from a certain classical paternalism – springing perhaps from his noble forebears – of liberalism and moralism, which make him the incarnation of the Italian liberal Catholic. So in the story of a Milan riot, which the Spanish governor Ferrer tries to negotiate:

S'aiutava dunque co' gesti, ora mettendo la punta delle mani sulle labbra, a prendere un bacio

He needed to help himself with this gesture, and that is what he did, sometimes by putting the tips of his

che le mani, separandosi subito, distribuivano a destra e a sinistra in ringraziamento alla pubblica benevolenza; ora stendendole e movendole lentamente fuori d'uno sportello, per chiedere un po' di luogo; ora abbassandole garbatamente, per chiedere un po' di silenzio. Quando m'aveva ottenuto un poco, i più vicini sentivano e ripetevano le sue parole: 'pane; abbondanza; vengo a far giustizia; un po' di luogo di grazia.'

Alessandro Manzoni,
I promessi sposi

fingers on his lips to take there a kiss which his fingers, immediately open again, distributed to right and left to pay back public benevolence; sometimes by stretching his hands out and waving them out of the carriage doors slowly, to ask for a little room, sometimes lowering them with a gracious air to solicit a bit of silence. When he had obtained some, those who were nearest to him heard and repeated his words: 'Bread; abundance; I come to do justice; a little more room, please.'

Russia constituted a case apart, because of its censorship. After the death of Alexander I in 1825, Nicholas I came to power – the progressives, known as Decembrists, had not succeeded in installing a constitutional regime – and applied a policy of repression for thirty years. To avoid accusations of subversion, writers had to place their tales in a period of history sufficiently remote. On the other hand, despite its success, in 1830 the historical genre underwent the influence of realism, which had its moment of glory during the second half of the nineteenth century. In 1835, Gogol published two volumes of stories called *Mirgorod*. Taking as its starting point the war between the Cossacks and the Poles, *Taras Bulba* (1835), written in a highly colourful style, became transformed into a Romantic epic, sacrificing historical truth to patriotic idealism. Some of Goethe's other stories dealt precociously with a theme close to realism: that of everyday life, 'pochlost'. The most famous of these stories is *Šinyel'* (*The Overcoat*, 1842). Dostoyevsky is said to have declared: 'We all came from Gogol's *Overcoat*,' testifying to the important role Gogol played in the introduction of the realist novel in Russia – in spite of his visionary temperament, characteristic of Romanticism.

The author of several works on the history of his country and of idyllic tales of rural life,

Conscience became, in his time, the most read writer of Flemish literature. He was known, above all, for *De Leeuw van Vlaanderen* (*The Lion of Flanders*, 1838), a national epic celebrating the Battle of the Golden Spurs (1302) which ended with the defeat of the French nobility. His taste for myth made Conscience an incomparable writer of historical novels, in a class of his own.

The verse tale

The first half of the nineteenth century saw the birth of the verse tale, one of the most characteristic and flourishing genres developed by Romanticism. While the epic tale adopted an elevated tone, verse tales favoured the familiar and the everyday, with an apparent prosaicness mitigated by idealism, sensibility and imagination. The most important works appeared in 1830. Byron projected his complex and contradictory personality in *Childe Harold's Pilgrimage* (1812), an autobiographical poem inspired by his travels in Spain, Greece, Italy and the East, and in the demystificatory *Don Juan* (1819–1824), a long epic–burlesque poem and a model of Romantic irony.

In the same league, Pushkin's *Evgeny Onegin* (*Eugene Onegin*, 1825–31), half-lyrical, half-nonchalant, broke with previous Russian literature in its form and content. The verse tales by Byron, Romantic but rooted in daily life, served as a model for Italian writers (Prati), Slavic (Sládkovič, Mickiewicz), French (Musset and Gautier) and Hungarian (Arany).

The realist novel

> You can with thirty printed witticisms, at the rate of three a day, cause a man to curse himself for being alive.
>
> Balzac,
> *Lost Illusions*

The realist novel appeared a short time after the historical novel. This narrative genre reached its zenith. In Europe it manifested itself in its perfected form during the second half of the nineteenth century, after the 1848 bourgeois revolution was over and Europe's political, literary and intellectual situation had been transformed. The forerunners of realism, however, appeared in the first half of the century.

In France, Romanticism and Realism appeared at the same time. In 1831, a year after mounting *Hernani*, Balzac recorded his opposition to the historical novel and to exoticism in his preface to *The Wild Ass's Skin*, a fantasy in a realistic setting. The year 1831 coincided with the establishment of a new political regime which, by conferring power on the bourgeoisie, favoured the growth of new mentalities and artistic tastes. In his series of novels, *The Human Comedy* (1829–1850), Balzac evoked reality in painstakingly meticulous detail, constructing totally believable characters. His technique of composition, the stylised nature of the world he recreates and the simplicity of his style, perfectly adapted to his intentions, made him the father of the realist story. Endowed with a Romantic sensibility offset by critical intelligence, **Henri Marie Beyle**, known as **Stendhal (1783–1842)**, gave us in *Scarlet and Black* (1830) his 'art of living' based on individualism, passion and the struggle against prejudice. We find the theme of happiness discovered again in solitude in *The Charterhouse of Parma* (1839):

There was a moon that day, and, just as Fabrice was entering his prison, it rose up majestically on the horizon to his right, above the Alps, towards Treviso. It was only half past eight in the evening, and on the other side of the horizon, to the west a brilliant red sunset tinged with orange picked out perfectly the contours of Mount Viso and the other Alpine peaks extending from Nice in the direction of Mount Cenis and Torino; without even thinking of his misfortune, Fabrice was moved and ravished by this sublime spectacle. 'So, it is in this ravishing world that Clelia Conti lives! With her pensive and serious soul she must enjoy this view more than anyone; here it's like being in solitary mountains a hundred leagues from Parma.' It was only after having spent over two hours at the window, admiring this horizon that spoke to his soul, and frequently stopping to look at the pretty Governor's Residence that Fabrice suddenly cried out: 'But is this a prison? Is this what I was so afraid of?'

Stendhal,
The Charterhouse of Parma

In England 1832 was marked by the death of Walter Scott and, symbolically, by the end of the Romantic movement. Almost everywhere in Europe, the situation developed in the same way: at the end of a brief period of transition which saw Romanticism's final effulgence, objective reality was definitively integrated into narration. The new movement took root as reality became more complex and Romantic idealism, worn threadbare, could no longer provide a satisfactory response.

Queen Victoria's accession to the throne marked the beginning of a long period of relative stability, the Victorian era (1837–1901), characterised by strong industrial expansion arising from the entrepreneurial capitalist spirit of a wealthy middle class. This rapid period of industrialisation, marked by the exploitation of the weak and the misery to which they were reduced, because of the absence of legal protection for them, led eventually to a serious crisis. Hunger was the cause of violent social unrest which culminated in the 1840s. The novel echoes this situation and, in a more or less critical way, makes its victims a part of the literary world. All the great storytellers of the period described and even went as far as to denounce the fate suffered by these victims. With humour and tenderness, the novels by **Charles Dickens (1812–1870)** recall a childhood bruised by the selfishness of a bourgeois society which grinds people down. Made popular by the newspapers that published them in serial form, these novels were appreciated for their authenticity: for example, *David Copperfield* (1849) and *Oliver Twist* (1838).

> Everybody knows the story of another experimental philosopher, who had a great theory about a horse being able to live without eating, and who demonstrated it so well, that he got his own horse down to a straw a day, and would unquestionably have rendered him a very spirited and rampacious animal on nothing at all, if he had not died, just four-and-twenty hours before he was to have had his first comfortable bait of air. Unfortunately for the experimental philosophy of the female to whose protecting care Oliver Twist was delivered over, a similar result usually attended the operation of her system.
>
> Charles Dickens, *Oliver Twist*

Along with Romantic features, realist elements appeared in the work of certain Russian authors, as in *Mertvye duši* (*Dead Souls*, 1842) by Gogol and *Póvesti Bielkina* (*Tales of Bielkin*, 1830) by Pushkin.

The Danes Peter Andreas Heiberg (1758–1841), with *Rigsdalers Sedlens Haendelser* (*The Adventures of a Banknote*), published in serial form from 1787 to 1793, and Steen Steensen Blicher (1782–1848), with *Brudstykker af en landsbydegns dagbot* (*Fragments of the Journal of a Country Sacristan*, 1824), the pessimistic realism of which is frequently placed in an ironic light, and the Swede Almqvist with his feminist novel *Det Går an* (*It Can Work*, 1838) bear witness to this gradual adoption of realism.

Romanticism disappears as it appeared: asynchronously. German Romanticism continued during the first half of the century, by which time realism was already well established in France, England and Russia.

The 'appendici' – Italian serialised novels – found it difficult to gain favour with the reading public, who were used to stories with a moral. In Spain, the realist novel knew its hour of glory after 1850, with the one exception of *La Gaviota* (*The Seagull*, 1845) by Cecilia Böhl de Faber, known as Fernán Caballero (1796–1877). *The Seagull* put an end to a long period in Spain dominated by 'costumbrismo' (a literary form specialising in genre painting), more geared to the past and the picturesque than to social criticism.

In the Balkans and in Portugal, the introduction of realist elements into literature was much slower. In Poland, Hungary and Bohemia the 1850s and 1860s were marked by the deaths of four famous writers: Mickiewicz, Słowacki, Vörösmarty and Božena Němcová (1820–1862). The latter, by creating a fine example of Czech womanhood in *Babička* (*Grandmother*, 1855) signalled the end of Czech Romanticism.

JOURNALISM

Journalism was not only an instrument for the distribution of many literary texts, it was also a literary genre in its own right. The greatest writers of the period forged their sensibility, their creativity and their political ideas as journalists. The German *Athenäum*, the French publication *Le Globe* and the English *The Liberal* had many writers as collaborators.

In the nineteenth century the press became a medium for communicating to the masses in Europe and an opportunity to showcase the talents of young writers, as the Hungarian poet, Charles Kisfaludy (1788–1830) did in his review *Aurora*. In Russia, Karamzin founded *The European Messenger* (1802). Ramón López Soler (1806–1836), the herald of Romanticism in Spain, created *The European* (1823–1824), distributed in Catalunya. Included among other founders of French newspapers, Félicité Robert de Lamennais (1792–1854), 'a soldier of the press', according to his own description, impressed his readers with his articles and with his *Paroles d'un croyant* (*Words of a Believer*, 1834).

The German editor **Johann Joseph von Görres (1776–1848)** invented committed journalism by publishing incisive articles against Napoleon. In 1849, Mickiewicz went to war against the oppressors of peoples and established a mouthpiece for his revolt: *The Peoples' Tribune*. Two years later censorship forced him to publish his articles anonymously.

The 1840s were distinguished in Bohemia and Slovakia by the activities not only of the literary press with Tyl, but the political press with **Karel Havlíček-Borovsky (1821–1856)**, a man with Voltaire's spirit, a radical liberal democrat who turned his sights first on ill-defined 'pan-Slavism'. The founder of the journal *Národní noviny* (*The National Gazette*, 1848–1850), he took part in revolutionary events and attended the first Slav Congress in 1848 in Prague. All these activities were savagely suppressed by the Austrian authorities. Havlíček-Borovsky was deported to the Tyrol and wrote long satirical poems, such as *Tyrolské elegie* and *Tyrolian Elegies*, which circulated under the counter until the 1860s.

Herculano dedicated a large part of his activities to encyclopedic journalism. His reviews *Panórama* and *Repositório Literário* (*Literary Repository*) played a major part in the dissemination of the Romantic aesthetic in Portugal. The Spaniard **Mariano José de Larra (1809–1837)**, endowed with a highly complex personality, was ceaselessly torn between exalted feelings and rationalism. His articles, signed Figaro, were the expression of his literary opinions, acute sensitivity and frustrated patriotism. They devoted most of their space to the satire of manners and to personal themes. This extract from *El Día de los Difuntos* (*The Day of the Dead*, 1836) alludes to the disappointment of a woman's rejection, which drove him to suicide three months later:

> - ¡Necios! – decía a los transeúntes -. ¿Os movéis para ver muertos? ¿No tenéis espejos por ventura? [. . .] ¿Vais a ver a vuestros padres y a vuestros abuelos, cuando vosotros sois los muertos? Ellos viven, porque ellos tienen paz; ellos tienen libertad, la única posible sobre la tierra, la que da la muerte [. . .].

Mariano José de Larra,
El Día de los Difuntos

> 'Fools,' I said to the passers-by, 'are you in a hurry to see dead people? Don't you have mirrors? [. . .] Is it for you to go to see your parents and your grandparents, dead as you are? They are alive because they have peace; they have freedom, the only freedom possible on earth, that given by death [. . .].

Was there a Romantic revolution?

Was there a Romantic revolution? In the first half of the nineteenth century, when Larra fell down dead, a new personage, the Romantic, asserted himself in Europe. He broke with classical tradition. He had his roots in the Middle Ages, in which his country's genius was forged. Scott and Balzac increased the range of literary types, making of the novel a consecrated genre in which a swineherd (Ivanhoe) and a vermicelli-maker (Old Goriot) step to the fore. Romanticism was lived as a liberation from false dogmas: for Heine, all the thinkers who paved the way for his emergence in Germany were milestones along the road where German thought blossomed. Mickiewicz and Pushkin also shared this national consciousness. But, for the first, to be a Pole was to be open to universal cultural values, to prepare for the peoples' liberation of. Pushkin created a national literature in Russia on the basis of the conscious assimilation of contributions from a wider Europe. Did the new spirit blowing through Europe herald a happy future? Andersen's ugly duckling tempered this optimism with irony. Grotesque characters and situations in Gogol cast off the ropes of Romanticism: the way is open for other types of exploration.

The first decades of the nineteenth century were those of Romanticism's triumph. Its various and even contradictory manifestations reflected the exaltation of the ego, a search for truth and freedom, a vision of the world founded on metaphysical idealism, creative imagination and the humanisation or divinisation of nature.

Romantic polymorphism and certain artistic successes which we cannot discount explain its impact on later literary movements as diverse as realism, symbolism and surrealism. Realism, whose gestation began in France c.1830, and which fully came into its own with positivism and after the failure of the revolution of 1848, has its point of departure in Romanticism. Even if, it eventually questions it, it is, nevertheless, the natural heir of Romanticism. It will take the direct observation of reality to its logical conclusion, the search for truth and the conflict of the artist with society while rejecting elements fundamental to Romanticism such as subjectivism and metaphysical idealism.

The *'Bildungsroman'*

P. Dahl

Wilhelm began to have a premonition that things in the world happened differently to how he had imagined them happening.

Goethe, *Wilhelm Meister's Years of Apprenticeship*

Preoccupied with a hero's adventures for many years, the novel began to be interested in the effects of those adventures on the psychological and social make-up. The German term *'Bildungsroman'* – a novel of education – explicitly referred to the apprenticeship that a character has to undergo to find his own 'form', his identity in society. Far from being the education of a picaro, that of the hero of a *'Bildungsroman'* is a social education the purpose of which is to make it possible for him to live in harmony with society.

A theory of education

In 1792, Wilhelm von Humboldt (1767–1835), a philosopher and future pedagogue and diplomat, published a thesis, *Ideen zu einem Versuch, die Grenzen der Wirksamkeit des Staates zu bestimmen* (*An Essay to determine the Limits of the Action of the State*). The title explicitly indicates a liberal conception of the State: the latter must limit its interventions in human activity, confining itself to making available and safeguarding a framework for the operation of free and equal competition, for civic activities and for the education of individuals.

According to Humboldt, one of the basic themes for any reflection on education is the fact that, like culture, education tries, with the help of work and a process of maturation, to control what comes from nature, as much human nature as the surrounding environment. Thanks to his will and his common sense, man becomes free and independent of his subjection to nature and necessity. Guided by his common sense, the man's true aim is the highest and best thought-out education of human forces tending towards a balanced and organic whole. Individuality must not be uniform: it must take account of variety and universality.

But so that all his talents can rise to the challenges that stimulate them, during the time he is being educated a free man must be brought up against different types of situation. An encounter with life in all its diversity is the declared objective of the 'Grand Tour' or the 'educational journey' (*'Die Bildungsreise'*) which, through a series of situations and episodes conceived of in pedagogical and classical fashion, plunge the individual into the world. For people speaking English, German or a Scandinavian language, to undertake the Tour usually meant going from north to south, in order to discover places listed in ancient culture. It also sometimes meant setting out in search of a life driven by passion and an absence of restraint. It was easy for the heedless tourist to give himself up to this life, while the returning traveller is forced to channel his passion into more productive and more lasting forms.

The enlightened bourgeoisie who found its place in society in the nineteenth century favoured the idea of knowing oneself, the deepening of this self-knowledge with the 'Grand Tour' and the ensuing period of reflection. This self-knowledge allows the individual to step back, to leave his own personal needs and his private interests on one side to fulfil the requirements of all needs and interests. The *'Bildungsroman'* or novel of apprenticeship thus retraces the education of an individual, at the end of which he finds his place in the world and his sphere of activity by morally submitting himself to the community represented by the State.

The process of writing a *'Bildungsroman'*

Independently of the specific viewpoints taken for national or temporal reasons, the basic process involved in the novel of apprenticeship may be subdivided into three phases throughout which an omniscient narrator concentrates attention on the world's main action. The process of psychological evolution is present in the continual and normally fruitful interchange between the hero and the world in which he lives and moves. The main action does not exclude multiple secondary actions, any more than it does many secondary characters of symbolic significance. But from the very fact of its reflecting on and harking back to the actions and development of the main

character, the essential subject matter of the *'Bildungsroman'* is always clear and definite.

The first phase goes through childhood years with growth situated in a harmonious and secure environment, whose circumscribed frontiers are never overstepped or questioned. The hero is 'in the family' according to the expression used in one of the longest novels of apprenticeship of the period, *Without a Family* (1857) by the Dane Meir Goldschmidt.

The second phase depicts the youth or the years of wandering during which the hero is 'without a family', often caught up in a conflict situation that reveals a lack of harmony in the hero's relationship to his environment, as well as a battle between the inner forces of the 'self'. Alternatively, the self is submitted to a variety of situations: because of its opinionated will to take the initiative and its need for emancipation, it must needs find itself confronted with society and its severe limitations which prompt the individual to evolve.

In the final phase, a Utopian perspective can open up for the hero, or else close upon a more or less harmonious recognition that it is possible to achieve things within the established order.

After his long inner and outer journey of apprenticeship, the hero finally returns home. A period of reflection succeeds the intermediary phase of expansion. The hero can see once more his mistakes and the trials that he has successfully negotiated. He understands in this way that he has matured: he can henceforth enter into the human community and actively play a part in it.

Goethe composed the first major example of this genre with *Wilhelm Meisters Lehrjahre* (*Wilhelm Meister's Years of Apprenticeship*, 1795–1796). This was the story of a theatrical vocation. In the final analysis, the hero, learning the lessons of his mistakes and failures, finds his blossoming not in an individual conquest, but in harmoniously developing his personality in a society whose rules and regulations he accepts.

Wäre ich ein Edelmann, so wäre unser Streit bald abgetan; da ich aber nur ein Bürger bin, so muß ich einen eigenen Weg nehmen, und ich wünsche, daß Du mich verstehen mögest. Ich weiß nicht, wie es in fremden Ländern ist, aber in Deutschland ist nur dem Edelmann eine gewisse allgemeine, wenn ich sagen darf, personelle Ausbildung möglich. Ein Bürger kann sich Verdienst erwerben und zur höchsten Not seinen Geist ausbilden; seine Persönlichkeit geht aber verloren, er mag sich stellen, wie er will. Indem es dem Edelmann, der mit den Vornehmsten umgeht, zur Pflicht wird, sich selbst einen vornehmen Anstand zu geben, indem dieser Anstand, da ihm weder Tür noch Tor verschlossen ist, zu einem freien Anstand wird, da er mit seiner Figur, mit seiner Person, es sei bei Hofe oder bei der Armee, bezahlen muß, so hat er Ursache, etwas auf sie zu halten und zu zeigen, daß er etwas auf sie hält.

If I was a noble, our discussion would soon be over; but as I am only a bourgeois, I need to take a certain tack and I want you to be quite clear with me on this. I don't know what it's like in other countries, but in Germany, only a noble is in a position to acquire culture and a general and, if I may say so, a personal education. A bourgeois can acquire merit and, at best, cultivate his mind; but whatever he does, his personality will fade away completely. Whereas a noble, who frequents the most distinguished men, sees it as his duty to achieve a supreme distinction, a distinction which becomes with him – for he is well received everywhere – a personal distinction, since he must pay it with his person and with what his person represents, either in time of war or at a court: he therefore has his reasons for making a big thing of it and for showing that it really does mean something to him.

The Grand Tour

Despite its autobiographical elements, *Anton Reiser* (1785–1790) by Karl Philipp Moritz was still quite a long way from a novel by Goethe. *Franz Sternbalds Wanderungen* (*The Wanderings of Franz Sternbald*, 1798) by Ludwig Tieck and *Heinrich von Ofterdingen*

(1799–1800, published in 1802) by Novalis are typically Germanic: the Middle Ages and medieval art, that of Albrecht Dürer, among others, play an important part in them. *Titan* (1800–1803) by Jean-Paul and *Ahnung und Gegenwart* (*Premonition and Presence*, 1815) by Eichendorff take a critical look at the pragmatic and efficient hero that is Goethe's Wilhelm. These novels emphasise the genius of subjectivity and internalise the problems of personal education, deviating from the normal and the universal perspective that we find in Goethe. In these novels, as in those by Hans Christian Andersen, the artist rejects the action and the practice that Goethe had given as the aims of education; this rejection shows in itself the latent criticism formulated by the artistic genius of an education which is too narrow.

Because of the evolution of society in the nineteenth century, it became increasingly difficult to put into practice the neo-humanist ideals about education. These problems are mentioned in works like *Der Grüne Heinrich* (*Green Henry*, 1854–1855) by Gottfried Keller, *Soll und Haben* (*Debit and Credit*, 1855) by Gustav Freytag (1816–1895), *Der Nachsomme* (*Saint Martin's Summer*, 1857) by Adalbert Stifter (1805–1868), as well as *Der Hungerpastor* (*The Hunger Pastor*, 1864) by Wilhelm Raabe and especially his later novel *Stopfkuchen* (1891). The heroes are left to their own devices and never succeed in coming to terms with the world.

The evolution of the genre

Novels of apprenticeship, of which there were many in Germany when the genre first made its appearance, gradually fell out of fashion. On the other hand, in Scandinavian literature, a series of representative works appears, created under the very strong influence of naturalism and modern thought. *Niels Lyhne* (1880) by Jens Peter Jacobsen and *Lykke-Per* (*Lucky Peter*, 1898–1904) by Henrik Pontoppidan had something in common: the apprenticeship was now no longer directed towards a particular end. Attention is focused on the elements that make the hero an isolated entity. These novels, in this sense, lead us to *Die Auszeichnungen des Malte Laurids Brigge* (*The Notebooks of Malte Laurids Brigge*, 1910) by Rainer Maria Rilke, *Die Verwirrungen des Zöglings Törless* (*The Perplexities of the Pupil Törless*, 1906) by Robert Musil, and later to novels by Thomas Mann and Hermann Hesse. The modern version of the novel of apprenticeship, the 'novel-centred-on-the-self', is reduced to being no more than a story centred on the self's states of mind. Reflections on educational problems gradually replaced the epic plot of the classic 'Bildungsroman'.

Outside Germany and Scandinavia, the 'Bildungsroman' did not play a decisive part in European literature. In England, Thomas Carlyle translated Goethe's *Wilhelm Meister* in 1824 and, without them being dominant features, we find elements of the apprenticeship novel in *Vivian Grey* (1826) and *Contarini Fleming* (1832) by Benjamin Disraeli (1804–1881) as well as in Edward George Bulwer-Lytton (1803–1873). More significant examples appear later with Charles Dickens, *David Copperfield* (1849–1850) and *Great Expectations* (1860–1861), with William Thackeray, George Meredith and George Eliot. Nevertheless the social criticism in English novels was, in general, more direct and more severe; their description of society is only rarely a dialectical element in a positive interaction with the individual at the heart of the 'Bildungsroman'.

In French literature, there was a lack of the prerequisite interest in the psychological development of the 'Bildungsroman' hero. The typical hero of the French novel of this period was determined in advance: Rousseau, in his *Confessions*, had already produced a form of apology for a writer's life rather than a tale based on the story of an individual's development. Occurrences, for instance, in Balzac's *Old Goriot*, cover or uncover the character of Rastignac, but do not constitute him in the sense of a 'Bildungsroman'.

The Life of Henry Brûlard (published in 1890) by Stendhal, *The Disciple* by Paul Bourget and *Jean-Christophe* by Romain Rolland are closer to the apprenticeship novel – and to biography. The growing crisis of how to present education because of the confrontation between the expanding sciences and society's evolution, of which they are constituent parts, provoked reaction. The personal transformation of the impersonal observations of positivism is sought after in a desperate attempt to have education retain its active aspect. In the private form of undertaking, the individual can still vouch for the universality of education, but not its fruit: action, intrigue. Culture splits and divides: on the one hand, a concept of the personality tinged with religion or self-contemplation of the soul emerged. On the other, a cult of the man of action, full of personal initiative, the 'original' man as he appears in Nietzsche in his revolt against cultural 'philistinism', or in the regionalist literature of the end of the nineteenth and the beginning of the twentieth century, or again in the heroes of proletarian literature.

The structure of the intrigue of the 'Bildungsroman' is hidden in the first great proletarian novels by Gorki and Martin Andersen Nexoe. In *Pelle Erobreren* (*Pelle the Conqueror*, 1906–1910), by Nexoe, we find – according to the terms of the preface – 'the long march of the worker on earth, in his infinite and half-conscious quest for the light'. While the original apprenticeship novel had a precise aim and described the very achievement of the hero himself in his relationship to this end, its heirs find themselves increasingly up against crises, renunciations and weak, resigned heroes. At the beginning of the century the proletarian novel appears with a new type of character in it, the proletarian, and a new working-class environment, as well as a new theme: the social struggle. This theme refers back to the optimistic vision of man to be found in the 'Bildungsroman', to a belief in the possible evolution of man, for he possesses the faculty of learning and using his experiences in the class struggle, which is, at the same time, a struggle for his own self-realisation. The representative and symbolic connection between the class struggle and his own realisation makes the hero an example to imitate because it has a declared relevance to his education and training.

In the last part of the nineteenth century, the European apprenticeship novel and education began to take the form of cynical tales and novels of personal crisis. It does so increasingly in an architectonic and stylistic context that is confused: neo-classical, neo-rococo, neo-Renaissance. Characteristics of the *'Bildungsroman'* then appeared in the historical novel in which cultural thought, toppled from its throne, found one of its final refuges. This was especially the case with the historical and biographical novel. The birth of biography, its growth and dominant position in the nineteenth and twentieth centuries, are inversely proportional to the decline and fall of the *'Bildungsroman'*; above all that of historical, spiritual and cultural biography, with its hidden sublimations of bourgeois melancholy, its nostalgia, its suppressed protest and its aesthetic opposition to contemporary values.

Byron (1788–1824)

F. Robertson

'Whoever you are, Byron, good or evil genius.'
Lamartine,
Second Meditation

'One hates an author that's *all author*', Lord Byron declared haughtily, and provocatively, in his comic poem *Beppo* (1818). It is appropriate therefore that his place in European culture should be as much a consequence of his tempestuous life and his political idealism as of his poetry. The personality of Byron, on a literary level as well as on a social one, is both complex and fascinating. For his contemporaries, he was the epitome of the Romantic poet: detached and contemplative, and full of a sense of his own significance. Such is the picture suggested in his first major work, in which he created the dark peripatetic hero –

the knight errant, Harold, 'the wandering outlaw of his own dark mind'. Soon after followed his poems featuring 'satanic' heroes: *The Giaour*, *Lara* and *The Corsair*. In *Manfred* (1817), Byron shrouds in Romantic mystery the crime of incest of which he himself had been accused, and which had led to the breakdown of his marriage and precipitated his departure from England the previous year. He experimented with several competing literary styles before perfecting in *Don Juan* (1819–1824) the seemingly spontaneous colloquial, knowing tone that suited him. In the end it is the ironic but compassionate accents of *Don Juan* that earned him his special place in literature: he is, at one and the same time, the symbol of idealistic Romanticism and its most penetrating critic. If Byron is a personality of European stature, it is because he deliberately cultivated this image. He despised what he saw as provincial mediocrity and the complacency of several of his English contemporaries, and fought, in his life as in his poetry, to recover classical detachment, balance and urbanity. For example, he chose to turn his back on traditional English prosody by adapting the 'ottava rima' for *Don Juan* and *Beppo*, that celebration of Venetian style and manners which explicitly rejects what it defines as characteristic English 'coldness'. He also perfects an adaptation of the narrative form of the travel journal in two of his great works, *Childe Harold's Pilgrimage* (4 cantos; 1812, 1816, 1818) and *Don Juan* (unfinished, 17 cantos), so as to create a comparative perspective on various states in Europe and the East. Byron's criticisms of insularity and intolerance constitute a questioning of the tastes of his own nation, and are addressed to the wider European audience for whom he wrote.

For Byron, poetry and politics were inseparable. He did, of course, write poetry with specifically political aims in mind, including satirical poems such as *The Vision of Judgement* (1821). But the struggle for social and political freedom was connected much more fundamentally with poetic creativity itself. In his Ravenna Journal (1821), Byron meditated on the political subjection to which the Italian states had fallen victim: 'It is no great matter, supposing that Italy could be liberated, who or what is sacrificed. It is a grand object – the very *poetry* of politics. Only think – a free Italy!!!' The '*poetry* of politics' was to prove an energising and influential conjunction, and the death of Byron in Missolonghi in 1824, during the struggle for Greek independence, was the perfect symbol of this vital interaction. The commemorative ceremonies organised in Greece after his death anticipated the mythical role that Byron was to play in other countries fighting for their freedom in post-Napoleonic Europe.

Scott (1771–1832)

F. Robertson

History, you know, is half fiction.

Walter Scott,
The Betrothed

The works of Scott played an essential role in the development of the European novel in the nineteenth century and helped to define Europe's sense of its own history. Although he was best known as a poet and a novelist, Scott also published collections of ballads, plays, critical essays and assessments of contemporary writers (including Hoffmann), political reflections and historical works, the most important of which were *The Life of Napoleon Buonaparte* (1827) and *The Tales of a Grandfather* (1827–1828), a history of Scotland for children. His fictional works, themselves influenced by varied and diverse literary traditions, furthered the development of a distinctly European sensibility.

A European by education

The tone was set at the start of Scott's literary career: his first published works (at the end of the 1790s) were translations of Bürger's ballads and Goethe's play *Götz von Berlichingen*. Scott was particularly inspired by late eighteenth-

century German literature: closely connected to his interest in the primitive and the sensational, in Ossian and in the plays of John Home, German literature was one source of his life-long devotion to the idea of a natural, 'untamed' imagination. His enthusiasm for European literature, based on sound knowledge, was never to fade. According to J. G. Lockhart, Scott's son-in-law and biographer, 'those who observed him the most constantly, were never able to understand how he contrived to keep himself so thoroughly up to the stream of contemporary literature of almost all sorts, French and German, as well as English'.

Among the authors of the past, Ariosto and Cervantes were particular favourites of Scott's. He was also fascinated by folk literature, the ballad and the saga. Scott was one of the first to transcribe and to try to conserve Scottish ballads and legends in his 1802–3 collection *Minstrelsy of the Scottish Border*.

Poetry, picturesque and sublime

Scott's celebrity began with the series of long narrative poems inaugurated by *The Lay of the Last Minstrel* in 1805. These poems consolidate and experiment with his long-standing interest in popular literature. They enjoyed resounding success. *The Lady of the Lake* (1810), in particular, awakened in the reading public a lively curiosity about the ways and customs of the Scottish Highlands. The picturesque and the sublime were always central to Scott's work, but what captivated the public was, above all, the quality of the story-telling, rapid in pace and moving seamlessly from local legend or popular superstition to the battlefield and political stratagem.

The best example of this narrative art is probably to be found in *Marmion* (1808), which culminates in an impressive account of a battle central to Scottish national consciousness, the battle of Flodden Field. After experimenting with a melodramatic story of brigands in *Rokeby* (1813) and with pseudo-Arthurian legend in *The Bridal of Triermain* (1813), Scott returned to the great legends of Scottish history and national identity, tracing the career of Robert the Bruce in *The Lord of the Isles* (1815). In all his narrative poetry, Scott started to develop the technique of the historical tale which he was to perfect in his novels. In all his work, the popularisation of history is a self-conscious and self-critical process.

Many of Scott's fictions are in part elegiac, conjuring up the lost image of an independent Scotland. At the heart of the idea of a Scotland governed by clan loyalty is the reciprocal nature of duty, a theme to which Scott repeatedly returns. But Scott's narrational perspective on all these tales reminds readers that this ideal community is a construct, created not in Scotland's past but in Scott's present, and for the benefit of an early-nineteenth century readership which no longer had to face the political threat of an independent Scotland.

The novels of Walter Scott

After the success of his first novel, *Waverley*, in 1814, Scott focused his creative energies on prose fiction. The long series of novels which followed taught other writers how to imagine and present a national history and identity. This is why many of Scott's works, which seem specifically Scottish in terms of subject matter and locality, nevertheless had a huge influence on the rest of European literature. In *Waverley*, the author declares his intention of awakening an interest in the customs of Scotland comparable to the interest in those of Ireland aroused by the novels of Maria Edgeworth. But Scott recreated the Scottish national character in an increasingly impressionistic and imaginative way, a way which was to generate its own myths. His contemporaries were particularly struck by the diversity of class types in his novels. By depicting beggars, fishermen, shopkeepers and thieves – relegated in previous fiction to the subplot or serving merely as comic relief – Scott gradually defined aspects of the Scottish popular consciousness which were to be a source of inspiration for other Scottish writers, especially Galt, Hogg and Stevenson.

Scott's rustic and artisan characters have an idiosyncratic conception of life and history which challenges and ironises the interpretations offered by official historians. In *The Antiquary* (1816), for instance, Scott mocks the efforts of an antiquary, Jonathan Oldbuck, whose passion is to collect and classify different versions of popular legends and ballads which only make sense when set in their natural context: working-class lives and their struggles. In *Redgauntlet* (1824), the mannered and derivative style of the two heroes is in stark contrast to the fantastic story 'Wandering Willie's Tale' told in Scottish dialect by a blind old fiddler. The Waverley novels demonstrate that historical information always consists of an interweaving of texts, stories and personal interpretations which may contradict one another. As Jonathan Oldbuck declares, in the introduction to *The Betrothed* (1825), 'history, you know, is half fiction.'

Scott's fame

Scott's novels quickly won a large readership throughout Europe and North America. His popularity increased further when, with *Ivanhoe* (1819), he started writing about historical subjects prior to the seventeenth century, and set outside Scotland. Apart from its obvious attractions – its historical spectacles, jousts, conspiracies and last-minute escapes – *Ivanhoe* clearly shows the effectiveness of Scott's central technique. This is the analysis of historical change by juxtaposing distinct social groups during periods of struggle. Among Scott's other medieval novels, *Quentin Durward* (1823) is of special interest, being the first of his novels to take place wholly outside Scotland, in the fifteenth-century France of Louis XI and Charles the Bold, Duke of Burgundy. While plotting the course of the evolution of modern political ideas by contrasting the machinations of Louis with the decadent chivalry of Charles, *Quentin Durward* also deals with events that dominated French political life during Scott's own lifetime. At the climax of the action, the narrator depicts the execution of Louis de Bourbon, Bishop of Liège, by a frenzied crowd, and describes in his introduction the ruined château of a French nobleman, a victim of the French Revolution. Scott shows that historical fiction can be a powerful medium for the analysis of contemporary politics. In the unjustly neglected novel *Anne of Geierstein, or the Maiden of the Mist* (1829) he focuses on the struggle of Swiss burghers for freedom from Burgundian rule, setting this tale alongside a sketch of the troubadour court of René de Provence. *The Talisman* (1825) further develops the technique of *Quentin Durward*, which uses the experiences of a Scot in exile to portray the struggles of a society with which he is entirely unfamiliar, and which is riven by political and ideological crises. Once again, the ideology of chivalry is central.

Scott's subject matter was to become increasingly European as his career as a novelist progressed. Appropriately, his last, unfinished, novel, *The Siege of Malta*, was inspired by the Knights Hospitaller of Malta. More generally, many of his novels set in medieval or Renaissance times deal with the problems generated by Christian (often, specifically Protestant) factionalism. So, novels such as *The Monastery* (1820), *The Talisman* and *The Fair Maid of Perth* (1828) examine the establishment of ways of life which had an impact on the whole of Europe, exploring Protestant, Capitalist and parliamentary values. These novels also bear the marks of contemporary European events. Scott focuses intently on great social upheavals, civil wars and ideological struggles, and ponders the theory and practice of monarchy. These themes are recurrent in novel after novel: *The Abbot* (1820) tells of the forced abdication of Mary, Queen of Scots; *Peveril of the Peak* (1822) traces the destinies of two families on opposing sides during the English Civil War; *Woodstock* (1826) moves to the times of Cromwell, lingering on the complicated political and emotional aftermath of the execution of Charles I.

Scott wrote five plays, but these never achieved the success enjoyed by the innumerable stage adaptations of his poems and novels made during his lifetime and for many years after his death. Scott actually sent the proofs of some of his works, prior to publication, to his friend the dramatist Daniel Terry, and, as a result of the popularity of stage versions of his work, his stories were disseminated simultaneously in different media. During the whole of the nineteenth century, the plays and operas inspired by his poems and novels contributed to the dissemination of his tales throughout Europe. When, in 1822, George IV, a Hanoverian monarch dressed up in tartan, paid an elaborately staged official visit to Scotland, it was an adaptation of *Rob Roy* (1817) that was chosen to celebrate the first night of his stay.

Scott's characteristic blend of history and fiction inspired writers all over Europe. In the field of historical research, Macaulay, Thierry and Michelet were enormously indebted to him. His work quickened interest in the theory and practice of historical study, and directly influenced the greatest writers of the century: Balzac, Hugo and Mérimée in France; Manzoni in Italy; Alexis in Germany; Pushkin, Gogol, then Tolstoy in Russia; Ingemann, Blicher and Andersen in Denmark; Munch in Norway; Stevenson in Scotland. For many later writers, Scott's interest in the folklore of their native countries was as important as his innovative contributions to the theory of history. For many others, and especially for those combining and exploring the techniques of historical fiction and the realist novel (including Flaubert, Thackeray and George Eliot), Scott's lasting legacy was to show how to analyse the present as if it were the past.

Balzac (1799–1850)

R. Kieffer

And as a first act of the defiance that he felt for Society, Rastignac went to dine at the home of Madame de Nucingen.

Honoré de Balzac,
Old Goriot

On 14 May 1935, Gide noted in his journal: 'Finished yesterday the reading of the long triptych which includes *Lost Illusions*, *The Splendour and Wretchedness of Courtisans* and *The Final Incarnation of Vautrin*, that Saint-Gothard of *The Human Comedy*, in which Balzac gives both of his best and his worst; he is incomparable at his best, but misses Zola by a long chalk at his worst and just in the things that Zola would have excelled at describing. Just like Hugo, Balzac has too much confidence in his genius; often, under the pressure of financial need no doubt, he makes a botch of things.' The familiarity with the work of Balzac of an educated Frenchman like André Gide appears to us as natural. But take the memoirs of the Soviet writer Ilya Ehrenbourg, called *Men, Years, Life* (1961–1965). Balzac is mentioned in them, and Ehrenbourg was also an assiduous reader of his work. Drawing our attention to Boris Pasternak's tragic situation in 1958, he points out that the latter treated above all the theme of art, that theme which, he said, 'gave rise to Gogol's *The Portrait*, Balzac's *The Unknown Masterpiece* and Chekhov's *The Seagull*. 'The ways of art are strange,' he writes further on. 'Cervantes wanted to turn into ridicule the novels of chivalry and created the character of a knight who was the only one to have survived his age. Balzac thought he was praising the nobility, though he had, in fact, come to bury it.' Then Balzac reappears in considerations on capitalism. In Ehrenbourg's eyes its upholders, in the twentieth century, are madmen, whereas in Balzac's lifetime, though they were hard-headed, they nevertheless contributed to economic progress. Balzac expressed his thoughts, his desires and his passions in his books. Even though he had compiled political pamphlets, elaborated plans for financial schemes to eliminate his debts, and ardently wanted to be a deputy, these things were really superficial. Balzac only got excited when he spoke about his characters.

Balzac fever

Born in Tours in 1799, Balzac experienced a melancholy childhood before undergoing a strict pedagogical regime at the Collège de Vedôme, injurious to his delicate, dreamy personality. As an adolescent, he was taken to Paris, a city he judged severely in his work. He studied law, but plunged into philosophical meditation: in his eyes, thought has a marvellous, awesome energy. It leads to crime and is a source of exploits. He took part in affairs whose adventurous side corresponded to the vivacity of his imagination, and certain dark novels became his first literary attempts. For a time, solitary, ambitious, passionate, he lived at his printer's on the rue Visconti. On 24 September 1924, the German romanist Ernst Robert Curtius reported on his meeting with Marcel Bouteron, the author of *The Cult of Balzac*. The French host showed his German guest the rue Visconti, prompting the latter to write: 'And pensively we contemplate the dark façade behind which young Balzac's years of struggle and suffering gradually passed. He would have collapsed had it not been for the *dilecta*, who was for him a friend, a lover, a mother and an angel.' In his study, Bouteron showed Curtius a treasure-trove of Balzac relics: 'This is the sanctuary of the cult offered up to Balzac,' Curtius noted, 'to the visionary genius of *The Human Comedy*.' Marcel Bouteron attracted young literary researchers to Paris so that they could become involved in exploring Balzac's work. Among them were many Americans. 'Send me Germans,' he said to his visitor, 'I want all countries to participate in this great work.' 'Balzac fever caught hold of us,' Curtius wrote at the end of *Impressions of Paris*, 'and, like a magnet, it blends in with the smell of the summer night, with the Parisian night, with the rhythm of the town where millions of inhabitants live.'

For his part, the French Germanist Robert Minder was adept at placing Balzac's genius in its Parisian setting. In an essay called *Paris in French Literature, 1780–1960*, Minder evoked the young unknown writer, all the way from Touraine and defying the capital with the defiance he will put into the mouth of Rastignac: 'Now it's just you and me.' Minder characterised Balzac's gifts by emphasising his mystical temperament; this mystic, however, possessed a speculator's gifts, was a 'born entrepreneur', a 'maker of plans' and a clever crook. His house had two exits so that he could flee his creditors. He loved in a romantic and almost religious way a woman who for a long time had lived far away from him, whom he marries in 1850 and whom he installs in Paris in a luxurious house, shortly before his premature death.

A titanic enterprise

For Minder, Balzac had a 'volcanic nature'; he underlines the mysticism of the novelist, the attention the latter gave to the works of a Swedenborg or a Louis Claude de Saint-Martin. Curtius did the same. Scientific research opens to man the portal of mysteries, and it inspired Balzac with an enthusiasm for great scientific discoveries and systems testifying to audacious logic. He dedicated to Étienne Geoffroy Saint-Hilaire his novel *Old Goriot* (1833), and set out to order and classify social types in the same way in which the great man of science ordered zoological species.

As was his wont, the novelist signed the dedication 'De Balzac'. The noble particle, which appeared for the first time in his sister Laure's birth certificate in 1802, seems to be close to his heart – his political ideas led him to attribute sterling qualities to the nobility. As for the name 'Balzac', did the writer, sensitive to secret influences, transfer it to that of Z. Marcas? 'MARCAS,' wrote Balzac. 'Repeat to yourself this name composed of two syllables; do you not find it has a sinister ring to it? Does it not seem to you that the man who bears such a name has to end up a martyr?' Did Balzac himself die a victim or a martyr to his demigodly or titanic enterprise? An epicure, a traveller curious to see the world, he is no less familiar to us in his guise as a literary worker or a convict whose ball and chain were literature. A prolific journalist, a dramatist, a novelist and, as such, the creator of a world parallel to ours, Balzac has been portrayed in a spirit of admiring understanding by

the Austrian Stefan Zweig. An emulator of Napoleon Bonaparte, who had submitted Europe to his sovereign will, Balzac raised up a world in order to dominate it. He brought together, Zweig declared, all singular appearances and, on the basis of their multiplicity, in the furnace of creativity, flame in hand, he fashioned a system as Linnaeus did, who was able to situate thousands of plants in the framework of his concepts, like the chemist who breaks up innumerable compounds and resolves them into 'a handful of elements'.

In the great overall composition of scenes of Parisian life, provincial life, military life, analytical and philosophical works, Balzac the creator carries his characters like a mother feeds her child. He possesses the power of living the life of another person in the present and the past, even perhaps in the future. In a letter addressed to Balzac in February 1842, George Sand pointed out that he was 'an exceptional ego', 'infinitely powerful and endowed with the memory that other poor devils have lost'. She believes him capable of seizing hold of life in 'the eternal past', 'there where we see only dead people and darkness'. In recreating the outside world, to make of it his hallucinatory world, Balzac plunged into the lower depths of life, exploring the abysses of the human conscience. In August 1850, Hugo walked to the cemetery with Balzac's bier. He gave a speech in which he spoke of a real Balzacian universe which bore the imprint of the horrible: 'All his books are only one book, a living, luminous, profound book, in which we see people coming and going and walking around and moving, with I know not what about them that is frightened and terrible mixed in with what is real, the whole of our contemporary civilisation.'

The man, however, the artist who descended into the gulfs of human desires, felt in himself an aspiration which he communicated to some of his characters, a passionate desire for elevation. In *Air and Dreams*, Gaston Bachelard was led to quote a key sentence borrowed from *Séraphita* (1835): 'Man alone has the feeling of verticality placed in a special organ.' This psychic dynamism of Balzac animated characters endowed with a superior strength of thought. Thanks to this strength, *The Human Comedy* comes close to the end of the *Divine Comedy*.

In this creative urge, genius went beyond duality, in a fertile dialectic, but its conservative opinions sometimes surprise us. Doctor Bénassis, in *The Country Doctor* (1833), does not want the right to vote for the poor. He assures us that power structures are not open to discussion and thinks that the proletariat consists of minors in need of a guardian. In his dedication to Charles Nodier in *La Rabouilleuse* (1842), Balzac complained of 'the diminution of paternal authority'. In a striking reflection, he mentions the ravages caused by the power of money, which authorises men to use any means to solidly establish their success.

In a letter to Madame Hanska, dated 26 October 1834, and in which he expounded the plan of *The Human Comedy*, this strict judge of society compared it to a temple, to a palace. At the end he observed: 'And, on the foundations of this palace, I, a child and a prankster, will have traced out the huge arabesque of the *Hundred Droll Tales!*'

So, with laughter, this defender of 'the established values' undermined the edifice that he appeared to want to stubbornly protect. The author of a remarkable work on Rabelais, the Russian Mikhail Bakhtin thought that laughter delivers us from external censorship and the internal censor who, over the centuries, has appeared in human beings, on the basis of the fear of what has been declared sacred, the authoritarian ban, the past, power. A supporter of the *status quo*, Balzac also knew how to differ from it.

Balzac rose above the conflicts, surmounting them with his genius. He is expressed in two symbols which serve to complement each other: that of the pelican feeding its young, the 'Christ of fatherhood', who feeds his children from his own entrails; and that of the phoenix perishing in a fire kindled by its own body heat, whose ashes give birth to a new being, more beautiful than that which has just been consumed in the flames. Thus we have Balzac, a beacon to literature, who died of his work, and was reincarnated in the work itself!

Heine (1797–1856)

M. Windfuhr

A German nightingale nesting in Voltaire's wig.

Heinrich Heine

This jest, put about by Heine himself, and which was already being repeated during his lifetime, sums up with marvellous accuracy the life of this German poet with the gift of potent language who chose exile in Paris. He was of Jewish origin at a time marked by anti-Semitism. After having studied law and social sciences in the universities of Bonn, Berlin and Göttingen, he knew that his chances of professional success were reduced. Shortly before he took his doctorate in law, Heine was converted to Lutheranism in 1825. But it was to be a waste of time: he never had a steady job, unless we count the six months he spent in Munich as an editor. Most of his income came from his work as a writer, his main activity. He visited Poland in 1822, the North Sea in 1823, the Harz mountains in 1824, England in 1827 and the north of Italy in 1828. All these places inspired him to write. Meanwhile, his links grew stronger with the publishing house of Julius Campe, a Hamburg man opposed to the regime, who after 1826 published most of his books in German, and with Cotta, for whom he wrote review articles. Very early on, Heine openly adopted a stance for the new democratic ideas and against the Restoration politics of Metternich. His works were censored mercilessly. Despite his growing reputation, in 1831 this conflict with the authorities drove him to go to Paris, where liberal ideas had been in the air since the 1830 July Revolution. With Börne, Marx and Engels, Heine formed a part of the German opposition in France, even though literary activity was his main concern. For twenty-five years, he published his writings in German and in French. In 1835, the tensions between Heine and the authorities in his native country were such that the writer and four of his friends who were part of the movement 'Junge Deutschland' (Young Germany) were banned from publishing their works in Germany. This ban, which relaunched the polemic against Heine in his native land, had little effect on the work itself.

The Parisian shop assistant Crescence Eugénie (known as Mathilde) Mirat, whom he married in 1841, did much to reinforce his fondness for France. In 1848, a medical problem with his bone marrow, in combination with an atrophying of the muscles, make him a bedridden invalid for the eight years preceding his death. However, Heine did not stop writing.

'The poet is only a small part of myself'

Despite this declaration by Heine, poetry, together with his critical works, was his speciality. He made his début in lyrical poetry in 1817, when he published in a small Hamburg review *Zwei Lieder der Minne* (*Two Songs of Courtly Love*) under the pseudonym of 'Sy Freudhold Riesenharf', poems in the Romantic style which give no indication of the mixture of sentimentalism and irony which later characterised his style. Ten years later, *Das Buch der Lieder* (*The Book of Songs*) (1827), one of the most republished, translated and set to music poetry collections in the nineteenth century, established his fame as a lyrical poet throughout Europe. These songs of unrequited love, in the tradition of Petrarch's *Canzoniere*, reveal from one poem to the next the dissatisfaction of a nineteenth-century man. The poet's only dramas, *William Ratcliff* and *Almansor* (1823) also date back to this early period; the second offers a meaningful interpretation of the relationship between Islam and Christianity.

During his Parisian period, Heine tackled political themes; the style became harder, more dissonant in dealing with erotic themes. The *Neue Gedichte* (*New Poems*, 1844) called

together love poems in which, despite the sensual possession of the beloved, there is a lingering nostalgia for a total love, and satirical poems, 'Zeitgedichte', which strongly attacked the representatives and ideas of the Restoration. The verse epic, *Deutschland, ein Wintermärchen* (*Germany, A Winter's Tale*, 1844), written after a short trip to Hamburg, had the same aim. In this poem – Heine's most critical about Germany – he depicts his country anaesthetised by its illusions about its past and its chauvinist ideas. *Atta Troll* (1843–1847), a second verse epic in the style of Ariosto, conjured up a picture of Germany as a political dancing bear. With *Romanzero* (*Romancero*, 1851) and *Gedichte* (Poems, 1853–1854), the lyrical poems of his old age, Heine, marked now by illness and death, portrayed with a resigned irony the unavoidable defeat of men of good will. The gaze he directed at his own past and at the Jewish people was charged with melancholy. A third epic, composed at the same time, reflected the same disappointments: having set off in search of the fountain of youth on a wonderful island off the coast of Central America, the traveller hero of *Bimini* (1853) only encounters Hell, the country of death. These belated poems herald the symbolism of the next generation.

A writer all the richer

In German literature, Heine achieved the transition from being a traditional poet to being a modern writer interested in all areas of life and knowledge, who expressed his opinions in newspapers. What was often disdained as journalism proved, on closer inspection, to be an experience of political and intellectual systems formulated with wit and clarity.

The four volumes of *Reisebilder* (*Travel Pictures*, 1826–1831) are Heine's best known works. In them, with an agreeable tone and some twisting of the truth, Heine described his travels in the 1820s. Above all he was interested in national movements, in the transition from the Ancien Régime in Europe to a Europe of free peoples. In the chapter on Marengo in the 'Journey from Munich to Genoa', he formulated his political programme: 'But what is that great task of our time? Emancipation. Not only the Irish, the Greeks, the Jews of Frankfurt, the Negroes of the West Indies and other oppressed peoples, but the emancipation of the whole world, particularly of Europe who has now attained the age of majority and is breaking the chains of privilege and aristocracy.' Some parts of *Travel Pictures* are set out in short works like *Das Buch Legrand* (*The Book of Legrand*), a mixture of Napoleonic legend and love story, or *Die Bäder von Lucca* (*The Baths of Lucca*), in which Heine criticised society. Not all Heine's tales are travellers' tales: *Der Rabbi von Bacherach* (*The Rabbi of Bacherach*) gives a glimpse of the martyrdom of Jews in the Middle Ages; *Die Memoiren des Herrn von Schnabelewopski* (*The Memoirs of Mr Schnabelewopski*) is a fragment of a picaresque novel; *Die Florentinischen Nächte* (*Florentine Nights*) is a new form of dialogue in the style of Boccaccio's *Decameron*. The latter appeared between 1833 and 1840, though they were written earlier. Their principal interest is not in the fascinating storyline on an epic scale, but in the clever arrangement, in the mixture of observations and reflections, of witty episodes and in-depth analysis.

Heine and the theory of art

The 1830s saw the gestation of the great essays on culture and art, in which Heine explained to both the Germans and the French the history and current reality of the two neighbouring countries. In contrast to Madame de Staël, he did not interpret the history of religion and German philosophy as a progression towards idealism, but as an intellectual preparation for a revolution, as a process of freeing oneself from false dogmas. From Luther via Lessing to Kant and Hegel, Heine saw a rising vertical line recording the coming to fruition of the German mind. He summed up the opposition between asceticism, hostile to the senses and the pleasures of the senses in the terms 'spiritualism' and 'sensualism', or

even 'Nazarene' and 'Hellene'. He suggests a modified form of pantheism as the purpose of religious and social evolution. In the footsteps of the Utopia of Saint-Simonianism, in 1834 he wrote in *Zur Geschichte der Religion und Philosophie in Deutschland* (*The History of Religion and Philosophy in Germany*): 'We are not fighting for people's human rights, but for the divine rights of man . . . We do not want to be *sans culottes*, thrifty citizens, cheap presidents; we are founding a democracy of gods who have the same majesty, the same sanctity, the same felicity.'

Heine's main ideas on the theory of art are expressed in *Die romantische Schule* (*The Romantic School*, 1836). This first appeared in French, like some of his other works, then in German. In this work he criticised the historicism of German Romanticism and the aestheticism of Goethe's school. Ancient literature is referred to in it as a period of art which needs to be replaced by a modern critical poetry, a synthesis of art and commitment. He praised young authors because 'they refuse to make a distinction between life and writing, do not separate politics from science, art and religion, and because they are simultaneously artists, tribunes and apostles.'

In certain mythological writings like *Elementargeister* (*Elementals*, 1835–1837), Heine pointed out that there is already a natural pantheism in popular European cultures, which can be used as a departure point for desired renewal. Nature and mind are combined in simple representations of the spirits of water, fire, air and earth.

Heine evoked artistic life in France in the series of articles 'Französische Maler' ('French Painters', 1831–1833), 'Französische Zustände' ('The Situation in France', 1832) and 'Über die französische Bühne' ('The Theatre in France', 1837), written above all for the reviews edited by Cotta. These articles aimed to make German readers familiar with the changes which had taken place in France: the system of constitutional monarchy, the interest of modern French painters in politics, and the social foundation of the Parisian theatre.

His book *Ludwig Börne* (1840) was a brilliant polemic against a former friend who later became an adversary. It was also a self-portrait: Heine explained why he had to distance himself from Börne's short-term republicanism and nationalism, preferring to see a wider emancipation in Europe and a revolution in men's minds.

In the 1840s, Heine continued his reports on France in a voluminous series of articles for Cotta's *Allgemeine Zeitung* (1840–1843). In the meantime the parliamentary system continued to develop in Paris and communism made its appearance in the extra-parliamentary opposition. Heine was the first well-known author to describe communism, which he admired, with a prophetic force and to analyse its significance and also its dangers. However, he decried the equalising constraints of communism, particularly in the field of the arts and sciences. Culture and the new art call for a renewal of society's foundations. The mere proclamation of the rights of man formulated in 1789 is not enough. It needs a patient process of democratic education, the 'incarnation of liberty in the people: the sowing of liberal principles has only done good in an abstract way and it must first of all be quietly rooted in the most rough and ready of concrete realities. Liberty which, up till now, has only grown to manhood sporadically, must be received by the masses themselves, by the lowest layers of society and become the people.'

Heine spent the last years of his life retrospectively, on his poetry as well as his prose. He described some of his memories in *Geständnisse* (*Confessions*, 1854). Here he recognised that he had turned away from the pantheism of the 1830s and rediscovered his faith in a personal God. He also wrote *Memoiren* (*Memoirs*), an unfinished text published in 1884, in which he painted a humorous, radiant picture of his family and his childhood years.

Heine was a complex person, situated midway between classical–Romantic and modern literature. In him were superimposed and mixed Romantic and rationalist traits, ele-

ments of popular and erudite poetry, trivial literature and the art of symbols. During his forty years of activity, he experienced moments of rupture. However, the constants in his work predominate, giving it cohesion and explaining the influence the style and subjects of his works have exercised on nearly all European countries. Symbolism and various movements have laid claim to him. He has sometimes been considered the greatest poet since Goethe, sometimes as a destroyer of literature, or the representative of 'non-poetry' (Benedetto Croce). These two extreme judgements have today been superseded. They have given way to more objective considerations, in which the lyric poet and prose-writer may be more serenely appreciated.

Mickiewicz (1798–1855)

B. Dopart

> A curse on peoples who stone their prophets!
> Adam Mickiewicz,
> *To Russian Friends*

The Polish writer Adam Mickiewicz personified a national Romanticism without nationalist deformations and open to universal cultural values. The Romantic creative principle which presided over his principal writings consisted in seeking a synthesis of different literary genres, of narrative historiography and of poetic myths. A man of action, by his personal example, his political writings and prophetic appeals, he gave his support to the cause of the liberty of peoples. He was born three years after the fall of the Polish State, the year in which Napoleon began his Egyptian campaign. He died carrying out a patriotic mission during the Crimean War, eight years after the January insurrection, a political action that marked the end of Romanticism in Poland.

The Romantic

The initiator of Polish Romanticism, Mickiewicz studied at the university of Vilnius, one of the main centres of Polish education. A difference in social status became an obstacle to a love affair in his youth; he gave artistic expression to that failure by reconciling profound idealism with an outburst of passion characteristic of Byron. He was imprisoned, judged by a Czarist tribunal and exiled to Russia for having taken part in a patriotic plot. After his involvement in this conspiracy, he felt torn between his attachment to an ethical code of chivalry and obligatory recourse to illegal methods. When he was able to leave the empire of the Czar, Mickiewicz travelled in Germany – where he visited Goethe and A. W. Schlegel – Switzerland and Italy. After 1832, he spent most of his time in Paris, recognised as the nation's spiritual mentor by a group of Polish émigrés. He understood the enthusiasm of creative passion and the feeling of power characteristic of the 'century of geniuses'. Paradoxically, he also doubted the power of poetic language in the areas of knowledge and morality. Twenty years before his death, he stopped publishing his works, hiding among his manuscripts some excellent poems and lyrical fragments. Critical about academic knowledge, he nevertheless accepted the post of teacher of Latin literature in Lausanne, then the post of Professor of Slavic Literature at the Collège de France where, with Michelet and Quinet, he opposed the July monarchy and professed Messianic hopes. He followed up his democratic, independent-minded ideas by participating in the Springtime of the Peoples and by editing *La Tribune des Peuples* (*The Tribune of the Peoples*), a newspaper which preached a radical social programme and used revolutionary European slogans.

Mickiewicz's Romanticism, which knew neither pessimism nor escapism, was imprinted with the fascination the poet felt for Napoleon. In this he was close to Byron: he conceived of historical experience as an existential intervention, like a myth animating the collective conscience. He modelled the relationship of the individual to the nation in a heroic direction, which had as its ultimate consequence a Messianic representation of a character who was simultaneously martyr,

liberator and religious prophet. Mickiewicz's poetry revealed his need to know everything, his nostalgia for a universal sacred order, his desire to reconcile the ethical with his image of the world or the truths of faith with the results of experimental science.

An eschatological vision

This cognitive project (opposed to the idea of 'physical and moral order' peculiar to the Enlightenment) was already present in one of Mickiewicz's first works, the drama *Dziady* (*Ancestors*, parts II and III in 1823). The poet referred to the religious and philosophical sources of Antiquity, to the still extant idea of the Eastern Slavs that the sacrosanct represented the cosmos. He made the eschatological beliefs of these people into a poetic adaptation: he transported the modest ceremony to commemorate the dead which, according to custom, takes place in houses and cemeteries, to a chapel where he gave it the dimension of a rite, a symbolic reproduction of the process of the creation of the world. Souls in purgatory appeared in it, who formulate a primitive and sublime moral code, based on an affirmation of human destiny and on the commandment of charity. There was even a trinity of ghosts who make visible the physical order of the cosmos, revealing a link, ungraspable for the lay spirit, between the order of nature and ethical law. Introduced into the same rite, the posthumous confession of a fourth spectre unveiled the reasons for Romantic individualism. The story of an unfulfilled love and a suicide are transformed into a treatise on the soul enslaved by the temporal world and the suffering which impregnates the whole of existence. The interpenetration of a popular vision of man and a tragic anthropology made of the second and fourth parts of *Ancestors* a unique work in its genre.

The third part of *Ancestors* (1823) is justifiably considered as the manifesto of Polish Messianism in solidarity with enslaved peoples. Mickiewicz tried to claim for European culture a symbol that would clearly show the links between the individual, the nation, humanity and God. The story of the drama's protagonist was based on the myth of Adam, in which the elevation of the first man and his domination of nature are followed by his rebellion against the Creator and the fall, then penitence and transfiguration. The myth of Adam was also manifestly linked to the eschatological concept of history and the Messianic prophecy announcing a new humanity, the New Church and the triumph of the Gospel spirit in political and social life.

Mickiewicz's Adamism, with its Biblical sources, is above all that of the mystics and theosophers; far removed from ecclesiastical orthodoxy, it is, on the other hand, close to the Romantic philosophy of activism and the basic literary problems of the period. The poet criticised the Promethean character of the Enlightenment which, according to him, did not give a satisfactory response to the question of the reciprocal links between human nature and historical evil. The idea of man expressed in the drama, which takes account of the antinomies of Byronic metaphysical revolt, seems to have been conceived as an alternative to Goethe's Faustian humanism.

Master Thaddeus

Pan Tadeusz (Master Thaddeus, 1834), the national Polish epic, re-established links with accumulated noble traditions from the end of the sixteenth century to the middle of the eighteenth. These traditions, which were called Sarmatism, included a range of values, chivalrous, property-owning, moral, religious and republican. The Polish Romantics had a way of dealing with them which reminds us of German Romantic medievalism. Unlike writers with a conservative tendency, Mickiewicz tried to bring these values up-to-date in a democratic context.

The poem depicts the domestic life of the provincial nobility in the years 1811 and 1812. The legions, a Polish army of liberation which headed for Russia to Napoleon, form a touch of historical pathos. The hero is a humble monk, a converted adventurer and criminal

who, through his patriotic merits, expiates his faults and saves his soul. The main significance of the work comes from the narrator's situation in the world portrayed; it resides in the aesthetic symbolism of Romanticism. We can identify the 'person' of the narrator, fictionally absent, but made concrete by lyrical means, like a Romantic creator – the poet – who empties the world from his soul and, moved by religious inspiration, proclaims a solar theodicy. *Master Thaddeus*, the work of a poet who venerated Dante, is one of the great manifestations of a valiant faith in European poetry:

Ksiega XI, Rok 1812
Wojna! Wojna! – nie było w
Litwie kąta ziemi,
Gdzieby jej huk nie doszedł.
Pomiędzy ciemmemi
Puszczami, chłop, którego dziady
 i rodzice
Pomarli, nie wyjrzauszy za lasu
granice,
Który innych na niebie nie
 rozumiał krzyków
Prócz wichrów, a na ziemi prócz
 bestyi ryków,
Gości innych nie widzial oprócz
 społ-leśników:
Teraz widzi na niebie dziwna
łuna pała.

Book XI, Year 1812
The war! The war! There is
not on Lithuanian soil
a single acre which this apocalyptic
rumbling does not reach.
In the forests, the peasant whose
ancestors and father
died without even having
crossed the border of
their land,
who never heard in the sky
any noise but that of the wind,
on earth
any noise but that of
animals howling,
he who has never seen
humans apart from those, familiar

to him, coming from the woods,
now he sees in the sky
strange lights that
flash.

Among Mickiewicz's other works, *Ballady i romanse* (*Ballads and Romances*, 1822) introduced Polish Romanticism under the sign of popular traditions; a Romantic orientalism pervaded *Sonety Krymskie* (*Crimean Sonnets*, 1826); the lyrical poems of Lausanne (1839–1840) were a cycle of mystical poems ahead of their time; *Graøyna* (*Grazyna*, 1823) is an epic poem with a medieval ring; the hero of the poetic novel *Konrada Wallenroda* (*Konrad Wallenrod*, 1828) makes a tragic sacrifice for his homeland, and *Księgi narodu i pielgrzymstwa polskiego* (*The Books of the Nation and of Polish Pilgrims*, 1832), are written in Biblical prose. *The Books*, composed in Paris for his émigré compatriots, and above all *Master Thaddeus*, made Mickiewicz extremely popular among all the Slavs.

Pushkin (1799–1837)

A. Monnier

The words of a poet are already tantamount to actions.

Gogol, *Selected Correspondence with Friends*

When Pushkin appeared, Russian literature, the last son and heir of European letters, was still a vast piece of fallow land broken up here and there by recently cultivated plots. At the end of Pushkin's brief career, cut off in full flow by a duel at the age of thirty-seven, Russia could boast of having an authentic national literature.

French influence

Born into an aristocratic family in Moscow, steeped in the French culture of the Enlightenment, Pushkin soon had access to the great French works in their original language. This is why his poetic vocation, which began when he was thirteen at the grammar school of Tsarkoïe Selo, quenched his thirst first and foremost quite naturally at this source.

Until 1820, Pushkin took inspiration in large doses from poetry by Parny, Millevoye, Delille, Lebrun or Marie Joseph Chénier, eclectically going from elegy to satire, from Anacreontic lyricism to romance and from the eclogue in letter form to heroic or epic songs. His relationship to these models nevertheless excluded all mimicry: the young poet only borrowed his subjects or the overall tone of his works to indulge in stylistic exercises, often of astonishing virtuosity, working with the material offered by Russian language and prosody. He tried to pull Russian literature away from the archaic ponderousness of the eighteenth century. In the company of reforming writers clustered together in the Arzamas Association, he broke lances with the adepts of a classicism petrified by stylistic rules. French influence was equally perceptible in the political liberalism derived from the Encyclopédistes which pushed a certain number of poems to express 'civil' revolt directed against autocracy and all forms of oppression against the citizen: 'Oda na vol'nost' ' (Ode to Liberty), 'Derevnya' (The Country), 'Čaadaevu' (To Tchaadaev). A virulent hostility against Czar Alexander and his entourage forced even Pushkin to write epigrams of a dangerous audacity that earned him a long period of exile in the southern provinces of Russia from 1820.

Despite his openness to European culture, the young Pushkin remained unaffected by German Romanticism, which Zhukovsky had already acclimatised to Russian taste and which had a certain fascination for a section of young Russian people. His first narrative poem, *Ruslan i Ljudmila* (*Ruslan and Ljudmila*, 1820), was a tongue-in-cheek parody of Zhukovsky. It substituted a malicious fairyland for the dark motifs of Germanic ballads and lined his lyrical outpourings with Voltairean humour.

Enthusiasm for Lord Byron

From the beginning of his exile in southern Russia, Pushkin was seized by a lively admiration for the work of Byron, whose characteristic themes henceforth reverberated in his verse. The poem *Kavkazskij plennik* (*The Prisoner of the Caucasus*), published in 1821, began this new phase in his career. We can see in this poem the main ingredients of Byronic Romanticism: the flamboyant exoticism of the natural setting, the disenchantment of a hero whose existential unhappiness no passion can eradicate, the pathetic ending. The whole poem is carried forward by a flow of uninterrupted lyricism. The theme of *Baxtĕisarajskij fontan* (*The Fountain of Baxtechisaraï*, 1824), centred on the murderous jealousy of the favourite of an oriental prince towards a European captive, also pays obvious tribute to Byron, even if the melancholy accents of the epilogue have a truly Pushkinian tone.

It is to the same source that the haughty desperation of shorter pieces refers, such as 'Pogaslo dnevnoe svetilo . . .' ('The Daystar has gone out . . .'), 'Demon' ('The Demon') and 'Svobody sejatel' pustinnyj . . .' ('The Sterile Sower of Liberty').

Pushkin's first original masterpiece, *Cigany* (*The Gypsy Women*), finished in 1824, also borrows a Byronic theme as it presents the insurmountable opposition between nature and civilisation. An antagonism from which there is no way out pits the possessive passion of the Russian Aleko against the 'primitive' need for boundless liberty felt by the young nomad with whom he falls in love. But Pushkin revamps this commonplace with important formal innovations, notably subordinating lyrical writing to a dramatic structure that replaces monologue by authentic dialogue, while his narrative style becomes increasingly sober.

Poetic maturity

A period of extraordinary poetic creativity began up for Pushkin after his second period of exile, which led him to stay for two years in Mikhaïlovskoïe before being set free by Nicholas I in 1826. Having achieved perfect mastery of his creative faculties, Pushkin shook off the Byronic influence, having paid him one last homage, in 1824, in the poem *K Morju* (*To the Sea*). From then on Pushkin's personal lyricism became purer and deeper. From now on Pushkin tended to give prominence to the objectivity of his vision and to the simplicity of stylistic means for translating all stirrings of sensibility. This is how the concrete truth of a landscape often became the favoured means of expressing a state of soul, as in 'Zimnij Večer' ('Winter Evening'):

> *The storm that rages,*
> *White swirling fog,*
> *Howls at the sky, a wild animal,*
> *Whimpers softly, a small child;*
> *And the wind, the wind penetrates*
> *The old broken-down thatched cottage,*
> *The wind knocks on the window*
> *Like a traveller lost at night.*

His narrative poetry evolved along the lines laid down by *The Gypsy Women* combining all types of writing in long stretches. The poem *Poltava* (1828) reflected this syncretist ambition. The grandiose evocation of the battle in which Peter the Great triumphed over the Swedes constitutes the epic crowning of the work. But this denouement actually resolved a political and sentimental intrigue of which the Cossack hetman Mazeppa is the tragic hero, and which mixes lyricism, drama and forms of writing inspired by popular tales.

The same desire to decompartmentalise genres and to harmonise the most varied styles shows itself to stunning effect in the 'verse novel' begun in 1825 and finished in 1831, *Evgenij Onegin* (*Eugene Onegin*). The two protagonists, Eugene and Tatiana, a couple who never get together, are sketched on the basis of easily identifiable literary materials. Pushkin endows them with a singularly poetical life which transcends his models. His heroine, in particular, is depicted in such subtle communion with her country's nature and national customs that Dostoyevsky later saw in her the archetypal figure of Russian womanhood. An omnipresent narrator, who sometimes lends his voice to the characters, sometimes detaches himself from them ironically, gives the tale an allegro tempo, while the evocation of Russia in all its aspects, including the humblest, gives this work a realistic colouring, although it serves above all as a pretext for many poetic variations.

During the same period, Pushkin injected fresh blood into the Russian theatre's repertoire. Dazzled by Shakespeare, like his Western contemporaries, in 1825 he wrote a historical tragedy on a national theme taken from the time of troubles at the beginning of the seventeenth century, *Boris Godunov*. The real hero is not the infanticide Czar, Boris, tormented by remorse, nor the usurper Dmitri, who ends up by stealing his throne from him, nor even the Russian people, a collective character with a surprisingly dramatic stage presence, but History itself and its procession of violence and iniquity that the play imposes as a modern portrayal of destiny. Five years later, Pushkin composed a cycle of four short tragedies, dramas in miniature, in which an action even more pared down than that of classical tragedy is played out in a concentrated way over a very short period of time. Pushkin's laconic power of suggestion was placed at the service of a tragic vision of the human condition. Beyond the destructive passions which seem to motivate the characters, these dramas explored the depths of being and unveiled a world of hidden impulses in which the dizziness of death fused with an irrepressible need for absolute values.

The predominance of prose

During the last phase of his literary career, Pushkin showed his preference for prose. He revealed his opposition to the sentimental, romantic prose of his time with a collection of five short stories, *Povesti Belkina* (*The Tales of Belkin*, 1830). These are characterised by the dynamism of the narration, the rigour of the composition and a form which is shorn of

all decorative ornament. Pushkin abandoned himself to a humorous parody of literary conventions, letting us see how real life is linked to the imaginary.

Pikovaya Dama (*The Queen of Spades*), written in 1834, is more solemn in tone. Its hero heralds Dostoyevsky's Raskolnikov in his 'Napoleonic' amorality, in the service of a will to power that will lead him into madness. Pushkin has him evolve in an ambiguous universe, located at the limits of the real and the supernatural, where the past never stops symbolically interfering with the present, so that the mystery of souls is thereby deepened and the irony of destiny acquires a demonic dimension.

Two more voluminous works made him a novelist. If *Dubrovsky* (*Dubrovsky*, 1832), too indebted to the eighteenth-century adventure novel, was left unfinished, *Kapitanskaja dočka* (*The Captain's Daughter*), published in 1836, represented an original success in the realm of the historical novel. Set in the reign of Catherine II, the novel depicts the Cossack usurper Pugatchev, who had raised up an army of peasants against the powers-that-be. Pushkin gave his material a historian's objectivity, keeping himself aloof as much from apology as from caricature in the portrayal of his hero. But this impartiality did not prevent him from bringing the period to life with the fascinating reality of portraits and descriptions, and without giving in to Romantic exaggeration.

The visible decrease in poetic production over this period was in no way a synonym of decline. Pushkin enlarged the area covered by his creative activity by composing a series of tales which, in a juicy style, copy popular poetry. His last great poem, *Medny vsadnik* (*The Bronze Horseman*), written in 1833, gives free course to his visionary imagination to express the tragic conflict which always opposed Russian history and the Russian citizen. With its infinitely rich and contrasting images of Peter the Great's the metropolis, this poem began the famous myth of St Petersburg in Russian literature.

The poetics of Pushkin

Pushkin had a marked ability to assimilate foreign borrowings. He distinguished himself in all literary genres and was in permanent contact with all European literature, both classical and modern. He also knew how to express his own personality and the intimate relationship he maintained with Russian culture.

Varied in its forms and in its themes, Pushkin's work presented remarkably constant aspects which gave it a vigorous originality. Whatever the subject or the type of writing, Pushkin's text is subtle and balanced. To this elegant consistency of architecture, Pushkin adds a lightness of touch. In the middle of a period of verbosity, Pushkin worked at being laconic and economical, always preferring allusion or suggestion to exaggeration and pomposity. He is justifiably considered to be the real founder of literary language in Russia, whatever the occasional merits may have been of his predecessors in the century of Catherine. He was the first Russian writer to use the riches of his national language in all its fullness, reconciling various stylistic registers within his poetic creations in which they fuse together with an ease and a naturalness which indicate the greatest victory of his art. At the same time, he admirably mastered the possibilities of Russian verse and its tonic metre to create diverse melodic effects.

His genius never prostrated itself to the pre-established demands of any idea, for he loathed didacticism in art. His work never failed to express in depth a coherent vision of the world in which a tragic consciousness of individual destiny or the collective destiny of man does not manage to do away with an obstinate aspiration to happiness, which can only be realised in communion with Beauty. Pushkin's 'realism' has been discussed too often and superficially, because the most ordinary beings and things can become objects of poetry.

Andersen (1805–1875)

P. E. Sœrensen

There's nothing wrong with being born in a farmyard when you hatch out of a swan's egg.
Hans Christian Andersen,
The Ugly Duckling

Andersen was a major writer whose work covered most genres. Whatever the chosen form, his texts all had an ambivalence which was an obstacle to the stability of the worlds he created. His works were an incomplete staging of himself, drawn between two incompatible poles: a miserable childhood in Odense and an adult life in cultivated bourgeois circles. He lacked solid roots in either of these two milieux, yet had a constant need to be recognised by them. Andersen openly celebrated the petit bourgeois civil servants he mixed with. He kept his childhood secret, spent as it was with the proletariat, although he anonymously praising the them as being a natural focus for goodness. His work was a constant masquerade, Behind each mask lay hidden a multitude of others. For this reason, Andersen is as much an ironic Romantic as a legitimate interpreter of bourgeois culture. We constantly find these ambiguities between different works and within a single work.

A plant of the marshes

Andersen was born a son of the people and understood the conditions of life in the proletariat. He was always short of money as a child. This frightened him. He hated a poverty: as a 'plant of the marshes', he wanted to be able to flower in the light and fulfil his dream of security. But without means, without education and without a family he could be proud of, security seemed impossible. Helped by an unbelievably tenacious will to survive, he found all that outside his own social milieu. After a series of failures in the theatrical world, he finally became the protégé of cultivated bourgeois do-gooders, which admitted him to the world of culture and sinecures: higher education. Social recognition, however, never succeeded in reducing Anderson's feelings of insecurity. He lived through a roller-coaster ride of peaks and troughs, making them the constant themes of newspaper articles, biographies, novels and stories. At Christmas 1825, during a stay as a student in a family in Copenhagen, he noted in his diary, having first presented himself as a 'fortunate chosen one', that he was at his window looking at the street below: 'Five or six years ago I too was in the street below, I knew no one in the town and now I can, above all that and in the bosom of a loved and respected family, treat myself to gobbets of Shakespeare.' The 'above all that' is revealing. The person who wrote it was torn between an 'above' and a 'below'. He tried unsuccessfully to reconcile these two poles. His diary continued: 'Oh, how good God is, a drop of the honey of happiness makes me forget all my bitterness. He has made me so happy.' Simultaneously happy and bitter, torn and chosen, impossible to reconcile and reconciled with the world, that was Andersen's situation as a writer.

All his autobiographies contained this tragic evocation of a divine reconciliation. Not the God of the Christians, but the medieval wheel of fortune – this is what makes a unity of his overstretched self. Whether his memoirs were authentic or fictitious, they were all marked by an intense desire for happiness which gave the guarantee that, in spite of all his trials, he was 'a chosen one'. This motif was already in his first autobiography *Levnedsbogen* (*The Book of My Life*, 1831), and was much more developed in the later *Mit Livs Eventyr* (*The Story of My Life*, 1855). He passionately pursued this theme in a whole series of autobiographical texts, for example the tale *Den grimme Aelling* (*The Ugly Duckling*, 1843) and the novel *Improvisatorem* (*The Improviser*, 1835). His novels were all built around one autobiographical kernel. *O.T.* (1836) and *Kun en Spillemand* (*Just a Fiddler*, 1837), for instance, have heroes from the underprivileged classes of society. And, like Andersen's alter egos, they try to climb the social ladder. The model here is Goethe's *Wilhelm Meister*, who never

managed to bring the action to a convincing conclusion, for the antagonisms were too strong. In the legitimate discourse of the 'Bildungsroman', there is always a contradictory rhetoric which shows us everything that must be repressed for happiness to be possible. Exactly as in *The Ugly Duckling*, the masked narrator tells us that other than a story of reconciliation: the story of an incurable social, personal and aesthetic tearing. This ambiguity, associated with descriptions of exotic backgrounds, fascinated a European public, and Andersen was known internationally before he was known in his own country. His many travelogues, *Billedbog uden Billeder* (*The Picture Book without Pictures*, 1840), *En Digters Bazar* (*A Poet's Bazaar*, 1842), *I Sverige* (*In Sweden*, 1851) and *I Spanien* (*In Spain*, 1863), cultivated the impressionistic exoticism in the wake of the Italian travel pictures of *The Improviser*.

The ambivalence of Andersen's world

Andersen began with a tale of a fictitious journey, in the German Romantic style, *Fodrejse fra Holmens Kanal til Østpynten af Amager* (*The Journey on Foot from the Holm Canal to the Eastern Point of Amager*, 1828). Here he played on a fractured fantasy in the style of Tieck and Hoffmann and, like a new Friedrich Schlegel, carried out experiments with Romantic irony. Written between 1835 and 1872, first under the title *Eventyr, fortalter for Børn* (*Tales told to Children*), then under the simpler title of *Tales or Stories*, Andersen's tales are imaginative, original works. In his plays and novels he used recognised genres which already enjoyed the critical appreciation of the cultivated bourgeois public, but he wrote his tales in a form which had no 'official' sanction. This allowed him to write more freely. In 125 stories, his ambivalence blossomed in a bewildering, limitless ludicity: childhood was simulated, naïveté was well thought out, spontaneity was a sham. In children's stories, he dealt with the most horrendous knowledge: 'truly the world is ignoble', he said in *Skyggen* (*The Shadow*). Toys, plants and animals appear everywhere as carnival parodies of the rigid, problematic adult world. These fragments of culture evoked a nature that was absent and a repressed childhood. Under the childish mask of naiveté, this fair culture implodes, even in tales like *Klokken* (*The Bell*) which try to promote its values. In texts that seem closer to his optimistic cultural ideals, like *Den lille Havfrue* (*The Little Mermaid*), *Snedronningen* (*The Snow Queen*) and *Den lille Pige med Svovlstikkene* (*The Little Matchgirl*), the story is continually undermined from within by implicit negations. Other stories, such as *Hjertesorg* (*Heartache*), *Tante Tandpine* (*Aunty Toothache*), *Den standhaftige Tinsoldat* (*The Brave Tin Soldier*) and *Tårnvoegteren Ole* (*Ole the Watchman*), erode all trace of optimism even though they constantly dream about it. In these tales the world is an unstable place. In *The Shadow*, this ambivalent game is staged in a profound reflection on splits in relationships. The fine culture of the elite is embodied by 'the Scholar' who talks and writes about 'the Good, the True and the Beautiful', without having any connection to the real world around him. Everything he cannot or does not want to understand takes the form of a shadow, of his shadow which, little by little, comes to lead a 'life' which is increasingly autonomous and makes a lot of money by unmasking many hypocritical forms of kindness. Under the surface of culture, in this real world that the Scholar does not want to bother with, baseness reigns. The Shadow throws itself wholly into this bourgeois hypocrisy and, in the end, marries the princess, while the Scholar is decapitated: culture is dead and the future belongs to shadows. The irony here takes 'high culture' as its target and its problematic offspring; but this irony is linked to what it destroys. Behind *The Shadow* stretch the burnt-out landscapes of nihilism, like an uninhabitable region:

Den lærde Mand havde det slet ikke godt, Sorg og Plage fulgte ham, og hvad han talte om det Sande og det Gode og det Skjønne, det var for de Fleste ligesom Roser for en Ko! -

han var ganske syg tilsidst.
«De seer virkelig ud ligesom en Skygge!» sagde Folk til ham, og det gjøs i den lærde Mand, for han tænkte ved det.
«De skal tage til Bad!» sagde Skyggen, som kom og besøgte ham, «der er ikke andet for! Jeg vil tage Dem med for gammelt Bekjendtskabs Skyld, jeg betaler Reisen og De gjør Beskrivelsen og er saadan lidt morsom for mig paar Veien! Jeg vil til et Bad, mit Skjæg groer ikke ud som det skulde, det er ogsaa en Sygdom, og Skjæg maa man have! Vær De nu fornuftig og tag imod Tilbudet, vi reise jo som Kammerater!»

The Scholar was not at all well, unhappiness and cares were dogging his footsteps and all he said to people about the True, the Good and the Beautiful was, in the majority of cases, like throwing pearls before swine: and finally he became really ill.
'You really look like a shadow!' people said to him; and the Scholar shivered because he was thinking.
'You should go to take the waters!' said the Shadow when it paid him a visit. 'There's no other solution! I'll take you with me in the name of our old friendship: I'll pay for the journey, you can describe it and you can divert me a bit on the way! I want to take the waters as my beard doesn't grow as it should, and that's an illness too for one ought to have a beard! Come on, be reasonable and accept my offer and we'll be travelling companions, naturally!'

Apart from this total irony, there is only a vague, Utopian concept of poetry: neither the Scholar, nor the Shadow, nor the narrator can really know it as it is, but perhaps they can imagine it. The Shadow is the formulation of a new poetics *per se* in which the beautiful is not necessarily 'beautiful' or 'good', but true for all that. It is only in a few rare tales, like *Elverhøj* (*Elf Hill*), that the narrator throws himself into the experience of the comically Utopian, but the story is then sent 'underground'. Andersen's irony is basically that of an orphan. But in this captive, exiled irony there is an irremediable vitality, an almost unbelievable 'still more'. This excess of irony represents Andersen's discredited inheritance. Discredited because posterity, essentially, will choose the child in Andersen without recognising the intention of the irony. But he is still read and reread because the openings towards an unspoken something else, which are silently present in the fissures of the work, continue to fascinate us.

Gogol (1809–1852)

D. Fanger

A word from the heart cannot be hacked out with an axe.

> Nikolai Vasilievich Gogol,
> *Dead Souls*

Gogol is universally recognised as the greatest Russian comic writer. He is also one of the creators of the modern Russian novel. Born in the Ukraine, he chose to write in Russian. His literary output, immediately appreciated for its originality and expressive power, nevertheless disconcerted his contemporaries who wanted clear, unambiguous messages. Because his mature works gave unusual emphasis to the prosaic details of everyday life and to characters who are worryingly banal, he was for a long time considered in Russia to be a realist, despite a constant violation of the principles on which all realism rests. In the same way, he is held traditionally to be a satirist, though the mysterious poetry of his creations largely transcends the purpose of satire. In fact, the entire Gogol phenomenon is a paradox: his temperament, his biography and his career, no less than his work and his artistic heritage were fundamentally excentric. The challenge, faced by translators and critics, has been to do justice to his weirdness; for a long time, most of them, educated to expect something more conventional, had great difficulty in recognising what they had before their very eyes.

The art of displacement

One of the reasons for this strangeness is the persistent, subtle displacement to be found in Gogol's most characteristic works. Things are rarely where we think they are and rarely what they seem to be. When, in the novel *Mĕrtvyje duši* (*Dead Souls*, 1842), the prosecutor dies, we read: 'We perceived then that the prosecutor had a soul: out of modesty no doubt, he had never shown it before.' the smug, self-satisfied Major Kovaliov, the protagonist of *Nos* (*The Nose*, 1835), without doubt the most enigmatic of Gogol's tales, wakes up one fine morning to find that his nose has disappeared from his face. He ends up by surprising this mobile appendage in the process of paying a visit, 'wearing a uniform embroidered with gold, with a big stiff collar, chamois leather trousers and a sword at his side, his two-cornered hat with feathers giving to understand that he had the rank of state councillor'. Kovaliov follows the usurper to a cathedral to find that 'the nose had completely hidden its face in the great stiff collar and was praying with an expression of enraptured piety'! When he dares to protest: 'After all, you are my own nose!' the nose replies: 'You are mistaken, sir, I only belong to myself.' Identities with Gogol are rarely stable. In *Revizor* (*The Government Inspector*, 1836), the corrupt administrators of a small Russian provincial town persuade themselves that a young man passing through is a government inspector sent to make a report on them; when the postmaster discovers their error by unsealing a letter, the governor asks him:

Городничий. Да как же вы осмелились распечатать письмо

такоĭ уполномоченноĭ особы?
Почтмеĭстер. В том-то и штука,
что он и не унолномоченньıĭ и не
особа!
Городничиĭ. Что же он, по-вашему,
такое?
Почтмеĭстер. Ни се ни то! черт
знает что такое!

THE GOVERNOR But how could
you have dared to open a letter to
such a great personage?
THE POSTMASTER Because,
in fact, he is neither great nor
a personage!
THE GOVERNOR Well then,
what do you say he is?
THE POSTMASTER Neither
one thing nor the other . . . The devil
only knows who he is!

The postmaster's words must be taken literally.
People are not what they seem. This displacement technique is also in the structure of the
work, which tends to circularity. A meaningful
experience is visibly denied to the characters;
the reader must discover the sense of the text.

According to an often-quoted formula,
Gogol talked about producing in his readers
laughter through invisible tears. In fact,
laughter, tears and terror (often associated
with the erotic) together constitute the scale
of responses striven for. Romantic and inclined
to hyperbole by nature, Gogol combined
grand artistic aspirations with a leaning towards what Flaubert called 'the melancholy of
matter', and this combination distils in his
work a unique poetry. Reality appeared to
Gogol as intrinsically devoid of sense, and he
set himself the task of giving it meaning by the
sole force of his art.

Creative energy

The active period of Gogol's career was
remarkably brief, and was framed by two
works which were radically distinct from his
main achievements. *Hans Küchelgarten*, a
long narrative poem, was published under a

pseudonym in 1829; *Vybrannye mesta iz
perepiski s druz' jami* (*Selected Correspondence
with My Friends*, 1847) is a patchwork of
moral, social and literary essays, written in
epistolary form and offered, after five years of
silence, to a public impatient for the second
volume of his epic novel *Dead Souls*. Between
these two works lay an intensely prolific period
of eleven years, from 1831 to 1842. His first
tales were collected as *Večera, na khutore bliz'
Dikan'ki* (*Village Evenings near Dikanka*,
1831–1832). Set in a Ukraine of light opera,
their content varies from popular farce,
Soročinskaja jamarka (*Sorochintsky Fair*) to the
sombre opera of *Strašnaja mest'* (*A Terrible
Revenge*) by way of the strange comedy of *Ivan
Fedorovič Špon'ka i ego tetuška* (*Ivan Fyodoro-
vich Shponka and his Aunt*). *Mirgorod* (1835),
on the face of it, continued these tales, but,
in reality, it showed that Gogol had reached
maturity and was abandoning Ukrainian
themes. Together with the early historical epic
Taras Bul'ba (*Taras Bulba*, 1835), this volume
also contained the pseudo-folkloric *Viy*, with
its suggestions of perverse eroticism, the
brilliant opener, *Starostvetskie pomeščiki* (*Old-
World Landowners*), a masterpiece of ambivalence, and *Povest' o tom kak possorilis' Ivan
Ivanovič s Ivanom Nikiforovičem* (*The Story of
How the Two Ivans Quarrelled*), another variation
on the comedy of human mediocrity.

In 1835, Gogol published a new volume,
Arabeski (*Arabesques*), a mixture of essays
and fiction which included *Nevskij prospekt*
(*Nevsky Prospekt*), *Portret* (*The Portrait*) and
Zapiski sumasšedšego (*Notes of a Madman*)
belong to the Petersburgiskie povesti (St
Petersburg Tales), Then came *The Nose* and
his masterpiece in the short-story genre,
Šinyel' (*The Overcoat*, 1842). The main character in this cycle is Saint-Petersburg, depicted
as a place of absurdity and diabolical malevolence, where sensitive, innocent souls are
condemned and soulless beings prosper.
Dostoyevsky pursued and developed this
portrayal, as also did the symbolists at the turn
of the century.

In 1836 the premiere of *The Government
Inspector* took place, in which creation and

confession went together. The accidental impostor Khlestakov rivals with the mayor and his associates in an orgy of imaginary accomplishments which escalate and only crumble in the final scene with the announcement of the arrival of the real government inspector. When the primitive habits of Russian actors had transformed Gogol's subtle art into broad farce, he left Russia for Italy, resolved to give up the pursuit of glory and only to write for posterity.

The project to which he devoted himself was the novel *Dead Souls*, begun in 1835 on Pushkin's insistence, who reminded him that Cervantes would no doubt be no longer remembered had he not undertaken *Don Quixote*. The initial situation, as for *The Government Inspector*, was given to him by Pushkin himself. When Pushkin was killed in 1837, Gogol treated it as a sacred trust laid on him. Located in the heart of Russia, the story is centred on Tchitchikov, a scoundrel who had undertaken to redeem dead serfs who were still included in the official population census, the 'dead souls' of the title. His stay in the town of N. brings him into contact with a series of landowner caricatures, maniacs whose principal obsession is reflected in the organisation of their estates as well as in their conduct. Subtitled a 'poem', the novel abounds in authorial digressions on the theme of Russia and its destiny. This theme makes full sense of a constant emphasis on absence, absurdity, banality and non-sequiturs of all sorts in arguments and narrative. Like Pushkin's verse novel, *Eugene Onegin, Dead Souls* is an exercise in Romantic irony, a novel on the writing of a novel.

A spiritual guide

In 1842, when *Dead Souls* appeared, Gogol thought of it as 'only the rather pale threshold of the great poem which is being constructed in it, and which will finally resolve the problem of its existence', somewhat along the lines of Dante's *Divine Comedy*. The manner was different in each of its parts. Gogol believed that his own spiritual education was a prerequisite for the accomplishment of his work. Increasingly anguished, he gave up comedy and disowned all his previous work. To the public who were waiting for volume two of *Dead Souls* he offered *Selected Passages from Correspondence with My Friends*, a series of short sermons on Russian life and literature, in which he outlined the duties that a Russian spiritual leader and educator should have for society. There was a role which only the new generation would be able to assume. When he died, most of those about to create the golden age of the Russian novel had started to publish, confirming his forecasts.

'We all came out of Gogol's Overcoat'

What a contemporary had noted during Gogol's lifetime – namely that everyone saw in his work what they wanted to see, rather than what was really there – remained true after his death. Always considered as a classic, he appeared to the nineteenth-century as a realist writer. At the beginning of the twentieth century, the emphasis was placed rather on the strangeness and grotesqueness of his work, in which anticipations of symbolism and surrealism were seen. As much can be said of his influence on later Russian writers. 'We all came out of Gogol's *Overcoat*' is a remark often attributed to Dostoyevsky, but it could have been made by any one of the writers of the latter's generation. In the same way, many major writers of the period 1890–1930 might have said, thinking of their bold experiments in the field of style: 'We all came out of Gogol's *Nose*.' In Western Europe, the difficulties of translation, coupled with a certain predisposition (as in Mérimée) to see Gogol through already familiar ways of seeing, led to his constant underestimation. Kafka was an exception: *The Nose* was one of his favourite stories, and his own *Metamorphosis* shows his indebtedness to Gogol. Fiction by Nabokov and Siniavsky represented an extension of the techniques which Gogol pioneered.

13 *The Second Half of the Nineteenth Century: Realism and Naturalism*

H. MARMARINOU

They call me a psychological novelist, which is false; I am merely a realist in the highest sense of the word, which is to say that I depict the human soul in all its depth.

Dostoyevsky

The literary production of the second half of the nineteenth century, the era of positivism and scientism which are exclusively linked to actual facts, was characterised by realism, a literary trend which left a deep mark on the history of European letters. In the middle of the nineteenth century, a new wind of liberalisation blew throughout Europe. This had an effect on absolutist States like constitutional monarchies, and lively people still deprived of liberty and national unity with a nationalist spirit. This liberalism reached its zenith in 1848, when a series of revolutions of a complex nature occurred which historians have called the 'springtime of the peoples'. At the same time the Industrial Revolution, which began in England, spread through Europe. On the philosophical level, the positivist and scientific spirit of the epoch was wholly contained in the works of Auguste Comte and Herbert Spencer (1820–1903).

The failure of the revolutions that took place in 1848 came as a huge disappointment. They an end to Romantic dreams of liberty and led to a profound crisis of conscience: man was henceforth confronted by a new reality he could no longer ignore. The different aspects of this reality, the consolidation and prosperity of the bourgeoisie, the entry of materialism into everyday life and the radical modification of the scale of values arising from it found theoretical support in the utilitarianism of the English philosopher John Stuart Mill (1806–1873). These different elements ended up by undermining literary Romanticism, which gave way to a new aesthetic: realism. It was a bourgeois art form, the product of a liberal conscience, permanently vigilant before the reality that surrounded it, prolonged towards the end of the nineteenth century by the naturalist movement.

AN ATTEMPT TO DEFINE REALISM

Realism, strictly speaking, was neither a movement nor a school. It was rather a general tendency in literature that developed during the second half of the nineteenth century, spread through Europe and expressed itself in the novel. It also influenced the theatre and poetry. In contrast to Romanticism, linked to the idealism of German philosophy, European realism began in France where, according to Auerbach's categorical formula, 'it blossomed earlier and more vigorously'.

Literature and reality

In the nineteenth century, the term 'realism', used to designate an aesthetic that was the diametrical opposite of Romanticism, was used for the first time in painting: the painter Gustave Courbet (1819–1877) created an art which, by the choice of its themes, taken from modest provincial reality, by the simplicity and fidelity of its representation, rejected the Romantic idealism of Delacroix and the dominant academicism of Ingres as bourgeois conventions. His canvases (*An Afternoon in Ornans*, 1849; *The Burial in Ornans*, 1850), pejoratively qualified as 'realist', caused a scandal. However, Courbet, who affirmed that art in painting could only consist in the representation of visible and tangible objects by the artist, placed a board with the words 'Du réalisme' ('Realism') in the room where he exhibited his canvases in 1855. According to Baudelaire, this exhibition took on 'the appearance of an insurrection'. The only saving grace for the realist painter, Courbet, to whom Baudelaire meted out severe criticism, 'is a reactionary spirit [. . .] which is sometimes salutary'.

A group of artists and men of letters formed around Courbet for whom realism was not a school but a reaction to Romanticism. For the defenders of this aesthetic of the 1850s, in the realm of realism, the novelist chose some salient facts, grouped them together, distributed them and framed them, freeing himself from fine language, which was not in keeping with the subjects to be treated.

The two great names of this period, Baudelaire and Flaubert, were opposed to this simplistic conception of reality. Baudelaire asked 'if realism has a meaning', since 'all good poets were always realists'. Flaubert declared: 'I loathe everything that people are agreed on calling realism.' He said *Madame Bovary*: 'Do you think that this ignoble reality that we find disgusting to reproduce does not make us want to heave as much as you? If you knew me better, you would know that I detest ordinary life. I have always personally kept myself from it as much as I could. But aesthetically, I wanted this once, if only this once, to practise it in depth.'

Realist themes and writing

The realist writer took his themes from polymorphous reality as fashioned by social history. In 1851 Thackeray wrote in one of his letters: 'The art of the novel is to represent Nature: to communicate as strongly as possible a feeling of reality.' The Russian literary theorist, Tchernichevsky, in his work on the aesthetic relations of art to reality, was still more categorical: 'the first aim of art is the reproduction of reality', while Fontane looked for 'the reflection of all real life, of all true strength in the element of art'.

Among the many facets of reality, the realists focused their attention on the social aspect: on the relationship of the individual to society. The heroes of realist works have nothing heroic about them. On the contrary, they are ordinary people, caught up in the rat-race, in everything insignificant and tragic about it, treated, for the first time, seriously. The psychological dimension of the characters is also taken seriously. Reacting to a blinkered realism, Dostoyevsky said of himself: 'They call me a psychological novelist, which is false; I am merely a realist in the highest sense of the word, which is to say that I depict the human soul in all its depth.'

The writer, through the discourse of fiction, manipulates time and space and the characters of his tale, so that everything he describes may be probable with respect to external reality, and possess an internal reference, a spatio-temporal motivation and a systematic psychological motivation peculiar to it. From this viewpoint, the realist work is coherent and self-sufficient without need of external verification. It is sometimes so complete, so motivated and so persuasive that it forms an addition to reality either by modifying or complementing it: 'Everything we invent is true, there are no two ways about it,' claimed Flaubert. 'My poor Bovary no doubt suffers and weeps in twenty villages of France simultaneously by now.'

THE NOVEL: THE MAIN GENRE OF REALISM

Realism, being *a priori* representative of a reality by nature linked to time, adopted the tale, as its way of expressing itself. The tale takes into account the dimension of time (narrating a story) and the dramatic staging of a story (hence the frequent use of dialogue). Realism therefore appropriates prose to itself. Prose is more appropriate in representing everyday reality, thus marking its opposition to lyrical, subjective and static Romantic poetry. The novel then became the dominant genre.

Aesthetic realism: Gustave Flaubert

French realism found its roots in Stendhal and Balzac, for whom the desire to 'depict actual ways of life' when Romanticism was in full flow, already heralded the beginnings of realism. **Gustave Flaubert (1821–1880)** spent most of his life in the provinces, dedicating himself to art with the faith of an adherent to the dogma of 'art for art's sake'. His following proclamations bear witness to this: 'The morality of art consists in beauty itself, and I value above all style, and then Truth'; 'style being, in itself a way of looking at things'. However, if Flaubert shared the cult of beauty with the Parnassians, he differed from them in his deliberate choice to observe his age with careful and objective scrutiny. The subject of his first novel, *Madame Bovary* (1857), is indeed taken from the provincial reality of his age. Emma, the main character, the daughter of a small landowner, was raised, as was then customary, in a convent. She starts out in life with a head full of dreams and illusions. Her marriage to Charles Bovary, a clumsy country doctor, and her stifling life with him in a claustrophobic provincial society are unbearable. Disappointed, she hopes to live out her dreams with her lover, Rodolphe, but the latter abandons her. In debt and terrified at the idea of a double scandal, she kills herself by taking arsenic. Her daughter, poor and orphaned, gets a job, after her father's death, in a cotton mill. This coming back to earth with a bump completes the vicious circle.

Realist objectivity is shown in the way in which the banality of provincial society is portrayed and in the apparent eclipse of the author's subjectivity. But this realism is an aesthetic realism: Flaubert, as a creator, is always present in his work. When it comes to the famous scene of Emma and Rodolphe's walk in the forest, when the young woman abandons herself for the first time to her love, Flaubert describes in a lively way a new process of literary creation: 'It is a delightful thing to write, to no longer be oneself, but to put oneself about in the creation one is describing. Today, for instance, man and woman simultaneously, lover and mistress together, I rode my horse through a forest strewn with yellow leaves on an autumn afternoon and I was horses, leaves and wind.' Here is a description which associates observation and a love of detail with the distance the narrator takes from the theme of his description:

> But above all it was at meal times that she could no longer put up with it, in that little room on the ground floor, with the smoking stove, the creaking door, the walls running with condensation, the stone flags damp; all the bitterness of existence seemed to her served up on her plate, and, with the steam of the boiled food, there came up in her soul other languorous vapours. Charles took a long time over his meals.
>
> Gustave Flaubert, *Madame Bovary*

Moral realism

English Romanticism, unlike French or German Romanticism, already had realist aspects in Wordsworth, Scott and Dickens. This is why the realist reaction in England was not excessive as in other countries. On the other hand, Victorian society, with its Puritan morality, was not so inclined to accept, through an overly realistic literature, a radical revelation of its weaknesses. The combined effect of these reasons tempered the harshness of English realism.

Most important novelists of this period took care over the realism of the plot. Elizabeth Gaskell (1810–1865), who lived in Manchester for many years, set her novels in highly industrialised regions of northern England (*North and South*, 1855). The aristocracy is the subject of George Meredith's ironic scrutiny (1828–1909) in *The Ordeal of Richard Feverel* (1859). Later, by adopting a style of writing which anticipates reported speech, Meredith made highly credible sallies into the depths of the female psyche (*The Egoist*, 1879).

The simplicity of daily country life was another favourite subject of English realism. In the novels of **George Eliot** (aka **Mary Ann Evans, 1819–1880**), we have a procession of small landlords, country people and clergy from her own native area – in *Scenes of Clerical Life* (1857), *Adam Bede* (1859), *The Mill on the Floss* (1860) and *Middlemarch* (1872) – which is marked by the quality of the detailed psychological description of its characters. Anthony Trollope (1815–1882) also described provincial life. He was particularly concerned to depict ecclesiastical activity and influence (*Barchester Towers*, 1857; *The Last Chronicle of Barset*, 1867).

Nevertheless these realist themes are mingled with elements of Romantic origin: with Dickens the presentation of reality was modified by poetic imagination and a passionate tone; the virulence of the indictment is sharpened, paradoxically, by the introduction of comic and burlesque elements. Moreover, he used symbolism and allegory, notably in *David Copperfield* (1849) and *Great Expectations* (1861), to throw moments of high pathos into sharp relief. Thackeray, the most realistic of all English authors, in spite of his irony tinged with cynicism, was frightened of outraging the social conventions of his time (*The Newcomes*, 1853–1855). Sentimentality, emotion and pity towards the victims of a society obsessed by money encountered in all these authors – from Dickens to George Eliot and Elizabeth Gaskell – have nothing to do with the objectivity and distance of pure realism.

English realism was always accompanied by a qualifying adjective: 'romantic', 'emotional', 'symbolic' 'comic'. It was above all a moral realism: the novelists of this period were above all moralists. Thackeray and George Eliot were openly didactic, and Dickens was undoubtedly the instigator of the social novel with moralising aims. All his work was a call to goodness, to greatness of soul, an invitation to put into practice the divine commandment: 'Love one another.'

Philanthropic realism

Russian realism was related to realism in the rest of Europe, apart from one element which made it different and gave a new dimension to its general trend: its philanthropy. This can only be interpreted in the specific framework of Orthodox Christian ideology, for which each man before God has the same value as an indivisible, unique individual.

Unlike positivist Western Europe, which became increasingly atheistic, the soul of holy Russia was sealed by its Christian faith. It was not by accident that Gogol died as an ascetic to punish himself for having created an immoral work, if work by **Fyodor Mikhail-ovitch Dostoyevsky (1821–1881)**[*] is shot through by a message of Christian love and suffering, forged by Dostoyevsky in Siberian prisons, or if, finally, **Leo Nikolaievich Tolstoy (1828–1910)**[*] ended his life as a prophet of a personal and Christian morality.

Journalistic criticism made its definitive appearance on the scene with Vissarion Grigorievitch Bielinsky (1811–1848). Head of the Western faction – of those who were opposed to the Slavophiles and officialdom and made claims for the modernisation of Russia in all areas – he devoted himself, from 1841, in particular, to radical criticism. He fought for a modern literature which, freed from the heritage of the past, would answer the needs of current modern society. His ideas found great sympathy in the writers of his generation who took their inspiration from Gogol, Dickens and George Sand.

The social aspect of Russia's reality retained the interest of its writers. So the work of Turgeniev and Gontcharov introduced contemporary social problems into the treatment of realist themes. **Ivan Sergeivich Turgenev (1818–1883)** was the most 'Western' of the great Russian realist novelists because of his culture and his long stays in France (he corresponded with Flaubert), because of his elegant style, his love of restraint and short forms (tales, novellas) and his anti-prophetism. *Zapiski ochotnika* (*A Huntsman's Sketches*, 1852), a moving picture of serfdom's human tragedy, is also a hopeful work, a poetic evocation of the charm of the Russian countryside and its people's poignant grandeur. In *Rudin* (1856), an admirable portrait of an intellectual incapable of action, in *Dvorjanskoe gnezdo* (*A Nest of Gentlefolk*, 1858), and in *Otcy i deti* (*Fathers and Sons*, 1862), he became not only the chronicler of the intelligentsia, but also the judge of revolutionary fanaticism. The undisputed master of 'classical' language at its finest, who inspired many writers, including Chekhov and Bunin, in his short stories, Turgeniev managed to move away from the insipidity of an art too close to the censor's blue pencil for having flirted with the fantastic and manifested an existential pessimism, obvious only in *Senilia (Stichotvoreniya v prozé, Poems in prose*, 1879–1883), but underlying all his work. **Ivan Aleksandrovitch Gontcharov (1812–1891)** created *Oblomov* (1859), one of the masterpieces of the Russian novel. Oblomov is a young, apathetic nobleman who takes pleasure in a lazy life. He gives up the love of the over-active Olga, and dies prematurely, worn out by inactivity. A borderline case, the product of a patriarchal Russia sunk in serfdom, Oblomov carries in himself the historical condemnation of this Russia faced with another Russia represented by Olga and her future husband, the dynamic Stolz. But this condemned country is also magnified by Oblomov's dreams of it. Going well beyond moral lessons, Gontcharov's slow prose created one of the great myths of Russian literature and culture.

Mikhail Saltykov-Shtchedrin (1826–1889), a publicist and satirist engaged in the revolutionary struggle, published two cycles of tales whose unity lies in the extraordinary force of their denunciation: *Istoria Odnogo Goroda* (*The History of a Town*, 1869–1870) and *Gospoda Golovlevy* (*The Golovlevs*, 1876–1880). *The History of a Town*, under cover of the burlesque chronicle of the town of Gloupov (Dafttown), is a parody of Russian history. *The Golovlevs*, the history of a noble provincial family, is above all the analysis of the putrefaction of a dying class of social parasites.

Nikolai Leskov (1831–1895) knows all the languages of Russia that he has travelled through in every direction; he is also *au fait* with Old Russian literature and its literary traditions. His novel *Soborjane* (*Church Folk*, 1872) is an amused, tender account of humble country clergy.

Regional realism: The short story

The literatures of the period all possess, in greater or lesser measure, their regional and rural production as provincial life constitutes one of the facets of contemporary reality. However, in some countries like Germany and the German-speaking territories, Bohemia, Hungary, Serbia, Croatia and Greece, writers turn to their province mainly because it is a focus for national identity and the purest and most complete expression of the national soul. Also, in the literatures of these countries, regional themes are predominant, combined with outbursts of nationalist fervour and Romantic sentimentalism.

In Germany, Wilhelm Raabe (1831–1910), in *Die Chronik der Sperlingsgasse* (*The Chronicle of Sparrow Street*, 1857), *Der Hungerpastor* (*The Hunger Pastor*, 1864) and *Der Scudderump* (*The Plague Cart*, 1870), describes life in the German provinces with warmth and sympathy. He placed at the centre of his novels a hero who cannot preserve his integrity unless he remains isolated from society. In the short stories by Theodor Storm (1817–1888), *Pole Poppenspaler* (*Paul the Marionettist*, 1874) and *Der Schimmelreiter* (*The Rider of the White Horse*, 1888), which contained detailed descriptions of landscapes typical of Northern Germany, elegant patriotism and an elegiac tone describe the background, family life and its problems within the framework of an idyllic provincial town. The Swiss–German writer **Gottfried Keller (1819–1890)** concentrated into his novel *Der grüne Heinrich* (*Green Henry*, 1854–1855, then 1879) the whole of Swiss cultural tradition. He realistically describes the psychology of his character: an individual at odds with his environment, who is led to renunciation and failure. His many village tales, *Romeo und Julia auf dem Dorf* (*A Village*

Romeo and Juliet, 1856), for example, or urban ones such as *Züricher Novellen* (*Tales of Zurich*, 1877), are distinguished by their humorous realism.

Regionalism became an outlet for nationalist dreams and for the existential anxieties which the bourgeois world experienced after the failure of the 1848 revolution. In novels by **Theodor Fontane (1819–1898)**, the most realist of German writers and an objective observer of Prussian society, resignation and relativism are developed even more strongly than in the balanced idylls of Keller or Raabe. His humour, like that of other realists, has a tragic foundation: it is a response to an ungrateful era. The central theme of his work is impossible love among young people of different social backgrounds (*Irrungen, Wirrungen, Labyrinths,* 1887) and bourgeois marriage (*Effi Briest*, 1895), a theme which brings him close to writers such as Flaubert, Ibsen and Tolstoy.

From a literary point of view, two generations mark Czech literary output: the so-called generation of 'May' – Hálek, Neruda, Světlá, Arbes – and the following generation which is divided between two different schools: the national school (Čech, Krásnohorská), traditionalist in its orientation, and the cosmopolitan school (Sládek, Zeyer, Vrchlický).

While the great narrative art of **Jan Neruda (1834–1891)** plunges us with *Malostranské povídky* (*Tales of Malá Strana*, 1878) into working-class life in the part of Prague under Prague Castle and Karel Sabina (1813–1877), **Jakub Arbes (1840–1914)**, and others establish the Czech social novel, regionalism was represented by the female novelist Karolina Světlá (1830–1899). Living the battle between dying Romanticism and emergent realism, she created, with idealism and moral conviction, female characters who make their mark with sacrificial love (*Vesnický román, A Village Novel*, 1867). However, the regional novel and tale dramatically expanded after 1880 thanks to writers who had much in common with the national school. They were the natural expression of the strong conviction that the peasantry, alone faithful to ancestral language and traditions, constituted the solid base of the Czech national community. So **Josef Holeček (1853–1929)** elaborated a truly peasant epic of Southern Bohemia (*Naši, Our People*, 1888–1913), while **Teréza Nováková (1853–1912)**, whose adoptive country was Eastern Bohemia, extracted from her deep knowledge of the people of this region and a genuine ethnographic interest in them five remarkable novels, mostly centred around a popular figure (1885–1909).

Regionalism may not have been the fundamental characteristic of Hungarian realism, but together with psychological analyses by Zsigmond Kemény (1814–1875) in *A rajongók* (*The Fanatics*, 1859), we find the same Romantic atmosphere in *Egy régi udvarház utolsó gazdája* (*The Last Owner of an Old Manor House*, 1857) by Pál Gyulai (1826–1909), a novel of lost illusions, while the '*Bildungsroman*' in verse *A délibábok hőse* (*The Hero of Mirages*, 1872) by László Arany (1844–1898), the son of the poet János Arany, casts a critical and nostalgic sideways glance at what Arany called the 'mirages' of the Romantic attitude.

Regionalism and rural themes predominated in Serbian realism, however, which expressed itself especially in 'peasant stories' like those by **Laza Lazarević (1851–1891)**. These stories, depicting peasant Utopias, include psychological realism. A specific trait is added to regional Serbian realism by the fantastic stories of Radoje Domanović (1873–1908) which contain the beliefs and superstitions of popular tales. Svetozar Marković (1846–1875), under the influence of realism and Russian socialism, engaged in a literature which 'will present the life of the people'.

The local colour of the native country is fully present in the fantastic, mystical stories by the Croatian writer, Ksaver Sandor Djalski (1854–1935). In Greece, realism appeared *c.*1880, a crucial year for the economic, social and cultural life of the country, a year which brought to a close the Romantic post-revolutionary period of the free State (1830). Nevertheless, even at the heart of Greek Romanticism, Pavlos Kalligas (1814–1896) declared in the preface to his novel *Thanos*

Vlekas (1855) his realist intention of giving 'sketches in miniature of our up-to-dateness', whereas the novel that draws attention to itself is by **Emmanuel Roïdis (1836–1904)**, *I papisa Ioana* (*Pope Joan*, 1866). The detailed documentation which underlies the book fully justifies its subtitle: 'A study of the Middle Ages'.

The massive production of realist works began in the 1880s with the appearance of the new school of Athens. At the instigation of Palamas, this school wanted to break free of a sterile attachment to the past, preached a definitive turning towards modern reality and its objective representation, and used as its medium of expression the colloquial language, Demotic. The publication of the story by Dimitrios Vikélas (1835–1908), *Loukís Laras* (1879) and above all, in 1883, that by **Georgios Vizyinos (1849–1896)**, *To amartima tis mitros mou* (*My Mother's Sin*) and *Pios iton o phonefs tou adelphou mou* (*Who was my Brother's Murderer?*) mark the official beginnings of Greek realism. Vizyinos was unquestionably their leader. He was a writer open to European influences since, between 1875 and 1884, he lived and studied mainly in Germany, but also in France and in England. In his prose we see for the first time all the fundamental characteristics of this first Greek realism: short forms (short story or tale), an attentive observation of modern rural life, the disappearance of taboo subjects (for the first time Turkish characters are treated with sympathy and attention to detail), an absence of national pride and the detailed psychological description of characters.

The conservative review with the symbolic title of *Estia* (*Hearth*), as a reaction to the Greek translation of Zola's novel *Nana* (1879), which introduced 'bad' foreign habits, into Greek literature and society, launched a story competition in May 1883. Its influence on Greek letters of the future would be decisive. The condition was that the works had to be inspired by national, social and historical life and that they must not be written just to please, but also to teach and strengthen the love of one's own country. This competition

also led to the appearance of a typically Greek literary genre, the 'ithographia', whose principal representatives were Georgios Drossinis (1859–1951), Argyris Eftaliotis (1849–1923), Kostas Krystallis (1868–1894) and Yannis Vlachoyannis (1867–1945), as well as **Ioannis Kondylakis (1862–1920)**, an author known for his descriptive power and humourous style. His story *Patoukhas* (1892), and the one by the poet Palamas *O thanatos tou palikariou* (*The Death of Pallicarus*, 1891) are the best examples of 'ithographia'. This term, which literally means 'genre painting', in the works of those who wrote according to the precepts laid down in *Estia*, eventually meant the 'superficial, optimistic, idyllic, calming and edifying representation of noble Greek manners, kept intact in village life'. The term refers to a hybrid genre at the heart of which the superficial claims of realism and the profound ideological function of Romanticism met.

During the realist period, at the same time as the novel, there was a significant output of short works in prose, called 'short story', although, for some of them, their authors deliberately chose the form of the short tale. The short story, the reading of which was favoured by the development of the periodic and daily press, appeared to realists the most appropriate means of describing slices of life, short, true, but faithful, able to function as synecdoche. Regional realism preferred this type of story: German novella, Czech rural tale, Greek 'genre painting'.

Bourgeois and petit-bourgeois realism

In Spain the second half of the nineteenth century was a time of great internal political tensions. These were the result of opposition between the traditional and the modern spirit. The first novelists – Pedro Antonio de Alarcón (1833–1891), Juan Valera (1824–1905), José María de Pereda (1833–1906) – represent a strong regional realism, closely linked to the landscape, people and customs of the Spanish province. The theme of Valera's novels was essentially religious even more than it was regionalist (*Pepita Jiménez*, 1874). The 'naturalist' generation took over from them (Bazán, Clarín, Palacio Valdés), but between the latter and the former stood a writer of real stature: **Benito Pérez Galdós (1843–1920)**. A committed journalist and a radical politician from Gran Canaria, as a writer he decided to paint a picture of nineteenth-century Spain, centred on Madrid, in the immense forty-six volume compilation of *Episodios nacionales* (*National Episodes*, 1873–1879, 1890–1912), a romantically fictionalised chronicle of recent history in Spain. After his first novels (*La fontana de oro*, *The Golden Fountain*, 1871; *Doña Perfecta*, 1876; *Gloria*, 1877), he went on to the second stage of his creation, that of his maturity, with a series of works written between 1881 and 1889 which he described as 'contemporary novels'. Dickens and Balzac were his models, Comte and Taine his guides, Zola his catalyst and Cervantes his undisputed master. *Fortunata y Jacinta* (1886–1887) deals with the subject of bourgeois marriage and the eternal triangle – husband, wife and lover – around which a whole world gravitates: the political reality of his time, aristocracy and the plebs, the bourgeois economy based on trade and loans, intellectual debates in cafés, institutions such as the Church and convents, organised charity and a series of characters and secondary episodes which, taken together, have made it possible to describe this fresco of life in Madrid as a 'forest of interlinked novels'.

The society within which Belgian realists lived and worked was that of a well-off and conformist bourgeoisie, attached to material wellbeing, for whom laziness was the cardinal sin. In Flanders, the realist movement remained faithful to art 'which teaches and which has a civilising influence', playing a utilitarian role in the rise of national aware-ness. However, in the autobiographically inspired pictures of *Ernest Staes, advocaat* (*Ernest Staes, Lawyer*, 1874), **Anton Berg-mann (1835–1874)** rejected the temptation to edify and to express a political message. Virginie Loveling (1836–1923), who started her literary career with her sister Rosalie (1834–1875), dealt in her last novels (*Sophie*, 1885; *Een dure eed, A Solemn Oath*, 1892) with

new problems such as the quarrel between education, religion and heredity.

In The Netherlands the first realists emerged *c*.1850, and their work contained, above all, novels of 'Dutch manners'. The example had been set by the preacher **Nicolaas Beets (1814–1903)** who, under the pseudonym of Hildebrand, humorously described typically Dutch situations and characters in *Camera Obscura* (1839), a fre-quently reprinted work whose influence extended to the twentieth century. Van Lennep, notably influenced by Balzac's *The Physiology of Marriage*, composed *Klaasje Zevenster* (1865–1866), a novel of Dutch manners in five volumes. The short story *Fabriekskinderen* (*Factory Children*, 1863), by Jacobus Jan Cremer (1827–1880), revealed the blatant contrast between the poverty of textile workers in Leyden and the student élite.

Critical realism

In Scandinavia, a bourgeois democracy succeeded autocracy and despotism but, as soon as it came to power, liberalism became reactionary and aligned itself with the right in politics. The reaction of intellectuals unavoid-ably led first to a political rupture, then to an aesthetic and cultural one: the modern Breakthrough (1870–1890) opened up the way to realist literature. Earlier than 1870, liberal realism had broken away from idealism, Romanticism and anti-feminist prejudice.

The problem of faith opposed to positive and scientific knowledge had been prudently tackled by Andersen in his novel *At vaere eller ikke vaere* (*To Be or not to Be*, 1857) and by Viktor Rydberg (1828–1895) in *Den sista Athenaren* (*The Last Atheneum*, 1859). Above all, Kierkegaard's philosophy provoked the final break with idealism, as we find it in Ibsen, Bjørnson and Brandes. The conflict between exacerbated idealism and atheism was the recurring theme in several novels: *Ein Fritenkjar* (*A Free Thinker*, 1878) by Arne Garborg (1851–1924) and *Niels Lyhne* (1880) by Jens Peter Jacobsen (1847–1885). The latter created an impressionistic style, very precise in the description of situations, which had considerable influence on Scandinavian and German authors at the turn of the century.

The break with the ideas of Romanticism was already glaringly obvious in *Phantasterne* (*The Phantasts*, 1857), a psychological realist and ironic novel by Hans Egede Schack (1820–1859). The condemnation of the exploitation of woman, in a society dominated by men and full of anti-female prejudices, expressed itself in a more subtle way in Denmark with Mathilde Fibiger in *Clara Raphaël. Tolv Breve. (Clara Raphael. Twelve Letters*, 1851), in Sweden in *Hertha eller En själs historie* (*Hertha, or the History of a Soul*, 1856) by Fredrika Bremer (1801–1865), and in Norway with Camilla Collett (1813–1895) in *Amtmandens Doettre* (*The Prefect's Daughters*, 1855). The battle of modernism quickly became women's: they organised themselves into a precocious feminist movement. The problems linked to their difficult situation and to their emancipation were to become the major themes of Scandinavian literature a few years later.

The yardsticks of the politico-cultural and literary movement that was the modern Breakthrough in Scandinavia were put in position by the Danish critic **Georg Brandes (1842–1927)**. He discovered modern philosophy and literary criticism thanks to Stuart Mill and Taine. With his series of lectures *Hovedstroemninger i det nineteen de Aarhundredes Litteratur* (*The Major Literary Currents of the nineteenth Century*, 1871) in which, by setting himself apart from the ruling class, he showed himself to be a free, independent spirit, Brandes considerably influenced the aesthetics of contemporary authors. Favouring realism, he insisted that a modern, living literature is one which 'brings a problem under discussion'. Thanks to his links with Poland, Russia, Bohemia and Armenia, he introduced the question of minorities on to the international scene, and made of the modern Breakthrough an influential united front, above all in German-speaking countries. In Scandinavia, the radical ideas launched by the modern Breakthrough nurtured, towards 1880, a critical realism. This is a literature which, supported by a strong Russian and Danish influence, revealed itself to be in a lively, active way concerned by the growing rift between countryside and town, between the peasant and bourgeois worlds, after rapid industrialisation and urbanisation. It was marked by a knowledge of modern psychology and the use of minute, naturalistic description.

OTHER LITERARY GENRES

The theatre and poetry did not flourish during this period. It was only at the end of the nineteenth century, thanks to the combined contributions of naturalism and symbolism, that a theatrical revival took place of which **Henrik Ibsen (1828–1906)*** was the culmination. Similarly, poetry* only regained prominence after having shaken off its realist principles. **Charles Baudelaire (1821–1867)*** made poetry finally evolve towards naturalism and symbolism.

The realist theatre

Realism in the theatre was represented by **Alexander Ostrovsky (1823–1886)**. Because of the abundance of his work and influence, he was the great classic of the Russian stage. Born in the 'trans-Moskova', the commercial quarter of Moscow where the old guild traditions still survived, Ostrovsky described this milieu whose customs, psychology and language he knew intimately. In *Svoi ljudi-sočtëmsja* (*With Friends you can always Work Something Out*, 1850), he depicted the struggle between generations, equally rapacious but in different ways, while in *Bednost' ne porok* (*Poverty is not a Vice*, 1854) the 'samodour', appeared a typically Russian character. Ostrovsky's sympathy for the humble, the denunciation of an anachronistic moral order, but also the aspiration to freedom and beauty were merged in a powerful popular tragedy, *Groza* (*The Orange*, 1859). In France, the theatre of the period depicted the manners of the bourgeoisie: Eugène Labiche (1815–1888) used comedy as a formidable weapon to track down Pharisaism and the peccadilloes of a bourgeoisie led astray by pleasure and leisure (*Un chapeau de paille d'Italie, An Italian Straw Hat*, 1851; *Le Voyage de M. Perrichon, Mr Perrichon's Journey*, 1860). Alexandre Dumas *fils* (1824–1895), in *La Dame aux camélias* (*The Lady with the Camellias*, 1852), brought to the stage the raw reality of consumption in a drama in which the manners of a twilight world were depicted.

The peasant theme, which nurtured Czech prose, was also present in the theatre. The play *Naši furianti* (*Our Boastful Peasants*, 1887) by Ladislav Stroupežnický (1850–1892) was epoch-making. It brought face-to-face the rich and poor in a Southern Bohemian village with realism and great psychological finesse. Gabriela Preissová (1862–1946) emphasised this vision in her drama *Její pastorkyňa* (*Her Goddaughter*, 1890), which will achieved fame thanks to the opera Leoš Janáček adapted from it. The summit of realist drama was attained with the tragedy *Maryša* (1893), a work jointly written by *Vilém Mrštík (1863–1912)* and his brother, Alois.

In Rumania, Ion Luca Caragiale (1853–1912) put on stage two facets of Rumanian reality: the peasant – whose life and social relationships conformed to the Christian rules of a popular civilisation deeply attached to the soil (*Napasta*, 1889) – and the internal struggle of a society trying to become Europeanised by adopting Western habits and ideas (*De ale carnavalului, Carnival Adventures*, 1885).

Poetry, between Romanticism and symbolism

During the period of realism dominated by prose, poetry seems to have lost its vital spark. Influenced of necessity by the realist literary ideal, it rejected Romantic subjectivity. Leconte de Lisle (1818–1849) declared in the preface to his collection of *Poèmes antiques* (*Ancient Poems*, 1852): 'Personal emotions have left but little trace here.' Poets (Coppée, Browning, Nekrassov, Verde) described the reality that surrounded them often satirically (Carducci, Palamas, Nekrassov). But their essential inspiration was everything that they themselves considered to be permanently real: nature, 'an eternal reality to be described' (Carducci), the history of their country and nation, the prehistory of the European mind and civilisation (Tennyson, Carducci, Palamas, Leconte de Lisle), the eternal meta-physical questions that man asks (Leconte de Lisle, Carducci, Vrchlický, Palamas) and art as creation in its own right ('art for art's sake').

If their themes recalled those of Romantic lyricism, they drew near to the spirit of their time by the often conscious interaction in them of science and poetry. Leconte de Lisle posits this position in the 1852 preface: 'Art and science for a long time separate [. . .] must have a tendency to come close together, even to coalesce.' Forty years later, Palamas, in a text just as important with the evocative title *Pos enooumen tin piisin* (*How we Hear Poetry*, 1890), continued to affirm that 'the poet studies the true in order to create the beautiful [. . .]; he takes his inspiration from science not when he sings the praises of physiology [. . .] but when he represents beings and things [. . .] according to scientific research and discoveries'.

There was a veritable revival of metrics and a systematic heightening of the rhythmical possibilities of traditional verse; poems in fixed forms, mainly sonnets, but also terza rimas, sestinas and pantoums were preferred to free forms.

The theoretical yardsticks of this poetry were established by Théophile Gautier, who formulated his theory of 'art for art's sake' by proclaiming poetry's freedom from all political, moral and social opportuneness and by underlining the primordial importance of the form.

The generally pessimistic, poetry by Leconte de Lisle (*Ancient Poems; Barbaric Poems*, 1862; *Tragic Poems*, 1884) was basically epic in nature and reconstituted with the help of static imagery, the ancient Greek past or the Indian, Biblical or Celtic past. *La Légende des siècles* (*The Legend of the Centuries*, 1859, 1877, 1883) by Hugo, an epic which exerted considerable influence on the rest of Europe, probably owed something to the epic cycles of short poems by Leconte de Lisle.

Les Trophées (*The Trophies*, 1893) by José Maria de Heredia (1842–1905) brought to a close the cycle of Parnassian poetry: erudite, static and cold. In Greece, the 1880 New School of Athens liberated poetry from the rhetorical mannerism that characterised Romanticism and brought it closer to reality. Following the example of Solomos and the folk song, it adopted Demotic to replace the katharevussa, the learned language of the Romantics, and opened up to the fertility of Western European literature. Among its representatives, Aristomenis Provelegios (1850–1936), Georgios Drossinis, Nikos Kambas

(1857–1932), Ioannis Polemis (1862–1924) and Georgios Stratigis (1859?–1938), the poet and critic **Kostis Palamas (1859–1943)** loomed large. His monumental poetic work developed over half a century and contained more than twenty collections: *Ta traghoudhia tis patridhos mou* (*Songs of my Homeland*, 1886), *Ta matia tis psikhis mou* (*The Eyes of my Soul*, 1892), *Iamvi ke Anapesti* (*Iambs and Anapests*, 1897), *I Asalefti Zoï* (*Immutable Life*, 1904). Often containing a Romantic tone, this poetry was totally pervaded by a philosophical reflection whose central axis was the idea of ancient, Byzantine and modern Hellenism. Thanks to this final ingredient, Palamas, like Solomos and Kalvos, was given the title of national poet.

Μόνος. ’Εγώ; Δὲν εἶμαι μόνος,
ὄχι.
Στὸ φτωχικὸ σκοταδερὸ κελλί μου
ἥρωες ἄνθρωποι, θεοί
σὰ φωτοσύγνεφα σαλεύουν ἀντικρύ
μου.
Ταιριάζουνε μὲ ὀνείρατα σὰν τὰ
ροδοχαράματα
στοιχιὰ ποὺ μαυροφέρνουνε. Κι ἀπὸ
μιὰ κώχη
κάτι σὰν ἄγγελος μὲ βλέπει κι
ὅλο βλέπει με.
Μόνος. ’Εγώ; Δὲν εἶμαι μόνος.
Ὄχι.

Kostis Palamas,
I Asalefti Zoï

Alone, me? No, I am not
alone.
In my cell, here very near,
down there very far,
Men, heroes, gods
and goddesses,
like a golden cloud, go and
writhe ceaselessly.
Genies all dressed in black
go past looking strange,
like dreams of dawn. And
in a corner,
Sometimes, I think that a beautiful
Archangel is looking at me.
Alone, me? No, I am not
alone.

The work of the Czech poet **Jaroslav Vrchlický (1853–1912)** was legendary. Thanks to his many translations from other languages, he introduced the average Czech reader to universal literature, beginning with French. He introduced at the same time 'exotic' forms like the ghazel, the sestina and the pantoum. The poetic genius of this 'brother of Goethe, Victor Hugo, Carducci and Leconte de Lisle' was essentially lyrical and meditative: *Z'hlubin* (*Out of the Depths*, 1875), *Sny o štestí* (*Dreams of Happiness*, 1876), *Hudba v duši* (*Music in the Soul*, 1886) are good examples. Reflection applied to the evolution of humanity unfolds in twenty collections of

poems under the general title *Zlomky epopeje* (*Fragments of an Epic*), in which he looks for the sense of the march of the human spirit, taking up Hugo's ideas.

The Polish poet **Cyprian Kamil Norwid (1821–1883)**, with his collection of lyrical poems *Vade mecum* (*Come with Me*, 1865), left the Romantic tradition thanks to the lean, laconic nature of his language, but perpetuated it through the great themes of homeland and civic duty. The work of the poet *Cesário Verde (1855–1886)* was linked to town life in Portugal and industrial civilisation; it is a poetry that is plastic and anti-lyrical in its objectivity with a new sensibility learned from

Baudelaire: *O Livro de Cesário Verde* (*The Book of Cesário Verde*, published in 1901).

The reality of Russia, the sad life of the peasants, served as a background to poetry by **Nikolaï Nekrassov (1821–1878)**, a friend of Bielinsky. His philanthropic attitude confronted by a suffering populace (*Moroz krasnij nos, Frost with a Red Nose*, 1863) found its aesthetic consecration in the popular style of the realist satire *Komu na rusi žit' xorošo?* (*Who can Live Happily in Russia?* 1863–1876).

English poetry was dominated by **Alfred Tennyson (1809–1892)** and **Robert Browning (1812–1889)**. Important differences existed between them, although both were deeply influenced by Romanticism. Tennyson (*Poems*, 1842; *In Memoriam*, 1850; 'Enoch Arden', 1864; *Idylls of the King*, 1857–1885) found his inspiration in ancient Greece for 'The Lotus-Eaters' (1833) and 'Ulysses' (1842), as well as in the legends of the epic of King Arthur, showing his concern for the dilemma of faith versus science. His permanent attachment to the aesthetic beauty of his poetry recalls the analogous efforts of the Parnassian adepts of 'art for art's sake'. There was a close connection between the Parnassians, as well as Poe's aestheticism, and the Pre-Raphaelites: Dante Gabriel Rossetti, 1828–1882; his sister Christina Rossetti, 1830–1894; William Morris, 1834–1896. There is also a connection with the audacious, sensational **Algernon Charles Swinburne (1837–1909)**, who gained fame with *Poems and Ballads*, 1866. Browning (*Dramatic Romances and Lyrics*, 1845; *Men and Women*, 1855; *Dramatis Personæ*, 1864; *The Ring and the Book*, 1868–1869) was the poet–thinker who unveiled his soul in his dramatic monologues. His work had great lyrical qualities, despite his tendency to philosophise.

The Italian **Giosue Carducci (1835–1907)** simultaneously sought to oppose Romanticism and crude verism. Deeply involved in Italian political life, he felt the pathos of great historical events. His work was usually classically inspired. Carducci cultivated literary tradition, which he tried to renew in complex metres. *Rime Nuove* (*New Poetry*, 1877) and *Odi Barbare* (*Barbaric Odes*, 1877, 1882, 1889) celebrate the values of a peaceful, active life, love and the great myths of the classical period.

NATURALISM, IN THE WAKE OF REALISM

The gap between the bourgeoisie, accumulating wealth in a provocative fashion, and the working class, pushed into dire poverty, dangerously increased. The start of a two-speed Europe, in conformity to the current North–South, East–West, dates back to this period. The German naturalist Arno Holz (1863–1929) defined the world around him: 'Our world is no longer classical / Our world is only modern.' Faced with this new reality, socialism promoted the interest of society by opposing it to the interest of the individual (Marx, *Das Kapital, Capital*, 1867). The working class became aware of the situation and actively advocated strike action and growing unionisation for the protection of its rights and interests (the First Workers' International, 1864).

After the impressive progress of the physical sciences during the first decades of the century, it was the turn of biology and medicine with works by Charles Darwin (1809–1882) and Claude Bernard (1813–1878). Their progress directly concerned human evolution. Naturalism's mission was to put literature in contact with this new social and scientific reality.

The naturalist school and its relationship to realism

The undisputed founder of naturalism was **Émile Zola (1840–1902)**. From France, where it appeared for the first time in the 1870s, naturalism spread throughout Europe, over the next twenty years, polarising analogous research that already existed in different national literatures.

For some, naturalism was only a second stage of realism. It was more intense, but no new term was necessary. For others naturalism constituted a major tendency and embraced authors like Balzac and Flaubert, Tolstoy and Chekhov. Most people used the terms realism and naturalism interchangeably, indifferently or in convenient but confused association. This confusion was caused by the absence of a clear theory of what realism was. It may also be traced back to Zola who, in his desire to annex prestigious names to naturalism, called writers like Balzac, Stendhal and Flaubert naturalists (*The Naturalist Novelists*, 1881) and subtitled the English edition of *La Terre, The Soil, a Realistic Novel* (1889). We will take it here that realism and naturalism constitute notions of which one is contained in the other, at least as far as literary dogma is concerned; realism constitutes the broad notion, while naturalism is the more restricted notion since it uses and takes as its premise all realism's basic principles and themes. Over and above a realist and positivist attitude, if we adhere to Zola's theory the naturalist school demanded that while he was producing his work the writer applied a strictly scientific method, close to those put into practice by the natural sciences and which had for the first time been used by Sainte-Beuve and Taine in the positivist criticism of literary phenomena.

Positivist criticism and the scientific novel

Hippolyte Taine (1828–1893), philosopher, historian and critic, set out to discover the laws which, like every living organism and in conformity to the relation of cause to effect, govern literature. He claimed that race, the natural, social and political environment and the moment at which a literary work is created, define its specific traits and evolution (*Introduction to the History of English Literature*, 1863–1864).

The brothers **Edmond (1822–1896)** and **Jules (1830–1870) de Goncourt** published *Germinie Lacerteux* (1865), preceded by a preface that became just as famous as the work itself. In this novel two of the basic characteristics of naturalism appeared for the first time: the heroine is a maid of all work from the lowest class in society, and her behaviour is studied and dissected impartially with a pen which bears a strong resemblance to the magnifying glass of the clinician, the biologist, the anatomist. Zola's *Thérèse Raquin* (1867) was the first naturalist novel. Taine's aphorism that 'Vice and virtue are products like vitriol and sugar' formed the book's starting point. The naturalism of the novel did not result from its plot (Thérèse and Laurent, her lover, kill her husband, Camille. They commit suicide because of the remorse they subsequently feel), but from the interpretation of the actions of the characters and their personal development. The inner, blind impulses which cause them to act determine their choices and reactions, and leave no room for morality, 'dominated' as they are 'by their nerves and their blood, devoid of free will'.

Émile Zola and the experimental novel

The novelist is made up of an observer and an experimenter.

Émile Zola,
The Experimental Novel

In the preface to *Thérèse Raquin*, and in *Naturalism in the Theatre* and *The Naturalist Novelists* (1881), above all in *The Experimental Novel* (1880), Zola formulated his theory on the novel which he described as 'experimental'. He wanted to confer on naturalism the status of a scientific doctrine and to bequeath to writers the tool of a strict method. Taking as his model, including his title, the Doctor Bernard of *Experimental Medicine* (1865), and following his method step by step, Zola expounded the theory according to which 'the novelist is made up of an observer and an experimenter'. The observer chooses his subject (alcoholism, for example) and puts forward a hypothesis (alcoholism is hereditary or caused by the influence of the environment). The experimental method rests on the fact that the novelist 'intervenes in a direct way to place his character in circumstances' which will reveal the workings of his passion and verify the initial hypothesis. 'In the end, there is knowledge of man, scientific knowledge of man, in his individual and social action.'

However, long before *The Experimental Novel*, in which he justifies himself and lays the foundations of naturalism as a whole, Zola had already begun to apply these ideas to a cycle of twenty novels with the overall title *Les Rougon-Macquart*. He related in these 'the national and social history of a family under the Second Empire', following the development and evolution of its members from all social classes over five successive generations: *La Fortune des Rougon* (1867), *L'Assommoir* (1877), *Nana* (1880), *Germinal* (1885), *La Terre* (1887), *La Bête humaine* (1890), *Le Docteur Pascal* (1893). Zola's main aim in this project was to show the decisive role of the environment (nature, society) and heredity in the life of man who, at the end of the day, cannot be held responsible for his moral depravity. In this way the decline of Zola's morally and physically wretched characters constituted another form of *J'accuse*. His highly-coloured, daring descriptions bring to mind the drama of the individual that indifference and social injustice progressively demote to the level of an animal. In *Germinal*, Madame Hennebeau, the mine manager's wife, and Negrel, the engineer, shut in a barn with their friends, witness the march of the striking miners:

> And the men made a bee-line for the place, two thousand angry men, thrutchers, cutters, menders, a compact mass moving as one, serried, intermingled to the point that it was no longer possible to distinguish either the faded breeches or their woollen sweaters hanging in tatters, mixed together as they were in the same earthy uniformity. Their eyes were burning, only the black holes of their mouths were visible, singing the Marseillaise, whose stanzas were lost in an indistinct roaring, accompanied by the striking of clogs on the hard earth. Above their heads, amid the bristling iron bars, an axe stood out, carried vertically; and this one axe, which was like the group's rallying point, had, against the clear sky, the sharp presence of a guillotine's blade.

> 'What atrocious faces!' Madame Hennebeau stammered.
>
> Negrel muttered: 'The Devil take me if I recognise a single one of them! Where have they all come from, those bandits?'
>
> > Émile Zola, *Germinal*

The French naturalist group

In 1880, when Zola was already the undisputed leader of naturalism, some young novelists published a collection of stories called *Les Soirées de Médan* (*Evenings at Médan*, 1880), a title which contains a reference to Zola's country house where they were used to meeting. Their subject was common to them all: the Franco-Prussian War of 1870.

> And we are sitting at Émile Zola's table in Paris, Maupassant, Huysmans, Céard, Alexis and myself, for a change. We talk about this and that and the subject of the war comes up, the famous war of '70. Several of us had been volunteers or mobilised. 'Wait a minute,' said Zola, 'why not bring out a book on it, a book of short stories?'
>
> Alexis: 'Yes, why not?'
>
> – Subjects to write on?
>
> – We'll find some.
>
> – The title?
>
> Céard: 'Evenings at Médan.'
>
> > Léon Hennique, 1930 introduction to the collective stories of *Les Soirées de Médan*

Guy de Maupassant (1850–1893) made his first literary appearance with his short story *Boule de Suif* (1880). Maupassant's talent was immediately recognised and he quickly became famous thanks to a series of stories which took as their subject provincial life in Normandy, his native area (*La Maison Tellier*, 1881; *Contes de la bécasse*, 1883; *Contes du jour et de la nuit*, 1885; *Yvette*, 1885). His universe is sometimes traversed by mysterious forces which terrorise his neurotic characters (*The Horla*, 1887). A pessimistic vision of the human condition emerged from his work: 'Everything is re-enacted over and over again lamentably,' Maupassant himself remarked.

Paradoxically, French naturalism, apart from Zola, seems to be limited to Maupassant and maybe Alphonse Daudet (1840–1897). The other members of the group of Médan, Paul Alexis (1847–1901), Henri Céard (1851–1924) and Léon Hennique (1851–1935) are now almost forgotten.

The novelty of naturalism quickly wore off in its country of origin and was rapidly abandoned by its practitioners. Huysmans, in *À rebours* (*Against the Grain*, 1884), broke with Zola's school and turned towards a spiritualism tinged with the supernatural (*Là-bas*, *Over There*, 1891). In 1887, Maupassant, in the introduction to his novel *Pierre and Jean* (1888) stressed that objectivity is impossible in literature. The same year, the *Figaro* published the *Manifesto of the Five*, five writers protesting, in the name of their literary conscience, against Zola's extremism in *The Soil*. In 1891, all men of letters agreed that naturalism is dead. Only the former collaborator in the writing of the *Soirées*, Alexis, sent a telegram to Huret, who was commissioned to investigate the question: 'Naturalism not dead. Letter follows.' And he was right.

The European reception of naturalism

Unlike the rather cold, not to say negative reception given him by the critics, and his minimal effect on other French writers, Zola experienced enormous success with the general public, starting with *L'Assommoir* (*The Drinking Den*), augmented by the success of *Nana* and *Germinal*: a success that never wavered. About the same time, Zola's work and ideas began to spread to other European countries. In Russia, for example, translations of his works were published simultaneously in six reviews from 1873. *Germinal* was serialised in six German-language dailies at the same time as it appeared in *Gil Blas*; the same was true of *Nana*. Between 1879 and 1881, translations of Zola can be found in Danish, Greek, Italian, Dutch, Polish, Russian and Swedish.

Even though criticised, more on the basis of its theoretical foundation, it is true, than as

a literary act, naturalism excited interest everywhere. So the viewpoint that claims it might be possible, even desirable, for an author to adopt methods of scientific exactitude in the elaboration of his work was hotly debated. Protests arose over the materialism of naturalism, the determinism of heredity and the environment, while the assimilation of man to an animal provoked a general outcry. Polish critics pointed out, not without humour, that if the naturalists had observed that 'man is all animal', they have not said that 'not all of man is in the animal'. On the other hand, naturalism had a positive response, for it enriched the subject matter of the novel genre with the introduction of new subjects such as the influence of the environment on human behaviour or even social injustice, and it perked up novel-writing with the pictorial and colourful liveliness of description.

If Zola's work has survived and influenced many other writers, it is precisely because the theorist understood how to let the writer penetrate his novels: 'A work of art is a corner of nature seen through an individual temperament'; or even: 'The novelist intervenes in his work in a direct way to place his character in circumstances over which he is still master.'

The evolution of naturalism on the European front

In Victorian England and Christian Russia, naturalism was unable to take root, doubtless for the same reasons that made the realism of these countries moralistic and philanthropic. So the efforts of George Moore (1852–1923), a solitary figure in English literature, to transplant Zola to an English climate were fruitless, and Tolstoy's *Vlast' t'my* (*The Power of Darkness*, 1886) was unique in Russian literature.

In the last twenty-five years of the nineteenth century, Dutch naturalists published their works under the influence of Zola. Marcellus Emants (1848–1923) defended Zola's ideas in the introduction to *Drietal novellen* (*Three Stories*, 1879): he composed naturalist novels (*Een nagelaten bekenntnis*, *An Inherited Confession*, 1894) under the influence of Gogol and Dostoyevsky. Louis Couperus' work (1863–1923), *Eline Vere* (1889), stems from the same tradition. Eline, elegant and charming, is an indolent woman, living in the aristocratic, decadent milieu of The Hague. She sees herself as a victim of heredity and her social surroundings and ends up by committing suicide. The campaigns in favour of *L'Assommoir*, then of *Germinal*, which coincide with the discoveries of social realities, permitted Belgian naturalism to begin a period of rapid expansion with the work of **Camille Lemonnier (1844–1913)**. His novels, which are never merely works to prove a thesis, nevertheless show that he was familiar with the ideological debates of the time. The naturalism of his world of peasants and workers stands in contrast to the naturism of his final period of literary output, a Utopian vision of the reconciliation between man and nature. After *Un mâle* (*A Male*, 1880), a lyrical work, and *L'Hystérique* (*The Hysteric*, 1885), the psychological study of a neurotic, the naturalist Lemonnier published *Happe chair* (*Catch Flesh*, 1886), dedicated to Zola, a novel about the workers in the iron foundries of central Belgium, and *La Fin des bourgeois* (1893), which recounted a family epic in the manner of the *Rougon-Macquart*. **Georges Eekhoud (1856–1927)** was interested in all social *milieus*. *New Carthage* (1888) was a veritable social fresco and an audacious criticism of triumphant capitalism. The most important naturalist author in Flanders was **Cyriel Buysse (1859–1932)**. He began in 1890 with his short story *De biezenstekker* (*The Bastard*), in which he applied Zola's experimental method. He dealt with the fate of the rural poor, whose sordid, bestial, hopeless condition is attributed to social injustice. A visionary imagination and a sense of typical detail characterise his best-known works, which include *Het recht van den sterkste* (*Might is Right*, 1893).

Luigi Capuana (1839–1915), short-story writer, novelist, writer of comedies and esteemed literary critic, was the first Italian to become interested in French naturalism. His influence on the choice of his colleagues and friends, Verga and De Roberto, was considerable. In his novels *Giacinta* (*Hyacinth*, 1879), which he dedicated to Zola, and *Profumo* (*Perfume*, 1899), he applied the clinical methods of naturalism to the study of pathological cases, even venturing into the realm of parapsychology before realising the limits of scientism.

Giovanni Verga (1840–1922), after early works written in the wake of patriotism and Romanticism, arranged his verist novels within an unfinished cycle of novels called *I Vinti* (*The Vanquished*), which portrays the struggle for life which always ended in bitter failure. His most famous novels – the only two complete volumes of *The Vanquished* – *I Malavoglia* (*The Malavoglias*, 1881) and *Mastro Don Gesualdo* (*Master Don Gesualdo*, 1889) are both set in Sicily among the poor fishermen and peasants on the one hand and the upwardly mobile bourgeoisie and decadent nobility on the other. The determining influence of the environment played an important part in the character of the Sicilian rustics. Federico de Roberto (1861–1927) and Matilda Serao (1856–1927), a committed journalist, short-story writer and novelist, also belong to the Italian verist movement, while Grazia Deledda (1871–1936), despite her description of the rural world, remained isolated because of her mystic inspiration which reminds us of Tolstoy and Dostoyevsky.

Although Galdós' *La Desheredada* (*The Disinherited Woman*, 1881) a work in which heredity weighs down on the schizophrenic heroine, is generally considered to be the first naturalist novel in Spanish literature, it was Leopoldo Enrique García de Alas y Ureña, better known under his pen-name as a journalist **Clarín (1852–1901)**, who got Zola's name known in Spain through translations and criticism. He himself was influenced by naturalism in both his short stories (*Pipá*, 1886) and his novel *La Regenta* (*The Regent*, two volumes, 1884, 1885). Here Clarín conformed to a naturalist aesthetic without sharing its philosophy: his characters remained in charge of their destiny and their actions are the fruit of their own free will.

In Portugal, **Eça de Queirós (1845–1900)**

created an original work which, although pointing out the essentials of realism and naturalism, did not identify with either of these trends. If his naturalism (determinism, heredity, detailed psychological analysis, anticlericalism) is evident in his novels *O crime do Padre Amaro* (*The Crime of Father Amaro*, 1875) and *O Primo Basílio* (*Cousin Basílio*, 1878), in the novels *O Mandarim* (*The Mandarin*, 1880), *A Relíquia* (*The Relic*, 1884) and above all *Os Maias* (*The Maias*, 1888), the story of a family and a panorama of decadent Portuguese society, this same naturalism is undermined by the introduction of elements such as the rejection of ineluctable determinism and the role of chance in the development of the novel's action. It is also undermined by irony and caricature and the permanent emphasis on the symbolic. This dual attitude to naturalism is clearly reflected in the debate that certain characters in *The Maias* have on this burning issue:

Carlos declarou que o mais intolerável no realismo eram os seus grandes ares científicos, [. . .] e a invocaçao de Claude Bernard, do experimentalismo, do positivismo, de Stuart Mill e de Darwin, a propósito duma lavadeira que dorme com um carpinteiro! [. . .] Ega trovejou: justamente o fraco do realismo estava em ser ainda pouco científico, [. . .] A forma pura da arte naturalista devia ser a monografia, o estudo seco dum tipo, dum vício, duma paixão, tal qual como se se tratasse dum caso patológico, sem pitoresco e sem estilo! . . .	*Carlos, on the other hand, declared that the most unbearable defect of realism was its great scientific airs, [. . .] that way of invoking Claude Bernard, experimentalism positivism, Stuart Mill and Darwin, with regard to a washer woman who is sleeping with a carpenter! [. . .] Ega could not contain herself. The weak point of realism was precisely that it was still too unscientific, [. . .]. The purest form of naturalist art ought to be the monograph, the basic study of a type, of a passion, as if this were a pathological case, without picturesqueness and without style! . . .*

Eça de Queirós,
Os Maias

Polish criticisms of Zola focused, among other things, on the indifference of naturalism to the historical past that Poland was never to forget. The work of Prus and Eliza Orzeszkowa (1841–1910) can only be described as naturalist because of the manner in which certain subjects were treated, while Sienkiewicz distinguished himself by his historical novels. **Boleslaw Prus (1845–1912)** depicted in his stories the sinister blocks of flats in the poor parts of Warsaw, where his characters fight daily against the spectre of hunger. In his novel *Placówka* (*The Forward Post*, 1886), he studied with much sympathy and warmth, but without the slightest hint of glamour, the hard living conditions of a poor Polish village. Even if in the novel *Lalka* (*The Doll*, 1887), the story is transferred to Warsaw, the basic subject was the same: the inertia of Polish society proved fatal to national progress. Many characters, representing all social classes, revolve around the two protagonists whose tales, memories and flashbacks include recent events in Polish history, which constitute the real background of the work. Eliza Orzeszkowa always took her inspiration from Polish villages and small provincial towns. She described the harshness of the environment which had an effect on her modest characters, wrote pointedly about the oppression to which women and the Jewish religious minority are subject, and, rejecting naturalist neutrality, with lyrical and often poetic tones, she showed sympathy for her unfortunate heroes (*Silny Samson, Samson the Strong*, 1877; *Cham, The Peasant*, 1888; *Nad Niemnen, On the Niemen*, 1888). Among Polish writers who faithfully followed Zola's model (Antoni Sygietynski, 1850–1923; Gabriela Zapolska, 1860–1921), **Adolf Dygasinski (1839–1902)** was the most representative. He wrote many stories about rural Poland, in which the decline in manners, misery, antagonism and the underprivileged conditions of the peasants are almost photographically observed. His short story *Wilk, psy i ludzie* (*Wolves, Dogs and Men*, 1883–1884) presents a cruel vision of nature, derived from Darwinism, in which human beings and animals are on the same footing.

The social problems posed by industrialisation in Bohemia are at the heart of novels by Jakub Arbes: *Moderní upíři* (*Modern Vampires*, 1882), *Mesiáš* (*The Messiah*, 1883) and *Anděl míru* (*The Angel of Peace*, 1890). Zola found his greatest propagator in Mrštík, whose novel *Santa Lucia* (1893) is an implacable portrayal of Prague, a large town that devours the weak.

After the first glimmerings of realism with **Ján Kalinčiak (1822–1871)**, a lucid gaze at the reality of Slovakia was the rule in novel by Svetozár Hurban Vajanský (1847–1916), *Suchá ratolest'* (*The Dried-up Offspring*, 1884), and in the stories of several female prose writers. All these culminated in **Martin Kukučin (1860–1928)** and *Dom v stráni* (*The House on the Hill*, 1904).

In Scandinavia, critical realism had already prepared the ground for naturalism, present in novels by the Norwegian Alexander Kielland (1849–1906). Herman Bang (1847–1912), using a scenic presentation to shorten his tale, revealed the problem of sexual passion in *Ved Vejen* (*On the Road*, 1886), while novels by the writers Amalie Skram (1846–1905) and Victoria Benedictsson (1850–1888) broached taboo areas such as the psychiatric treatment of women. **Henrik Pontoppidan (1857–1943)**

came close to naturalism with his novels *Det forjacttede Land* (*The Promised Land*, 1891–1895), the story of a thwarted secret ambition which, with a great deal of irony, reveals the latent antagonisms of peasant life and *Lykke-Per* (*Lucky Peter*, 1898–1904). German naturalists, influenced by foreign writers (Zola, Taine, Darwin, Scandinavian and Russian writers), revolted against the temperate 'poetic' realism of the bourgeoisie, which cannot or does not want to face up to the grave problems generated by industrial society, and eventually created a much more radical art than Zola's. This is how German naturalism, successfully called 'logical naturalism', came to be the most extreme in Europe. Circles of young writers, united around the brothers Heinrich (1855–1906) and Julius Hart (1859–1930), Holz, Hauptmann and Herman Sudermann (1857–1928), progressively elaborated their naturalist theory in a series of theoretical texts, the first of which was *Kritische Waffengänge* (*Critical Passages of Arms*, 1882) by the Hart brothers. This theory was summed up in Holz's celebrated formula: Art = nature - x, where the factor x represents the subjectivity of the artist. Holz and Johannes Schlaf (1862–1941) created between them a style of writing known as 'Sekundenstil' (second-by-second style), thanks to which the distance between things and the narrative is abolished and in which the time of the narrative coincides with the time taken by the story.

The three stories of their collection *Papa Hamlet* (1889) were the most characteristic sample of this technique. Here the discourse of the characters in the form of an everyday, natural dialogue is acoustically reproduced with great fidelity: incomplete words and phrases, hesitations, pauses, grammatical errors and peculiarities of accent and individual articulation, repetitions – everything was included in a text in which dialogue is the main element and in which what the narrator says, jammed into the gaps of the dialogue, is often related to the stage directions given by a director for a theatrical performance:

«Na? Willst du – nu, oder *nich? Bestie!!!»* *«Aber-Niels! Um Gottes* *willen! Er hat ja wider* *den-Anfall!»* *«Ach was! Anfall! – Da!* *Friss!!»* *«Herrgott, Niels . . .»* *«Friss!!!»* *«Niels!——* *«Na? Bist du-nu still? –* *Bist du-nu still? Na?!* *Na?!»* *«Ach Gott! Ach Gott, Niels,* *was, was-machst du denn* *bloss?!* *Er, er-schreit ja gar nicht* *mehr! Er . . . Niels!!»*	*'Right! Do you want to or* *not Bastard!!!'* *'But, Niels! For God's* *sake! He's having a fit* *again!'* *'What? A fit? Yes!'* *'Friss!!!'* *'Oh my God! Niels . . . .'* *'Friss!!!'* *'Niels!——* *'Right? Are you calm* *now? Are you calm?* *There, there!'* *'My God! My God, Niels,* *but what are you doing?!'* *'Hey! He's not shouting any more!* *Hey . . . Niels!!'*

Arno Holz and Johannes Schlaf,
Papa Hamlet

In Croatian naturalism, which simultaneously underwent the influence of Russian realism and Italian verism, Romantic overtones survived that reflect the national aspirations of a country under Austro-Hungarian domination. Eugen Kumičić (1850–1904) created a Rougon-Macquart cycle of sorts, but his stories unfold along sentimental and Romantic lines. Vjenceslav Novac (1859– 1905) used in his works of a national character urban and the first proletarian themes. Ante Kovačić (1854–1888) in his novel *U Registrature* (*In the Clerk's Office*, 1888), described urbanisation, savage industrialisation and the proletarisation of the peasants, a consequence of the 1873 great land reform.

In Greece, naturalism was complex phenomenon. The translation of *Nana* in serial form (1879) provoked violent reactions, especially from readers of the *Estia* review. The publication of the novel was interrupted, but in 1880 the whole work was translated and appeared as a book with an enthusiastic introduction about Zola, considered as the manifesto of Greek naturalism. Meanwhile, the publication in 1888 of *To taxidhi mou* (*My Journey*), a novel by Ioannis Psichari (1854–

1929), marked a stage that was not only linguistic but literary. The writers who put Psichari's lessons into practice adopted Demotic, the spoken language of the people; much more expressive, Demotic contributed to the rapid expansion of naturalism. A short story by **Andreas Karkavitsas (1865–1922)**, *O Zitianos* (*The Beggar*, 1896), denounced and criticised society, constituting the purest expression of Greek naturalism. The action is set in a typical village in Thessaly. Karkavitsas reveals the passions, instincts and needs, but also the ignorance and superstitions which inevitably govern the actions of the members of this circumscribed society. **Alexandros Papadiamandis (1851–1911)**, taking advantage of naturalist subject matter to a certain extent, took the subjects for his tales and stories from the life of his native island of Skiathos from the indigent suburbs of Athens; he tackled burning social issues. His heroes are working class, poor, marginal, failed individuals. However, the basic character of his work was defined by his deep Orthodox religious faith which lends to his tortured characters, often sinners and sometimes criminals, the aura that surrounds Dostoyevsky's characters. His work and his art went well beyond naturalism. The endings of many of his stories deviated in a typical way from naturalist poetics. They do not refer the reader back, like those of Maupassant, for instance, to the contemporary reality of the historical process and the human drama which continues to unfold outside the text, but rather to the timeless world of God's love. In his story *O Erotas sta khionia* (*Love in the Snow*, 1896), the hero, an old wandering sea captain with an eye for the ladies, who has frittered away all his money on prostitutes in Marseilles, finds a dead body frozen in the snow one night, when, coming home drunk, he trips and falls in the snowy street:

Κ' ἐπάνω εἰς τὴν χιόνα ἔπεσε
χιών. Καὶ ἡ χιὼν ἐστοιβάχθη,
ἐσωρεύθη δύο πιθαμάς, ἐκορυφώθη.
Καὶ ἡ χιὼν ἔγινε σινδών,
σάβανον.
Καὶ ὁ μπάρμπα–Γιαννιὸς ἄσπρισεν
ὅλος, κ'ἐκοιμήθη ὑπὸ τὴν χιόνα,
διὰ νὰ μὴ παρασταθῆ γυμνὸς καὶ
τετραχηλισμένος, αὐτὸς καὶ ἡ ζωή
του καὶ αἱ πράξεις του, ἐνώπιον
τοῦ Κριτοῦ, τοῦ Παλαιοῦ Ἡμερῶν,
τοῦ Τρισαγίου

Alexandros Papadiamandis,
O Erotas sta khionia

And onto the snow more snow fell.
And the snow built up; it rose
to a height of two spans;
it got as high as it could.
And the snow was a winding sheet and
a shroud.
Barba Yannios had fallen asleep forever
under the snow. He had become
all whiteness so as not to
show himself naked and
bare-chested, himself, his life and his
works, before the Judge, the Three-Times-Holy
Ancient of Days.

In this way Papadiamandis goes beyond the philosophical starting point of naturalism to encounter symbolism and poetry.

Naturalism and the theatre

Writing for the theatre, into which the 'logical' naturalism of Holz and Schlaf in *Papa Hamlet* had finally been channelled, made obvious the internal organic relationship of naturalist theory to the theatre. The transfer of naturalist principles towards drama contributed to its renewal. First, as far as plays were concerned, new themes were introduced: heredity was the subject of Ibsen's *Ghosts*; the working class that of Hauptmann's *Die Weber* (*The Weavers*, 1892). From the technical point of view, naturalist dramatists were obliged to look for new solutions of setting, structure and plot which would allow them to show the characters' past, which weighs so much on their present, as they have, no opportunity to describe this past in detail, like their novelist counterparts.

Methods of staging were renewed and mod-ernised. The development of the naturalist theatre overall was favoured by the creation of 'independent' theatres: the Théâtre Libre founded in 1887 in Paris by André Antoine (1858–1943), the Freie Bühne in Berlin in 1889. The performance of first-class naturalist plays by Tolstoy, Ibsen, Strindberg and Hauptmann impressed the public enormously and sometimes even scandalised it.

The theatre was Germany's most important contribution to European naturalism. German theatre was influenced by the models of the two great Scandinavians, Ibsen and Strindberg, to whom we may add **Bjørnstjerne Bjørnson (1832–1910)** for his works *Leonarda* (1879), *En Hanske* (*A Glove*, 1883) – which led to a 'quarrel over decency' – and *Over Aevne* (*Beyond Strength*, 1883). The first great success of **Gerhardt Hauptmann (1862–1945)** was the play *Vor Sonnenaufgang* (*Before Dawn*, 1889), a success which was not stemmed by *The Weavers*. This social drama depicted the Silesian textile workers' revolt in 1844, condemned to mass unemployment by industrialisation, whom Heine had depicted in his poem 'Die schlesischen Weber' ('The Silesian Weavers', 1847). Hauptmann contrasts the poverty stricken workers and the class of the rich oppressors. In the second Act the insurgents burst into song:

> *Nun denke man sich diese Not*
> *und Elend dieser Armen,*
> *zu Haus oft keinen Bissen Brot,*
> *ist das nicht zum Erbarmen!*
> Gerhardt Hauptmann
> *Die Weber*

> *Think of the misery*
> *And the distress of these poor people,*
> *At home, there is often not*
> *a bite of bread,*
> *It makes you feel for them!*

Nevertheless, the revival of the European theatre, despite important, purely naturalist contributions to it, such as the stage adaptation of Tolstoy's *Power of Darkness* in 1886) only happen when Ibsen, and later Chekhov, associate naturalism with symbolism.

SURVIVALS OF AN ALTERED ROMANTICISM

Romanticism did not disappear, but, in the works it continued to inspire, it was altered by historical, ideological and literary changes. Poetry continued to be the privileged genre. It retained a hangover from the Romanticism of old: a predilection for historical subjects.

Romanticism in poetry

In France, poetry by **Victor Hugo (1802–1885)**[*] – *Punishments* (1853), *The Legend of the Centuries* (1859–1883) and especially *Contemplations* (1856) – far from maintaining the sentimentality of a Lamartine or a Musset, reached a symbolic level and was nourished by living metaphors.

> *Do you think that nature in its enormity*
> *mumbles,*
> *And that God, in his immensity, would*
> *only*
> *Have given himself the pleasure, for all*
> *eternity,*

> *Of listening to the stammerings of a deaf-*
> *mute?*
> *No, the abyss is a priest and the shadow is*
> *a poet;*
> *No, everything is a voice, everything an*
> *odour;*
> *Everything in the infinite says something* to
> *someone;*
> *One thought fills the tumultuous wonder.*
> *God did not make a noise without mixing*
> *in the word;*
> *Everything, like you, moans, or sings like*
> *me;*
> *Everything speaks. And now, man, do you*
> *know why*
> *Everything speaks? Listen, it is because*
> *wind, sea, flames,*
> *Trees, reeds, rocks, everything is alive!*
> *Everything is full of souls.*
> Victor Hugo, 'The Mouth of Shadow',
> *The Contemplations*

Work by the Flemish poet **Guido Gezelle (1830–1899)** was based on Romantic ideas of nature, reinforced by religious inspiration: *Gedichten, gezangen en gebeden (Poems, Canticles and Prayers*, 1862), *Tijdkrans (Crown of Hours*, 1893), *Rijmsnoer (Necklace of Rhymes around the Year*, 1897). His specificity resulted from the rural and rustic framework of his poems, in which nature acquires a symbolic value. The personal aspect of Gezelle's poetry is that much stronger because many poems were dedicated to his favourite pupils.

> *Ofschoon, zo wel voor mij als u,*
> *– wie zal dit kwaad genezen?*
> *– een uur bij mij, een uur bij*

> *Although for me as for*
> *you – who could render it*
> *immortal? – an hour next to*

u, niet lang een uur mag
wezen; ofschoon voor mij,
ofschoon voor u, zo lief en
uitgelezen,
die roze, al was't een roos van u,
niet lang een roos mocht wezen,
toch lang bewaard; dit zeg ik u,
't en ware ik't al verloze,
mijn hert drie dierbre beelden: u,
dien avond – en – die roze!

Guido Gezelle,
Gedichten, gezangen en gebeden

me, an hour next to you cannot
for a long time remain just that;
although for me, although
for you this fair chosen flower
– even though I received it
from you – will soon lose its petals
and wither, my heart, nevertheless,
I say it to you now, will keep open
for a long time the flower of a triple
memory: You, That night and . . . that
Rose.

In Spain, the simplicity and limpidity of poetry by **Gustavo Adolfo Bécquer (1836–1870)** in *El Libro de los gorriones* (*The Book of Sparrows*) reminds us of Heine, while that of Rosalía Castro (1837–1885), both in Galician (*Cantares gallegos, Songs of Galicia*, 1863 and 1872) and Castilian (*En las orillas del Sar, On the Banks of the Sar*, 1884), steeped in pain and sadness, deeply expressed the soul of her native land.

In Portugal, in the mid-1860s, the climate of bourgeois euphoria arising from the Regeneration was on the wane. In literature, the change became perceptible through the literary polemic called 'The Coïmbra Question' (1865–1866). At the heart of this polemic was a new concept of art in society, which *Odes modernas* (*Modern Odes*, 1865) by **Antero Tarquínio de Quental (1842–1891)** illustrate. With his famous *Sonetos* (*Sonnets*, 1886), Quental evolved in the direction of a metaphysical and somewhat pessimistic poet. Three other Portuguese poets, Guilherme de Azevedo (1839–1882), Gomes Leal (1848–1921) and Guerra Junqueiro (1850–1923) oscillated between social Romanticism, Baudelairian Satanism and indistinct realist or symbolist touches.

Poetry by the Czech Jan Neruda, half-way between Romanticism and realism, tackles with emotion and fervour, often with humour, social, national and philosophical themes (*Knihy veršů, Books of Verse*, 1868; Písně Kosmické, Cosmic Songs, 1878), translated with apparent simplicity and a precise economy of expression.

In Slovakia, Romanticism persisted with **Ján Botto (1829–1881)** in his poem *Smrt' Jánošikova* (*The Death of Jánošik*, 1861), a rebel and a legendary dispenser of justice, and with Samo Chalupka (1811–1884), the author of the poem-cry for freedom *Mor ho*! (*Destroy them*! 1864).

Tyutchev is considered to be the precursor of Russian symbolism. Nourished on Goethe, Schelling and Heine, he translated his philosophical Romantic inspiration into a vision of nature close to pantheism, but which opposed the cosmos – a world of order and beauty – nocturnal chaos, lying just beneath the surface. This opposition developed into a Manichean vision of good/evil, day/night, love/death, a source of thoughts and images derived from symbolism (*Silentium, Silence*, 1833). In the lyrical work by Afanasy Fet-Shenshin (1862–1911), love and eroticism dominate (Vecérnye ogni, Evening Fires, 1883). A contemplative poet, a poet of the ephemeral and hence a poet of suggestion, of the almost ineffable, he was interesting to the symbolists because of his acute awareness of the poet's power to make great metaphysical intuitions tangible. However, the most abundant Romantic production of this period appeared in countries who were fighting for their national independence and the strengthening of their national consciousness: Hungary, Poland, Rumania, Bulgaria. Norway. The literature of these countries found in Romanticism a means of expression which allowed them to better externalise their love of liberty and homeland, exploiting subjects which belonged to their historical past, to their popular legends and to their national mythology. This patriotic Romanticism sometimes came under the influence of realism.

Sweden was celebrated in the collection of historical poems *Svenka Bilder* (*Pictures of Sweden*, 1886) by Carl Snoilsky (1841–1903), which recalled the great moments of national history. Just as popular, the work of his fellow countryman **Viktor Rydberg (1828–1895)** contained the poem *Tomten* (*The Goblin*, 1877) which is still read by Swedes today. **János Arany (1817–1882)** forged with realism a national poetry, Romantic in conception, nourished on Hungary's historical past, with the aim of unifying his country and ensuring its future survival. His epic trilogy *Toldi* (1847, 1847–1848, 1879), his epic poem *Buda Halála* (*The Death of Buda*, 1863), his ballads – an expression of national soul and morality – and his lyrical poems warmed the heart of his compatriots, affirming their belief in their nation's historical and moral greatness. However, Arany did not abandon himself to a deceitful Romanticism; thanks to his precise expression, psychological analysis and positivist vision of history, he oscillated between the ideal and reality, often illustrating this tension in a tragic way.

The belated Romanticism of Svatopluk Čech (1846–1908) was corrected by his liberal humanism and his interest in the working man. His patriotism underpinned historical epics (*Adamite, The Adamites*, 1873; *Václav z Michalovič, Václav from Michalovice*, 1882) or was inspired by contemporary events (*Lešetínský kovář, The Blacksmith of Lešetín*, 1883). By virtue of his poetic themes, **Josef Vaclav Sládek (1845–1912)** could be ranked as a member of the national school, if his patriotism were not part and parcel of his modern democratic ideas and if he were not the theoretical defender of cosmopolitanism. His poetry, sober, dense and melodic in its verse, is elegiac, but it also addressed manly calls to the national community in *Selské písně a České znělky* (Peasant Songs and Czech Sonnets, 1889). In three collections, he founded Czech poetry for children, poetry of

a high calibre and devoid of didacticism. **Julius Zeyer (1841–1901)**, a cosmopolitan and great traveller, a solitary, sensitive and cultivated poet, lived in search of a spiritual and artistic absolute. His idealism attracted the Decadents and the Symbolists. His favourite method consisted of taking and paraphrasing foreign or national themes in a personal, free way, and in composing 'revitalised pictures' as an epic poet. So mythical periods of Czech history were recreated in *Vyšehrad* (1880), *Čechův příchod* (*The Arrival of the Czechs*, 1886).

In Rumania, Nasile Alecsandri (1821–1890), laid the foundations of modern Rumanian poetry with the ballad *Miorita* (*Lamb*, 1852). But the most important poet of the period was **Mihail Eminescu (1850–1889)**. Published in its entirety in 1883, his work is full of nostalgia for the lost world of the 'Doinas' (Rumanian popular songs). It is steeped in legends from all the Rumanian provinces.

In Bulgaria, Romanticism, which delved extensively into patriotic popular epic, remained just as closely linked to the idea of national liberation, embodied in poetry by Georgi Sava Rakovski (1821–1867), that 'Bulgarian Garibaldi', and by Petko Slavejkov (1827–1895). But it was, above all, the poetic genius of **Hristo Botev (1848–1876)** that contributed to the achievement of a national renaissance and distinguished the Bulgarian poetic tradition. A revolutionary and publicist, a poet and national hero (killed at the age of twenty-seven in a battle against the Turks), the author of a mere twenty odd poems, and famous nevertheless, Botev celebrated the drama of rebellion, a thirst for liberty and justice, the fascination of sacrifice. Poetry by the Croat Silvije Strahimir Kranjcevic (1865–1908) combined patriotic Romanticism and philosophical reflection.

Patriotic and historical prose

The Romantic prose of the period, much less in evidence than poetry, possessed, to all intents and purposes, the same characteristics:

it was historical, patriotic and national, and its realist tendencies were revealed in the representation of social and psychological reality.

Midway between Romanticism and realist criticism, the novel by **Multatuli (Eduard Douwes Dekker, 1820–1887)**, *Max Havelaar* (1860), was a bitter satire of the Dutch colonial politics of his time.

Ook aan de europesche beambten	*And European civil servants too*
wordt een belooning uitbetaald	*receive a bonus*
in evenredigheid met de	*proportionate to the yield of*
opbrengst.	*their sector.*
Wel wordt dus de arme Javaan	*The poor native of Java is, of course,*
voortgezweept door dubbel gezag,	*driven by the whip*
wel wordt hy dikwyls	*of a dual authority, and is, of course,*
afgetrokken van zyn rystvelden,	*often turned aside from his paddies*
wel is hongersnood vaak 't	*and, of course, famine is a*
gevolg van deze maatregelen,	*frequent consequence of such*
doch . . . vroolyk wapperen te	*measures, but . . . in Batavia, in*
Batavia, te Samarang, te	*Semarang, in Surabaya, in*
Soerabaja, te Passaroean, te	*Passaruan, in Bezuki, in*
Bezoeki, te Probolingo, te	*Probolingo, in Patjitan, in*
Patjitan, te Tjilatjap, de	*Tjilatjap, the flags flap*
vlaggen aan boord der schepen,	*joyfully on the masts of the*
die beladen worden met de	*ships wherein are laden*
oogsten die Nederland ryk	*the harvests which enrich the*
maken.	*Netherlands!*

Multatuli,
Max Havelaar

The paroxystically Romantic side of **Camilo Castelo Branco (1825–1890)**, who attained sublimity in the Romantic expression of love and hate, and in the tragic perception of life as a struggle against fate in *Amor de Perdição* (*Love of Perdition*, 1862), did not prevent him from taking an interest in the social reality of typically northern Portugal and from devoting himself to the satire of manners. The novel *A Brasileira de Prazins* (*The Brazilian Woman of Prazins*, 1882) even reveals a partial assimilation of naturalism. In Portugal, Julio Dinis (1839–1871) also unearthed the psychological mechanisms of his characters, and mixed realism with Romantic idealism. The sickness of civilisation was condemned in the work of the Norwegian Kielland who preferred the sailor's life. His novel *Steipper Worse* (*Captain Worse*, 1882) depicted his countryman's destiny, dedicated to trade and the sea. Ljuben Karavelov (*c.*1834–1879) is also a Romantic by virtue of his idealism and the hyperbole and

pathos of his stories. At the same time, he was the first Bulgarian realist to introduce a social theme into his works (*Bălgari ot staro vreme*, *The Bulgarians of Yesteryear*, 1872). Historical novels by Jakov Ignatovic (1822–1889), of picaresque inspiration, highlighted the typical traits of Serbian Romanticism: heroism and sentimentalism. August Senoa (1838–1881), father of the Croat historical novel, combined Romantic elements with a solid historical documentation and a realist description of characters and settings in *Zlatarevo zlato* (*The Treasure of the Goldsmith*, 1871).

The Hungarian **Mór Jókai (1825–1904)** in the tradition of Hugo, seems to represent the three principal tendencies of the European Romantic novel of the second half of the nineteenth century: the representation of a social reality *(Egy magyar nábob, A Hungarian Nabob*, 1853), the representation of the historical past (*A kôszívü ember fiai, The Sons of Men with Hearts of Stone*, 1869) and deep psychological description (*Az arany ember, A Gradely Man,* 1872).

Historical prose by Alois Jirásek (1851–1930) brought with it an overall vision of Czech national history, which is that of the historian Palacký. The same scientific precision also characterised great historical novels by the Hungarian Kemény: *Az özvegy és leánya* (*The Widow and her Daughter,* 1855).

The beginnings of the Czech social novel are linked to work by Karel Sabina (1813–1877), while *Z malého světa* (*The Little World,* 1864) by Gustav Pfleger-Moravský described the first wildcat strike in Bohemia.

The Romantic prose of central European countries was also inspired by their historical past and, like poetry, this inspiration was caused by the same political and national factors. In this case, realism consisted of being lively and precise in historical representation. Work by **Henryk Sienkiewicz (1846–1916)** was characteristic from this viewpoint. He was a novelist who, despite the criticism of his positivist contemporaries, was awarded the title of national representative of Polish letters. The heroic trilogy of his great historical novels (*Ogniem i mieczem, With Iron and with Fire,* 1883; *Potop, The Deluge,* 1886; *Pan Wolodyjowski, Mister Wolodyjowski,* 1888) was merely the glorification and the apotheosis of Poland's struggles over the centuries to ensure its national survival. He obtained a worldwide reputation for his novel *Quo Vadis?* (1896).

The eternal tragedy of man

The tragic position of the Romantic artist of the period, who took on himself the moral burden of not turning a blind eye to harsh reality, was expressed in the dramatic poem in fifteen acts by the Hungarian **Imre Madách (1823–1864)**, *Az ember tragediaja* (*The Tragedy of Man,* 1860). This play, which made its author known throughout Europe and raised the most contradictory interpretations, had Adam, Eve and Lucifer as its protagonists. This is an isolated, complex work, profoundly philosophical, in which Adam and Lucifer coexist, together with Romanticism and

positivism, a teleological and optimistic philosophy of history and a determinist vision of the world.

On the edge of '-isms'

European literature presented a certain number of convergences during this period, realism and naturalism or survivals of Romanticism, which lend an indisputable homogeneity. Two authors, however, defy all classification and remain marginal to these tendencies.

For many years considered as a second-rate writer of children's literature, ignored by the critics, **Jules Verne (1828–1905)** – *Journey to the Centre of the Earth* (1864), *The Children of Captain Grant* (1867–1868), *Twenty Thousand Leagues under the Sea* (1870), *Around the World in Eighty Days* (1873), *The Mysterious Island* (1874) – has only recently been regarded seriously. We have now discovered his literary and visionary value. His work must be placed alongside that of his reader Jakub Arbes, *Newtonův mozek* (*The Brain of Newton,* 1877), which marked the birth of Czech science fiction.

Yet again it is the twentieth century that did justice to another work of this period: *The Legend of Eulenspiegel and the heroic, joyful and glorious adventures of Eulenspiegel and Lamme Goedzak in the country of Flanders and elsewhere* (1867), by **Charles De Coster (1827–1879)** is more like an epic than a novel. Eulenspiegel, a legendary and popular hero from Belgium, initially lazy, jocular and mischievous, avenges his father's death – on whom the Spanish occupier has inflicted burning at the stake – and the occupation of Flanders.

Towards symbolism

The realist ideal of an objective, faithful representation of the world, transformed by the naturalists into an obligation to give a scientific report on things, led to an essentially pictorial art. Rarely before naturalism had literature, from which poetry had been excluded by definition, found itself so close to painting. It is enough to remember Zola's pictorial talent, whose descriptions have been compared to seventeenth-century Flemish painters. We only need to consider the real interest of Belgian writers of this period for painting and the plastic arts in general (Lemonnier), and its literary realisation in *The Road of Emerald* (1899) by Eugène Demolder (1862–1919), a narrative transposition of art in the area of painting, in which the best-known scenes of the paintings of the Dutch school form the subject of the story.

Beyond the almost scientific representation of reality that naturalist works offered, naturalist theory, potentially, contained the abolition of the difference between reality, natural and social, objectively existing, and its literary representation. 'Logical naturalism' and the 'Sekundenstil', extreme but theoretically feasible possibilities, placed the very existence of literature in mortal danger. In effect, if literature did nothing more than repeat or verify a given reality, already known, scientifically as it happens, what good was it? Faced by this danger that he had already seen in a simplistic realism, Baudelaire took it himself to save literature: 'Poetry is what is most real, what cannot be completely true except in another world. This world is a dictionary of hieroglyphs.'

Following in his footsteps, symbolism, helped by a growing scepticism about the opportunities that science offered for clearing up the mysteries of this 'dictionary of hieroglyphs' – Renan himself admitted in his introduction to *The Future of Science*, a work written in 1848–1849 but only published in 1890, that 'the mistake that pervades these old pages is an exaggerated optimism' – undertook to ensure the survival and autonomy of literature. It will succeed by giving precedence to poetry over prose and over the metonymic description of the world, and to the transfer to another plane that poetry can realise with the use of metaphor. The assimilation of poetry to music, the least representative and most suggestive of all the arts, came about as an inevitable result.

This is why, at the height of realism, after *The Flowers of Evil* (1857), which brought poetry into a new era – that of modernity – we see the blossoming of the first symbolist poems: in 1866 *Poèmes saturniens* by Verlaine, *Petits Poèmes en prose* by Baudelaire, *Les Chants de Maldoror* by Lautréamont; in 1873 *Une saison en enfer* and *Les Illuminations* by Rimbaud; in 1874 *Romances sans paroles* by Verlaine. Symbolism open the door of European literature.

Poetry: the Birth of Modernism

J.E. Jackson

Over lake and over vale,
Woods and mountains, clouds and seas,
Beyond the sun, air rarefied,
Beyond the limits of the starry spheres,
You move, my spirit, with agility.
Charles Baudelaire, *Elevation*

The years 1850 to 1880 represented a decisive epoch in European poetry's development. This is the period that witnessed the establishment of what was later to be called modernism. Modernism was linked with three names: Baudelaire, Rimbaud and Mallarmé. This preponderance of Frenchmen – Walter Benjamin planned to call his great work *Paris, Capital of the nineteenth Century* – should not mislead us about to the European significance and extent of this movement. Modernism which set itself up between *The Flowers of Evil* and the *Throw of the Dice* was going to inform modern poetry from Rilke to Ungaretti, from Trakl to Pessoa, from Eliot to Mandelstam, to Seferis or to Aleixandre, in almost all the great works of the twentieth century. The gaze that different national poetries henceforth cast at their own past were also modified. The creative paradox of modernism is that it redesigned the face of its prehistory: it was only after the First World War that a poet like Friedrich Hölderlin, whose output ceased about 1805, was rewarded with the eminent place which was his by right in European poetry's order of merit.

The Flowers of Evil, charter for modernism

It is commonly held that the poetic charter for modernism emerged in 1857 with the publication of Baudelaire's anthology *The Flowers of Evil*. This book was important for several reasons. First, it was important because of the divorce in it between a subjective approach in love with the absolute and dreaming of mastery over it and the resistance on the part of reality to let itself be pinned down by the poet's desire. Whether this was in the form of a swan that had 'escaped from its cage', of a 'ridiculous hanging man', even 'a shade of Hamlet imitating his posture', the images or allegories which Baudelaire used to refer to the situation of the writer in the society of his time have as their common denominator an alienation of awareness to a reality henceforth recognised by its power to move us. This power is so strong that with Baudelaire poetry changes scene: from pastoral (Wordsworth, Brentano, Leopardi), mythic (Hölderlin, Nerval) or historical (Hugo), it became urban. Baudelaire was not just the poet of Paris, he was the singer of a humanity that knows that its destiny is henceforth linked to big towns. The disproportion between the poet's ego and the dimensions of the reality into which he is thrown will get larger. There will result from it an accentuation of the gap between internal and external. In effect, confronted by the indifference or hostility of his social surroundings, the poet will tend, initially, to fall back on himself, on the pride or ambition inside him, opposing the depth of his own resources to the flat, external nature of what is opposed to poetry. But this movement, already perceptible with the Romantics, was backed up in Baudelaire by the awareness that this interiority is only a lure, and that reality has alienated the self to the point of having broken down its defences: the poet in the 'Seven Old Men', for example, having gone home to flee the terrifying apparition of the multiplied image of the Old Man he has met in the street, can only note: 'Vainement ma raison voulait prendre la barre;/ La tempête en jouant déroutait ses efforts,/ Et mon âme dansait, dansait, vieille gabarre/ Sans mâts, sur une mer monstrueuse et sans bords!'. ('In vain my reason wanted to take the helm;/ The playful storm defeated its best efforts,/ And my soul danced and danced, an old freighter/ Dismasted, on a monstrous and limitless sea!'). Hence a melancholy which must be understood, more than something personal, as the expression of a lost integrity which both haunts contemporary consciousness and places it in exile. For Baudelaire, Paris became the scene of a historical drama in which, from the swan to the little old women, from prostitutes to beggars or to blind men, the pathetic figures of an interminable and tragic procession go past in which he recognises doubles of his own feelings of dispossession. This is a feeling all the stronger in that it contrasts with the rapid expansion of an imagination in which a desire for limitless sovereignty expresses itself.

Indeed, it is perhaps the very admission of this division or this contradiction that made *The Flowers of Evil* the book that founded modern poetry. Baudelaire, with all his desire for mastery, was too much in love with truth, too irrepressibly lucid either to renounce his dreams or to try to hide his failure in making them come true. Hence the two great tendencies of his book: the euphoric tendency, which is often confused with dreams or with amorous memory, and the painful, anguished tendency which marks so many poems. In the first case, the poem becomes an autonomous universe, the beloved becoming both the present microcosm of a beneficent distance and the starting point for a reverie about this distance. So it is, for example, in 'La Chevelure' ('The Head of Hair'), where, speaking of his mistress's curls, Baudelaire exclaims:

I will plunge my head in love with giddiness
Into this black ocean where the other is
*   enclosed;*
And my subtle mind caressed by the roll of
*   her hair*
Will be able to find you, oh fertile laziness,
Infinite cradlings of leisure
*   embalmed!*

In the second instance, the 'Parisian Dream', for example, the way out of the dream only makes the less than ideal state of the reality that the dream left behind even worse:

Opening my eyes full of passion again
I saw the horror of my hovel,
And felt, going back to my soul,
The edge of cursed worries;
The clock with funereal tones
Brutally chimed twelve noon,
And the sky shed darkness
On a sad world benumbed.

This 'clock with funereal tones' not only recalls the dreamer to reality, but fixes him too in a time marked by the onward journey towards death. If Paris is the background to the *Flowers of Evil*, above all in the second edition (1861), death is the presence that hovers over this background, and modernism has close links to death: it is in order to consent to its power, to recognise its finiteness as an intervention that a new mode of poetry invented itself. Rilke remembered this in *Die Aufzeichnungen des Malte Laurids Brigge* (*The Notebooks of Malte Laurids Brigge*, 1910), the whole of the beginning of which can be read as a sort of gloss on the section in *The Flowers of Evil* entitled *Tableaux parisiens* (*Parisian Pictures*) and in which, moreover, it is explicitly stated that the means of modern poetic expression was founded in the poem 'Une charogne' ('Carrion'). Later, T.S. Eliot, in *The Waste Land* (1922), made use of the introductory verses of 'Les Petites Vieilles' ('The Little Old Women') to make them the symbol of a modernity coinciding henceforth with a sort of *Hell* which Baudelaire took over from Dante to delineate the barrenness of a society deprived of transcendence, or, at the very least, of certainties. Closer to our own day, Yves Bonnefoy always referred to *The Flowers of Evil* as the book in which, named for the first time in its inevitable physical reality, death opened up to poetry the ways of an authentic truth sealed in finite form in the so often timeless language of traditional poetic diction. After all, the last verses of the book ('Plonger au fond du

gouffre, Enfer ou Ciel, qu'importe?/ Au fond de l'Inconnu pour trouver du *nouveau!*' ['To dive to the bottom of the abyss, Hell or Heaven, what does it matter?/ So long as, at the bottom of the Unknown, we find something *new!*']) are addressed to that 'old captain' who is an archetypal allegory of death on the initiatory journey that will lead the poet to his destination.

Rimbaud the poet-seer

No one had this appetite for the 'new' more than Arthur Rimbaud, whose famous 'Letter of the Seer' (15 May 1871) made of Baudelaire a 'true God'. Rimbaud, in all honesty, only wanted to retain of the work of this 'God' the part likely to confirm him in his desire to submit the real to what he calls an 'alchemy of the word' designed to awaken unexplored possibilities in it. The dichotomy between wounded subjectivity and wounding reality is thus transcended into a movement which aims to transform one and the other into a process of a reinvention as exalted as it is vertiginous: it was not by accident if Rimbaud considered 'Le Bateau ivre' ('The Drunken Boat') to be the passport that would earn him his official naturalisation as a poet with his Parisian colleagues. This poem, which took up where Baudelaire's 'Voyage' left off, prolongs the search, not in the realm of the dead, but in the imaginary space of a clairvoyance in which all the resources of poetic invention are conjured up. Drunk on his new-found freedom, the poetic 'I', sailing like a rudderless boat without its grappling irons, can create for itself a totally unconventional world:

I saw the sun low, stained with mystical
horrors,
Illuminating long and purple coagulations,
Like actors in very ancient dramas
The waves rolling far away their shivered
shutters!

I dreamed the night was green with
dazzling snow,
A kiss mounting to the eyes of slow-moving
seas,

The circulation of unknown saps,
And the yellow and blue awakening of
singing phosphorus!

These unprecedented stanzas say more than the incandescent giddiness of a true poetic talent. They mark the godlike ambition to submit the world to a vision and a word that redistribute and recreate its constituent parts according to a 'learned music' orchestrated by the imagination, which Baudelaire already used to refer to as 'the queen of the faculties'. We can understand, under these circumstances, that Rimbaud in his turn became one of the 'gods' of European surrealism to which he offered the example of a matchless freedom, in which the part that was dream, or even an hallucination, became the pass key to a 'surreality' which could triumphantly be opposed to the real. There is, in fact, in his work such a pull, such a power of invention, such conviction in the substitution of the world of the clairvoyant for the conventional world that the surrealists could see in it, quite rightly, their literary programme realised. There was a pull so great, in fact, that it survived the abandonment of poetic practice and René Char could exclaim: 'You were right to go off, Arthur Rimbaud!' by celebrating in his departure the leaving of 'bars where piss-pot poets would congregate' where too many so-called poets would immure themselves.

Rimbaud, however, unlike many of his surrealist disciples, was too lucid not to notice how the godlike taking-off of clairvoyance encountered the resistance of a reality refractory to his desire to transform it. Thus already, at the end of his drifting, the subject of the 'Bateau ivre' rediscovered himself in the nostalgia of a child's memory deprived of all the prestige of the imaginary: 'If I want European water, I'll take the puddle/Black and cold where towards the odorous twilight/ A crouching melancholy child lets go of/ A boat as flimsy as a straw bottle-holder.' And, in the same way, at the end of *A Season in Hell* (1873), after having expressed the full extent of his creative aspirations ('[. . .] to invent new flowers, new stars, new flesh, new languages'),

the poet has to recognise that he must 'bury his imagination and his memories' and that he has 'come back to earth with a duty to search and a rough reality to grasp!' This awareness of the negative was certainly not alien to the predilection that Georg Trakl had for the poetry of his predecessor, even if for him the dream part tends to assume more importance than the eruptive power of the word. But the associative logic of Trakl's poems was hardly thinkable without the model of *A Season in Hell* or the *Illuminations* (1871–1875).

Mallarmé or words of incantation

This disillusionment, this fall from grace which seem, paradoxically, to belong to Rimbaud's poetic consciousness, on a par with his desire to fly away and to be transformed, define, at the very least, a relationship between subject and the language of this subject to a doubter. It is because he has pushed this doubt to an exaggerated level that Stéphane Mallarmé took poetry in a direction that was even more singular. Here, all hope of building a relationship between words and things as between the subject and the world has given way to a gesture of separation and a fall-back position all the more radical in that it sees itself as deliberate and thought-out; since words fail to express the world other than in an imperfect way, poetry will be the world, taking itself as object. Like Herodiad reflected in the 'severe fountain' of a mirror, poetry with Mallarmé becomes the auto-celebration of a word which discovers its space by affirming its reflexivity. Where Baudelaire was expressing his alienation from a reality that could not be mastered, where Rimbaud was portraying the drama of his godlike passion, Mallarmé made himself the celebrant of a position in which the act of poetry, first of all the simple and sovereign affirmation of the freedom of a spirit delighted by its own great power to fictionalise will end up growing to fill the universe: 'yes, *I know*, we are only vain material forms, but sublime by virtue of having invented God and our soul. So sublime, my friend, that I want to feast my eyes on this matter, conscious of it and yet throwing ourselves headlong into the Dream that it knows it is not, singing the Soul and all the similar divine impressions which have accumulated in us from the beginning, and proclaiming, before the Nothingness that is truth, these glorious lies!' This is what he wrote in April 1866 to his friend Cazalis. This 'glorious lie' is made up of words which know that they are only in truth exalting themselves, whatever they do, as if they were speaking about an object or a reality distinct from themselves, and as if this object had its own reality, ontologically recognised. This pretence demands, in order to be used, that the language that supports it be freed in turn from every referential function to let it turn in on itself. Mallarmé, in another letter to Cazalis, formulated this thought initially by saying that he wanted 'to depict, not the thing, but the effect that it produces', adding later that the verse 'of several syllables imparts a word that is total, new, foreign to the language and like an incantation', before concluding that 'the world is made to yield a fine book'. As may be gleaned from these brief quotations, Mallarmé's concern aimed at nothing less than to enthrone poetic language in a position of absolute sovereignty which subordinates the ontological dimension to the text. *Un coup de dés jamais n'abolira le hasard* (1897) is there to attest to the fact that he himself had the lucidity to admit the impossibility of his enterprise just when he was bringing it to its highest level of realisation. The dice of the work will never abolish the gratuitousness of matter. It is no less true that from Valéry to Claudel, from Rilke to Celan, from Eliot to Montale, many of the major works of twentieth century European poetry will meditate on the depth of the challenge with which Mallarmé had confronted the poetic adventure of words. Almost all major works will feel called on to take up a position about the absolute nature of language and Mallarmé's famous sonnet in YX became its unforgettable symbol.

Hugo (1802–1885)

G. Fontaine

The century was two years old.
Rome replaced Sparta,
Already Napoleon showed under Bonaparte,
And in many of his features, already,
The imperial brow broke the mould
of the First Consul's
narrow mask.
Then, in Besançon,
an old Spanish town,
Was born.

Victor Hugo was born in 1802. He who perceived his century as a legendary time, in which he himself, a hero of legend, was charged with a fabulous mission; this is what the above verses of 'Feuilles d'automne' ('Autumn Leaves') prompt us to think.

To express the fable of the world, to elevate everything he saw, everything he lived, to the level of epic: the whole of his work, Hugo's biography, could be called 'The Legend of the Centuries'. At the heart of Franche-Comté, not far from Switzerland, is, Besançon, where Victor was born, because his officer father had been stationed there. The Hugo 'seed', which gave birth to *Hernani* (1830), and *Ruy Blas* (1838), inseminated the real and makes it bring forth colourful children.

We have, for instance, the flamboyant sonority of a landscape in fourteen syllables: 'Mounts of Aragon! Galicia! Extremadura!' Then a staggeringly understated picture of a sad, frozen, cotton-wool landscape: 'It was snowing, still snowing . . .' Then the death in vermilion of a street urchin in 1830, Gavroche, whose magnanimity cuts a mythological figure: 'There was something of Anteus in this pygmy; for the urchin, to make contact with the pavement is the same as for the giant to make contact with the earth; Gavroche had only fallen down to get up again; he remained seated, a long trickle of blood ran down his face . . .'

Hugo's genius also lay in guiding the hand of his future biographers: a right-winger till the age of forty-six, he was later hailed as one of the first socialists. He was held to be the model of the persecuted intellectual and forced into exile, so that, from Jersey or Brussels, he could get off parting shots against Napoleon III without ever putting more than a hundred kilometres between himself and France. He was also the horny old gentleman who, in Guernsey, dragged his young maids into a corner of his house he himself had baptised 'kiss me quick' and was presented, in histories of literature, as a perpetual lover.

But Victor Hugo was, first and foremost, the poet who knew how to contemplate the humble; in *The Contemplations*, a poor man walks past his door, he makes him come in and places his coat in front of the fire:

> And I gazed, deaf to what we were
> saying,
> At his homespun cloak in which I could see
> constellations.

On 31 May 1885, two million French people, among whom were delegations of workers from all over France, accompanied the author of the *Misérables* (1862) to his final resting-place: the Pantheon.

Baudelaire (1821–1867)

M. Gosselin

I have found the definition of Beauty, of Beauty for me, it is something ardent and sad, something slightly vague, giving free course to conjecture.

Charles Baudelaire,
Rockets

Although he did not invent the notion of the writer as a beacon, in *The Flowers of Evil* Baudelaire gave definitive form to the image of the artist as a torch for humanity from age to age, bearing witness to man's ability to transcend himself and to leave behind his wretchedness by transfiguring it into an expectant sensitivity:

> A cry reiterated by a thousand sentries,
> An order circulated by a thousand mega
> phones:
> A beacon lit in a thousand citadels,
> A horn-blast from hunters lost in great
> woods.
> For it is truly, Lord,
> the best testimony
> That we can give of our dignity,
> This ardent sob which rolls
> from age to age
> And comes to fade out on the edge
> of Your eternity!

Nearly the whole of Baudelaire's aesthetics appears in this poem. An artistic heritage is assumed in it through set-pieces devoted to painters, engravers or sculptors from different parts of Europe. The classical rhythm of the alexandrine praises in it the Baroque profusion of Rubens, the sad rebelliousness of Puget's convicts, the physical strength of Michelangelo's statues of Hercules and Christ, and the pathetic mysticism of Rembrandt. The Romanticism of Delacroix encounters the 'sigh' of Weber; the graceful fantasy of Watteau brushes against the absurd yet feasible monsters of Goya. There is the dizzy Baroque poetry of d'Aubigné and the rebellious dandyism of Byron; the light in paintings by Veronese and Delacroix, and music according to Hoffmann and Wagner. Baudelaire was like that: his work assembled and renewed a whole European tradition, even transcending that by his translations of Poe which were his first claims to fame. His work constitutes perfection achieved by an innovatory aesthetic founded on a tamed Romanticism, a poetry of the imagination and not of the heart, on hard work not just on inspiration. There is the introduction of dissonance at the heart of the poem, of the symbol at the heart of the vision in a paradoxical work that combines blasphemy and Satanism with a certain religious faith, an aspiration to ideals and the awareness of an ineluctable fall which Baudelaire called the double postulation towards God and Satan.

Must we, as Sartre did, seek in his life the source of his choice of evil against good, or ought we to seek, in a different critical tradition, the source of his love poems? Without pretending to explain these choices, we can at least point out the critical moments at which his life seems to have 'taken a turn', those that he himself gave us to read in his work in which he apparently half-opens his heart and his room to the reader – 'Hypocrite lecteur, mon semblable, mon frère.' ('Hypocritical reader, my fellow creature, my brother.')

A dandy's life

The author of the *Parisian Pictures* had a father who was already old, cultured, enthusiastic about Enlightenment ideas, a lover of painting and a painter himself, a priest who was able to be defrocked thanks to the Revolution. We can imagine what his father passed on to the poet, the father that he lost at the age of six. His mother remarried in November 1828 to Brigadier Aupick and secretly had a daughter, who died on 2 December of the following year. What could young Charles have felt about this, prudently sent away at the time? His letters to his family already testify to literary gifts, but not to rebelliousness. In his final year at school (1839), he was expelled from high school for a trivial matter. From this moment he chose to live a life in opposition to the bourgeois values embodied by his mother and his stepfather. Officially enrolled on a law course, he lived a Bohemian life, searching with his mistresses, such as Sarah La Louchette, the satisfaction of sensual pleasures. He got into debt and a family council suggested that he went to the Indies on *Le paquebot-des-mers-du-Sud* (*The Steamship of the Southern Seas*). He went in fact to Mauritius where he wrote the sonnet 'À une dame créole' ('To a Creole Lady') and gathered images which nurtured his vision of a former life or an exotic elsewhere. But, having reached Reunion, he sailed back to France.

In 1842, he claimed the use of his fortune, half of which he spent in two years. He met at this time the quadroon Jeanne Duval with whom he knew all the charms and the bitterness of passion. Both a bibliophile and an art lover, he lived surrounded by friends who all dabbled in writing, but knew how superior his verse was. By 1843 he had already written several poems in *The Flowers of Evil*, working, at the same time, as a satirical journalist and an art critic. In 1844, Madame Aupick, frightened by the scale of his spending, made him a ward of court. This did not stop Baudelaire from leading the life of a dandy, who promoted artifice and singularity, despising the bourgeois 'philistine' and his edifying morality. He was influenced by the black Romanticism of Petrus Borel (1809–1859) and the fantasy of Hoffmann. It was from this that the character of Samuel Cramer emerged in *La Fanfarlo*, a short story published in 1847, whose text ended on the satire of a poetry based on the hatred of self, contempt for others and the sophistication of the heart.

The art critic

As an art critic, Baudelaire, in the Salons of 1845 and 1846, fought against the exalted forms of 'Romanticism which is not exactly in the choice of subject nor in exact truth, but in a way of feeling. Whoever says Romanticism says modern art, i.e. intimacy, spirituality, colour, aspiration towards an infinite expressed by all means that the arts afford'. In 1837 Baudelaire published a short story called *The Young Magician*, translated without permission by the English writer Croly, and he announced a collection of poems with a fashionable title, *Les Lesbiennes*. He got hot on the barricades during the 1848 revolution, but he is above all intent on shooting Aupick! His revolutionary Romanticism soon made way for a certain conservatism taken from Joseph de Maistre as he affirmed in his *Intimate Diaries*: 'De Maistre and Poe taught me how to reason.' His encounter with Poe gave rise to a penetrating study, *Edgar Poe, His Life and His Works* (1853), then to notices that introduce his translations of Poe's *Stories* and *New Extraordinary Stories*. He found in Poe's *Poetic Principle* – which he translated – an aesthetic of pure poetry which was not a striving after art for art's sake but a search for beauty as perceived by the imagination.

The alchemy of the word

No more poetry from the heart according to Musset! No more moral utilitarianism! The world is 'hieroglyphic' as he stated in *Romantic Art* (1868); the poet is a decipherer. To manipulate language is to practise 'an evocative sorcery', an 'alchemy' that gives access to the world's secrets, without being able to abolish the vision of modernism.

We cannot elude either dissonance or clandestinity. By 1851, Baudelaire had published 'Wine and Hashish', the first part of what became *Artificial Paradises* (1860) and eleven poems under the supernatural title of *Limbo*. In 1852 he starts to pay court to 'Chairwoman' Appollonie Sabatier, whom he idealised the more for having only known her physically for a short time. In 1855 he took up again with Marie Daubrun, 'the golden-haired beauty' he was already friendly with in 1847.

The first edition of *The Flowers of Evil* was published in 1857, and on twenty August of that year, on the order of the same judge Pinard who had banned Flaubert, Baudelaire and his publisher were in their turn condemned for immorality, while six of the finest poems of the collection were banned. A new edition, without these poems, but largely augmented and modified in its structure, appeared in 1861. Meanwhile, Baudelaire published 'Aesthetic Bric-a-Brac' (1858), the original title of *Aesthetic Curiosities* (1868). At the same time he composed his first poems in prose and his great study on *Richard Wagner and Tannhäuser in Paris* (1861). This was a productive period, but full of bitterness and despair, as he confessed in *My Heart Laid Bare* (1862–1864): 'I cultivated my hysteria with enjoyment and intoxication. Today twenty-three January 1862, I felt a singular warning. I felt the wind of imbecility pass over me.' His half-brother died in April 1863 of general paralysis – the only thing they probably had in common. In the same year, Baudelaire revealed his prophetic views on modernism in

Le Peintre de la vie moderne (*The Painter of Modern Life*), in which he praised Constantin Guys, and in an obituary for Delacroix. The title *The Spleen of Paris* appeared with the publication, in 1864, of six new poems in prose. Baudelaire then went to Belgium, staying in Brussels where he prepared a pamphlet against that country which was in his eyes a caricature of bourgeois and Voltairean France. He died of aphasia and general paralysis on thirty-one August 1867, having asked for the last rites.

The Flowers of Evil

Even the title *The Flowers of Evil*, in which there is a kind of oxymoron, reveals the paradoxical idea of unveiling as well as denouncing the beauty of evil. A spiral structure placed *The Flowers of Evil* at the centre of the collection, between on the one hand the longer section, *Spleen and Ideal* and, on the other, *Revolt, Wine and Death*. We leave the luminous region of the ideal, an original homeland from which the poet feels himself to be exiled, to encounter spleen, that modern and piercing form of boredom which can only be expressed by a word recently imported from England. The poet has us enter with him all the circles of love, that of a sensual passion which oscillates between the happy intimacy of 'The Balcony', the warm eroticism of 'The Jewels' and the violence of 'Duellum', a love for which Jeanne Duval was the paradigm. Then there is the circle of love pulled between reverence and profanation which inspired 'She Who is Too Gay', Madame Sabatier.

Finally, there is the circle of a love in which tenderness and sensuality are reconciled with the symbolic Christian name of Marie (Mary). This cycle takes in the two others, thus revealing that the thread is less biographical than initiatory. We journey to it looking for sovereign beauty at the height of love and voluptuousness with a sister-spouse, as in 'The Invitation to the Voyage'.

Beyond futile diversions, the journey takes us to the hell of evil and self-destruction, driving the poet to curses and blasphemy to aspire at length to death, 'the supreme hope'.

Alas! The second edition reveals a deeper descent into evil and despair with 'The Irremediable' and 'The Irreparable', two of the thirty-five poems among which he had introduced the *Parisian Pictures*.

Baudelaire's melancholy quest haunts the regions of the fantastic, of a hate and a beauty which are, perhaps, hellish, but whether it be from Satan or God, what does it matter? This disillusioned inspiration will be bitterer still in the little poems in prose, written for many at the same time as the second edition, whose parody they often constitute. It is as if Baudelaire had wanted to translate in parallel the dissonance and the sarcasm of a modernism enslaved by vulgarity or stereotypes. There are sometimes texts containing black humour ('The Bad Glazier'), or tenderness and compassion ('The Old Acrobat'), but also whimsy: 'So as not to be the martyred slaves of time, get drunk incessantly on wine, on poetry or virtue, as you wish!' There is sometimes a dream-like quality too: 'Whoever looks from outside through an open window never sees as many things as someone who looks at a window which is closed. There is no object more profound, more mysterious, more fertile, darker or more dazzling than a window lit by a candle.'

The reverberations of Baudelaire's work

This work strikes us by the fusion of its diverse influences: the colours of Veronesi and the engravings of Goya combine with Shakespearean drama and the frenzy of Gothic novels. Traces may be found in it of readings in Byron and Dante. In the poem 'Le Guignon' ('Bad Luck') Baudelaire mixed quatrains, one borrowed from Thomas Gray, one from Longfellow, and we can appreciate how he transforms them, the structure, the sense and the range of these verses. What he took from elsewhere has often been what his readers best understood in him: he took from the Swede Swedenborg and the German

Hoffmann 'that reciprocal analogy' which made of nature a vast 'dictionary'. From this came the poem 'Correspondences' whose symbolism was all over Europe in 1890.

Nature is a temple
where living columns
Sometimes allow to escape
muffled words;
Man walks there through
forests of symbols
Which observe him with
familiar looks.

Like long echoes
which from afar are mingled
In a dark
and deep unity
Vast as night
and brightness
Odours, colours
and sounds complement each other.

Baudelaire's concept of a poetry wholly based on music came in part from Hoffmann, but Baudelaire must, no doubt, have 'had a better aim' for it is of him that people normally think. From 1860, Baudelaire was disseminated and often translated by poets who had found in his work the source of their own creativity. This was the case for the German poet Stefan George, in Hungary for Gyula Reviczy and Endre Ady. Translated by Loïnc Szabo and Mihály Babits in Hungary, and in Bohemia by the poet Vrchlický, *The Flowers of Evil* had a knock-on effect. In Greece it was revealed in 1873 by the critic Roïdis and translated in 1880 by the poet from Smyrna Argyropoulos. Some people, such as the Portuguese poet Cesário Verde, lay claim to him to put into practice a realist and plastic aesthetic he would perhaps not have recognised. Around 1890 his work was garlanded with laurel wreathes. He then appeared as the father of symbolism, the first seer for Rimbaud, the first modern for Mallarmé. In Scandinavia, Johannes Jurgensen and Sophus Clausen introduced him, *c.*1893–1894, in the Danish review *The Spectator* and in the symbolist review *The*

Tower, in which they published translations of Baudelaire. He was translated in Greece by Simiriotis (1917) and Kanelis (1928). He inspired even more directly the poet Ouránis, as the titles of the collections *Spleen* and *Nostalgia* indicate. Along with the symbolist, the creator of the poem in prose is clung on to, as also is the creator of a bold aesthetic based on dissonance and conjecture, His Satanism and sadism were also retained. In the 1920s we see in him, as did Gide, Mauriac, Green and Jouve, the poet of sadness and remorse, while the poet Sigurd Svanes recreated *The Flowers of Evil* in Danish. If his glory was afterwards overshadowed by Mallarmé and surrealism, he remained the great poet of modernism, the poet of the poem in prose and the user of a prosody able to translate all the moods and motions of the soul. But he was also the master of a classical rhetoric in which the alexandrine and the sonnet are bent to all the audacities of sound. He was the one who reconciled the unsurpassable perfection of a tradition and a Romanticism with Baroque elements still in it. The kind of Romanticism that made Sainte-Beuve discover 'at the bottom of our Romantic Kamchatka, the madness of Baudelaire'.

Dostoyevsky (1821–1881)

J. Catteau

> Mankind is to be found in men.
> Fyodor Mikhailovich Dostoyevsky

Dostoyevsky first appeared on the literary scene in 1843 with a translation of Balzac's *Eugénie Grandet*. This fact alone shows just how much Russia, in spite of her great writers, Pushkin, Lermontov and Gogol, still looked towards Europe for ideas. With one or two rare exceptions, however, Europeans took no notice of Russian literature. A quarter of a century later, *Crime and Punishment* and *War and Peace* appeared, soon to be followed by *The Idiot*, *The Possessed*, *The Brothers Karamazov* and *Anna Karenina*. These were enormous, powerful novels which were received with enthusiasm in Russia. The two giants of the Russian novel, Tolstoy and Dostoyevsky, began to see their works published in the West, especially after 1880. They fascinated European readers with the depth of their psychological insights, their spontaneous sublimity and their lofty contempt for conventional plot-construction. They began to be mentioned in the same breath as Homer, Dante, Montaigne, Cervantes, Shakespeare, Goethe and Balzac, having been able, in less than half a century, to conquer Europe and to turn its eyes on themselves.

The fallout from this historic explosion of Russian creative genius is still with us today. Many modern writers are avowed admirers of Dostoyevsky: Nietzsche, Gide, Proust, Claudel, Mauriac, Zweig, Thomas Mann, Virginia Woolf, Faulkner, Camus, Malraux and Nathalie Sarraute, among others.

The novel as tragedy

Dostoyevsky's universe is stifling. It oppresses the soul. The passage of time for its protagonists results in the pain of living under too much pressure: a quicksand of nightmares and recurring dreams out of which suddenly emerge implacable crescendos of violence and scandal culminating in lethal storms. The setting for these events is both tragic and expressionist at the same time. In yellow and misshapen bedrooms a fallen woman and a murderer read scripture (*Prestuplenie i nakazanie*, *Crime and Punishment*, 1866). There are shadowy and greasy flights of stairs where terrible things are confessed to in a whisper, where Rogozhin lurks with a knife in his hand (*Idiot*, *The Idiot*, 1868). There are dark and windy nights on which the hero tries to avoid his own double (*Dvojnik*, *The Double*, 1846), on which Svidrigailov kills himself after having been tormented by sinister, erotic dreams (*Crime and Punishment*), on which Chatov is murdered (*Besy*, *The Possessed*, 1871–1872) while fires are breaking out as a result of arson. There is a gathering storm that breaks just as Rogozhin lifts the knife or Prince Myshkin has an epileptic fit (*The Idiot*).

Dostoyevsky's world, despite its radiant visionaries and its great holy men who talk to God, is full of fools, swindlers, spies, debauchees, criminals, women who have been ill-used, young girls who have been humiliated and epileptics. It is a world devoid of stability. Lovers harry each other until their love turns to hate. Those who want to do good suddenly do harm. One minute someone is dreaming of a golden age, of mankind's future happiness, the next this idyllic picture is obscured by blood. A desire to believe is reason enough for breaking a crucifix or an icon. No sooner are you lost in meditation, like Ivan Karamazov, than the devil comes to make fun of you.

Everything here is dangerous, a threat oozing up from cracks in the ground where the poor and the ineffectual are eating their hearts out, oozing up from human passions, from obsessions under the burden of which man is crushed, from all manner of cunning and intrigue. There is, for example, the individual who undermines himself (Golyadkin in *The Double*). There is Raskolnikov, ambitious and Napoleonic, who conspires against the female practitioners of usury (*Crime and Punishment*, 1866). There are atheistic terrorists who conspire against Mother Russia (*The Possessed*). There are the brothers who conspire against the father they hate (*Brat'ya Karamazovy, The Brothers Karamazov*, 1878–1879). Aggression is the bottom line in this tragic universe that certain critics have described as pathological and from which we return, according to E.M. de Vogüé, 'with moral aches and pains', despite the attempted deployment of copious supplies of love for his characters on Dostoyevsky's part.

The extremity of genius

This tragic universe is theatrical: it is a metaphor for what Dostoyevsky is exploring in his work. We should not be surprised at the aesthetic excess and extravagance of Dostoyevsky's genius. His genetic and psychological make-up gave him a predisposition for dramatic outbursts, for the portrayal of violence as experienced in his own life. His father died

of unnatural causes in 1839, possibly murdered by the serfs on his estate. Dostoyevsky himself was arrested, imprisoned and the victim of a mock execution in 1849 for his involvement in a political plot against the ruling autocracy. Then came the years he spent in a penal fortress (1850–1854), the harsh experience of military service in Siberia, his humiliating struggle to secure a pardon.

He developed epilepsy in its latent form from 1846 to 1848 and, by 1851, was being regularly afflicted by it. Then he was to suffer a series of bereavements: his wife, his brother and a friend of his all died in 1864. His debts forced him into European exile with his second wife, Anna, from 1867 to 1871 and he had a serious addiction to roulette from 1863 to 1871. These were the rare, sad privileges of a life filled with chronic anxiety and eventually written down. They are all there in his writing: the contemplation of death in front of the aimed rifles of a firing squad, the feeling of exaltation before the sudden onset of his epileptic fits and, during remission, one of 'mystical terror', the feeling of being a criminal, the burden of a great sin unknown to him. He perceived gambling as flying in the face of God and calling on fate to decide. Dostoyevsky's soul craved storms, explosions, solutions to problems requiring a total catharsis of all inner tensions. His creative energy, paradoxically strongest in his moments of greatest distress, converted this tendency to paroxysm into a powerful literary corpus.

Psychology in depth

At the age of eighteen, Dostoyevsky had already defined his aims as a novelist: 'Man is a mystery. We must penetrate this mystery and, even if it takes us a lifetime to do it, let it not be said of us that we wasted our time' (letter to his brother Mikhail, sixteen August 1839).

The whole of his work from *Bednye lyudi* (*Poor Folk*, 1846), his first novel, to *The Brothers Karamazov*, his last, is a delirious exploration of the enigma that is man. From the first, Dostoyevsky made the discovery that each person is fundamentally two people, that each and every one of us is both the wound and the knife, the slap and the cheek, the life-giving idea and the germ of the idea carrying within it its own destruction. We are, in short, the tragic dialectic of human aspiration, oscillating between falling and getting up again, embracing both conformity and non-conformity to moral law. Like Kierkegaard, Dostoyevsky found man's true greatness in his angst, beyond both the natural and the supernatural, beyond all borders and limits. His underground man declares heightened awareness to be an affliction and perversely claims this affliction as a way to enjoy 'great suffering and great pleasure', thus giving pride of place to the superego in the overall scheme of things. In the great novels *Crime and Punishment*, *The Idiot*, *The Possessed* and *The Brothers Karamazov*, Dostoyevsky's heroes take the plunge: they enter into actions, bad as well as good, which define their freedom, they experience in the reality of *pro* and *contra*, in angst and in suffering the duplicity of their consciousness, their 'vastness' of soul to quote from *The Brothers Karamazov*.

Towards the end of his life, Dostoyevsky distilled the essence of his art into the following celebrated formula: 'While I continue to be at all times a realist, mankind is to be found in men [. . .] They call me a psychological novelist, which is not true; I am merely a realist in the highest sense of the word, which is to say that I depict the human soul in all its depth.'

A philosophy of freedom

Dostoyevsky made a clean sweep of all philosophical systems based on the rational from the ancient Greeks to Hegel by affirming that 'real life' cannot exist without desire, free will and suffering. Rationally speaking, being is an irreducible mystery: we find it 'where parallel lines come together and opposites intersect' in the eternal struggle between good and evil. It is precisely this that constitutes its prophetic grandeur and its philosophical impact on the denizens of our modern world who today

challenge, with leaps of faith and overt religiosity to the point of fundamentalism, the model of civilization inherited from the European Enlightenment and nineteenth-century scepticism in the shape of Marx, Nietzsche and Freud, who had officially certified God as dead, and, in so doing, had done as much for man and ushered in an era of totalitarianism. The most penetrating vision of man in utopian leading strings is vouchsafed to us by the Grand Inquisitor in *The Brothers Karamazov*. Christ the Liberator is silent in his presence and the corollary of this silence is that man himself must accept full responsibility for his actions. To put it another way: 'All of us share in a common guilt.'

Dostoyevsky's modernity as an artist and a thinker

Dostoyevsky, though a thinker and a 'spiritual clairvoyant', did not write philosophical novels as such. His heroes, part of an overall harmony analysed and attested to by M. Bakhtin, feel in themselves, in their own flesh and blood, the ideological battles that consume them, even if the methods chosen to evoke these battles – tense dialogues, dreams of all descriptions, murderous outbursts, psycho-drama – create an almost fantastic atmosphere of mounting tension (Dostoyevsky himself referred to this as 'fantastic realism'). Yet there is nothing unreal in the initial inspiration. In this sense Dostoyevsky is a modern writer. The whole of his creation is rooted in reality as we know it: there are journalistic human interest stories which he lapped up in a big way, the dominant role played by money, big-city violence (unlike his contemporaries he wrote about towns), a fascination with current affairs, both social and political, an interrogation of what motivates 'modern man, highly-strung, complex and deep as the sea'. When we add Dostoyevsky's explosive force, the sheer pace of his writing, the brutal, insistent, declamatory nature of his prose, devoid of all affectation, a picture emerges of a novelist and great intellectual who belong to our own time.

If his novels perpetuate the asking of metaphysical questions through the ages, from Plato to Schopenhauer, they also contain the great twentieth-century themes: the death of God and the existence of the superman, the desire to be rid of one's father and psychoanalysis, grand inquisitors and totalitarian regimes, the existentialist revolt of Sisyphus, organised terrorism and revolutionary dogma, the twin Utopias of the Crystal Palace and mankind as a great garden. Writers as diverse as Vladimir Soloviov (1853–1900), the Symbolists and Russian idealists such as Berdiyayev and Chestov, Nietzsche, Freud himself (probably influenced by Dostoyevsky in the writing of *Totem and Taboo*), Camus, Gabriel Marcel, Sartre (a genuinely Dostoyevskian hero according to Czeslaw Milosz) were all indebted to their famous Russian predecessor. His work, which questions more than it prescribes, both anticipates and elucidates recent history. Dostoyevsky always makes us feel uncomfortable. Under Stalin, this herald of personal freedom was condemned as an 'enemy of the people' and his work was censored out of all recognition. Today in Russia, since the coming of *glasnost* and *perestroika*, he has become someone to whom that same people are turning more and more.

Ibsen (1828–1906)

G. Ueberschlag

For the essential lie is the true stimulant, you see.

Henrik Ibsen,
The Wild Duck

Henrik Ibsen was born on 20 March 1828 in Skien, a small port in southern Norway. His father was a well-off merchant who did not know how to run his business and who lived in a disorganised household. Rather than pay for Henrik to study medicine, he sent him to a chemist in Grimstad. Considered as a poor relation and treated as such, young Ibsen experienced isolation and social rejection. This only served to sharpen his rebellious spirit. In 1848, he sympathised with all the revolutionaries in Europe, but that was all he could do at the time. In effect, Norway, which had only just discovered its own internal autonomy, was still turned in on itself, looking for its national identity, dominated by an austere Lutheranism. This society was be the stage from which Ibsen plucked his dramatis personæ.

The dramatist

How could Ibsen assert himself under these circumstances? How could he succeed in such an environment? For a while he thought of becoming a painter, because of his fascination with colours, but he decided very quickly to become a dramatist. This was a surprising decision, for Norway had established no tradition in this field and for a long time Danish had been the official language. But writing, for the young Ibsen, was 'getting rid of venom' and that he was not without it is proved by his regular and abundant dramatic production: a drama nearly every two years.

Having published his first tragedy *Catilina* (1848) at his own expense, fortune smiled on him. Ibsen was taken on as adviser to the theatre in Bergen, which wanted to create a national theatre in Norway. He learnt his craft as a dramatist there, as well as in Christiania where he collaborated a few years later with Bjørnstjerne Bjørnson, his great rival and a future Nobel Prize winner. However, he was completely estranged from his approach, beginning with his sympathy for modernism and the Norwegian workers' movement.

Despite beginning to earn money, Ibsen decided to live abroad in voluntary exile for twenty-seven years, from 1864 to 1891, a decision which would lead him to live mainly in Germany and Italy. This was an indispensable literary precaution, necessary to the further development of his genius. He wanted to escape the boredom of the North and have contact with the great centres of European intellectual life. Thus he created a distance from Norwegian society, in which almost all his great plays are situated, that the sharpness of his imagination and memory allow him to reconstruct and recapture faithfully.

With the regularity of a civil servant, his face like that of a Daumier magistrate, with its well-trimmed beard, Ibsen produced twenty-five plays in fifty years of writing for the theatre. He developed successively from the national theatre of his early years to social drama, then to a theatre more orientated to psychological analysis. His youthful experiments, in which he tried to adapt to a Scandinavian nationalist version of Romanticism that was all around him, lasted for more than ten years. The rediscovery of the sagas and old Norwegian tales did not prevent him from imitating the ready-made formulas of Scribe and looking for his own technique of writing, already testing the first symbolist elements of his theatre, as in *Kongsemnerne* (*Pretenders to the Crown*, 1863), the last of a series of historical plays, and the most successful. Coming a year after the realist drama *Kaerlighedens Komedie* (*The Comedy of Love*, 1862), a violent satire against the social institution of marriage which had caused a scandal, it already looked forward to one of Ibsen's essential themes, the dissolving strength of doubt and the damage it does to the soul of man.

This period was marked by two master-pieces: *Brand* (1866) and *Peer Gynt* (1867). These plays, still Romantic in inspiration, were above all tracts. Ibsen had already started to pour out his venom, for Brand and Peer Gynt are two faces of one and the same character: Ibsen himself, who denounced in one the apathy of Scandinavians confronted by the modern world, and caricatured in the other their political Romanticism. Solitary and mad in the eyes of the people around him, Brand is an individual who lives by and for his mission, while the life of Peer Gynt, that Nordic *bon viveur*, is a succession of strange adventures designed to stimulate the imagination, beginning with that of the musician Edvard Grieg. In contrast to the uncompromising moralist of Brand, Peer Gynt is someone who has not gone beyond the

aesthetic stage of existence – for Ibsen had already studied Kierkegaard!

Listening to the world

Educated by Georg Brandes, Ibsen began to listen to the world. He wanted to live in the here and now, as shown by his comedy *De unges forbund* (*The Union of the Young*, 1869), in which he pilloried political opportunism, and even by *Kejser og Galilaeer* (*Emperor and Galilean*, 1873), in which the character of Julian the Apostate serves as a pretext to depict the transformation of the modern world that has broken away from Christianity.

This historical fresco, however, was an exception, for Ibsen went on to definitively abandon the mask of history to begin to sound his own time. In the first of his social plays, *Samfundets stotter* (*Pillars of Society*, 1877), he judged the actions of an unscrupulous businessman, Consul Bernick.

Having already several times asserted his feminist convictions, Ibsen made feminism the major theme of his play *Et Dukkehjem* (*A Doll's House*, 1879). Nora, the heroine, wants to be free of a partner unworthy of her and to gain her independence:

NORA *Da jeg var hjemme hos pappa, så fortalte han meg alle sine meninger, og så hadde jag de samme meninger; og hvis jeg hadde andre, skjulte jeg det. [. . .] Han kalte meg sitt dukkebarn, og han lekte med meg som jeg lekte med mine dukker. Så kom jeg I huset til deg. [. . .]*

HELMER *Hva er det fort uttrykk du bruker om vårt ekteskap?*

NORA (uforstyret) *Jeg mener, så gikk jeg fra pappas hebder over i dine. [. . .] Nar jeg nu ser på det, synes jeg jeg har levet her som et fattig menneske. [. . .] Men du ville ju ha det så. Du og pappa har gjort stor synd imot meg. I er skyld i at det ikke er blitt noe av meg.*

NORA *When I lived with my father, he would tell me everything he thought, and I shared his opinions. If I had other opinions,*

*I kept them to myself [. . .] He called me
his little doll and he played with me like I
played with my dolls. Then I came to you,
to your house. [. . .]*

HELMER *That's a strange way of saying we
got married!*

NORA (imperturbable) *I mean I passed
from daddy's hands to yours. [. . .] When I
think about it now, it seems that I lived
here like a poor relation. [. . .] But that
was what you wanted, wasn't it? You and
daddy both treated me badly. It's your fault
if I've grown into a good-for-nothing.*

Nora realises that she has made a big mistake
with her husband. She can no longer either
look up to him or love him when a woman's
vocation in life, according to Ibsen, is the love
of a good man. The play gives us an insight
into the tragedy of two married people. It
has retained its interest, while the feminist
message has, to some extent, lost its topicality.

The feminist struggle

The feminist struggle that Ibsen headed
continued in his next play *Gengangere* (*Ghosts*,
1881), in which he stigmatised a marriage
of convenience, a social screen to allow an
old man to satisfy his instincts with a young
woman. The theme of physical heredity is at
the centre of this work, at a period when
Darwinism was triumphant and when biology
had become the most important of the human
sciences. Just like Zola, whom he disliked,
Ibsen analyses the psychology of his characters
as a function of their heredity. By doing this,
however, he did not succumb to fatalism.
His real objective, beyond feminism, was to
liberate the whole of humanity from despotism
by denouncing demagogues. *Et Folkefiende* (*An
Enemy of the People*, 1882) is a harsh illustration
of this desire on Ibsen's part. Although Ibsen
presents it as a tranquil play 'which can be
read by ministers, big businessmen and their
wives', it basically calls into question power
in all its forms. Alone against everyone, Doctor
Stockmann, a character in love with truth
and freedom, finds himself confounded by

careerists, conservatives and so-called men of
the left, and shouted down by the people he is
defending. A subversive work, *An Enemy of
the People* exalts the individual opposed to
the masses and their tyranny, and cultivates
nostalgia, even a taste for anarchy. Ibsen's
contemporaries were not wrong about the
play's subversiveness, given its success at a
time of anarchy.

New ways

With his next play, *Vildanden* (*The Wild
Duck*, 1884), Ibsen turned away from his committed dramas. Henceforth he plumbed the
depths of souls, put on stage interior dramas,
'found new ways' and leant over the shoulder
of complex, even disturbing characters.
The psychologist took the place of the
pamphleteer.

If the search for the secret springs which
make men act constituted one of the outstanding features of this play, it is nevertheless
true that the irrational had already erupted,
and brutally, in Scandinavian theatre, thanks
to Strindberg. He raised the idea of a 'clash
of minds' into an almost scientific theory – one
that would be magnificently illustrated in
Ibsen's new play, *Rosmersholm* (1886), which
he analysed as a veritable psychic murder. This
drama, which Freud admired as a fine example
of psychoanalysis, shows the cruel, unavoidable confrontation between two characters,
Pastor Rosmer and his young housekeeper.
Since the death of Beate, the pastor's wife, they
live in seclusion in the manor of Rosmersholm,
in a small provincial town where the representatives of socialism and conservatism are
locked in merciless struggle. Rebekka West has
succeeded in converting the pastor to modernist ideas and in taking the place of Beate in his
heart, driving the latter to suicide by a veritable
power of suggestion. But because they end
up by knowing too much about each other,
Rosmer, a distinguished but weak man, loses
his bearings, and Rebekka, the anti-authori-
tarian, allows herself to be beset by scruples
which undermine her. Their personalities are
undone, and they throw themselves together

down the waterfall, in the same place that Beate committed suicide.

The women in this theatre of psychology are no longer strong and sure of themselves like Nora, but ambiguous figures like Rebekka, or fatal and perverse like Hedda Gabler, or even mystical like Ellida in *Fruen fra havet* (*The Lady of the Sea*, 1888).

In *Hedda Gabler* (1891), Ibsen continued with a series of heroines tormented by strange passions and struggling against their neuroses. Hedda is one of two women who surround the successful writer Eilert Lövberg. Wanting, at least once, to rule over the fate of a man, as she arrogantly proclaims, she ends up by suggesting to Lövberg he should kill himself by offering him one of her father's pistols. A psychic murder no doubt – we think of the character of Jean in *Miss Julie* by Strindberg. As life offers her nothing worth having after that, Hedda also blows her brains out.

The strangely Strindbergian atmosphere of these plays, where decadent characters come to grief by not being able to resist the suggestions of the stronger, is also to be found in Ibsen's last plays, a phase that opens with *Bygmester Solness* (*Solness the Master Builder*, 1892), and which could be described as the confessional phase of Ibsen's theatre. The playwright takes stock of what he has done and tries to justify himself in the eyes of the younger generation, which he is afraid will turn away from him, drawn by Strindberg's more exclusively self-centred theatre. He depicts himself on stage. Solness is self-educated, as Ibsen was, a builder, but for whom the time has come to retire. His will to power has remained intact. This is the theme that dominates all others in this complicated play, next to the theme of the solitude of the rebel. Genius can only be realised by crushing what is around it, and, like Solness, Ibsen, as he grew older, felt terrible scruples because of this.

The lesson life teaches us is that we always have to pay, sooner or later. *John Gabriel Borkman* (1896) traces the portrait of a banker who reached the dizzy heights of holding in his hands the destiny of his fellow creatures. Now

in old age, he goes over his feelings of rancour and disappointment, for he has also experienced dishonour. This is the price he must pay, in addition to his solitude, just as the old sculptor Anton Rubeck must pay what he owes in Ibsen's last play, *Når vi døde vågner* (*When We Dead Awaken*, 1899), which he also called *Dramatic Episode*.

Ibsen's genius

Will genius always have to take, without ever experiencing exchange? Ibsen's final question prolongs the pessimism that his critics have underlined and which is illustrated by the fact that all his great dramas recount the story of a failure: the failure of idealism. Idealistically, Ibsen had given himself the task of decrying the prejudices and hypocrisy on which society founded its morality, but, at the same time, he continually shows us how this idealism only ends in disaster. Perhaps, beyond his rebellion against lying, he never had that many illusions on the happiness to be conquered for oneself. His own morality is neither traditional nor revolutionary. The upholders of the class struggle can expect no support from him, for he hated 'compact crowds'. His pose as a well-off bourgeois anarchist was, in fact, real. But the anarchist sketches no new social model. He simply wants to set man free, and, to begin with, free those few rare individuals who help humanity to progress.

Ibsen himself lived like a bourgeois, anxious above all for sophistication and honours, enjoying his little court of admirers, but always very reserved, very reticent. His life therefore contrasted strangely with his convictions as a writer and his egalitarian dreams which lead him to burn what he himself is satisfied to be, from a lack of courage, no doubt, and through natural timidity. But does that take away anything at all from his greatness?

Belonging to the generation of Victorien Sardou, Octave Feuillet, Dumas Junior and Strindberg, Ibsen is the only one, along with Strindberg, to have stayed modern, by the accuracy of his ideas and his consummate art of dialogue. His influence in Europe on the naturalist and symbolist theatre was already important during his lifetime. In France, where he was introduced by the Théâtre Antoine and by Lugné-Poe, he was considered a master, and his disciples in Germany often took him on board unconditionally, performing his plays on the stages of the courts of all the princedoms. Struck down by epilepsy in 1900, Ibsen dragged out the last years of his life in an enforced sterility. He died on twenty-three May 1906, considered a national treasure by Norway which had just recently won its independence.

Tolstoy (1828–1910)

M. Aucouturier

There are thousands of people suffering throughout the world. Why are there so many around me?

Leo Tolstoy

'But this is Shakespeare, this is Shakespeare!' Flaubert exclaimed when reading *War and Peace*. With this monumental work that launched him in the West, Tolstoy, the barbarian from the East, immediately entered into the constellation of great classics of European literature. 'This is not a novel,' he explained for his part in a draft of an abandoned introduction to justify his disobedience to the rules of the genre. It is, in fact, a veritable transformation of the novel, whose status, towards the middle of the century, was not entirely that of a great classical genre. More than anyone else, Tolstoy helped to give it this status: it was only after *Vojna i mir* (*War and Peace*, 1863–1869) that Lukács could define the novel as the epic of modern times, even if the definition was afterwards applied to its predecessors.

The novel of reality

Paradoxically, Tolstoy gave its letters patent of nobility to the novel by cutting the umbilical cord of the romanesque, of the so-called literature of the imagination, whose mainspring was complacent abandonment to fantastic games. Tolstoy never invented. His first writings were autobiographical. In *Detstvo* (*Childhood*) which marked his triumphal entry on the literary scene in 1852, then in *Otročestvo* (*Boyhood*, 1854) and *Junost'* (*Youth*, 1857) which formed its sequels, he created the character of a young Russian gentleman of the 1840s by calling on his own memories. The tales of the Caucasus (1853–1855) and of Sebastopol (1855–1856), which established his reputation as a 'military writer' are frontline reports in which the author, a volunteer, appears among his comrades in arms. *Metel'* (*The Blizzard*, 1856) and *Lucerne* (1857) are episodes taken from his travels in Russia and Europe. *Utro pomeščka* (*A Landowner's Morning*, 1856) tells of the clumsy attempts of the young gentleman-farmer that Tolstoy wanted to be when he left university to make his peasants happy in spite of themselves. The most ambitious of his early works, *Kazaki* (*The Cossacks*, 1863), based on the most poetic of his memories of the long sojourn in the Caucasus that followed this unfortunate experience, is merely a sequel to the autobiographical trilogy, turned into a novel by the rough sketch of a love interest. Sometimes, it is true, autobiography itself becomes imaginary: so in *Semejnoe ščast'je* (*Wedded Bliss*, 1859), in which, hesitating to get married, he tries to guess the future; but here too the creative imagination serves to slow the fantasy down rather than to give it free rein. In *War and Peace*, even when he wants to conjure up the period of the Napoleonic Wars, he took as the background for his tale the life of his parents when they were young.

In this, it is true, Tolstoy was not original: just emerging realism, at a time when his literary tastes were being formed, came as a challenge to convention and romantic ideas, and researched social archives. In Russia, under the influence of French literature, 'physiology' was fashionable. Tolstoy knew who he was writing to when he sent *Childhood* to the poet Nekrassov, editor-in-chief of *The Contemporary*, leader of the 'naturalist school'.

But he also had more obscure masters, ones who were closer to his heart: the author of the *Sentimental Journey* and *Tristram Shandy*, Laurence Sterne, and the author of the *Stories of Geneva*, Rodolphe Töpffer. They were the ones who taught him that the description of any day in the life of any single human being could be an inexhaustible source of fascinating observations and unexpected discoveries. *The Story of What Happened Yesterday*, Tolstoy's first literary essay, undertaken and abandoned in 1851, was a bold attempt on his part to systematically apply that lesson.

Imagination in search of the truth

Tolstoy the novelist did not need exceptional characters, actions of note, extraordinary events: the lifestyle of average individuals gave him enough subject matter to awaken the reader's curiosity and maintain their interest. He submitted society and the world around him – its hierarchies, its values, its language – to the aesthetic criteria of authenticity, spontaneity and naturalness. These criteria, in one of his most important early efforts, *Tri smerti* (*Three Dead People*, 1859), presented the peasant as superior to the noble lady, and the tree to the peasant: this was his basic criterion of all moral judgement.

This is how the novel became much more than a social document, creating the character types and conflicts through which the material and moral structure of a society is expressed, as in Balzac, Dickens and Thackeray, and as in the work of his contemporaries and compatriots, Turgeniev, Alexei Pissemski (1820–1881) and Gontcharov. We certainly have this being expressed in Tolstoy's novels: *War and Peace*, *Anna Karenina* (1873–1877), *Voskresenie* (*Resurrection*, 1899), with their vast gallery of characters, typical of nineteenth-century Russia at three quite distinct moments of her history. But, unlike the heroes of Turgeniev or Gontcharov, their main character is less a social type than a wakened consciousness, applying the criterion of authenticity with as much obstinacy to itself as to others, and seeking, through the determinism of history

and society, an answer to the eternal question 'What is there to do?' Thanks to this, Tolstoy's novels are, above all, stages in an obstinate quest for moral truth.

History demythologised

In Napoleon's invasion of Russia, the fiftieth anniversary of which was celebrated in 1862, Tolstoy had a subject tailor-made for his strengths: a vast national movement dragging into itself the whole of a collective organisation in the great European whirlwind started by the French Revolution that made Russia mature and enter the assembly of nations as an equal. The subject fascinated Tolstoy because it posed the major philosophical problem of the nineteenth century under its two aspects: that of the role of the individual in the collective destiny of the nation, and that of the historical dimension of human existence.

Such a subject gave Tolstoy the opportunity to manifest the requisite creative power and epic grandeur to set into motion fifty characters, simultaneously develop several plots, take in with a sweep of the eye a space extending from Vienna to St Petersburg and from Tilsitt to Tula. But the method was always the same: history is lived from day to day, whether it be the conversations in a St Petersburg salon, the family life of a Muscovite squire, the unchanging rituals that govern the way a proud aristocrat spending his retirement on his estate makes use of his time, or even the confused chaos of bodies where a soldier rushes forward, strikes with his rifle or bayonet, falls down, flees without knowing, like Fabrice at Waterloo, that he is taking part in a historical event which is going to be called the battle of Austerlitz or of the Moskova. Seen from close to, mixed up with the heroes of the novel, observed in the same prosaic situations, Napoleon, Alexander I, Kutuzov infect these moments with their historicity and receive in return their human dimension. By bringing the historical event in line with everyday life, Tolstoy made the novel an attempt to understand history by the concrete mechanisms of human behaviour. We may draw the following conclusion: the hold that man has over events is greater when he is less aware of his role in these events. The instinct of the simple peasant, apparently deaf to the patriotic speeches of the enlightened nobility, did more than the latter to free Russia from foreign invaders. Kutuzov, the Russian generalissimo who falls asleep during councils of war, triumphs over the strategist Napoleon, who only embarrasses those he believes he commands. And an even more general conclusion drawn by Tolstoy from his strategic analyses in the last part of the work: all rational explanation of history implies determinism; we are free because we are alive and because we act; there is an essential part of reality which eludes our reason – and History as we can know it. The final scene of *War and Peace* shows the heroine, Natasha, whom we have seen as a mischievous adolescent, then a young, romantically inclined woman, and who is now a happy young mother, contemplate with joy her baby's dirty nappy. How could it be said more clearly that battles like Austerlitz and Borodino are merely the epiphenomena of an everlasting history which takes place in the human family, and whose chapters are birth, love and death? A novel about history more than a historical novel, *War and Peace* is, in fact, a novel against history out of which the nineteenth century made an idol.

Existence laid bare

Tolstoy's second great masterpiece, *Anna Karenina*, is closer to a traditional novel: it is the story of a young married woman in St Petersburg high society whose passion leads her into adultery and then to suicide. However, here again, the novelist's work of creation does not consist in inventing a plot, but in questioning reality by means of the imagination. It was a real-life drama, whose ending he knew about, which led Tolstoy to reflect on love, woman, the couple and the family. To do justice to the heroine, to understand her gesture, to apportion blame, we have to situate her in her world, recreate her universe; we must, in particular, compare her story with

that of a happy couple, whose existence, far from the madding crowd, is based on agricultural labour and harmony with nature. The novel thus acquires, like *War and Peace*, and despite the absence of a historical subject, the human dimension and the majestic movement of an epic, punctuated this time by the succession of the seasons and the work of the fields, forming the stable basis of an existence in which drama is an anomaly.

But this epic serenity does not manage to stifle the rumblings of a tragic fatality displayed in Anna's triumphant vitality by a passion which results from it. Contrary to expectation, she is shaken by it. At the centre of a cloudless married life, the 'happy' man, Levin, who is in this novel the voice of conscience, is present without understanding why it happens at the annihilation of all his reasons for living, and holds on as if to a lifebelt to one reason he discerns in a sentence spoken in his presence by a peasant.

It is this discovery of a tragic dimension to existence, hidden till then by the vital power of his energy, which, when Tolstoy finished *Anna Karenina*, took hold of his mind and dominated his thought. It steered him towards a search for a faith strong enough to impose on him an absolute rule of life, and, on the basis of that uncompromising rule of life, towards a radical critique of society at the end of the nineteenth century, all of whose institutions only serve, in his opinion, to justify the domination of a class of parasites over those who live from the only work that is useful, that of farming the earth.

Art as he practised it himself he henceforth saw as a rich man's diversion: he denied it and only took up his pen to lay bare the mortality of man (*Smert' Ivana Il'iča, The Death of Ivan Illitch*, 1886), to denounce the trickery of marriage (*Krejcerova Sonata, The Kreutzer Sonata*, 1891), the hypocrisy of a judicial, penitentiary, politico-administrative and ecclesiastical system which only defends and protects the privileged (*Resurrection*), the pitfalls of a whole corrupt civilisation that the Russian royal family took to the mountain-dwellers of the Caucasus (*Hadji-Murad*,

1904). If not to denounce, he took up his pen to call to conversion and to the spiritual life (*Xozjain i rabotnik, Master and Servant,* 1895; *Otec Sergij, Father Sergei,* 1898). But his mastery remained intact, and his last works show no sign of his faculties having dimmed: without the epic serenity, it is still the same plastic vision of reality, the same pitiless lucidity of gaze, accentuated now by clarity and the vigour of the satirical trait. For the moral justification which is henceforth indispensable to him is only different in degree and not in nature from the demand for truth which always inspired his work and which has ensured its permanence.

14 *The Fin de Siècle*

A. VARTY

All art is quite useless.

Oscar Wilde,
The Portrait of Dorian Gray

On the border between two worlds, the end of the nineteenth century is marked by tendencies which can seem contradictory. On the one hand there was an extreme aestheticism which it was possible to describe as decadent and which was reflected by the works of Wilde, Huysmans and Strindberg. On the other, there was the symbolist tendency, which grouped around Mallarmé and which, with Maeterlinck, opened the way to the theatre of silence. Along with these major currents literature across Europe began to concern itself with themes heralding the twentieth century: literature and politics, literature and the 'Woman Question'.

THE *FIN DE SIÈCLE* SPIRIT

In the last decades of the nineteenth century, a new sensibility appeared as a reaction against positivism and naturalism. While this last movement had described reality in the most brutal of its trivial details, the *fin de siècle* spirit sought out sophistication, beauty and art. Three works explored, almost simultaneously and in exemplary fashion, the possibilities of the decadent: Wilde's *The Picture of Dorian Gray*, Huysmans's *Against the Grain*, and Ibsen's *Hedda Gabler*. The aestheticism they exhibited found an enthusiastic audience in select circles, coteries and literary reviews.

'All art is quite useless'

The insolence of **Oscar Wilde (1854–1900)** erupted in the 1891 'preface' to *The Picture of Dorian Gray* (1890), and, the *fin de siècle* spirit triumphed on the Munich stage with Ibsen's *Hedda Gabler* (1891). For decades, Théophile Gautier and the 'art for art's sake' movement had paved the way for the decadent: 'I would give up most gladly my duties as a Frenchman and a citizen to see a genuine picture by Raphaël or a beautiful nude woman – Princess Borghese, for instance, when she posed for Canova' (introduction to *Mademoiselle de Maupin*, 1835). In the preface to *Dorian Gray*, Oscar Wilde proposed an analysis of the intoxicating but pernicious effects that the influence of such an aesthetic can have, in the personal as well as the literary realm:

> The artist is the creator of beautiful things. There is no such thing as a moral or an immoral book. Books are well written, or badly written. That is all. No artist desires to prove anything. Even things that are true can be proved. All art is quite useless.
>
> Oscar Wilde, preface to *The Picture of Dorian Gray*.

The work of art has more influence on the aesthete than life itself. Thus the reading of a small 'yellow book' is a turning point for the young Dorian Gray. In it, Dorian recognises and embraces the idealised representation of his own conduct and destiny. This book could well be Pater's *Studies in the History of the Renaissance* (1873) or Huysmans' *Against the Grain*.

The gem-like flame

The Renaissance by **Walter Pater (1839–1894)** collected a series of essays devoted to subjects in the history of art which seek to redefine the Renaissance not as a historical period, but as a state of mind liable to reappear during any period of history, and particularly at the end of the nineteenth century. The 'conclusion' to this study, actually written in 1868, caused a scandal, for this manifesto of 'art for art's sake' implicitly preached atheism and amorality. To burn always with this hard, gem-like flame is the attitude of inspired criticism: such is Pater's credo when he speaks of aesthetic ideology and 'wisdom':

> Of such wisdom, the poetic passion, the desire of beauty, the love of art for its own sake, has most. For art comes to you proposing frankly to give nothing but the highest quality to your moments as they pass, and simply for those moments' sake.
>
> Walter Pater,
> *The Renaissance*

Commenting on Pater's text, the Austrian poet and dramatist Hugo von Hofmannsthal wrote: 'One way or another we are all in love with a past which has been perceived and stylised by the intermediary of art. It is, so to speak, a way of falling in love with an ideal or, at the very least, an idealised sort of life. This is aestheticism, one of those words that are famous in England; it is also an important and pervasive element in our culture as dangerous as opium.'

A poisonous book

This love of the past, which supports and stimulates the imagination, was shared by **Joris-Karl Huysmans (1848–1907)** in his novel *Against the Grain* (1884). Many recognised this as the 'yellow book' presented to Dorian Gray by his mentor Lord Henry Wotton.

> The style in which it was written was that curious jewelled style, vivid and obscure at once, full of argot and of archaisms, of technical expressions and of elaborate paraphrases, that characterises the work of some of the finest artists of the French school of Symbolistes. There were in it metaphors as monstrous as orchids, and as subtle in colour. The life of the senses was described in the terms of mystical philosophy. One hardly knew at times whether one was reading the spiritual ecstasies of some medieval saint or the morbid confessions of a modern sinner. It was a poisonous book.
>
> Oscar Wilde,
> *The Picture of Dorian Gray*

When *Against the Grain* appeared, Huysmans had already published several novels in the naturalist tradition. *Against the Grain* was the second volume of a trilogy, the first of which was called *Down the Drain* (1882) and the third *In Harbour* (1887). These three titles allude to a state of drifting or the impossibility of running away, to the three faces of a new *mal du siècle* which manifested itself in the appearance of lassitude. *Against the Grain* can be considered as the charter of the decadent movement, overturning the traditions of naturalism.

Des Esseintes, the central figure of the novel, is above all a dandy who worries about the cut of his clothes, the shape of his shoes and whose sartorial elegance harmonises with the elegance of his furniture. But – and this is one of the fundamental laws of the decadent movement – Des Esseintes uses dandyism against itself. He lives like a dandy in his solitary retreat of Fontenay, but without a public, being both the subject and the object of his fads. Everything he likes is, of necessity, artificial and man-made. Nature can only repeat herself and cannot compete with human creativity and imagination. This is why he contrasts feminine beauty (the work of Nature and generally held to be her most original and most perfect achievement) with the beauty of locomotives; and he then describes the beauty of two locomotives (the Crompton and the Engerth) in terms normally reserved for describing women. Decadence is misogynist: it considers femininity as a force inimical to man. So the myth of Salomé develops on the basis of the pictures of Gustave Moreau and *fin de siècle* literature. 'After such a book,' wrote Barbey d'Aurevilly, 'all that is left to the author is to choose between the barrel of a gun and the foot of the cross.' 'The choice is made,' Huysmans added in conclusion to the 1903 introduction: he retired to the Trappist monastery of Notre-Dame d'Igny.

The audience for *Against the Grain*

In 1889, five years after the publication of *Against the Grain*, *Il Piacere* (*Pleasure*) by Gabriele d'Annunzio was published. As in Huysmans, in Wilde, and in the sensualist dogma preached by Pater, we can find in this decadent novel the affirmation of the primacy of pleasure.

Jules Barbey d'Aurevilly (1808–1889), like **Auguste Villiers de l'Isle-Adam (1838–1889)**, harboured a contempt for the century comparable to that of Des Esseintes. The best-known work by the former, *The Diabolical Ones*, was censored as soon as it was published in 1874, and could not appear again until 1882. Villiers, one of the accursed poets dear to Verlaine, also opposed positivism in his humorously disturbing *Cruel Tales* (1883). **Maurice Barrès (1862–1913)** inherited another legacy of Huysmans: that of the 'cult of self', the only cult that Des Esseintes knew how to celebrate; he made it the title

of his trilogy *Under Barbarian Eyes* (1888), *A Free Man* (1889) and *The Garden of Berenice* (1891). The freedom called for by Huysmans' hero was also one of Gide's key concepts, even if it had to be an immoral freedom. In Couperus' short novel *Noodlot* (*The Irrevocable*, 1890), the main character is a consummate dandy. Couperus' short stories and novels, written between 1890 and 1900, are steeped in an atmosphere heavy with obsession and aestheticism.

The most typical of the Czech decadents was **Jiři Karasek ze Lvovice (1871–1951)**. In his poems (*Honory se smrti*, *Dialogue with Death*, 1904), in his novels (*Goticka duse*, *A Gothic Soul*, 1950), in his plays and in his impressionistic prose sketches, he captured perfectly the atmosphere of this twilight period.

The art of the 1890s can be felt as a dialectic of aesthetic introspection and naturalism. These two tendencies are opposed to the ponderous, narrow and bourgeois attitude which developed in a century of industrialisation and utilitarianism. The death of Hedda, in the late naturalist play *Hedda Gabler* (1891), could be taken to symbolise the failure of innovation and regeneration in the art of this period, a reminder that this period was dubbed that of the 'tragic generation' by Yeats. Hedda may be seen as a corrupt and corrupting female dandy; her choice of an aesthetic lifestyle is manifest when she gives her former lover, Eilert Løvborg, a pistol with which to shoot himself.

HEDDA *Eilert Lovborg, – hor nu her – kunne De ikke se til at – at det skjedde i skjonnhet?* LOVBORG *I skjonnhet?* (smiler) *Med vinlov i håret, som De for i tiden tenkte Dem.* HEDDA *A nei. Vinlovet – det tror jeg ikke lenger på. Men i skjonnhet allikevel! For en gangs skyld! – Farvel!*	HEDDA *Eilert Lovborg, listen to me. Let it be beautiful: finish beautifully.* LOVBORG *Beautifully?* (He smiles.) *With a crown of vine leaves? That's what you already suggested to me, a long time ago.* HEDDA *No, I no longer believe in the crown. But I still believe in beauty. Farewell!*

Henrik Ibsen,
Hedda Gabler

Hedda, like Dorian, scandalised her contemporaries with her apparent amorality and her inability to live according to the conventions of her class. But, in provoking Løvborg, an exceptional being like herself, to commit suicide 'elegantly', she only asks of him what she herself is prepared to do, for she is far removed from the provincial middle-class mentality of her husband, colleagues and friends. Hedda, world weary, is bored like Des Esseintes and plays out her life like a dangerous game; but her toys are pistols, people, lives and ideals. In this play the decadent elements bring, paradoxically, new life to the theatre as they are framed by naturalism. Influenced by Ibsen and breaking with Romantic theatre, the dramatist **Ivo Vojnovic (1857–1929)** was the founder of Croatian symbolist theatre. For the background of his plays (*Dubrovacka trulogija*, *The Dubrovnik Trilogy*, 1900), he took his home town of Dubrovnik.

The evolution of naturalism

> Naturalism not dead. Letter follows.
> Paul Alexis

The output of naturalism was not affected by this *fin de siècle* atmosphere. **Maxim Gorky (1868–1936)** took an interest in the world of the working classes with *Na dne* (*The Lower Depths*, 1902). In *A dajka* (*The Wet Nurse*, 1902) by the Hungarian **Sándor Bródy (1863–1924)**, we find a certain affinity with Gorki's *Lower Depths*, but the lyrical atmosphere is more Chekhovian. Henri Becque (1837–1899) clearly opted for the naturalist theatre, ready to denounce the vicious manners of the ruling classes (*The Crows*, 1882). With the innovative *Poil de Carotte* (*Carrot Hair*, 1900), Jules Renard (1864–1910) preferred to put his realist and impressionist talent into creating believable characters rather than working on the coherence of the plot. The plays by the Dutchman **Herman Heijermans (1864–1924)**, founder and director of the socialist periodical *De Jonge Gids* (*The Young Guide*, 1897–1901), met with success all over Europe, in particular *Op hoop van zegen* (*By the Grace of God*, 1900), in which he analyses social injustice.

Novelists throughout Europe remained faithful to naturalism, each giving it a characteristic twist. The Scot **Robert Louis Stevenson (1850–1894)**, a stylistic disciple of Balzac and Flaubert, preferred the short story and novella form. His best-known works such as *Treasure Island*, 1881–1882) and *The Strange Case of Dr Jekyll and Mr Hyde* (1886) show his sense of dynamism in narrative construction, at the same time as his desire to discover and describe unknown areas of geography, psychology or ethics. **Rudyard Kipling (1865–1936)**, Anglo-Indian, also viewed his contemporaries with detachment. *The Jungle Book* (1894–1895), a collection of short tales taken from the life of Mowgli – a wild child raised by animals in the jungle – shows the kingdom of the beasts as more virtuously governed than the cruel, savage human society which had rejected him. The disciples of the Greek novelist **Psichari, Alexandros Pallis (1851–1935)** and Eftaliotis, adopted the Demotic and exploited its linguistic potential to give a new thrust to Greek naturalism.

At the same time, however, catharsis came in the shape of liberating laughter: 'Merdre!' shouts Old Ubu at the opening of *Ubu roi* (1896) by Alfred Jarry (1873–1907). These 'oaths', 'the belly, the bread-basket, the gut' of Old Ubu are a 'ginormous' raspberry to the theatre of naturalism (Zola, Becque, Synge) and to the psychological realism of Stanislavski, the director of Chekhov and Gorki.

COSMOPOLITANISM, COTERIES AND LITERARY CIRCLES

Ibsen was living in Munich when he wrote *Hedda Gabler*, and Wilde found his inspiration for *Dorian Gray* during a stay in Paris, in the course of which he frequented literary circles. Across Europe many artists went into exile to rally round a man, an idea, a movement, forming coteries in which fruitful debates reached an audience on a European scale: the Tuesday meetings at Mallarmé's in the rue de Rome; the Friedrichshagen circle, enthusiastic about psychology; the German cabarets; the Griensteidl café in Vienna.

Evenings in the rue de Rome

In Paris the most important literary meeting place was situated in the rue de Rome at the home of Stéphane Mallarmé (1842–1898). Over the years many famous names were to be encountered there at the 'causeries du mardi': Symons, Wilde, Mockel, Huysmans, Valéry, Moréas, Verlaine, Maupassant, Khan, Ghil, George, Maeterlinck, Verhaeren, Claudel, Gide, among ones. The painters Morisot, Whistler, Manet, Gauguin, and the composer Debussy also frequented the salon of the 'master'. The English writer **Arthur Symons (1865–1945)** remembered those receptions:

Invaluable, it seems to me, those Tuesdays must have been to the young men of two generations who have been making French literature . . . Here was a house in which art, literature, was the very atmosphere, a religious atmosphere, and the master of the

house . . . a priest . . . It was impossible to come away from Mallarmé's without some tranquilising influence from that quiet place, some impersonal aspiration towards excellence, the resolve, at least, to write a sonnet, a page of prose, that should be in its own way as perfect as one could make it, worthy of Mallarmé.

The Belgian symbolist **Albert Mockel (1866–1945)**, founder of the poetic review *La Wallonie* (*Wallonia*), expressed the same sentiments in his obituary of Mallarmé written for *Le Mercure de France* (*The French Mercury*): 'We spent there hours that were unforgettable, the best no doubt that we will ever experience . . . And the man who received us was the ABSOLUTE TYPE OF THE POET'.

However, his quest for perfection was such that Mallarmé wrote very little. He himself never identified with symbolism: 'I hate schools,' he declared. In 1860 he read Baudelaire's *The Flowers of Evil* which had a powerful effect on him. His first collection of ten poems was printed in the *Parnasse contemporain* in 1866. 'Sea Breeze' reproduced Mallarmé's aspiration for spiritual perfection, both encouraged and held back by the attraction of 'the sailor's song':

La chair est triste, hélas! et j'ai lu tous les livres.
Fuir! là-bas fuir! Je sens que des oiseaux sont ivres
D'être parmi l'écume inconnue et les cieux!
Rien, ni les vieux jardins reflétés par les yeux
Ne retiendra ce coeur qui dans la mer se trempe
Ô nuit! ni la clarté déserte de la lampe
Sur le vide papier que la blancheur défend
Et ni la jeune femme allaitant son enfant.
Je partirai!

Stéphane Mallarmé,
'*Brise marine*'

The flesh is sad, alas! and I've read all the books.
To run away! To run away down there! I feel that birds are drunk
to be among the unknown spray and sky!
Nothing, neither old gardens reflected by the eyes, oh night, will hold back this heart which is drenched by the sea,
nor the deserted clearness of the lamp on the empty paper protected by whiteness, nor the young woman breast-feeding her baby . . .
I will leave!

To purify the dialect of the tribe

Mallarmé was dissatisfied with language as a means of poetic expression: when the English

journal *Equinox* wanted to disseminate the poet's ideas, it published an edition that was wholly blank. 'To purify the dialect of the tribe,' as Mallarmé wrote in 'The Tomb of Edgar Poe' (1877), was his main idea. His method for transforming ordinary language into ideal poetic language included the use of 'sound symbolism' (which he described in *English Words*, 1877): 'sneer' and 'snake' have the same phoneme 'sn', a 'sinister digraph'.He thought that the sounds of words themselves should contain their sense, and complained that, in French, the word for 'day', 'jour' had a dark vowel, and the word for 'night', 'nuit' had a light vowel, which contradicted their meaning. To this sonorous quality of language, the poet added the art of metre: 'I'm making music,' he would say. Mallarmé manufactured neologisms, used archaisms and disrupted traditional French syntax: 'Poetry is a language in a state of crisis.' He breathed into the younger generation the fundamental idea that 'to name an object is to take away three quarters of the pleasure of a poem written to be understood little by little; to suggest something is the ideal. It is the perfect use of this mystery that constitutes symbolism: making a theme evolve in stages to show a state of mind or, conversely, taking a theme and detaching a state of mind from it by a series of unveilings'.

It could be taken as a definition of symbolism, which is primarily an art of evocation and suggestion. While there are as many definitions of symbolism as there are symbolist poets, it is nevertheless possible to identify some common trends. As early as 1834 the Scot **Thomas Carlyle (1795–1881)** had pronounced 'In the symbol proper . . . there is ever, more or less distinctly and directly, some embodiment and revelation of the Infinite; the Infinite is made to blend itself with the Finite, to stand visible, and as it were, attainable there'. Yet even retrospectively, Valéry in 1924, acknowledged the lack of consensus about the term: 'We are in the process of constructing symbolism . . . definitions are not lacking; each of us put forward our own and was quite free to do so.'

The first symbolist manifesto

Jean Moréas (the pseudonym of **Jean Papadiamantopoulos, 1856–1910**), a French poet of Greek origin, published the first 'symbolist' manifesto in *Figaro litéraire*:

> Symbolist poetry, inimical to education, declamation, false sensibility and objective description, tries to clothe the idea in a tangible form which, nevertheless, should not be its aim per se, but which, in serving to express the Idea, should be secondary.
>
> Jean Moréas,
> *The Symbolist Manifesto*

Moréas considered Baudelaire to be the precursor of the 'current movement', Mallarmé as its high priest, and Verlaine and Théodore de Banville as its main interpreters. How far is symbolism from decadence? The polemics around these two concepts was developed by competing reviews in the same avant-garde sphere of influence: *The Literary and Artistic Decadence* by René Ghil (1862–1925) was countered by *The Symbolist* by Moréas. The only point on which critics and writers seem to be agreed is the place Baudelaire occupied as the precursor of this new art. His *In Praise of Cosmetics* had everything to attract the younger generation (and here we are back with Huysmans and Wilde again): Nature, fallen and intrinsically bad, can only be improved by artifice. Only art can redeem nature. So the slogan 'art for art's sake' inherited from Gautier finds itself equipped with a moral dimension. The more a life or a work of art is artificial or aesthetic, the better it is morally. This is a perverse view, but it offers a spurious moral licence to decadence. The first publication of the English avant-garde review, *The Yellow Book* in April 1894, included an article by Max Beerbohm (1872–1956) which began:

> This era of cosmetics is our own. . . . Artifice is the strength of the world.
>
> Max Beerbohm,
> *In Defence of Cosmetics*

The 'sweet song' of European symbolism

The profusion of literary reviews was one of the *fin de siècle's* most salient traits. 'Little reviews' became an art form in themselves, giving an international impulse to the artistic avant-garde. Thanks to them, symbolism found a European audience. These reviews saw in **Paul Verlaine (1844–1896)** ˟ – who, as far as he was concerned, did not belong to any school – one of the architects, with Mallarmé,

of the symbolist movement. 'To him,' wrote Symons, 'physical sight and spiritual vision, by some strange alchemical operation of the brain, were one.' 'Rien de plus cher que la chanson grise, / Où l'indécis au précis se joint' ('Nothing is dearer than the grey song, / In which the unclear and the precise are joined together') say the nonasyllables of his 'Art of Poetry'. What Pauvre Lélian, alias Paul Verlaine, wants is 'music before everything else'.

Les sanglots longs	Tout suffocant	Et je m'en vais
Des violons	Et blême, quand	Au vent mauvais
De l'Automne	Sonne l'heure	Qui m'emporte,
Blessent mon coeur	Je me souviens	De çà, de là,
D'une langueur	Des jours anciens	Pareil à la
Monotone.	Et je pleure.	Feuille morte.
(The long sobs	(Suffocating	(And I go off
Of the violins	And livid, when	In the bad wind
Of Autumn	The hour strikes,	That carries me,
Wound my heart	I remember	Here and there,
With monotonous	The old days	Similar to
Languor.)	And I weep.)	The dead leaf.)

Paul Verlaine,
'Song of Autumn',
Saturnine Poems (1866)

More dazzling and syntactically bolder than work by Verlaine, poetry by **Arthur Rimbaud (1854–1891)** ˟ expressed adolescent revolt.

> Poetic old-fashionedness counted for a lot in my verbal alchemy. I got used to straight-forward hallucination: I could see very clearly a mosque in the place of a factory, a school for drummer boys made by angels, stately coaches on the roads to heaven, a living-room at the bottom of a lake; monsters, mysteries; a vaudeville billboard showed me its terrors.
>
> Then I explained my magical sophistry with the hallucination of words! I ended up by finding my mind's disorder sacred.
>
> Arthur Rimbaud, 'Delirium II',
> *A Season in Hell*

The work of Verlaine and his contemporaries spread throughout Europe. Even in Russia, by 1892, Zinada Vengerova had studied his work as well as that by Rimbaud, Mallarmé, Laforgue and Moréas in an article for *Vestnik Evropy* (*The European Messenger*). Thanks to this publication, as well as to the interest given to Baudelaire by Constantin Dimitrievitch Balmont (1867–1943) and Valeri Iakovlevitch Briussov (1873–1924), a new spirit entered Russian poetry. These two poets translated Verlaine's *Romances without Words* (1874). In Bohemia, the poet Vrchlický created a new school of poetry based on Czech translations of French innovators. **Karel Hlaváček (1874–1898)** introduced a musicality like that of Verlaine into Czech poetry; he left behind several collections, including *Pozdě k ránu* (*Late towards Morning*, 1896) and

Mstivá kantilená (*Vengeful Cantilena*, 1898). In Hungary, before the review *Nyugat* (*The West*, 1908–1941) was published, modernism in poetry was represented by a few great isolated figures, in particular by János Vajda (1827–1897). Romantic in his individuality, he used objects, which he progressively deformed, as symbols to interpret existence. Another poet whose Romanticism was visionary, obsessed with total freedom, was **Jenö Komjáthy (1858–1895)**, who expressed his metaphysical 'revelations' with successions of symbols. Poetry by Gyula Reviczky (1855–1889) is elegiac and impressionistic in its musicality. Also an impressionist poet, József Kiss (1843–1921) founded, the review *A Hét* (*The Week*) in 1890. It expressed the *fin de siècle* sensibility.

In Portugal, in 1888, there appeared the reviews *Os Insubmisos* (*The Unruly*) and *Bohemia Nova* (*New Bohemia*). However, it was, above all, the review *Arte* (*Art*), founded in 1895 by Eugénio de Castro (1869–1944) and Manuel da Silva Gaio (1860–1934), which followed with interest the evolution of French literature.

In Greece, the symbolist movement, introduced there thanks to the review *Art* (1898–1899), edited by **Konstantinos Hadjopoulos (1868–1920)**, reflected innovations from Great Britain, Scandinavia and Russia. The poets Miltiadis Malakassis (1869–1943), John N. Gryparis (1870–1942), Lambros Porphyras (1879–1932) and Zacharias Papantonious (1877–1940) also contributed. The review *Dionisios* (1901–1902), published by Yannis Kambyssis and Dimitrios Hadjopoulos, offered the same programme, which would carry the fruits of Greek symbolism into the first decades of the twentieth century.

The Danish poet Johannes Jørgensen (1866–1956) published a series of portraits of Poe, Verlaine, Mallarmé and Huysmans in 1893. He continued his work by founding *Taarnet*, the most influential avant-garde literary review in Scandinavia. This monthly publication offered a hotly disputed manifesto, 'Symbolism', translations of Baudelaire, Flaubert, Mallarmé and Maeterlinck, as well as poems by Jørgensen himself and by the Danish decadent Sophus Clausen (1865–1932), whose first collection *Naturborn*, published in 1887, brought a new figurative and formal language to Scandinavia. The Norwegian decadent poet Sigbjørn Obstfelder (1866–1900) also contributed to *Taarnet*, in which his prose poem 'Natten' ('Night') was particularly noticed. His first collection *Digte* (*Poems*, 1893) owed something to the influence of Verlaine and Maeterlinck. Rilke gave it high praise in Vienna in 1904, and his own novel *The Notebooks of Malte Laurids Brigge* derived from Obstfelder's lyrical prose, which may be found in his short story *Korset* (*The Cross*, 1896). In Sweden, the tendencies of French symbolism were found in the poet **Vilhelm Ekelund (1880–1949)**, a close neighbour to the artistic circle of Tua in Lund. Ekelund took his inspiration from Verlaine, George, Hölderlin and Nietzsche, notably in his collection *Syner* (*Mirages*, 1901), which contains *Verlaine Stamming* (*Verlaine's Stammering*), and in *Melodier i skymning* (*Twilight Melodies*, 1902).

Stefan George (1868–1933) began his literary career in 1889, by participating in Mallarmé's Tuesday evening meetings. In 1892 he founded the literary review *Blätter für die Kunst* (*Pages for Art*), whose purpose was to satisfy the literary needs of the artistic circle gravitating around him. We find in this review translations of Baudelaire, Mallarmé and Verlaine, often by George himself, as well as poetry by Dauthendy, Gerardy, Gundolf and Hofmannsthal. The review enjoyed increasing success, and continued publication until 1919. George's poetry was divided into cycles that reflect the superior order of the 'All'. His first unrhymed symbolist verse, was accented according to the rules of German metre, and evoked serene pastorals of ancient Greece peopled by mythical beings. In the cycles *Hymnen* (*Hymns*, 1890), *Pilgerfahrt* (*Pilgrimage*, 1891) and *Algabal* (1892), the pared-down syntax and archaic morphology strengthen the impression of sophistication. The life of Algabal, based on that of the Roman emperor, Heliogabalus, who introduced sun-worship to Rome, allowed him to set up a comparison with the situation of the poet: because the poet is close to the gods, he is marked with a religious and imperial dignity. The poems of the cycle *Das Jahr der Seele* (*The Year of the Soul*, 1897) move away from linguistic and symbolist stylisation. Nature like a garden reflects the state of mind in which the 'I' responds to the 'you': 'The *I* and the *you* have rarely belonged as much to a single soul as in this book.' The motifs, the delicate sophistication and the hermeticism show the proximity of Jugendstil. With the cycle *Der Teppich des Lebens* (*The Carpet of Life*, 1900), George left the realm of art and set himself up as a visionary, claiming through poetry 'the glorious rebirth that neither the art of the State nor the art of society are able to offer'. The cycle *Der siebente Ring* (*The Seventh Ring*) laid claim to the validity of literary fiction as a new religion in a feudal State system. Influential representatives of German culture considered themselves his disciples. The celebration of his irrational works and concepts such as 'the celebration of power', 'the struggle' and 'heroic action' made George appear an increasingly significant representative of an hieratic world, and explained the use of his ideas by national socialism.

The culture of the Austro-Hungarian Empire extended to almost all the provinces of the empire. In the Czech lands, however, in the middle of the 1890s, a culture developed which was interested in foreign literature. This generation rejected the preciosity of the school of Vrchlický, while retaining the cosmopolitanion he had introduced. The Decadents, the Symbolists and the neo-Romantics initially found themselves under the banner of the *Moderní Revue* (*Modern Review*), and rallied to the 'Manifesto of Czech Moderns' in 1895: 'We want the truth in art, not that of a photograph of external things, but the honest internal truth can only be found in he or she who assumes it – the individual.' This manifesto was signed by Šalda, Machar, Březina, Sova, Mrštík and many others.

The founder and co-editor of the *Modern Review* was the poet, translator and prolific essayist **Arnošt Procházka (1869–1925)**. His co-editor was Jiři Karásek ze Lvovice, the most prominent Decadent of the decadent movement. In his poems, novels and plays, he painted decadent psychology to perfection: nostalgia, exhaustion, escapism and sincere emotion, morbid eroticism, extreme subjectivity, all gathered together by stylised formalism and aristocratic aestheticism.

In 1895 symbolism triumphed with the avalanche of symbols and metaphors in the first collection by **Otokar Březina (1868–1929)**, *Tajemné dálky* (*Mysterious Distances*):

Pro tajemství bolesti, smrti a
znovuzrození sladko je žíti!
[. . .]
Pro hvězdný duchový pohled
zem ze všech stran současně
objímající:
krystalné samoty pólů, pravěku,
prahor, zákona, čísla;
ticha moře zkvetlého světla,
štěstí, klasu a nocí;
horečné zahrady tropů, krve,
zízně a knížecích snení;
[. . .] sladko je žíti!

Okokar Březina,
Tajemné dálky

For the mystery of pain, death and
rebirth, life is sweet!
[. . .]
For the spiritual and stellar
gaze embracing everywhere,
at the same time, the earth:
the crystal solitudes of the poles,
of mountains and centuries past,
of laws and of numbers;
the silent seas of light,
happiness, ears of corn, night;
the feverish gardens of the
tropics, blood, thirst, and
dreams of princes;
[. . .] life is sweet!

The rest of his work, developing into hymnic free verse, marked the stages of his spiritual development: *Svítání na západe* (*Dawn at Sunset*, 1896), *Větry od pólu* (*Polar Winds*, 1897), *Stavitelé chrámu* (*Builders of the Temple*, 1899) and *Ruce* (*Hands*, 1901).

Elek Gozsdu (1849–1919) had symbolist and lyrical elements in the foreground of his short stories and in his novel *A köd* (*The Fog*, 1882). The trend called Moderna opened up Serb literature to Western influences, particularly those of the Parnassus and of French symbolism. Aestheticism and formalism predominated in poetry. Many poets took part in this movement, following Ilić, and undertook research into poetic form. Aleksa Santic (1868–1924) was a lyrical poet faithful to the popular Serb and Eastern tradition. Jovan Ducic (1874–1943) sang of love, God and death in a solemn style and proclaimed himself above all as a nature poet. Milan Rakic (1876–1938) introduced intellectual scepticism and Baudelairean existentialist angst into his poetry. Sima Pandurovic (1883–1960) followed this meditative vein and added a nihilist spirit to his verses. Poetry by Vladislav Petkovic Dis (1880–1917) was made up of cosmic visions and metaphysical suffering.

The Croatian Moderna movement presented itself as a synthesis of the *fin de siècle* Viennese spirit, of impressionism, symbolism and expressionism. Literature was set free from national and social utilitarianism to the benefit of aesthetic research. Antun Gustav Matos (1873–1914) inaugurated modern Croat literature. Exiled in Belgrade and Paris, he expressed the *mal du siècle* in his first poems, only to burst forth subsequently in a poetry mingling images and colours. Poems by Vladimir Vidrić (1875–1909) were steeped in associations of ideas and music.

The Slovene Moderna movement affirmed itself in 1899 with the publication of two collections of poetry: *Erotika* by Ivan Cankar (1876–1918) and *Casa opojnosti* (*A Cup of Drunkenness*) by Oton Zupancic (1878–1949). In his poetry, marked by a subtle lyricism, strong symbolism and a melodious rhythm, Cankar showed himself to be close to the symbolists and impressionists.

In Bulgaria the talent of the national poet and writer Ivan Vazov (1850–1921) flowered. He was the author of a work of twenty volumes, translated into twenty-four languages.

In Holland, the principal literary review *De nieuwe gids* (*The New Guide*) was created in 1885. Albert Verwey (1865–1937), one of its founder editors, published the *Tweemaandelijksch tijdschrift* (*The Bimonthly Magazine*) in 1894. Interested in how Europe was evolving, he contributed to Stefan George's *Pages for Art*. He studied Verlaine's *Epigrams* in 1894. In 1895 his co-editor, Lodewijk Van Deyssel, published a critical essay on Zola and Maeterlinck, rejecting naturalist prose in favour of aestheticism, a movement which a few years later announced its adherence to symbolism. As in France, where Baju had forged links between avant-garde artistic and political movements, *The Bimonthly Magazine* made its contribution to the socialist movement in Holland.

There were strong links between Belgian and French symbolists which came through in their collaboration for the *Wallonia* review. The motto 'Be Ourselves', which served as a preface to the review *Young Belgium*, expressed a desire to reject old models rather than to show signs of literary nationalism. But the writers of this new generation could not prevent their movement from being exploited by the upholders of nationalism. A new impetus had also been given to the visual arts, architecture and literature. This renaissance was the work of artists who had broken away from *Young Belgium*, the Parnassian and classical position of which seemed to them retrograde in the light of innovation by Mallarmé. Paradoxically for many countries, the movement of *Young Belgium* remained the model for innovation as for instance, in *Young Poland*, strongly influenced by its Belgian precursor. Even so, in Schönberg's *Pierrot lunaire*, taken from Giraud's poem, the revolution inaugurated by the composer was certainly not to the taste of the poet who respected classical versification.

The four principal tendencies of the Belgian symbolist movement, merged in the practice of its leaders, were as follows. First, there was an idealist reaction against the then dominant positivism. Schopenhauer had a decisive influence on **Émile Verhaeren (1865–1916)**, on Charles Van Lerberghe (1861–1907) and on Georges Rodenbach (1855–1898). Discouragement and melancholy were the common language of all these men who departed from the ideological norms of bourgeois society. Death, madness, masks, and the character of Pierrot were themes used to 'externalise' the despair of the rebellious soul. Mockel went so far as to speak of a 'trilogy of suffering' in referring to Verhaeren's collections of poetry published after his parents' death, *Evenings* (1887), *Fiascos* (1888) and *The Black Torches* (1889).

> En sa robe, couleur de fiel et de poison
> Le cadavre de ma raison
> Traîne sur la Tamise.

Émile Verhaeren, 'Death',
The Black Torches

> In its dress the colour of gall and posion
> The corpse of my reason
> Floats slowly down the Thames.

Second, debates took place about the verse form influenced by Mallarmé. Violent arguments ensued between Giraud and Verhaeren on the legitimacy of 'free verse'. Third there was innovation in the realm of drama. Finally, the fervent political commitment of artistic innovators led them to take part in meetings of the Belgian Workers' Party: Verhaeren, the architect Horta and the art critic Maus were present at these meetings. Most Belgian symbolists were Dreyfusards and in favour of progress. A poetry of the modern world was born of industrial power: Verhaeren's *The Hallucinated Countryside* (1893) and *The Towns with Tentacles* (1895) found an echo in Apollinaire, 'las de ce monde ancien' ('weary of the ancient world').

> C'est la ville tentaculaire
> La pieuvre ardente et l'ossuaire
> Et la carcasse solennelle
>
> Et les chemins d'ici s'en vont à l'infini
> Vers elle.

Émile Verhaeren,
Les Campagnes hallucinées

> It is the town with tentacles
> The ardent octopus and the ossuary
> And the solemn carcass
>
> And the roads from here go on endlessly
> Towards it.

The symbolist theatre

The work of **Maurice Maeterlinck (1862–1949)**[*] quickly found admirers in Paris. His *Pelléas and Mélisande* (1892), orchestrated by Debussy in 1902, is a work of apparent simplicity in which the dialogue reveals the premonitions of the characters, correspondences are established between the separate physical and spiritual states, and silence plays a vital part.

Most of the Belgian symbolists, Verhaeren in *The Dawns* (1898) or Van Lerberghe in *The Sniffers* (1889), used this genre. The theorist behind these innovations was Edmond Picard, author of *Discourse on the Revival in the Theatre* (1897), who invited Lugné-Poe to Brussels, the director of experimental theatre in Paris. In the realm of experimental theatre, the Belgians launched a movement which developed in Paris and Vienna, then throughout Europe. The atmospheric theatre of **Anton Chekhov (1860–1904)**,[*] in which the unstated and silence are so important (*Čajka*, *The Seagull*, 1896), or the slow unfolding of the poetic phrasing of Claudel (*The Exchange*, 1893), recall that of Belgian symbolist theatre.

The Friedrichshagen meetings

The mixture of aesthetic and political sympathy, so marked in current Belgian cultural achievements, was also found in the small, influential and rather bohemian circle which was established in Friedrichshagen in Germany. This village near Berlin attracted a group of artists who were looking for rural tranquility not far from the busy metropolis, home to their mentor, Hauptmann. Friedrichshagen thus became the centre of a North European literary avant-garde.

The first 'colonisers' of this town, in 1888, were Bruno Wille (1860–1928) and Wilhelm Bolsche (1861–1939). Soon, other writers in literary circles in Berlin like Erich Mühsam (1878–1934) and Gustav Landauer (1870–1919) joined those in Friedrichshagen, trying to set up a group identity based on Bakunin's ideas of anarchy and socialist Utopia, on Schopenhauer's nihilism and on revolutionary socialist ideas about the aesthetic contained in Richard Wagner's first essays. They lived in great poverty and experienced the disappointment of seeing their literature rejected by the very working class with whom they wanted to form a Utopian alliance. The Swede **Ola Hansson (1860–1925)** and his wife were among the first to settle in Friedrichshagen. They brought a contagious radicalism to art and politics. Hansson also attracted many other Scandinavians: the Norwegian novelist Garborg and his wife, the Danish poet Holger Drachmann (1846–1908), the Norwegian painter Edvard Munch, the dramatist Gunnar Heiberg (1857–1929), the poet Obstfelder, the Norwegian sculptor Gustav Vigeland and the Finns Axel Gallen Kalleva and Sibelius, the Scandinavians who 'discovered' Nietzsche.

Hansson rejected old-fashioned naturalism and, in its place, attracted writers' attention to authors such as Huysmans, Bourget, Poe, Barbey d'Aurevilly and the painter Böcklin. Alongside his collections of poetry and his erotic short stories, Hansson published texts in German monographs on contemporary Scandinavian writers such as Strindberg, Hamsun, Garborg and Jacobsen, thus counterbalancing the overly great importance attached to Ibsen and Bjørnson. The leading idea of Hansson's criticism was to replace the interest of the naturalists for the outward appearances of life with a fascination for inner and psychological conditions. The novel *Sult* (*Hunger*, 1890), by **Knut Hamsun (1859–1952)**, was an example of this new style, both in form and content: the novel, whose narrative perspective varied according to whether the narrator identifies with the hero or not, has neither action nor a traditional plot; it offers us the ironic, subtle and tragic portrait of an unpredictable writer who, a combination of dandy and tramp wanders through the streets of Christiania (Oslo), increasingly sinking into mental and physical decay. The hero's physical hunger represents a metaphysical hunger and an appetite for spiritual adventure. Lost, the hero wanders through the social jungle of the town, confusing hallucination and reality.

Så fremmed som jeg i dette oieblik var for mig selv, så fuldstœndig et bytte for usynlige indflytelser, foregik intet omkring mig uten at jeg la mœrke til det. En stor brun hund sprang tvœrs over gaten, henimot lunden og ned til tivoli; den hadde et smalt halsbånd av nysolv. Hoiere op I gaten åpnedes et vindu i anden etage og en pike la seg ut av det med opbrœttede œrmer og	*For all that I was a stranger to myself at that moment, and wholly prey to invisible influences, I nevertheless noticed everything that was going on around me. A big brown dog ran across the street near Lund Square and went down towards the* Tivoli; *he was wearing a narrow white metal collar. Further up the street a window opened on the first floor; a maid*

> *gav sig til å pusse ruterne på*
> *yttersiden. Intet undgik min*
> *opmærlsombet jeg var klar og*
> *åndsnærværende, alle ting*
> *strommet ind på mig med en*
> *skinnende tydelighet som om det*
> *pludselig var blit et stærkt lys*
> *ombring mig.*

Knut Hamsun,
Sult

> *leaned out, and started*
> *to clean the windows*
> *outside. Nothing escaped*
> *my attention. I was compos mentis*
> *and had all my wits about me, the flow*
> *of things penetrated me with*
> *a sparkling clarity as if*
> *a bright light had suddenly been switched*
> *on around me.*

Hunger (1890) was the first modernist Scandinavian novel, and Hamsun developed this with *Mysterier* (*Mysteries*, 1892), *Pan* (1894) and *Victoria* (1898). Other Scandinavians took up the challenge of the modernist urban novel, such as Strindberg with *Inferno* (1897) and Jensen with *Einar Elkaer* (1898). Rilke, influenced by Hamsun, made his contribution with *The Notebooks of Malte Laurids Brigge*. To some Jacobsen appeared as a decadent sentimentalist, languid, dreamy, with morbid ideas, who gives vent to all his humours in his poetry; to others he seemed a writer of naturalist novels. The subtle psychological novel by Jacobsen, *Niels Lyhne* (1880), fascinated and inspired the young Rilke.

One of Friedrichshagen's most celebrated inhabitants was the master of Polish Satanism, **Stanisław Przybyszewski (1868–1927)**, who had become the leader of Young Poland, a movement of artistic and political renewal spearheaded by the journal *Zycie* (*Life*), published in Cracow in 1898. Przybyszewski studied architecture and psychiatry in Berlin and, starting as a critic, published a study in German in 1892 on Chopin and Nietzsche, in which he identified the inspirational impulses of modern creativity.

On 1 January 1899, this admirer of Huysmans published his manifesto 'Confiteor': 'Art has no aim, it is an aim in itself; it is the absolute for it reflects the absolute. Art is higher than life.' His vision of man, the plaything of his instincts and the desires of his subconscious mind, came from his studies in psychology: man's hidden, primitive forces are governed by Satan, and the individual must confront them 'bare-souled' to discover their

creativity. Przybyszewski's ideas linked the positivism of the beginning of the century with the aestheticism of the end of the century: he believed that only art can truly delimit life, prey as it is to uncontrollable forces.

> Art is higher than life.
> Stanisław Przybyszewski

When **August Strindberg (1849–1912)** settled at Friedrichshagen for a short time towards the end of 1892, his interest in chemistry, alchemy and the occult, which led to his 'Inferno' period, was enthusiastically supported by Przybyszewski. Despite the eccentricity of these preoccupations, the two men created works of a psychological subtlety that anticipated Freud's discoveries. In 1893, Strindberg returned to live in Berlin and was a regular customer at the restaurant Zum Schwarzen Ferkel (The Black Pig, whose original name, The Cloister, had been changed at his request). He separated from his Polish drinking companion, but reappeared under the name of Popoffsky, the hero of the novel by Przybyszewski, *Opactwo* (*The Abbey*).

The dramatist **Frank Wedekind (1864–1918)** was an occasional visitor to Friedrichshagen. The story of his somewhat original family explains his precocious maturity. His parents were influenced by the revolutionary spirit of 1848 and, in their Swiss place of exile, Schloß Lenburg, gave their children an education free of all restraint. Wedekind's literary isolation manifested itself in his rejection of the prevailing naturalist norm, and set back recognition of his first dramas by at least ten years. Wedekind adopted the pseudonym

'Hieronymus Jobs' (a name equally used by the Baroque poet Karl Arnold Kortum) as a cover for the political poems he published in *Simplicissimus*, a satirical weekly edited in Munich by his friend Albert Lange. A satire on the political incompetence of the 'travelling emperor', Wilhelm II, on the occasion of his trip to Palestine in 1898, got him sent to prison for three and a half months for treason. From the cabaret The Black Cat that he went to in Paris, as well as other clubs (that were difficult to find in Prussia with its rigid Protestant mores), from 1891 to 1896, Wedekind borrowed elements to construct the reviews, songs and drinking songs of *Lautenlieder*. Through mime and dance, he rediscovered forms of expression forgotten by the bookish culture of the nineteenth century. He wrote the pantomimes *Die Fürstin Russalka* (*Princess Russalka*, 1897) and *Die Flöhe* (*The Fleas*) which, despite their grotesque side, were at the fountainhead of his most productive literary style.

The *Lulu* plays, written between 1892 and 1905, abandon the psychological motivation of action and character and the representation of struggles between individuals or groups. Lulu, the 'Real', 'the noble and beautiful animal', is not an active subject but a passive object who dies when confronted by men because they project on her their expectations of a certain type of social behaviour and cannot accept her as an elemental life force. The shock between sensual desire and rational constraint leads to Lulu's death in the second part of *Die Buchse der Pandora* (*Pandora's Box*, 1904). In 1953 Alban Berg composed an opera, *Lulu*, based on these plays, and the anti-naturalist style of Wedekind inspired the expressionists Georg Kaiser, Carl Sternheim, and later Brecht, as well as the surrealists. His experimental style lent dignity to the cabaret as an art form.

Little revue theatres were created throughout Europe: Schall und Rauch (Noise and Smoke) in Berlin, under the direction of Max Reinhardt, Zielony Balonik (The Green Balloon) in Cracow under the direction of Jan August Kisielewski in 1905, Els Quatre Gats (The Four Cats) in Barcelona in 1897 under the direction of Miguel Utrillo, who had previously belonged to the circle of the Black Cat in Paris, Letushaya Mysh (The Bat) in Moscow in 1908.

The Griensteidl café: the joyful Viennese apocalypse

The Griensteidl café in Vienna, the capital of the Austro-Hungarian Empire, rivalled Friedrichshagen in importance as a *fin de siècle* literary centre. Rich upper-middle-class children, more often than not from old assimilated Jewish families, were brought up in the pretentious structures of an outmoded monarchy and the problems of a multi-ethnic community. They gave themselves over to a joyless hedonism, coloured by an impotence full of regret, a consciousness of the ephemeral nature of things and a dysfunctional life. The work of **Hugo von Hofmannsthal (1874–1929)**, in particular, reflected this vision of existence. *Brief des Lords Chandos* (*The Letter of Lord Chandos*, 1902), his imaginary letter from a Renaissance poet to Francis Bacon, explains why he found it impossible to continue to write. It became a manifesto for a generation dominated by scepticism and a fascination for language, who could only look on the world as a series of sensations and sensual impressions. Among the writers who met at the Griensteidl Café and promoted *Young Vienna*, were Felix Salter (1869–1947), Schnitzler, Richard Beer-Hofmann (1866–1945) and the cultural critic Herman Bahr (1863–1934). From time to time Karl Kraus also came. Together they contemplated 'the joyful Viennese apocalypse'.

Hofmannsthal, influenced by George until 1906, published the dramatic fragment *Der Tod des Tizian* (*The Death of Titian*) in *Pages for Art* in 1892. He wrote his most important verse before 1900; their sounds and images, which exist independently, reflect a symbolist attraction towards the Absolute, signalled by the very titles of the poems: 'Lebensleid' ('The Pain of Life'), 'Weltgeheimnis' ('The Mystery of the World'), 'Ballade des äußeren Lebens' ('Ballad of the Outer Life'), 'Terzinen über Vergänglichkeit' ('Terza Rimas on the Ephemeral'), and his best-known poem, 'Manche freilich' ('More than One, no doubt').

Manche freilich müssen drunten sterben,	More than one, no doubt, will die down there,
Wo die schweren Ruder der Schiffe streifen,	There where the heavy oars of the ships glide,
Andre wohnen bei dem Steuer droben,	Others have their dwelling near the tiller, up above,
Kennen Vogelflug und die Länder der Sterne.	Know the flight of birds and the countries of the stars.
Manche liegen immer mit schweren Gliedern	More than one, with all the weight of his members, lies forever
Bei den Wurzeln des verworrenen Lebens,	Near the roots of mixed-up life;
Andern sind die Stühle gerichtet Bei den Sybillen, den Königinnen,	For others, seats are set out Near the Sibyls, near the queens,
Und da sitzen sie wie zu Hause, Leichten Hauptes und leichter Hände.	And there they are seated as at home, Head light, hands light.
Doch ein Schatten fällt von jenen Leben	However a shadow of these lives Falls on other lives,
In die anderen Leben hinüber, Und die leichten sind an die schweren	And the lightest are joined to the heavy
Wie an Luft und Erde gebunden:	As to the air and the earth.
Ganz vergessener Völker Müdigkeiten	The weariness of peoples fallen into a deep neglect,
Kann ich nicht abtun von meinen Lidern,	I cannot stop them from making my eyelids heavy,
Noch weghalten von der erschrockenen Seele	Nor keep away from my scared soul
Stummes Niederfallen ferner Sterne.	The silent collapse of far-off stars.
Viele Geschicke weben neben dem meinen,	Many are the destinies which are woven next to mine:
Durcheinander spielt sie alle das Dasein,	Existence makes them all vibrate at once,
Und mein Teil ist mehr als dieses Lebens	And my lot is not confined to this life,
Schlanke Flamme oder schmale Leier.	A thin flame or a frail lyre.

Hugo von Hofmannsthal,
'Manche freilich'

His first plays *Der Tor und der Tod* (*The Fool and Death*, 1893), *Das kleine Welttheater* (*The Little Theatre of the World*, 1897) and *Der weiße Fächer* (*The White Fan*, 1897), are elegies on the ephemeral nature of things. They express the bad conscience of aestheticism by revealing the gap between the active life and sterile aesthetic contemplation. The short story *Das Märchen der 672en Nacht* (*Tale of the 672nd Night*, 1895) describes the useless but necessary death of an aesthete who abandons his retreat and returns to live in the threatening world of society. Hofmannsthal continued to write throughout his life and was famous as the librettist for Richard Strauss' operas *Elektra*, 1909; *Der Rosenkavalier*, 1911 and *Ariadne auf Naxos*, 1912.

Arthur Schnitzler (1862–1931) continued to practise medicine all his life, observing his patients and diagnosing disease; as a writer he deployed the same skills in his critique of Viennese society. His plays and stories are psychological studies of a culture in decline. In a conversational tone, he expounds the potential proximity of death; the rigid structure of the dialogues reveals a spiritual coldness; social inertia and restraint are suggested by recourse to cyclical models. In *Anatole* (1890), erotic adventures are denounced as false experiences. In his most celebrated play, *Reigen* (*La Ronde*, 1896), five couples

from different social classes play out a game of relationships analogous to a dance of death, thus showing their common vulnerability to the power of eroticism. Schnitzler was the first writer in German to use the stream-of-consciousness technique in his story *Leutnant Gustl* (*Lieutenant Gustl*, 1901).

Peter Altenberg (also known as **Richard Engländer, 1859–1919**) was the most celebrated personality among the members of the Bohemian group who gathered in Viennese coffee houses. He called his many prose sketches and aphorisms *Extracte des Lebens* (*Life's Telegrams*, 1898–1919). Experiences are visualised and expressed in an impressionistic manner. **Karl Kraus (1874–1936)**, the humorist of the Viennese apocalypse, was a remarkable eccentric who moved heaven and earth to lead this community into the twentieth century. His subtle political vision, pure literary tastes and boundless energy made him a pitiless satirist of the corrupt, moribund Austro-Hungarian Empire – and, indeed, of the Western world. His main weapon was the journal *Die Fackel* (*The Torch*), which he launched in 1899 edited after 1912, and sustained for twenty-two years as sole author. His brilliant aphorisms show how much the fashionable style of egocentric aesthetes could be subverted into an instrument of violent polemic.

Krieg ist zuerst die Hoffnung,	*War is first of all the hope*
daß es einem besser gehen wird,	*that one can better one's own*
hierauf die Erwartung, daß es	*situation, then the hope that the situation*
dem andern schlechter gehen	*of someone else will get worse, then*
wird, dann die Genugtuung,	*the consolation that others have suffered*
daß es dem andern auch nicht	*a fate at least as bad*
besser geht, und hernach die	*as ours, and finally the surprise*
Überraschung, daß es beiden	*that we have both suffered*
schlechter geht.	*a very bad fate.*

Karl Kraus,
Magie der Sprache

The feeling of belonging to a moribund period, present in Viennese literature, appeared in comparable form in Spain, Portugal and Italy.

The generation of 1898: Spain, Portugal, Italy

Disillusionment invaded the Iberian peninsula after the 1898 disaster which marked the end of the Spanish Empire overseas. Confronted with the Spain of official speeches, the intellectuals of 1998 – Unamuno, Azorín, Baroja, Maetzu, Valle-Inclán, Ortega y Gasset, Antonio Machado – assiduously sought the real Spain, the eternal genius of the Spanish people. They thought they could find it in medieval and Renaissance Spain and in the folklore which they identify with rural Spain. Castille, once the most powerful kingdom in the peninsula, latterly the most ruined, lent itself admirably to the symbolists, to the expression of desolation, sterility and the individual's solitude. But it was not only Castille that interested the generation of 1898. Its writers roamed all over Spain and Portugal (Unamuno, *Por tierras de Portugal y España*, *Through the Lands of Portugal and Spain*, 1911), looking for old villages, old towns, monuments, landscapes, human types, evocative memories of Spain's essential characters they wanted to resuscitate. Hence the importance

of travel literature. 'We made excursions in space and time, we visited the ancient cities of Castille. We discovered in these towns the durability of the nation, they were the proof of it,' wrote Azorín. The landscape art of the Generation of 1898 can be interpreted as an escape from the demands of real life.

Miguel de Unamuno (1864–1936) and **Azorín** (the pen-name of **José Martínez Ruiz, 1873–1967)**, both essayists and philosophers, took particular interest in rethinking and reinterpreting *Don Quixote*: Unamuno, *Vida de Don Quijote y Sancho* (*The Life of Don Quixote and Sancho Panza*, 1905), Azorín, *La ruta de Don Quijote* (*Don Quixote's Route*, 1905).

The desire to forge a new Spanish literary identity was difficult to achieve because of the strong influence of French literature, in particular that of Baudelaire. Azorín, in *Diario de un enfermo* (*The Diary of Someone Sick*, 1901), was violently opposed to urbanisation:

Hoy, un tranvía ha atropellado a un anciano en la Puerta del Sol. Louis Veuillot abominaba del telégrafo, de los ferrocarriles, de la fotografía, de los barcos de vapor [. . .] ¿Por qué no abominar? Hay una barbarie más horrida que la barbarie antigua [. . .] Me ahogo, me ahogo en este ambiente inhumano de civilización humanitaria.	*Today a tram crushed an elderly man at the Puerta del Sol. Louis Veuillot hated telegraphs, railways, photography, steamships [. . .] And why should we not hate all that? There is a barbarity more horrible than ancient barbarity [. . .]. I'm choking, choking in the inhuman atmosphere of this civilisation which calls itself human.*

Azorín,
Diario de un enfermo

In Portugal, there was equal attachment to the values of the countryside, less corrupt than towns. Eça de Queirós, in *A Cidade e as Serras* (*Town and Country*, 1901), praised the Portuguese countryside, as did José Francisco Trindade Coelho (1861–1908) whose *Os Meus Amores* (*My Loves*, 1891) evoke memories of a rural childhood. In the poetry of the 1890s, António Nobre (1867–1900) was influenced by a neo-Romanticism that preached national values and gave free rein to emotion and deep

desire, to the nostalgic longing of Portuguese 'saudade'.

The result of the declaration of Italian unity in 1861 was the domination of cultural life at every level by the problems of nationalism. The scholar and poet Carducci was the fervent interpreter of a patriotic pride of his country's past; he thought that traditions should be maintained in order to favour the glorious renewal of the homeland. His metrically experimental collection of poems *Barbaric*

Odes influenced the young D'Annunzio in his collection *Primavera* (*Spring*, 1879). Through D'Annunzio, nationalist preoccupations became more general questions on the relationship between man and place, while this chivalrous poet delved into French poetry and German philosophy (Novalis, Schopenhauer, Nietzsche) to forge his own artistic identity. The spirit of modernism was pursued by the novelist and poet Antonio Fogazzaro (1842–1911), who expressed his views in *Ascensioni Umane* (*Human Ascents*, 1899).

The Flemish revival

The main review which inspired the literary revival in Flemish-speaking Belgium was *Van Nu en Straks* (*Now and Just Now*). The first ten editions (1893–1894) were published by Emmanuel de Bom, Cyriel Buysse, Prosper Van Langendonck and August Vermeylen. Henry Van de Velde, director of typography, established an important connection with the group Les XX (later called the Free Aesthetic) which represented both the avant-garde and the Modern Style in Brussels.

Van Nu en Straks was illustrated by Theo Van Rysselberghe, James Ensor, Georges Minne and Jan Toorop. The review did not present itself as a manifesto, but was, in fact, placed at the cutting edge of avant-garde publications. Its authors preached a global vision of the 'total man' and of 'life': they rejected the 'art for art's sake' movement. Ideal art must be a form of life nurtured at the heart of the community which would give individual emotion a universal meaning.

The second series of *Van Nu en Straks* manifested not only a particular interest in art and literature, but also a growing concern with social and political questions. In this series of the magazine, anarchist essays written by Mesnil, the verse drama *Starkadd* (*Flotsam and Jetsam*, 1898) by Alfred Hegenscheidt and the novel *Wrakken* (1898) by Emmanuel de Bom (1868–1953) appeared side by side. Streuvels, Van de Woestijne, Teirlinck and Van Boelaere collaborated in its publication. The ethical and aesthetic diversity of the magazine was such

that the reforming liberal and anarchist August Vermeylen could publish items alongside those by the Catholic reactionary Prosper Van Langendonck (1862–1920), by the symbolist Van de Woestijne and by the dilettante Hermann Teirlinck (1879–1967). **August Vermeylen (1872–1945)** was the co-founder and artistic director of the review. His novel *De Wandelende Jood* (*The Wandering Jew*, 1906), strongly influenced by Flaubert, tells the symbolic story of a man searching for truth. After a violent crisis of metaphysical anguish, he discovers it can only be found in an earthly and atheistic humanism in which love of life and the ethical responsibilities of social solidarity are balanced and in harmony with one another. Vermeylen exerted an enormous influence on the Flemish movement and its cultural life, in particular before the First World War, with his famous slogan: 'We want to be Flemings in order to become Europeans.'

The Hungarian 'secessionist' tendency

In Hungary the 'secessionist' tendency, present above all in architecture and painting, marked by an artistic interest in popular traditions – Malonyay Dezsö (1866–1916), *A magyar nép müvészete* (*The Art of the Hungarian People*, 1907–1922) – an interest that guided Béla Bartók's (1881–1945) first steps. The latter, together with Zoltán Kodály (1882–1967), undertook research into authentic folklore, basing himself on peasant oral traditions. This investigation ended with the publication of the famous *Magyar népdalok* (*Hungarian Popular Songs*, 1906).

In literature, apart from the nationalism of a certain political class that would brand the imagination of other countries in the Austro-Hungarian Empire (eventually neighbouring countries of Hungary itself), the period belonged to solitary individuals. The detailed historical descriptions by Géza Gárdonyi (1863–1922), which later proved to be very popular, were written in retreat from all literary life, in the author's provincial home (*Egri csillagok*, *The Stars of Eger*, 1901). Solitude in a remote province was the prerogative of many *fin de siècle* authors, for the most part short-story writers. Having retired to his native Transylvania, István Petelei (1852–1910) celebrated the sensitivity of marginal populations. But the truly symbolic figure was the prose writer **Kálmán Mikszáth (1847–1910)**. Beginning with populist short stories (*Tót atyafiak, Our Good Slovaks,* 1881), he became a master of irony and the portrayer of eccentrics in the style of Don Quixote (*Beszterce ostroma, The Siege of Beszterce,* 1895; Új zrinyász, The New Zriniad, 1898). The biographer of Jókai (1907), the author of a few great novels, social frescos of the nineteenth century (*Különös házasság, A Strange Marriage,* 1900; *A Noszty-fiú esete, Tóth Marival, The Story of Young Noszty with Maria Tóth,* 1908), Mikszáth had recourse to anecdote to create and parody his characters, and to the novel to preserve, at the same time, the privileged position of the narrator as both the peripheral and main witness of events in a universe where reality and appearance intermingled (*A gavallérok, High Society,* 1897).

TWO NEW THEMES: WOMAN AND MYTH

The sensibility of this *fin de siècle* divided between lucid rationalism and visionary escapism, allowed two themes to dominate literature: 'the woman question' and myth. Just as this period can be viewed simultaneously as regenerative and degenerative, so the literary treatments of women and myth are often inextricably linked. The political thinking that motivates literature of women's emancipation is enmeshed in myth, and the literary significance of myth can be politically driven.

The woman question

Whether or not the aim of texts written about the 'new woman' was to furnish literature with arguments about sexual equality or to give a picture of experience from a female viewpoint, women learned to express themselves during this period in a provocative manner. When Nietzsche could ask: 'Has woman lost her seductive side? Is she gradually becoming boring?' or stated: 'When a woman is interested in the things of the mind, there is generally something wrong with her sexuality', it seemed high time for women to answer with their own voice, like Nora in the final scene of Ibsen's *A Doll's House.* And they did. In Norway, Amalie Skram, with a whole series of novels, contributed to the debate on the position of woman in society and marriage: *Constance Ring* (1885), *Hellemystefolket* (*The Hellemyr People,* 1887–1898) and *Lucie* (1888). Callirrhoè Parrin (1861–1940) was the first Greek woman to become a journalist. She founded *I ephimeris ton kirion* (*The Ladies' Journal*) in 1888 and organised the first National Congress for Greek Women, who first met at the Acropolis in Athens in 1898. She also wrote the novels *I khiraphetimeri* (*The Emancipated Woman*), *I maghisa* (*The Witch*) and *To néon simvóleon* (*The New Contract*) in order to promote her liberating ideas. French novelists, Gabrielle Réval (1870–1938), for instance, in her *Lycée de jeunes filles* (*High School for Young Ladies,* 1901) and Colette Yver in *Helle* (1898) or Marcel Tinayre in *La Rebelle* (*The Female Rebel,* 1904–1905), described the psychological and political difficulties of emancipation. Its ideal was embodied in Poland during the era of modernism by the poet Maria Komornicka (1876–1948), who expressed a feminine eroticism up till then absent from Polish literature and came close to an expressionist aesthetic. She enthusiastically embraced certain elements of Nietzschean philosophy. Her poems, in the collection *Skice* (*Sketches,* 1894), often written in free verse or in prose, became an apology for total freedom for the individual and for woman.

In Great Britain, the emancipation of women was perceived as a human rights issue, suggested by the very title of the book by the liberal philosopher John Stuart Mill *The Subjection of Women* (1869). Eleanor Marx (1855–1898), Karl Marx's, daughter, published with Edward Aveling *The Woman*

Question: from a socialist point of view (1886). She spoke in this work of 'sexual slavery' and developed an analogy between the fate of married women and that of Black slaves.

Close relations existed between politics and fiction. The English author 'George Egerton' (1859–1945) wrote about her work: 'I realised that in literature, everything had been done better by man than woman could hope to emulate. There was only one small plot left for her to tell: the *terra incognita* of herself, as she knew herself to be, not as man liked to imagine her – in a word to give herself away, as man had given himself away in his writings.' Her first collection of stories, *Keynotes*, dedicated to Hamsun, was published in 1893, rapidly followed by another, *Discords* (1894). In a mixture of impressionist, realist and Utopian styles, she throws down an unmistakable challenge to a patriarchal society.

The works of English female novelists are often characterised by stilted and theory-laden speeches, a specific feature of these novels which contrasts oddly with their particularly careful stylistic realism. The collection of allegorical stories by Olive Schreiner (1855–1920), *Dreams* (1891), gives a mythical dimension to feminist Utopian visions. *The Heavenly Twins* (1893) by Sarah Gand (1854–1943) unveils the hypocrisy which exists with regard to women by examining attitudes to venereal disease. *TheSuperfluous Woman* (1894) shows how choices are limited, socially as well as sexually, for upper-class women. *The Daughters of Danaus* (1894) by Mona Caird (1858–1932) looks at the fate of creative women of independent means.

Male novelists were also interested in the theme of the sexual and social emancipation of women. *Tess of the D'Urbervilles* (1891) by **Thomas Hardy (1840–1928)** retraces the life of Tess, the daughter of a villager whose head has been turned by the idea of being a distant relation of the D'Urberville family. She also experiences the misfortunes of the seduced maid, the abandoned wife and a woman pushed to commit a crime of passion by a cruel twist of fate before being sentenced and hanged. *Jude the Obscure* (1895) presents us

with another complex female character. Hardy added some explicit preliminary remarks to this work in 1912: 'After the issue of *Jude the Obscure* as a serial story in Germany, an experienced reviewer of that country informed the writer that Sue Bridehead, the heroine, was the first delineation in fiction of the woman who was coming into notice in her thousands every year – the woman of the feminist movement – the slight, pale 'bachelor' girl – the intellectualized, emancipator bundle of nerves that modern conditions were producing, mainly in cities as yet . . . the regret of this critic was that the portrait of the newcomer had been left to be drawn by a man, and was not done by one of her own sex, who would never have allowed her to break down at the end.'

The indignant hostility with which the literary 'establishment' received Hardy's novel, and its representation of marriage as an outmoded social construct, showed the violence of the literary debate then raging in Great Britain on the subject of sexual emancipation. The denunciation of social hypocrisy and the appropriation of literary space by women to express their needs were nevertheless features of the art of this period which exerted a real and lasting effect.

This polemic also existed in other countries. In The Netherlands, Cornelie Huygens (1848–1902), after having studied economy, played an active role in the Sociaal-democratische Arbeiderspartij; she also used the novel to publicise her radical views on marriage, feminism and socialism in *Barthold Meryan*, (1857). As for the novel by Cecilia Goekoop (1866–1944), *Hilda Van Suylenburg* (1898), it provoked a political response, the pamphlet *De liefde in de vrouwenquestie* (*Love in the Woman Question*, 1898) by Anna de Savornin Lohman (1866–1930), which advised women to exercise restraint.

A free-thinking woman who defended the emancipation of women and rejected as a false dichotomy the choice between a husband and a career was **Lou Andreas-Salomé (1861–1937)**. In 1892 she published *Henrik Ibsens Frauen-Gestalten* on Ibsen's female characters, and, in 1899, addressed the 'woman question' in her essay *Der Mensch als Weib* (*The Human Being as Woman*), in which she opposes fashionable theorising. Woman must realise her potential by *being*, the man by actively *doing* something. She developed these views in an essay, *Gedanken über das Liebesproblem* (*Thoughts on the Problem of Love*, 1900) and in *Die Erotik* (*The Erotic*, 1910). In her novels too, *Ruth* (1895), *Fenitschka* (1898) and *Aus fremder Seele* (*From Foreign Souls*, 1901), she repeats that women will only find their satisfaction and emancipation by recognising and cultivating their own personal qualities.

Literature and myth

> Myths are at the very heart of our actions. We cannot act or live without walking towards a ghost.
>
> Paul Valéry (1871–1945)

> *Górgone antica ne la grande chioma,*
> *ella avea la potenza originale del Sesso. Era colei che non si noma.*
>
> *Ella era Circe ed Elena ed Onfale,*
> *Dalila meretrice da le risa terribili, Erodiade regale.*

D'Annunzio,
'Preludio', *Intermezzo*

This single multifaceted character takes the reader towards a more abstract category and makes individual identification harder. The reader approaching each one of these *femmes fatales* will be transfigured by the fear of the divine power with which they are endowed. Flaubert's novel *Salammbô* (1862) and his tale *Herodias* (1877) sparked off the literary use of the story of Salomé in the nineteenth century. In 1864, when Mallarmé began to write *The Wedding of Herodias*, this theme was addressed from a specifically symbolist perspective. Only

The end of the century was also characterised by a revisiting of ancient myths, reinterpreted by writers as various as Nietzsche, Renan or Mallarmé, and also by the creation of new mythologies. Greek myths structured works by **Friedrich Nietzsche (1844–1900)**,* Germanic myths those by Wagner, Hebrew and Christian traditions *The Life of Jesus* (1863) by Ernest Renan (1823–1892), mythological visions those by the symbolists. Sigmund Freud (1865–1939) researched on the origin of myths in the subconscious mind (*Über den Traum*, *On the Interpretation of Dreams*, 1900): the end of the century is haunted by myths.

Out of the wealth of mythological texts of this period a character detached herself who symbolised the ambiguity of the era, the *femme fatale*, who appeared in many guises: Circe, Helen of Troy, Pasiphaé, Galatea, Eurydice in the Greek tradition and, in the Hebrew tradition, Eve, Lilith, Judith, Dalilah and Salomé. D'Annunzio also introduces us to Herodias:

> *An ancient Gorgon with her long flowing hair*
> *she possessed the original power of the Sex. She was the one no-one named.*
>
> *She was, at one and the same time, Circe, Helen, Omphales*
> *and Dalilah, the courtesan with the terrible laughter, and the royal Herodias.*

a part of the dramatic poem that we have was published by Mallarmé in his lifetime, in the *Contemporary Parnassus* (1870). Huysmans, greatly impressed by it, refers to it in *Against the Grain*. Mallarmé was haunted by this story: he composed many fragments, subsequently gathered together under a single title. The way in which this work was conceived clearly changed in the course of thirty-five years. In 1864, Mallarmé had the idea of writing a verse tragedy, *Herodias*, but, abandoned the idea in 1865. In 1889, his description of the traditional events of the story were eclipsed by his personal expression of the subject of creative ideals. He wrote: 'The subject of my work is beauty . . . the obvious subject is only an excuse to go towards Her.' Wilde pursued this in his own *Salomé* (1892).

The creation of personal mythologies multiplied during this period: there is *Algabel* by George, for instance, and *Stichi o prekrasnoj dame* (*Verses on a Beautiful Lady*, 1901–1902) by Alexandr Alexandrovitch Blok. The Irish poet Yeats placed the character of Salomé at the heart of his personal mythology: as a young poet, he pillaged the myths of Ireland to enrich his poetry, associating images with it predominantly of the 1890s. He explains the poem 'The Hosting of the Sidhe' in *The Wind among the Reeds* (1899) by speaking of the gods of ancient Ireland (the 'Sidhe') who still comb the country as they did in days of yore. 'Sidhe' is also the Gaelic term for wind, and the 'Sidhe' do indeed have a lot in common with the wind. They move about in a tornado, and these winds were called in the Middle Ages the dance of the daughters of Herodias, who took the place of some ancient goddess.

During this period the theme was treated in different ways, as much in the visual arts as in literature and music. Wilde's play was illustrated by Aubrey Beardsley in 1893 and by Marcus Behar in 1903; it was set to music by Richard Strauss in his opera *Salomé* in 1905; Laforgue's story, *Salomé*, published in *Vogue* in 1885, was illustrated by Lucien Pissarro in 1897; in Portugal, Eugénio de Castro wrote four songs called *Salomé* in 1896, and the same year the Czech Alfons Mucha designed a colour lithograph, *Salomé*, for *L'Estampe*. Many women had their portrait painted as Salomé: Franz von Lenbach in 1894 painted *Mary Lindpainter als Tochter der Herodias* (*Mary Lindpainter as the Daughter of Herodias*, currently in the Neue Pinakothek in Munich); in 1894, Pierre Roche cast a bronze statue of *Loïe Fuller als Salome* (*Loïe Fuller as Salomé*, in the Museum of the Decorative Arts in Paris); Adolf Münzer showed Isadora Duncan as Salomé in the 1904 journal *Jugend* (*Youth*).

Decadence or transition?

The myth that underpins the whole of this period, the one that guides artists and politicians alike and which engenders a mixture of anxiety, profound pessimism and an optimism tinged with Utopianism, is that of the historic status of this *fin de siècle*. Is it an age of decadence and degeneration in every sense of the word or, on the contrary, an era of transition which, through its richness and complexity, heralds the new life of the twentieth century?

Aestheticism, decadence, symbolism are perhaps just so many ways of escaping from the same malaise: the paths of realism and naturalism, which made it possible to explore the world, but also exposed their own limitations. Science calls into question ideas considered stable and tries to impose its own dogmas. What is left to the writer so that he can escape from his 'materialistic penitentiary' in which Claudel would say that people tried to imprison his youth?

The cult of the senses, the interest taken in the body, give pride of place to Eros in literature*, making eroticism one direction forward. Verlaine and, above all, Rimbaud based their poetry on the 'deregulation of all the senses' in their quest for new forms. Nietzsche preached the transcendence of self and a rejection of all metaphysical idealism. But is man capable of leading his own life? No, says Chekhov with humour and tenderness. No, says Strindberg in despair. Poetic and introspective, the theatre of Maeterlinck does not have a positive answer either.

Eros in Literature

C. Purkis

In the beginning was sex. Sex is the basic substance of life, the stuff of evolution, the most intimate essence of individuality. Sex is the eternally creative principle, the force of destruction and disorder.

Stanisław Przybyszewski,
Mass for the Dead

Do we even have to say that literature, like other arts, has, since its origins, celebrated 'Eros'? The Old Testament, with the *Song of Songs*, celebrated the sacred in very sensual terms. Sappho, from her Greek isle of Lesbos, and Anacreon expressed the rapture of hetero and homosexual love. In Rome , Catullus and Propertius exalted the discourse of desire. One of the first French troubadours, Wilhem IX, Duke of Aquitaine, evoked both the modesty of courtly love and the excesses of physical passion, as later did Ronsard and Louise Labé. Hand-in-hand with this erotic strain of writing, the tradition of bawdiness was perpetuated in the *Decameron*, the *Canterbury Tales, Pantagruel and Gargantua,* who mingle the most serious moral commentaries with the crude celebration of joyful sexuality. The work of Lord Wilmot followed on in this tradition.

The evolution of eroticism

Although there are erotic works of great literary value, like *Fanny Hill* (1748) by Cleland or *Justine or the Misfortunes of Virtue* (1791) by the Marquis de Sade, it is not easy to make eroticism a real literary genre, with fixed characteristics. Sexuality is perceived culturally in different ways according to the period, and this diversity of perception leads to a different output and reception. In the nineteenth century, Eros played an increasingly prominent role, especially towards the end of the century, when it became one of the distinguishing marks of the decadent aesthetic. The erotically inspired fiction written during this period was described as 'pornographic' and hence belonged to an area that was unlike that of other literary genres. Works such as Baudelaire's *The Flowers of Evil* (1857) in France, or Swinburne's *Poems and Ballads* (1866) in England, allowed an erotic genre to emerge that was distinct from pornography. In order to express all aspects of human experience in new ways, the artist availed himself of Eros as a powerful weapon, an instrument of his revolt against the established values of

bourgeois culture. He needed to defy a *fait accompli*: the bourgeoisie controls sexuality by excluding it from highbrow art. The dominant ideology feared the strength of the 'natural' and the potentially anarchic energy of sexuality which can only be in opposition to the civilising forces of science, for example. Literature, more than any other art form, puts sexuality at the heart of artistic debate, refuses censorship and opposes the secret conspiracy that has gradually turned into an institution since the seventeenth century.

In the same way that before the 1890s, eroticism had its ups and downs, *fin de siècle* reactions to the challenge of eroticism varied considerably from country to country. In France, by virtue of a literary tradition dating back to the Middle Ages, the welcome extended to erotic works is more liberal than that in Germany or Italy. In England, on the other hand, where freedom of writing was strictly limited, a book like *The Picture of Dorian Gray* (1891) was stigmatised for its immorality although sex is hardly mentioned in it. French novels like *Nana* (1880), in which Zola deals with prostitution in the corrupt world of the Second Empire, had a considerable influence abroad. Reading such books in the original made it possible to defeat censorship and to discover how language, beyond realism, could convey the eroticism of desire.

During the 1890s the question of sexuality was debated more widely, both in scientific and sociological discussions and in international forums on art and its tendencies. Erotic literature was no longer limited to the description of physiological functions or purely physical passions. It began to analyse how sexual relationships work between men and women, socially and culturally. It also underlined the emotional, intellectual and aesthetic characteristics of desire and of the reactions it provoked. This literature proclaimed an awareness that Eros is a libidinal force which influences all human activities and can lay down the conditions for a new experience.

Wagner's influence

All over nineteenth-century Europe the same views on sex developed as a counterpoint to industrial society. Wagner's operas which became a veritable cult, made possible a collective awareness of eroticism. They sublimated desire within the conventions of a higher art form, and brought a message of redemption through erotic love. Their influence throughout Europe was obvious, despite the diversity of cultural traditions: in *Modernus* (1904) by Lilienfern, the unbridled sensuality of the decadent hero is aroused by the mystical discovery of the erotic effects of Wagner's music. The *Liebestod* of *Tristan and Isolde* (1859), evocative of an orgasm, has the effect of an aphrodisiac on the hero of *Zo'har* (1886) by Mendes, and has the same effect on the protagonists of *The Husband's Victory* (1889) by Péladan, *Evelyn Innes* (1898) by George Moore, *The Triumph of Death* (1899) by D'Annunzio and Thomas Mann's *Tristan* (1903).

Even more clearly, in *Wälsungsblut* (*Blood Set Apart*, 1906) by Thomas Mann, as in *The Twilight of the Gods* (1884) by Elemir Bourges, the music of the *Walkyrie* leads to the birth of a desire so uncontrollable and dangerous that the twins, Siegmund and Sieglinde, are impelled to reproduce the incest they have seen acted out on stage. Also inspired by Wagner, *Venus and Tannhäuser* (1907) by Aubrey Beardsley portrays an erotic fantasy on the mythical mountain of Venusberg, a pornographic Utopia poised between the good and evil of a conventional morality in which all perversions are permitted.

Naturalism

Naturalist writers, interested by the social organisation of sexuality and its implications, contributed, with some of their works, to the movements of emancipation which developed at this time. The constraints that civilisation imposed on the needs and desires of individuals are at the heart of Zola's *Thérèse Raquin* (1873) and Ibsen's *Rosmersholm* (1886) and

Hedda Gabler (1891). The most sordid aspects of sexuality also arrest the attention of writers: Ibsen's *Ghosts* (1881), a highly controversial play, dealt with the effects of syphilis, the most important sexual taboo of the period, and emphasised society's hypocrisy on this subject. The tragic consequences, for adolescents, of a poor sexual education are the subject of Wedekind's *Spring Awakening* (1891), a play considered to be too provocative to be performed in Germany until 1906. *A Doll's House* (1879) by Ibsen, *Mrs Warren's Profession* (1894) by Shaw, *Earth Spirit* (1895) and *Pandora's Box* (1904) by Wedekind are just so many realisations that sex, in marriage as in prostitution, is an object of exchange which the demands of conventional morality handle roughly.

Eros and death

A pathological Romanticism which associated sex with sin, suffering, degeneracy and death, had favoured the representation of the *femme fatale*, the embodiment of sexuality. This image continued to influence *fin de siècle* writers. A whole literature sprang up portraying women as sexually obsessed and therefore essentially diabolical. It acted as a catalyst to the apprehensions and morbid fantasies of a sexual nature on which patriarchal society was founded, the latter feeling itself at risk of being destabilised by female kind, the incarnation of the forces of nature. In *Salomé* (1892) by Wilde, for example, the death of the heroine appears as the direct consequence of an erotic passion that goes beyond the pale of what is socially acceptable. Bram Stoker's novel, *Dracula* (1897), in which the undead (who just happen to be women) personify masculine sexual aggression in a disturbing way because they are female, accentuates the fatal character of sexual instinct and the erotic character of the death wish. This duality is one of the characteristics of the individual and collective fears of the nineteenth century. It is found again in Przybyszewski's *Mass for the Dead* (1893) and in *The Other Side* (1909) by Kubin.

A morality of asexuality

While the novels of the beginning of the nineteenth century present marriage as the road to heaven and sex as the road to hell, *fin de siècle* literature presents a negative vision of all male–female relationships. We only have to read the vitriolic description of marriage in *The Dance of Death* (1901) by Strindberg. Huysmans in *Against the Grain* (1884), Rachilde in *Mister Venus* (1889), Joséphine Péladan in *Hymn to the Androgynous* (1891) and Przybyszewski in *The Androgynous One* (1906) sought to avoid being confronted by the other sex: in order to do this, they created a concept of 'asexual morality', a mixture of hermaphrodism, different sorts of chastity and homosexuality, which, until then, because of a certain voyeurism, were usually thought of as perversions.

The Utopia of a liberated eroticism

Next to the morbid vision of Eros, to the temptation to flee all relationships with the opposite sex, the *fin de siècle* found a third way to cope with its sexual difficulties: letting itself indulge in the fantasies of a liberated eroticism. Sex, emancipated from love and sin, was celebrated in Schnitzler's play, *La Ronde* (1897) in particular, and in the poems of Altenberg. The followers of Nietzsche ranged themselves against writers like Sacher Masoch who had described the pleasure taken in committing scandalous sins: in *Venus in a Fur Coat* (1870) he had affirmed that only masochism can produce sexual satisfaction. In *The Immoralist* (1902) Gide (1869–1951) gave a Utopian vision of a sexuality regenerated by total freedom and Stefan George sang a hymn to erotic homosexual love. Both went beyond the almost neurotic feeling of guilt which haunted the literary visions of sexual liberation of a Schnitzler or a Strindberg, for example. Written by women as well as by men, novels belonging to what was called a literature of 'the new woman' made war on the iconography of the time, in which feminine sexuality was represented in a negative and conventional way. They defended their different idealised visions of a sexual revolution which, in the spirit of the regenerative philosophy of the time, defied patriarchal morality and tended to develop a real relationship between human beings, which would serve as a foundation for a progressive humanitarian society.

Eros and criticism

More recently, erotic desire and sexuality have become objects of study in more and more varied fields. Criticism has picked up on them to use them as objects of cultural and philosophical analysis as with Georges Bataille, Marie Bonaparte, Michel Foucault, Peter Gay, Stephen Heath, Julia Kristeva, Kate Millett, Roger Scruton and Elaine Showalter.

Verlaine (1844–1896) and Rimbaud (1854–1891)

G. Fontaine

The poet–sage, the rebel, was seventeen. 'Oh let my keel shatter! Let me go into the sea!' his drunken boat screams. He has as his shipmate his elder by ten years who leaves behind his wife, his son and his job in Paris. Arthur Rimbaud (1854–1891), 'Husband from hell', drags off with him Paul Verlaine (1844–1896), 'Foolish virgin'.

Two years of frenzied human and literary adventure then began. 'Indeed I had, in all sincerity, committed myself to restoring him to his natural state as a son of the Sun, and we roamed around, nourished on the wine of cellars and the biscuit of the road, with me in a hurry to find the place and the formula.' ('Tramps' *Illuminations*).

The scandalous liaison is poetically fertile, but soon takes on the aspect of 'a season in hell'. It leads to separation: 'the noise of taverns, the mud of pavements' for Verlaine and for Rimbaud a time of poetic silence. The 'thief of fire' was now twenty.

Verlaine's limp

In the 1890s, after the death of Rimbaud, Paul Claudel, then a student, came across the elderly Verlaine in the street in Paris, and remembered 'the shock on the asphalt of the stick and the limping foot of the poor pilgrim, which seemed to my ears to scan the advice of his art of poetry: Prefer, poet, prefer, prefer, prefer unevenness!'

'Verlaine's limp, that wounded presence between heaven and earth' defined for Claudel both the work and the man.

It was not a case of 'ambiguity', but of 'duality': 'the angel' and 'the drowsy beast' were trying to live together. The adventure of Verlaine, the Catholic and the débauché, was all too human.

The wind-worn soles of Rimbaud

'You did well to leave, Arthur Rimbaud! Some of us believe without proof happiness possible with you,' exclaimed the poet René Char.

Verlaine, bewitched by 'Satan as a young man', Claudel, who received like a revelation the poetry of the 'saint of Charleville', Germain Nouveau, Drieu La Rochelle, Genet and Char all believe Rimbaud without proof.

That alchemist of poetry had definitely struck gold: 'Poetry has been touched,' Mallarmé announced during a lecture in Cambridge. But Rimbaud's true desire was to outdo Prometheus, to succeed where Christ had, according to him, failed. 'Jesus could say nothing to Samaria', 'to transform life'.

Did 'the departure in new noise and affection' celebrated by the *Illuminations* (1886) result from a perception of failure, serving as a prelude to Rimbaud's choice to be silent? The young man who turned his back on the world at the age of thirty-seven, after only a few years of public life, knew how pregnant with meaning was his enigma. The communist André Breton reproached him with this in the *Second Surrealist Manifesto* (1924): 'It's

no good continuing to discuss Rimbaud. We think him guilty of having allowed, of not having rendered quite impossible certain dishonourable interpretations of his thinking.'

Nietzsche (1844–1900)

J.-E. Andersen

> You must live so as to be master of your life and to wish for it to be made ever new.
>
> Friedrich Nietzsche,
> *Thus Spoke Zarathustra*

Is the Mediterranean haunted by the concept of a superman? Perhaps. The novel *The Virgins on the Rocks* (1895) by the Wagnerian Italian 'decadent' D'Annunzio gives us the portrait of Claudio Cantelmo, a nationalist epicure attracted by a certain type of necrophilia. His relationship with decadence and death are supposed to culminate in the resurrection of a 'superman'. In Marinetti's allegorical novel *Mafarka the Futurist* (1910), the character Mafarka embodies the superman as a futuristic technologist, while the heroes of the Cretan writer Kazantzakis, Zorba and his opposite Boss, personify the superman as a politically committed, existentialist celebrant of life on earth. These three very dissimilar portraits, all inspired by Nietzsche, are at the same time very different from the Nietzschean concept of the 'superman'. There is a difference between Nietzsche's philosophy and the ideas it inspired.

In the 1890s, Nietzsche was the subject of many debates, but his writings remained little known. In the twentieth century, Thomas Mann and Robert Musil were influenced by Nietzsche. Unlike the work of many other writers, their work seems to be more in keeping with his philosophy, the imprint of which influenced their style and their themes. Nietzsche's influence on European literature, from the 1890s on into the twentieth century, was indisputable.

Life and work

The critic Georg Brandes gave a series of lectures on the subject of Friedrich Nietzsche in Copenhagen, in April and May 1888. The following year he published a long article in German called 'Aristocratic radicalism. A study of Friedrich Nietzsche'. Brandes' article, together with the biographical portrait of Nietzsche written by the Swedish poet and critic Ola Thausson both greatly helped to dissipate the shadows round this still little known German philologist and philosopher. From the 1890s, he became a subject of controversy and a fashionable talking-point in *fin de siècle* culture.

Nietzsche and Brandes kept up a correspondence from 1887, and the latter was among those who received one of the mad letters at the time of Nietzsche's attack of dementia in Turin in January 1889: 'Having discovered me, it was not necessary to be a genius to find me! The hardest thing now is for you to rid yourself of me. The crucified one.'

Nietzsche was born in Roecken on 15 October 1844. After studying classical philosophy, he was appointed a philosopher at Basle in 1869, where he worked until he resigned for health reasons in 1879. Afterwards he lived mostly in Italy and Switzerland, where, often ill and alone, he wrote many of his major works before his personal crisis in Turin. After January 1889 and until his death in August 1900, he lived in mental and physical isolation, looked after in his mother's home in Namburg and, from 1897, at his sister's in Weimar.

Among the people who were significant for Nietzsche – Erwin Rohde, Jacob Burckhardt, Franz Overbeck, Paul Rée, Peter Gast, Lou Andreas-Salomé – Richard and Cosima Wagner were, without doubt, the ones who had the greatest influence on his life and thought.

Between Apollo and Dionysus

In 1866 Nietzsche read *The World as Repre-* *sentation and Will* by Schopenhauer which changed his self-image as a philologist and philosopher. In *Die Geburt der Tragödie oder Griechentum und Pessimismus* (*The Birth of Tragedy or Hellenism and Pessimism*, 1871), taking as his starting point the dichotomy Apollo–Dionysus, he traced the path of a watershed between reason and will, a break which had been a part of philosophy since ancient Greek times. The effort of the philosophical tradition to cultivate principles of rationality, the Apollonian aspect to Socratic dialogue, are, according to Nietzsche, the result of a degeneration which, far from healing the break, tries to hide it by means of illusions and new interpretations so as to repress the principle of Dionysian will. For Nietzsche the only way out is to let himself be inspired by the cult of Dionysus and pre-Socratic philosophy (Heraclites and Empedocles). The asceticism of Schopenhauer, the abnegation of life in Christian love and the morality of humanism, however, do not permit this. It can only come about as the result of a new aesthetic, such as is found expressed in the music of Wagner and his 'total' art.

This body of work constituted an important point of departure for Nietzsche's future philosophy. But deep transformations came into operation. So art, for example, lost its superior status: from *The Birth of Tragedy*, in which art was 'the highest duty and the most metaphysical, in the full sense of the word, activity of life', to the later works in which art is often, but not wholly, described as an illusion and a lie, there is evidence of this loss. In 1878 all this provoked a break with Wagner, whose late Romantic traits and Christian turn of thought will henceforth be described as lies and mystifications, continuing the same function as religion had for centuries.

After *Menschliches, Allzumenschliches* (*Ein Buch für freie Geister*) [*Human, All Too Human*, 1878–1880] and *Morgenröte* (*Dawn*, 1881), Nietzsche developed his aphoristic style. His style became refined and his thought split into radical and composite forms.

The 'will to power'

The concept of will that appeared in *The Birth of Tragedy* was transformed into a wider concept of 'will to power'. Where there is life, a will expresses itself. Interpretation is the will to give sense to the world. The more perspectives a particular interpretation suggests, the greater is the will to make sense of the world. Such an exploit is not for the weak. The latter take refuge in the illusion that there is only one sense to give to absurdity – faith in God is one of the most common of these illusions. Breaking with illusory all-encompassing interpretations means, above all, breaking with the asceticism of Christian thought, decreeing that God is dead and taking it upon oneself to re-evaluate all values.

Apart from 'the will to power', Nietzsche's concepts of a 'superman' and an 'eternal return' remained central to his philosophy and appeared in *Also sprach Zarathustra* (*Thus Spoke Zarathustra*, 1883–1885).

The idea of a superman does not have its source in the ideals of a race of 'aristocratic' lords, fair and muscular. The superman does not despair when faced with the absence of meaning that the 'death of God' can generate. On the contrary, he offers the possibility of winning and, in doing so, of mapping out an independent understanding of oneself and of the world without metaphysical constraints. This victory is permanent: it has no end, it repeats itself. Thus the superman can be – at least in several interpretations of him – associated with the concept of the eternal return: 'You must live so as to be master of your life and to wish for it to be made ever new.' The zenith of this new 'Kosmodicy' (justification of the world) is symbolised by an 'annulus æternitatis' (the ring of eternity): 'The sun of knowledge shines again on the southern meridian and the serpent of eternity coils up in its light – this is their time, my brothers of the south.' 'The will to power', 'the superman' and the 'eternal return of the same things' do not constitute 'the essence' of Nietzschean philosophy. These elements are in perpetual movement on the horizon of an anti-metaphysical and anti-pessimistic vision of the world. Nietzsche's readers are thus encouraged to create for themselves one or more readings of his texts and the world.

The influence of *Zarathustra*

The 'superman' was perceived in the 1890s as the central idea of Nietzschean philosophy, and many representations of the 'superman' blossomed in decadent art and literature.

The idea was formulated for the first time in *Zarathustra*. This work was received as the global expression of Nietzsche's 'teaching'. Philosophical in its prose, poetic in its style, 'Biblical' in its parables and 'prophetic' in its tone, the work seduced the literary élite of the 1890s. A 'new man' was portrayed in it who, 'by playing, flying and dancing', overcomes the metaphysical distress and sufferings of a people enslaved by a superhuman individuality, and a creative force, re-shaping values, becomes the image of a 'new' type of artist. Christianity and morality are also called into question in the works of the 1880s: *Die fröhliche Wissenschaft* (*The Gay Science*, 1882) describes, among other things, a new and freer type of man; *Jenseits von Gut und Böse* (*Beyond Good and Evil*, 1886) analyses the game of masking truth; *Zur Genealogie der Moral* (*The Genealogy of Morals*, 1887) satirises the Christian 'slave mentality'. Christianity and morality are also called into question in the late works: *Götzendämmerung* (*The Twilight of the Idols*, 1888–1889), which hammered home its philosophy, and *Der Antechrist* (*The Anti-Christ*, 1888). *Ecce homo*, Nietzsche's 'autobiographical' work, only appeared in 1908.

Because *Zarathustra* is a philosophical work filled with often hidden metaphors and symbols that are difficult to interpret, Nietzsche is regarded as a poetic philosopher – a fate he shares with Kierkegaard. But Nietzsche's style of writing is not, in the traditional sense of the word, 'poetic'; poetry is a constituent part of his manner of understanding philosophy. This is how his style appears in *Zarathustra*, in his aphorisms, in *Dionysos-Dithyramben*

(*Dithyrambs for Dionysus*, 1888) as well as in his short drama *Empedokles* (*Empedocles*, 1870–1871) inspired by Hölderlin. The language expresses a mind in revolt against moral, scientific and religious values. His theory of 'perspectivism' says it all: the world can be interpreted in a thousand different ways. The interpretations themselves give no inkling of eternal truth; they are rather provisional perspectives alongside other perspectives just as relevant.

Paradoxically, we are totally ignorant of the way in which Nietzsche – notably in *Zarathustra* – castigates poets with irony: in their desire to be 'radical', they precisely reproduce the conditions that the 'superman' is supposed to learn to overcome. Many writers influenced by Nietzsche seem to have been content to go through his texts, only seeking elegant, evocative and 'radical' formulations on everything and nothing. Stefan George seems to use his texts in this way, and above all *Zarathustra*, like an arbitrary mirror of his own ideas. 'Apart from his madness, Nietzsche's greatest misfortune was his success. For several years he was fated to be a fashionable thinker, an oracle of literature, a furnisher of phrases destined to be repeated in the circles of aesthetes. Many are those who thought they understood the philosopher because they liked the artist and this "literary" admiration rendered him suspect in the eyes of true philosophers. And neither side was entirely wrong,' Giovanni Papini pointed out in 1904 in *Criticism*.

A game of masks

Many serious readers of Nietzsche avoid designating a single character or a single thought as being the 'essence' of his philosophy. On the contrary, they constantly emphasise that his texts positively refuse to fit together. 'I am not so blinkered as to adhere to a system – and not even my own,' wrote Nietzsche. His task might rather be construed as designating possible ways of saying yes to life rather than saying what is implied by the fact that we do live. The strength of his texts is justly perceived as a sort of opposition to unity. Jacques Derrida raised the question of knowing if 'Nietzsche was not, like Kierkegaard, one of those rare people to reproduce his name and to play with signatures, masks and identities.'

Strindberg (1849–1912)

P. Stounbjerg

The question without an answer, doubt, uncertainty, mystery constitute hell for me.
August Strindberg

August Strindberg had the reputation of being a madman, a misogynist, someone who in his sinister dramas did not scruple to expose his own private life and that of others. It is all too often forgotten that he himself created the myth of Strindberg.

A life full of contradictions

According to his own words, Strindberg was born in the good old days, when there were oil lamps, stagecoaches and eight-volume novels. He died in his home town of Stockholm, having discovered the age of steam and electricity and having lived a nomadic existence. After his university entrance exam, he studied art, letters and medicine without finishing any of the courses. He tried unsuccessfully to be an actor. For most of his life, Strindberg lived by writing, first as a journalist, then, after the success of *Röda rummet* (*The Red Room*, 1879), as a novelist. For a time he was also employed by the Royal Library, in charge of the departments of the History of Art, Cartography and Sinology. Strindberg loved Stockholm and its coast fringed with islands, but nevertheless went into voluntary exile for more than ten years in Paris, Berlin and Copenhagen. Not one of his three wives was Swedish, and none of them corresponded to his concept of the ideal woman.

Strindberg never worked with his hands and understood nothing of nature; the experiences he described came rather from the sphere of personal intimacy: couples, sex and sensuality.

This narrow choice of theme was in contrast to a ferocious curiosity. His acute sense of journalistic observation complemented by wide reading gave him an eclectic range of knowledge, from chemistry to psychology, from linguistics to the occult. A constant and productive anxiety made him always change his mind. He was an atheist, an anarchist, a socialist, an alchemist, a Christian mystic, and always an ardent polemicist, always on the move and in contact with the latest ideas. His erudition has been compared to that of Goethe, but he was a hysterical version of Goethe and not an edifying model for others. He was an anxious and divided modern man.

The social observer

Strindberg published over a period that lasted more than forty years. His colossal work shows him to be a cultural historian, a philologist, a painter, a poet, a novelist and a dramatist. He wrote about religion, politics – and women. He wrote in many registers: didactic, realistic, historical, for example, in the novels *Den romantiska klockaren på Rånö* (*The Romantic Bellringer of Rånö*), which conjures up the intoxication of the senses, and *Hemsöborna* (*The People of Hemsö*, 1887), a humorous description of ordinary people's lives. But it was above all as a dramatist that he became famous in world literature, with more than fifty plays, magical compositions, dramas of religious pilgrimage, psychological studies, spectacular historical plays and short one-act plays.

Strindberg began by calling into question social and religious institutions: his decisive works were steeped in the radical and democratic ideal of freedom and in fundamental scepticism. *Mäster Olof* (*Master Olof*, 1872), written with the Paris Commune in mind, takes place during a period of social reform in Sweden, a period of transition in which oscillate the concepts of reason and error, truth and untruth. Olof, Strindberg's first great sceptical character, is torn between the revolutionary Gert Bokpräntare, who ends up by describing him as a 'traitor', and the pragmatic king, Gustav Vasa. This play breaks

with the conventions of historical drama: the action is not led by ideas and the characters are not monolithic.

Like an explorer, Arvid Falk, the disenchanted character in *The Red Room*, takes us through society's 'tissue of lies'; this novel, which satirised society in general, introduced the Modern Breakthrough in Sweden. Strindberg preferred a quickfire, natural prose to the breadth of an epic treatment, a prose born of precise observations which often tended towards grotesque caricature. This tendency cropped up again in the surrealist scenes of the pamphlet *Svarta fanor* (*The Black Flags*, 1907). In *Giftas* (*Married Couples*, 1884–1886), the stories are meant to show the importance of society in relationships between the sexes, and also the cost of fighting against it. After *Nya riket* (*The New Kingdom*, 1882), Strindberg became *persona non grata* in respectable Swedish society which put him on trial for blasphemy. At the same time, his anti-feminist portrayals of couples shocked and alienated many of his supporters. When the scandal had died down, Strindberg abandoned the criticism of democratic society for psychological studies of aristocratic and intellectual circles (*Vivisektioner*, *Vivisections*, 1887).

Taking his inspiration from the psychology of suggestion, Strindberg set out to present in minute detail and objectively 'the clash of heads'. *Fadren* (*The Father*, 1887), *Fröken Julie* (*Miss Julie*, 1888) and *Fordringsägare* (*The Creditors*, 1890) all have the battle of the sexes as their central theme. The manifesto of these basic works of naturalist theatre was written by Strindberg in the prologue to *Miss Julie*. *I havsbandet* (*On the Shore of the Great Sea*, 1890), the last novel of this first phase of Strindberg's work, in which Borg, a highly sensitive superman, dies at sea, 'the Mother of us all', was very influential.

Doubts and uncertainties

In the middle of the 1890s, Strindberg went through a violent crisis in which he totally revised his view of the world. From this emerged a strange written record of a conversion *Inferno* (1897). Strindberg believed himself to be persecuted and dominated by evil forces. He put his problems into a religious and occult perspective, preserving his sensations in a clear-cut way thanks to 'naturalist clairvoyance'. Strindberg's hell is a very modern one. In spite of its religious framework, the world has no coherent centre: in the place of God are diffuse 'powers' which are sometimes absolute authorities, sometimes nondescript vanities. But everything can change, and in the end, this book hesitates between doubt and faith: 'The question without an answer, doubt, uncertainty, mystery constitute hell for me.'

The poetic essays of the following years returned to a religious and mystical literary tradition, but in a dissolute and unstable world. They made Strindberg the creator of the modern, if not modernist, drama, hinting at surrealism and even the theatre of the absurd. In *Till Damaskus* (*The Road to Damascus*, 1898), everything and everyone bathe in an indefinable half-life. The characters are pawns in an obscure game in which nothing can be identified or fixed, in which changes of scale and transformations efface the solid co-ordinates of the legible world: action, space, time, the individual. Strindberg is also a contemporary of Einstein's theories: 'Where am I? Where have I been? Is it spring, winter or summer? What century am I living in? What world do I inhabit? Am I a child or an old man, a man or a woman, a god or a demon? Who are you? Are you you or are you me? Are these my intestines that I see around me? And are these stars or nervous reflections in my eyes? Water or tears?'

Strindberg's last plays were deeply influenced by ontological doubt. In *Ett drömspel* (*The Dream Play*, 1901), the use of repetitions, transformations and scene-shifting becomes systematic. Dream, poetry and reality are relocated in this panorama of passion. The pictures are not gathered around one single plot, they gravitate in a rhetorical fashion around the theme of 'Humanity is to be pitied'.

In *Dödsdansen* (*The Dance of Death*, 1900), the apparently realist marital conflict goes round in circles. The Captain, on the other hand, learns something of life and death. His apprenticeship is revealed by tell-tale signs. Stylised visual procedures break up the realism and make one divine the existence of a metaphysical conflict behind this hell on earth. Even the historical dramas like *Karl XII* (*Charles XII*, 1901) have allegorical overtones. In the Intimate Theatre of Stockholm, *Oväder* (*Storms*), *Brända tomten* (*Burnt-out House*), *Pelikanen* (*The Pelican*) and *Spöksonaten* (*The Ghost Sonata*), written in 1907, the principal role is played by houses, sinister houses. Strindberg is experimenting here with new dramatic forms which anticipate the theatre of the absurd.

Autobiographies

Strindberg the dramatist occupies an obvious place in world literature. He deserves another as an autobiographer. He intended to publish under a single title a dozen of his plays that he considered autobiographical. *Tjänstekvinnans son* (*The Servant's Son*, 1886) is the naturalist tale of a life founded on intellectual and artistic evolution. *Le Plaidoyer d'un Fou* (*A Madman's Plea*, 1887–1888), with its French title is a disturbing and dazzling novel about love, with a complex narrative. Strindberg's lucid self-portrait *Ensam* (*Alone*, 1903) avoids all explicit narration, and *Han och Hon* (*Him and Her*, 1906) constructs autobiographical fiction with an epistolary novel. This great series of self-representations weaves its way indecisively between fiction and genuine human document. The August Strindberg myth constitutes the raw material for writing which refused to respect the frontiers between different genres.

In the autobiographies, which reflect Strindberg's path towards modernism, the world increasingly falls apart as life is rewritten. *The Servant's Son*, in the end, refuses to identify the main character: it advises the reader to create his own character from one thousand pages of text. The maniac who speaks in

A Madman's Plea has still not learned anything about women or himself: in the final analysis, he becomes the plaything of suspicions, rumours and doubts. As for the *Inferno*, here the whole world dissolves in mobile energy and incomprehensible signs. In *Alone*, the poet is finally capable of accepting this situation. Doubt and versatility turn into productive methodology and impulse. Liberation is aesthetic: the poet as an artist is henceforth no longer the victim of a tormented life. Memories can, like 'building blocks', 'show their different colours on the surface'. We are now quite near to a dream poetic which is the aesthetic answer to a complex, multifaceted modern world.

Chekhov (1860–1904)

B. Kataev

To the devil with the philosophy of the great of this world!

Anton Pavlovitch Chekhov

'To the devil with the philosophy of the great of this world!' Chekhov wrote one day in a letter. This remark was addressed in the main to his senior and contemporary, the great Leo Tolstoy. 'Such a philosophy is not worth [. . .] even a mare from "Kholstomera".' In literature, no amount of theorising is worth a living artistic image. Literature, Chekhov asserted, must depict 'life as it is in reality', but it is 'easier to write about Socrates than about a young girl or a cooker'. To depict real life, then, is the aim that Chekhov set himself in his literary work, deliberately choosing the difficult in the name of the interest it would generate.

Depicting real life

In comparison with the intellectual giants and extraordinary characters of Tolstoy's novels, and even more so those of Dostoyevsky, Chekhov's heroes surprise us. More down to earth and ordinary figures, they are less interesting and more representative than Tolstoy's characters, and they could be anyone. The man in the street and the everyday are the principal subjects of Chekhov's work, who tries each time to show 'what a hotchpotch everyday life is' and to unravel the knots of tiny details that make up human relationships. Here is one of the secrets of the universality of his work, totally based on the reality of Russia at the end of the nineteenth and the beginning of the twentieth. Objectivity and justice are the most precious things for an artist. Chekhov thought that the most important thing for a writer was not to find, or even to look for, answers to the questions that he asked, but to ask 'the right questions'. This idea was foreign to the Russian literary world of the time, which included many professors and prophets. Critics never tired of accusing Chekhov of relativism and even of indifference. Chekhov's work, however, was not motivated by a refusal to answer questions *per se*, but by the desire to work out what was right in the way in which questions were phrased. And it was above all in the way he asked questions, in his vision of the world, that Chekhov's originality was revealed.

Tales, short stories, theatre

Chekhov chose to write in genres that Tolstoy and Dostoyevsky considered to be secondary: instead of writing novels he wrote hundreds of tales and short stories. He also wrote plays (seven major ones and ten lesser ones), on the subject of which he recognised 'that they show no respect at all for the rules of dramatic art'. But his originality and creative stamina made him the equal of the greatest of his contemporaries, and served for many as an inspiration for twentieth century prose and drama all over the world.

The choice of these three genres was only partly caused by chance. Chekhov began to write while he was still in high school: a great drama which fits perfectly into the tradition of the Russian novel and is characterised by its problems. Platonov, the hero, is a teacher in the provinces, a reluctant Don Juan, frivolous in his habits and with a provocative attitude, but nevertheless eager to discover his reason for being. In his monologues, Platonov puts himself, as well as those around him, on trial. This youthful work was still very much influenced by French melodrama (as a child Chekhov was passionately interested in the theatre), but beyond the shape of the play, it is already possible to detect what will motivate him throughout his work.

Chekhov's grandfather was a serf. His father was a grocer in provincial Taganrog. Chekhov studies at Moscow's Faculty of Medicine, cherishing a dream of entering Russian literary life by the main door. But his play was turned down by the Imperial Theatre of the Mali and he was unable to stage it. Twenty years old, a complete unknown, Chekhov began to work for small humorous journals.

His second major play only saw the light of day seven years later. But during those seven years, Chekhov never stopped working. Needing to struggle to survive, he multiplied the number of his minor literary labours. His meagre income not only had to allow him to live and study, but also to help his parents, his brothers and his sister. During these hard times he wrote works that are most imbued with joy and gaiety, often short and comic: about five hundred tales, sketches, parodies and farces. Having become a journalist and a doctor, he gradually enlarged his field of observation. He preferred to deal with 'more serious subjects' (although humour was never lacking). He began to write longer stories which amount to psychological portraits, case studies and character studies. By writing tales which were published in newspapers, he learned the art of brevity (which he called 'the sister of talent') and how to use the telling detail. He depicted scenes from everyday life and built dialogues on the most banal subjects, finding in this an inexhaustible source of inspiration.

Chekhov's descriptive prose offered an exceptionally wide cross-section of Russian life. It showed many aspects of it through many characters and situations. However, Chekhov always adopted the same point of view, thus creating a new type of action. In effect, Chekhov was especially interested in his hero's consciousness, in the attempts made by an ordinary man to 'find his way in life': he made the dawning of awareness the main action of his tales and then his plays. Rejecting his past ideas and illusions, a character suddenly discovers a new, unexpected aspect to his life. Arguments, betrayal, shots, duels and major revelations are now just appearances, pretexts which all converge on that moment of awareness. Hence the impression of 'inaction' given by his works. The action is there, though, but different. It is no longer so much about events or incidents, but about the consequences these can have on the hero who experiences them and on his awareness, about the change in attitude that is produced in him about different phenomenon, about the transition from 'impression' to 'certainty'.

So, Ivanov, the leading character in the play of the same name, considers himself as 'definitively dead' simply because the values which had served him hitherto as yardsticks are no longer valid and he has not found others to replace them. His conscience cannot allow him to live without 'belief, without love and without purpose', and he commits suicide on his wedding day. With *Ivanov* (1887), Chekhov depicts a situation taken directly from his age. For him, all respectable Russian society of the 1880s had, like his hero, in twenty years lost all its past beliefs; it had gone from being 'bubbly' to 'jaded'. The play, put on in 1887, was received with applause interspersed with whistles and had a mixed critical reception.

The psychological study of the hero

During these ten first years of writing, Chekhov perfected his technique of studying the hero psychologically. He was influenced in his analysis by Darwin, by the school of science that he attended at university, and by his experience as a doctor which taught him to 'think medically'. For Chekhov, it was important not to speak about an illness, but about particular cases, about each patient who exhibits a whole series of special individual peculiarities. Chekhov thought that complications make an illness interesting. So he tried to apply a medical principle which consisted in 'individualising each particular case', to literature and, through literature, to the study of life, psychological processes and human consciousness.

Where Tolstoy generalised, uttering necessary and universal truths, Chekhov particularised: he showed that life, in all its real complexity, can unexpectedly turn a man's destiny around. To the 'simple truth' valid for all Tolstoy's characters he opposes the multiplicity of circumstances which make truth more complicated and make it lose its absolute and universal character. Tolstoy himself appreciated Chekhov's talent and thought that he had created a 'new and original form of writing'. He liked Chekhov, but did not want to admit his refusal of the moral values that had been inculcated in him.

In his next major play, *The Wood Demon* (1890), Chekhov denounced the evil caused by men's habit of passing judgement on each other on the basis of prejudice, of labelling others, of making final judgements, of building their life on clichés and worshipping idols. But the play was a flop: it was said that Chekhov did not know the rules of dramatic construction and that it was more like a short story than a play. Later Chekhov reworked it more successfully and rechristened it *Dyadya Vanya* (*Uncle Vanya*).

In the meantime, Chekhov acquired the reputation for being the most talented writer of his generation and received the Pushkin Prize. Many people at the time did not understand that why, at the height of his success, Chekhov suddenly embarked on a journey of several months through Siberia to the penal colony on Sakhalin Island. In fact, Chekhov was motivated by a feeling then quite common among Russian writers: he felt himself responsible for all the misery in the world, to which the vast majority of people remained indifferent. 'We are all to blame,' he answered one day when he was asked why millions of people die in prison or penal colonies. He was so devastated by what he saw in Sakhalin that, as he himself, admittedly, the whole of his work was from then on imbued with this image.

Unfortunately this journey only served to make Chekhov's health worse – he knew he had tuberculosis – and strengthened the principles elaborated in his work. At home on his small estate of Melikhovo, not far from Moscow, he continued to write stories that his contemporaries saw as descriptive of the whole of Russia, such as *Palata n° 6* (*Room 6*).

But in 1896, nine years after *Ivanov* and seven years after *The Wood Demon*, he decided to return to the theatre with *Čajka* (*The Seagull*, 1896), a comedy whose hero commits suicide! Performed in the Alexander Theatre in St Petersburg, the first night was a total failure: the play, misunderstood by the actors, was mocked by the audience. We have to wait another two years for the opening of the New Moscow Art Theatre to see *The Seagull* triumph and become at one fell swoop the favourite item in that theatre's repertoire and a symbol of theatrical innovation. Chekhov married Olga Knipper, one of the Art Theatre's actresses, about this time. The letters they exchanged – Chekhov was obliged by his illness to live in Yalta – give us a lively picture of this last and greatest love of Chekhov's life.

Dramatic conflict according to Chekhov

The Seagull, then *Tri sestry* (*The Three Sisters*, a play written in 1901 for the Art Theatre), illustrate Chekhov's theory of dramatic conflict. This is not a conflict caused by ill will or malevolence in one of the characters. What Chekhov most often describes is antagonism born out of mutual incomprehension. This incapacity to understand others stems from the fact that everyone is blinded by their own 'questions', their own 'truth' and their own 'erroneous conceptions'. So where others would only have seen incompatibility and disharmony, Chekhov reveals the identity of two antagonists: in *The Seagull*, the characters seem to have diametrically opposite ideas about love and art, and yet discover points in common hitherto hidden. The same is true of *The Three Sisters*, in which the main theme of Chekhov's work (man's aptitude to 'make his way in life', and not only in the bosom of his family) is taken up throughout the play by each of the main characters through their thoughts, words and actions. So the author's vision of life is not just revealed by the play's leading character, but shared out equally among several characters, and sometimes even among all of them. Conscientious readers of *The Seagull* will have been struck by 'the drama and the tragedy which are hidden behind each of the characters'. It was necessary for the theatre to modify its approach so that the troupe could act harmoniously, and so that the things hinted at and left unsaid in the play could be understood.

Chekhov was already battling with death when he wrote *Višněvyj sad* (*The Cherry Orchard*, 1904). The themes of the dying orchard and a love which is silent and ignored are closely linked and give to the play a poetic veneer of sadness. Chekhov, however, insisted that it was not a drama but a comedy, even in places a farce. The play's comic aspect does not just stem from the characters. The relationships between the protagonists and the dialogues they exchange almost always indicate the mutual ignorance they have of their divergent opinions and the illogicality of their deductions. To this must be added unexpected repartee, funny reiterations and subplots. All these imperfections in reasoning and action lend themselves to laughter. The moving and pathetic monologues that almost all the characters utter are systematically followed by a comic effect, itself tied into a lyrical note which allows us to understand the subjective conviction and emotion of the character, whose blindness once more leads to mockery. Throughout his work, Chekhov's characters clash with reality, with the author reaffirming through the conflicts that all his characters share a common fate and resemble one another despite appearances to the contrary, blown to and fro by a life they cannot control. It was in *The Cherry Orchard*, Chekhov's last great play, that he created the quite singular genre which suits the demonstration of this principle.

Шарлотта (в раздумье). У меня нет настоящего паспорта, я не знаю, сколько мне лет, и мне все кажется, что я молоденькая. Когда я была маленькой девочкой, то мой отец и мамаша ездили по ярмаркам и давали представления, очень хорошие. А я прыгала *salto-mortale* и разные штучки. И когда папаша и мамаша умерли, меня взяла к себе одна немецкая госпожа и стала меня учить. Хорошо. Я выросла, потом пошла в гувернантки. А откуда я и кто я - не знаю . . . Кто мои родители, может, они не венчались . . . Не знаю. (Достает из кармана огурец и ест.) Ничего не знаю.

CHARLOTTA (dreamily) I don't have a real passport, I don't know my age, and it always seems to me that I am very young. When I was very young, my father and my mother did fairs, they gave performances, very good performances. I would perform the salto-mortale and all sorts of tricks. And when mum and dad were dead, a German lady took me in, and she it was who brought me up. Well. I grew up and then I was placed as a governess. But where I come from, and who I am – I don't know . . . Who my parents were, if they were married . . . I don't know. (She takes a cucumber out of her pocket and bites into it.) I don't know anything about anything.

Chekhov died in Badenweiler, a German spa town in which he was taking the waters, leaving many writing projects unfinished. The day after his death, Tolstoy, evaluating the importance of Chekhov's work for Russian and world literature, declared: 'He was a writer without equal, a painter of real life . . . What makes the value of his work is that not only Russia, but the whole world can understand it and see itself reflected in it . . . And that is the most important thing.'

Maeterlinck (1862–1949)

M. Otten

They're poisoning someone in the garden!
The enemies are giving a great feast!
Maurice Maeterlinck,
'Hospital'

Maeterlinck's early work – his only work that really counts – is vital for symbolism. Probably better than anyone the author of *Serres chaudes* (*Greenhouses*, 1899) fulfilled a part of the promise of post-Mallarmean aesthetics: he endowed symbolism with a theatre which is still staged and introduced into poetry the vertigo of surrealist imagery.

Maeterlinck owed his superiority over most of the symbolists of his generation to his ethnic origin. A Belgian, a French-speaking writer from Flanders, with a reading knowledge of German and English as well as Dutch, he was able, unlike most Frenchmen, to make contact with the genuine roots of symbolism: German idealism and its remote source, Rheno-Flemish mysticism (Master Eckhardt, the Admirable Ruysbroeck).

The mysterious side to things

Born in Ghent in 1862, Maeterlinck studied law without any great conviction: he was only interested in literature. Between 1885 and 1886, during a stay in Paris, he visited the circles of Mallarmé's young disciples. He had the opportunity to meet Villiers de l'Isle-Adam, who steered him towards 'the spiritual, poetic and mysterious side to things' and introduced him to the riches of German idealism (Fichte, Hegel, Schopenhauer).

At the same time, Maeterlinck discovered a fourteenth-century Flemish mystic, the Admirable Ruysbroeck, and decided to make him known. In 1891 he published a translation of *The Adornment of a Spiritual Wedding*. In a long introduction, he declared that Ruysbroeck allowed him to trace the symbolism which was then emerging in Paris and which he subscribed to himself to its source. 'Since I read Ruysbroeck,' he pointed out, 'our art no longer seems to me suspended in a vacuum.' In Ruysbroeck, he also made the discovery that, beyond reason, there exists 'the abyss of the soul', that 'dark' sea in which the mystic can 'touch' his God.

From then on, Maeterlinck only had faith in the intuitive riches of the Germanic world; he wanted to break with the spirit of French literature which seemed to him to be dominated by a narrow rationalism. In order to go deeper into the way opened up by Ruysbroeck, he devoted himself to Novalis whose *Fragments* and *The Disciples at Saïs* he translated. Through Novalis he entered into contact with the great themes of the Romantic school of Jena, that innovative aesthetic of which symbolism is a direct derivative. Novalis also made him sensitive to the importance of a subconscious life and permitted him to grasp the true nature of the symbol, an intuitive interpretation of worldly forms, opposed to the more inflexible and more stereotyped procedure of allegory.

The works published between 1889 and 1896 all bore the mark of this particular formation, leaning towards things Germanic and the Germanic world.

A theatre of the soul

The originality of Maeterlinck's first theatrical productions must be placed in the context of the evolution of the European drama at the end of the nineteenth century. In his *Theory of Modern Drama*, Peter Szondi has shown that after 1880 five great dramatists – Ibsen, Chekhov, Strindberg, Maeterlinck and Hauptmann – transformed the classical drama, until then devoted to the relationships which opposed human beings to each other.

However, among these five innovators, Maeterlinck occupies a place apart: he is the only one to have created a radically new dramatic form. He alone dared to execute a theatre of pure inwardness (a theatre of the soul), such as symbolism had dreamed of.

In the eight plays that appeared between 1889 and 1894, Maeterlinck's aim was clear: he wanted to portray on stage a dimension of man which, up until then, had only been sporadically suggested by the greatest of dramatists (like Shakespeare in *Hamlet*): the soul in its most mysterious inner life, that 'transcendental self' whose existence Ruysbroeck and Novalis revealed to him and that only begins where reason leaves off.

He established a theatre of the soul and tried to make perceptible the dialogue of the soul with its destiny.

Theatrical innovations

Such an experimental programme, which Maeterlinck only realised in three plays – *Intérieur* (*Interior*, 1894), *L'Intruse* (*The Female Intruder*, 1890) and *Les Aveugles* (*The Blind*, 1890) – led him to a radical transformation of the concept of classical drama. He proposed a series of innovations which he defined in a few key concepts: the sublime character, the static drama, everyday tragedy. To make the soul of the world tangible, Maeterlinck introduced what he called the third character or 'sublime character'. He defined this as an invisible, omnipresent power, a sort of 'unknown character without a face' which is introduced into the action and weighs down on humans who are disarmed by it. Only those whose soul is awake can perceive it. It is, if you like, Destiny or Fate. Striving to make this sublime character concrete, Maeterlinck made it in turn death (*L'Intruse*), unhappiness (*Intérieur*), anguish (*Les Aveugles*), the old cruel queen that no one has ever seen (*The Death of Tintagiles*, 1894), a character who has been too quickly identified with death and who is perhaps the premonition of a power more cruel and more obstinate than death. In his masterpiece, *Pelléas and Mélisande* (1892), love forces its way in; but it is a love that leads of necessity to death. Love and death are therefore, here too, at the service of an inscrutable destiny.

The second concept, the static drama, can be summed up as follows: only the sublime character is active, the others are stationary because they are impotent, frozen in expectancy, but mainly because their immobility is the best way of making them receptive to the Unknown which steps forward in the darkness. Maeterlinck was convinced that the essential can only rise to the surface when human agitation, adventures and struggles have stopped. He dared to imagine that the spectacle most charged with humanity would be that of 'an old man sitting in his armchair, simply waiting under a lamp'. This is the extreme form of a static theatre, in which Maeterlinck claims to find the germs of Aeschylus and Sophocles, and in the character of Hamlet, he who does not act.

This static drama must moreover portray ordinary situations and perfectly banal characters. It is the simple fact of being alive which is tragic. To portray heroic exploits, some of the mighty of this world, prestigious action is ultimately superficial, for it is not in paroxysm that the soul awakes, but in the simplicity of the everyday. *Intérieur* and *L'Intruse* will dare to go as far as this stripping everything bare.

Like all the symbolists, Maeterlinck tried to replace the classical actor. This was because the individual actor, with his distinct personality, his psychology, his body, acted as a screen for the deep meaning which he is supposed to manifest. The human presence stops the symbol from emerging. Maeterlinck dreamed of 'a theatre of androids' and explicitly subtitled three of his plays 'short dramas for marionettes'. As Rilke observed, he wanted a more abstract actor, who by a simple and stylised method of acting would suggest the major attitudes of the soul confronted with destiny.

Another way of avoiding the cumbersome individuality of the actor is to dilute the individual character in a group which reacts more anonymously to disturbing manifestations. These groups recall the ancient Greek chorus in tragedies. For example, there are the three sisters in *L'Intruse*, the various groups of blind people in the same play, the family in *Intérieur*.

Since action has almost been eliminated, words will acquire even more importance. But not just any words. Maeterlinck expects nothing from ordinary dialogue, which accompanies and explains actions; it is necessary, but it does not touch the deeper meaning of the drama. The ideal, for him, would be to keep to a bare minimum this external dialogue to favour 'dialogue of the second level'. The latter seems at first sight superfluous, because it is unexpected, out of place in relation to appearances; but only this type of dialogue is 'in conformity with a deep-seated truth and incomparably closer to the invisible soul which sustains the poem'. Much more powerful than the deepest word, active silence is the true language of the soul and essential encounters. In the same way that he postulated a static theatre, Maeterlinck dreamed of a drama that would only consist of silence: an encounter with the unknown. In concrete terms, he limited himself to inserting tense silences into his dialogues, often themselves only made up of snatches of conversation. In *Les Aveugles*, for instance, these silences allow us to perceive the worrying noises which signal the approach of threatening powers:

> – *Can you hear the dead leaves?*
> – *I think someone is coming towards us . . .*
> – *It's the wind. Listen!*
> – *No-one else will come now!*
> – *The big freeze is coming . . .*
> – *I hear someone walking in the distance.*
> – *I can only hear the dead leaves!*
> – *I can hear someone walking along way off!*
> – *All I can hear is the north wind!*
> – *I'm telling you someone's coming towards us!*
> – *I can hear a noise of very slow footsteps. . . .*
> – *I think the women are right!*

Critics who have placed the accent on the omnipresence of death in Maeterlinck's plays are not wrong, but, in doing so, they have unfortunately reduced his theatre to a banal philosophy and have obscured the novelty of his dramatic construction. For death is only one possible manifestation (admittedly the most compelling) of the 'sublime character'; there are others. The fact that death has the last word in all the dramas must not make us forget that the essential thing in the drama is the slow approach of the sublime character; or, in other words, the soul's awakening to its destiny.

Maeterlinck's influence

Such theatre could not be performed immediately according to the aesthetic that had inspired it. Nineteenth-century directors and actors, brought up to quite a different style of acting, more often than not failed to understand this almost abstract drama. Some twentieth-century productions, more sensitive to this minimalist art, make us think that we are gradually getting closer to the theatre envisaged by Maeterlinck, but the latter still has to be invented.

None of this prevented Maeterlinck's first plays from exerting a profound influence on European theatre from the end of the nineteenth century. Nearly all the great dramatists of the first half of the twentieth century have gone through their Maeterlinck period and have composed short dramas 'in the manner of' *L'Intruse* or *Les Aveugles*. It is as if access to a certain theatrical modernity had to pass through a sort of Maeterlinck stage – we could cite Rilke, Hofmannsthal, Trakl, Strindberg, Crommelynck, Ghelderode, D'Annunzio. Wispianski, Pessoa, Lorca and Azorín. All in all, it is in France that the influence of Maeterlinck has penetrated least and lasted least.

Maeterlinck's poetry fits in its entirety into two slim volumes: *Serres chaudes* and *Douze Chansons* (*Twelve Songs*, 1896), later to become *Quinze Chansons* (*Fifteen Songs*). From this conglomeration the seven poems in free verse of *Serres chaudes* emerge, surprising in their modernity. In 'Hospital', for example, an unusual proliferation of images gives birth to a dream world in which the soul seems to grope for contact with a reality which shies away from view and in which 'nothing is in its right place':

> They're poisoning someone in a garden!
> The enemies are giving a great feast!
> There are stags in a town under siege!
> And a menagerie in the middle of the lilies!
> There is tropical vegetation at the bottom of a coal field!
> A flock of ewes crosses over an iron bridge!
> And the lambs of the plain go sadly into the meeting room!

With the years, the contradictions became more accentuated, but Maeterlinck accepted them. If his thought was increasingly orientated towards a philosophy of agnosticism, his mystique remained essentially a mystique of waiting.

These images set free had a decisive effect on Apollinaire, on the French surrealists (Breton, Éluard, Artaud), and on some of the German expressionists (Benn, Trakl, Heym).

Maeterlinck's work as a prolific essayist, (twenty volumes) met with a good reception from the general public. *The Life of Bees* (1901) went through innumerable reprints and as many translations. The book still has its supporters. But we must consider as peerless *The Treasure of the Humble* (1896), a collection of essays contemporary with the symbolist period. In a style which owes more to suggestion than analysis, Maeterlinck develops an essentially mystical series of meditations. By means of a few special experiences (silence, everyday tragedy, femininity), he tries to define the deep life of the soul, of that transcendental self that Novalis had revealed to him. In the essays which follow, despite certain hesitations which have led to Maeterlinck being taken for an agnostic, he remained faithful to what he wrote in 1897: 'The deepest thing in man is his desire for God.' His long investigation into man's limits and the enigma of the world oscillates constantly between discouragement and recourse to an unknown God that he wants to safeguard against any mutilating definition.

15 *The First Decades of the Twentieth Century*

M. BOUSSART

Art in one sense has its revenge on life, for what it creates is real creation in the sense that it is not dependent on time, or freaks of fate or obstacles, and has no other end but itself.

Luigi Pirandello,
Tonight we Improvise

The beginning of the twentieth century is a period in which intellectual sparkle and cosmopolitanism go together. In Paris, where the Universal Exhibition opens its doors, a new world seems to emerge, a world of opulence and audacity. Confrontations between the great colonial powers and nationalist tensions in the Balkans do not appear to tarnish the colours of the Belle Époque. However, some years later, in spite of the universalist ideas which began to see the light of day, the First World War breaks out, a conflict without precedent out of which Europe will emerge in a state of total upheaval and exhausted. The revolutionary movement which shook Russia in 1917 had repercussions in many Western countries.

These different events made a deep impression on European literature which went, not without fits and starts, from rediscovered classicism to modernism, and even as far as avant-gardism.

TRANSFORMATION AND CONTINUITY

The twentieth century resolutely turned its back on positivism, but it did not shake off the past altogether. In the case of many literary trends, we can talk in terms of the transformation of traditions. The areas of symbolism, classicism, romanticism and realism were re-explored.

The movement of ideas

The beginning of the century was marked in the history of ideas by the desire to limit the ascendancy of the scientific method and of positivism, which symbolism and the decadent movement had already weakened at the end of the nineteenth century. In Germany, Wilhelm Dilthey emphasised that the methods of the natural sciences were not applicable to the social sciences, in which intuition and sympathy had their part to play. In France, Ferdinand Brunetière, converted in 1900 to Catholicism, Maurice Barrès and Paul Bourget, in Italy, Benedetto Croce and Giovanni Gentile rose up against the abuses of positivism. European letters became richer with the ideas of Kierkegaard and Dostoyevsky and with their attraction for the irrational side of human behaviour. The pessimism of Schopenhauer, the exaltation of Nietzsche's vital urge, the intuitions of Bergson, his theories on memory and subjective time, broadened literature's investigative scope. Freudian psychoanalysis, and William James' exposure of the 'current of consciousness', of the role of the subjective in the apprehension of reality, made a deep difference to the psychological novel. The phenomenology of Husserl placed the accent on the *a priori* data of experience and on intentionality.

A number of writers exalted life forces and rediscovered the power of desire, instinct and sexuality: Gide in France, Przybyszewski in Poland, Dehmel in Germany, D'Annunzio in Italy, Kazantzakis in Greece and Lawrence in England. This vitalism was often linked to a vision of the unity of beings and things beyond frontiers.

Work by the Cretan writer and thinker **Nikos Kazantzakis (1885–1957)** bear the stamp of a deep spiritual restlessness and an indefatigable search for God (*Askitiki, Asceticism*, 1927). He went beyond the currents of thought that traversed the first decades of the century, regarding them as so many necessary stages to attain the highest summit: salvation of the spirit. This summit can be conquered in two ways: by the way of the flesh and the way of spiritual asceticism. The two types of man who follow these courses have in common a constant striving for perfection, the heroic attitude of the combatant, pride and intransigence and, last but not least, freedom from all hope of consolation, man's highest freedom.

The inner life is something too that Paul Bourget (1852–1935), Léon Bloy (1846–1917) and **Charles Péguy (1873–1914)** actively advocate. In verses inspired by the Bible and the rhythms of the litany, Péguy exalts Christian virtues and celebrates the land of France in *La Tapisserie de Notre-Dame* (*Our Lady's Tapestry*, 1912) and *Ève* (*Eve*, 1914). Poetry and drama by **Paul Claudel (1868–1955)**, with its mystical accents, speak of the struggle between hope and the temptation of despair, the being torn between attachment to the flesh and the call of the sacred: in both his lyrical work (*Five Great Odes*, 1910) and his drama (*Partage de midi*, 1906; *The Hostage*, 1911; *The Tidings brought to Mary*, 1912; *Hard Bread*, 1918; *The Satin Slipper*, 1929). An analogous mystical renewal appears in many other European countries: in England, Flanders, Germany, Hungary, Bohemia and Russia.

The exaltation of national and patriotic values asserts itself at the turn of the century with **Gabriele D'Annunzio (1863–1938)**[*] in Italy, Barrès and Charles Maurras (1868–1952) in France. George opposes to the mediocrity of his age the greatness of the German emperors, while Kipling celebrates the British Empire. The great poetic syntheses of Palamas, the prose works of Pinelopi Delta (1872–1941) sing of Hellenism. In Portugal *c.*1912 'saudosismo' develops, born in Porto around **Joaquim Teixeira de Pascoais (1877–1952)**, who tries to define 'the national soul', whose most important trait is the untranslatable 'saudade' (the juxtaposition of 'salutatem' and 'solitatem': memory, regret occasioned by absence). A vehement nationalism drives work by the Rumanian Octavian Gogá (1881–1938) and that by the Hungarian Dezsö Szabó (1879–1945).

In Italy, the humanism of **Benedetto Croce (1866–1952)** stands in contrast to D'Annunzio's nationalism. His aesthetics (*De Estetica*, 1902; *Poesia e non poesia*, 1921–1922) define art as a form of knowledge based on intuition and slanted towards the individual.

In France, to the slogans Nation, King, Army, Church by Barrès and Maurras correspond the universalist thought, the pacifism and the tolerance of Anatole France (1844–1924), Romain Rolland and Alain (1868–1951). Ortega y Gasset (1883–1955), leading light and driving force behind *novecento-*ism, influenced by the vitalism of Dilthey, reinforces with his *Review of the West* that opening-up of Spain to the rest of Europe – to German culture in particular – and to the civilisation of America.

Of quite a different order is the influence exerted by 'the disturber', 'the awakener' **André Gide (1869–1951)** on many minds between the wars. The calling into question of conventional moral values, egotism and the cult of novelty are received as an exhortation to independence of spirit and a refusal of 'rootedness'.

The heritage and superseding of symbolism

Turn of the century literature cannot be thought of without the ground-breaking efforts of symbolism. It went on in Belgium till the eve of the First World War, opening up to the world of that period and becoming orientated to a vitalist symbolism perceptible from the 1890s. It is there in the great collections of Verhaeren, *Les Forces tumultueuses* (1902), *La Multiple Splendeur* (1906), *Les Heures d'après-midi* (*Afternoon Hours*, 1905) and *Les Heures du Soir* (*Evening Hours*, 1911), in *La Chanson d'ÈE[lac]ve* (*The Song of Eve*, 1904) by Van Lerberghe, in work by Max Elskamp (1862–1931) and by Mockel. Just after the war, various poetry collections by

Elskamp, by Mockel, as well as the first works by Franz Hellens (1881–1972), Jean de Boschère (1878–1953) and Charles Plisnier (1896–1952) continue in this vein.

As far as Flemish poetry goes, collections of poems before 1909 by **Karel Van de Woestijne (1878–1929)** constitute a sort of lyrical autobiography characterised by a diffuse melancholy and a musicality caused by a subtle dosage of assonance.

Het huis mijns vaders, waar de dagen trager waren, was stil, daar't in de schaduwing der tuinen lag en in de stilte van de rust-gewelfde blaeren.	*The house of my father, where the time passed slowly, rested peacefully in the shade of gardens and the quiet dome-like silence of the leaves.*

Karel Van de Woestijne,
Het Vaderhuis

In the following works, more sober, sometimes hermetic, the inner life of the poet appears to be dominated by the dichotomy between a sensualist vitalism and mystical asceticism (*De Modderen Man, The Man of Mud*, 1920), only to become calmer later on (*God aan Zee, God at the Seaside*, 1926; *Het Bergmeer, The Mountain Lake*, 1928).

In Germany, George, the youthful Rilke and even Hofmannsthal remained faithful to the symbolist aesthetic at the turn of the century. Afterwards they evolved in the direction of a more sober style. George's lyricism after *The Seventh Ring*, became more solemn when he condemned the bourgeois civilisation of his time (*Das neue Reich, The New Reign*, 1928). Rilke's first collections are characterised by a diffuse pantheism and preciosity of style. Certain recurring themes emerge from *Das Buch der Bilder* (*The Book of Pictures*, 1902) and *Das Stundenbuch* (*The Book of Hours*, 1905): evocations of young women and pages, angels, madonnas and gardens. Rilke afterwards tended towards a less emotional style of writing, although symbolist and decadent traits were not wholly eliminated.

Hungarian symbolism is represented by Ady and Babits. **Endre Ady (1877–1919)** had

a unique literary destiny. A poet accursed and a national poet, he feels himself to be at one and the same time the rebellious victim and the hero of 'the Hungarian hell'. The leader of the innovators of the review *Nyngat* (*West*), influenced by the French symbolists, his *Új versek* (*New Poems*) and his subsequent works (*Az eltévedt lovas, The Lost Horseman*) were received with as much hatred as enthusiasm. His work constitutes a watershed in modern Hungarian letters. Dezsö Kosztolányi (1885–1936) retains for a long time the decadence and fluidity of Rilke's language, before developing a sparser style of writing. Musicality also characterises tales of Gyula Krúdy (1878–1933).

The Dane **Johannes Vilhelm Jensen (1873–1950)**, whose first works still contain a great deal of symbolism, undergoes a veritable change of heart in theme and style in his historical novel set during the time of the Revival, *Kongens Fald* (*The Fall of the King*, 1900–1901). It places the accent on the fragility of man as subject and is innovatory in the intensity of its style and the priority given to atmosphere. In the years that followed, Jensen and Hamsun concentrated on confronting man with industrialisation and

'Americanism'. The reaction was enthusiastic to Jensen's *Madame d'Ora* (1904) and *Hjulet* (*The Wheel*, 1905), and there was critical rejection on the part of Hamsun, notably in his trilogy of novels (*Landstrykere, The Vagrants; August, August the Sailor; Men livet lever, And life goes on*, 1927–1933). Jensen shared with Hamsun a fascination for myth and the purity of origins.

The collection by **Antonio Machado (1875–1939)**, *Soledades. Galerías. Otros poemas* (*Solitude. Tunnels. Other poems*, 1907), shows a strong feeling of the temporal expressed with the help of symbolic words mingling dream and reality, in which the 'Tunnels' are the imaginary spaces within solitude. With *Campos de Castilla* (*Castilian Landscapes*, 1912), the poet passes from the subjective sphere to ethical and social reflection to denounce the backwardness of Spain. **Juan Ramón Jiménez (1881–1958)** also begins with decadent sensibility in *Ninfeas* (*Water Lilies*, 1900) and *Almas de violetas* (*Souls of Violets*, 1900) before teaching a more rigorous poetry in *Eternidades* (*Eternities*, 1917): 'Intelligence, give me / the exact name of things!' He

abandons the poetry of suggestion for that of precision, retaining the worship of Beauty as absolute. A characteristic trait of literary evolution in Spain, this poetry by no means excludes popular tradition. Machado and Jiménez also look towards the romanceros and pass this taste on to the poets of the Generation of 27. In Portugal symbolist poetry finds its happiest expression in the only collection by Camilo Pessanha (1887–1926), *Clepsidra* (*Water Clock*, 1922). Napoleon Lapathiotis (1888–1944), Romos Philyras (1888–1942), Costas Ouranis (1890–1953) and Tellos Agras (1899–1944) created a Greek symbolist poetry dominated by melancholy reverie and musicality. For most of these poets, poetry was above all a refuge.

The autumn of poetic language is proclaimed in work by **Costas Karyotakis (1896–1928)**, in whose work symbolism and realism coexist, the search for the absolute and sarcasm, traditional versification and metrical innovation (*O ponos ton anthropon ke ton praghmaton, The Pain of Man and of Things*, 1919; *Nipenthi, Nepenthe*, 1921; *Eleghies ke Satires, Elegies and Satires*, 1927).

Ε'ίμαστε κάτι ξεχαρβαλωμένες κιθάρες. Ο άνεμος, όταν περνάει, στίχους, ήχουσ παράφωνους ξυπνάει στίς χορδές πού κρέμονται σάν καδένες.	*We are sorts of smashed-up guitars. The wind, when it goes past, wakes up verses, dissonant sounds on the strings which hang like chains.*

Costa Karyotakis,
Imaste Kati

With Viatcheslav Ivanov (1866–1949), and especially with **Alexander Blok (1880–1921)**, rhythms, alliterations, images and symbols are employed to grasp a mystical world hidden behind the world of appearances. *Stixi o prekrasnoj dame* (*The Verses of the Beautiful Lady*, 1904) by Blok bathe in an ethereal

atmosphere and *Gorod* (*The Town*, 1904–1908) evokes St Petersburg, an apocalyptic vision. The famous poem *Dvenadcat'* (*The Twelve*, 1918) marks the passage of the twelve murderous apostles of the revolution and ends on the ambiguous vision of Christ:

Так идут державным шагом Позади – голодный пес, Впереди – с кровавым флагом, И за вьюгой невидим, И от пули невредим,	*And so they walk with the gait of victors, Behind them the starving dog In front of them, under the bloody flag, Invisible beyond the wind, Invulnerable to bullets, Hardly touching the ground,*

Нежной поступью
навьюжной,
Снежной россыпью
жемчужной,
В белом венчике из роз –
Впереди – Исус Христос.

Alexander Blok, *Dvenadcat'*

Dripping with pearls of snow,
Crowned with white roses,
In front of them –
Jesus Christ.

The most famous work by **Andrei Biélyi (1880–1934)**, *Petersburg* (1913), imparts a mythical and malevolent dimension to the town of Peter the Great, which becomes, in spite of its perfect geometry, a place of delirium and revolutionary madness. The structure and the rhythm of the language and its leitmotifs contribute to the reinforcement of the novel's expressive power. In Poland, the symbolist movement only finds a feeble echo, except in dramas by **Stanisław Wyspiański (1869–1907)**, *Wesele* (*Wedding*, 1901) and *Wyzwolenie* (*Liberation*, 1903), poems by Jan Kasprowicz (1860–1926) and the poetic programme of Bolesław Lésmian (1878–1937).

In the wake of Břežina, Jakub Deml (1878–1961), singer of flowers, of the female soul and of Christian love, is the author of a labyrinthine tale, *Hrad smrti* (*The Castle of Death*, 1912) which the surrealists later invoked. Antonin Sova (1864–1920) went from egotistical and naturist lyricism to socialist visions of fraternity. Slovakian poetry carries the incantatory accents of the symbolist Yvan Krasko (1876–1958).

Alexander Macedonski (1854–1920) introduces symbolism to Rumania while Ovid Densusianu (1873–1938) becomes the movement's theorist. Poetry by Ion Pillat (1891–1945), Ion Minulescu (1881–1944) and George Bacovia (1881–1957) mixes neo-Romantic features with symbolist tendencies. Evocative and musical, Bulgarian symbolism is closer to Verlaine than Mallarmé. Pejo Javorov (1878–1914) speaks of an obsession with death, solitude and revolt against his time. Teodor Trajanov (1882–1945) marries symbolism and expressionism. The most European of Bulgarian symbolists, Nikolaj Liliev (1885–1960), flees from reality, seeking refuge in a world of harmony and beauty. Dimčo Debeljanov (1887–1916) overcomes excessive individualism and hermeticism.

Towards a modern classicism

The classical heritage is gathered in Greece by Palamas, close to the Parnassian ideal by the classical form of his poetry that celebrates ancient beauty. Apart from lyrical poems, he composed poetry of a national and philosophic nature (*I asálefti zoï, Immutable Life,* 1904; *I politia ke i monaxia, The City and Solitude,* 1912; *Soneta, Sonnets,* 1919). Palamas, whose style is sometimes pompous, nevertheless influenced Greek poetry. He extended the thematic and rhythmic repertoire of Greek verse.

With **Angelos Sikelianos (1884–1951)**, the author of lyrical poems (*O alaphroïskiotos, The Visionary,* 1909; *Mitir Theou, Mother of God,* 1917; *Prologhi sti zoï, Prologues to Life,* 1915–1917) and tragedies, classicism takes on visionary dimensions. Brought up on the myths of Greek antiquity, Sikelianos attaches special importance to Orphism and preaches the union of man with nature and the union of the universal soul with God by the worship of Beauty and the practice of Good. Kazantzakis composes an *Odhisia* (*Odyssey*) of 33,333 verses, which was not published until 1938. His Ulysses wanders the oceans of the world, alone and liberated, beyond Good and Evil.

In Portugal, Texeira Gomes (1860–1941) practises a would-be classical language and even transforms his homeland into a sort of Greece of the heart (*Gente Singular, Peculiar People,* 1909). The same ideal of rigour and starkness characterises the drama and epic poetry by the German Paul Ernst (1866–1933), and odes, elegies and sonnets by Rudolf Alexander Schröder (1878–1962).

Hofmannsthal, the supporter of a conservative humanism, found a source of inspiration in ancient theatre (*Elektra*, 1904; *Ödipus und die Sphinx, Oedipus and the Sphinx*, 1906), before turning to the Baroque period and the cultural traditions of old Austria. It was also perfection of form, clarity and mastery of language that were sought in The Netherlands by Pieter Cornelis Boutens (1870–1943), the translator of Aeschylus and Homer, who incorporated Platonic contemplation into his own work (*Carmina*, 1912; *Sonnetten, Sonnets,* 1920), Jan Hendrik Leopold (1865–1925), Jacques Bloem (1887–1966) and Adriaan Roland Holst (1888–1976). The classical tendency represented in Italy by the group of the review *La Ronda* (Bachelli, Cardarelli, Cecchi, Rome, 1919–1923) was not limited to simply rejecting avant-garde ideologies; it included a revision of the very concept of tradition itself, ending in a 'metaphorical and double-bottomed classicism' rich in the expressive resources granted to the modern period.

Russian acmeism took its name from the Greek word 'acme' meaning apogee. It sets out to be a return to the concrete and to classical clarity. As Gumiliev, the leader of the movement, emphasises, the poet is no longer a wise man or a prophet, he is a craftsman giving to that word his exact meaning. Work by **Anna Akhmatova (1889–1966)** corresponds to this ideal because of its purity, sobriety and technical perfection. Her first poems (*Večer, Evening,* 1912; *Čëtki, The Rosary,* 1914) are

short lyrical dramas, partly autobiographical. Ossip Mandelstam (1892–1943) also takes on board the principles of acmeism. His collection *Kamen'* (*Stone*, 1915) adopts the tone of an ode, and *Tristia* (1921) is made up of elegiac poems, evocative among other things of St Petersburg, Europe and the freedoms suppressed by the revolution. Mythological images, ancient motifs and prosaic expressions mingle, while the border between poetry and prose tends to disappear.

English Imagism, close to acmeism, is a poetic current expounded by Thomas Edward Hulme (1883–1917), then by the Americans Ezra Pound and Amy Lowell (1874–1925). The exposition of the objectives of imagism by Pound and F.S. Flint in the review *Poetry* (1913) constitutes a sort of manifesto reacting to Romanticism. The authors call for a direct treatment of subject matter, reject abstraction and the superfluous word, and place the accent on rhythm, advocating a precise poetry, not effusive, close to everyday speech and concrete reality. The essential element of the poem is the image, conceived as an 'intellectual and emotional complex', like a spontaneous equivalent of perception.

Having devoted himself to intellectual speculation, **Paul Valéry (1871–1945)**, in his long poem *La Jeune Parque* (1917), then in *Charmes* (1922), developed a poetics based on the primacy of mind. But far from turning away from the senses, he gave an important place to sight, smell and touch.

Comme le fruit se fond en jouissance,	*As fruit melts into pleasure,*
Comme en délice il change son absence	*As into delight it changes its absence*
Dans une bouche où sa forme se meurt,	*In a mouth in which its form is dying,*
Je hume ici ma future fumée,	*I breathe in here my future smoke,*
Et le ciel chante à l'âme consumée	*And the sky sings to the soul consumed*
Le changement des rives en rumeur.	*The alteration of the humming banks.*

Paul Valéry,
'Le cimetière marin', *Charmes*

Close to Valéry, whom he translated, the Spaniard **Jorge Guillén (1893–1984)** wrote hermetic poetry distinguished by very rigorous composition, notably in *Cantico* (*Canticle*, 1928). His works run the gamut from the most

simple phenomena to the greatest abstractions in a desire to grasp the first shapes of things, the plenitude and underlying structure of Being. Landscapes, for example, are dematerialised, dehumanised and reduced to networks of tensions and relationships. The simplicity of the syntax forms a contrast with the hermetic nature of the content. An analogous esoteric phenomenon is found in Italy with **Eugenio Montale (1896–1981)**, whose first collection, *Ossi di Seppia* (*Cuttlebones*, 1925), contains in embryo some of the elements of his ambitious poetic programme: to join with post-romantic and post-symbolist poetry in order to transcend the abrupt breaks of the avant-garde. Montale takes on board certain borrowings from nineteenth-century English and American poetry, from the poetry of D'Annunzio and the 'twilight brigade', who put the brake on romantic subjectivity to end up with a poetry of the object, which is accompanied by a renewal of stylistic procedures.

The Hungarian **Mihály Babits (1883–1941)** was also considered to be a representative of pure poetry. As early as 1909 (*Levelek Irisz koszorújából, Leaves of the Crown of Iris*), his works reveal his desire to endow poetry with a rigorous architecture by exploiting the musicality of its language. Babits is one of the masters of objective poetry, who place 'words in the impeccable order that the Mind desires'. The 'Ding-Gedichte' ('thing-poems') by **Rainer Maria Rilke (1875–1926)** try to focus on an object, an animal, a flower in its authentic being, to grasp it from the inside, to seize its essence. Poetic language in *Neue Gedichte* (*New Poetry*, 1907–1908) becomes more concise, more exact and more abstract. The writer takes another step towards being esoteric with *Duineser Elegien* (*The Duino Elegies*, 1923), begun in 1912 in the Castle of Duino on the Adriatic and finished in Muzot, in the Swiss canton of Valais, where *Die Sonette an Orpheus* (*Sonnets to Orpheus*, 1923) were also composed.

> *Here is the time for things tellable, here is*
> *their home.*
> *Speak and proclaim.*
> Rainer Maria Rilke, *Duineser Elegien*

Rilke's complaint about the ephemeral nature of human life becomes transformed into an attachment to life which includes the acceptance of death:

Erde, ist es nicht dies, was du	*Earth, is this not what you*
willst: unsichtbar	*want: invisible*
in uns erstehn?	*in us to be reborn?*
– Ist es dein Traum nicht,	*– Is it not your dream*
einmal unsichtbar zu sein? –	*to be for once invisible? –*
Erde! Unsichtbar!	*Earth! Invisible!*
Was, wenn Verwandlung nicht,	*What mission do you lay down, if it*
ist dein drängender Auftrag?	*is not transformation?*
Erde, du liebe, ich will.	*Earth, my beloved, I want it.*
Rainer Maria Rilke,	
Duineser Elegien	

In prose, many European authors hark back to the literary tradition of the novel of analysis: Gide gives us tales of spiritual adventures with *The Immoralist* (1902), *Strait is the Gate* (1909) and *The Pastoral Symphony* (1919). *The Devil in the Flesh* (1923) by Raymond Radiguet (1903–1923), is written in a subtle, precise style, and *The Ball of the Count of Orgel* (1924) recalls *La Princesse de Clèves* with the purity of its form. François Mauriac (1885–1970) and **Julien Green** (born in 1900) re-establish the Christian novel by conferring on it tragic, Dostoyevskian characteristics. Mauriac evokes the clashes between the individual and the family in the framework of provincial life (*A Kiss for the Leper*, 1922; *Genitrix*, 1924; *Thérèse Desqueyroux*, 1927). Green's characters seem impelled to do evil by an obscure fatalistic force and embody a deep-seated metaphysical anxiety (*Mont Cinère*, 1926; *Adrienne Mesurat*, 1927; *Leviathan*, 1929). Convinced of the shortcomings of analytical psychology,

Georges Bernanos (1888–1948) conjures up the discontinuity of spiritual life in his novels with a metaphysical dimension (*Under Satan's Sun*, 1926).

The first important work by the Austrian **Robert Musil (1880–1942)**, *Die Verwirrungen des Zöglings Törless* (*The Perplexities of Pupil Törless*, 1906) indicates the role of the irrational and of sado-masochistic impulses in the psychology of the boarders of a provincial boarding school. In Bohemia, Růžena Svobodová (1868–1920) was one of the first to react against naturalism (*Milenky, Women in Love*, 1902) with her subtle portraits of young women confronting the world and love, while in 1919 Ivan Olbracht (1882–1952), in his novel *Podivné přátelství herce Jesenia* (*The Actor Jesenius's Strange Friendship*), demonstrates a rare command of introspection. The creator of the Slovakian psychological novel, Milo Urban (1904–1983), describes a village during the First World War (*Živý bič, The Living Plague*, 1927).

In *Komen en Gan* (*The Female Visitor*, 1927), by Maurice Roelants (1895–1966), the setting, the social circle and the action have only limited importance: the emphasis is on a brief crisis in the life of the protagonists torn between their desires and their moral values.

Neo-Romantic tendencies

Various components of Romanticism reappear at the beginning of the century: the exaltation of nature and elemental forces, a return to popular values, exoticism: In Germany, for instance, these are present in the fantasy-laden narratives by Ricarda Huch (1864–1947), who rediscovered the tone of the short tale, and above all in **Hermann Hesse (1877–1962)**. His *Romantische Lieder* (*Romantic Songs*, 1899) bathe in an atmosphere of melancholy on the border of dream and reality, while his stories (*Peter Camenzind*, 1904; *Knulp*, 1915) take up the themes of wanderlust, of the freedom of the artist, of escape into a dream world and of openness to nature. His subsequent novels *Demian* (1920), *Siddhartha* (1922), *Der Steppenwolf* (*The Wolf of the Steppes*, 1927) and

Narziß und Goldmund (*Narziß and Goldmund*, 1930) describe the diametrically opposite pulls of sensuality and spirituality. It is not until the end of a long quest for self that the tormented heroes finally attain inner equilibrium. With Verner von Heidenstam (1859–1940), **Selma Lagerlöf (1858–1940)** is the leading representative of Scandinavian neo-Romanticism. In contrast to her didactic tale *Nils Holgerssons underbara resa genom Sverige* (*The Marvellous Journey of Nils Olgersson through Sweden*, 1906–1907), she relates in *Kejsaren av Portugallien* (*The Emperor of Portugal*, 1914) the mad love of a father for his daughter.

Neo-Romantic accents are also perceptible in England with the 'Georgian poets' Edward Thomas (1878–1917) and Robert Graves (1895–1985), in Portugal with the poet Florbela Espanca (1895–1930), and in France with Paul Fort (1871–1960), Francis Jammes (1868–1938) and Anna de Noailles (1876–1933). The poetic novel by Alain Fournier (1886–1914), *Le Grand Meaulnes* (1913), retraces the initiation of an adolescent to love and evokes a sensibility which transfigures everyday reality with wonders and dreams.

Some writers seek a way out of their Weltschmerz in the charms of a different world: the Dutch novelist Arthur Van Schendel (1874–1946) set his first works in medieval Italy (*Een Zwerver verliefd, A Vagabond in Love*, 1904; *Een Zwerver verdwaald, A Vagabond Lost*, 1913). This exoticism takes on more tragic overtones and a more modern form with the poet Jan Jacob Slauerhoff (1898–1936).

In the face of English culture, the Celtic revival asserts the originality of the Irish temperament characterised by a visionary dimension, by a predisposition to dreaming, melancholy and mysticism. In his lyrical dramas, **William Butler Yeats (1865–1939)** exalts the heroic suffering of Ireland (*Cathleen Ni Houlihan*, 1902; *Deirdre*, 1907) in a dreamlike and mysterious atmosphere akin to Ossian. The poet and dramatist **John Millington Synge (1871–1909)** recounted popular superstitions and dramatic tales of the sea (*Riders to the Sea*, 1904). If some of his plays are worthy of Greek tragedy (*Deirdre of the Sorrows*, 1910), others give an important place to the element of comedy (*The Well of the Saints*, 1907; *The Playboy of the Western World*, 1907; *The Tinker's Wedding*, 1907).

> In a good play every speech should be as fully flavoured as a nut or an apple.
>
> Synge, *The Playboy of the Western World*

Synge's manner will find its prolongation in drama by **Sean O'Casey (1884–1964)**, which alternates brutal irony with pathetic accents, creating a sombre, sometimes sordid realism (*Juno and the Paycock*, 1925; *The Plough and the Stars*, 1926). Plays by Yeats, Synge and O'Casey helped to consolidate the reputation of the Abbey Theatre, Dublin.

The neo-Romantic revolt of Bohemia's poets is directed against bourgeois society and the Austrian state. Stanislav Kostha Neumann (1875–1947), still a 'decadent' in his 1896 collection, became the editor of the anarchist review *Novy Kult* (*The New Cult*, 1897–1905), revealing himself as a 'naturist' in *Kniha lesu vold a stráni* (*The Book of Forests, Streams and Hillsides*, 1914), before celebrating, *c*.1918, modern civilisation and the Bolshevik revolution. The decadent humours of Viktor Dyk (1877–1930) lead to a totally romantic ambiguity between delusions of grandeur and disenchantment faced with a down-to-earth society. About the same period there flourished what was called Scythism, the poetry of Russian nature and the countryside, illustrated by Nicholas Kliuiev (1885–1937) and **Sergei Essenin (1895–1925)**. Both were disappointed by the Russian Revolution, which they hoped would lead to the resurrection of the old peasant Russia. Kliuiev's poem *Derevnya* (*The Countryside*, 1927), which earned him the name of counter-revolutionary, ends by calling for a new revolution for the peasantry. His work links the traditions of the peasants of Northern Russia and the sophisticated culture of the Decadents (*Pesnoslov*, *The Book of Songs*, 1919). With Essenin, the Messianic predominates (*Prišestvie*, *Advent*, 1917; *Preobpaženie*, *Transfiguration*, 1917), particularly in *Inonia* (1918), the evocation of a Utopian city, in which the poet prophetically announces the coming of a new Saviour. Anguish and despair dominate Essenin's late work and the poet committed suicide in 1925.

A literature of the native land with nostalgic and rebellious overtones was created by three great poets from Transylvania: Georg Cosbuc (1866–1918), the author of ballads and idylls, Stefan Iosif (1875–1913), a writer of elegies, and the ardent 'national poet' Gogá. Nicholas Yorga (1871–1940) exalts in his tales and historical dramas the world of the peasants and village traditions, while novels by Mihail Sadoveanu (1880–1961) evoke the Rumanian people's past through a multitude of characters: soldiers, peasants and boyars. In Bulgarian literature the same values are asserted: Jordan Jovkov (1880–1937) delves happily into folklore. Romantic ideals also leave their mark on one of the most popular Bulgarian writers, **Kiril Hristov (1875–1944)**, the author of nature and passionate love poetry in which the self is liberated from conventions and norms to give free rein to an unbounded sensuality.

The realist vein: the novel as king

In France several multi-volume novels were published including *Jean-Christophe* (1904–1912) by Romain Rolland (1866–1944), a fictional biography of a composer who greatly resembles Beethoven; and *Les Thibault* (1922–1940) by Roger Martin du Gard (1881–1958), a picture of French social and political reality from the eve to the aftermath of the First World War. In the same way John Galsworthy (1867–1933), in *The Forsyte Saga* (1906–1927), evokes the rise and fall of the upper middle classes through several generations, from the Victorians to the 1920s. Arnold Bennett (1867–1931) with small precise brushstrokes paints a picture of the drab existence of the 'middle class' and the workers in the industrial areas of the Midlands (*Anna of the Five Towns*, 1902; *The Old Wives' Tale*, 1908; *Hilda Lessways*, 1911). Herbert George Wells (1866–1946) tackles, not without humour, the problems of the middle classes at the dawn of the century (*Love and Mr Lewisham*, 1900; *The History of Mr Polly*, 1910). In Germany *Buddenbrooks, Verfall einer Familie* (*Buddenbrooks*, 1901) by **Thomas Mann (1875–1955)*** also belongs to those novels covering several generations which give an accurate image of current society. In Denmark, Jensen composes a long novel cycle, *Den lange Rejse* (*The Long Journey*, 1908–1922) exalting the myths of humanity.

Ivan Alekseïevitch Bunin (1870–1953) retraces in his stories the last days of the Russian landed aristocracy and paints a picture of peasant life before 1917 (*Derevnya, The Village*, 1910). His *Gospodin iz San Francisco* (*The Man from San Francisco*, 1915) is an incisive satire of socialite circles in which life is like death.

Wacław Berent (1873–1940), in *Ozimina* (*Winter Plants*, 1911) paints a picture of pre-First World War Polish society. The revolution of 1905 inspired the critic of Polish provincialism, Stanisław Brzozowski (1878–1911). In *Płomienie* (*Flames*, 1908), he develops a philosophy reconciling Marxism with Catholic thought and, in this respect, he has had a great influence. During and after the First World War, the most important realist stories were those by Stefan Zeromski (1864–1925), *Przedwiośnie* (*Before Spring*, 1925), Juliusz Kaden Bandrowski (1885–1944), Andrzej Strug (1871–1937) and Zofia Nałkowska (1884–1954), stories which evoke the beginnings of Polish independence and occasionally underline the gap between the dream of a free Poland and the application of that freedom. *Siréna* (*The Siren*, 1935), by Marie Majerová (1882–1967), again brings to life three generations of a working-class family in an industrial basin close to Prague. Anna Maria Tilschová (1873–1957) depicts the bourgeois, intellectual and artistic circles of the capital, and Karel Matěj Čapek-Chod (1860–1927) comes close to naturalism with his pitiless, grotesque evocations of the lower depths of Prague and the salons of suspicious characters. In Slovakia, the realist trend continues to be affirmed in the last great novel (1904) by Martin Kukučín (1860–1928) and in Jozef Nádaši

Jégé (1866–1940), the author of historical frescoes, who grasps, in an equally satirical way, aspects of contemporary life. In Hungary, Babits retraces the life of a family and a town beyond the Danube (*A halálfiai, The Sons of Death*, 1927), while **Zsigmond Móricz (1879–1942)** gives a critical panorama of the gentry and notables (*Uri muri, These Gentlemen are Enjoying Themselves*, 1928; *Rokonok, The Family*, 1930), and brings back to life Transylvania's golden age in the seventeenth century, under the reign of a Protestant prince who reconciled religions and nationalities (*Erdély, Transylvania*, 1922–1939).

Carlos Malheiro Dias (1875–1941) sets out to elucidate the events which overwhelmed the Portugal of his time and of which he himself, a monarchist in exile and a persecuted writer, was a victim. His novel *Os Teles d'Albergaria* (*The Teles of Albergaria*, 1901) describes the fortunes and misfortunes of a family at the time of the struggles of liberalism, and *A Paixào de Maria do Céu* (*The Passion of Maria do Céu*, 1902) retraces life in Lisbon when Napoleon's army tried to conquer Portugal. Aquilino Ribeiro (1885–1963), a supporter of the Republican cause, knew how to depict provincial life without falling into pure regionalism (*Terras do Demo, Lands of the Demon*, 1919). Some of his novels are centred on heroes who add panache to courage (*O Homem que matou o diabo, The Man who Killed the Devil*, 1930).

Grigorios Xenopoulos (1867–1951), also a playwright, is not content with a detailed, relatively superficial representation of the reality of modern Greece, but asks questions about the psychological and social reasons for situations (*Margharita Stefa*, 1906; *O kokinos vrakhos, The Red Rock*, 1915; *Laoura*, 1921; *Mistiki aravones, Secret Engagement*, 1929). He sets his novels in very diverse frames, often in Athens, whose atmosphere Konstantinos Christomanos (1867–1911) also evokes.

The satirical vein

Between 1900 and 1930, the novel and the theatre were the breeding-ground of biting criticism of the current social and political situation. In England a great figure dominated the scene: **George Bernard Shaw (1856– 1950)**. His vision of the world, informed by the thought of Darwin and Nietzsche, was distinguished by his optimistic belief in a 'life force' determining evolution (*Man and Superman*, 1905; *Back to Methuselah*, 1922) which impels certain individuals to want social progress. His theatre is above all a theatre of ideas, characterised by fascinating plots, often contrived, and by brilliant dialogue, laced with witticisms and paradox. Shaw normally gives us a demonstration of a political idea (*Caesar and Cleopatra*, 1901; *Pygmalion*, 1913; *Saint Joan*, 1924) and the preface to each of his plays is designed to clarify his message. He tackles subjects as diverse as religion, marriage and love, education, parent–child relationships and property. He denounces the hypocrisy of a society founded on money, in which poverty is the worst vice of all (*Major Barbara*, 1905).

Lucidity and sarcasm triumph in prose with **Aldous Huxley (1894–1963)** who satirises postwar intellectual circles: *Crome Yellow* (1921), *Antic Hay* (1923), *Point Counter Point* (1928). Huxley laughs at the futility and moral anarchy of his time, denouncing the quest for a superficial happiness, the ignorance and the mediocrity which are hidden under pretensions. Learned discussions between characters constitute the essence of his novels, for the essayist often wins out over the novelist.

After an initial period still dominated by *fin de siècle* sensitivity and aestheticism, the prose of **Heinrich Mann (1871–1950)** denounced the faults of artist circles at the time, and above all the hypocrisy and conformism of the world of Kaiser Wilhelm (*Professor Unrat oder Das Ende eines Tyrannen*, *The Blue Angel*, 1905). His magnum opus was the trilogy of *Das Kaiserreich* (*Empire*) consisting of *Der Untertan* (*The Subject*, 1918), *Die Armen* (*The Poor*, 1918), *Der Kopf* (*The Head*, 1925). *The Subject* reveals the gullibility, nationalism and thirst for power of the Prussian bourgeois. The outrageous character of the satire, which sometimes slides into caricature and grotesqueness, is reminiscent of expressionism.

The novels and short stories by the Swede Hjalmar Södeberg (1869–1941) are representative of a realism tinged with irony and scepticism.

Political and social satire is one of the weapons of the Slovaks, who lampoon the Hungarian oppressors and the mentality of their fellow countrymen before and after the liberation of 1918 (Joseph Gregor Tajovský, 1874–1946; Janko Jesenský, 1874–1945). In the same way the Czech brothers Josef Čapek (1887–1945) and **Karel Čapek (1890–1938)** denounce human follies in their plays. *Lásky hra osudná* (*Love's Fatal Game*, written in 1908–1910, published in a literary magazine in 1911) by both brothers is an amusing, lyrical and grotesque variant of the commedia dell'arte. The 'comedy' on all-conquering youth, *Loupežník* (*The Brigand*, 1920), joyfully dashed down during their stay in Paris, was afterwards taken up and situated by Karel in a new, even more satirical perspective. **Jaroslav Hašek (1883–1923)**, in *Dobrý voják Sveik* (*The Good Soldier Shveik*, 1921–1923), criticises the State, the 'system' which crushes the individual. He creates an 'unknown and modest' hero, a picaro with an innocent face who carries out all his orders to the letter. Is he a simpleton, a 'congenital idiot', a cynical, dangerous pretender, or simply an individual anxious to save his own skin? This difficult-to-pin-down anti-hero is above all the man who tries to escape from alienation and who, in doing so, knocks out the cogs in the apparatus of coercion. Satirical verve is equally alive in Poland in 1913–1914 with Strug, Stanisław Ignacy Witkiewicz (1885–1939) and Roman Jaworski (1883–1944), as well as in Russia with **Evgeni Zamiatin (1884–1937)**, the leader of 'Serapion', a group that had borrowed its name from Hoffmann's hermit embodying the independence of artistic creativity. In his first books, he stigmatised the triumph of mediocrity and conformism (*Uezdnoe*, *The Provinces*, 1913; *Na Kuličkax*, *The Back of Beyond*, 1914), then the enslavement of the individual in the name of the masses (*Peščera*, *The Cave*, 1920; *My*, *We*, 1921). In **Mikhail Bulgakov (1891–1940),** satire takes on a fantastic colouring. In his short stories, whether set in Moscow or on collective farms, he unmasks the pettifogging nature and greed of the average Soviet, the power of bureaucracy and the danger of unnatural scientific experiments (*Sobačje serdce*, *A Dog's Heart*, 1925; *Rokovye jajca*, *The Fateful Eggs*, 1925). With Mikhail Zoščenko (1895–1958), short, highly stylised narratives give a veritable Soviet comedy of manners, based on anecdotes told in a pithy way by a man of the people who was limited, petty and attached to collectivism. The satirical vein is illustrated by drama by **Vladimir Maya-kovsky (1893–1930)**[*] who in *Klop* (*The Bug*, 1929) criticises Soviet bureaucracy.

Literature and socialism

From the beginning of the century, the work of various European authors bore the mark of their socialist convictions. In The Nether-lands, **Henriette Roland Holst-Van der Schalk (1869–1952)**, traced her spiritual itinerary through her collections of poetry, from her adoption of socialism (*De Nieuwe Geboort*, *The Second Birth*, 1903; *Opwaartsche Wegen*, *The Rising Roads*, 1907) to her diffi-culties with communism (*De Vrouw in het woud*, *The Woman in the Wood*, 1912; *Tussen twee werelden*, *Between Two Worlds*, 1923). In Flanders, the socialist struggle was often duplicated by a struggle for the Flemish cause, attested to by the poetry of René de Clercq (1877–1932).

Martin Andersen Nexoe (1869–1954) created in his novel cycle on *Pelle Erobreren* (*Pelle the Conqueror*, 1906–1910) the first Proletarian hero in Denmark. He described, from a communist and Utopian viewpoint, the evolution of the character from his childhood as the son of a day labourer to his activity as a trade unionist.

> *Pelles Barndom havde været*
> *lykkelig i Kraft af alt; en*
> *graadblandet Sang til Livet*
> *havde de, været. Graaden gaar*
> *paa Toner saa vel som Glœden,*
> *hørt paa Afstand bliver den til*
> *Sang. [. . .]*
> *Og nu stod han her sund og*
> *kraftig – udstyret med*
> *Profeterne, Dommerne,*
> *Apostlene, Budene og 120*
> *Salmer! – og satte en aaben,*
> *svedig Erobrerpande ud mod Verden.*

Martin Andersen Nexoe,
Pelle Erobreren

> *Pelle's childhood had been*
> *happy, in spite of everything. A*
> *song to life, mingled with tears,*
> *that is what it had been.*
> *Tears make music as well*
> *as joy, and from a distance, it sounds*
> *like a song. [. . .] And*
> *now, there he was, sturdy*
> *and healthy, armed with the prophets, the*
> *judges, the apostles, the*
> *commandments and 120*
> *psalms and, bareheaded and*
> *covered with sweat, he was setting out to*
> *conquer the world.*

In Russia, after the Revolution, a committed art developed. It was the period of the 'Prolet-kult' (1918–1923), a cultural organisation whose role was to educate the proletariat. The Proletkult movement rapidly spread to Germany, Poland and Czechoslovakia.

Militant socialism infringed on the studies of manners of two Greek novelists, Hadjo-poulos (*O pirghos tou Akropotamou*, *The Castle on the Riverbank*, 1915) and Constantinos Theotokis (1872–1923), *I timi ke to khrima* (*Honour and Money*, 1912), *Sklavi sta dhesma tous* (*Slaves in their Chains*, 1922).

War literature

The horrors of the First World War affected many writers: psychological shock left lasting traces on their work. For example, Henri Barbusse (1873–1935), *Le Feu* (*Under Fire*,

1916), Roland Dorgelès (1886–1968), *Les Croix de Bois* (*The Wooden Crosses*, 1919); poems by the English poets Rupert Brooke (1887–1915), whose early death at the front made of him a very popular hero, Robert Graves (1895–1985), Siegfried Sassoon (1886–1967) and Wilfred Owen (1893–1918). In Germany there are many accounts of those dark years, in particular *Der Streit um den Sergeanten Grischa* (*The Quarrel about Sergeant Grischa*, 1927) by Arnold Zweig (1887–1968), and the controversial novels by Ernst Jünger (born in 1895), who celebrated the grandeur of war in *In Stahlgewittern* (*Storms of Steel*, 1920), *Der Kampf als inneres Erlebnis* (*The Struggle as Inner Experience*, 1922).

The war of the 'legionaries', Czech and Slovak volunteers in the allied armies, was evoked in a realist and critical fashion by the novelist Josef Kopta (1894–1962) with *Treti rota* (*The Third Company*, 1924–1934) and in an epic and heroic fashion by the poet Rudolf Medek (1890–1940) in *Anabaze, Anabasis* (1921–1927). Vladislav Vančura (1891–1942) rebels against militaristic folly in *Pole orná a válečná* (*Fields under Cultivation and under War*, 1925). With the Slovaks, the war initially inspired horror in sonnets by Pavel Hviezdoslav (1849–1921); then there was the consciousness of a decisive struggle for national liberation (Jesenský, Tajovský, Urban). In Poland the end of the war coincided with rediscovered independence; the only great witnesses to pacifism were poems by Jósef Wittlin (1896–1976), in particular *Hymny* (*Hymn*, 1920).

The theme of the land

The regionalist novel and peasant realism represent a trend which was extremely strong in Flemish literature. *De Vlaschaard* (*The Field of Flax*, 1907), by Stijn Streuvels (1871–1969), evokes the elemental passions which fire the peasants on the banks of the River Lys, a father and his son whose story is placed in parallel to the life of nature and thus acquires a cosmic dimension. In Scandinavia, certain

aspects of peasant realism are found in the works of many writers, including Johan Skjoldborg (1861–1936), Jeffe Aakjaer (1866–1930) and Johan Falkberget (1879–1967). Marie Bregendahl (1867–1940), the author of a sequence called *Billeder af Södalsfolkenes Liv* (*Scenes from the Life of People in Södal*, 1914–1923), describes, in a critical way, the living conditions of Danish peasants and day labourers confronted by modern society. The same theme is taken up in Hungarian letters by István Tömörkeny (1866–1917) and Ferenc Móra (1879–1934), in Poland by **Władysław Reymont (1868–1925)**, *whose impressive fresco of peasant life in four volumes, Chłopi (The Peasants, 1904–1909)*, won him the Nobel Prize in 1924. **Maria Dąbrowska (1889–1965)** writes about similar things in *Ludzie Stamtad* (*The People from Over There*, 1925), and Władysław Orkan (1875–1930), was a peasant writer. The folklore and wild nature of the Tatras Mountains, tales and customs of mountain-dwellers, inspire Kazimierz Przerwa-Tetmajer (1865–1940) with *Legenda Tatr* (*The Legend of the Tatras*, 1912). In Czechoslovakia, Josef Knap (1900–1973) publishes his novel *Muži a hory* (*Men and Mountains*, 1928). Peasant themes, present in the Slovak writer Kukučin, are one of the favourite subjects of the Bulgarian **Elin Pelin (1887–1949)**, hostile to the world of the town which was destroying a patriarchal society.

The French rural novel came rather from a poetic realism which did not exclude the marvellous. Autobiography and romantic storytelling, the evocation of the realities of the countryside and psychological analysis are mingled together in *Les Vrilles de la Vigne* (*The Tendrils of the Vine*, 1908), *La Maison de Claudine* (*The House of Claudine*, 1922) and *Sido* (1930) by Colette (1873–1954). Maurice Genevoix (1890–1980) created with *Raboliot* (1925) the character of a poacher motivated by instinct; he manages to communicate, in a juicy style, the fascination exerted by the landscapes of Sologne. This tendency was reinforced by the 'mountain tragedies' of Charles-Ferdinand Ramuz (1878–1947). *La Grande Peur dans la montagne* (*The Great Terror in the Mountain*, 1926) portrays the anguish of a man before his own perceptions deformed by the power of the imagination. The tales that followed emphasise the spell that the mysteries of the mountain cast over simple souls. In the long short-story tradition, they are steeped in fantasy, though the language is modelled on the peasants of Vaud.

From realism to fantasy

Science fiction, with many realistic details that give an authentic ring to the weirdest settings and events, is orientated towards a denunciation of Utopias, as in tales by the Russian Zamiatin, who inspired Orwell, and in the 'lunar' trilogy of the Polish novelist Jerzy Zuławski (1874–1915), *Na srebrhym globie* (*On the Silver Sphere*, 1903), *Zwyciezca* (*The Conqueror*, 1910), *Stara ziemia* (*The Old Earth*, 1911). *The First Men in the Moon* (1901), *The Food of the Gods* (1904) and *The War in the Air* (1908) by H.G. Wells do not just tell fascinating adventure stories, as Jules Verne did: they also warn against the dangers of science.

The novel by Antoni Słonimski (1895–1976), *Torpeda Czasu* (*The Torpedo of Time*, 1924), shows us an attempt to rewrite history by transporting us to the time of the French Revolution.

Another type of fantasy appeared with Witkiewicz, whose works are rooted in the catastrophic. His novel *Pozegnanie jesieni* (*Farewell to Autumn*, 1927) evoked a society which, the victim of one upheaval after another, ended up totally levelled. The last intellectuals wear themselves out with arguments and give themselves over to all sorts of experiences to stimulate their metapsychic potential and creativity. Similarly, Karel Čapek warns against the mechanisation and uniformity of modern societies. He caught the popular imagination with his play *R.U.R.* (*Rossum's Universal Robots*, 1920). His artificial men, the 'robots', a word coined by Josef Čapek on the basis of the Czech noun and verb which means the work of / to work like a slave, endowed with men's technical expertise but not their feelings, release people from physical work. Increasingly numerous, they rebel and eliminate the human race. The novels that followed, *Krakatit* (*Krakatite*, 1924), *Ze Žnvota hmyzu* (*The Life of Insects*, 1921) and *Válska s mloky* (*The War of the Salamanders*, 1926) were so many warnings to men intoxicated by their scientific powers. The premonitions of the Czech Jan Weiss (1892–1972) are psychopathological in nature with their hallucinated visions of a soul traumatised by the horrors of war.

The minute detail of realist description is associated in certain cases with the use of varied symbols, with the expression of a deep existential anguish and a wholly subjective vision of the world. The enigmatic work by **Franz Kafka (1883–1924)**[*] is the best example.

In Russia, folk wisdom steeped in the marvellous and the Jewish tradition give a fantasmagorical dimension to a world anchored in reality. Isaac Babel (1894–1941), in *Konarmija* (*The Red Cavalry*, 1926), relates in a rapid, expressive style the Cassacks fight against the Whites during the 1920 Russo-Polish War. He evokes a brutal world with garish colours, overflowing with vitality. The Portuguese novelist, Paul Brandão (1867–1930), inspired by Dostoyevsky, creates a pathetic world characterised by deformation and eccentricity (*Húmus*, 1917), in which life appears as a tragic farce.

In Belgium, larger-than-life drama by Fernand Crommelynck (1886–1970) and the Baroque universe of Michel De Ghelderode (1898–1962) in *Escurial* (1927) and *Barrabas* (1928), are intruded on by fantastic elements sometimes close to the grotesque which derive from popular sources and have outrageous, expressionistic features. Francophone Belgium seems to have been a land peculiarly suited to the blossoming of magic realism. Poetry by Elskamp, in his second period, illustrates this with its evocations of far-away journeys and legendary figures. Disillusion, a feeling of solitude and failure, and nostalgia for transcendence are the dominant features in his work (*Cynical Songs, The Song of the rue Saint-*

Paul, 1922, *Aegri Somnia, Remembrances*, 1924). Hellens, a novelist and poet, makes plenty of space in his work for a world of dreams. His novel *Mélusine* (1921) is the transcription of a series of dreams revolving around a female figure. A climate of fear and anguish is created by the fantastic tales of Jean Ray (1887–1964) in *Whisky Tales* (1925). In Italy magical realism will be the subject of a theoretical elaboration by Massimo Bontempelli (1878–1960) and those who collaborate in the review *Novecento* (1926–1929). The failure of the transition to Bontempelli's practice, guided by the idea of universal fascism, cannot make us forget the influence he had on writers such as Moravia, Alvaro, Buzzati and Landolfi.

The poetic prose tale

The tales of adventure (*Typhoon*, 1903; *Lord Jim, The Secret Agent*, 1907; *Tales of the Sea*, 1910; *The Shadow Line*, 1917) by Joseph Conrad (1856–1924) show a predilection for the seafaring world and far horizons. Conrad was a naval officer. But they go well beyond the limits of the genre in the place he reserves for the characters' inner life and in the crisscrossing of different points of view. His novels acquire thereby a poetic dimension.

The work of **Edward Morgan Forster (1879–1970)** shifts traditional realism with a sense of poetry and smiling irony (*Where Angels Fear to Tread*, 1905; *A Room with a View*, 1908). His masterpiece, *A Passage to India* (1924), is centred on the difficult relationship between Indians and the British and bears witness to a liberal spirit rejecting the notion of racial superiority. **David Herbert Lawrence (1885–1930)** gives the language of the novel a symbolic, lyrical dimension. His powerful prose, made rhythmical by numerous repetitions, evokes exotic countries and 'dark gods', it exalts physical love and vital forces (*The Rainbow*, 1915; *Women in Love*, 1921; *Lady Chatterley's Lover*, 1928; *The Plumed Serpent*, 1928).

In France the poetic novel is tinged with cosmopolitanism and modernism in **Valéry**

Larbaud (1881–1957), whose writing is fragmented into an infinity of impressions (*Fermina Marquez*, 1911; *Barnabooth*, 1913).

MODERNISM AND AVANT-GARDE

In some countries, the rejection of literary tradition went as far as a radical, provocative and shocking break with the past. The bias of novelty, of modernism, is linked to an overall rejection of materialism and bourgeois society. Futurism, expressionism and dadaism will go even further. Art is not a reproduction but a process of deconstruction and reconstruction of the real, governed by relationships of analogy and association. It makes possible a deeper penetration of life, of which it reveals aspects previously obliterated.

> *In the end you are weary of that ancient*
> *world*
> *Shepherdess oh Eiffel Tower*
> *the flock of bridges bleats this morning*
> *You have had enough of living in Greek*
> *and Roman antiquity.*
>
> Guillaume Apollinaire,
> *Zone*

Poets and novelists try to pick up on the frenzied rhythm, the chaotic flow of heterogeneous and simultaneous impressions, the effects of discontinuity and shock that characterise the great modern metropolis. In order to do this, they have recourse to a technique of montage. This introduces advertising slogans, names of streets, extracts from newspapers or snatches of popular songs into the literary text. Characterised by intense dynamism and life, the town is also a place of misery and solitude, where violence and vice break out. This is how Dublin, London, Berlin and St Petersburg *inter alia* appear in works by Joyce, Eliot, Döblin, Biélyi, Zamiatin, Hamsun and Jensen. **Alfred Döblin (1878– 1957)**, in his novel *Berlin, Alexanderplatz* (1929), directly refers to the Babylon of the Apocalypse:

| *Und nun komm her, du, komm, ich will dir etwas zeigen. Die grosse Hure, die Hure Babylon, die da am Wasser sitzt. Und du siehst ein Weib sitzen auf einem scharlachfarbenen Tier. Das Weib ist voll Namen der Lästerung und hat sieben Häupter und zehn Hörner.* | *And now, come, I want to show you something. The great whore of Babylon, the prostitute, sitting by the side of the water. And you can see a woman sitting on a scarlet-coloured beast, covered with blasphemous names and with seven heads and ten horns.* |

Alfred Döblin,
Berlin Alexanderplatz

Between 1905 and 1925, aesthetic theories circulate round Europe, impelled by reviews which are as interested in literature as in the visual arts, which therefore favour the development of more than one talent: Oskar Kokoschka (1886–1980), painter and dramatist, Lajos Kassák (1887–1967), poet, novelist and painter, Burliuk, Mayakovsky, Krutchenykh, Khlebnikov, poets and futuro-cubist painters.

Modernism in France

The 'new spirit' asserted itself in France before 1914 with **Guillaume Apollinaire (1880–1918)**. He advocated a revolution in poetry similar to that which had occurred in painting with Cézanne (*The Cubist Painters, aesthetic meditations*, 1913). After 1912, rejecting the decorative and descriptive style, he recommends forceful formulas and surprise effects, new images to seize the complexity of modern life. Like the simultaneous art of Delaunay in the realm of painting, he created the 'synthetic poem', which had to look like the page of a diary in which the most varied information came to light (*The New Spirit and Poets*, 1917). If the collection *Alcools* (1913) still contains traditional elements, *Calligrammes* (1918) took experimentalism further, playing with typography, substituting rhythm and stanza breaks for punctuation and traditional prosody. Apollinaire was also a pioneering figure for the stage. *Les Mamelles de Tirésias* (*The Breasts of Tirésias*, 1917), rich in burlesque invention, was described by its author as a 'surrealist' drama.

Close to Apollinaire, Max Jacob (1876–1944) devoted much space to the unexpected image and 'the liberated word' (*Le Cornet à dés, The Dice Cup*, 1917), while Pierre Reverdy (1889–1960) created various typographical games and 'the plastic poem' (*La Lucarne ovale, The Oval Skylight*, 1916). Blaise Cendrars (1887–1961) practised the simultaneous poem and the poem-object (*nineteen Poèmes élastiques, nineteen Elastic Poems*, 1919). A similar experimentalism can be seen in tales by Raymond Roussel (1877–1933), *Locus Solus* (1914) and *Impressions of Africa* (1928), whose unreality and artificial procedures had little influence at the time, but which were hailed by the surrealists. The novel went through a sea change. Gide has recourse to a 'story within a story' and inserts into the novel a reflection on the art of the novel; he started to do this in 1895 in the anti-novel *Paludes* (*Swamps*). The technique became more clearly defined in the 'sotie' *Les Caves du Vatican* (*The Vatican Cellars*, 1913), culminating in *The Counterfeiters* (1925) which was described as a 'pure novel'.

À la recherche du temps perdu (*In Search of Time Past*), by **Marcel Proust (1871–1922)**, published from 1913, is the story both of an era and of a consciousness. It chronicles the world of high society and analyses human passions in the clan of wealthy social upstarts – the Verdurins – and the circle of the Princess of Guermantes. Proust underlines their vanity and snobbishness, often with ferocious humour. But he is also keen to show the inner workings of affective memory and the perception of time. He describes those privileged instants when, thanks to certain sensations, a past world suddenly resurfaces. There is the famous episode of the madeleine. The composition of the novel, often described as musical, does not depend on the working out of a plot, but on the interlinking of certain themes – love, time lost and found again, art – repeated with subtle variations and progressively intensifying. Proust's edifice translates once and for all his faith in art as the only way of escaping from time and of overcoming the vanity of the world. Thus, by its style, by its architecture and by the wealth of its themes, Proust's work represents a major landmark in the evolution of the modern novel.

Modernism in England

The English and Irish modernist trend reached its zenith in 1922, the year in which Joyce's *Ulysses*, Virginia Woolf's *Jacob's Room* and T.S. Eliot's *The Waste Land* were published. The English modernist novel of those years was tremendously influenced by Henry James, but decisively transformed by **James Joyce (1882–1941)**.*

The daughter of the critic Leslie Stephen, familiar with the philosophy of Bergson and the works of Proust, **Virginia Woolf (1882–1941)** launched with her essay *Modern Fiction* (1919) a sort of manifesto in which she lays claim to Joyce and rejects traditional realism as unable to seize the truth of life.

> Life is a luminous halo, a semi-transparent envelope surrounding us from the beginning of consciousness to the end.
>
> Virginia Woolf,
> *Modern Fiction*

Renouncing both plot and continuous narrative, like Gide and Proust, Woolf concentrates on rendering the 'stream of consciousness' without submitting it to a rational, and logical ordering which would deform it (*Mrs Dalloway*, 1925; *To the Lighthouse*, 1927; *Orlando*, 1928; *The Waves*, 1931). Built around inter-subjective relationships about the experience of time and death, her novels proceed in little touches so as to grasp the tiny, fleeting

elements which make up everyday experience. This technique is evidently linked to her concept of human identity which appears to her as diffuse, on the move and elusive. Past and present intermingle as the conscious and the subconscious mind interpenetrate. This vision of experience is expressed in a flexible style, which has frequent recourse to interior monologue and a musical structure.

> Nothing should be named, for fear that the name might transform it.
>
> Virginia Woolf,
> *The Waves*

Modernist poetry was dominated in England by **Thomas Stearns Eliot (1888–1965)**. Born in the United States, living in Britain from 1915 and a naturalised British citizen, this admirer of Baudelaire, of the French symbolists and of the 'Metaphysical' poets was as deeply influenced by them as Ezra Pound (1885–1972) who, having come from America in 1908, deviating from the ritual forms of poetry, introduced to it reminiscences borrowed from various cultures. *The Waste Land* is presented as a series of scenes from contemporary life, full of quotations in several languages and laden with multiple allusions which take the reader on a journey through time and space. Eliot expresses in it his scepticism in the aftermath of the war and his nostalgia for a spiritual revival. The same climate is to be found in *The Hollow Men* (1925) before being laid to rest in *Ash Wednesday* (1930). Fragmentation is the major characteristic of this poetry, which combines heterogeneous elements in a sort of montage from which comes an impression of incoherence and unreality, the only way of restoring original emotion, as the following extract shows:

The Burial of the Dead

Winter kept us warm, covering
Earth in forgetful snow, feeding
A little life with dried tubers.
Summer surprised us, coming over the
  Starnbergersee

With a shower of rain: we stopped in the
  colonnade,
And went on in sunlight, into the
  Hofgarten,
And drank coffee, and talked for an hour.
Bin gar keine Russin, stamm' aus Litauen,
  echt deutsch.
And when we were children, staying at the
  arch-duke's,
My cousin's, he took me out on a sled,
And I was frightened. He said, Marie,
Marie, hold on tight. And down we went.

T.S. Eliot,
The Waste Land.

Yeats, from about 1914 and in contact with
Ezra Pound, renewed the making of poetry: its
language became more intense and more
hermetic, laden with symbols borrowed from
spiritualism and theosophy as well as classical
Antiquity. This eclectic mythology reflects the
poet's philosophical anxiety and his aspiration
to more spirituality. His poems, however, have
lost none of their musicality and their power to
fascinate.

Leda and the Swan

A sudden blow: the great wings
beating still
Above the staggering girl, her
thighs caressed
By the dark webs, her nape

caught in his bill.
He holds her helpless breast upon
his breast.

William Butler Yeats

Other modernist tendencies

Characteristics similar to these are to be found
in *The Notebooks of Malte Laurids Brigge*
by Rilke, *The Magic Mountain* by Thomas
Mann, and *Berlin Alexanderplatz* by Döblin.
La coscienza di Zeno (*The Conscience of Zeno*,
1923), by **Italo Svevo (1861–1928)**, comes
close to them in its treatment of time and its
use of the interior monologue. However, the
solutions of the Italian novelist, sustained by
an epistemological reflection on the subject-
character, on the unconscious and writing, are
both more contradictory and more open. The
interference of different points of view which
make the narration advance produces an ironic
ambiguity which makes all knowledge relative.

Giuseppe Ungaretti (1888–1970), with
Allegria di naufragi (*Shipwrecks*, 1916–1919),
begins a search for the 'absolute word' which
will evolve towards finding orphic and
hermetic solutions. Poetic language appears as
the destruction and reconstruction of rhythms,
metres, syntagmatic elements and stylemes.
The short verse, devoid of punctuation, is conceived of as a central element in a reinvention
of poetic language:

Veglia	*Vigil*
Un'intera nottata	A whole night
buttato vicino	thrown alongside
a un compagno	a comrade
massacrato	killed
con la sua bocca	his mouth
digrignata	grating
volta al plenilunio	turned to the full moon
con la congestione	his flushed hands
delle sue mani	having entered
penetrata	my silence
nel mio silenzio	I have written
ho scritto	letters full of love
lettere piene d'amore	I have never been
Non sono mai stato	more
tanto attaccato alla vita	attached to life

Giuseppe Ungaretti,
Allegria di naufragi

The strange, tormented drama by **Luigi Pirandello (1867–1936)*** is set in the modernist sphere of influence because of the themes it tackles. It is in effect constructed on the disintegration of the personality, on the problem of identity, whose instability is constantly emphasised.

The Greek poet **Constantin Cavafy (1863–1933)*** is one of the precursors of modern poetry.

In Portugal, **Fernando Pessoa (1888–1935)**,* **Mario de Sá-Carneiro (1890–1916)**, *Dispersão (Dispersion*, 1914) and **José de Almada-Negreiros (1893–1970)** transformed poetic language. Mario de Sá-Carneiro, who died prematurely, haunted by death and anguish, willingly makes use of derision, while the poetry of Almada-Negreiros is more violent, more provocative.

¡Indigesta- te na palha dessa tua civilizaçao!	*Vomit into the straw of your civilisation!*
¡Desbesunta-te dessa verméncia!	*Get rid of that vermin!*
¡Destapa a tua decéncia, o teu imoral pudor!	*Bare your decency, your immoral chastity!*

José de Almada-Negreiros,
A cena do ódio

In Spain young novelists like Francisco Ayala (born in 1906) and Benjamín Jarnes (1888–1949) chose a new way of dealing with time and with the dissolution of action. The poetry of the end of the 1920s represents a compromise between the avant-garde and tradition. The assimilation of literary cubism via 'ultraism' and 'creationism' brought with it a predilection for bold metaphors and unusual images, notably in Lorca. Vincente Aleixandre (1898–1984), Luis Cernuda (1902–1963) and Lorca and Rafael Alberti (born in 1902) came close to surrealism. The example of Valéry and Jiménez led Pedro Salinas (1892–1951) and Guillén to a poetic 'of the essential gaze'.

The Danish modern novel comes into its own with Harald Kidde (1878–1918) who adopted the 'stream of consciousness' technique (*Jaernet, Iron*, 1918) and Tom Kritensen (1893–1974) whose work, set in an urban milieu, underlines the chaotic character of the inner life (*Haervaerk, Mortar*, 1930). Poetry, liberated from formal constraints by Jensen and Clausen, the latter favouring free verse (*Evil Spells*, 1904), was given a new look in the 1920s and 1930s by Ekelund and the Finno-Swedish poets Gunnar Björling (1887–1960), Elmer Diktonius (1896–1961) and Rabbe Enckell (1903–1974) who formed part of the Helsingfors group close to the avant-garde. The poetess Edith Södergran (1892–1923), who was in direct contact with symbolist and futurist circles in St Petersburg, wrote poems inspired by Nietzsche reminiscent of expressionism (*September lyran, September Lyre*, 1918; *Rosenaltaret, The Altar of the Rose*, 1919).

In Russian literature, Marina Tsvetaeva (1892–1941) practises all kinds of formal experiments: her poetry, characterised by the expression of extreme feelings, by a sense of mysticism and a taste for myth, intent on seizing the essence of things, borrows certain procedures from cinematography, enjoys stylistic jolts and develops the syntactic and semantic possibilities of the Russian language. Poetic prose by Boris Pilniak (1894–1938) also shows novel features, notably in *Golyj god (The Naked Year*, 1922), whose dynamic and musical style is inspired from Biélyi. His novels develop from an 'aesthetics of chaos' and a montage similar to that of Joyce. Lexical inventions, phonic repetitions, an extreme use of metaphor and musical structure are the essential characteristics of the art of **Vladimir Nikolaievitch Nabokov (1899–1977)**, in which the imaginary element has an important place (*Stixi, Poems*, 1916; *Korol', dama, valet,*

King, Queen, Jack, 1928). Next in importance to Słonimski and Wierzyński were the popular Julian Tuwim (1894–1954), who created a poetry characterised by variety of rhythm and verbal inventiveness, and Jan Lechoń (1899–1956). In Cracow there was a more radical avant-garde. It included Julian Przybós (1901–1970) and Tadeusz Peiper 1891–1969), whose work was close to the spirit of Apollinaire, Max Jacob, constructivism and even ultraism. Vančura takes for his model the Renaissance short story, Rabelais and Cervantes; he favours a somewhat archaic-sounding language, writes long periods, leading to a majestic and monumental style in his novels of the 1920s. In Hungary, Milán Füst (1888–1967), dramatist, novelist and literary theorist, combines the traditions of the recitative and modernism in a poetry characterised by philosophical abstraction and sensual imagery. Bulgarian letters, whose attachment to German and French literature gets stronger, experience at this particular moment a spectacular flowering, above all in the field of poetry, thanks to the reviews *Missăl (1892–1907),* Hyperion (1922–1931) and *Zlatorog* (1920–1943).

Modernist accents were introduced into Rumanian poetry by Ion Barbu (1895–1965), whose 'abstract' art is above all a game, imagery, pure music and a search for the absolute, while the novel genre is dominated by **Ionel Teodoreanu (1897–1954)** with his prodigious fresco *A Médéleni (The Medeleni Woman,* 1925–1927). This text, marked by the Moldavian patriarchal tradition, uses symbolist and Proustian procedures and constitutes one example of the confluence of traditionalist and modernist trends.

The futurist revolt

Futurism opened the way for the most audacious experiments in form. Between 1909 and 1914, **Filippo Tommaso Marinetti (1876–1944)** launched a series of manifestos in France and Italy. Provocative in tone, they were directed against the *status quo,* calling on artists to exalt a new beauty: that of the machine, speed and dissonance. Dynamism, violence and simultaneity were henceforth the key words of the movement. Repudiating logic, Marinetti preached an aesthetic creed founded on intuition and analogy, a language which eliminated traditional punctuation, adjectives and adverbs. Nouns, verbs in the infinitive form and onomatopoeia are its essential elements. Syntactical order is abolished in favour of 'words at liberty'. Marinetti's novel *Mafarka il futurista (Mafarka the Futurist,* 1909) and texts like *Battaglia Peso Odore* (1912) and *Zang Tumb Tumb* (1914) all serve to illustrate these theories. Marinetti also demands a 'synthetic theatre', in which the action on stage would continue into the auditorium.

Futurism took on singular dimensions in Russia. The virulent manifesto of 1912, *Poščecina obščemu bkusu* (A Slap in the Face for Public Taste) creates a scandal: it spares neither the symbolists, nor Pushkin, nor even Dostoyevsky or Tolstoy. Founded by Mayakovsky, **Velimir Khlebnikov (1885–1922),** Alexander Krutchenykh (1886–1968) and David Burliuk (1882–1967), the movement is close to Italian futurism in many respects, as much with its nationalism and themes as in its revolution in language and the role played by 'the word as such' (1913 manifesto). Two poets dominated the movement: Mayakovsky and Khlebnikov. The former attached primary importance to phonic and pictorial elements, seeking dissonance and semantic or phonetic deformation. Khlebnikov was called 'the liberator of the word': the root of the word, the sound, became the essential poetic unit as the following verses demonstrate:

Заклятие смехом	***The Conjuration by Laughter***
О, рассмейтесь, смехай!	*Laugh, you laughers!*
О, засмейтесь, смехай!	*Lighten loads, laughers!*

Что смеются смехами, что
смеянствуют смеяльно!
О, засмейтесь усмеяльно!
О рассмешищ надсмеяльных
– смех усмейных смехачей!
О, иссмейся рассмеяльно
смех надсмейных смеячей!

Velimir Khlebnikov, *Zaklijatie smexom*

*Laughers of laughs, laughing
laughingly.
Smile at your lightened loads!
Smiling irony – laughter of
ironical smilers!
Exploding laughter – laughter of
mocking mockers!*

The futurists invented a 'transmental' language, 'zaoum', whose essence is a game of sounds supposedly corresponding to the direct apprehension of reality. Less radical than futuro-cubism, ego-futurism, founded by Igor Severianin (1887–1941), whose work combines hedonism with experimentalism, achieved the acceptance of the avant-garde by the public at large. On the margin of futurism, the poet **Boris Pasternak (1890–1960)** was initially influenced by Khlebnikov and Mayakovsky, but soon escaped this influence. Receptive to the art of Blok and Rilke, he tried to capture the flashes of sensations, the vital flux, in the manner of the impressionists.

Expressionism

Expressionism developed in the main in the German-speaking lands, from 1910 to *c.*1920. The expressionist were not a group closely united by a theory and precise objectives, but rather a number of individual manifestations linked by tendencies they held in common. Characterised by hatred of the bourgeoisie and materialism, expressionism pleaded for values of the spirit and the soul. Unlike impressionism, it aspired to penetrate the essence of reality by an eminently subjective way of looking at things, which went well beyond the impression produced by the external world and cultivated deviance. Expressionist language is characterised by its outrageousness and violence, by the explosion of syntax and

the condensation of formulas. Expressionist theories, related to those of futurism, found their most convincing application after 1913 in poetry and plays by August Stramm (1874–1915), *Du* (*You*, 1915), *Sancta Susanna* (*Saint Susan*, 1914). These reduce verse to its most expressive elements: the isolated word, sound and rhythm. Poets express the feeling that the world is coming to an end and of 'the twilight of humanity', according to the title of the famous anthology by Kurt Pinthus *Menschheitsdämmerung* (1919). Among the most brilliant of these poets were apart from Else Lasker-Schüler (1869–1945) and the Alsatian Ernst Stadler (1883–1914), Georg Heym (1887–1912) with *Umbra Vitæ* (1912), whose apocalyptic visions lend a mythical dimension to certain phenomena in the modern world and evoke, among other pagan gods, the 'God of the City', 'red-bellied Baal'. With his first collection *Morgue* (1912) Gottfried Benn (1886–1956) created a poetry whose brutal cynicism derives from an aesthetic of ugliness, to which his experience as a doctor has made him familiar. But the works that follow are dominated by a nostalgia for Dionysiac drunkenness and Mediterranean beauty. The most hermetic poems by the Austrian **Georg Trakl (1887–1914)** owe their particular tonality to a whole network of leitmotifs and a colour symbolism that goes with a very personal vision of nature, the evocation of suffering, solitude and death:

*Elis, wenn die Amsel im
schwarzen Wald ruft,
Dieses ist dein Untergang.
Deine Lippen trinken die Kühle
des blauen Felsenquells.*

Georg Trakl, 'An den Knaben Elis'

*Elis, when the blackbird sings
in the dark forest,
your end will be near.
Your lips drink in the freshness
of the blue spring in the rocks.*

The expressionist drama by Georg Kaiser (1878–1945), *Die Bürger von Calais* (*The Burghers of Calais*, 1914), Ernst Toller (1893–1939), *Die Wandlung* (*The Conversion*, 1919), *Masse Mensch* (*Man and the Masses*, 1920) and Franz Werfel (1890–1945) translated in pathetic terms the Messianic dream of a nobler humanity. The characters are carriers of ideas; they are types rather than individuals. The psychological dimension fades to reveal a tendency towards abstraction. The battle between generations, the battle of the sexes are the themes of Kokoschka's novels (*Mörder, Murderer, Hoffnung der Frauen, Hope of Women*, 1907), as they are of those by Walter Hasenclever (1890–1945), *Der Sohn* (*The Son*, 1914) and Carl Sternheim (1878–1942), *Aus dem bürgerlichen Heldenleben* (*The Heroic Life of the Bourgeoisie*, 1908–1922). The expressionist novel portrays pathological cases, conjures up problems of identity, states of folly and anguish (Heym, Döblin). It is oriented towards 'absolute prose' influenced by cubism with Carl Einstein (1885–1940) in *Bebuquin* (1912).

Flemish literature was receptive to expressionism, as much to its humanitarian trend as to its formal experimentation. **Paul Van Ostaijen (1896–1928)**, the poet of the modern city and of unanimism (*Music Hall*, 1916), dreams of a new man (*Het Sienjaal, The Signal*, 1918). But, at the beginning of the 1920s, disenchantment and nihilism give way to the hope of universal brotherhood (*De Feesten van Angst en Pijn, Feasts of Anguish and Suffering*, 1921, *Bezette Stad, Occupied Town*, 1921). His writing also reveals the influence of Apollinaire's typographical experiments, dadaism and futurism.

Teirlinck introduced expressionist theatre to Flanders. His dramatic works, influenced by vitalism, put the masses before the individual and tend to be a 'total' theatre, mixing song, dance, pantomime and film (*De Vertraagde Film, Film Slowed-Down*, 1922); *De Man zonder lijf, The Man without a Body*, 1925; *Ave*, 1928). In The Netherlands, expressionist writers gathered around the reviews *Het Getij* (1916–1924) and *De Vrije Bladen* (1924–1931). The trend's dominant figure, with the exception of Herman Van den Bergh (1899–

1967), is Hendrik Marsman (1899–1940), who seeks above all to be intense. His poetical works reflect his vitalism and are distinguished by their visionary character (*Verzen, Poems*, 1923, *Penthesileia*, 1925, *Paradise Regained*, 1927). A similar orientation can be seen in Bohemia dating from before the First World War in plays by Jaroslav Hilbert (1871–1936) and the first works by the Čapek brothers as well as in prose by Richard Weiner (1884–1937) and Ladislav Klima (1878–1928). In 1921, an expressionist group is formed in Moravia which includes the dramatist and prose writer Lev Blatný (1893–1981) and the novelist Cestmír Jeřábek (1894–1930). They insist on ethical values and cosmic brotherhood, but reject Marxism.

The Balkans were heavily influenced by expressionism. In Bulgaria it became the strongest and most well-structured tendency, although it only developed in the Balkans relatively late. The tendency was especially prominent in two writers who had lived in Germany, the poet and theorist Geo Milev (1895–1925), *Zestokijat prăsten* (*The Terrible Ring*, 1920), and the prose-writer Čavdar Mutafov (1889–1954), the author of the collection *Marionettes, Impressions* (1920). In Croatian letters, in which the avant-garde began in earnest *c*.1916 with the review *Kokot* (*The Cock*), short stories by Uderiko Donadini (1894–1923), poems by Antun Branko Simić (1898–1925), *Preobrazenja* (*Metamorphoses*, 1920), and above all work by Miroslav Krleža (1893–1981), bear the stamp of expressionism. Krleža's war poetry forcefully expresses his revolt and despair. A similar theme is in the novel *Seobe* (*Migrations*, 1929) by the Serb Miloš Crnjanski (1893–1977), who traces the history of the Serbian population of the Voïvodina.

The revolt of dadaism

Every product of disgust capable of becoming a negation of the family is dada.

The Dada Manifesto

Dada was born in 1916 in Zurich, in the Cabaret Voltaire, within a cosmopolitan group that had as its leaders the Rumanian **Tristan Tzara (1896–1963)**, and the Germans Hugo Ball (1886–1927) and Richard Huelsenbeck (1892–1974). They did not develop a coherent programme, but their provocative and iconoclastic attitude expressed itself in a series of aggressive manifestos, in noisy and subversive happenings. The war made them aware of the universality of absurdity and of the vanity of the Messianic Utopianism of the expressionists. They proclaimed their integral doubt, their refusal of all culture, of all established systems, and practised an art of mockery. Their texts boil down to associations of words, sounds and onomatopoeia regulated by rhythmical imperatives and reflecting a gratuitous aesthetic. In this way they created a non-referential language, free of all syntax, that has been compared to abstract art. The 'Lautgedichte' (1916) of Ball, the texts by Huelsenbeck (*Schalaben, Schalabai, Schalamezomai*, 1916; *Phantastische Gebete, Fantastic Prayers*, 1916) and by Tzara (*The First Celestial Adventure of Mr Antipyrin*, 1916; *Twenty-Five Poems*, 1918; *The Cinema Calendar of the Abstract Heart*, 1918) were the first important manifestations of literary dadaism.

From Zurich the movement spread to Germany, when Huelsenbeck settled in Berlin in 1917. He founded the Club Dada there, published an important manifesto in 1918 and collaborated with Raoul Hausmann, Wieland Herzfelde and Johannes Baader. For his part, the Strassburger Hans Arp (1887–1966), after having participated in the manifestations in Zurich, founded a dadaist centre in Cologne (1919–1920). His polyglot poetry (*Die Wolkenpompe, The Cloud Pump*, 1920) ushers in the automatic writing of the surrealists. In Hanover, between 1918 and 1923, an apolitical dadaism, fantastic and constructivist, made its appearance, the *Merz* of Kurt Schwitters (1887–1948). In a spirit of parody, Schwitters introduced the principle of collage in poetry (*Anna Blume*, 1919; *Ursonate*, 1932). In Yugoslavia, dadaism established itself in 1921 under the name of 'Zenitizam', associating futurist and constructivist ideas with its programme.

Surrealism

Preceded in 1919 by the coterie of the review *Literature*, founded by Philippe Soupault (1897–1990), **Louis Aragon (1897–1982)** and **André Breton (1896–1966)**, the surrealists are formed in Paris in 1924 around Breton, considered as 'the Pope of surrealism'. He published his first manifesto at the end of that same year, presenting surrealism as a 'way of totally freeing the spirit'. Breton and his followers denounce all mutilation of man and condemn reason, morality, religion, society. The spontaneous surge of images is to be found at the heart of artistic creation and will be stimulated by fortuitous juxtapositions of words or phrases ('objective chance') and by automatic writing, a principle which had already been put into practice by Soupault and Breton in *Fields of Magnetic Force* (1921). In the eyes of the surrealists, the artist has a political and moral responsibility; his work is capable of transforming mankind. This principle leads to political commitment – writers who join the Communist party.

The works of the surrealists situated on the border of the rational and the irrational, of real life and dreams, exalt love and eroticism subsumed under the fusion of the self into universal life: Soupault, *Rose of the Winds* (1920); Breton, *Clair de terre* (1923), *Nadja* (1928); Aragon, *Libertinism* (1924), *The Peasant of Paris* (1926), *Perpetual Motion* (1926); **Paul Éluard (1895–1952)**, *Dying of not Dying* (1924), *Capital of Pain* (1926), *Love, Poetry* (1929).

To the surrealist sphere of influence also belong Benjamin Péret (1899–1959), René Crevel (1900–1935), Michel Leiris (born in 1901) and Robert Desnos (1900–1945), celebrated for his practice of self-induced hypnotic sleep (*Freedom or Love*, 1927, *With All Hands*, 1930). On the margin of surrealism, Jean Cocteau (1889–1963), closely associated with bohemian life in Paris, is a Proteus, while Antonin Artaud (1896–1948), excluded from the surrealist group in 1926, composes a poetic prose which has been correctly described as psychedelic.

Surrealism fared particularly well in French literature in Belgium. **Paul Nougé (1895–1967)**, (*A Few Writings and a Few Drawings*, 1927), founded a surrealist centre in Brussels in 1924 with the poets Camille Goemans (1900–1960), *Round Tours* (1924) and Marcel Lecomte (1900–1966), *Demonstration* (1922). Belgian surrealism distanced itself from the automatic writing, the Messianism and the political commitment of the Paris group. The writer and maker of collages E.L.T. Mesens (1903–1971), who was a friend of Magritte, the poets Paul Colinet (1898–1957), Louis Scutenaire (1905–1987) and André Souris (1899–1970), also belonged to the Belgian surrealist trend.

Surrealism will have a stimulating effect on the development of Spanish poetry, but only at the end of the 1920s and despite the distrust aroused by the inherent irrationality of the notion of automatic writing. Ramón Gómez de la Serna (1888–1963) defines his unexpected juxtapositions, 'greguerías' as 'humour + metaphor'. The ultraist trend brought about a change of tone in the poets of the Generation of twenty-seven: Lorca, Alberti, Aleixandre and Cernuda.

Surrealist principles are found in Scandinavia and in the USSR with Nikolaj Zabolockij (1903–1958) and Daniil Kharms (1905–1942). In Central Europe, surrealism is present for a few years in the works of the Hungarians Kassák, Attila József (1905–1937) and Gyula Ills (1902–1983). Czech poetise can be considered as a first phase of surrealism. It was established in 1924 with a manifesto published by Karl Beige (1900–1951), who conceived of poetry as an integral creation, giving free rein to the imagination and a sense of fun. Its most eminent Czech representatives were Jaroslav Seifert (born in 1901), *Na vlnách TSF* (*On the Airwaves of the TSF*, 1925), *Slavík zpívá špatně* (*The Nightingale Sings Badly*, 1926), and especially Nezval, of whom Soupault underlined the audacity of imagery and symbol (*Most, The Bridge*, 1922). The Serbian surrealist movement had close contacts with the French one thanks to Marko Ristić (1905–1986).

Constructivism

In the USSR, constructivism was born out of the practices and style inspired by cubism, valuing the making of the object. The theorist of literary constructivism, the critic **Kornelij Zelinsky (1896–1968)** brought out his programme on Constructivism and poetry in 1924. The poet is a builder who has recourse to logical procedures and a rational organisation of his material. Constructivists proclaimed that they belonged to urban, industrial and technical civilisation, rejecting all ties with peasant and rural Russia. The dominant figures of the movement were the poets Ilya Selvinsky (1899–1968) and Tchitcherin. If they both started out from the same basic theories, they nevertheless ended up with very different results: while Selvinsky preserved a popular raciness, Tchitcherin was geometrical to the point of being hermetic. His poetry reads like a musical score laden with new signs and is sometimes reduced to pure graphics. Thus a tendency appears to 'deverbalise' poetic construction and to make of it a visual art which will have an influence on the theatrical experiments of the Bauhaus.

Back to the future

Looking back at this period overall, we are struck by the importance of the innovations which mark the main three literary genres from one end of Europe to the other. Poetry will be characterised henceforth by a predilection for free verse, and for typographical and phonic games. The manipulations and deformations which poets inflict on language result in one which is pure and 'transrational'.

Among the transformations which touch the novel, we should retain, first and foremost, from Proust to Witkiewicz, the rejection of linear narration, of causal linking and of traditional psychology. The proof of the discontinuity of the self leads to the disintegration of the 'hero', while a more fluid and subjective treatment of time imposes itself. The theatre also embarks on new ways, opened by Strindberg in Sweden and Wedekind in Germany at the turn of the century. These ways were marked out by a rejection of character psychology and a taste for provocation and the grotesque. Distancing techniques also emerged and disillusion which was fully exploited later on. The dream of the 'Gesamtkunstwerk' (total work of art) seems to re-emerge to exert its fascination in different sectors of literary life.

Theatre, Circus, Music Hall and Marionettes

M. Otten

The theatre possesses a surprising peculiarity: a talented actor will always encounter an intelligent spectator.

Vsevolod Meyerhold,
The Theatricality of the Theatre

From the end of the nineteenth century, especially in symbolist circles, the idea appears that the theatre has reached such a point of inertia that recourse was needed to certain forms of popular spectacle in order to regenerate it. To bring about this life-saving transplant, the pioneers of the avant-garde will addressed themselves in turn or simultaneously to marionettes, the circus and the music hall.

Giving the theatre a new look

Maeterlinck (1891), then Jarry (1896), asserted the superiority of the marionette over the human actor. Before long, Edward Gordon Craig (1872–1966) put forward his concept of the super-marionette.

In 1891 in Paris, Wedekind discovered the magic of the circus and introduced many grotesque elements into his plays and pantomimes. Later, the poets of the New spirit (Apollinaire, Pierre Albert-Birot, Cocteau) tried to venture into the realms of 'theatre in the round', exploiting to its maximum the burlesque elements peculiar to the circus.

However, neither marionettes nor the circus interacted constructively with traditional theatre. Their respective aesthetics were too incompatible. For example, the circus can only exist in its own space, the ring, which is based on quite a different spatial logic to the Italian stage.

Music hall, on the other hand, combined easily with the traditional theatre: it makes use of the human actor, and it operates on an Italian stage. This popular art, much more recent and less traditionally hidebound than marionettes or circus, shoot traditional stage-craft to its foundations and produces a series of works which were epoch-making in the history of avant-garde theatre.

Music hall was born in big industrial towns at the end of the nineteenth century. Though it has no traditions, it is nevertheless related to the theatrical past. Innovators perceived that, in the free, carnival spirit which reigned in the music hall, something of the essence of the old popular theatre had crept in: the rough humour and dynamism of the Italian commedia dell'arte, the flavour of the Russian 'balagan' (fairground theatre). In Germany, very early on, there was an interest in the aesthetic virtues of the music hall, which at that time was known as the variety theatre. In 1896, Oskar Panizza, encouraged by Wedekind, advocated the intrusion of 'variety' into the theatre as into the visual arts. At the beginning of the twentieth century, the project became more radical: theatre is to be given a new look by using the variety stage, according to Otto-Julius Bierbaum, Ernst von Wolzogen and Georg Fuchs. The decisive impulse came from two major texts by extraordinary personalities: the long polemic study by Meyerhold, called *Balagan* (*Fairground Theatre*), published in 1912, and Marinetti's virulent futurist manifesto, *Music Hall*, launched in 1913.

Meyerhold's 'balagan'

In this study Meyerhold began by stating his opposition to all forms of realism, to the psychological drama as well as to plays with something to prove. In his opinion, this 'literary' theatre, in which speeches predominate, had lost all contact with what he considers to be the very essence of the theatre: the dynamism of the body in motion as it was found in dance or mime. For Meyerhold, over and above the word there is the gesture. This is why he has the highest praise for the clown, the jester and even the ham actor who trod the boards of fairground theatre. Unfortunately, he notes, the contemporary stage has lost all the principles of fairground theatre; these principles 'have taken refuge for the time being in French *cabarets*, [. . .] in *music halls* and *variety theatres* all over the world'. This is why the great director turned to the music hall to find a style and forms capable of regenerating the theatre of his time.

A second aspect of the 'balagan' which interested Meyerhold, its carnival atmosphere, he described as 'grotesque', which was much more than comic incongruity. Like Hoffmann, from whom he derived his inspiration, he saw a structure of sharp contrasts which abruptly brought together the most disparate elements: comic and tragic, ordinary and sublime, real and supernatural, everyday and fantastic, even life and death. In these 'montages of conflict', we are to see a determined attempt to render the real in all its complexity.

Marinetti's music hall

Marinetti's manifesto is much more violent and radical in its questioning of all the theatre's past incarnations. It was animated by the destructive spirit peculiar to the twentieth century avant-garde.

First, Marinetti systematically analysed in nineteen points the virtues of the music hall, considered as the most modern form of art, worthy of the century of speed and electricity. The music hall is exalted because it encourages the permanent invention of the new, because it glorifies motion, speed, rhythm, physical beauty and physical effort, because it refuses all serious and inner values, and ignores 'that disgusting thing: psychology'. Above all, Marinetti saw in it a place in which the burlesque is predominant: all forms of laughter, mockery and satire meet in it. This is why, second, music hall is considered as the

weapon which will make it possible to do away with all the principles of the classical theatre and, in this way, to regenerate drama: 'We find in it [in the music hall] the ironic breakdown of all the worn-out prototypes of the Beautiful, the Great, the Solemn, the Religious, the Fierce, the Seductive . . .'

Marinetti even envisages, thanks to multiple procedures, mocking all past masterpieces: 'We must . . . systematically prostitute all classical art on stage.' How? By burlesque combinations of clowns and tragic actors, by condensations of caricature ('putting the whole of Shakespeare into a single act'), by the paradoxical assignment of roles ('having *The Cid* played by a black man').

The ultimate aim of this theatrical revolution is explicitly stated: to bring about the reign of 'hyperphysicality' on stage and, better still, to plunge the play and the audience into a sort of Dionysian fury.

This manifesto launched, like all of Marinetti's, with an acute sense of the marketplace, was translated almost immediately into English, French and Russian and from 1913 exerted a considerable influence over European avant-garde circles. Meyerhold's text, for its part, contributed to orientating the Russian theatre in the direction of a characteristic form of staging which spread throughout Europe after 1918.

Hyperphysicality at work

In Italy, the great novelty of the futurist theatre was the 1915 production of many dramatic 'syntheses'. These were very short plays reduced to an essential message, which was, more often than not, treated in an illogical, satirical or farcical way. The aesthetic of the music hall mainly intervened when, to put together a 'futurist soirée', Marinetti and his friends accumulated a whole series of syntheses. Montage itself was, of necessity, devoid of sense and only rested on a law of rhythm and escalation of comic tension. In fact, the futurists found it very difficult to execute their productions in the music-hall style, mainly because traditional actors were not prepared to present plays in this manner, and music-hall artistes refused to take part in dramatic spectacles which they found disconcerting.

In among the abundant theatrical production of futurism, it was without doubt *Cocktail* (1926), a Marinetti pantomime choreographed by Prampolini, which came the closest to the ideal formulated in the 1913 manifesto. This mechanical ballet, in which the dancers mimic the various liquors, celebrates the joy and triumph of drunkenness. The absence of text, the supremacy of dance and syncopated music perfectly express the vitality which is the soul of futurism.

In his search for a new form of drama, Marinetti rejects circus which he regards as too bound up with the past. It was not like that in other European countries where the influence of circus was sometimes closely allied to that of music hall. The two arts are not unconnected: the music hall took from the circus its clowns (Coco rather than his all-white counterpart), jugglers and tightrope-walkers.

In France, circus and music hall came together to bring about a revival in theatrical forms, mainly in Apollinaire and Cocteau. Apollinaire began things in 1917 by mounting *Lees Mammals de TireéSiam* (*The Breasts of Tierces*), a surrealist drama. This farce, reminiscent of Jar, accumulates the procedures of the cabaret revue in the vein of the aesthetics of surprise dear to the futurists. The same year, Cacti put on *Parade*, with sets by Picas and music by Sate, a ballet in which three music-hall numbers show off a fairground theatre; but the curtain did not go up on the play announced. Circus, music hall and jazz furnished heterogeneous elements, abruptly juxtaposed. In 1920 Cacti staged *The Ox on the Roof*, a farce mimed by a troupe of clowns, including the famous Fratellini, and in 1921, *The Newly-Weds of the Eiffel Tower*, a burlesque montage of stereotyped scenes, interpreted by the Royal Swedish ballet company with music by the Group of Six. Many of the Paris productions of the Swedish ballet (1920–1925) can be included in this aesthetic trend. The reason for this is simple: the new theatre tried to replace the verbiage of the literary play with an art based on gesture and body rhythms.

The ballet, especially when renewed by the introduction of 'free dance', offered dramatists the chance to plan spectacles based purely on movement. Thanks to their collaboration with avant-garde musicians and painters, they even added the magic of sound and colour. Two pieces are worth remembering: *Skating Rink* (1922) by the futurist Canudo, with music by Honegger and sets and costumes by Fernand Léger, which mimed the Dionysian frenzy that possessed a crowd of roller-skaters, and *The Creation of the World* (1923) by Blaise Cendrars, with music by Darius Milhaud and sets and costumes by Fernand Léger, an 'abstract' ballet derived from African myths and rhythms. Won over by the movement, Antonin Artaud and Charles Dullin also saw in variety theatre the model for a renovated theatre. In June 1923, Dullin put on in his theatre a curious show called *Workshop-Music-Hall*, a series of parades and parodies by Marcel Achard, followed by mimes and songs. In Germany, futurist theses crept into dadaism, which remained for a long time a force to be reckoned with. The most representative work of this trend was *The Collision* (1927) by Kurt Schwitters, sub-titled *a grotesque opera*. Like many avant-garde works, *The Collision* depicted the theme of the end of the world, but in a burlesque way, 'to disarm the apocalyptic pathos of expressionism'.

With the Bauhaus, the tendency was quite different. Its experimental theatre derived from the techniques of popular shows (music hall, variety and circus) to build up an action on stage conceived first and foremost as a study of forms in which the body played a central role. *Musical Clown* (1926) by Oscar Schlemmer, *Circus* (1924) and *All-Female Rehearsal* (1925) by Xanti Schawinsky mined this vein, while Laszlo Moholy-Nagy, in an important manifesto (*Theatre, Circus, Variety*), dreamed of a 'total stage action', which would not have any particular meaning, but which would seduce spectators by contemporary rhythms and forms.

Political theatre took a different tack. With Brecht and, above all, with Piscator, elements borrowed from cabaret broke up the artificial unity of classical drama, destroying the illusion of realism in conformity with the alienation effect. But above all these elements retained a didactic, non-playful function. *Red Fairground Review* by Piscator, for example, distilled social criticism by making use of cabaret: 'sketches, songs, boxing matches, sessions of physical culture alternate with one another'.

In Russia, the trend began much earlier and had a greater influence. In 1913, Krutchonykh and Matiushin (for the music) and Malevitch (for the sets and costumes) created a veritable scandal by putting on *Victory over the Sun*, an opera which saw itself as futurist: all classical forms of theatre are tortured, all the ideals of the past are laughed to scorn in a series of sketches which mingle song with dance. But soon the October Revolution completely transformed the aesthetic climate. In the eyes of left-wing artists, the opposition between elevated genres (theatre, ballet, opera) and inferior or minor genres (circus, variety, music hall) was no longer tenable. In 1919, a freedom of circulation and many cross-pollinations between all the dramatic arts was noticeable: dance, theatre, circus, cinema, variety.

Avant-garde theatre became politicised without ceasing to find sustenance in circus or music hall. One of the most remarkable plays, from this point of view, was *Misterija-Buff* (*Mystery-Bouffe*, 1918) by Mayakovsky. A futurist spectacle mounted as a cabaret revue, *Mystery-Bouffe* taunts the enemies of the people and backward-looking theatre in equal measure.

Productions

But much more than through authors' it was through the extremely creative work of brilliant directors that the burlesque style inspired by music hall invaded the stage. Between 1921 and 1924, Nicolas Foregger, for example, in his Workshop Mast For, embarked on a process of radical carnivalisation of the theatre.

Suppressing the plot as a mainstay of the show, he practised a 'montage of attractions' in which mechanical dances, jazz improvisations and joyous parodies of all serious Moscow theatre became interlinked. Particularly in the frame were *The Tidings Brought to Mary* by Claudel and *Dawns* by Verhaeren that Meyerhold had just directed.

Between 1919 and 1925, excentrism was also developed, a sort of radical futurism: a series of young and enthusiastic directors – Kosintsev, Iurkevitch, Trauberg – put on several shows dominated by the clown of the excentrists: the whey-faced clown in check trousers. These productions were inspired by the circus and the music hall, and also by cartoons and burlesque cinema: Charlie Chaplin was their idol. The most brilliant representative of this trend was undoubtedly Sergei Mikhailovitch Eisenstein, better known for the films he went on to direct. His 1923 direction of a rewritten classical play, *The Wise Man* by Ostrovsky prefigured De Ghelderode's work on the myth of Faust. The plot of Ostrovsky's play was first simplified to the point of demystification, fragmented, parodied. This rewriting served as a pretext for a free-wheeling montage of attractions inspired by the music hall: farcical interludes contradict, in a burlesque way, what could still be thought of as serious in the text. The montage was corrosive, then, a montage that 'unites the unreunitable' as Chlovsky pointed out. Eisenstein subsequently mounted two plays by Sergei Tretiakov, politically committed, but no less 'a mixture of heroic pathos and grotesque buffoonery'. The sub-titles of these plays are interesting, for they suggest the emergence of totally hybrid genres. *Can you hear me, Moscow?* (1923) is sub-titled '*agitated guignol*' and *Gas Masks* (1924), 'agitated melodrama'.

Meyerhold's work as a director was important for the evolution of the theatre in Russia and in Europe. He came closest to the futurist aesthetic when he put on *Mystery-Bouffe*; but in 1922 he pioneered constructivist directorship with his original adaptation of Crommelynck's *The Magnificent Cuckold*. The acrobatic and burlesque acting that he foisted on the actors, according to the principles of biomechanics, transformed the play into an enormous farce. In his radical rewrite of Ostrovsky's *Les (The Forest)*, Meyerhold accentuated the role of buffoonery by using music-hall elements: pantomime, magic tricks, choruses linked with certain roles, abracadabra and slapstick.

In Belgium, the Vlaamsche Volkstooneel (VVT), helped by the Dutch director Johan de Meester, very much attracted to Russian futurist and constructivist theatre, sought the formula for a modern eclectic theatre capable of appealing to the masses. This theatre was a combination various popular traditions: 'kermesse procession, circus clowning, tragic farce, pantomime, marionettes, masks in the style of Ensor'.

De Meester introduced the Flemish dramatist Teirlinck to the research conducted in the Russian theatre (Meyerhold and Taïrov), encouraging him to write in this way to swell the repertory of the VVT. In the same way, in 1926, he encouraged Michel de Ghelderode to persevere with the formula the latter has just discovered: a theatre entirely informed by the spirit and form of music hall. De Ghelderode was a unique case in this tradition. More often than not, theatrical performances influenced by music hall were either very short plays (the syntheses of the futurists) or ballets without texts (*Cocktail* by Marinetti, *Parade* by Cocteau). Long-haul plays are rare. De Ghelderode is probably the only person, in the space of three years (1926–1928), to have taken literary advantage of the research of the 1920s by producing four long original plays: *The Death of Doctor Faust. Music Hall Tragedy* (1926), *Don Juan or the Chimerical Lovers. Drama-Farce for Music Hall* (1928), *Pictures from the Life of Saint Francis of Assisi* (1926) and *Christopher Columbus* (1928). These four modernist plays, neglected today, illustrate two of the great orientations of the formula: either the radical demystification of values by the exaggeration of burlesque elements (Faust and Don Juan), or the glorification of the solitary hero (Columbus) or the saint (Francis of Assisi) who has to grapple with the mass of grotesque characters who do not belong to their world.

Around 1930–1931, quite abruptly, the burlesque vein seemed to run dry. Theatre became serious again, returning to realism and unity of tone. But the virtues of the circus and the music hall were not forgotten. Each time the theatre experiences the need to regenerate itself, it returns to delve into the popular arts. This was the case with the theatre of the absurd in the 1950s (Beckett, Ionesco, Adamov), with Gombrovicz, Tadeus Kantor and many others.

Mayakovsky (1893–1930)

C. Dalipagic

April 1930. Vladimir Vladimirovitch Mayakovsky, born in 1893, consecrated by Stalin as the poet of the Revolution, has just committed suicide: 'No-one is to blame . . . the boat of love has run aground on conventions.' An exemplary and tragic destiny? A symbol of the increasing gulf between the intelligentsia and political power or the logical end of a paradoxical poetic itinerary?

Dominating the first few years of the twentieth century, Mayakovsky concentrated within himself the contradictions of revolutionary Russia on its way to the terror of Stalin. An immensely lyrical poet, he gave himself to the revolution heart and soul. 'This is my revolution,' he would say: in order to serve it, he consciously stifled his lyrical self, 'hurts himself by walking on the throat of his own song' and, an employee of the State, he became one of the perfect practitioners of social manipulation.

Down with tenderness, long live hate

A Christ crucified by the crowd, Mayakovsky was ready to love those who had offended him, like 'a dog who licks the hand of the person who beats him'. But soon he called for the unending struggle, class hatred. He tore out his soul and trampled it underfoot to make it a bloody flag offered to the crowd (*Oblako v štanax*, *The Cloud in Trousers*, 1915).

In his always unsatisfied quest for love, Mayakovsky mingled hate and passion. Personal love, betrayed by conventions, teamed up with universal love whose reign was retarded by the petit bourgeois mentality: 'When will the earth deprived of love finally go back to the first shout of a comrade?' he exclaimed. While he waited for this to happen, the watchword was hate, 'the hate that cements solidarity', the hate of the 'fat he has learned to hate from infancy', of daily life, capitalism and the bourgeoisie, obstacles to love.

The herald of future truths

Mayakovsky wanted to be seen as a prophet of the revolution. He saw coming 'beyond the mountains of time [he] whom no oneelse can see' and saw the approach of the year 1916 in the 'crown of thorns of revolutions'. The thirteenth apostle, the original title of the poem, soon found in the person of Lenin the 'combative and vengeful God of punishment' of his materialistic religion in *Vladimir Il'ič Lenin* (*Vladimir Ilitch Lenin*, 1924).

Wearing his provocative yellow smock, the futurist poet advanced, 'insolent and caustic', 'deafening the world with the thunder of his voice': 'But Raphaël, have you forgotten him? / You have forgotten Rastrelli / It is time / For the bullets / To riddle the walls of museums. / Execute what is old with the cannons of throats.' It is the town's turn to speak, the turn of the crowd, of the masses.

Eager for immortality, he wrote topical verse and propaganda destined for oblivion. His great lyrical poems did not have the backing of the authorities. The poet who contemplated his double about to throw himself off a bridge in a pre-revolutionary poem had carried out his prediction.

In this final act of Mayakovsky's tragedy, life had been reunited with poetry. Like destiny in Greek plays, death had resolved the contradictions. The new time being ushered in is not made for poets.

D'Annunzio (1863–1938)

P. Puppa

'Mister User' was France's nickname for Gabriele D'Annunzio. Moved, in effect, by the desire to take from the *fin de siècle* culture of 'Little Italy' its provincial character, to open it up to Europe, this writer from the Abruzzi became a veritable laboratory, inexhaustible and mannered, delving into the literary heritages, libraries and even the art galleries that he encountered along his way. Moreau's Herodias and Orpheus, Kleist's Penthesilea and Wilde's Salomé, the Psyche recumbent of Burnes Jones, Khnopff's Medusa, the Muses of Dionysius adapted by Maeterlinck, Rosetti's Beatrice and Mallarmé's faun, Swinburne's Cleopatra, Flaubert's Salammbô, Sartorio's sibyl, Pater's beautiful young man and the whole languid and voluptuous iconography, the Anglo-Byzantine 'garden of delights and horrors' all appear in D'Annunzio's stories.

A laboratory

In the realm of poetry, the fan opens with the 'hard core' elements that came out of Hellenic, Parnassian and Carduccian imagery – *Primo vere* (1879) and *Canto novo* (*New Song*, 1882). It closes with the tender tremblings and splenetic delicacies of *Poema paradisiaco* (*Paradisiac Poem*, 1894) to afterwards dilate into the frenzies and metamorphoses of *Laudi* (*Praises*) and, above all, *Alcyone* of 1903.

The area of narrative covered is just as varied, but the diversity of registers is even more obvious in his tormented drama: the word out of place, positively declaimed, contains in its violent allergy to the bourgeois salon and the 'well-made play' the changes of the immediate postwar period, futurist aggression and the bizarre behaviour of 'grotesques', the surrealist myths of Pirandello and the metaphysical anxieties of a Bontempelli and a Rosso di San Secondo. D'Annunzio's theatre strays into the world of faery with the first *Sogni* (*Dreams*). There are the Ibsen-like arguments on art and life of *La*

Gioconda (*Mona Lisa*, 1899), pastoral scenes, the Sacra rappresentazione, art deco exoticism and eroticism in *The Martyrdom of Saint Sebastian* (1911), ideological stances on 'the masses and power' in *La Gloria* (*Glory*, 1899) and in *La Nave* (*The Ship*, 1908), in which the theme of the *femme fatale* goes hand-in-hand with that of the orgiastic, undisciplined crowd.

The destiny of a 'dux'

Collective myths and individual myths: the self-promoting strategy of the poet who transforms each one of his private gestures into a public event tends towards their interaction. It becomes indispensable to modify his own image as a function of the evolution of the spirit of the age. What unites the perverse and polymorphous Alexandrine Orpheus of the early years to the interventionist and bellicose orator of the period 1915–1920 or to the irritated and stoical King Lear of the final years in the Victorial? Is it not that exhibitionist writing, capable itself of turning into action, as for example when the poet buries ships under the grass (a metaphor of classical poetry turned into a domestic ornament), when he takes part in the *Beffa di Buccari* or in the 'parades' in Fiume which announce fascism by their emblems and their ceremonial, a mixture of aesthetics and politics, a general rehearsal for a tactless form of persuasion today entrusted to electronics?

Kafka (1883–1924)

H. Ch. Graf von Nayhauss

We are in the situation of passengers on a train involved in a derailment in a long tunnel.

Franz Kafka

THE KAFKA. The Kafka is a splendid blue mouse like the moon which has not often been seen. It does not eat meat but feeds on bitter herbs. It looks fascinating because it has human eyes.

Franz Blei, *The Great Bestiary*

The Stateless person

Franz Kafka was born in Prague into a Jewish family. He grew up, worked and wrote in German in this bilingual town, a citizen of the multinational State of Austria-Hungary, then a citizen of the Republic of Czechoslovakia. This existence of citizen of the world (in appearance only), determined by the political situation of the period between the wars, hid the fundamental condition of being Stateless.

Kafka was marked by his linguistic Statelessness divided between Yiddish, Czech and German. Solitude, a dearth of relationships, exile and a lack of identity characterise his heroes, who are merely called K., or who have no name, and cannot be defined by their temporal or geographical existence. In his texts, Kafka speaks to man in general, to the whole world. Like Rilke, he is one of those cosmopolitan frontiersmen of Europe who elude national classification.

It is not surprising therefore if various nations, including France, should have tried to spiritually naturalise this Kafka from nowhere in particular. Kafka thought of himself as a German writer, even though in the circle of German writers he belonged to with members like Franz Werfel and Max Brod, his friend and future editor, he occupied a singular position: he spoke fluent Czech and was among that country's intellectuals. In comparison to Rilke or Werfel, the writers of the future 'school of Prague', Kafka's language was overly sober, almost poor. However, with Kafka the narrator, as with Rilke the lyrical poet, German literature reached new heights. According to Kurt Tucholsky, 'Kafka wrote the clearest and most beautiful prose ever written in German.' His bare, concentrated style, with rhetorical overtones, ranged from bureaucratic dryness to the committed note of impassioned pleading. After 1945, with Thomas Mann, Kafka became in Germany and throughout the world the most commented on German language writer.

The father's verdict and K's imagination

Kafka's imaginary world had its origin in his Prague childhood. By dint of hard work, Kafka's father, a small trader in a village in southern Bohemia, became an important business man in Prague. He sent Franz, the eldest of his six children, to the German primary school, the German high school in Altstadt and the German Karl Ferdinand University in Prague. He wanted his son to succeed, but Kafka hated this town influenced by German in which he could find no love and which made him ill. At the age of nineteen, he wrote to his university classmate Oskar Pollak: 'Prague doesn't let go . . . One has to adjust or else –. We should set fire to it at both ends . . . then it might be possible to pull oneself away from it.' His famous *Letter to My Father* (1919) shows how much Kafka suffered from his father's desire to make him 'a strong and courageous young man', well integrated into the German bourgeoisie. Kafka's dream world reflects the tensions of his family environment: on the one hand the trial, the stern tribunal of the father, mistrust that destroys all communication, which is self-destructive and which searches for 'salvations'; on the other, struggle, tracking down. His father is the one he struggles against, his mother becomes a hunter who hunts within the family. In 1921, he notes: 'Finally I have the idea that, as a small child, I was vanquished by my father and that now, out of vanity, I cannot abandon the place where the struggle took place, after all these years, even though I am always beaten.' This is where the key to Kafka's 'the inner dream world' is to be found. He was familiar with Freud's theory of dreams as a desire to realise personal ambitions. Freud considered the writer as an alert dreamer to whom the world of dreams serves as a refuge.

Another key to the absurd and labyrinthine universe in which Kafka's characters move must be sought in the legal world where he worked. For want of anything better, Kafka studied law and, after a short period of court practice, he was employed in 1907 by the Italian insurance company, Assicurazioni generali, for a meagre pittance. He despised this gainful employment which kept him a prisoner 'from 8 o'clock in the morning to 7 o'clock at night, bah' stealing from it the time necessary for his writing, the most fertile part of his existence. In 1908 he joined the Prague Arbeiter-Unfall-Versicherungs-Anstalt where he worked until he took early retirement in 1922, rising to become first secretary (section head). In this job work finished at 2 o'clock in the afternoon. However, Kafka only began to write a little before midnight, when everything is calm, leading 'a terrible double life, which one can only get away from by going mad'. The legal world with its court proceedings, authorities, opaque hierarchies and ways of doing things was found in his prose, even down to the choice of titles (*The Verdict, The Trial*). During this period Kafka published eight short prose tales in the review *Hyperion*.

Love life and correspondence

In 1912, Kafka met Felice Bauer, a twenty-five-year-old Berlin executive secretary, at Max Brod's. An intense five-year correspondence (Letters to Felice) followed, and a complicated relationship which lead twice to their being engaged, then to breaking it off (1914, 1917). Kafka's awareness of his vocation as a writer was intimately linked to the beginning of this relationship. Two days after the first letter to Felice, he wrote during the night of twenty-two to twenty-three September 1912 the story *Das Urteil* (*The Verdict*), in which he transposed his own feelings (a possible marriage to Felice) to the main character, Georg Bendemann, who announces to a friend and his father his forthcoming marriage to Frieda Brandenfeld. The same year in which *The Verdict* appeared, Kafka's first book, *Betrachtung* (*Contemplation*), was published, containing eighteen prose sketches. Inspired by Felice's letters, he compiled his principal works in 1912: apart from *The Verdict*, he wrote *Die Verwandlung* (*Metamorphosis*) and most of the novel fragment *Der Verschollene* (*The Missing Person*) which appeared in 1927 under the title of *Amerika*.

Kafka left his parents' home and in 1914 began a second novel, *Der Prozeß* (*The Trial*), in which Felice Bauer appears under the name of Mademoiselle Bürstner. The end of Kafka's relationship with Felice was linked to the first warning signs of his tuberculosis. He became engaged for the third time in 1918, despite his father's opposition to the match, to Julie Wohryzek, a cobbler's daughter who was 'more funny than sad'. The engagement lasted until 1920. As their married couple's apartment is still not free on their wedding day, Kafka sees in this a sign of fate and immediately stops the wedding preparations.

Kafka now became acquainted, during a holiday in Merano, in 1920, with the Czech journalist Milena Jesenská, with whom he begins a new 'epistolary love'. His love for Milena and the free time afforded him by his early retirement encouraged him to write a third novel, *Das Schloß* (*The Castle*, 1926). This time the setting is not Prague, but a nameless village for which Zurau acted as the model.

Kafka's correspondence with Milena is literally remarkable: 'Writing letters means making oneself naked before ghosts who are eagerly waiting for that to happen. Kisses written down do not reach their destination but are drunk *en route* by ghosts.' The fact that his different fiancées did not live in Prague is typical of the panic fear Kafka felt about forming attachments: 'This desire on the part of my family which translates into fear when it is realised only operates during holidays.'

Kafka's genius

During the summer of 1923, while Kafka was on holiday on the Baltic coast, Kafka met an eighteen-year-old woman, Dora Diamant. In September 1923 he rented an apartment with her in Berlin-Steglitz. Against his parents' will,

he left Prague. Kafka described this getting away from his parents, from his father and from Prague as 'the greatest exploit of my life'. All his attempts to marry were 'the greatest and most promising attempt to find redemption, though it was true that the failure to do so was on the same scale'. Kafka blamed his father for the failure of these attempts. He wrote in his *Letter to My Father*: 'in these attempts were assembled on the one hand all the positive forces at my disposition, on the other all the frantic negative forces that I described as being the consequence of your education, i.e. weakness, lack of confidence, feelings of guilt, and all these things literally formed a barrier between me and marriage.' From Berlin he wrote to Max Brod: 'I have escaped the demons, this move to Berlin has been magnificent, now they are looking for me, but not finding me.' But he could not escape illness. Almost a year later, he spent the last weeks of his life in sanatoria. Dora Diamant accompanied him to the sanatorium at Kierling, where he died in March 1924. He was interred in the Jewish cemetery in Prague on eleven June 1924.

Four years before his death, Kafka noted: 'The reason why the judgement of posterity on an individual is more just than that of his contemporaries is to be found in the dead person – one's character develops only after one's death.' This declaration had a prophetic significance for Kafka's work. Almost fifty years later, the world recognised his genius. Kafka escaped oblivion because his friend, Max Brod, did not respect his wishes to 'burn without exception' his manuscripts. Like Thomas Mann, Brod thought that they formed part of 'what is worthiest to be read among all the works of world literature'.

'I would be hard put to say what I admire most [in Kafka],' André Gide wrote in his journal on twenty-eight August 1940, 'the "naturalist" notation of a fantasy world, but which a detailed depiction renders real in our eyes, or the sure audacity of his swerves towards strangeness. There is in this a great deal to learn. The anguish that this book breathes out is, occasionally, almost intolerable, for, how can one not say to oneself incessantly: this hunted individual is me?'

In these affirmations we already find the different attempts at interpretation of Kafka's work: philosophical, existential, religious, sociological, psychoanalytical. Following the critical editions of Kafka in Germany and France, interest again focused on the texts in the sense of a strict philological analysis. We think of Hermann Hesse's observation in a letter to a young student: 'Kafka's stories are not treatises on religious, metaphysical or moral problems, but works of poetry . . . Kafka has nothing to say to us as a theologian or a philosopher, but only as a writer.'

The writer paints, from an insider's viewpoint, a life of isolation, uncertainty and exile. The following picture attests to this:

> Seen through eyes stained by earthly filth, we are in the situation of passengers on a train involved in a derailment in a long tunnel, and just at that point where we can no longer see the light at the entrance, but where the light from the exit is so slight that our gaze must always seek it and invariably lose it; the entrance and the exit are not even certain entities. But around us, in the confusion of our senses or in their exacerbated sensitivity, we only have monsters and, depending on the humour and the injuries of each of us, a kaleidoscopic vision which is ravishing or wearisome. What should I do? or: Why should I do that? are not questions that exist in these regions.

In such a poetic context, and in order to depict this inner life of dreams, the author uses a particular narrative style, which does not allow the narrator to distance himself from the telling of the story and forbids him any reflection on the characters or their actions. This is what is called personal narration in the third person. Kafka always writes by placing himself in the same perspective as his characters. Because of this, the reader is condemned to suffer the obsessions, fixations and eccentricities of the characters without being able to draw away from them. This is

why Kafka's readers are so subjugated by the dream-like logic of these characters inexorably pushed towards the abyss and who '[lose] consciousness without losing life'.

Pirandello (1867–1936)

P. Puppa

> But yes, that is where all the evil is! In words!'
>
> Luigi Pirandello,
> *Naked Masks*

Luigi Pirandello was born in Agrigente in 1867 into a bourgeois family of the Risorgimento which owned land and sulphur mines. Initially he wanted to be a philologist and dialectologist (he upheld in Bonn a thesis in phonetics and in morphology a thesis on the speech of his home town) and a gentleman poet. His first publications were small twilight and romantic volumes of lyrical poetry, in particular *Mal giocondo* (*Discontent*, 1889), *Pasqua di Gea* (*Easter in Gea*, 1891) and *Elegia renane* (*Rhineland Elegies*, 1895), composed along the lines of the *Roman Elegies* by Goethe which he translated in the following year. The economic crisis and madness which affected his young wife, Antonietta Portulano, radically modified his life. Pirandello became a professor of stylistics, then of Italian literature, but also a critic, an essayist, and above all a collaborator on daily papers and reviews, in which he published stories which allowed him to refine his narrative technique.

The theatre: a marginal exercise

The theatre therefore for Pirandello was a marginal exercise. And even in the theoretical production of his début, from *L'azione parlata* (*Action Spoken*, 1899) to *Illustratori, attori e traduttori* (*Illustrators, Actors and Translators*, 1908), he showed a very clear aversion for the bringing to the stage of a narrative work; translation to the stage constituted a betrayal pure and simple as he points out in *Teatro e letteratura* (*Theatre and Literature*) in 1918: 'The literary work is the drama and the comedy conceived of and written by the writer: what we can see in the theatre is not and cannot be anything other than a translation to the stage. There are as many translations as there are actors, always and necessarily inferior to the original.'

This primacy accorded to the written text was not, however, devoid of contradictions. The character, for example, goes backwards and forwards between the charisma aroused by his mythical autonomy, fixed *ab æterno* by the poet's imagination, and the neurotic, naturalist and petit bourgeois framework within which his anxious and precarious existence unfolds. Sad settings, the pitiless hostility of institutions, wretched incomes, the heavy responsibility of the head of a family, unpredictable illnesses – all in all, everything comes together to overwhelm this 'penpusher', to isolate him from History, during this period of underdevelopment in the south of Italy and of the proletarisation of the lower classes, and to prevent him from understanding the social mechanisms that crush him.

Persecution mania, vague impulses and diabolical resentments, escapes into dreams and madness constitute the desperate and impotent response of the protagonist faced by a domestic hell, to the alienating work and the terrorism of a hierarchy.

The prehistory of the novels accumulates insults and provocation, from *Il professore Terremoto* (*Professor Earthquake*, 1910) to *Il treno ha fischiato* (*The Train Whistled*, 1914), from *La trappola* (*The Trap*) and *Tu ridi* (*You're Laughing*), both from 1912, to *Rimedio: la geografia* (*Remedy: Geography*, 1920), from *Visitare gli infermi* (*Visiting Sick People*, 1896) to *La camera in attesa* (*The Room in Waiting*, 1916) . These insults and provocation are directed against the unfortunate character for whom *La morte addosso* (*Death Hot on One's Heels*, 1918) appears as the most coherent, liberating ending, the exit from the stage of the world, a glimpse of the life beyond, a single and unique form of compensation or revenge.

The creature, made lighter by being dissociated from its earthly links, tends to become disembodied, to become transformed into a mysterious shadow, a strange phantom painfully leaving the page to seek, outside and beyond the text, its own fulfillment by being incarnated in the body of actors as in the *Colloqui coi personaggi* (*Conversations with Characters*, 1915):

Qualcosa brulicava in quell'ombra, in un angolo della mia stanza. Ombre nell'ombra, che seguivano commiseranti la mia ansia, le mie smanie, i miei abbattimenti, i miei scatti, tutta la mia passione, da cui forse erano nate o cominciavano ora a nascere. Mi guardavano, mi spiavano. Mi avrebbero guardato tanto che alla fine, per forza, mi sarei voltato verso.

Something was swarming in that shadow, in a corner of my bedroom. Shadows in the shadow, following compassionately my anxiety, my agitation, my depressions, my tensions, the whole of my passion, from which perhaps they had emerged or were beginning to emerge. They were watching me, they were spying on me. They were watching me so much that, in the end, of necessity, I would turn towards them.

Actors in search of characters

But if Pirandello recommends to actors that they serve their characters rather than make use of them, if he encourages them to lose themselves in evoking another, he also shows the risks that we run in effecting this walk outside ourselves, this journey towards death; it is enough to remember *Questa sera si recita a soggetto* (*Tonight we improvise*, 1930) and the delightful short story which comes in the middle of the play *Il pipistrello* (*The Bat*, 1920). All the more so because, while Pirandello's vocation as a dramatist is coming to fruition, followed by his vocation as a theatre manager, he is going from strength to strength. From *Il fu Mattia Pascal* (*The Late Mattia Pascal*, 1904) via *Si gira* (*We're going round*, 1915, which later became *The Notebooks of Serafino Gubbio, Operator*) up to and including *Uno, nessuno e centomila* (*Somebody, Nobody and a Hundred Thousand People*, published in 1926), he allows the narrating 'I' to speak in monologues, to dissolve, to founder in the multiformity and vagueness of paranormal and schizoid states, which no interpreter, however pure and available, ascetic and detached from his own ego, could, even with difficulty, make explicit.

And this is how the 'ineffable' emerges, that which exists subliminally, and a Freudian psychopathology of everyday life takes shape, as is noted in the essay *Umorismo* (*Humourism*, 1908): 'Do we not often feel springing from our inner selves strange thoughts, almost flashes of madness, inconsistent thoughts, unspeakable, even to ourselves, as if sprung in fact from a soul different to the one that we normally recognise? Hence, in humour, all that searching for the most intimate and minor details, which can even seem vulgar and trivial when they are confronted with the idealising syntheses of art.'

This variety is difficult to represent (on stage), as it is made up of sensations and identifications ceaselessly changing. This is compensated for by the presence, on this same stage, of logical 'reasoners', characters who play no part in the plot, but who limit themselves to watching other people live, modelled on the memory of the Franco-English drawing rooms of Dumas Junior and Wilde, but with a much greater burden of transgression.

In effect, their dialectical rage is no longer just directed against conventions, the commonplaces of the public, the concepts of honour and respectability, but rather against the foundations of logic and the exchange on the basis of which interpersonal relations are regulated. Lamberto Laudisi in *Così è* (*se vi pare*) (*As you like it*, 1917), Angelo Baldovino in *Il piacere dell'onestà* (*The Pleasure of Being Honest*, 1918), Leone Gala in *Il Gioco delle parti* (*The Game of Parts*, 1919) are the heroes of nihilist *pièces à thèse*, heads without viscera, empty shells who bask in their own lack of being.

Problematic and relativist, there is the anti-character angry with the institution of marriage mocked in the comic contract of *Pensaci, Giacomino!* (*Watch out, Giacomino!* 1916), lost among the animal caricatures of *L'uomo, la bestia e la virtù* (*Man, Beast and Virtue*, 1919) orientates, by dint of speaking, the theatre of Pirandello towards silence and night. These are metatheatrical solutions, solutions that will make the writer world famous and serve to mediate between two moments.

Characters in search of authors

In *Il berretto a sonagli* (*The Beret with Bells*, 1917) and *Enrico Quarto* (*Henry IV*, 1922).

In these two works, we end up with the solitude of the creator, in a triumphant farewell, but a farewell tinged with anguish and melancholy, to daily existence and to its fascinating vanities. In *Sei personaggi in cerca d'autore* (*Six Characters in Search of an Author*, 1921), autism reaches its zenith. The key scene, that in which the father is surprised in the brothel on the point of copulating, without knowing it, with his daughter-in-law, is continually interrupted by returns to the 'vigil', to the falsity and the banality of the attempts at staging which conspire to make us forget the taboo involved in the scene. During this time, fragments of poetry are hammered home obsessively which deny that different characters share the same communicative code. Gestures no longer represent the person who accomplishes them, they are acts without responsibility, almost like words, corroded and empty, no longer belonging to the same semantic order (*Maschere Nude, Naked Masks*):

Ma se è tutto qui il male! Nelle parole! Abbiamo tutti dentro un mondo di cose! E come possiamo intenderci, signore, se nelle parole che io dico metto il senso e il valore delle cose come sono dentro di me; mentre chi le ascolta, inevitabilmente, le assume col senso e col valore che hanno per sé, del mondo come l'ha dentro? Crediamo di intenderci, non ci intendiamo mai.

566

But yes, that is where all the evil is! In words! We all have in us a world of things! And how can we understand each other, sir, if in the words that I say I put the sense and the value of the things that are in me, while whoever listens to them, inevitably, gives to them the sense and the value that they have for him, in the world that he has inside himself? We think we understand each other and we never understand each other.

For *Six Characters in Search of an Author*, we can speak of a penetration into the dramatic and cynical imagination of Europe, of a sort of event setting off from different starting points in various national cultures; of the production by Pitoeff in 1923 to the plays of Reinhardt in 1924. In the final stages of the theatre within the theatre, *Ciascuno a suo modo* (*Each in His Own Way*, 1924) and *Tonight we Improvise*, we can see the asymmetry of the internal articulations, of the syntactic joins, the separation between actor and spectator, between actor and character, between critic and performance, in a fragmentation of time and space which takes in the stalls and the foyer and is manifested on the walls of the way in and in the street itself. But such a futurist and vitalist revival emphasises in reality the impasse of the stage surrounded by the new mass media or affected by forms of urban spectacle, from lyricism to jazz, from the religious service to variety. Drama sinks into the chaotic Babel of the metropolis where the 'crisis' of the 'self' calls for other techniques, more rapid and more flexible, to express incoherent and bewildering impulses. It was Hinkfuss, the vendor of sensations and of finds, the director of *Tonight we Improvise*, who regulated the flux and the intersection of shocks and redemptive awakenings between the stage and the auditorium; he was the prototype of the man who sets out to amuse, the contemporary of the hero of *Mario and the Magician* by Thomas Mann, and announced at the same time the irresistible rise of the enactment of television.

From then on all that remains to be done is to leave the town, to go in the direction of magical and fatal places, going over old roads, with the joyous and shabby intrepidity of fairground jugglers in search of unknown audiences: such is the grace or disgrace reserved for the ramshackle troupe that gets lost in the mysterious island of *I giganti della montagna* (*The Giants of the Mountain*), the manuscript and final testament of Pirandello, whose publication set in motion in 1931 was stopped by the writer's death in 1936.

The mythical theatre

The theatre became mythical, in osmosis with European surrealism, seeking prodigious and baroque shock effects, and such effects are found, apart from in *The Giants*, in *La nuova colonia* (*The New Colony*, 1928) and *Lazzaro* (*Lazarus*, 1929).

However, in the stories of this period, like *Di sera un geranio* (*One Evening a Geranium*) and *I piedi sull'erba* (*Feet on the Grass*), both from 1934, or the 1936 stories *Effetti di un sogno interrotto* (*Effects of an Interrupted Dream*) and *Una giornata* (*A Day*), the indeterminacy of perception is at its height: mirrors, windows, pictures are the magical agents of a ludic saraband in which we can no longer tell the difference between the person watching and the person being watched, between what is actual and what is dream, between the present and the past. So it is in the arsenal of apparitions, controlled by the Scalognati, the unfortunate and nevertheless privileged hosts of *The Giants*, desire appears on the stage. While the 'reasoner' disappears, the word is transformed: it becomes a 'construction', the evocator and creator of reality, able to cure the paralysed child of *Lazarus* or to make the island of the wicked disappear, submerged by a tidal wave in *The New Colony*. Marta Abba, the young actress discovered by the dramatist in 1925, at the beginning of his activities as leader of the company at the Art Theatre of Rome, was the high priestess of that religious dimension, of that hieratic and evocative pronunciation. For her Pirandello created female roles filled with a relentless tension between animality and spirituality, between physiological maternity and aesthetic maternity: Tuda in *Diana e la Tuda* (*Diana and Tuda*, 1927), Marta in *L'amica delle mogli* (*The Confidante of Wives*, 1929), the Sconosciuta (Unknown Woman) in *Come tu me vuoi* (*As You Want Me*, 1930), Donata in *Trovarsi* (*Finding Each Other*, 1932), Verotcha, the exotic Russian woman of *Quando si è qualcuno* (*When You are Someone*, 1933), the young girl that an old poet, all of a tremble, falls in love with, but ends up by leaving because she could be his daughter. Motherhood, so often integrated into the work of Pirandello as a theme, now becomes a dramatic form. The dual couple, held together by the solidarity of devotion mother/child, as in the closing catastrophe of *The New Colony*, or in the journey of initiation in *La favola del figlio cambiato* (*The Fable of the Changeling*, 1933), conquers the isolation to which a person is condemned, i.e. the individual mask, and 'the other' is no longer a wall one walks away from. Whether it be a prostitute like Spera in *The New Colony*, or an adulterous and rebellious woman like Sara in *Lazarus*, the process of transforming matter into spirit rises to even more astonishing levels: fathers disappear and poets kill themselves (so, in the prologue to *The Giants*, a technological society which does not care about motherhood, seems doomed to extinction), but, on the other hand, the Sicilian-expressionist regression back to the great Mediterranean mother can take place fully.

Cavafy (1863–1933)

C. Storghiopoulos

Imperceptibly, I have been walled away from the world.

Constantinos Cavafy,
'*Walls*'

An original character, Cavafy, isolated from the Hellenic world, devoted himself exclusively to poetry and reading history, apart from one or two works in prose. He is the poet of our present rather than the poet of his time and of the past. If we remember the European cultural environment with which he identified the most, we have to recognise that there are many correspondences with the European present. Beyond the links he had with his own time, his work contains so many modern elements and shows itself so close to the psychology of postwar man that he is, rightly, considered today to be the 'number one precursor' of modern poetry – and not just in Greece.

The precursor of modern poetry

The ninth and last child of Petros Cavafy and Chariklia Fotiadis, Constantinos Cavafy was born in Alexandria in April 1863 and died there in April 1933. He made his first appearance in the world of letters in 1886 as a collaborator to the review *Hesperos* in Leipzig. From then on, his works were published in different reviews, annual almanacs and newspapers in Athens, Alexandria and Constantinople. But he is especially in the habit of having one or two poems at a time printed on loose-leaf pages, of bringing them together afterwards in brochures and of finally having them published in loose-sheet format, bound or stuck together to circulate them 'uncommercially'. The first edition presented by Rika Segopoulou containing one hundred and fifty-four poems that he had himself 'recognised' took place in Alexandria, two years after his death. The body of his poetic work is swollen by the publication of *Ta Apokirighmena* (*The Disowned Poems*, published in 1983), while his prose output consisted of the *Anekdhota peza* (*Texts in Prose*, published in 1963), the *Anekdhota peza kimena* (*Unpublished Texts in Prose*, published in 1963), and the tale *In the Light of Day* (published in 1979), a peripheral work. By introducing in his work the realism of 'everyday life' and by taking the first step towards new modes of expression, Cavafy brought into the writing customs of his time singular elements which strayed from the beaten tracks of traditional versification and, more generally, from the paths of the neo-Hellenic tradition.

A 'difficult' poet in the understanding that Seferis had of that term, he hammered the form of his work into a mixed language peculiar to him based on a purist language tinged with demotic. His strategy not only aimed at producing a surprise effect, it was also the expression of an existential originality connected to his unstated sexual penchants. A scholarly writer, particularly when it came to history, he added to the anachronistic originality of his language the singularity of his sources: he took his inspiration from the Byzantines and the authors of the Hellenistic period, above all from historians and chroniclers, the Church Fathers and the Alexandrines, those makers of epigrams quoted by Constantine Cephalas in the *Palatine Anthology*, as well as in more recent historians. Afterwards he matched his finds with those of Dante and of certain English writers, with Wilde and with his theories on aestheticism, with the Parnassians and with the French symbolists and the cultured Greek poets of the first Athenian school – all this at a time when his brother poets were fighting in Greece to impose demotic without differentiating themselves from the poetic tradition. That is why Cavafy clashed so visibly with his peers.

Introspection

Cavafy's poetry is an evocative, hemmed-in poetry, centred on man and anti-rational despite his intellectualism and his absence of spontaneity, often prosaic, with rare moments of lyricism. It had its roots in the Hellenistic era to express an experience at once individual and social. Sometimes didactic, it ranges from extreme subjectivity to universality. It is characterised by realism and aestheticism, scepticism and irony, sobriety of expression and a certain preciosity. However, forbidden love, immurement within 'walls' as in the poem of the same name, and introspection crystallise poetic sensibility into a modern form of expression.

ΧΩΡΙΣ περίσκεψιν, χωρίς λύπην,
χωρίς αἰδὼ

μεγάλα κ'ὑψηλὰ τριγύρω μου
ἔκτισαν τείχη.

Καὶ κάθομαι καὶ ἀπελπίζομαι
τώρα ἐδὼ.
Ἄλλο δὲν σκέπτομαι: τὸν νοῦν μου
τρώγει αὐτὴ ἡ τύχη.

Διότι πράγματα πολλὰ ἔξω νὰ
κάμω εἶχον.
Ἀ ὅταν ἔκτιζαν τὰ τείχη πως νὰ
μὴν προσέξω.

Ἀλλὰ δὲν ἄκουσα ποτὲ κρότον
κτιστῶν ἤ ἦχον.
Ἀνεπαισθήτως μ' ἔκλεισαν ἀπὸ τὸν
κόσμον ἔξω.

Walls

Without consideration, without pity, without modesty,
around me, big and high, they have built walls.
And now here I am, here, plunged into despair.
I can only think of this fate which is eating away at my spirit;
for I had so many things to accomplish outside.
When these walls were going up,
How is it that I took no notice?
However, I heard no noise
of stonemasons, nor echoes.
Imperceptibly I have been walled away from the world.

Outside there is the 'town' and the urban environment from which nature is totally absent. All that exists is 'a little of that town so much loved, / a little of the movement of the street and of shops'. What counts most is what is going on inside when the poet, turning in on himself to avoid the impasse created by social imperatives, has to face another impasse:

ΣΥΤΕΣ τὲς σκοτεινὲς κάμαρες,
ποὺ περνὼ
μέρες βαρυές, ἐπάνω κάτω
τριγυρνὼ
γιὰ νἄβρω τὰ παράθυρα. –

Οταν, ἀνοίξει
ἕνα παράθυρο θάναι παρηγορία. –
Μὰ τὰ παράθυρα δὲν βρίσκονται,
ἢ δὲν μπορῶ
νὰ τἄβρω. Καὶ καλλίτερα ἴσως
νὰ μὴν τὰ βρῶ.
Ισως τὸ φῶς θάναι μιὰ νέα
τυραννία.
Ποιὸς ξέρει τί καινούρια
πράγματα θὰ δείξει.

The Windows

In these dark rooms, where I pass
oppressive days, I roam about
trying to find windows. –
When one of them is open,
it will be a consolation to me. –
But there are no windows, or it is I
who cannot find them. Perhaps
it is better this way.
Perhaps the light would only be
a new kind of tyranny.
Who knows what new things conjure up . . . it
  would

So Cavafy is the first writer of neo-Hellenic poetry to experience a double impasse by being a prisoner in the realm of the conscious. Certain supernatural forces – Necessity, Fate, Destiny, 'the mysterious noise / of events as they happen', 'the footsteps of the Furies' – prolong his world towards zones of 'shadow', make it existentially less cramped, but do not manage to open it up to a transcendental realm, nor to indicate clearly to it, in spite of its 'underlying' religiousness, the path of metaphysics. However, to Fate, Destiny and Necessity, Cavafy opposes human dignity; against Ephialtes and the Medes, who will 'end up by getting through', Cavafy leads a desperate resistance which opposes his vision of life to the whole of the neo-Hellenic poetic tradition.

Poetry is born from things

Up till then neo-Hellenic poetry was the fruit of words and feelings. With Cavafy, poetry is born from things and ideas, while feelings are expressed by reflection. We are present, thanks to silence, at a 'transformation of thought into feeling', or rather it is feeling which is transformed into thought. The poet is not in the habit of unveiling his feelings. And yet their masking cannot suppress the latter, and their mental transfiguration confers on them an important dimension which envelops the work with an increased dramatic aura, the fruit of philosophical reflection. The moral of 'Walls' and its evocative aesthetic do not allow its dramatic character to express itself; they relegate it to the realm of the implied and pass over it in silence. The latter is crystallised by 'its firmly forbidden, frowned upon erotic penchant'. Not very demonstrative by nature, Cavafy has recourse to artifice and masks.

In so doing, he sketches an intellectualised reality and relies on history to transpose this reality into the past; he thus creates a multitude of masks to hide his face, fictions to conceal his eroticism, adding to real historical characters other imaginary characters, which allow him to complete the image of an idealised and sensual world. At the same time, he has recourse to his own past and strives to resuscitate intellectually his erotic sensations, and in so doing resuscitates an atmosphere of confinement. Characteristic in this respect is the fact that a number of his sensual poems were written when he had stopped, or almost stopped having a sex life. For this reason, in fact, most of the beautiful young men in his poetry are, like those on tombs, ghosts of the past, and suggest an awful feeling of being worn. In effect, the return of Cavafy to the past does not constitute a romantic reverie but a 'retrospection', as he liked to say himself. By means of a mirage in time and correspondence in space, the poet proceeds to an intellectualised resurrection of the past in the present, quite conscious that everything that is lost is lost forever.

Cavafy uses history and mythology in a similar way to create the impression that the past and the present identify with each other in time; this temporal fusion feeds his erotic passion and a reflection on social questions.

To treat time in this way, to show its face by hiding it or by using its reflection in a mirror, to enter into a subject through a crack and to generalise on the basis of a detail, but also to refer to authors and events, to borrow phrases from them, are all things which appear for the first time in Cavafy, before being adopted by Ezra Pound and by T.S. Eliot. These things constitute characteristics of modern poetry and are part of those 'difficulties' that the reader meets from time to time. It is because of these difficulties that modern poetry has been described as cerebral and accused of being unintelligible, while all it was doing was illustrating a different function of poetic thought.

Pessoa (1888–1935)

A. Saraiva

I do not intend to enjoy my life; [. . .]
I merely want to make it great.

Fernando Pessoa

Fernando Antonio Nogueira Pessoa was born in Lisbon in 1888 while the town was celebrating the feast of his patron saint, Saint Anthony, from whom he received one of his Christian names. He is considered to be one of the most important Portuguese writers. Roman Jakobsen included him in 'the list of world-class artists born during the 1880s along with Picasso, Joyce, Braque, Stravinsky, Khlebnikov and Le Corbusier'.

Profession: commercial correspondent

Pessoa's mother belonged to a great family in the Azores: she was the daughter of a jurisconsult and director general of the Kingdom's ministry, spoke several languages and wrote verse. Pessoa's father, a music critic for Lisbon's main newspaper, was descended from an aristocratic Jewish family (Pessoa one day drew its coat of arms), one of whose ancestors was persecuted by the Inquisition. Having become an only child – his brother

died at the age of one, a few months after the death of their father – Pessoa was suddenly faced with being alone, which no doubt explains why he felt the need, from his earliest years, to invent different names for himself. Towards the end of 1895, his mother married the Portuguese consul in Durban. From this union five half-brothers were born with whom Pessoa did not get on particularly well.

Pessoa was a pupil in the Catholic convent, then at the high school in Durban. Later, at the school of commerce and Cape University, he was a brilliant student. However, he decided to return to Lisbon to follow the courses of the faculty school of letters. But he lost interest in it two years later, when he began to work for a company as a commercial correspondent. He carried out these duties to the end of his days; his other efforts – publisher, astrologer, mine prospector and museum curator – failed.

Once settled in Lisbon, which he looked on as his home, Pessoa had many friends, particularly Sá-Carneiro. He lived for literature (but not, unfortunately, from literature), which led, twice, to his breaking off his engagement with his fiancée and work colleague, Ofelia. He was aware of his genius (which, he knew, would only be recognised after his death) and of the 'mission' that he owed it to himself to accomplish: 'I do not intend to enjoy my life; I do not even think about enjoying it. I merely want to make it great . . . I just want it to belong to the whole of humanity, even if, in order to achieve that, I have to lose it as my own.'

If, from his childhood days, he wrote texts and invented characters and journals, it was only in 1912 that he published for the first time in the review *A Águia* (*The Eagle*), an essay on the new Portuguese poetry in which he predicted the coming of a 'super-Camões'. From then on and until he died, he published many poems (two hundred and ninety-nine) and texts in prose (one hundred and thirty-two). He signed these with different names in newpapers and reviews, founded by himself or to the creation of which he had contributed, among others the reviews *Athena* and *Orpheu*, whose two published editions and the third, which will not be distributed, represented the end of the Portuguese modernist movement in 1915. On the other hand, he never tried to publish his books, apart from those he wrote in English (*thirty-five Sonnets*, 1918; *Antinous*, 1918; *English Poems I–II*, 1921; *English Poems III, Epithalamium*, 1921). Similarly, apart from a few brochures, all he published in Portuguese was the collection *Mensagem* (*Message*) a year before his death.

An enormous work

Pessoa, however, never stopped planning to publish things. He ordered and classified with that aim in view his papers that he kept in a chest: more than twenty-seven thousand of them. These original texts are today at the National Library of Lisbon where, duly catalogued, they are the object of specialist attention and of the attention of the official team responsible for the critical edition of Pessoa's work. It is indeed an enormous work, especially when we consider that Pessoa only lived for forty-seven years. It is an eclectic and complex work, as if Pessoa had wanted to prove that he had been 'a whole literature to himself'. It is made up of poems in Portuguese, English and French, of different genres (epic and popular, bucolic and futurist poetry), but also fictional texts (the fragmentary novel *Livro do Desassossego*, *The Book of Untranquillity*, 1913–1934), in which Pessoa questions himself on the fate of man:

> Somos quem não somos, e a vida é prompta e triste. O som das ondas á noite é um som da noite; e quantos o ouviram na propria alma, como a esperança constante que se desfaz no escuro com um som surdo de espuma funda! Que lagrimas choraram os que obtiveram, que lagrimas perderam os que conseguiram! E tudo isto, no passeio á beira-mar, se me tornou o segredo da noite e a confidencia do abismo. Quantos somos! Quantos nos enganamos! Que mares soam em nós, na noite de sermos, pelas praias que nos sentimos nos alagamentos da emoção!

We are those that we are not and life is swift and sad. The noise of waves at night is a night noise; and how many have not heard it in their own soul as a constant hope which unravels in the dark with a muffled sound of thick spray! What tears have not been shed by those who have arrived, what tears have not been cried by those who have succeeded! And all that, while I was walking by the side of the sea, became in me the secret of the night and the confidence of the abyss. How many there are among us! How many there are among us who are not mistaken! What seas do not resound in us, in the night of being, on the beaches that we feel in waves of emotion!

'Philosophical' stories and 'reasoning' ones exist alongside essays to do with different areas of knowledge (literature, aesthetics, philosophy, politics, religion, astrology, the esoteric, economy, commerce), theatre plays (*O Marinheiro, The Sailor*, 1915, *Primeiro Fausto, Faust One, Salomé*), journals and pages of self-interpretation, manifestos and committed texts, chronicles and correspondence, including the *Cartas de Amor* (*Love Letters*), introductions and translations.

If many texts still need to be edited and others to be established with critical variants, what we know of Pessoa's output is enough for him to be considered a great creative writer. The success his work has had recently in various countries of all continents confirms it. Although throughout his life he was engaged in patriotic cultural action, the Portugal of his time went through various crises. There was the English ultimatum, the proclamation of the Republic, fights between monarchists and republicans, a military dictatorship under Salazar which Pessoa mocked and criticised, the decadence of Empire. Pessoa, in spite of everything, always considered his country to be 'the present school of the future supernation' and strove to 'contribute to the evolution of humanity'.

A contemporary of the instigators of the First World War and the first theories of fascism and totalitarianism, Pessoa was radically opposed to them by his stern antidogmatism, his paradoxical intelligence but, above all, by virtue of the theory of creative plurality, illustrated so originally in the flurry of names which he took on the year in which war broke out: Alberto Caeiro, Álvaro de Campos, Ricardo Reis, Vicente Guedes, Bernardo Soares, Alexander Search, António Mora, Raphael Baldaia . . . were as many assumed names which, not being him, were him, or being him, were not him, because they were his alter ego. They do not just reflect a great ideological and stylistic versatility, but also an effort, never taken as far before, to capture the slightest sensations and perceptions, to surprise what was theatrical or mystifying or sham in social relations, even in creation, to wander through the labyrinths of the human condition, especially in its most fragile and solitary areas, evoked by the following short poem entitled 'Autopsicographia' or 'Self-psychography':

O poeta é um fingidor.
Finge tão completamente
Que chega a fingir que é dor
A dor que deveras sente.

The poet knows the art of pretence
He pretends so completely
That he ends up by pretending to be in
  pain
The pain that he is in fact feeling.

Joyce (1882–1941)

T. Purdue

Using for my defence the only arms I allow myself to use – silence, exile and cunning.
James Joyce, *A Portrait of the Artist as a Young Man*

It was in 1882, in Dublin, in a family of well-to-do Catholics, that James Joyce was born. His date and place of birth, as well as the religion that he practised and the social class to which he belonged, were all important elements in his life. To be a Catholic in Ireland at the end of the nineteenth century meant to be a part of a people who were dispossessed, in a colonial society that had lived under British rule for a long time, and to be excluded from the predominant Protestant culture. Belonging to the bourgeoisie in Joyce's Ireland also entailed the same type of exclusion. But the Catholic bourgeoisie of the time nevertheless formed a social group whose power and political influence increased during the whole of the nineteenth century, from 1829 onwards, the year of Catholic emancipation. This social group discovered that it could express itself in all its originality. To be a native of Dublin was to be a city-dweller and to live in ignorance of rural Ireland, of the peasantry in particular. But to be born in 1882, above all, was to enter into an extraordinarily fertile period of Irish history, during which all political and social cleavages would be smashed to smithereens. During this period Ireland witnessed the fall of Charles Stewart Parnell, leader of the Irish group in parliament, in 1890. Then in 1891, his death seemed to deal a mortal blow to the fervent hope for Irish independence he had kindled. A period of disillusionment followed, during which passions and conflicts were expressed no longer in the political but in the cultural arena. Nevertheless this trend was quickly reversed with the resurgence of Irish nationalism leading to the Easter Rising in 1916, and finally to the creation of the Irish state in 1921. Was there a better moment for the first writer of genius produced by Irish Catholic culture to appear? However, he was not destined to become Catholic Ireland's favourite son.

This reaction of rejection was in part caused by the juvenile disdain shown by Joyce, his rebellious and uncompromising pride which made him mock all doctrines. Joyce's father was a ambitious man, but also 'a drinker, a fine fellow' who was so extravagant that he led his family to ruin. All this is hardly calculated to encourage arrogance. The young Joyce, a brilliant student, benefited from excellent educational facilities, first in Catholic schools, then at Dublin's Catholic University College. The education he received served to enhance his sterling personality, and a mind suited to looking at Catholicism critically and at the poverty, in certain areas, of the culture that

Catholic Ireland had to offer. Joyce was hostile to the Philistine morality of his milieu and to its new nationalist aspirations. But neither was he taken to the bosom of an Anglo-Irish culture which, under the influence of Yeats, Synge, Moore, Russell and Lady Gregory, was then in the ascendant. Cut off from all the major currents in contemporary Irish culture, Joyce repeated the gesture, already hallowed by usage, of more than one Irish intellectual or political refugee: he went into exile in Europe.

Silence, exile and cunning

This voluntary exile helped Joyce to accept Ireland and its culture in his own way, and also to celebrate his country's existence in his work. At the end of *A Portrait of the Artist as a Young Man* (1916), Stephen Dedalus, who represents Joyce, wants 'to forge in the smithy of my soul the uncreated conscience of my race'. Such a declaration should not be taken lightly, for it conveys the author's real intentions. 'Our national epic is still to be written,' proclaims a character in *Ulysses* (1922). Joyce saw himself as the creator of that 'epic'. The Irish, he says, are 'the most backward race in Europe', and deserve that the reflection of their 'meanness' be sent back to them in what Joyce calls his 'well-polished mirror'. The book that he describes in these terms was in fact his first important work, a collection of short stories called *Dubliners* (1914), in which he tried to write a 'chapter of the moral history' of his 'country', and, at the same time, to take 'a first step' towards its 'spiritual liberation'. Such objectives can appear incompatible with the 'style of scrupulous mischievousness' in which, according to Joyce, the book is written. Similarly, we are disconcerted by Joyce's declaration that a 'smell of corruption', 'of a cesspit, old grass and rubbish', hovers over these stories. But we must read *Dubliners* first and foremost as a cultural anatomy. The stories often show in a highly subtle way that lack of will, dryness of soul and an inability to act freely in Farrington, Eveline, Mr Duffy, and other characters of this ilk and are deeply

revealing when it comes to the colonised Irish state of mind.

But Joyce soon abandoned contemporary history for another kind of writing which he had already tried: fictional autobiography. Apparently he set off in a direction in contrast to that he had chosen for *Dubliners*. In reality, all this came down to the same project: Irish contemporary history viewed by a character who has transcended it without eluding it, rather than by those who are completely immersed in it. *A Portrait of the Artist as a Young Man* unfolds as an inexorable march until the final declarations of Stephen Dedalus who shows a fierce desire for independence.

Stephen is determined to resist the pressures that the characters in *Dubliners* unfortunately yield to. He insists on the vital importance that all the things they lack have for him: freedom, creativity, sincerity, the ability to defend the integrity of their personality. Without being presented by Joyce as a necessarily sympathetic character, or as someone above reproach, Stephen is nevertheless exemplary. Disconcerted and discouraged by what he sees as the 'infamy' of his people, he nevertheless identifies with the latter. He knows that he shares 'the thoughts and desires of the race' to which he belongs. But he will not let himself fall into the same pitfalls as the others: 'When the soul of a man is born in this country there are nets flung at it to hold it back from flight. You talk to me of nationality, language, religion. I shall try to fly by those nets.' Stephen finally decides to leave Ireland so as to be truly capable of assuming and expressing his Irish identity and also so that he can learn 'far from his family and friends what the heart is and what it feels'.

Begun in 1914 and published in 1922, *Ulysses* can be read in several ways. First it is a great realist novel which traces all Stephen Dedalus' movements and the hero, Leopold Bloom, in Dublin, on 16 June 1904. It is also a sort of anthology in which Joyce experiments with various techniques and styles. He is the first to use the interior monologue in a systematic way in the modern novel. In the second part of *Ulysses*, Joyce devotes himself to an extraordinarily inventive game with language and literary forms. He is taken to be the precursor of what T.S. Eliot calls 'the mythical method': a text, taken from classical mythology, Homer's *Odyssey* in the case of *Ulysses*, serves as the infrastructure to a work particularly interested in the pulse of modern life. Moreover, *Ulysses* is, in its encyclopedic way, a fiercely Irish work. The work is in large part modelled by the Irish past which crops up in the thoughts, conversations and experiences of the different characters through the course of the day.

At the same time, *Ulysses* is characterised by an awareness of European culture and its traditions which is manifested in many allusions. It is not that Joyce exchanged his national identity for that of a European and cosmopolitan aesthete. We must see in this European preference the way found by the author to bring his 'backward race' into the swing of European culture, and *Ulysses* is a long way from taking it easy on Ireland and the Irish. The hero of the book, for example, is a man of Hungarian Jewish origin, who gives us his own picture of Ireland; this picture, not being that of a native, is often funny and full of salutary lessons.

'I do not write in English'

The same desire to encompass everything is even more apparent in Joyce's last work, *Finnegans Wake* (1939), which he worked at from 1923 to 1938. Initially Joyce had a very clear idea of his characters and the plot of his book. But characters and plot gradually became secondary to a language composed of elements deriving from a large number of existing languages, a breathtaking myriad of multilingual plays on words. Joyce himself seems to provide a commentary on the effect that the use of such language has on the subject and the significance of the book, when he writes: 'in this scherzarade of one's thousand one nightinesses that sword of certainty which would identinfide the body never falls'. It is probably in terms of its literary and linguistic practice that this work is best understood. 'It is from my revolt,' Joyce would one day declare, 'against English conventions, whether literary or whatever else in nature, that the main part of my talent is derived. I do not write in English.' *Ulysses* was already a challenge and an act of defiance 'to English conventions'. But when this text was published, Ireland had recovered its liberty. *Finnegans Wake* took the revolt much further. It was Joyce's ultimate refusal to continue to write 'in English' – this triumphant repudiation of the language of the conqueror also constitutes for this language itself a form of punishment, eliminating 'alley english spooker, multaphoniaksically spuking, off the face of the erse'. At the same time, it is still Ireland and things Irish which make up the central theme of this book. But this Irish whirlwind latches on to many foreign elements: European languages, but also literature, history and European culture, and a whole range of materials from various and more distant sources. *Finnegans Wake* goes all round the world and its 'unfortunate inhabitants' looking for resources. But where Joyce reigns supreme in the matter of culture, no one element can dominate the others, neither text, nor culture, nor voice, nor language. 'Here comes Everyone,' we are told, for such is the surname of the book's protagonist, Humphrey Chimpden Earwicker.

We could describe various novelists from various countries and backgrounds as 'post-Joycean': Arno Schmidt, Claude Simon, Gabriel García Márquez. Joyce aroused the interest of philosophers like Derrida and musicians like John Cage. It is above all the modernist who has been praised, the man who had the audacity to question not only the conventions of Western literary tradition, but also the epistemological premises of these conventions. Modern humanists have often underlined his talent for depicting characters, his moral concerns, his humane vision and tolerance for ordinary men and women in their banal lives. But this is not the main thing. Researchers who see in Joyce a selfish person are mistaken. If Joyce went into literature, it was for a race which, he thought, 'would wake up to a consciousness of itself'. This awakening took place during Joyce's lifetime and this is the consciousness that he tried to make sharper by the bias of his writing. The prominent place which his works occupy shows that, better than anyone, Joyce succeeded in putting his native Ireland in the forefront of modern world culture.

Thomas Mann (1875–1955)

G. Pilz

He dedicated himself unconditionally to the power that he thought the most sublime in the world . . . the power of the Mind and of the Word, which sits in triumph, smilingly, above unconscious and mute Being.

Thomas Mann,
Tonio Kröger

'A great deal of admiration, a great many critics . . .' The gamut of appreciations of Thomas Mann stretches from one extreme to the other: the fascination inspired by the master stylist, the 'magician' who knew how to make the most of the possibilities of the German language; respect for the representative of German and European culture, that prince of poets of the Weimar Republic, the living embodiment of that other Germany, the human, acceptable face of those who emigrated; admiration for the man whose 'gurgling spring exorcised Imperfection' and who left behind a gigantic collected works; but, on the other hand, there was coldness, distance as from a relic relegated to a museum, a feeling which could go as far as outright hostility.

An ambivalent personality

This internal contradiction came, at least partially, from the ambivalence of his personality: Thomas Mann was, first and foremost, a representative of his time who possessed, even when an émigré, the financial means requisite for a brilliant lifestyle, which are ceaselessly applied to consolidate the effect produced on the public by his work as a man of letters and an essayist, and who, for that very reason, undertook, at an advanced age, long and tiring lecture tours. He was the 'poet laureate', who lacked virtually no seal of approval and no conspicuous honour. Now his correspondence and especially his journals published since 1977 show us quite a different aspect of his personality: the man who so much wanted to be appreciated reveals himself to be a solitary man, whose desire for human warmth was hardly ever satisfied. While he seems to have been looking for glory and honours, his intimate writings reveal that he was morbidly hypersensitive and narcissistic. If he can face in a sovereign manner any public, he was not less frequently divided between extreme feelings, and his physiological equilibrium was not always perfect. This father of six children, who led a bourgeois life, was constantly subject to sentimental problems of a homosexual nature.

Literary beginnings

Born in Lübeck on six June 1875, the son of the merchant and senator Johann Heinrich Mann and Julia da Silva-Bruhns, a Brazilian with an artist's temperament, Thomas Mann had an early break from his studies. We find him in 1894 in Munich where his mother settled after her husband's premature death. At the end of a placement he thought of as 'a provisional second-best' with an insurance company, he enrolled as an unregistered student allowed to attend lectures at the university.

He then wrote his first story which met with moderate success. After a stay in Italy with his brother, Heinrich, he managed to break decisively into literature in 1898 with a collection of short stories *Der kleine Herr Friedemann* (*Little Herr Friedemann*). The story that gave its name to the collection was the prelude to a characteristic theme in his work: that of the sublimation of erotic impulses into the life of an aesthete. The distress provoked by a repressed sexuality and the fragility of what Nietzsche had called 'the aesthetic ideal' lead the hero into humiliation which results in his self-destruction.

Thomas Mann decided very early to make a career as a writer, and his activity as a proof-reader at *Simplicissimus*, a satirical periodical, was only temporary. All these years were in fact influenced by his novel *Die Buddenbrooks* (*Buddenbrooks*, 1901), the first plan for which dates from his stay in Italy in Palestrina in 1897. The sub-title, *Verfall einer Familie* (*The Decline of a Family*), illuminates the theme of the novel: taking as his example four succeeding generations, Thomas Mann depicts 'the spiritual history of the German bourgeoisie' as he put it. The economic decline of the family firm and the physical decadence of the Buddenbrooks, from generation to generation, may be attributed to the development of individual reflection. In Nietzsche's mind, access to knowledge was accompanied by a loss of vitality. Hanno Buddenbrook, who searches in vain, in crises of musical intoxication, to make up for his disgust with reality, is symbolic in this sense. In 1929, Thomas Mann received the Nobel Prize for this novel.

Literary success

Having finished *Buddenbrooks*, Thomas Mann went back to short and epic tales. In 1903 a collection of stories appeared with the title of one of them, *Tristan*, in which a particularly well-appreciated story appeared, *Tonio Kröger*. These two stories deal with the antagonism of art to life, of the artist to the bourgeois, the first in the shape of a satirical parody, while the tone of the second is sentimental and elegiac. According to the author, it is a 'mixture of melancholy and criticism, of tenderness and scepticism, of atmosphere and intellectualism' which characterises *Tonio Kröger*.

Mann's literary success opened up the paths of social success: henceforth, he was received in Munich salons like the home of the Pringsheim where he met Katja, their only daughter. By marrying her in 1905, Thomas Mann laid the foundation for a bourgeois existence.

The principal protagonist of *Der Tod in Venedig* (*Death in Venice*, 1912), Gustav Aschenbach, is a writer who enjoys high official esteem and who forces himself to work with ascetic dedication. In the course of a period of convalescence in Venice, because of his attraction for a young Polish boy, Gustav Aschenbach does not leave the town in which an epidemic of cholera has broken out. Ravished by the beauty around him, Aschenbach consciously accepts contamination and death. Like most German writers, Thomas Mann is enthusiastic about the outbreak of the First World War, which marks the beginning of an increasingly heated quarrel with his brother, Heinrich. The latter resolutely takes up a position on the side of international pacifism and courageously defends this position in an essay on Zola (1915). Thomas Mann responded to this essay in 1918 with a conservative and nationalist counterblast, *Betrachtungen eines Unpolitischen* (*Reflections of Someone Who is Apolitical*, 1915–1918). Here he depicts his brother as the archetypal Francophile and 'civilised scribbler', believing in progress, convinced of being able to plan the future, while he describes himself as a non-political poet, the supporter 'of culture, soul, freedom and art'. Relations between the two brothers will remain tense until 1922, when, in his speech *Von der deutschen Republik* (*On the German Republic*), Thomas Mann revealed his new political orientation.

The Magic Mountain

The extremely varied spiritual concerns that we may note in the *Reflections* were one of the essential preliminaries to the sketching out of Mann's great epic work, which he saw first as a simple dramatic tale, but which became, as things turned out, a great novel in tune with the years 1913 to 1924, *Der Zauberberg* (*The Magic Mountain*). A reflection of the epoch which preceded the First World War in Europe, this novel was also philosophical, as the theme of empirical knowledge of the period became the very object of the story, because of the author's digressions and the reflections of the hero on the sense of this period, and because of the symphonic composition of the overall layout of the novel: in effect, on the basis of events which are spread out in time, there is a thematic weave which endeavours to suppress the course of time. If we accept Mann's optimistic interpretation and read *The Magic Mountain* as a novel 'of cultural education', its hero, Hans Castorp, the son of a patrician family in Hamburg, appears to us as a belated successor of Goethe's Wilhelm Meister, a man always serving an apprenticeship. The sanatorium at Davos, where Castorp at first only intends to stay the length of time it takes to visit his cousin Ziemssen, who has tuberculosis of the lungs, fascinates him so much that, instead of the three weeks he anticipated staying, he remains for seven years. Seen from this point of view, the sanatorium becomes transformed into a centre of cultural education which allows the hero to have contact with the spiritual trends and the most disparate manifestations of human nature: the humanism of Settembrini, a Democrat, a writer imbued with civilised values who firmly believes in progress; the dark fanaticism and dyed-in-the-wool conservatism of the Jesuit Naphta; the moribund, enchanting beauty of a Russian lady, Claudia Chauchat, and the vital power, consisting in intoxication and silence, of Mynheer Peeperkorn. In this novel, the action seems to follow an upward curve, and the true message would therefore seem to be the maxim which, in the chapter entitled 'Snow', is detached in italics: '*In the name of Good and of Love, man must not give death any power over his thoughts.*' However, such an interpretation is contradicted by the tendency towards disintegration which is reinforced at the end of the novel, above all with the anonymous loss of the hero in the chaos of the First World War. If we think about its ending, *The Magic Mountain* appears to be a novel not of cultural education, but 'of cultural disintegration'.

With this novel, which on publication, was very successful, Mann reached the summit of his career in Germany. The increasingly threatening triumphs of National Socialism prompted him to set himself up as an active defender of the Weimar Republic. In 1930, he expressed his disagreement with fascism in the story *Mario und der Zauberer* (*Mario and the Magician*), in which Cipolla, a sinister hypnotist and perverse showman is the embodiment of the seducer of the masses. In 1933, his speech on the fiftieth anniversary of the death of Richard Wagner provoked a violent campaign against him; he took advantage of a lecture tour to leave Germany. It was the beginning of a long exile: from 1933 to 1938 in Switzerland, then from 1938 to 1952 in the United States.

The Joseph cycle

'We must take from intellectual fascism that mythical character which must function afresh in a human sense.' This statement, taken from a letter to Karl Karényi, expressed one of the intentions of Thomas Mann's biggest work, a tetralogy of novels, *Joseph und seine Brüder* (*Joseph and his Brothers*), which was published between 1926 and 1942 as *Geschichten Jakobs* (*The Stories of Jacob*, 1933), *Der junge Joseph* (*The Young Joseph*, 1934), *Joseph in Ägypten* (*Joseph in Egypt*, 1936) and *Joseph der Ernährer* (*Joseph the Breadwinner*, 1943).

The theme of this work, inspired from the story of the Old Testament, describes the hero's origin, life and path, whose awareness of being chosen and the narcissism that results from this twice brings about his fall into a pit from whence, fully aware of the mythical archetype his situation implies, he manages each time to extricate himself. Joseph, in his role as universal 'breadwinner', finally becomes the saviour of humanity and the incarnation of that reconciliation of myth and reason that Thomas Mann opposes to the irrationalism of the mythical cult of the Third Reich.

Even before he had finished the Joseph cycle, Thomas Mann published a novel about Goethe in 1939, *Lotte in Weimar*, a literary homage to a poet whose personality and work have influenced all subsequent creative periods and who, particularly during Mann's years of exile, embodied for him the cultural substance of Germany. In this novel, Goethe first appears indirectly in a series of reflections on his background before becoming, in Chapter seven, the centre of the action. He manifests himself in an internal monologue which is, in part, a montage of quotations. To the coldness and the distance that his meeting with Charlotte Kestner, ex-Charlotte Buff, the now older model for Werther's Charlotte, provokes in him during a stiff and conventional dress dinner, succeeds, like a contrapuntal voice, the nocturnal conversation of two former lovers, in which dream and reality are mingled in an extraordinary way. Thomas Mann lends his hero many features of his own, characteristic of the idea he has of the artist, his solitude, his coldness, as well as the reserve and the distance he feels about others.

Doctor Faustus

Mann finished the most important of his late works, *Doctor Faustus*, in 1947 started in 1943 during the final phase of the Second World War. Adrian Leverkühn, the modern Faust, has a rare intelligence and possesses the faculty of being able to direct his gaze directly to the heart of matters. He abandons the study of theology to devote himself to music, fascinated by its mathematical orderliness and by the sensual intoxication it affords. Conscious of living at the end of a period in which the traditional methods of art have been used up and can only be used at best to parody what was, he is led to enter into a pact with the devil who, in exchange for his soul, promises him, for a limited time, the experience of the thrill of enthusiasm and the ecstasy of inspiration. After having created his musical work, the verbal evocation of which, penetrating and suggestive, is one of Thomas Mann's great poetic successes, Adrian Leverkühn, after a fit of hysterical paralysis, spends the last years of his life in a mentally alienated state.

The postwar years will unfold with Mann's turning in on himself and increasing hostility to the world that surrounds him: the intolerant and anti-Communist America of McCarthy. He also experiences reserve towards Germany and is opposed to what has been called 'internal emigration'. He decides in 1952 to settle in Switzerland. There he finished the first part of a picaresque novel, *Bekenntnisse des Hochstaplers Felix Krull* (*The Confessions of the Confidence Trickster Felix Krull*, 1954), whose title is an ironic allusion to some autobiographical tradition.

Thomas Mann died in Zurich on twelve August 1955, shortly after his eightieth birthday. More than his literary reputation, history has kept of him the image of a man who, as his brother Heinrich wrote, represented 'more than himself: a country and its tradition, more, a whole civilisation, a supranational consciousness of man in general'.

16 *The era of ideologies (1930–1945)*

R. ALTHOF

There will always be a Castellion to rise up against every Calvin and to defend the sovereign autonomy of thought against all the violences of violence.

Stefan Zweig, *Conscience versus violence, Castellion versus Calvin*

European literature from the 1930s to the Second World War was a period determined more than any other by the history of its age. If committed literature and totalitarian temptations dominate this period, the 1930s were equally characterised by the evolution of the history of ideas: socialism continued to advance theories, while psychology and philosophy experienced profound renewals. Ideological violence and the violence of war left their mark, but literature was also a place for surrealist experiments, for a return of religion and mythology, for the opening up of new ways in poetry.

THE RADICALISATION OF IDEOLOGIES

The ideological evolution of the Soviet Union under Stalin was characterised by the application of the ideology of 'the building of socialism in a single country'. In this way the USSR strayed from the idea of world revolution in socialism to tend towards the principle of Soviet nationalism. After the wave of terror following the 'great purge', from 1936 to 1938, *The History of the Communist Party of the Soviet Union – a Short Treatise* was published. It contained many simplifications and massively dogmatic statements, stereotyped formulas such as 'the history of the party shows . . .', and aimed to strengthen the links between the party and the people in a simplistic way and to prepare ideologically the 'doctrine of revolution from the top downwards' later proclaimed by Stalin.

By its dictatorial and totalitarian nature, Stalinism presented obvious parallels with Hitler's national socialism, which was also accompanied by a return to the idea of nationhood, assimilated to that of the people. The ideological basis for the notions of 'people' and 'nation', closely associated to those of race and blood, appeared in Hitler's *Mein Kampf* (*My Struggle*, 1925–1926) and in *Der Mythus des Zwanzigsten Jahrhundert* (*The Myth of the twentieth Century*, 1930) by Alfred Rosenberg (1893–1946). The Churches, in particular, rose up *en masse* to oppose the attempt at a theological justification of racist ideology undertaken by Rosenberg who proclaimed the superiority of the Germano-Aryan race, a race of leaders whose mortal enemies were the Jews. His book was placed on the Index of forbidden books. National socialism, for which communism was the second sworn enemy, also proceeded to regiment culture and to eliminate all opposition to the regime. This regimentation, made apparent by the parades, mass demonstrations and dissolution of the individual in the people, facilitated the political manipulation of the latter by a dictator. The study of that mass phenomenon – the 'people' – that of the role of the individual, and the question of the possible relationship between the two became the main themes of the psychology and philosophy of the period.

Psychology

The Swiss psychologist **Carl Gustav Jung (1875–1961)** contributed in a major way to the progress of psychological theory, which was subsequently to influence literature, literary criticism and philosophy. Under the title *Psychologische Typen* (*Psychological Types*), Jung published in 1921 his treatise on the eight basic psychological types, which result from the combination of two fundamental psychological types, 'extrovert' and 'introvert', with thought processes, feeling, sensation and intuition. These processes are not conceived as fixed states, but as constantly changing characteristics, of which the individual becomes aware during the process Jung calls 'individuation'. In *Die Beziehungen zwischen dem Ich und dem Unbewußten* (*Dialectic of the Self and the Unconscious*, 1928), the fruit of fifteen years research, Jung developed his ideas on the process of individuation, in particular its relation to the unconscious. He goes further than Freud to the extent that, next to the personal unconscious, he discovers the content of an unconscious common to all: the 'collective unconscious'. This content refers to thousand-year-old human experiences, preserved in primitive images of the human psyche, which he calls 'archetypes' from 1919. During the process of individuation and the development of his personality, the individual liberates himself from the domination of archetypes. Subsequently, Jung extended his analysis, notably in *Über die Psychologie des Unbewußten* (*The Psychology of the Sub-conscious*, 1942) and in *Psychologie und Religion* (*Psychology and Religion*, 1939), in which he integrates religion with his own personal reflections.

The emergence of existentialism

Two German philosophers **Martin Heidegger (1889–1976)** and **Karl Jaspers (1883–1969)** placed the concept of human 'existence' at the centre of philosophical interest, thus concentrating on a theme that would become, mainly though the input of the French existentialists, an important area of postwar philosophy and literature. In 1931 Jaspers had already noted in *Die geistige Situation der Zeit* (*The Spiritual Situation of Our Time*):

> The philosophy of *existence would be lost if it imagined that it too could know what man is*. It too would lay down frameworks for the study of types of human and animal life and would become in its turn anthropology, psychology and sociology. It can only be meaningful if it refuses to be fixed in its object. It awakens possibilities that it does not know about, it enlightens and starts moving, but does not fix things. It is the means which allows man in search of himself to keep going in the right direction and to achieve the highest moments of his life.

From this work, as from his *Philosophy* (1932), for example, it emerges that existence, for Jaspers, is not something finite or perfect; on the contrary, it is always in flux and constantly tends to perfect its own possibilities. Jaspers calls this process of constant making perfect 'the illumination of existence'. He conceives of a human being as a synthesis of two things: intellectual reason and instinctive existence, which, taken individually, cannot by themselves allow for a satisfying life. Such a philosophy, even when it is turned towards communication and concretely opposed to all excessive subjectivity, attributes a central position to the individual, to the existence of a particular man, thus dissenting from all discourse that values the masses.

Technik und Masse haben einander hervorgebracht. Technische Daseinordnung und Masse gehören zusammen. Die große Maschinerie muß eingestellt sein auf die	*Technology and the masses have reciprocally given birth to each other. The technical organisation of existence and the masses belong together. The great Machine Age must be adapted to*

Masseneigenschaften: ihr Betrieb auf die Masse der Arbeitskräfte, ihre Produktion auf die Wertschätzungen der Masse der Konsumenten. Die Masse scheint herrschen zu müssen, aber es zeigt sich, daß sie es nicht vermag.

Karl Jaspers,
Die geistige Situation der Zeit

the properties of the masses: its functioning must be established as a function of the mass of the work force, its products must conform to the appreciation of the mass of consumers. The mass seems to have to establish its domination, but it is evident that it is incapable of doing so.

As in *La Rebelión de las masas* (*The Revolt of the Masses*, 1930) by the Spaniard Ortega y Gasset, the concept of the masses for Jaspers appears to be clearly negative. It is easy to understand why the Nazis banned him from teaching from 1937 to 1945. In Heidegger, existence also had a central position. He considers it to be the quintessence of man's Being and, like Jaspers, as a blossoming of individual possibilities in communicative relations and the processes of understanding the world; he sees it above all in its relation to temporality, as the title *Sein und Zeit* (*Being and Time*, 1927) suggests. Heidegger rightly reproaches previous philosophy with its lack of reflection on the temporal factor. According to him, the concerns of philosophy have always been limited to the person doing the being, not, as they made out, to Being itself, for the latter is fugitive in its 'essence', and only indirectly bears witness to itself, when man seizes it in thought and word, and thus reveals it. Sartre took this interpretation to the point of identifying man with Being, and claiming there is no transcendence: man will be sent back to his own 'naked' existence, so to speak, and will only win his freedom by accepting and recognising nothingness.

TRANSITIONS AND CONTINUITY: SURREALISM AND NEO-REALISM

The year 1930 marked the beginning of a decade during which literature was increasingly influenced by politics.

Surrealism

The year 1930 marked surrealism's definitive farewell to its purely literary and artistic phase. This was partly because of the publication of the *Second Surrealist Manifesto* (1930) by Breton, but also because of the abolition of the central committee that published all surrealist texts, including *The Surrealist Revolution* (1924–1930) and *Surrealism in the Service of the Revolution* (1930–1933). Although the surrealists later wanted to support communism by adopting its political orientation, the marriage of their world views was almost impossible to bring about as they were so different. Aragon was the only one to separate from the surrealists and devote himself totally to communism: in 1930 he published a poem with a significant title, *'Front Rouge'* ('Red Front'). The communists' attitude to Breton became increasing by distant when the French government refused Trotsky the right to political asylum, thereby recognising that Stalinism was the only official form of communism in France. Breton and the communist party were in agreement in denouncing national socialism as the greatest of the dangers threatening culture and social evolution freely brought about. In 1935 the International Congress for the Defence of Culture took place, the initiative of certain international artists to combat fascism. Although the surrealists wanted to take part, they were excluded after the Soviet delegate Ehrenburg condemned them in the following terms: 'The surrealists agree with Hegel, with Marx and with the revolution, but what they do not want to do is work. They study, for example, pederasty and dreams . . . The theme 'Women' is already old-hat as far as they are concerned, and the programme they have elaborated is quite different: onanism, pederasty, fetishism, exhibitionism and even sodomy. In addition . . . they employ Freud as a sign, and the most common perversions are hidden under the veil of the incomprehensible. The more stupid it is, the better it is!'

This denigration of surrealism's aims was caused by the slap that Breton had publicly administered to Ehrenburg a week before the congress opened. The communists decided to exclude Breton, but admired him for giving his explanation in public. This appreciation of Ehrenburg and his objections had some foundation, for the surrealists, transcending the realm of dreams, try to attain that of hallucinations and transcribe them into literature by means of automatic writing. They build up almost into a principle their conviction that true authenticity is impossible without the removal of all mental control. More than exploring the territory of dreams, they cross over into madness, as much by their attempts to attain to hallucinatory states as in trying to imitate the forms of language used by the mentally ill and lunatics. Breton related this kind of experience with Éluard in *The Immaculate Conception* (1930). Éluard also wrote surrealist love poems published in *The Immediate Life* (1932), *The Public Rose* (1934), *Easy* (1935), *The Fertile Eyes* (1936) and *The Open Book* (1947). A surrealist group, in French-speaking Belgium, included writers assembled around Nougé, whose poems were source material for Magritte's paintings and titles of works. Nougé wrote *René Magritte or Forbidden Images* (1943). His poems, which appeared above all in small reviews, were afterwards collected in *Histoire de ne pas rire* (*No Laughing Matter*, 1956). The second group in Belgium had as its leader Achille Chavée (1906–1969), who in 1934 founded a group he called Rupture, then in 1938, Fernand Dumont (1903–1945), the surrealist group of Hainault. In 1947, he took an active part in the movement of Revolutionary Surrealism and published *For a Definite Reason*

(1935), *The Ashtray of Flesh* (1936), *Once and For All* (1938) and *The Question of Confidence* (1940). Dumont composed *Open to the Elements* (1937) and *The Region of the Heart* (1939). While this last work contains romantic poems, those of *Open to the Elements* are mainly the result of the use of automatic writing. In 1935, Dumont started work on *The Dialectic of Chance at the Service of Desire* (1942), his last writing, since he was arrested in 1942 by the Gestapo and disappeared into a concentration camp.

We can connect to the surrealist movement the works of the Pole **Bruno Schulz (1893–1942)**, *Sklepy cynamonowe* (*The Shops of Cinnamon*, 1934) and *Sanatorium pod Klepsydrą* (*The Sanatorium under the Water Clock*, 1937), as well as the works of a Greek poet who was a friend of Breton, **Andreas Embiricos (1901–1975)**, who wrote *Ipsikaminos* (*High Furnace*, 1935) and *Endhokhora* (*Inner Land*, 1945). Greek poetry bears the imprint of surrealism, in particular that of Nikos Engonopoulos (1907–1985) with *Mi omilite is ton odhigon* (*Don't Talk to the Driver*, 1938) and *Ta klidhokimvala tis siopis* (*The Pianos of Silence*, 1939).

The first collection by **Odysseas Elytis (1911–1976)**, *Prosanatolismi* (*Orientations*, 1940), also bearing the stamp of surrealist elements, is a veritable mythogony: we are present at the very birth of myth. Creating an original lyricism, Elytis glorifies the world, life and essence of man. He finds his vision of the world made concrete in the long history of the Greek people, the orthodox religion, omnipotent love, beauty and the light of Greek nature.

Yugoslav and Slovak surrealists take the name 'Nadrealisti'. Towards the end of the 1920s and the beginning of the 1930s, they also practise automatic writing: **Aleksandar Wuco** (born 1897), the author of *Koren Vida* (*The Root of Vision*, 1928), and Oskar Davičo (born 1909), who also wrote essays, manifestos and dream arrangements. Despite the dissolution by the police of the 'Nadrealisti', some of them wrote surrealist texts until the end of the 1930s, like Ristic (*Turpituda*,

Turpitude, 1938). The Slovak 'Nadrealisti' publish collective anthologies, such as *Ano a nie* (*Yes and No*, 1938). The Rumanian Tzara published in France *L'Homme approximatif* (*The Nearly Man*, 1931) and *Sur le Chemin* (1935). The Czech surrealist, **Vítězslav**

Nezval (1900–1958), the author of Žena v množném čísle (*Woman in the Plural*, 1936), and *Absolutní hrobař* (*The Absolute Gravedigger*, 1937), compared, in *Praha s prsty deště* (*Prague with Fingers of Rain*, 1936), the towers of Prague to fingers:

Stověžatá Praho	*Prague with the hundred towers*
S prsty všech svatých	*with the fingers of all the Saints*
S prsty klamných přísah	*with the fingers of all the perjuries*
S prsty ohně a krupice	*with the fingers of fire and the*
S prsty hudebníka	*powder of snow*
S oslnivými prsty naznak ležících	*with the fingers of a musician*
žen	*with the burning fingers of*
S prsty dotýkajícími se hvězd	*women asleep on their back*
Na počitadle noci	*with fingers touching*
S prsty.	*the stars*
	on the abaci of the night
	with fingers.

Vítězslav Nezval,
Praha s prsty deště

In Portugal, surrealism had a belated welcome. It did not really emerge until the foundation of the Lisbon surrealist group with José-Augusto França (born 1922). **Mario Cesariny de Vasconcelos** (born 1923) was the author of *Corpo visível* (*Visible Body*, 1950), **Alexandre O'Neill (1924–1986)** of *Tempo de Fantasmas* (*The Age of Ghosts*, 1951), and Antonio Pedro (1909–1966), the author of the

first Portuguese surrealist text composed in automatic writing, called *Apenas una narrativa* (*Scarcely a Tale*, 1942), and of the *Proto-poema de Serra d'Arga* (*The Proto-Poem of Serra d'Arga*, 1948). The literary surrealist movement continued until after 1950 and its multiple influence on writing carried on even after that.

Não faz mal abracem-me	*It doesn't hurt*
os teus olhos	*kiss me*
de extremo a extremo azuls	*those eyes which are yours*
vai ser assim durante muito	*from one extreme to the other blue*
tempo	*it will be like this for*
decorrerão muitos séculos antes de	*a long time*
nós	*many centuries will pass*
mas não te importes não te	*before us*
importes	*but don't let that matter to you*
muito	*at least not much*
nós só temos a ver	*we just have to*
com o presente	*worry*
perfeito corsários de olhos de gato	*about the perfect*
intransponível	*present*
maravilhados maravilhosos únicos	*about your pirate inimitable eyes*
nem pretérito nem futuro tem	*like a cat*
o estranho verbo nosso	*marvelling marvellous unique*
neither past nor future has	*the strange verb which is ours*

Mario Cesariny de Vasconcelos,
De profundis amamos

Neo-realism

Neo-realism might be considered as the opposite of surrealism, for it is very close to journalism and the technique of reporting: it is primarily about stating the 'fact' itself, and therefore representing the object as it is and not its literary form. This concentration on facts and on things is already in itself a programme. However, this is only a branch of neo-realism, designated by the name of verism. The neo-realist desire to state the facts had already reached its height by the 1920s, especially in Russia and Germany. During the 1930s, **Sergei Tretyakov (1892–1939)** enjoyed some fame with *Den Si-chua* (1930), *Polnym skol'zom* (*As fast as possible*, 1930) and *Vyzov* (*Challenge*, 1930). *Den Si-chua* offers the most celebrated example of this factual literature. This book was born out of the conversations that Tretyakov had had daily for a semester with a student from Peking, while he was spending two years as a teacher in China. He mingles the biography of Den Si-chua, or rather the point of view he has on it, with many facts of Chinese life, geographical data, translations of terms, elements of traditional Chinese culture, even information that he had himself noted in China and events in which he had personally been involved. The publication of *Den Si-chua* brought a wave of neo-realism in its wake, particularly in Germany.

The technique of the bio-interview used by Tretyakov was also used by Ernst Toller, Hans Marchwitza (1890–1965), Egon Erwin Kisch (1884–1958) and Hans Fallada (1894–1947). Fallada describes the consequences of the worldwide economic crisis on ordinary people in *Kleiner Mann was nun?*(*Little Man what now?* 1932). In this novel, the facts are those of the living conditions of the Pinneberg family, but the couple's relations constantly interfere with the description of reality and fragment it.

Another particular aspect of this neo-realism is the adaptation for the cinema of many literary works by the writers themselves (especially French writers). Jean Cocteau directed the cinematic adaptation of his work *The Blood of a Poet* (1930), Marcel Pagnol that of *César* (1933) and Malraux that of *Hope* (1938). In Dutch neo-realist literature the names of W.A. Wagener (1901–1968), with *Sjangai* (1932), and Johan Hendrik Stroman (1902–1985), the author of *Stad* (1932), stand out. Ferdinand Bordewijk (1884–1965) had great success with *Blokken* (*Blocks*, 1931), *Bint, roman van een zender* (*Bint, the Novel of a Prophet*, 1934) and *Karakter* (*Character*, 1938). In Flemish-speaking Belgium, **Willem Elsschot (1882–1960)** presented the most straightforward realities, the facts of everyday life, in *Tsjip* (*The Ship*, 1934) and *Kaas* (*Cheese*, 1933). This last novel is the story of an accountant who sets up in the cheese business, but fails and has to become an accountant again just to be able to survive. The Czech neo-realist Karel Poláček (1892–1944) paints a picture of the petite bourgeoisie in *Okresní město* (*The Provincial Capital*, 1936–1939). Karel Nové (1890–1980) depicts the life of workers in the 1930s and observes the evolution of a proletarian family in his trilogy *Železný bruh* (*The Iron Circle*, 1927–1932); Olbracht made the discovery of sub-Carpathian Russia in *Nicola Šuhaj Loupežník* (*Nicola Šuhaj the Bandit*, 1933). In Slovakia, Josef Cíger-Hronský (1896–1960) and Urban relaunched the realist story devoted to peasant life. Neo-realism also emerged in Poland with the group Przedmieszie (Preface), of which Helena Boguszewska (1886–1978) and Jerzy Kornacki (1908–1981) were members.

In 1932 the Pole Ksawery Pruszyński (1907–1950), constructed a sort of bridge between this factual research, coming out of the First World War, and the new conflict it is feared will soon come about. In his works *Sarajewo* (1914), *Szanghai* (1932) and *Gdansk* (1931), he used the technique of reportage, in the last-mentioned to imagine the outbreak in Gdansk (Danzig) of a Second World War several years before it actually happened. But it was principally the First World War which was, at the end of the 1920s and the beginning of the 1930s, the source of many novels.

Killing was the first profession we had in life.

Erich Maria Remarque,
All Quiet on the Western Front

Novels on the First World War

During the First World War and its immediate aftermath, it was mainly English poets, the best-known of whom were Owen and Sassoon, who recorded their experiences of the slaughter. But at the end of the 1920s, many novels

Er fiel im Oktober 1918, an einem Tage, der so ruhig und still war an der ganzen Front, daß der Heeresbericht sich nur auf den Satz beschränkte, im Westen sei nichts Neues zu melden.

Erich Maria Remarque,
In Westen nichts Neues

represented the horrors of war in all its atrocity, with the aim of bearing witness to its inanity. This stupidity, with its unending sea of mud, the immobility of tactical war, its arsenal of weapons, the equality of value in human terms chivalrously credited to the enemy characterise all these novels, in which, despite the horror, we discover a depth of human dignity. Erich Maria Remarque (1898–1970) comes first to mind with *In Westen nichts Neues* (*All Quiet on the Western Front*, 1929).

He fell in October 1918,
on a day that was
so peaceful over the whole front that
the military communiqué limited itself to
pointing out that in the West nothing
new had happened.

This ending not only explains the book's title, it brings out the unimportance and anonymity of an individual death in relation to the importance given to events of a collective nature. The hero, who tells his story in the first person, and who becomes in this way a character familiar to the reader, is suddenly transformed into an anonymous third party whose death is unimportant. On this death which closes the book, the circle described since the warning given at the beginning closes too: 'This book is not meant to be either an accusation or a confession. It is only meant to be an attempt to report on a generation destroyed by the war, even though it escaped its shells.'

This thesis of the 'lost generation' is found in most novels about the war: in Remarque's second novel, *Der Weg zurück* (*The Way Back*, 1931), in *Krieg* (*War*, 1930) by Ludwig Renn (1889–1979), and in *Erziehung vor Verdun* (*Lesson before Verdun*, 1935) by Arnold Zweig.

In Great Britain novels about the war that had just ended appeared in large numbers. The poet Sassoon evoked its horrors in *Memories of an Infantry Officer* (1930). If Sassoon's poetry was written directly under

the influence of the war, his novel recalls these events already ten years away from them. This second volume of Sassoon's trilogy, which also includes *Memoirs of a Fox-hunting Man* (1928) and *Sherston's Progress* (1936), is one of those anti-war novels which deals with the lost generation. In France, Jean Giono (1895–1970), in *Le Grand Troupeau* (*The Great Flock* (1931), also vehemently attacked the warrior mentality.

In Greece, **Stratis Myrivilis (1892–1969)** described the unbearable conditions in the trenches in *I zoï en tapho* (*Life in the Tomb*, 1930). He emphasised the impotence of the individual trapped in a system which threatens all human values. **Ilias Venezis (1904–1973)** depicted the war in Asia Minor and his imprisonment by the Turks in *To noumero 31328* (*Number 31328*, 1925–1932). Stratis Doukas (1895–1983) related the fiasco of the Greek expeditionary force in Asia Minor in *Istoría enos ekhmalotou* (*The Story of a Prisoner of War*, 1929).

In 1930 the Italian Corrado Alvaro (1895–1956) wrote the novel *Vent'Anni* (*Twenty Years*), tracing the life and feelings of a young peasant torn from his youthful dreams, who finds himself dragged into the world of a war from which he cannot escape. Carlo Emilio Gadda (1893–1973) published *Il castello di Udine* (*The Castle of Udine* in 1924), a collection of his memories as an Alpine chasseur during the First World War. *Srpska trilogija* (*Serbian Trilogy*, 1937) by the Jugoslav Stevan Jakovlievic (1890–1962) is also an autobiographical novel opposed to the very idea of war. *Sol Ziem* (*The Salt of the Earth*, 1935) by the Polish writer Wittlin, described the loss of identity suffered by a simple peasant obliged to adapt to a soldier's life. The action, despite all the tragedy of the war, is often treated with humour. Stanislav Rembek (1901–1985), in *W Polu* (1937) he depicted the condition of a Polish soldier captured in the 1920 Russo-Polish War during the Polish retreat which stopped just before Warsaw.

In Czech literature, the final testimonies to the First World War are critical, in particular those by Karel Konrád (1899–1971), *Razchod!* (*Break!* 1934) and by Benjamin Klička (1897–1943), *Generace* (*A Generation*, 1928–1938).

The Hungarian Aron Tamási (1907–1966) having become, with the change of frontiers, a Hungarian in Rumania, took his inspiration from popular ballads. He described the consequences of the war and the peace. In Hungary, Jenö Tersántsky (1888–1969) described the fate of a young girl behind the front in *Viszontlátásra, drága* (*Goodbye, Darling*, 1916).

Russian literature experienced a thematic evolution in subject matter, for it was less involved in the course of the First World War than in that of its own civil war.

In the realm of the drama, besides the Englishman **William Somerset Maugham (1874–1965)**, who wrote *For Services Rendered* (1932), the Irish playwright Sean O'Casey (1880–1964) wrote on the theme of the world war *The Silver Tassie* (1928). The main character in the play is a footballer, a star player, who goes to war a hero and returns an invalid.

COMMITTED LITERATURE AND TOTALITARIAN TEMPTATIONS

When the crisis of the 1930s occurred, literature became increasingly politicised and committed. Two major tendencies can be distinguished in the spheres of socialism and fascism. At the same time, anti-Soviet and anti-fascist literatures emerge.

Workers' literature

Around 1930, European workers' poetry flourished mainly in the Soviet Union, in the Scandinavian countries, in Germany, Austria, Spain and Hungary, although the International Union of Revolutionary Writers, called the International Bureau for revolutionary literature from 1926 to 1930 also maintained sections in Poland, Bulgaria, Czechoslovakia and Holland. In Slovakia a lasting proletarian poetry was created around the review *Dav*, with Laco Novomesky (1904–976). In the USSR, literature was influenced by the Russian Association of Proletarian Penmen, the RAPP, which questioned avant-garde literary forms.

It was on the model of this association that all foreign sections were formed: in Germany, Willi Bredel (1901–1964), the author of *Maschinenfabrik N. u. K.* (*Machinery Factory N & K*), and Marchwitza with *Schlacht vor Kohle* (*The Battle for Coal*, 1931). The Czechs Marie Majerová, with *Siréna* (*The Siren*, 1935), and Marie Pujmanová (1893–1958), with *Lidé na Křižovace* (*Men at the Crossroads*, 1937), come close to socialist realism.

For Barbusse and Charles Plisnier, the most important criterion needed to define workers' literature was the origin of the writer. Like the Belgian miner Constant Malva (1903–1969), the author of *Ma nuit au jour le jour* (*My Night from Day to Day*, 1938), he must have come from the workers' world. Paul Nizan (1905–1940), the author of the novels *Antoine Bloyé* (1933), *The Trojan Horse* (1935) and *The Conspiracy* (1938), political pamphlets, *Aden-Arabia* (1932) and *The Guard Dogs*

(1932), did not come from this world. Neither did Simone Weil (1909–1943), although this intellectual chose to work in the Renault factories, an experience she recounts in *The Condition of the Workers* (1936).

Workers' literature found a particularly favourable area of development in the Scandinavian countries. In these countries, above all in Sweden, the first decades of the twentieth century witnessed the emergence of a working class made up of day labourers and agricultural workers. These agrarian societies were transformed into industrial ones. This process was by no means finished around 1930. Up until 1945, a system survived in Sweden known as 'statary' (from the Swedish 'statare': a worker paid mainly in kind). Wretched living conditions are penetratingly described at this time in novels called 'collective', since their main theme is these statary collectivities, whose authors are, for the most part, formerstataries or day labourers. The Swede Ivar Lo-Johansson (born 1901) wrote about this literary school in what we could consider to be a programme: *Statarskolan i literaturen* (*The Statary School in Literature*). Jan Fridegård (1897–1968) was the author of *Lars Hard* (1933), the first volume of a trilogy; he contrasts the world of the 'stataries', from which the protagonist has come, to that of the dominant class, to which the young girls that he carries off belong. Fridegård's trilogy is autobiographical, as are the novels by Harry Martinson (born 1904), *Nässlorna blomma* (*Flowering Nettles*, 1935) and *Vägen ut* (*The Way Out*, 1936). Martinson describes the degradation and anguish of agricultural workers: the peasants who are their masters only see them as a factor of production, a mere workforce, and not as human beings. Among the best known Swedish working-class were Carl Arthur Vilhelm Moberg (1898–1973) with *Manns kvinna* (*The Man's Wife*, 1933) and *Soldat med brutet gevär* (*The Soldier with a Broken Gun*, 1944), Eyvind Olof Verner Johnson (1900–1976) with *Regn i gryningen* (*Rain at Dusk*, 1933) and *Romanen om Olof* (*The Novel of Olof*, 1934–1937) and *Krilon Trilogi* (*The Krilon Trilogy*, 1943). The Danes

Hans Christian Branner (1903–1966) with *Legetoej* (*Toys*, 1936), Hans Kirk (1898–1962) with *Fiskerne* (*The Fishermen*, 1928) and *De ny tider* (*New Times*, 1939), William Heinesen (1900–1991), from the Faeroe Islands, with his first novels, in particular *Noatum* (1938), also belong to this category of writers of collective novels. The Icelandic writer **Halldór Killjan Laxness** (born 1902) may also be included with them, a writer who collected under the title *Salka Valka* (1931–1932) two novels which take place among working and fishing people.

In Norway, in *En dag i Oktober* (*A Day in October*), Sigurd Hoel (1890–1960) called into question the moral conventions of bourgeois marriage which appear to be sacrosanct. **Aksel Sandemose (1899–1965)** wrote *En flyktning krysser sit Spor* (*A Fugitive Rediscovers his Own Scent*) in 1933. This novel reissued in 1955, reworked and modified, shows the importance of childhood for the future development of a human being.

Idealism and optimism

The literature of the Soviet Union certainly remained socialist, but the changes in Soviet political reality, and above all the replacement of Leninism with Stalinism, prevented many writers in other countries from continuing to consider the USSR as a model. The centre of gravity of the literary debate moved away from the classic divide of left and right towards a confrontation between supporters of totalitarian literature and the upholders of a democratic, freedom-loving one. The latter, the Revolution's 'travelling companions' known as 'Poputčiki', were immediately prey to the growing attacks of the party, and therefore of the RAPP Their works spread, while, following from the Stalinist orientation of politics, the doctrine of 'socialist realism' developed.

Emerging from Gorki's school, several writers broke away from it immediately, including **Veniamin Kaverin** (born 1902), Olga Forš (1873–1961), Vsevolod Ivanov (1895–1963), Lev Lunc (1901–1924) and **Konstantin Fedin (1892–1970)**. Fedin's works are characterised by an heroic optimism which appears in *Poxiščenie Evropy* (*The Rape of Europe*, 1935) as well as in his polemical response to Thomas Mann's *The Magic Mountain*: *Sanatorii 'Arktur'* (*The 'Arcturus' Sanatorium*, 1939), in which he opposes the vitality of socialism to the morbid symptoms of the decadence of the Western world. In the novel *Dva Kapitana* (*Two Captains*, 1938–1944), which is especially aimed at children, Kaverin describes the life of the pilot Captain Aleksandr Gregorev: raised by the State in a socialist society he becomes a hero. He manages to explain what has happened to an Arctic explorer, a captain like himself.

Vsevolod Vižnevskij (1900–1951) finally decides, after many modifications, to give to a drama he had had performed in 1933 the paradoxical but encouraging title of *Optimističeskaja Tragedija* (*An Optimistic Tragedy*). Entirely in the pro-Soviet spirit, this optimistic appreciation of the cause of socialism is in contrast to the tragedy of individuals. For this work, Vižnevskij obtained several honours. The evolution of socialism in the Soviet Union led to the appearance of many travellers' tales, like those of the Austrian Roth, the Rumanian Panaït Istrati (1884–1935), the Pole Melchior Wańkowicz and the British philosopher Bertrand Russell (1872–1970). However, among these apologies for Soviet realism, criticisms may be heard: the Frenchman André Gide, for example, in his *Return from the USSR* (1936), judged severely this art dependent on the State and on the Soviet regime. Pierre Herbart (1904–1974), who went with André Gide to the USSR, in his autobiography (*The Line of Force*, 1958), relates the feeling of unease that came over him when he was made 'to admire a huge picture showing Stalin surrounded by members of the Central Committee. As soon as I looked at this picture, I was struck by a feeling that Gide would have called *estrangement*.'

Socialist realism

The creation of socialist realism is attributed to **Andrei Zhdanov (1896–1948)**. In 1934,

during the First United Congress of Soviet writers, Zhdanov referred to Gorki's theoretical reflections and to Stalin's declaration – 'Writers are the engineers of the human soul' – in order to give this definition of socialist realism: 'Moreover, artistic representation conforms to truth and, historically concrete, must be linked to the task of transforming and ideologically educating active people in the spirit of socialism. This is the method that, in belles-lettres and criticism, we designate as socialist realism.' Thus, from the beginning, it was a matter of a programme of education and training for human beings as socialist workers. In conformity with this doctrine, **Anton Semenovitch Makarenko (1888–1939)** wrote, from 1933 to 1936, a *Pedagogičeskaja Poema* (*Pedagogical Poem, the Path towards Life*) which, without the support of Gorki, would doubtless never have been published, as the following dedication indicates: 'With devotion and love, to our godfather, friend and master, Maxim Gorki.' In this work, Makarenko describes his own teaching activity dedicated to the re-education of juvenile delinquents turned into criminals in the Gorki colony during the 1920s. This re-education, whose aim was to nurture personal and common responsibility by means of collective work, results, not without authoritarianism, in the transformation of young criminals into socialist men. The very life of **Nikolai Ostrovsky (1904–1936)** influenced socialist realism with *Kak zakaljalas' stal'* (*How the Steel was Tempered*, 1932–1935). Ostrovsky created with Kortchagin the type of the positive and optimistic hero of socialist realism, who never stops fighting for the establishment of a better society. The hero of his novel, having become blind like himself, writes a book to teach his fellow men that we must never lose heart, even in the most desperate situations, and that we must continue to fight for the good of mankind and society.

To be an engineer of the human soul is to stand erect on one's own two feet on the ground of real life.

Andrei Zhdanov,
Discourse on Soviet Literature

In France, Aragon made the central theme of his tetralogy of novels the evolution of man towards socialism: *The Real World* included *The Bells of Bâle* (1934), *The Beautiful Suburbs* (1936) and *Travellers Upstairs on the Double-Decker* (1941).

Portugal offered the example of a semi-clandestine literature. Salazar having created the 'Estado novo', the new State which suppresses all opposition to the União nacional, it was impossible to use the term 'socialist realism'; Portuguese socialist writers speak of 'neo-realism'. **Alves Redol (1911–1969)**, who wrote *Gaibéus* (1939) *Avieiros* (1943) and *Fanga* (1943), made a strong attack during a 1934 lecture on the aesthetic beliefs of the group Presença, which he describes as subjectivist literature. Among the neo-realists, Joaquim Soeiro Pereira Gomes (1909–1949) was *Esteiros* (1941), Oliveira published *Turismo* in 1942 and *Máe pobre* (*The Poor Mother*) in 1945, and Fernando Namora (1919–1989) brings out *Fogo na noite escura* (*Fire in the Night*) in 1943.

Socialist literature and commitment

What do you understand by human dignity?
– The opposite of humiliation, replied Kyo.
André Malraux,
The Human Condition

Because of their marked ideological perspectives, many socialist realist works amount to 'politically committed literature'. Yet other works indicate a commitment which is ruled by a socialist or communist viewpoint, without taking socialist realism as its predominant model.

André Malraux (1901–1976) wrote *The Conquerors* in 1928. The work was based on the experience of various witnesses of events which took place during the Chinese Revolution, in which Malraux had participated along with the Guomindang. The revolution is again present in *The Human Condition* (1933) – which introduces us to Kyo, a communist who has organised uprisings and commando raids in Shanghai – but it is not the main theme

of the novel. Through the tragic destiny of his heroes, Malraux shows that nothing is greater than Man, that no cause, however fine, can make it possible for man to escape from his condition.

In Denmark, **Kjeld Abell (1901–1961)** renewed the Danish theatre, up till then mainly naturalist, with *Melodien, der blev vaek: Larsens komedie i 21 Billeder* (*The melody that vanished: the comedy of Larsen in 21 Scenes*, 1935). These scenes, rather light and accompanied by music, highlight the character of Larsen, a petit bourgeois bureaucrat and married man. He has lost the 'melody' of freedom, of zest for life, which his wife tries to find again for him. After a total criticism of society and of all the institutions which pretend to represent the true 'melody', he finds it in a child and a workman. Because Larsen, during the course of a nationalist reunion, revolted against the 'melody' of war, he was arrested. This exclusion from society leads him to identify with the child and the workman and to understand that man can only find fulfillment in a socialist society.

In The Netherlands, Theun De Vries (born 1907) wrote *Stiefmoeder Aarde* (*Stepmother Earth*) in 1936 and, two years later, *Het Rad der Fortuin* (*The Wheel of Fortune*). In this historical novel, the author transfers his personal commitment to socialism to the nineteenth century. Jef Last (1898–1972), the author of *Zuidersee* (1934) and Henk Van Randwijk (1909–1966) with *Burgers in nood* (*Citizens in Need*, 1935) are also committed to socialism.

Alongside this literature committed to socialism, there appear, between 1930 and 1945, works in which authors take up a position in favour of humanity in general or for certain ethnic groups, without direct reference to the principles of socialism: Kisch, the author of novels-cum-reportages, *Bei Ford in Detroit* (*With Ford in Detroit*, 1929), *Asien gründlich verändert* (*Asia Fundamentally Transformed*, 1932) and *Landung in Australien* (*Landing in Australia*, 1937); Gide, who opposes colonial power and oppression in *Voyage au Congo* (*Journey to the Congo*, 1927) and *Retour du Tchad* (*Return from Chad*, 1927), and **George Orwell (1903–1950)**★ in his first works, *Down and Out in Paris and London* (1933), in which he raises the subject of the consequences of the world crisis, and *The Road to Wigan Pier* (1937), which deals with the situation of the unemployed in the north of England.

The way things developed in the 1930s and 1940s would justify even more a committed literature for the common struggle against totalitarian systems, especially in the context of anti-fascism and under the banner of international socialism, first during the Spanish Civil War (1936–1939), then during the Second World War.

The five-year plan and historical novels

In the Soviet Union, writers' political commitment to socialism or State organisations produced a literature with specific characteristics. The optimism of the Soviet hero, which the regime later made into an article of faith, was manifested by 1925 in the novel by **Fedor Gladkov (1883–1958)** called *Cement*, in which the hero Gleb Tchumalov manages to put back on its feet a cement works whose productivity then serves as a shining example

to socialism. In the same way, Pilniak, who was later disgraced, reworked his novel *Volga vpadaet v Kapijskoe More* (*The Volga Flows into the Caspian Sea*, 1930), to make of it a 'production-line novel' in the fashion of the time. The evolution of this novel genre was so closely linked to the organisation of the Soviet economy based on five-year plans that it was possible to classify all these works of the 1920s as 'novels of the Five Year Plan'.

The acceleration of production, the triumph of collective effort over the obscure forces of nature, the rejection of all private life, this tone is set by the extract we give from *Den' vtoroj* (*The Second Day*, 1934) by **Ilya Ehrenburg (1891–1967)**. Together with *Sot'* (1930) by Leonid Leonov (born 1899), *Gidroelektrocentral'* (*The Hydroelectric Plant*, 1930–1931) by Mariette Chaginian (born 1888), *Vremya, vpered!* (*Forward, Time!* 1932), *Energija* (*Energy*, 1932–1938) by Valentin Kataev (born 1897), and *Ljudi iz zaxolust'ja* (*People from Far-Flung Places*, 1937–1938) by Alexander Malyshkin (1892–1938), he represents the industrial variant of works which had as their agricultural pendant novels of collectivisation such as *Podnjataja Celina* (*Virgin Soil Upturned*, 1930–1931) by Mikhail Sholokov (1905–1984) and *Brouski* (1928–1937) by Fyodor Panfiorov (1893–1960).

Люди жили как на войне. Они взрывали камень, рубили лес и стояли по пояс в ледяной воде, укрепляя плотину. Каждое утро газета печатала сводки о победах и о прорывах, о пуске домны, о новых залежах руды, о подземном тунеле . . .	*Me lived like they were at war. They blew up rocks, knocked down trees, stood up to their waists in freezing water to repair a dyke. Every morning, the newspaper published communiqués which mentioned victories and breaches, the launching of a blast furnace, new deposits of minerals, the piercing of a tunnel . . .*

Ilya Ehrenburg,
Den' vtoroj

The new conformism which emerged in Stalinist society after 1936 was particularly clear in the area of the historical novel, then in its heyday. On the margin of this genre,

works on the civil war illustrated, after the broken forms of the first half of the 20s, the triumph of monumental realism and of the epic novel as in *Xoždenié po mukam* (*The*

Road of Torments, 1921–1941), by Alexei Nikolaievitch Tolstoy (1883–1945), and in *Tixij Don* (*Quiet Flows the Don*, 1927–1940) by Sholokov. Written in four parts, *Quiet Flows the Don* has often been described as a tragic 'epic', for it relates the tragedy of a people and of a time, through the fate of a couple during the Revolution and the Civil War.

The historical novel in the true sense of the word continued to describe the great rebels of the past, such as *Emelian Pugachev* (1938–1945) by Vyatcheslav Shishkov (1873–1945). But the development of the 'cult of the personality' and the rise of patriotic values promote new heroes, the great builders of a strong, centralised State which official historiography was simultaneously rehabilitating.

Critical voices: the literature of silence

At the end of the 1930s and during the 1940s, more and more voices were raised in the socialist camp to express their scepticism about the evolution of socialism. In the Soviet Union this type of literature was immediately repressed on a massive scale: some books were banned and their authors sent to concentration camps. In the West, Orwell and Koestler became the critics of socialism. In *Animal Farm* (1945), Orwell imagined that the farm animals, moved by feelings of idealism, freed themselves from man's yoke. Starting from idealist declarations of the type 'All animals are equal', the pigs manage to impose a new principle: 'All animals are equal, but some are more equal than others.' In the end, the pigs take to walking on two legs and deal with men as equals, thus closing the vicious circle.

> Twelve voices were shouting in anger, and they were all alike. No question, now, what had happened to the faces of the pigs. The creatures outside looked from pig to man, and from pig to man again; but already it was impossible to say which was which.
>
> George Orwell,
> *Animal Farm*

In his novel *1984*, Orwell went even further in his criticisms and creates genuine neologisms like 'ingsoc' and 'doublethink'. In *Darkness at Noon* (1940) **Arthur Koestler (1905–1983)** used the protagonist Rubahov to show how the communist regime renews itself by dint of internal liquidations. Just like Orwell, Koestler reveals the danger which threatens every socialist or communist State: that of betraying its own ideals. In Czechoslovakia, well-known poets such as Josef Hora (1891–1946), Vančura, Seifert and Olbracht left the party which was becoming increasingly Bolshevik. The communist Jiři Weil (1900–1959) provoked the fury of his comrades with his reportage-style novel on the Soviet regime *Moskva-hranice* (*Moscow-Border*, 1937). Since it was impossible to express such criticisms in the Soviet Union, there developed what has been called 'the literature of silence'.

This underground literature bore witness to the aesthetic and moral resistance of poets and prose-writers whose work, destined for a long time for silence, was only published decades later. Such was the case of Anna Akhmatova who, banned from being published from the middle of the 1920s, composed the great poems *Rekviem* (*Requiem*, 1935–1940) and *Poema bez geroja* (*The Poem without a Hero*, 1940–1962). Such was also the case for Mandelstam, whose 1930s poems remained unpublished for many years. Pasternak, who continued to publish until 1936 (*Vtoroe roždenie*, *Second Birth*), fell silent in his turn and worked on a novel which became *Doctor Zhivago*.

Two marginal writers, Bulgakov and Platonov, spared by the terror, secretly brought the richest contribution to 1930s prose. At the same time as several plays and novels dedicated to the tragic destiny of a creator, Bulgakov wrote his novel *Master i Margarita* (*The Master and Margarita*) all through the 1930s. In it, social satire, Hoffmannesque fantasy, the Romantic legend of a poet and a debate on art and power are intertwined. In this text, the work of the hero forms a 'novel within a novel', a sort of apocryphal gospel which a Mephisopheles who is a dispenser of justice and a patron of the arts brings back to birth from its ashes.

From a very different horizon, **Andrei Platonovitch Klimentov**, known as **Platonov (1899–1951)**, depicts in his 1930s novels the hijacking of proletarian Utopia by the new power, which at first had attracted him: *Tchevengur* relates the construction and tragic end of an ideal communist society in a little town in the steppe. *Kotlovan* (*The Excavation*, 1930) shows workers ceaselessly digging the foundations of the great mansion of the proletariat; the hero of *Djann* (1936) drags in his long wandering through the desert the remnants of his dying people to try to save it. These philosophical fables are written in a very unusual language, in which are closely built together the simple speech of heroes and the phraseology of the new power, Utopia and its perversion, which all make Platonov a profoundly original writer.

The literature of the totalitarian right

Diametrically opposed to all the literature inspired by socialism, fascist literatures developed, equally steeped in the awareness of their mission. But while, even in the Soviet Union, it took years for a progressively rigorous Stalinism to succeed in imposing a type of art that was manipulated and controlled in a totalitarian manner, this was not the case under fascist regimes. Literature there was from the beginning treated with the greatest brutality, above all in Germany, by the National-Socialist party. Certainly, in England, France and other countries, there were fascist authors and in Italy Mussolini tried hard to use literature to reach his ends.

But the spirit of consistency with which the Germans attacked every problem explained how after Hitler's coming to power in January 1933, the destructive measures taken not only in the political arena (dissolution of existing parties and suppression of trade unions), but also in the cultural arena, reached a level unknown in other European States.

In Germany, the whole of cultural life, like the whole of business life, became the object of global 'regulation': the State defined and immediately checked what it considered to be 'literature'. Already in April 1933 there was a 'black list' on which figured, among many others writers as eminent as Brecht, Döblin, Heinrich Mann, Schnitzler, Toller and Stefan Zweig. On 10 May 1933, the Nazis offered the world an unprecedented spectacle: the burning of books that belong to the category of 'undeutsche' (un-German) literature. All Jewish and Marxist authors became un-German, as did pacifists, so works by Heine, Feuchtwangler, Remarque and Tucholsky and many others were thrown to the flames. A massive exodus of artists and intellectuals immediately took place.

Fascist literature, all propaganda, found its expression in Germany in a series of lyrical forms, like the poems of praise addressed to the 'people' and the Führer, songs of soldiers, marching songs, and exhortations to the supreme sacrifice, composed, among others, by Baldur von Schirach (1907–1974), Heinrich Anacker (born 1901), Hans Johst (1890–1978) and Erwin Guido Kolbenheyer (1871–1962). These lines, taken from Kolbenheyer's poem, 'Der Führer' (1937), give an idea of his ideological orientation:

Und Grenzland Sehnsucht schärft ihm das Gesicht.
Er weiß, hoch über allem Ränkespiel
wird sich sein Volk als Führervolk erweisen:
Das weite Volk, geeint durch Blut und Eisen!

Erwin Guido Kolbenheyer,
'Der Führer'

And his passionate regret for border territory hardens his face. He knows that high above all these machinations,
His people will show that it is a people of leaders:
A great people, united by blood and iron!

The National-Socialists favoured the drama, for this genre accorded with their instinct to direct 'mass spectacles'. Johst's drama, *Schlageter* (1933), first performed on Hitler's birthday, depicts a hero who sacrifices himself for his people. The age saw the appearance of a new type of spectacle, the 'Weihespiel' or 'Thingspiel', a kind of open-air ceremony, essentially mythical and cultural: *Deutsche Passion* (*A German Passion Play*, 1933) by Richard Euringer (1891–1953), *Das Frankenburger Würfelspiel* (*The Frankenburg Game of Dice*, 1936) by Wolfgang Möller (1906–1972). Hans Zöberlein (1895–1964), Franz Schauwecker (1890–1964) and Werner Beumelburg (1899–1963) wrote novels which glorified the war.

The negative expression 'undeutsch' corresponded in fascist Italy to the programme of 'italianità'. Like the Nazis, the Italian fascists tended to exclude not only what was foreign, but every form of avant-garde literature. **Vitaliano Brancati (1907–1954)**, the author of *L'amico del Vincitore* (*The Friend of the Victor*), D'Annunzio, who published in 1932 *Carmen votivum* and *Cento e cento e cento pagine del libro segreto di Gabriele D'Annunzio tentato di morire* (*A hundred and a hundred and a hundred pages of the secret book of Gabriele D'Annunzio tempted to die*, 1935), Aldo Palazzeschi (1885–1974) with *Le sorelle Materassi* (*The Materassi Sisters*, 1934), Elio Vittorini (1908–1966), and Marinetti, the founder of futurism, were all attracted to fascism. For the latter, war was a natural consequence of industrial production, which he continued to celebrate in *Spagna veloce e toro futurista* (*Rapid Spain and Futurist Bull*, 1931), *Manifesto del romanzo sintetico* (*The Manifesto of the Synthetic Novel*, 1939), *La grande Milano tradizionale e futurista* (*The Great Traditional and Futurist Milan*, 1943) and *Una sensibilità italiana nata in Egitto* (*An Italian Sensibility born in Egypt*, 1943).

In France, the situation of pro-fascist writers was fundamentally different. At least until the German occupation, they did not write under the pressure of an already established political system, but freely obeyed their own convictions. Nor did they allow themselves to be impressed by the will to action, or by the aesthetic of the mass movements of the German National-Socialists: in a way they considered shows of force as spectacles. **Pierre Drieu La Rochelle (1893–1945)** in 1934 gave in *Fascist Socialism*, an apology for fascism, in which he saw after the failure of all other systems an ideology of salvation. In his novel *Gilles* (1939), fascism (that of Franco's Spain) appears to his hero, Gilles Gambier, as the only solution to a life in which nothing satisfies him. **Robert Brasillach (1909–1945)**, took up a position in *The Seven Colours* (1939) in which fascist man is presented as the one who will regenerate European nations. *Our Prewar Days* (1941), another of Brasillach's works stemming from fascism, is a critical analysis of civilisation between the wars. **Louis-Ferdinand Céline (1894–1961)**, a doctor to the poor and a writer, made a name for himself in 1932 with *Journey to the End of the Night*, a novel with a strong autobiographical content. He subsequently published two pamphlets of fascist derivation *Bagatelles pour un massacre* (*Trifles for a Massacre*, 1937) and *L'École des cadavres* (*The School for Corpses*, 1939). *Trifles for a Massacre* was composed of quotations from different sources ranging from the Bible to newspaper articles: the only thing they have in common is a violent anti-semitism.

In Spain, just before the beginning of the Civil War, the fascists tended to conjure up a concept they call 'the People': Azorín, for instance, in *Una hora de España* (*An Hour of Spain*, 1934), and Ramiro de Maetzus (1874–1936) with *Defensa de la Hispanidad* (*a Defence of Spanishness*, 1931). With the Civil War, the glorification of this armed conflict became one of the tasks of fascist literature, which made bloodshed an unavoidable necessity, linking it to ancient, glorious traditions. Of the 15,000 poems or so which were published in Spain on the events tearing the country apart, a third were inspired by fascism. Rafael de Balbin-Lucas, in a collection of poems called *Romances de cruzada* (*Crusading Poems*), used the word crusade to justify this 'absolutely necessary' war against the 'red barbarians'. The parties of the right appropriated another theme to integrate it into their ideology; it is remarkable that many writers, who did not belong politically to the right, should also have made use of it, and done so throughout Europe: we are talking about the theme of peasant workers.

The peasant, a central theme

There has always been a poetry whose central theme is the evocation of the work of the fields and of peasant society. In the 1930s, this theme was taken up by extreme right-wing literature in Germany and Yugoslavia; it was also taken up in the USSR, where it formed an integral part of the programme of socialist realism. In other countries, in which its position was far from negligible, in Scandinavia, The Netherlands and Belgium, it was not linked to any kind of political commitment.

In National Socialist Germany, there was a transfer of the notion of the 'German people' to the myth of the peasant and the land, which was supposed to exalt the race's consciousness of its 'Germanic roots', of the native land: Hans Grimm (1875–1959), Josefa Berens-Totenohl (1891–1969), Friedrich Griese (1890–1975) and the Austrian Heinrich Waggerl (1897–1973). This literary genre also received an evocative nametag: that of 'Blut und Boden' (the poetry of blood and soil). It was the same in Croatia, in submission to an independent state, under fascist control, where a peasant poetry developed, strongly influenced by politics. For writers like Mile Budak (1889–1945), it was most important to describe national characteristics and to preserve Croat traditions.

Apart from a 'nationalised' peasant mythology, the radioscopy of rural society in the work of Hungarian writers – Gyula Illyés Zoltán Szabó (1912–1984) – was a powerful undercurrent, half-way between literature, sociology and political anthropology. Its principal theorists were Lázló Németh (1901–1975), a dramatist and essayist in search of a

'third way' between two dictatorships and István Bibó (1911–1978), the analyst of the 'wretchedness of the little Eastern European countries'.

Whereas in Nazi Germany peasant poetry was a form of literature encouraged by the State, in the Soviet Union it quickly became the expression of conflicts. The socialist transformation of the State brought about the destruction of a purely peasant social class: that of the Kulaks. Aleksandr Tvardovsky (1910–1971) described this process in *Strana Moravija* (*The Land of Moravia*, 1934–1936). While he received the Stalin prize for this work in 1941, Pavel Nikolaevitch Vassiliev (1910–1937), whose poems in verse *Soljanoj bunt* (*The Salt rebellion*, 1932–1933) and *Kulaki* (*The Kulaks*, 1933–1934) were considered by the regime as favourable to the Kulaks, was arrested and executed. The regime also criticised the somewhat Utopian representation of the total freedom enjoyed in a peasant village by all living beings, as in *Toržestvo zemledelija* (*The Triumph of Peasant Agriculture*, 1929–1932) by Nikolai Alekseievitch Zabolotsky (1903–1958).

The Pole Leopold Buczkowski (born 1905) dealt with the problem of Polish-Soviet territories and borders in his experimental novel *Vertepy* (1938), and Jalu Kurek then wrote *Grypa szaleje w Naprawie* (*Influenza causes Havoc in Naprawa*), the most famous novel in Polish peasant literature.

In Scandinavia, Norwegian authors wrote their works in the peasant dialect: Kristofer Uppdal (1878–1961) and Olav Dunn (1876–1939), as well as Tarjei Vasaas (1897–1979). All of them describe the pitiless harshness of peasant living conditions, though they also idealise peasant life, as for example in the work of Vasaas *Det store Spelet* (*The Great Game*, 1934–1935).

The Flemish novelist **Gerard Walschap (1898–1989)** also wrote on the world of the peasant, in works like *Volk* (*People*, 1930), *De dood in het dorp* (*Death in the Village*, 1930), *De wereld van Soo Moereman* (*The World of Soo Moereman*, 1941). This is what the author himself has to say about it: 'This is how . . .

we describe, by means of banal and rustic stories, the complexity, the modernity and the tragedy, in what we have called the Flemish people, simple and Christian folk.' The Belgian Maria Gevers (1884–1975) evoked in French, Flanders, her native land, in realist novels. *The Countess of the Dykes* (1931) is the story of the unhappy love and marriage of a young woman from Escaut, also the framework for *Madame Orpha or the Serenade in May* (1933) and *The Great Wave* (1943). The Dutchman Antoon Coolen (1897–1961) was interested in the life of village communities. In *Kinderen van ons Volk* (*Children of Our People*, 1928), he described points of social tension, conflicts between believers and unbelievers, between old and young, between tradition and progress. His novel *Dorp aan de rivier* (*Village on the River*, 1934) was very successful. The German Oskar Maria Graf (1894–1967) and the Austrian Hermann Broch (1886–1951) described the peasant world torn between the ideology of the fascist right and the anti-fascist struggle of writers. While in *Anton Sitinger* (1937) Graf brings to life, in a Bavarian village, petit bourgeois behaviour and a context which had made possible the evolution of Germany from 1918 to 1933, *Der Bergroman* (*The Novel of the Mountain*) by Broch, published in fragments after his death, described the collective madness that took hold of a mountain village in the Austrian Tyrol. Comparable themes lay at the origin of many anti-fascist works.

ANTI-TOTALITARIAN LITERATURE

To fight against totalitarianism, to mobilise words against ideological perversions of all types: there are many ways in which writers find themselves caught up in this struggle, from the realist novel to the mythological tale, from theatre to poetry.

Anti-fascist literature

Anti-fascist literature devoted itself to a veritable political exegesis to strengthen the convictions of fascism's opponents, to give yardsticks to those who were undecided, to shake fascist certainties. Opposition writers who lived under the direct domination of a fascist regime had to make a choice: to go into exile or to stay where they were and write works of resistance which will be subject to political bans and persecutions, or again to limit their efforts to the framework of what was called in Germany 'the literature of inner migration'.

In France, in 1932, writers grouped themselves within the ranks of the Association of Revolutionary Writers and Artists, in which Barbusse, Gide, Romain Rolland, Paul Vaillant-Couturier (1892–1937), Aragon and Nizan held dominant positions. In 1935 this association organised the Writers' World Congress for the defence of culture under the presidency of Malraux, Gide and Louis Guilloux (1890–1980). This congress was the basis of an effective collaboration between liberal and communist writers: among others, it included the French philosopher Julien Benda (1867–1956), the Germans Brecht, Ernst Bloch (1885–1977), Jan Petersen (1906–1969) and Erich Weinert (1890–1953), the British writers Forster and Huxley, the Austrian Musil, the Dane Nexoe, the Soviet writer Ehrenburg and the Czech Nezval.

From 1935 to 1938, **Bertolt Brecht (1898–1956)*** portrayed, in *Furcht und Elend des 3. Reich* (*The Fear and Misery of the Third Reich*), the reality of Germany under the yoke of National Socialism: it was a veritable panorama of German society. Two physics teachers, X and Y, cannot manage to solve a problem without turning to Einstein, whose name they do not dare to pronounce, until X inadvertently lets it slip:

X – *Aber was sagt Einstein zu . . .*	X – *But what does Einstein say about . . .*
(Am Entsetzen Y's merkt X seinen Lapsus und sitzt starr	(Faced with Y's horror, X realises his mistake and remains rooted to the

vor Entsetzen, Y reißt ihm die
mitgeschriebenen Notizen aus
der Hand und steckt alle
Papiere zu sich.)
Y (sehr laut zur linken Wand
hinüber). – Ja, eine echt
jüdische Spitzfindigkeit! Was
hat das mit Physik zu tun?
(Erleichtert nehmen sie ihre
Notizen wieder vor und
arbeiten schweigend weiter,
mit allergrößter Vorsicht.)

Bertolt Brecht,
Furcht und Elend des 3. Reichs

spot in fear. Y grabs
the notes from his hands and stuffs
all the papers into his pocket.)
Y (very loud, to the left-hand
wall). – Yes, pure Jewish
subtlety! What does that have to do
with physics?
(Relieved, they take up their notes
again and continue to work in
silence, as prudently as they are
able to.)

During her exile, Anna Seghers also wrote anti-fascist novels, but from an exclusively communist viewpoint: *Das siebte Kreuz* (*The Seventh Cross*), for example, published in 1942 in Mexico. After the war, she and Brecht went to live in the German Democratic Republic. In the meantime, in France, Malraux also committed himself to the fight against fascism. In 1935, in *The Time of Scorn*, he described the arrest of and the torture undergone by the communist Kasner engineered by the National-Socialists. In 1933, the Swede **Pär Lagerkvist (1891–1974)** published *Bödeln* (*The Executioner*), one of the most striking testimonies to Scandinavian anti-fascism. *The Executioner* was adapted for the theatre in 1934, and Lagerkvist had his executioner appear on stage dressed completely in red, initially before a crowd dressed as they would be in the Middle Ages, but replaced in the second part of the drama by a contemporary audience. The Czech Karel Čapek, in his last plays *Bíla nemoc* (*The White Sickness*, 1937) and *Matka* (*The Mother*, 1938), launched an impressive call to resistance against the fascists. In this last play we see a mother talking to the shades of her husband and her children, who are all dead with one exception. The play is a condemnation of the various ideologies which call for revolutions and lead men to their death. But this observation is only a preparation for the play's dramatic ending: the mother finally gives her one remaining child the weapon with which he is to fight

against fascism. The Czech anti-fascist front included many other authors and poets, but also the famous 'Liberated Theatre' (1927–1938) of Jiří Voskovec and Jan Werich.

In Italy anti-fascist literature had as its active centre a periodical, *Solaria*, which never proclaimed itself to be one, practising an anti-fascism of content rather than programme. Its collaborators were the poet Montale, Umberto Saba (1883–1957), Vittorini, whose novel *Il garofano rosso* (*The Red Carnation*) appeared initially in 1933 in this review, Gadda, the author of *La Madonna dei filosofi* (*The Madonna of the Philosophers*, 1931), and Pavese, whose first collection of poems *Lavorare stanca* (*Work Fatigue*) was printed in 1936.

Up until the start of the Civil War in Spain there were many anti-fascist publications. During the war, the 'romances', whether Republican or Franquista, occupied a central place in literature. Many foreign writers defended the Spanish Republic, either in their writings or by taking an active part in the armed struggle. Nevertheless, the most famous novel to emerge from the Spanish Civil War was not European in origin but American: Ernest Hemingway (1898–1961) published *For Whom the Bell Tolls* in 1940. In Spain itself, José Ramón Sender (1902–1982) wrote *Contrataque* (*Counter-attack*, 1938). In Czechoslovakia, František Halas (1901–1949) published *Dokořán* (*Wide Open*, 1936), and Zdeněk Němeček *Dábel mluví spand´lsky* (*The Devil Speaks Spanish*, 1939). In *Homage to*

Catalonia (1938), Orwell raised a cry of alarm: because of the rivalries between Republican factions, and above all because of the brutality of the methods of communists who were faithful to the Moscow party line, it is almost impossible from this point in time to make a distinction between Republicans and Phalangists. In his novel *L'Espoir* (*Hope*), Malraux had also described how, on the Republican side, internal quarrels and the use of the enemy's methods, like the moral confusion of the concepts 'killing' and 'dying', had made all idea of justice disappear. Bernanos challenged the religious side of right-wing totalitarianism in *The Big Cemeteries Under the Moon* (1938). First he militated in favour of Franco and the Phalangist cause, but he changed his viewpoint when he saw the servile support the Catholic Church gave to the fascist state.

The literature of exile

In Spain, one of the consequences of the civil war was the voluntary migration of many artists and intellectuals from both camps. Franco's victorious regime tried to repatriate many of them, but only a few accepted the invitation. Two essential characteristics mark this Spanish literature in exile: on the one hand, some continue to discuss the civil war and its aftermath, like Sender; others become detached from the culture of the mother country and adopt an internal concept of politics, like Cernuda in his poetry. The exile of French writers was brief, even for those who, like Breton, only returned to France after the war, as well as for others, who chose to take an active part in the liberation of France, like Éluard, Malraux or Antoine de Saint-Exupéry (1900–1944) who, after having published *Terre des hommes* (*Man-Made Earth*, 1939), emigrated to the United States. This cultural bleeding dry had a worse effect on Germany, from which country nearly all writers and intellectuals were obliged to flee for a long time. Because of this Germany and Austria also witnessed the blossoming of this literature characteristic of exile, though this term covers

the output of a host of very different writers: Thomas Mann, Remarque, Brecht, Friedrich Wolf (1888–1953), Johannes Robert Becher (1891–1958), Bredel, Heinrich Mann, Klaus Mann (1906–1949), Toller, Döblin and Stefan Heym (born 1913). What they all have in common is an obvious anti-fascism and the frequent use of archive material, whose aim was to give a positive picture of democracy, which can be opposed to the negative characteristics of totalitarianism.

Leon Feuchtwangler (1884–1958) was one of the first to describe the situation of the Jews in Nazi Germany in a novel which appeared in 1933 under the title of *Die Geschwister Oppenheim* (*The Oppenheim Brothers and Sisters*). The name Oppenheim in subsequent editions became 'Oppermann'. The theme of the novel is the uprooting of this great family, which includes merchants and writers, and which is finally driven to suicide. This novel is the second volume of the trilogy *Der Wartesaal* (*The Waiting Room*, 1939). The two others, *Erfolg* (*Success*, 1929) and *Exil* (*Exile*, 1939), were devoted to emigration to Paris and Moscow. In 1935 and 1937, Heinrich Mann wrote a two-volume novel, *Henri IV*. He paints in this book the portrait of a man whose humanity can only be realised in the coming together of mind and action, and by the pooling of the spiritual and cultural achievements of two countries: France and Germany. In conformity with this thesis, each of the chapters of the first novel ends with a sort of morality written in French. While the first half of this biography was primarily concerned with describing the replacement of religious terror by a reign full of humanity and goodness, the second book concentrates on the old king's plan to reunite all European countries in a confederation of Christian peoples – which never happened as Henri IV was assassinated.

Politically and spiritually close to German intellectuals, some Austrian writers also found themselves exiled. Musil in exile continued to write *Der Mann ohne Eigenschaften* (*The Man without Qualities*), a monumental work begun in 1930 and left incomplete. Hermann Broch

(1886–1951) and Werfel also left Austria. Josef Roth (1894–1939), just before his premature death from alcoholic poisoning, evoked his life of exile in Paris in the *Legende vom Heiligen Trinker* (*The Legend of the Holy Drinker*, 1939). But it was above all **Stefan Zweig (1881–1942)** who knew how to rise up against

the fascist terror. In *Ein Gewissen gegen die Gewalt, Castellio gegen Calvin* (*Conscience versus Violence, Castellio versus Calvin*, 1936), Zweig evoked the struggle that Castellio, dismissed from Bern by Calvin, waged in favour of religious tolerance. Here are the last words of this work:

Denn mit jedem neuen Menschen wird ein neues Gewissen geboren und immer wird eines sich besinnen seiner geistigen Pflicht, den alten Kampf aufzunehmen um die unveräußerlichen Rechte der Menschheit und der Menschlichkeit, immer wieder wird ein Castellio aufstehen gegen jeden Calvin und die souveräne Selbständigkeit der Gesinnung verteidigen gegen alle Gewalten der Gewalt.	*For with each new human being, a new conscience is born, and there will always be one of these consciences to remember its spiritual duty, that of taking up again the old fight for the inalienable rights of the human race and human goodness, there will always be a Castellio to rise up against every Calvin and to defend the sovereign autonomy of thought against all the violences of violence.*

Stefan Zweig,
Ein Gewissen gegen die Gewalt,
Castellio gegen Calvin

Zweig was not to see the victory of conscience over violence, nor to live that of democracy over fascism. In 1942, he committed suicide in Brazil where he had gone into exile, drawing the same conclusion from his situation as Hasenclever, Toller and Walter Benjamin (1892–1940). During and after the Second World War, Polish writers also fought in a banishment that must have seemed endless; their main theme then rejoined the Romantic heritage of the Polish migrations of the nineteenth century and was expressed in nostalgic poems like those by Stanislav Balinski in *Postoj w Parysu* (*Stopping in Paris*, 1941) and by *Kazimierz Wierzynski* (1894–1969) in *Barbakan warszawski* (*The Warsaw Barbican*, 1941). Among the Czech exiles were the novelist **Egon Hostovský (1908–1973)**, who wrote *Listy z vyhnanství* (*Letters from Exile*, 1941) and *Ukryt* (*The Shelter*, 1943), the dramatist František Langer (1888–1965) and the poet Viktor Fischl (born 1912), who published *Evropské Žalmy* (*European Psalms*, 1941).

In Russia, the political troubles of 1917 and those of the 1920s forced many writers to emigrate. Bunin, exiled in France, was the first Russian writer to receive the Nobel Prize for literature in 1933 for his short stories and his autobiographical work. Exile took Nabokov first to Germany, then England, then France and then to the United States.

The literature of inner migration

Inner migration allowed several writers to survive within totalitarian systems. This literature which developed in Germany, in Czechoslovakia, in Belgium and in The Netherlands expressed itself, above all in Germany, in lyrical poetry inspired by nature which we could equally think of as a sort of 'magic realism'. In it, nature takes on the triple role of curer, liberator and redeemer. The creator of harmony in the chaos of time, it is in her direction – that of a promised land – that all human aspirations turn. The poem which gives its title to the collection of poems by **Oskar Loerke (1884–1941)**, *Im Wald der Welt* (*In the Forest of the World*, 1936), uses the motif of the forest to represent the refuge of inner migration in an atrocious world. The forest offers sanctuary to those whose soul is pure and who are not sure of being able to continue to live in a world in which they are constantly pursued; it remains inaccessible to the masses who, in the din and laying about them with their swords, imagine they dominate the world; its magic is such that it dissolves under the eyes of its pursuers:

Erblickt ihr hinter mir die	*Can you see behind me the*
Flüchtlingspur	*trace of the fugitive*
Und trifft euch ein gehetzter	*And can you hear the breath of*
Atemstoß?	*a hunted animal?*
Ihr sucht und horcht umsonst.	*You look and listen in vain.*
Ich lächle nur:	*I merely smile.*
Der Wald der Welt ist groß.	*The forest of the world is vast.*

Oskar Loerke,
Im Wald der Welt

To this poetry of inner migration belong works by Wilhelm Lehmann (1882–1968), *Antwort des Schweigens* (*The Answer of Silence*, 1935), *Der grüne Gott* (*The Green God*, 1942), and those by Ina Seidel (1885–1974), Elisabeth Langgässer (1899–1950) and Benn. The latter, who had hailed the coming of the National Socialist State in 1933, was quickly 'banned from writing'. Horst Lange (1904–1971) wrote *Schwarze Weide* (*Black Pasture*, 1937).

The best-known work of the inner migration, *Das einfache Leben* (*The Simple Life*, 1939) by Ernst Wiechert (1887–1950), takes place in the forest of Mazuria, a haven of peace for the man who has taken refuge in it. There is a similar blossoming of the inner migration in Czech literature, which reacts by turning to the past: the novelist Vančura stoops over ancient chronicles, *Obrazy z dějin národa českeho* (*Historical Pictures of the Czech Nation*, 1939–1940). Next to this symbolic author who was executed by the Nazis there are also novels by Durchy and poetry with allegorical evocations by Seifert and Halas, as well as existential poems by Jiři Orten (1919–1941).

With the Flemings, **Maurice Gilliams (1900–1982)**, Roelants and Filip De Pillecyn (1891–1962), it is not nature or history which constitutes the centre of gravity of their novels, but the inner life of human beings. Roelants describes people looking for their own convictions and their true identity in his novels *Het leven dat wij droomden* (*The Life We Dreamed of*, 1931), *Alles komt terecht* (*Everything Comes Right*, 1937) and *Gebed om een goed einde* (*Prayer for a Happy End*, 1944). Gilliams also deals with the inner experiences of human beings – he does not consider life as a struggle, but as the achievement of a definite objective, of the experience we must acquire for ourselves – in his poems *Het verleden van Columbus* (*Columbus's Past*, 1937), in his short stories, *Oefentocht in het luchtledige* (*Maiden Voyage into Emptiness*, 1937) and in his novel *Elias of het gevecht met de nachtegalen* (*Elias or the Fight with the Nightingales*, 1937), the sub-title of which indicates his struggle against the dreams that attract him.

The return of religion

The reappearance of a religious content in literature was brought about through the movement known as the 'Catholic renewal', even if Catholicism was not the only religious orientation of the writers who were part of it. The Catholic renewal appeared *c.*1900, so we cannot talk of the movement's being anti-totalitarian in the strict sense of the word, all the more so as this literature was not characteristic of the 1930s. But in this context, because of their religious opinions, writers took up a position against the increasing importance of politics and the politicisation of literature. This literature was not only the preserve of authors who were already Catholic, but above all of unbelievers who were converts to the Catholic faith.

The first collection of poems that T.S. Eliot published after his conversion to Anglo-Catholicism in 1927 was *Ash Wednesday* (1930). In 1935 he composed a religious play in two acts, *Murder in the Cathedral*, which evokes the conflict between Church and State. In 1940, he expounded his ideas in an essay, *The Idea of a Christian Society*. **Graham Greene (1904–1991)** converted to Catholicism in 1927 and in *The Power and the Glory* (1940) also deals with the conflict between Church and State.

In the 1930s, in France, Bernanos, Claudel and Mauriac belonged to the Catholic renewal. At the end of the 1920s, Bernanos had already published a first novel about a clumsy priest. During the 1930s, he again took up the theme of the demon which, ensconced in the human heart, constantly fights with God to conquer it. In *The Diary of a Country Priest* (1936), an idealistic young priest from the Flanders countryside wants to communicate the knowledge of true Christianity to his little village community. In 1932, *The Nest of Vipers* makes famous the name of Mauriac, whose novels, for the most part, were religiously inspired. In *The Woman of the Pharisees* (1941), the heroine, infatuated with herself, has created difficulties, all through her life, for those who have approached her. She finally understands that, for God, it is not personal merit that counts, but the love that we give to others. In 1930, Claudel published *The Book of Christopher Columbus*, a monumental play inspired by religion. In it, he uses all the registers of dramatic creation – music, songs, choruses, dances and pantomimes – , and even those of the mystery play, the film and the revue. Two other dramas follow, in the form of medieval mysteries: *Joan at the Stake* (1938), and *The Story of Tobias and Sarah* (1938).

In Werfel's writings of the 1930s and 1940s, the effect of his conversion to Catholicism is noticeable: after *Barabara oder die Frömmigkeit* (*Barbara or Piety*, 1929) in *Die Geschwister von Neapel* (*The Brothers and Sisters of Naples*) Werfel presents the relationship which exists in Italian life between the Catholic religion and family ties. His novel *Der veruntreute Himmel* (*Heaven Misappropriated*, 1939) contained anti-fascist declarations. Its heroine, Teta Linek, a cook, discovers that only a spiritual experience, that money cannot buy, allows us to reach God. Werfel's most famous book is *The Song of Bernadette* (1942), a novel about the miracles at Lourdes and the canonisation of Bernadette. Werfel swore he would write it when he managed to escape the German troops of occupied France. A renewal of Catholic spirituality appeared in the Czech lands: Jaroslav Durych (1886–1962) wrote a trilogy on the Thirty Years' War, *Bloudĕni* (*Wanderings*, 1929), Karel Schulz (1899–1943) wrote about the age of Michelangelo, *Kamen a bolest* (*The Stone of Suffering*, 1942), and there were the poets Jan Zahradníček (1905–1960), *Karouhve* (*Battle Standards*, 1940) and Zdeněk Rotrekl (born 1920), *Kyvalda duše* (*The Pendulum of the soul*, 1940). Slovakia experienced the same renewal with works by the 'Catholic modernists' and those by the Protestant Emil Boleslav Lukáč (1900–1970), *Malach* (1938) and *Babel* (1944).

In Poland, the same religious themes appear in the novel by **Jerzy Andrzejewski (1909–1983)**, *Lad serka* (*The Order of the Heart*, 1938), as well as in the collection of poems that Jerzy Liebert published in 1930 under the title *Gusła* (*Mysteries*), evoking the profound religious experiences of a poet dying of tuberculosis. Attracted by the spirituality of Eastern Christianity and Buddhist mysticism, finally transcending all ideologies, Kazantzakis created his own philosophical synthesis in the centre of which is located the unceasing quest for spiritual salvation and, through this, God's salvation. There are two ways to pass the test: that of going through the torments of the bleeding flesh and that of spiritual asceticism. Kazantzakis's heroes, borrowed from myth, religion, everyday life, are the incarnation of proud, free and fighting man: *Vios ke politia tou Alexi Zorba* (*Zorba the Greek*, 1946), *O Teleftéos pirasmos* (*The Last Temptation*, 1951).

Mythological materials

Christianity played a part in the literature of this period, as did ancient myth. The use made of it was not always explicitly inspired by anti-totalitarianism, but it was very often in this sense that writers concerned with the destiny of humanity used ancient myths. Thomas Mann's tetralogy of novels, *Josef und seine Brüder* (*Joseph and His Brothers*, 1926–1943) is a good example. Throughout this work, Thomas Mann dug into the many myths in Bible stories. He connects this mythology to the psychological discoveries of Freud and Jung to rip the mask from fascist ideology: 'For a long time, I have been an enthusiastic proponent of this combination; for, in fact, psychology is a way to rip the myth from the hands of the fascists, those men of darkness, and to put it once again at the service of humanity. This link represents for me the world of the future, a human world, blessed by the spirit on high, and which will emerge from the depths which are below us,' he wrote in a letter to Kárdy Kerényi.

This use of myth is found again in Germany in drama, and particularly in a work by the ageing Hauptmann. While *Die Finsternisse* (*The Darkness*), a work that he wrote in 1937 after the death of a Jewish friend, was banned, the Nazis, mistaken about the meaning of the last part of his tetralogy of the Atridae, *Iphigenie in Delphi* (1941), saw in it a work favourable to the regime and allow it to be performed. Another play in this tetralogy, *Iphigenie in Aulis* (1943), was also performed in the author's lifetime, while the two remaining plays, *Agamemnons Tod* (*The Death of Agamemnon*, 1946) and *Elektra* (1947), were only performed after his death. In this tetralogy, Hauptmann made the figure of Iphigenia an ideal for human beings to work towards, in stark contrast to a world of madness and chaos.

In France, in 1929, **Jean Giraudoux (1882–1944)** took his inspiration from mythology to write *Amphitryon 38*. In *The Trojan War will not Take Place* (1935), Hector and Ulysses try to prevent the war which is threatening to break out between the Trojans and the Greeks, but just as they have come to an agreement that this war will not take place, an incident, which costs the hawkish Demokos his life, takes on such proportions that it is no longer possible to avoid the conflict. In 1937 Giraudoux made further use of a figure from mythology in *Électre* (*Electra*). Jean Anouilh (1910–1987), after having written *Eurydice* in 1941, staged *Antigone* in 1944, written in 1942. The heroine, the niece of King Creon, buries her brother despite her father's expressly forbidding it. *Antigone* was then praised and understood as a play that celebrated resistance to an oppressor, even though, when Antigone opposes Creon's interdiction, she does not invoke as the motive for her act any lofty ideal, but simply declares that she has acted of her own free will. In *The Flies* (1943), Sartre renews the theme of the *Oresteia*, in a very special way: his Orestes does not obey any superior force, he acts fully aware of his freedom and responsibility.

The Greek **George Seferis (Giorgos Seferiadis, 1900–1971)★** wrote a collection of mythical poems in 1935 *Mithistorima* (*Mythology*). These poems, imagined during a trip at sea and inspired from various ancient myths, in particular that of the *Odyssey* and the *Oresteia*, are filled with a feeling of sadness elucidated, in the background, by the recent history of the Greek nation.

Yeats and Joyce rekindled the central themes of Irish Gaelic mythology. In his last one-act play, *The Death of Cuchulain* (1939), Yeats evokes this Celtic hero who, a vassal of Conchobar, the King of Ulster, kills his own child without knowing it, and dies himself shortly afterwards. Irish Gaelic mythology also formed the background to the poetry by the Dutchman Holst. His collection of poems *Een wereld aan Zee* (*A World in the Sea*, 1937) was inspired by Yeats' poetry.

In Spain, **Federico García Lorca**

(1898–1936)* used mythical archetypes in his play *Bodas de sangre* (*Blood Wedding*, 1933) which depicts the revenge of an ex-fiancé rejected because of his poverty. He abducts the young bride. The husband finds him and they both fight in the forest and kill each other. This drama unfolds under the influence of ancient and mythical divinities. The Moon and Death appear in the shape of two woodcutters and the young woman's mother corresponds to the archetype of the Earth mother.

SOCIETY IN THE LITERARY MIRROR

The literature of the period between the wars is a mirror: a mirror of society, the mirror of an epoch, often a distorting mirror. Even in works less clearly committed, the ideologies of the 1930s are present, notably through a certain vision of society.

Pictures of an epoch

Between 1930 and 1945, there were many attempts to paint a romantic picture of the historical and cultural evolution of the end of the nineteenth and the beginning of the twentieth. **Jules Romains (1885–1972)** wrote a novel cycle in twenty-seven volumes, *The Men of Good Will*, published from 1932 to 1946. This panorama of French society stretched from 6 October 1908 to 7 October 1933 and revolved around the central point represented by the First World War.

In Poland, Maria Dabrowska wrote a tetralogy *Noce i dnie*, which included *Bogumil i Barbara* and *Wieczne zmartwienie* (published together in 1932 under the title *Everlasting Care*), *Milosc* (*Love*, 1933) and *Wiatr w oczy* (*Wind in the Eyes*, 1934). This cycle depicts, through the opposite opinions of Bogumil and his wife Barbara, the decline of the Polish landed aristocracy before the First World War.

O'Casey stages, in 1943, *Red Roses for Me*, whose background is the railway strike in Dublin in 1911. The protagonist of this play, Ayamonn, will be shot, but Sheila, the woman

he had left behind, identifies with the female figure in the song which serves as a leitmotif to the play, 'Red Roses for Me', and thus poetically symbolises a new hope for Ireland. In Great Britain, Orwell, in his novel *Coming Up for Air* (1939) compares the confident, well-ordered life of pre-First World War days to the chaotic situation in 1939: the protagonist, Browning, returned to his hometown, where he sees that everything has changed, as if dissolved into anonymity. In his novel *Brighton Rock* (1938), Greene shows us the dark side of modern civilisation by plunging us into the criminal underclass of a great English seaside resort. In the Soviet Union, Aleksei Nikolayevitch Tolstoy describes what Russian society had been like during the years of the Revolution and the Civil War in his trilogy *Xoždenie po mukam* (*The Way of Torment*, 1920–1941). This between-the-wars period is also described by the Dane Knud Soenderby (1909–1966) in *Midt i en jazztid* (*In the Middle of a Jazz Age*, 1931). The hero, Peter Hasvig, is a normal young man, plunged into a world devoid of sense. He can only bear it with the use of alcohol, jazz, dancing: in a word, all the anaesthetics of the period. The situation of Germany in Berlin before the seizure of political power by the National Socialists, already suggested by Döblin's novel, *Berlin Alexanderplatz*, is again evoked by the English writer, Christopher Isherwood (1904–1986) in *Goodbye to Berlin* (1939), a combination of autobiograpy texts, reportage and fiction, by means of which the author relives his Berlin experiences. Klaus Mann describes the period in which National-Socialist Berlin made people completely oblivious to its previous incarnations in *Mephisto, Roman einer Karriere* (*Mephisto, the Novel of a Career*, 1936), which symbolises the decline of the actor Hendrick Höfgen.

Roth takes the collapse of the Hapsburg monarchy, Emperors of Austria and Kings of Hungary, as the theme of his novel *Radetsky-marsch* (1932). Captain Hans Trott hears this famous march played every Sunday in front of his house. This leitmotif scans the existence of the monarchy until the First World War, which announces the death of the Emperor and therefore of the monarchy itself and of the book's hero. The background of Musil's *The Man Without Qualities* is the same as that taken by Roth – the 1920s and 1930s in Austria – but, for Ulrich, the protagonist, the world can now only perform mindless actions because it is dominated by technology and matter; because of this, he is only able to consider himself as a man without qualities.

Greek writers of the 1930s also experienced this sensation of absurdity in the world, but for other reasons: in 1922, the Turks conquered the old Greek town of Smyrna, annihilating its population in a blood-bath which prompted the exodus of two million Greeks from Asia Minor. **Giorgos Théotokas (1906–1966)** evoked this tragedy in *Elefthero Pnevma* (*The Free Spirit*, 1929). In Greece, a whole generation lost faith in ethical, national and human values. The reaction was a blossoming of novels and poems in which the authors sought to define once and for all the very essence which made their country 'Greece': Théotokas, *Argo* (1933), Venezis, *Ghalini* (*Serenity*, 1939), Angelos Terzakis (1907–1979), *I prinkipessa Isabo* (*The Princess Isabeau*, 1945) and Pantelis Prevelakis (1909–1986), *To Khroniko mias politias* (*Chronicle of a Town*, 1938). Their ideological position is summed up by the concept of 'Romios', a term which designates the Eastern Roman Empire and Greekness, alluding to the nationalist ideas and the collective convictions linked with the nineteenth-century movements of emancipation in their country. This concept also served all these writers as an aesthetic justification, and contained the essence of all that is 'Greek'. It is to be found in works by Seferis and by Elytis and includes the ideas of personal liberty and social justice, as in the poetic syntheses by Yannis Ritsos (1909–1990) *Epitaphios* (*Epitaph*, 1938) and *Romiosini* (*Greekness*, 1947). This concept assumes a certain religious form and a humanist optimism in poetry by Nikiphoros Vrettakos (1912–1991).

Social criticism and social satire

Apart from those works whose primary intention was to paint a faithful picture of the period, there were others whose aim was not to take up a position on a political subject, but to devote themselves to a criticism of society, sometimes even to satirise social criticism is an important aspect of the work of three British women writers: Jean Rhys (the pseudonym of Ella Gwendolyn Rees Williams, 1894–1979), Virginia Woolf and Dorothy Richardson (1873–1957). They consciously opposed their female viewpoint to the descriptions of reality to be found in works of fiction by male authors. Virginia Woolf, in her essay *A Room of One's Own* (1929) proclaimed that the emancipation of women depended on a regular personal income and on the use of a room of one's own, representing private woman's space. *The Waves* (1931) and *Between the Acts* (1941) yield new critiques of society obliquely, through highly innovative portrayals of mental landscapes and inner lives. The central figures of the novels of Jean Rhys are solitary and embittered women, as, for instance, in *After Leaving Mr Mackenzie* (1930) and *Good Morning, Midnight* (1939).

Noel Coward (1899–1973), deploys comedy of manners to call into question the words and customs of the period in plays such as a *Private Lives* (1930) and *Design for Living* (1933). But the great master of British wit and social satire was **Evelyn Waugh (1903–1966)** with *Vile Bodies* (1930), *Black Mischief* (1932), *A Handful of Dust* (1934), *Scoop* (1938), *Put Out More Flags* (1942) and *Brideshead Revisited* (1945).

Like Evelyn Waugh, De Ghelderode indulged in ironic and satirical criticism of the interests and positions of world politics in his drama *Pantagleise* (1930). The Dutchman Simon Vestdijk (1898–1971) had recourse to satire in his novel *Else Böhler, Duitsch dienstmeisje* (*Else Böhler, the German Chambermaid*, 1935) to make fun of the debates called forth by the Nazification of Germany. Such was also the case for a number of German writers like Tucholsky, Walter Mehring (born 1896) and

Erich Kästner (1899–1974), the author of the parody of Goethe's famous Mignon song written which begins with the verse: 'Kennst Du das Land wo die Zitronen blühn?' ('Do you know the land where lemons are in bloom?')

> Do you know the land where cannons are in bloom?
> You don't? You're going to!
>
> Erich Kästner

In 1941 the Italian Moravia published a satirical story called *La mascherata* (*The Quadrille of the Masks*), which he later made into a tragi-comedy. In it he portrayed the dictator of an imaginary republic as so much of a caricature that Mussolini personally intervened to ban it.

In the USSR in 1930, Mayakovsky wrote a Utopian and satirical play, *Banja* (*The Baths*), in which, to overcome the slowness of socialist bureaucracy, the characters make use of a 'time machine'. Just as satirical are the plays *Zolotoj telenok* (*A Millionaire in Soviet Russia*), by Ilya Ilf (1897–1937) and Evgenii Petrovitch Petrov (1903–1942). Stanisław Dygat (born 1914) undertook a satire of the national and popular myths of Poland in *Jezioro Bodénskie* (*Lake Constance*, 1946). While *Mieszkańcy* (*Lodgings*, 1933) by Tuwim is a satire, his poem *Bal w operze* (*Ball at the Opera*, 1936) is a grotesque critique of Poland's politics and social organisation. In his novel *Granica* (*The Wardrobe*, 1935), Zofia Nałkowska complained of the 'dirty tricks' and 'scurrilous compromises' that were unavoidable in making a political career. Another Polish novel, *Mateusz Bigda* (1933), by Juliusz Kaden-Bandrowski (1885–1944) has as its theme the political rise to power of a leader of the peasant movement.

In Spain, social criticism was strongly linked to the importance of the family, as in *La familia de Pascal Duarte* (*The Family of Pascal Duarte*, 1942) by Camilo José Cela.

In a new, deliberately 'slipshod' style, Céline, a marginal doctor-cum-novelist, close to ordinary, suffering people, sounds out his time. He lists the symptoms of the 1930s crisis: capitalism, nationalism, misery, colonialism and Taylorism, notably in *Voyage au bout de la nuit* (*Journey to the End of the Night*, 1932).

> It was right what he'd been telling me about them taking anyone on at Ford. He hadn't lied. I didn't quite trust him though, because seedy people are prone to fantasize. There is a moment in being wretched when the spirit is no longer in tune all the time with the body. It really doesn't feel at home in it. It's almost like somebody's soul talking to you. A soul is not responsible for its actions. They made us strip off to begin with, of course. The visit took place in a sort of laboratory. We moved along slowly. 'You're not up to much,' said the male nurse after looking me up and down, 'but never mind.'
>
> Louis-Ferdinand Céline,
> *Voyage au bout de la nuit*

Anti-Utopia

Utopian works are the other face of social criticism and satire and this genre proliferated during this period. Most Utopian novels that appeared were no less anti-Utopian for all that, for they painted imaginary states that were far from paradise. In all these works, totalitarian systems ruled the earth; the liberty of the individual, as Western civilisation had conceived it and created it, was always curtailed. The Utopian novel, stylistically experimental, *Nienasycenie* (*Insatiability*, 1930) by Witkiewicz, had as its backdrop the confrontation between Europeans and Asiatics. The story ends with the collapse of the personality and moral values of the Western hero, Genezyp Kapen, who, after Poland's defeat, takes sides with the Chinese.

In *Blocks* by Bordewijk, written in a neo-realistic style, there is no hero. Bordewijk describes a state in which everything conforms to the ideal form of a rectangle and in which the blossoming of the personality is considered a threat for this type of collective organisation. But the power of subversion of other geometrical forms and the individuality of the

605

human being finally show themselves to be impossible to uproot. In 1932, the British writer Huxley published *Brave New World*. In this dystopic vision, the American industrialist Ford has replaced 'the Lord God', and the new era is calculated 'in years after Ford'. Human beings are no longer 'born' or 'brought up', but genetically engineered and developed in jars. To avoid all problems they have the drug 'soma' available at all times:

> Swallowed half an hour before closing time, that second dose of *soma* had raised a quite impenetrable wall between the actual universe and their minds.
>
> Aldous Huxley,
> *Brave New World*

Válka s mloky (*The War against the Salamanders*, 1936) by Karel Čapek is a novel constructed like a collage of diverse elements. We can identify in this work many resemblances to current events: the weakness of the reactions of humans attacked by salamanders and the aggressors' decisiveness and bellicose behaviour.

The Swedish writer Karin Boye (1900–1941), on a visit to Russia, had been struck by the totalitarianism of the Stalinist state and by its similarity to the fascist and National-Socialist State. This impelled her to write an anti-Utopian work, *Kallocain Roman fran 2000-talet* (*Callocaine, a Novel of the Year 2000*, 1940), before committing suicide in 1941. Callocaine is a drug which permits a totalitarian State to explore the most secret recesses of man's mind in order to dominate it completely. But after the first trial of the drug, it is discovered that human beings have dreams that are so unreal that, if they were known, they could be dangerous to the State.

> The Glass Bead Game is also played with all the contents and all the values of our culture.
>
> Hermann Hesse,
> *The Glass Bead Game*

The Swiss-German Hesse, at the other end of the spectrum from anti-Utopia, showed that it was possible to create a peaceful social order: in his enigmatic work *Das Glasperlenspiel. Versuch einer Lebensbeschreibung des Magister Ludi Josef Knecht samt Knechts hinterlassenen Schriften* (*The Glass Bead Game. An Attempt at Describing the Life of the Magister Ludi Josef Knecht, including his Posthumous Writings*, 1943), he tried to make a synthesis of the world around him and the imaginary and perfect world of Castalia, a sort of ideal city in which the mind reigns supreme. The development of Josef Knecht, a student, then a model disciple of the province of the Order of Castalia, and, last but not least, the master of the Glass Bead Game, shows the road to follow to gain admittance to a spiritual élite. The contemplative, remote life led by this elite is not complemented by an active life, with its pulsations and seething, without which it is impossible to attain to the outward intellectual blossoming of the Western spirit, which Hesse opposes to totalitarian systems and their mass movements.

A NEW EXPERIENCE OF WAR

In texts which attempt to reconstitute the events of the Second World War, there are three overlapping trends: the representation of war, the description of Resistance struggles and attempts at discussion and persuasion between different camps and tendencies.

War diaries

The personal diaries compiled during the Second World War which have become the best known are those by the German evangelical theologian Dietrich Bonhoeffer (1906–1945) and that by **Anne Frank (1929–1945)**, a Jewish adolescent who hid from June 1941 to August 1944 in a house overlooking an interior courtyard in Amsterdam. This journal, kept until she was deported to a concentration camp, was published for the first time in 1946 in The Netherlands under the title *Het Achterhuis* (*The House on the Courtyard*). Also published in The

Netherlands in 1946 was *Doortocht* (*The Passage*) by Bert Voeten (born 1918). And in 1981, under the title *Het verstoorde Leven* (*A Troubled Life*), the journals and letters of Etty Hillesum (1914–1943), written between 1941 and 1943, were also published. In 1950 Alvaro's journal, *Quasi una vita, Giornale di uno scrittore* (*Almost a Life, the Journal of a Writer*) appeared, made up of notes taken between 1927 and 1947. Finally, the Warsaw Ghetto lives again in the drawings and text of Adam Czerniakov's journal and in *Dzienniki czasu wojny* (*Journal of Wartime Days*) by Zofia Nałkowska, which appeared in 1970.

War literature

In the USSR events of the Second World War and the immediate postwar period nearly always found a literary echo. The Red Army's heroism at Stalingrad is the main theme of a novel by Konstantin Simonov (1915–1979), *Dni i noči* (*Days and Nights*, 1944). Viktor Nekrassov (1911–1987) also took Stalingrad as the keystone for his novel *V okopax Stalingrada* (*In the Trenches of Stalingrad*, 1936). Seifert put into words the feelings of the Czech people, abandoned and crushed, in *Zhasněte světla* (*Put Out the Lights*, 1938) and *Přilba Hlíny* (*The Helmet Full of Clay*, 1945).

The Second World War became one of the great themes of Polish literature. From the beginning of the conflict, many Polish war stories was published, written in the tradition of nineteenth-century Polish exiles. Although the sufferings of the Polish people were infinitely worse during the last war and authors had tried to free themselves from the influence of nineteenth-century concepts, the past was 'automatically' present in stories of this period. That is why this literature constantly oscillates between two poles: on the one hand, there is a passionate consent to the very idea of war, on the other, an ironic distancing with regard to events. Many works deal specifically with the 1939 German-Polish, such as the collection of poems *Poky my zyjemy* (*As Long As We Live*) by Przybós, and the tales that Wierzynski published in 1944 called *Pobojowisko* (*Battle-field*). With his novel *Droga wiodla przez Narvik* (*The Road Went through Narvik*, 1941), Ksawery Pruszyński (1907–1950) celebrated another battlefield, in a documentary style. Melchior Wańkowicz described the battle of Monte Cassino in which the Poles were involved in *Bitwa o Monte Cassino* (1945–1947).

The heroic struggle of Greek soldiers fighting for months on the mountains of Epirus against the fascist armies inspired, among others, Angelos Vlachos (born 1916) in *To mnima tis ghrias* (*The Old Woman's Grave*, 1945), Yannis Beratis (1904–1968) in *To plati potami* (*The Big River*, 1946) and Loukis Akritas (1909–1965) in *Armatomeni* (*Armed*, 1947). In The Netherlands, Bert Schierbeek (born 1918) wrote a war novel *Terreur tegen Terreur* (*Terror for Terror*, 1945), as did Frank Wilders (1917–1977) with *Grensconflict* (*Border Struggle*, 1948).

In his poems, some of which were found in the common grave of deportees where he was buried, the Hungarian Miklós Ranóti (1909–1944) became the chronicler of a time when 'men killed joyfully without needing to be told to'.

Resistance literature

In The Netherlands, Greece, France and Slovakia, the Resistance found a particular way of expressing itself in literature. The ideological contradictions which had characterised the prewar era, in The Netherlands as well as in France, were neutralised by the struggle against their Nazi occupation. Nazi attempts to exercise total control over The Netherlands had been reinforced in 1942 by the creation of a 'Kulturkammer' or 'Chamber of Culture'. But publications described as 'illegal' rose up openly against the Occupation, and 'clandestine' publications also appeared without the authorisation of the Chamber of Culture. In this Dutch Resistance literature, the predominant genre was poetry. These poems were inspired by the Royal Family, the predicament of the homeland and hatred of the occupying forces. Jan Campert (1902–1943), in the title of his poem *De achttien doden* (*The Eighteen Dead*), was referring to fifteen members of the Resistance network De Geuzen, and three communists, who were all executed in March 1941. Like many others, this poem was hugely popular during the years that followed the drama of war.

Part of this literature's function was to raise money for the Resistance and for artists, writers and Jewish children who were being hidden from the Germans. The texts of most Dutch resistance poems were collected in various anthologies. Many writers paid for their commitment with their life, including Johan Brouwer (1898–1943), Adrianus Michael de Jong (1888–1943) and Etty Hillesum. Most of them were executed or disappeared into concentration camps.

In Greece, the Resistance epic was celebrated in Bertis' *Odhiporiko tou 43* (*The Itinerary of 43*, 1946) and in *Photia* (*Fire*, 1946) by Dimitris Hadjis (1914–1981). Many French writers took part in the struggle against the German occupation, like the group of surrealists clustered round Éluard. Together they published in 1942 'Poetry and Truth', a collection of sixteen poems that allied planes dropped over occupied France. Aragon wrote 'Rhyme in 1940' and 'The Lesson of Ribérac or French Europe' in 1941. **René Char (1907–1991)** composed *The Sheets of Hypnos* on the basis of notes taken during his Resistance days. Also with the Resistance were Pierre-Jean Jouve (1887–1976), Pierre Emmanuel (born 1916) and Malraux, whose manuscript *The Struggle with the Angel* (1943) was partly destroyed by the Gestapo. He only retained *Les Noyers d'Altenburg* (*The Walnut Trees of Altenburg*). Bernanos published in exile several Resistance texts. Vercors (the pen-name of Jean Bruller, 1902–1991) wrote *The Silence of the Sea* (1942), one of the best-known texts of the French Resistance, on a par with Eluard's poem 'Freedom'. For the Slovaks, the principal theme of Resistance literature was the 1944 national insurrection, conjured up by Vladimír Mináč (born 1922), Dominik Tatarka (1913–1989), Alfonz Bednár (1914–1989), Rudolf Jašík (1919–1960) and Cíger-Hrouský.

> Bitter future, bitter future, ball among the rose trees.
>
> René Char,
> *The Sheets of Hypnos*

The literature of the camps

There were many attempts to explain the Second World War, its atrocities and the frightening events which took place in the concentration camps. Shortly after the war, it is possible to read *Mote ved milepelen* (*Encounter at the Milestone*, 1947) by the Norwegian Sigurd Hoel, the twenty-five poems by Dylan Thomas (1914–1953), *Deaths and Entrances* (1939–1945), the play *Oak Leaves and Lavender* (1946) by Sean O'Casey, and stories by Borchert. Literary descriptions of events in the concentration camps occupy a place apart in Polish literature. Tadeusz Borowski (1922–1951), a survivor of Auschwitz, has described what life was really like there in his two collections of tales and stories, both of which appeared in 1948: *Pożegnanie z Marią* (*Farewell to Mary*) and *Kammieny świat* (*The World of Stone*). He notes that the moral paranoia of the death camp universe contained its own rules, impossible to understand from the outside. His tales describe the camp from the inside; he gives us a picture of himself helping the Nazi camp police to give a better understanding of the influence that the system finally had on prisoners:

> *Ciało wykorzystali, jak się da:*
> *wytatuowali na nim numer,*
> *żeby zaoszczędzić obroży, dali tyle*
> *snu w nocy, żeby ozłowiek mógł*
> *pracować, i tyle czasu w dzień,*
> *aby zjadł. I jedzenia tyle, żeby*

> *They made use of one's body as much as*
> *possible: they tatooed numbers*
> *on it to be able to do without*
> *a collar tag, they gave it so much*
> *sleep a night so that a*
> *man could work, and so much*

bezproduktywnie nie zdechł.

Tadeusz Borowski,
U nas, w Auschwitzu . . .

*freedom during the day so that he
had time to eat. And enough food
for a man not to die
in an unproductive manner.*

Alongside these texts written to try to exorcise the haunting memories of German concentration camps, other Polish tales evoke Russian camps, forced crossings of the USSR, with many cynical comments about Soviet society; so *Inny Świat. Zapiski sowieckie* (*The Other World*, 1951) by Gustaw Herling-Grudziński (born 1919), one of the first tales about Soviet labour camps to appear in the West, presented Soviet society as a sort of demoralised prison, disorientated and full of suffering. The most poignant of Czech testimonies to the Nazi concentration camps is still *Básně z koncentračního tábora* (*Poems from a Concentration Camp*, 1946) by Josef Čapek. The martyrdom of the Jews later found its greatest witnesses in Norbert Frýd (1913–1976) and Arnošt Lustig (born 1926).

Particular manifestations of poetry

Certain special developments of poetry which do not fit into any of the preceding contexts or belong to one of the great literary trends of this period deserve separate mention. At the beginning of the 1930s, an aesthetic movement, 'Presença', began to dominate Portuguese literature. This movement had developed thanks to the support of the periodical of the same name (1927–1940), and of particular interest because of the relationship between art and the personality of the artist. **José Régio (1901–1969)** wrote, with others, three anthologies of poetry: *Jogo de Cabra Cega* (*The Game of the Blind Goat*, 1934), *O príncipe con orelhas de burro* (*The Prince with Ass's Ears*, 1942) and *Mas Deus é grande* (*But God is great*, 1945). In his appeal programme called 'Literatura viva' (living literature), he demanded that poetry be original, and that the style of the poet be expressive and correspond to their personality. The opposite, negative pole, of this living literature for him was 'literatura livresca' (bookish literature), which

in his opinion lacked originality and serious objectivity. Régio's work is characterised by his analyses of the contradictions inherent in the human psyche and by an aspiration to divine grace. The personality of Miguel Torga (born 1907) was marked by his peasant origins and his experiences as a child. Although he was politically committed, his poems never lost a mythical and idyllic vision of life in the countryside. Adolfo Casais Monteiros (1908–1972), Branquinho da Fonseca (1905–1974), Carlos Queiros (1907–1949), Antonio de Navarro (1902–1980), Edmundo de Bettencourt (1889–1973), Alberto de Serpa (born 1906), Cabral do Nascimento (1897–1978) and Pedro Homen de Melo (1904–1984) were also members of Presença.

The Netherlands initially experienced a period of distrust during the 1930s with respect to 'fine language'. Colloquial language made its way into poetry and there was a considerable widening of Dutch poetry's lyrical possibilities. The periodical *Forum* (1931–1935) created a favourable climate for the publication of *Parlando* (1930) by Eddy du Perron (1899–1940) and *Poems* (1934) by Jan Gresshoff (1888–1971). They wanted to make poetry accessible, to democratise, to some extent, Dutch lyrical poetry. Though they kept to traditional forms, their poems, like the sonnet, had a truly realistic tendency which is still characteristic of Dutch poetry. The opposition united a round the review *Criterium* (1940–1942) to try to bridge the gap between the realistic style of colloquial language and Romantic and symbolist lyricism.

The Italian poetry called 'Ermetismo' followed a path almost diametrically opposite to that of Dutch poetry in the 1930s. Its writers took the French symbolists and the Italians of the previous generation as their particular models: Montale, Ungaretti and Salvatore Quasimodo (1901–1968). Ermetismo developed around the periodical *Il Frontespizio*, in which, during the 1930s, certain religious elements in Florence dealt with literary questions and Catholic's relationship to literature. Starting from a purely literary platform, Ermetismo gave poetry a religious value. The poets belonging to this group sought to oppose truth, the fortress of the soul's existence and of its dark secrets, to the individual's despair and the confusion when faced with recent developments in history and politics, confronted by the weakness of official morality and the uncontrollable movements of the masses. The principal themes of writers like Mario Luzi (born 1914), Alfonso Gatto (1909–1976) and Vittorio Sereni (1913–1983) are solitude, absence, expectancy and memory, but also the uncertainty inspired by the lack of all direction in life. The questions the poet asks on the value of the symbolic expression of the word, on the dark and mysterious being which is hidden behind the world of appearances, are close to the questions that existentialism itself asked. The start of the Second World War and the resulting need to be committed spelt the end of Ermetismo's development.

The value of life

The question of the value of human existence, of which the poets of Ermetismo had hardly scratched the surface, was asked again during the war and especially in the immediate postwar period, which witnessed the collapse of all extremist ideologies, at least right-wing ones. The importance of this question established itself throughout Europe as much on the plane of practical everyday life as on a philosophical and literary one. In 1938, Sartre wrote *La Nausée (Nausea)*, whose protagonist, Antoine Roquentin, feels a growing disgust, a feeling of nauseousness with human existence. In two essays looking towards the future, Sartre laid out a programme of thought and action: with *Being and Nothingness, an Essay on Phenomenological Ontology* (1943) and *Existentialism is a Form of Humanism* (1946), he touched the depths of the problem of this era by postulating that man's destiny is nothing

more than his existence. Sartre saw this existence as the obligation to constantly recreate oneself, to permanently reject the Being one has been up to and including the present moment. Man, according to Sartre, possesses nothing else and is nothing else apart from his own life.

The period of mass movements, collectivism and ideology had come to an end. It ends with a full-stop; the free and solitary existence of the human being at 'Stunde Null', zero hour.

Poetry and music

R. Horville

It's the poetry of the poor, the poetry that is needed like bread for every dawn.

Gabriel Celaya, sung by Paco Ibañez

'The history of literature,' Paul Claudel wrote in 1937, 'compiled by narrow-minded and prejudiced people, contains surprising gaps and monstrous injustices that distort it.' Among these, there is primarily the small amount of space set aside for songs. 'The heart of children, like that of men and women, is obstinately deaf to all these stilted declamations, all these pseudo-heroic harangues, all the preciosity and artifice which people have tried to fill them up with. But let them only hear refrains like *Au pont du Nord* or *Auprès de ma blonde* or *Le Chevalier du guet*, and immediately the soul is stirred, the eye lights up and the divine gates of dreams, of fantasy and of what Dante called "fair love" open up before us.' 'Poetry and music', Claudel continued, 'no more than drawing, must not be the prerogative of the cultivated and of those unemployed of the writing desk that Rimbaud calls *The Seated*.'

Lyre and lyricism

There are many links between literature and music: writers, particularly poets, sensitive to the harmony of a phrase, look for musicality, try to find words suited to the evocation of sounds. Alternatively, literature sometimes devotes passages to music, when it describes characters in the process of playing an instrument, or again when the action of a novel takes place during a concert or a ball whose atmosphere it depicts, summoning up a whole network of sensations. Literature and music can also work together, together making up one and the same work. This alliance then gives birth to complex genres like opera, comic opera, operetta, even musical comedy, or shorter compositions like songs. Popular or scholarly, at the confluence of writing and the oral tradition, songs appear as favoured vehicles for poetry in the literary history of Europe.

A great richness of inspiration

The song is not a monolithic genre. On the contrary, it is distinguished by great variety. In the Middle Ages, for example, along with the song of deeds which derives from epic, a lyrical inspiration based on love develops: the foundation of the art of the troubadours and trouvères, it spread throughout Europe. It was particularly noticeable in the Limburger poet Hendrik Van Veldeke, who, in work composed between 1170 and 1190, plays the part of intermediary between the Provençal tradition and the German 'Minnesänger'.

During the Renaissance and the seventeenth century, many varieties of song coexisted. Religious song went through a considerable period of evolution: poets, Catholics as well as Protestants, composed hymns in which they praised their faith. Historical events were also an important source of inspiration. In the northern Netherlands, the Reformation and the repression that followed produced martyrs' songs, gathered together in the collection *Het offer des Heeren* (*The Sacrifice of the Lord*, 1562). The current national anthem of The Netherlands, *Een nieuw christelick liet* (*A New Christian Song*), composed at the beginning of 1568, recalls the failure of the campaign of the Meuse. At the same time, is a prayer, a plea in the spirit of the rhetorical poets of The Netherlands. This is a unique mixture and the only national anthem which does not deal with glorious exploits, but a defeat. The love song blossomed, marked by courtliness, practised by great authors and composers, like the Frenchmen Clément Janequin (*c.*1480–1558) and Pierre de Ronsard. The popular tradition asserted itself in songs with various themes to accompany daily life – drinking songs, wedding songs, marching songs, satirical songs or lullabies.

This wealth of popular song took on a particularly interesting aspect in Greece. Until the nineteenth century, versified oral language was a daily practice, building up a culture marginal to the complex written word, the scholarly and ecclesiastical tradition. In this perspective, several types of songs gradually developed from the eleventh and twelfth centuries. The court life of the potentates of Asia Minor encouraged the development of epic songs which exalted the strength, valour and glory of the Greek magistrates, described their confrontations with the Emperor, their battles against the Saracens, their encounters with mythical creatures: the dragons and monsters that made concrete the hostility of nature. From these songs, known as 'akritic', the ballads developed which described human behaviour against a mythical background. Another group of songs, the 'klephtic', appeared in the eighteenth and nineteenth centuries, exalting the bravery of brigands or armed gangs of Greek Christians, the Klephts, in their struggles against Albanian Muslims. Through these centuries, songs of lamentation, wedding songs, love songs, lullabies were woven of the same thread of a rural tradition, little seduced by metaphysics, founded on social reality.

In Germany, the Lied gave a good account of the complexity of song-writing. Originating in the Middle Ages and continuing until the nineteenth century, illustrated by musicians of the calibre of Schubert, Schumann or Brahms and poets like Opitz, Novalis or Brentano, Lieder can be songs of religion, love and satire. We can also make distinctions between them based on the subjects treated: songs having to do with history, society, metaphysics, journeys (the *Carmina Burana*). They can also be divided according to their origin, their popular character or their artistic complexity, bearing in mind reciprocal influences.

In many countries specific forms of song developed like the flamenco in Spain or the fado in Portugal. One form has a particular significance: the English ballad. The definition of the genre stirred up much controversy. In *The Ballad of Tradition* (1932), Gordon Hall Gerrould suggests: 'A ballad is a folk song which tells a story by emphasising the basic situation, which tells it by letting the action unfold with the speaking of it, which tells it in an objective way, without commentary, without intrusion, without personal bias.'

There is a difference between anonymous popular ballads designed to be sung and those written by poets who, while respecting the spirit of the genre, did not necessarily compose them to be sung. Many popular ballads circulated in Great Britain after the end of the eighteenth century. In the Romantic period, they had a profound influence on the work of poets such as Wordsworth, who adapted them by trying to imitate the spontaneous language of the ordinary people. In 1892, Kipling's *Barrack-Room Ballads* had a rougher edge to them, influenced by street ballads, expressive of the life of the colonial soldier.

During the Romantic period, several poems were marked by the style of the ballad: *The Ancient Mariner* (1798) by Coleridge or *La Belle Dame sans Merci* (1819) by John Keats. The best known of the nineteenth century ballads was *he Ballad of Reading Gaol* (1898) by Oscar Wilde. In Scotland, the ballad had a comparable influence on poets: *Auld lang syne* by Burns remains, even today, a traditional song for the New Year, and Walter Scott produced a series of Scottish ballads called *The Minstrelsy of the Scottish Border* (1802–1803).

The political songs of the 1930s

The cabaret song was born between the wars and developed apace. It often took on a realist aspect, as with Koos Speenhoff (1869–1945) in The Netherlands, who wrote melodramatic works with a direct, popular tone. In Germany, where it flourished, this mode of expression was soon taken up by dramatists, who integrated it into their works to make it a tool in the questioning of the traditional working of theatre and a political weapon. Frank Wedekind, a writer and singer, opened the way, soon followed by the great names of the German theatre: Piscator, Toller and Brecht. To these dramatists way of thinking, the incorporation of popular songs in their plays was designed to attract working-class spectators, while the use of jazz made it possible to evoke the new, progressive world of America. In Ernst Toller's play, *Hoppla, wir leben* (*Hey, We're Alive*, 1927), technology, radio and 'upbeat' music all play their part in creating an atmosphere of touching modernity in a Germany reduced to the nadir of political instability by the devastation and humiliation of the First World War.

For Brecht, the integration of the song into the dramatic text was an essential ingredient of epic theatre. He considered it to be a calming element which broke up the text and created a distancing effect, prompting the audience to adopt an attitude of calm reflection about the action on stage. Brecht collaborated with several composers, including Hans Eisler and Kurt Weill, representatives of a musical concept which included the language of jazz and rejected the style of Mahler and Strauss in favour of clarity and lightness of expression. Brecht and Weill produced short operas, like *Mahagonny* (1927–1929) and *Happy End* (1929). Their best-known work was *Die Dreigroschenoper* (*The Threepenny Opera*, 1928). In order to avoid the clichés of traditional opera, they included in it ballads by Villon and Kipling. Songs were interpreted in a harsh style, designed to isolate the words from the music. The singers were recruited in theatres and cabarets rather than from opera. One of Brecht's singer–actresses, Lotte Lenya, took pains to point out that she was chosen for a play because she did not know how to read music. Brecht resolutely wanted to avoid the style of song associated with traditional bourgeois theatre. The songs were to be completely separate from the dialogue and serve as commentaries on the text; the singer was gave a summary of the action rather than a description of their feelings.

Contemporary diversity

Since the Second World War, the development of the song has diversified, helped by audio-visual techniques. A preponderance of Anglo-Saxon songs took over most of Europe, but national identities were not erased.

Brassens, Trenet and Ferré gave new life to poetic texts by putting them to music. Songs by Theodorakis create a bridge between the Greece of yesterday and the Greece of today. Those by Okudjava are instruments with which to contest official Soviet ideology. In Spain, Paco Ibañez sings about the suffering of his oppressed people.

Born in Brussels, Jacques Brel (1929–1978) expressed nostalgia for the poetry of land-scapes and people (*Le Plat Pays*, 1962), life's difficulties (*Vieillir*, 1977), the disillusion and the sufferings of love (*Ne me quitte pas*, 1959), the realism of a generous, dramatic life (*Amsterdam*, 1964), but also the banality of a limited and mediocre bourgeois existence (*Les Bourgeois*, 1962).

Georges Brassens (1921–1981) composed poems that were anti-conformist in accent and popular in tone. A writer–composer and singer, he gave the French chanson tradition a wide scope with *Le Gorille*, *L'Auvergnat* and *Les Copains d'abord*. Born in Monte-Carlo in 1916, Léo Ferré was a fully-fledged writer. A novelist, in 1970 he published *Benoît Misère*, in which he mixed dreams and reality. A poet, he manifested a verbal virtuosity, a sense of imagery which made him a successor to the surrealists. He knew how to renew the lyrical themes of the passing of time, death, revolt. He sings of love and anarchy, which he defines in *Testament phonographe* (1980), as 'the poli-tical formulation of despair'. A composer, he practised all the genres and all the rhythms of popular tradition to that oratorio of his

composed on the basis of *La Chanson du mal aimé* by Apollinaire.

An admirer of great poets, Ferré contributed towards making them accessible to the general public thanks to his musical settings of many texts by Rutebeuf, Villon, Baudelaire, Verlaine, Rimbaud, Apollinaire and Aragon. He was an entertainer with a compelling voice and a moving presence. Some of his texts are among the great poems of the twentieth century. The explosion of words and images which characterises Ferré's language is revealed in this stanza of *De toutes les couleurs*:

De toutes les couleurs
Du jaune à l'étalage
Et dans la déraison quand Vincent
  la partage
Quand la vitrine du malheur tourne
  la page
Comme tournent les sols devant la
  Vérité
Du jaune dans le vent quand le
  pollen peluche et
À l'heure exacte fait danser le rock
  aux ruches
Quand une abeille a mis son quartz
  à l'heure-miel
Quand le festin malin semble venir
  du ciel
Pour rire jaune enfin dans le
  supermarché

Every colour
Yellow in the display case
And in irrationality when Vincent
  shares it
When the plate-glass window of
  misfortune turns the page
Like sunflowers turn in front of
  Truth
Yellow in the wind when the
  pollen fluffs up and
Punctually makes the beehives
  dance the rock
When a bee has placed its quartz
  at honey-hour
When the sly feast seems to come

from heaven
To laugh yellow at last in the
supermarket

The poetic chanson also flourished in Greece. Born after the Second World War, it came fully into its own after 1960, under the impulse of two composers, Manos Hadjidakis (born 1925) and especially Mikis Theodorakis (also born 1925). Basing themselves on the Greek musical tradition, they set literary texts to music: they themselves had written the text or borrowed it from the poets of previous generations (Solomos, Palamas, Karyotakis), or from contemporary poets (Seferis, Elytis, Ritsos). This musical setting familiarised the wider public with modern poetry, functioning, to some extent, as a commentary. During dictation, these songs, conveying a whole national, political and social content, became a way of fighting repression. The new generation of composers, among whom were Yannis Markopoulos, Yannis Spanos, Dionyssis Savopoulos and Christos Leondis, followed this tradition and knew how to develop an original manner by concentrating on the lyrical themes of love and nature.

In the USSR, official songs of the people took pride of place. They gave an essential role to music, whose affective charge was designed to play on the mass psyche of the audience. The words, simple and laconic, were often summed up in formulas bordering on slogans, liable to be fixed in the collective memory. Held in by the music, deprived of all personal characteristics, the text was conceived to unite the population. At the end of the 1950s, songs in which the lyrics are important develop as a reaction to this musical tradition. In what is called 'the song of the bard', music was reduced to an unostentatious backing on the guitar, which underlines the content of the text, now of primary importance. This new concept did not develop in large-scale performances, but appeared in friendly gatherings. So professionalism gave way to the sincerity of amateurs. These songs were destined not for the impersonal masses but for friends, for the initiated. The individual and individuality

became the artistic dominant of this mode of expression whose the themes and forms they define. This bard's song was inspired from genres rejected by officialdom, like the urban romance, the gypsy romance, the hooligan's song, the oral tradition of anecdotes. Three names illustrate this aspect of Soviet culture: Aleksandr Galitch (1919–1977), the creator of satirical song-spectacles, Vladimir Vyssotsky (1938–1980), who, in his sung monologues, presents a whole portrait gallery of Soviet citizens, and Bulat Okudjava (born 1924), whose works appear like lyrical poems in the manner of urban romances.

The literary song is not limited to these different countries. It forms a general phenomenon throughout Europe. In Spain, we can single out for special mention Joaquin Diaz, Mari Trini, Alberto Cortez and Paco Ibañez. The latter has notably set to music poems of yesterday (Quevedo, Góngora) and poems of today (Alberti, Celaya, Blas de Otero).

In The Netherlands, the chanson often conveys a humour which, as in the work of Annie Schmidt (born 1911), emphasis the tragi-comic elements of daily life. In Italy, after the end of the last war, a new wave of singer-writer-composers emerged, the 'cantatori', to whose ranks Paolo Conte belonged.

García Lorca (1898–1936)

J.-C. Rosales

I am neither a man, nor a poet, nor a leaf, but a wounded pulse that has a premonition of the beyond.

Federico García Lorca,
Poet in New York

Lorca: myth and reality

Pablo Neruda said there were two Lorcas, the legendary one and the real one. To study the work of Federico García Lorca, we must not allow ourselves to be taken in by the atmosphere of legend which, maintained by the poet himself, surrounded his life and work from the beginning and which was reinforced by his violent death at the age of thirty-eight. Lorca's execution and the scattering of his original writings during the Spanish Civil War (1936) explain why there is still no complete edition of his considerable work and why original manuscripts keep reappearing at regular intervals.

Born into a middle-class family, Lorca spent his early years in the plain of Granada. There he learned about nature, the customs and the popular songs which are reflected in many of his works. Later, he collected and harmonised some folksongs from Granada which would probably have vanished without him. The music lessons that he had while still a child, a sharp sense of rhythm and harmony, his friendship with the composer Manuel de Falla will mean that he never forgot, when he wrote, the melodic, rhythmical dimension of his verse. In Granada, Lorca began to study law, letters and philosophy. He lived in the Student Hall of Residence in Madrid where he met other writers and intellectuals with whom he formed the Generation of 27.

Lorca the poet

It is possible to plot, from Lorca's first works, *Libro de poemas* (*Book of Poems*, 1921), *Canciones* (*Songs*, 1927), *Poema del cante jondo* (*Poem of the 'Deep Song'*, 1931), three tendencies in his poetry: tradition, renovation and populism or scholarly tradition, popular tradition and the avant-garde. Prolonged, modulated, jockeying for position, they were present throughout his work and, mutually conditioning themselves, manage to create that personal, enigmatic world, in which love and desires, frustration and death show themselves or hide themselves, are assertive or self-effacing.

The best example of the scholarly tradition is in *Los Sonetos de amor* (*Love Sonnets*), an unfinished work which Lorca began in 1935 and which is sometimes called *Sonetos del amor oscuro* (*Sonnets of Dark Love*): a direct allusion to a theme already evoked by St John of the Cross (1542–1591) in his poem *The Dark Night of the Soul*.

Soneto de la dulce queja

Tengo miedo a perder la maravilla
de tus ojos de estatua y el acento
que de noche me pone en la mejilla
la solitaria rosa de tu aliento.

Tengo pena de ser en esta orilla
tronco sin ramas y lo que más siento
es no tener la flor, pulpa o arenilla,
para el gusano de mi sufrimiento.

Si tú eres el tesoro oculto mío
si eres mi cruz y mi dolor mojado,
si soy el perro de tu señorío

No me dejes perder lo que he ganado
y decora las aguas de tu río
con hojas de mi Otoño enajenado.

Sonnet of the Sweet Complaint

I am afraid to lose the marvel
of your statuesque eyes and that accent
the night comes to place on my cheek
the solitary rose of your breath.

I am sorry only to be on this river bank
a trunk without a branch and my
greatest torment
is not to have the flower or the pulp or
the clay
which would nourish the worm of my
suffering.

If you are the treasure I am
concealing,
my sweet cross and my drowned grief,
and if I am your majesty's dog,

Do not let me lose the good that I have
gained
and take to embellish your river
these leaves of a desolate autumn.

Popular tradition and Andalusian folklore are another key to Lorca's poetry, especially in *The*

Poem of the 'Deep Song' and *Romancero Gitano* (*Gypsy Romancero*, 1928). It was with this book that Lorca achieved success. But his unprecedented popularity quickly became stifling: he felt himself imprisoned by a theme whose readers had not understood all its symbolic significance. The gypsy is primarily an archetypal 'victim of persecution' or 'marginal person'. Lorca often proclaimed his sympathy for the persecuted, be they gypsies, Negroes or Jews. Many readers, then and now, underestimate the expressiveness and aesthetic content of this book, seeing in it only the tragedy of the world of the Andalusian gypsy.

One of the romanceros, the *Romancero sonámbulo* (*Romancero of the Sleepwalker*), unites popular themes, dear to Lorca, and a subtle renovatory élan, discreetly surrealistic, which allowed Lorca to describe a scene that is a mixture of reality and nightmare. Characters, noises, words, everything is drowned in a green mist which only shows brief snatches of a story of love, pursuit and death. The wounded gypsy looks for a peaceful place to die and wants one last meeting with his beloved; the latter, leaning against the well, also seems to be dead, or perhaps simply tired by the wait. The double quest of the gypsy will be in vain: only death is certain.

From June 1929 to March 1930, Lorca lived in the USA and Cuba. He described the emotional impact that the observation of North American society produced on him in *Poeta en Nueva York* (*Poet in New York*). In this book, published in 1940, the influence of surrealism is obvious. However, even if gratuitous invention and automatic writing were constant factors, Lorca never falls into the purely mechanical use of surrealist techniques. Everything here is deliberate choice, and the most characteristic viewpoint is that of the 'European' faced with the hell of Wall Street. Lorca was present on 'Black Thursday' at the New York Stock Exchange in 1929; he knew the inhumanity of the streets and the windows from where, he said, no one had time any more to watch a cloud go by. European and cosmopolitan anti-Americanism

will be one of the characteristics of this work; in many poems devoted to the Black American cause, Lorca once again expressed his solidarity with the oppressed. In the final part of the collection, significantly called *Huida hacia la civilización* (*Flight towards Civilisation*), he nostalgically recalls a Europe symbolised by the town of Vienna. The allusions to a lost love are mingled with the evocation of a desolate landscape.

Lorca the dramatist

Intuition, a variety of registers and resources, interest in his period, the expression of universal emotions and situations, Lorca the dramatist had the same gifts as Lorca the poet. His poetic themes are found in his dramatic works: the desire to be loved, the frustration of solitude, the silent threat of death, the conflict between liberty and authority. In his first play, *El Maleficio de la mariposa* (*The Butterfly's Evil Spell*, 1919), the confrontation between dream and reality emerges, fundamental to all Lorca's theatre. From that moment on, and after some guignolesque plays, the style and anxieties of his plays make them an exception in the Spanish theatre of the time. In 1925, the success of *Mariana Pineda* (a heroine of the Liberal Party executed in Granada in 1831 for having embroidered a flag for the rebels), and, some years later, that of *Bodas de Sangre* (*Blood Wedding*, 1933) made Lorca a respected dramatist. Like *Blood Wedding*, *Yerma* (1934) and *La casa de Bernarda Alba* (*The House of Bernarda Alba*, 1936) are two tragedies that portray the rural world of peasants. Death is always here, one way or another, the inevitable outcome for individuals who desire an honest life. Most of the characters are women (one of the tragedies has as its subtitle 'a drama of women in the villages of Spain') and they symbolise, like gypsies and Negroes in the poetic work, marginalised, oppressed people, those who yield without eluding their dominant desire for freedom.

Two other works, unfinished and posthumous, *Comedia sin título* (*Play without a Title*) and *El Público* (*The Public*) with their formal research and more abstract, disembodied themes, reveal Lorca's maturity.

Seferis (1900–1971)

N. Vayenas

Let our souls seek to travel.

George Seferis

Among the poets of the 1930s who brought fresh energy to Greek poetic discourse and rescued it from the impasse of traditional poetry, George Seferis occupies a prominent position: he received the Nobel Prize in 1963 and his work has been translated into most European languages. Seferis was born in 1900 in Smyrna. He studied law in Paris (1918–1924) and embraced a diplomatic career in which he rose through the ranks to become an ambassador. He died in Athens in 1971.

The literary personality

The years Seferis spent in Paris were decisive for his artistic personality. Fascinated by Valery's poetry (which he read for the first time in 1922 before the 'quarrel' of pure poetry), it was only natural that his first poetic publications (*Strophi, Stanza*, 1931; *Sterna, The Water Tank*, 1932) should bear his influence.

However, his works of this period were not a Greek version of pure poetry. Such an assertion would tend to ignore the 'impure' poems of *Stanza*, as well as a number of other poems from this same period, written under the creative influence of the French symbolists (particularly Laforgue and Claudel), and published subsequently, along with other later poems, in his third book of poetry (*Tetradhio ghimnasmaton, Study Notebook*, 1940).

However, even among the most important poets of this period of pure poetry (*Erotikos Loghos, Erotic Words, The Water Tank*), the question of pure poetry is not just resolved by the application of a given theory of poetry, but becomes a question of artistic absolutes. The verses of *Erotikos Loghos*, a poetic study of the

subject love and time, are filled with the best moments of Greek poetry and form the swansong of the Greek decapentasyllable and the last red-letter day for Greek poetry in verse.

Seferis' efforts to write a poetry as harmonious as possible, at the risk of being hermetic, and his love for the tangible and concrete are reconciled after *The Water Tank*, without cancelling each other out. It is this phenomenon that Takis Sinopoulos describes when he speaks of the 'two alternating faces' of Seferis and his 'open' and 'closed' poems. One of the reasons for this phenomenon should be attributed to Seferis's more generalised schizophrenia alternating between the individualist and gregarious sides of his temperament.

Another key to his 'closed' poems must be sought in certain roots that the poet has in common with French symbolism. In the final analysis, this schizophrenia, which, in its extreme manifestations, is responsible for the weaknesses we may observe in Seferis, constitutes, at the same time, one of the sources of his expressiveness. In effect, most of his best poems, be they 'open' or 'closed', are those for which the intensity of their main emotive charge is due to the friction generated by the juxtaposition of the latter with an opposite point of view.

The renewal of Greek poetry

If *Stanza* immediately made Seferis's reputation in Greece as a major poet, his second work, *Mithistorima* (*Mythology*, 1935), established him as a modern poet, contributing to the renewal of Greek poetry. It was not just the free verse of this work which was the first effective freeing of Greek verse from rhyme; it was the use of ancient myth, different from the use that the Parnassians made of it, and that more global vision which gave to this text its pioneering character. Mythology is a collection of twenty-four poems reviving many ancient and modern characters, in a diachronic perspective which juxtaposes the ancient moment to the new. Seferis' 'mythical method' is analogous to the one used by T.S. Eliot in *The Waste Land* though Seferis' use of myth is clearly more homogeneous. Despite the intensely Greek colour imparted by its geography and choice of characters, this work is much more universal, since its deep theme is that of the search for man in man in a world ruled by fate. The aspiration to a happier life 'outside the broken marbles', the transcendence of the personal which characterises the poems of Seferis' first period, the evocation of the rifts in a country divided between East and West, gives his poetry a damatic tone:

> ΜΑ τί γυρεύουν οἱ ψυχές μας
> ταξιδεύοντας
> Πάνω σὲ καταστρώματα
> κατελυμένων καραβιῶν
> Στριμωγμένες μὲ γυναῖκες
> κίτρινες καὶ μωρὰ ποὺ κλαῖνε
> Χωρὶς νὰ μποροῦν νὰ ξεχαστοῦν
> οὔτε μὲ τὰ χελιδονόψαρα
> Οὔτε μὲ τ' ἄστρα ποὺ δηλώνουν
> οτὴν ἄκρη τὰ κατάρτια.
> Τριμμένες ἀπὸ τοὺς δίακους τῶν
> φωνογράφων
> Δεμένες ἄθελα μ' ἀνύπαρχτα
> τροσκυνήματα
> Μουρμουρίζοντας σπασμένες
> σκέψεις ἀπὸ ξένες γλῶσσες.

> *Let our souls seek to travel*
> *On damaged ships' bridges*
> *Piled up amid sallow-skinned women*
>   *and crying babies*
> *Without finding forgetfulness either*
>   *in flying fish*
> *Or in the stars that the spire*
>   *of the masts points to.*
> *Used up by the discs*
>   *of phonographs*
> *Linked in spite of themselves to non-existent*
>   *pilgrimages*
> *Muttering shreds of thought*
>   *in foreign languages.*

In reality, Seferis' use of myth is only a dramatic employment of symbol borrowed from the symbolists. The expression charac-

teristic of *Mythology* is a logical sequel to the evolution in musical form of the first period imposed by the realist tendencies of the poet which, despite his outward-looking gaze, will remain 'a closed book'.

Imerologhio katastromatos, A' (*Logbook I*, 1940) contains poems which illustrate both of Seferis' poetic tendencies. The 'open' poems clearly allow his anxiety about the forthcoming war to shine through, while in his 'closed' poems the pain of lost happincss is rcsolved in a problematic perception of time, which finds its most characteristic expression in *Piazza San Niccolo*, a commentary on Proust's idea that saw memory as a liberating function. Seferis did not share the viewpoint according to which lost time could be regained.

Seferis' experience during the wanderings of the Greek government in exile in North and South Africa during the Nazi occupation of Greece is reflected in *Imerologhio katastromatos, B'* (*Logbook II*, 1944). The inner adventure of the poet comes up against the reality of war and gives these poems a realism which proves to be the most potent in the whole of his work.

The poetic landscape changes in *Kikhli* (*The Thrus*, 1947), a composition in three parts which becomes a significant stage in Seferis' artistic development from the point of view of theme as well as that of form. The musical element and the realist element coexist harmoniously in this work, but the work remains hermetic. The poem is the last stage of Seferis' odyssey with Ulysses, Elpenor and Circe symbolising the basic elements of human reality. The relationship which the two men (the incarnation of the calculating and the concupiscent mind respectively) have with Circe (the symbol of voluptuousness and human desire) is described both lyrically and dramatically, in a psychological treatment that leads to an awareness of human tragedy and, at the same time, to a way of transcending it. The poem ends with the Proustian return of the modern Ulysses to Paradise Lost, through an experience of enlightenment during which the clash of absolute light with earthly reality is transcended to be resolved in an act of union in a dazzling and eternal moment of a lifetime.

The Thrush, more than any other poem by Seferis, shows his confidence in individual responsibility. This does not mean, however, that he does not recognise the power of 'necessity' and the limits imposed by fate. Seferis' final 'cosmotheory', if we want to consider it through a philosophical prism, is tinged with existentialist overtones.

Seferis' last two poetic works were written as a result of enlightenment, but the subjects treated remain the same. *Imerologhio katastromatos, C'* (*Logbook III*, 1955) includes poems that express the feelings inspired in him by a visit to Cyprus, a major area of Hellenism where 'each sensation does not evaporate as in the capitals of the great wide world'. Cyprus, perceived as a place 'where space still functions', becomes for Seferis the symbol of a 'higher Greece'. The form of certain poems in the collection show that they constitute a dialogue between Seferis and his two precursors and contemporaries, Cavafy and Sikelianos; these works illustrate his efforts to attain to a form of expression which will not just be the voice of a poet, but that of Greek poetry.

The short pieces which make up the poetic units of which the *Tria Kripha piimata* (*Three Secret Poems*, 1966) are comprised, are state-of-play poems. As the title suggests, we are present here at a return to the 'closed' form which follows on from the largely 'open' expression of the previous collection. Although the poems contain the essence of the poet's human adventure, their dry, asthmatic breath indicates that the verses of these final years are the fruit of a poetic senility. The work ends once again with a reference to a revelatory experience, a sort of epilogue which expresses the feeling of a just reward after a long and fruitful life in poetry:

φώναξε τὰ παιδιὰ νὰ μαζέψουν τὴ
στάχτη
καὶ νὰ τὴ σπείρουν.
Ὅ, τι πέρασε πέρασε σωστά.

Κι᾽ ἐκεῖνα ἀκόμη ποὺ δὲν πέρασαν
πρέπει νὰ καοῦν
τοῦτο τὸ μεσημέρι ποὺ καρφώθηκε

ὁ ἥλιος
στὴν καρδιὰ τοῦ ἑκατόφυλλου
ρόδου.

*Call the children to collect the
ashes and to scatter them.
All that has happened has happened
justly.
And what has not happened yet
must burn,
this noon to which the sun is nailed
in the heart of the rose with a hundred
petals.*

The prose work

It was only after Seferis' death that the breadth and the worth of his works in prose became better known. A novel (*Exi nikhtes stin Akropoli, Six Nights at the Acropolis*, 1974, written in 1926–1930 and 1954) and nine volumes of his personal and political diaries reversed the image of a not very productive writer that Seferis had acquired through his poetry. The novel, whose hero is the symbolist poet Stratis Thalassinos (a character in numerous poems by Seferis), does not succeed artistically because of the heaviness due to an insufficient working out of the material furnished by the writer's diary. The diaries more than anything reinforced the image that Seferis had already projected of an important prose writer in his critical essays. Written on the model of French intimate diaries, his personal journals (seven volumes) unveil many details of the poet's individual and artistic adventure, while his political diaries (two volumes, of which one remains unpublished) relate his participation in the major and minor events of Greek political history before and after the Second World War.

Of comparable importance to Seferis' poetic work is his work as a critic summed up in his fundamental essays on poetry (*Dialoghos pano stin piisi, Dialogue on Poetry; Monologos panostin piisi, Monologue on Poetry; I ghlosa stin piisi mas, Language in Our Poetry*), as well as in texts devoted to poets (Eliot, Kalvos, Palamas, Sikelianos, Cavafy, Cornaros and Dante) collected in *Dokimes* (*Essays*). At the beginning of his career, under the influence of French symbolism, Seferis had flirted with an idealist aesthetic; the importance of his critical work resides in new theories which he expounds on the nature of the poetic phenomenon.

Seferis' theories on criticism are the natural outcome of his aesthetic positions: as *a priori* there are no laws about beauty, similarly critical rules are created *a posteriori*. They derive from the principles imposed by great works over the centuries and by the emotional needs of each age. The relativism of Seferis's critical theory rests on his ideas about human values, the basis of which is psychological. There are no deathless works, but works with a short or long lifespan. Their longevity depends on the extent to which they satisfy the demands of each epoch, which are not always the same, but which are modified through the psychological scaffolding of their time. All effort made by the critic to endow his judgement with universality is condemned to failure, for the ground it is supported by is 'an ever shifting foundation'.

Orwell (1903–1950)

M. Miller

He had won the victory over himself. He loved Big Brother.

George Orwell,
1984

Born in 1903 in Bengal, where his father was a civil servant, Eric Arthur Blair did not become George Orwell until 1933, the year in which he published *Down and Out in Paris and London* under a pseudonym. In 1904, Orwell and his two sisters returned to England with their mother, while their father stayed in India until 1911. At the age of eight Orwell was sent to a prep school called Saint-Cyprian, on the subject of which another 'former pupil', Henry Longhurst, would later write: 'My brother wholly attributes the fact that he escaped, healthy in mind and body, from the five years

he spent as a prisoner of war, to the time he spent at Saint-Cyprian.' In 1916, Orwell won a scholarship to Eton; from 1922 to 1925 he worked in Burma for the imperial police. He relates this experience in his novel *Burmese Days* (1934) and in two essays, *A Hanging* (1931) and *Shooting an Elephant* (1950). The latter begins with the following words: 'In Moulmein, in Lower Burma, I was hated by large numbers of people – the only time in my life that I have been important enough for this to happen to me.'

Becoming one of the oppressed among the oppressed

After having handed in his resignation to the Burma police, Orwell decided to live by his writing. He described this period in *The Road to Wigan Pier* (1937): 'I felt that I had got to escape not merely from imperialism but from every form of man's dominion over man. I wanted to submerge myself, to get right down among the oppressed, to be one of them and on their side against their tyrants.' For a few years he was very ill and his health deteriorated.

Orwell looked on his work with the greatest modesty. Having read Joyce's *Ulysses*, he wrote to his friend Brenda Salkeld: 'When I read a book like that and then come back to my own work, I feel like a eunuch who has taken a course in voice production . . . but if you listen closely you can hear the good old squeak just the same as ever.' In 1936, Orwell married Eileen Maud O'Shaughnessy, a graduate of St Hugh's College, Oxford. The following year, he went to Spain to fight in the ranks of the POUM. Bob Edwards, his comrade in arms, who was later to become a labour MP, describes Orwell in the trenches – an easy target with his tall stature – as a man who was 'resolutely bold', and suffering from a phobia of rats, like Winston Smith, the hero of *1984*. Eileen joined Orwell in Spain where she worked as a secretary in the office of the International Workers' Party in Barcelona. Orwell got a bullet in the throat: his voice was never the same again. He was demobilised and left Spain. He had lost his illusions: many of his anarchist friends had been arrested by the Communists.

In 1938, Orwell spent six months in a sanatorium after a serious pulmonary haemorrhage. Although he was extremely critical about the events that led to the Second World, when the conflict broke out Orwell remarked in *My Country Right or Left*, an essay published in 1940: 'I was patriotic at heart, would not sabotage or act against my own side, would support the war, would fight in it if possible.' Orwell was devastated when the army rejected him on health grounds. During the war, he made broadcasts for the BBC and began to be quite famous, while remaining very poor. In 1944, he and his wife adopted a baby, Richard; the following year, Eileen died suddenly during an operation.

Animal Farm

When *Animal Farm* (1945) appeared, the book thrilled the critics, who compared Orwell to Swift. Its publisher, Fred Warburg, declared some years later: 'It is to *Animal Farm* that I owe my first success as a publisher.' In an essay published in 1946 called *Why I Write*, Orwell described his concept of writing: 'What I have most wanted to do throughout the past ten years is to make political writing into an art.' He added: 'And looking back through my work, I see that it is invariably where I lacked a political purpose that I wrote lifeless books and was betrayed into purple passages, sentences without meaning, decorative adjectives and humbug generally.' In 1946, after a fresh pulmonary haemorrhage, Orwell took his son Richard to the island of Jura, renowned for its mild climate. There he finished the first manuscript of *1984*, but his health deteriorated and he was forced to stay in a sanatorium.

1984 and Orwell's world

1984 was published in London and New York in June 1949. Like *Animal Farm*, this book has never stopped selling, and has been translated into almost every languages.

In October 1949, Orwell married Sonia Brownwell, a collaborator on the literary magazine *Horizon*. After another haemorrhage, Orwell died on 21 January 1950.

His reputation as a writer has grown considerably since his death. 'Orwellian' is an adjective whose international connotations by far transcend the framework of literary criticism. In 1984, the Council of Europe, in collaboration with the European Foundation for Science, Art and Culture, organised a conference in Strasbourg on the subject '*1984: Myths and Realities*'. In the introduction to the collection of essays called *And he loved Big Brother*, the closing session of the conference was summed up: 'The starting up of powerful intellects whose role would be to evaluate modern cultural processes by reference to the Orwellian apocalypse.' In the same work, Simone Veil, then president of the European Parliament, wrote: 'The European idea is above all a militant idea, which cannot take on its full meaning without the background, past or future, of Orwellian totalitarianism.'

In Eastern Europe, Orwell is one of the most appreciated of English writers, although his books were banned in all countries of the Soviet bloc, with the exception of Yugoslavia, until quite recently. His works have been abundantly commented on: Victor Tsoppi, for example, wrote in 1984 in the news weekly *Novoye vremya* that '*1984* . . . is a severe warning for bourgeois democratic society, which, as he [Orwell] emphasised, is founded on anti-humanism, destructive militarism, and the negation of the rights of man . . . But not a single one of the Western commentators of *1984* could find the necessary wisdom, courage or honesty to finally admit that George Orwell, with his prophetic talent, was describing the syndrome of current capitalism with which we are forced to coexist, for want of a better solution, while resisting with all our strength its pathologically militarist ambitions in the realm of nuclear missiles.'

In 1984 an exhibition called 'Orwell in Eastern Europe' was organised at the British Library in London. According to the explanatory notes that accompanied this exhibition, 'in Latvia a certain Gunars Astraa was recently condemned to seven years of close detention and five years of internal exile for having copied out a Latvian version of Orwell's *1984* and for other crimes against the Soviet state.' In Poland, Orwell was particularly popular, and his face was even chosen to adorn a clandestine postage stamp issued by Solidarity. It is perhaps this ability to lend himself to various interpretations with various audiences which justifies Orwell's reputation as a great writer.

Brecht (1898–1956)

G. Cepl-Kaufmann

The curtain down and questions open.
Bertolt Brecht,
The Good Woman of Sizuan

Eugen Berthold Friedrich Brecht, who called himself Bertolt Brecht or Bert Brecht according to the fashionable Americanism of the 1920s, made his mark in a decisive manner on twentieth-century European theatre, as much by his dramatic work as by his staging techniques.

Literary debut

Brecht's literary début coincided with the collapse of the bourgeois world at the end of the First World War. From his early works, his non-conformist socialism appears entire, as if condensed, in his first drama *Baal* (1919). His experience of anarchist groups, his socialising, among others, with Caspar Neher, the future set designer, and his love of nature which came to him from his wanderings in the meadows studded with canals in the charming countryside round Augsburg, the town in which he was born in 1898, are to be found in the zest for life and anti-bourgeois attitude of Baal. Verlaine, with his life of debauchery and vagrancy at the side of Rimbaud, and Villon were the godparents of the 'anti-life' that Baal chooses for himself: his demand for happiness

and his search for pleasure lead him to refuse a writer's career in bourgeois society and seek out marginal groups. The lyricism of Villon's ballads and Wedekind's Lieder influenced Brechtian poems of this period, which appeared in 1927 in a collection called *Die Hauspostille* (*Household Sermons*).

The Berlin period

In 1924, Brecht abandoned Munich and his sporadic medical studies, and left for Berlin, the 'Mecca' of the 1920s, with its explosive political climate, its heavy atmosphere of sensual greed, its pro-American delirium and its tumultuous life of pleasure. For Brecht, influenced by his reading of Kipling, Berlin became an exhausting jungle, his 'Chicago'. This period, however, was a period of heightened creativity, especially after 1922 when he was awarded the Kleist prize. He thus benefits from early fame while his first theatrical works made an impression, in which he gave himself over to 'a nihilist critique of bourgeois society'.

There was already a characteristic anti-illusionism in his plays. In the text which accompanies *Trommeln in der Nacht* (*Drums in the Night*, 1920), he recommends putting up a poster in the auditorium: 'Do not make such big romantic eyes!', a provocative gesture which forbids the spectator any identification with the work based on sentimentality and pathos. In this 'comedy', Brecht depicts for the first time through this 'hero' the petit bourgeois whose political ignorance he henceforth denounced. While street fights have started in Berlin, Kragler prefers to muse on his limited petit bourgeois idyll: 'My flesh should rot in the stream for an idea to reach the sky? You're crazy!' In the following play, *Im Dickicht der Städte* (*In the Jungle of Cities*, 1921), Brecht's preference for grotesque characters, full of vitality and sensuality, but devoid of any reflection on the meaning of life, dominates 'this duel of two men in the giant town of Chicago'. In *Die heilige Johanna der Schlacht-höfe* (*Saint Joan of the Stockyards*, 1929–1930), Chicago becomes a synonym for the cold, cynical greed for profit which animates these 'asphalt jungles'. Joan of Arc, transported to the wretched reality of the stockyards, understands the brutalising laws of capitalist society.

It was at this point that Brecht's image of mankind became radical. In his play *Leben Eduards des Zweiten von England* (*The Life of Edward II of England*, 1924), Brecht, while keeping a critical distance, tries once more to depict the heroic age of individualism: Edward II tries to make his own personal interests prosper at the expense of reasons of State. He fails and plunges his country into a bloody civil war.

The operas

Brecht had his greatest success with the operas that he created in collaboration with Kurt Weill: *Aufstieg und Fall der Stadt Mahagonny* (*The Rise and Fall of the Town of Mahagonny*, 1928) and especially *Die Dreigroschenoper* (*The Threepenny Opera*, 1928), based on *The Beggar's Opera* by John Gay, which he enlivens with texts by François Villon and elements taken from Kipling. We observe the struggle for life of the London robber Macheath, known as 'Mack the Knife'. He is behind the robbings and muggings committed on the London streets, while his enemy and father-in-law directs the order of beggars. After a plot has been hatched to capture him, Mack the Knife is condemned to death. He is saved by a king's messenger who arrives on horseback. Ennobled, Mack the Knife receives a chateau and a pension in keeping with his position. Brecht thought this fable would unmask the real essence of social relationships: misery treated as merchandise, a robber who is merely a bourgeois, and vice versa. Such is the morality expressed by Mack's song: 'First comes the food, then comes the moralising.' But the hope that Brecht had in the public to understand the criticism contained in *The Threepenny Opera* was not realised.

The disenchantment of the world

After this point Brecht's political motivation and his solidarity with the proletariat characterised his lyrical, epic and dramatic work. He preferred the form of the ballad and the Lied in all their variants, from the lullaby and the cry of the revolutionary song to the 'song' and the chorus that had come to Germany from America. Later he reverted to the didactic poem. He then used the sonnet and the elegy forms. *The Büchower Elegien* (*Büchow Elegies*, 1953), which take their name from the little village that was Brecht's last place of residence, near Berlin, reflect the ambivalence of his feelings about the workers' uprising of 17 June in East Berlin. The last poem of the elegies has as its satirical theme the people deprived of democratic elections, which expressed Brecht's growing disenchantment with the German Democratic Republic.

Brecht's prose stayed in the shadow of his other works, which is also explained by the fragmentary character of his two great works in prose: a novel, *Die Geschäfte des Herrn Julius Caesar* (*The Business Affairs of Mr Julius Caesar*, 1937–1939) and the project *TUI* (the acronym of Brecht's satirical 'Tellekt-Uell-In' for 'intellectual'). With this project, he returned to one of his great themes: the doubt and scepticism that intellectuals, the 'TUIS', inspired in him. By dint of schematising his characters, changing perspectives, superimposing different literary types ranging from the thriller to the love story, and by renouncing all psychological and moral motivation, he made a frontal attack on the idea that a reader had about a novel. His works in prose were more popular when they were shorter, above all his tales, for example *Kalendergeschichten* (*Calendar Tales*, 1948) and *Geschichten vom Herrn Keuner* (*The Tales of Mr Keuner*, 1926–1956). Keuner, that imaginary character, whose consciousness is that of Brecht, is like him a thinker capable of discussing dialectics and materialism. His often provocative questions, succeed, like those of Socrates, in stating certain facts:

Wenn Herr K. einen Menschen liebte

'Was tun Sie, wurde Herr K. gefragt,
wenn Sie einen Menschen lieben?'
'Ich mache einen Entwurf von ihm,
sagte Herr K., und sorge, daß er ihm
ähnlich wird.'
'Wer? Der Entwurf?'
'Nein, sagte Herr K., der Mensch.'

When Mr K. liked a person

'What do you do,' someone asked Mr
K., 'when you like a person?'
'I make a sketch of him,' replied Mr
K., 'and I make the two similar to
each other.'
'What? The sketch to the man?'
'No,' said Mr K. , 'the man to the
sketch.'

In their dialogues, Kennedy's stories are close to Brecht's plays.

Didactic and epic theatre

In 1928, Brecht perfected his aesthetic-cum-political concept of 'didactic theatre'. His political interest in the theatre extended to the actors themselves. He expounds his theories in *Zur Theorie des Lehrstücks (On the Theory of the Didactic Play,* 1937), in which he says that 'the didactic play educates by the very fact of its being performed, not by reason of its being seen. In principle no spectator is necessary for a didactic play, but can naturally take advantage of it. What lies at the basis of the didactic play is the hope that he who performs it can be socially influenced by the execution of quite precise modes of action, the adoption of particular attitudes, the restitution of particular speeches.'

During Brecht's exile, which began in February 1933, immediately after the Reichstag fire, he was working on a huge collection of his epic plays. He stayed in Denmark until 1939, and *Svendborger Gedichte (The Svendborg Poems,* 1939) bear witness to this period. They are a political-cum-lyrical attack on National Socialism and on his Führer Hitler, the 'house painter'.

Brecht went through Sweden (up until 1940), Finland (until 1941) and Moscow, finally reaching the United States where he lived in Santa Monica until 1947. Disturbed by being summoned to appear before the committee of enquiry on un-American activities during the MacCarthy era, Brecht returned to Europe. He set up house at first in Zurich, then, after 1949, in East Berlin. He rejected the gradual restoration of the Federal Republic of Germany, but his relations with the German Democratic republic did not develop without conflict. With his Berliner Ensemble – he had at his disposition in 1954 his own theatre, Am Schiffbauerdamm – he managed to realise on stage the logical conversion suggested by his theory on epic theatre and to perform the plays written during his exile. From the middle of the 1950s, Brecht would no longer be there to take in the triumph of his epic theatre on the great European stages: he died in Berlin in 1956.

Brechtian aesthetics

The great problems of his period, the perils of fascism and the changes in social structure brought about by the levelling of the masses and their impoverishment, had led Brecht to Marxism. The aim of his aesthetic theory was to use the theatre to give an exact view of social relations and to bring about in everyone a change of behaviour. The essential principles of this aesthetic theory figure in fragments of the dialogue *Der Messingkauf (Buying Brass,* 1939–1940) and in the texts of the *Kleines Organon für das Theater (Little Organon for the Theatre,* 1948). For Brecht, the theatre had to be 'the theatre of a scientific age'. The parable is his favourite means of analysing the age, as in *Der aufhaltsame Aufstieg des Arturo Ui (The Resistible Rise of Arturo Ui,* 1941), in which Brecht unmasked American gangsters as well as the Hitler regime. Dialogue became the means of asserting a truth the evidence for which is strengthened during the theatrical performance, as in *Das Leben des Galilei (The Life of Galilei,* 1938). In this drama's three versions, Brecht shows the necessity and the possibility of displacing such experience into different time periods: Galileo, in 1938–1939, succeeds, by a stratagem, in making his knowledge safe. But we see him, after Hiroshima, in 1945–1946, accuse himself of murder. Finally, in the third version, which takes place in 1954–1955, after the perfecting of the H-bomb, he launches an appeal to humanity.

With his dialectical plays, Brecht wanted to triumph over traditional ideas: the stage should no longer be the place for conflicts of soul, spiritual problems and individual anxieties, nor that of symbolic escape-routes which take us away from reality. It should be a battlefield for ideas and political concepts. In *Buying Brass*, the confrontation of the characters gives us a basic example of this dialectic: in a succession of nocturnal dialogues between Art (the Actor) and Science (the Philosopher), old and new theatre confront each other. The interest of the philosopher is comparable to that of the trader in brass who wants to buy a trumpet for an orchestra because he is interested in its 'material value'. During the fourth night the synthesis of practice and theory takes place: this is when 'the philosopher's plan to highlight the didactic nature of art meets up with the artist's plan to give to art his knowledge, his experience and social problems'. If, with his 'didactic plays', Brecht seems to have abjured all sensuality in the theatre, his aesthetic form of the game states its claims more and more loudly, and theatre thus regains an appeal which is exerted over the intelligence but also over the sensibility. Above all it is the dramas of his period of exile which seduce us by the effectiveness of their scenarios, the charm of their parables and their characters full of contradictions. His female figures are often striking. Brecht uses them to give personal messages, especially where war is concerned, and this is a dominant theme for the pacifist that he is. Señora Carrar and Mother Courage are the epitome of war-affected victims. In the play *Die Gewehre der Frau Carrar* (*Señora Carrar's Rifles*, 1937–1938), this mother, whose son is one of the victims of Franco's fascism, recognises that it is not by refusing rifles that we can be freed from fascism in the middle of a civil war, but by forming an active front with a view to solidarity of action. With *Mutter Courage und ihre Kinder* (*Mother Courage and her Children, a Chronicle of the Thirty Years' War*, 1939), Brecht wrote a milestone in the history of the theatre, if only because of the magnificent acting of his wife, Helena Waigel. In this play, the female type is very different to that of Señora Carrar: Anna Fierling, the female tramp who is called 'Mother Courage', is prey to a moral conflict: she would like to protect her children from the troubles of the war and at the same time profit from this war 'to feather her own nest'. Finally this 'hyena of the battlefield' will pursue her route alone: her children are dead, but that has not 'taught her anything'. It is for the spectator to draw the lesson from this didactic piece. In the epilogue of another drama, *Der gute Mensch von Sezuan* (*The Good Woman of Sezuan*, 1941), an actor expounds the problem to the audience who are waiting for a positive conclusion to the play; his way of formulating the problem reveals the essential idea and the world view of all Brecht's theatre:

Wir stehen selbst enttäuscht und sehn betroffen
Den Vorhang zu und alle Fragen offen. [. . .]
Verehrtes Publikum, los, such dir selbst den Schluß!
Es muß ein guter da sein, muß, muß, muß!

Overcome we too stare disappointed
The curtain down and questions open.
Honourable audience, away and work the end out for yourself!
There must be a good one there somewhere, there must, must, must be!

17 *The Postwar Era: 1945–1968*

M. DE CLERCQ, H. BOUSSET

Nell *Nothing is funnier than unhappiness, I grant you that, but . . .*

Nag *Oh!*

Nell *Yes, yes, it's the most comical thing in the world.*

Samuel Beckett,
Endgame

Germany, 1945: with the fall of the Third Reich came a desire to build a new world out of the rubble. The past will be erased. This is zero hour, 'Stunde Null'. France, 1968: 'Nothing will be the same again,' President Georges Pompidou declared. More than twenty years had gone by, culminating in an uprising in Czechoslovakia – the Prague spring – student revolts in Louvain, Berlin, Rome and Paris. For more than twenty years, progress was believed possible, starting from new foundations, politically as well as culturally. The intellectual debate rises from 'degree zero', to which Hans Magnus Enzensberger alludes when he speaks of 'the death of the novel'.

In the countries of the 'Eastern bloc', the Zhdanovian model of 'socialist realism' developed with Sovietisation. Defined in the Hungarian and German writings of György Lukács (1885–1971), realism is subordinated to the ideological control of the Communist Party, faithful to Soviet directives. The symptoms of socialist realism, enumerated for the first time in 1953 by the Polish émigré **Czeslaw Miłosz (born 1911)** in his essay on 'popular logocracies', *Znielwolony umys*

(Captive Thought), were rife in the 1950s. In the West, people were looking for something new: the 'Trümmerliteratur', literature of the rubble, developed from a reflection on war and the coming of a new era. We could say, to characterise their cultural context, that two decades took Europe from 'year zero' to 'degree zero'. The war called reality into question again. The world was perceived as something absurd. Angst made its appearance. For the existentialists, man was only defined by his actions in a lawless, morality-less, godless world. He was condemned to be free and to construct his own destiny. In 1945 **Jean-Paul Sartre (1905–1980)*** founded *Les Temps modernes (Modern Times)*, not to start a school of thought, but to create an atmosphere, a certain way of life in which non-conformism was applicable. In this way he opened the debate on the literature of combat and its vocation to transform society. Until 1960, existentialism was at the heart of intellectual discussions. A philosopher of the absurd in *The Outsider* (1942) and *The Rebel* (1951), **Albert Camus (1913–1960)** developed in *The Plague* (1947) a humanism of solidarity, in which is asserted the will 'to be a saint without God'. Gabriel Marcel (1877–1973) participated in the advent of a Christian existentialism with the German philosopher Jaspers. Pierre Teilhard de Chardin (1881–1955) rejected the divorce between science and religion. After Camus' deaths, the structuralist method, in the wake of the school of Prague, developed in France with the works of the ethnologist Lévi-Strauss. From 1960 the group Tel Quel took particular

care to isolate structures of thought on the basis of language study. Structural analysis was applied in several areas: philosophy (Foucault), semiology and psychoanalysis (Lacan), the new criticism (Barthes). Man gave way to things. Towards the end of the 1960s, in the line of postwar Marxist theories (Horkheimer, Adorno), then of those of Lucien Goldmann, literary criticism* was primarily concerned with social and political commitment.

VARIATIONS ON TRADITION

After the break caused by the war and the flourishing of committed literature, there was a return to the narrative tradition. In France, the desire to assert the very finality of literature was rediscovered: narrative. Hence there was a return to aestheticism and tradition.

The traditional novel

In France, next to committed literature, a fresh enthusiasm for Stendhal and his narrative technique may be observed: 'egotism' and a certain aristocratic and nonchalant cynicism developed. At the instigation of Roger Nimier (1925–1962) a battalion of 'hussars' was formed, a group of writers who took their name from the title of his novel *The Blue Hussar* (1950), in which war lost its sacred aura. Michel Déon (born 1919), Antoine Blondin (1922–1991) and Jacques Laurent (born 1919) gave free rein to their sensitivity. The anchoring of the novel in a story or in history is noticeable before, during and after the arrival of the 'nouveau roman' in France. Telling a story is what **Julien Gracq** (born 1910) did in a lucid way in *Un balcon en forêt* (1958). Close to Breton without being a surrealist, he used a rich language in sumptuous novels which play with myth (*Le Rivage des Syrtes*, *The Sandy Shore*, 1951).

Marguerite Yourcenar (1903–1987), even before she wrote her great historical novels, *The Memoirs of Hadrian* (1951) and *The Abyss* (1968), had put together a narrative and autobiographical *magnum opus*, strolling through the gardens of history (*The Labyrinth of the World*, 3 volumes published between 1977 and 1978) outside movements and fashions.

> I have often thought about the mistake that we make, when we suppose that a man and a family necessarily have a share in the ideas or the events of the century they find themselves in.
>
> Marguerite Yourcenar,
> *The Memoirs of Hadrian*

The novels by Michel Tournier (born 1924) are so many incarnations of the predominant role of the story, of the narrative (*Friday or the Limbo of the Pacific*, 1967). History and autobiography coexist in the work of Albert Cohen (1895–1981), but *Belle du Seigneur* (1968), which depicts the political situation in the 1930s, is primarily the story of a passion. In England, the traditional novel dominated the literary scene. Works by Graham Greene and by **William Golding (1911–1993)** were characterised by 'a revolt against reductionism'. The novels by Greene (*A Burnt-Out Case*, 1961) and by Golding (*Rites of Passage*, 1980) were influenced by Conrad, whose exoticism they reflect, the compulsion to transgress human limits. Golding interprets his vision of evil as 'the terrible sickness of being human'. In *Lord of the Flies* (1954), young schoolboys, who have escaped from a plane crash, turn into bloodthirsty savages.

> Ralph looked at him dumbly. For a moment he had a fleeting picture of the strange glamour that had once invested the beaches. But the island was scorched up like dead wood – Simon was dead . . .
>
> William Golding,
> *Lord of the Flies*

From *The Power and the Glory* (1940) to *Monsignor Quixote* (1982), Greene, a convert to Catholicism, was concerned to fill a gap and create a territory, 'Greeneland', inhabited by exceptional beings. Golding, in *The Inheritors*

(1955), depicts Neanderthal times, delving into the deepest part of the history of humanity in the hope of rediscovering lost innocence but finds there a rising brutality. In *Pincher Martin* (1956), the central figure, a drowning man, is overwhelmed not simply by the tide but by the moral paradoxes of the life he is losing. The same desire to be a moralist is present in the work of Angus Wilson (1913–1991): *Hemlock and After* (1952), *The Old Men at the Zoo* (1961), *Late Call* (1964) are a questioning of the nature of good and evil. In *No Laughing Matter* (1967), we find chronicled half a century of English history as lived by the generations of the Matthews family from 1912 to 1967. Iris Murdoch (1919–1999) also participated in the great tradition of the psychological novel. In *An Unofficial Rose* (1962) and *The Unicorn* (1963), her characters, close to allegory, are submitted to painful initiations. Her universe tends towards the supernatural. Another female writer, Doris Lessing (born 1919), who espoused the cause of feminism, owes her popularity to a sort of 'Bildungsroman' in five volumes, which introduces us to South Africa before and after the Second World War (*The Children of Violence*, 1952–1969).

In Flanders, the struggle of the Christian in the dechristianised modern world, which Bernanos, Mauriac and Julien Green had described, haunts Flemish Catholic writers: André Demedts (born 1906) and Maria Rosseels (born 1916). History and autobiography coexist in Marnix Gijsen (1899–1984): the symbolic novel *Het boek van Joachim van Babylon* (*The Book of Joachim of Babylon*, 1947) is as much a moral as a philosophical tale. Work by Paul Lebeau (1908–1982) is located between the historical and the intellectual novel. Introspective analysis forms the essential weave of his *Xanthippe* (1959). This is also the case for Bernard Kemp (1926–1980), in *Het laatste spel* (*The Last Game*, 1957) and *De kater van Orfeus* (*The Disenchantment of Orpheus*, 1960). In French-speaking Belgium, Plisnier took pains to reconcile the message of Lenin with the words of the Gospel. In his great series of novels, he

takes the side of his rebellious heroes: Noël in *Murders* (1941), and Daru in *Mothers* (1947–1949). *Our Shadow Precedes Us* (1953), by Albert Ayguesparse (born 1900), is of the same ilk. After a literary début hailed by Cocteau, the novelist Dominique Rolin (born 1913) returns to the theme of the family drama in *Breath*. It is perhaps in the shadows, on the margin of Belgian society that authors appear who will come to enjoy a worldwide reputation. Félicien Marceau (born 1913), after *Urges of the Heart* (1955), left Belgium to begin a career in France which will bring him to the Académie Française. The convulsive and subversive writing of Marcel Moreau (born 1933) was revealed to the reading public in France by *Quintes* (*Fits of Coughing*, 1962). Another son of emigrants to France, Hubert Juin (born 1926) devotes an entire cycle of novels to the Belgian side of the Ardennes with *Les Hameaux* (*The Hamlets*, 1963).

The Bulgarian Dimităr Talev (1898–1966) traced the evolution of a family in Macedonia at the end of the nineteenth century. The 1960s witnessed the historical novel at its peak. *Legenda za Sibin* (*The Legend of Sibin*, 1968) and *Antichrist* (*The Anti-Christ*, 1969) by Emiljan Stanev (1907–1979) pose the fundamental problem of the struggle between the flesh and the spirit. The novel *Tjutjun* (*Tobacco*, 1951), by Dimităr Dimov (1909–1966), deals with Bulgaria's national destiny on the eve of the Second World War, during a short period in which the bourgeoisie at last played an effective role. In 1945, the Yugoslav Ivo Andrić (1892–1975) published the novels *Na Drimi ćuprija* (*Bridge over the Drima*) and *Travnička kronika* (*The Chronicle of Travnik*), differing from socialist realism by their theme, an eventful rather than heroic story, and by their narrative technique. The Bosnian Meša Selimovic (1910–1982) also returned to historical themes in the shape of an interior monologue. Several writers, still attached to the theme of the war, broke with realist clichés to concentrate on psychological after-effects: Dobrica Cosić (born 1921) with ethical accents, and Davičo in the tradition of surrealism. Antonijé Isaković (born 1923) gazed a trifle unconventionally at the war; Mihajlo Lalic (born 1914) emphasised the contemplation of the human condition.

In Czechoslovakia, a first attempt to give a synthesis of this sombre postwar period came from Vladimír Pazourek (1907–1987): *Česká trilogie* (*Czech Trilogy*, 1947–1949) presents the complex evolution of Czech society under the heel of the Germans. In 1958, Jan Otčenášek (1924–1979) published a short story, *Romeo, Julie a tma* (*Romeo, Juliette and Darkness*, 1958). This work, which relates the tragic encounter of two pure beings, marks the beginning of his ideological detachment. In the novel that followed, *Kulhavý Orfeus* (*The Limping Orpheus*, 1964), he is sensitive to the disastrous experience of his generation during the years of the German occupation. The renewal of prose is announced in novels by Josef Škvorecky (born 1924) including *Zbabělci* (*The Cowards*, 1958), characterised by a return to psychology, to the individual, to human problems.

In Poland, Andrzejewski showed how the mechanisms of history are reflected in the individual consciousness (*Ciemności kryją ziemę*, *Darkness Covers the Earth*, 1957; *Bramy raju*, *The Gates of Paradise*, 1961). Konwicki detached himself after 1956 from the communist tendency. His novel on guilt, *Sennik współczesny* (*The Key to Contemporary Dreams*,

1963), established as a major Polish writer. In *Sława i Chwała* (*The Honour and the Glory*, 1956), Jaroslaw Iwaszkiewicz (1894–1980) depicted the Polish intelligentsia through several decades of war. In Tadeusz Breza (1905–1970), narrative prose falls between the essay and fiction (*Spiżowa brama*, *The Gate of Bronze*, 1960). Lesze Kołakowski (born 1927) parodied celebrated messages from the Bible in his novels (*Klucz do niebios*, *The Key to Heaven*, 1964). Stanisław Lec (1909–1966) wrote *Myśli nieuczesane* (*Dishevelled Thoughts*, 1965), aphorisms highly representative of the satirical tone of the years 1956–1966. The work of Tadeusz Parnicki (born 1908) is marked by great complexity: *Słowo i ciło* (*The Word and the Flesh*, 1959) is a collection of letters and imaginary dialogues relating to the world of Hellenism. *Glosy w Ciemności* (*Voices in the Darkness*, 1956), by Julian Strykowski (born 1905), depicted the Jews of Galicia. The question of cultural identity within the Austrian Empire was posed by **Andrzej Kuśniwicz (born 1904)** in his novel *W drodze do Koryntu* (*The Road to Corinth*, 1964). He also evoked a return to the country of his childhood (the Ukraine), the famous 'Triangle of Big Fields' near the 'Two Rivers'. However, the narrator warns the reader not to be taken in by the illusion of geographical names, which do not figure on any map.

> *[. . .] zrósl się z faktów i ich interpretacji, ze strzępów krajobrazu i fragmentów rozmów, ówiat utkany z prawdy i zmyślenia, gdzie części zmyślone bywają trwalsze i cenniejsze, wydają się rzetelniejsze od rzeczywistości prżezytej, która służy im tylko za kanwę i tło.*

Andrzej Kuśniéwicz,
W drodze do Koryntu

> For there exists *[. . .]* a world that agglutinates events and their interpretations, scraps of landscape, fragments of conversations, a world woven of truth and fiction, in which it happens that the made-up bits are the most lasting and the most precious, so that they seem more solid than the lived-through reality which serves as their canvas and their background.

The existentialist novel

Historical events also furnished raw material for many Greek novels and novellas, but their authors wrote from a revolutionary ideology and consciousness: Camus and Sartre left their mark. **Alexandros Kotzias (born 1926)** studied the metaphysics of evil in its totality in his first book, *Poliorkia* (*Siege*, 1953), which is set under Nazi occupation. Realism and lyricism interact in novels by Kostas Taktsis (1927–1988), through whose pages process all of the Greek petite bourgeoisie of the first half of the twentieth century (*To trito stephani*, *The Third Ring*, 1962). The novelist **Stratis Tsirkas (1911–1980)**, a Greek born in Cairo, depicted the atmosphere of intrigue in the Jerusalem of the period in his trilogy *Akivernites Polities* (*Cities Drifting*, 1961–1965). He belonged to the avant-garde by virtue of the modernity of his writing. George Ioannou (1927–1985) also evoked Greek society and reality, but mingled it with personal experiences (*Ghia ena philotimo*, *Out of Self-Respect*, 1964; *I Sarkophagos*, *The Sarcophagus*, 1971). The universality of his themes and his heroes entitled **Antonis Samarakis (born 1919)** to be translated into twenty-five languages; his characters are representative of modern man crushed between the mechanisms of the State and indifference in *Sima Kindhinou* (*Distress Signal*, 1961) and *To Lathos* (*The Mistake*, 1965). Vassilis Vassilikos (born 1933) – known in Greece and abroad for his novel *Z* adapted for the big screen by Costa Gavras – posed the question of human solitude in his trilogy *To philo, To pighadhi, T'angheliasma* (*The Leaf, The Well, The Annunciation*, 1961). He often leaves his stories 'open', without an ending, and experiments with the different possibilities of writing.

In Portugal, **Vergílio Ferreira (born 1916)** was strongly influenced by Sartre and Malraux. After a neo-realist period, in the 1950s and 1960s he was concerned with the contemplation of 'extreme moments', linked to the experience of the mystery of birth and death (*Apariçao, Apparition*, 1959; *Cantico final*, 1960).

At the beginning of the 1960s, Yugoslavian literature discovered existentialism and French and American techniques of narrative deconstruction. Petar Segedin (born 1908) published two novels in 1946 and 1947 in which he devotes himself to an autopsy of primitive mentality and existential reflection. The novel essay *Proljece Ivana Galeba* (*The Spring of Ivan Galeb*, 1957), by **Vladan Desnica (1905–1967)**, relates the thoughts of a sick musician. He makes his hero say, in a parody of the rules of socialist realism: 'Who is there to still take an interest in the story of a young man cultivating green beans and walking off with the prize at a regional exhibition? . . . Sociologists and pragmatists plead for an optimistic literature, a literature of "perspective" as they call it. They believe in meteorology provided they are told the weather will be fine tomorrow.'

In Dutch literature, prose and poetry are also touched by an atmosphere of existentialism, not without a breath of scandal. The novel *De avonden* (*The Evenings*, 1947), by **Gerard Reve (born 1923)**, develops the story of the psychic evolution of an adolescent to adulthood, in the spiritual climate of the 1930s and the war years. His epistolary novels *Op weg naar het einde* (*On the Way to the End*, 1963) and *Nader tot U* (*Closer to You*, 1966) tackle the themes of homosexuality and religion freely and from a personal viewpoint. **Willem Frederik Hermans (born 1921)** wrote nihilist novels in defiance of convention with *Ik heb altijd gelijk* (*I am Always right*, 1951) and on the absurdity of life in *De donkere kamer van Damocles* (*The Black Room of Damocles*, 1958): here we do not know if the main character is a hero of the Resistance or the plaything of hallucinations.

We find a comparably problematic existentialism, combined with humanitarian concern, in *Rytteren* (*The Horseman*, 1949) by the Dane Branner, and in *De dömas ö* (*The Island of the Damned*, 1946) by the Swede Stig Dagerman (1923–1954). The theme of the war is ever present. In *Syv fantastiske Fortaellinger* (*Seven Gothic Tales*, 1958), **Karen Blixen (1885–1962)** gives a description of characters placed in a fatal situation, half-way between fantasy and tradition. Blixen's work, simultaneously symbolic and mythical, set a pattern.

The problems of existentialism are found in the novels *Roerloos aan zee* (*Rudderless at Sea*, 1951) and *Negatief* (*Negative*, 1958) by the Fleming Jan Walravens (1920–1965). *De witte muur* (*The White Wall*, 1957) by Maurice

D'Haese (1919–1981) is an echo of Camus' *The Outsider*.

The tragic solitude of modern man forms the main theme of work by **Alberto Moravia (1907–1991)**, who was the husband of the novelist Elsa Morante (1912–1985). He took his inspiration from Sartre's ideas in *Il Conformista* (*The Conformist*, 1957) and *La Noia* (*Boredom*, 1960), full of 'nausea'. From one text to another, he 'harps on' the same topic, but, from year to year, his way of reconciling scorn and disillusion changes. For the Hungarian Miklós Mészöly (born 1921), Camus' work is an ethical and political reference. He is concerned by the situation of the individual who wants to make something of himself, like the athlete in his novel *The Death of an Athlete* (published first in French in 1965; *Az atléta halála*, 1966). *Iskola a határon* (*A School on the Border*, 1959) is the novel that the younger generation in Hungary raved about, a generation for whom **Géza Ottlik (1912–1990)** became a mentor.

A traditional poetic aesthetic

In the modern world, being socially and politically committed is reflected in the themes of contemporary poetry. But many poets continue to exploit neo-classical themes. In The Netherlands, reviews with very different ideological orientations develop a traditional poetic aesthetic: *Maatstaf* (*The Measure*, founded in 1953), *Tirade* (founded in 1957) and *Hollands Maandblad* (*The Dutch Monthly*, founded in 1959). The title of the poem 'Laat het zo blijven' ('Let Everything Stay the Same') by **Rutger Kopland (born 1934)** illustrates this vision of the world (*Onder her vee*, *Under the Livestock*, 1966).

In Flanders, next to the avant-garde, there was a poetry of classical manufacture, which speaks to us of the present: 'an agitation that is modern in classical verse'. The collections *Gedaanten* (*Figures*, 1954) and *Azuren holte*

(*The Azure Hole*, 1964) form the kernel of work by **Jos de Haes (1920–1974)**, in which pain is dissected in the context of Greek antiquity. He also takes his inspiration from Baudelaire and Hölderlin, and in his turn inspires work by Christine D'haen (born 1923). Works by poets such as Herwig Hensen (1917–1988), Karel Jonckheere (born 1906), Hubert Van Herreweghen (born 1920) and Anton Van Wilderode (born 1918) were published in the major literary reviews (*Nieuw Vlaams Tijdschrift*, *The New Flemish Review*; *Dietsche Warande en Belfort*, *The Theux Garden and Belfry*; *De Vlaamse Gids*, *The Flemish Guide*). Such reviews, standing aside from political debate and taking their inspiration from the masters of previous decades, are also one of the characteristics of Portuguese poetry. The lyricism and the personality of artists like David Mourão-Ferreira (born 1927) and Sophia de Mello Breyner (born 1919) blossom in the review *Tavola Redonda* (*Round Table*). This same rather Catholic orientation is found in *Graal* and *Tempo presente* (*Present Time*). Portuguese poets like **Jorge de Sena (1919–1978)**, Ramos Rosa (born 1924) and Carlos de Oliveira borrow from Rilke, Pessoa, Pound and Lorca both their intoxication with life and their spleen before undergoing the influence of the new tendencies which were now defining themselves.

In Hungary, there was a tendency towards individual poetic experience. György Rába (born 1924) brought together in his poems the clarity and plasticity of sometimes dreamlike visions. Also linked to the tradition of Babits and Rilke, Ágnes Nemes Nagy (born 1922) was a master of writing poems about objects. This same trend finds an echo in poetry by János Székely (born 1929), a Hungarian prose-writer and poet from Rumania, and that by János Csokits (born in 1928). A Catholic fascinated by Simone Weil's philosophy and experience, **János Pilinszky (1921–1981)** expressed the vertigo of the essential:

Isten az Isten.	God is God.
Virág a virág.	The flower is a flower.
Daganat a daganat.	The tumour is a tumour.

Tél a tél.	*Winter is winter.*
Gyüjötábor a körülhatárolt	*The fenced-in land a*
bizonytalan formájú terület.	*concentration*
János Pilinszky, *Költemény*	*camp, vaguely shaped.*

In poetry by the Greek Costas Sterghiopoulos (born 1926), existential and social concerns intersect with the symbolism of his early writing.

In England, poetry engaged with society. This is particularly evident in the work of **Philip Larkin (1922–1985)**, whose poetry was inspired by that of Thomas Hardy. *The Less Deceived* (1955) and *The Whitsun Weddings* (1958) vividly evoke the atmosphere of Britain in the 1950s.

Realism in poetry and the socialist perception of the world found a spokesman in the Danish review *Dialog* (1950), poles apart from the review *Heretic*. Eric Knudsen (born 1922) and Ivan Malinowski (1926–1990) both wrote for *Dialog*.

The political temptation in poetry

The Greek political situation generated various types of poetic commitment: the themes developed by Tassos Livaditis (1921–1988) in his collections *Makhi stin akri tis nikhtas* (*Battle at the End of the Night*, 1952) and *Phisaï sta stavrodhomia tou kosmou* (*It is Windy at the Cross-roads of the World*, 1953) are an echo of his political awareness. But ideological scepticism gradually took over from militant optimism. The same leftist enthusiasm animated Titos Patrikios (born 1928). His poetry is structured round three principal axes: nature, love and political hope (*Mathitia, Apprenticeship*, 1963).

Manolis Anagnostakis (born 1925) represents the disappointment of left-wing supporters who between 1940 and 1950 witnessed the failure of their efforts, the betrayal of their hopes and the abandonment of their dreams. Distancing himself from the Communist Party, he transformed his political morality into poetic morality: *Epokhes* (*Seasons, Seasons 2*, 1945, *Seasons 3*, 1948), and *Sinekhia* (*Suite*, 1954), followed by *Suite*

2 (1956) and *Suite 3* (1962). The strategy of Aris Alexandrou (1922–1978), poet and prose-writer (*To Kivotio, The Chest*, 1975) is comparable: he went from orthodox Marxism to the debunking of communism and the defence of the autonomy of poetry.

In Hungary, the poet Ferenc Juhász (born 1928) was discovered under the new communist regime at the end of the 1940s. He was later criticised for his sovereign vision and the baroque complexity of his language. László Nagy (1925–1978), following a similar path, became a model for poetry and ethics.

The Bulgarian regime conferred on poetry a social and political vocation, which aroused a solid opposition to all dogmatic concepts of the world, the individual and art. Stefan Canev (born 1936) declared: 'The poet is not a servant but a sword at the service of the people.' Konstantin Pavlov (born 1933), using the aesthetic effect of the absurd, underlined the paradox of an existence entirely subordinated to repressive ideology. In *Satiri* (*Satirical Poems*, 1960), his irony is transformed into annoyance and even anger. The poet Radoj Ralin (born 1923) joined him in being satirical.

In 1955, the Spanish poet Blas de Otero (1916–1979) wrote: 'I ask for peace and to be allowed to speak.' For him, as for Gabriel Celaya (born 1911) and for all of the 'Generación de los 50', regional poetry and its historical roots are the battle flag of dispute.

In Italy, the idea of a neo-realist cinema appeared at the same time as contemporary prose or the cinema of Rossellini and De Sica. A literature was founded that formally recorded the end of the war, and described the Renaissance of man after the negative experience of fascism. The new poetry responds to the new era's demands for truth, humanity and justice. Quasimodo formulated in a quite hermetic way a revolt against war. Vittorio Sereni left a long elegiac poem on the decadence of European civilisation under

Nazism and fascism; then he tackled the theme of the dehumanisation of man within the industrial age in *Gli strumenti umani* (*Human Instruments*, 1953). Luzi wonders in desperation about the confusion and desolation of the modern world in *Nel magma* (*In the Magma*, 1963). Franco Fortini (born 1917), a non-communist ideologist of the left, opts for sarcasm and prophecy after contact with Brecht's poetry (*Poesia ed errore, Poetry and Error*, 1959). Montale, the greatest of the hermetic poets, wrote many collections including *La Bufera* (*The Storm*, 1956).

Theatre between court and garden

The temptation on the one hand to social commitment, on the other to neo-realism divided the theatre. Sheltered from all activities of the avant-garde, young Francophone Belgian dramatists construct a neo-classical work: Suzanne Lilar (born 1901) wrote *Tous les chemins mènent au ciel* (*All Roads Lead to Heaven*, 1947), Charles Bertin (born 1919) scored with *Don Juan, les Prétendants* (*Don Juan, the Suitors*, 1947) and, above all, Georges Sion (born 1913) gained success with *Charles the Bold* (1944). Heir to the great symbolists, **Paul Willems (born 1912)** offered surreal theatre of high quality; in Antwerp, in *La Ville à voile* (*The Town with Sails*, 1967), there is no longer a house with sails, only 'television aerials everywhere, like little ships'.

In France, a real theatrical revolution is born of the close collaboration between Claudel and the director Jean-Louis Barrault: the latter systematically put on the plays that this dramatist had, for the most part, written during the age of symbolism. For Henry de Montherlant (1895–1972), to put on stage the world of the Mediterranean, in the twentieth century, was to discuss a cultural model valid for all eternity. In a France traumatised by the Algerian crisis, turning its back on the present, he brought to the theatre an episode of the history of Castille (*The Spanish Cardinal*, 1960) or the ancient quarrel of Caesar and Pompey in *The Civil War* (1965). The virtuosity and grating humour of *Pauvre Bitos* (*Poor Bitos*, 1956) and *La Foire d'Empoigne* (*The Free-for-all*, 1962), by Anouilh, assured these plays real popular success. Despite the accuracy of the shots they fired and the effectiveness of their comedy, *The Head of Other People* (1962) by Marcel Aymé (1902–1967), *The Ostrich Eggs* (1948) by André Roussin (1911–1987), and *The Invoice* (1968) by Françoise Dorin (born 1928) were labelled pejoratively by the critics as 'West End plays', but met an enthusiastic reception from the general public.

A new style in English theatre erupted onto the London stage in 1956 with *Look Back in Anger*, the first play by **John Osborne (1929–1994)**. The play addresses issues of class divisions and political complacency through the aggressively disruptive monologues of its iconoclastic hero Jimmy Porter. Designed to disturb the social and aesthetic values of its audience, *Look Back in Anger* initiated a phase of political engagement by 'angry young men' and women writing for the English theatre in the 1950s and 1960s. Arnold Wesker (born 1932), Shelagh Delaney (born 1939) and John Arden (born 1930), who adopted Brechtian elements in his work, followed Osborne's lead.

To circumvent censorship the Hungarian novelist and essayist Németh elaborated a metaphorical and allusive theatrical language, which brought back to life the trial of *Galilei* (1954). The poet and prose-writer Illyés, who evoked the Revolution and the fight for independence of 1848–1849 in *Fáklyaláng* (*The Glow of Torches*, 1952), used the same indirect approach. Writers from the Hungarian minority in Rumania also had recourse to this language: András Sütö (born 1927) and Géza Páskándi (born 1933) in *Vendégség* (*The Host*, 1969). In Hungary, István Örkény (1912–1979), the adept of a minimalist art, was the dramatist of the tragi-comic and everyday grotesque.

The Spanish social theatre found its theorist in Alfonso Sastre (born 1926). The author who dominated the whole of this generation was undoubtedly **Antonio Buero Vallejo (born 1916)**. He went from the 'existential' theatre to social and political theatre in which he denounced injustice and lack of liberty (*Hoy es fiesta, Today is a Holiday*, 1955).

REALISM: AN OBLIGATORY PATH

The Yalta conference did not draw a line under the Second World War. The decades which followed 1945 bear the imprint of this conflict which remained engraved on people's minds and inspired a whole spate of realist literature.

'Trümmerliteratur'

In the strict sense of the word, 'Trümmerliteratur', 'rubble literature', inspired only a limited number of works of fiction in England. The most notable was the Evelyn Waugh trilogy, *Sword of Honour* (1965). *Officers and Gentlemen* (1955), the second in the trilogy and the best-known book of this genre, presents us with unforgettable characters and describes the most absurd military situations. In Germany, on the other hand, war literature is in the ascendancy. In 1945, those who went abroad returned and internal migrants were able to make themselves heard. In 1949 Anna Seghers' second great novel appeared, *Die Toten bleiben jung* (*The Dead Stay Young*). At the beginning of the 1950s, 'rubble literature' came into its own. **Wolfgang Borchert**

(**1921–1947**), with *Draussen vor der Tür* (*The Man Outside*, 1947), is its most famous representative.

From 1947 to 1967, writers gather around Group 47, created by Hans Werner Richter (born 1908). Martin Walser (born 1927) describes the Germany of the end of Nazism and the beginning of the FRG; Siegfried Lenz (born 1926) evokes his childhood memories under the Nazis in *Deutschstunde* (*The German Lesson*, 1968); *Die Blechtrommel* (*The Tin Drum*, 1959) drummed on by little Oskar Matzerath, the hero of **Günter Grass (born 1927)**[*], recalls, in incantatory fashion, the terrible memories of the Nazi period. One of the members of Group 47 was **Heinrich Böll (1917–1985)**, who also starts from his experience of the ruins and tries to understand and express postwar reality, often perceived as a period of restoration. The whole of his work, steeped in personal Catholicism, protests against the constraints of a purely pragmatic society. His novels are an appeal for human solidarity, for the respect of others. *Haus ohne Hüter* (*A House Without Hats*, 1954) describes the dispersion of families. In his most famous novel, *Ansichten eines Clowns* (*The Clown*, 1963), a person excluded from society claims in vain his right to live outside the hypocritical limitations of social morality.

> *[. . .] hält vor amerikanischen Frauenklubs Reden über die Reue der deutschen Jugend, immer noch mit ihrer sanften, harmlosen Stimme, mit der sie Henriette wahrscheinlich zum Abschied gesagt hat. 'Machs gut, Kind.' Diese Stimme konnte ich jederzeit am Telefon hören, Henriettes Stimme nie mehr.*
> Heinrich Böll, *Ansichten eines Clowns*

> *[. . .] she gives lectures to American women's clubs on the remorse of German youth, in that same sweet and innocent voice that she probably used to say to Henriette at the moment of her departure for the army: 'Work well, child.' The voice of my mother I can hear on the telephone as often as I want to. That of Henriette I'll never hear again.*

From the moment of its publication in Paris in 1952, the novel *The 25th Hour* by the Rumanian **Constantin Virgil Gheorghiu (1916–1992)** is received with great interest: it stimulates legitimate debate about the rights of the citizen, about his basic liberties, and questions the bad conscience of Western man, truly liberated from fascism and racism, but closing his eyes to the practice of fascism and racism in others.

Another war, the civil war in Greece, also encouraged literary works. In 1950, Renos Apostodolis (born 1924) published *Piramidha '67* (*Pyramid 67*), which included texts and letters written on the battlefields between 1947 and 1949. His originality is found in the neutral attitude of the author to the two warring factions, denouncing the absurdity of a civil war. Dido Sotiriou (born 1909) evoked the adventures and the struggles of the left-wing partisans in her first novel *I nekri perimenoun* (*The Dead Are Waiting*, 1959). In *Matomena khomata* (*Bloodied Earth*, 1962), she takes up the theme of the tragic story of the Greeks of Asia Minor between 1919 and 1922.

In Italy, **Giorgio Bassani (1916–1989)** traced the history of Ferrara, and particularly of the Jewish community that lived through fascism in *Il giardino dei Finzi-Contini* (*The Garden of the Finzi-Contini*, 1956). We are also indebted to him for the publication of *Il Gattopardo* (*The Leopard*, 1958) by **Giuseppe Tomasi di Lampedusa (1896–1957)**, famous for this portrait of post-Risorgimento Sicily.

Neo-realism

The reaction against fascism produced a new kind of literature, faithful to the directions of the Marxist aesthetic: neo-realism. *La macchina mondiale* (*The World Machine*, 1965) by Paolo Volponi (born 1924) gives an apoca-lyptic reflection of daily life in Italy through an existential enquiry into the condition of the working class. Carlo Bernari (born 1909), in *Prologo alle tenebre* (*Prologue to Darkness*, 1947), and Francesco Jovine (1902–1950), in *Le Terre del Sacramento* (*The Lands of the Sacrament*, 1950), transcribe, with a dearth of expressive means, the reality of war, still so close (prison, deportations, resistance of the partisans), and the immediate postwar period (workers' struggles, the misery of the peasants).

Left-wing critics, who preached neo-realism, wanted its political theses to be embodied in novel form. *Il Metello* (*Metello*, 1955), by Vasco Pratolini (born 1913), is the first novel in a series which sets out to represent the evolution of Italian history through typical characters – in this case a mason who becomes a socialist. Influenced by the situation emerging from the war, **Elio Vittorini (1908–1966)** and **Cesare Pavese (1908–1950)** are tempted, in the beginning, by neo-realism: in *Uomini e no* (*Men and Others*, 1945), Vittorini makes the fascists the monsters of the civil war, then creates extraordinary and Utopian stories (*Le città del mondo*, *The Cities of the world*, 1969). *Il Compagno* (*The Comrade*, 1947) by Pavese is a pro-communist novel, inspired by the Resistance. But immediately afterwards, Pavese calls into question the Manicheism which was the basis of postwar left-wing ideology. He then devotes himself to the analysis of the break-up of the bourgeoisie in *Il diavolo sulle colline* (*The Devil on the Hills*, 1954) and *La bella estate* (*The Beautiful Summer*, 1949):

Eppure una di loro, quella Tina ch'era uscita zoppa dall'ospedale e in casa non aveva da mangiare, anche lei rideva per niente, e una sera, trottando dietro gli altri, si era fermata e si era messa a piangere perché dormire era una stupidaggine e rubava tempo all'allegria.	*And one of these girls even, Tina, who had come out of hospital with a limp and who didn't have enough to eat at home, used to laugh too for something and nothing and, one evening when she was hobbling behind the others, she had stopped and had begun to cry because sleeping was ridiculous and because it was time taken away from having fun.*

Cesare Pavese,
La bella estate

In Portugal, Redol, **Carlos de Oliveira (1921–1981)** with *Uma Abelha na Chuva (A Bee in the Rain*, 1953), Manuel da Fonseca (born 1911) with *Scara de vento (Harvest of Wind*, 1958) are in solidarity with the oppressed working classes in their struggle against dictatorship. The decadence of the rural bourgeoisie appears in the work of Agustina Bessa Luís (born 1922), whose exuberant power of evocation gives her writing an almost hallucinatory precision.

Between 1950 and 1960, Portuguese neo-realism went through a second phase during which it becomes urbanised. The writing becomes more dialectical, more contradictory, more critical, influenced by the climate of existentialism. Man with his angst, prey to a sort of desperate hope (partly provoked by the consolidation of Salazar's dictatorship): this is what neo-realism henceforth wants to analyse. The witnesses of this change are Fernando Namora with *O Homen Disfarçado (The Man in Disguise*, 1957), José Cardoso Pires (born 1925) with *O Anjo Ancorado (The Anchored Angel*, 1958) and Augusto Abelaira (born 1926) with *A cidade das Flores (The Town of Flowers*, 1959).

The portrayal of urban life is also present in Spanish social realism, the theory of which is provided by Goytisolo. *La Colmena (The Beehive*, 1951) by **Camilo José Cela (born 1916)** is the living picture of the grey, difficult existence of Madris's inhabitants. The style adopted is direct, almost journalistic:

La mañana sube, poco a poco, trepando como un gusano por los corazones de los hombres y de las mujeres de la ciudad; golpeando, casi con mimo, sobre los mirares recién despiertos, esos mirares que jamás descubren horizontes nuevos, paisajes nuevos, nuevas decoraciones.	*Morning comes gradually, climbing like a worm over the heart of men and women in the town; knocking, almost gently, on the gazes which have just woken up, those gazes which never discover new horizons, new landscapes or new decors.*

Camilo José Cela,
La Colmena

We owe to **Miguel Delibes (born 1920)** the evocation of the life of peasants in Castilian villages through the eyes of three children discovering the world around them (*El Camino, The Road*, 1950). A news item, a tragic picnic by Madrid shop assistants, becomes an essential element in the exploration of the mixed-up consciousness of the other characters in *El Jarama (The Little River*, 1956) by Rafael Sanchez Ferlosio (born 1927).

The Hungarian **Tibor Déry (1894–1977)**, the author of a realist fresco, *A befejezetlen mondat (The Unfinished Sentence*, 1947), adopts the sceptical attitude of someone who has had to go through the dictatorships of this century, and reaches the ironic impartiality sought in the novel of his life: *Ítélet nincs (No Sitting in Judgement*, 1969). The tradition of the social novel is taken up in Hungary by Ferenc Sánta (born 1927) in *Húsz óra (Twenty Hours*, 1964), a picture of a village from 1945 to 1960.

The Bulgarian novel of the 1960s tackles contemporary problems through the evocation of memories. Taking her inspiration from the technique of cinematographic montage, **Blaga Dimitrova (born 1922)** is provocative. The main theme of her novels *Pătuvane kăm sebe si (Journey into Oneself*, 1965) and *Otklonenie (Deviation*, 1967) is the balance sheet of a life, told with several variants and many psychological confrontations. Ivajlo Petrov (born 1923) occupies a particular place with an original work, *Predi da se rodja . . . i sled tova (Before my Birth . . . and Afterwards*, 1968). The retrospective, associative and demystifying narration freely intermingles realism and fantasy, visual representation and reflection.

We owe to the Rumanian author **Marin Preda (1922–1980)** *Morometii* (*The Morometos, I*, 1966, *II*, 1967), a social naturalist novel which describes peasant life in the years before the war, then after the war, covering the period of agrarian collectivisation. To the new sociopolitical discourse the old father, evicted from his acre of land, opposes his victim's credo: 'As for me, Mr Towny, I have always been independent, with my head and with my arms.' The author also takes inspiration from the urban milieu, events which 'freeze' or 'defreeze' contemporary history from time to time: *Risipitor* (*The Prodigals*, 1962) and *Delirul* (*Delirium*, 1975).

The Greek novelist **Dimitris Hatzis (1913–1981)** has the same concern for the social reality of the postwar period (*To telos tis mikris mas polis*, *The End of Our Little Town*, 1952). Spyros Plaskovitis (born 1917) describes life in Greek towns and the Greek countryside; *To fragma* (*The Dam*, 1961) evokes machinery, its problems, its dangers.

English society did not escape from the criticisms of 'the angry novelists'. They were convinced that the individual only exists as a social person, and, in the wake of John Wain (1922–1994), Kingsley Amis (1922–1995) and Alan Sillitoe (born 1928) attack the 'establishment'. We owe to Alan Sillitoe the emergence of a true English proletarian novel.

In Flanders, social realism is primarily represented by **Louis Paul Boon (1912–1979)**. Boon wanted to rewrite the history of the Flemish people, from the viewpoint of the ordinary people, first with the monumental diptych *De Kapellekensbaan* (*The Road to the Chapel*, 1953), *Zomer te Ter-Muren* (*Summer at Ter-Muren*, 1956), then in a triptych: *Pieter Daens* (1971), *De Zwarte Hand* (*The Black Hand*, 1976), *Het Jaar 1901* (*The Year 1901*, 1977). A similar humanitarian commitment characterises the work of Ward Ruyslinck (born 1929), in novels which are frightening anti-Utopias (*Het reservaat*, *The Reservation*, 1964). The individual, prey to a world of robots, is a central theme for Jos Vandeloo (born 1925). The documentary novel appears following Boon, in Hugo Raes (born 1929) who describes disarray through extracts from terrifying journals in *De vadsige koningen* (*The Idle Kings*, 1961). Eroticism, death, decadence and vitalism are themes which also appear in colonial novels by Jef Geeraerts (born 1930), including *Gangreen I* (*Black Venus*, 1968) and in the therapeutic writing of the Dutchman Jan Wolkers (born 1925) in *Terug naar Oegstgeest* (*Return to Oegstgeest*, 1965).

At first sight, we could also take *Les Choses* (1965) by the Frenchman **Georges Perec (1936–1982)** for a documentary tale that catalogues the joys and sorrows of the consumer society. In fact, we need to read this book both as an experiment in writing and an art of living.

Do you read a lot, a little, not at all?

Georges Perec,

Things

Směšne Lásky (*Laughable Loves*, 1963, 1965, 1968), published in 'three notebooks', already contain the specific features of the Czech Kundera's vision of things human – tragicomic, ironic, philosophical – through erotic relationships which reflect the moral state of an 'abnormal' society, formally subject to burdensome rules. In 1967, Kundera published his novel *Žert* (*The Joke*), a radical denunciation of this society that grinds down individuals. It was only at the age of forty-nine that **Bohumil Hrabal (born 1914)** could publish his former stories in collections: *Pábitelé* (*The Chatterers*, 1964) and *Inzerát na dům ve kterém už nechci bydlet* (*Sell the House in which I can no longer Live*, 1965) and *Ostře sledované vlaky* (*Closely Observed Trains*, 1966). These apparently straightforward stories are full of ordinary people with naturalistic gestures; they talk a lot, with an imagination that spills over; their meeting places are most often welcoming hostelries, far from party gatherings. These 'Hrabalian' figures live their real life on the edge of society.

Několik kanadských křečků pracuje ke svobodě ve vysokém komínu akvária. Jednou jsem se za tři sta korun stal na chvíli světcem. Skoupil jsem všechny stehlíky a z vlastní ruky jsem jim dal svobodu. Jejej, ten pocit, když z dlaně vám vzlétá ustrašený ptáček! A pak jdu do tržnice, kde babičky prodávají na talířcích sedlou krev. Je to zvláštní, že velké svátky odnesou zvířátka. Vánoce ryby, velikonoce kůzlata a jehňata.	*In an aquarium as high as a chimney, several Canadian hamsters are preparing to escape. One day, for a few minutes and with the help of three hundred crowns, I changed into a saint. I bought all the goldfinches and personally gave them their freedom. Ah, that sensation of the panicky bird which flies out of one's hand! Afterwards, I went to the market where old women sell saucers of coagulated blood. Strange that, for all the great feasts, it has to be animals that suffer. Fish at Christmas, kids and lambs at Easter.*

Bohumil Hrabal,
Inzerát na dům ve kterém už nechci bydlet

Socialist realism and dissidence

During that part of the postwar period which extended to the 1960s, on the other side of the Iron Curtain, few authors and literary works escaped the dogma of socialist realism.

In the GDR the 'Bitterfeld programme' stipulated that writers and intellectual workers should mingle with manual workers to create 'a socialist culture that is nation-wide'. Christa Wolf took her inspiration from this programme in her novel *Der geteilte Himmel* (*Heaven Divided*, 1963). The Kuznica (Forge) movement, the expression of socialist realism in Poland in the 1950s, was replaced by the review *New Culture*, which imposed nineteenth-century models. Yugoslavia went its own way outside the 'Soviet bloc'. Krleža advanced the idea of 'freedom of artistic creation and a multiplicity of styles', and rejected 'the mask of political propaganda'. His intellectual and poetic influence marked a whole generation of Croatian writers. In Rumania, socialist realist dogmas are metamorphosed into a nationwide socialist ideology in the 1970s and 1980s via a discourse 'of committed art' at the service of building a new society. Tastes and reading must match the sweat and enthusiasm of workers in factories and countryside. However, some young artists do not with this: they assert themselves in the ambiguity of their 'sayings' and 'non-sayings'. Their sayings preach revolution; their non-sayings are incomplete and implied 'stylistic exercises' which deny the political discourse of a rootless society, without traditions or a memory of the past. **Nicolae Labis (1935–1956)** sings of the love of the native soil mutilated by the foreign invader:

Seceta a ucis orice boare de vînt Soarele s-a topit si a cura pe pamînt A ramaa cerul fierbinte si gol Ciuturile acot din fîntîna namol Peste paduri tot mai des focuri, ocuri	*Drought has killed the least breath of wind The sun has melted and run over the earth Leaving behind the burning, naked sky Of the well, sludge is gathered*

> Dansraza salbatice, satanice
> jocuri.
>
> Nicolae Labis,
> *Moartes caprioarsi*

> Above the woods, ever more
> frequent, fires, fires
> Dance savage and
> satanic rounds.

The career of the 'poet accursed' of Rumania **Ion Caraion (1923–1987)**, the author of *Cînteca-negre* (*Black Songs*, 1946), will develop primarily after the 'thaw' of the 1960s: the writer is 'an ear of sweetness and an ear of venom'. **Anatol Baconski (1925–1977) is a** baroque poet and prose-writer (*Poezii, Poems*, 1950; *Fluxul memoriei, The Flux of Memory*, 1957; *Echinoxul nebunilor, The Equinox of Madmen*, 1967). His parables take sustenance from the 'empty corpse' of the decadent everyday, terrifying in its aggression and funny in its grotesqueness. Petru Dumitriu (born 1924) sought sanctuary in the West where he published *Incognito* (1962), a novel with a key, revealing the occult morals and practices of the communist society he had just left behind. The years 1960–1965 are favourable for Rumanian letters that a new generation had taken under its wing: Nikita Stanescu and Marin Sorescu in poetry and plays; Stefan Banulescu in artistic prose and the Ana Blandiana in poetry.

Between 1945 and 1948, Czechoslovakia knew a brief period of liberty. Between 1960 and 1969 the literary renewal expressed itself first in poetry and the theatre, then in novels by Edvard Valenta (born 1924) and by Škvorecký. The return to the individual as a centre of interest and a rejection of ideology appears in these words. Next to the poets Vladimir Holan (born 1905) and Seifert, from the older generation, and next to the dramatist **Václav Havel (born 1936)**, prose-writers are in the majority: Kundera, Hrabal, Škvorecký, Kohout. When Seifert reappeared with his collections *Koncert na ostrově* (*Concert on the Island*, 1965), *Odléváni zvonu* (*The Casting of Bells*, 1967) and *Halleyova kometa* (*Halley's Comet*, 1967), he is a long way from his melodious, regular poetry. The harshness of his words and of the images of his free verse are shocking.

In the USSR, some great writers who were still alive, such as Pasternak and Anna Akhmatova, were reduced to silence. But after Stalin's death, there was an awakening of literary life in the Soviet Union, a sort of return to 'reality' as a reaction to the lies of Stalinist literature. A literature develops on the horrors of war (Vassili Bykov, born 1924), on the countryside and its miserable living conditions (Fyodor Abramov, 1920–1983), on the Stalinism of the camps and the terror described by **Alexander Solzhenitsyn (born 1918)**[*] and on the Stalinism of daily life and its omnipresent fear (Yuri Trifonov, 1925–1981). With a more open attitude to the West, young writers in particular Hemingway, discover American literature. The stories and the novels that they write have a young rebel for hero who is at the same time the narrator (Vassili Axionov, born 1932; Anatoly Gladilin, born 1935; Gyorgy Vladimov, born 1931). The will of the entire social body to link up with its past encourages the publication of memoirs. Ehrenburg adopts this genre and takes up a position on all kinds of problems. The literary life of these years is marked by an alternation between periods of ideological openness – which permit the publication of *Odin den' Ivana Denisoviča* (*A Day in the Life of Ivan Denisovitch*, 1962) by Solzhenitsyn, for example – and moments of closing up which spark off campaigns like the one against Pasternak. Censorship remained vigilant, and there was a big difference between the literature being written and the literature being published. The phenomenon of 'samizdat' (clandestine literature) and publication abroad only developed in the 1970s. A certain social and political optimism perhaps explains the fact that the traditional forms of 'great Russian literature' are only rarely called into question. We might believe that writers and readers have confidence that literature can help to reform society. In the middle of the 1960s, there is a calling into question of mimesis and a blossoming of works which use the fantastic and grotesque; this is how **Andrei Siniavsky (born 1925)** writes, whose trial in 1966 marked the end of the thaw in Russia.

Literature in exile

Alongside official Soviet literature, represented by the political novel and literature of the 'grey' area, there are dissident writers and writers, who chose to live in exile: Josef Brodsky (1940–1996), Vladimir Maximov (born 1932), Mikhail Sokolov (1905–1984) and Maramzin, the writer of fantasies.

George Markov (1929–1978) represented Bulgarian literature in exile. In his many plays, he had the courage to oppose the stereotypes imposed by sociological determinism and explored the path of Western thought and art.

Emigration from Hungary happened in two major waves: the first at the end of the 1940s, with the exile of Lajos Zilahy (1891–1975), Sándor Márai (1900–1989), the author of *Egy polgár vallomásai* (*The Confessions of a Bourgeois*, 1934), László Szabó (1905–1984), the essayist Zoltán Szabó, as well as the short-story writer Gergely Lehoczky (1930–1979). The second wave of emigration followed the 1956 revolution, with the exile of the poet György Faludy (born 1910) and the poet-novelist-dramatist Gyözö Határ (born 1914). Another form of emigration was internal exile: the prose-writer Béla Hamvas (1897–1968), after 1948, published nothing during his lifetime in Hungary (his best-known works are the novel *Karnevál, Carnival*, 1985 and the essays of *Scientia sacra*, 1988).

Two great Polish voices made themselves heard from their place of exile: **Witold Gombrowicz (1904–1969)**,* who cast his pitiless gaze on Poland, and Miłosz who, in *Rodzinna Europa* (*A Different Europe*, 1958), wrote the autobiography of an East European. Between 1962 and 1965, Miłosz composed *Gucio Zaczarowany* (*Bloke Transformed*). The first poem of this group presents us with a character taken from his childhood reading. A naughty scamp, turned into a fly, explores reality: omnipresent, he can see things inaccessible to men's eyes. This metamor-

phosis made it possible to know the world's multiple facets.

Abroad, notably in France, works by **Eugène Ionesco (1912–1994)** appeared in Rumanian and in French, and by Cioran.

While Hostovský, with *Všeobecné spiknutí* (*The General Conspiracy*, 1957) ended his 'Ahasuerian' destiny in New York, his friend Jan Čep (1902–1974) ended his life in Paris, his second 'spiritual' home. The personal and literary itinerary of **Ivan Klíma (born 1931)** is exemplary. As a child he spent three years in the Terezín concentration camp. He thought communism would provide a solution to man's major problems, an attitude attested by his first tales. His disillusionment is soon complete. Klíma then became interested in existentialism, in the theatre of the absurd, in Kafka. He wrote several plays which denounced the ravages caused to spirits and souls, *Porota* (*The Jury*, 1968), and collections of short stories, *Milenci na jednu noc* (*Lovers for One Night*, 1964) and *Lod' jménes naděje* (*A Boat named Hope*, 1969), focusing on the difficulties of establishing true relationships between people in love. The book that followed was partially destroyed and then he only published in secret and abroad.

From realism to fantasy

In the countries of the East, fantasy was often a kind of escape-route from the iron collar of socialist realism. It took the form of science fiction in Poland with Stanisław Lem (born 1921) in *Solaris* (1961). In the Bulgarian writer Radičkov, it developed in the shape of grotesqueness and parody in *Svirepo nastroenie* (*Fierce Humour*, 1965) and *Baruten bukvar* (*Primer for Gunpowder*, 1969). The Slovene Ciril Kosmac (born 1910), with his novel *Balada o trubi i oblaku* (*The Ballad of the Trumpet and the Cloud*, 1957), introduced a synthesis between fantasy and realism. *Crveni petao leti prema nebu* (*The Red Cockerel*, 1959) and *Vuk i zvono* (*The Wolf and the Bell*, 1958) by **Milorad Bulatovic (born 1930)** rescued from oblivion 'negative heroes', marginals, thugs and criminals in a tragic/grotesque vision of a reality that turns into fantasy. This prefigures 'negative realism', an expression of the 'black wave'. In Czechoslovakia, about 1960, the tale and science fiction novel reappeared with **Josef Nesvadba (born 1926)**: he turned his profession of doctor–psychiatrist to good use in order to invent fantastic and scientific stories. The detective novel was also resurrected with the series of books by Škvorecké about *Lieutenant Boruvka* (1966).

The German-speaking Prague writer Leo Perutz, with *Nachts unter der Steinernen Brücke* (*Night under the Stone Bridge*, 1953) gives us a narrative with keys, made up of fourteen short stories, half-way between the historical tale (the book traces the history of the Jewish quarter of Prague in the sixteenth and seventeenth centuries), and the fantastic and satirical tale.

In the work of the English writer **J.R.R. Tolkien (1892–1973)**, verisimilitude gives way to fantasy, above all in the trilogy *The Lord of the Rings* (1954–1955) which depicts a world of gnomes and goblins, dragons and wizards. The collection of tales of the fantastic by Dino Buzzati (1906–1972) opens with *K.*, a story full of metaphysical resonance. His Italian compatriots, Vittorini and especially Pavese headed in the direction of fantasy with a mythical and magical/religious dimension. **Italo Calvino (1923–1985)** received his education at the school of Pavese. After writing the partisan novel *Il sentiero dei nidi di ragno* (*The Path the Nest of Spiders*, 1947), which Pavese hailed as a book 'smelling of fantasy', Calvino, forsaking his first track, wrote philosophical tales, *Il visconte dimezzato* (*The Pierced Viscount*, 1952), *Il barone rampante* (*The Rampant Baron*, 1957), then science fiction texts, *Le cosmicomiche* (*Invisible Cities Cosmicomics*, 1965) and Utopian dialogues such as *Le città invisibili* (*Invisible Cities*, 1972). **Leonardo Sciascia (1921–1989)** delved into Enlightenment philosophy to reconstruct many ancient and modern episodes of the history of Sicily and Italy, which describe crime and political violence (*Il giorno della civetta*, *The Day of the Owl*, 1964; *Gli zii di Sicilia*, *The Sicilian Uncles*, 1966).

The Swedish poet and sailor Martinson devoted a cycle of 'poems' (*Aniara*, 1956) to evoke a day in space some time in the future. The fantastic element distinguished the work of the Dutch writer **Harry Mulisch (born 1927)**. The collection *De versierde mens* (*The Illustrated Man*, 1959) takes place in an atmosphere of magical realism and myth. The principle of alchemy is obvious in the combination of science and myth (*Het stenen bruidsbed*, *The Bride's Bed of Stone*, 1959).

In Flanders this atmosphere is also found in **Johan Daisne (1912–1978)**. Dream and reality encounter each other in the metaphysical novel *De man die zijn haar kort liet knippen* (*The man who Had his Hair Cut Short*, 1947). In *De komst van Joachim Stiller* (*The Arrival of Joachim Stiller*, 1960), **Hubert Lampo (born 1920)** evoked an enigmatic world.

THE NEW LITERARY FORMS

Literary research in the postwar years was fertile with innovations: from the heritage of surrealism to the new novel, writing became a veritable research laboratory in which authors rival one another in inventiveness.

The reclaiming of the avant-garde: surrealism

'Quand je serai mort / J'veux un suaire de chez Dior' ('When I'm dead / I want a Dior shroud') Boris Vian sang (1920–1959) in 1954. **Raymond Queneau (1903–1976)**, with his saucy heroine, Zazie, who 'does not want to go with the mister' is also provocative (*Zazie in the Underground*, 1959). Both the first and the second owe to surrealism a taste for the unusual, for 'free' writing (Vian, *L'Arrache-coeur*, *The Heartrender*, 1953; Queneau, *Exercices de style*, *Stylistic Exercises*, 1947–1963).

There were many surrealist titles: Char's first works want to transform life, having learnt the lesson of Breton and Éluard. Char used language with precision: he is primarily the poet of the fragment, of the aphorism, close to painters and philosophers (*Fury and Mystery*, 1948, *The Early Risers*, 1950, *The Word in the Archipelago*, 1952).

Terre à bonheur (*Land of Happiness*, 1952) by Eugène Guillevic (born 1907) bears the stamp of the declared will of modern poetry: to consider language as a raw material. **Jacques Prévert (1900–1977)**, *Words* (1946), **Henri Michaux (1899–1984)**, *Elsewhere* (1948), and Queneau explore the path of verbal invention. This game over the object, both material and linguistic, is the very fabric of poetry by Francis Ponge (1899–1988): the 'object' is at the centre of *The Bias of Things* (1942) and *Pieces* (1961). Sickened by ideologies, which make language and therefore the world unnatural, Ponge 'will choose to talk about the ladybird out of disgust for ideas'. If the surrealists are affected by political concerns, English poets claiming this influence are interested in man.

Mysticism and eroticism clash in poetry by George Barker (1913–1991), in that by David Gascoyne (born 1916) and by Dylan Thomas (1914–1953), whose work celebrates the innocence of childhood, the corruption of the world, the majesty of death. One of his prose poems evokes a day in a small Welsh town called Llareggub which, spelt backwards, gives us 'bugger all'. A dionysiac ardour spreads throughout his poems, *Deaths and Entrances* (1946) and in his radio play, *Under Milk Wood* (1954).

Coming from surrealism, **Takis Sinopoulos (1917–1981)** and **Miltos Saktouris (born 1919)** move away from it to produce a poetry of the absurd: *Metekhmio* (*Between the Two*, 1951) and *Nekrodhipnos* (*Funeral Feast*) by Sinopoulos express the painful experience of modern man. Saktouris creates a poetic system that is closed, sober and hermetic, in which poetry simplifies the world, restores it in an immediate fashion, often tragic or sarcastic (*Me to prosopo ston tikho*, *Facing the Wall*, 1952):

Η ΣΚΗΝΗ	**The stage**
Σπάγγοι διασχίζαν το δωμάτιο	*Strings traversed the room*
ἀπ' ὅλες τὶς πλευρὲς	*all over the place*
δὲ θὰ 'ταν φρόνιμο κανεὶς	*it would not have been prudent*
νὰ τούς τραβήξει	*to pull them*
ἕνας ἀπό τούς σπάγγους ἔσπρωχνε	*one of the strings prompted the bodies*
τὰ σώματα	*to make love*
στόν ἔρωτα	
Ἡ δυστυχία ἀπ' ἔξω	*Misery from outside*
ἔγδερνε τὶς πόρτες	*scratched the doors*

Miltos Saktouris,
Me to prosopo ston tikho

The Dutch painter, designer and poet **Lubertus Jacobus Swaanswijk (known as Lucebert, born 1924)** showed himself off in the periodic press of the Movement of the Fifty. All his works are characterised by a style and a vision of man which resemble dadaism and surrealism in their rejection of conventions (*Apocrief. De analphabetische naam*, *Apocryphal. The Illiterate Name*, 1952).

Herfst der muziek	*Musical Autumn*
oh oor o hoor	*ear listen ear*
maar eentonig het eenzame zingt	*the solitary man sings his monotonous song*

de dag breekt en de nacht smelt	*the day breaks the night melts*
de zon en de maan gaan heen	*the sun the moon go away*
het woord zingt alleen	*the word alone sings*
Lucebert, *oh oor o hoor*	*listen ear listen*
Van de afgrond en de luchtmens	

Lucebert belongs to the Cobra group (1949–1950), founded by artists from Copenhagen (Co), Brussels (br) and Amsterdam (a). Painters like Appel, Constant, Corneille and Asger Jorn work for this movement and for the review *Cobra*, a mouthpiece for experimental painters and writers, with a Marxist orientation, but not politically doctrinaire. Out of eight issues, the fourth was the Dutch issue. In it we find, among other things, children's drawings, amateur painters – modern primitives – poetry by **Hugo Claus (born 1929)***, by **Gerrit Kouwenaar (born 1923)**, who chose poetry itself as a subject for poetry (*Het gebruik van woorden*, The Use of Words, 1958) and Corneille's aphorisms: 'Aesthetics is one of civilisation's tics', 'Art has nothing in common with beauty', 'Imagination is a means of experiencing reality'. The experimental poets inspired by the Cobra group's paintings provoked many undercurrents: Simon Vinkenoog (born 1928), Remco Campert (born 1928), Schierbeek, Leo Vroman (born 1915), Sybren Polet (born 1924), Hans Andreus (1926–1977), as well as the poetry theorist Paul Rodenko (1920–1976), editor of an important anthology of twentieth-century avant-garde poetry, *Nieuwe griffels, schone leien* (*Tabula Rasa*, 1954). All these authors tried to use a highly associative and inventive language, while neglecting traditional syntax and prosody.

After 1950, an experimental poetry which fitted into the European tradition of the avant-garde developed around the Flemish review *Tijd en Mens* (*Time and Man*, 1949–1955); the first experimental generation abandoned traditional poetry. Claus and Jan Walravens were its most representative authors. Jan Walravens (1920–1965) produced a particularly innovative collection with *Waar is de eerste morgen?* (*Where is the First Morning?* 1955).

The poets of the second experimental generation belonged to the review *Gard Sivik* (*Civil Guard*, 1955–1964), including **Paul Snoek (1931–1981)**, who explored the possibilities of an art of the absurd of dadaist inspiration in *De heilige gedichten* (*The Holy Poems*, 1959), but, above all, those of an opulent and associative use of metaphor in, for example, *Hercules* (1960) and *Nostradamus* (1963). **Hugues C. Pernath (1931–1975)** went further still in the direction of experimentalism and hermeticism. His poetry, which inspired Leonard Nolens (born 1947), was dominated by the problem of communication – it is under the sign of 'difficulty being', which is first expressed in a dislocation of the syntactic order (*Instrumentarium voor een winter*, *Instrumentarium for a Winter*, 1963).

In Francophone Belgium, we witness the blossoming of what the review *Phantomas* will one day call 'wild Belgium'. A series of authors assumed the heritage of surrealism: Christian Dotremont (1922–1979), and his Cobra friends, Colinet, Noiret, Puttemans, and the most obscure of the poets of this period, François Jacqmin (born 1929). These men worked in the shadow and only emerged from it during the period that followed. Between 1945 and 1968, academic Belgium ignored them; they produced for all that a sizeable amount of work which remains a laboratory for language and a place of expression for a demanding ethics of literature.

The Hungarian Zoltán Jékely (1913–1982), the heir to surrealism, kept a diary for his dreams throughout his life, letting his great poems feed on this source.

István Kormos (1923–1977) cultivated an original variant of surrealism: 'populist surrealism' whose acquired characteristics also appeared in the Hungarian poet from Rumania, Domokos Szilágyi (1938–1976).

After fifteen years of secret activity, the Prague group went public again with exhibitions, conferences and publications) under the abbreviation UDS (1963–1968), led by Vratislav Effenberger (1923–1986). Next to the plastic surgeon, scriptwriter and director Jan Švankmajer (born 1934), Effenberger's most influential collaborator after 1950 was the great surrealist painter Mikuláš Medek (1926–1974), who also wrote poetry (published abroad in 1963 and 1976).

In the early 1950s Portuguese poetry witnessed surrealism: the review *Unicornio*, O'Neill and Vasconcelos attest to the importance of this influence. In 1951 a second series of the *Cadernos de Poesía* (*Poetry Notebooks*) appeared, supervised by Jorge de Sena among others, maintaining the eclecticism of the first series: 'There is only one poetry.'

Innovations: the new novel

Two other mannequins are still visible in the mirror above the chimney: one in front of the first window section, the narrowest, completely on the left, and the other in front of the third (which is the furthest on the right). They are not facing each other; the one on the right is showing her right side; the one on the left, slightly shorter, her left side. But it is difficult to be certain at first sight, for the two images are orientated in the same way and both of them seem to show the same side – the left one probably.

Alain Robbe-Grillet,
Snapshots

Breaking with a certain novel tradition, the new novel inherits from past avant-garde work by Proust, Joyce, Kafka and Faulkner. The movement that literary criticism called 'nouveau roman' after some hesitation between 'antiroman' (anti-novel), 'école du regard' (school of looks), 'nouveau réalisme' (new realism) and 'littérature littérale', brought together various French writers by the things they rejected rather than their plans. **Nathalie Sarraute (born 1902)** cuts the figure of a precursor when she introduced a collection of

brief texts which appeared in 1939 *Tropismes* (*Tropisms*), a new narrative perspective derived from interior monologue that she called 'sub-conversation'. In 1948, her first novel, *Portrait of an Unknown Man*, was supported by an introduction from Sartre who described its being an 'anti-novel'. But it was at the beginning of the 1950s that the informal constellation of 'new novelists' started to form around Jérôme Lindon, a publisher with Éditions de Minuit, and another precursor of the genre, the Irishman **Samuel Beckett (1906–1989)**★ with *Murphy* (1947), *Molloy* (1951) and *Malone meurt* (*Malone Dies*, 1952). They have in common the searching out of 'roads for the novel of the future' and the condemnation of old-style novels which favour the psychological study of a character and the simple narration of their story. In *Martereau* (1952), *The Planetarium* (1959) and *The Golden Fruits* (1963), Nathalie Sarraute continued her investigation of the disturbed bits of the subconscious, in which imperceptible movements take place that she calls 'tropisms', and satirised bourgeois platitudes. **Alain Robbe-Grillet (born 1922)** published novels that only a virtuoso could have constructed (*The Rubbers*, 1953, *The Voyeur*, 1955, *Jealousy*, 1957, *In the Labyrinth*, 1959) around a theme which is often enigmatic, borrowed primarily from the detective novel, then abandoned to a fantasy world. **Michel Butor (born 1926)** explores the possibilities of simultaneity (*Passage de Milan*, 1954; *Degrés*, 1960) and tracks the wanderings of a consciousness that is getting to grips with time (*L'Emploi du temps*, 1956) or with itself (*La Modification*, 1957). Claude Simon produced a work irreducible to formal concerns, in which writing, consubstantial with the search for identity which underlies the proposition, asks major questions about man, history, culture and their tragic and derisory conflict. No doubt closer to Beckett, **Robert Pinget (born 1919)**, with *Mahu ou le Matériau* (1952), *Graal flibuste* (1956), *L'Inquisitoire* (1962), *Quelqu'un* (1965), tried to find in his novels the uninterrupted flow of repetitive words, sometimes to disconcert the reader with his fantasies. A later recruit to the movement, Claude Ollier (born 1922), with *La Mise en scène* (*The Production*, 1958) and *Le Maintien de l'ordre* (*The Maintenance of Order*, 1961), brought the new novel into the realm of new science fiction. Other writers, including Louis-René des Forêts (born 1918) with *Le Bavard* (*The Chatterbox*, 1946), and **Marguerite Duras (born 1914)** with *Moderato cantabile* (1958), *Le Vice-Consul* (*The Vice-Consul*, 1966), followed similar directions, without becoming associated with the group's organised demonstrations.

A series of articles expressed these novelists' theoretical positions. To the general refusal to accept 'out-dated notions' (Robbe-Grillet) constituted by 'psychology', 'characters', committed literature and the illusion of realism may be added appreciable differences in each one's choices, as asserted in *L'Ère du soupçon* (*The Age of Suspicion*, 1956) by Nathalie Sarraute, *Pour un nouveau roman* (*For a New Novel*, 1963) by Robbe-Grillet and in the *Essais sur le roman* (*Essays on the Novel*, 1969) by Butor. The commentaries that **Roland Barthes (1915–1980)** soon made on Robbe-Grillet's work, then on the theoretical exposés by Jean Ricardou (born 1932), whose articles are taken up in *Problèmes du nouveau roman* (*Problems of the New Novel*, 1967), and *Pour une théorie du nouveau roman* (*For a Theory of the New Novel*, 1971), in combination with the influence of *Tel Quel* and novels by its main driving forces including Philippe Sollers (born 1936) *Le Parc* (*The Park*, 1961), *Drame* (*Drama*, 1965) progressively propel the new novel down a road more attentive to language games. Robbe-Grillet, who, like Marguerite Duras, had experience of the cinema, published *Project for a Revolution in New York* (1970), then *Topology of a Phantom City* (1976), slipping increasingly towards fantastic and playful eroticism. Simon, with *La Bataille de Pharsale* (*The Battle of Pharsalis*, 1969) and *Les Corps conducteurs* (*Conductive Bodies*, 1971), and Ricardou with *La Prise de Constantinople* (*The Capture of Constantinople*, 1965), as well as Butor, explored more radical experimental lines. Butor abandoned novel writing

and produced serial texts, divorced from all literary genres. After 1980, some of these novelists returned to less marginal forms, sometimes casting at their work a retrospective glance which today authorised a critical re-evaluation of this original movement. At the same time as the development of the new novel in France, some other European writers produced texts which were sometimes quite close to the new novel. Gadda, in *Quer Pasticciaccio brutto de via Merulana* (*The Awful Maze of Via Merulana*, 1957), certainly practised a narrative subversion of the detective-novel plot of which some echoes recall *Les Gommes* and *L'Emploi du temps*, but his verbal inventiveness and vigour bring him closer to Joyce and Céline than to his French contemporaries.

The effective influence of the new novel is not, however, negligible, either in France – on writers like Jean-Marie-Gustave Le Clézio (born 1940) and Perec – or in Europe.

In more general terms, the movement in France was the source of questions, unexplored paths in the novel which other writers adopt and transcend. In Spain particularly, its penetration was favoured by the affinity it had with the recommendations of Ortega y Gasset, very much adhered to by the Generation of 27. **Juan Benet (born 1927)** in the cycle *Volverás a Región* (*You will Return to the Region*, 1967) rediscovered the equivalent of the county of Yoknapathawpa, and in *La Otra casa de Mazón* (*Mazón's Other House*, 1970) the technique of telling stories contrapuntally and the alternation of drama and narration Faulkner experimented with in *The Wild Palms* and *Requiem for a Nun*. He also presents us with the theme of the generalised degradation of beings and the world similar to Simon's. Death and time – without chronology, immobilised in a fixed past (*Una meditación*, *A Meditation*, 1970) – occupy a central place in his work. The very varied work of **Juan Goytisolo (born 1931)**, *Senas de identidad* (*Identity Papers*, 1966), for instance, appears as a neo-romantic effort in which the author frees himself from social realism. He lifts the interior monologue technique and reconstructs the past on the basis of a photo album. From *Las Horas* (*The Hours*), his first novel, Juan Carlo Trulock (born 1932) rediscovered the random narration of an absolute and infinitely friable present. Over taken by uncertainty, the reader no longer knows what is and is not happening. Reality dissolves, the character becomes impersonal: the 'out-dated notions' of which Robbe-Grillet used to speak are given a hard time. *Inventario base* confirms this technique by bogging the tale down in an inordinate timespan. As in the majority of 'new novels', the passages of dialogue and narration can no longer be distinguished from each other: all yardsticks of rationality and chronology are abolished in favour of a generalised 'de-realisation'. In fact, the new novel above all allowed Spanish literature to strengthen its calling into question of socialist realism. We should note in this connection the importance of Manuel García-Vino's work and the influence of *Tiempo de Silencio* (*The Time of Silence*, 1962) by Luis Martin-Santos (1924–1964).

In Italy, literature listened to the new novelists. In the style of Butor, Oreste del Buono (born 1923) concentrated action into a limited time-period, superimposing various temporal strata and fragmenting a character's soul between memories and present experiences (*Un intero minuto*, *A Whole Minute*, 1959, *L'amore senza storie*, *Love Without Stories*, 1958). Gruppo 63, the movement that launched the idea of the experimental novel, shared in the repudiations of the French and, in so doing, rediscovered certain futurist practices. But work by Foloarolo Sanguinetti (born 1930), like that by Butor after *Degrees*, went beyond the notion of the novel. Most of the group's members were closer to *Tel Quel*

than to the stable of authors of the Éditions de Minuit. The other Italian echoes of this experimentation in the novel are moreover attenuated by a sort of natural mistrust about pure rationality and by the will to conserve an emotional participation in narrative content.

In Greece, the new novel is primarily represented by work by Tatiana Gritsi-Milliex (born 1920), like *Kai idou ippos kloros* (*And Here is the Green Horse*, 1963), which belong in the main to the 'school of looks'. Kostovla Mitropoulou, in *O Enokos* (*The Guilty Party*, 1966) is particularly interested in exploring the depths of the female soul.

According to Lars Gustafsson (born 1936), Robbe-Grillet's principal merit is to have induced Nordic writers to think again about the question of realism. In the same way, the Cologne school, of which Dieter Wellershoff (born 1925) made himself the theoretical champion (*Ein schöner Ta*, *A Lovely Day*, 1966), developed 'new realism' within the new novel's sphere of influence. Flemish novels retained its mistrust of fiction. The subject of writing has become the criticism of the means of expression employed to arrive at it: this is the case for *Aankomen in Avignon* (*Arrival in Avignon*, 1969) and for *Praag schrijven* (*Writing Prague*, 1975) by Daniël Robberechts (1937–1992). Mark Insingel (born 1935) makes constructivist books in prose including collages of different registers (*Dat wil zeggen*, *It Means*, 1975). The questioning of novelistic practices that began with *Het boek Alfa* (*The Book Alpha*, 1963) by **Ivo Michiels (born 1923)**, depicts the interior monologue and the transformation of a sentry contending with the rhythm of orders:

Wist je 't An? Wits je dat ik	*Did you know, Ann? Did you know*
naar je toe zou komen? Ja ik	*that I would come to you? Yes,*
wist het wel. Dat ik zou komen	*I knew it for a fact. That I*
ook wanneer er de doodstraf op	*would come even under pain of*
stond? Zelfs dan? Ook dan, ja.	*death? Even then? Even*
Zoals ik kwam die keer bij het	*then, yes. When I came*
bos toen je hard van me wegliep	*the other time near the wood, when*
en je onderweg je schoen verloor,	*you ran off and you*
en je andere schoen ook? Ja. En	*lost your shoe on the way and*

ik de schelp van je lichaam
nam? Ja. Neerknielde in het
gras en roerloos met mijn hoofd
op je buik de aarde in leven
hield?

Ivo Michiels,
Het boek Alfa

your other shoe too? Yes.
And when I cleared away the shell
of your body? Yes. And when I
knelt down in the grass and,
unmoving, my head on your
belly, I kept the earth alive?

Holland offered an experimental procedure of the same nature after 1951: *Het boek ik* (*The Book Me*, 1951) by **Bert Schierbeck (born 1918)** was conceived according to an associative method designed to reproduce 'the space of an entire life' by the juxtaposition of diverse styles. Jacq Firmin Vogelaar (born 1944) criticised the language which is the reflection of the reigning ideology and which deformed reality in *Anatomie van een glasachtig lichaam* (*Anatomy of a Worm-Eaten Body*, 1966). Reality is the object of reflections conducted by the review *Komma* (1965–1969) around the autobiographical writing made famous by Paul De Wispelaere (born 1928), with *Paul-tegenpaul* (*Paul-antipaul*, 1970) and Willy Roggeman (born 1934) with *Opus finitum*.

The English writers Alan Burn (born 1929) and Gabriel Josipovici (born 1940) applied this new technique to exploring mental topologies. Brian Aldiss (born 1925) enriched English science fiction with work arising from new novel practices. An attentive critic of the new novelists, Christine Brooke-Rose (born 1926), after 1964, began an experiment inspired by French innovations a tetralogy devoted to computers.

Studied in an important article by Handke – whose personal work takes account of certain formal innovations advanced by French novelists, notably in *Die Hornissen* (*The Hornets*, 1966) – Robbe-Grillet's influence was also passed on to Austrian writers like Gert Friedrich Jonke (born 1946) and Friederike Mayröcker (born 1924). Peter Weiss (1916–1982) was influenced by this type of writing for a time (*Der Schatten des Körpers des Kutschers*, *The Shadow of the Body of the Coachman*, 1960). His theoretical importance

in Portugal at the beginning of the 1960s is perceptible in work by Almeida Faria (born 1943), particularly in early novels *Rumor branco* (*White Noise*, 1962) and *A paixao* (*The Passion*, 1965). The Greek **George Cheimonas** (born 1938), a psychiatrist, took from this profession a novel form which never ceased to be reflected and to question its own limits (*Mithistorima*, *Novel*, 1966). His wilfully broken up, cobbled together and contradictory writing (*Peissistratos*, *Pisistratos*, 1960, *I ekdromi*, *The Excursion*, 1964), recalls the efforts of Robbe-Grillet and Simon; it also sometimes reveals that taste for the oral that reminds us of Pinget. In Hungary, **György Konrád (born 1933)**, introduced a sort of new novel with *A látogató* (*The Visitor*, 1969). Poland was sensitive to the influence of the new novelists. Zofia Romanowicz (born 1922) combined her reading of the new novel with the fertile perspectives offered by existentialism (*Przejście przez morze czerwone*, *The Crossing of the Red Sea*, 1960). Kuśniewićz primarily solicited from the new novel its techniques, such as the superimposition of temporal strata and of different points of view around the same central event, writing in the future tense and above all the use of the second person suggested by *The Modification*.

We do not find elsewhere in Europe straightforward imitations of the French new novel. It did not create disciples any more than it was a school. But it led novelists to look at their work with a different eye and made possible creative revisions of novelistic procedures and their end-products. It also contributed powerfully to reflecting on writing itself. Its importance has to be measured by that of the writers it stimulated.

The poetic exploration of modernity

Danish poetry was characterised by a tension between tradition and novelty. The immediate postwar period was dominated by the circle that formed around the review *Heretica* (1948–1953), a period often considered as the first phase of modernism in Danish literature, even though this period can hardly be called 'modern'. On the contrary, it helped to retard evolution by its insistence on the existential responsibility of the individual, often coloured in a religious manner: *Stjaernen bag gavlen* (*The Star behind the Façade*, 1947) by the lyric poet Thorkild Bjoernvig (born 1918), *Fragmenter af en dagbog* (*Fragments of a Diary*, 1948) by Paul La Cour (1902–1956), and *Loegneren* (*The Liar*, 1950) by the novelist **Martin A. Hansen (1909–1955)**. What is called 'the second phase of modernism' in Danish literature, and can truly be called 'the prelude to modernism' was established as a sort of revolt against tradition. The short stories *Saere historier* (*Strange Stories*, 1953) by Villy Soerensen (born 1929) give the signal: they plunge the reader into an absurd universe in which the subject (in the traditional sense of the term) is alienated and fragmented, notably in the poetry of **Klaus Rifbjerg (born 1931)**, for example, in *Konfrontation* (*Confrontation*, 1960) and *Camouflage* (1961):

Ville klarheden som en drøm	Wanting clearness like a dream
af taerger over vandet sådan ser	of boats on water so it is,
det ud alene og ansigtet	alone and your face
drejet ind i stimer af øer	turned toward swarms of islands one's
pupiller	pupils
gennemflojet af goplernes	crossed by double traces
dobbeltspor i ensom demokrat	of solitary democratic
Klaus Rifbjerg,	jellyfish
Camouflage	

Poems by the Finn Björling and the Swede Gunnar Ekelöf (1907–1968) are close to Danish modernist trends. The truly innovative work by Peter Seeberg (born 1925) appears in his short novels, extremely cold in their objectivity: *Bipersonerne* (*Secondary Characters*, 1956) and *Fugls føde* (*Bird-feed*, 1957).

In the middle of the 1960s 'the third phase of modernism' ('systemdigtning') appeared, which can be perceived as another form of deconstruction of the subject as centre of the universe: arbitrary systems structure expressions themselves constructed like machines, understanding their own relativity in constructions which merely repeat themselves. The main work of 'systemdigtning' in the strict sense of the word is the collection of poems called *Det* (*That*, 1969) by Inger Christensen. During this period, poetic works by Per Hoeholt (born 1928) appear, *Cezannes metode* (*The Method of Cézanne*, 1967) and *Turbo* (1968), and Peter Laugesen (born 1942) with *Landscab* (*Landscape*, 1967). Madsen dominated the following period with *Tilfoejelser* (*Additions*, 1967). Away from this trend, Rifbjerg created novels and short stories (*Arkivet*, *The Archive*, 1961). On the material and spiritual ruins of the war, German writers want to practise a policy of 'slash and burn', to rid language of the demagogic jumble of Nazism. Lyricism tried to rediscover the authenticity of language. Günter Eich (1907–1972) and **Paul Celan (1920–1970)** tried to recreate a world where beauty and love reign. 'Be the grain of sand and not the oil in the machinery of the world,' said Eich. In this spirit he wrote his poem 'Inventur', while Celan fled the horrible world of the Holocaust. At the beginning of the 1950s, 'Konkrete Poesie' (concrete poetry) appeared in several countries. Though opposed to the poetic forms of the moment, this new poetry was nevertheless based on a tradition of visual poetry according to **Eugen Gomringer**

(born 1925), one of its creators. It is an element in a philosophy that is critical of contemporary language, which it calls into question, and is also an element in communication theory and semiotics. This poetry, international in scope, was initially multilingual. After visiting the main art gallery in Zurich, Gomringer began to formulate his poetics, and with Marcel Wyss and Diter Rot he founded the review *Spirale*. The same year, he published his first poems under the title *Konstellationen (Constellations)*. In 1954 he left for Ulm and became Max Bill's secretary at the Academy of Art (Gestaltung), one of the principal meeting places for adepts of concrete poetry, including Helmut Heissenbüttel (born 1921). Apart from visual poetry, 'Sehpoesie', concrete poetry also inspired an auditory poetry, 'Lautpoesie'.

In Italy, Pier Paolo Pasolini (1922–1975) and the neo-experimentalists of *Officina* abandon hermeticism; Pasolini experimented with poetry in dialect (*La meglio gioventù*, *The Flower of Youth*, 1954) in Friulian, a multilingual poetry (*Le Ceneri di Gramsci*, *The Ashes of Gramsci*, 1957), and a poetry which is expressed a kind of return to religion (*Poesia in forma di rosa*, *Poetry in the Shape of a Rose*, 1964).

The road was open for the neo-avantgardists of Gruppo 63. Sanguinetti, against both old and modern hermeticism, proclaimed polemically that he belonged to the school of Pound in his way of representing the hell of capitalist society.

At the beginning of the 1960s, artists in Portugal took an interest in renewing the language of poetry in reviews like *Árvore* (*Tree*) and *Cadernos do Meio-Dia* in which pieces by Eugenio de Andrade (born 1923) appeared, the poet of purity and nature, of the body and memory, and Ramos Rosa, the poet of the senses and the questioning of the power of words. **Herberto Helder (born 1930)** was first influenced by surrealism before he came to promote experimentalism. He went beyond simple experimentation, always imparting a rich sense of hermetic potentiality to his texts (*O Amor en Visita*, *Love on a Visit*, 1958).

Dai-me uma jovem mulher com sua harpa de sombra e seu arbusto de sangue. Com ela encantarei a noite. Dai-me uma folha viva de erva, uma mulher. Seus ombros beijarei, a pedra pequena do sorriso de um momento.	*Give me a young woman with her harp of shadow and her shrub of blood. With her I will charm the night. Give me a living leaf of grass, a woman. I will kiss her shoulders, the little stone of the smile of a moment.*

Herberto Helder,
O Amor en Visita

Influenced by the experiences of Bense, Pound and Brazilian trends in concrete poetry and praxis poetry, authors like Ernesto Melo e Castro (born 1932) perfected a new form of writing to be called experimental poetry. In his book A Proposição 2.01 (*Proposition 2.01*) and *Poesia Experimental (Experimental Poetry)* he defined this new form of writing: 'It is the aesthetics of the signifier, of puzzles, of word games, of graphemes, of images, of the computer.'

At the crossroads of several tendencies, the Hungarian Sándor Weöres (1913–1989), a secret, Protean personality who delved into the world of dreams and the mysterious East, tried to exploit all the musical and semantic possibilities of language. At the end of the 1950s, the Czech poet Jiři Kolř (born 1914) undertook experiments which left the realm of language behind and projected poetry into the realm of visual expression, to render it 'obvious'.

Work by the Bulgarian Nikolaj Kăncev (born 1937) took on a philosophical aspect in *Kolkoto sinapeno Zărno* (Like a Mustard Seed, 1968). He was a poetic innovator who used complex, surprising associations, an extreme synthesis of thought.

The English poet Ted Hughes (1930–1998), fascinated by animals, tried to express the 'essence' of beings and things that an exceptional gift of 'empathy' allows him to apprehend: *The Hawk in the Rain* (1957), *Wodwo* (1967). His bestiary symbolises the violence of human instincts and impulses.

'Concrete' audiovisual poetry, which evolved as a mixture of music, graphic art and poetry, gazed critically at society: Paul de Vree (1909–1982) and the review *De Tafelronde* (*The Round Table*) in Flanders. The hermeticism of experimental poets provoked a reaction of rejection. A neo-realist poetry appeared in England, in The Netherlands and in Flanders (Roland Jooris, born 1936; Eddy Van Vliet, born 1942; Herman De Coninck, born 1944), as did the evolution of the visual arts in new realism and pop art. The defining characteristics of this poetry are simple and un-metaphorical language, attention to anecdotal, everyday, perceived reality, and, at the same time and paradoxically, the calling into question of the separation between reality and fiction.

The return to realism developed in The Netherlands by the review *Barbarber* (1958–1971), and *De Nieuwe Stijl* (*The New Style*, 1965–1966) manifested itself in part with new forms of expression ('ready-made' and documentary texts) close to French neo-realism and early Dada: J. Bernlef (born 1937) gathered and observed the most banal data. His poems became collages by means of which reality becomes much less of an everyday thing.

The theatre comes close to dramatic modernity

Sartre and Camus depicted on stage the recurrent themes of their philosophy, but did not give new life to theatrical language. In England a veritable 'theatre of the absurd' developed: **Harold Pinter (born 1930)** gives us to understand that there is in man a fundamental difficulty about communication. Repetitions, jerky rhythms, interspersed with pauses and silences, form the central style and theme of his dialogue. Pinter writes plays open to many different interpretations. A mysterious atmosphere reigns in his first works (*The Room*, 1957, *The Birthday Party*, 1958). In *The Caretaker* (1960), he brings out of the shadow the 'terra incognita' that each of us hides in our innermost being, while perverse eroticism colours *The Homecoming* (1965). The protagonists of *The Collection* (1961) evolve in an atmosphere which is half-real and half-dream. *Landscape* (1968) and *Silence* (1969) plunge the spectator into the fascinating, mysterious world of memory. Impotence and inaction are an integral part of Pinter's theatre. **Tom Stoppard (born 1937)** in his early work also develops a theatre of the absurd while depending on literary intertextuality of parody. *Rosencrantz and Guildenstern are Dead* (1967) is a modern version of *Hamlet* set in an absurd universe.

'Normal existence' is, for the Polish poet and dramatist **Tadeusz Rożiewicz (born 1921)** an intolerable concept. From 1956, he was the driving force behind the theatre of the absurd in Poland. One of his concerns is to erase the borders that separate people. *Kartoteka* (*Card Index*, 1961) and *Swiádkowie* (*Witnesses*, 1962) denounce language, a very imperfect instrument of communication. Influenced by Kafka, Sławomir Mrożek (born 1930) opposes his absurd humour to the inflexibility of the regime, which is deployed in political tragi-comedies (*Policiada*, *The Police*, 1958, *Tango*, 1965).

'When there's a ring at the door, sometimes there's someone there, other times there's no-one,' the fire-chief affirms sagely in *La Cantatrice chauve* (*The Bald Prima Donna*, 1950) by Ionesco. The mixture of the grotesque and the everyday is the favourite theme of this farcical theatre (*The Bald Prima Donna*), baroque (*Rhinoceros*, 1959) or tragic (*The King is Dying*, 1961).

Every tongue, miss . . . is basically a language system, which necessarily implies that it is composed of sounds.

Eugène Ionesco,
The Lesson

Klíma, Vyskočil and above all Havel are the principal representatives of the Czech variant of the theatre of the absurd. The denunciation of totalitarian phraseology, of the cliché, of bureaucracy as an end in itself and of the mechanisation that results is masterly. Havel's third play, *Ztížená možnost soustředění* (*The Increasing Difficulty of Concentration*, 1968), criticises man's duplicity – in this case that of the scholar Huml who, on the one hand, dictates to his secretary fine phrases on the fundamentals of life with respect to inscrutable metaphysics, and who, on the other, just as rationally and cynically, leads a serial sex life which includes his secretary.

In Flanders, the first works by **Tone Brulin (born 1926)** depict the impossibility of communication, the absurd status of man: *Horizontaal* (*Horizontally*, 1955), *Vertikaal* (*Vertically*, 1955) and *Dromen vanijzerdraad* (*Dreams of the Wire*, 1955). *De honden* (*The Dogs*, 1960) voices strong recriminations against the apartheid regime in South Africa. His later work took on a new orientation. From the middle of the 1960s he communicated with the great innovator of the Polish theatre, Jerzy Grotowski (born 1933). In his plays we find body rituals, inspired by Asian tribesmen.

An attraction to the Far East is also one of the motors of theatrical creation in **Jean Genet (1910–1986)**: to the realism of the Western theatre – theatre as diversion – he opposes a ceremonial theatre; his ambition is to exalt evil. Blasphemy, sacrilege and scatology feed his powerful lyricism. Like Antonin Artaud, he gives life to the theatre of cruelty (*The Maids*, 1947, *The Blacks*, 1959), sometimes pushing theatricality to its limits (*The Screens*, 1961, twenty-five tableaux, 100 characters).

Under the influence of Artaud, the Portuguese dramatist **Bernardo Santareno**

(1924–1980), despite the censorship of institutions, brings to the stage *O crime da Aldeia Velha* (*The Crime of the Old Village*, 1959), and a play inspired by Brecht, *O Judev* (*The Jew*, 1966). In the collections *Teatro de Novos* (*Theatre for New People*, 1961), *Novissimo Teatro Português* (*Brand New Portuguese Theatre*, 1962) and *Teatro 62* (*Theatre 62*), the typical experimentalism of the period intersects with a desire for social realism.

Brecht's influence favoured the renewal of the theatre in Switzerland. **Friedrich Dürrenmatt (1921–1990)** represents in 'his tragic comedies' the grotesqueness of a world in which comedy tips over into horror, the 'danse macabre of ideologies'. The most famous of his works is *Der Besuch der alten Dame* (*The Visit*, 1956), which reveals how the power of money corrupts justice and humanity. In *Die Physiker* (*The Physicists*, 1962), the future of the human race is in the hands of a madwoman. *Porträt eines Planeten* (*Portrait of a Planet*, 1970) ends with the explosion of the Sun, which stamps out to the grotesque carnival of humanity. **Max Frisch (1911–1991)**, in *Biedermann und die Brandstifter* (*Biedermann and the Fire-Raisers*, 1958), describes the cynicism with which dictators seize power, and caricatures the cowardice of solid burghers. In *Andorra* (1961), a young man is declared to be a Jew; he is forced to accept this image of himself till he dies. The problem of identity is a recurring theme in Frisch's work.

As in Switzerland, the themes of dictatorship and madness haunt the German theatre: in the documentary theatre, reflection on the past is deeper. Rolf Hochhut (born 1931) in 1963 stages *Der Stellvertreter* (*The Representative*), in which he levels accusations against the attitude of the Catholic church confronted by the Nazis. 'An oratorio in eleven parts', *Die Ermittlung* (*The Investigation*, 1965) by Peter Weiss (1916–1982), investigates what went on at Auschwitz. *Marat-Sade*, a dialogue on revolution and madness in which the two main protagonists are locked up in a lunatic asylum, had already made him famous in 1963.

'Oh, happy days!'

The literature of Western Europe, from just after the war to 1968, oscillated between humour and despair, in a world which was looking for values to cling to: 'Oh, happy days!' is the bitterly ironic remark by Beckett. In 'the other Europe', the interwoven pettiness of life and its absurdity constitute work by Gombrowicz. Solzhenitsyn's voice repeats the message of humanism, in an implacable indictment of Soviet tyranny. At the same time, literature put itself under the microscope. The genre of literary criticism explored new possibilities for interpretation.

Literary Criticism

H. Bousset

How many critics have read only to write?
Roland Barthes

In the twentieth century the status of the literary work of art, like that of criticism and the critic, underwent such a profound change that Gérard Genette wrote in *Figures II*: 'The work of criticism could well appear as a sort of creativity highly characteristic of our time.'

The text as a unique point of reference

The exaggerated amount of attention given to the author's life and the work of literature reduced to an ideological content ('Gehalt') in traditional criticism brought about c.1920 a reaction in many 'critical schools' that thought their duty lay in examining the work itself rather than what was extraneous to it. These schools tackled the work as an autonomous whole, an object in its own right. Internal relations like form and structure ('Gestalt') benefitted from particular attention.

Towards the end of the 1920s, in America (William Empson) and in England (I.A. Richards), an autonomous movement revealed itself initiated by J.E. Spingarn and called the 'New Criticism'. The 'New Critic' made the work the central element and questioned himself on his capacity to demonstrate the sense of the work by the help of a scrupulous stylistic analysis, by applying a method of pure formalism. This method is called 'Close Reading'.

In Russia too, in the first quarter of the twentieth century, an important and influential independent movement began to appear. Emerging from the Linguistic Circle of Moscow (1915, with Roman Jakobson) and the Society for the Study of Poetic Language (1916, abbreviated to OPOÏAZ, with Boris Eikhenbaum, Yuri Tynianov and Boris Tomashevsky), this Russian formalism became famous in Western Europe just after the Second World War. The formalists began with the principle that the literary quintessence of something is hidden in the work, and more especially in the work's aesthetic. With the help of the concept of 'literarity', they try to understand the aesthetics of the literary language and to define it by reference to the natural language. The reader of literary texts is confronted by a complex, artificial linguistic form, the word 'artificial' containing, of course, the word 'art'. 'Poetry is organised violence, exercised on natural language,' thinks Jakobson. There is no doubt that the reader encounters certain difficulties, for his attention is distracted by and towards the form. The formalist Victor Chlovski describes this basically literary system as *'ostranenie'* or distancing. To the extent that a literary work distances us from it, it engenders a phenomenon of breaking norms and innovation, both artistic and literary. Around the 1930s, formalism was slowed down in its evolution by the pressure of Marxism and was only introduced to the West after the Second World War.

Certain literary theorists, among whom were Jakobson and Tynianov, uncovered imperfections and described formalism as 'a childhood illness of structuralism'. Jakobson emigrated to Czechoslovakia and took part in the creation of the Prague Circle of Linguists (1926–1948). Jakobson (who devoted himself mainly to linguistics), Jan Mukařovský (aesthetics), Felix Vodická (literary trends) and

Bohuslav Havránek were the representatives of this Prague structuralist school. On the tracks of the formalists, the structuralists adhered to the idea of autonomy and the principle of distancing. However, they introduced important modifications. Later, they became aware that individual elements (phonological, syntactic or semiotic) cannot be treated in themselves, but only in relation to the function they each have and to the internal workings of the latter. Structure takes precedence. The structuralist subscribes to this concept along with the theory of the linguist Ferdinand de Saussure, who affirms that 'language is a raft of functions that must be studied like a system in its totality'.

Shortly afterwards another form of literary criticism in Germany (1939–1945). The critic developed a method immanent to the work and interpretative, called 'Werkinterpretation'. The autonomy of the work of art becomes obvious through the nature of things. However, the precise interpretation of all the individual materials of the work, in interpenetration and relation with the whole predominates. So the demands of an ideological interpretation imposed by the Nazis can be rejected. Günther Müller (theorist) and Wofgang Kayser (exegetist and theorist) were the leaders of the 'Werkinterpretation' movement which dominated German literary criticism primarily in the 1950s.

In The Netherlands, several critics of the structuralist tendency (J.J. Oversteegen, Kees Fens and H.U. Jessurun d'Oliveira) rallied round the review *Merlyn* (1962–1966).

A house with many mansions

The polemic begun by and around Sartre illustrates the arrival of structuralism in France in the 1950s and 1960s. In his essay *What is Literature?* (1964), Sartre expounds the idea that novelistic language possesses an instrumental function which can unveil and modify the structure of the world in a particular historical situation. The ethical demand of commitment is imposed on the writer. The structuralists will reject this idea for, in the real

world, and in point of fact, there are fixed structures which determine human existence. There is even a polemical debate about this: Sartre reproaches the structuralists with misunderstanding historical materialism.

Whatever the true state of affairs, on the margin of university criticism a critical literary trend develops which Raymond Picard calls patronisingly *Nouvelle Critique ou Nouvelle Imposture* (*New Criticism or New Deception*, 1965), and which will be identified under this name. Contrary to other schools, that of new criticism does not have one precise definition: it is a house with many mansions.

The structuralists occupy pride of place. The French structuralists study how the work of literature, which is a system of signs, acts as a linguistic object, how a meaning can be attributed to certain configurations, and how this meaning is constructed. It is a purely semiotic point of view. Apart from the school of semiotics in France (A.J. Greimas, Roland Barthes, Julia Kristeva), there is also the important school of Tartu (Yuri Lotman) in the Soviet Union and the American School (Charles S. Peirce), who influenced the Italian Umberto Eco. In his celebrated essay *Opera aperta* (*The Open Work*, 1962), Eco already insists on the open character of the literary work towards the creative reader. These schools develop a theory of writing which culminates in the creation of the review *Tel Quel* (1960) with Philippe Sollers, Jean Ricardou, Julia Kristeva, Jacques Derrida and others. They set themselves up as defenders of the new novel, very well thought of at this time, and in which they see their thought given a boost. In this type of novel, the storyline is reduced to the language, to a structure which carries in it its own meaning and which does not of necessity refer to the 'real world'. French structuralism reached the conclusion that a work conceals in itself several meanings, it is by definition ambiguous, multidimensional and subject to many different interpretations. So literary criticism is a subject that adds its own value to the work.

From this point of view, it is not surprising that the psycho-criticism of Charles Mauron

(*From Obsessive Metaphors to Personal Myth*, 1962) should be catalogued as a relevant form of the new criticism. Mauron elaborated an analytical and interpretative model which leant essentially on Freud's traditional psychoanalysis. He put forward texts (by a particular author) and, on the basis of textual data, reduced the words, the motifs and the characters constantly returning to the conscious or unconscious personality of the writer so as to explain them afterwards on the basis of psychoanalytical concepts.

In a more recent, post-structuralist version of psychocriticism (Jacques Lacan), this ambition is abandoned: the equivalent of an author's personality reconstructed from texts does not exist, for an author's personality is determined by the 'discourse of the Other'. Lacan's concepts have points in common with deconstructionism and intertextuality.

Gaston Bachelard, it is true, uses many Freudian terms, but is careful to avoid an overstrict and heavy-handed application of any system whatsoever. When all is said and done, the artistic imagination cannot be analysed on the basis of a ready-made theory. This explains Bachelard's advocacy of the phenomenology of the imagination. He wants to experience poetic intentionality as if it were his own work, a criticism of the imaginary. Like Jean-Pierre Richard, he hovers around the frontiers of phenomenology, psychoanalysis and structuralism. Gilbert Durand, Bachelard's pupil and influenced by Jungian thought, took the study of the personal and artistic imagination in the direction of the examination of traditional myths in the writer's imagination. The mytho-criticism of the school of Chambéry analyses in this way the transformations of original myths (which have their roots in the human unconscious) under the influence of the personality of the writer and the sociocultural situation.

The fact that the researcher always gives himself more methodological freedom appears especially in the criticism of consciousness, nurtured by the German critic Friedrich Gundolf, introduced by Georges Poulet's manifesto (*The Critical Consciousness*, 1971),

and taken up by the 'genetic critics' Marcel Raymond, Jean Rousset, Maurice Blanchot, Jean Starobinski and Albert Béguin of the Geneva School. For them, the work of art is an expression of human existence, and that calls for a subjective approach on the part of the critic. Criticism is thus a meeting between two subjects in which the critic must lay bare 'the consciousness inherent to the work' by means of an intuitively descriptive metatext. This criticism of consciousness is, to a certain extent, the precursor of deconstructionism.

The pen as a weapon

In the 1950s, and even more in the 1960s, the approach to literature, often reductionist, of the structuralists, who concentrate all their attention on the text and on the textual process, provokes reactions from German critics of the sociological, neo-Marxist and 'materialist' sphere of influence. In the materialist theory of literature, ideology played a primordial role in the significance of the 'world vision'. Ideology is the intermediary link in the chain between literature and history as well as the socioeconomic sector. Materialism consists of two tendencies. With 'orthodox' Marxists like the Hungarian György Lukács, who in 1920 had already published *Theorie des Romans* (*Theory of the Novel*), we note the presence of the theory of reflection: literature becomes a sort of 'materialisation' of a particular ideology, a 'reflection' of a vision of the world. For Lukács this leads to an aversion to 'decadent' avant-garde movements.

In 1958 the German Theodor W. Adorno attacked Lukács, whose position had meanwhile become even more rigid. For most neo-Marxists, literature expressed a formulation of ideology, even a denunciation, a taking away of ideology. Instead of understanding the literary work as a reflection of the collective consciousness, the French critic Lucien Goldmann, born in Bucharest, saw it rather as a material of consciousness. So he wants to place the work in the context of collective structures and individual biography. The British Raymond Williams aspired to a reconciliation between the individual and the collective, between social Marxism and liberal humanism. With other materialist critics, the dominant discourse is also studied critically. The American Herbert Marcuse, born in Berlin, cult figure for the student revolts in May 1968 (Paris, Rome, Berlin, Louvain), explains that the uniform and functional discourse of the capitalist consumer society is the discourse of a one-dimensional thought which leaves no room for critical or transcendent concepts. In a period of intellectual decline and of elimination of alternative thought, the task of art, according to Adorno, is to criticise reality and to constitute the expression of 'aesthetic difference'. Adorno belongs, with Jürgen Habermas among others, to the Frankfurt School linked with the Institute for Social Research, reincorporated in 1950 by Max Horkheimer.

Later, the progressive optimism of sociology and of the vision of neo-Marxist literature was received with scepticism by the French critic Michel Foucault, for all theories are themselves fragments of reality which therefore cannot be entirely controlled.

Reading in order to write

In the 1970s the interest taken in the study of literature increased and altered its orientation. The text remained the fundamental point of departure, but, from a different perspective, it was also a part of a system of communication inside which the author, the text and above all the reader (and, by extension, the critic) had a proper function to carry out. The text thus lost its validity as an autonomous object (of study). The merit of having studied the process of interaction between the text and the reader is mainly to be credited to the Konstanzer School.

Wolfgang Iser, in *Der implizite Leser* (*The Implied Reader*, 1972), under the influence of the phenomenologist Roman Ingarden, mainly studied those elements of the text which have to do with content and form and communication with the reader. He concluded that the aesthetic reach of a text rests essentially on

a form of 'Unbestimmtheit' (indetermination): the impossibility of expressing with words what we really want to say. This is why the reader must (re)construct for himself in a creative way the effective meaning. Subsequently, Iser showed interest in 'Leerstellen', in empty spaces (like a change of perspective or an ellipsis in time) which the reader must complete for himself to discover the text in its full import. The 'Leerstellen' therefore arouse the aesthetic reaction of the reader. The work generates an 'Appellstruktur' (a calling structure).

In addition to Iser's reception aesthetics, another member of the Konstanze School, H.R. Jauss, introduced the concept of the history of reception (*Literatur als Provokation*, *Literature as Provocation*, 1970). For Jauss, the history of literature is a process of production and reception which he is interested above all to elucidate how a work is received by the reader (contemporary or historical). To make this process objective, he introduces the term 'Erwartungshorizont' (horizon of expectation), thanks to which the reader can compare the 'literary' text with previous experiences of reading in order to come to a value judgement on this text. The Frenchman Jacques Derrida radically concluded that the frontiers between literary and non-literary texts are intangible: all texts are in essence rhetorical and intertextual. This conclusion introduces a totally new approach to literature and culture, revolutionary and subversive, called deconstruction.

For a deconstructionist, each text is in principle liable to many interpretations: one single and definitive interpretation is not possible and not even desirable. It is not part of his intention to master the polysemy of a text. However, he will study how the architecture of a text undermines the direct giving of a single message. Derrida defends the following opinion: a text does not 'reproduce' a meaning but a 'product'. A text does not represent reality, but on the contrary it constructs it. According to him 'there is no outside the text'. As the text does not constitute an entity with a coherent meaning: the critic–reader must cut out the latter by showing that each text is intrinsically involved with other texts and refers back to this intertextual evidence. Literary criticism signifies in this context asking questions rather than formulating answers.

Derrida's theory of deconstruction largely influenced, deconstructionists like J. Hillis Miller, Paul De Man, Harold Bloom and Geoffrey Hartmann, at the American University of Yale, and cannot be described as 'postmodern' bearing in mind the deep mistrust about all established principles.

Subsequently, Barthes tried to localise the text in an infinite game of differences (the 'plural text'). This 'founding evaluation' is only possible on the basis of practice and 'textual writing' thanks to which he aims not only at the writer but also at the activity of the reader. His essay *S/Z* (1970) constitutes an eminent example of this creative reading–writing (metatextuality). What is truly at stake in literature is no longer the idea of reducing the reader to a consumer (the text reduced to the 'readerly'), but to rechristen it as a producer participating in the future deployment of the text (the text become 'writerly'). The reader–critic then becomes a writer of metatexts.

Let us end on the paradox of the current (and future?) literary criticism with a quotation from Barthes: 'With the writer for pleasure (and his reader) begins the untenable text, the impossible text. This text is beyond pleasure, beyond criticism, *unless it is reached by another text for pleasure*: you cannot speak "about" such a text, you can only speak "in" it, *in its way*.'

Sartre (1905–1980)

J. Deguy

He fired on the handsome officer, on all Beauty on earth, on the street, on the flowers, on the gardens, on all that he had loved . . . He fired: he was pure, he was all-powerful, he was free.

Jean-Paul Sartre,
Iron in the Soul

'A whole man, made up of all men and who is worth them all and that anyone is worth,' is how the author of *Words* defines himself in the last sentence of this text. One year later, Jean-Paul Sartre was awarded the Nobel Prize: a curious snub for an apostle of anonymity. He refused it. The Nobel Prize jury, however, did not betray their role in consecrating the man who was perhaps the last total intellectual after Albert Camus. The leader of French existentialism, Sartre was also and at the same time a major writer who expressed himself in novels, in plays and criticism. After 1945, he wanted to extend to politics the field of experience of his philosophy: this won for him in France, then in Europe and the rest of the world, an enthusiastic audience that obscured for a moment the altogether literary quality of his work. This new Socrates could not care less, only too happy to allow detractors to go round in circles and to bring down on himself the enmity of conformists of whatever persuasion.

A philosophy of existence

A tree and an object sum up the genesis of Sartrian existentialism, which, for the generation after the Second World War, will be a dominant thought pattern (fashion?) applied to life. The tree is the celebrated chestnut tree of *Nausea* (1937). In a letter to Simone de Beauvoir in October 1931 (they discovered each other in 1929), Sartre tells how, sitting down on a bench in a park in Le Havre, he allowed his glance to rest on that tree with trim little leaves whose name he, notebook at the ready, asks his correspondant. This is the point of departure for the main scene in the novel in which the hero, Antoine Roquentin, discovers 'contingency', the immediate and frightening relationship of conscience to objects and to the world.

The gaze of the novelist is doubled in these pages by the philosopher's gaze. An iconoclastic philosopher, to whom his comrade Raymond Aron revealed one day, while they were sitting outside at a café table in Paris, that one could talk philosophically of the apricot cocktail they were going to drink. Sartre wanted only that: to philosophise about an object, a glass of alcohol, a pebble, a dirty piece of paper. In this way he was initiated to German phenomenology. Aron summed up for him the works of Husserl, and Sartre went off to read in the original text during the winter of 1933–1934 at the Institut Français in Berlin. Making his own the postulate that 'all consciousness is consciousness of something', he later said: 'Husserl put back horror and charm into things' (*Situations I*). The old French analytical tradition that Sartre hated, Bergson, whom he hated less, everything was swept away by this return to the concrete operated by phenomenology. The reading of Heidegger (from whom he will take the notion of 'Dasein', 'being there') and of Kierkegaard completed the theoretical foundations of *Being and Nothingness*, which appeared in 1943. This Bible of French existentialism deals with several notions which have become almost popular, first and foremost the notion of contingency, illustrated in *Nausea* by Roquentin's experience. Nothing justifies existence, no rational or metaphysical legitimation is to be expected: this is the Sartrian, and just as atheistic version, of the absurd simultaneously unveiled by Camus.

Satre's second major concept is freedom. He makes war on all those systems which make man a product: a product of society, a product of history, a product of his temperament or his unconfessed impulses. The individual freely determines himself on the basis of an 'original project' and in constant choices, depending on the 'situations' in which he finds himself. Sartre is opposed to the Freudian unconscious, where he detects strong undercurrents of mechanical psycho-physiology. He prefers to speak of 'bad faith': of realities buried in consciousness, of which the subject does not 'wish' to be aware. When it becomes permanent, this lying to oneself prompts some people to become 'bastards', like the notables whose portraits hang in the museum of Bouville: they turn to stone in their own statue, forgetting the person at the expense of the personage they want to portray. The aim of a new morality will be to fight against this

petrification, founded on authenticity, and the treatise on which, promised at the end of *Being and Nothingness*, was never completed.

We also owe to Sartre a reflection on the existence of others and the risks that existence makes each individual run. Like that of freedom in *The Flies* (1943), this theme was popularised by the pessimistic reply was *In Camera* (1944): 'Hell is other people.'

After 1950, Sartre, relying more on Hegel and on Marx, extended the reflections in his 1943 treatise to society. In 1960, the *Critique of Dialectical Reason* denounced the masses who have been 'serialised' by capitalism, to which he opposes the revolutionary ideal of 'group in fusion'. In his last great unfinished work, *The Idiot of the Family* (1971–1972), Sartre put to the test, in the particular case of Gustave Flaubert's literary vocation the notion of 'universal singular' presented in the critique. 'What can one know of a man today?' he asks in his introduction. In order to answer this question, he articulated a non-determinist Marxism and a non-Freudian psychoanalysis in a 'progressive-regressive' methodology which advocates moving between the particular and the general, analysis and synthesis. Existentialism *per se* has disappeared at the expense of the dialectical viewpoint of social sciences constituted, but always subject to being rethought, to make room for human freedom. Structuralism which emerged in the 1960s did not forgive Sartre for leaving the subject and consciousness at the centre of his reflection in this way.

A baroque writing

From his youth, Sartre dreamed of being both Spinoza and Stendhal, not making a distinction between literature and philosophy. Refusing, in a way which is entirely modern, to make the time-honoured distinctions between genres, he practised a plural writing in which there are no watertight compartments between words and concepts, between the novel and criticism, between journalism and fiction.

The literary expression of a primary anarchy which he himself calls an 'aesthetic of opposition', this writing allows itself to be well defined, as Geneviève Idt suggests, by the notion of the baroque, as it was normally used for European artistic productions of the sixteenth and seventeenth centuries.

This Sartrian baroque shows itself for instance in a taste for images and the power. The architects of the Counter-Reformation wanted to make the majesty of God tangible to the faithful. In *Nausea*, Sartre does the same thing for contingency: he wants to make the experience of God's absence tangible to the point of dizziness. With the episode of the pebble, the portrait of the Self-Taught Man, the depiction of the places and rituals of Bouville, the visit to the museum and, finally, Roquentin's 'awful ecstasy' before the root of the chestnut tree, the reader makes the concrete discovery of this naked and 'obscene' existence that disorders the hero's everyday order. With paradoxical profusion, since the writer's task is to paint fear before the emptiness of meanings, images impose themselves before concepts, in a writing of visual and tactile 'Erlebnis'.

Sartre showed in *Words* another aspect of what Mikhail Bakhtin has called, with regard to Rabelais and Dostoyevsky, the carnival aesthetic, whose baroque nature can pass for the ultimate in expressiveness. This tale of childhood, which its author wanted 'to write as well as possible' because it had for him the value of a 'farewell to literature', plays with the genre itself of the tale of childhood: it is written against childhood, against the child that he was, 'a poodle of the future', a monkey or parrot mystified by 'the family comedy', and against the tender stereotypes proper to this autobiographical form. Sartre enjoys himself as a virtuoso of fine language, language such as his grandfather, Charles Schweitzer, was able to teach him, multiplying rhetorical effects in the interests of perpetual surprise.

This taste for surprise, this writing of reversal is sometimes marked in the working-out of plots. The short story *Le Mur* (*The Wall*, 1937) ends with an unlikely melodramatic effect: the patriot really is hidden in the cemetery where the hero, after a night of anguish, sends the Phalangists for a joke. Set during the Spanish Civil War, this text curiously makes use of one of the mainsprings of action which ensured the success of Spanish short stories in the Europe of the Baroque age. Sartre's theatre abounds in such turnarounds: in *Le Diable et le Bon Dieu* (*The Devil and the Lord*, 1951), the hero Goetz successively embodies demons and saints before accepting the supreme renunciation of military action. Baroque is finally for Sartre the writing of parody. He tells in *Words* how much he sacrificed to plagiarism in his first essays. In his mature works, he often plays with intertextuality, not without irony. At the end of *Nausea*, Roquentin, having arrived at the end of his discovery of 'existence' evokes a possible literary vocation by listening to a worn record. It has been possible to read into this a parody of Proust. Sartre's interest as a writer also resides in these games of mirrors. At the heart of often pessimistic fiction, writing manifests a distance, the optimistic revenge of the lightness of words against the weight of the world.

A commitment to Europe

In the game of the intertext, we have said how much, in his philosophy Sartre escaped, the exclusively French tradition, drawing inspiration explicitly from Husserl and Heidegger. Of Alsatian origin on his mother's side of the family (the branch of the Schweitzers, who alone have the honour of *Words* being dedicated to them, while the Sartres, written in the heart of deepest France, are hidden), Sartre was familiar with German language and culture. A number of novels and plays carry the marks of this. *Nausea* owes something to *The Notebooks of Malte Laurids Brigge* by Rilke. Its first title was *Melancholia*, from the name of the celebrated engraving by Dürer. *Le Diable et le Bon Dieu* recreates an episode of the Thirty Years' War, while Sartre's last play, *Les Séquestrés d'Altona* (*The Prisoners of Altona*, 1959), depicts a great German family traumatised by Nazism. During the phoney war, Sartre, a soldier at the front, read the biographies of Heine and Kaiser Wilhelm with interest. In the French twentieth century, he shared with Romain Rolland and Jean Giraudoux an interest in Germany that appears directly in his work.

The originality of Sartre's relationship to Europe, however, does notreside in these literary and philosophical influences. In consequence of the 'commitment' to literature that he advocated in the review *Les Temps modernes* (*Modern Times*) in 1945, he also wanted to act politically on the fate of the Old Continent by adopting stances, travelling and making contacts with intellectuals and leaders. The European Sartre was Sartre coming to grips with postwar history, the splitting of Europe into two ideologically opposed blocs, whose walls and iron curtains he crossed. Exerting an influence from the Atlantic to the Urals, his work will reunify, in its way, what had not been. We may see as a symbol the joint publication, in 1965, of the same German translation of *Words* in both Federal and Democratic Germany.

Returning after 1950 to the French Communist Party, 'converted' to Marxism, Sartre seems to choose his side. For a time Vice-President of the Association France-USSR, he travelled regularly to the Soviet Union from 1954 to 1966. Soviet readers will be entitled to an introduction to *Words*, the only one he wrote for this book. But existentialism remains suspect to party ideologists. Fighting for a Marxism which will not scrap individual freedom, the author of *Nausea* wins more and more sympathy from dissidents.

In Western Europe, where he was translated and read as few twentieth-century French writers were, Sartre took from his communist comrades his later 'leftism' the contested image of an uncompromising militant.

Well received in Belgium and in Switzerland (these two countries have provided respectively 'Sartrians' as eminent as Pierre Verstraeten and Michel Contat), Sartre found a second home in Italy, where he spent most of his summers (in Rome) from 1953. Of all the European communist parties, it is the Italian that best corresponds to his desire to reconcile

socialism and freedom. The day after his death, the Italian daily *Il Manifesto* headlined with 'A wonderful life.' A life which, in effect, achieved his ambition to be read and commented on outside his own country, often with more warmth and generosity than in France.

Gombrowicz (1904–1969)

J. Jarzebski

The man that I am putting forward is created externally, he is in his very essence in-authentic.

Witold Gombrowicz, *Diary*

Witold Gombrowicz was born on 4 August 1904 in Małoszyce, a small village in Central Poland, where his parents had an estate. His father's family came from Lithuania, where it had lost its property after having taken part in the January uprising 1863. Witold felt superior to the middle nobility, but inferior to the aristocracy. When he settled with his close kin in Warsaw in 1911, he could not choose between the bourgeois spelling Gombrovicz and the 'peasant' form Gombrowicz; this feeling of not belonging to a group as well as the resulting conflicts with those around him had a profound effect on his personality and literary work.

Memoirs of Immaturity

Having finished his law studies, Gombrowicz made his literary debut by publishing a collection of short stories called *Pamiętnik z okresu dojrzewania* (*Memoirs of the Period of Immaturity*, 1933); an extended edition appeared after the war with the title *Bakakaj*. Here Gombrowicz revealed his heroes in conflict with social stereotypes: they are divided between the will to be superior, to have a role to play in the world, and a mysterious impulse which drags them towards humiliation and suspect passions in which they give free course to an eroticism that is complicated and burdened with complexes. These short stories were not understood by literary critics who only gave the young writer vague approval and unimportant advice. This rather indifferent reception sparked off a kind of revolt or passion in Gombrowicz who, in 1937, published his best-known novel, *Ferdydurke*. It was the story of a thirty-year-old man who, like Gombrowicz, remained incomplete, not yet formed, an individual who did not belong to any particular social group. This struggle against immaturity, already told in part in *Memoirs of the Period of Immaturity*, aroused malevolent comments from the author's family and literary critics. The hero, Jojo, wants to create a work which will prove his maturity, but just at this moment the arch-teacher Pimko appears who, in the name of Culture, mercilessly reveals the gaps in Jojo's knowledge and sends him back to school in a most brutal fashion. In the following three sections of the book, Jojo confronts three milieux which force him to return the world of childhood to pin it down: first school, then the home of the Jouvencels – a couple obsessed by the idea of modernity – and finally the home of very conservative landowners. However, after each liberation there follows immediately a 'new being trapped': we cannot escape from either the stereotype of form or the imposition of childhood. The person who looks for authenticity can only snatch successive masks from his face which are created in the game between individuals.

Later, Gombrowicz wrote in *Dziennik* (*Diary*, 1957–1960): 'The man that I am putting forward is created externally, he is in his very essence inauthentic since he is never himself, merely a form which is born among men. . . . He is an eternal actor, but a natural actor, by reason of his being a man; to be a man means to be an actor.'

This inauthenticity is also the main feature of the artist in whom literary convention imposes the stylistic attributes of a work. So *Ferdydurke* is a sort of challenge thrown down to the traditional form of the novel: we find in it three disparate sections which constitute the parody of different literary models; between these three parts are interpolated two stories

apart, in a grotesque parable form, themselves preceded by introduction-manifestos by the author which imitate each other.

A philosopher who used mockery

While *Ferdydurke*, with his refusal of conventions, heralds the post-modernist novel, Gombrowicz's philosophy recalls Sartre's postwar existentialism; both offer a vision of Godless world devoid of traditional values. We can also see in it the apotheosis of freedom of being and the primacy of existence over essence-Form. Gombrowicz adds to this the opposition Form / maturity, divinity – and Chaos / youth, immaturity; these ideas thus take on a more concrete and more carnal form and, because they are embodied in daily life, a more caustic one. Gombrowicz's attitude towards values and authority remains ambivalent: they fascinate him. Gombrowicz owes much to Rabelais, Montaigne, Shakespeare, Dostoyevsky, Kierkegaard, Schopenhauer, Nietzsche, Mann and, in Poland, Mickiewicz and Słowacki, but he prefers to measure himself against them, to parody their values and to make fun of them. This is what he did in his first play: *Iwona, Księżniczka Burgunda* (*Yvonne, Princess of Burgundy*, 1938), in which the Shakespearean motif of the heir to the throne who revolts against their parents is used in the form of a farce: the prince Philippe wants to take Yvonne as his wife, a mediocre girl born into a different social class. Her pusillanimity and refusal to take part in court rituals risk bringing about the annihilation of the royal family's majesty. The courtiers, aggrieved, give vent to their lower instincts – until now carefully dissimulated – then, to maintain the established order, they kill Yvonne. Gombrowicz, while he is already enjoying a certain amount of fame, commits, all through the 1930s, a sort of 'sin of immaturity': his novel *Opętani* (*The Bewitched*, 1939), serialised in a large circulation newspaper, in which may be distinguished certain traits borrowed from Gothic novels, is a mixture of turns of phrase suited to a wide and relatively undemanding public and literary procedures heralding writers' future works.

An immigrant's fate

During the war and until 1963, Gombrowicz lived in Argentina. Initially he found himself at the bottom of the social ladder and explored new cultural spaces, appropriating new tones of immaturity and irresponsibility. At the same time, he was firmly persuaded that with the war the old world will disappear forever with its values and its hierarchies. The annihilation of the old order and attempts to create a new one were the principal themes of his postwar works. In *Ślub* (*The Marriage*, 1953), a play whose action takes place in the main character's dream, he tries to create on the ruins of divine-paternal power 'the interhuman church' in which values will emerge from a social game. However, the impunity of this game shows itself to be illusory at the end of the play: Henry the dictator, who had wanted to set the demons free, must suffer the consequences of his action. In *Trans-Atlantyk* (*The Ocean Liner*), published in Polish together with *The Marriage* in 1953, Gombrowicz brings a mythical dimension to his desertion. With *The Ocean Liner*, as well as in the two novels that followed it – *Pornografia* (*Pornography*, 1960), and *Kosmos* (*Cosmos*, 1965) – the writer is the principal hero of the fictitious tales. The extent of the destruction of the traditional world develops gradually in it: in *Pornography*, it first touches on the social order, religion and ethical ideals, while in *Cosmos* the writer attacks the whole structure of the meaning we give to reality. At the same time the author's nonchalant smile, of the rebel, becomes transfixed: in the first of these works, it is the erotic fascination of young and old which prevents the eruption of the void; in the second, there is only the building and demolition of structures that give a meaning to reality. These structures, composed of occasional elements, come from the impact of complex erotic fascinations and a strange attraction to death. Gombrowicz's last play *Operetka* (*Operetta*, 1966) is a more optimistic work: after the

destruction of the old regime and the folly of totalitarian ideologies comes the triumph of young, spontaneous nakedness.

From 1953 until his death, in Vence, on 25 July 1969, Gombrowicz published in *Kultura*, a Parisian monthly for Polish immigrants successive chapters of his *Diary* which, in the view of many critics, is his most impressive work. The *Diary* is both a sort of confession and an autobiography in which fictional elements interfere. But also, and perhaps essentially, it is an essay on culture, a look at philosophy, literature and different approaches to the world under the angle of usefulness to the individual. This confrontation with people and ideas is intermingled with scenes from the writer's life, stories constructed with great mastery and a great sense of drama; the struggle with the sacred and profane is one of the dimensions. The author places himself before evil and suffering while trying to grasp the sense of his own life.

Before the war, in Poland, Gombrowicz was considered a very promising beginner. Then his destiny became that of every immigrant: first banned in his own country, then, for several years after 1956, imitated and idolised, he only reappeared officially in 1986, the date of the publication of *Dzieła* (*Works*). Gombrowicz is one of the legends of Polish literature, an undisputed master for his successors, Brandys, Dygst, Lem, Kuśniéwicz, Mrożek and Konwicki. Many expressions or key words that he invented henceforth figure in everyday language.

Gombrowicz became famous in the 1960s in France, Germany and the Scandinavian countries. He belonged to the ranks of authors who were difficult and élitist, even if the force of his liberating laughter drew young rebels to him. Without being politically committed, he contributed indirectly to the demolition of beliefs and totalitarian or national authority by taking up the defence of the individual. No less important was his contribution to the field of novelistic form, philosophical discourse found itself implanted in the literary game, the hero, the narrator and the author united under the same name, mutually creating and interpreting one another, keeping their own 'self' and the world around them in a state of constant change. None of these forms turned out to be definitive, and the pursuit of a hierarchy and a form is always accompanied by a destructive parody.

Grass (1927–)

G. Cepl-Kaufmann

A whole credulous people believed in Father Christmas. But Father Christmas was, in fact, the gasman.

Günter Grass,
The Tin Drum

'Such a reconstruction allows one to posit the existence of a foregoing loss,' remarked Hans Magnus Enzensberger when the novel *The Tin Drum* appeared, a work subsequently reissued together with the short story *Cat and Mouse* and the novel *Dog Years* under the title of *The Danzig Trilogy*. This is where we find brought together the first prose texts by Günter Grass. The town of Danzig where he was born in 1927, his youth in the petit bourgeois surroundings of the Langfuhr suburb, that mixture of people from Poland, Germans and Kachubs settled on the shore of the Baltic and in the basin of the Vistula, the influence of Catholicism and especially of National Socialism in full flow influenced the Grass's youth.

The Danzig Trilogy

This is the background that characterises the world of Oskar Matzerath, the anti-hero, who, at the age of three, refuses to grow any more and decides to stand aside from the traditional line of the petite bourgeoisie. A child's drum varnished in red and white – the colours of Poland whose painful history reinforces the literary value of *The Tin Drum* – becomes a remedy for this marginal, while he observes the society around him as closely as a scientific researcher.

With *Die Blechtrommel* (*The Tin Drum*, 1959), Grass had immediately found his themes: the inability of individuals to admit their involvement in the rise of fascism, the resulting impossibility, when they finally become aware of their guilt, of assuming social responsibility for it.

Pilenz, the narrator of *Katz und Maus* (*Cat and Mouse*, 1961), unable to be aware of the present in a fitting fashion, experiences a feeling of guilt which prompts him to write, 'for what started with the cat and the mouse torments me today like a crested grebe on a pond surrounded by reeds'. He tells the story of his classmate, Mahlke, analysing the perversion of the humanist ideal by Nazi ideology. The amalgam between the model of the father and the institutions of school and army which have taken in and trained heroes has no room for Mahlke. He tries to compensate for his marginality – emphasised by a huge Adam's apple symbolising the mouse – by a valorous military action which will earn him a knight's cross. Naturally, he fails. This motivation of the story by the game of accepting or refusing historical responsibility is manifested even more forcibly in the novel *Hundejahre* (*Dog Years*, 1963). This is a complex composition in three sections, each section with its own narrator and style. The relationship between the victim and the guilty party is presented in this even more dialectically than in *Cat and Mouse* by an odd couple of friends, Eddi Amsel and Walter Matern. Eddi is an artist who transposes reality into a scarecrow; Walter is an actor who, guilt-ridden, collapses into the pathos of a role without ever recognising the historical reality he is living through. The worldwide resonance of *The Danzig Trilogy* was not because of the topicality of its subjects: the rise of fascism, the war and its dramatic consequences. What is striking is a form of realism animated by fantastic, fairy, satirical and grotesque elements. The trilogy also combines lyrical and dramatic elements, and the tale, with its many brusque changes in tone, corresponds to the requirements of the concept of alienation with which Lukács wanted to embrace reality. Before the linguistic complexity of the author, contemporary criticism proceeded to make several historical and literary comparisons, categorising Grass among the poetic creators of myths. In reality, Grass is a craftsman who accurately prepares his plan of work. He transfers his training as a sculptor to the overall composition of a literary work, to the structure of its surface and the treatment of language. In *The Tin Drum*, he begins by getting to know his material: he touches it, sounds it out, enriches it to better make use of it in a critical way:

'Glaube – Hoffnung -Liebe' konnte Oskar lesen und mit den drei Wörtchen umgehen wie ein Jongleur mit Flaschen: Leichtgläubig, Hoffmannstropfen, Liebesperlen, Gutehoffnungshüte, Liebfrauenmilch, Gläubigerversammlung. Glaubst du, daß es morgen regnen wird? Ein ganzes leichtgläubiges Volk glaubte an den Weihnachtsmann. Aber der Weihnachtsmann war in Wirklichkeit der Gasmann.

'Faith – Hope – Love' Oskar was able to read and he could juggle with these three little words as with bottles: credulous, pink pills, acid drops, soup kitchens, Virgin's milk, credit union. Do you think it will rain tomorrow? A whole credulous people believed in Father Christmas. But Father Christmas was, in fact, the gasman.

My dream is light grey

Grass gave secondary place to his work as a sculptor because it interfered with his work as a novelist. He replaced sculpting with drawing and engraving. Graphic art, in addition to the meticulous approach required of the craftsman, is close to literary work. In both procedures, Grass finds the same concrete character. Fish, mushrooms, keys, worn shoes and pens are his favourite motifs. But with him things also have a referential, allusive function; each of them is the centre of many relationships, like the drum, the Adam's apple and the dog. In addition to its role as leitmotif,

each thing has its own objective correlation. Grey is the colour of Grass's graphic design, grey is the vitiated air of the petite bourgeoisie whom he describes, grey is his anti-ideological attitude, 'but his dream is light grey':

Du sollst mit einem spitzen Blei
die Bräute und den Schnee
schattieren, du sollst die graue Farbe
lieben, unter bewölktem Himmel
sein.

You must, with a sharpened pencil,
shade in the brides-to-be and the snow,
you must love the colour grey,
being under a cloudy sky.

In a situation of dialectical tension, the artist falls back on the restricted world of the concrete and on the huge, some might even say monumental, project that a prose work can become. *Siebenkäs* by Jean-Paul and *Wilhelm Meister* by Goethe, that Grass took as his models, are the milestones of such a tension. In his first prose works, Grass constantly referred to the European novel tradition and not only the picaresque novel that he discovered with Rabelais, the reading of whom Celan had recommended to him during his stay in Paris (1956–1960). We must also cite Joyce and Dos Passos among the moderns; and the relationship of the new novel with objects was equally fascinating for him. But it was, above all, Baroque literature that influenced him, and he erected a veritable monument to the poets of this period by imagining that he encounters them, in *Das Treffen bei Telgte* (*The Meeting in Telgte*, 1979). In the meantime, Döblin had become the most important of his literary guides: in 1969 Grass published an essay, *Über meinen Lehrer Döblin* (*On my Master Döblin*), in which he recognises that he learned a great deal from Döblin's ability to reconstruct reality in his prose. Like Berlin in Döblin's novel *Berlin Alexanderplatz*, Danzig is for Grass a microcosm, the exemplary hero of an exemplary story. Just like Döblin, he pursues a moral and didactic purpose which he develops unceasingly. *The*

Danzig Trilogy is the first literary work in which Grass takes an anti-Hegelian position, from the point of view of the philosophy of history. Instead of making of the individual a victim of history, he posits in principle the necessity of moral categories, which are as many maxims for an act for which an individual is responsible. He finds these categories in a return to the Sermon on the Mount, and confirms them by relying on the lights of reason: we must not let the past fall into oblivion and thus we can guarantee the fertility of the future; this is the dominant factor of the consciousness that Grass has of himself as a writer and citizen. In 1960 he set off for Berlin.

The social-democrat

Influenced by the personality of Willy Brandt and the events which would lead to the construction of the Berlin Wall, Grass abandoned the sphere of purely personal production to intervene in what was happening under his eyes, a change revealed in several collections of poems. *Die Vorzüge der Windhühner* (*The Advantages of Headless Chickens*, 1956) is the title of the first, in which the absurd predominates under the influence of Apollinaire, followed in 1960 by *Gleisdreieck* (*Railway Junction*), in which the poem which gives its title to the collection evokes the problematic situation of Berlin.

His dramatic work also reflects this change: after two absurd one-act plays, *Hochwasser* (*The Flood*, 1957) and *Onkel, Onkel* (*Uncle, Uncle*, 1958), came politically motivated plays, *Die Plebejer proben den Aufstand* (*The Workers Rehearse the Insurrection*, 1966) and *Davor* (*Faced with This*, 1969). With his 'open letters', his series of articles and speeches (electoral in favour of the Socialist Party), Grass positions himself with Böll in the vanguard of a movement of understanding oneself to put an end to the fatal dichotomy marking, in modern literature, the relations between society and the writer.

For several months, Grass made it his business to make known in Federal Germany the movement 'Initiative of Social Democrat

electors' (1969), which allows him to plead for a reconciliation with Poland and Israel. Certainly a growing scepticism invaded the writer about the effectiveness of his 'call to reason'. But we may consider this call as a change of model in his political and literary work, which takes him from the promises of the future during the electoral contest of 1961 to *Aus dem Tagebuch einer Schnecke* (*From the Diary of a Snail*, 1972), where he promises no more than a minimum of progress, to end up with the vain existentialist efforts of Sisyphus in *Kopfgeburten oder Die Deutschen sterben aus* (*Headbirths or the Germans are Dying Out*, 1980).

This confrontation with today's problems also informs his last two great novels. From the point of view of form, the simultaneity and the parallelism of some of his ways of telling tales became almost mannered. In the autobiographical work of fiction *Der Butt* (*The Flounder*, 1977), in which the hero tells his story in the first person and the author does not leave the present period, taking his inspiration from an old German folktale, *The Fisherman and his Wife*, he tries to oppose to the principle of male domination the history of woman seen from the angle of the history of cookery, and to demonstrate in this way the practical, sensual superiority of femininity.

In the novel *Die Rättin* (*The Rat*, 1986) as in *The Flounder*, the lyrical feeling works with the prose in a kind of counterpoint in which a subjective emotion is often expressed. While maintaining the dual structure of the storyteller and his period, *The Rat* also possesses a power to evoke the future tinged at the same time by experiences of the past and present. Next to the part played by the creative imagination appears the argument raised by the threat of the destruction of the environment and an atomic catastrophe. All that leaves hardly any room for the dialectics of Utopia and melancholy, of dream and reality, which until then had dominated all Grass' work. Even though it announces itself in a vague way, this change is noticeable: the Baroque fullness of the story mingles with the explanatory argument of the political work. In all the acts of submission to 'the misery of intelligence' and to 'the absurdity of the historical process', shines like a feeble light what one may discern in the work of Jean-Paul, *Speech of Christ who died on top of the building of the world, in which he proclaims that there is no God*, which Günter Grass has put in a contemporary setting in his speech of the rat 'on top of her mountain of rubbish'. And that light is that of the hope given by Utopia.

Beckett (1906–1989)

M. De Clercq

Thing always and memories I say them as I hear them murmur them in the mud.

Samuel Beckett,
How It Is

In 1945 Samuel Beckett wrote *The World and the Trousers* on the occasion of an exhibition of the work of two Dutch painters, the brothers Abraham and Gerardus Van Velde. The text begins with a dialogue between a customer and his tailor. The former exclaims: 'God made the world in six days, and you are not damn well capable of making me a pair of trousers in three months.' The latter replies: 'But, sir, look at the world, and look at my trousers.'

In this little dialogue we discover the whole of Beckett's world: God, the world, the look and the trivial expression 'damn'. This discrepancy between the registers of language accentuates Beckett's particular humour and engenders paradox, his distinguishing mark. Further on in this same work, Beckett states his aesthetic and poetic sensibility: 'It's the *thing* alone *isolated* by the *need* to see it . . . The thing *motionless* in the *void* . . . This is the point where we finally begin to see in the *darkness*.'

Sight and hearing

Beckett's work was influenced by that desire to 'see', that aspiration to be able to 'speak' of this view of the world. It is also this permanent questioning of the 'saying' of the word, which takes itself for an object, which becomes the thing in isolation. It becomes the voice which is ever vigilant, murmuring in the silence and the darkness the desire to be finished. The aforementioned dialogue is repeated in the play *Fin de partie* (1957, translated by Beckett himself into English in 1958 under the title *Endgame*):

(*Customer's voice.*) 'God damn you to hell, Sir, no. it's indecent, there are limits! In six days, do you hear me, six days, God made the world. Yes Sir, no less Sir, the WORLD! And you are not bloody well capable of making me a pair of trousers in three months!'

(*Tailor's voice, scandalized.*) 'But my dear Sir, my dear Sir, look – (*disdainful gesture, disgustedly*) – at the world – (*pause*) – and look – (*loving gesture, proudly*) – at my TROUSERS!'

(*Pause. He looks at Nell who has remained impassive, her eyes unseeing, breaks into a high forced laugh, cuts it short, pokes his head towards Nell, launches his laugh again.*)

HAMM. – Silence!

(*Nagg starts, cuts short his laugh.*)

NELL. – You could see down to the bottom.

HAMM. (*exasperated*) – Have you not finished? Will you never finish? (*With sudden fury.*) Will this never finish?

In this play, as in so many other works – *La Dernière Bande* (1959, translated into French by Beckett from the English, *Krapp's Last Tape*, 1958) and *Pour finir encore* (1976), right up to his last writing published in 1989, *Soubresauts* (the translation of *Stirrings Still*) – we find that same acute desire to be done with things. From the beginning, this sense of the end is constantly present. Each time, from the 1930s onwards, he has always started and restarted. In this movement he is looking for 'un temps énorme' ('an enormous time') (*Comment c'est*, 1961, *How It Is*, 1964), in search of *Compagnie* (1980, translated from the English), hoping to find a way towards the voices, towards the ultimate voice that leads to oneself, *Solo* (1981, the translation of *A Piece of Monologue*). But each time there is the admission of failure, the double failure of hearing and sight, as in *Mal vu mal dit* (1981; *Ill Said, Ill Seen*) and *Catastrophe* (1982).

The palimpsests

In the beginning, we could still classify some of his writings in the category of novels, *Murphy* (in English in 1938, in French in 1947), *Watt* (in English in 1953, in French in 1968) and the trilogy *Molloy, Malone meurt* (*Malone Dies*), *L'Innommable* (*The Unnamable*), written between 1947 and 1953. Beckett is also known for his plays: *En attendant Godot* (1952; *Waiting for Godot*, 1954), *Fin de partie, Oh, les beaux jours!* (1963; translation of *Happy Days*, 1961).

If in his first novels a plot of sorts can still be found, a statement, a tale, after the 1960s the texts become fragments, in which the statement becomes increasingly dominant.

Novels, theatre, short stories, essays and poetry start to make way for 'pochades', 'foirades' (1975), 'mirlitonnades' (1978). The characters resemble thinly disguised shadows; their murmurs become extenuated breaths (*Le Souffle*, 1971; the translation of *Breath*). Nevertheless, they continue to stammer, driven by an inner force which leaves them no peace, constantly looking for an identity expressed by and in words, language being the only refuge.

Relationships, contacts with others are almost impossible. In *Le Dépeupleur* (1970; *The Lost Ones*, 1971), in which some of the characters are looking for the others in a large cylinder, this is the case; there is the same absence of relationship in *Comment c'est*, in which some of the characters are victims, the others torturers.

Space becomes empty: a room of whatever description, an undefined spot, an interminable cylinder, the unfathomable darkness. The characters wait (the well-known duo of Vladimir and Estragon in *Waiting for Godot*, Hamm and Clov in *Endgame*), or else they get

excited in novels, move about in the mud, stammering and panting to be able to say something (*How to say it*, his last writing), to utter some sounds, well knowing that the world shrinks with each step, with each sound, becoming more and more *The Unnameable*, more and more abstract (*How it is*).

If Beckett's work appears to get more and more pessimistic and minimalist, it is all the stronger for the essential bits – the palimpsests. His world is the expression of an infinite melancholy, of the human suffering of a solitary being in an absurd world. But in this universe there shines a 'black sun' (Julia Kristeva) from which shines forth a very peculiar light – the light of a lighthouse.

Word, image and sound

Beckett has often been associated with Ionesco. He has been compared to Sartre for his existentialist vision and the experimental form of his writings. But the European canvas is even broader. Beckett also pays tribute to Proust (*Proust*, 1931) as well as to Joyce, his spiritual father.

Whistled at, caricatured, the continental philosophies of Descartes, Geulincx, Schopenhauer and Vico form the pattern for all Beckett's theatre, with Ireland in the background. Human beings find themselves alone, vulnerable, depraved and nevertheless majestic in their nothingness, singing from one stanza to another, in *How it is*, the rhythm of life: 'past moments old dreams that come back again or fresh like those that pass or thing thing always and memories I say them as I hear them murmur them in the mud'. As simple as it may appear, Beckett's text lends itself to games of intertextuality: it refers to the works of Dante (the figure of Belacqua in *Dante and the Lobster*), of Cervantes, of Diderot, of Sterne.

Beyond the text, Beckett weaves links between the image and the word by associations with the painters Tal Coat, Staël, Giacometti and the Van Veldes. He also searches for musical affinities. Finally he practises an intertextuality with different media: the cinema (Buster Keaton in *Film* in

1964 in New York), radio and television. Moreover, there is that other intertextuality quite typical and colourful of this author–translator who, every time, makes a gift not only of himself, but of French and Anglo-Irish culture and literature; so the last phrase of *Watt*, 'no symbols where none intended', becomes in French 'honni soit qui symboles y voit'.

Solzhenitsyn (1918–)

G. Nivat

Someone that you have deprived of everything is no longer in your power. He is once again completely free.

Alexander Solzhenitsyn,
The First Circle

Alexander Solzhenitsyn dominated our time like Leo Tolstoy dominated his. Once again Russian literature has not been content to be just literature, it has also been resistance to evil, 'dissidence'. It was the dissident ex-convict who fascinated the world when, in 1962, with the personal permission of Kruschev, then Secretary General, there appeared in the Soviet review *Novyj Mir* (*New World*) a story called *Odin den' Ivana Denisoviča* (*A Day in the Life of Ivan Denisovitch*). What hundreds of testimonies of survivors of Soviet camps, of denunciations of terror by Westerners like David Rousset and Robert Conquest, had not been able to accomplish was now accomplished in a few weeks: the readers of this story that was classical in its respect of the three unities became aware of the Soviet prison system, and, beyond that, of the organic relationship which had became established between the communist Utopia in power and a gigantic system of slave labour designated by the acronym 'gulag', to which Solzhenitsyn, after the publication of *A Day*, began to devote a huge work. It has been compared to Dante's *Divine Comedy*, and was called *Arxipelag Gulag* (*The Gulag Archipelago*, 1973–1976).

Solzhenitsyn has thus entered the ranks of European literature with a story-documentary, without any plot, reduced to a limited time-span: twenty-four hours in the life of a Soviet 'zek' (convict). The strict economy of artistic means corresponds to a more general philosophy on the part of the writer, that we could call an economy of abstinence. Ivan's companion, a Baptist called Alyosha (their two Christian names obviously recall those of Ivan and Alyosha Karamazov), says to Ivan: 'What good will freedom be to you? Set free your last vestige of faith will be choked by thorns.' His eulogy of prison echoes that of the apostle Paul and corresponds to a whole Judeo-Christian tradition of the strengthening of oneself in captivity, prison, or in this case the camp, being the very image of the captive of the finite time period of his story. This eulogy has nothing fortuitous about it. Ivan Denissovitch, who is only prisoner number CH852 in the camp, recovers his human dignity in the celebrated scene of the wall that he builds in twenty degrees of frost, with the mortar freezing before it is slapped on, and all gestures needing to be precise and quick. From being a passive object of historical study, little Ivan Denissovitch finds himself not only a mason, but a creative subject of history, thanks to the wall he has built.

The First Circle

The novel *V kruge pervom* (*The First Circle*, 1955–1958), which describes three days in the lives of privileged zeks, in a prison-laboratory or 'charachka', busy making a voice decoder for their jailer-tyrants, also describes the strengthening of the self under a regime of extreme privation. But these are scholars and mathematicians, and Solzhenitsyn's cultural references are made more precise: those called to the ark of the 'charachka' are stoics who have read Seneca and La Boétie, Rosicrucians who are carrying out the secret work of the spirit. As for the form of their dialogue, it freely evokes that of the first great intellectual dialogues of humanity: those of Socrates and his disciples, as Plato relates them to us. In other words, they are an exercise in philosophical dialectics on the free will and liberation of man. In this text for the strengthening of the self, we discover a systematic recourse to irony, the book's true cement. One of the best pages is the ironical updating of the theme of the medieval epic of the *Slovo o polku Igoreve* (*Lay of the Regiment of Igor*): the zeks resting imagine the trial of Prince Igor according to the rudimentary legality of the Soviet system, and we end up with a piece of grotesque legal bravura reminiscent of Rabelais.

Cancer Ward

Solzhenitsyn is a mathematician by education. The heroes of *The First Circle* are mathematicians in a penal colony (of which there were many, including the celebrated Tupolev), and the construction of the book also possesses a mathematical rigour, to such a point that we can make a geometrical plan of the action. Its principal protagonist is Gleb Nerjin, the 'seeker after truth', both a scientist and tormented by the enigma of history: when did the dream of liberation become transformed into slave labour? Solzhenitsyn's second favourite character in this book is the little moaner who resists his fate out of orneriness: such is the case of the former zek Oleg in the novel *Rakovyj korpus* (*Cancer Ward*, 1968), a novel that brings together a cross-section of Soviet society in a room full of sick people, all subject, as in the tales of Tolstoy, to the questions posed by death. But the tale reaches glorious heights in the nightmares of Russanov, the KGB man in charge of population control, who dreams of a young woman crawling towards a spring. This hidden living water, this hidden spirituality, may be found in the words of the old woman Stephanie to young Diomka, in the wisdom of the Kadmins in exile in Central Asia, and in the customs and even the habitat of the Usbeks, completely inward-looking. *Cancer Ward* is not a simple metaphor for the cancer which is eating away at the country, it is also a tale full of freshness and dramatic heightening about the condition of man afflicted by an incurable illness, one of

the finest tales inspired by the dialogue of man with death coiled up in his own body. And it corresponds to an experience endured by Solzhenitsyn himself, while he was exiled to Central Asia. In 1968 he addressed the Congress of Writers which will open just as his two great novels, banned in the Soviet Union, appear abroad, and he protested against the banning of *Cancer Ward*. He also protested about censorship and demanded the re-establishment of publicity in public life: in other words 'glasnost', a word that will be pressed into new service twenty years later.

The Gulag Archipelago

The Gulag Archipelago, written in secret, while hiding in various retreats, never seen in its entirety by the writer on his desk, is an extraordinary cathedral of writing which contains confessions on the initial indoctrination of the author, his pride as a Soviet officer, his cowardice when he himself was arrested, his going into his first cell, his transfers from one camp to another, a potted history of concentration camps in the world and in Russia, an encyclopedia of penitentiary conditions before and under Stalin, a philosophical reflection on the relations between Utopia and violence, and, in particular, a burning meditation on the positive and negative effects of the camps on men. Taking the opposite view to Varlaam Chalamov, the author of *Tales of the Kolyma*, who describes the inevitable dehumanisation of man in the camps, Solzhenitsyn, though he hides nothing of human depravity in the factories of the inhuman, evokes in Book V, *The Soul and the Barbed Wire*, cases of sainthood in the camps which are the spire of his cathedral, the central argument in that vast quest for salvation which constitutes *The Gulag Archipelago*. The biting irony, a constant sarcastic parallel with the 'embryonic' violence before totalitarianism, intense moments of lyricism, burning confessions and outcrops of prayer make this work one of the greatest in Russian literature, a monument to prisoners even larger than

Tolstoy's *Resurrection*, than Chekhov's *The Island of Sakhalin*, and even Dostoyevsky's *Memories of the House of the Dead* – three works to which it is natural to compare *The Archipelago*. The link with *A Day in the Life of Ivan Denissovitch* is obvious, all the more so as in *The Archipelago* the author addresses little Ivan as Dante addresses Virgil in *The Divine Comedy*, asking him to be his guide.

The Red Wheel

The seizure of the manuscript of *The Archipelago* in 1973 sparked off the last episode in the duel between Soviet authority and the writer. But another project was already haunting Solzhenitsyn: that of a vast historical attempt to go back to the sources of totalitarianism in Russia, and to understand when exactly the country went off the rails. This project referred to as *R-17* (Revolution 17) in Solzhenitsyn's coded language has given us the historical 'nodes' of *August 14, October 17* and *March 18*, three enormous volumes whose pace is cleverly varied. *August 14* alternates scenes of civil peace and prosperity (already troubled nevertheless by terrorism and the corruption of minds) with the first scenes of the war, dominated by the defeat of General Samsonov, Commander of the Russian First Army in the forests of Prussia. Two great metaphors order the romance and tragedy of this book: that of the circus acrobat during the great scene of the assassination of Prime Minister Stolypin in 1911 in Kiev, seen in flashback, and wheat threshed on the threshing-floor of war, the wheat being the men, the human family of Russia. This Russian family is itself symbolised by a small group of survivors who escape from the German pincer movement, galvanised as they are by a young colonel, Georgi Vorotynsky. The latter has kept his sense of honour and he takes on the feelings of the Russian family precisely with these survivors, in particular with a young peasant, Arseni Blagodariov. The pace becomes deliberately slow in *October 17*: the front is stable, individuals have fallen prey to remorse and are looking for repentance.

Finally, in *March 18*, despite the enormity of the tale, the pace is jerky, each moment is pregnant with renunciation and treason. Dreams, intellectual discussions, the rites of the Church alternate with astonishing probes into the psychology of the Czar and his family, intrusions into Lenin's world of intolerance and fevered monologue, long didactic digressions, in small print, that furnish panoramic views of events, or summaries of parliamentary debates, and curious 'chapter-screens'. These correspond to a veritable visual obsession on Solzhenitsyn's part. He has a director's gaze and a pronounced taste for the theatre and the potent symbolism of dramatic action (he wrote five plays, three on the camps, one on the war and one on the ethics of science).

The publication of the enormous block of writing contained in *The Red Wheel* indicates something paradoxical: Solzhenitsyn makes himself the advocate of a kind of asceticism or fasting for Russia, but to implement this fasting he accumulates masses of narrative; he deplores the loss of the natural sense of things and the organic growth of history. But the more his own historical novel advances, the more the document grows at the expense of the fable, and the less clear the central hypothesis of this investigation appears: is it really the loss of honour in each of us that can explain such a going off the rails? Can the parliamentary game in the Duma (a Russian assembly constituted before the Revolution of 1905), highlighted with mordant irony in the book, really explain just by itself the rise of lies in the country? Solzhenitsyn, as he goes forward, seems to lose confidence in his sense of direction. Like the survivors of the Samsonov catastrophe wandering about in the Prussian forest, so he wanders in a labyrinth of events that he has counted day by day and even sometimes minute by minute. The only things that remain are islands of significance: the Orthodox church and its liturgy, the soul of certain pure ones (including the Bolshevik Chliapnikov in whom is to be found the austere heritage of a family of 'old believers'), the dreams of certain wise men like the 'astrologer' Varsonofiev, a central philosophical figure who seems to be inspired by the orthodox gnostic thinker, Nikolai Fedorov, Tolstoy's friend.

The polemicist

The third great panel of Solzhenitsyn's work is its polemical panel: from *Pis'mo voždjam* (*Letter to the Leaders of the Soviet Union*, 1974–1976) to the brochure *Kak nam obustroit' Rossiju?* (*How Can We Reorganise Russia?*) published in 1990, the writer tries to trace a programme for his country. He is one of the first to truly break free from the progressive plans invented by the Russian intelligentsia at the end of the nineteenth century. A Slavophile in the search for the perfection of the individual rather than society, he looks at the Swiss cantons and the local 'zemstvos' created by the local government reform of Alexander I, a federal principle which allowed for freedom of speech in Russia.

For this reason, because he wants to break free of the model for revolution that the West has always wanted to impose on Russia, he is more European than many give him credit for. In wishing to dissolve Russian unity to give it a diversity that it has hardly known politically apart from in the twelfth and thirteenth centuries, he has given his country a 'Helvetic' vision of the future: a surprising challenge for the country of wide-open spaces, which he himself has so mystically described in *The First Circle*. This observation must colour the classic political diptych formed by the positions of Sakharov and Solzhenitsyn as they stood in relation to each other at the beginning of the 1970s, particularly as summed up in *My Country and the World* by Sakharov, and *Iz pod glyb* (*Voices from the Ruins*, 1970) by Solzhenitsyn and a group of his friends. One of them more democratic than the other, the other more religious, they form a model couple as far as opposition goes between the Slavophile and the Occidentalist. But Slavophiles and Occidentalists were originally brothers, and they became so again in the struggle against totalitarian communism. In his memoirs, *Kak bodalsja telenok s dubom* (*The Oak and the Calf*, 1975), we find a very fine portrait of Sakharov.

The Russian language

One of the most important characteristics of Solzhenitsyn's work and style is his recourse to proverbs: his borrowings from the syntax of the Russian proverb make his own syntax quite different from the logically articulated language based on French that we find in the great Russian nineteenth-century novels. Far from living in the past, which he is sometimes accused of doing, Solzhenitsyn is a bold linguistic innovator; in this respect he can be compared to the prose-writer Remizov and the poetess Marina Tsvetaieva. He has in common with the first a taste for a popular style, the singing rhythm of his prose, always couched in long or short lyrical breaths which resemble verses of poetry. He has in common with Marina Tsvetaieva an extraordinary speed of syntactic modulation, permanent recourse to anacoluthon, an exploitation of all the etymological resources of the Russian language in a state of dormancy. The dictionary of 'Russian expressions worth reviving' that Solzhenitsyn had just published in Moscow is wholly necessary to understand the language reform inseparable from his work. He is therefore a poet, even if almost all his work is in prose. He is a poet who has created moments of intense poetic and religious contemplation. Such is his portrait of Matriona, the old landlady in the story *Matrënin dvor* (*Matriona's House*, 1963), a simple soul, but one who can distinguish a Glinka melody on the radio without having the least idea about the history of Russian music, and who, by her sing-song speech, peppered with proverbs, gives back peace of mind to the former zek who has come to live with her. 'We all lived next to her, and did not understand that she was the Just one mentioned in the proverb, the one without whom the village would not be able to stand. Or the town. Or the whole earth.'

Claus (1929–)

P. Claes

I will not see it, but it will come, the white day of the world's end.

Hugo Claus,
Phaedra

Hugo Claus or 'the Flemish giant': if the name given to him by his admirers is tinged with irony, it is, nonetheless, deserved since Claus, the author of more than 100 books, is the most prolific writer of his generation, and, by virtue of his creative and polymorphous genius, the great master of that Dutch language spoken in Belgium and The Netherlands by some twenty million people.

'Noble Flanders, where the chilly North warms itself up / In the sun of Castille and couples with the South': Victor Hugo well recognised the hybrid character of Flanders, which is found at the intersection of Germanic and Latin cultures: a position which has made it the battlefield of Europe, but also a commercial and industrial crossroads inclined to internationalism and multilingualism. This knowledge of languages allows the Flemings to absorb the most diverse foreign influences. Hugo Claus is one such Fleming.

The cosmopolitan

The son of a printer who moved house dozens of times, Hugo Claus was born on 5 April 1929 in Bruges, which became for him the symbol of traditional, Catholic and folkloric Flanders. After a childhood spent in Courtrai, a commercial and petit bourgeois town, he ran away from his father's house and became a seasonal worker in Northern France. In Paris he met Antonin Artaud, whom he considers to be a second father. Together with the modernist painters of the Cobra movement and the experimental Dutch poets who then lived in Paris, he took part in the avant-garde revolution of postwar art. Henceforth his work will be influenced by surrealism and political commitment. With his partner, the Dutch woman Elly Overzier, who starred in some French films, under the name of Norden, he left for Italy in 1953 where he became familiar with cinematic circles. He stayed in Ibiza, then returned to Flanders, where he began a dazzling career as a poet, a novelist, a dramatist, a scriptwriter, a director, a film-maker, a painter and a designer.

In 1960, in the company of authors like Claude Simon and Italo Calvino, he undertook a study journey to the United States and Mexico. Until 1966 he lived in Ghent, the nineteenth-century industrial town and centre of revolt, which is a stark contrast to Bruges, a medieval and unchanging place. Then he settled down for a few years in the countryside of eastern Flanders.

At the end of the 1960s, Claus played a leading role in the anti-establishment movement which tried to reform social and cultural policy in Flanders. In 1967, at the experimental festival of Knokke, he shocked public opinion by having appear on stage three naked men in the role of the Holy Trinity. In 1968 he visited Cuba, whose revolution he celebrated in his *Free Cuba*. In his play *Het leven en de werken van Leopold II* (*The Life and Achievements of Leopold II*, 1970) he attacked the Belgian royal family. In 1970 he left for Amsterdam, the centre of the progressive movement in Europe. There he became involved with the Dutch actress Sylvia Kristel, 'Emmanuelle'. Accompanied by her he travelled the world and settled in Paris. After their break-up he returned to Ghent. In 1990 this perpetual nomad settled in the south of France.

Despite criticism on the part of conservative critics, Claus's talent was recognised very early. Approval from abroad was not slow in coming: in 1955 the young writer had already receive the Lugné-Poe prize from the hands of Françoise Sagan for his play *Een bruid in de morgen* (*The Betrothed in the Morning*). French translations of his novels, plays and poems followed. In collaboration with the British author, Christopher Logue, Claus produced an English translation of his play *Vrijdag* (*Friday*, 1969). An appearance in the television programme 'Apostrophes' noted by Bernard Pivot along with some particularly flattering reviews make his novel *Het verdriet van België* (*The Suffering of the Belgians*, 1983) a best-seller in France. After the German translation, the English version of the novel appeared in New York in 1990.

The rural poet

If Claus belongs to a cultivated petit bourgeois milieu on his father's side of the family (his great-grandfather was a bailiff, his grandfather an inspector of primary schools), he is above all fascinated by the agrarian background of his mother's side of the family. Claus' merit is to have been able to reconcile this traditional theme with the surrealist technique which up till then had favoured the portrayal of urban life. In one of his first experimental collections, *Tancredo infrasonic* (1952), he addressed an ode to his native land, Western Flanders. This poem is a synthesis of regionalism and social criticism, something that falls half-way between an evocation of nature and individual expression, between tradition and modernism.

In 1954, just twenty-five years old, Claus published his first good volume, *De Oostak-kerse gedichten* (*The Poems of Oostaker*). The agricultural theme is deepened by a mythology of vegetation and self-analysis with Freudian echoes. After the model of T.S. Eliot's *The Waste Land*, Claus interprets the myths of vegetation in an anthropological and existential framework, opposing liberating and enlivening nature to alienating and destructive culture. The Oedipus myth, omnipresent in Claus' work, is projected on to the myths of nature, so that the mother finds herself assimilated to the Earth, the father to the sterile, dying god of vegetation, the son to the resuscitated god, the mother's new lover. Joined together in a fight to the death, mother and father are symbols of nature and culture. The son–man, though instinctively attracted to his mother, finally realises he must incorporate the paternal component into his process of maturation.

The intertextual dramatist

A self-taught man, Claus is well-read and keeps himself informed of the latest international developments. It is above all in his theatrical work that this constant interest in literary tradition and current trends manifests itself. He had translated and adapted a number of foreign dramatists: Georg Büchner and Christian Dietrich Grabbe from German; Cyril Tourneur, Ben Jonson, William Shakespeare, Noel Coward, Samuel Beckett, Christopher Logue from English; Fernando de Rojas and Federico García Lorca from Spanish; Fernand Crommelynck and Jacques Audiberti from French. The modernist Claus surprises us with his adaptation of classical plays. Using intermediary translations, he adapts plays by Sophocles, Euripides and Aristophanes; avoiding banal updating, he manages to make this theatre relevant to a modern audience. The theatrical instinct of the author reveals itself above all in his adaptations of Seneca. The grandiloquent tragedies of the Roman, exalted by the Renaisance and the Baroque and detested by Classicism and Romanticism, have new life breathed into them by his modern approach. Like the adaptation made by Antonin Artaud in 1933, Claus staged *Thyestes* in 1966. In this 'mixture of grand-guignol and formalism', as Claus describes it, he does not avoid either the grotesque horror or the sententious language of Seneca, thus revealing the affinity of Roman 'decadence' to contemporary sensationalism.

Related to the ritual theatre of Peter Brook and Peter Weiss, the adaptation of Seneca's *Oedipus* (1971) presents the story of the Theban hero as an elimination of anti-social and even criminal tendencies by the interposition of a scapegoat. The poetic version of *Phaedra* (1981) underlines the Oedipal structure: Hippolytus, a latent homosexual, recoils before an act of incest with his mother-in-law and is condemned by his father to a terrible death. In these three tragedies, Claus replaces the affected morality of Seneca, which preaches a composite attitude towards human suffering, by a morality of existential despair.

Claus' theatrical adaptations form part of an intertextual practice which is found in his poetry and novels. A postmodern writer, he considers literature to be a treasure-trove of themes and techniques into which he can dip. Contrary to classical imitation, this game of quotations and allusions can fulfil a critical, even destructive function. The dialectic of affirmation and negation of the European tradition was one of the most interesting aspects of Claus' work.

The political novelist

Before the Second World War, the writer August Vermeylen had already advocated a transcendence of all provincial attitudes: the Flemish movement owed itself to integrate its ambitions to be independent in a vast European synthesis, without denying its individuality. This principle is summed up in the slogan: 'We want to be Flemish in order to become European.' Claus' novels fit into this framework.

Claus is primarily the critic of the traditionalism and the provincialism which dominated Flemish society. Thus the novel *Omtrent Deedee* (*All About Deedee*, 1963) depicts the decline of the main character, an introverted adolescent in a hypocritical milieu in which the cretinism of the petit bourgeois family is, nevertheless, less exasperating than the hollow intellectualism of the parish priest.

The novel *De verwondering* (*Surprise*, 1962) presents us with an intellectual, a language teacher, who has become a victim of the fascist authoritarian tendencies which still flourish in postwar Flanders. The hero, who wants to tear himself away from his mother's influence, and who is looking for a strong father, identifies with a mythical leader. When he realises the inanity of this ideal, he loses all hope and descends into madness. He will be rejected by those who live in the complacent illusion of the established order:

Soms gebeurt het dan, dat wij, wanneer wij keurig wandelen over de kade van Oostende, de koningin der badsteden, een man zien die ons tegenkomt, en zijn gezicht is vervaarlijk, gekweld, gebrandmerkt. Vaak schrijven wij dit toe aan een overmaat aan drank of vrouwen. Soms niet. Soms, zonder dat die man daarom vies is of ongeschoren of in lompen, herkennen wij hem niet als een der onzen. Als iemand eerder die in de klem zit. Dit kennen wij niet. Wij zitten in geen klem. Wij houden niet van viezeriken, onverant-woordelijken, eenzamen.

Sometimes, walking elegantly along the pier at Ostend, queen of beach resorts, we see a man coming towards us with a haggard, afflicted, withered face. Often we attribute this kind of thing to an excess of alcohol or women. Sometimes we don't. Sometimes, without the man being disgusting or badly shaven or in rags, we do not recognise him as one of us. More like someone who is trapped. We do not know about that kind of thing. We never find ourselves trapped, We do not like disgusting, irresponsible, solitary people.

In *The Suffering of the Belgians*, Claus depicts in a way as debunking as it is disconcerting the behaviour of his fellow countrymen during the Second World war. The portrait he gives of the typical Fleming – profiteering, hypocritical, a collaborator, an imbecile, a glutton, a trader, a conformist, a coward, a simpleton, a boaster, a black marketeer and a liar – recalls the realistic caricature of a Breughel or an Ensor. Nevertheless this *'Bildungsroman'* also shows how a talented individual can escape from such a stifling background. An intelligent and skilful boy, the hero gets a freer and more open vision of the world by discovering and exploring the European avant-garde. The 'degenerate art' rejected by the Nazis and by the representatives of Flemish culture will serve as a model for the young author. Like the Joyce of *A Portrait of the Artist as a Young Man*, the Claus of *The Suffering of the*

Belgians impugns the pettiness of his country of origin to take refuge in art's 'silence, exile and cunning'. But, like Joyce, he remains fascinated by this mother country that he will try to recreate in the form of a myth. Such a transubstantiation of trivial reality presupposes a rare combination of realism and imagination, of sensitivity and objectivity, of intuition and intelligence.

18 *Contemporary Figures and Trends*

M. KYNDRUP

The present is not history yet. It only becomes 'History' after the distance of time has made it possible to determine the trends and movements which have had an influence, and those which have turned out to be ripples on the surface. So it is with literature. That is why today we cannot write a 'history' of European literature after 1968. What we will rather set out in this chapter is a selection of trends and personalities so as to give an idea of the range and vitality of European literature being written and read now today.

When we ask the question 'What comes after modernism?', we are far from thinking that we can bring together all these trends and contemporary figures under the label of 'postmodernism' – nor under any other designation, whatever that might be. But the theories which since 1968 have highlighted the last three decades of the twentieth century have had a crucial part to play. It has never been possible to agree on what can be subsumed under postmodernism. But the idea of a 'break', provoked by the adoption of new points of view and different concepts of existence, including of art and of literature, has always been recognised.

WHAT COMES AFTER MODERNISM?

The history of this notion is complex and full of contradictions. After having been used to designate a particular style, in the 1970s, postmodernism became, a banner for those who started, in the overall context of the Western world, to call into question the dominance of 'modernist' functionalism. This is why after cubic, symmetrical and severe constructions, erected solely from an economic and functional viewpoint, 'superfluous' ornamentation was used in a mixture of styles and architectural expressions borrowed from different epochs.

However, it was not until the end of the 1970s, thanks to the work *La Condition postmoderne* (*The Postmodern Condition*, 1979), translated into most European languages and written by the French philosopher and theoretician of aesthetics Jean-François Lyotard, that the postmodern appeared as a fundamental 'condition' for every exchange of meaning, and particularly in art and literature. Does the postmodern represent a new epoch? To this question various answers have been given, and all the more varied for us being in a society of transition. However, everyone agrees to recognise that significant shifts have taken place in society and in the world of ideas.

The change is complex and twofold: on the one hand, art seems to be in the process of 'losing' part of its traditional significance of being a favoured domain in the scheme of knowledge, a higher phenomenon than the predominantly rational. On the other hand, it has acquired new importance: by its limitless power to dispose of all aesthetic and stylistic processes, art turns into a semantic game and plays at revealing that it is a game. It reconquers the public that the élitist, but necessary experimentation of modernism had rejected, or spurned.

All this is that much more true for literature. The fact that 'grand narratives' have in general lost their credibility as far as their implicit allusiveness is concerned, confers a wholly different status on local stories. Narration re-experiences its hour of glory: not as a simple return to the classical form of the nineteenth-century novel, but as a utilisation of qualities and important features which this novel form contains, including its entertainment aspect. So, new perspectives seem to be offered to literature, which ironic recourse to intertextuality serves to enrich.

However, this image is not completely one-sided. In the literature of each nation, and in each nation's history, different forms coexist which, in reality, should be linked to very different registers historically. In many European literatures, for example, the first generation of modernists is still alive, and in many instances, still productive. They are perhaps even faithful to their initial pro-gramme. It is precisely this 'simultaneous non-simultaneity' which has led to significant deviations between the validity of concepts of 'postmodernity' and 'postmodernism'. For some, postmodernism served as a triumphant symbol of liberation from the repressive and meticulous rationality of the modern, which could only lead to a philosophical and even physical of the subject. For others, it served as an injury founded on the collapse of values and the absence of morality that characterised the superficial media image of the post-industrial era, in which appearance has replaced substance.

Without concluding the debate, we offer here a more neutral image of the emergence of these contrasting trends in various Euro-pean countries.

Postmodernism in Europe

The debate on postmodernism opened in

France over *The Postmodern Condition*. The work is not so much a reflection on aesthetics as on ideological 'grand narratives'. The author observes that, in his knowledge or his actions, postmodern man no longer believes in these legitimising tales. Apart from this work, it is philosophy in particular which has reflected on the concept of postmodernity. Polemics goes beyond borders, and Lyotard enters into debate with, for example, the German Jürgen Habermas. But polemical exchanges also involve Anglo-Saxons (the Americans Barth and Hassan), the Italians (Vatimo, Eco) and the Dutch. The Germans are the most opposed to Lyotard's theses. The question also arises in relation to aesthetics, architecture and art criticism (Catherine Millet, Jean Clair, Guy Scarpetta). But the debates do not quite reach the realm of literature, not theoretically anyway. However, literary output attests to a postmodern aesthetic.

Apart from France, Italy is frequently cited as the cradle of postmodern European thought and art (Perniola and Vattimo). In concrete terms, Italian postmodernism comes to fill the gap created by the disappearance of com-mitted literature, great ideological syntheses having, at the end of the 1960s, revealed their theoretical and practical fragility. After an ultra-avant-gardist transition, postmodernism appears to be linked to theoretical trends like post-structuralism and deconstruction. Two works are emerging, despite their complexity, as new postmodern classics, as much in Italy as in the rest of Europe. One of these works is *Se una notte d'inverno un viaggiatore* (*If on a Winter's Night a Traveller*, 1979) by Italo Calvino. Its theme complex relationship or dynamic of is the author-reader-fiction, and this is objectified in the very form of the novel:

Lettore, drizza l'orecchio. E un sospetto che ti viene insinuato, ad alimentare la tua ansia di geloso che ancora non s'accetta come tale. Ludmilla, lettrice di più libri in una volta, per non lasciarsi sorprendere dalla delusione che può riservarle ogni storia, tende a portare

Reader, prick up your ear. You are beginning to suspect something, and your suspicion is augmenting your jealous anxiety, which has not yet accepted itself as such. Ludmilla, the reader of many books at once, so as not to let herself be surprised by the disappointment that

avanti insieme anche altre storie . . . (Non credere che il libro ti perda di vista, Lettore. Il tu che era passato alla Lettrice può da una frase all'altra tornare a puntarsi su di te. Sei sempre uno dei tu possibili. Chi oserebbe condannarti alla perdita del tu, catastrofe non meno terribile della perdita dell'io? Perché un discorso in seconda persona diventi un romanzo occorrono almeno due tu distinti e concomitanti che si stacchino dalla folla dei lui dei lei, dei loro.)

Italo Cavino,
Se una notte d'inverno un viaggiator

each story can have in store for us, had a tendency to carry on with several stories at once. (Don't think that the book has lost sight of you, Reader. The you that was passed on to a Female Reader, can, from one sentence to the next, return to focus on you. You remain one potential you. Who would dare to condemn you to the loss of your you, a catastrophe no less terrible than the loss of one's I? For a second person narration to become a novel, we need at least two distinct and concomitant yous, which stand out from the crowd of hes, shes and theys.)

The other classic postmodern novel is by Umberto Eco,* *Il nome della rosa* (*The Name of the Rose*, 1980), which, in the outward form of a detective novel set in the Middle Ages, deals with the beginnings of Western thought, notably on the basis of a discussion about universal semiotic abduction. These two works are in the Italian narrative tradition, whose contents are not at any moment freely available to the public. In most other European literatures, evolution did not, in the same way, engender postmodern 'models'; the models, on the contrary, were provided. For example, in Francophone Belgian literature, which almost entirely neglected the new novel or 'nouveau roman' and most of the forms created from 1950 to 1970, and which bolstered up its autonomy against the Parisian cultural milieu, a whole generation of writers began to have a new relationship with traditional literary codes. The current renewal presents itself primarily in the form of attention being given to language and narrative procedures, in the theatre (with Jean Louvet and René Kalisky) as well as in poetry and the novel. There is a sort of delayed reaction in this literature: after the classical forms of a generation made up of Charles Bertin, Georges Sion, Albert Ayguesparse and Constant Burniaux, writing, after 1968, embraced every aspect of modernity, at a time when the latter had become a prime target for deconstructive ideology. But this encounter produces the positive shocks that we receive with the novels by Pierre Mertens*, Marcel Moreau and Jean-Louis Lippert.

Dutch-language Belgian literature was, after 1968, deeply influenced by postmodern characteristics. The traditional novel based on mimesis was called into question. Daniël Robberechts tried to distance himself from it by establishing a distinction between the total work (in which writing attacks all subjects suitable for narrative, among others the narrative 'I') and 'pseudo-prose' (in which the author chooses to write without a subject as such). The first category mingles novel, document, essay and autobiography in an attempt to escape from the separation of genres. The second category uses writing which is radically independent, which has no recourse to an event, but which is, in itself, a creation or, even more, which constitutes an event. This type of prose text is very close to poetry and borders on philosophy.

In The Netherlands, critics have shown themselves generally to be very reserved and sceptical about postmodernism and the new development of literature: the postmodern artist is the pillager of the huge warehouses of history; the postmodern thinker is a horrid pluralist; the postmodern writer uses different styles and genres in the same text, quotes his predecessors unscrupulously, discusses the truth of language with the help of absurd techniques, as, for instance, the blowing up out of all proportion details from everyday life. But, despite these positions, postmodernism seems to be on the point of becoming literary theorists' favourite subject. Hans Bertens and Theo D'haen published the essay *Het postmodernisme in de literatuur* (*Postmodernism in Literature*, 1988). The anthology *Het Barbarberalfabet* (*The Barbarber Alphabet*, 1990) is a good example of the artistic position of the postmoderns. The contents of the neo-realist and neo-dadaist review *Barbarber* is re-organised in alphabetical order, selected and finished off by the review's first three editors. Readers must choose their own route in this voluminous collection which offers them about four hundred and fifty very different contributions to choose from, signed by writers who are internationally known such as Beckett, Satie, Schwitters, Cendrars, Ponge, Borges, Calvino, Reuterswärd, Duchamp and Marianne Moore. In this perspective, we must also mention the collective work of Martin Bril and Dirk Van Weelden, *Arbeidsvitaminen. Het ABC van Bril & Van Weelden,* 1987), which contains many essays and literary and philosophical notes with everything arbitrarily listed under one of the first three letters of the alphabet.

The question of postmodernity has had a fairly modest part to play in Germany. The period that followed 1968 was marked by a documentary tradition (with among others Günther Wallraff) which, in the 1970s, was replaced by what has been called the 'new subjectivity'. From a philosophical viewpoint, however, there have been many discussions on postmodernism, most of them devoted to criticism of the very notion of posmoderns to, a view most dominant amongst different pupils of the Frankfurt School. But, in the 1980s, we see the appearance in literature of a 'decisive farewell to dialectics, evolution and progress': with authors like Botho Strauß*, fantasy, narration as well as the self-referential nature of texts start to be important.

We find these tendencies in Scandinavian literature. After a certain domination of documentary socio-realism in the 1970s, we see in the following decade a renaissance of literature which is presented as 'poetry'. A narrative and peculiarly creative literature flourishes in Denmark with writers like Svend Åge Madsen* and Per Højholt, as well as Peter Høeg (whose career started in 1989). We can also mention the Norwegian Dag Solstad*, who went beyond the limits of social realism, and especially Jan Kjaerstad, whose choice of themes puts him at the heart of today's postmodernist Scandinavian novel.

> *Antennene lignet hvite muslinger, ører som vendte ut mot himmelrommet. En av de få tingene som virkelig kunne hisse opp en nordmann, var når parabolantennene ble ødelagt av en syklon og landet lå uten TV-forbindelse i dagevis. I disse timene kunne ingen slippe unna det faktum at Norge var en øde øy, fullstendig isolert fra omverdenen.*
>
> Jan Kjaerstad,
> *Det store eventyret*

> *The aerials looked like white mussels, ears raised up towards outer space. One of the things that could really irritate a Norwegian was when the dishes were destroyed by a cyclone and the country found itself in this way deprived of television for days on end. At moments like those, no-one could ignore any longer that Norway was a desert island. Completely cut off from the world.*

Kjaerstad, editor of the review *Vinduet* (*Window*), made the first move, in 1987, in an important debate on postmodernism in literature. In Denmark, and partly in Sweden, a similar debate was at first prevented by entrenched positions 'for or against'. A Danish cultural review of a 1970s Marxist persuasion published in 1986 an issue called *What was Postmodernism?*, to show that this awful phenomenon was well and truly over. Conspiracies of silence about the concept itself, however, have not prevented the appearance of an art and literature of great richness, linked in an explicit way to postmodernism, and developing in parallel with the trends to be found elsewhere.

The connection of British fiction with the name and evolution of postmodernism is probably more tenuous than for many other parts of Europe, perhaps stemming from the country's isolation in general and a traditionally conservative vision, which still plays a major part in its literature and criticism. Most of the movements of the 1950s were opposed to experiment or modern innovations, and a certain amount of that kind of thinking still survives today, though things did evolve a great deal in the 1960s. Since 1968, in Great Britain as elsewhere, emancipatory forces in society and art have been more and more obviously present; certain English novels of this period, *The French Lieutenant's Woman* (1969) by John Fowles, for instance, deal with political freedom, both sexual and textual, and reflect these changes. Fowles' work also possesses the characteristics of postmodernism: self-reference, the calling into question of the text within the text itself, art becoming itself its own subject for reflection, the creation with words of imaginary worlds, going hand-in-hand with the questioning of whether language itself can reflect a 'real world'.

The river of life, of mysterious laws and mysterious choices, flows past a deserted embankment; and along that other deserted embankment Charles now begins to pace, a man behind the invisible gun-carriage on which rests his own corpse. He walks towards an imminent, self-given death? I think not; for he has at last found an atom of faith in himself, a true uniqueness, on which to build; has already begun, though he would still bitterly deny it, though there are tears in his eyes to support his denial, to realize that life, however advantageously Sarah may in some ways seem to fit the role of Sphinx, is not a symbol, is not one riddle and one failure to guess it, is not to inhabit one face alone or to be given up after one losing throw of the dice; but is to be, however inadequately, emptily, hopelessly into the city's iron heart, endured.

And out again, upon the unplumb'd, salt, estranging sea.

John Fowles,
The French Lieutenant's Woman

Many British authors – Christine Brooke-Rose, Rayner Heppenstall, John Berger and Muriel Spark, for example – who are experimenting in the field of the structure of fiction and its ability to reflect on itself, are influenced, like Fowles, by foreign literature, often French literature. Many postmodernist elements do not come from the new novel but from Irish modernism – from Joyce by way of Flann O'Brien and Beckett.

Despite a stronger resistance on the part of social and cultural traditionalism than in other European countries further down the post-industrialist road, neo-Hellenic literature has radically differentiated itself, since 1970, from the modernism that was predominant in the 1930s. However, although there have been changes afoot, neo-Hellenic prose is above all characterised by a more or less traditional and 'realist' tendency.

The evolution of the situation in Portugal is more along the lines of French and Italian models: the modern Portuguese novel has recourse to almost all the forms that this genre has known, to the extent that it partly reinvents them without, however, destroying their traditional nature. It becomes the end-product of various aesthetics: on the one hand, those inherited from the 1950s and 1960s (neo-realism, the Portuguese version of socialist realism, existentialism, the new novel), on the other, there is the revival of techniques that have come out of the traditional novel, like a taste for plot development and for a sort of hyperrealism manifesting itself thanks to the attraction of fictional forms that call into question the traditional organisation of the logic of fiction, like fantasy and first-person narratives (diaries, chronicles). In Spain, too, literature experiences a positive development in the same direction, with a remarkable rebirth of artistic creativity since Franco's death and the country's return to democracy. After the first postmodern experiments dominated by a metaliterary thought of almost cult proportions, the experiments were no longer an end in themselves: today works are being created whose special effects serve the overall design of the work, and more especially their ability to retain the reader's attention. Literary criticism is also interested in the new conditions governing art and literature. *La cultura como espectáculo* (*Culture as a Spectacle*, 1988) by Eduardo Subirat is a good example.

In the countries of former Eastern Europe, the situation was, generally speaking, different, mainly because the role of literature in totalitarian systems was quite alien to its role elsewhere. Opposition to official literature often led to a rejection of 'meaning' and 'coherence'. Progressive literature was closer to the avant-garde or classical modernism than to postmodernism. This was the case in Poland, where modernism was synonymous with 'Young Poland'. The concept of postmodernism does not square with the fundamental problems of Polish literature during this period. The same is true for literary movements in the Soviet Union (where literature consists of a great many different national literatures), although the term has been used for literary experiments by Prigov and Sorokin, with, nevertheless, a different meaning to that in Western Europe.

There are exceptions to this 'divergence' between Eastern and Western Europe: opposition to official literature can also take ironic and self-referential forms as in the work of Milan Kundera* in Czechoslovakia. The concept of 'the unbearable lightness of being' in Kundera has become practically a classical metaphor for experience of the world lived by the subject in the perspective of the postmodern condition. But it is clear that the postmodernist Kundera is also influenced by his new surroundings, in his case France. In Serbian literature, we can see the precocious development of a literature of postmodern aspect. Inspired by Ionesco, Beckett, Nabokov and also Borges, we can observe the emer-

gence of a tendency to 'deconstruction' of which Danilo Kiš,* Borislav Pekic, Mirko Kovac and Milorad Pavic are the chief representatives. Romantic irony is being rediscovered by the Hungarian Rumanian poet, prose-writer and dramatist, János Székely. The concept of 'anecdotal prose' of a younger generation, that of Peter Esterházy* in Hungary, and of the Hungarian novelist of Czechoslovakia Lajos Grendel, with *Éleslövészet* (*Rifle Range*, 1981) borders on Romantic irony. Bulgarian literature presents an identical tendency. While the 1970s were above all characterised by moral compromises and silent opposition, the 1980s saw the emergence of a literature that was more structured from the point of view of art and criticism of the system. Authors like Jordan Radičkov*, Dimităr Korudžiev, Ivailo Dičev and Viktor Paskov are openly supporters of an anti-mimetic art, but, unlike modernists, they are also interested in history and politics. Thanks to them we can talk today of a specific Hungarian 'postmodernism'; traditional realism just like classical modernism is considered to be a thing of the past.

It is therefore clear that, since 1968, many significant traits in European literature can be understood in the light of the idea of a postmodern condition of change. On the other hand, a number of differences are clearly apparent and, in certain literatures, a number of elements elude this type of criticism.

We have therefore chosen, in order to describe the evolution of contemporary European literature, certain angles of approach which represent significant general tendencies in that evolution – in the framework of a postmodern perspective and outside this: the renarrativisation and refictionalisation of prose literature; the different trends in women's writing; 'autofiction' – changes that have come about in (auto)biography; the complex connections maintained in the theatre between text and theatricality; the presence of poetry at the end of the twentieth century; and, finally, fragmentary aesthetics.

RE-NARRATIVISATION AND REFICTIONALISATION: ESSENTIAL DEVELOPMENTS IN PROSE

With avant-gardism, neo-avant-gardism and the new novel, novel writing lost contact with the reading public. During the last decades, the reverse seems to have happened with European and even world literature. This is not just about a return to the narrative forms of traditional realism which have always existed, and played, in the shape of documentary, some part in many European national literatures in the 1970s. It is indeed all about a resurgence of narrative, a revival in the use of the elementary forms of audience appeal in stories. But this happens at the same time as fiction and solid construction, which modernism had the merit of formalising in its novels, are kept in the forefront of creativity. Thus we are in the presence of a new type of novel which reuses the qualities of the traditional novel form, for instance its potential to be structured and eye-catching, but which, on the other hand, concentrates on its own nature as a linguistic game in performance. The result is a great many hybrid forms, mingling 'realism' with stories, myths and self-reference; forms that want both to make an appeal to the reader's ability to emotionally identify with them and to keep the reader at an objective distance; forms which dare to unfold and represent the 'real' world and, simultaneously and in a definitive, deliberate and obvious way, to be joined to the limits of their own constructive nature.

Novels and tales in French literature

If these tendencies are particularly visible in French literature it has as much to do with the philosophical context as with the historical and literary presuppositions in 1960s experiments. Narration is currently characterised by a manifest fiction (which is no longer theoretical as in the 1960s and 1970s, though it is not immune from the masquerades of rewriting and of quotations that give it a somewhat

ironical side); texts are highly readable (in contrast to the complicated constructions of the 1960s and 1970s). Moreover, fiction is rarely encased in its own system of reference; the text thus offers a certain amount of 'deconstruction'. Novels by Renaud Camus, *Roman roi* (1983) and *Roman furieux* (1986), constantly undermine, by means of allusion, the fiction that they are on the point of orchestrating; novels by Jean Échenoz, *Le Méridien de Greenwich* (*Greenwich Meridian*, 1979), *Cherokee* (1983) and *Lac* (*Lake*, 1989), are veritable detective novels which somehow 'do not work'.

Without totally reverting to nineteenth-century forms, there is research into constructing new tales, with other methods, often more ironical, thanks, for instance, to 'rewriting', different from the parody by virtue of its more allusive and playful link to the original text. Michel Tournier rewrote Defoe's *Robinson Crusoe* in *Man Friday or the Limbo of the Pacific* (1967), and dealt with all categories of narration in *Le Médianoche amoureux* (*The Amorous Midnight Feast*, 1989). Novels by Jean-Philippe Toussaint and Échenoz carry out deconstruction work on the popular 'detective novel'.

The development of the historical novel represents a parallel phenomenon: the genre enjoys great success with the general public, who avidly read authors like Jeanne Bourin (*The Ladies' Room*, 1979), Jean d'Ormesson (*The Glory of the Empire*, 1971), Françoise Chandernagor (*The King's Avenue*, 1981), Michel Tournier (*Gaspard, Melchior et Balthazar*, 1980). There are several reasons for the popularity of the historical novel. The avant-garde novels of the 1960s and 1970s had turned away from the general public by exhibiting hermetic tendencies and a criticism of the very essence of the novel genre. At the same time, historians went out to meet the public by publishing their research in the shape of tales. Most of these works (for example those by Georges Duby) had a big impact. Simultaneously there was a rise in the number of documentary tales, notably on the difficulties of peasant life or the memoirs of industrial workers: Georges-Emmanuel Clancier (*A Halt in Summer*, 1976). This fact is related to the development of the historical novel, to a return to narrative, but also to a return to the subject, which is revealed in biographies and autobiographies of all types.

Camouflage works just as well in this area; the success of 'false' historical novels no longer needs to be proved: *L'Être et le Géant* (*Being and Greatness*, 1989) by Bernard Fauconnier depicts an encounter between De Gaulle and Sartre that did not happen. We can no longer totally erase the past. We are living in the reign of the quotation, as it is nowadays normal to go back to old systems of aesthetics (Baroque, classical).

The postmodern novel thus appears as a repertoire of signs, itself generative of signs. It no longer tries to produce meaning or to denounce the absence of it, but is satisfied with the representation of signs and dreams that they can engender. If the novelist demonstrates great virtuosity in the game of implicit references, allusions and transformed quotations. French novel-writing today thus reveals impressive knowledge, perhaps more impressive than the message it has to convey.

The authors of postmodern French novels do not argue with the progress and the critical potential of the new novel (with the exception of some conservatives who are jubilant because they think they are present at a return to old literary models); in fact, the postmodern tale uses the techniques of the new novel: Renaud Camus owes much to Robbe-Grillet and to Claude Simon[*], whose works he cites as a connoisseur. In the same way Danièle

Sallenave recognises his debt to Nathalie Sarraute. Thus it is possible to read the new novel in a different light through these works – and to see a resurgence of something in it which its founders had already put there, but which had gone unnoticed. So the last texts by Robbe-Grillet (*The Returning Mirror*, 1985) and by Nathalie Sarraute (*Childhood*, 1984) make it possible to rediscover the subject we thought was lost in their first novels.

Fiction in Scandinavia

Identical perspectives appear in Denmark and in Scandinavia. For example, a liberating metatextual self-irony came to light very early in novels by the Danish writer Klaus Rifbjerg. His important output in the 1970s and 1980s contains genres as different as pamphlets, pastiches, studies of manners and personal diaries. This return to narrative manifests itself in Svend Åge Madsen who broke with an almost systematic modernist position, including with regard to its readership, in *Tugt og utugt i mellemtiden* (*Luxury and Punishment in the Meantime*, 1976), a great novel in two volumes which is inspired as much by the detective novel as by science fiction to give a fascinating story, making the readers catch their breath. Madsen pursues this evolution with *At fortaelle menneskene* (*Saying Mankind*, 1989). The very act of narration becomes one of the themes developed by the ingenious putting together of tales. Madsen creates a network of reappearing characters which reminds us, in postmodern discourse, of Balzac's project in *The Human Comedy*.

'Det vil sige, at den verden jeg troede at have skabt, I virkeligheden stammer fra dig', sagde han rystet.
Han stillede skakspillet fra sig på baenken og så ud som om han slet ikke havde lyst til at fortsaette med det projekt, som for et øjeblik siden havde fået ham til at se så ivrigt på uret. 'Du tager fejl', svarede Jaina efter en pause, hvori drengen gennemtaenkte muligheden. 'tanker ligner verden og drømme. De er der muligvis når

'This means that the world I thought I had created, was in fact created by you,' he said in an anguished tone of voice. He put the game of chess on the bench; he seemed as if he no longer wanted to go on with this project which, not so long beforehand, was making him constantly direct his gaze towards the clock.

'You're wrong,' Jaina replied after a moment during which he had reflected on this possibility, 'thoughts are like the world

øjnene op, men først når man giver dem ord, får de facon og bestandighed. Uden at blive fortalt videre ville de øjeblikkelig ophøre med at existere. Men det har vi vist allerede fortalt en gang.'

Svend Åge Madsen,
At fortaelle menneskene

and like dreams. They are probably there when we open our eyes but it is only when we furnish them with words that they take on form and duration. If they are not spoken, they immediately cease to exist. But we've already said that once before, I think.'

The influence of the great traditions, of H.C. Andersen and Karen Blixen among others, shines through in two notable works by Peter Høeg, *Forestilling om det tyvende århundrede* (*The Representation of the twentieth Century*, 1989) and *Fortaellinger om natten* (*Tales of the Night*, 1990). The Norwegian novelists Kjartan Floegstad, Dag Solstad and Jan Kjaerstad had a great part to play right up until the 1980s. Solstad looped the loop, from an 'incomprehensible' modernism to political and socio-realist literature, and even a new realism that was ambiguous and imaginative, for example in *Novel 1987* (1987). It has been said of Kjaerstad, perhaps exaggeratedly, that his intellectual range made other Norwegian authors look like cows chewing the cud! But it is undeniable that with his three novels, *Homo Falsus* (1984), *Det store eventyret* (*The Great Adventure*, 1987) and recently *Rand* (*Limit*, 1990), he has produced works that delicately analyse the subject-object dichotomy of postmodern man. The novel form he adopts borrows elements from detective fiction, thus creating suspense, while practising literary self-deconstruction. In Swedish literature, Per Olov Enquist[*] attempted literary experiments very early on, playing with the 'authenticity' of prose.

Dutch, Flemish and Francophone Belgian literature

A new group of authors, including Frans Kellendonk, collected around the review *De Revisor* (founded in 1974). Their prose is characterised by polyphonic stratification and by intertextuality. In other writers, the return to conventional narrative is striking, for example in the novel by Harry Mulisch which

traces the course of a love affair between two women, *Twee vrouwen* (*Two Women*, 1975). Work by Maarten 't Hart is significant in the renewal of the traditional art of narration (*De Jacobsladder*, *Jacob's Ladder*, 1986). The female novelist Hella Haasse prolongs her work with a certain number of historical documentary novels and romantic chronicles of women's lives, all based on archive material. Cees Noteboom writes novels steeped in a fascination with nothingness (*Rituelen*, *Rituals*, 1980). J. Bernlef fights against the fearsomeness of time in *Hersensshimmen* (*Chimeras*, 1984).

Discontinuity in the characters and radical insecurity are typical elements in three postmodern novels: *Een weekend in Oostende* (*A Weekend in Ostend*, 1982) by Willem Brakman, an intertextual game based on a traditional novel about a family; *Turkenvespers* (*Turkish Vespers*, 1977) by Louis Ferron, an author of books in which fiction and history intermingle for the purely mimetic expression of reality is impossible; last but not least, *Maurits en de feiten* (*Maurice and the Facts*, 1986) by Gerrit Krol. With the intention of sending it up, the author writes an anti-detective novel in the style of Robbe-Grillet and Échenoz.

In Flemish prose, the accent is on the renewal and evolution of the traditional novel which is accused of not confronting the real questions posed by the genre by having recourse to realist illusions. The postmodern Flemish novel covers two categories: the autobiographical novel, in which the line of demarcation between the facts and fiction is effaced, and the philosophical and musical novel as conceived by Claude Van de Berge, Herman Portocarero, Patricia De Martelaere and Stefan Hertmans. All of them write stratified novels. In *Ruimte* (*Space*, 1981), Hertmans tries to suggest a feeling of serenity and of contemporaneousness in the world by introducing the formal structure of Gabriel Fauré's sonatas into his work. The main characters in his collection of tales *De grenzen van woestijnen* (*Frontiers of the Desert*, 1989) endure with pride and desperation an existence which is unliveable; they are sometimes intoxicated with the immensity of the moment. The mystical novels by Claude Van de Berge, like *Het bewegen van het hoge gras op de top van de heuvel* (*The Rustling of the High Grass at the Top of the Hill*, 1981), are inspired by variations in repetitive music, and the second novel by Patricia De Martelaere, *De schilder en zijn model* (*The Painter and his Model*, 1989) is based on Bach's Goldberg variations.

In Francophone Belgian literature, biographical interest is primarily concentrated on foreign characters. In this way, Mertens systematically uses a series of doubles to define his connection with Belgium. Similarly, Anna Geramys, a discreet pseudonym, puts her name to one of the rare novels on the Belgian version of colonisation (*The Rest of the World*, 1989) and Jean-Louis Lippert mobilises his *alter ego* Anatole Atlas to dictate to him his astonishing *Full Moon on the Existence of the Young Rascal* (1990). In this light we may read *The Black Regiment* (1972) and *Oedipus on the Road* (1990) by Henri Bauchau, which show that the playwright who wrote *Gengis Khan* (1960) knew how to breathe new life into the fascinating problems of power, coming back to certain very ambiguous characters. The character of Elvis Presley dominates in *A Young Man Who Was Too Fat* (1978), a short novel by Eugène Savitskaya who, in his other works, cultivates the weak and the uncertain, fog and indecisiveness, as in *Memoirs of a Clumsy Angel* (1984) by Francis Dannemark. Another 'extreme' is found in the old, classical flight of French-speaking Belgians to Paris and later to Germanic areas – not Flemish, for Flemings are the enemy, but German-speaking. Mertens, for example, discovered Gottfried Benn. Thierry Haumont sets in one of these areas *Keeper of the Shadows* (1987), a

novel on decomposition in general. *The Three Brothers* (1987) by René Swennen tells the story of a family of Austro-Hungarian origin. The intense musical work of Gaston Compère is inseparable from German Romanticism (from *Seven Machines for Dreaming*, 1974 to *I the undersigned, Charles the Bold, Duke of Burgundy*, 1985).

Prose literature in southern Europe

Neo-Hellenic prose is characterised above all by a somewhat traditional and 'realist' tendency. Usually it touches on particular events and phenomena which have had a marked effect on Greek sociocultural development since the Second World War. Narrative technique is compact and balanced, underlining the importance of allusive indications and of the omniscient narrator (Tolis Kazandzis). Another trend advocates a break with the norms, for literature can reject all forms of codification; thus we obtain a hybrid novel form, half-way in the ambivalent relationship between fiction and history, which establishes a distinction between two types of novels. On the one hand the novel, the essay, the document, the journal (the individual's and the traveller's), correspondence, parodies of literary texts and historical genres, in which are underscored the fusion of writing and the genre and the interdiscursiveness of a Bakhtin (Thanassis Valtinos, G. Aristinos, G. Panou). On the other hand, there is the singularity of the writing, the autonomy of a 'cosmic' order (trans-human discourse / the end of myth), hence the creation of 'textual happenings' (Georges Cheimonas, D. Dimitriadis, A. Deligiorgi, E. Sotiropoulou).

In Portugal, we observe from the end of the 1960s the development of an experimental tendency, fascinated by the materiality of the text, heavily influenced by structuralism, but having at the same time kept the taste of the surrealists for liberty of metaphor and the imagination in language: Nuno Bragaça, *A Noite e o Riso* (*Night and Laughter*, 1969), Maria Gabriela Llansol, *O Livro das Com-*

unidades (*The Book of the Communities*, 1977) and *Um beijo dado mais tarde* (*A Kiss Given Later*, 1990), and Maria Velho da Costa, *Maina Mendes* (1969), *Casas Pardas* (*Dark-brown Houses*, 1977), *Lucialima* (1983). Two vital themes dominate in the modern Portuguese novel. The first is the colonial war or memories of an Africa haunted by colonial ghosts which are evoked by Lobo Antunes, *Memoria de Elefante* (*The Memory of an Elephant*, 1979) and José Manuel Mendes, *Ombro, Arma*! (*Shoulder Arms*! 1978). The second burning issue is the emigration which depopulated Portugal during the 1960s portrayed in *A Floresta de Bremerhaven* (*The Forest of Bremerhaven*, 1975) by Olga Gonçalves, *Gente Feliz com Lagrimas* (*Happy People in the Midst of Tears*, 1988), and *Os cus de Judas*! (*The Arse of Judas*! 1979) by João de Melo.

> Ai, durante um ano, morremos nao a morte da guerra, que nos despovoa de repente a cabeça num estrondo fulminante, e deixa em torno de si um deserto desarticulado de gemidos e uma confusao de panico e de tiros, mas a lenta, aflita, torturante agonia da espera, a espera dos meses, a espera das minas na picada, a espera do paludismo, a espera do cada vez mais improvável regresso, com a família e os amigos no aeroporto ou no cais, a espera do correio [. . .].

João de Melo,
Os cus de Judas!

> [. . .]. There, for a year, we died, not, however, of the death people die in war which often depopulates our skull in an explosion and leaves around one an inarticulate desert of groaning and a confusion of panic and of gunshots, but dying from the slow, agonising, excruciating agony of waiting, waiting for months, waiting for mines on the trail, for swamp fever, waiting for the each-time-more-improbable return, with family and friends at the airport or on the platform, waiting for the post [. . .].

Magical or fantastic realism, out of which sprang a certain type of modern historical novel, is one of the most authentic tendencies of contemporary Portuguese fiction. Three names are linked with this phenomenon: José Saramago*, who takes up certain very prolific myths in Portuguese history to transplant them and rewrite them in novels that have become best-sellers, Lídia Jorge from her first book *O Dia des Prodigios* (*The Day of Miracles*, 1980) and Mário de Carvalho who has made a name for himself as a story-teller. We are present at a re-evaluation of the traditional novel, the historical novel and the biographical novel, connected with a certain taste on the part of the general public for hyperrealism: Américo Guerreiro de Sousa, Paulo Castilho.

In Italy, alongside postmodern novels by Calvino and Eco, an overall 'classical' tendency asserts itself. After the 'destruction' of the novel that neo-avant-gardist writers of the 1960s had advocated, narration was once again favoured in the novel which turned in two main directions: there was an anthropological perspective – *Corporale* (*Corporal*, 1975) by Paolo Volponi, and *La Storia* (1975) by Elsa Morante – and a paradigmatic one, *The Moro Affair* (1978) by Leonardo Sciascia, and Giuseppe Pontiggia, who enjoy using the structure of a detective novel plot. Narrative literature, feigning to evoke various historical situations, calls into question the world of today; this intention seems to explain the rise of historical novels. Younger writers work in this direction: Daniele Del Giudice (*Lo stadio de Wimbledon, Wimbledon Stadium*, 1983, and *Atlante Occidentale*, 1985) on the relationship between life and literature; Antonio Tabucchi uses the literary tradition as a raw material in his search for himself (*Il gioco del rovescio, The Game of Tails*, 1981, *Il filo dell'orizzonte, The Thread of the Horizon*, 1987).

In Spain it is also the narrative genre which is currently the most productive and the most innovative. The history of its evolution is similar to that which took place in France, in Portugal and in Italy: we have gone from the radical formal experiments of the 1960s (the 'novisimo') to today's hybrid novel – a mixture of traditional realism and experimental modernism – while respecting the fundamental qualities of the traditional novel, above all in its relation to the reader: Eduardo Mendoza*, with masterly works like *La verdad sobre el caso Savolta* (*The Truth about the Savolta Affair*, 1975) and *La ciudad de los prodigios* (*The Town of Prodigies*, 1985). Manuel Vásquez Montalban is one of the first to use the detective novel form with *Tatuaje* (*Tattoo*, 1975), in which he returns to fiction of a more traditional form appreciated by the reading public. His novels are chronicles of Spanish history, presented in the form of detective novel plots, in the heart of which are found description of and reflections by the hero on society. Vásquez Montalban is at the same time one of the most well-known Spanish journalists. Like him, many journalists have enriched the novel with their knowledge of the Spanish mentality (Rosa Montero, who deals with male–female relationships). Antonio Muñoz-Molina, like so many other novelists of his generation, has created a solitary hero. The world of memories, intimate feelings and personal reflections thus becomes the very raw material of the narrative in *El invierno in Lisboa* (*Winter in Lisbon*, 1987) and *Beltenebros* (1989). The blossoming of narrative prose in Spanish literature is marked by a general return, in new contexts, to traditional genres and themes: the detective novel is one example, but there is also the erotic novel; history is a source of inspiration, under the influence of foreign writers like Marguerite Yourcenar and Umberto Eco.

Great Britain between tradition and modernity

A leading tendency in British fiction of the last twenty-five years is the product of a combination of tradition and modernity. Martin Amis talks of writing like Robbe-Grillet and Jane Austen. But we find in him and in some of his contemporaries, such as Julian Barnes, Graham Swift, Peter Ackroyd, Iain Banks and Ian McEwan, the signs of a new vitality, orientated less towards traditional modernism than towards a radical postmodernism. In the name of their femininity Eva Figes and Angela Carter find new modes of discourse and undermine conventions. There are other motifs in the British context which indicate that English writers are on the road to post-modernism. Cultural and linguistic conflicts do not occur simply between Great Britain and its European neighbours, but also and mainly inside the country itself, between Scottish, Irish and Welsh minorities, those of former colonies, the Indian subcontinent and the West Indies, and predominant English culture. The increasing financial dominance of the south-east of England, conservative and urban, increases the feeling of cultural and political isolation of most of these minorities. The latter are developing a critical vision of authority and are opposed to the formal conventions defended by the dominant culture. Formal radicalisation is a consequence already evident in Scotland in work by Alasdair Gray and James Kelman. Conventional realism seems insufficient to Salman Rushdie or Timothy Mo to transmit their versions of British colonial experiences. They have recourse to magical realism or to other innovative strategies. Many signs indicate that this tendency, beyond convention and realism, and on the way to something more radical and postmodern, will continue in years to come.

Germany and the literatures of Central and Eastern Europe and the Balkans

In West Germany, in the 1970s, documentary literature dominates, emanating in the main from the celebrated Group 61 (Max von der Grün). Günther Wallraff has become famous for his own special method of 'the mole's eye view': he gets himself taken on incognito in a place to work in the real working conditions experienced by employees and then describes his experiences in documentary novels. Written in 1966, his collection of short stories *Wir brauchen Dich* (*We Need You!*) was published for the first time in 1970 in pocket paperback format under the title *Industriereportagen* (*Reports on Industry*). Wallraff writes here in a remarkable way of how hard production-line work is, the effects of a constant struggle against the clock with, among other things, the risks of having an accident at work. As the author calls for 'genuine' experiences, told in the first person, his work comes close to autobiography. After *Reports on Industry*, he published in 1977 a report on a period of work for the German magazine *Bild*. Then, under the title *Ganz unten* (*Turk's Head*), he describes the experiences he had when, passing himself off as a Turkish immigrant, he worked at McDonald's as a guineapig to test new medicines, as an illegal worker on a big building-site and as a temp for Thyssen. Wallraff's project shows how much literature and writers can be used in a 'transliterary' way. However, at the end of the 1970s, a new subjectivity emerges, and interest is directed above all at a literature whose links with reality are looser. At the end of the 1980s, with Botho Strauß, we head for a new wave of fictionalisation parallel to the main trends in the rest of Western Europe.

In Eastern Germany, literature obviously finds itself in quite a different situation. The official doctrine of 'socialist realism' formally advocated the traditional realism of previous generations and, for the most part, literature adhered to that. But from the fact of literature's status as a 'mouthpiece' in a social debate that was anyway censored, we witness the appearance of works which play an important part in intellectual discussion in the country. Christa Wolf* is an example of this; she also experimented with traditional form. But even in this framework, writers like Gerti Tetzner (*Karen W.*, 1974) have spoken with conviction and authority of the problems of the individual.

In Eastern Europe, experimentalism increasingly takes over. In Croatian literature, we can see the influence of Borges in Goran Tribusan, Pavao Pavici and Dubravka Ugresic in the shape of a reappropriation of the fan-

tastic, of a leaning to the metatextual, of a new and original attitude to literary tradition, both national and international. The transformation into irony and parody of these genres poses the question of the limits between good and bad literature. The postwar generation of Bulgarian writers also presents signs of a return to narration. Jordan Radičkov places an omniscient narrator at the centre of a cycle of stories; Viktor Paskov, in his astonishing novel *Balada za Georg Henih* (*Ballad for Georg Henig*, 1988), maintains that art is the only salvation in a society sick with materialism. Tadeusz Konwicki,* in Poland, and András Simonffy, in Hungary, direct the tale to the origins of the past of both the individual and the nation. These two pasts are very often mixed up, as in the work of the Hungarians Imre Kertész, *Sorstalanság* (*Deprived of a Destiny*, 1975) and Peter Lengyel. *Emlékiratok könyve* (1986) by Peter Nadas is a novel of three stories, memoirs of three different periods – the present, the recent past and the last century. In a particular current of Soviet literature, the novel dissolves into a prose that uses official aesthetics as the raw material only to inflict on it a premeditated distortion (Sorokin). But it is the traditional form of the novel which dominates Soviet literature in the 1980s, whether it be dissident writing (novels by Solzhenitsyn) or official literature. The 1970s were distinguished by the success of the historical novel. This success was renewed by the coming of perestroika by a new appropriation of the past (Rybakov). Faced with this trend, Vassili Belov and Victor Astafiev glorify traditional and patriarchal Russian peasant life, contrasting it with the decadent character of modern 'socialist' civilisation. Astafiev is one of the leaders of Siberian literature, a literature which emerged in the 1960s and 1970s, after a long period of silent maturation. Particularly original, the works of 'Siberian' writers have been translated in large numbers in the West, and their authors have quickly been recognised as dominant figures in contemporary Russian prose. The place of Siberia in Russian literature is on the same scale as the part that this region plays in Russian culture: an immense province in comparison to Moscow, with its forests and its limitless steppes it inspires a feeling of unlimited freedom; but, a land of unspeakable suffering, it is also the symbol of the Gulag. It is the product of all the country's contradictions, born of its forced development, which are tearing modern generations apart. Other tendencies are asserting themselves: a more 'modern' existential prose (Vladimir Makanin), a feminist tendency (Liudmila Petrushevskaïa*) and a tendency towards the grotesque in the tradition of Gogol (Vladimir Voïnovitch, Iuz Alcchkovsky).

Even split into three sections – official, clandestine, from exile – Czech narrative literature continues its astonishing revival. Josef Škvorecký has revived the tradition of Karel Čapek that he enriches with Anglo-American additions to give a strongly auto-biographical series of novels and psychological and biographical stories, almost detective stories. Under the guise of celebrating every-day life, Bohumil Hrabal has recourse to a very elaborate style of narration (*Obsluhoval jsem anglického krale, I served the King of England*, 1975, *Příliš hlučná samota, An Overly Noisy Solitude*, 1976). Milan Kundera looks for new ways forward in the contemporary philosophical novel. This precarious situation lends itself to the production of short genres in the great tradition of Neruda, Hašek and Čapek: tale, short story, serial, cultivated by Hrabal, Kundera, Škvorecký and Klíma. Ludvík Vaculík is the undisputed master of the serial to which he gives a poetic and semantic micro-structure.

But it is precisely the link between the evolution of Western and Eastern Europe which shows the full importance of frame-works in which a given literature can develop. In other contexts, the function of literature is different. The fall of the Iron Curtain will undoubtedly mean a more lively exchange of views and a greater 'simultaneity' in the tendencies proper to each country.

WOMEN'S WRITING, FEMINIST LITERATURE

During this period and almost everywhere, a specific women's literature develops, which, in its very conception, constitutes a realm apart; it was during the 1970s that this evolution seems to have been most marked. There is a whole literature written by women, which often takes as its theme female experience although it docs not basc its distinctness on this fact. At the same time a militant and radically feminist literature is published in stark contrast to the rest of literature (male) which is based on the concept of there being something quite distinct about women writing.

The point of departure for this sudden growth in literature by women has been, in most cases, a growth in awareness of the oppression of woman in the traditional division of male and female roles. This oppression then became quite naturally the main theme of women writing. A redefinition of women's writing has therefore been sought just on the basis of this theme. Others have wanted to see in writing by women a genetically conditioned distinctness. The delimitation of the world of women's writing is a question has not been resolved in a satisfactory manner. It would be absurd to place on the shelf of women's writing every book written by a woman: the outcome of this would be to discriminate against this literature, which would be quite contrary to the declared intention of the women writers' manifesto. This problem crops up everywhere where the deliberate marginalisation of an element supposedly suppressed is encountered.

This is not the place to tackle different theoretical struggles concerning the internal and external limits of women's writing. It is even too early to evaluate its impact on the evolution of literary production. It is, however, indisputable that this literature has contributed very positively to the articulation, and therefore to the manifestation, of a certain number of female experiences in a male-dominated world; and that alone represents an important contribution by women's literature to the cultural development of the last twenty-five years.

The pace of the evolution as well as its importance have varied from one country to another. In Great Britain, we have the feeling – currently very deep-rooted within British academic institutions and their curricula – that there is a need for a different analysis of women's writing. We have also recognised the need for a female point of view on the concept of the nature and the strategy of writing by men. Most university publishers today have a department specialising in 'women's studies' or 'women's criticism'. Publishing policy has shed new light on part of what has given women's literature its strength and power both today and yesterday: Rosamund Lehmann, for example, tells how, after years of neglect, she experienced being republished by Virago Press as a sort of exhumation. The re-appearance of female authors on the literary scene is a general phenomenon: women's writing past and present has found a much bigger audience than could be foreseen only fifteen years ago. British women's literature works more and more directly on experiences and ways of thinking normally attributed to women: Margaret Drabble, Anita Brookner, Marina Warner. Some tackle these questions from a political point of view. Doris Lessing, Emma Tennant and Fay Weldon move into action to voice their opposition, their desire for change and their social stance. From the need of women authors to find a discourse and to define their own experience is born a willingness to experiment with different ways of writing. Doris Lessing, Eva Figes, Emma Tennant and others have thus made women's literature one of the most lively and prolific forums in the current development of British literature.

'Free women,' said Anna, wryly. She added, with an anger new to Molly, so that he earned another quick scrutinising glance from her friend: 'They still define us in terms of relationships with men, even the best of them.' 'Well, *we* do, don't we?' said Molly,

rather tart. 'Well, it's awfully hard not to,' she amended, hastily, because of the look of surprise Anna now gave her. There was a short pause, during which the women did not look at each other but reflected that a year apart was a long time, even for an old friendship. Molly said at last, sighing: 'Free . . . Do you know, when I was away, I was thinking about us, and I've decided that we're a completely new type of woman. We must be, surely?'

Doris Lessing,
The Golden Notebook

In The Netherlands, in the wake of Hella Haasse, women's literature also played a vital part. Philosophy, social commitment and an unconventional narrative style are the appendages of Andreas Burnier; a philosopher, a feminist and a university professor of criminology, she writes under a male pen-name. With verbalisation and fiction, she casts doubt on the ability of language to describe and analyse reality in a series of neo-Platonic and intellectual novels, like *De reis naar Kithira* (*The Journey to Cythera*, 1976). She also demonstrates a very marked stand against machismo, anti-semitism and technocracy, in essays and research work. However, she cannot be described as a militant feminist in the political sense of the word, as can socialist authors like Anja Meulenbelt, *De schaamte voorbij. Een persoonlijke geschiedenis* (*Beyond Shame. A Personal Story*, 1976). Hannes Meinkema (the male pen-name of Hanne-mieke Stamperius), publishes book criticism as well as theoretical studies of literature, but she is especially known as an author of feminist novels and short stories written in a naturalist style. Meinkema is the co-founder of the first feminist literary review in The Netherlands, *Chrysallis* (1978–1987). Independently of feminist literature, there exists a growing number of freelance women writers (Tessa De Loo and Hermine De Graaf).

Dutch-speaking Belgian literature has produced influential works in women's literature: Monika Van Paemel,[*] with *De vermaledijde vaders* (*The Cursed Fathers*, 1985), and Kristien

Hemmerechts with *Een zuil van zout* (*A Column of Salt*, 1987), which achieves a perfect equilibrium between the chaos of the inner life and a writing marked by apparent coldness, an absence of compassion, and the conjuration of existential fear. Most of the tales in his work *Weerberichten* (*Weather Forecasts*, 1988) derive their strength from an opposition between the 'hyper-realist' registering an unknown reality and a whirling maelstrom of evil, pain and distress.

The trilogy by the Norwegian woman writer Herbjoerg Wassmo, *Huset med den blinde glasveranda* (*The House with the Blind Glass Verandah*, 1981), *Det stumme rum* (*The Silent Room*, 1983) and *Hudlos himmel* (*Hypersensitive Sky*, 1986), adopts a more realist form. This tale of childhood goes a very long way into the description of incest and ensuing psychosis. The Finnish female novelist known under the pen-name of Rosa Liksom,* presents an image of femininity in an extremely hard style, which might traditionally be attributed to male writers. In Denmark, novels by Jette Drewsen and Kirsten Thorup belong to women's literature without going as far as to defend militant feminist viewpoints. It is true that these viewpoints flourished in the 1970s, but even though they were important with regard to 'sexual politics', their literary outreach does not seem to have been long-lasting. Kirsten Thorup created, in a feminine perspective, a long novella which resembles a study in manners, *Himmel og helvede* (*Heaven and Hell*, 1982).

In Central Europe and the Balkans, the picture is far from being homogeneous. In certain regions (in Serbia, for instance), female perspectives give the impression of having been hidden by more general questions on freedom; elsewhere, notably in the ex-GDR, the theme of feminism has been a favoured route in this area. Women's literature has oscillated between the 'political' and 'aesthetic' aspect of its creation. In Croatia, women's writing (above all work by Vesna Krmpotic, Irena Vrkljan and Slavenka Drakulic) is characterised by a poetic language and a fictionalisation of biographical material.

On the other hand, no real women's literary movement has shown itself in Hungarian literature; the main works are those by Anna Kiss and Katalin Ladik, who lives in Yugoslavia. Women's liberation was initially one of the favourite themes of classical Polish modernism, but, after the Second World War its importance lessened because of new social and political conditions. In Polish poetry, Anna Świrszczyńska develops the sentimental space of a woman in *Szczęśliwa jak psi ogon* (1978). Russian women's literature finds its voice in work by Liudmila Petruchevskaïa and Tatiana Tolstaïadahs. In Czech literature, psychological, intimate and erotic female problems appear mainly in poetry, but also in tales by Eda Kriseová and Lerka Prócházková. Politics rears its ugly head in work by Zdena Salivarová and Eva Kantůrková, the author of *Přítelkyně z domu smutku* (*Girlfriends in the House of Sorrows*, 1984) – prison. In Bulgaria, the literary landscape is dominated by Blaga Dimitrova, a pioneer of modern 'synthetic' prose which we find notably in her novel *Lice* (*The Face*, 1981), banned only a few days after it was published. The concept of women's literature seems somewhat diffuse in Germany. The review *Emma* presents itself as an 'instance of evaluation', feminist with one voice. But when it tackles the question of the role of the sexes, women's literature also covers a very large palette of sensibilities. On the one hand, we find, for example, Karin Struck who, in *Trennung* (*Separation*, 1978), fought against the right to abortion, on the other Christa Reinig who, in her novel *Entmannung* (*Castration*), underlines that, for a woman, there are only three possibilities in a world where the norms are established by men: to fight and to find oneself in prison, not to fight and go mad, and lastly to give in to men and fall ill. Between these two poles, there are in Germany a good many women writers of renown who have made a strong contribution to specific female worlds, such as Christa Wolf and Sarah Kirsch.

Greek women's literature favours refinement and aesthetics; the self-referential texts A, Deligiorgi and E, Sotiropoulou, as well as poetry by M. Kirtzaki and P Pampoudi involve the reader; the imaginary nature of the dichotomy (body/sex) as well as the chaotic flux of wild imagery coming from the 'interior landscape' reach a strangely emphatic equilibrium in this discontinuous universe. The balance of this writing is reached by a cyclical organisation of the sentence and the text, divided into rhythmic sequences. The 'status of reality' is in this way penetrated and recalled into question.

The feminist discourse in Portugal, formal and thematically very varied, is linked to the 'new' Portugal born out of the ashes of the April 1974 Revolution: Maria Ondina Braga and Maria Velho da Costa with *Maina Mendes*. The second Maria, working in collaboration with Maria Isabel Barreno and Maria Teresa Horta, published *Novas Cartas Portuguesas* (*New Letters from Portugal*, 1972) in which 'the three Marias' decry women's condition by parodying the eighteenth-century *Letters from Portugal*, a text in which the author, Mariana Alcoforado, breaks the law and symbolises in her imprisonment the 'imprisonment' of all women. The book was seized and its authors risked imprisonment, giving rise to an unprecedented mobilisation of Portuguese feminism. In Spain, formal innovations are not what dominate either in women's literature which is highly fashionable. Its themes are most often concerned with moral freedom, notably in work by Anna Rossetti who, in *Los Devaneos de Erato* (*Erato's Frivolity*, 1980), describes the female libido in particular through a series of erotic images. We should also mention *Las Diosas Blancas, Antología de la joven poesía española escrita por mujeres* (*The White Goddesses, An Anthology of Modern Spanish Poetry Written by Women*, 1985), including, among the women poets represented, Blanca Andreu and Amalia Iglesias.

In Italy, militant feminist literature developed in parallel to the strong politisation of intellectuals, at the end of the 1960s and the beginning of the 1970s (Dacia Maraini, Giuliana Morandini, Bianca Maria Frabotta). Even women writers who had been on the literary scene for some time (Elsa Morante,

Ortese, Sanvitale) started to adopt specifically female points of view, in their description of the mother–son relationship, for example. However, it seems that at the end of this century Italian women's literature is changing. While historical feminism is gradually losing its polemical and aggressive character, and looking for cognitive yardsticks, certain authors are coming closer to an 'androgynous' model, which, in its thematics as well as its stylistics, has lost the most obvious characteristics of women's writing. The youngest women writers, Marta Morazzoni and Paola Capriolo, write stories in which visions, analysis and nightmares are no longer clearly distinguishable from their male equivalents. Dacia Maraini and Giuliana Morandini try to create veritable historical and atmospheric reconstructions. It appears anyway that there is here a convergence in which what is first experienced by women's literature also becomes the experience of literature in general.

France has been the cockpit of a fruitful debate on women's literature which has influenced the whole of Europe, especially in theoretical terms. The distinction between feminist literature and women's literature (apart from the category of female writers) seems to be relevant today. Feminist literature, which has its roots in the work of Simone de Beauvoir (1908–1986), *The Second Sex* (1949), regroups works opening up to women new fields of discourse. Psychoanalytic discourse is taken up by Luce Irigaray in *Speculum*. In the 1970s the idea of a 'male' writing claimed successfully by women emerges. Works by Catherine Clément, *The Young Child* (1975), and by Hélène Cixous are located somewhere between the themes of women's literature and feminist commitment. In *La Venue à l'écriture* (*Coming to Writing*, 1977), Hélène Cixous asks herself questions on the relationship between women and writing: she wants to venture into this 'forward march', this dialogue with the 'burning bush', she whom fairy-tales imprison in household chores, and that Judeo-Christian society excludes:

But to you the tales announce a destiny of restriction and neglect, the brevity, the lightness of a life which only leaves your mother's house to make three little detours which bring you back quite dazed to the house of your grandmother who will swallow you down in one. For you, little girl, little milk jug, little honeypot, little basket, experience shows and history promises this short alimentary journey which takes you back quite quickly to the bed of the Jealous Wolf, your ever insatiable grandmother, as if the law wanted your mother to be forced to sacrifice her daughter to expiate her audacity in having enjoyed the good things of life in her little red offspring. A vocation of one who is gobbled up, a scybalus.

For the Sons of the Book, research, the desert, inexhaustible space, discouragement, encouragement, the forward march. For the daughters of the house, getting lost in the forest. Deceived, disappointed, but jumping with curiosity. Instead of the great enigmatic duel with the Sphinx, the dangerous set of questions addressed to the body of the Wolf: what good is the body? Myths murder us. The Logos opens its great maw, and swallows us.

Hélène Cixous,
La Venue à l'écriture

These women writers are also interested in psychoanalysis and, moreover, militate in the critical avant-garde within writing. According to them, the 'female text' is more subversive than the male text, or at least, is characterised by a subversive power. Women's literature takes on purely female themes like the body and pregnancy without producing a literature of struggle: *Parole de femme* (*A Woman's Words*, 1974) by Annie Leclerc, considered to be a manifesto, Chantal Chawaf, *Retable* (*Altarpiece*, 1974). Finally, in French literature, there are many high-calibre women writers whose works cannot be specifically linked to being female. Texts by Marguerite Duras, Marguerite Yourcenar and Nathalie Sarraute do not just deal with feminine themes. Some women would go as far as to condemn a work like *The Memoirs of Hadrian* for its 'virile docility'. Other women observe that women's writing has existed for centuries and that it is nothing more than a writing in which women express things with their own sensibility. It is also hard to think of texts by Annie Ernaux, *The Square* (1984) and *A Woman* (1988), and those by Danièle Sallenave, *The Gates of Giubbio* (1980) and *Farewell* (1988) as specifically women's texts; the problems envisaged by these two women transcend the limits of the limited territory of women's writing. In the last resort, it is a problem of definition: if it is correct that women's writing always presents a specifically feminine character, the territory embraced by this writing is then determined. But in this case, fortunately, it is not closed to readers of the opposite sex.

AUTOFICTION, NEW BIOGRAPHY

For some years now, more or less all over Europe, we have been present at the emergence of a writing that resembles the genres of biography and autobiography. But it seems there has been a change. Some particular forms of self-portrayal have become popular. We are no longer talking about traditional, 'honest' autobiographies; a biographical 'I' is nevertheless often found at the centre of the theme. This phenomenon, which plays specifically on the link between authenticity and fictionalisation, may be called autofiction. At the same time, a 'new style of biography' has appeared which no longer consists of 'honest' portraits of the people who form the subject of the book. The facts are openly flouted; very often these works with a biographical orientation are, in reality, more or less autobiographical in their spirit and intention. The fact that these genres are developing precisely now is due to a complex set of reasons. But it would be quite natural to see a connection with the global modification of the image of the subject which is one of the movements in meaning that some would call postmodern.

The new biography in Germany

In Germany, after the heyday of the documentary in the 1960s and the beginning of the 1970s, the new biography appears in the shape of a 'new subjectivity'. Henceforth individuals, their lives and surroundings begin to play a leading role again. In his novel *Mars* (1977), Fritz Angst, under the pseudonym of Fritz Zorn, depicts the long process of his own death through cancer, a death that he attributes in essence to his education. According to Angst, his overly great adaptation to the conventions that society imposed on him indirectly brought about his death. While *Mars* is primarily an example of the reciprocal effects of social norms and conventions and the story of an individual, many autobiographies attempt to show us historical time in each individual biography. In *Gestern war heute, one hundred Jahre Gegenwart* (*Yesterday was Today, one hundred Years of Present*, 1978), Ingeborg Drewitz tells the story of a family during five generations. She shows how private and individual autobiography is always determined by social conventions and the overall political situation.

The characteristic writing of the 'new biography' – fictionalised biographies – also became more prevalent. We may remember here the novel by Peter Härtling, *Hölderlin* (1976), *Mozart* (1977) by Wolfgang Hildesheimer, the biography of Oswald von Wolkenstein by Dieter Kühn, *Ich Wolkenstein* (*I Wolkenstein*, 1977), or *Kohlhaas* (1979) by Elisabeth Plesse.

These autofictional elements, among others the theme of individual involvement in the recent past under national socialism, appear both in the literature of the GFR and GDR in the 1970s and 1980s. This parallel – and other factors like the 'Ausbürgerung' (expatriation) of a certain number of authors in the GDR – makes us wonder if there are two German literatures or just one. *Kindheitsmuster* (*Childhood's Web*, 1976) by Christa Wolf, for example, is at the heart of a new history of literature common to both Germanies. Christa Wolf describes how little Nelly grows up in Nazi Germany. Even though her family does not really support this party, she adapts to the new political situation and bows to the demands of the authorities by displaying the swastika and giving the Hitler salute. Nelly can but follow this model. The presentation of Nelly's experiences is interrupted by the author's reflections, who tries to transmit history as lived through and remembered by her daughter. This type of subjective and authentic writing is fundamentally different from the 'official' style of socialist realist writing in the GDR in those days.

Dutch and Flemish prose

In The Netherlands and Dutch-speaking Belgium, biographical literature plays an influential part throughout this period. In Flemish prose in particular, the autobiographical novel represents an important tendency in the shape of mixed genres in which the line of demarcation between fiction and reality is erased. Walter Van den Broek creates a hybrid work consisting of elements of the documentary novel, of the family chronicle, of history and autobiography, composed in a systematic way. Van den Broek obtains his first popular successes with his trilogy *Aantekeningen van een stambewaarder* (*Annotations of a Genealogist*, 1977), *Brief aan Boudewijn* (*Letter to Baudouin*, 1980) and *Het beleg van Laken* (*The Siege of Laeken*, 1985), in which he examines the facts and events which are the foundation of his education as a man and as a writer. His enquiry is conducted first at the historical level, then at the geographical level, then at the level of textual analysis. The last part resembles a subtle anthology of allusions to works by Kafka and Dante. In work by Willy Spillebeen, the writing of the 'I' is an effort to fight against the absurdity of existence and the scarcities of the human condition. Leo Pleysier achieved an autobiographical triptych consisting of *De razernij der winderige dagen* (*The Anger of Windy Days*, 1978), *De weg naar Kralingen* (*One-Way Paths*, 1981) and *Kop in kas* (*Leapfrog*, 1983). The characters of Pleysier's novels are often described on the basis of old photographs (illiterate peasants and proletarians of days gone by, for instance). Another key novel is *Wit is altijd schoon* (*White Always Looks Nice*, 1989), a musical monologue of a hundred pages; the title at the same time is his mother's motto, by then deceased. *Een schoon bestaan* (*Life is Good*, 1989) by Pol Hoste, offers an indiscreet autobiography in which the young hero cannot make contact with his parents. Unhappiness is here contrasted with beautiful dream sequences.

In The Netherlands in the 1930s, Adriaan Morriën begins a career as a poet, but becomes a literary critic and translator. He is fully accepted in 1988 with the publication of his autobiographical novel *Plantage Muidergracht* (*The Muidergracht Plantation*). This novel is not an autobiography in the usual sense of the word, but a mosaic of fragments without much coherence. Other young writers have published autobiographical works, notably Jan Siebelink with *Nachtschade* (*Nightshade*, 1975) and *Weerlos* (*Weaponless*, 1978) and A.F.Th. Van der Heijden with *De tandeloze tijd* (*Toothless Time*), four volumes begun in 1983; the 'toothless time' is that of the new generations, of their evolution from the 1950s to the 1980s, of their progressive disengagement.

Free-form autofiction in Scandinavia

Elsa Gress favours the 'free' autobiography of herself and her time in *Fuglefri og fremmed* (*Free and Foreign*, 1971). But the biographical portrait also played a very important role in Danish literature. Thorkild Hansen, with *Processen mod Hamsun* (*The Trial of Hamsun*, 1978), stirred up a great deal of controversy both in Denmark and Norway, for he was accused of exonerating Hamsun from having been a Nazi quisling. The most interesting contribution to the biographical novel, and one that was translated into many languages, was made by Henrik Stangerup who, with *Vejen til Lagoa Santa* (*Lagoa Santa*, 1981) and in particular *Det er svaert at dø i Dieppe* (*It is Hard to Die in Dieppe*, 1985) and *Broder Jacob* (*Brother Jacob*, 1992), shows, with the aid of the destiny of concrete historical characters, fundamental problems linked in particular with the 'outside' and 'inside' of the individual in the widest sense. These problems are depicted in the light of history and presented as quite up-to-date because they implicitly provide a direct parallel with the existential problem of the writer himself.

Og Kierkegaard er borte, som hvirvlet ud ad døren af en orkan, efterladende sin spanskrorsstok I sofaen, mens Møller mobiliserer alle vredens legioner imod sig selv. Han griner hånligt og får pigerne til at grine med – og foler leden vokse i sig, som vaelling der ikke kan fordojes, mens Norske-Kate irriteret, idet hun saetter sig ned foran et afhaendet empirespejl og reder håret frem, fortaeller hvordan den lille snurretop havde sat sig på hendes sengekant og bare kigget på hende da hun la med udstrakte arme, naesten afklaedt, og ventede – indtil han pludselig gik amok, kyssede hende til vanvid med kys der havde mere med abebid at gore for så, nu selv naesten afklaedt, at fare op, klaede sig på i en

Leaving his cane on the sofa. Kierkegaard disappears abruptly, as if carried off by a tornado, while Moller is mad with rage at himself. He sneers, he makes fun and makes the girls laugh with him, but disgust repeats on him like an indigestible puree, while Norway Kate, now settled with her comb in front of an Empire mirror bought cheap, tells what has happened. Sat on the edge of the bed, the little client had been content to observe her while she waited for him, her arms outstretched and almost naked. On this, he had suddenly covered with her with kisses that were more like monkey-bites then, himself almost unclothed, had jumped up and got dressed and then run off as if an earthquake had

fart og løbe som var den en jordrystelse under vejs. Intet interesserer Moller mindre.

Henrik Stangerup,
Det er svaert at do i Dieppe

started. Nothing could interest Moller less.

In the same genre, Dorrit Willumsen writes her novel on Marie Tussaud, *Marie* (1983), and Peer Hultberg, in his way stubborn and deep, intense and brutal, recently wrote something 'on' Chopin's childhood in *Praeludier* (*Preludes*, 1989). In Sweden, Jan Myrdal publishes his autobiographical trilogy *Barndom, En annan värld* and *Tolv på det trettonde* (*Childhood, Another World, Twelve out of Thirteen*, 1982–1986). The most widely read and most translated Scandinavian biography was also Swedish: the moving but more traditional story of Ingmar Bergman, *Lanterna Magica* (*Magic Lantern*, 1987). Per Olov Enquist also makes use of biographical material in his theatrical works: *Tribadernas natt* (*The Night of the Lesbians*, 1976) suggests Strindberg. In Norway, Kjartan Flogstand devotes to the Norwegian poet Claes Gillson his *Portrett af eit magisk liv* (*Portrait of a Magical Life*, 1988).

A general revival of the genre

In Southern Europe, there is a revival of the genre. In Greece, autobiography comes across as a palimpsest in which different levels of the autobiographical 'I' are superimposed on each other. Texts by Thanassis Valtinos are constructed with the help of all kinds of discourse: from 'authentic' correspondence to instructions for use and advertisements. Going through all these materials, the autobiographical 'I' intervenes and discovers the traumatic condition of postwar life for each individual. G. Aristinos slips other literary texts into his works (Rabelais, Shakespeare, Pound and Borges among others) which are distinguished by a painful quest for identity. G. Panou, in his novel . . . *opo to stoma tis palias Remington . . . by the Mouth of Old Remington*, 1981) intertwines the different levels of the text. The author is here trying to construct the

world of the years 1930–1950, as his dearly beloved uncle saw and experienced it.

In Portugal, this form of fictional biography and autobiography generates new interest. Marío Cláudio, with his trilogy *Amadeo, Guilhermina* and *Rosa* (1984–1988), found in more or less imaginary biography a form of research on the identity of artistic Portugal. In Spain, there is currently a huge development in the genre, still linked with a revival of interest in the 'I', the subject, characteristic of our era. Next to the written memoir of established writers like Francisco Ayala, Miguel Delibes or Juan Goytisolo, more innovative texts have appeared over the last few years: *Mundinovi* (1987) by Miguel Sanchez-Ortiz and *El gato encerrado* (*The Trapped Cat*, 1990) by Andrés Trapiello.

The Swiss writer Max Frisch,[*] in his final works (for example *Montauk*, 1976), uses a particularly mature and ambiguous form of autofiction, with very complex narrative tenses.

We also find a quasi-autobiographical movement in modern Polish literature, for instance in Tadeusz Konwicki and Jerzy Andrzejewski who, in *Miazga* (*Pulp*, 1979), intertwine a bitty discourse, built around the I-narrator, with elements of a personal diary and personal notes by the author. *Pamietnik z powstania warszawskiego* (*Diary of the Warsaw Uprising*, 1970) by Miron Biatoszewski offers an interesting formula for a biographical novel. The story, devoid of the pathos endemic to chroniclers of the Second World War, explores the authentic linguistic variants of human societies dragged into the bloody whirlpool of history. A quite different autofictional way of going about things characterises the novel *Bohiń* (*Bohini, a Manor in Lithuania*, 1990) by Tadeusz Konwicki, who invents a biography for himself that exploits the past of his Lithuanian ancestors:

I juz jestem nad brzegiem Wilii, ciemnozielonej rzeki z niebieskimi zmarszczkami na łagodnej toni. Juz przedzieram się przez chaszcze jakichú roślin, traw i ził, których imion nie pamietam, bo nie musiłem zapamiętac. Poznaję z trudem wielkie dzikie mięty, zaczynające juz wonieć pod naporem słońca, omijam drzewa durnapianu, zwanego gdzie indziej blekotem, glaszczę krzaki porzeczek z pozasychanymi juz owocami. Ale nie mam czasu, bo spieszę do mojej babki, która dziś obchodzi swoje urodziny w nieduzym rodzinnym folwarczku, zwanym chyba Korzyscia, skromnej sadybie szlacheckiej odległej o kilkanaście wiorst od kolei nie tak dawno zbudowanej.

And there I am on the bank of the Wilia, a dark green river streaked with the blue wrinkles of its peaceful waves. I walk not without difficulty through the brushwood of plants, grass and vegetables whose name I have forgotten for I did not have to remember it. I recognise just about the great stems of wild mint which, under the constraint of the sun, begins to exhale its aroma, I go past the absinthe shrubs which are actually called artemisia, I brush past the gooseberry bushes with dried-up fruits. But I don't linger because I'm in a hurry to find my grandmother who is celebrating today her anniversary in a not very big manor house, called I think Korzysc, a modest noble dwelling a few versts away from the railroad only just constructed.

Tadeusz Konwicki,
Bohiń

Autobiographical writing itself has a metaphorical significance for the Hungarian Deszö Tandori (born 1938), who transformed his whole life into a literary laboratory, a kind of 'work in progress', an autofiction from start to finish (approximately fifty books, including the novel *A meghívás fennáll, The Invitation Still Stands,* 1979).

In England as well as in Italy, genre plays an insignificant role. The only exception to this might be Moravia, who, in 1971, sketched his autobiography in an interview granted to his writer friend Enzo Siciliano (*Alberto Moravia, vita, parole e idee di un romanziere, The Life, Words and Ideas of a Novelist*) who, in 1990, took up his biography again with Alain Elkann (*Vita di Moravia, The Life of Moravia*). However, we cannot really speak of a notable revival of this genre in Italian literature. In France, on the other hand, we can see a development in first-person narratives (Annie Ernaux). Most of these are aimed at no genre in particular: 'It is not a biography, not a novel, of course, perhaps something half-way between literature, sociology and history,' writes Annie Ernaux. Under the title

of the self-analysis that he calls *Biography,* Yves Navarre adds the word 'Novel'. These works defy the traditional theory of genres; they endeavour to suppress borders and being one thing rather than another. 'Autofictions' are ever more numerous. The term itself appears in a text by Serge Doubrovsky, *Fils (Threads,* 1977). But, in fact, the existence of autofiction goes back further than that: *Je me souviens (I Remember,* 1978), *W ou le Souvenir d'enfance (W or the Childhood Memory,* 1975) by Georges Perec, *Livret de famille (Family Archive,* 1977) by Patrick Modiano, as well as Marguerite Yourcenar's trilogy, *Le Labyrinthe du monde (The Labyrinth of the World,* 1974–1988) or *La Fête des pères (Father's Day,* 1989) by François Nourrissier. *L'Immortalité,* by Milan Kundera, gathers together many 'historically real' characters, from Goethe to Hemingway, in a fiction which centres on an authentic I-narrator. And we find the following strangely fragmented discourse, which transcends discourse, and which can both be deeply reflective of the individual and reach very precisely to his world:

More than Goethe drinking wine on the sly, it is Bettina who seems to me interesting: she doesn't behave like you or I would, for we would have watched Goethe with amusement, but in discreet and respectful silence. Telling him what others would not have ('your breath smells of alcohol! Why have you been drinking? Why do you drink on the sly?') was her way of extorting from Goethe part of his intimacy, of finding herself face to face with him. In this aggressive indiscretion, which in the name of her childish spontaneity she had always hung on to, Goethe immediately recognises the Bettina who, thirteen years earlier, he had decided never to see again. Without saying a word, he got up, took a lamp to signify that the conversation was over and that he was going to see his visitor back down the dark corridor as far as the door.

Milan Kundera,
Immortality

THE PRESENCE OF POETRY AT THE END OF THE TWENTIETH CENTURY

At the opening of the Congress of the World Organisation of poets in Florence in 1986, the poet Mario Luzi declared in substance: 'so as to be present at this meeting, poets have said goodbye to their creative contemplation, but not in order to listen to some "Messiah" have they come, but, on the contrary, to exchange all their personal experiences.' In fact, the participants at this congress agreed to bring out the anthology *Spaces – In Search of an Ecology of the Spirit* which bears witness to the vitality of poetry today. The scholar André Lichnerowicz described mathematics as 'the royal game of the spirit'. For many poets, poetic creativity also became a subtle diversion for the intelligence and they reached in that ascetic exercise a higher plane of art. Is access to their work thereby rendered difficult?

Many other poets share our life. Ancient Greek poets had already testified to life in all its states, to darkness and to light. Today's Greek poets remain attached to ancient traditions. In his book *The Greek Summer*, Jacques Lacarrière devotes a chapter to the different forms of the Greek language and congratulates himself on the victory that Demotic has won over its 'rivals', while assimilating their virtues: 'George Seferis, in his speech in Stockholm for his award of the Nobel prize, quoted a good example. Homer said: 'phaos iliou' to say: the light of the sun. Greeks today say: 'phos tou iliou'; is it not still the same language?' In this ancient and ever young language, poets experience grief and celebrate life. When Elytis praises the beauty of the world, his poetry becomes a song of hope and liberty for his oppressed compatriots.

If Greece reveals to us this thousand-year-old continuity, Europe, during this century, has seen new poetry being born. In certain regions of the Soviet Union, peoples have forged a literature for themselves out of their own national language. In Gennadi Aïgui the Tshuvash people have discovered a poet of remarkable delicacy. In the area of Slavic languages, a national poetry has blossomed in Macedonia during the second half of our century. The Lapps have made an appearance on the literary scene: the anthology *Modern Scandinavian Poetry* that Martin Allwood published in Sweden in 1982 opens with a chapter presenting the poetry of a country called 'Kalâtdlit-nunat', or Greenland. We find in this volume another chapter on 'Saame Poetry', the poetry of the Laplanders. The poet Isak Saba invites his readers to rediscover in their mother tongue the strength of their ancestors. Paulus Utsi sings of the incantation of the word *per se*. Ailo Gaup looks for the 'hidden knowledge', the wisdom of shamanism.

The Latvian poet Mâris Caklais, director of the weekly review *Literature and Art*, has said: 'Whoever has no past has no future either.' Formerly condemned to seven years hard labour for anti-Soviet activity, Knuts Skujenieks has been able to contemplate in his library the long line of weighty tomes carrying the swastika on their cover, the svastika, the Indo-European symbol for the sun, and containing the 'dainas', popular poems. Lithuania, a land of 'ponds and meadows', possesses a popular poetry of similar inspiration and still living. Estonians and Finns, for their part, turn towards their epics: 'Our national epic, the Kalevala, is full of vitality . . . it has influenced, in many ways, the art and culture of our country,' says Irjö Varpio. In the same way, the Hungarian authoress Ágnes Gergely, in *Focus*, wrote: 'Everything is source. The source is everything.'

The works of the past form an earth in which new creations germinate and grow, quite often in the bad weather of adversity. Anna Akhmatova – as her friend Lidia Tchukovskaïa tells us – used to carry her manuscripts in her handbag when she went out, for fear of her house being searched by the police. But she knew that she was anchored in the great poetry of Alexander Pushkin, who was also persecuted and yet triumphant.

The Swedish poet Lasse Söderberg organised meetings in Malmö during which poets went from one building to another, everywhere reciting their poems.

All through the nineteenth and twentieth centuries, Estonian poetry is marked by the presence of three women, Lydia Koidula, Marie Under and Betti Alver. During this century, German language poetry has been stimulated by a tonic élan emanating from four Jewish women poets: Else Lasker-Schüler, Nelly Sachs and, closer to us in time, Rose Ausländer and Hilde Domin. In their works, the experience of suffering and death has given life a peculiar beauty. In her collection *Der Traum hat offene Augen* (*A Dream Keeps Its Eyes Open*), Rose Ausländer uses the expression 'grüne Kräfte' (green forces). Together with her, many contemporary poets experience the need to preserve the Earth thanks to their words. In 'French Poets of Europe' (1990), René Welter, a disciple of René Char and an enemy of nuclear power plants, writes: 'Is there still an island on the Sorgue? It is in vain that they bring lorries, bulldozers, cranes, pneumatic drills, that they dig, uproot, carry off, lay asphalt, concrete, tar: the underground work of a single snowfall and there, in the first

crack: a clump of grass. There's no getting round it.'

German booksellers have created a literary peace prize, the 'Friedenspreis des Deutschen Buchhandels'. In 1990, they gave it to a Slavic scholar Karl Dedecius, and during 1991, at the instigation no doubt of Dedecius, the town of Frankfurt-am-Main awarded its Goethe prize to Wisław Szymborska, a woman poet writing in Polish. In the wake of certain social and political events in the years 1968 and 1970 – student uprisings in the West, Soviet repression in Prague, a strike in Gdansk – a new poetic movement was born in Poland; in a purified language, it sought to signal the degradation of human dignity by daily mockery. In a 'poetic autobiography', *Lebenslauf aus Büchern und Blättern*, Karl Dedecius informs us of this satirical surge. But it was above all Wisława Szymborska who was said, with an almost metaphysical humour, in a context of Baroque depiction of the world, to unveil the hard seriousness of our condition under the light veil of a serenity tinged with sadness.

Poets refuse in effect to be integrated into a fixed framework and reject any temptation to paralysis; they are faithful to their personal vision, to such an extent that Gherasim Luca, a Rumanian in Paris, was able to write in 'The prey is shaded': 'To be an outlaw / That is the question / And the only way to carry on the quest.' Codes established by tyrants stifle poetry and the poet, but the latter blossoms in life and in the word. The Portuguese poet Eugenio de Andrade (in his homeland, a very strong accent is placed on the study of one's mother tongue) explains why, in his poetry, he likes 'words which have the taste of earth, water, fruits of the fire of summer', why he likes 'words smooth like pebbles, rough like rye bread. Words which smell of hay and dust, clay and lemon, resin and the sun.' He adds: 'I could limit my answer to a quotation from Merleau-Ponty: "It is by my body that I understand others." But I would add: the importance of the body in my poetry comes from the desire to give dignity to what has been the most insulted, humiliated, despised and corrupted thing in man, at least from Plato down to the present day.'

'And the Poet also is with us, on the road of the men of his time', wrote Saint-John Perse (1887–1975) in *Winds* (1946). In looking at all the European literatures, we perceive, in big countries as in small ones, the living presence of poetry. Seizure of the object, the dramatic expression of the human condition, the sophisticated science of language, the different elements of poetic creation are nowhere lacking. From the Iberian peninsula to Cyprus, to the Caucasus, from the Crimea to Iceland, Europe expresses itself in the language of poetry. Like the knight in search of the Grail, the poet accomplishes a quest for formal perfection, spiritual elevation, human solidarity, communion with the divine. The French poet Jean-Claude Renard aspires to 'A land mature enough, a people deep enough to receive the god, / To become the bed of lightning and the river / And to allow the Spirit to make everything new!' ('The Land of the Sacred Oath', 'Psalm for Advent'). Whereas, in the English-speaking world, and let us not forget that so many European languages are written far from our own continent, a W.H. Auden (1907–1973), in his 'Ode to Terminus', thanks that pagan god for having assigned to men 'limits', rules of prosody, grammar, metrics. But out of this experience he conjures up the miracle of Pentecost, the faculty of mutual comprehension through language!

THEATRE AND THEATRICALITY

The temptation – a legitimate one? – exists to describe theatre as an autonomous genre which has cast off all that moors it to literature. 'If I were to write a book on the theatre . . .', 'in any book I would write on the theatre . . .', writes Daniel Mesguich: theatre and text have something to say to each other.

A theatre without theatricality does not exist

Barthes, as we know, called 'theatricality' everything in the theatre which was not text. Theatre may be supposed to consist of, on the one hand, a text, and on the other, theatricality; on the one hand an essential axis, the taking away of 'it was written', writing as a law unto itself, on the other a contingent axis, constantly different, relative, a troupe of actors, projectors arranged according to the configuration of the scene. On one side the absolute nature of the book, of the trail; on the other the relative values of the troupe, of physical presence. And theatre sways unceasingly from one of these sides to the other, rubbing against the improbable string that separates them. The string is called the stage and the swaying is called acting.

From time immemorial – perhaps this is more than a characteristic – the art of the theatre has been attracted by its 'limits', dangerously playing at approaching one of these sides to the point of being swallowed up by it. And there will always be a certain type of theatre which will try to confound text and theatricality, reducing or trying to reduce theatricality to zero, and a certain type of theatre which will try to confound theatricality and text, reducing or trying to reduce the text to zero. But these limits never allow themselves to be reached; neither of these sides ever completely disappears.

A theatre without theatricality does not exist, in spite of the sometimes peremptory assertions of those who, from time to time, claim to operate a return to the text by itself (a return which is only underlain by an ideological belief in its supposed purity, when it is not in the purity or the predominance of the intentions – taken for granted – of the author):even though scarcely 'said', the text is already 'played'; the empty space is only a 'certain' concept of props management; a simple lights up is equivalent to a 'certain' concept of lighting; remaining static amounts to a 'certain' kind of movement; the innerness of the acting, the absence of form is a 'certain' type of form. On a stage, with reference to the absolute nature of the written choreography, even a minor adjustment is always too much; and often this minimal theatricality, even to the extent that, taking it as insignificant, we do not 'work' on it, do not 'highlight' it on stage, do not 'open' it up, do not 'suspect' it, comes over as that much more full, that much more solid, that much more spectacular.

Text and theatricality

A theatre without a text does not exist either. We are coming out of a period – which began with Antonin Artaud, but we could take it back to the Italian futurists, and perhaps even to the ancient bacchanalia – in which the text in the theatre has seemed to recede in importance. Theatricality has reigned supreme. But it also seems – with some, sometimes magnificent, exceptions: the shows of Bob Wilson, for instance, or those of Pina Bausch – that we were starting to come out of this overly simplistic way of doing things. Not everything, in the theatre as elsewhere, is audible, catchable, intelligible except through signs which only hark back, to language, otherwise they would not be signs. Without language no sign makes sense. There is no theatricality without text in the same way that there is no sign without language, and shows without a text are, unknowingly, often only stagings of invisible texts, rather mediocre in comparison to those by Shakespeare or Beckett. The pleasure of the images alone in the theatre increasingly shows itself for what it is: an illiterate pleasure, a form of deafness.

The finest adventures in the contemporary theatre are a sounding – by the eye 'as well' – of the sense, of the meanings trapped between the lines, a bringing to a crisis – by this improbable mixture of book and actor, flesh and blood and ink – an 'overture'. The theatre, when it is not mutilated, enriches both text and theatricality.

LITERATURE IN EUROPE TOWARDS THE YEAR 2000

What comes after modernism? we asked at the beginning of this chapter. Let us begin at the end: we are not maintaining that a term such as postmodernism will serve as a symbol or a new designation for the literature of future decades. This notion and what it contains are much too closely linked, as we have seen, to a time which seems to be in the process of disappearing.

Moreover, there are also genres and potential trends which will perhaps turn out to be more important than those we have already dealt with. With the destruction and the ordinary crossing of limits between traditional genres, we are witnessing the emergence of hybrid forms, half-way between literature and philosophy, philosophy becoming literature and vice versa. In France, Maurice Blanchot, Jean-Paul Sartre and Claude Lévi-Strauss in the 1960s, Michel Foucault, Gilles Deleuze, Jean-François Lyotard, Jacques Derrida, Michel Serres and Jean Baudrillard in the 1970s and 1980s infringe the limits of traditional discourse and come closer to literature. It is not by chance if it is precisely these names which are linked with thought about the postmodern condition in different ways. The transcendence by these authors of the formal limits of genres has had an effect throughout Europe.

The limits of traditional genres are crossed 'in the other direction' by literature, as the evolution of the novel in Italy shows us. The two novels by Umberto Eco, *The Name of the Rose* and *Foucault's Pendulum*, both pose fundamental philosophical questions. Italo Calvino constantly makes use of in his later texts, especially in *Mr Palomar* (1983) and *Sotto il sole giaguaro* (*Under the Jaguar Sun*, 1986), points of view orientated towards philosophy, in a 'muted' discourse which seems to be linked to what he calls 'weak thought' (*Il pensiero debole*, 1983). This philosophical thematisation also has to do with poetry.

We must also evoke the special role that literature has played in European countries which have been submitted to different types of authoritarian regimes in which it was not able to develop freely. In countries like this it has played a very particular role: that of an echo chamber for a debate on society which could not be otherwise expressed. According to the term used by the Hungrian novelist György Konrád, it has become an 'antidote to politics', placed therefore at the opposite pole to State politics. With this aim, literature, in the prolongation of a secular tradition concentrated on the subversive potential hidden in literary works, has had to use a specific range of sophisticated means of action, as well as rhetoric, to express what it wanted. In these countries, literature has been divided into an official literature, of which a part tried to do what it could within the framework of official limits, and a literature of exile, which, to compensate for its 'freedom', had to cut itself off from its original national audience. In literary terms, the collapse of authoritarian systems gives rise to surprising paradoxes: Christa Wolf, an author of the former GDR, who, in a constantly critical way, brought the system up against its own ideals of humanism, hears herself today, after the reuniting of the two Germanies, being reproached with not having fought enough against the oppression of the old regime. The choice was not easy for a great many writers from these countries to stay where they were and, in often difficult conditions, to try to fight on with their pen. To malignly reproach them with not having known what everyone knows today is, quite often, to be historically knowledgeable after the event.

A European literature?

Is it conceivable that the social and economic integration of Europe should contribute to the formation of a new authentically European literature? Two elements must be emphasised here. First, a European literature cannot 'spring up': it has always existed *per se*. The phenomenon that we call 'literature' developed throughout Europe; even important contributions which came from elsewhere, for example those of North American writers from Poe to Auster, were, one way or another, elements in this movement.

If we examine the history of European literature, there has always been a decisive interplay between similarity and difference. We find the the similarity in the fundamental concept of the aesthetic function itself, which has progressively formed and developed the concept of 'literature', and a similarity in certain general historical tendencies. But literature has also been marked by an effervescence of differences, from one work to another, from one subject area to another, from one country to another. And if there is the prospect of integration, nothing in history has until now indicated that this sort of integration implied uniformity or falling into line. We can see this in bilingual societies like Belgium, but also in Great Britain, where autonomous national literatures flourish.

Literature will know how to survive in tomorrow's Europe much longer than its anxious guardians. Nor will it necessarily need special subsidies to survive. But it may be desirable to 'artificially' maintain literature at least in one sense: translation. If the readers and poets of the new Europe are to be able to profit from the multiplicity, the calibre and the heterogeneous nature of this literature, it is no doubt necessary to contribute financially to its dissemination beyond borders. Multilingualism will be and must be henceforth the special defining characteristic of Europe. Literature is one of the reasons for this multilingualism. It is also one of its consequences. So European literature appears overall as a multiplicity of differences. There are a great many literatures and a single Literature.

The Aesthetics of the Fragment

D. Viart

Hack [the work] into many fragments, and you will see that each fragment can have a separate existence.

Charles Baudelaire,
The Spleen of Paris

The fragment and fragmentary writing are not particularly linked with any one period, but came especially into favour in the twentieth century. We must make a distinction between the fragment that remains of a complete work, the whole of which is not known to us, and that produced deliberately by the writer. The fortuitous forms of fragments are only important in this connection in the reception and reading that other writers who take them as the models for their own works give to them: 'A book is only beautiful when skilfully adorned with indifference to ruins,' wrote Georges Bataille. Often confused with the aphoristic form, which gives us brief but complete and self-contained texts, fragmentary writing cannot break free of this parentage: from the German Romantics to Cioran or René Char, the writer who espouses fragmentary outburst often has recourse to 'Witz' (wit) and aphorism. In the seventeenth century, Pascal's *Thoughts* already offer an example of this mixture of maxims and unfinished bits.

The nineteenth century makes a particular space for this literary form in its enterprise of renewing and contesting classical models of thought and writing. From the beginning of the century, the Schlegel brothers (*Athenäum, Critical Fragments*) and Novalis (*Pollens*) gave German Romanticism its most polished fragments. With them this form acquired a new status in which may be measured the crisis of classical concepts of the work. Philosophers like Kierkegaard and Schopenhauer find in it a means of getting round linear rationality, and Nietzsche uses it as a weapon against metaphysics. In poetry, after Baudelaire had laid claim to textual fragmentation in the dedication of the *Spleen of Paris* – 'Hack [the work] into numerous fragments, and you will see that each fragment can have a separate existence' – *Un coup de dés* (*A Roll of Dice*) by Mallarmé inaugurated the typographical fragmentation that the twentieth-century avant-garde will seize on, an avant-garde for whom the fragment can also be cultivated in the shape of collages, whether cubist, futurist or surrealist.

The fragment and modernity

Fragmentary writing is thus solidly linked to the great myths and the breaks of modernity, which, playing at sketching out work and avoiding completeness, looks for a suitable way of expressing its rejections (literary genres, completeness, a certain form of discursive rationality.). It is unceasingly worked at, in a variety of forms, during the first half of the twentieth century, some writers favouring, in this practice, the unfinished aspect that it lends to a work, others the surprising encounters it allows in the game of collage. The names of Valéry (*Cahiers, Tel Quel*), of Kafka, of Ramón Gómez de la Serna (*Greguerías*), of Ezra Pound (*Cantos*) suffice to indicate the widespread nature of the phenomenon. Fragmentary writing is still very much admired by some of the major postwar literary figures (Georges Bataille, *The Inner Experience*, 1943), it triumphs in the field of a certain kind of poetry (René Char, *The Sheets of Hypnos*, 1945, *The Word in the Archipelago*, 1962). For many writers, the fragment bears witness to the failure of global discourse (Cioran, *Summary of Decomposition*, 1949).

In the 1960s and 1970s, the practice of writing in fragments and, above all, the theory underpinning it, go through their halcyon days. Maurice Blanchot, for whom 'words in which are revealed the demands of the fragmentary do not contradict the whole', harps on it in *The Infinite Conversation* (1969), *The Step Further* (1973), right up to *The Writing of Disaster* (1980). Roland Barthes gives us his *Roland Barthes by Roland Barthes* in this deliberately fragmented form. In its broken spontaneity, the fragment is potentially the finished work that it nevertheless impugns by its incompleteness. It designates that absence towards which it tends without deciding to enter, in an enterprise which smacks of 'idling'. Several English experimental authors, occasionally influenced by the 'cut up' of William Burroughs, have recourse to similar practices: Alan Burns pursues a task of writing novels dominated by the requirement of fragmentation. Eva Figes, from

Equinox (1966) to *Waking* (1983), constructs her stories like broken mosaics. Giles Gordon pieces together short syncopated stories (*100 Scenes from Married Life: A Selection*, 1976) and Penelope Shuttle deploys a proliferation of aphorisms in *Rainsplitter in the Zodiac Garden* (1972). The Spaniard Sánchez-Ortiz radical-ises experimental fragmentation in works like *P(royecto) De M(onólogo) A 3 S(oldados)* (*P(lan) Of A M(onologue) To 3 S(oldiers)*, 1973) and *O* (1975). Innovative work by Torrente Ballester also turns towards this type of experience in *Fragmentos de apocalipsis* (*Fragments of Apocalypse*, 1977). We must also mention, within the 'Viennese group', the poem-montages of Hans-Carl Artmann, which combine collages, neologisms and segments of dialect, and the work of many European experimentalists of this decade. Production in general tends to offer a frag-mented representation of the subject which, no longer being able to shelter under the sign of a unique, stable identity, exhibits an irreducible bittiness. The presentation on the page of the poems of André du Bouchet, *Laisses* (1975), *Incoherence* (1979), inherited from Mallarmé and Reverdy, shows us that scattered effect that no linear discourse can assume.

The calling into question of the modernist trend and the return of the subject in the 1980s does not appear to have indicated the immi-nent demise of the fragment. Just when the end of the century seems to herald the twilight of this aesthetic aggression, its survival in literary production remains manifest. Even if it sometimes evokes *A Technical Embarrassment with Regard to Fragments* (Pascal Quignard, 1986), the postmodern aesthetic, in its pronounced taste for the composition of heterogeneous fragments, its deliberate prac-tice of having recourse to quotations, leads to the reactivation of fragmentary writing. The latter finds other justifications for itself: far from appearing as the weapon of cultural rupture, it becomes the mode of writing of a reality apprehended in its irreducible dispersion and enters *a contrario* in virtuoso compositional games and constructions.

The image and its fragmentation

In the 1980s, Bulgarian poetry willingly favours the fragment to render a particular viewpoint or an isolated image. In the same way, in Hungary, the work of Gyorgý Petri turns towards a concerted fragmentary poetry, designed to depict social decomposition, the reflection of a world breaking up, a wounded society, deprived of its values and cohesive-ness. Constructed more often than not around an image, Petri's strongly elliptical verses prefer allusions to any kind of development. Suitable for critical use, this dense, concise writing is also that of the Finno-Swedish writer, Willy Kyrklund, who only uses short forms to express himself in short stories, novellas or aphorisms. Such enterprises are not very different in the way they are executed from those that preceded them, but they increasingly eschew the legitimisation of a use of the fragmentary which belongs henceforth to the order of straightforward statement, of the seizure and immediate transcription of a reality that no discourse can organise or put into perspective.

Our epoch has persuaded itself that writing can only now capture fragments of reality. The Polish poet Miron Bialoszewski, who since 1955 has been exploring and exploiting the verbal dross of daily conversational exchanges, comes over as a precursor. He nurtures his poems like his prose works (*Rustlings, Collages, Series*, 1976) in this unworked-on manner, giving a literature close to what the visual disciplines call 'art in the raw'. Similar ele-ments are sometimes found in the theatre of Franz Marijnen and Tadeus Kantor, who reproduce in this way the recurrent fragments of personal traumas fixed in a wounded memory. In Greece, Thanassis Valtinos wrote short texts, mingled with silence (*Three Greek Plays in One Act*, 1978). His book *Elements of the 1960s* (1989) combines fragments of newspaper advertisements and articles, many letters and news-in-brief items, juxtaposed without commentary. The Italian poet Mario Luzi tries to bring together these fragments offered by the world by pursuing the vital principle which underlies them in *For the Baptism of Our Fragments* (1985). Edoardo Sanguinetti is happy just to note down snatches in his *Postkarten* (1978). *Vlaanderen, ook een land (Flanders, Also a Country,* 1987), one of the volumes in the *Diary in the Raw* by Ivo Michiels, is characteristic of the stratified, fragmented novel: an ambiguous evocation of Flanders, intertextuality, an essay on memory and especially on the gaps in it.

The virtuosity of fragmentary composition

But efforts at composition, mainly 'montages', based on principles sometimes inherited from modernism, are everywhere having a new lease of life: in Germany, *Leben und Abenteuer der Trobadora Beatriz (The Life and Adventures of the Troubadour Beatrice,* 1974), a voluminous and polyphonic novel by Irmtraud Morgner, in which a hundred varied tales are inter-mingled, is composed like a patchwork of mythological fragments, current affairs and various humorous testimonies. In Spain, Julián Rios follows a similar path with *Larva, Babel de una noche de San Juan (Larva. Babel on St John's Night,* 1983), in which various languages, quotations, footnotes (sometimes with secondary footnotes appended) and photos all contribute to a hotchpotch, inspired by Pound, as another work by Rios explicitly recognises: *Poundemonium. Homenaje a Ezra Pound (Poundemonium. A Homage to Ezra Pound,* 1986). In The Netherlands, for Gerrit Krol, the spaces between the fragments are almost more important than the fragments themselves: the reader has the chance to create their own novel.

The case of Serbian literary output, which concurrently presents the multiple facets of fragmented experience, is perhaps the most archetypal example: Bora Cosic takes from the avant-garde the technique of collage in his novel *Uloga moje porodice u svetskoj revoluciji (The Role of my Family in World Revolution,* 1969). *Zivotopis Malvine Trifkovic (The Biography of Malvina Trifkovic,* 1979) by Mirko Kovac limits itself to the listing of verbal statements, expert medical or legal opinions, wills, testimonies and the contents of letters. In the previous year, his fragmentary novel *Vatra od utrobe (The Gate of Entrails,* 1978) intertwined the fragmented tale of a family breakdown, jointly conducted by a narrator who is half-child, half-adult and by a chronicler, with metatextual commentaries on novel writing. *Hazardski recnik (Khazar Dictionary,* 1984) by Milorad Pavic is the surprising story of a lost civilisation and its enigmatic conversion to one of the three monotheistic religions – Judaism, Christianity and Islam respectively – reported in the shape of three juxtaposed dictionaries. The frag-ments are therefore a collection of notices and articles in which the reader is free to organise his own stroll. Developing an ambiguous game in which the rejection of all traditional linearity is contrasted with a concern for underlying order, both neutral (alphabetical order) and compositional (the triptych, the echoes and the internal references), this text develops a dimension of parody which fragmentary writing, up until this point rather serious, was hardly acquainted with. The same organ-isational principle borrowed from lexis may be found elsewhere, but with noticeably different intentions. In France there is the publication of the essays, *Fragments of an Amorous Discourse* (1977) by Roland Barthes, and in Denmark of the poems, *Alfabet* (1981) by Inger Christensen.

The option of fragmentary writing does not exclude the internal composition of the work, whatever that is. Renouncing linearity, the latter becomes a montage or a dictionary. Collages continue to fascinate writers from several countries: the Dane Klaus Rifbjerg, Peter Laugesen and his 'spontaneous' poetry, Rodolfo Wilcock, born in Buenos Aires of an English father and an Italian mother, who similarly mixes in his works in Italian pictures, sketches and narrative collages inspired by Kafka and Swift. In the collections by the Flemish writer Stefan Hertmans, *Zoutsneeuw (Snow of Salt,* 1987) and *Bezoekingen (Afflic-tions,* 1988), the description of the inner world is interspersed with allusions to cultural heritage and mythology. This fragmentation is also characteristic of work by Dirk Van Bastelaere. In the field of autobiography, the fragment also has a certain amount of success, with, for example, the triptych (1978–1983) by Leo Pleysier where room is allowed for papers stuck in, assembled from letters, scraps of intimate diaries, bits of history or cinema. Sometimes the composition is more kaleidoscopic, as in the Dutch novel *Vincent of het geheim van zijn vaders lichaam* (*Vincent or the Secret of His Father's Corpse*, 1981) by Rudy Kousbroek, who mingles and permutes different texts.

The ingeniousness of such compositions borders in some works on virtuosity; in Italy, Giorgio Manganelli presents in his novel *Centurie* (1979) 'a hundred long sagas in miniature', in which 'the hasty reader will only see texts made up of sparse and spare lines'. On a slightly different model, the Dane Peer Hultberg published *Requiem* (1985), a work which combines five hundred and thirty-seven brief tales, picked out of the internal monologues of anonymous characters whose isolation is made apparent by the confrontation of fragments. This work of fragmentary composition characterises the contemporary epoch which thus affirms the power and agility of artistic creation without subscribing to aesthetic theories that modernism has gone some way towards calling into question. The choice of using fragments also allows us to borrow what seems good from works of the past without necessarily adhering to the principles which motivated them.

The triumph of the use of quotations and parody indicates a new stage in the literary management of the fragment: the latter is justified both as a borrowing or throwback to an artistic form of which only one aspect is chosen to be saved, and as a presentation of a reality which is definitively plural and broken up. In its rejection – and its criticism – of all synthetic conceptualisation of the varied, postmodern writing can only offer the orphans of collapsed ideologies disenchanted virtuosity at work in these surprising fragmentary compositions. Whether sceptical or cynical, critical or playful, the fragment constitutes one of the main resources of the literature of the end of this century. If it has, to a large extent, stopped being the instrument of a definite break wielded by defunct modernity, it remains the only atom of reality or discourse on the basis of which it is still possible to write.

Writers of the Late Twentieth Century

Vizma Belševica (1931–)

During the years of Soviet occupation, Vizma Belševica, with other poets like Ojárs Vacietis, Imants Ziedonis, Knuts Skujenieks and Egils Plaudis, counted as one of the most noteworthy writers in Latvia. Born of working-class parents, she finished her literary studies at the Gorky Institute in Moscow in 1961. She belongs to that category of Soviet authors who know all about spying, censorship and interrogations from personal experience.

Vizma Belševica has published many collections of poetry, including *Visu ziemu šogad pavasaris* (*For the Whole of Winter This Year Spring*, 1955), *Jura deg* (*The Sea is Burning*, 1966), *Dzeltu laiks* (*The Season that Bites*, 1987), and her collection for young people *Ievziedu aukstums* (*The Cold of the Wild Cherry Trees*, 1988), Among her prose works mention may be made of *Kikuraga stasti* (*Kikurags's Tales*, 1965) and *Nelaime majas* (*Misfortune in the Home*, 1979). She has also written screenplays and translated English, Russian and Ukrainian works into Latvian.

Vizma Belöevica was the first Latvian writer to set little store by the imperatives of 'socialist realism' and to try to describe reality in the full complexity of its contradictions. As her approach did not fit the straitjacket of official literary ideology, exalting hate, revenge and pathos, she was deemed a 'heretic'. She showed herself capable of breaking with this ideology by indicating that man, with all his affective and intellectual peculiarities, occupies a relatively small place in the dynamics of life in the world. She has known how to combine life and vitality with the emotions of peace and silence, arousing dramatic effect in this way. Thus she has revived the Latvian literary tradition by adding to it a seeking after new ideas and by practising at the same time a realism reinvigorated by classicism – ideas that come naturally – simplicity, clarity; she has brought together all these constituents in a particular overall vision, also characterised by the inspiration of the grotesque, paradox and passion.

The poetic space in which Vizma Belševica works plays on contrasts – mountains / valleys, silence / cries, thirst / the quenching of thirst – which, at a pinch, can be transformed into thirds – sky / earth / marsh, thirst / quenching / drying up. Spatial harmony is symbolised by the heart, flowers, a cross. In order to explore the subconscious mind, she has recourse to the language of surrealism.

Under the Soviet occupation, Vizma Belševica was the first writer to have the courage to proclaim that art allows a nation to become aware of itself.

For this author the road that leads to freedom goes through non-conformity, moral rectitude, the use of a language rich in symbols, analogies and images. The cross occupies the main focus of her imagination, but there is no divorce between the cross and ancient Baltic nature symbols: fire, water, the tree, the bird. Her vigorous imagination expresses itself best in personification when this is combined with hyperbole and a recourse to symbols. Thus she is able to integrate into the image the gradual transition from myth to an epic age. Vizma Belševica is a love poet, capable of seeing what is typical and universal in what is unique and personal. The aim of her demanding love is the same as that of the Renaissance masters – a love that remains unappeased – not only that but it can only be expressed in imagery which is laconically harsh and concrete.

In the context of Latvian fiction of the period following the Second World War, we must remember Vizma Belševica's contribution to the revival of the short story, in which she insists on grotesque and tragi-comic elements. Her short stories take the form of monologues, having as their centre strong, colourful middle-aged women who have the admirable ability to face up to all the situations imaginable. In poetry as in prose, Vizma Belševica handles the Latvian language with an extraordinary mastery.

Caryl Churchill (1938–)

Caryl Churchill is a British dramatist who is not afraid of breaking the rules, a fact to which her plays bear witness. Among her characters are to be found seventeenth-century witches, a dancing Dionysos and the ruthless speculators of the 1980s. She has written about sexuality and politics, social injustice, violence and crime as well as about personal relationships. Sometimes sarcastic and funny, sometimes austere and moving, her plays invite reflection and discussion; their unravelling is unpredictable. The dramatic form that she uses is unconventional, whether the action is placed in colonial Africa or in a London stockbroker's office. She often mingles irrational elements with realism and sometimes songs and dances are an integral part of the text.

Caryl Churchill began writing during her student years at Oxford University, but was only recognised as a dramatist in the 1970s. She describes *Traps* (1978) as an 'impossible object' which can only be real in the theatre. Her characters have a variety of opportunities to do things, whether in the field of personal relationships or in terms of acquiring skills. While she started her career as a solitary writer

who only showed people her work when it was finished, she subsequently collaborated with several theatre companies. She has written some of her plays with other dramatists. The plays *Light Shining in Buckinghamshire* (1976) and *Vinegar Tom* (1976) were both collaborative efforts, the first with the Joint Stock theatre company and the second with Monstrous Regiment. Thanks to workshop discussions and improvisations in which the actors, the director and the playwright worked together, it was possible to formulate new ideas.

Probably because of these working methods, the individuality of the characters is often considered as unimportant and one actor often plays two parts. *Vinegar Tom* relates a witch-hunt perpetrated in the seventeenth century. The contemporary songs that accompany the play link the fate of the witches to that of women today: 'Who are the witches now? / Ask how they're stopping you now.' Another play about sexuality and gender roles is *Cloud Nine*, a comedy in which a parallel is traced between sexual oppression and imperialism. The first Act takes place in an African colony at the time of Queen Victoria and the second Act in present-day London, showing the evolution of attitudes about sexuality. In 1982, Caryl Churchill wrote *Top Girls*, a play whose characters are all women and which describes the success of women in Margaret Thatcher's Britain. In the beginning, the praises are being sung of the main character who has just been appointed the director of an employment agency, but the play goes on to consider the question of the cost and nature of success in a world which is still dominated by men. One of the most remarkable passages in this work is the first Act, in which an extraordinary dinner-party is given at which famous women, historical, artistic and literary figures, talk about their lives. Caryl Churchill returned to the theme of material success in a satire composed entirely in verse *Serious Money* (1987). Considered as 'a comedy about the City', it deals with the greed and ruthlessness of a group of 1980s speculators who play the financial markets. One of the characters, a woman, says of herself: 'I'm greedy and totally amoral', which admirably sums up the nature of the characters in this play.

Caryl Churchill's talent is to know how to mix social conscience with an original theatrical form which makes her one of the most interesting contemporary British dramatists.

Emil Mihaï Cioran (1911–1995)

Cioran was born in 1911 in Rashinari, a large Transylvanian village on the outskirts of Sibiu, in Rumania. His father was an Orthodox priest. His mother was a saintly woman. His memory of her underlies his writing and gives it a lyrical feel. There are two types of writing, two periods in Cioran's work: from 1930 to 1940 the author thinks, plans and writes in Rumanian, his native language; after 1949 (the year when his *Summary of Decomposition* was published in Paris), he chose French as the language of his writing and will be henceforth a writer who expresses himself in French.

Cioran's first philosophical essay is called *Pe culmile disperarii* (*On the Summits of Despair*, 1934). It already contains the themes of his meditation on God, on Creation, on existential anguish and on the 'drawback of having been born'. Men go off the rails falling prey to the feeling of nothingness which is the negation of God. Everything collapses around them. Cioran notes in the margin of a chapter: 'It gives me a strange feeling to think that at my age [he is twenty-two] I have become a specialist on the problem of death!' The tone is feverish, nurtured by the lyrical resources of subjectivity. It is interesting to note, twenty-two years later, in *The Temptation of Existence* (1956), how his propositions are being refined through writing in French: the desperate confession before the 'nothing' that is death changes to cerebral doubt under the sardonic smile of the moralist. The lyricism of subjectivity is a barbaric outburst 'of blood, sincerity and flames'. In 1936 *Schimbarea la fata a României* (*The Transfiguration of Rumania*) appears, an unusual work for a young man who had chosen a 'metaphysical exile' and decided to distance himself from the political

morality and culture of the masses. Cioran engages in a sort of cultural Messianism which germinates in the strength of soul of the Rumanian people, armed with potent myths and the will to assert itself in the universality of enlightened humanism, but bearing primarily the stamp of a creativity peculiar to a nation. 'A people becomes a nation when it affirms its spiritual values as universal values.' In *Lacrimi si sfinti* (*Tears and Saints*, 1937), Cioran returns to his stoical meditation contemplating man and his precarious condition within a limited and finite world that rejects him. Man's 'salvation' will come out of his passions, more precisely from tears 'of blood and flames', from heroic adventures that miscarry, from asceticism. Cioran's passions are music, female saints, hesychastic mystics. He also has a soft spot for iconoclastic madmen, nihilists and pessimists who make out that life is a dream. He has something to do with all these people, out of fear of death which is matter and terror: 'We cannot die elegantly without going round it.' Going round it with the art of living. Since 1949, Cioran has continued to pursue his 'philosopher's' quest, to write his moralist's essays in French, including *The Summary of Decomposition*, *Syllogisms of Bitterness* (1952), *The Temptation of Existence, History and Utopia* (1960), *The Fall in Time* (1965), *The Evil Demigod* (1969), *The Drawback of Having Been Born* (1973), *Quartering* (1979), *Confessions and Anathemas* (1981) and *Exercises in Admiration* (1985). He goes on with a 'nihilistic work', according to some, and produces stimulating irony in which he underlines; with delicate touches, the sometimes delightful absurdity of man floating aimlessly, of his mortal passions and of his being prey to the feeling of nothingness which is the negation of God. Stylistically may be added the trembling 'phrasing' of a latter-day Pascal: a flower from a cultivated French garden. It has been grown and tended lovingly. It still has the grace of the flower of the fields that Cioran picked in his native land. 'Born in Cyprus, Zeno, the father of stoicism, was a hellenised Phoenician who retained his foreignness right until the end of his life!' says

Cioran, speaking of another exile. A superb metaphor.

Umberto Eco (1929–)

Born in Alexandria in 1932, Umberto Eco currently works as a teacher of semiology at the Italian university of Bologna. An essayist, a story-teller, a journalist (he works for *L'Espresso* and *La Repubblica*), he directs the review of semiotic studies *versus*. He has held and continues to hold important editorial functions. Attracted primarily by medieval aesthetics, in 1956 he published his doctoral thesis, *Il problema estetico in San Tommaso* (*The Aesthetic Problem in St Thomas Aquinas*), and in 1985 *Arte e belleza nell'estetica medievale* (*Art and Beauty in Medieval Aesthetics*).

With *Opera operta* (*The Open Work*, 1962), his attention is focused on the problems of contemporary literature and justifies his participation in the debates of the neo-avant-garde, which is called Gruppo '63 (in 1966, he published *Le poetiche di Joyce*, *The Poetics of Joyce*). His interest in the language leads him to think about the problem of mass communication (*Apocalittici e integrati*, *Apocalyptics and the Integrated*, 1964) which prompts him both to do research on the popular novel in the nineteenth century (*Il superuomo di masa*, *The Superman of the Masses*, 1976) and to test his opinions against the themes of structuralism. However, Eco refuses the *a priori* and onto-logical basis of structuralism (*La struttura assente*, *The Absent Structure*, 1968) and launches semiological research that will result in 1975 in the *Trattato di semiotica generale* (*General Treatise on Semiotics*), on pragmatic foundations inspired by the positions of Peirce. His reflection on the problems of art (*La Definizione dell'arte*, *The Definition of Art*, 1968, *Le Forme del contenuto*, *The Forms of the Content*, 1971) is located not only in a more general philosophical perspective (*Semiotica e filosofia del linguaggio*, *The Semiotics and Philosophy of Language*, 1984), but also leads him to investigate the role of the reader (*Lector in fabula*, 1979) who is not the passive beneficiary of the text, but collaborates in the construction of its meaning and participates in the process of interpretation.

A first attempt to leave the area of criticism in the direction of a more independent exercise of literary writing is the inspiration behind *Diario minimo* (*Minimal Diary*, 1963), a collection of ironical and debunking digressions on various aspects of literature and manners, in a movement of fantasy which links up with extremes of parody and the 'nonsense' of Borges. This diary has been completed by a second *Minimal Diary* (1992). But the whole of Eco's theoretical and cultural reflection will be summed up in 1980 by his novel *Il nome della rosa* (*The Name of the Rose*). Conceived as an imitation not of reality but of literature, *The Name of the Rose* operates a grandiose and original synthesis of avant-garde procedures and the demands of traditional narration, in the classical and nineteenth-century sense of the term. In 1971, Eco was busy with an anthology of novels in instalments called *Il ritorno dell'intreccio* (*The Return of the Plot*). The plot consisted in the quest for a murderer who commits several crimes in a fourteenth century monastery and its labyrinthine library (books play an essential role here as they are both a symbol of freedom and carriers of death). On this historical foundation, and following the clues of a murder enquiry, the cloistered walks of a novel in the shape of a philosophical essay develop which, to represent the ideological and social contrasts of the end of the Middle Ages, is transformed into an allegorical projection of the contradictions of the present, as a conflict between the forces of progress and those of reaction, of the rational and the irrational (personified by William of Baskerville and his adversary Jorge de Burgos). *The Name of the Rose*, which can be read on different levels (and which we can then characterise according to the level chosen as an open or closed work), can also be defined as a semiotic and intertextual novel, composed, in large measure, of echoes and quotations from other books, in a chain of references which, without neglecting to set up values, do not aim at giving consoling and problem-solving certainties. The same literary 'game' also maintains a background of dark tragedy which is revealed particularly in the symbolic final apocalypse (we could say that the great theme of the death of God is accompanied by the possibility of living without Him), allowing an anguish to persist which escapes from all rational solution. It is not by chance if Eco, paraphrasing Wittgenstein, wrote: 'What one cannot theorise about must be told.' In some respects, *Il pendolo di Foucault* (*Foucault's Pendulum*, 1988), uses the same methods of composition as those used in *The Name of the Rose*. But the field here seems enlarged and, overturning temporal realtionships, the novel starts in the present to go back to the past (the three protagonists, editors in a firm of publishers, are hot on the trail of a mysterious plan which goes back to the medieval order of the Templars and try to decode it with the help of a computer). The presence of a more anxious and tormented autobiographical element (the tale is told in the first person), finds its response in the deepening of a theme of horror and the irrational, burdened with inextricable references to esoteric, magical and cabalistic traditions.

Per Olov Enquist (1934–)

Per Olov Enquist is the most representative writer of the new generation of Swedish writers of the 1960s which, while criticising the psychological realism and the autocracy of Sweden's authors, wanted to experiment with the possibilities inherent in writing. Enquist is the saboteur of uniformity in one of the most discussed prose experiments of the age, *Hess* (1966) in which the novel and the meta-novel play with the reader, asking him if, rhetorically, it is possible to find in the text a single human being. In *Magnitisörens femte vinter* (*The Mesmerist's Fifth Winter*, 1964) Enquist had made the hero of a novel out of a criminal; he comments indirectly in the following manner on his role as a creator: 'The novel is a deception, but a necessary deception.'

It is with such formal exercises practising the art of uncertainty and an attack on the monopoly of truth that Enquist builds up his role as a writer in the 1960s, years marked by ideology and confessions. His novel on the highly controversial loss of the Baltic provinces in 1946, *Legionärerna* (*The Legionaries*, 1968), is much noticed. This time the documentation is authentic and the book, which calls into question the conventional Swedish writing of history, has a strong political impact. This novel devoted to a dramatic period of contemporary history simultaneously indulges in how the narrator, influenced by his story, colours it with his own judgements. As the author tries to elucidate the past, it is he himself who is elucidated by the present.

In his next novel *Sekonden* (*The Witness*, 1971), the role of the narrator Enquist is that of an investigator, a questioner, any individual who leads a discussion on truth, morality and politics. The main character is a hammer-thrower who cheats; he is also the social democratic reformer who breaks with the message of solidarity.

Opposite his pitiful distress there stands, politically orthodox and ready for the class struggle, the worker hero from the East. The novel's contradictions make concrete a Swedish dilemma. A sympathetic and un-problematic worker allows himself to be invaded by the myths of success and thus becomes a traitor to himself. This compromise is much too a high price, according to Enquist. Confronted by the excesses of idealism, he ends up by accepting the human deception of the hammer-thrower. With ideological positions more explicit than before, Enquist abandons absolutist formulations and recognises the necessity of compromise, of moderate demands. This means a renewal of interest in the individual at a point in time when, on the contrary, collective responsibility was being preached.

The real discovery of Enquist by the reading public happened in the 1970s and 1980s: it was then he made his stage debut with *Tribadernas natt* (*The Night of the Lesbians*, 1976), his play about August Strindberg and Siri von Essen, whose success very quickly assumed international proportions. *Till Fedra*

(*For Phaedra*, 1980) and *Från regnormarnas liv* (*Scenes from the Life of a Worm*, 1981) consolidate his place in Swedish literature. The naturalist construction of his plays is perfectly adapted to the popular, rich Swedish theatrical tradition by virtue of his choice of themes (the ups-and-downs of love), even if Enquist perseveres in his search for form, always opposed to aesthetic realism. His one-act play *I lodjurets timma* (*Unloading Time*, 1988) represents a formal departure as, questioning himself about the integrity of the individual, the answer comes as love. In the short story *Nedstörtad ängel* (*The Fallen Angel*, 1985), the search to understand an unfathomable love is stripped of all narcissism. We have reached man's limits.

José Ensch (1942–)

A French-language poet, José Ensch was born in Luxembourg. Through her family first of all, and thanks to the special structure of education in Luxembourg, she was initiated into Germanic civilisation as much as into the culture of France.

In Germany, Bonn, and in France, Nancy and Paris, José Ensch undertook an in-depth study of literature. At the end of her higher education, she decided to devote herself to the study of French language and literature. Back in Luxembourg, she completes her formation as a future teacher in secondary and higher education, and she defends before a Luxembourg jury a literary memoir on the sister of the painter Mario Prassinos, Gisèle Prassinos-Fridas, whose poetic gifts from adolescence had dazzled the surrealists.

José Ensch entitled her work 'Gisèle Prassinos – From the Child Prodigy of Surrealism to Today's Novelist. Evolution, Correspondence.' Out of this work was born a deep friendship between a woman from Luxembourg and the whole of the Prassinos family. José Ensch has never stopped being passionately interested in the creative evolution of Gisèle Prassinos. After having taught French literature in a high-school in Luxembourg, she returned to Paris to further her research in the field of surrealist poetry. After she returned to her own country, she undertook, for the Canadian publisher, Antoine Naaman, the compilation of a study of the poetic work of Gisèle Prassinos: a veritable in-depth exploration of the act of creation, of the birth-process of a work of art: *Listening to Gisèle Prassinos – a Greek Voice* (1986).

In parallel with these various activities, José Ensch wrote poetry that she kept locked up at home, allowing it to mature in silence. A gifted musician and painter, excelling in artistic 'odd jobs', José Ensch lays hold of the world's reality with ears, eyes and hands. This experience of life contributes to the enrichment of her own poetry. With Gisèle Prassinos, she did exercises in 'writing with the left hand': creative expression seems to change its character when the poet, in order to write, changes hands. Very sensitive to vocal expression, she studies diction and dramatic art – and this factor is not without influence on the voice of this artist.

She travels to Greece and the Romanic lands, Italy, Spain, Portugal. It is, however, Provence that becomes her second home, the maritime Alps and the beaches of the Mediterranean breathe into her poetry the force of air and water.

Her first collection of poems, appearing in 1984, was called *The Tree*. The author, very attached to her roots, her family and her country tends to wax lyrical. The creative endeavours of José Ensch, characterised by meticulousness – a painful struggle 'with the angel' – tend towards the transcendence evoked by the title of her second collection: *Elsewhere . . . for sure* (1985). Labouring under a desire for the absolute, José Ensch has experienced the suffering of serious illnesses, the tragedy of sterility, the crossing of the 'desert': she continues, nonetheless, to believe in the existence of that 'elsewhere' which, first and foremost perhaps, consists in the happiness of giving birth to a finished work.

Representing Luxembourg at various international poetry meetings, she publishes her poems in numerous reviews both in Luxembourg and abroad. Two of her most recent collections are *The Profile and the Shadows* and *In the Cages of the Wind*. The form of these poems which initially was pregnant and concise has expanded into long streams of blood, tears or salt water. Suddenly there springs up the cry of deliverance, of giving birth: 'Your womb is rich / with ink limpid in the blood / like a bird in the fountain of the sky.' Her human experience, her French culture, though nurtured by a certain amount of Germanic sap, guarantee José Ensch her place in European letters.

Péter Esterházy (1950–)

'Our countries are in the process of changing,' wrote the Hungarian Péter Esterházy in one of his essays, written towards the end of 1989. 'We believed – at least, I believed – that never, never ever, that habit of lying, that I grew up with, would change, that there would always be that constant pulling; there are worse things, it's true, but that practice itself is completely corrupt. But, there we are, things have changed, something we can see from Moscow to here. Like the new joke has it: it's an insane system, but at least we can speak freely.'

For Esterházy, it is a sort of literary game worthy of OULIPO to be a spokesman in a country 'of the East' after the Soviet takeover. The absurdity which reigned there was made worse by the practice of lying, an amalgam, officially, of a new Orwellian language, and, more or less privately, of the weariness that comes from being pulled at: in everyday life, should one speak or shut oneself up in a silence without complicity? A trained mathematician, this particular prose-writer settled into a world of games, phrases one inside the other, indirect expression and allusiveness. The latter becomes scholarly and ironical, because it is inviting a whole library, 'its' works and 'its' writers, to participate in the modulation of his words so as to be able to hide behind them. He conjures them up as so many guests in the tragedy and futility of his existence described with the help of the bourgeois values of a repressed past, still alive, in spite of everything, but living in internal exile. Esterházy is a representative figure for his generation for whom these values, 'European' ones they say, were part of a heritage transmitted through literature, the arts in general, a few furtive nods towards the West – idealised as a repository of ideals held up to ridicule in the East – and through an oral tradition coming from the family. The experience of these values being partly verbal, partly linked to the intimacy of a circle of family and friends ever under threat, this descendant of an illustrious Hungarian family became a craftsman with words, an intimist both sentimental and grotesque in his descriptions. He discovers. or rediscovers, the anecdote, the little stories told in the salons and cafés of former times. This was also a source of inspiration for one of his masters from the end of the previous century, the novelist Kálmán Mikszáth, evoked in his first novel *Termelési regény* (*Three Angels Watch Over Me*, 1979). He parodies the novel of production, a genre imposed by socialist realism (the first part of the book), and a cycle of anecdotes (the second part), by means of which the daily life and intimacy of a family are revealed thanks to the narrator, the Master, whose words are reported by a certain E. – E. for Eckermann or Esterházy. The anecdote recovers its original sense, its 'secret story' in another novel, *Kis Magyar Pornográfia* (*A Small Hungarian Pornography*, 1984), a series of incidents which relate the doings of members of the secret police.

The point of view adopted to describe this small 'porno set-up' may remind us of a whole tradition of absurdist literature, from Bulgakov to Gombrowicz and Hrabal (to whom is dedicated *Hrabal könyve*, *The Book of Hrabal*, 1990). Other texts can be suggested for a parallel reading with the books of Georges Perec or Peter Handke, like the tale of someone in their death throes in *A szív segédigéi* (*The Auxiliary Verbs of the Heart*, 1985), or the evocation of Agnes in *Ki szavatol a lady biztonságáért?* (*Who can Guarantee the Safety of Lady?* 1982), the story of a love and of a town both real and fictional, the Berlin of the Wall. The sprightly yet melancholic tone of *Tizenkét hattyúk* (*Twelve Swans*, 1987) brings even more strongly into focus the fundamental problem of narration with Esterházy: that of the fragment.

The anecdotal point of departure comes from a tradition of literature and values transmitted orally, but it is an element that forms part of Esterházy's aesthetics when the writer brings together in a single book under one cover several works already published separately. The eloquent title of the collection *Bevezetés a szépirodalomba* (*An Introduction to Belles-Lettres*, 1986) suggests a conception of literature that is both modern and traditional: the tales and the novels, just like the anecdotes, those fragments of life, are merely pieces perhaps of an unknown work in the process of being accomplished. But their fragmentary unity forms an introduction to something that comes after them, perhaps transcends them, and which is called literature or, with a hint of irony, belles-lettres.

Hans Faverey (1933–1990)

During the summer of 1990, the Dutch poet Hans Faverey died. The week of his death his last book of verse appeared which he had written with an eye to the end of his life, and which must be read in that light, however unexplicit the poetry is about his imminent death. Just before he died, the Constantin Huygens prize had been awarded to him for the whole of his work which had come together over some twenty-five years. The many obituaries constantly cast light on the greatness of his poetry which has been interpreted differently by different people: we find Buddhist elements in it as well as pre-Socratic ones, and references to the absolute poetry of Mallarmé.

The greatness of Faverey's poetry and its unique character are undeniable. It does not let itself be confined to a tendency or a trend. His first collections were compared with the poetry of Gerrit Kouwenaar, because of the evident autonomy of these verses which seem to have very little to do with the outside world. The conviction is gaining ground according to which these poems, in which there is a ceaseless alternation between construction and destruction, and which seem to end up in nothingness and silence, have a life of their own. In this Faverey's poetry is characteristic of twentieth-century Dutch poetry which consists of independent works by a few great writers. It is only by observing them from a very lofty vantage-point that it is possible to establish connections between some of them, and only this loftiness allows us to observe certain influences on other poets. But this effort is quickly revealed to be artificial. Poets rise up in their solitude, even if some are considered as belonging to what we call a 'movement'.

Faverey is the last of the group. His disappearance seems to mark provisionally the end of Dutch poetry. What best defines Dutch poetry is that, with each great poet, it seems to start anew. A school of poetry or a poetic movement can form, but always rapidly dissolves to leave room for individual poets whose works have virtually nothing in common.

Hans Faverey is a true Dutch poet. He represents poetry in what is best in it. To enter into the life of his poems shows paradoxically how death touched Dutch poetry at the same time as it touched him.

Max Frisch (1911–1991)

The Swiss writer Max Frisch was born on 15 May 1911 in Zurich, where his father was an architect. After matriculating, he decided to be a writer and began to study literature, a study that the death of his father obliged him, however, to cut short. He became a journalist to earn a living. His first literary efforts, fruitless, as well as the reading of Keller's *Green Henry*, convinced him that it was better to make sure of his future with a 'manly' occupation. He remembered his father and took up architecture.

But the desire to write continued to burrow eat away at him, and, when he had finished his studies, in 1941, Frisch divided his time between architecture and literature. He wrote for the theatre and kept a 'Diary', a form which ended up influencing his style and his vision, both in *Blätter im Brotsack* (*Sheets of Paper in the Bread Bag*, 1940) or the various volumes of his *Journal* (1946–1949), 1966–1971), and in his great novels, *Stiller* (1957), *Homo Faber* (1957) and *Mein Name sei Gantenbein* (*Let My Name Be Gantenbein*, 1964, published under the title *Le Désert des Miroirs, The Desert of Mirrors* in 1966).

'I try on stories like clothes,' says Gantenbein. 'Trying on' and 'stories': neither images, nor language, not the most intimate confessions are able apparently to do anything other than to 'dress differently', and provisionally. In his *Journal*, Frisch notes in 1946: 'Language pushes the void, the sayable, in the direction of the mysterious, the living.' The kernel, the 'I', however, remains intact. It is with this logic that Stiller, coming home after a long absence, rejects biography, and, therefore the existential prison that everyone wants to confine him to; a prison in which Andri, the young hero of *Andorra* (1961), will find himself well and truly trapped: by dint of his being suspected of being a Jew, he will end up by believing it himself; and as far as Gantenbein or his avatar Enderlin are concerned, they are not 'revealed' by the accumulation of phantasms and dreams that the author piles up round them.

'To know what is right!' exclaims Don Juan (*Don Juan oder Die Liebe zur Geometrie, Don Juan or the Love of Geometry*, 1953) in his fear of being caught in a world of feelings. And Walter Faber, the technocrat, also hangs on to the solidity of facts. The only problem is that facts, like stories, are only ever the 'hollow' shavings of being, and Faber, in wishing to reject the world of deep feelings, will fall into them as into a trap, His attempt to hang on to the 'verifiable' world is as absurd as that of old Geiser in *Man Appeared During the Quaternary Period* (1979), surrounded by his pile of mini-encyclopedias.

Nothing, in fact, establishes with certainty that we are alive; everything has two sides to it, of which one is hollow. It is not just the structure of the works that draws attention to this 'hollow' in Frisch: it is in each step, in each sentence, in which doubt is implicit in whatever assertion (a dimension of the style which makes all translation of this work extremely problematic). On this level, language is also a void, and the 'I' remains anonymous and solitary, washed up on the banks of a twentieth century which carries in its waters more images and words than ever before. Max Frisch's work, in the light that it sheds, seizes this desperate confrontation with perfect acuity.

Rea Galanaki (1947–)

Born in Heraklion, in Crete, in 1947, Rea Galanaki is a professional historian: she studied history and archaeology in Athens, during a period deeply influenced by the political and social crisis of the dictatorship of the colonels. She has published two collections of poetry, *Plin efkaris* (*Even Though Happy*, 1975) and *Ta orikta* (*Minerals*, 1979), two more or less narrative texts, *To keik* (*The Cake*, 1980) and *Pou zi o likos?* (*Where Does the Wolf Live?* 1982), three stories collected together in one volume, *Omokentra dhiighimata* (*Concentric Tales*, 1986) and a historical novel, *O vios tou Ismaïl Ferik Pacha* (*The Life of Ismaïl Ferik Pacha*, 1989). From the collection of poems in 1975 onwards in which Rea Galanaki formulated the demands of 'verb symmetry', the whole of her work has evolved gradually towards bigger narrative units like the myth, the tale, the historical narrative. The move from poems to prose is obvious from the first collection. The reader is led to discover a closed universe of correspondences between constituent elements which, arranged in a spiral, take up the insistent theme of the author: the limits of writing, and more precisely of female writing, the disappearance of the great tales of modernity, the eclipse of the myth.

The perspective in which modernism apprehends the myth associates the Greece of dreams and the real Greece, the interior vision and the historical fact. In Rea Galanaki's work, the authoritarian discourse of the 'male hunter who kills myths' and the female body which is reborn to life through writing forbid such an association. The search for a unique, mythical or historical centre is demonstrably impossible to achieve, Utopian. There is no way back to lost innocence; this statement bowls the reader over at the end of the novel whose main character, of Greek origin, has lived, after the destruction of his village, in the entourage of the sultan of Egypt and has become Ismaïl Ferik Pacha: 'That night he wanted to give himself to eternity, for he felt that he had risen above gestures and words to attain supreme knowledge. For years he had believed he would find there his lost innocence; he was not worthy to enjoy the death of innocents if he was not like them. That night then, in his old house, innocence smiled like the rediscovered guardian angel of memory. Hesitating to believe in the miracle, he stretched out his child's hand to touch the angel. It was only then that he saw the black snakes twisting in the shining curls and he recoiled. His spirit was suddenly illuminated and he understood that there is no, nor never has been any, lost innocence, and therefore that there is no, nor ever has been any, way back.

'He got up. He approached the hearth and took the stone out of the hole. He kissed Antonis's letter, without rereading it, and tore it to shreds. Then he took the old dagger and stabbed himself in the heart with it.'

Peter Handke (1942–)

All the works by the Austrian Peter Handke aim at getting to the 'true feeling' common to the author and the reader beyond and within all cultures. From the very first novels and plays, his writing tries to liberate words from what they mean to make them rediscover their object. The 'tales' thus pierce the metaphorical layer of language to restore to it its sensory dimension. Language is the only means at our disposal to talk about what we feel, and ceaselessly language is distracted from this aim to more mundane ends.

What makes human beings recognisable to themselves is not the traces that cultural acquisitions have left behind in them – these are found by introspection – but, says Handke, the initial unease which manifests itself in spite of culture and which is described in *Die Stunde der wahren Empfindung* (*The Moment of True Perception*, 1975), for example. A quite different way of seeing emerges from this, both new, as if the unease made us see everything for the first time, and just a way of seeing so that everything becomes apparent and unexpected. From then on, the world is reconstructed at the pace of this 'slow return' which rediscovers the bedrock of sensation as built by *Die Lehre der Sainte-Victoire* (*The Lesson of Sainte-Victoire*), and Cézanne now no longer belongs to culture but to the arranging of the world.

For this is what it is all about now in the work of Handke, a work whose unfolding he fixes in *Das Gewicht der Welt* (*The Weight of the World*, 1977) and *Die Geschichte des Bleistifts* (*The History of the Pencil*, 1983) making a note of the main perceptions around which the work of the writer is arranged to the extent that all his effort consists in formulating the world of the reader. It is always through the latter that the author writes, he never preaches to him, but takes the time to open his eyes.

From the beginning, through tales, films or theatre, Handke's work is the same in the diversity and the constant renewal of writing and themes. Everything that daily forgetfulness allows to escape, everything that daily life evades, reappears forcefully in the texts that Handke constructs with what surrounds him or with what he feels.

Confined to one place in particular (Paris or Salzburg), the exploration of perception extends to all the world, as it can reveal itself anywhere, here, Alaska or Slovenia. Before it had been a case of defining human beings, in *Die linkshändige Frau* (*The Left-Handed Woman*, 1976) or *Kindergeschichte* (*Children's Story*, 1981). It is because beings are inseparable from the places in which they find themselves that travel is one of the basic motifs of Handke's work. Walking, looking and listening allow us to rediscover the world and to give to writing its sharpness and intensity.

His more recent books – *Die Abwesenheit* (*Absence*, 1987) and *Versuch über die Juke-box* (*Essay on the Juke-Box*, 1990) – trace this journey to the heart of the visible, which is revealed in its precision and its breadth to become both the matter of which the world is made and the most intimate part of each of us.

Seamus Heaney (1939–)

The stable rural community into which Heaney was born has kept its presence in his poetry, rubbing shoulders with the vitiated and unstable political system of Northern Ireland which started to disintegrate while he was growing up. His first books, *Death of a Naturalist* (1966) and *Door into the Dark* (1969) explore the immediate world of his childhood; he knows instinctively that familiar elements, names, places and even lands can have a mysterious side. After *Wintering Out* (1972), the detailed examination of the world and its names intensifies until in *North* (1975) Heaney returns to the places of his childhood and discovers there, through the Viking past of Ireland, the sacrificial victims which become a symbol for contemporary violence.

Even though Heaney's poetry is supposed to bring comfort, in reality this is not possible. His peaceful evocation of rural landscapes, traditions, popular customs and ancient times is indeed moving. However, the search for a balance is undermined by the realisation that this is merely insubstantial. And there exists an insubstantiality that death renders even more intense, in particular the death of his mother and of several victims of terrorism commemorated in the elegy *Field Work*. In *North*, Heaney illustrates this problem by describing the opposition between Anteus, the one who embraces the earth which is the source of his strength, and Hercules, who can vanquish Anteus by lifting him up in the air.

The act of poetry is a Herculean effort to grab the visions that transcend the austere and rational representations of the terrestrial embrace, holy and violent, like Anteus' embrace taken towards the kigdom of the air and of fire. Heaney's art is knowing how to unite air and earth to achieve the vision while escaping from abstraction.

Ismail Kadaré (1936–)

Kadaré's career began one day in 1936 in a little town in Southern Albania, Gjirokastër, which he has described in *Kronike ne gur* (*Chronicle of the Town in Stone*). At the age of seventeen, this son of a humble postman received a poetry prize in Tirana, which earned him official permission to go off to study at the Gorky Institute in Moscow. He will be driven out of there in 1961, at the severing of relations between Moscow and Tirana. During this time, he wrote *Gjenerali i ushtrise* (*The General of the Dead Army*), which reaches France where it quickly becomes a success. Kadaré praises the Albanian resistance against Italian fascism, while singing of the magic of a mountainous country, lost in the mist beyond the Adriatic, a country whose enigma will be unintelligible to every invader.

Like this first novel, all Kadaré's books are a huge parable, a gigantic allegory taking to task the world of totalitarianism. But the basis of the novel is never directly political: Kadaré hates militant literature. He belongs instead to the family of great oriental story-tellers, reanimating by himself the whole saga of the Balkans. With the breath of a rhapsodist and an ethnographer's rigour, he goes in one squirt of ink all through Albanian collective memory, from the Turkish invasions to the Maoist 'occupation' of the 1970s. Embroidering thousand-year-old legends on historical realities, mixing dream and epic, Kadaré resembles a Gorky singing after the fashion of old Homer, and with a sense of tragic destiny like Aeschylus, that 'eternal loser' to whom he has dedicated a remarkable essay.

Everything that relates to Albanian tradition is grist to the mill for him, but this tradition is constantly transcended by a metaphysical perception of our destiny. Every time he can, Kadaré also shows the superiority of popular wisdom over the wooden tongue of those who orchestrate the destiny of States. His irony is then more biting than ever, for he has

Chaplin's sense of the grotesque and of caricature. His most famous books are all rooted in a very precise historical reality: the divorce between Albania and the Soviet Union in *Dimri i madh* (*The Big Winter*) and *Perendemi i zotave te stepes* (*Twilight of the Gods of the Steppe*), the fight against the Ottoman invasion in *Ura me tri harqe* (*The Bridge with the Three Arches*) and *Daullet e shiut (Keshtjella)* (*The Drums of the Rain*), the Albanian uprising in Kosovo in *Kortezhi I krushqeve te ngrire* (*The Wedding Procession Got Stuck in the Ice*), the cruel rivalries between Catholics and Orthodox in *Kush e salli Doruntinen* (*Who Took Doruntine Home?*), the breaking off of relations between Tirana and Peking in *Koncerti* (*The Concert*), a marvellous novel in which Mao becomes a crazy megalomaniac clown.

One of Kadaré's finest novels is *Prilli i thyer* (*Broken April*). The story takes place around the 1930s, on the top of a range of mountains, in a world which is dark and violently feudal. A bloody vendetta sets two families against each other, dragging them into a frightful trail of carnage. But a few pages are enough to transform this banal manhunt into a tragedy, a tragedy which gives to old Albanian ancestor worship an epic, even cosmic dimension. In a world of sanguinary men's men, the most universal of regional writers produces a lament in which death appears as a kind of superior wisdom.

Kadaré's masterpiece, *Pallati endrave* (*The Palace of Dreams*), which appeared in France just before the novelist asked for political asylum there, is a massive parody of totalitarian perversion. We find in it a diabolical tyrant, so Machiavellian that he has conceived the monstrous idea of manipulating men's dreams, so as to enslave them and keep an eye on them even while they sleep, at dead of night. Kadaré coldly dissects the mechanisms of dictatorship, when, by dint of sophistication, it reaches the height of perfidy. A journey to the end of a nightmare, this novel gives a glimpse of what the fascism of dreams or the Stalinism of the unconscious might be like. It is this visionary aspect that imparts such masterly strength to the twenty or so books by Kadaré, a novelist who sweeps through history with a great Shakespearean breath. His work appears like a tragic *opera buffa*, in which we see a procession of all the ghosts and all the terrors which shake our time.

Einar Kárason (1955–)

A genre that was old-fashioned in the 1980s, the family saga, close to televised screenplays, disconcerting heroes (an eccentric clairvoyant and an incongruous caricature of Marlon Brando) – an anachronistic fairy-tale for adolescents? – it was with these ingredients that Einar Kárason became one of the great names of Icelandic literature in the 1980s.

His trilogy devoted to an Icelandic family of the 1950s, with flashbacks and expectations, *Djævelsøen* (*The Island of the Devil*, 1983), *Guldøen* (*The Island of Gold*, 1985) and *Det forjættede land* (*The Promised Land*, 1989) was tremendously successful both in Iceland and Scandinavia. Despite a theme close to the television serial, the work was perceived as serious literature and adapted for the stage. Why? To the avant-garde or modernist temptations of the 1960s, to the socialist realist sirens of the 1970s, Kárason preferred a traditional but not simplistic narrative art, which favours the telling of a story. The action takes place in Reykjavik in a shanty town in which various losers have sought refuge: drunkards, rootless peasants, ageing prostitutes, thieves, honest paupers, all rejected by urban life. They have created an anarchist village in the middle of the rapidly developing capital. As in so many other books in postwar Icelandic literature, there is a brutal encounter between the old peasant culture and American mass culture; but, in contrast to many other works, without the least desire to draw moral lessons.

With an irony close to that of Hamsun, but without disdain for human beings, the tale describes a people who look lost; poverty is talked about without accusing society, tragic destinies with a touching absence of sentimentalism. Heroes are mentioned whose heroism only exists two-dimensionally, like the out-dated heroes of sagas played by Humphrey Bogart or Elvis Presley. It is no doubt there that the force of the tale resides: Einar Kárason creates a novelistic universe apparently based on historical elements. He awakens a certain nostalgia in readers who know that in Reykjavik, for a long time now, shanty towns have been replaced by modern lodgings, that culture shock has become culture fusion.

However, the reader, as well as the author, knows that all this is only false nostalgia: the world whose passing we would like to mourn was never like that: both of them are in cahoots with each other. And the reader, once abandoned, finds themselves alone with an indefinable languor. So in the last volume of the trilogy, years later, the alter ego of the author goes to the USA with one of the descendants of the clairvoyant, to look for the last survivor of the family who left a very long time ago for the Promised Land. It becomes the tale of a chaotic, absurd journey, an indeterminate quest for a dream that ends with an unforgettable scene: the characters say goodbye to their artificial ideals on an Indian reservation. In this book, Einar Kárason's most personal, the journey is that of the author; it resembles a pilgrimage without Jerusalem, a children's crusade in which only our illusions disappear.

Danilo Kiš (1935–1989)

Jewish on his father's side, Montenegrin on his mother's, Danilo Kiš spent his childhood on both sides of the border between Hungary and Yugoslavia. He writes in Serbian and has a working knowledge of Hungarian, French and Russian. Through his work, Kiö shows himself to be the heir to the culture of Central Europe, above all in his quest for a lost identity, but he is equally the heir to the bookish and erudite inspiration of a Borges and documentary technique proper to the new novel.

In his first work, *Mansarda* (*The Garret*, 1962), Kiš unveils his argumentative spirit about novel narration and indicates an innovative penchant in the tradition of Proust,

Gide, Beckett, Nabokov and Borges. He creates a sort of anti-novel centred around the myth of Orpheus and Eurydice (the paradigm of the novel of love) which he subjects to so many variations that we are unable to say if he is reinterpreting it, parodying it or simply reminiscing out loud. The myth is lost, replaced by the dynamic of the text and the rhythm of its fragments and sequences. His works obey a single rule: each new text calls for a new way of writing. He creates a tale as an event, as a form, explaining, in *Homo Poeticus* (1973), this obsession: 'The form could contribute to our fatal and fateful failure being less painful and less insane, a Form which could give a new content to our emptiness, a Form which could do the impossible, place the work beyond the reach of darkness and the void, make it cross the Lethe.'

The family trilogy *Family Circus* is a 'work in progress.' The first volume, *Rani jadi* (*Precocious Grief*, 1969), 'a tale for children and the sophisticated', explores the principal themes (love, memory, fear, father) which will be pulverised, as if held in a mirror in the second volume, *Bašta, pepeo* (*Garden, Ashes*, 1965), an interrupted myth, carried by an elegy. These same themes are reinterpreted in the third volume, *Peščanik* (*Hourglass*, 1972), in a 'hyperrealist' fashion, through a series of authentic and apocryphal documents, a bas-relief of miniaturisation. More than an ordinary hero, the character of the father is a literary instrument which links the three volumes. For Kiš is not writing a biography, he is using biography to show that it can function as 'a subversive work'. It is the first layer of a palimpsest, written and effaced, completed and reconstructed with the help of literary references, parables taken from the Bible, but also from Cervantes, Goethe and Joyce, into which it settles in order to continue another life, both new and already lived. The presence of quotations, of catalogues and Rabelaisian inventories constantly diverts the tale and enriches its semantic content, eliminating the limits between fiction and reality.

After this cycle, the author has a look at contemporary history, laying claim to a document that confirms it, if only apparently. Two collections of short stories, *Grobnica za Borisa Davidovica* (*A Grave for Boris Davidovitch*, 1976) and *Enciklopedija mrtvih* (*Encyclopedia of the Dead*, 1984), are variations on the theme of death, 'that neighbour to art', in 'several chapters of the same story'. In relating the tragic destiny of his characters, for the most part children of the October Revolution, Jews and victims of the Stalinist purges, who have 'never become famous and whose name is not mentioned in any encyclopedia' (one has to be invented for them), Kiš transforms them into a global metaphor for the end of a civilisation marked by a symmetrical arrangement of totalitarian regimes, whether it be the Inquisition, the Holocaust, the Gulag, concentration camps or anti-semitism. History is presented as political and ideological staging, mobilising erudition, figures of style, irony and paradox which are alone capable of showing without betraying themselves. With Kiš, reality is called into question by the book. He derives this inspiration from books – let us quote the author – 'has as its purpose the correction of human injustice and giving to every creature of God an equal share in eternity.' A difficult task, but one of the finest tributes to twentieth-century literature.

Tadeusz Konwicki (1929–)

'The good fortune and misfortune of peoples often recall the good fortune and misfortune of ordinary individuals, normal people lost in the crowd, the lustreless existence of every day,' observes the narrator of *Kompleks polski* (*The Polish Complex*, 1977). This brief sentence lends itself well to its Polish creator, also lost in the anonymity of a large town. The fate of a writer, even one famous in his own lifetime, cannot escape from the implacable laws of History.

Tadeusz Konwicki, sitting in an armchair in the company of his cat, Iwan, gazes out from the top of his apartment block in the suburbs of Nowy Świat, both severely and tenderly at Warsaw, at his friends, at his family, at the police who spy on them, the censors who mutilate his books – in a word at all those who have made up, the world that is closest to him over a period of years. The last will and testament of a novelist? Memories from beyond the grave? It is true that for some time now the author of *Nowy Świat i okolice* (*Nowy Świat and Surrounding Areas*, 1986) has been preparing to say goodbye to his readers. We may suspect a certain amount of coquettishness from someone whose life has been a zigzag full of ambushes and paradoxes: armed struggle against the Soviets and the Germans, the temptation of communism, opposition to the Marxist system, voluntary literary exile, a return to official literary life. The impossible definition of the Pole of our time has been this writer's major concern. He was born in Nowa Wilejka, in Lithuania, which he evokes by means of mythical landscapes, but his work was born in the People's Republic of Poland.

In 1950, he is one of the happy recipients of the State Prize for Literature given to young and talented practitioners of socialist realism. However, little by little, the author of *Władza* (*Power*, 1954) links up with the prewar literary tradition censured by Marxist ideology, he publishes his books clandestinely, openly denouncing the abuses of the regime.

With *Dziura w niebie* (*Hole in the Sky*, 1959), Konwicki goes back to the days of his childhood to stay. At the same time, his novels conceal many allusions to the colourlessness of Polish daily life and the political impasse of a society groaning under the burden of its illusions. The theme of the insurrection of 1863, a crucial date in the history of Poland, is constantly caught up in events being described. However, what the author expresses is not the faith of the Romantic poets to whose charm he is susceptible, but a tragic consciousness manifested by the interposition of grotesque clowning and sublime grandeur.

Konwicki's books obey the laws of a Romantic poetics which could almost derive from an anti-epic manifesto. The same motifs, the same characters, the same places crop up to importune: the suicide of an unknown man, pebbles taken from a river-bed or cards formerly dealt, with which we can predict the future or revel in the past.

The lyrical tone often gives way to mordant sarcasm. But these bitter and ironical accents, which we encounter time after time in *Mała Apokalipsa* (*The Little Apocalypse*, 1979), in *Wschody i Zachody* (*The Risings and Settings of the Moon*, 1981), or again in *Rzeka podziemna, podziemne ptaki* (*The Underground River, Nightbirds*, 1984), sometimes fade away before the search for a spirituality which transcends the world of primitive beliefs. Mythical Lithuania is a favoured meeting-point for reality and metaphysics. The reader is led to wonder incessantly about this far-off, mysterious country where people pray to an Orthodox God, fear Dewajtis and Peroun (pagan gods formerly venerated by the Lithuanian people) and feverishly celebrate the Day of the Dead, as is the case in *Bohiń* (*Bohini, a Manor in Lithuania*, 1987).

Many of the author-narrator's own interventions in the tale take the form of passionate reflections, provocative professions of faith on the destiny of peoples and freedom. But what remains at the centre of the work is the tireless quest for the identity of a writer who strives less to represent the world than to represent himself: 'Where is my homeland? Where is the homeland of the gods? I would like to go back there, even were it to prove similar to this country of men where I have endured exile.'

Milan Kundera (1929–)

Although he studied in Prague, at the film school which would later employ him as a teacher, Milan Kundera has always had a soft spot for Moravia and its capital, Brno, where he was born on 1 April 1929. The musical culture that he received from his father, a pianist, and which his native region is steeped in, will influence him even in the formal composition of his novels. But his intellectual curiosity, despite the isolation in which Czechoslovakia found itself in the 1950s, stimulates his interest in foreign literatures (Apollinaire, the avant-garde, Austrian literature, the European Romantic tradition).

Before finding his own mode of expression in the novel, he will publish three collections of poetry, an essay on Vladimir Vančura, a Czech novelist of the period between the wars, and in 1962, he will have his first play produced, *Majitelé klíčů* (*The Keyholders*). During the political thaw, which ended with 'the Prague spring', he was among the reformist writers grouped around *The Literary Gazette*, writers who entered into open conflict with the powers-that-be at the Fourth Congress of the Union of Writers (1967). Known as a prose-writer for the short stories of *Směšné lásky* (*Laughable Loves*, 1963), which has already been reissued twice, he ensured a reputation as a great novelist not only in Czechoslovakia, but also abroad thanks to *Žert* (*The Joke*, 1967), the last of his books to be published in Czechoslovakia before going into exile.

Kundera was, in fact, one of the first victims of 'normalisation'. Banned from being published, he was authorised in 1975 to go to France, where he established himself in Paris after a brief sojourn at the University of Rennes.

Život je jinde (*Life is Elsewhere*, 1973) and *Valčík na rozloučenov* (*The Farewell Waltz*, 1976), written in Czechoslovakia, contain, with *The Joke*, most of the major themes that Kundera will subsequently deal with: *Kniha smíchu a zapomnění* (*The Book of Laughter and Forgetting*, 1979); *Nesnesitelná lehkost bytí* (*The Unbearable Lightness of Being*, 1984); *Nesmrtelnost* (*Immortality*, 1990): man is betrayed by history, yet he cannot live outside it. Eroticism, cynicism, exile, Utopia and revenge make up the pattern of the tragic farces of his life and get substituted for its 'meaning' whose existence is itself only illusory. From Stalinism in Czechoslovakia to the France of today, the mechanisms in which the destinies of his protagonists are summed up bear a striking resemblance to each other. Kundera gives us the key to interpret them: kitsch, going round in circles, lyricism, violated intimacy, immortality, forgetfulness, infantocracy. Many authorial observations which accompany the story sometimes take the form of a dialogue which the reader gets dragged into. These give to Kundera's novels not only humour and a nonchalant charm, but also an extra dimension, which he has developed separately in his essays. These, published piecemeal before being collected under the title *The Art of the Novel* (1986), have played a major role in the recognition of Eastern European historical and cultural specificity, the tragedy of which has been, for Kundera, an omen for the destiny of the whole of Europe. If he has not expressed an opinion about the chances of its survival after the political upheavals of 1989, there is nevertheless the shining example of his contribution to contemporary literature.

Rosa Liksom (1958–)

The Finnish writer who writes under the pen-name of Rosa Liksom has published with the photographer Jukka Uotila a book called *Go Moskova Go* (*Go Moscow Go*, 1988), It contains portraits of young people in the town of Moscow: 'The bride and groom are dressed as one ought to be in the space age. The bride is wrapped in a costume which comes straight from Ziggy Stardust and the groom sports a Starway Swordsman garment. These clothes both socialist and romantic in appearance have been designed by the groom himself.' Rosa Liksom writes about life on the margins of modern towns as if the experiences were genuine, influenced by Georges Bataille, Ambrose Bierce and Jean Cocteau. This young Finnish woman seems to be perfectly at ease in the settings of rural Siberia (*Väliasema Gagarin, Stop Gagarin!* 1987).

When Rosa Liksom exhibited her own works in Helsinki, she wore a military uniform. This style of clothing as well as dark glasses are useful to her in a game of hide-and-seek that has been going on for some years. We know that this young woman who is hiding behind her pseudonym was born in Lapland, that she has travelled all over the world and that she lived for a few years in Copenhagen.

In her short stories, young people set off on pilgrimages to Copenhagen, earn their living by working in a Norwegian fish factory or settle down in a nameless town. They can also live in small villages in the wastes of Lapland, gateway to Europe. 'Tamed by hunger, the reindeer gather along the roads and at the entrance to villages. Many of them put themselves out of their misery by throwing themselves after dark under the wheels of lorries transporting wood. Bones and bleeding carcasses are strewn in ditches and over the approaches to fields. . . . It had died immediately. The body was already frozen when Elli discovered it after the evening news' (*Yhden yön pysäkei, Stopping the Night*, 1985).

Rosa Liksom has strong ties with big European cities, but always comes back to Finland, to her roots which are in that Lapland set on the edge of the world, only to find the same type of human relationships there as in the inhabitants of towns, relationships based on violence and destruction.

Her short laconic texts are stories that tell of bizarre, comic or tragic lives. She prefers to write about men, soldiers, monks, hermits. When she talks about love and eroticism, she chooses situations in which relationships are hopeless or coming to an end. People who are alone are always telling horrible real-life experiences, in laconic monologues in which a life is totally condensed into a few pages: 'I got hold of that bloody carving knife and I stabbed him with it two or three times. The bastard didn't say a word, damn it, and fell down dead on the only bed I had. I rang the loony-bin and told them that my husband had committed suicide, that he had stabbed himself in the vicinity of the heart and went out to see some friends' (*Unohdettu vartti, The Hollow of Oblivion*, 1986).

Svend Åge Madsen (1939–)

Since he started writing in 1962, the Dane Svend Åge Madsen has published eighteen novels and collections of short stories, not counting an equally large number of theatre plays and radio plays.

During this period, his work has evolved considerably while preserving within it a meditation on epic form and narrative. Known plots and ordinary methods of narration are constantly parodied or given an unexpected twist; fresh output is in constant thematic dialogue with previous output, and is so always with a liberal dose of humour.

As for a whole generation of Danish writers, the work of Svend Åge Madsen rests on an international ingredient, the modernism of the radical calling into question of writing in the 1960s, and more especially on the theatre of the absurd and the new French novel. In novels which fall apart as a result of the destruction of the coherence of the narration, he shows that the closed stories of tradition only create the illusion of a meaning and a wholeness that no longer exist in the modern world (*Besoeget, The Visit*, 1963).

Basing himself on this relativistic position, at the end of the 1960s, Svend Åge Madsen published a series of pastiches of popular genres, myths and classical novel types. These are the texts in which the characters of novels try to liberate themselves from their narrow roles and their closed concept of reality, as suggested by classical narrative models and the traditional concepts of being. The plays on words and the stylistic games underpin the theme, thus breaking with all the reader's expectations about the genre and reality (*Saet verden er til, Imagine that the World Exists*, 1971).

In the 1970s, historical and social realities begin to play a bigger part in his novels. Time and space become concrete to the point that years and places (Aarhus) are mentioned. It is also the period when the public discovers the use that Svend Åge Madsen makes of the effects of comic relief and suspense appertaining to recognisable genres. Themes like the loss of innocence, hate and revenge are presented as the result of social oppression and the constraints of the system. The tale has become existential: man's identity is asserted in the reciprocity created between the freedom of story-telling, and the constraint of being told by others (*Tugt og utugt i Mellemtiden, Lechery and Punishment in the Meantime*, 1976). This process intensifies and, during the 1980s, Svend Åge Madsen constructs an idiosyncratic fictional world, in which all his characters are attached one to the other beyond individual books; the stories criss-cross in a labyrinthine manner while they comment on, contradict or reproduce each other (*At fortaelle menneskene, Expressing Mankind*, 1989).

In this deliberate fabrication of a writing, the author illustrates the way in which the real is tacked on to the narration. And the more things we tell, the more possibilities there are to bring them into existence. The story has then, over the years, been rehabilitated, and the words of Wittgenstein – 'the limits of my language are the limits of my world' – have become for Madsen: 'The limits of the narrative represent the limits of my world.'

The fictional world of Svend Åge Madsen has a life of its own, and we can today, with justification, call it a 'novel of the world'. There are continually rising up in it new worlds, full of ironical games and numerous ambiguities, which put the conceptual horizon of the reader to the test. But, as we begin to dive into this work, we find, as a reader, food for bewildering discoveries.

Eduardo Mendoza (1943–)

Born in Barcelona, Eduardo Mendoza may be considered as an author representative of contemporary Spanish literature, as much by his work as by his chosen genre, the novel. As if providentially, it was in 1975, the year of Franco's death, that he published his first novel, *La verdad sobre el caso Savolta* (*The Truth about the Savolta Case*). This date has acquired a symbolic value and marks the beginning of a new era for Spanish society and culture, an era which will see the coming of democracy and the flowering of letters. This rapid development coincides with a new vision of the past: the young have taken from tradition the best it had to give them, without leaving out the aftermath of the Civil War. The distance Mendoza puts between himself and socialist realism and experimental techniques of writing, for example, stares us in the face; but at the same time, his attachment to certain forerunners like Juan Marsé is obvious. Both of them use Barcelona as a backdrop: the town almost becomes a character in its own right.

Mendoza studies law, then lives in New York from 1973 to 1982, where he works as an interpreter for the United Nations Organisation. He is currently living in Barcelona. *The Truth about the Savolta Case* made him known and marked the emergence of a new way of conceiving the relationship between narrative innovation and tradition. He did not abandon experimentation, but it was discreet and, above all, subordinated to the interests of history; an equilibrium is established between the construction of the story and the way it is told on the one hand and the seduction of the reader on the other. The narrator's games become plot devices and factors that add tension for whoever is following the argument. Behind Mendoza's work, we divine what he calls 'the great Spanish novel': Cervantes, the picaresque novel, the novel of chivalry, Perez Galdós. He is acquainted with the narrative power of Pío Baroja and the talent for the angst-laden satire of Valle-Inclán. Finally, he uses the contemporary American novel, which he parodies in *The Truth about the Savolta Case*. The story's point of departure is the statement of the hero, Javier Miranda, to a judge, a statement that retraces his memories of the murder of the industrialist Savolta, starting from ten January 1927. Other violent deaths, sentimental sub-plots, political tensions derived from history, and a very detailed description of the life of Barcelona at the time are superimposed on the central theme.

Mendoza afterwards publishes *El misterio de la cripta embrujada* (*The Mystery of the Bewitched Crypt*, 1979) and *El laberinto de las aceitunas* (*The Labyrinth of Olives*, 1982), works in which, still with a political backdrop, he accentuates the satirical character of the situations and deepens the description of the characters. In *La ciudad de los prodigios* (*The Town of Miracles*, 1986), Mendoza returns to an argument in which urban chronicle, political history and novel fiction are intermingled. Set between two universal exhibitions, organised in 1880 and 1929 respectively,

Barcelona is the scene for the rise of Onofre Bouvila, poverty-stricken as a child, a militant anarchist as an adolescent, then a gangster, the self-confident and aggressive manager of his own business and, a few years later, a millionaire made rich by his business interests: property speculation and gun-running during the First World War. Mendoza plays with history, makes of it an element indissociable from the story, exploits, for the argument as for the description of the people, situations as disparate as the first anarchist revolts to happen in Catalonia, the cinema in its infancy, the dictatorship of Primo de Rivera and the first adventures in aviation.

Pierre Mertens (1939–)

Born in Brussels in 1939 of a journalist father and a mother who was a biologist, the Belgian writer Pierre Mertens is a jurist and an expert on international law. A researcher at the Sociological Institute at the Free University of Brussels (where he is currently director of the department of literary sociology), he wrote between 1964 and 1966 *Une leçon particulière*, a first text which arouses the interest of Jean Cayrol and Claude Durand. For twenty years, he divides his attention between two passions, literature and law, twenty years that end with the victory of the first after the award of the Médicis Prize in 1987 for *Les Éblouissements* (*Dazzling Sights*). Mertens has travelled in the Near East, in Greece, in Portugal, in Chile, in Cyprus: these missions as a legal observer help him to acquire a sensitive awareness of the world. He will take from this the foundations of an active notion of literary intervention, which is resolutely at odds with the introspective tendencies of his fellow countrymen. Contrary to the alternatives normally observed by Belgian writers – to base oneself on inwardness or to blend into the literature of France – Mertens wishes to preserve the rights of the historical memory of his own country, while opening on to a world larger than that of France. He has thus played a decisive role in the change of mentality that Francophone Belgium experienced in the 1980s. Mertens tries to escape from the role of the simple witness which is normally granted to an author, in order to participate wholeheartedly in debates as an intellectual. This transition from being a writing 'specialist', which he nevertheless is, to an overall reflection is precisely what sets him apart and makes him, functionally, and not just by vocation, a writer.

His first novel, *L'Inde ou l'Amérique* (*India or America*, 1969) was a book that was immediately one of the sources of his inspiration: a way of inventing his survival by giving density to an imaginary biography. *La Fête des anciens* (*The Feast of the Ancients*, 1971) follows the same path. But in *Les Bons Offices* (*Good Actions*, 1974), *Terre d'asile* (*Land of Sanctuary*, 1978) and *Dazzling Sights*, this personal dimension is mingled with the rehabilitation of history. These three novels established a sort of hierarchy of exteriority. Heroes are successively a mediator who is half Quixote (Don Quichotte in French) and half Sancho Panza: Paul Sanchotte, a Chilean émigré and the expressionist German poet Gottfried Benn. Every time Belgian history sees itself subjected to a foreign gaze, which bursts its apparent simplicity, but in so doing gives it back an existence which national amnesia tends to deprive it of. At the same time, Mertens' writing is transformed. A deeper search for the well-phrased remark succeeds the temporal breaks and the unexpected metaphors of the first books. The gap, initially solicited in narrative discontinuity, now finds its place in the sinuosity of the writing.

From childhood, Mertens has been influenced by music. Leitmotifs permeate the whole of his literary work (the figure of the tiger, music itself). He is also the author of an opera libretto, *La Passion de Gilles* (*The Passion of Gilles*, 1982), set to music by Philippe Boesmans. Apart from several collections of stories, this attentive and highly cultivated reader has a regular 'column' in the daily paper *Le Soir*. His critical works, collected notably in *The Double Agent* (1989), try to make visible the topicality of works. They derive from the same formula in which Mertens gives an admirable definition of the need for him to create: 'To conceive a book is not so much to add another volume to one's own library – a pathetic ambition – as to pull out that book in particular from all libraries.'

Liudmila Petruchevskaïa (1938–)

For a long time a familiar name in Russian literary circles, Liudmila Petruchevskaïa only found an audience quite recently, when, in 1987 to 1988, her plays were performed and her stories, banned or scattered in reviews, were brought together in a collection. The Soviet public knows her mainly as a playwright. With *perestroïka*, young theatre studios and theatrical institutions fought for her plays. She became in this way one of the younger generation's most popular dramatists (with Slavkin and others). In Činzano (*Cinzano*, 1985) she traps in camera three friends who are alcoholics; their delirium tremens in a descent into hell constitutes the play. In *Tri devuški v golubom* (*Three Young Ladies in Blue*, 1987), an evocation of a Chekhov play, the heroine, despite or because of a mad search for happiness, experiences failure, then catastrophe.

With Liudmila Petruchevskaïa, the misfortune that afflicts her characters is not social or political: she does not denounce the wounds of the people or the perversions of the regime. It is rather a difficulty in living, a daily horror, impossible relationships between human beings and, above all, between men and women. Her plays and stories have nothing in common with the 'committed' literature which is shown today on stage. No light compensates for the shadows in the picture, no transcendence (God, history, man) comes to impose a meaning or to establish an order in the chaos of events and feelings of a world that has crumbled to bits. But neither are we dealing with a by-product of the theatre of the absurd for, and here Liudmila Petrushevskaïa joins up with mainstream Russian literature, she loves her uprooted and wandering characters – both literally and metaphorically – without landmarks or homes. 'In my work I have never fled from horrible things,' she says, 'but I never write without loving my characters. I love then all.' This love has nothing sentimental about it, but it allows her to talk about her heroes from the inside, and thus to avoid the trap of being moralistic about them. We should not be surprised that her first collection is called *Bessmertnaja ljubov'* (*An Undying Love*, 1988).

One of the reasons for the success of her theatre is her sensitivity to street language with its shifts of meaning, its unarticulated syntax, its repetitions and confusions. 'My greatest joy is the language people speak in the street. I take in all the time what I hear around me. I do not make any notes of anything, but the best things stick.' In her prose, Liudmila Petruchevskaïa has recourse to two procedures: the uninterrupted interior monologue or what Russian formalists used to call 'skaz' (the narrator speaks the language of his characters in a sort of reported speech). More often than not we are told a story which has already happened and which is already being forgotten. *An Undying Love* begins like this: 'What the ultimate destiny of the heroes of our story was . . .' In a story which caused a scandal in Moscow, called *Svoj Krug* (*His Circle*, 1989), a typical group of Muscovite intellectuals is described by their most stupid female member, despised by all the others; her narrow vision ends up giving a cruelly lucid picture of what the semi-dissident milieu of the 1970s was like. The author sometimes makes a personal appearance in her work and allows her sadness when faced with the misery of human existence to come through, but, normally, it is precisely the apparent neutrality of the author (in which we can trace a connection with Chekhov) which, more than the blackness of characters and situations, came as a shock to the reigning moralism of the Soviets.

Jordan Radičkov (1929–)

Since 1959, when his first collection of tales appeared, Radičkov has occupied a special position in Bulgarian letters. From the beginning, his works, written in a traditional way, stand out for their humour and lyricism. After 1963 the results of his innovative research become manifest; the subject disappears and the narrative is subjected to a game of associations and assembling the more or less autonomous fragments which sum up in a mosaic the spiritual experience of the author, his vision of life, his lyrical reflection and his attempt to know and appreciate himself: *Neosvetenite dvorove* (*Dark Courtyards*, 1966). Radičkov quickly goes beyond this introspection, real but very discreet, and replaces, in many tales, stories and plays, the lyrical element with irony, caricature and the grotesque: *Svitepo nastroenie* (*Fierce Humour*, 1965), *Sumatoha* (*Agitation*, 1967) and *Barupen bukvar* (*A Primer for Lightning*, 1969). Thanks to his unbounded and Baroque imagination, through play and gaiety, the author trains an innocent and observant gaze on life so as to translate the conflict between the old-fashioned principles of the peasant and the modern spirit of life here and now. We must look for the key to this work in the historical destiny of the Bulgarian village. With the transformation of villages into towns, many age-old psychological and spiritual elements from the past, transposed into today's reality, create conflicts which are grotesque and carnival-like. Through myths, very ancient ones, but new in function and content, Radičkov, neither an ideologist nor a moraliser, charts, in original writing, the decline of a morality and a way of life as well as the disappearance of the village, and more precisely of the patriarchal mentality, like a tragi-comedy, the absurd aspects of which are rendered by laughter.

Radičkov, as a chronicler of his village, wrote the story of a worldwide phenomenon and dealt with a problem that is still with us today (and even fundamental in certain countries): the urbanisation of the planet.

José Saramago (1922–)

To make one's mark indisputably in the world of the Portuguese and European novel, then in full flow, to make one's mark in the 1980s, the decade of the 'yuppies', when one is over fifty, such is the claim to fame of José Scaramago.

He had his first success in 1980 with his epic about the agricultural labourers of the latifundio, *Levantados do Chão* (*Brought Up on the Land*). At fifty-eight years of age, Scaramago was an experienced writer even though unknown: he had already published poems, tales and above all chronicles. But it was thanks to the novel that he found the mode of expression suited to the effusion of his imagination and would go on to become a successful writer. The five novels he has written since reveal the living force of his creativity. On the basis of a kernel of realism, historically delimited and probable, he can captivate the reader over hundreds of pages, dragging him tirelessly from reality to fantasy, from the known to the supernatural; he confronts him with many and contradictory human truths, in a fullness of allegories close to magical realism.

The central theme of his work seems to be that of wandering, linked to a quest that gives a meaning to the human adventure. The voyage – which has long been a part of Portuguese culture – and wanderings, real and symbolic, structure his books, issuing a challenge to individual and collective immobility. They are the link, the dialogue between differences. *Mémorial do Convento* (1982), from which Azio Corghi took the opera *Blimunda*, is a surprising picture of a Baroque-age Portugal, the gesture of the construction of a convent and a pedestrian suspension bridge. Blimunda, the companion of Baltasar Sete-Sóis, the typical convent builder, possesses unusual gifts of clairvoyance. She contributes something towards realising the heretical dream of flight of Friar Bartolomeu de Gusmão by bringing together 'wills' able to make the flying machine take to the air.

The wealth of descriptions and the author's taste for digressions make the tale a continuous, captivating, original recital. The narrator integrates the dialogue with the narrative, crossing sentientiousness with irony; out of this is born a writing close to Baroque prose.

In his three other novels, Saramago holds the reader's attention from the first lines with an unexpected idea which is at the source of a fable. *O Ano da morte de Ricardo Reis* (*The Year of the Death of Ricardo Reis*, 1984) brings about the meeting of the poet Pessoa, already dead, with his borrowed name, Ricardo Reis, still alive. In *A Jangada de Pedra* (*The Raft of Stone*, 1986), he imagines a wonderful love story, while the Iberian peninsula gets detached from the continent and floats oddly across the Atlantic. *História do Cerco de Lisboa* (*The Story of the Siege of Lisbon*, 1989) rewrites another version of the siege laid by the Christians, in 1147, to Lisbon being held by the Moors, on the basis of a 'not' that a proof-reader decides, gratuitously, to put in at a crucial moment in the historical narration of the siege.

In the meantime, Saramago's journey reveals other worlds to us.

Claude Simon (1913–)

The work of the Frenchman Claude Simon, who proclaims that 'he has no imagination' delves widely into family memories and personal experience. But, far from giving a long autobiography of himself, the novelist, having gone through the experimental stage of the new novel, delivers this material up to the transforming work of his writing. Placed from the outset under the sign of a certain amount of research, aimed at shaking off traditional forms, the first novels by Claude Simon (*The Cheater*, 1945, *Gulliver*, 1952, *The Rite of Spring*, 1954) betray Faulkner's influence. The author is mainly interested in mediocre, clumsy characters who are ill at ease. A veritable 'thematic reservoir' of the work, *La Corde raide* (*The Tightrope*, 1947) sketches a meditation on art, inspired by Cézanne, dominated by a critique of representational art that the work will not omit to develop: 'Writing does not allow one to represent what is called reality, but, on the contrary, to say something which bears to reality the same sort of relationship that an apple painted in a picture (i.e. an infinitesimal layer of colour spread over a canvas) bears to an apple that one can get hold of and eat.'

The pictorial model meditated on at length by Claude Simon allows a veritable growth in awareness of artistic reality, and suggests fertile techniques, collages, a description of the real in the shape of a restitution of images.

The author is quickly associated by critics with the 'new novelists', with whom he has certain affinities. But he develops in a very personal direction, with *Le Vent* (*The Wind*, 1957) and even more with *L'Herbe* (*Grass*, 1958), a form which allows him to link an attempt to restore the past – or a particular past – the troubles and the movements of perception or consciousness to the distortions imposed on them by writing. A memory, taken from an image fixed by a ubiquitous present participle, becomes a pretext for all sorts of speculations, reveries and questionings. The main preoccupations of the work are deepened by combining the 'family saga' (*Grass; The Road to Flanders*, 1960; *Story*, 1967) and the war. Already present in his previous novels, the Spanish Civil War is to be found in *The Palace* (1962); the Second World War in *The Road to Flanders*. Out of these major conflicts between the beliefs and dramas of history is born a necessary criticism of the values of humanism and progress that our century has inherited. The philosophy of the Enlightenment, a primitive Rousseauism, faith in progress or in better tomorrows: the ideologies our post-modern period has registered the death of were already dying more than forty years ago in this major work (from *The Tightrope* to *The Invitation*, 1987).

With *La Bataille de Pharsale* (1969) a new period opens up: after the description of fragmentary and fixed scenes, collage effects and the seizure of a broken-up present triumph for a time over the exploration of a consciousness and the restoration of a past. *Triptych* (1973), *General Science* (1975) and even *Women* (1966), written about the paintings of Miró and published under the title *The Hair of Bérénice* (1984), concentrate their efforts on a writing which is deployed in terms of its potentiality, words that are cross-roads for meanings, and along the lines of the painters Simon lays claim to: Cézanne, Rauschenberg, Poussin (*Blind Orion*, 1970).

After a silence of six years, *The Georgics* (1981) were both the end of experimentation and Simon's return to his basic preoccupations. The rhythms of war and the earth, those of life and history ferment in a total form shared experiences, coalescing and confounded, of men of different generations. The movement of the phrase, which never stops correcting itself and leaping off into new analogies, pursues the traces and the wanderings of a general under the Empire, a member of the Convention and a regicide, of a young man fighting for the Spanish Republicans and of a horseman caught up in the fiasco of 1940. Nearer perhaps to the memories of its author, *The Acacia* (1989) displays an astonishing mastery of the art of writing. The work turns back on itself, works over afresh the same images and the same themes, but in a more refined sort of sentence structure. From the family saga and the novel of the war again intimately intermingled, the image of an absent father becomes detached from the rest (Claude Simon's father, a career army officer, was killed in 1914, when his son was only one) whose dark presence is an obsession for the writing and for its disorientated quest.

Another way of looking at the world is elaborated in the textual space of this work which shows an interest in the real that noble themes can no longer measure up to.

Every object, even the most banal or vile, can tap into the deepest of reflections as well as gain glimpses of the unconscious and experience waking dreams. One of Simon's sentences gets hold of something and nothing, and weaves around it, in its infinite development, the questions, the anguish and the most fundamental enthusiasms of existence. However, the author teaches us that we never know the world – and we never live our own lives except through stored blueprints and cultural knowledge, whatever the violence with which we affect to reject them. The novelist himself is implicated in this phenomenon, as Simon recalls by quoting *Henry Brulard* in which Stendhal, thinking to describe the crossing of the Alps by Napoleon's army, finds out after the event that he has described an engraving picturing the scene. 'Postmodern' literature has known how to be aware of this 'Brulard syndrome', and we can read, in its avowed taste for quotation and pastiche, an elegant way of assuming a heritage that we cannot get rid of. We are always taken in by the very thing that makes us ourselves and that we think we dominate. It is therefore not surprising that the majority of Simon's novels set themselves in the final analysis a veritable quest for identity, often led with a nostalgia for origins, like an investigation carried out on ancestors, the experience of which redoubles that of the narrator, and allows him to narrate himself, even if he cannot know himself. This strong, uncompromising work, crowned in 1985 by a Nobel prize, asks the European literature of today the question, constantly repeated: 'How do we know what to know?'

Dag Solstad (1941–)

The young Norwegian writer Dag Solstad held a prominent position in the legendary 'Profil-Gruppen' (Group Profile) of the 1960s. Because they despised conventional novel narration, these young Norwegian authors introduced and experimented with different ideas of late modernism. A bias towards systematic pathos is one of the keys to the success of this institutional revolt against traditionalism and provincialism. These writers were then emulating their enlightened contemporaries of the most up-to-date avant-garde of Paris, New York and Buenos Aires, while seeking marginalised heroes in the history of Norwegian literature.

The change, abrupt when it arrived, came in the 1970s: Solstad was once again in the front line. Modernism ceases to be an avant-garde tendency and now becomes a banner for socialist realism which thus obtains, belatedly, a great success in Norway. Norwegian Maoism, a moralising movement, after a long and involuntarily comic journey, sees itself as literature. The break with this political literature is consummated in 1980 by Dag

Solstad. There followed a series of remarkable novels signalling the break rather than a reaction.

We find in these novels obvious traces of a literary master, Knut Hamsun. There are resemblances between Hamsun and Solstad: both of them acted at times as extremist political thinkers and as writers with ambiguous messages. Solstad's writing is that of a master, transparent but difficult to imitate and translate.

To formulate with delicacy the creative dynamic at the heart of this multifaceted work is to undertake a wager. Let us try, however. In the novel *Arild Asnes 1970* (1971), we are present at a double conversion: first the evolution of Arild Asnes, who goes from being an independent writer to being a Maoist militant, then the change of writing which passes from a modernist register to a realist register. In contrast to Joyce's *A Portrait of the Artist as a Young Man*, the movement, in Solstad, goes from art to politics, like a road that leads to the real world, away from an art that has become totally insignificant. The paradoxical role of art is then, by becoming an anti-art, to fill the gap that separates it from life. This choice leads to history. Hence the trilogy of novels on the Second World War, a genuine but failed attempt to place the subject in a context where the present is part of a perspective leading to the past and the future. This appears in the more recent novels of Solstad as a tragic and metaphysical aim: the present merely consists of reiterated pasts.

The texts register this break as being inevitable. To prefer art to life is then as impossible as to prefer life to art. At the risk of repeating ourselves, the work becomes an immense intertext inhabited by an enormously sinister comicalness. *Novel 1987* (1987) deals with history and a historian. It ignores the future, as much as it does the jubilation that there is to be experienced in freeing oneself from Time. In this deliberately retrospective text, the previous novels of Solstad form a hall of mirrors where perspective is replaced by an objectless melancholy. Here, more clearly than ever, Dag Solstad reveals himself to be an ironist in the Kierkegaardian sense: 'We encounter here the ironic subject. For him, reality has lost absolutely all validity; for him it has become an imperfect form which is always importunate. A new reality does not suit him any better.'

A new twist: Solstad's last book was published after the writer had signed a contract for three years with the industrial giant Aker. The literary maestro has become the historian of big business. Is it by chance that this book is called *Medallens forside* (*The Reverse Side of the Medal*, 1990)? Solstad makes out that he wanted to write a non-Christian work and that he became a court painter in the sense in which Velázquez and Goya were. Has Solstad capitulated? Or is this something quite different?

Botho Strauss (1944–)

Botho Strauss, born on 2 December 1944 in Naumburg an der Saale, Germany, may be numbered among the most important dramatists in the German language of our era, though he is not exclusively confined to this genre. Wanting to hold up a mirror to society as to the individual, and to have an effect through his plays more than through his person, Strauss avoids interviews and all forms of what could amount to a personality cult. After his first play, *Die Hypochonder* (*The Hypochondriacs*, 1972), he rapidly makes a name for himself with *Bekannte Gesichter, gemischte Gefühle* (*Familiar Faces, Mixed Feelings*, 1975). From his first plays, we can recognise the stylistic devices and themes that are his trademark: identity, roles and social behaviour, but also inner points of view, emotions and reflections: in brief, the tension between social and personal identity. To make this tension obvious, Strauss frequently associates everyday situations and apparently banal dialogues, but loads them down with extraneous and surrealist elements, enigmas, allusions to myths to the point of obscurity, so as to prevent any superficial or hasty reading, proceeding on purely realist assumptions.

The problem of identity, treated with a distancing effect by the introduction of dreams and surrealist perceptions, constitutes the theme of the story *Marlenes Schwester* (*Marlene's Sister*, 1975). *Theorie der Drohung* (*The Theory of Menace*, 1975) analyses the conditions and opportunities for writing in the area of tension between reality and unreality. Strauss is also interested in loving relationships which fail and break down, as in the story *Die Widmung* (*The Dedication*, 1977). In the following works, he analyses the questions of being and appearing, of supposed importance and real impotence (*Trilogie des Wiedersehens, The Trilogy of Seeing Again*, 1976), of co-existence based on humanitarian feelings (*Groß und Klein, Big and Small*, 1978) and failure (*Pumo*, 1980). *Kalldewey Farce* (1981) is a play whose content eludes logical interpretation and any attachment to a definite genre.

After *Paare, Passanten* (*Couples, Passers-By*, 1981), Strauss writes the novel *Der junge Mann* (*The Young Man*, 1984) and the play *Der Park* (*The Park*, 1984), before reverting, with *Niemand anderes* (*No-one Else*, 1987), to rapid narrative sketches. In 1988, he composes three new plays: *Besucher* (*Visitors*), *Die Zeit und das Zimmer* (*Time and the Room*) and *Sieben Türen* (*Seven Doors*). If the latter are 'narrations of the everyday', as the title already indicates, the play *Visitors* is devoted to the world of the theatre, to the actors and the audience.

After a new prose work, *Kongreß, die Kette der Demütigungen* (*Congress, the Chain of Humiliations*, 1989), Strauss is one of the first to depict on stage the reuniting of West and East Germany. The title of this play is pregnant with meaning: *Schlußchor* (*Final Chorus*, 1991). It is notably possible to see an allusion to Beethoven's *Ninth Symphony* with the final chorus taken from 'The Ode to Joy' by Friedrich Schiller chosen as the European national anthem; it would be typical of Strauss to indicate in this way the need to see Germany above all in the wider European context. The play, composed of Acts that are relatively self-sufficient, traces in the memory of the first Act for one 'last' time the portrait of the society of the Federal Republic. In the mirror that the second Act literally holds out to this society, are reflected the history of the period and banalities, failed love affairs and the lives of artists, while the third Act tackles the theme of the inadequacy of myths and traditional symbols of German history when confronted with the problem posed by the necessity for Germany to overcome its immediate and its most remote past.

Monika Van Paemel (1945–)

The autobiographical and feminist novel in five parts *De vermaledijde vaders* (*The Cursed Fathers*, 1985) by the Flemish-speaking Belgian Monika Van Paemel is a novel in layers permitting several readings according to the viewpoint that the reader is invited to follow. With fragmented tales, interior monologues, scattered extracts from personal diaries, historical chronicles and litanies, Monika Van Paemel treats among other themes that of the ambiguous exploration of her country of origin, of the diminished influence of woman in society, of eroticism and of 'how to live'.

She also asks herself questions about the violence of the times we live in and the impulses our world has to self-destruct, and she is still surprised at her power to write and live in spite of this violence and death-wish.

As regards the problem of female emancipation, the plural in the novel's title is significant: the fathers, the 'gentlemen' are responsible for the wretched history of human beings, which has been written in tears and blood. But it is above all the language of the 'gentlemen' which is analysed critically: in effect they speak the language of command, of violence, of monologue, of non-communication. But the author's vision of the world is very subtle. Mothers also are responsible for their situation by reason of the hysterical complaints they give voice to and their predilection for the victim's role. Monika Van Paemel tries to write for a future worth living, in which the relationship between men and women might be built on a foundation of equality. There is in this work no

petrified ideology, but a writing permeated by intelligence.

In the following extract, the author addresses her father and the 'gentlemen' through the voice of her main character: 'I have not become a crazy pacifist. (We adore that little dish.) Nor a consenting victim. I always want to give blows back. (A good reflex, no?) Turn the other cheek? Of course, but for a kiss! I don't want an agitator next to me. Nor an oppressor in my bed. Nor a destroyer in my kitchen. Nor a father who spies on his chidren. What I'd like is to pound them to a pulp, those gentlemen, scatter the pernicious seed of discord. . . . I do not have the impression that prayers and supplications will serve any useful purpose.'

Christa Wolf (1929–)

Christa Wolf was born on 18 March 1929 in Landsberg on the Warta (today Gorzów Wielpolski in Poland). In 1949 she joined the East German communist party and, from 1949 to 1953, studied German at Jena and Leipzig. Since 1962 she has been living from her writing in Berlin and near Güstrow in Mecklenburg, a region whose countryside has served as a setting for some of her novels and stories (*Nachenken über Christa T.*, *Christa T.* 1968, *Störfall*, *Incident*, 1986, *Sommerstück*, *Scenes of Summer*). From 1955 to 1977 she was a member of the committee of the Union of Writers. From 1963 to 1967 she was a candidate for the central committee of the SED, a member of the German Democratic Republic's Academy of Arts, of the Academy of Language and Literature in Darmstadt, of the Acaemy of Arts in West Berlin. She has won many literary prizes in East Germany, West Germany and Austria. Christa Wolf can be described as a 'pan-German writer', for there is no other writer whose work has been so warmly welcomed in West and East Germany. Her themes, like the personal flowering of the individual in a society which strives for collective responsibility (*Christa T.*), subjection to the marks left by childhood (*Kindheitsmuster*, *Childhood's Pattern*), reflections on the role of women (*Kassandra, Cassandra*, 1983) and the nuclear threat menacing mankind with self-destruction (*Incident*), as well as her many memberships of political and artistic organisations show clearly that she has always considered her literary activity as a conscious reflection of her responsible stand on current problems.

Christa Wolf's work is an example of the development of the literature of the former GDR. Her first story *Moskauer Novelle* (1959) and the novel *Der geteilte Himmel* (*Heaven Divided*, 1963) are still entirely written in the spirit of the 'Bitterfeld conference' which wanted literature to contribute to the development of socialism. The work that followed already heralded the end of the 'Bitterfeld way'. Her novel *Christa T.* has brought down on her head the reproach of engaging in unproductive personalism. In this novel, as in the tale *Juninachmittag* (*An Afternoon in June*) published a year previously, in response to a new interpretation of Romanticism in the GDR, Christa Wolf intermingles sense impressions, imagination and reflections. *Childhood's Pattern* strengthens this subjective tendency. The subject of the novel is an interrogation on the causes of fascism, its repercussions on people and the crucial question: 'How did we get to be what we are?'

Wolf's principal work is the story *Cassandra*: 'With this story I walk towards death,' she wrote in the introduction. Here she collects all her themes and makes them converge in the light of ancient myth: power and abuse of power, language as an instrument of domination, the war, its logic, as well as the internal preparation and role of a woman. She calls on us to overcome the manicheism of friend-enemy, the antagonistic nature of blocs, and, using precise tools of analysis, brings out the relationships between aggression, violence and male domination.

Her text *Was bleibt* (*What Remains*, 1990), which recalls the surveillance of the author by the GDR's secret service, sparked off a literary polemic. She has been accused of not having had the courage to publish her text at a time when the Communist Party was in power. This polemic has again shown the difficult situation in which writers were caught up in the GDR. 'But we have not yet reached the end. And anyway: getting older means ceasing to hold someone else responsible for what befalls you,' she wrote in *Scenes of Summer*. May she be equally able to stick to her guns in a united Germany!